Malaysia

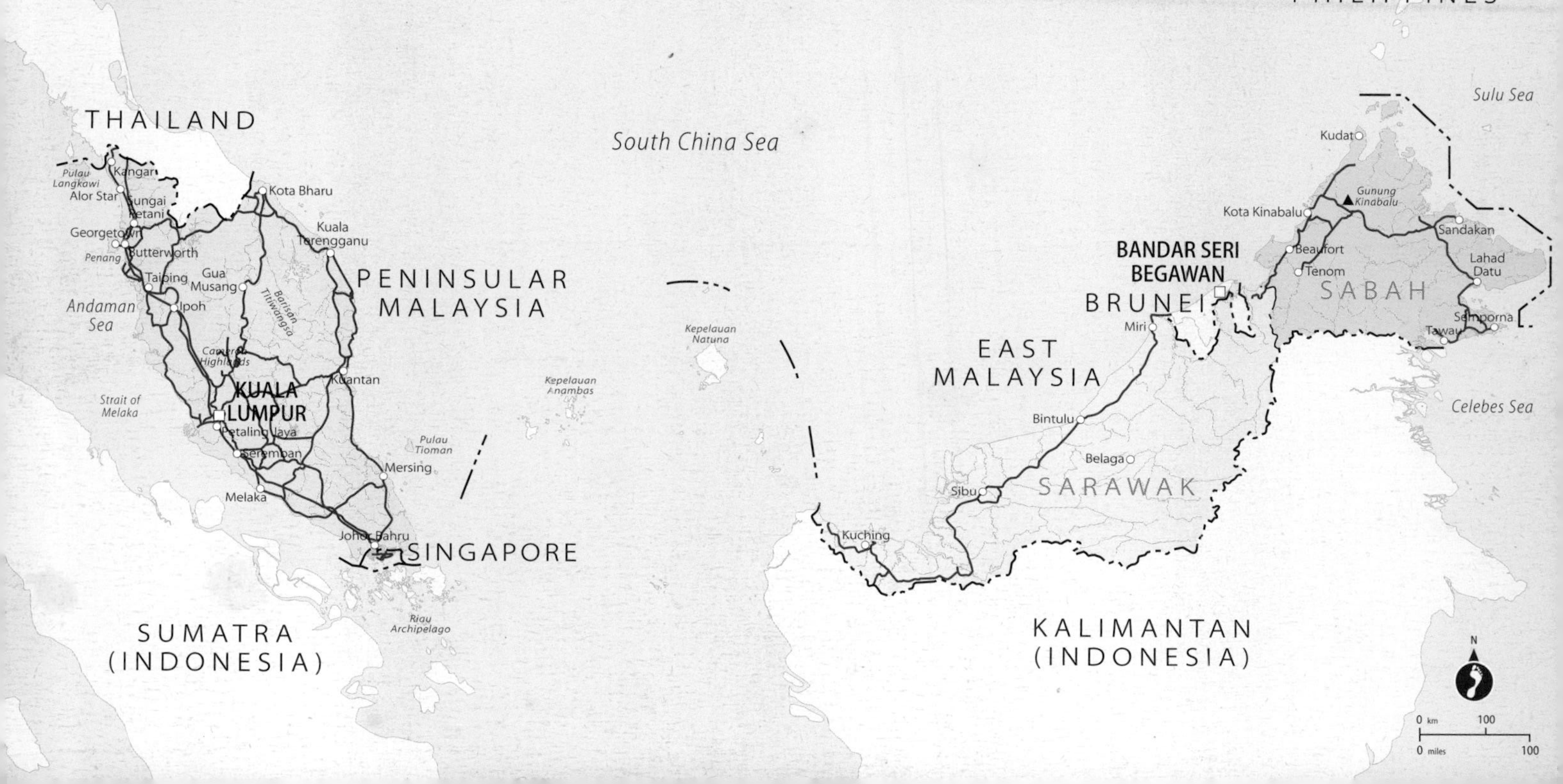

PHILIPPINES

Sulu Sea

Celebes Sea

N

0 km 100
0 miles 100

Kudat

Gunung Kinabalu

Lahad Datu

Sandakan

Semporna

Tawau

SABAH

Kota Kinabalu

Beaufort

Tenom

BANDAR SERI BEGAWAN

BRUNEI

Miri

Belaga

Bintulu

SARAWAK

EAST MALAYSIA

Sibu

KALIMANTAN (INDONESIA)

Kuching

South China Sea

Kepulauan Natuna

PENINSULAR MALAYSIA

Kepulauan Anambas

THAILAND

Kota Bharu

Kuala Terengganu

Pulau Langkawi

Alor Star

Sungai Petani

Georgetown

Penang

Butterworth

Taiping

Gua Musang

Ipoh

Banjaran Titiwangsa

Kuantan

Cameron Highlands

KUALA LUMPUR

Petaling Jaya

Pulau Tioman

Mersing

Melaka

Johor Bahru

SINGAPORE

Riau Archipelago

Andaman Sea

Strait of Melaka

SUMATRA (INDONESIA)

Malaysia Handbook
Third edition
© Footprint Handbooks Ltd 2000

Published by Footprint Handbooks
6 Riverside Court
Lower Bristol Road
Bath BA2 3DZ. England
T +44 (0)1225 469141
F +44 (0)1225 469461
Email discover@footprintbooks.com
Web www.footprintbooks.com

ISBN 1 900949 52 0
ISSN 1363-7363
CIP DATA: A catalogue record for this
book is available from the British Library

Distributed in the USA by
Publishers Group West

Credits

Series editors
Patrick Dawson
Rachel Fielding

Editorial
Editor: Jo Williams
Maps: Sarah Sorensen

Production
Pre-press Manager: Jo Morgan
Typesetting: Richard Ponsford and
Emma Bryers
Maps: Kevin Feeney, Robert Lunn
and Claire Benison
Proof reading: John Work

Design
Mytton Williams

Photography
Front cover: Pictures Colour Library
Back cover: Impact Photos
Inside colour section: Robert Harding
Picture Library; Pictures Colour Library;
Eye Ubiquitous; Pictor International;
James Davis Travel Photography

Print
Manufactured in Italy by LEGOPRINT

Malaysia

Footprint

Handbook

Joshua Eliot, Jane Bickersteth, Kate Renshaw
& Dan Harlow

*The more you eat of it, the less you feel inclined to
stop. In fact, to eat durians is a new sensation
worth a voyage to the East to experience.*

Alfred Russel Wallace in *The Malay Archipelago*
(1869), as his disgust of the foul-smelling durian
turns to delight.

Contents

Left: *Jalan Petaling in Kuala Lumpur's Chinatown wakes up during late afternoon for the frenetic night market.*

Right: the vast karst limestone cavern at Batu Caves, north of Kuala Lumpur.

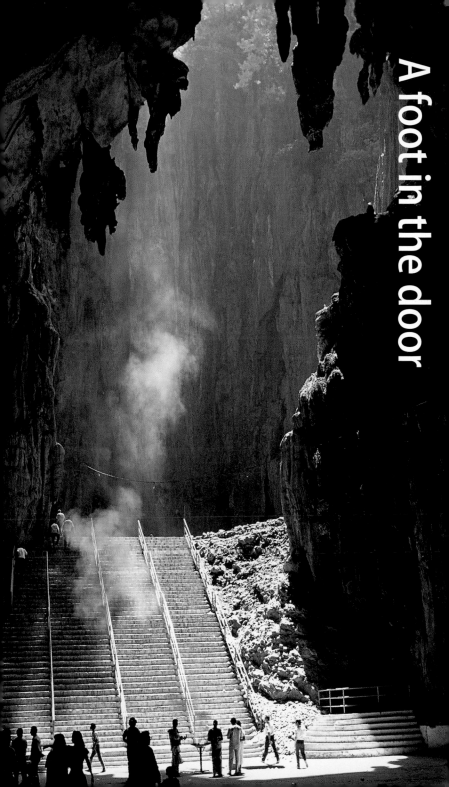

A foot in the door

Highlights

The 'Malay Archipelago' is a term intimately associated with the mystery of the East. It conjures up images of sultans, head-hunters and pirates; munificent jungles brimming with exotic life; clippers cutting through the warm waters of the South China Sea; and of explorers discovering new tribes while planters sit on verandahs taking tiffin and, later, a pink gin laced with quinine to keep malaria at bay.

Today's Malay Archipelago is somewhere very different. Singapore's godowns have been replaced by towering glass and steel office blocks. The rickshaw pullers, who rarely lived long enough to see middle age, have become English-speaking workers with incomes among the highest in the world and a health system that sustains them well into old age. Malaysia, thrusting and self-confident, is following where Singapore has been, with a mission to transform itself into a developed country by 2020 - and notwithstanding its brush with the Asian economic crisis.

Malaysia divides into two different worlds. West - or Peninsular - Malaysia is the industrial, political and economic heartland of the country. While East Malaysia is a territory of forests and rivers, mountains and caves, tribes and abundant wildlife.

Sandwiched between Singapore to the south and Thailand to the north, the Peninsula states support the great bulk of the country's population. And just as Malaysia itself is a country of two halves, so the Peninsula too can be broadly divided into two: a vibrant western side and a bucolic east. Between the two is the Barisan Titiwangsa, the Peninsula's jungled spine. Kuala Lumpur, the capital, and most of the country's main urban centres are to be found on the western side of the Peninsula. Tin was discovered here, so roads and railways were built, a development that also favoured the growth of the rubber industry. Malays proved reluctant to leave their kampungs to assist Britain develop the Malaysian colonial economy so Chinese and Indian labourers were shipped in. So was born Malaysia's plural society. The east coast of the peninsula, in the process, became a half-forgotten backwater.

Malaysian Borneo or East Malaysia, encompassing the states of Sabah and Sarawak, dovetails more closely with the romantic vision of 'Malaya'. While cities like Kuching and Kota Kinabalu have been colonised by the people (Malays, Chinese) and ideas of the Peninsula, the countryside remains dominated by tribal groups, collectively known as Dayaks, like the Iban, Kelabit, Kenyah, Bidayuh and Kayan, and much of it is still forested. Beyond the coast and the main towns, roads are limited and often air or river transport are the only sensible ways to travel in the interior. While the headhunters that so terrified the early colonists - and the Japanese during the Second World War - may be consigned to the history books, the territory is still mightily imposing. The country's finest national parks, indeed some of the world's finest protected areas, can be found here.

Singapore Singapore is a world city with world-class attractions - and only the barest whiff of the East. When the Old Orient does appear it has invariably been sequestered by New Singapore. Hundred year-old shophouses have been converted into drinking holes and edgy design studios while the bumboats which used to ferry cargo from freighter to godown now carry tourists up and down the restaurant-lined Singapore River. Renowned for its epicurian delights, Singapore is also aiming to become a regional centre for the arts too.

Left: Kuala Lumpur's skyline with the world's tallest building, the distinctive Petronas Twin Towers, which stand 452m high.
Below: boats are the best way to get from one kampung to another on Pulau Tioman, off the east coast of Peninsular Malaysia.

Above: monks blessing a shophouse in Jalan Hang Jebat, Chinatown, Kuala Lumpur.
Left: Pulau Sipadan off the coast of Sabah, East Malaysia, is a protected marine area, surrounded by the best coral reef in Malaysia.
Overleaf: the market in Johor Bahru.

12

Right: the temperate climate of the Cameron Highlands, the biggest and best known of Malaysia's hills stations, is ideal for growing tea.
Below: Penang's largest Thai monastery, Wat Chayamangkalaram, is just one of the island's many religious buildings that reflect its rich cultural heritage.

Above: trishaws are a popular form of transport for tourists in the colonial town of Melaka, in southern Peninular Malaysia.
Right: despite the growth in hotels, Pulau Tioman on Peninsular Malaysia's east coast is still an ideal destination for anyone looking for a deserted beach, a touch of diving and some superb seafood.

Peninsular Malaysia

Malaysia's capital, Kuala Lumpur, is a colonial creation that owes its existence to the rich tin deposits found in the area in the 1850s. So the historical claims of Kuala Lumpur, or KL, as it is more commonly known, date back little more than a century. Chinatown, the Moorish-style railway station and one or two other notable buildings represent the old; the new is showcased in the 88-storey, 421 metre-high Petronas Twin Towers, the world's tallest building(s).

The modern west

The far more venerable city of Melaka - or Malacca - has churches and trading houses that reflect its mixed parentage, dating from the Dutch and Portuguese periods. It also has a fine Chinatown. But an even better array of colonial-era Chinese shophouses are to be found in Georgetown, Penang, a town which vied briefly with Singapore in the early 1800s for the honour of trading capital of the Melacca Straits. It lost. Today conservationsists are battling to protect its architectural inheritance from rapacious developers. Ipoh is a rarely visited town which deserves more attention. Another tin-rush settlement colonised by Chinese, Ipoh has a well preserved Old Town and some of the best Chinese restaurants in Malaysia.

As the French did in Indochina and the Dutch in the East Indies, the British hunted out hill retreats where they could escape the heat and humidity of the lowlands. The Cameron Highlands was converted into a tropical version of the home counties with beamed cottages and rose gardens in the 1920s, as was the less well known Fraser's Hill. While the developer's hand is evident in the profusion of golf courses and luxury hotels it is still possible to settle down to a cream tea or roast beef and Yorkshire pudding and imagine, just for a brief moment, that the British never left.

The development of the west coast's beaches and islands had to await the invention of the bikini and suntan oil, as well as the fascination for tanned bodies. Penang island is the west coast's best known and most developed beach resort - now linked to the mainland by one of the world's longest bridges. Langkawi and Pangkor islands are altogether more beautiful although no longer the idyllic retreats they once were.

To truly escape it is necessary to travel over the Barisan Titiwangsa to the East Coast. It is sold by Tourism Malaysia as the 'real Malaysia' using rather hackneyed PR images of a coastline fringed by coconut palms, beaches and sleepy fishing villages. The West may be the industrial and political core of Malaysia, but the East is regarded as the heartland of Malay culture and tradition. Malay sports from top-spinning to kite-flying and crafts like batik-making and silverwork remain vibrant. Islam, particularly in Kelantan and Terengganu, strongly influences public behaviour and private morals.

The (half-)forgotten east

The densely forested Tioman island, once rated as one of the world's top 10 desert islands escapes by *Time* magazine, is fringed by white coral-sand beaches. Tropical islands such as Tioman, along with stretches of quiet (and not-so-quiet) coastline and beach like those of Kampung Cherating, Merang and, confusingly, Marang, offer far more diving possibilities than the west coast. While the coral around offshore islands like Pulau Redang and the Perhentian group is not world class, this is a good area to learn to scuba dive. There is also the additional attraction of turtles, including the endangered Giant Leatherback, which come ashore to lay their eggs at numerous locations including Rantau Abang. Inland are the Peninsula's finest national parks, Endau Rompin and Taman Negara. Fishing, hiking and swimming, waterfalls, rapids and 1,500m-peaks, along with wildlife from Sumatran rhinoceros to civets, wild boar, hornbills and the (very) odd tiger add to their allure.

14

Right: the rafflesia is the world's largest flower, but it only blooms for a few days every year.
Below: Mount Kinabalu in Sabah, East Malaysia, is probably the most impressive sight in Borneo, particularly at sunrise.

Above: Danum Valley's virgin jungle, the largest expanse of undisturbed lowland dipterocarp forest in Sabah, East Malaysia, contains over 2,000 species of tree.
Right: one of the most important turtle breeding spots in Southeast Asia is the Turtle Islands National Park in Sabah, East Malaysia, an area famous for its green turtles.
Overleaf: Kek Lok Si Temple, Penang Island, took 20 years to build and is fashioned on a monastery in China.

Malaysian Borneo

The Skrang, Belaga, Rejang and Baram rivers with their trading settlements, tribal villages, rapids and terrifyingly fast river boats are the entrees into inland Sarawak and the state's magnificent natural heritage. It is an area well worth exploring by boat. There is an array of 14 protected areas from the tiny, coastal Tanjung Datu National Park to the vast and inaccessible Lanjak-Entimau National Park. Not only do these sanctuaries protect arguably the world's most diverse terrestrial ecosystem - the lowland tropical rainforest - but there is also trekking, rafting and climbing to entice the adventurous traveller.

Of particular note are the stupendous caves of the Gunung Mulu National Park and the archaeologically significant Niah Caves. The latter have revealed evidence of early human settlement in bones and cave paintings while the former are simply part of what is one of the world's most extensive cave systems stretching over nearly 200 kilometres and including the world's largest cavern. For those who like some more human contact with their jungles, caves and wildlife, Sarawak's 1,500-odd longhouses, lining the rivers which are often the only way to travel, are a fascinating insight into a fast-disappearing way of life and living.

Kuching, Sarawak's capital, supports arguably Malaysia's finest museum, the Sarawak Museum, with an incomparable ethnographic collection. About 35 km outside Kuching on the Damai Peninsula, and at the opposite extreme, is the 'living', but in reality expensively - and skilfully - contrived, Sarawak Cultural Village where well-trained 'tribal' men and women (some, reportedly, not tribal at all!) act out their allotted roles.

Like its sister state to the south, Sabah is a natural wonderland with nearly 20 protected areas. From the state capital of Kota Kinabalu it is easy to see Malaysia's highest mountain, Gunung Kinabalu, which rises to more than 4,000m. It is not the 'highest mountain in Southeast Asia', as it is continually billed, but is nonetheless a wonderful, invigorating climb. Early morning on the summit is an incomparable experience. The world's largest flower, the Rafflesia, grows here although few get to see it - the plant only flowers for a few days a year. Sandakan is Sabah's second city and within easy reach of the town is another of the state's more popular protected areas: the small Sepilok Orang Utan Rehabilitation Centre. Here domesticated and half-domesticated orang utans are weaned off their unnatural diets of pizza, beer and such like and reintroduced to the wild.

Two of Sabah's most memorable protected areas are marine. The Turtle Islands National Park, 40 km from Sandakan, is Southeast Asia's most important turtle-breeding area. Here it is possible to see the kings of Malaysia's reptile population, Green and Hawksbill turtles, laying their eggs on three tiny islands. The second, the Sipadan Island Marine Reserve off Sabah's northeast coast, rises on a stalk 200m from the bed of the Celebes Sea. When Jacques Cousteau visited Sipadan in 1989 he was dumbfounded. "Now", he remarked, "we have found an untouched piece of art". The diving here is the best in Malaysia - indeed, some of the best in the world.

Essentials

2

Essentials

Planning your trip

Getting around Peninsular Malaysia and Singapore is not difficult and even making the trip from Kota Bharu at the northern extremity of the east coast, down to Melaka, towards the southern end of the west coast, need only take a day's travelling by road. Air links between the major towns are clearly faster still. However, many visitors with only a fortnight, say, in the area wonder whether it is possible to combine a trip to Peninsular Malaysia and Brunei. This requires a little more thought. There are regular domestic air connections between the Peninsula and the major cities of East Malaysia and Brunei, and from there with smaller towns in the Bornean interior. For those intending, for example, to fly to Kota Kinabalu, stay a few days at Tanjung Aru Beach, and then return, taking in East and West Malaysia should pose no difficulties. However, if intending to do more than this, such as climbing Mount Kinabalu, travelling upriver on the Baram, Rejang or Skrang rivers, or hiking through one of the national parks, then a little more leeway in terms of time is required. A minimum period to just scratch the surface would be one week; preferably 10 days to two weeks. Of course some people spend many weeks in just one area and still profess to have seen only a fraction of what is on offer.

Hill stations   Fraser's Hill and the Cameron Highlands offer a taste of colonial Malaya, **Where to go** and there are good walks around the Cameron Highlands. The Genting Highlands is more ersatz and kitsch, a favourite haunt of Kuala Lumpur's nouveau riche. Maxwell Hill is the quietest of the hill stations.

Wildlife and jungle   The national parks of the peninsula do not compare with those of East Malaysia. Nonetheless, Taman Negara and the Endau Rompin National Park are both well worth visiting. Rantau Abang on the east coast is a stretch of shoreline where turtles come to lay their eggs. In East Malaysia, Sarawak and Sabah offer a wealth of parks and conservation areas. Some, like the Semonggoh Orang Utan Sanctuary and the Bako National Park outside Kuching, and the Sepilok Orang Utan Rehabilitation Centre and the Turtle Islands National Park outside Sandakan are accessible as day trips. Other parks, like the Niah and Gunung Mulu national parks for example, require several days to explore properly.

Natural features   The caves at the Niah and Gunung Mulu national parks and Gunung Kinabalu, Malaysia's highest mountain, are stupendous natural features worth visiting for themselves. There are many islands you can visit off both the west and east coasts of the Peninsula. Penang has a wide selection of hotels and facilities, and some may view it as over-developed. Langkawi, though more recently 'discovered', has also developed rapidly in recent years. Also off the west coast is Pulau Pangkor. Tioman, off the Peninsula's east coast, is less developed than Langkawi and Penang and there are also numerous other islands which are less touched by the hands of humans still. On the Peninsula itself, Kampung Cerating is the best known beach resort, which still has a backpacker-feel to it, although it is hardly off the beaten track. There are also other groups of hotels and chalets dotted up and down the east coast. Sabah and Sarawak do not have beach 'resorts' to compare with those at least in scale of the Peninsula. However, there are some fine beaches and excellent snorkelling and diving, especially in the Tunku Abdul Rahman National Park and at Sipadan Island Marine Reserve. Small resorts include those at Damai, north of Kuching; Tanjung Aru, outside Kota Kinabalu; and Labuan.

Historical sites Melaka is one of Malaysia's two historic gems. There are buildings dating from the Portuguese and Dutch periods, as well as some fine Chinese shophouses. Georgetown, the capital of Penang, is Malaysia's second city of architectural and historical note with probably the finest assembly of Sino-colonial architecture in the region.

For information on visiting longhouses in Sarawak, see page 339

Culture Traditional Malay culture is best preserved on the east coast of the Peninsula and especially in the Malay heartland of Kelantan (Kota Bharu), with its rural kampongs and thriving craft industry. The Sarawak Cultural Village near Kuching offers an anaesthetized vision of tribal life and culture; the upriver 'tribes' and longhouses give a taste of the real thing. The Rajang, Skrang, and Kinabatanagan rivers, dotted with towns and small tribal settlements, are all worth exploring by boat.

Shopping KL is the best place to buy the full range of handicrafts from batik to blowpipes, although prices are higher than at their source. The east coast is the centre of the Peninsula's Malay handicraft industry, particularly Kelantan (Kota Bharu). Sabah and Sarawak are the places to find tribal handicrafts. Many are on sale in the main towns, although smaller communities potentially offer the best buys.

Museums KL's museums are less impressive than those in Singapore but are still worth visiting. Surprisingly, perhaps the best museum in East Malaysia is the Sarawak Museum in Kuching with its superb ethnographic collection.

The above is only a selection of places of interest and is not exhaustive. It is designed to assist in planning a trip to the region. Any 'highlight' list is inevitably subjective.

When to go
For more information on climate, see page 515

The rainy seasons should be borne in mind when planning itineraries in Malaysia; the best time to visit the Peninsula's east coast is between March and September. Trips along the east coast and interior jungles are not advisable between November and February, during the northeast monsoon. The east coast suffers flooding at this time of year, and it is inadvisable and also impossible to take fishing boats to offshore islands such as Pulau Tioman as the sea can be very rough. Taman Negara National Park is closed from November to the end of January. Other parts of Peninsular Malaysia can be visited year round as the rainy season is not torrential, although it is fairly wet during the northeast monsoon period. Rainfall is worst from May to September on the west coast of the Peninsula, but it is never very heavy.

In East Malaysia March and June are the best times to visit the interior, the worst rains are usually from November to February and some roads are impassable in these months. Conversely, in the dry season, some rivers become unnavigable. In recent years the onset of the wet and dry seasons in both Sabah and Sarawak have become less predictable; environmentalists ascribe this to deforestation, although there is no scientifically proven link.

NB School holidays run from mid- to late February, mid-May to early June, mid to late August and late November to early January. During these periods it is advisable to book hotels.

Tours & tour operators

Abercrombie & Kent Travel, 1520 Kensington Road, Oak Brook, Illinois, 60523-2141 USA, www.aandktours.com. Global company with 32 offices worldwide offering a large range of tours in and around Malaysia.

Borneo Eco Tours, Shoplot 12a, 2nd Floor, Lorong Bernam 3, Taman Soon Kiong, 88300 Kota Kinabalu, Sabah, Malaysia, www.borneoecotours.com. Specializing in environmentally aware tours.

Eastern Oriental Express, www.orient-expresstrains.com. Offices worldwide. Offering luxury train trips between Thailand, Malaysia and Singapore.

Exodus Expeditions, 9 Weir Road, London SW12 0LT, www.exodus.co.uk. Wide range of trips in Southeast Asia including Malaysia. The Borneo Explorer tour includes river journeys and the caves at the Niah National Park.

Explore Worldwide, 1 Frederick Street, Aldershot, Hampshire, GU11 1LQ, T01252-760000, www.explore.co.uk. Arranges small group tours (average 16 people) with any different types of trip offered including cultural excursions, adventure holidays and natural history tours.

Flightbookers, UK, T020-77572444, sales@flightbookers.co.uk. Organizes anything from airfares to self-drive trips and cruises, to jungle treks.

Ideal Holidays, No 4, Ground Floor, Jalan Api-Api, Off Jalan Gaya, PO Box 21490, 88772 Luyang, Kota Kinabalu, Sabah, Malaysia, www.ideal-borneo.com. Another Malaysian based tour operator. Four set tours with the option of creating your own tailor-made tour.

Intrepid Travel, 12 Spring St, Fitzroy, VIC, Austrailia, www.intrepidtravel.com.au. Australian company with agents all over the world. Offers three different tours of Malaysia.

Kuoni Travel, www.kuoni.co.uk. Consistently high-quality service tour operator which organises trips all over Southeast Asia.

Magic of the Orient, 2 Kingsland Court, Three Bridges Road, Crawley, West Sussex, RH10 1HL, www.magic-of-the-orient.com. Specialists in tailor-made tours to Asia.

Silk Steps, 83 Quakers Rd, Downend, Bristol, BS16 6NH, UK, T0117-9402800, F0117-9406900, info@silksteps.co.uk, www.silksteps.co.uk.

Symbiosis, 113 Bolingbroke Grove, London, SW11 1DA, T020-79245906, F020-79245907, info@symbiosis-travel.co.uk, www.symbiosis.co.uk. An environmentally aware company that offers expeditions respecting traditional values and cultures. It specializes in tailor-made tours.

Essentials

Essentials

 Malaysian tourist board offices overseas

Australia, 65 York St, Sydney, NSW 2000, Tÿ02 2994441/2/3; 56 William St, Perth, WA 6000, T09-4810400

Benelux Countries, c/o Malaysia Airlines System Bhd, Westeringschans 24A, 1017 SG Amsterdam, T020-6381146/020 6381189

Canada, 830 Burrard St, Vancouver, BC, V6Z 2K4, T604-6898899

France, Office National du Tourisme de Malaisie, 29 Rue des Pyramides, 75001 Paris, T331-42974171

Germany, Rossmarkt 11, 60311 Frankfurt Am Main, T069-283782

Hong Kong, Gd Flr, Malaysia Bldg, 47-50 Gloucester Rd, T2528-5810

Italy, Secondo Piano, Piazza San Babila 4/B, 20122 Milano, T02-796702

Japan, 5F Chiyoda Bldg, 1-6-4 Yurakucho, Chiyoda-Ku, Tokyo 100, T 03 3501 8691; 10th Flr, Cotton Nissay Bldg, 1-8-2 Utsubo-Honmachi, Nishi-Ku, Osaka 550, T06-444 1220

Singapore, 10, Collyer Quay, 01-06 & 18-02, Ocean Bldg, Singapore 049313, T02-5326321

South Africa, 1st Flr, Hutton Court, CNR Jan Smuts, Avenue and Summit Rd, Hyde Park 2196, Johannesburg, T 2711 327 0400

South Korea, 1st Flr, Han Young Bldg, 57-9 Seosomun-dong, Chung-ku, Seoul, T02-7794422

Sweden, Sveavagen 18, Box 7062, 10386 Stockholm, T46-8249900

Thailand, Ground Flr, 315, South East Insurance Bldg, Silom Rd, Bangkok 10500, T236-7606

UK, 57 Trafalgar Square, London WC2N 5DU, T020-79307932

USA, 818 Suite 804, West Seventh St, Los Angeles, CA 90017, T213 6899702; 595 Madison Ave, Suite 1800, New York, NY 10022, T212-754 1113.

Thomas Cook Holidays, PO Box 5, 12 Conigsby Rd, Peterborough PE3 8XP, www.tch.thomascook.com. Organized tours as well as beach holidays all over Southeast Asia.

Specialist interest travel

Trekking and climbing There are good jungle treks in Taman Negara and in the Endau Rompin National Park and hiking in the Cameron Highlands. There are numerous opportunities for climbing, especially in East Malaysia. Most of East Malaysia's parks offer hiking trails, but the best are in the Niah, Gunung Mulu and Gunung Kinabalu national parks. Climbing Mount Kinabalu in Sabah, to be at the summit for sunrise, is one of the most popular hikes.

Diving Dive sites off the Peninsula are not world class although there are some very good places to learn to scuba dive including Pulau Paya, Pulau Pangkor, Tioman, the Pulau Sibu archipelago, Pulau Redang and Pulau Perhentian. There are some world class dive sites in East Malaysia including Pulau Sipadan, Pulau Layang-Layang, the Tunku Abdul Rahman and Turtle Islands national parks, Pulau Tiga and Labuan.

West coast Generally, the diving off the west coast of Peninsular Malaysia is the least spectacular in the country. However, as the bulk of Malaysia's population live near here, it is the most accessible from KL and other important centres. The islands of the **Paya archipelago**, to the north of Penang and south of Langkawi (see page 188), offer the best diving opportunities. It is now protected as an underwater reserve, having being gazetted in 1985. The principal islands are Paya, Kacha, Lembu and Segantan and they support a marine flora and fauna that includes 36 genera of hard corals, 92 other marine invertebrates and 45 genera of fish. On Pulau Paya itself, the waters off the rocky southwest tip offer the best diving; the corals here are particularly good (with semi-precious black coral in deeper waters). Barracuda, grouper, jack and garfish are regularly seen in deeper waters. Facilities include an information centre and bathroom

Diving seasons in Malaysia

West coast, Peninsular Malaysia	November-May
East coast, Peninsular Malaysia	March-October
East Malaysia (Sabah & Sarawak)	March-September*

** **NB** Diving conditions at Pulau Sipadan are generally good year-round.*

facilities. Camping is allowed (if the authorities are informed beforehand; see Paya, Langkawi for further information), but there is no accommodation available; the nearest hotels are on Langkawi to the north, or Penang to the south. Further expansion is planned however.

Other west coast dive sites: less well-known and developed dive sites off the west coast of the Peninsula include Pulau Sembilan, Pulau Pangkor and Pulau Pangkor Laut, situated not far from the town of Lumut, see page 142.

East Coast The waters around **Pulau Tioman** have been devastated in recent years through over-fishing and the uncontrolled activities of tourists. However, it is a convenient base to visit islands in the area including Pulau Tulai, Labas, Chebeh and Sepoi (see page 240). **Pulau Sibu Archipelago** is a group of islands off Mersing in Johore province and includes Pulau Rawa (see page 252), Babi Hujung, Babi Tengah, Babi Besar, Tinggi, Mentinggi and Sibu (see page 252). They are all included within a single marine park and with the exception of Babi Hujung and Mentinggi, offer basic accommodation. **Pulau Tenggol** is the largest of a small group of islands, still relatively undeveloped and unspoilt. The range and number of fish here is impressive. Particularly noteworthy are the spectacular sunken cliffs. There is no accommodation available (see page 290). Like Pulau Perhentian, **Pulau Kapas** is an area suited to snorkelling and shallow dives (3-10m). The beaches are good and there is accommodation available (see page 281).

The dive sites around the protected **Pulau Redang** island group, consisting of nine islands 45 km off the Terengganu coast, are numerous and varied and are considered some of the best in Malaysia. There are an estimated 500 species of coral, 1,000 species of bivalves and some 3,000 species of fish, and the star of the show is a resident whale shark. There are also large schools of red snapper and other fish. The beaches of the islands that constitute the Pulau Redang Marine Park are nesting sites for the hawksbill and rarer green turtles. A fishing village on stilts occupies one end of the island, but there is no dedicated tourist accommodation (see page 291 and box on page 280).

Shallow water snorkelling is excellent around **Pulau Perhentian**, and in July and August dolphins and pilot whales migrate through the waters fringing the island. Accommodation in 'A'-frame huts available (see page 291).

Distant islands: Pulau Aur and **Pulau Pemanggil** are situated 15 km apart about 65 km off the east coast of the Peninsula to the south of Tioman. Their remoteness has meant that they are the least disturbed diving locations in the area (see page 252).

East Malaysia The most memorable feature around **Pulau Layang-Layang** is a 2,000m sea wall; the oceanic position means that sharks and pelagic fish are common (see page 415). **Tunku Abdul Rahman Park** includes five pristine islands Gaya, Sapi, Manukan, Mamutik and Sulug. The beaches are excellent and the coral and marine life good. They are also the most easily accessible dive spots of quality from Kota Kinabalu, lying about 20 mins by boat from the state capital. Accommodation is available on two of the islands, Mamutik and Manukan. **Pulau Mantanani** is a group of islands off Sabah's west coast of which Pulau Mantanani is the largest. Sharks and large pelagic fishes abound and the area is also a renowned fishing location. **Pulau Mengalum** is 70 km west of Kota Kinabalu and fish include marlin and sail fish along with the more usual grouper, wrasse and snapper. **Pulau Tiga** dive spot comprises three islands that lie within the boundaries of a 15,864 hectare park gazetted in 1978, 50 km southwest of Kota Kinabalu. Marine life includes turtles, tuna, dolphin and stingrays. The islands themselves support populations of monkeys and monitor lizards, as well as a mud volcano (see page 434). The park is primarily a research area for naturalists and so tourist facilities are intentionally kept to a minimum. Camping is allowed, but visitors need to bring their own food. **Turtle Islands National Park** was created in 1977 and encompasses three islands: Pulau Selingaan, Gulisan and Bakkungan Kecil. As the popular name of the park suggests, it was gazetted to protect the rare green and hawksbill turtles. The peak period for egg laying is August to October for the green turtle and February to April for the hawksbill. Pulau Selingaan is the only island with accommodation (see page 458). The duty free island of **Labuan** is a good base for visiting surrounding islands and dive spots. Because Labuan was a focus of military activity during the Second World War, there are a number of wrecks here including Japanese and US warships (the latter probably the US *Salute*). **Sipadan** is probably the best-known dive site in east Malaysia because of its stunning 700m sea wall. Because Sipadan is an oceanic island, fish such as manta rays and large schools of barracuda are commonly seen here while they are rare elsewhere (see page 468).

Other popular activities include rafting, which is becoming increasingly popular, especially in East Malaysia, and cultural tours. Again, East Malaysia offers the greatest possibilities; trips to explore longhouses in upriver settlements are your best bet.

Finding out more
A good source of information is the internet; for websites on Malaysia and Southeast Asia, see page 67. For a list of tourist boards overseas, see box on page 22; see also box on embassies and consulates, page 25.

Before you travel

Getting in

Visas
Passports should be valid for 6 months beyond the period of intended stay

No visa is required for a stay of three months if not working for citizens from Commonwealth countries (except India, Bangladesh, Sri Lanka and Pakistan), Albania, Algeria, Austria, Bahrain, Belgium, Britain, Czech Republic, Denmark, Egypt, Finland, Germany, Hungary, Germany, Iceland, Republic of Ireland, Italy, Japan, Jordan, South Korea, Kuwait, Lebanon, Liechtenstein, Luxembourg, the Netherlands, Norway, Morocco, Oman, Qatar, San Marino, Saudi Arabia, Republic of Slovakia, Sweden, Switzerland, Tunisia, Turkey, United Arab Emirates, USA and North Yemen.

Citizens of France, Greece, Poland and South Africa, as well most African and Latin American countries, are permitted to stay for one month without a visa.

On arrival visitors normally receive a one or two month visitor's permit (Commonwealth citizens get two months). Usually those arriving by air get two months; overland, one month. If you intend to stay longer, permits can be painlessly extended to three months at immigration departments in Kuala Lumpur, Penang or Johor Bahru.

Citizens of ASEAN countries (Brunei, Indonesia, Laos, Myanmar/Burma, Philippines, Singapore, Thailand, Vietnam), do not need visas for visits not exceeding a month – they are issued on arrival. Nationals of most other countries including Afghanistan, Iran, Iraq, Libya, Syria and South Yemen may stop over in Malaysia for up to 14 days without advance visas but it is preferable to have proof of outward bookings. Citizens of Bulgaria, Rumania and Russia may stay for seven days without a visa. Applications for visas should be made well in advance to the nearest Malaysian diplomatic mission, or, in countries where there are no Malaysian representatives, to the British Consular Representative.

Malaysian embassies and consulates

Australia, High Commission, 7 Perth Ave,
Yarralumla, Canberra, ACT 2600,
T06-2731543

Austria, Prinz Eugenstrasse 18, A-1040
Vienna, T5051042

Bangladesh, High Commission, No Four
Rd No 118, Gulshan Model Town,
Dhaka-12, T600291

Belgium, 414A, Ave de Tervuren, 1150
Brussels, T7626767

Brunei, High Commission, No 473 Kg
Pelambayan, Jln Kota Batu, PO Box 2826,
Bandar Seri Begawan, T228410

Canada, High Commission, 60 Boteler St,
Ottawa, Ontario KIN 8Y7, T613-2375182

China, 13, Dong Zhi Menwai Dajie, San Li
Tun, Beijing, T5322531

CIS, Mosfilmovskaya Ulitsa 50, Moscow,
T1471514

France, 2 Bis Rue Benouville, Paris,
T45531185

Germany, Mittelstrasse 43, 5300 Bonn 2,
T0228-376803

Hong Kong, 24th Flr, Malaysia Bldg, 50
Gloucester Rd, Wanchai, T5270921

India, High Commission, 50-M, Satya
Marg, Chanakyapuri, New Delhi, 110021,
T601291; No 287, TTK Rd, Madras –
600018, T453580

Indonesia, 17, Jln Imam Bonjol, 10310
Jakarta Pusat, Tÿ336438; Consulate:
Medan, T511233

Italy, Via Nomentana 297, Rome,
T8415764

Japan, 20-16, Nanpeidai-Machi,
Shibuya-ku, Tokyo 150, T34763840

Laos, Route That Luang, Quartier Nong
Bone, PO Box 789, Vientiane, T2662

Myanmar (Burma), 82, Diplomatic
Quarters, Pyidaundsu Yeikhta Rd, Yangon
(Rangoon), T20248

Netherlands, Runtenburweg 2, 2517 KE
The Hague, T070-3506506

New Zealand, High Commission, 10
Washington Ave, Brooklyn, Wellington,
T852439

Pakistan, No 224, Nazimuddin Rd, F-7/4,
Islamabad, T210147

Singapore, 301, Jervois Rd, Singapore
1024, T2350111

Spain, Paseo de La Castellano 91-50,
Centro 23, 28046 Madrid, T341-5550684

Sri Lanka, High Commission, 47/1
Jawatta Rd, Colombo 7, T94-1508973

Sweden, Engelbrektsgatan 5, PO Box
26053, 100 41 Stockholm, T08-6795990

Switzerland, Laupenstrasse 37, 3008
Berne, T252105

Thailand, 35, South Sathorn Rd, Bangkok
10120, T2861390; Consulate: Songkhla,
T311062

UK, High Commission, 45, Belgrave Square,
London SW1X 8QT, T020-72358033

USA, 2401, Massachusetts Ave NW,
Washington, DC 200008, T202-3282700;
Consulates: New York, T212-4902722; Los
Angeles, T212-6212991

Vietnam, Block A-3, Van Phuc, Hanoi, T53371.

Essentials

Visitors arriving by air and who are staying less than 72 hours in the country are eligible for visa-free entry.

Visit passes issued for entry into Peninsular Malaysia are not automatically valid for entry into the East Malaysian states of Sabah and Sarawak. On entry into East Malaysia from Peninsular Malaysia visitors have to go through immigration even though the flight is an internal one. You get a new stamp in your passport and it may actually reduce the time you can stay in Malaysia. A month's stamp is usual – if you want more, then you must ask the official. (The reason for this odd state of affairs is that Sabah and Sarawak maintain control over immigration and even Malaysian visitors from the 'mainland' are required to obtain a travel permit to come here.) Apply to the immigration offices in Kota Kinabalu and Kuching for an extension. There are certain areas where permits are necessary in East Malaysia, eg for upriver trips in Sarawak permits are obtained from the residents' offices (see appropriate sections). All national parks in Peninsular and East Malaysia require permits from the national or state parks offices.

ISIC　Anyone in full-time education is entitled to an International Student Identity Card (ISIC). These are issued by student travel offices and travel agencies across the world and offer special rates on all forms of transport and other concessions and services. The ISIC head office is: ISIC Association, Box 9048, 1000 Copenhagen, Denmark, T45-33939303.

Customs　**Duty-free allowance**　200 cigarettes, 50 cigars or 250g of tobacco and one litre of liquor or wine. Cameras, watches, pens, lighters, cosmetics, perfumes, portable radio/cassette players are also duty-free in Malaysia. Visitors bringing in dutiable goods such as video equipment may have to pay a refundable deposit for temporary importation. It is advisable to carry receipt of purchases to avoid this problem.

Export restrictions　Export permits are required for arms, ammunition, explosives, animals and plants, gold, platinum, precious stones and jewellery (except reasonable personal effects), poisons, drugs, motor vehicles. Unlike Singapore, export permits are also required for antiques (from the Director General of Museums, Muzium Negara, Kuala Lumpur).

Vaccinations　A certificate of vaccination for yellow fever is necessary for those coming from
See also page 55　endemic zones except for children under one year of age.

What to take　Travellers usually take too much. Almost everything is available in the main towns and cities – and often at a lower price than in the West. Remoter areas are inevitably less well supplied.

Suitcases are not appropriate if you are intending to travel overland by bus. A backpack, or even better a travelpack (where the straps can be zipped out of sight), is recommended. Travelpacks have the advantage of being hybrid backpacks-suitcases; they can be carried on the back for easy porterage, but they can also be taken into hotels without the owner being labelled a 'hippy'. **NB** For serious hikers, a backpack with an internal frame is still by far the best option for longer treks.

In terms of clothing, dress in Southeast Asia is relatively casual – even at formal functions. Suits are not necessary except in a few of the most expensive restaurants. However, although formal attire may be the exception, dressing tidily is the norm. Women particularly should note that in many areas of Malaysia and Brunei, they should avoid offending Muslim sensibilities and dress 'demurely' (ie keep shoulders covered and wear below-knee skirts or trousers). This is particularly true on the east coast of the Peninsula, especially in Kelantan, but does not generally apply in most beach resorts.

There is a tendency, rather than to take inappropriate articles of clothing, to take too many of the same article. Laundry services are cheap, and the turn-around rapid.

Checklist　Bumbag, earplugs, first aid kit, insect repellent and/or electric mosquito mats, coils, international driving licence, passports (valid for at least 6 months), photocopies of essential documents, short-wave radio, spare passport photographs, sun protection, sunglasses, Swiss Army knife, torch, umbrella, wet wipes, zip-lock bags.

Those intending to stay in budget accommodation might also include: cotton sheet sleeping bag, money belt, padlock (for hotel room and pack), soap, student card, toilet paper, towel, travel wash.

For women travellers: a supply of tampons (although these are available in most towns), a wedding ring for single female travellers who might want to help ward off the attentions of amorous admirers.

Unlike Indonesia and Thailand, camping grounds do exist pretty widely in Malaysia, both in Peninsular Malaysia and in Sabah and Sarawak. If intending to camp, then all the usual equipment is necessary: a tent, stove, cooking utensils, sleeping bag etc.

Exchange rates (March 2000)

	US$1	£1	DM1
Malaysia (ringgit)	3.80	6.00	1.87
Singapore (dollar)	1.71	2.70	0.84
Brunei (dollar)	1.71	2.70	0.84

For the very latest exchange rates, try www.oanda.com/converter/classic

Also useful are: pollution mask if travelling to large cities, a basic tool kit including a puncture repair kit, spare tubes, spare tyre, pump, a good map of the area, bungee cords, a water filter.

Money

Currency
See also box above

The Malaysian dollar (RM), is called the **ringgit**, and is divided into 100 **sen** (cents). Bank notes come in denominations of RM1, 5, 10, 20, 50, 100, 500 and 1,000. Coins are issued in 1, 5, 10, 20 and 50 cent denominations. As a rough guideline, US$1= RM3.80 (March 2000). Note that the ringgit is pegged to the US dollar, which was Prime Minister Mahathir's response to the Asian economic crisis (see Background, page 508). In early 2000, most economists believed that the currency was undervalued and that its true value was somewhere between US$3.20 and US$3.30. But it seems that, for the time being at least, the government will try to keep the US$3.80 peg, although later in 2000 the ringgit may be allowed to appreciate.

Currency regulations have been in a state of flux, not that they have had an impact on most visitors though. The government introduced currency controls in 1998 as a means to stabilize the economy and prevent currency speculation. For non-residents the last of these controls was lifted in October 1999.

Credit cards

Most of the bigger hotels, restaurants and shops accept international credit cards, including American Express, BankAmericard, Diners, MasterCard and Visa. Visa and MasterCard are the most widely accepted. Cash advances can be issued against credit cards in most banks, although some banks – notably Bank Bumiputra – limit the amount that can be drawn. A passport is usually required for over-the-counter transactions. It is also possible to draw cash from ATMs (Automatic Teller Machines) if you have a PIN number (Personal Identification Number). Maybank, with branches in most towns, will accept both Visa and MasterCard at its ATMs.

Travellers' cheques

These can be exchanged at banks and money changers and in some big hotels (often guests only). Money changers often offer the best rates, but it is worth shopping around. Banks charge commission on travellers' cheques. Those from all major issuing companies and denominated in just about any major currency are widely accepted. But, as elsewhere, US dollars are probably best.

Cost of living

Prices have been relatively stable and because the ringgit has been held down at a lower-than-market exchange rate, Malaysia is cheaper for overseas visitors than a few years ago. Inflation in 1999 was just 2.8% and because consumption in 1998 and 1999 was weak because of the economic crisis businesses, including hotels, have struggled to maintain their rates rather than pushing them up.

Having said all that, Malaysia was no longer a cheap place to live even before the 1998 recession and people wanting to stay in accommodation other than that pitched at the pocket of the budget traveller will find the country more expensive than neighbouring Thailand and (especially) Indonesia.

But all is not lost. It is still possible to travel on a relatively low budget. Cheaper guesthouses charge around RM15-50 a night for two – which at the early 2000 rate of exchange translates into a US dollar figure of about US$4-13. Dorm beds are available in many towns, and these are priced at around RM10-15, or US$2.50-4. It is usually possible to find a simple a/c room for RM50-80 or US$13-21. Eating out is also comparatively cheap: a good curry can be had for as little as RM2-4, or around US$1. Finally, overland travel is a bargain. Although private car ownership is rapidly spreading, many ordinary Malaysians still travel by bus and consequently the bus network is not only extremely good, but fares are very good value.

Getting there

Air

See also box below for air connections with Kuala Lumpur

KL's new international airport is open at Sepang 72 km from the city, see page 112. Some international flights also go direct to Penang, Kota Kinabalu and Kuching. Smaller airlines also run services between Singapore and island resorts such as Langkawi and Tioman. More than 25 international carriers serve Kuala Lumpur.

Non-Malaysian passport holders are eligible for the **Discover Malaysia Pass**, if they fly into the country on Malaysian Airlines (MAS). It offers significant savings on domestic air travel. The pass is valid for any five sectors within the peninsula, or within Sabah or Sarawak as well as the peninsula. It must be purchased outside Malaysia. Not surprisingly, the pass makes most sense when travelling on longer sectors. **NB** Flights between Singapore and Malaysia cost the same dollar figure whether bought in Malaysia or Singapore; it saves money buying a return ticket in Malaysia. There are flights from KL to most Asian destinations.

From Europe Approximate time from London to KL (non-stop): 12½ hours. From London Heathrow British Airways and Malaysia Airlines (in a joint service with Virgin) are two carriers. From Amsterdam: Malaysia Airlines and KLM. From Frankfurt: Malaysia Airlines, Lufthansa and China Airlines. You can fly from Zurich with Malaysia Airlines, Royal Brunei and China Airlines. From Paris: Malaysia Airline. From other cities a change of plane is often necessary *en route*.

From the USA & Canada Approximate time from LAX (Los Angeles): 20 hours. Malaysia Airlines fly from LA via Tokyo and Canada.

From Australasia You can fly direct from Sydney, Melbourne, Brisbane, Darwin, Cairns and Perth (flight times range between five and nine hours), with Qantas, British Airways, Malaysia Airlines and many others. From Auckland, Malaysia Airlines.

From South & Southeast Asia From Delhi, Malaysia Airlines and Air India. From Colombo, Air Lanka. From Dhaka with Biman Bangladesh Airlines and from Karachi (PIA and Malaysia Airlines). Flights via other cities available from Male and Kathmandu. There are flights to KL from all regional capitals in Southeast Asia.

From the Far East There are many flights from Hong Kong, Manila and Tokyo.

....

Connections by air in the region with Kuala Lumpur

To	Connections/Week
Bangkok	numerous
Rangoon	2
Hanoi	2
Saigon	daily
Manila	twice daily
Phnom Penh	3
Singapore	numerous
Jakarta	numerous
Bali	numerous

....

Train

Keretapi Tanah Melayu (KTM) run express trains daily between Singapore and the
major cities on the west coast of Malaysia. There is a daily express train between
Bangkok and Butterworth, which connects with Kuala Lumpur; KL-Singapore.
Bangkok to Singapore via Malaysia. Another railway line runs from Gemas (halfway
between KL and Johor Bahru) to Kota Bharu, on the northeast coast.

*For details on fares &
schedule see tables
pages 646-647 & map
on page 36*

The most luxurious way to journey by train to Malaysia is aboard the *Eastern &
Oriental (E&O) Express*. The a/c train of 22 carriages including a salon car, dining car, bar
and observation deck and carrying just 132 passengers runs once a week from
Singapore to Bangkok and back. Luxurious carriages, fine wines and food designed for
European rather than Asian sensibilities make this not just a mode of transport but an
experience. The journey takes 43 hours with stops in Kuala Lumpur, Butterworth and
Padang Besar. But such luxury is expensive. For information call Bangkok T2514862;
London T020-79286000; USA T800- 5242420; and Singapore T065-2272068.

Road

It is possible to travel to and from Malaysia by bus or share taxi from Thailand and
Singapore. Direct buses and taxis are much easier than the local alternatives which
stop at the borders. Singapore is six hours by taxi from KL (via Johor Bahru) and about
seven hours by bus (see page 112). Taxi fares are approximately double bus fares.

There are direct buses and taxis to destinations in Thailand from most major towns in
northern Malaysia (see relevant sections) and six border crossing points. For those using
the north-south highway – which is most people – the crossing point is at Bukit Kayu
Hitam, which links up with the Thai city of Hat Yai. On the western side of the Peninsula
there are also crossings at Wang Kelian and Padang Besar. The Wang Kelian crossing (to
Satun in Thailand) is convenient if driving oneself; it is quiet and usually pretty rapid. The
Padang Besar is an easy crossing on foot and makes sense if travelling to or from Pulau
Langkawi. In Perak the crossing is at Pengkalan Hulu, and in Kelantan, on the eastern side
of the Peninsula there are two more crossing points, the more important at Pengkalan
Kubar, and the second from Kota Bahru to Rantau Panjang/Sungai Golok (see page 295).
The more popular of this is the Rantau Panjang crossing; few people cross at Pengkalan
Kubar. Local buses and taxis terminate at the border crossing points, but there are
regular connections to towns and cities from each side.

It is also possible to cross overland from the East Malaysian states of Sarawak and
Sabah to Kalimantan (Indonesian Borneo) and Brunei. The main crossing point is in
the west, between Kuching in Sarawak and Pontianak in Kalimantan and regular
buses run between these two towns.

Boat

Most passenger ships and cruise liners run between Port Klang, west of Kuala Lumpur,
Georgetown (Penang), Singapore, Kuantan, Kuching and Kota Kinabalu. Feri Malaysia
connects these Malaysian ports and Singapore. Deluxe cabins are also available.
Schedules change annually; contact *Tourism Malaysia* for bookings, see page 30.

There are also regular ferry services from Melaka to Dumai in Sumatra and from
Georgetown (Penang) to Medan, also in Sumatra (see relevant sections). Passenger
boats connect Langkawi Island with Satun in South Thailand (see page 178).
High-speed catamarans connect Singapore with Pulau Tioman (off the east coast of
Peninsular Malaysia), 4½ hours. Small boats also run between Johor state and
Singapore's Changi Point. In East Malaysia, there are connections between Tawau and
Tarakan via Nunukan (see page 473).

Essentials

Touching down

Essentials

Emergencies *Ambulance, police or fire, T999.*

Business hours *Banks: 0930-1500 Mon-Fri and 0930-1130 Sat. **NB** For Kedah, Perlis, Kelantan and Terengganu banks are open 0930-1130 on Thur and closed on Fri.*
Government offices: *0800-1245, 1400-1615 Mon-Thur, 0800-1200, 1430-1615 Fri, 0800-1245 Sat. In the states of Kedah and Terengganu, 0800-1615 Sat-Wed, 0800-1245 Thur, closed Fri. In Kelantan 0800-1645 Sun-Wednesday, 0800-1245 Thursday, closed Fri and Sat.*
Shops: *0930-1900, supermarkets and department stores 1000-2200.*
  In the former Federated States, which were under the British (Selangor, Melaka,

Penang, Perak, Pahang and Negri Sembilan), there is a half day holiday on Sat and full day holiday on Sun. The former Unfederated States of Kelantan and Terengganu retain the traditional half day holiday on Thur and full day holiday on Fri. Sat and Sun are treated as weekdays. In the other former Un-federated States – Johor, Kedah and Perlis – the half day on Thur is often observed, but most businesses now observe the Sat/Sun weekend.
Official time *Eight hours ahead of GMT.*
Voltage *220-240 volts, 50 cycle AC. Some hotels supply adaptors.*
Weights and measures *Metric, although road distances are marked in both kilometres and miles.*

Touching down

Airport information
The new KL International Airport (KLIA) is at Sepang, 72 km from the city. Glitzy and high tech, reflecting Malaysia's 2020 vision, it has lots of restaurants, shops, banks and such like. A helpful *Tourism Malaysia* desk dishes out lots of pamphlets on KL and beyond. The old airport at Subang (confusingly similar to Sepang), 24 km southwest of KL, is still used for some domestic departures such as AirAsia. For details of other international airports, such as Penang, Kota Kinabalu and Kuching, see relevant sections.

Airport tax
Airport departure tax is RM5 for domestic flights, and RM40 for all other countries.

Tourist information
Tourism Malaysia (headquarters), 24-27 Flr, Menara Dato' Onn, Putra World Trade Centre, 45, Jln Tun Ismail, 50480 Kuala Lumpur T03-2935188, F03-2935884. There is an information centre on Level two of the Putra World Trade Centre (in the convention centre). For practical advice, visitors are better advised to contact Malaysian Tourist Information Centre (MATIC), 109 Jln Ampang, Kuala Lumpur T2423929. There are several other tourist information bureaux in KL (see page 114) and regional tourism offices in state capitals, all of which are reasonably efficient.
  Tourism Malaysia has a tourist information bureau in most large towns; it is very efficient and can supply further details on tourist sights, advise on itineraries, help place bookings for travel and cultural events and provide updated information on hotels, restaurants and air, road, rail, sea and river transport timetables and prices. If there is no Tourism Malaysia office in a town, travel agents are usually helpful.

Rules, customs & etiquette
Clothing Malaysians dress for the heat. Clothes are light, cool and casual most of the time, but also fairly smart. Some establishments, mainly exclusive restaurants, require a long-sleeved shirt with tie or local batik shirt and do not allow shorts in the evening. Those visiting the Cameron Highlands or other upland areas are advised to bring a light sweater. For jungle treks, a waterproof is advisable, as are canvas jungle boots, which dry faster than leather. Although many Malaysian business people have adopted the Western jacket and tie for formal occasions, the batik shirt, or *baju*, is the traditional formal wear for men, while women wear the graceful *sarung kebaya*.

Malaysian manners – as learned from a princess

In modern, cosmopolitan Malaysia, traditional customs and cultural conventions are alive and well and rigorously adhered to. In Malaysia's multi-ethnic melting pot, Malays, Chinese, Indians, Eurasians and expatriates have discovered that cross-cultural etiquette and the art of obliging another's sense of decorum is the essence of racial harmony. The trouble is that for many visitors, committing a Malaysian-style faux pas is one of life's inevitabilities. Or it was, until Datin Noor Aini Syed Amir published her practical handbook to Malaysian customs and etiquette in 1991. As a Malay princess, Datin Noor – Malaysia's Miss Manners – should know. "While the Malays are very generous and forgiving with foreigners who make Malay faux pas, those who do not make such blunders will be highly admired and respected," the Datin says.

Her catch-all advice to visitors is to utter "a profuse apology in advance to the person you may offend". For those who forget to absolve themselves before they slip up, her social observations cover every conceivable situation mat sallehs – the local nickname for foreigners – might find themselves in. When eating with chopsticks, warns Datin Noor, avoid crossing them and never stick them vertically into your ricebowl so they resemble joss sticks. Do not be offended by enthusiastic belches and slurps around the dinner table either: Malaysians live to eat and like to share their appreciation.

Visitors must also learn to distinguish between flabby handshakes and Malay salams. "Unlike the Western handshake, which is a rather vigorous up and down movement… the Malay handshake is a simple palm-to-palm touch", she writes. The most important part of the gesture is immediately touching your hand to your heart as a signal of sincerity. And, she adds, "never use your left hand in Malay company!" Datin Noor goes on to warn newcomers not to touch people's heads, when to take their shoes off and to think before they kiss a lady's cheek – in greeting. Dazzling, long-sleeved batik shirts are what you wear to formal dinners and black is taboo for happy occasions. She explains what Tunkus, Tuns, Datuks, Dato's and Datins are and notes that the King's title 'Yang Di-Pertuan Agong' means 'He Who is Made Supreme Lord'.

Malaysian Customs & Etiquette: A Practical Handbook by Datin Noor Aini Syed Amir. Times Books International, 1991.

Conduct Dress: Malaysians dress smartly, particularly in cities; tourists in vests, shorts and flip-flops look out of place in modern cosmopolitan KL. Dress codes are important to observe from the point of view of Islamic sensitivities, particularly on the peninsula's east coast. In some places such as Marang, bikinis are banned and wearing them will cause great offence. Topless bathing is completely taboo in Malaysia; this should be remembered even where tourists have started doing it, such as on Pulau Tioman. Dress modestly out of respect for Muslim tradition.

Malaysia's cross-cultural differences are most apparent on the streets: many Chinese girls think nothing of wearing brief mini-skirts and shorts, while their Malay counterparts are clad from head to toe. The tudung (or telukung) veil signifies adherence to the puritanical lifestyle of the fervently Islamic dakwah movement; during the 1980s, this almost became a fashion among women at universities as well as among blue-collar workers in factories. Some women began to dress in the full black purdah until it was forbidden by the government. Much of this was the result of peer pressure and reflected a revival of strict Islamic values in Malaysia during and after the 1970s.

Eating When picking up and passing food, do not use the left hand in Muslim company. It is worth remembering that Malays do not make pork satay and that Hindus do not make beef curries.

Essentials

Drugs trafficking – stiff punishment

Malaysia is well known around the world for its stringent laws against drugs. As they fill in their immigration forms, visitors cannot fail to notice the bold block capitals reading: "BE FOREWARNED – DEATH FOR DRUG TRAFFICKERS UNDER MALAYSIAN LAW". At entry points to Malaysia there are prominent posters repeating this warning, the words emblazoned over an ominous picture of a noose. World attention focuses on Malaysia whenever Westerners go to the gallows, but they represent a tiny fraction of those hanged for drug trafficking offences. Since 1983 about 150 prisoners have been hanged and about 4,000 arrested under Section 39(B) of the Dangerous Drugs Act; about a quarter of those face execution within the next few years. Malaysia's biggest-ever mass-hanging of traffickers took place at Taiping jail in May 1990 when eight Hong Kong people were executed.

The Dadah Act - dadah is the Malay word for drugs – stipulates a mandatory death sentence upon conviction for anyone in possession of 15 or more grams of heroin or morphine, 200g of cannabis or hashish or 40g of cocaine. Those caught with more than 10g of heroin or 100g of cannabis are deemed to be traffickers and face lengthy jail sentences and flogging with a rotan cane. Following the execution of two Australians in 1986, the then Australian Prime Minister, Bob Hawke, branded the Malaysian government 'barbaric'. A similar outcry resulted from the hanging of a Briton in 1987; the British opposition even called for a trade embargo of Malaysia. But Malaysian Prime Minister Dr Mahathir Mohamad, who is a medical doctor and as such has taken the Hippocratic Oath, has consistently refused to bow to international pleas for clemency. In a British television documentary in 1991, The Prime Minister, the junkie and the boys on death row, he said: "We have to carry out this death penalty because it would not be fair to those who had already been hanged and their families."

Pointing Using the index finger to point at people, even at objects, is regarded as insulting. Use the thumb or whole hand to indicate something, or to wave down a taxi.

General Everywhere in Southeast Asia, 'losing face' brings shame. You lose face if you lose your temper, and even in a situation like bargaining, using a loud voice or wild gesticulations will be taken to signify anger. By the same token, the person you shout at will also feel loss of face too, particularly if it happens in public. It should also be noted that in Muslim company it is impolite to touch others with the left hand and other objects – even loose change. Although men shake hands, for a man to shake a woman's hand is not the norm outside KL. Indeed excessive personal contact should be avoided: Malays, especially, do not tend to slap one another on the back!

Private homes Remove shoes before entering a private home; it is usual to bring a small gift for the host.

Religion Remove shoes before entering mosques and Hindu and Buddhist temples; in mosques, women should cover their heads, shoulders and legs and men should wear long trousers.

Tipping Tipping is unusual in Malaysia as a service of 10% is added automatically to restaurant and hotel bills, plus a 5% government tax. Nor is tipping expected in smaller restaurants where a service charge is not automatically added to the bill. For personal services, porterage for example, a modest tip may be appropriate.

Hotel prices and facilities

L RM500+ **Luxury**: hotels in this bracket are few and far between. KL's splendid Carcosa Seri Negara is one such hotel. The Datai on Langkawi is another and the Pangkor Laut Resort on the private island of Pangkor Laut is also in the top league. Most **AL** grade hotels have luxury presidential suites.

AL RM260-499 **International class**: impeccable service, beautifully appointed, offering a wide array of facilities and business services. Malaysia's AL grade hotels, most of which are grouped towards the bottom end of the price category, are regarded as among the best value in the region.

A RM130-259 **First class**: good range of services and facilities. Very competitively priced, given standards of service.

B RM65-129 **Tourist class**: hotels in this category will have swimming pools; most provide just a basic range of services and facilities although all will have a/c.

C RM40-64 **Economy**: while there are some excellent economy hotels in this category, few provide much in the way of services. Guests will usually have the option of a/c or fan-cooled rooms and a choice of attached/shared bathrooms. Government rest houses (rumah rehat) offer the best value for money in this grade.

D RM20-39 **Budget**: most hotels in this class are Chinese-run and located in town centres. They are therefore often noisy and not just because of the traffic; they also seem to be busy much later into the night because of the arrival and departure of the long distance drivers who use them. At the upper end, rooms have a/c and attached bathrooms; cheaper rooms have fans and communal bathrooms (with mandi). Some fine old tumbledown colonial relics in this range offer good value for money. Youth hostels also fall into this price range.

E RM10-19 Lodging house/guesthouse/hostel: rooms are rarely a/c; shared mandi with squat toilet; few facilities. Lodging houses (rumah tumpangan) sometimes double as brothels. Tourist-orientated guesthouses usually offer more value and a better atmosphere; there are a few exceptionally good places in this category.

F under RM10: there is little accommodation in this category in Malaysia, although many guesthouses and hostels in the **D** and **E** categories provide the option of bottom-dollar, cramped dormitory accommodation. In some beach resort areas it is sometimes possible to find simple 'A'-frame accommodation in this range.

Safety

Normal precautions should be taken with passports and valuables such as cameras; many hotels have safes. Pickpocketing is a problem in some cities. Women – if not accompanied by men – usually attract unwarranted attention, particularly in more Islamic areas, such as the east coast. Mostly this is bravado, however, and there have been no serious incidents involving foreign tourists.

The trafficking of illegal drugs into Malaysia carries the death penalty (see box, page 32).

Where to stay

Malaysia offers a good selection of international class hotels as well as simpler hotels, rest houses and hostels. Room rates are subject to 5-10% tax. Many of the major international chains have hotels in Malaysia, such as Hilton, Regent, Holiday Inn and Hyatt plus local and regional chains such as Merlin, Ming Court and Shangri-La; most of these are on the west coast. Room rates in the big hotels, particularly in KL, rose steeply during the early and mid-1990s but have been stable for the last few years. The

For our quick reference price guide to hotels, see the inside front cover of the book

number of four and five star hotel rooms has doubled over the last four years or so and this has helped to keep prices stable. By world standards, even the most expensive hotels are good value for money. It is also possible to rent condominiums in some cities, mainly KL and Georgetown.

There are youth hostels in KL, Georgetown (Penang), Port Dickson, Fraser's Hill, Cameron Highlands, Kuantan, Kota Bahru, Kota Kinabalu and Pulau Pangkor. There are also scores of government rest houses (*rumah rehat*) around the country; these often offer well-maintained, reasonably priced rooms, although they can become heavily booked, particularly during public holidays. On the east coast of Peninsular Malaysia and in East Malaysia, it is often possible to stay with families in Malay *kampungs* (villages), the so-called Homestay programme (contact local tourist office or travel agent for more information). The most popular place to do this is at Kampung Cerating, north of Kuantan, although it has become increasingly touristy in recent years; it is also possible to stay in a kampung house in Merang. Along many of Malaysia's beaches and on islands, there are simple atap-roofed 'A'-frame bungalows.

Accommodation in East Malaysia does not offer such value for money as hotels on the peninsula, although, again, there are some bargains. As on the peninsula, there are government rest houses in many of the main towns. For accommodation in national parks, see relevant sections: it is necessary to book in advance. In Sarawak it is possible to stay in longhouses, where rates are at the discretion of the visitor (see page 339).

NB In the more popular holiday destinations like the Cameron Highlands, accommodation can become scarce during the school holidays – April, August and December. During these months it is worth booking ahead.

Camping   There are not many sites in Malaysia, but 'wild camping' is easy. In Sabah camping is a much cheaper option and you get to stay exactly where you want to be, for example at Tunkul Abdul Rahman Marine Park, Danum Valley, and the islands around Semporna.

Getting around

Transport around the East Malaysian states of Sabah and Sarawak is not as easy as it is on the peninsula since there are fewer roads and they are not in a good state of repair. There are excellent coastal and upriver express boat services in Sarawak and the national airline, MAS, has an extensive network in both states; flying is relatively inexpensive.

MAS domestic network

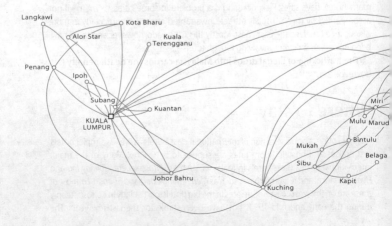

Pelangi Airways network

Air

Malaysia Airlines (MAS) operates an extensive network to domestic destinations: KL, Ipoh, Penang, Alor Star, Langkawi, Kota Bharu, Kuala Terengganu, Kuantan, Johor Bahru, Kota Kinabalu, Sandakan, Lahad Datu, Labuan, Kuching, Sibu, Bintulu, Tawau, and Miri (plus many more internal flights in Sabah and Sarawak) and flights to Singapore. Local MAS offices are listed under each town; the head office is at Bangunan MAS (opposite *Equatorial Hotel*), Jln Sultan Ismail, 50250, Kuala Lumpur. For fares, see table. Domestic flights from KL leave either from its new international airport, KLIA, 72 km from the city, or Subang, 24 km from the city, so check your ticket. **NB** Flights get very booked up on public holidays.

For a map showing MAS domestic routes, see page 34
For details of the MAS air pass, see page 28

Pelangi Air, a solely domestic airline, operates services to certain resorts and smaller towns. It flies to/from: Kuala Lumpur, Ipoh, Penang, Alor Setar, Melaka, Kerteh, Kuantan, Tioman Island, Johor Bahru, Kota Bharu, and Kuala Terengganu. There are reductions for night flights, group and advance bookings.

A start-up airline is Airasia which still has a relatively limited network (check their website – www.airasia.com/airlines/ ttable.html) offering services between KL's Subang airport and Kuching, Langkawi, Kota Kinabalu and and Labuan.

Train

In August 1992 the Peninsular Malaysian Railway System or Keretapi Tanah Melayu (KTM) was privatized and became the Keretapi Tanah Melayu Berhad or KTMB. Their corporate mission statement declared: "We strive to provide excellent rail and related transport services in Malaysia, utilizing our resources to optimize financial performance whilst meeting stakeholder expectations."

See also map & tables on pages 36 & 647 respectively

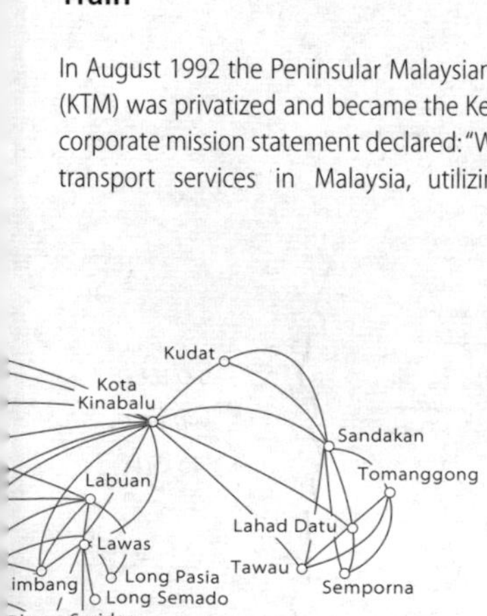

Notwithstanding the tendency to hyperbole in any mission statement, the KTMB is an economical and comfortable way to travel round the peninsula. Privatization has pumped much needed investment into the system which, in 1981, the *New Straits Times* was predicting would "collapse into one mass heap of worthless metal".

There are two main lines. One runs up the west coast from Singapore, through KL, Ipoh and Butterworth, connecting with Thai railways at Padang Besar (where a half of the extra-long platform is managed by Malaysian officials and the other half by Thais) and from there continues to Hat Yai in Southern Thailand

and north to Bangkok. The other line branches off from the west coast line at Gemas (halfway between KL and Singapore) and heads northeast to Kota Bahru. From Kota Bahru it is possible to take buses/taxis to Rantau Panjang/Sungai Golok for connections with Thai railways. The express service (Ekspres Rakyat or Ekspres Sinaran) only stops at major towns; the regular service stops at every station but is slightly cheaper. All first and second class coaches have sleeping berths on overnight trains and all classes have a/c. Reservations can be made for both classes. Visitors should note that the a/c on Malaysian trains is very cold. First and second class carriages are equipped with videos. In East Malaysia there is only one railway line, running from Kota Kinabalu to Tenom, via Beaufort (see page 417).

Rail passes for 10 and 30 days are available to all foreign visitors, except those from Singapore, for every class and there are no restrictions other than seat availability. Passes are available from railway stations in Singapore, KL, Johor Bahru, Butterworth, Padang Besar, Rantau Panjang, Wakaf Bahru (Kota Bahru). A 30 day pass in 1999 cost US$120 (adult), US$60 (child); and a 10 day pass, US$55 (adult), US$28 (child). Students with a valid ID card (eg ISIC) can also buy an ISSA Explorer Pass which provide unlimited second class travel for seven days (US$38), 14 days (US$50) or 21 days (US$60) on KTM railway services in Peninsular Malaysia, Thailand and Singapore. There are also concessions offered (including for foreigners) to family groups (4 people or more), 25%; groups of 10 or more, 25%; handicapped persons, 50%; and senior citizens (65 years+), 50%. If travelling overnight, berth charges are RM70 (lower a/c), RM50 (upper a/c) for deluxe; and RM14 (lower a/c), RM11.50 (upper a/c) for second class. There are additional charges for international express services.

Train information   T032738000, 032747435, 032747442, 0630-2230. Email: passenger@ktmb.com.my. Website: www.ktmb.com.my. Transport to town: Taxis from KL's magnificent Moorish

Malaysian Railways

railway station also run on a fixed-price coupon system; coupons must be bought in advance from the booth next to the taxi rank.

Bus

Peninsular Malaysia has an excellent bus system with a network of public express buses and several privately run services. A/c express buses (and VIP buses on the more popular routes) connect the major towns, seats can be reserved and prices are reasonable. Prices quoted are for a/c buses. The a/c on Malaysian buses is, like the trains, very cold. There are also cheaper non-a/c buses that ply between the states and provide an intra-state service. Prices vary according to whether the bus is a/c or non a/c, express or regular, and between companies. The largest bus company is MARA, the government service. In larger towns there may be a number of bus stops; some private companies may also operate directly from their own offices. Travelling up the east coast of the Peninsula is often quicker as the roads are less congested; west coast travel is very slow but will be improved with the completion of the north-south highway.

During school holiday time, it can be difficult to get bus tickets & it is worth booking ahead

Buses in East Malaysia are more unreliable because of the poorer road conditions. But even in East Malaysia, roads are a good deal better than in Indonesian Borneo (Kalimantan). In Sarawak, the Sibu-Bintulu and Bintulu-Miri roads are rough and often impassable in the wet season, as is the road connecting Kota Kinabalu and Sandakan in Sabah.

Car and motorbike travel and hire

Car hire companies are listed in individual towns under **Local transport**. Visitors can hire a car provided they are in possession of an international driving licence, are over 23 and not older than 65 and have at least one year's driving experience. Car hire costs from RM100 to RM250 per day approximately depending on the model and the company. Cheaper weekly and monthly rates and special deals are available.

See also distance chart below

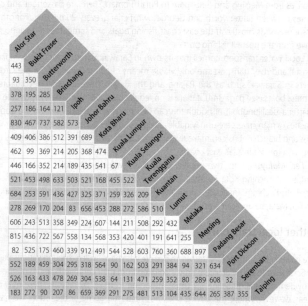

Malaysia distance chart (km)

Essentials

 Important road signs to note

awas caution	*jalang bahaya* dangerous road ahead
beri laluan give way	*jalan licin* slippery road
berhenti stop	*jalan sehala* one way
dilarang berhenti no stopping	*kawasan kemalangan* accident area
dilarang meletak kereta no parking	*kurangkan laju* slow down
dilarang memotong no overtaking	*utara/selatan* north/south
ikut kiri keep left	*timur/barat* east/west

Driving is on the left; give way to drivers on the right. Within towns the speed limit is 50 km per hour; the wearing of seat belts is compulsory for front seat passengers and the driver. Most road signs are international but *awas* means caution. Petrol costs a little over RM1 a litre. Road maps are on sale at most petrol stations; Petronas (the national oil company) produces an excellent atlas: *Touring Malaysia by Road*. Road conditions are good when compared with Indonesia and Thailand: most are kept in good repair and local drivers are generally safe. However during the monsoon season, heavy rains may make some east coast travel difficult and the west coast roads can be congested. In Sarawak the road network is extremely limited: air or water transport are the only option in many areas. In Sabah, four-wheel drive vehicles are *de rigeur*; they are readily available, but expensive. On some islands, such as Penang, Langkawi and Pangkor, motorbikes are available for hire for around RM20-25 per day. If bringing your own car into the country, no carnet or deposit is required. The vehicle is allowed to stay in the country as long as the owner has permission to stay.

Boat

In Peninsula Malaysia, there are regular scheduled ferry services between the main islands, Pulau Pangkor, Penang and Pulau Langkawi, and the mainland. There are services from Mersing and Singapore to Pulau Tioman. There are passenger and car ferries between Butterworth and Georgetown, Penang, every 20 minutes. For other offshore islands, mostly off the east coast, fishing boats, and sometimes regular boats, leave from the nearest fishing port.

Local water transport comes into its own in Sarawak, where lack of roads makes coastal and river transport the only viable means of communication. On the larger rivers in Sarawak, such as the Rajang and the Baram, there are specially adapted express boats (see page 344). If there is no regular boat, it is nearly always possible to charter a local longboat, although this can be expensive. In the dry season the upper reaches of many rivers are unnavigable except by smaller boats. In times of heavy rain, logs and branch debris can make rivers unsafe. Some river transport still operates on rivers on the peninsula's east coast.

Feri Malaysia runs two routes, both on a weekly schedule. 1) Port Klang-Singapore-Kuching-Kota Kinabalu-Singapore-Kuantan-Port Klang. 2) Kuantan-Kota Kinabalu-Kuching-Singapore-Port Klang. Tourism Malaysia offices have information on Feri Malaysia and can place bookings. For price guidelines, see page 262.

Other local transport

Cycling   We have had a number of letters from people who have cycled through various parts of Southeast Asia. The advice below is collated from their comments, and is meant to provide a general guideline for those intending to travel by bicycle. There may be areas, however, where the advice does not hold true. Some of the letters we have received even disagree on some points.

Bike type   Touring, hybrid or mountain bikes are fine for most roads and tracks in Malaysia – take an ordinary machine; nothing fancy.

Spares   These are readily available for most machines. Mountain bikes have made a big impact in the country, so accessories for these are also widely available. What is less common are components made of unusual materials – titanium and composites, for example. It is best to use common accessories.

Attitudes to bicyclists   Cycling is becoming more common in Malaysia, and clubs are springing up across the country. Unlike Indonesia and Thailand, a foreigner on a bike is not such an object of interest.

Road conditions   The maps in this guide are not sufficiently detailed for bicycling and a good, colour map is useful in determining contours and altitude, as well as showing minor roads.

Road users attitude to bicyclists   Cars and buses rarely give way to a bicycle. Be very wary, especially on main roads.

Taking bikes on buses   Non-a/c, cheaper buses are more accommodating of bicycles; a/c tour buses may refuse to carry a bike.

Bicycles on airlines   Many international airlines take bicycles free-of-charge, provided they are not boxed. Take the peddles off and deflate the tyres.

In general   Avoid major roads and major towns.

It is easy for foreigners to hitch in Malaysia; look reasonably presentable and it shouldn't **Hitchhiking** be long before someone will stop. Hitching is not advisable for single women.

There are two types of taxi in Malaysia – local and 'out-station' – or long distance. The **Taxi** latter – usually Mercedes or Peugeot – connect all major towns and cities. They operate on a shared-cost basis – as soon as the full complement of four passengers turns up the taxis set off. Alternatively, it is possible to charter the whole taxi for the price of four single fares. Taxi stands are usually next door to major bus stations. Fares are fixed by the government and posted at stands, so there is no need, or point, in bargaining. If shared, taxi fares usually cost about twice as much as bus fares, but they are much faster. For groups travelling together taking a taxi makes good sense. Note that it is easier to find passengers going your way in the morning than later in the day.

Local taxi fares in Malaysia are among the cheapest in Southeast Asia. Most local taxis in major towns are now metered and a/c. Turning the a/c on costs an additional 20%. If there is no meter, or, as is more often the case, the meter is broken, fares should be negotiated in advance.

In KL it has long been too dangerous for trishaws, apart from around Chinatown and **Trishaws** suburban areas. In towns such as Melaka, Georgetown and Kota Bharu, as well as in many other smaller towns, they remain one of the best, and certainly most pleasant, ways of getting around, particularly for sightseeing. It is necessary to negotiate fares in advance. As Malaysia becomes more affluent, so trishaws are disappearing; before long, presumably, it will be like Singapore: an expensive way to travel for well-heeled tourists.

Keeping in touch

Malaysia's post is cheap and reasonably reliable, although incoming and outgoing **Postal services** parcels should be registered. To send postcards and aerograms overseas costs RM0.50, letters, RM0.90. Post office opening hours are 0800-1700 Monday-Friday, 0800-1200 Saturday. Fax and telex services are available in most state capitals. Poste Restante is a reliable service available at general post offices in major cities.

Telephone services

Operator for 'outstation' (trunk) calls: T101
Enquiries: T102
Directory: T103
International IDD assistance: T108

Local There are public telephone booths in most towns; telephones take RM0.10 and RM0.20 coins. Card phones are now widespread. There are two types of card: Kadfon and Unicard. Kadfon can only be used at Telekom phone-booths, Unicard can be used at Uniphone phone-booths. Cards are available from airports, petrol stations and most outlets of *7-eleven* and *Hop-In*. Telekom cards are sold at post offices, Telekom offices, and some shops. On most public phones it is necessary to press the release button once the other person responds.

International There is an international telephone exchange in KL and calls can be booked to most countries in the world. Calls may be booked in advance. Collect calls can be linked to destination countries without delay (the operator will call you back). Direct calls can be made from telephones with IDD (international direct dialling) facility (007 plus country code plus area code plus number). Direct international calls can be made from most Kedai Telekom and telephone booths in major towns.

Media

Newspapers The main English-language dailies are *The New Straits Times*, *Business Times*, *The Star*, *The Daily Express* and *The Malay Mail* (afternoon). The main Sunday papers are *The New Sunday Times*, *The Sunday Mail* and *The Sunday Star*. The English-language dailies are government-owned and this is reflected in their content which tends to be relentlessly pro-government. *Aliran Monthly* is a high-brow but fascinating publication offering current affairs analysis from a non-government perspective. *The Rochet* is the Democratic Action Party's opposition newspaper, and also presents an alternative perspective. Both are available at news outlets. International editions of leading foreign newspapers and news magazines can be obtained at main news stands and book stalls, although some of these are not cleared through customs until mid-afternoon (notably *The Asian Wall Street Journal*). In East Malaysia the main English language newspapers are the *Sabah Daily News* and the *Sarawak Tribune*.

If you are looking for any alternative line to the government's then it would be best to check the welter of opposition websites. A couple of years ago Prime Minister Mahathir assured high-tech investors that he wouldn't attempt to control or censor the Web. This was all part of his attempt to create a MMSC or Multi-Media Super Corridor, a sort of Asian Silicon Valley. The best web-based newspaper is Malaysiakini.com, to be found at malaysiakini.com/columntoday.htm.

Radio There are six government radio stations which broadcast in various languages including English. Radio 1 broadcasts in Bahasa Melayu; Radio 2 is a music station; Radio 3 is mainly Bahasa but broadcasts a special programme for tourists every day at 1800; Radio 4 is in English; Radio 5, Chinese; Radio 6, Tamil. In KL you can tune into the Federal Capital's radio station and elsewhere in the country there are local stations. The BBC World Service can be picked up on FM in southern Johor, from the Singapore transmitter. Elsewhere it can be received on short-wave. The main frequencies are (in kHz): 11750, 9740, 6195 and 3915.

Short-wave radio British Broadcasting Corporation (BBC, London)   *Southeast Asian service* 3915, 6195, 9570, 9740, 11750, 11955, 15360; *Singapore service* 88.9MHz; *East Asian service* 5995, 6195, 7180, 9740, 11715, 11750, 11945, 11955, 15140, 15280, 15360, 17830, 21715.
Voice of America (VoA, Washington)   *Southeast Asian service* 1143, 1575, 7120, 9760, 9770, 15185, 15425; *Indonesian service* 6110, 11760, 15425.
Radio Beijing   *Southeast Asian service* (English) 11600, 11660.
Radio Japan (Tokyo)   *Southeast Asian service* (English) 11815, 17810, 21610.

Learning the language: a practical alternative

Malaysian English, which has been dubbed 'Manglish', as opposed to Singaporean English ('Singlish'), has evolved its own usages, abbreviations and expressions. Its very distinctive pronunciation can be almost unintelligible to visitors when they first arrive. The first thing many visitors notice is the use of the suffix lah *which is attached to just about anything and means absolutely nothing. English has been spoken in the Malay world since the late 18th century, but over time, it has been mixed with local terms. The converse has also happened: English has corrupted Malay to such a degree that it is now quite common to hear the likes of* 'you pergi-mana?' *for 'where are you going?' In abbreviated Malaysian-Chinese English,* can *is a key word.* 'Can-ah?' *(inflection) means 'may I?';* can-lah *means yes;* cannot *means no way; also* can *means 'yes, but I'd prefer you not to' and* how can? *is an expression of disbelief.*

The man who first applied the term Manglish to mangled Malaysian English was Chinese-Malaysian satirist Kit Leee, in his book Adoi *(which means ouch). It gives an uncannily accurate and very humorous pseudo-anthropological rundown on Malaysia's inhabitants. His section on Manglish, which should be pronounced exactly as it is written, is introduced:* Aitelyu-ah, nemmain wat debladigarmen say, mose Malaysians tok Manglish... Donkair you Malay or Chinese or Indian or everyting miksup... we Malaysians orways tok like dis wan-kain oni. *Below are extracts from his glossary of common Manglish words and phrases (which will help decipher the above).*

atoyu (wat) *gentle expression of triumph: 'What did I tell you?'*

baiwanfriwan *ploy used mainly by shop assistants to promote sales: 'If you buy one you'll get one free'.*

betayudon *mild warning, as in 'You'd better not do that'.*

debladigarmen *contraction of 'the bloody government'; widely used scapegoat; for all of life's disappointments, delays, denials, and prohibitions.*

hauken *another flexible expression applicable in almost any situation, eg 'That's not right!', 'Impossible!' or 'Don't tell me!'.*

izzenit *from 'isn't it?' but applied very loosely at the end of any particular statement to elicit an immediate response, eg* Yused you will spen me a beer, izzenit?

kennonot *request or enquiry, contraction of 'can or not': 'May I?' or 'Will you?' or 'Is it possible?'*

nola *a dilute negative, used as a device to interrupt, deny or cancel someone else's statement.*

oridi *contraction of already.*

sohau *polite interrogative, usually used as a greeting, as in 'Well, how are things with you?'*

tingwat *highly adaptable expression stemming from 'What do you think?'*

wan-kain *adjective denoting uniqueness; contraction of 'one of a kind'. Sometimes rendered as* wan-kain oni *('only').*

watudu *rhetorical question: 'But what can we do?'*

yala *non-committal agreement, liberally used when confronted with a bore.*

yusobadwan *expression of mild reproach: 'That's not very nice!'*

With thanks to Kit Leee and his co-etymologists: Rafique Rashid, Julian Mokhtar and Jeanne MC Donven. Leee, Kit (1989) Adoi, *Times Books International: Singapore)*

Essentials

☞ *Malaysian words and phrases*

Basic phrases

Yes/No *ia/tidak*
Thank you *Terimah kasih*
You're welcome *Sama-sama*
Good morning/Good afternoon
(early) *Selamat pagi/Selamat tengahari*
Good afternoon (late)/Good
evening/night *Selamatpetang/Selam*
at malam
Welcome *Selamat datang*
Goodbye (said by the person
leaving) *Selamat tinggal*
Goodbye (said by the person
staying) *Selamat jalan*
Excuse me/sorry *Ma'af saya*
Where's the...? *Dimana...*
How much is this...? *Ini berapa?*
I [don't] understand *Saya [tidak]*
mengerti
I want... *Saya mahu*
I don't want *Saya tak mahu*
My name is... *Nama saya...*
What is your name? *Apa nama anda?*

Sleeping

How much is a room? *Bilik berapa?*
Does the room have
air-conditioning? *Ada bilik yang ada*
air-con-kah?
I want to see the room first please *Saya*
mahu lihat bilik dulu
Does the room have hot water? *Ada*
bilik yang ada air panas?
Does the room have a bathroom? *Ada*
bilik yang ada
mandi-kah?

Travel

Where is the railway station? *Stesen*
keretapi dimana?
Where is the bus station? *Stesen bas*
dimana?
How much to go to...? *Berapa harga*
ke...?

I want to buy a ticket to... *Saya mahu*
beli tiket ke...
How do I get there? *Bagaimanakah*
saya
Is it far? *Ada jauh?*
Turn left / turn right *Belok kiri /*
belok kanan
Go straight on! *Turus turus!*

Time and days

Monday *Hari Isnin (Hari Satu)*
Tuesday *Hari Selasa (Hari Dua)*
Wednesday *Hari Rabu (Hari Tiga)*
Thursday *Hari Khamis (Hari Empat)*
Friday *Hari Jumaat (Hari Lima)*
Saturday *Hari Sabtu (Hari Enam)*
Sunday *Hari Minggu (Hari Ahad)*
Today *Hari ini*
Tomorrow *Esok*
Week *Minggu*
Month *Bulan*
Year *Tahun*

Numbers

1 satu
2 dua
3 tiga
4 empat
5 lima
6 enam
7 tujuh
8 lapan
9 sembilan
10 sepuluh
11 se-belas
12 dua-belas...etc
20 dua puluh
21 dua puluh satu...etc
30 tiga puluh
100 se-ratus
101 se-ratus satu
150 se-ratus limah puluh
200 dua ratus...etc
1,000 se-ribu

Television RTM1 and RTM2 are operated by Radio Television Malaysia, the government-run broadcasting station. Apart from locally produced programmes, some American and British series are shown. Three other channels are commercially run. There is a broad mixture of content, from Chinese kung-fu movies to Tamil musicals and English-language blockbusters and series. On the three commercial

2,000 dua ribu...	**I/me** saya
100,000 se-ratus ribu	**ice** air batuais
1,000,000 se-juta	**island** pulau
	male lelaki
Basic vocabulary	**man** laki
a little sedikit	**market** pasar
a lot banyak	**medicine** ubat ubatan
all right/good baik	**milk** susu
and dan	**more** lagi/lebeh
bank bank	**open** masuk
bathroom bilek mandi	**please** sila
beach pantai	**police** polis
beautiful cantik	**police station** pejabat polis
bed sheet cadar	**post office** pejabat pos
big besar	**railway station** stesen keretapi/tren
boat perahu	**restaurant** restoran/kedai makanan
broken tak makan/rosak	**room** bilik
bus bas	**sea** laut
bus station setsen bas	**ship** kapal
buy beli	**shop** kedai
can boleh	**sick** sakit
cannot tak boleh	**small** kecil
cheap murah	**stand** berdiri
chemist rumah ubat	**stop** berhenti
cigarette rokok	**sugar** gula
clean bersih	**taxi** teksi
closed tutup	**tea** teh
coffee kopi	**they** mereka
cold sejuk	**that** itu
crazy gila	**ticket** tiket
day hari	**toilet (female)** tandas perempuan
delicious sedap	**toilet (male)** tandas lelaki
dentist doktor gigi	**town** bandar
dirty kotor	**trishaw** beca
doctor doktor	**very** sangat
drink minum	**wait** tunggu
eat makan	**water** air
excellent bagus	**we** kami
expensive mahal	**what** apa
fruit buah	**when** bila
he/she dia	**woman** perempuan
hospital rumah sakit	**you** awak/anda
hot (temperature) panas	
hot (chilli) pedas	

Essentials

stations, all programmes are liberally interspersed with advertising, most of it for cigarettes, and leading tobacco companies sponsor film shows. Programmes for all channels are listed in daily newspapers. Singapore Broadcasting Service programmes can be received as far north as Melaka and are often listed in Malaysian papers. The government has long resisted the arrival of satellite TV, believing it to be a cultural polluter. To supplement local TV news, CNN was rebroadcast for an hour every night and since March 1994, BBC World Service Television has also been allowed in. It too is rebroadcast however, enabling government censors to review the output.

Internet cafés   Malaysia has embraced the web with enthusiasm and most towns now have internet cafés, which are listed under Communications in the Directory of individual towns. Increasingly hotels have email addresses and websites too, which are listed in the text.

Language   *Bahasa Melayu* (the Malay language, normally just shortened to *bahasa*) is the
For a list of words &   national language. It is very similar to Bahasa Indonesia, which evolved from Malay,
phrases, see page 42   and can be understood in southern Thailand, throughout Borneo and as far afield as the Moro areas of the southern Philippines. All communities, Malay, Chinese and Indian, as well as tribal groups in Sabah and Sarawak, speak Malay, as most are schooled in the Malay medium. Nearly everyone in Malaysia speaks some English, except in remoter rural areas, although the standard of English has declined markedly in the past 10 years. Realizing this, and because good English is essential for business, the government has sought to reverse the decline. The other main languages spoken in Malaysia include the Chinese dialects of Mandarin, Cantonese and Hokkien as well as Tamil and Punjabi.

For those wanting to get a better grasp of the language, it is possible to take courses in KLr (enquire at *Tourism Malaysia* offices) and other big cities. The best way to take a crash course in Malay is to buy a 'teach-yourself' book; there are several on the market, but one of the best ones is *Malay in 3 Weeks*, by John Parry and Sahari bin Sulaiman (Times Books, 1989), which is widely available. A Malay/English dictionary or phrase book is a useful companion too; these are also readily available in bookshops.

Basic grammar and vowels   Basic grammar is very simple: there are no tenses, genders or articles and the structure of sentences is straightforward. Plurals are also easy: one man, for example is *laki*, men" is *laki-laki*, often denoted as *laki*. Pronunciation is not difficult as there is a close relationship between the letter as it is written and the sound. Stress is usually placed on the second syllable of a word. For example restoran (restaurant) is pronounced *res-TO-ran*. For pronunciation of vowels and consonants: *a* is pronounced as *ah* in an open syllable, or as in *but* for a closed syllable; *e* is pronounced as in *open* or *bed*.; *i* is pronounced as in *feel*; *o* is pronounced as in *all*; *u* is pronounced as in *foot*. The letter *c* is pronounced as in *ch* as in *change* or *chat*. The *r*'s are rolled.

Food and drink

Food

For our quick reference   Malaysians, like neighbouring Singaporeans, love their food, and the dishes of the three
restaurant price guide,   main communities, Malay, Chinese and Indian, comprise a hugely varied national menu.
see the inside front   Even within each ethnic cuisine, there is a vast choice; every state has its own special
cover of the book.   Malay dishes and the different Chinese provincial specialities are well represented; in
For health matters   addition there is North Indian food, South Indian food and Indian Muslim food. Nyonya
relating to food,   cuisine is found in the old Straits Settlements of Penang and Melaka. Malaysia also has
see page 56   great seafood, which the Chinese do best, and in recent years a profusion of restaurants, representing other Asian and European cuisines, have set up, mainly in the big cities. In the East Malaysian states of Sabah and Sarawak, there are tribal specialities.

As in Singapore, good food is not confined to restaurants; some of the best local dishes can be sampled at hawker centres, which are cheap and often stay open late into the night. Hotels regularly lay on buffet spreads, which are good value at about RM20-30, often much cheaper than the price of a room would suggest. **NB** Many restaurants charge an extra 15% service and tax.

With a large ethnic Indian population, vegetarian food is usually available, especially on the Peninsula. In East Malaysia it can be harder to find vegetarian alternatives. There are also numerous Chinese and Malay vegetarian dishes although it is not unusual to find slivers of meat even when a vegetable dish is specifically requested. In tourist areas and more cosmopolitan towns vegetarian restaurants are becoming popular.

The best Malay food is usually found at stalls in hawker centres. The staple diet is rice and curry, which is rich and creamy due to the use of coconut milk. Herbs and spices include chillis, ginger, turmeric, coriander, lemongrass, anise, cloves, cumin, caraway and cinnamon.

Malay
During Ramadan many Malay restaurants close during daylight hour

Essentials

Rice dishes *nasi campur* – Malay curry buffet of rice served with meat, fish, vegetables and fruit.

nasi goreng – rice, meat and vegetables fried with garlic, onions and *sambal*.

nasi lemak – a breakfast dish of rice cooked in coconut milk and served with prawn sambal, *ikan bilis*, a hard boiled egg, peanuts and cucumber.

nasi padang – plain rice served with a selection of dishes.

nasi puteh – plain boiled rice.

nasi dagang – popular on the east coast for breakfast; glutinous rice cooked in coconut milk and served with fish curry, cucumber pickle and *sambal*.

Soup *soto ayam* – popular for breakfast in Johor and Sarawak, a spicy chicken soup served with rice cubes, chicken and vegetables.

lontong – popular in the south, particularly for breakfast. Cubed compressed rice served with mixed vegetables in coconut milk. *Sambal* is the accompaniment.

Meat *satay* – chicken, beef or mutton marinated and skewered on a bamboo, barbecued over a brazier. Usually served with *ketupat*.

Noodles *kway teow* – flat noodles fried with seafood, egg, soy sauce, beansprouts and *kuchai* (chives).

laksa johor – noodles in fish curry sauce and raw vegetables.

mee goreng – fried noodles.

mee jawa – noodles in gravy, served with prawn fritters, potatoes, tofu and beancurd.

mee rebus – noodles with beef, chicken or prawn with soybean in spicy sauce.

Curries *rendang* – dry beef curry (a Sumatran dish).

longong – vegetable curry made from rice cakes cooked in coconut, beans, cabbage and bamboo shoots.

Salad *rojak* – Malaysia's answer to Indonesia's *gado gado* – mixed vegetable salad served in peanut sauce with *ketupat*.

Vegetables *sayur manis* – sweet vegetables; vegetables fried with chilli, *belacan* and mushrooms.

Sweets *(kueh) apam* – steamed rice cakes.

pulut inti – glutinous rice served with sweetened grated coconut.

nyonya kueh – Chinese kueh, among the most popular is *yow cha koei* – deep-fried kneaded flour.

Cantonese and Hainanese cooking are the most prevalent Chinese cuisines in Malaysia. Some of the more common Malaysian-Chinese dishes are Hainanese chicken rice (rice cooked in chicken stock and served with steamed or roast chicken), *char kway teow* (Teochew-style fried noodles, with eggs, cockles and chilli paste), *or luak* (Hokkien oyster omelette), *dim sum* (steamed dumplings and patties) and *yong tow foo* (beancurd and vegetables stuffed with fish). Good Chinese food is available in restaurants, coffee shops and from hawker stalls.

Chinese
Each province of China has its own distinct cuisine. A balanced meal should contain the five basic taste sensations: sweet, bitter, salty, spicy and acidic to balance the yin & yang

Cantonese Light and delicately flavoured dishes are often steamed with ginger and are not very spicy. Shark's fin and birds' nest soups, and *dim sum* (mostly steamed delicacies trolleyed to your table, but only served until early afternoon) are Cantonese

Restaurant prices

4 RM40+   Hotel and exclusive restaurants
3 RM12.50-40+   Restaurants in tourist class hotels and more expensive local restaurants
2 RM5-12.50   Coffee shops (kedi kopi) and basic restaurants
1 under RM5   Hawker stalls

classics. Other typical dishes include fish steamed with soya sauce, ginger, chicken stock and wine; wan ton soup; blanched green vegetables in oyster sauce; and suckling pig.

Hainanese Simple cuisine from the southern island of Hainan; chicken rice with sesame oil, soy and a chilli and garlic sauce is their tastiest contribution.

Hakka Uses plenty of sweet potato and dried shrimp and specializes in stewed pigs' trotters, yong tau foo (deep-fried beancurd), and chillis and other vegetables stuffed with fish paste.

Hokkien Being one of Singapore's biggest dialect groups means Hokkien cuisine is prominent, particularly in hawker centres, although there are very few Hokkien restaurants. Hokkien Chinese invented the spring roll and their cooking uses lots of noodles and in one or two places you can still see them being made by hand. Hokkien cuisine is also characterized by clear soups and steamed seafood, eaten with soya sauce. Fried Hokkien mee (yellow wheat noodles stir-fried with seafood and pork), hay cho (deep fried balls of prawn) and bee hoon (rice vermicelli cooked with prawns, squid and beansprouts with lime and chillies) are specialities.

Hunanese Known for its glutinous rice, honeyed ham and pigeon soup.

Peking (Beijing) Chefs at the imperial court in Peking had a repertoire of over 8,000 recipes. Dumplings, noodles and steamed buns predominate, since wheat is the staple diet, but in Singapore, rice may accompany the meal. Peking duck, shi choy (deep fried bamboo shoots), and hot and sour soup are among the best Peking dishes. Peking duck (with the skin basted with syrup and cooked until crisp) is usually eaten rolled into a pancake and accompanied by hoisin sauce and spring onions. Fish dishes are usually deep-fried and served with sweet and sour sauce.

Shanghainese Seafood dominates this cuisine and many dishes are cooked in soya sauce. Braised fish-heads, braised abalone (a large shellfish) in sesame sauce, and crab and sweetcorn soup are typical dishes. Wine is often used in the preparation of meat dishes, hence drunken prawn and drunken crab.

Steamboat The Chinese answer to fondue is a popular dish in Singapore and can be found in numerous restaurants and at some hawker centres. Thinly sliced pieces of raw meat, fish, prawns, cuttlefish, fishballs and vegetables are gradually tossed into a bubbling cauldron in the centre of the table. They are then dunked into hot chilli and soya sauces and the resulting soup provides a flavoursome broth to wash it all down at the end.

Szechuan Very spicy (garlic and chilli are dominant), Szechuan is widely considered the tastiest Chinese cuisine. Szechuan food includes heaps of hot red peppers, traditionally considered to be protection against cold and disease. Among the best Szechuan dishes are smoked duck in tea leaves and camphor sawdust; minced pork with beancurd; steamed chicken in lotus leaves; and fried eels in garlic sauce.

Teochew Famous for its muay porridges. This is a light, clear broth consumed with side dishes of crayfish, salted eggs and vegetables.

Indian Indian cooking can be divided into three schools: northern and southern (neither eat beef) and Muslim (no pork). Northern dishes tend to be more subtly spiced, use more meat and are served with breads. Southern dishes use fiery spices, emphasize vegetables and are served with rice. The best-known North Indian food are the tandoori dishes, which are served with delicious fresh naan breads, baked in ovens on-site. Other pancakes include roti, thosai and chapati. Malaysia's famous mamak-men are Indian Muslims who are highly skilled in everything from teh tarik (see Drink below) to rotis.

Essentials

A Malay food glossary

assam sour	*minum* drink
ayam chicken	*nasi* rice
babi pork	*roti canai* pancakes served with lentils
belacan hot fermented prawn paste	and curry
daging meat	*roti john* baguette filled with sardine/
garam salt	egg mixture
gula sugar	*roti kosong* plain pancake
ikan fish	*sambal* spicy paste of pounded chillis,
ikan bakar grilled fish	onion and tamarind
ikan bilis anchovies	*sayur* vegetables
ikan panggang spicy barbecued fish	*sayur manis* sweet vegetables
kambing mutton	*sayur masak lemak* deep fried
kerupak prawn crackers	marinated prawns
ketupat cold, compressed rice	*sejuk* crab
kueh cakes	*soto ayam* spicy chicken soup
lemang glutinous rice in bamboo	*sotong* squid
limau lime	*tahu* beancurd
makan food	*telur* egg
manis sweet	*udang* prawn
mee noodles	

Essentials

Other dishes include *roti canai* – pancakes served with lentils and curry.
murtabak – a thick *roti*-pizza with minced meat, onion and egg.
nasi biriyani – rice cooked in ghee, spices and vegetable, served with beef or chicken.
nasi kandar – Mamak's version of nasi campur.
daun pisang – a Malay/South Indian *thali* – curry and rice, with poppadoms and chutneys all served on a banana leaf.

Nyonya
See page 210 for information on the history of the Nyonyas

Through inter-marriage with local Malays a unique culture evolved and with it, a cuisine that has grown out of a blend of the two. Nyonya food is spicier than Chinese food, and it uses pork. Nyonya dishes in Penang have adopted flavours from neighbouring Thailand, whereas Melaka's Nyonya food has Indonesian overtones. In traditional Straits Chinese households, great emphasis was placed on presentation and the fine-chopping of ingredients.
    Typical dishes include *kapitan* – chicken cooked in coconut milk.
otak otak – minced fish, coconut milk and spices, steamed in a banana leaf.
laksa – rice noodles in spicy coconut milk and prawn-flavoured gravy blended with spices and served with shellfish, chicken, beancurd and *belacan*.
assam laksa – the specialized Penang version – rice noodles served in fish gravy with shredded cucumber, pineapple, raw onions and mint.

Sabahan

The Kadazans form the largest ethnic group in Sabah. Their food tends to use mango and can be on the sour side.
    Popular dishes include *hinava* – marinated raw fish.
sup manuk on hiing – chicken soup with rice wine.
tapai – chicken cooked in local rice wine.
pakis – ferns, which are fried with mushrooms and *belacan*. Sometimes ferns are eaten raw, with a squeeze of lime (*sayur pakis limau*).
sup terjun – jumping soup – salted fish, mango and ginger.
hinompula – a dessert made from tapioca, sugar, coconut and the juice from screwpine leaves.

Distinctive fruits

Custard apple (or sugar apple)   Scaly green skin, squeeze the skin to open the fruit and scoop out the flesh with a spoon. Season: June-September.

Durian (Durio zibethinus)   A large prickly fruit, with yellow flesh, about the size of a football. Infamous for its pungent smell. While it is today regarded by many visitors as simply revolting, early Europeans (16th-18th centuries) raved about it, possibly because it was similar in taste to Western delicacies of the period. Borri (1744) thought that "God himself, had produc'd that fruit". But by 1880 Burbridge was writing: "Its odour – one scarcely feels justified in using the word 'perfume' – is so potent, so vague, but withal so insinuating, that it can scarcely be tolerated inside the house". Banned from hotel rooms throughout the region, and beloved by most Southeast Asians, it has an alluring taste – some maintain it is an addiction. Durian-flavoured chewing gum, ice cream and jams are all available. Season: May-August.

Jackfruit   Similar in appearance to durian but not so spiky. Yellow flesh, tasting slightly like custard. Season: January-June.

Mango (Mangifera indica)   A rainforest fruit which is now cultivated. Widely available in the West; in Southeast Asia there are hundreds of different varieties with subtle variations in flavour. Delicious eaten with sticky rice and a sweet sauce. The best mangoes in the region are considered to be those from South Thailand. Season: March-June.

Mangosteen (Garcinia mangostana)   An aubergine-coloured hard shell covers this small fruit which is about the size of a tennis ball. Cut or squeeze the purple shell to reach its sweet white flesh which is prized by many visitors above all others. In 1898, an American resident of Java wrote, erotically and in obvious ecstasy: "The five white segments separate easily, and they melt on the tongue with a touch of tart and a touch of sweet; one moment a memory of the juiciest, most fragrant apple, at another a remembrance of the smoothest cream ice, the most exquisite and delicately flavoured fruit-acid known – all of the delights of nature's laboratory condensed in that ball of neige parfumée". Southeast Asians believe it should be eaten as a chaser to durian. Season: April-September.

Papaya (Carica papaya)   A New World Fruit that was not introduced into Southeast Asia until the 16th century. Large, round or oval in shape, yellow or green-skinned, with bright orange flesh and a mass of round, black seeds in the middle. The flesh, in texture and taste, is somewhere between a mango and a melon. Some maintain that it tastes 'soapy'. Season: Year round.

Pomelo   A large round fruit the size of anything from an ostrich egg to a football, with thick, green skin and pith, and flesh similar to grapefruit, but less acidic. Season: August-November.

Rambutan (Nephelium lappaceum)   The bright red and hairy rambutan – rambut is the Malay word for 'hair' – with its slightly rubbery but sweet flesh is a close relative of the lychee of southern China. The Thai word for rambutan is ngoh, which is the nickname given by Thais to the fuzzy-haired Negrito aboriginals in the southern jungles. Season: May-September.

Salak (Salacca edulis)   A small pear-shaped fruit about the size of a large plum with a rough, brown, scaly skin (somewhat like a miniature pangolin) and yellow-white, crisp flesh. It is related to the sago and rattan trees.

Tamarind (Tamarindus indicus)   Brown seedpods with dry brittle skins and a brown tart-sweet fruit which grow on a tree introduced into Southeast Asia from India. The name is Arabic for 'Indian date'. The flesh has a high tartaric acid content and is used to flavour curries, jams, jellies and chutneys as well as for cleaning brass and copper. Elephants have a predilection for tamarind balls. Season: December-February.

Ternbok – fish, either grilled or steamed.
pan suh manok – chicken pieces cooked in bamboo cup and served with *bario* (Kelabit mountain rice).

For those wishing to learn more about Malaysian cuisine, several state tourist boards offer short courses in curry-making, etc. Enquire at Tourism Malaysia information centres. **Tourism Malaysia** publishes a glossy pamphlet called *Malaysian Common Recipes* providing an introduction to spices and ingredients and easy-to-follow recipes to 16 succulent dishes, see page 30 for contact information. A wide variety of Malaysian cookery books is available at leading bookshops.

Drink

Soft drinks, mineral water and freshly squeezed fruit drinks are available. Anchor and Tiger beer are widely sold, except in the more Islamic states of the east coast, especially Kelantan, and is cheapest at the hawker stalls (RM5 per bottle). A beer will cost RM8-12 per bottle in coffee shops. Malaysian-brewed Guinness is popular, mainly because Chinese believe it has medicinal qualities as it has been successfully sold on the 'Guinness Stout is good for you' line. Malaysian tea is grown in the Cameron Highlands and is very good. One of the most interesting cultural refinements of the Indian Muslim community is the Mamak-man, who is famed for *teh tarik* (pulled tea), which is thrown across a distance of about a metre, from one cup to another, with no spillages. The idea is to cool it down for customers, but it has become an art form; mamak-men appear to cultivate the nonchalant look when pouring. Malaysian satirist Kit Leee says a tea-stall mamak "could 'pull' tea in free fall without spilling a drop – while balancing a *beedi* on his lower lip and making a statement on Economic Determinism". Most of the coffee comes from Indonesia, although some is locally produced. Malaysians like strong coffee and unless you specify *kurang manis* (less sugar), *tak mahu manis* (don't want sugar) or *kopi kosong* (empty coffee, black, no sugar), it will come with lashings of condensed milk.

Shopping

Most big towns now have modern shopping complexes as well as shops and markets. Department stores are fixed-price, but nearly everywhere else it is possible – and necessary – to bargain. In most places, at least 30% can be knocked off the asking price; your first offer should be roughly half the first quote.

The islands of Langkawi and Labuan have duty-free shopping; the range of goods is *For Langkawi & Labuan see pages 185 & 428 respectively* poor, however. In addition to the duty-free shops, cameras, watches, pens, lighters, cosmetics, perfumes and portable radio/cassette players are all duty-free in Malaysia. Film and camera equipment are still cheaper in Singapore, which offers a wider selection of most products – especially electronics and computer products.

Kuala Lumpur and most of the state capitals have a Chinatown which usually has a few curio shops and nearly always a *pasar malam*. Indian quarters, which are invariably labelled 'Little India', are only found in bigger towns; they are the best places to buy *sarungs*, *longuis*, *dotis* and *saris* (mostly imported from India) as well as other textiles. Malay handicrafts are usually only found in markets or government craft centres.

The Malaysian arts and crafts industry used to enjoy much more royal patronage, but when craftsmen went in search of more lucrative jobs, the industry began to decline. The growth of tourism in recent years has helped to reinvigorate it, particularly in traditional handicraft-producing areas, such as the east coast states of Terengganu and Kelantan. The Malay Arts and Crafts Society has also been instrumental in preventing the decline of the industry. In 1981, Malaysian Handicraft and Souvenir Centres (*Karyaneka* centres), were set up to market Malaysian arts and crafts in KL and some state capitals. Typical Malaysian handicrafts which can be found on the peninsula include woodcarvings, batik, *songket* (cloth woven with gold and silver thread), pewterware, silverware, kites, tops and *wayang kulit* (shadow puppets). For more detail on Malaysian crafts, see page 552.

Other than the peninsula's east coast states, Sarawak is the other place where the traditional handicraft industry is flourishing (see page 398). The state capital, Kuching, is full of handicraft and antique shops selling tribal pieces collected from upriver; those going upriver themselves can often find items being sold in towns and even longhouses *en route*. Typical Sarawakian handicrafts include woodcarvings, *pua kumbu* (rust-coloured tie-dye blankets), beadwork and basketry. Many handicraft shops on Peninsular Malaysia also sell Sarawakian handicrafts – particularly those in KL – although there is a considerable mark-up.

Holidays and festivals

Tourism Malaysia has dates of movable holidays & festivals, see page 30 for contact information

Note that Islamic holidays, which are listed separately below, may vary significantly in their timing during the year. Chinese, Indian (Hindu) and some Christian holidays are also movable. To make things even more exciting, each state has its own public holidays when shops close and banks pull down their shutters. This makes calculating public holidays in advance a bit of a quagmire of lunar events, assorted kings' birthdays, and tribal festivals. But federal and state public holidays, including movable religious holidays, are listed (albeit in Malay) at http://202.184.140.111/cuti/cutiNegri.asp.

School holidays   Schools in Malaysia have five breaks through the year, although the actual dates vary from state to state. They generally fall in the months of January (one week), March (two weeks), May (three weeks), August (one week), and October (four weeks).

January-February   **New Year's Day** (1 January, public holiday except Johor, Kedah, Kelantan, Perlis and Terengganu).

Thaipusam   (movable: public holiday Johor, Negeri Sembilan, Perak, Penang and Selangor only, January 2001) celebrated by many Hindus throughout Malaysia in honour of their deity Lord Subramanian (also known as Lord Muruga); he represents virtue, bravery, youth and power. Held during full moon in the month of Thai, it is a day of penance and thanksgiving. Devotees pay homage to Lord Subramanian by piercing their bodies, cheeks and tongues with sharp skewers (*vel*) and hooks weighted with oranges and carrying *kevadis* (steel structures bearing the image of Lord Muruga). There are strict rules the devotee must follow in order to purify himself before carrying the kevadi; he becomes a vegetarian and abstains from worldly pleasures. Women cannot carry kevadis as they are not allowed to bare their bodies in order to be pierced. Although a kevadi carrier can have as many as a hundred spears piercing his flesh he only loses a small amount of blood in his trance. Each participant tries to outdo the others in the severity of his torture. At certain temples fire-walking is also part of this ceremony. Many Hindus disapprove of the spectacle and believe that their bodies are a gift from Siva; they should serve as a temple for the soul and should not be abused. This festival is peculiar to Hindus in Malaysia, Singapore and Thailand and is a corruption of a Tamil ceremony from South India. The biggest gatherings are at Batu Caves just outside KL, when thousands of pilgrims congregate in a carnival-like atmosphere (see page 86); there are also festivals held in Melaka, Penang and Singapore.

Chinese New Year (movable: public holiday, two days in most states, one day in Kelantan and Terengganu) a 15-days lunar festival celebrated in late January/early

Festivals in East Malaysia

Besides those celebrated throughout the country, Sabah and Sarawak have their own festivals. Exact dates can be procured from the tourist offices in the capitals. State public holidays are listed on page 53.

Kadazan Harvest Festival or **Tadau Keamatan** (movable: public holiday, Sabah and Labuan only) marks the end of the rice harvest in Sabah; the magavau ritual is performed to nurse the spirit back to health in readiness for the next planting season. Traditionally, the ritual world would have been performed in the paddy fields by a bobohizan (high priestess). Celebrated with feasting, tapai (rice wine) drinking, dancing and general merry-making. There are also agricultural shows, buffalo races, cultural performances and traditional games. The traditional sumazal dance is one of the highlights of the festivities.

Gawai (movable: public holiday Sarawak only) is the major festival of the year for the Iban of Sarawak; longhouses party continuously for a week. The Gawai celebrates the end of the rice harvest and welcomes the new planting season. The main ritual is called magavau and nurses the spirit of the grain back to health in advance of the planting season. Like the Kadazan harvest festival in Sabah, visitors are welcome to join in, but in Sarawak, the harvest festival is much more traditional. On the first day of celebrations everyone dresses up in traditional costumes, singing, dancing and drinking tuak rice wine until they drop.

Gawai Burung (Sarawak) is biggest of all the gawais and honours the war god of the Ibans. Gawai Kenyalang is one stage of Gawai Burung and is celebrated only after a tribesman has been instructed to do so after a dream.

Gawai Antu (Sarawak), also known as Gawai Nyunkup or Rugan, is an Iban tribute to departed spirits. In simple terms, it is a party to mark the end of mourning for anyone whose relative had died in the previous six months.

Gawai Batu (Sarawak) is a whetstone feast held by Iban farmers in June.

Gawai Mpijong Jaran Rantau (Sarawak) is celebrated by the Bidayuh before grass cutting in new paddy fields.

Gawai Bineh (Sarawak) is an Iban festival celebrated after harvest. It welcomes back all the spirits of the paddy from the fields.

Gawai Sawa (movable) is celebrated by the Bidayuh in Sarawak to offer thanksgiving for the last year and to make the next year a plentiful one.

Essentials

February. Chinatown streets are crowded for weeks with shoppers buying traditional oranges which signify luck. Lion, unicorn or dragon dances welcome in the New Year and, unlike in Singapore, thousands of firecrackers are let off to ward off evil spirits. *Chap Goh Mei* is the 15th day of the Chinese New Year and brings celebrations to a close; it is marked with a final dinner, another firecracker fest, prayers and offerings. The Chinese believe that in order to find good husbands, girls should throw oranges into the river/sea on this day. In Sarawak the festival is known as *Guan Hsiao Cheih* (Lantern Festival).

Easter (movable) celebrated in Melaka with candle-lit processions and special services (see page 221). *Good Friday* is a public holiday in Sabah and Sarawak.

March-April

Labour Day (1st: public holiday).

May

Kurah Aran (1st) celebrated by the Bidayuh tribe in Sarawak (see page 395) after the paddy harvest is over.

Wesak Day (movable: public holiday except Labuan, 18 May 2000) the most important day in the Buddhist calendar, celebrates the Buddha's birth, death and enlightenment. Temples throughout the country are packed with devotees offering incense, joss-sticks and prayers. Lectures on Buddhism and special exhibitions are held. In Melaka there is a procession at night with decorated floats, bands, dancers and acrobatics.

June **Birthday of His Majesty the King** (first Saturday of the month: public holiday) mainly celebrated in KL with processions.

Dragon Boat Festival (movable) honours the suicide of an ancient Chinese poet hero, Qu Yuan. He tried to press for political reform by drowning himself in the Mi Luo River as a protest against corruption. In an attempt to save him fishermen played drums and threw rice dumplings to try and distract vultures. His death is commemorated with dragon boat races and the enthusiastic consumption of rice dumplings; biggest celebrations are in Penang.

August **Hari Kebangsaan** or **National Day** (31st: public holiday) commemorates Malaysian independence (*merdeka*) in 1957. Big celebration in KL with processions of floats representing all the states; best places to see it: on the Padang (Merdeka Square) or on TV. In Sarawak, Hari Kebangsaan is celebrated in a different divisional capital each year.

Mooncake or **Lantern Festival** (movable). This Chinese festival marks the overthrow of the Mongol Dynasty in China; celebrated, as the name suggests, with the exchange and eating of mooncakes. According to Chinese legend secret messages of revolt were carried inside these cakes and led to the uprising. In the evening, children light festive lanterns while women pray to the Goddess of the Moon.

August- **Festival of the Hungry Ghosts** (movable) on the seventh moon in the Chinese lunar
September calendar, souls in purgatory are believed to return to earth to feast. Food is offered to these wandering spirits. Altars are set up in the streets and candles with faces are burned on them.

October **Festival of the Nine Emperor Gods** or **Kiew Ong Yeah** (movable) marks the return of the spirits of the nine emperor gods to earth. The mediums whom they are to possess purify themselves by observing a vegetarian diet. The gods possess the mediums, who go into trance and are then carried on sedan chairs whose seats are comprised of razor-sharp blades or spikes. Devotees visit temples dedicated to the nine gods. A strip of yellow cotton is often bought from the temple and worn on the right wrist as a sign of devotion. The ceremonies usually culminate with a fire-walking ritual.

October- **Deepvali** (movable: public holiday except Sarawak and Labuan, 26 October 2000) the
November Hindu festival of lights commemorates the victory of light over darkness and good over evil: the triumphant return of Rama after his defeat of the evil Ravanna in the Hindu epic, the Ramayana. Every Hindu home is brightly lit and decorated for the occasion.

December **Christmas Day** (25th: public holiday) Christmas in Malaysia is a commercial spectacle these days with fairy lights and decorations and tropical Santa Clauses – although it does not compare with celebrations in Singapore. Mostly celebrated on the west coast and ignored on the more Muslim east coast. Midnight mass is the main Christmas service held in churches throughout Malaysia.

Islamic holidays

The timing of Islamic festivals is an art rather than a science and is calculated on the basis of local sightings of various phases of the moon. Thus dates are approximations and can vary by a day or two. Muslim festivals move forward by around 9-10 days each year. To check on dates for 2001, see the following websites: www.regit.com/malaysia/holiday/holiday.htm or www.asianinfo-by-cj.com.

March **Hari Raya Haji** (movable: public holiday; in Kedah, Kelantan, Perlis and Terengganu *Hari Raya Qurban* is also a public holiday) celebrated by Muslims to mark the 10th day of Zulhijjah, the 12th month of the Islamic calendar when pilgrims celebrate their return from the Haj to Mecca. In the morning, prayers are offered and later, families hold 'open house'. Those who can afford it sacrifice goats or cows to be distributed to the poor. Many Malays have the title Haji in their name, meaning they have made the pilgrimage to Mecca; men who have been on the Haj wear a white skull-hat. The Haj is one of the five keystones of Islam.

Maal Hijrah (**Awal Muharram**) (movable: public holiday) marks the first day of the Muslim calendar, marking the Prophet Muhammad's journey from Mecca to Medina on the lunar equivalent of 16 July 622 AD. Religious discussions and lectures commemorate the day. Wesak Day (movable, public holiday).

Birthday of the Prophet Muhammad (**Maulidur Rasul**) (movable: public holiday, June 15 June 2000) to commemorate Prophet Muhammad's birthday in 571 AD. Processions and Koran recitals in most big towns.

Hari Hol Almarhum Sultan Ismail (movable, 4 October 2000, Johor). *Israk and Mikraj* October (movable, 25 October 2000, Kedah and Negeri Sembilan).

Nuzul Quran (movable, Kelantan, Pahang, Perak, Perlis, Selangor and Terengganu, 13 December December 2000).

Awal Ramadan (movable: public holiday Johor and Melaka, 27-28 December 2000) the first day of Ramadan, a month of fasting for all Muslims – and by implication, all Malays. During this month Muslims abstain from all food and drink (as well as smoking) from sunrise to sundown – if they are very strict, Muslims do not even swallow their own saliva during daylight hours. It is strictly adhered to in the conservative Islamic states of Kelantan and Terengganu. Every evening for 30 days before breaking of fast, stalls are set up which sell traditional Malay cakes and delicacies. The only people exempt from fasting are the elderly as well as women who are pregnant or are menstruating.

Hari Raya Puasa or **Aidil Fitri** (movable: public holiday, 27-28 December 2000) marks the end of the Muslim fasting month of Ramadan and is a day of prayer and celebration. In order for Hari Raya to be declared, the new moon of Syawal has to be sighted; if it is not, fasting continues for another day. It is the most important time of the year for Muslim families to get together; Malays living in towns and cities balek kampung (return home to their village), where it is 'open house' for relatives and friends, and special Malay delicacies are served. Hari Raya is also enthusiastically celebrated by Indian Muslims.

State holidays

Only sultans' and governors' birthday celebrations are marked with processions and festivities; state holidays can disrupt travel itineraries – particularly in east coast states where they may run for several days.

Sultan of Kedah's birthday (30 January 2000, Kedah). **Sultan of Tereengganu's** January **birthday** (22 January 2000, Terengganu).

Federal Territory Day (1 February 2000, KL and Labuan). February

Installation of Sultan of Terengganu Day (4 March 2000, Terengganu); **Sultan of** March **Selangor's birthday** (11 March 2000, Selangor); **Sultan of Kelantan's birthday** (30 & 31 March 2000, Kelantan).

Sultan of Johor's birthday (8 April 2000, Johor); **Declaration of Melaka as Historic** April **City** (15 April 2000, Melaka); **Sultan of Perak's birthday** (19 April 2000, Perak).

May **Rajah of Perlis' birthday** (6 May 2000, Perlis). **Pahang Hol Day** (7 May 2000, Pahang); **Harvest Festival** (30 & 31 May 2000, Sabah and Labuan).

June **Dayak Day** (1 & 2 June 2000, Sarawak).

July **Governor of Penang's birthday** (second Saturday of the month, 8 July 2000, Penang); **Yang Di-Pertuan Besar of Negri Sembilan's birthday** (19 July 2000, Negri Sembilan).

September **Governor of Sarawak's birthday** (9 September 2000, Sarawak); **Governor of Sabah's birthday** (16 September 2000, Sabah).

October **Governor of Melaka's birthday** (second Saturday of the month, 14 October 2000, Melaka); **Sultan of Pahang's birthday** (24 October 2000, Pahang).

Health

With the following advice and precautions, you should keep as healthy as you do at home. In Southeast Asia the health risks are different from those encountered in Europe or the USA, especially in the tropical regions, but the region's medical practitioners have particular experience in dealing with locally occurring diseases. There is an obvious difference in health risks between the business traveller who tends to stay in international class hotels in large cities and the backpacker trekking through rural areas. There are no hard and fast rules to follow; you will often have to make your own judgements on the healthiness or otherwise of your surroundings.

Medical facilities Malaysian health care is excellent and private clinics are found in most small towns and there are good government hospitals in major cities. All state capitals have general hospitals and every town has a district hospital. If you are in a city it may be worthwhile calling on your embassy to provide a list of recommended doctors. Big hotels have their own in-house doctors who are extremely expensive. Other doctors are listed in the telephone directory. Most doctors speak English, but the likelihood of finding this and a good standard of care diminishes very rapidly as you move away from the big cities. On the whole it is inexpensive to visit a private doctor (about RM30-50), and a sojourn in a government hospital is cheaper than most hotels (no a/c or pool).

Pharmaceuticals are available from numerous outlets including shopping centres, supermarkets and hotels. Most pharmacists are open 0900-1800 Monday-Saturday. A number of drugs that can only be obtained on prescription in Western countries can be bought over the counter in Malaysia. Traditional Chinese pharmacies, mostly found in Chinatowns, also dispense Chinese medicines, and will advise on traditional remedies for most ailments. Facilities in East Malaysia are not as good as those on the Peninsula. There are systems and traditions of medicine wholly different from the Western model especially in rural areas and you may be confronted with less orthodox forms of treatment such as herbal medicine and acupuncture. At least you can be sure that local practitioners have a lot of experience with the particular diseases of their region.

Medicines If you are a long way away from medical help, a certain amount of self-administered medication may be necessary and you will find many of the drugs available have familiar names. However, always check the date stamping (sell-by date) and buy from reputable pharmacists because the shelf life of some items, especially vaccines and antibiotics, is markedly reduced in hot conditions. Unfortunately, many locally produced drugs are not subjected to quality control procedures and so can be unreliable. There have, in addition, been cases of substitution of inert materials for active drugs. With the following precautions and advice you should keep as healthy as usual. Make local enquiries about health risks if you are apprehensive and take the general advice of European, Australian or North American families who have lived or are living in the area.

Before you go

Take out medical insurance. You should also have a dental check-up, obtain a spare glasses prescription and, if you suffer from a long-standing condition, such as diabetes, high blood pressure, heart/lung disease or a nervous disorder, arrange for a check-up with your doctor who can at the same time provide you with a letter explaining details of your medical disorder. Check the current practice for malaria prophylaxis (prevention) for the countries you intend to visit.

Visiting the peninsula's west coast does not require any medical precautions other than some insect repellent. Those travelling to national parks, rural areas and to Sabah and Sarawak are advised to have vaccinations against cholera, typhoid and polio, hepatitis A, tetanus and Japanese encephalitis. Smallpox vaccination is no longer required. Neither is cholera vaccination, despite the fact that the disease occurs, but not at present in epidemic form. Yellow fever vaccination is not required either, although you may be asked for a certificate if you have been in a country affected by yellow fever immediately before travelling to Southeast Asia.

Vaccination & immunization

Infectious hepatitis This is less of a problem for travellers than it used to be because of the development of two extremely effective vaccines against the A and B form of the disease. It remains common, however, in Laos. A combined hepatitis A and B vaccine is now licensed and has been available since 1997 – one jab covers both diseases.

Typhoid (monovalent) One dose followed by a booster 1 month later. Immunity from this course lasts 2-3 years. An oral preparation is also available.

Poliomyelitis This is a live vaccine generally given orally but a full course consists of three doses with a booster in tropical regions every 3-5 years.

Tetanus One dose should be given, with a booster at 6 weeks and another at 6 months. Ten yearly boosters thereafter are recommended.

Meningitis and Japanese B encephalitis (JVE) There is an extremely small risk of these rather serious diseases; both are seasonal and vary according to region. Meningitis can occur in epidemic form; JVE is a viral disease transmitted from pigs to man by mosquitoes. For details of the vaccinations, consult a travel clinic.

Children should, in addition to the above, be properly protected against diphtheria, whooping cough, mumps and measles. Teenage girls, if they have not had the disease, should be given a rubella (German measles) vaccination. Consult your doctor for advice on BCG inoculation against tuberculosis: the disease is still common in the region.

You may find the following items useful to take with you from home: suntan cream, insect repellent, flea powder, mosquito net, coils or tablets, tampons, condoms, contraceptives, water sterilizing tablets, anti-malaria tablets, anti-infective ointment, dusting powder for feet, travel sickness pills, antiacid tablets, anti-diarrhoea tablets, sachets of rehydration salts, a first aid kit and disposable needles (also see page 59).

Basic supplies

Information regarding country-by-country malaria risk can be obtained from the World Health Organization (WHO) or in Britain from the Ross Institute, London School of Hygiene and Tropical Medicine, Keppel St, London WC1E 7HT which also publishes a highly recommended book: *The Preservation of Personal Health in Warm Climates*. The Centres for Disease Control (CDC) in Atlanta, Georgia, USA will provide equivalent

Further information

Essentials

information. The organization MASTA (Medical Advisory Service for Travellers Abroad) also based at the London School of Hygiene and Tropical Medicine (T020-76314408) will provide up-to-date country-by-country information on health risks. Further information on medical problems overseas can be obtained from *Travellers Health: How to Stay Healthy Abroad*, edited by Richard Dawood (Oxford University Press, 1992). This revised and updated edition is highly recommended, especially to the intrepid traveller. A more general publication, with hints on health and much more besides, is John Hatt's *The Tropical Traveller* (Penguin, 1993).

Staying healthy

Water is clean and safe to drink in major cities on the peninsula but in other areas it should be boiled or sterilized. Mineral water can be bought fairly easily. With food, normal precautions should be taken with shellfish; ensure stall food is properly cooked and avoid unpeeled fruits.

Intestinal upsets
Practically nobody escapes intestinal infections, so be prepared for them. Most of the time they are due to the insanitary preparation of food. Do not eat uncooked fish, vegetables or meat (especially pork), fruit without the skin (always peel fruit yourself), or food that is exposed to flies (particularly salads). Tap water may be unsafe, especially in the monsoon seasons and the same goes for stream water or well water. Filtered or bottled water is usually available and safe but you cannot always rely on it. If your hotel has a central hot water supply, this is safe to drink after cooling. Ice should be made from boiled water but rarely is, so stand your glass on the ice cubes instead of putting them in the drink. Dirty water should be strained through a filter bag (available from camping shops), then boiled or treated. Bringing the water to a rolling boil at sea level is sufficient. In the highlands, you have to boil the water a bit longer to ensure that all the microbes are killed (because water boils at a lower temperature at altitude). Various sterilizing methods can be used and there are proprietary preparations containing chlorine or iodine compounds. Pasteurized or heat-treated milk is now fairly widely available as is ice cream and yoghurt produced by the same methods. Unpasteurized milk products, including cheese, are sources of tuberculosis, brucellosis, listeria and food poisoning germs. You can render fresh milk safe by heating it to 62°C for 30 mins followed by rapid cooling or by boiling. Matured or processed cheeses are safer than fresh varieties.

Fish and shellfish are popular foods throughout island Southeast Asia but can be the source of health problems. Shellfish which are eaten raw will transmit food poisoning or hepatitis if they have been living in contaminated water. Certain fish accumulate toxins in their bodies at certain times of the year, which give rise to illness when they are eaten. The phenomenon known as 'red tide' can also affect fish and shellfish which eat large quantities of tiny sea creatures and thereby become poisonous. The only way to guard against this is to keep as well informed as possible about fish and shellfish quality in the area you are visiting. Most countries impose a ban on fishing in periods when red tide is prevalent, although this is often flouted.

Diarrhoea
Diarrhoea is usually the result of food poisoning, but can occasionally result from contaminated water. There are various causes – viruses, bacteria, protozoa (like amoeba), salmonella and cholera organisms. It may take one of several forms coming on suddenly or rather slowly. It may be accompanied by vomiting or severe abdominal pain, and the passage of blood or mucus (when it is called dysentery).

All kinds of diarrhoea, whether or not accompanied by vomiting, respond favourably to the replacement of water and salts taken as frequent small sips of some kind of rehydration solution. There are proprietary preparations consisting of sachets of oral rehydration electrolyte powder which are dissolved in water, or make up your own by adding half a teaspoonful of salt (3.5 grams) and 4 tablespoons of sugar (40 grams) to a litre of boiled water. If it is possible to time the onset of diarrhoea to the minute, then it is probably viral or bacterial and/or the onset of dysentery. The treatment in addition to rehydration is Ciprofloxacin (500 mgs every 12 hrs). The drug is now widely available as are various similar ones.

If the diarrhoea has come on slowly or intermittently, then it is more likely to be protozoal, ie caused by amoeba or giardia, and antibiotics will have no effect. These cases are best treated by a doctor as should any diarrhoea continuing for more than 3 days. If there are severe stomach cramps, the following drugs may help: Loperamide (Imodium, Arret) and Diphenoxylate with Atropine (Lomotil). The drug usually used for giardia or amoeba is Metronidazole (Flagyl) or Tinidazole (Fasigyu).

The linchpins of treatment for diarrhoea are rest, fluid and salt replacement, antibiotics such as Ciprofloxacin for the bacterial types, and special diagnostic tests and medical treatment for amoeba and giardia infections. Salmonella infections and cholera can be devastating diseases and it would be wise to get to a hospital as soon as possible if these were suspected. Fasting, peculiar diets and the consumption of large quantities of yoghurt have not been found useful in calming travellers' diarrhoea or in rehabilitating inflamed bowels. Oral rehydration has, especially in children, been a lifesaving technique and as there is some evidence that alcohol and milk might prolong diarrhoea they should probably be avoided during, and immediately after, an attack. There are ways of preventing travellers' diarrhoea for short periods of time when visiting these countries by taking antibiotics but these are ineffective against viruses and, to some extent, against protozoa. This technique should not be used other than in exceptional circumstances. Some preventatives such as Enterovioform can have serious side effects if taken for long periods.

Sunburn & sunstroke The burning power of the tropical sun is phenomenal, especially in highland areas. Always wear a wide-brimmed hat, and use some form of sun cream or lotion on untanned skin. Normal temperate zone suntan lotions (protection factors up to 7) are not much good. You need to use the types designed specifically for the tropics or for mountaineers or skiers, with a protection factor between 7 and 15 or higher. Glare from the sun can cause conjunctivitis so wear sunglasses, particularly on beaches.

There are several varieties of heat stroke. The most common cause is severe dehydration. Avoid this by drinking lots of non-alcoholic fluid, and adding salt to your food.

Heat & cold Full acclimatization to tropical temperatures takes about two weeks and during this period it is normal to feel relatively apathetic, especially if the humidity is high. Drink plenty of water (up to 15 litres a day are required when working physically hard in the tropics). Use salt on your food and avoid extreme exertion. Tepid showers are more cooling than hot or cold ones. Large hats do not cool you down but do prevent sunburn. Remember that, especially in highland areas, there can be a large and sudden drop in temperature between sun and shade and between night and day so dress accordingly. Loose-fitting cotton clothes are best for hot weather. Warm jackets and woollens are often necessary after dark at high altitude.

Insects These can be a great nuisance. Some, of course, are carriers of serious diseases such as malaria, dengue fever or filariasis and various worm infections. The best way of keeping mosquitos away at night is to sleep off the ground with a mosquito net and to burn mosquito coils containing Pyrethrum. Aerosol sprays or a 'flit gun' may be effective as are insecticidal tablets which are heated on a mat which is plugged into the wall socket. If taking your own, check the voltage of the area you are visiting so that you can take an appliance that will work; similarly, check that your electrical adaptor is suitable for the repellent plug; note that they are widely available in the region.

Essentials

You can, in addition, use personal insect repellent of which the best contain a high concentration of diethyltoluamide (DET). Liquid is best for arms and face; take care around eyes and make sure you do not dissolve the plastic of your spectacles. Aerosol spray on clothes and ankles deter mites and ticks. Liquid DET suspended in water can be used to impregnate cotton clothes and mosquito nets. The latter are now available in wide mesh form which are lighter to carry and less claustrophobic to sleep under.

If you are bitten, itching may be relieved by cool baths and antihistamine tables (take care with alcohol or when driving), corticosteroid creams (use with great care and never use if any hint of septic poisoning) or by judicious scratching. Calamine lotion and cream have limited effectiveness and antihistamine creams have a tendency to cause skin allergies and are therefore not generally recommended. Bites which become infected (a common problem in the tropics) should be treated with a local antiseptic or antibiotic cream such as Cetrimide, as should infected scratches. Skin infestations with body lice, crabs and scabies are unfortunately easy to pick up. Use gamma benzene hexachloride for lice and benzyl benzoate for scabies. Crotamiton cream alleviates itching and also kills a number of skin parasites. Malathion lotion is good for lice but avoid the highly toxic full strength Malathion which is used as an agricultural insecticide.

Bites & stings If you are unlucky enough to be bitten by a venomous snake, spider, scorpion, centipede or sea creature, try (within limits) to catch or kill the animal for identification. Reactions to be expected are shock, swelling, pain and bruising around the bite, soreness of the regional lymph glands, nausea, vomiting and fever. If in addition any of the following symptoms should follow closely, get the victim to a doctor without delay: numbness, tingling of the face, muscular spasms, convulsions, shortness of breath or haemorrhage. Commercial snake-bite or scorpion-sting kits may be available but these are only useful against the specific type of snake or scorpion for which they are designed. The serum has to be given intravenously so is not much good unless you have had some practice in making injections into veins. If the bite is on a limb, immobilize it and apply a tight bandage between the bite and the body, releasing it for 90 secs every 15 mins. Reassurance of the victim is very important because death from snake bite is very rare. Do not slash the bite area and try to suck out the poison because this sort of heroism does more harm than good. Hospitals usually hold stocks of snake-bite serum. The best precaution is not to walk in long grass with bare feet, sandals or in shorts.

When swimming in an area where there are poisonous fish such as stone or scorpion fish (also called by a variety of local names) or sea urchins on rocky coasts, tread carefully or wear plimsolls/trainers. The sting of such fish is intensely painful. This can be relieved by immersing the injured part of the body in water as hot as you can bear for as long as it remains painful. This is not always very practical and you must take care not to scald yourself, but it does work. Avoid spiders and scorpions by keeping your bed away from the wall, look under lavatory seats and inside your shoes in the morning. In the rare event of being bitten, consult a doctor.

Intestinal worms are common and the more serious ones, such as hookworm, can be contracted by walking barefoot on infested earth or beaches.

Influenza and **respiratory diseases** are common, perhaps made worse by polluted cities and rapid temperature and climatic changes – accentuated by air-conditioning.

Prickly heat is a very common itchy rash, best avoided by frequent washing and by wearing loose clothing. It can be helped by the use of talcum powder, allowing the skin to dry thoroughly after washing.

Athlete's foot and other fungal infections are best treated by sunshine and a proprietary preparation such as Tolnaftate.

Other risks and more serious diseases

The main symptoms are pains in the stomach, lack of appetite, lassitude and yellowness of the eyes and skin. Medically speaking there are two main types. The less serious, but more common is hepatitis A for which the best protection is the careful preparation of food, the avoidance of contaminated drinking water and scrupulous attention to toilet hygiene. The other, more serious, version is hepatitis B which is acquired usually as a sexually transmitted disease or by blood transfusion. It can less commonly be transmitted by injections with unclean needles and possibly by insect bites. The symptoms are the same as for hepatitis A. The incubation period is much longer (up to six months compared with six weeks) and there are more likely to be complications.

Infectious hepatitis (jaundice)

Hepatitis A can be protected against with gamma globulin. It should be obtained from a reputable source and is certainly useful for travellers who intend to live rough. You should have a shot before leaving and have it repeated every six months. The dose of gamma globulin depends on the concentration of the particular preparation used, so the manufacturer's advice should be taken. The injection should be given as close as possible to your departure and as the dose depends on the likely time you are to spend in potentially affected areas. The manufacturer's instructions should be followed. Gamma globulin has really been superseded now by a proper vaccination against hepatitis A (Havrix), which gives immunity lasting up to 10 years. After that boosters are required. Havrix monodose is now widely available as is junior Havrix. The vaccination has negligible side effects and is extremely effective. Gamma globulin injection can be a bit painful, but it is cheaper than Havrix and may be more available in some places.

Hepatitis B can be effectively prevented by a specific vaccine (Engerix) – three shots over six months before travelling. If you have had jaundice in the past it would be worthwhile having a blood test to see if you are immune to either of these two types, because this might avoid the necessity and costs of vaccination or gamma globulin. There are other kinds of viral hepatitis (C, E etc) which are fairly similar to A and B, but vaccines are not available as yet.

AIDS in Southeast Asia is increasingly prevalent. Thus, it is not wholly confined to the well known high risk sections of the population ie homosexual men, intravenous drug abusers, prostitutes and the children of infected mothers. Heterosexual transmission is probably now the dominant mode of infection and so the main risk to travellers is from casual sex. The same precautions should be taken as when encountering any sexually transmitted disease. In some Southeast Asian countries, Thailand is an example, almost the entire population of female prostitutes is HIV positive and in other parts intravenous drug abuse is common. There is possibly less of a problem in Malaysia. The AIDS virus (HIV) can be passed via unsterile needles which have been previously used to inject an HIV positive patient, but the risk of this is very small indeed. It would, however, be sensible to check that needles have been properly sterilized or disposable needles used. The chance of picking up hepatitis B in this way is much more of a danger. Be wary of carrying disposable needles. Customs officials may find them suspicious. The risk of receiving a blood transfusion with blood infected with the HIV virus is greater than from dirty needles because of the amount of fluid exchanged. Supplies of blood for transfusion are supposed to be screened for HIV in all reputable hospitals so the risk should be small. Catching the virus which causes AIDS does not necessarily produce an illness in itself; the only way to be sure if you feel you have been put at risk is to have a blood test for HIV antibodies on your return to a place where there are reliable laboratory facilities. However, the test does not become positive for many weeks.

AIDS

Essentials

Essentials

Dr Watson solves the Malayan malaria mystery

The word 'malaria' was first used in the 18th century and comes from the Italian mala aria – or 'bad air' – because it was thought to be caused by unwholesome air in swampy districts. It was not until 1899 that Dr Ronald Ross, a medical officer in Panama during the construction of the canal, discovered that the real culprit was not the air, but the swamp inhabitants themselves – mosquitos. The following year a young Scotsman, Dr Malcolm Watson, was appointed as a government medical officer in Malaya, where malaria was the biggest killer. Dr Watson was posted to Klang where a malarial epidemic was wreaking havoc. In September 1901 nearby Port Swettenham (now Port Klang) opened for business; by Christmas 118 out of the 176 government employees had been struck down by the disease.

Armed with the knowledge of the recent Panama discovery, Dr Watson set about draining the coastal swamplands, spraying them and improving the water-flow in streams. It worked, and the doctor became known as the 'White Knight of Malaria Control'. Historian Mary Turnbull writes that "it was said of Watson that 'he could probably have claimed to have saved more lives than any other physician in history', and Ronald Ross described his work in Malaya as 'the greatest sanitary achievement ever accomplished in the British Empire'". The methods used in his battle against the nyamuk – the menacing and almost onomatopoeic Malay word for mosquito – became standard practice in the colony. Combined with the increased use of quinine, malaria was controlled, which is one of the reasons why colonial Malaya's plantation economy began to take off in the early 1900s. The planting of rubber estates in the coastal lowlands – greatly encouraged by the zealous director of Singapore's Botanic Gardens, 'Mad' Henry Ridley – would otherwise have been a much more hazardous occupation.

Malaria
See also box
This is not a problem in main cities but it is advisable to take malaria pills if you are going to rural areas. Malaria is more prevalent in East Malaysia, particularly in the jungled interior of Sabah. It remains a serious disease and you are advised to protect yourself against mosquito bites as above and to take prophylactic (preventative) drugs. Start taking the tablets a few days before exposure and continue to take them 6 weeks after leaving the malarial zone. Remember to give the drugs to babies and children, pregnant women also.

The subject of malaria prevention is becoming more complex as the malaria parasite becomes immune to some of the older drugs. In particular, there has been an increase in the proportion of cases of falciparum malaria which are resistant to the normally used drugs. It would not be an exaggeration to say that we are near to the situation where some cases of malaria will be untreatable with presently available drugs.

Take the advice of a reputable agency on prophylaxis but be prepared to receive conflicting advice. Because of the rapidly changing situation in the Southeast Asian region, the names and dosage of the drugs have not been included. But Chloroquine and Proguanil may still be recommended for the areas where malaria is still fully sensitive. Doxycycline, Metloquine and Quinghaosu are presently being used in resistant areas. Halofantrine Quinine and tetracycline drugs remain the mainstays of treatment.

It is still possible to catch malaria even when taking prophylactic drugs, although this is unlikely. If you do develop symptoms (high fever, shivering, severe headache, and sometimes diarrhoea) seek medical advice immediately. The risk of the disease is obviously greater the further you move from the cities into rural areas, with primitive facilities and standing water.

This is present in most of the countries of Southeast Asia. It is a viral disease transmitted by mosquito and causes severe headaches and body pains. Complicated types of dengue known as haemorrhagic fevers occur throughout Asia but usually in persons who have caught the disease a second time. Thus, although it is a very serious type it is rarely caught by visitors. There is no treatment, you must just avoid mosquito bites. **Dengue fever**

Remember that rabies is endemic in many Southeast Asian countries. If you are bitten by a domestic or wild animal, do not leave things to chance. Scrub the wound with soap and water and/or disinfectant, try to have the animal captured (within limits) or at least determine its ownership where possible, and seek medical assistance at once. The course of treatment depends on whether you have already been satisfactorily vaccinated against rabies. If you have (and this is worthwhile if you are spending lengths of time in developing countries) then some further doses of vaccine are all that is required. Human diploid cell vaccine is the best, but expensive: other, older kinds of vaccine such as that derived from duck embryos may be the only types available. These are effective, much cheaper and interchangeable generally with the human derived types. If not already vaccinated then anti-rabies serum (immunoglobulin) may be required in addition. It is wise to finish the course of treatment whether the animal survives or not. **Rabies**

Essentials

When you return home

On returning home, remember to take anti-malarial tablets for 6 weeks. If you have had attacks of diarrhoea, it is worth having a stool specimen tested in case you have picked up amoebic dysentery. If you have been living rough, a blood test may also be worthwhile to detect worms and other parasites.

Pentes, Tina and Truelove, Adrienne (1984) *Travelling with Children to Indonesia and South-East Asia*, Hale & Iremonger: Sydney. Wheeler, Maureen *Travel with Children*, Lonely Planet: Hawthorne, Australia. **Further information**

Travelling with children

Many people are daunted by the prospect of taking a child to Malaysia. Naturally, it is not something to be taken on lightly; travelling is slower and more expensive and there are additional health risks for the child or baby. But it can be a most rewarding experience, and with sufficient care and planning, it can also be safe. Children are excellent passports into a local culture. You will also receive the best service, and help from officials and members of the public when in difficulty.

Children in Malaysia are given 24-hour attention by parents, grandparents and siblings. They are rarely left to cry and are carried for most of the first 8 months of their lives since crawling is considered animal-like. A non-Asian child is still something of a novelty and parents may find their child frequently taken off their hands, even mobbed in more remote areas. This can be a great relief (at mealtimes, for instance) or most alarming. Some children love the attention, others react against it; it is best simply to gauge your own child's reactions.

What to take

These can be bought in Malaysia but are often expensive. If you are staying any length of time in one place, it may be worth taking Terry's (cloth) nappies. All you need is a bucket and some double-strength nappy cleanse (simply soak and rinse). Cotton nappies dry quickly in the heat and are generally more comfortable for the baby or **Disposable nappies** child. They also reduce rubbish; many countries are not geared to the disposal of nappies. Of course, the best way for a child is to be nappy-free like the local children.

Baby products Many Western baby products are now available in Southeast Asia: shampoo, talcum powder, soap and lotion. Baby wipes can be difficult to find.

Checklist Baby wipes; child paracetamol; disinfectant; first aid kit; flannel; immersion element for boiling water; Kalvol and/or Snuffle Babe or equivalent for colds; instant food for under-one-year-olds; mug/bottle/bowl/spoons; nappy cleanse, double-strength; ORS/ORT (Oral Rehydration Salts or Therapy) such as Dioralyte, widely available in the countries covered here, and the most effective way to alleviate diarrhoea (it is not a cure); portable baby chair, to hook onto tables - not essential but can be very useful; sarung or backpack for carrying child (and/or light weight collapsible buggy); sterilizing tablets (and an old baby-wipes container for sterilizing bottles, teats, utensils); cream for nappy rash and other skin complaints such as Sudocreme; sunblock, factor 15 or higher; sunhat; Terry's (cloth) nappies, liners, pins and plastic pants; thermometer; zip-lock bags for carrying snacks, powdered food; wet flannel.

Practicalities

Sleeping At the hottest time of year, air conditioning may be essential for a baby or young child's comfort. This rules out many of the cheaper hotels, but air conditioned accommodation is available in all but the most out-of-the-way spots. When the child is bathing, be aware that the water could carry parasites, so avoid letting him or her drink it.

Food & drink The advice given in the health section on food and drink (see page 56) should be applied even more stringently where young children are concerned. Be aware that expensive hotels may have squalid cooking conditions; the cheapest street stall is often more hygienic. Where possible, try to watch food being prepared. Stir-fried vegetables and rice or noodles are the best bet; meat and fish may be pre-cooked and then left out before being re-heated. Fruit can be bought cheaply right across Southeast Asia: papaya, banana and avocado are all excellent sources of nutrition, and can be self-peeled ensuring cleanliness. Powdered milk is also available throughout the region, although most brands have added sugar. But if taking a baby, breast feeding is strongly recommended. Powdered food can be bought in most towns, the quality may not be the same as equivalent foods bought in the West, but it is perfectly adequate for short periods. Bottled water and fizzy drinks are also sold widely. If your child is at the 'grab everything and put it in mouth' stage, a damp cloth and some Dettol (or equivalent) are useful. Frequent wiping of hands and tabletops can help to minimize the chance of infection.

Transport Public transport may be a problem; trains are fine but long bus journeys are restrictive and uncomfortable. Hiring a car is undoubtedly the most convenient way to see a country with a small child. Back-seatbelts are rarely fitted but it is possible to buy child-seats in capital cities.

Health

Younger travellers seem to be more prone to illness abroad, but that should not put you off taking them. More preparation is necessary than for an adult and perhaps a little more care should be taken when travelling to remote areas where health services are primitive. This is because children can become more rapidly ill than adults (they often recover more quickly however).

Diarrhoea and vomiting are the most common problems so take the usual precautions, but more intensively. Make sure all basic childhood vaccinations are up to date as well as the more exotic ones. Children should be properly protected against diphtheria, whooping cough, mumps and measles. If they have not had the disease, teenage girls should be given rubella (German measles) vaccination. Consult your doctor for advice on BCG inoculation against tuberculosis: the disease is still common in the region. Protection against mosquitos and drug prophylaxis against malaria is essential. Many children take to 'foreign' food quite happily. Milk may be unavailable outside big cities. Powdered milk may be the answer; breast feeding for babies even better.

Upper respiratory infections such as colds, catarrh and middle ear infections are common – antibiotics could be carried against the possibility. Outer ear infections after swimming are also common, antibiotic ear drops will help. The treatment of diarrhoea is the same as for adults except that it should start earlier and be continued with more persistence. Children get dehydrated very quickly in the tropics and can become drowsy and unco-operative unless cajoled to drink water or juice plus salts. Oral rehydration has been a lifesaving technique in children.

Emergencies Babies and small children deteriorate very rapidly when ill. A travel insurance policy which has an air ambulance provision is strongly recommended. When planning a route, try to stay within 24 hours' travel of a hospital with good care and facilities. Many expatriats fly to Singapore for medical care, which has the best doctors and facilities in the region.

Sunburn NEVER allow your child to be exposed to the harsh tropical sun without protection. A child can burn in a matter of minutes. Loose cotton clothing, with long sleeves and legs and a sun-hat are best. High-factor sun-protection cream is essential.

Further reading

Malaysia

Novels Burgess, Anthony: Burgess lived in Malaysia between 1954 and 1957, learnt Malay, and mixed with the locals to a far greater extent than Maugham or Conrad, and this is reflected in a much more nuanced understanding of the Malay character. After leaving Malaya in 1957, he taught in Brunei until 1960. Among his books are *Time for a Tiger* (1956), *The Enemy in the Blanket* (1958) and *Beds in the East* (1959) which were later published together by Penguin as *Malayan Trilogy*.

Conrad, Joseph: Perhaps the finest novelist of the Malay archipelago, books include *Lord Jim*, the tale of Jim, who abandons his ship and seeks refuge from his guilt in Malaya, earning in the process the sobriquet Lord, and *Victory*, arguably Conrad's finest novel, based in the Malay Archipelago. Both are widely available in paperback editions from most bookshops. Also worth reading is *The Rescue*, Penguin: London. Set in the Malay Archipelago in the 1860s; the hero, Captain Lingard, is forced to choose between his Southeast Asian friend and his countrymen.

Keith, Agnes (1969) *Land below the Wind*, Ulverscroft: Leicester. Perhaps the best-known English language book on Sabah. See page 452.

Maniam, KS (1983) *The Return*, Skoob Books: London. The novel, by a Indian Malaysian, is about the difficulties a Hindu has in finding a home in Malaysia, especially since the Indian in question is educated at a British colonial school.

Maugham, William Somerset (1969) *Maugham's Malaysian Stories*, Heinemann: London and Singapore. Another English novelist who wrote extensively on Malaysia.

Essentials

These stories are best for the insight they provide of colonial life, not of the Malay or Malay life.

Theroux, Paul (1979) *The Consul's File*, Penguin. A selection of short stories based on Malaysia.

Travel   Bird, Isabella (1883 and reprinted 1983) *The Golden Chersonese*, Murray: London, reprinted by Century paperback. The account of a late 19th century female visitor to the region who shows her gumption facing everything from natives to crocs.

Bock, Carl (1985, first published 1881) *The Headhunters of Borneo*, OUP: Singapore. Bock was a Norwegian naturalist and explorer and was commissioned by the Dutch to make a scientific survey of southeastern Borneo. His account, though, makes much of the dangers and adventures that he faced, and some of his 'scientific' observations are, in retrospect, clearly highly faulty. Nonetheless, this is an entertaining account.

Charles, Hose (1985, first published 1929) *The Field Book of a Jungle Wallah*, OUP: Singapore. Hose was an official in Sarawak and became an acknowledged expert on the material and non-material culture of the tribes of Sarawak. He was one of that band of highly informed, perceptive and generally benevolent colonial administrators.

King, Victor T (edit). (1992) *The Best of Borneo Travel*, OUP: Oxford. A compilation of travel accounts from the early 19th century through to the late 20th. An excellent companion to take while exploring the island. Published in portable paperback.

Mjoberg, Eric: *Forest Life and Adventures in the Malay Archipelago*, OUP: Singapore.

O'Hanlon, Redmond (1984) *Into the Heart of Borneo*, Salamander Press: Edinburgh. One of the best recent travel books on Borneo. This highly amusing and perceptive romp through Borneo in the company of poet and foreign correspondent James Fenton, includes an ascent of the Rejang River and does much to counter the more romanticized images of Bornean life.

History   Harrisson, Tom (1959) *World Within*, Hutchinson: London. During the Second World War, explorer, naturalist and ethnologist Tom Harrisson was parachuted into Borneo to help organize Dayak resistance against the occupying Japanese forces. This is his extraordinary account.

Barber, Noel (1971) *The War of the Running Dogs: Malaya 1948-1960*, Arrow Books. This is one of numerous accounts of the Malayan Emergency and the successful British attempt to defeat the Communist Party of Malaya.

Turnbull, Mary C (1989) *A History of Malaysia, Singapore and Brunei*, Allen and Unwin. A very orthodox history of Malaysia, Singapore and Brunei, clearly written for a largely academic/student audience.

Chapman, F Spencer: *The Jungle is Neutral*. An account of a British guerrilla force fighting the Japanese in Borneo — not as enthralling as Tom Harrisson's book, but still worth reading.

Payne, Robert: *The White Rajahs of Sarawak*. Readable account of the extraordinary history of this East Malaysian state.

Natural history   Briggs, John (1988) *Mountains of Malaysia: a Practical Guide and Manual*, Longman: London. He has also written *Parks of Malaysia*, useful for anyone intending to especially visit the country's protected areas (Longman: Kuala Lumpur).

Cranbrook, Earl of (1987) *Riches of the Wild: Land Mammals of South-East Asia*, OUP.

Cubitt, Gerald and Payne, Junaidi (1990) *Wild Malaysia*, London: New Holland. Large format, coffee table book, lots of wonderful colour photos, reasonable text, short background piece on each national park.

Hanbury-Tenison, Robin (1980) *Mulu, the Rain Forest*, Arrow/Weidenfeld. This is the product of a Royal Geographical Society trip to Mulu in the late 1970s; semi-scholarly and useful.

Payne, Junaidi et al: *Pocket Guide to Birds of Borneo*, World Wildlife Fund/Sabah Society.

Payne, Junaidi et al: *A Field Guide to the Mammals of Borneo*, World Wildlife Fund/Sabah Society. Good illustrations, reasonable text, but very dry.

Tweedie, MWF and Harrison, JL (1954 with new editions) *Malayan Animal Life*, Longman.

Wallace, Alfred Russel (1869) *The Malay Archipelago*. A classic of Victorian travel writing by one of the finest naturalists of the period. Wallace travelled through all of island Southeast Asia over a period of some years. The original is now re-printed. Wallace, Alfred Russel (1869).

Leee, Kit (1989) *Adoi*, Times Books: Singapore. An amusing book of Malaysian attitudes to most things.

Craig, Jo Ann: *Culture Shock Malaysia*. One in a series of Culture Shock books, this examines and assesses the do's and don'ts of Malaysian and Singapore society. Useful for those going to live or spend an extended period in the region.

Lat: Lat is Malaysia's foremost cartoonist. His images of the effects of social and economic change on a simple kampung boy are amusing and highly perceptive. His cartoons are compiled in numerous books including *Kampung boy* and *Town boy*, published by Straits Times Publishing.

Other books

Essentials

Southeast Asia

Buruma, Ian (1989) *God's Dust*, Jonathan Cape: London. Enjoyable journey through Burma, Thailand, Malaysia and Singapore along with the Philippines, Taiwan, South Korea and Japan; journalist Buruma questions how far culture in this region has survived the intrusion of the West.

Caufield, C (1985) *In the Rainforest*, Heinemann: London. This readable and well-researched analysis of rainforest ecology and the pressures on tropical forests is part-based in the region.

Clad, James (1989) *Behind the Myth: Business, Money and Power in Southeast Asia*, Unwin Hyman: London. Clad, formerly a journalist with the Far Eastern Economic Review, distilled his experiences in this book; as it turned out, rather disappointingly – it is a hotch-potch of journalistic snippets – but is worth taking along to dip into.

Dingwall, Alastair (1994) *Traveller's Literary Companion to South-east Asia*, In Print: Brighton. Experts on Southeast Asian language and literature select extracts from novels and other books by Western and regional writers. The extracts are annoyingly brief, but it gives a good overview of what is available.

Dumarçay, Jacques (1991) *The Palaces of South-East Asia: Architecture and Customs*, OUP: Singapore. A broad summary of palace art and architecture in both mainland and island Southeast Asia.

Fraser-Lu, Sylvia (1988) *Handwoven Textiles of South-East Asia*, OUP: Singapore. Well-illustrated, large-format book with informative text.

King, Ben F and Dickinson, EC (1975) *A Field Guide to the Birds of South-East Asia*, Collins: London. Best regional guide to the birdlife of the region.

Osborne, Milton (1979) *Southeast Asia: an Introductory History*, Allen & Unwin: Sydney. Good introductory history, clearly written, published in a portable paperback edition and recently revised and reprinted.

Reid, Anthony (1988 and 1993) *Southeast Asia in the Age of Commerce 1450-1680*, Yale University Press: New Haven. Perhaps the best history of everyday life in Southeast Asia, looking at such themes as physical well-being, material culture and social organization; meticulously researched.

Rigg, Jonathan (1991) *Southeast Asia: a Region in Transition*, Routledge: London. A thematic geography of the ASEAN region, providing an insight into some of the major issues affecting the region today.

SarDesai, DR (1989) *Southeast Asia: Past and Present*, Macmillan: London. Skilful but at times frustratingly thin history of the region from the first century to the withdrawal of US forces from Vietnam.

Savage, Victor R (1984) *Western Impressions of Nature and Landscape in Southeast Asia*, Singapore University Press: Singapore. Based on a geography PhD thesis, the book is a mine of quotations and observations from Western travellers. Hard to get hold of as it is out of print.

Sesser, Stan (1993) *The Lands of Charm and Cruelty: Travels in Southeast Asia*, Picador: Basingstoke. A series of collected narratives first published in the *New Yorker* including essays on Singapore, Laos, Cambodia, Burma and Borneo. Finely observed and thoughtful, the book is an excellent travel companion.

Steinberg, DJ et al (1987) *In Search of Southeast Asia: a Modern History*, University of Hawaii Press: Honolulu. The best standard history of the region; it skilfully examines and assesses general processes of change and their impacts from the arrival of the Europeans in the region.

Tarling, Nicholas (1992) *Cambridge History of Southeast Asia*, CUP: Cambridge. Two volume edited study, long and expensive with contributions from most of the leading historians of the region. A thematic and regional approach is taken, not a country one, although the history is fairly conventional.

Waterson, Roxana (1990) *The Living House: an Anthropology of Architecture in South-East Asia*, OUP: Singapore. Illustrated, academic book on Southeast Asian architecture, fascinating material for those interested in such things.

Young, Gavin (1991) *In Search of Conrad*, Hutchinson: London. This well-known travel writer retraces the steps of Conrad; part travel-book, part fantasy, it is worth reading but not up to the standard of his other books.

Magazines *Asiaweek* (weekly). A lightweight Far Eastern Economic Review; rather like a regional *Time* magazine in style.

The Far Eastern Economic Review (weekly). Authoritative Hong Kong-based regional magazine; their correspondents based in each country provide knowledgeable, in-depth analysis particularly on economics and politics, sometimes in rather a turgid style.

Maps & guides A decent map is an indispensable aid to travelling. Although maps are usually available locally, it is sometimes useful to buy a map prior to departure to plan routes and itineraries.

Regional maps Bartholomew Southeast Asia (1:5,800,000); Nelles Southeast Asia (1:4,000,000); Hildebrand Thailand, Burma, Malaysia and Singapore (1:2,800,000); ITM (International Travel Map) Southeast Asia.

Country maps Bartholomew Singapore and Malaysia (1:150,000); Nelles Malaysia (1:1,500,000); Nelles West Malaysia (1:650,000); Nelles Singapore (1:22,500); Nelles Indonesia (1:4,000,000).

City maps Nelles Singapore; Bartholomew Singapore.

Other maps Tactical Pilotage Charts (TPC, US Airforce) (1:500,000); Operational Navigational Charts (ONC, US Airforce) (1:500,000). Both of these are particularly good at showing relief features (useful for planning treks); less good on roads, towns and facilities.

Locally available maps Maps are widely available in Malaysia and Singapore. Both the Singapore and Malaysian tourist boards produce good maps of their respective capital cities and in the case of Malaysia a series of state maps, rather poorer in quality. The Sabah and Sarawak tourist boards also publish reasonable maps.

Map shops In London, the best selection is available from Stanfords, 12-14 Long Acre, London WC2E 9LP, T020-78361321; also recommended is McCarta, 15 Highbury Place, London N15 1QP, T020-73541616.

Malaysia Nelles Map; Shell Map of Malaysia (available from Shell stations in Malaysia). Concertina Road Maps – Peninsula Malaysia and Sabah, Sarawak and Brunei, published by Falcon Press.

Useful websites

Malaysians are pretty Internet savvy so there is a fair amount of information on the web. The tourist boards have websites which are OK for a browse but tend to be rather generalized. The best, oddly, are those for the East Malaysian states of Sabah and Sarawak.

tourism.gov.my/default11.1.html   The website for *Tourism Malaysia*.
www.sarawak.gov.my/   The Sarawak Tourism Board's own website, with 20 pages of information, mostly commercial.
www.asiainfo-by-cj.com   A good and informative non-commercial website on Malaysia and some other parts of Southeast Asia.
www.kiat.net   A website set up by a young Malaysian with excellent material on things like Putrajaya, Cyberjaya, KLIA and transport systems in Malaysia.
headlines.yahoo.com/full_coverage/world/malaysia/   An excellent news site for Malaysian current affairs.
www.jaring.my/   For general information on the country.
www.yahoo.com/regional/countries/[name of country]   Insert the name of country to access practical information including material from other travel guides.
www.singapore.com/   Pacific Asia Travel Association's website with stacks of information on travel in the Pacific Asian region including statistics, markets, products etc.
www.malaysiaairlines.com   Malaysia Airlines.
www.pelangiair.com   Pelangi Airlines.
www.ktmp.com.my   Homepage of *Malaysia Railways*.

www.sg/   Links to homepage with good information on events, health, sports, business and more.   **Singapore**
www.singnet.com.sg/~leeahkee/   Good links to government, educational, travel, employment, leisure and food sites.
www.ste.com.sg   A bulletin board for businesses to post notices and adverts; also a directory of licensed travel agents in Singapore.

www.mdx.ac.uk/www/hap/brc.html   Contents of the Borneo Research Bulletin and list of members of the Borneo Research Council.   **Sites with an indigenous peoples focus**
www.halcyon.com/FWDP/help.html   Site of the Centre for World Indigenous Studies; focus tends to be rather America-centric, but still a good place to start for those interested in Fourth World (tribal) issues.
www.ics.bc.ca/ica/member.html   Site of the Indonesia-Canada Alliance NGO Partnerships; focus is on indigenous peoples in Indonesia and Canada – has material on Dayak of Borneo.
www.pip.dknet.dk/~pip1917/publicat.html   Site of the International Work Group for Indigenous Affairs (IWGIA); good links with related sites and good source of articles.
www.icppgr.fao.org/links/2.html   Focus on traditional and indigenous knowledge; good links with related sites.

Essentials

General Asia   Listed below are internet addresses which access information on Asia generally, or the Southeast Asian region. Websites offer a whole range of information on a vast variety of topics. Below is only a selection. Note that websites on Asia are multiplying like rabbits and this makes searching a sometimes frustrating business.

www.city.net/regions/asia   Pointer to information on Asian countries.

www.branch.com:80/silkroute/   Information on hotels, travel, news and business in Asia.

www.agora.stm.it/politic   Information on political parties and organizations, good links, by country or by region.

www.aseansec.org   Homepage of the Asean Secretariat, the Southeast Asian regional organization of which Singapore is a founder member. Lots of government statistics, acronyms etc.

Kuala Lumpur

3

Kuala Lumpur

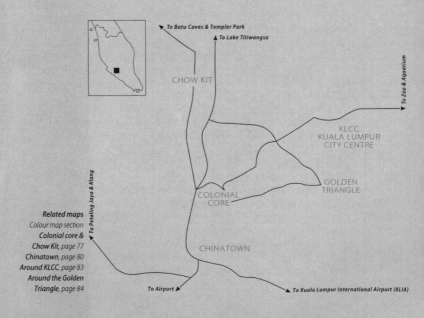

To Batu Caves & Templer Park

To Lake Titiwangsa

To Zoo & Aquarium

CHOW KIT

KLCC
KUALA LUMPUR
CITY CENTRE

To Petaling Jaya & Klang

GOLDEN
TRIANGLE

COLONIAL
CORE

CHINATOWN

Related maps
Colour map section
Colonial core &
Chow Kit, page 77
Chinatown, page 80
Around KLCC, page 83
Around the Golden
Triangle, page 84

To Airport

To Kuala Lumpur International Airport (KLIA)

In the space of a century, Kuala Lumpur grew from a trading post and tin mining shanty town into a colonial capital. Today, it is a modern, cosmopolitan business hub and the centre of government.

The economic boom that started in the late 1980s has caused a building boom that rivals Singapore's. In downtown Kuala Lumpur, old and new are juxtaposed – and the digger and piledriver seem to be nowhere far from eyesight or earshot. The jungled backdrop of the copper-topped clock tower of the Supreme Court of a century ago has been replaced by scores of stylish high-rise office blocks, dominated by the soaring, angular-roofed Maybank headquarters. The Victorian Moorish and Moghul-style buildings, the Art Deco central market and cinemas and the Chinese shophouses stand in marked contrast to these impressive new skyscrapers. The most recent addition to the modern skyline is the Petronas Twin Tower, also known as KLCC (Kuala Lumpur City Centre), the tallest building in the world.

Ins and outs

Getting there
See also Transport,
page 110

As befitting Malaysia's capital, KL is well linked to both other areas of Malaysia and to the wider world. The new international airport at Sepang provides a slick entrance to the country, although there is no rail link (yet) with the city, over 70 km to the north. There are domestic air connections (including to Sabah and Sarawak) from both Sepang and a handful from the old international airport at Subang. Visitors arriving by train or bus are deposited right in the city centre. From KL's stylish colonial railway station there are train connections with Bangkok (Thailand), Singapore and with destinations on the Malaysian peninsula. Puduraya bus station also has international connections south to Singapore and north to Bangkok, as well as to many towns on the Peninsula.

Getting around
Population: nearly 1.5
million
Phone code: 03
Colour map 2, grid A2

Kuala Lumpur is not an easy place to get around and its sights are spread thinly over a wide area which makes life difficult for the visitor. The pedestrian is not very high on the list of priorities for the Malaysian urban planner. Many roads, especially outside the central city, are built without pavements, making walking both hazardous and difficult. In addition, with the exception of the area around Central Market, Chinatown and Dayabumi, distances between places are too great to cover comfortably on foot because of lack of pavements, heavy pollution and the humid hot climate. Like other Southeast Asian cities, with the notable exception of Singapore, the internal combustion engine rules and little consideration seems to be given to the lowly pedestrian, either by drivers or planners. The bus system is labyrinthine and congested streets means that jumping in a taxi can make for a tedious wait in a traffic jam. Do try and insist taxi drivers use their meters, although do not be surprised if they simply refuse point blank. The only solution in some cases is the LRT (Light Rail Transit).

Orientation

The streets to the north of the Padang – the cricket pitch in front of the old Selangor Club, next to the new Merdeka Square – are central shopping streets with modern department stores and smaller shops.

The colonial core is around the Padang and down Jalan Raja and Jalan Tun Perak. East of the Padang, straight over the bridge on Lebuh Pasar Besar is the main commercial area, occupied by banks and finance companies. To the southeast of Merdeka Square is KL's vibrant Chinatown.

To find a distinctively Malay area, it is necessary to venture further out, along Jalan Raja Muda Musa to Kampung Baru, to the northeast.

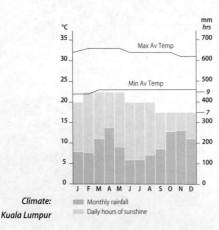

Climate:
Kuala Lumpur

Monthly rainfall
Daily hours of sunshine

To the south of Kampung Baru, on the opposite side of the Klang River, is Jalan Ampang, once KL's 'millionaires' row' – where tin towkays and sultans first built their homes. The road is now mainly occupied by embassies and high commissions. To the southeast of Jalan Ampang is KL's so-called Golden Triangle, to which the modern central business district has migrated. In recent years the city's residential districts have been expanding out towards the jungled hills surrounding the KL basin, at the far end of Ampang, past the zoo to the north, and to Bangsar, to the southwest. KL has become a city of condominiums, which have sprung up everywhere from the

Highlights

Museums and historical sights The centre of colonial Kuala Lumpur includes several Moorish-style buildings (page 78); National Art Gallery (page 78); Muzium Negara (the National Museum) (page 81).

Mosques and temples Masjid Jamek, the old Moghul-style mosque (page 76); the modern Masjid Negara (the National Mosque) (page 78); Sri Mahamariamman Hindu Temple (page 80); Chan See Shu Yuen Temple (page 81); Sze Ya Temple (page 81).

Other sights Chinatown, which retains much of its original turn-of-the-century architecture and comes alive each night with its pasar malam (night market) (page 80); Batu Caves, high on the

cliff-face of a limestone massif, and focus of Hindu pilgrimage (page 86); Templer Park, a 1,200-hectare tract of jungle (page 86).

Shopping Kuala Lumpur's Art Deco-style central market has been converted into a lively focus for the local artistic community and contains shops and stalls selling art and handicrafts (page 79); the Chinatown street market (pasar malam) sells everything from ten-cent trinkets and cheap T-shirts to inexpensive leather goods and copy watches (page 80).

Sport Royal Selangor Club for golf (page 109); a water theme park at Sunway Lagoon and adventure park at The Mines (page 109).

centre of town to these outlying suburbs. Greater Kuala Lumpur sprawls out into the Klang Valley, once plantation country and now home to the industrial satellites of Petaling Jaya and Shah Alam.

The most recent – and grandiose – development is Putrajaya, Malaysia's new administrative capital, which is being hacked out of plantations 35 km south of KL. When it is completed in 2005, Putrajaya's projected population will be 250,000, although its first bureaucrats were due to be relocated from congested KL as soon as 1998. The city will cost a cool US$8bn. Other developments in this area to the south of KL include the new international airport which opened in 1998 (45 km from KL) and the Cyberjaya, the heart of Malaysia's much vaunted Multimedia Super Corridor.

History

Kuala Lumpur means 'muddy confluence' in Malay – as apt a description today as it was in the pioneer days of the 1870s. This romantic name refers to the Klang and Gombak rivers that converge in the middle of the city – there is also some evidence that the *kopi-susu*-coloured Gombak was once known as the *Sungai Lumpur*. Kuala Lumpur, which nearly everyone knows as KL, has grown up around the Y-shaped junction of these rivers in the area called *Ulu Klang* – the upper reaches of the Klang River.

In 1857, members of the Selangor Royal family – including Rajah Abdullah, the Bugis chief of the old state capital of Klang – mounted an expedition to speculate for tin along the upper reaches of the Klang River. Backed by money from Melakan businessmen, 87 Chinese prospectors travelled up the river by raft to the confluence of the Klang and the Gombak. After trekking through dense jungle they stumbled across rich tin deposits near what is now Ampang. Sixty-nine miners on this first expedition died of malaria within a month.

This did not stop Rajah Abdullah from organizing a second expeditionary labour force, which succeeded in mining commercial quantities of tin, taking it downriver to Klang. Until then Malaya's tin-mining industry had been concentrated in the Kinta Valley near Ipoh, to the north. At about this time, the invention of canning as a means of preserving food led to strong world demand for tin. Spotting a good business opportunity, two Chinese merchants opened a small trading-post at the confluence in 1859. One of them, Hiu Siew, was later appointed *Kapitan Cina* – the first headman of the new settlement. But secret society rivalry between the Hai San (which controlled KL) and the Ghee Hin (which controlled a nearby settlement) retarded the township's early development. Malaria also remained a big problem and fires regularly engulfed and destroyed parts of the town.

By the mid-1860s, KL, which was still predominantly Chinese, began to prosper under the guiding hand of its sheriff, **Yap Ah Loy**. He was a Hakka gang leader from China, who arrived in Melaka in 1854, fought in Negri Sembilan's riots at Sungai Ujong (see page 199), then went to KL in 1862 where he became a tin magnate – or *towkay* – and ran gambling dens and brothels. But he emerged as a respected community leader and in 1868, at the age of 31, he was appointed *Kapitan Cina* of Kuala Lumpur by the Sultan of Selangor. He remained the headman until his death in 1885.

Frank Swettenham, the British Resident of Selangor, then took the reins, having moved the administrative centre of the Residency from Klang in 1880. The same year, KL replaced Klang as the capital of the state of Selangor; shortly after Yap's death, it became the capital of the Federated Malay States. Swettenham pulled down the ramshackle shanties and rebuilt the town with wider streets and brick houses. In the National Museum there is a remarkable photograph of the Padang area in 1884, showing a shabby line of atap huts where the Sultan Abdul Samad Building is today. By 1887 the new national

The town residence (in Jalan Pudu) of the last Captain China

The only legal Hash in Malaysia

Around the turn of the century, the annual dare in colonial KL involved swimming from the Royal Selangor Club terrace to the State Secretariat and back when the Klang River flooded the Padang. But the Spotted Dog, as the club was affectionately known, was also home to another eccentric sporting event which caught on around the world. The Hash, a cross-country chase – which is invariably followed by a drinking bout – was started in 1938, when the Selangor Club was the preferred watering hole for colonial bachelors. A Mr GS Gisbert, having drunk too much at the Long Bar, went for a jog around the Padang to sober up. In no time, Mr Gilbert's Hash had a band of disciples who took to the new sport with varying degrees of seriousness.

The run, named after the Club's dining room, the Hash House, ventured into the countryside surrounding KL where 'hounds' chased 'hares' – along a paper trail. The KL hash, known as the 'mother hash' to Hash House Harriers around the world (there are now 300 clubs in more than 60 countries) normally involves runs of 3-8 km, which are usually fairly jovial affairs. Most big Malaysian towns have a Hash and there are several branches in KL – men-only, women-only and mixed. Although popular among expatriates, many locals participate these days and visitors are welcome. For details, contact Kuala Lumpur Hash House Harriers, PO Box 10182, KL; T2484846.

Kuala Lumpur

capital had 518 brick houses and a population of 4,050. By 1910, when the magnificent Moorish-style railway station was completed, the city's population had risen more than 10-fold; nearly four-fifths of the population was Chinese. The town continued to grow in the following decades, becoming increasingly multiracial in character, as the British educated the Malay nobility, then employed them as administrators. The Indian population also grew rapidly; many were brought from South India to work on the roads and railways and the plantations in the Klang Valley.

In the Second World War, the city was bombed by the Allies, but little real damage was incurred. The Japanese surrendered in KL on 13 September 1945. Three years later, there was a massive influx of squatters into the city, with the start of the Communist Emergency. The city area quickly became overcrowded, so in 1952 Petaling Jaya, KL's satellite town, was founded to relieve the pressure. It subsequently went on to attract many of Malaysia's early manufacturing industries. Following the end of the Emergency, Malaya became the Federation of Malaysia on 31 August 1957. Independence was declared by the late Prime Minister Tunku Abdul Rahman ('Papa Malaysia') in the brand new Merdeka Stadium.

Modern Kuala Lumpur

In 1974, the 243 km² area immediately surrounding the city was formerly declared the Federal Territory of Kuala Lumpur, with a separate administration from its mother state of Selangor. Today, KL's population is approaching 1½ million, and although one of the smallest capitals in Southeast Asia, it is a rapidly growing business centre, its industrial satellites gaining the lion's share of the country's manufacturing investment. The most recent addition to the modern skyline is the Petronas Twin Tower, also known as KLCC (Kuala Lumpur City Centre), which when it was completed in 1996 was the tallest building in the world at 88 storeys and 421m. The bridge connecting the two towers claims the title of the highest bridge in the world. When it was under construction in 1995 and 1996 the contractors were completing a floor every four days – and were being paid RM2.2m a day. The structure was designed by American architect Cesar Pelli and the surrounding park by the Brazilian landscape artist Roberto Marx Burle.

There have been efforts to create a 'new Malaysian architecture', to lend the city a more integrated look and a national identity. Such buildings include the modern-Islamic National Mosque, the National Museum and the Putra World Trade Centre (the latter two have *Minangkabau*-style roofs) and the 34-storey Dayabumi complex, by the river, with its modern Islamic latticed arches. At the same time, KL has also been trying to cultivate a 'garden city' image like neighbouring Singapore; from the top of its sky scrapers, KL looks green and spacious, although green areas are fast being taken over by building developments. Despite all this, KL may not entirely have outgrown its pioneering tin-town mentality: rumour has it that the speculators were still looking for tin when the subterranean car park was built beneath the Padang at Merdeka Square in the mid-1980s.

Frankly, recent building development has done much to detract from what, just a few years ago, was a relatively quiet capital city. But as well as becoming increasingly noisy and congested, KL is also suffering from serious air pollution – or 'the haze' as it is known locally. The cause of the haze is widely thought to be the fires that burn uncontrollably in Sumatra and Kalimantan during the summer months, July to September. At the end of 1994, pollution levels at Shah Alam, a suburb of KL, reached '500' ('300' is deemed hazardous by the authorities). Visibility was down to 400m, making landings at KL's airport difficult. But though the root cause of the haze may be fires in Indonesia, it is when this smoke mixes with car fumes and other emissions that it becomes downright dangerous. Locals also note the convenience of being able to blame fires in another country for pollution problems at home: it means the authorities don't have to do anything about it. Whenever environmentalists have suggested ways to reduce pollution in the capital they have got nowhere. Instead, while KL hospitals fill up with children suffering from bronchial problems, the health ministry feebly recommends that Malaysians wear surgical masks and give up exercising outside. "But", as S Jayasankaran wrote in 1997, "the ministry can't advise them to stop breathing."

Sights

The Colonial Core

At the muddy confluence of the Klang and Gombak rivers where KL's founders stepped ashore, stands the Masjid Jamek, formerly the National Mosque (main entrance on Jalan Tun Perak). Built in 1909, the design by the English architect, AB Hubbock, was based on that of a Moghul mosque in North India. The mosque has a walled courtyard, or *sahn*, and a three-domed prayer hall. It is striking with its striped white and salmon-coloured brickwork and domed minarets, cupolas and arches. Surrounded by coconut palms, the mosque is an oasis of peace in the middle of modern KL, as is testified by the number of Malays who sleep through the heat of the lunchtime rush-hour on the prayer hall's cool marbled floors. ■ *Daily 0900-1100, 1400-1600*.

Behind the mosque, from the corner of Jalan Tuanku Abdul Rahman and Jalan Raja Laut, are the colonial-built public buildings, distinguished by their grand, Moorish architecture. All were the creation of AC Norman, a colleague of Hubbock's, and were built between 1894 and 1897. The photogenic former State Secretariat, now called the **Sultan Abdul Samad – or SAS – Building**,

Colonial core & Chow Kit

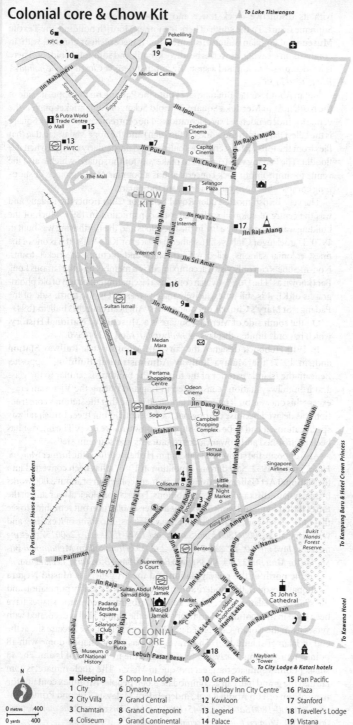

Kuala Lumpur

■ Sleeping

1 City	**6** Dynasty	**11** Holiday Inn City Centre	**16** Plaza
2 City Villa	**7** Grand Central	**12** Kowloon	**17** Stanford
3 Chamtan	**8** Grand Centrepoint	**13** Legend	**18** Traveller's Lodge
4 Coliseum	**9** Grand Continental	**14** Palace	**19** Vistana
5 Drop Inn Lodge	**10** Grand Pacific	**15** Pan Pacific	

5 Drop Inn Lodge
10 Grand Pacific
15 Pan Pacific

Related map
Colour map section

To Lake Titiwangsa

N

0 metres 400
0 yards 400

with its distinctive clock tower and bulbous copper domes, houses the Supreme Court. To the south of here is another Moorish building, the **Textile Museum**, at 26 Jalan Sultan Hishamuddin. It has excellent content, with an emphasis on weaving, as well as beadwork, batik and some embroidery. There is a video presentation and a shop. Recommended. ■ *Closed public holidays, RM1, T2917136.*

Sultan Abdul Samad Building faces onto the **Padang** on the opposite side of the road, next to **Merdeka Square**. The old Selangor Club cricket pitch is the venue for Independence Day celebrations. The centrepiece of Merdeka Square is the tallest flagpole in the world (100m high) and the huge Malaysian flag that flies from the top can be seen across half the city, particularly at night when it is floodlit. The Padang was trimmed to make way for the square, which is also the venue for impromptu rock concerts and is a popular meeting place. A shopping complex has been built underneath the square.

The very British mock-Tudor **Royal Selangor Club** fronts the Padang and was the centre of colonial society after its construction in 1890. Much of the building was damaged by a fire in the late 1960s and the north wing was built in 1970. The Selangor Club is still a gathering place for KL's VIPs. It has one of the finest colonial saloons, filled with trophies and pictures of cricket teams. Non-members can only visit if accompanied by a member and the famous Long Bar (known as 'The Dog') – which contains a fascinating collection of old photographs of KL – is still an exclusively male preserve. On the north side of the Padang is **St Mary's Church**, one of the oldest Anglican churches built in 1894.

On the south side of Merdeka Square is a **Museum of National History**, which has only limited displays. ■ *Daily 0900-1800, T2944590.*

In 1910 Hubbock designed the fairy-tale Moorish-style **Railway Station** and, in 1917, the **Malaya Railway Administration Building**, opposite. Beneath the Islamic exterior of the former, the building is similar to the glass and iron railway stations constructed in England during the Victorian era – except this one was built by convict labour. It is said that the station's construction was delayed because the original roof design did not meet British railway specifications; it had to be able to support snow a metre deep. The interior has been refurbished and now includes restaurants and souvenir stalls.

Also opposite the station on Jalan Sultan Hishamuddin is the former *Majestic Hotel*, built in 1932. Saved from demolition in 1983, it has been converted into the **National Art Gallery**, housing a permanent collection of about 2,000 works by Malaysian artists and touring exhibitions. For a chronological tour start at the top of the building and work down. It is a diverse collection but refreshing to see that most of the work retains a distinctively Malay spirit, some of it exciting and very original. ■ *1000-1800 Mon-Sun, closed 1200-1500 Fri, T2300157. Getting there: Sri Jaya bus 30, 47, 238, 247, 251, 252, 337 (from Sultan Mohammad Bus Station) or Mini Bus 22, 33, 35, 38 (from Bangkok Bank Bus Stand, Lebuh Pasar).*

To the north of the railway station and the art gallery is **Masjid Negara** (National Mosque), the modern spiritual centre of KL's Malay population and the symbol of Islam for the whole country. Abstract, geometric shapes have been used in the roofing and grillwork, while the Grand Hall is decorated with verses from the Koran. Completed in 1965, it occupies a five hectare site at the end of Jalan Hishamuddin. The prayer hall has a star-shaped dome with 18 points, representing Malaysia's 13 states and the five pillars of Islam. The 48 smaller domes emulate the great mosque in Mecca. The single minaret is 73m tall and the grand hall can accommodate 8,000 people. An annex contains the mausoleum of Tun Abdul Razak, independent Malaysia's second Prime Minister. ■ *0900-1800 Sat-Thur, 1445-1800 Fri. Muslims can visit the mosque from 0630-2200. Women must use a separate entrance.*

Close to the national mosque is the new Museum of Islamic Arts, still only partly open.

North of the mosque, back towards the Padang, is the 35-storey, marble **Dayabumi Complex**. Located on Jalan Raya, it is one of KL's most striking modern landmarks. It was designed by local architect Datuk Nik Mohamed, and introduces contemporary Islamic achitecture to the skyscraper era. The government office-cum-shopping centre used to house Petronas, the secretive national oil company, which has since moved to the even more grandiose Petronas Twin Tower. Try getting permission to stand on the 30th floor helipad where a superb, but fading (and increasingly obsolete) pictorial map of all the city's sights has been painted on the rooftop. Next door to the Dayabumi Complex is the General Post Office.

On the opposite bank to the Dayabumi complex, is the **Central Market**, a former wet market built in 1928 in Art Deco-style, tempered with 'local Baroque' trimmings. In the early 1980s it was revamped to become a focus for KL's artistic community and a handicraft centre – KL's version of London's Covent Garden or San Francisco's Fisherman's Wharf. It is a warren of boutiques, handicraft and souvenir stalls – some with their wares laid out on the wet market's original marble slabs – and is now a bit of a tourist trap, although it is definitely worth visiting for a one-stop buying spree. On the second level of the market are several restaurants and a small hawker centre.

Petaling Street on a quiet day; the processional route of Chinese feast

Kuala Lumpur

Chinatown

Southeast of the Central Market, lies Chinatown, roughly bounded by Jalan Bandar, Jalan Petaling and Jalan Sultan. It was the core of Yap Ah Loy's KL (see page 74) and is a mixture of crumbling shophouses, market stalls, coffee shops and restaurants. This quarter wakes up during late afternoon, after about 1630, and evening, when its streets become the centre of frenetic trading and haggling. Jalan Petaling and parts of Jalan Sultan are transformed into an open air night market, *pasar malam,* and food stalls selling Chinese, Indian and Malay delicacies, fruit stalls, copy watch stalls, music cassettes, leather bag stalls and all manner of impromptu boutiques line the streets. Jalan Hang Lekir, which straddles the gap between Jalan Sultan and Jalan Petaling, is full of popular Chinese restaurants and coffee shops. Off the north side of Jalan Hang Lekir, there is a lively covered fruit and vegetable market in two intersecting arcades.

South of Jalan Hang Lekir, tucked away on Jalan Tun HS Lee (Jalan Bandar) is the extravagantly decorated **Sri Mahamariamman Temple**, incorporating gold, precious stones and Spanish and Italian tiles. It was founded in 1873 by Tamils who had come to Malaya as contract labourers to work in the rubber plantations or on the roads and railways. Its construction was funded by the

Chinatown

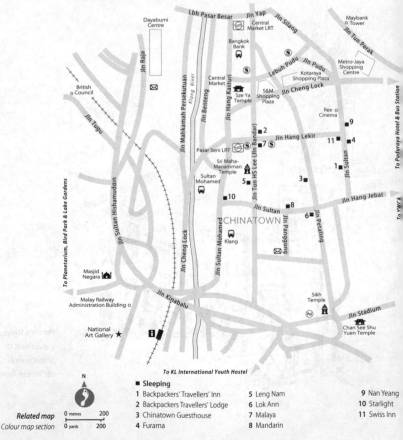

■ **Sleeping**
1 Backpackers' Travellers' Inn
2 Backpackers' Travellers' Lodge
3 Chinatown Guesthouse
4 Furama

5 Leng Nam
6 Lok Ann
7 Malaya
8 Mandarin

9 Nan Yeang
10 Starlight
11 Swiss Inn

Related map
Colour map section

0 metres   200
0 yards   200

wealthy Chettiar money-lending caste, and it was rebuilt on its present site in 1985. It has a silver chariot dedicated to Lord Murugan (Subramaniam), which is taken in procession to the Batu Caves (see page 86) during the Thaipusam festival, when Hindu devotees converge on the temple. The best time to visit is on Friday lunchtimes, from 1230, when Muslims head off to the mosques. Large numbers flock to the temple to participate in the ritual; this is usually preceded by about half an hour's chanting, accompanied by music. In testament to Malaysia's sometimes muddled ethnic and religious mix, it is not uncommon to find Chinese devotees joining in the ceremony.

There are two prominent Chinese temples in the Chinatown area. The elaborate **Chan See Shu Yuen Temple**, at the southernmost end of Jalan Petaling, was built in 1906 and has a typical open courtyard and symmetrical pavilions. Paintings, woodcarvings and ceramic sculptures decorate the façade. It serves both as a place of worship and as a community centre. The older **Sze Ya Temple**, close to the central market on Lebuh Pudu, off Jalan Cheng Lock, was built in the 1880s on land donated by Yap Ah Loy. He also funded the temple's construction and a photograph of him sits on one of the altars. Ancestor worship is more usually confined to the numerous ornate clan houses (*kongsis*); a typical one is the **Chan Kongsi** on Jalan Maharajalela, near the Chan See Shu Yuen Temple.

South of Chinatown, off Jalan Stadium, is the 50,000-capacity **Merdeka Stadium**, the site of Malaysia's declaration of Independence on 31 August 1957 (*merdeka* means 'freedom' in Malay). National and international sports events are held at the stadium (the famous Mohammad Ali vs. Joe Bugner fight was staged here in 1975) as well as the annual international Koran reading competition, held during Ramadan. ■ *RM1.*

Lake Gardens

Overlooking Jalan Damansara, near the south tip of the Lake Gardens, is the **Muzium Negara** (National Museum), with its traditional *Minangkabau*-style roof, and two large murals of Italian glass mosaic either side of the main entrance. They depict the main historical episodes and cultural activities of Malaysia. The museum's displays of photographs, models, artefacts and dioramas (with English-language texts) are excellent introductions to Malaysia's history, geography, natural history and culture. A Straits Chinese house from Melaka has been reconstructed in one gallery and the possessions and collections of various sultans are on show in another. The *Kris* exhibit is worth seeing and the fauna section is good. Over the next few years there is talk that the present museum building will become the Museum of Culture and a Museum of Natural Science may open near Titiwangsa Lake Gardens, on the city's north outskirts. ■ *0900-1800 Mon-Sun, closed 1200-1430 Fri, RM1, T2826255.*

Close to the museum is the south entrance to the man-made **Lake Gardens** (Taman Tasek Perdana), a park of around 90 hectares, a joggers' paradise and popular city escape. Pedal boats can be hired on the main lake, Tasek Perdana, at the weekend. The Gardens also hold a Hibiscus Garden, Taman Bunga Raya, with over 500 species; an Orchid Garden, Taman Bunga Orkid, which has over 800 species and is transformed into an orchid market at weekends; as well as children's playgrounds, picnic areas, restaurants and cafés, and a small deer park. At the north end of the Lake Gardens is the **National Monument**. Located at the far side of Jalan Parlimen, it provides a good view of Parliament House. The memorial, over 15m tall, with its dramatically posed sculpted figures, is dedicated to the heroes of Malaya's 12 year Communist Emergency (see page 498). The state of emergency was lifted in 1960, but members of the banned Communist Party managed to put a bomb under the memorial in

Kuala Lumpur

1975. Below the monument is a sculpture garden with exhibits from all over the Association of South East Asian Nations (ASEAN).

The showpiece of the Lake Gardens is the **Taman Burung** or **Bird Park**. Opened in 1991 in an effort to out-do neighbouring Singapore's famous Jurong Bird Park, this aviary is twice the size of Jurong, and encloses over 2,000 birds of 200 species, from ducks to hornbills. Spread out over eight acres of naturally landscaped gardens, most of the birds are free and very accustomed to being around people. The hornbill area is particularly exciting. It houses seven varieties of hornbill, most of which are local. A further 10 acres is under development and will eventually provide spacious enclosures for birds currently in cages. There is a reference centre, refreshment kiosk and binoculars for hire. ■ *0800-1800 Mon-Sun, RM3, child RM2.*

The Kuala Lumpur **Butterfly Park** is a five-minute drive from the main entrance of the Lake Gardens, coming in from Jalan Parlimen. It is a miniature jungle which is home to almost 8,000 butterflies, from 150 species. There are also small mammals, amphibians and reptiles, and rare tropical insects in the park. There is an insect museum and souvenir shop on the site. ■ *Daily 0900-1800, adult RM5, child RM2, RM1 admission to film.*

On the southeast edge of the park is **Tun Razak Memorial**, the former residence of Malaysia's revered second prime minister, the late Tun Abdul Razak, whose great, great, great, great, great grandfather, Sultan Abdullah of Kedah, ceded Penang to the British (see page 154). In recognition of his services – he is popularly known as the father of Malaysia's development – his old home has been turned into a memorial with the aim of preserving his documents, speeches, books and awards, including his collection of walking sticks and pipes. ■ *0900-1800 Tue-Sun closed 1200-1500 Fri, T2912111.* At the southern end of the Lake Gardens is the **National Planetarium**. The planetarium has a theatre with a 20m diameter dome screen where the Space Science Show (1100, 1400, 1600) and Sky movies are projected. Other facilities include an exhibition hall, an observatory, a viewing gallery and a 14in telescope. ■ *1000-1600 Tue-Fri, 1000-1900 Sat, Sun, closed 1200-1430 Fri. T22735484. Space Science Show adult RM3, child RM2, Sky movie adult RM6, child RM4, exhibition RM1.*

The modern 18-storey **Parliament House** and its Toblerone-shaped House of Representatives is on the west fringe of the gardens. When parliament is in session, visitors may observe parliamentary proceedings (permission must be formally obtained beforehand), and must be smartly dressed. In years gone by, many of the administrative arms of government were housed in the State Secretariat (now renamed the Sultan Abdul Samad Building) on the Padang. Most of the main government ministries are now situated in scruffy 1960s suburban office blocks off Jalan Duta, to the west.

Transport To get to the Lake Gardens, you can take buses 244 and 250 from Sultan Mohammed Bus Station and minibus 18, 21, 46, 48 from Jalan Tun Perak. Taxis away from the park can be difficult to obtain – it may be worth chartering one to wait for you or booking one in advance.

Jalan Ampang

Jalan Ampang became the home of KL's early tin millionaires and an important leafy adjunct to the colonial capital. The styles of its stately mansions ranged from Art Deco and mock-Palladian to Islamic. Today many of these buildings have become embassies and consulates. One of the lovelier **Art Deco-style buildings** now houses the **Rubber Research Institute**. Another of Jalan Ampang's fine old buildings is the old **Coq D'Or restaurant**, formerly the residence of a Chinese tin mogul, and still a great place for dinner and 'stengahs' on the terrace (*setengah* is Malay for 'half', and became the colonial term for shots of whisky and water). Further into town, another renovated house is now the **Malaysian Tourist Information Centre (MATIC)**, T2643929. It was the headquarters of the Japanese Imperial Army during the Second World War, but was originally built in 1935 by Eu Tong Seng, a wealthy Chinese rubber planter and tin mogul. Matic is a one-stop visitors' centre; as well as having a tourist information counter, it has money changing facilities, an express bus ticketing counter, reservations for package holidays, a souvenir shop, Malay restaurant, cultural shows every Tuesday, Thursday and Sunday at 1530, and audio visual shows 15 minutes long (closed until August 2000 due to renovations). The intersection of Jalan Ampang and the old circular road, Jalan Tun Razak, has become a booming shopping area in the shape of Ampang Park and City Square shopping centres.

The old Selangor Turf Club racecourse, which lies to the southeast of this intersection, is the focus of extraordinary redevelopment in the guise of the **KLCC** or **Kuala Lumpur City Centre** project – a 'city within a city'. High-rise development came late to KL but has rapidly gained a foothold; the city's offices, hotels and new shopping complexes are mostly concentrated in the Golden Triangle, on the east side of the city, near the former racecourse which is now being developed as the KLCC. When completed in another 10 years or so it will be one of the largest real estate developments in the world, covering a 40-hectare site. The first phase includes the construction of the Petronas Twin Towers (see box, page 85).

The Ampang Tower, a mere 50-storey office block, is part of phase one of the KLCC's development, as is Suria KLCC, a crescent-shaped retail and entertainment centre on the junction of Jalan Ampang and Jalan P Ramlee, the Esso Tower, a 20-hectare park with a children's playground and the Mandarin Oriental Hotel which will be a five-star establishment with over 600 rooms. Jalan Bukit Bintang and Jalan Sultan Ismail was where the first modern hotels and shopping complexes went up – the *Regent*, the *Hilton*, the *Equatorial*, *Holiday Inn*, *Shangri-La* and *Concorde*. More recently the area around Jalan Ampang and

Kuala Lumpur

Around KLCC

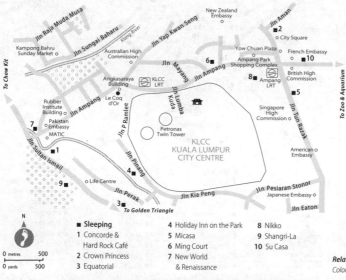

Sleeping

1 Concorde & Hard Rock Café	4 Holiday Inn on the Park	8 Nikko
2 Crown Princess	5 Micasa	9 Shangri-La
3 Equatorial	6 Ming Court	10 Su Casa
	7 New World & Renaissance	

0 metres 500
0 yards 500

Related map
Colour map section

Jalan Tun Razak has been transformed into a commercial centre; several towers have sprung up in the area in recent years, including the MBF building and the extraordinary hour-glass-shaped Pilgrims' Building, which co-ordinates the annual Haj and looks after the pilgrims' funds. There are several further developments including a new *Sheraton* and *Hyatt* both five-star tower block hotels. One of the newest shopping plazas in the Golden Triangle is *Star Hill Plaza* on Jalan Bukit Bintang, next to the new five-star *Marriott Hotel*.

A trip up to the observation deck is a must as the view is astonishing, giving an idea of the sheer scale of development taking place in the city, particularly in the KLCC area

Near the intersection of Jalan Ampang and Jalan Sultan Ismail atop Bukit Nanas stands the **KL Tower**, or **Menara KL**. This 421m-high teleBanks tower is the tallest such tower in Asia and the third tallest in the world – (viewing tower is at 276m) and, characteristically, the brain-child of PM Dr Mahathir Mohammed. There are 22 levels and 2058 stairs, so the lift is recommended! At ground level there are several shops and fast food restaurants and a mini amphitheatre. Above the viewing platform is the *Seri Angkasa* revolving restaurant. It has excellent Malay cuisine and one revolution every 60 minutes, so diners get to see the whole city between hors d'oeuvre and ice cream – should they remember to raise their heads from the trough. For reservations, T2085055. ■ *KL Tower is open daily 1000-2130, RM8, RM3 for children (4-12 years), free for children under 3 years, student RM6, T2085448, www.tm.net.my/menarakl. Getting there: no public transport – take a taxi or walk from one of the surrounding roads.*

Around the Golden Triangle

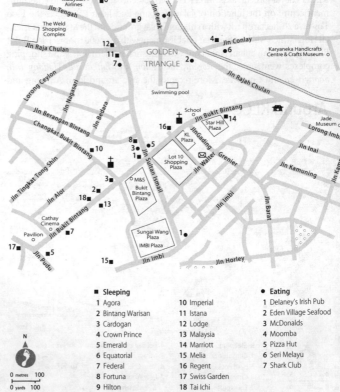

■ Sleeping		● Eating
1 Agora	10 Imperial	1 Delaney's Irish Pub
2 Bintang Warisan	11 Istana	2 Eden Village Seafood
3 Cardogan	12 Lodge	3 McDonalds
4 Crown Prince	13 Malaysia	4 Moomba
5 Emerald	14 Marriott	5 Pizza Hut
6 Equatorial	15 Melia	6 Seri Melayu
7 Federal	16 Regent	7 Shark Club
8 Fortuna	17 Swiss Garden	
9 Hilton	18 Tai Ichi	

N

Related map
Colour map section

0 metres 100
0 yards 100

Kuala Lumpur

The Petronas Twin Towers: a nation's pride and joy

Malaysians take enormous pride in the fact that the world's tallest building is found not in New York or Chicago - but Kuala Lumpur. The Petronas Towers comprise 88 storeys, and stand 452m above sea level. It has to be said that this makes it just a kangaroo leap taller than the Sears Tower in Chicago which is just 9m shorter. However, those crucial 9m have secured significant international coverage for Malaysia. Not only is the building, which was completed in 1997, a record breaker but it recently starred in the movie Entrapment *starring Sean Connery and Catherine Zeta Jones.*

The global attention is welcomed by Prime Minister Dr. Mahatir Mohamad, who strongly believes that the towers express the nation's great ambition to become a developed country. "A country needs something to look up to and we certainly have to look up to the towers", he commented at their official opening on 30 August 1999. Displaying a lack of sensitivity to the vertically challenged, he continued that "when one is short, one should stand on a box to get a better view. The twin towers is to our ego what the box is to the shorty". While the towers may symbolize the country's drive and ambition they have yet to prove an economic success. The steel and glass towers cost RM1.8bn to erect and are not yet fully occupied. One tower has been taken up wholly by Petronas, the national oil company, while the other tower is only one-third occupied.

The building was designed by the US-based Argentinean architect Cesar Pelli, who was also responsible for the design of Canary Wharf Tower in London. He has successfully created an imposing structure that strikingly looms over the capital - and sometimes above the smog. On the exterior the distinctive 58m double deck sky-bridge that links levels 41 and 42 is quite unique and make the towers instantly recognizable. Internally the skyscraper is believed to be the only one in the world with an Islamic floor motif. The geometric patterns, common in architecture of Islamic heritage, comprise two rotated and superimposed squares with circular infills. These figures symbolize unity, harmony, stability and rationality - all-important principles in Islam. It is unfortunate that the architect forgot about the visitor: there is no top floor restaurant, café or viewing platform.

The towers are just one of several significant building projects that have been undertaken in Malaysia over the last few years. These include the state of the art Kuala Lumpur International Airport at Sepang (KLIA) which opened in June 1998 at a cost of US$3.5bn; the new (and ongoing) federal government administrative centre in Putrajaya; and the creation of a multi-media super corridor south of KL which will have at its heart the new 'intelligent' city of Cyberjaya. While the Prime Minister has always enthusiastically supported these grand projects, they have also come in for some criticism as wasteful.

For information on the KLCC complex with the Petronas Towers at its heart see www.klcc.com.my. The website for the new multi-media super corridor is www.mdc.com.my.

Around the city area

The US$150m **Putra World Trade Centre** (Kompleks Seni Budaya, Jalan Conlay), to the north of the city centre on Jalan Tun Ismail, took nearly 15 years to materialize, but when it opened in 1985, Malaysia proudly announced that it was finally on the international convention and trade fair circuit. The luxurious complex of buildings includes the *Pan-Pacific Hotel*, a sleek 41-storey office block and an exhibition centre, adorned with a traditional *Minangkabau* roof. The headquarters of Prime Minister Dr Mahathir Mohamad's ruling United Malays National Organization (UMNO) occupies the top floor and there is a tourist information centre on the second floor.

The **Karyaneka Handicraft Centre** (Kompleks Seni Budaya) is on Jalan Conlay to the east of the city centre and is a popular tour group spot. A small museum illustrates batik, weaving and pottery processes. Craft demonstrations are held from 1000-1800. There is a selection of crafts for sale from each of the 13 states of Malaysia. ■ *0900-1800 Mon-Sun. Getting there: minibus or Intrakota no 40 from Jalan Tuanku Abdul Rahman.*

East of the Karyaneka Handicraft Centre, on Jalan Bukit Bintang, is the **Jade Museum**. This small museum houses a private collection of 80 jade artefacts from China. Replicas and jade souvenirs are for sale. Or, so it seems: in 1997 a case of tourists being sold fake rubies was under investigation by the police and it is likely that the authorities will take action against the museum. ■ *1000-1900 Mon-Sun, RM10. Getting there: Intrakota or minibus 40 from Klang Bus Station.*

Thean Hou Temple or the **Temple of the Goddess of Heaven** is situated at Jalan Klang Lama (off Jalan Tun Sambathan, to the southwest of the city). Perched on a hill, it has a panoramic view over KL. A contemporary Buddhist pagoda and Buddha images are enshrined in the octagonal hall. It stands between a sacred Bodhi tree and a Buddhist shrine, built by Sinhalese Buddhists in 1894. ■ *Getting there: minibus 27 from Kelang bus terminal to Jalan Syed Putra.*

Excursions

North

Batu Caves This system of caverns set high in a massive limestone outcrop, 13 km north of KL, were 'discovered' by American naturalist William Hornaby in the 1880s. In 1891 Hindu priests set up a shrine in the main cave dedicated to Lord Subramaniam and it has now become the biggest Indian pilgrimage centre in Malaysia during the annual Thaipusam festival (see page 50) when over 800,000 Hindus congregate here.

The main cave is reached by a steep flight of 272 steps. Coloured lights provide illumination for the fantasy features and formations of the karst limestone cavern. There are a number of other less spectacular caves in the outcrop, including the Museum Cave (at ground level) displaying elaborate sculptures of Hindu mythology. During the Second World War, the Japanese Imperial Army used some of the caves as factories for the manufacture of ammunition and as arms dumps; the concrete foundations for the machinery can be seen at the foot of the cliffs. ■ *RM1. Getting there: Intrakota or minibus 11 from Central Market. The caves are a short walk off the main road.*

Templer Park About 10 km further on up the main road from the turn-off to the Batu Caves is this park, which covers 500 hectares. It serves as Kuala Lumpur's nearest jungle playground, apart from the tiny Bukit Nanas Forest Reserve in the middle of the city. It opened as a park in 1954 and is named after the last British High Commissioner of Malaya, Sir Gerald Templer, 'the Tiger of Malaya', who oversaw the tactical defeat of the Communist insurgents during the Emergency (see page 498). The park is dominated by several impressive 350m-high limestone hills and outcrops, the biggest being **Bukit Takun** and **Bukit Anak Takun** (similar to the Batu Caves outcrop).

There are extensive networks of underground passages and cave systems within the hills, thought to have formed 400 million years ago. Unfortunately a huge new floodlit golf course has impinged on the north boundaries of the park making access to some of these massifs more difficult – and another 180hectare golf resort is being developed. The park has a wide variety of jungle flora and fauna. Templer Park is a popular venue for boy scout and youth camps and tends to attract swarms of day-trippers at weekends – although most of them do not venture much beyond the car park and picnic area. Nearby are the **Kanching Falls** (sometimes incorrectly referred to as Templer Park Falls) – a drop of 300m in several stages and a good place for swimming. ■ *Getting there: buses Len Omnibus 66, 78, 83 or 81 from Pudu Raya bus terminal (RM1.20).*

Ten minutes north of KL is this man-made lake with facilities for boating, horse riding, tennis, badminton, model car racetrack and a seafood restaurant.

Taman Tasek Titiwangsa

Situated 25 km north of KL on the old Gombak Road, this museum preserves the traditions of Malaysia's indigenous Orang Asli aboriginals, who number about 60,000 on the peninsula. Displays give the background on the 18 different tribes and their geographical dispersal. There are also models of Orang Asli village houses and a souvenir shop attached to the museum selling Orang Asli crafts. ■ *0900-1700 Sat-Thur, closed Fri, free, T6892122. Getting there: City Liner bus 174 from Lebuh Ampang terminus (RM1.50).*

Orang Asli Museum

It is possible to do this walk at the Forestry Research Institute of Malaysia (FRIM) at Kepong, some 30 minutes north of KL, on the Jabayan Perhutanan. However, it is important to book with the FRIM (T6357315), as it can be closed. Speak with Ms Terry Ong.

Jungle canopy walk

West and southwest

Located 15 km southwest of KL, this is a thriving industrial satellite and middle-class dormitory town for the capital and is known as PJ. It was initially built to provide low-cost housing for squatter resettlement but is now a city in its own right, with shopping and administration centres. The whole town, with its streets running in semi-circles, was planned on a drawing board, but despite its unimaginative street names (or rather, numbers), is not as sterile as it might sound. In recent years it has become quite lively, with its own nightlife scene and several gourmet restaurants, many of which cater for PJ's expatriate and wealthy Malaysian population. It is mainly frequented by businessmen, as the airport is close by. Buses to most parts of Petaling Jaya can be boarded at Bangkok Bank stop and Kelang bus terminal (RM0.60).

Petaling Jaya

Sleeping and eating AL *Allson Sunway Lagoon Resort*, Jalan Lagun Timur, Bandar Sunway, T7358886, F7365688. Brand new dazzling resort, the world's largest surf 'n wave pool, health and spa club, 3 tennis courts, squash, 170m man-made beach, annexed to Sunway Capitol Shopping Centre – one of the largest in Malaysia, and located near Sunway Lagoon water theme park, kiddy camp, shuttle service to KL, coffee house, Japanese restaurant, Chinese restaurant, American/Italian restaurant, poolside bar. Recommended. **AL** *Hyatt Regency Saujana Hotel & Country Club*, 2 km Subang International Airport Highway, T7461234, F7462789. Five minutes from the airport and 2 minutes from the golf course (it has two 18-hole championship courses), low-rise hotel set in landscaped gardens, it is a particularly convenient stop-over for early-morning flights, provides shuttle service to and from airport. **AL** *Pan Pacific Glenmarie Resort*, Jalan Sultan, T7039090, F7032728. New resort hotel with 300 rooms set in 450 acres, 10 minutes' drive from Subang Airport, all sports facilities include two golf courses, Olympic-sized swimming pool, squash and tennis courts.

Proton: driving the flag

Shah Alam is the production centre for Malaysia's national car company, Perusahaan Otomobil Nasional, better known as Proton. The huge manufacturing plant, located just off the highway from Kuala Lumpur, makes the only cars designed and built in Southeast Asia (although the Indonesian government announced its own national car programme in mid-1996). In 1995 140,500 Protons were sold in Malaysia, representing around two-thirds of the total car market of 225,000 vehicles. They have made an impact abroad too – Protons are now being sold in 12 countries. In Britain it was the only car to increase sales during the recession in the early 1990s and leading car magazines named it 'the best value car you can buy' and the 'rising star in the East'.

Profits at home and the company's success abroad seem to vindicate Prime Minister Dr Mahathir Mohamad's determination to launch the National Car Project in 1984. He wanted Proton to be the flagship of Malaysia's drive for industrialization but his brainchild coincided with a recession and was nearly written-off by inept management. The original car, the Proton Saga, is a locally customized and updated version of the 1982 Mitsubishi Mirage. "They say it's a boring car," the Prime Minister admitted. "On the other hand, it doesn't break down either." The Japanese company has a 17% stake in Proton. In reality Proton's cars are not as home-grown as Malaysians would like them to be, but the proportion of locally made components has been rising rapidly – in 1993, 65% by value of Proton's parts were sourced in Malaysia. In 1993, Proton unveiled its racey new Wira model – meaning 'warrior'. The car has been launched in Europe under the name 'Persona' and Proton's management hoped to sell 20,000 units there in 1996. The latest model to be unveiled is the Tiara which was launched amidst 7,000 tropical plants, a simulated tropical thunderstorm and a rainbow in April 1996. Significantly, the Tiara has been built without Mitsubishi's help – Proton went to Citroën for the basic design and technology. It seems that Mahathir and Malaysian executives at Proton have been disappointed at the level and rate of technology transfer from Mitsubishi and so have begun to look elsewhere for help.

In common with Malaysia's bumiputra Malay majority, the car enjoys certain privileges and advantages in the marketplace that other makes do not. It is exempt from the hefty duty other car assemblers pay on imported kits. The government has also set a compulsory profit margin on all car sales, which means no price wars and, for Proton, no competition. But with other cars competing with Proton on something close to a level playing field, as these protective measures are eroded, Proton's outdated technology and sometimes poor build quality may make Malaysia's roads a little more varied in terms of the cars they carry.

In December 1991 Dr Mahathir unveiled his wish to make an even cheaper 660cc Made-in-Malaysia saloon in conjunction with the Daihatsu Company of Japan. Production of the car, which is based on the Daihatsu Mira, and named the Kancil (Mouse Deer) began in September 1994. The Prime Minister did not ask Mitsubishi to help build the car but created a new firm – Perusahaan Otomobil Kedva or Perodva, literally the Second Vehicle Enterprise, in alliance with Daihatsu. In February 1995 Mahathir signed a deal with Japan's Kawasaki Heavy Industries to make 90cc motorbikes. And then, in October 1996, Proton bought the British sports car maker Lotus. In buying this world famous marque for just US$80 million, Proton and Malaysia Inc have gained access to a wealth of engineering and design expertise. Significantly, Proton have built a training centre near Lotus in Norfolk, England, so that its engineers and designers can learn from Lotus' years of experience. Presumably this will lead, in a few years, to a Lotus-derived Proton sports car.

Kuala Lumpur

AL *Petaling Jaya Hilton*, 2 Jalan Barat, T7559122, F7553909. A/c, restaurant, pool. **A** *Holiday Villa*, 9 Jalan SS 12/1, Subang Jaya, T7338788, F7337449. A/c, restaurant, pool. **A** *Merlin Subang*, Jalan 5512/1, Subang Jaya, T7335211, F7331299. A/c, restaurant, pool. **A** *Subang Airport Hotel*, Kompleks Airtel Fima, T7462122, F7461097. A/c, restaurant, pool. **B** *Shah's Village Motel*, 3 & 5 Lorong Sultan, T7569702, F7557715. A/c, restaurant. *Grand City* is a good Indian restaurant near the University Hospital.

The new state capital of Selangor is situated between KL and Port Klang. It has **Shah Alam** the reputation as Malaysia's best planned city and is an ultra-modern showpiece town. The skyline is dominated by the State Mosque, Masjid Sultan Salahuddin Abdul Aziz Shah, which has a huge blue aluminium dome, said to be the largest in the world. Completed in 1988, it is reputed to be the largest mosque in Southeast Asia and can accommodate up to 16,000. There is an interesting museum here and a *Holiday Inn* (**A**), on Plaza Perangsang, Persiaran Perbandaran, T5503696, F5503913. It is an ugly high-rise building, but is only 15 minutes' drive from Subang Airporth and has air conditioning, a restaurant and rooftop pool. Shah Alam is an hour from KL's Kelang bus station or you can take a taxi (RM20).

This royal town, 30 km southwest of KL, has a magnificent mosque and attractive **Klang** royal palace, the **Istana Alam Shah** set in well cared for grounds. It is closed to the public, but the palace can be seen from the road, Klang had been the capital of Selangor for centuries before the tin mining town of Kuala Lumpur assumed the mantle in 1880. Klang was the name for the whole state of Selangor at the time when it was one of the *Negri Sembilan*: the nine states of the Malay Federation. The town is also known as Kelang; it is thought to derive from an old Sumatran word for tin.

Today **Port Klang** (which used to be known as Port Swettenham, after former British Resident Frank Swettenham) is KL's seaport and is a busy container terminal. Klang is also an important service centre for nearby rubber and palm oil plantations, which, in the early decades of the 20th century, spread the length of the Klang Valley to KL.

The **Gedung Rajah Abdullah** warehouse, built in 1857, is one of the oldest buildings in the town. Rajah Abdullah was the Bugis Chief who first dispatched the expedition to the upper reaches of the Klang River, which resulted in the founding of KL. In 1991 it was turned from an historical museum into Malaysia's first tin-mining museum. ■ *0900-1600 Mon-Sun, closed 1200-1445 Fri.* There is also a **fort** in Klang, built by Rajah Mahdi (a rival of Raja Abdullah), which guarded the entrance to the Klang valley from its strategic position overlooking the river.

The town is well known for its seafood; most of the restaurants are close to the bus terminal. Ferries leave from Klang for offshore islands such as Pulau Ketam (see below), Pulau Morib (golf course, see page 109) and Pulau Angsa. Buses 51, 58, 225, *Kelang Bus Co*, leave from Kelang bus terminal (RM1.70) or you can take a train, 1½ hours.

Pulau Ketam (Crab Island), off Port Klang, is like a downmarket Venice, Malaysian-style, with the whole village on stilts over the fetid water. It is a good spot for seafood. Bus to Port Klang (RM2), ferry from Port Klang one hour (RM4), T3314713.

Kuala Selangor is on the banks of the Sungai Selangor, about 60 km north of Klang on the coast road. In the last century, it was a focal point of the Sultanate of Selangor. The Dutch built two fortresses there in 1784 which they used to blockade the river, Sungai Selangor, in retaliation for Sultan Ibrahim of Selangor's attacks on Melaka. Nearly a century later, in 1871, British gunboats bombarded the forts – then occupied by Malays – for several hours, marking the first British intervention in the Selangor Civil War, over the possession of the tin-rich Klang Valley. The two fortresses are on the hills overlooking the Sungai Selangor estuary. The larger of the two, **Fort Altingberg**, on Bukit Melawati, serves as a royal mausoleum and museum. ■ *Daylight hours Mon-Sun.*

The fort overlooks the **Kuala Selangor Nature Park**, 250 hectares of coastal mangrove swamp and wetland. It has several observation hides and more than 156 bird species, including bee eaters, kingfishers and sea eagles, have been recorded. There are also leaf monkeys. It is one of the best places to see Malaysia's famous synchronized fireflies – the only fireflies in Southeast Asia which manage to co-ordinate their flashing (see page 527). The fireflies are best observed on a moonless night, from about one hour after sunset. The actual riverside site is about 8 km from Kuala Selangor, near a village called Kampung Kuantan. A boat trip can be taken from Kampung Kuantan (RM2 each, 4 per boat), T8892403/8892294.

The Society runs chalets in the park, which is a short walk from the last bus stop. A-frames cost RM15 and accommodate two and chalets are RM25-30 for four people. These must be booked in advance (see below); a few days in advance for weekend visitors. There are also two small bus station hotels (**D-E**), rooms with bathrooms.

Transport There are regular direct buses from KL's Puduraya bus terminal (Platform 24) to Kuala Selangor (RM3.50). Taxis can be chartered from there to Kampung Kuantan (wait and return RM25-30; whole car). The *Malayan Nature Society*, which operates the park will also arrange private transport to Kampung Kuantan and back for about the same price. This must be pre-arranged by booking with their KL Office, T8892294 before 1700; T8892403 after 1700.

South

Mines Wonderland This adventure playground, next to the site of the new Sepang International Airport in Sungai Besi about 20 minutes south of KL, has been constructed on a 60 hectare plot which used to be the largest tin-mining lake in the world. Attractions include a Snow House, where you can see sculptures carved out of ice by artists from China. Alternatively, take a ride on a water taxi or see the Musical Fountain or any of the other sound and light attractions. The whole 'Mines Resort City' consists of a sizeable conference centre set within a five-star hotel, a 'Beach Resort' (although there is no beach here), a shopping mall, a business park, an international standard golf course, and a new residential development. ■ *1600-2300 Mon-Sun, RM25 adults, RM15 children. Batu 10 1/2, Jln Sungai Besi, T9425010. Getting there: minibus 65 from Kota Raya or Toong Foong Bus 110, or a taxi via the KL-Seremban Expressway. There are also all-in tours which service the major hotels with a special coach; T2488820 for more information.*

Sleeping AL *Palace of the Golden Horses*, Jln Kuda Emas, T9436633, F9436622, pgh_reservation@signature.com.my. Set on the old tin-mining lake, a 400 plus room hotel, with luxury fittings, range of cuisine, state-of-the-art conference centre, exquisite spa, fitness centre, free-form lagoon pool, children's camp. The closest 5-star hotel to the new airport. **AL** *Mines Beach Resort and Spa*, Jln Dulang, T9436688, F9435555, sales@mbr.com.my. Furnished to a high standard, the resort has even managed to achieve a sandy beach. Low-rise hotel in well landscaped gardens, a pleasant alternative to the bustle of KL. **B** *Mint*, 8th Rm, KL-Seremban Highway, T9438888, F9438889. New ugly block of over 400 rooms, sizeable pool, health centre, business centre, convenient for Mines Exhibition Centre and Wonderland, and for the new airport.

East

Malaysian Armed Forces Museum on Jalan Gurney, exhibits pictures, paintings and weapons, including those captured from the so-called Communists Terrorists (CTs) during the emergency. ■ *1000-1800 Mon-Thur and Sat. Getting there: minibus 19 (RM0.60).*

Royal Selangor Complex on Jalan Pahang, in Setapak Jaya, to the north of the city, is the biggest pewter factory in the world, employing over 500 craftsmen. Royal Selangor was founded in 1885, using Straits tin (over 95 percent) which is alloyed with antimony and copper. Visitors can watch demonstrations of hand-casting and pewter working. Visitors can also see jewellery making and the handpainting of bonded porcelain. One of the most photographed sights at the complex is the massive pewter tankard outside the building. It is in the Guinness Book of Records as the largest in the world. As well as the Setapak Jaya Complex, there are showrooms throughout the city (see page 107). ■ *0900-1600 Mon-Sun. Getting there: Len Seng Bus from Lebuh Ampang Bus Station 12 or 10 (RM0.70).*

National Zoo and Aquarium is 13 km from the centre of KL, down Jalan Ampang to Ulu Klang. The zoo encompasses a forest and a lake and houses 1,000 different species of Malaysian flora and fauna in addition to collections from elsewhere in the world. It also has an aquarium with over 80 species of marine life. ■ *0900-1700 Mon-Sun, adult RM4, child RM1. Getting there: Len Seng bus 170, Len Chee 177, Sri Jaya 255 from Jalan Ampang or minibus 17 from Chow Kit (RM0.50), T4083427.*

Tours

Many companies offer city tours, usually of around three hours, which include visits to Chinatown, Muzium Negara (the National Museum), the Railway Station, Thean Hou Temple, Masjid Negara (the National Mosque), the Padang area and Masjid Jame – most of which cost in the region of RM25. City night tours take in Chinatown, the Sri Mahmariamman Temple and a cultural show (RM55). Other tours on offer visit sights close to the city such as Batu Caves, a batik factory and the Selangor Pewter Complex (RM25) as well as day trips to Melaka, Port Dickson, Fraser's Hill, Genting Highlands and Pulau Ketam (RM40-80). Most of these tour companies offer tours to destinations around the peninsula. Helicopter tours of the city are now run by *Mofaz Air* from Bukit Lanjan, Taman Tun Dr Ismail on weekdays and from Taman Tasik Titiwangsa on Sunday. Trips last 15 minutes and cost RM100 per person, with a maximum of six people per helicopter. Another air tour company are *Asia Tenggara Aviation Services*, T6264613, offering tours seven days per week 0800-1830 – note that aerial photography is not allowed.

For a jungle tour with a difference there is *UBAT (Utan Bara Adventure Team)*, Unit 286-03-08, The Heritage, Jalan Pahang, T4225124, F4226125. The people who run this outfit are ex-security personnel and the names of their tours speak for themselves: 'Cross country jungle survival course' (four-seven days, US$180-350 per person), 'Jungle wilderness medicine camp' (five days, US$250), 'Mountain trekking' (five days, US$200), '35 km Taman Negara Jungle Trail' (US$200), 'Expeditions into the jungle to locate downed US and Japanese aircraft', etc.

See also Tour operators, page 110

Kuala Lumpur

Kuala Lumpur

Essentials

Sleeping

Price codes: see inside front cover

Room rates in KL's top hotels escalated as the economy boomed in the early 1990s. However the Commonwealth Games in 1998 led to the construction of many new hotels and the number of beds in 3, 4 and 5-star hotels has more than doubled between 1997 and 2000. Couple this with the economic crisis and the stagnation in tourism arrivals associated with the 'haze' and the political problems in the region, and in 1999 KL (and Malaysia more generally) faced a glut of rooms, low occupancy rates, and falling room rates.

By international standards KL's hotels are excellent value for money, but because of the city's traffic problems, the location of a hotel has become an increasingly important consideration. Most top hotels are between Jln Sultan Ismail and Jln P Ramlee, in KL's so-called 'Golden Triangle'. South of Jalan Raja Chulan, in the Bukit Bintang area, there is another concentration of big hotels. Corporate discounts of 10-15% are usually on offer; even if you are just on holiday, you are likely to qualify for the reduced rates by simply giving your company's name. This however may be out-weighed by the 'plus plus' that is quoted on top of rates by most hotels ('plus plus' is 10% service charge and 5% government tax).

NB In 1999 fantastic offers were available from most of the top class hotels. Expect to pay at least half the rack rate. Some prices quoted here are after discounts, others are not, so bargain hard. Some top hotels drastically reduce their room rates during the weekends. If you are staying in the larger, a/c hotels and are a non-smoker, it is possible to request a room on a non-smoking floor. Rooms with a/c generally have non-opening windows, making it difficult to freshen the air. Many of the cheaper hotels are around Jln Tunku Abdul Rahman, Jln Masjid India and Jln Raja Laut, all of which are within easy walking distance of the colonial core of KL, northeast of the Padang. There are also cheap hotels in the Chinatown area.

City centre
■ *on maps, pages 77 & 80*
Price codes: see inside front cover Most hotels are in & around Chinatown, a bustling area where KL's colonial roots have not been entirely obliterated. Fairly central for sightseeing but relatively distant from the CBD

A *Holiday Inn City Centre*, Jln Raja Laut, T2939233, F2939634. A/c, Szechuan restaurant, coffee house, pool, squash, health club, gymnasium, big enough hotel, but inside everything is rather bijou – the lobby is squashed, the swimming pool tiny and the fitness and business centres on the miniature side. A typical *Holiday Inn*. **A** *Malaya*, Jln Hang Lekir, T2327722, F2300980, hmalaya@tm.net.my; www.hotelmalaya.com.my. A/c, restaurant, 1970s hotel with central location in Chinatown, pretty characterless.

B *Furama*, Komplek Selangor, Jln Sultan, T2301777, F2302110, furamakl@tm.net.my. A/c, restaurant, health centre, another uninspired hotel with the benefit of a central location in the heart of Chinatown, reasonable rates, geared, as name suggests, mainly to Japanese visitors. Includes breakfast. **B** *Heritage*, Banguanan Stesen Keretapi, Jln Sultan Hishamuddin, T22735588, F22732842. Part of the magnificent Moorish-style railway station. It has recently been redeveloped and has managed to retain some of its colonial splendour, but disappointingly the standard rooms have been furnished in a contemporary style. **B** *Katari*, 38 Jln Pudu, T2017777, F2017911. A/c, restaurant, small hotel opposite Puduraya bus terminal, small, clean rooms, with showers only, price including American breakfast, reductions available, friendly staff, safe place to leave luggage. Breakfast included. **B** *Mandarin*, 2-8 Jln Sultan, T2303000, F2304363. A/c, restaurant, in Chinatown, used by business visitors, not as plush as its name suggests (it is not a part of the Mandarin group), but is clean, with an interesting location and is reasonable value for money. Good à la carte menu; tour organisation available. **B** *Puduraya*, 4th Flr, Puduraya Bus Station, Jln Pudu, T2321000, F2305567. A/c, restaurant, breakfast included, clean, spacious rooms, some with spectacular views overlooking the city centre. Residents have access to on-site healthclub. Also very convenient for bus station. Breakfast included. **B** *Swiss Inn*, 62 Jln Sultan, T2323333, F2016699, sikl@sgihotels.com.my. A/c, café, smart hotel, well run, 1930s Malaya-style furnishings, in good position in the heart of Chinatown. Good value breakfasts available.

C *Backpackers' Travellers' Inn*, 2nd Flr, 60 Jln Sultan (opposite *Furama Hotel*), T2382473. Some a/c, centrally and conveniently located in Chinatown next to excellent stalls/restaurants, popular and professionally run by Stevie. Rooms are small but generally clean, ranging from non-a/c dorm rooms to a/c rooms with attached showers, good facilities for the traveller including left luggage, washing and cooking facilities. Recommended. **C** *City Lodge*, 1st-4th Flr, 16 Jln Pudu, T2013725. Some a/c, small windowless rooms, some rooms with own bathroom, rather rundown, dorms (**E**). **C** *Kawana*, 68 Jln Pudu, T2386714. Some a/c, small barrack-like rooms equipped with small TVs, but very clean, communal toilets and showers, run by camp Indian fellow, some dorm beds (**E**). **C** *Lok Ann*, 118A Jln Petaling, T2389544. A/c, clean, large rooms, although shabby bathroom facilities, centrally located in Chinatown. **C** *Nan Yeang Hotel*, 83 Jln Sultan, T2387477, F2324611. Central location to Chinatown. Clean and tidy, some rooms with balconies over road. **C** *Starlight*, 90-92 Jln Hang Kasturi, T2389811, F2389776. A/c, spacious rooms with (basic) en suite facilities. Excellent staff. Well situated for Central Market, Chinatown, bus stations, eateries, shops, places of interest. Being opposite the Kelang bus station, it can be noisy. With breakfast. Recommended. **C** *YWCA*, 12 Jln Hang Jebat (to the east of Chinatown and south of Jln Pudu), T2383225. Fans. Hot/cold water, quiet, and clean with a friendly atmosphere. Also caters for couples. Restaurant, also access to TV and fridge. Recommended. **C-D** *Backpackers Travellers' Lodge*, 158 Jln Tun HS Lee, T2010889. Some rooms have a/c and attached bathrooms, clean and a good choice in this area, dorms. Three internet computers, several windowless rooms.

D *Drop Inn Lodge*, 1-3 Jln Tun HS Lee, T2386314. Some a/c, 13 rooms, basic and quite dirty – no windows in a/c rooms – but with the advantage of being very central. TV in some rooms and fresh towels provided. **D** *Leng Nam*, 165-167 Jln Tun HS Lee, T2301489. Small hotel, fan only, communal showers, very dirty with partitioned walls – only go if you are desperate! **D** *Travellers' Moon Lodge*, 36c Jln Silang, T2306601. Some a/c, conveniently located for Chinatown, Central Market and Puduraya bus station, popular with budget travellers, breakfast and bed bugs included in price, some dorm beds, dirty place with tiny cubicle rooms. **E** *Chinatown Guesthouse*, 2nd Flr, Wisma BWT, Jln Petaling (in the centre of the *pasar malam*), T2320417. Right in the middle of Chinatown, travel bulletin board, budget guesthouse, most rooms are quiet and have fans (RM24 with breakfast), very friendly. **E** *The Travellers Station*, right next to railway station, T22722237, station1@tm.net.my. One of the few backpackers' places left, basic but friendly, some dorm rooms (small), but showers available. Good selection of recent videos. Email is RM1 for 10 mins.

AL *Pan Pacific*, Jln Putra, T4425555, F4417236, aini@ppkl.po.my, www.panpac.com. A/c, restaurant, pool, gym, spa, attached to the Putra World Trade Centre, so favoured by convention delegates, good views over the city, excellent dim sum restaurant, next to the WTC LRT station. Big discounts being offered at present.

A *Grand Continental*, Jln Belia/Jln Raja Laut, T2939333, F2939732. A/c, restaurant, pool, not really in the big league, except insofar as it has 328 unremarkable rooms, impersonal atmosphere, but reasonable facilities, similar, but much larger, to nearby *Plaza Hotel*. Breakfast included. **A** *Legend*, 100 Jln Putra, T4429888, F4430700. A/c, Chinese, Japanese and health food restaurants (seven in total), pool, health centre,

Chow Kit area

■ *on map, page 77*
Price codes:
see inside front cover
A good choice for
business visitors using
the Putra World Trade
Centre. The Mall
Shopping Centre next
door provides a good
range of shops & fast
food outlets

like a monstrous creation out of Lego, this hotel is legendary in size, with 600 rooms and apartments, and a lobby on the ninth floor, the hotel was opened by Joan Collins and pursues a film-star image, all facilities and big reductions available. Next to the WTC LRT station, a very regal atmosphere.

B *City*, 366 Jln Raja Laut, T4414466, F4415379. A/c, no restaurant, 101 rooms, refurbished in 1993, does not look much from the exterior, but rooms are clean with good hot water showers, professional management, competitively priced, most guests are Malaysians. Recommended. **B** *City Villa* (formerly *Asia*), 69 Jln Haji Hussein, T2926077, F2935143. A/c, restaurant, established joint means it remains popular, karaoke bar, good value for money. Breakfast included. **B** *Dynasty*, 218 Jln Ipoh, T4437777, F4436688, resvn@dynasty.com.my, www.dynasty.com.my. A/c, pool, Chinese or Mediterranean restaurants, business centre, a short distance from the World Trade Centre, all the luxury you would expect for the price. Hugely discounted at present – price quoted was much less than half rack rate– and a rooftop heli-pad. Does 'The Ultimate Wedding Dynasty' for all religions; very tacky. Good value but inconvenient location. **B** *Grand Central*, 63 Jln Putra/Jln Raja Laut, T4413011, F4424758. A/c, clean but drab middle-market hotel with 138 rooms and little to recommend it bar reasonable room rates, very basic restaurant, nothing special. **B** *Grand Centrepoint*, 316 Jln Tuanku Abdul Rahman, T2933988, F2943688. A/c, Island Bar, café, two restaurants, 100-room hotel, very clean, stylish primary colour décor, good for business people on a tight(ish) budget. Price includes breakfast. **B** *Grand Pacific*, Jln Ipoh/Jln Sultan Ismail, T4422177, F4426078. A/c, restaurant, not very grand, but delightful views of the highway (drivers have good views into hotel bedrooms), an old hotel, rather the worse for wear, very inconvenient for foot access, on the edge of the city centre, with none of the facilities which one might expect from newer hotels. Not worth it given the location. **B** *Plaza*, Jln Raja Laut, T2982255, F2920959. A/c, restaurant, 160-room hotel offering competitive rates, price includes buffet breakfast and use of sauna. **B** *Stanford*, 449 Jln Tuanku Abdul Rahman, T2919833, F2936482. A/c, coffee house, business centre, on a lively thoroughfare with plenty of shops and stalls, small but comfortable rooms, discounts available in low season. Recommended. **B** *Vistana*, 9 Jln Lumut, off Jln Ipoh, T4428000, F4411400. A/c, *Thai Barn Restaurant*, coffee house, business centre, pool, classic business hotel of excellent standard but unpretentious, within easy walking distance of Putra World Trade Centre, a RM2 taxi ride from Chinatown, and close to Titwangsa STAR LRT station. **C** *Sentosa*, 316 Jln Raja Laut, T2925644. A/c, simple, Chinese-run, value for money, a great bargain.

Golden Triangle
■ *on map, page 80*
A big shopping and business area dominated by new high-rise hotels, shopping malls and office blocks

L *Istana*, 73 Jln Raja Chulan, T2419988, F2440111, istana@histana.po.my. A/c, Chinese, Japanese and Italian restaurants, pool, this striking, almost grotesquely, extravagant hotel in the heart of KL's business district, all facilities. **L** *Marriott*, 183 Jln Bukit Bintang, T9259000, F9257000, jwmh@po.jaring.my. Next to KL's most opulent shopping plaza *Star Hill*, has pool, fitness centre, conference facilities. Magnificent in its extravagance.

AL *Renaissance*, corner of Jln Ismail and Jln Ampang, T2622233, F2631122, reservations@renaissance-kul.com. A hotel with 400 rooms and an over-the-top lobby of massive black marble pillars. Furnishings in rooms are verging on the pretentious, but the bathrooms are nice, lovely pool makes up for all of this and there are two tennis courts. The ballroom seats 1,400. Also a total of nine lounges, bars and restaurants. Includes breakfast. **AL** *Shangri-La*, 11 Jln Sultan Ismail, T2322388, F2301514, slkl-res@shangri-la.com. A/c, Chinese, Japanese and French restaurants, small, rather old-fashioned pool, health club, sauna, jacuzzi, tennis, with its grand marble lobby and 720 rooms, the *Shang* has remained KL's ritziest hotel despite the arrival of swish upstart competition. Constantly hosting political leaders and assorted royalty for dinner, big bright rooms, good bar (styled after English pubs), but its best feature is its ground floor *Gourmet Corner* deli, which stocks a great variety of European food.

Recommended. **AL *Swiss Garden***, 117 Jln Pudu, T2413333, F2415555, sghkl@ sgihotels.com.my, www.sgihotels.com.my. A/c, Chinese restaurant, tiny pool, fitness centre with limited equipment, business centre, Blue Chip Lounge – a classy bar with live band and a computer terminal linked to the KL Stock Exchange, popular for their cocktail of the month, grand addition to first class hotels in KL, with 310 good sized rooms and 15 storeys, but disappointing facilities. Expensive for what you get.

A *Concorde*, 2 Jln Sultan Ismail, T2442200, F2441628, Chkl@ppp.nasionet.net. A/c, restaurant, decent sized lengths pool, gym, it is the old *Merlin* (the first big modern hotel in KL) masquerading behind a face-lift and rather sterile interior décor, 4 good restaurants and a coffee shop and the *Hard Rock Café* attached to it. **A** *Equatorial*, Jln Sultan Ismail (opposite MAS building), T2617777, F2619020, info@equatorial.com. A/c, restaurant (excellent Cantonese), pool, one of KL's earlier international hotels, the *Equatorial* has had several revamps over the years, its 1960s-style coffee shop has metamorphosed into one the best hotel coffee shops in town, open 24 hours (see below), with an international news agency in the basement, the hotel is the favoured repose of visiting journalists. Choose a room at the back to reduce disturbance by traffic noise, two no smoking floors. **A** *Federal*, 35 Jln Bukit Bintang, T2489166, F2482877. A/c, Indian restaurant, revolving restaurant, ice-cream bar, cafés, bowling, shopping arcade, business centre, pool. When it first opened in the early 1960s, it was the pride of KL: its *Mandarin Palace* restaurant was rated as the most elegant restaurant in the Far East, it is still good, but does not compare with the world-class glitz that KL has attracted of late. Breakfast included. **A** *Hilton*, Jln Sultan Ismail, T2482322, F2442157, info_kuala_lumpur@hilton.com. A/c, restaurant, pool, all facilities but not quite as good as others in this league, when returning to the hotel by taxi, specify *KL Hilton*, otherwise you are liable to end up in the *PJ Hilton* in Petaling Jaya. Recommended. **A** *Holiday Inn on the Park*, Jln Pinang, T2481066, F2481930, qscc@tm.net.my. A/c, restaurant, large pool and garden area, located across the road from a string of lively bars, '*Satay station*' restaurant is a train carriage in the forecourt. The 'Park' to which its title refers, is now a building site. Includes breakfast. **A** *Melia*, 16 Jln Imbi, T2428333, F2426623, melia@meliakl.com.my. Chinese and Spanish restaurants, over 300 rooms, pool, health centre, hairdresser, florist, business centre, not quite up to the standard of many of the other big hotels which charge around the same prices but nonetheless a very reasonable place to stay. **A** *New World*, 128 Jln Ampang, T2636888, F2631888. Five hundred and twenty rooms in this new horror. Good sized rooms and nice bathrooms but all a bit ostentatious. Shares its spectacular pool with the *Renaissance Hotel* next door. Includes breakfast. **A** *Park Royal*, Jln Sultan Ismail, T2425588, F2414281, sales@prkl.com.my. A/c, restaurant, pool, formerly called *The Regent*, the hotel underwent major cosmetic surgery in 1989, allowing it to charge more for its good range of facilities, although it often offers promotions for cheaper rooms. **A** *Regent*, 160 Jln Bukit Bintang, T2418000, F2421441, regentkl@tm.net.my. A/c, Western, Cantonese and Japanese restaurants, beautiful pool, gym with Roman baths, children's pool, a/c squash courts, health club, business centre (open until midnight), the ultimate hotel in KL – it won the 'Best Hotel in Malaysia' award the year it opened in 1990, all suites have butler service and the rooms and bathrooms are lavishly appointed, the enormous lobby is designed around a pool of cascading water. Recommended.

B *Agora*, 106-110 Jln Bukit Bintang, T2428133, F2427815. A/c, restaurant, small 50-room hotel, located on busy intersection in shopping area of Golden Triangle, rooms on the front tend to be noisy, interesting design incorporating Greek columns and elegant furnishings. Small but functional. **B** *Bintang Warisan*, 68 Jln Bukit Bintang, T2488111, F2482333, warisan@tm.net.my. A/c, coffee house, nice little hotel, limited number of standard price double bedrooms. Good, clean but quite basic small rooms, no extra facilities. **B** *Fortuna*, 87 Jln Berangan, T2419111, F2418237. A/c, coffee house with live band, health centre, just off Bukit Bintang, tucked away and slightly quieter than most, behind *McDonalds*, good value for money. Recommended. **B** *Imperial*, 76-80 Jln Changkat Bukit Bintang (Jln Hicks), T2481422, F2429048. A/c, restaurant, well priced Chinese hotel in an otherwise pricey part of town, well located for shopping centres but at this price don't expect a gem. **B** *Lodge*, Jln Sultan Ismail, T2420122, F2416819. A/c, restaurant, small pool, small hotel on busy junction, surrounded by tower blocks, large rooms with 1950s fittings. Like many other mid-range hotels in KL it is struggling to survive the Far Eastern depression. **B** *Malaysia*, 67-69 Jln Bukit Bintang, T2447733, F2428579. A/c, restaurant, a rather jaded hotel amidst all the glitz, faded wall-paper, limited facilities, but a lot cheaper than many. Iron railings over windows restrict view of the street. Unsuccessful attempt at international style. **B** *Noble*, 4th Flr, Jln Tuanku Abdul Rahman, T9257111, F9257222. Modern, clean and tastefully finished. Although without much character, this hotel offers reasonable value. Rooms include TV, have standing showers and a/c. Includes breakfast and a free paper. **B** *Sungei Wang*, 74-76 Jln Bukit Bintang, T2485255, F2424576. A/c, Thai restaurant, a small and very average hotel, but well-run, friendly and good value for money, discounts available.

C *Cardogan*, 64 Jln Bukit Bintang, T2444856, F2444865. A/c, coffee house, health centre, business centre, dark wood interior. It has 61 rather bare rooms and small shower rooms attached. Price includes tax and breakfast. Very good value. **C** *Emerald*, 166 Jln Pudu, T2429233, F2445774. A/c + TV, noisy location, on edge of Golden Triangle, reasonably maintained, considering this Chinese hotel is nearly 20 years old, strong Asian feel, attached bathrooms with hot water. Basic, you get what you pay for. **C** *Tai Ichi*, 78 Jln Bukit Bintang, T2427533, F2310162. A/c. Another little hotel in this strip. Nothing in particular to recommend it.

Jalan Ampang
■ *on map, page 83*
Price codes:
see inside front cover
A relatively new commercial district, running along the northern edge of the new KLCC (see box, page 83) making it a good position for anyone doing business here

L *Radisson Plaza*, 138 Jln Ampang, T4668866, F4669966, rphkl@po.jaring.my. Fantastically equipped new hotel. Facilities include a pool, tennis and squash courts, as well as a conference and business centre. **L-AL** *MiCasa Hotel Apartments*, 368b Jln Tun Razak (near junction with Jln Ampang), T2618833, F2611186, micasa@po.jaring.my. A/c, restaurant, pool, shopping arcade, hair salon, dentist and doctor, children's pool, jacuzzi, tennis, squash, gym, sauna, children's playhouse, business centre, first rate, especially for longer stays, KL's only apartment hotel with 240 suites which include fully equipped kitchen with utensils and sitting room, Italian restaurant, Tapas Bar. Recommended.

AL *Crown Princess*, City Square Centre, Jln Tun Razak, T2625522, F2624492, crownprincess@fhikl.com.my. A/c, on 10th floor is a pool and a restaurant good for 'High Tea' buffet, *Taj* Indian restaurant on 11th floor, lobby lounge with baby grand piano, cafés, Vietnamese restaurant on 11th floor, Szechuanese restaurant, business centre, adjacent shopping centre with 168 shops, opulent décor, over 500 spacious rooms with panoramic views. Recommended. **AL** *Ming Court* Vista Hotel, Jln Ampang, T2618888, F2623428, minvista@tm.net.my. A/c, restaurant, good pool, room rate includes a good buffet breakfast, spacious rooms, some with a view of the Petronas Twin Towers. **AL** *Su Casa*, 222 Jln Ampang, T4513833, F4521031. A/c, restaurant, pool, business centre, store, serviced apartment suites with fully equipped kitchens for business people intending a slightly longer stay than is usual, weekly and monthly rates are negotiable, prices are slightly cheaper here than at the sister hotel.

A *Century*, 17-21, Jln Bukit Bintang. T2439898, F4680880, cenkl@po.jaring.my. Opened 1998, very large, with restaurant, conference facilities and health club opened August 1999. **A** *MiCasa*. Relaxed atmosphere, although it is located near foreign embassies on road out of town. Recommended for long term visitors. **A** *Nikko*, 165 Jln Ampang, T2611111, F2611122, www.hotelnikko.com.my. A/c, pool, Japanese and Chinese restaurants, near city square and Ampang Shopping centres. Oriental atmosphere with very Japanese feel to it.

B *Kowloon*, 142-146 Jln Tuanku Abdul Rahman, T2934246, F2926548. A/c, coffee house, clean, value for money, rooms have mini-bar and TV, but those facing the main street are noisy. Residents can use health club on-site at a discounted rate. Recommended. **B** *Palace*, 40-46 Jln Masjid India, T2986122, F2937528. A/c, café, deli corner, shopping arcade, good lively location, but very average hotel. **C** *Chamtan*, 62 Jln Masjid India, T2930144, F2932422. A/c; although clean this small establishment offers little but a good location and is clearly in decline. **C** *Coliseum*, 100 Jln Tuanku Abdul Rahman, T2926270. Fans or a/c, restaurant, colonial hotel. If arriving outside hours, knock on one of the side doors. Large, simply furnished rooms and a famous bar and restaurant (see below) and friendly staff. No attached bathrooms. Rooms facing main street are very noisy. For those on a budget who want a taste of the 1920s it is certainly worth a try.

Little India
■ *on map, page 77*
Price codes:
see inside front cover

L *Carcosa Seri Negara*, Taman Tasek Perdana, T2821888, F2827888. A/c, restaurant, pool, former residence of the British High Commissioner and built in 1896, it is now a luxury hotel, where Queen Elizabeth II stayed when she visited Malaysia during the Commonwealth Conference in 1989 and where other important dignitaries, presidents and prime ministers are pampered on state visits, situated in a relatively secluded wooded hillside and overlooking the Lake Gardens there are just 13 suites served by over 100 staff. Recommended. **A** *Pan Pacific Glenmarie Resort*, T7031000, F7041000. A new golf resort in the suburbs of KL, close to the airport and 30 mins from the city centre, boasts two 18-hole golf courses, a pool and spa, business centre and guests will be able to use the Clubhouse, providing an Olympic size pool, tennis and squash courts, fitness centre etc. Just under 300 rooms in this low-rise resort, choice of dining and a quieter atmosphere away from the city centre. **AL-A** *Airside Transit Hotel*, KLIA, T6038787, F6038787. Hotel within the Satellite Building of the new aiport. Comfortable rooms along with gym, sauna and spa and business centre. The advantage for people in transit is that it is not necessary to pay the RM40 departure tax. Short stay possible at RM80 for up to 6 hours (standard room). **AL-A** *Wenworth*, Jln Yew, T9833888, F9828088, whkl@tm.net.my. asiatravel.com/wenworth. A/c, Chinese restaurant, café, roof pool, health spa, simple but comfortable rooms, good location for North-South highway – approaching KL from the south, it is one of the first hotels in the city. The surrounding Pudu area is fast being developed with old shophouses giving way to tower blocks and two new shopping centres (Phoenix Plaza and the Leisure Mall), in the pipeline. Breakfast is included in room tariff and there is a monthly food promotion, a taxi ride will get you to the city centre and Golden Triangle. Recommended.
 B *Concorde Inn*, Sepang, within the new airport site, T8431118, F8432118. A/c, TV, pool, tennis court, food court, restaurants, health and fitness centre, over 400 rooms. **B** *Matri Inn*, 235 Jln Tun Sambanthan, near KL-Klang Highway, 50470 Brickfields, T2731097, F2731569. A/c, café, run by an Indian family, good Indian food. Includes breakfast.
 C *Kuala Lumpur International Youth Hostel*, 21 Jln Kampung Attap. A/c, on the southeastern edge of KL, near the railway station and tucked in behind some big bank buildings, good hawker stalls nearby to serve office staff but reports are that the rooms are dirty and noisy – a last resort. **C** *Pan Pacific KL International Airport Hotel*, T87873333. A 450-room hotel, right next to the new airport at Sepang, should provide all the luxury you could demand, with pool, fitness centre, tennis court, spa, business centre, several restaurants. Incredible value. **C** *YMCA*, 95 Jln Padang Belia/ Jln Kandang Kerbau, T2741439, F2740559. Good facilities – sports facilities, language courses, shop – neutralized by inconvenient location in Brickfields district on the southwest outskirts, off Jln Tun Sambathan, it is, however, within sniffing distance of Raju's tandoori ovens (see *Sri Vani's Corner*, Eating), dormitory for men only (**D**) also private rooms. *Getting there*: minibus 12.

Others

Kuala Lumpur

Homes Away from Home programme Run by the Asian Overland Service, this programme gives visitors first-hand experience of Malaysian life by staying in fishing kampungs, rubber plantations, tin mines or pensioners' homes, RM45 per day including pick-up service, accommodation and two meals. Contact *Asian Overland Services*, 33M Jln Dewan Sultan Sulaiman Satu, T2925622, F2925209. *Village Home Stay*, 178 Jln Tuanku Abdul Rahman, T2920319.

Eating

Price codes: see inside front cover Many of KL's big hotels in the Jln Sultan Ismail/Bukit Bintang areas serve excellent value buffet lunches and offer a selection of local and international dishes. One of the best ways to sample various cuisines is to graze among the foodstalls.

Malay 3 *Nelayan Floating Restaurant*, Titiwangsa Lake Gardens, good but expensive. 3 *Seri Melayu*, 1 Jln Conlay, T2451833. Open 1100-1500, 1900-2300 (reservations recommended for groups of four or more – it seats 500), the best Malay restaurant in town in traditional Minangkabau-style building, the brain-child of Malaysian PM Datuk Seri Dr Mahatir Mohamad, beautifully designed interior in style of Negeri Sembilan palace, don't be put off by cultural shows or big groups – the food's still worth it, very popular with locals too, individual dishes expensive, buffet at RM35 (or RM70 for dinner) best bet (more than 50 dishes) with promotions featuring cuisine from different states each month, those arriving in shorts will be given a sarong to wear. Dinner show is still camp, food still superb, amazing variety, including regional specialities. Recommended. 3 *Seri Angkasa*, at the top of the KL Tower (see page 84), T2085055. A sister hotel to *Seri Melayu*. The tower revolves, achieving a full rotation in 60 mins. Good food, booking advisable for the evenings. There is also a good value buffet lunch available. 3 *Spices*, *Concorde Hotel*, 2 Jln Sultan Ismail, T2442200. Open 1130-1500, 1830-2300, closed Sun. Unlike its name, the food is not overly spicy, eclectic Asian cuisine as well as traditional Malay, four-piece band background music, a/c indoors or poolside outdoors, *se-tengah* – stiff whisky drink popular in colonial times – features on their varied drinks list. 2 *Jamal Bersaudara*, Jln Raja Abdullah, Kampung Baru. 2 *Rasa Utara*, Bukit Bintang Plaza, Jln Bukit Bintang. 2 *Wan Kembang* (Cik Siti), 24 Jln 14/22, Petaling Jaya (in front of the mosque), specializing in Kelantanese food. 1 *Satay Anika*, Ground Floor, Bukit Bintang Plaza, Jln Bukit Bintang, fast food satay. Recommended. 1 *Sate Ria*, 9 Jln Tuanku Abdul Rahman, fast food. 1 *Malay 'buffet'* Jln Gereja, opposite Jln Tun HS Lee. Very good value little restaurant.

Chinese 4 *Dynasty Garden Chinese Restaurant*, Lot M72-75, Mezzanine Flr, Plaza Yow Chuan, Jln Tun Razak. 4 *The Museum*, *The Legend Hotel*, The Mall, Putra Place, T4429888. Open 1200-1500, 1830-2230, aims to look like a museum, with Chinese antiques and columns everywhere, although many display cabinets still to be filled, Teochew and Cantonese cuisine, adventurous food promotions, winner of Malaysian Tourism and Promotion best Chinese award. 4 *Golden Phoenix*, *Hotel Equatorial*, Jln Sultan Ismail, T2617777. Open 1200-1430, gourmet Chinese establishment, mock Chinese courtyard setting. 4 *Lai Ching Yuen*, *The Regent Hotel*, Jln Bukit Bintang, T2418000. Set in mock Chinese pavilion, holder of four Malaysian Tourism Gold Awards for consistently fine cuisine, popular with Chinese gourmets, luxury table settings, revolving solid granite table centres. 4 *Shang Palace*, *Shangri-La Hotel*, Jln Sultan Ismail, T2322388. Open 1200-1430, 1900-2300, dim sum lunch of over 40 varieties costs around RM50, check food promotions for evening meals.

4 *Ampang Yong Tau Foo*, 53 Jln SS2/30, Petaling Jaya, T7753686. *Yong tau foo* (stuffed beancurd dishes) in a coffee shop. Recommended. Closed Mon. 4 *The Blossom*, *Swiss Garden Hotel*, 117 Jln Pudu, T2413333. Open 1130-1430, 1830-2230, 40 varieties of *dim sum*, tiger prawns a house speciality, good selection of pork dishes, abalone and birds' nests only for those on hefty expense accounts. 3 *Cha Yuan*

Teahouse, 5B Jln SS2/67, Petaling Jaya, traditional Chinese teahouse offers light meals and tea prepared by tea-master Paul Lim. Recommended. **3** *Hai Tien Lo*, *Pan Pacific Hotel*, Jln Putra, T4425555. Open 1200-1500, 1900-2300, excellent dim sum, steamed fish with suet. Recommended. **3** *Marco Polo*, Wisma Lim Foo Yong, 86 Jln Raja Chulan, T2412233. Open 1200-1500, 1900-2300, extensive menu, barbecue roast suckling pig recommended, 1970s style décor, very busy lunchtimes. **3** *Oriental Bowl*, 587 Leboh Pudu, T2025577. A/c restaurant above Chinese spice shop, convenient location for Central Market, rather formal atmosphere. **3** *Restoran Oversea*, G2, Central Market, Jln Hang Kasturi, T2746407. Cantonese restaurant, pleasant location, very popular with locals. Good range of dishes (*dim sum* particularly recommended, 0800-1500), excellent barbecue and roast meats, with unlikely looking 'vegetarian' dishes, which are about as vegetarian as chicken soup poured through a sieve can get. **3** *Tsui Yuen*, 5th Flr, *Hilton Hotel*, Jln Sultan Ismail, T2482322. Open 1200-1430, 1900-2230, main attraction is the lunchtime *dim sum*, weekend 'all you can eat' promotions also worth checking and good value set meals.

    2 Halfway to Kajang, near Sungai Besi (take Seremban highway, exit to left at Taman Sri Petaling – before toll gates, right at T-junction, over railway line and past Shell and Esso stations, turn left towards Sungai Besi tin mine, then branch right to Balakong, the restaurant is signposted), it is little more than a tin shed (with a fruit stall outside) but is famed among KL's epicureans for its deep-fried paper-wrapped chicken, wild boar curry and vinegar pork shank. Recommended. **2** *Cameleon Vegetarian Restaurant*, 1 Jln Thamboosamy (off Jln Putra, near The Mall and *Pan Pacific*), Thai and Chinese, good *kway teow*, but vegetarians with carnivorous instincts rate the soyabean roast duck and various other ersatz meat and fish dishes whose presentation (and sometimes taste) is convincing. **2** *Esquire Kitchen*, Level 1, Sungai Wang Plaza, Jln Sultan Ismail, T2485006. Dumplings and pork dishes good value, Shanghai dishes popular. **2** *Hokkaido*, 68 Jln Lumut, off Jln Ipoh, T4411316. Open 1800-0200, located at north end of town, opposite *Vistana Hotel*, good genuine fare, not fancy, tables outside, pleasant retreat from shopping plazas and hotel complexes. Recommended. **2** *Sin Kiew Yee*, Jln Hang Lekir (Jln Cecil, between Jln Petaling and Jln Sultan, Chinatown), mouthwatering dishes, good value for money, tables on pavement. Recommended. **2** *Westlake*, Jln Sultan, highly rated for its Hokkien *mee* and *mee hun*, mixed with raw egg. **2** *Yook Woo Hin*, 100 Jln Petaling, cheap dim sum in the middle of Chinatown – until 1400.

    1 *Nam Heong*, 54 Jln Sultan, Hainanese chicken rice. **1** *Seng Nam*, Lebuh Pasar Besar, Hainanese. The steamboats in the restaurant area of Chinatown are worth sampling at one of the outdoor tables.

4 *Baluchi's*, 3 Jln SS21/60, Petaling Jaya, T7190879 (advisable to take taxi; ask for Damansara Utama Shophouse Complex), North Indian cuisine, modest décor but excellent food; chicken tikka, tandoori chicken, prawn *masala* and *palak paneer* particularly recommended; freshly baked naan. Recommended.   **Nyonya**

    3 *Bangles*, 60A Jln Tuanku Abdul Rahman, T2986770. This is reckoned to be among the best North Indian tandoori restaurants in KL, often necessary to book in the evenings. Recommended. **3** *Bon Ton*, 7 Jln Kia Peng, T2413611. Open 1200-1500, 1900-2400, good Eastern Nyonya set menu, some Western dishes such as chicken pie, set in a 1930s colonial bungalow, just south of KLCC. Recommended. **3** *Dondang Sayang*, 12 Lower Ground Floor, The Weld, Jln Raja Chulan, T2613831; also branch at 28 Jln Telawi Lima, Bangsar Baru, T2549388. Popular and reasonably priced restaurant with big Nyonya menu. **3** *Kapitan's Club*, 35 Jln Ampang, T2010242. Open 1100-1500, 1800-2230, spacious restaurant decorated with Straits woodwork, staff in traditional outfits, 'top hats', the house speciality is a tasty pastry and egg dish, Kapitan chicken is popular, Malay dishes also available.

    2 *Sri Penang*, Lower Ground Floor, Menara Aik Hua, Changkat Raja Chulan (Jln Hicks), variety of Nyonya and North Malaysian dishes.

Indian & Pakistani

4 *The Taj*, *The Crown Princess Hotel*, 11th Flr, City Square Centre, Jln Tun Razak, T2625522. Open 1200-1500, 1900-2300, closed Sat lunch, stylish Anglo-Raj décor, live Indian muzak, open view kitchen, New Delhi chefs create first rate Indian cuisine, vegetable samosas and tandooris – meat and veg – are excellent. Recommended. **3** *Bombay Palace*, 388 Jln Tun Razak, next to US Embassy, T2454241. Open 1200-1500, 1830-2300, good quality North Indian food in tasteful surroundings with staff in traditional Indian uniform, menu including vegetarian section. **3-2** *Restoranua Jime*, next door to *Paradise B+B*, Jln Tunku Abdul Rahman, specializing in Moghul food and tandooris. Recommended.

2 *Annalakshmi*, 46 Lorong Maarof, Bangsar Baru, T2823799. Excellent Indian vegetarian restaurants run by the Temple of Fine Arts, dedicated to the preservation of Indian cultural heritage in Malaysia, the buffet is particularly recommended. **2** *Kampung Pandan*, 1st Flr, Central Market, specialist in fish-head curry. **2** *Sri Vani's Corner* (*Raju's*), Jln Tun Sambathan 4 (next to *YMCA* tennis courts), overgrown hawker stall rated among its dedicated clientele as the best place for tandooris and oven-baked nāan in KL. Recommended. **2** *Valentine Roti*, 6 Jln Semark (close to the National Library), this place was fortunate enough to be reviewed in the *Far Eastern Economic Review* and was billed as the best Roti restaurant in town, Ilango Arokias-amy's rotis are a treat, light and flaky, and as he says "I think God wanted me to do this".

1 *Alhmdoolilla*, 12 Jln Dang Wangi, rated for its rotis. **1** *Lay Sin Coffee Shop*, 248 Jln Tun Sambathan, banana leaf.

Japanese

4 *Keyaki*, Pan Pacific Hotel, Jln Putra, T4425555. Open 1200-1500, 1900-2300, good set meals, excellent sashimi and sushi made with fish flown from Japan twice weekly, highly rated, but extremely expensive. **4** *Nadaman*, Shangri-La Hotel, 11 Jln Sultan Ismail, T2322388. Shang quality and Shang prices.

3 *Chikuyo-Tei*, Plaza See Hoy Chuan, Jln Raja Chulan, T2300729. Open 1200-1500, 1830-2230, housed in a basement, good value set meals, quality teppanyak, seafood and steak. **3** *Munakata*, 2nd Flr, Menara Promet, Jln Sultan Ismail, T2417441. **3** *Tykoh Inagiku*, Ground Flr, Kompleks Antarabangsa, Jln Sultan Ismail (between Equatorial and Hilton hotels), T2482133.

2 *Sushi King*, Lower Ground Flr, The Mall, Jln Putra, T4428205 and 63 Jln Sultan Ismail, T2417312. Spotlessly clean sushi bar, prices from 50c to RM3 per sushi. **2** *Teppanyaki*, 2nd Flr, Sungai Wang Plaza, Jln Bukit Bintang and Lot 10, Jln Sultan Ismail, basement, excellent Japanese fast food, set meal for RM10.

Korean

3 *Koryo-Won*, Kompleks Antarabangsa, Jln Sultan Ismail, T2427655 (between Hilton and Equatorial hotels). Excellent barbecues, particularly when washed down with Jung Jong rice wine. Recommended. **3** *Korean Restaurant*, 24 Jln Medan Imbi, T2446163. Open 1100-1500, 1800-2300, small restaurant off Jln Imbi, lashings of garlic, friendly staff.

Thai

3 *Barn Thai*, 370B Jln Tun Razak (opposite MiCasa Hotel), T2446699. Open 1200-1430, 1900-0300, very tastefully decorated Thai style 'Jazzaurant' with excellent live music, extensive Thai menu, hot and sour sea bass and mango salad are specialities. Recommended. Also a more subdued but equally tasteful outlet in the Vistana Hotel, 9 Jln Lumut, off Jln Ipoh, T4428000. **3** *Sawasdee Thai Restaurant*, Holiday Inn on the Park, Jln Pinang, T2481066. **2** *Cili Padi Thai Restaurant*, 2nd Flr, The Mall, Jln Putra, T4429543. Soups and seafood are excellent, recommended speciality: King Solomon's Treasure (chicken wrapped in pandan leaves), closes 2200 sharp. Recommended. **2** *Restoran Miyako*, Level 5, Kota Raya Complex, Jln Cheng Lock, T2022822. Excellent Thai food, some of the best outside Thailand. Recommended. *Johnny's Thai Steamboat*, basement of Bukit Bintang Plaza.

4 *Mekong*, 11th Flr, Crown Princess Hotel, City Square Centre, Jln Tun Razak, **Vietnamese**
T2625522. Well-appointed, serving authentic Indo-Chinese cuisine with specialities
from Vietnam and Thailand. **3** *Restoran Sri Saigon*, 53 Jln 552/30, Petaling Jaya,
T7753681. Genuine Vietnamese dishes. **3** *Vietnam House*, 6th Flr Sogo Pernas,
T2941726. Open 1200-2100, genuine Vietnamese chef and many ingredients flown
from Vietnam, spring rolls and chicken with lemon grass are recommended.

4 *Carcosa Seri Negara*, Persiaran Mahameru, Taman Tasek Perdana (Lake Gardens), **International**
T2306766 (reservations). Built in 1896 to house the British Administrator for the Federated Malay States, Carcosa offers English-style high tea in a sumptuous, colonial setting,
expensive Italian lunches and dinners are also served in the Mahsuri dining hall on fine
china plates with solid silver cutlery, Continental and Malay cuisine, high tea (recommended) RM25 (1530-1800, Mon-Sun). **4** *Ciao*, 428 Jln Tun Razak, T9854827. Open
1200-1430, 1900-2230, closed Mon, authentic tasty Italian food served in a beautifully
renovated bungalow. Recommended. **4** *Flamenco*, 1 Jln U-Thant, T4517507. Open
1100-2400, excellent South Mediterranean food, good paella, daily specialities. **4** *Jake's*,
21 Jln Setiapuspa, Medan Damansara, off Jln Damansara, towards PJ, T2545677. Open
1200-1500, 1830-2300, Jake's steaks are highly rated in KL, served by cowboys and cow-
girls. Recommended. **4** *Lafitte*, Shangri-La Hotel, 11 Jln Sultan Ismail, T2322388. Open
1200-1500, 1900-2300, best French restaurant in Malaysia, but very expensive. Recommended. **4** *Melaka Grill*, Hilton Hotel, Jln Sultan Ismail, T2482322. Open 1200-1500,
1900-2300, closed Sat and Sun lunch, well-established, popular business lunch venue,
good quality international cuisine. **4** *Pour Toi*, 36 Jln Walter Grenier, T2455836. A new
Golden Triangle restaurant, French cuisine, fun décor, well-balanced menu, RM15 cork-
age if you bring your own wine. **4** *Sakura Café & Cuisine*, 165-169 Jln Imbi, excellent
variety of Malay, Chinese and Indian dishes including fish-head curry, located in an area
with many other good cheap restaurants. Recommended.

4 *TGI Friday's*, Life Centre, Jln Sultan Ismail, T2637762. Open 1130-2400, cocktails and
American food, good value for money, though lacks atmosphere perhaps because
they've been here for 30 years. **3** *Coliseum Café*, 100 Jln Tuanku Abdul Rahman (Batu
Rd), next door to the old Coliseum Theatre, long-famed for its sizzling lamb and beef
steaks, Hainanese (Chinese) food and Western-style (mild) curries, all served by frantic
waiters in buttoned-up white suits. During the communist Emergency, planters were
said to come here for gin and curry, handing their guns in to be kept behind the bar, it
is easy to believe it. Recommended. **3** *D'Ribeye*, Ground Flr, Central Market, Jln Hang
Kasturi. Good atmosphere and steak, offering great value, full of businessmen at
lunchtime. **3** *Hard Rock Café*, Ground Flr, Wisma Concorde Hotel, T2444062. Open
1130-0200, 2 Jln Sultan Ismail, one of the best places for top-quality American burgers, steaks and salads, good value. Recommended. **3** *Le Coq D'Or*, 121 Jln Ampang,
T2429732. European/Malay, former residence of a rich mining towkay with a porti-
coed veranda and Italian marble, Western, Chinese and Malay cooking, great atmosphere of crumbling grandeur now lost and in dire need of face-lift and improved
hygiene. **3** *Sam's Curry Lunch*, Indian buffet, Sun 1230-1400, excellent à la carte selection of Malaysian dishes, include nasi lemak and rendang, open 24 hrs. Recommended. **3** *Lot 253*, The Mall, 2nd Flr, 100 Jln Putra, T4431988. Open 1200-2200, good
set menu, and authentic French atmosphere. **3** *Marble Arch*, Hotel Grand Continental, Jln Raja Laut, T2939333. Open 1100-1500, 1800-2300, good buffet lunches (RM25)
and set meals during food promotions when chefs are on hand from the country
being promoted. **3** *The Jump*, Ground Flr, Wisma Inai 241, Jln Tun Razak, T2450046.
Open 1100-2230, American fare prepared by US chef, good value, popular with foreigners, good cocktail band and live music venue. **3** *The Ship*, 40 Jln Sultan Ismail, very
dark interior, extensive menu of steaks, chicken, salads. The stone grills are particularly
popular. Open from lunch until 0230. **3** *Uno's*, corner of Jln Kia Peng, reasonable

Kuala Lumpur

Kuala Lumpur

Italian pasta restaurant downstairs with disco/bar above which is the unchallenged nocturnal playground of KL's rich and famous. **3** *Moomba*, Ground flr, UOA Centre, 19 Jln Pinang, T2628226. Australian bar and restaurant, selection of sandwiches, ribs, pasta, pies. Trendy lunch spot for business people, but good value. **3-2** *Roadhouse Grill*, 42 Jln Sultan Ismail. Cheap and cheerful American fare. Open 1130-2400.

2 *Riverbank*, Ground flr, Central Market. 'Hearty American Fare', which just about says it all - burgers, sandwiches etc. **2** *Caleos*, 1 Jln Pinang, pastas and pizzas, Napoli-style seafood, upstairs bar and karaoke lounge. **2** *Equatorial Coffee Shop*, Basement, Equatorial Hotel, Jln Sultan Ismail. Malay curry buffets 1230-1400, Mon-Sat. Recommended. **2** *Federal Hotel Revolving Restaurant*, Jln Bukit Bintang. This was once one of KL's tallest buildings, now rather dwarfed but still a good spot for ice-cream sundaes with a view. **2** *Lodge Coffee Shop*, Jln Sultan Ismail. Good value for money, particularly local dishes: nasi goreng, curries and buffets. Recommended. **2-1** *Lakshmi Villas*, Leboh Ampang, excellent vegetarian food, try the dosai masala: pancakes stuffed with vegetables and accompanied by a lentil sauce.

Seafood
For additional seafood entries, see also Port Klang & Pulau Ketam (see page 89)

3 *Bangsar Seafood Village*, Jln Telawi Empat, Bangsar Baru, T254555. Open 1200-1430, 1800-2300, large restaurant complex with reasonably priced seafood, fresh from tanks that line the inside of the restaurant, specialities include crab in butter sauce and Thai-style tiger prawns (and a good satay stall). **3** *Eden Village*, 260 Jln Raja Chulan. Wide-ranging menu, but probably best known for seafood, resembles a glitzy Minangkabau palace with garden behind, cultural Malay, Chinese and Indian dances every night, less touristy outlet in PJ 25-31 Jln 5322/23, Damansara Jaya, T7193184. **3** *Hai Peng Seafood Restaurant*, Taman Evergreen, Batu Empat, Jln Klang Lama (Old Klang Rd). The smallest and least assuming restaurant in a row of Chinese shophouses (red neon sign), but one of the very best seafood restaurants in Malaysia, where the Chinese community's seafood connoisseurs come to eat (the other seafood restaurants in the cluster include Chian Kee, Pacific Sea Foods and Yee Kee, most of which are good, but not as good as Hai Peng). Its specialities include butter crab (in clove and coconut), belacan crab, sweet and sour chilli crab and bamboo clams, the siu yit kum (small gold-leaf tea) is a delicious, fragrant Chinese tea, which is perfect with seafood, open until 0100. Recommended. **3** *Studio 123*, 159 Jln Ampang. Easily missed - it's opposite the Ming Court Hotel - this is an unassuming place with friendly staff and excellent, good value food. Recommended.

2 *MASs*, 228 Jln Dua A, Subang, Selangor, T7461200. Well out of town, past Subang airport's Terminal 2, and strung out along the road running beside Runway One are about 10 seafood restaurants, they all do a brisk turnover, and there is not much between them; they all serve seafood and each has its own speciality, MASs is the one with the front end of an MAS jumbo jet on the roof. Recommended. **2** *New Ocean*, 29B Medan Imbi (off Jln Imbi and Jln Hoo Teik Ee). Good seafood restaurant just round the corner from the Sungai Wang and Lot 10 shopping complexes. **2** *Unicorn*, 1st Flr, Annex Block, Lot 10 Shopping Centre, Jln Sultan Ismail, T2441695. Open 1100-1500, 1800-0400, big, smart Chinese seafood restaurant in the Lot 10 complex, just by the footbridge to Sungai Wang, good stop for shoppers.

Teahouses
Traditional Chinese teahouse opposite Sungai Wang Hotel on Jln Bukit Bintang.

Foodstalls
Chow Kit is the best area for food stalls

Chow Kit On Jln Raja Muda Abdul Aziz there is a food court with great Indian and Afghan food. Jln Haji Hussien has a collection of superb food stalls, most open when the market closes at 1800 and stay open until 0200 and it is picturesque too. Walk up Jln Haji Hussien and turn right and there are some good cheap (**C-D**) hotels. The food court on the top floor of The Mall, built like rows of old Chinese shophouses, is run-down but has an attractive ambience. Indian, Malay and Chinese food, all good, but the majority of places to eat here close by 2000. It is cheap too: Tandoori chicken, Naan, Dal and drink, all for just RM8. Jln Raja Alang and Jln Raja Bot stalls, off Jln Tuanku Abdul Rahman are mostly Malay stalls.

East on Jln Datuk Keramat near Pasar Keramat are lots of Malay food stalls that stay open way after midnight. Next to *Keramat* supermarket there is a South Indian stall with good mutton soup. In the alleyway between *Keramat* supermarket and the Pakistani mosque are lots of good food stalls in the day. Kampung Baharu and Kampung Datok Keramat are Malay communities. On the river front behind Jln Mesjid India are good Indian and Malay night stalls.

Opposite the *Brisdale Value Inn* on the corner of Jln Hj Hussien and Jln Raja Bot is a block of flats. In front and behind are good Indonesian restaurants but they really only function during the day.

The top floor of the Central Market has a small restaurant with amazing Thai and Nyonya cuisine. On the same floor is an excellent, but small, centre with good nasi campur, open at lunchtime.

Ampang Park Shopping Complex (along Jln Tun Razak), popular, but small centre, with good variety of stalls. *Brickfields* (Jln Tun Sambathan), string of small outdoor restaurants. *Lorong Raja Muda Food Centre*, off Jln Raja Muda, on the edge of Kampung Baru, mainly Malay food. *Medan Hang Tuah*, The Mall (Top Floor), Jln Putra (opposite the Pan Pacific Hotel). *Munshi Abdullah Food Complex*, off Lorong Tuanku Abdul Rahman (near Coliseum), good satay. *Puduraya Bus Station*, Jln Pudu, good variety of stalls, open at all hours. Lot 10 Shopping Complex, Jln Sultan Ismail, excellent choice of food here, if you can tolerate the high volume music. *Sunday Market*, Kampung Baru (main market actually takes place on Sat night), many Malay hawker stalls, Jln Masjid India.

Bars

There is no shortage of good watering holes in KL; many have live Filipino and local cover bands, and others have discotheques attached. An increasing number of bars are now being taken over by karaoke.

Barn Thai, 370B Jln Tun Razak, T2446699. Self-styled 'Jazzaurant', Bangkok-type wooden bar with panelled interior and tasteful Thai décor, some of KL's best live acts with excellent jazz, drinks are expensive, also serves good Thai food. Recommended. *Betelnut*, Jln Pinang, T2416455. Thu ladies night, located in the ruins of a former colonial bungalow in a strip of bars and clubs which are not as good, disco in main house, but relaxed outdoor bar. Recommended. *Bull's Head*, Ground flr, Central Market, Jln Hang Kasturi, T2746428. Large bar with the darkened atmosphere of a London pub inside and with tables on the terrace outside, convenient for shopping in Central Market. *Bier Keller*, German pub and restaurant, Ground flr, Menara Haw Par (next to Shangri-La Hotel), Jln Sultan Ismail, T2013313. Authentic German draught beer served in stylish glasses, wide range of Shnapps, salty German food. Recommended. *Cathy's Place*, Wisma Stephen, Jln Sultan Ismail, T2481794. Cheap beer and a regular expat crowd; *Centrepoint*, Jln Setiapuspa, Medan Damansara, off Jln Damansara, lively bar with live music every night; *Coliseum*, 100 Jln Tuanku Abdul Rahman, the bar, which has a number of long term residents who never seem to move, is the haunt of Malaysia's star cartoonist, Lat (his Coliseum sizzling steak cartoon hangs on the wall along with his caricatures of regulars), the so-called Planters' Bar used to be the gathering point for colonial rubber planters and tin miners then became the hangout of war correspondents during the Malayan Emergency, the bar is frequented by everyone from diplomats and businessmen to backpackers, it is a pleasant old-time bar which opens for business before lunch and shuts at 2200 sharp. Recommended. *Delaney's Pub*, corner of Jln Imbi and Jln Pudu, quite expensive standard Irish pub.

Kuala Lumpur

English Pub, Shangri-La Hotel, not as naff as it sounds, and popular with visiting business people, happy hour 1730-1930, live band 2030-2230, full size pool table.

Hard Rock Café, Basement and Ground Floor Wisma Concorde, 2 Jln Sultan Ismail, T2444152. The Hard Rock, with its Harley Davidson chopper posing on the rooftop, opened in 1991 and quickly became one of the most popular and lively bars in town, good atmosphere and small disco floor. Recommended. *London Pub*, Lorong Hampshire, off Jln Ampang (behind Ming Court Hotel). Continuing KL's obsession with recreating English pubs, this one, part-owned by a London Cockney is not a mock-Tudor half-timbered mess, it has a good atmosphere and a regular darts competition. *Ronnie Q's Pub*, 32 Jln Telawi Dua, Bangsar Baru. Popular with expats and locals, great sporting moments with international cricket and rugby videos. *Shark Club*, 23 Jln Sultan Ismail, T2417878. Trendy bar and café open 24 hrs daily, live band in basement after 2030 Mon-Sat, American and Mexican food, giant screen for latest sports events, darts, and boasts the longest bar in KL. *Solutions*, City Square Centre, Jln Tun Razak, T2621689. Happy hours 1600-2200, popular after-work spot. *Tapas Bar*, MiCasa Hotel, 368b Jln Tun Razak (near junction with Jln Ampang), serves what are arguably the best margaritas in KL. Recommended. *Titiwangsa Bar*, Carcosa Seri Negara Hotel, Taman Tasek Perdana. *Traffic Lights*, 42 Jln Sultan Ismail (near Bukit Bintang junction), music (sometimes live) and attached grill.

Nightclubs and discos

Since the mid-1980s, with the rise of the local yuppy, KL has shaken off its early-to-bed image and now has a slightly more lively club scene. Several old colonial buildings have been converted into night spots. The Metro section in *The Star* is devoted to what's on where. Most nightclubs and discos in KL used to be open until 0300 during the week and until 0400 on Friday nights and weekends. But at the beginning of 1997 the government, worried at the proliferation of so-called 'social ills', introduced new regulations stipulating that nightspots must close by 0100. This has been a bit of a dampener on what was in danger of becoming a really zany club scene. In the past few years, Jln Pinang, once a backstreet of crumbling bungalows, has emerged as a late-night strip of bars. There are also hundreds of karaoke lounges around KL. Bangsar Baru to the west of the city centre, not far from the University of Malaya, is probably the hippest area of town with around 20 bars and nightclubs. It is frequented mostly by Malaysians.

Baze 2, Yow Chuan Plaza, Jln Tun Razak, popular for its R&B, acid jazz, and dance mixes, happy hour 2100-2300, Wed ladies night, RM30 cover charge. *Boom Boom Room*, 11 Lorong Ampang, off Jln Gereja, usually heaving by the weekend, disco plays up-to-the-minute tracks, busy upstairs bar with live show, dance and dirty jokes, RM15-20 cover. Recommended. *Betelnut*, Jln Pinang, very popular bar/disco complex, behind the disco clubhouse is a spacious outdoor bar area, Betelnut is the best in a strip of bars just down from the Holiday Inn on the Park, Thu ladies night. Recommended. *Cee Jay's*, Ground flr, Menara SMI, 6 Lorong P Ramlee (behind Shangri-La Hotel). Good bar and a restaurant, sports bar with screens, pool, darts, but is best known for its live music, with classy local acts playing covers. *Club Oz*, lower lobby, Shangri-La Hotel, Jln Sultan Ismail, professional DJs, predominantly Chinese control, not cheap, cover RM15-30. *Club Syabas*, 1 Lorong Sultan, Petaling Jaya, the club's renowned DV8 disco is very popular with KL ravers, as is the karaoke. Recommended. Cover charge RM12-15. *Faces*, 103 Jln Ampang. Also in an old colonial house, cover RM16. *Deluxe Nite Club*, Rooftop, Ampang Park Shopping Centre, Jln Ampang. Huge hostess bar ("every inch of the way we will make you feel like an Emperor"), Chinese bands (imported from Hong Kong and Taiwan) perform every night. *Legends*, 1 Jln Kia Peng. Particularly popular with local KL crowd and again, in an old converted bungalow. *The Jump* , Ground flr, Wisma Inai 241, Jln Tun Razak. One of the latest additions to the club scene, performance bartendering, live bands, jazz nights, popular Wed ladies night, RM20 cover. *Modesto's*, 1d Lorong Perak, off Jln P Ramlee. Trendy night spot, small dance floor, ladies night Wed, pizzas and Italian food. *Tin Mine*, Basement, KL Hilton, Jln Sultan Ismail. One of the few old nightclubs still going strong, small dance floor and backgammon for the less energetic, has a reputation as a hostess hangout. Recommended. Cover charge RM26.

Entertainment

KL is gradually becoming a centre for local and some international artists, but the art market is not exactly flourishing, and much of the art work around is mediocre. Some of the main galleries include: *Anak Alam Art Gallery*, 905 Pesiaran Tun Ismail off Jln Parliamen. *AP Art Gallery*, Ground Floor, Central Market, off Jln Hang Kasturi. *Artfolio Gallery*, 1st Flr City Square, Jln Tun Razak, T2623339. *Art House*, 2nd Flr, Wisma Stephens, Jln Raja Chulan, T2482283. *Balai Seni*, Menara Maybank, Jln Tun Perak, T2321416. *Fine Arts Gallery*, Yow Chuan Plaza, Jln Tun Razak. *Galericitra*, 1st Flr, Shopping Arcade, Shangri-La Hotel, Jln Sultan Ismail. *National Art Gallery*, Jln Sultan Hishamuddin, T2300157. Open 1000-1800, closed Fri 1245-1445, admission free. *Rupa Gallery*, Lot 158 Menara Dayabumi, Jln Sultan Hishamuddin. *Petronas Art Gallery*, Dayabumi Complex, Lower Ground Floor, Jln Hishamudin.

Contemporary Malaysian art can be seen at *Art Salon*, 4 Jln Telawi Dua, Bangsar Baru, open Tues-Sun. For information on the latest show, T2822601.

Art galleries

For What's On, the *Sun* paper publishes details. Tickets cost RM2-4. *Cineplex*, small cinema complexes, are increasingly popular and many are incorporated into the burgeoning shopping plaza, tickets cost RM8-10. Screenings listed in *The New Straits Times*, and the *Star*. Main cinemas: *Capitol*, Jln Raja Laut, T4429051. *Cathay*, Jln Bukit Bintang, T2429942. *Cathay Cineplex*, The Mall, T4426122. *Coliseum*, Jln Tuanku Abdul Rahman, T2925995. *Federal*, Jln Raja Laut, T4425014. *Odeon*, Jln Tuanku Abdul Rahman, T2920084. *Odeon Cineplex*, Central Square, T2308548. *President*, Sungai Wang Plaza, Jln Sultan Ismail, T2480084. *Rex*, Jln Sultan, T2383021.

Cinemas
Open daily from 1100. The first showing is usually a 1300 matinee with the last show at 2115 (midnight show Sat)

Eden Village, 260 Jln Raja Chulan, Malay, Indian and Chinese dancing every night. *Malaysian Tourist Information Complex* (Matic), 109 Jln Ampang, T2434929. Shows on Tue, Thu and Sun at 1530. *Seri Melayu Restaurant*, 1 Jln Conlay, traditional Malay folk dances and singing in KL's best Malay epicurean experience (see page 98), traditional music starts at 2000, dancing at 2045, ends 2130. *Temple of Fine Arts*, 116 Jln Berhala, Brickfields, T2743709. This organization, set up in Malaysia to preserve and promote Indian culture, stages cultural shows every month with dinner, music and dancing, the Temple organizes an annual Festival of Arts (call for details), which involves a week-long stage production featuring traditional and modern Indian dance (free, since "...the Temple believes art has no price"), it also runs classes in classical and folk dancing and teaches traditional musical instruments.

Cultural shows

Actor's Studio Theatre, Plaza Putra, underneath Merdeka Square.

Theatre

Shopping

As recently as the early 1980s Malaysians and KL's expatriates used to go on shopping expeditions to neighbouring Singapore as KL just was not up to it. These days however, the city has more or less everything, with new shopping complexes springing up every year. They are not concentrated in any particular area and ordinary shopping streets and markets are also dotted all around the city.

Kuala Lumpur

Antiques *Oriental Spirit*, northern end, 1st Flr, Central Market, T3272160. A stunning emporium of mostly mainland Southeast Asian treasures. Quite pricey but the interior is an Aladdin's Cave of goodies and is well worth a look for the imaginative way in which it's been laid out. Recommended. Bangsar Town Centre is also renowned for its antiques.

Artefacts For a general range of Southeast Asian artefacts, the best areas are Jln Ulu Klang, Jln Pudu and Bangsar Town Centre. *Tibetan Treasures*, 16 Changkat Bukit Bintang, for antique Tibetan furniture and paintings.

Batik *Aran Novabatika Malaysia*, 174 Ground Flr, Ampang Park Shopping Centre, Jln Ampang. *Batik Bintang*, Lobby Arcade, Federal Hotel, Jln Bukit Bintang. *Batik Corner*, Lot L1.13, The Weld Shopping Centre, 76 Jln Raja Chulan, excellent selection of sarong lengths and ready-mades in batiks from all over Malaysia and Indonesia. *Batik Malaysia*, 114 Jln Bukit Bintang, Mun Loong, 113 Jln Tunku Abdul Rahman. *Batik Permai*, Lobby Arcade, Hilton Hotel, Jln Sultan Ismail. *Central Market*, Jln Hang Kasturi, hand-painted silk batik scarves downstairs, many shops sell batik in sarong lengths. *Evolution*, G24, Citypoint, Dayabumi Complex, Jln Sultan Hishamuddin, T2913711. Fashionable range of readymades and other batik gift ideas by designer Peter Hoe. *Faruzzi Weld Shopping Centre*, Jln Raja Chulan (also at 42B Jln Nirwana, just off Jln Tun Ismail) exclusive and original batiks. Recommended. *Globe Silk Store*, 185 Jln Tuanku Abdul Rahman. *Heritage*, 38 1st Flr, has a big selection of very original Kelantanese batiks (RM15-90 per m), most ordinary batiks cost about RM7 per m. *Khalid Batik*, 48, Ground Flr, Ampang Park Shopping Centre, Jln Ampang. There are several shops on Jln Masjid India; there are two batik factories which welcome visitors - the East Coast Batiks Factory, No 1, 8½ mile, T6891948 and No 15, Jln Cahaya 15, Taman Cahaya, Ampang, T9840205.

Books *Berita Book Centre* and *MPH Bookstores*, Bukit Bintang Plaza, 1st Flr and Gd Flr respectively, Jln Bukit Bintang; *Bookazine*, Damansara Heights 8 Jln Batai; *Kinokuniya*, Isetan Dept Store, 2nd Flr, 50 Jln Sultan Ismail: *Minerva Book Store*, 114 Jln Tunku Abdul Rahman; *Popular Book Co*, Jln Petaling, Jln Hang Lekir, Sungai Way Plaza; *Times Books*, Yow Chuan Plaza, 6-7 Jln Tun Razak and Weld Shopping Complex, good selection of English language books; second-hand bookshop on first floor of Central Market.

Cameras *Sungai Wang Plaza*, Jln Sultan Ismail, Golden Triangle.

Carpets & rugs *KL Plaza*, Jln Bukit Bintang, Golden Triangle. *Ampang Park Shopping Complex*, Jln Ampang. *City Square*, Jln Tun Razak, northeast of Golden Triangle.

Clothing For designer clothing and accessories: *Starhill Shopping Centre*, Jln Bukit Bintang, Golden Triangle; Lot 10 on the corner of Jln Sultan Ismail and Jln Bukit Bintang, Golden Triangle. *Sogo*, Jln Tuanku Abdul Rahman. For custom-made clothing: *Sungai Wang Shopping Plaza*, Jln Sultan Ismail, Golden Triangle. For discount branded fashions: *Sungai Wang Plaza*, Jln Sultan Ismail; the *Weld Shopping Centre*, Jln Raja Chulan, near the KL Tower. *City Square*, Jln Tun Razak, northeast of Golden Triangle. **Shoes** Custom made shoes available from Jln Tuanku Abdul Rahman.

Computers *Imbi Plaza*, Jln Imbi, Golden Triangle.

Electrical items *Sungai Wang Plaza*, Jln Sultan Ismail.

Fabrics Jln Tuanku Abdul Rahman; *Lot 10*, Jln Bukit Bintang; *Semua House*, Lorong Tuanku Abdul Rahman (at northern end of Jln Masjid India); Ampang Shopping Complex, Jln Ampang.

Oriental Style, southern end of Central Market, 1st Flr and at 64 Jln Hang Kasturi, reproduction Asian furniture. Pricey. *Oriental Spirit*, northern end of Central Market, 1st Flr, antique furniture. Expensive but beautiful objects. Rattan furniture available from Bangsar Town Centre, Ampang Point and Wisma Stephens.

Furniture

Gold, pearls and precious gems: Petaling St; Lot 10, Jln Bukit Bintang; City Square, Jln Tun Razak; *Semua House*, Lorong Tuanku Abdul Rahman (at northern end of Jln Masjid India).

Gems

Semi-precious gems, jade and porcelain: *KL Plaza*, Jln Bukit Bintang. *Ampang Shopping Complex*, Jln Ampang. Petaling Street. Lot 10, Jln Bukit Bintang.

Much of the handicrafts are imported from Indonesia. *Aked Ibu Kota*, Jln Tuanku Abdul Rahman, shopping centre with wide variety of goods including local handicrafts. *Amazing Grace*, G-3P Yow Chuan Plaza, Jln Tun Razak. *Andida Handicraft Centre*, 10 Jln Melayu. *Central Market*, Jln Hang Kasturi, the old wet market is now full of handicrafts stalls, not always the cheapest but big selection. *Eastern Dreams*, 101A Jln Ampang. *Oriental Style*, Central Market, 1st Flr, selection of upmarket baskets, pots, brassware. Quite pricey but worth a look. *Golden Triangle*, Central Market, 1st Flr, Cornucopia of wooden figures. *Borneo Crafts*, Central Market, 1st Flr, mostly wooden pieces, good selection of puppets and boxes. *Karyaneka Handicraft Village*, Kompleks Budaya Kraf, Jln Conlay, government-run, exhibiting and selling Malaysian handicrafts. *Lavanya Arts*, 116A Jln Berhala Brickfields, run by the Temple of Fine Arts of Annalakshmi vegetarian restaurant fame, which aims to preserve Malaysia's Indian heritage, the shop sells Indian crafts: jewellery, bronzes, wood carvings, furniture, paintings and textiles. *Lum Trading*, 123 Jln SS2/24 SEA Park, Petaling Jaya, baskets and bambooware, 64 Jln Tun Perak. *Malaysian Arts*, 23 Jln Bukit Bintang. *South China Seas*, Level 4 Metro Jaya, Jln Bukit Bintang; for Chinese arts and handicrafts the areas to look are along Jln Tuanku Abdul Rahman and Bangsar Town Centre.

Handicrafts

Indian knick-knacks: incense, Indian silks, saris, jasmine, jewellery all available along Jln Melayu. Nepalese trinkets from Petaling St.

Third floor, Supermarket in the UDA Ocean Building. Camping stall in Central Market.

Mosquito nets

Sungei Wang Plaza, Jln Sultan Ismail; *Lot 10*, Jln Bukit Bintang; *KL Plaza*, Jln Bukit Bintang.

Optical goods

Dai-Ichi Arts and Crafts, 122 Mezanine Flr, Parkroyal Hotel, Jln Sultan Ismail/Jln Imbi; *KL Arts & Crafts*, 18 Ground Floor, Central Market, Jln Hang Kasturi; *Royal Selangor Pewter Showrooms*, 231 Jln Tuanku Abdul Rahman, T2986244.

Pewter

Lot 10, Jln Bukit Bintang; Sungai Wang Plaza, Jln Sultan Ismail; KL Plaza, Jln Bukit Bintang. Jln Petaling is the best place for the 'genuine copy' watch.

Watches

Central Market, next to Jln Hang Kasturi is a purpose built area with two floors of boutiques and stalls selling just about every conceivable craft. For example, pewter, jewellery, jade, wood, ceramics. Stalls of note include one which sells all kinds of moulds and cutters for baking, a wonderful spice stall, another one for nuts and a third for dried fruits. One shop called *Collectibles* sells old watches, brass pieces, bird cages - worth a look. See sections on antiques and furniture for details on other shops. *Chow Kit* (Jln Haji Hussein), just off Jln Tuanku Abdul Rahman, is a cheap place to buy almost anything - it doubles as a red light district, although this area is rapidly being developed and its image 'cleaned-up', the extensive wet market on Jln Haji Hussein is scheduled to be re-located to make way for building. *Jalan Melayu* is another interesting area for browsing - Indian shops filled with silk saris, brass pots and Malay

Markets & shopping streets

Kuala Lumpur

Kuala Lumpur

shops specializing in Islamic paraphernalia such as songkok (velvet Malay hats) and prayer rugs as well as herbal medicines and oils. *Jalan Tuanku Abdul Rahman* (Batu Rd) was KL's best shopping street for decades and is transformed into a pedestrian mall and night market every Sat after 1730, KL's original department store, Globe Silk Store, is on Jln Tuanku Abdul Rahman. *Kampung Baru Sunday Market (Pasar Minggu)* off Jln Raja Muda Musa (a large Malay enclave at the north end of KL) is an open air market which comes alive on Sat nights, Malays know it as the Sun market as their Sun starts at dusk on Sat (so don't go on the wrong night), a variety of stalls selling batik sarongs, bamboo birdcages and traditional handicrafts compete with dozens of food stalls, the Pasar Minggu has largely been superseded by Central Market as a place to buy handicrafts however. *Leboh Ampang*, off Jln Gereja was the first area to be settled by Indian immigrants and today remains KL's 'Little India', selling everything from samosas to silk saris. *Pasar Malam*, Jln Petaling, Chinatown is a night market full of copy watches, pirate cassettes and cheap clothes. *Pudu Market*, bordered by Jln Yew, Jln Pasar and Jln Pudu, is a traditional wet market selling food and produce, mainly patronized by Chinese.

Jln Sultan/ Jln Tun HS Lee for apparel, shoes, bags, textiles (nr. Klang bus station).

Petaling Street (Chinatown), barter for Chinese lanterns, paintings, incense holders, figurines. The nightmarket is good for a selection of imitation clothes and watches.

Shopping complexes　**Jln Sultan Ismail/Bukit Bintang**　The majority of KL's shopping complexes are to be found in this area, they include (east to west): *Star Hill Plaza*, Jln Bukit Bintang, prestigious marble clad shopping centre houses *Tang's Department Store* (of Singapore fame) and many designer boutiques. *Lot 10*, Jln Sultan Ismail, distinctive emerald green façade, Isetan Department Store, British India, Moschino, Knickerbox, other mid-range boutiques plus an excellent food court. *Bukit Bintang Plaza*, corner of Jln Bukit Bintang and Jln Sultan Ismail, houses the popular department store *Metrojaya*, a *Marks & Spencers* and a labyrinth of other shops, which lead into Sungai Wang. *Sungai Wang Plaza*, Jln Sultan Ismail, one of the largest complexes in KL, houses over 500 shops and *Parkson Grand Department Store*, food court in basement. *Imbi Plaza*, corner of Jln Sultan Ismail and Jln Imbi, good for computers.

Ampang　Centre of complexes on east edge of city: *Yow Chuan Plaza*, Jln Tun Razak, antiques, curios, souvenirs and designer goods, linked to City Square next door which has a *Metrojaya* department store and *Toys 'R' Us*. *Ampang Park*, Jln Tun Razak, opposite City Square, noted for its jewellery boutiques. Jln Tuanku Abdul Rahman: *Sogo Pernas Department Store*, largest department store in Southeast Asia on 10 floors. *Pertama Shopping Complex*, wide range of shops from souvenirs to fashion and a basement bazaar. Also photographic and electronic goods.

Jln Putra: *The Mall*, right across from Putra World Trade Centre, quite trendy, large shopping mall, good for fashion, *Yaohan Department Store*, Starlight Express indoor theme park, lots of fast food outlets, *Delifrance*, *Pizza Hut* etc.

Others　*The Weld*, corner of Jln Raja Chulan and Jln P Ramlee, quite a few food outlets here, large *Times Bookstore*, *Reject Shop*, art gallery and a selection of fashion/leather shops etc. *Subang Parade*, Subang Jaya, houses *Parkson Grand Department Store* and *Toys 'R' Us*, amusement park and fast food outlets. *Kota Raya Shopping Complex*, Jln Cheng Lock, cut-price goods.

Sports

Badminton　*Bangsar Sports Complex*, Jln Terasek Tiga, Bangsar Baru, T2546065. *YMCA*, 95 Jln Padang Belia, off Jln Tun Sambathan, Brickfields, T2741349, Jln Tun Razak Multipurpose Hall, T4231158.

Federal Bowl, Federal Hotel, Jln Bukit Bintang, T2489166. *Leisure Mall Bowling*, **Bowling**
Cheras Leisure Mall, Jln Manis, 6 Taman Segar, T9323866. *Miramar Bowling Centre*,
Wisma Miramar, Jln Wisma Putra, T2421863. *Pekeliling Bowl*, Yow Chuan Plaza, Jln
Tun Razak, T2430953.

Plaza Putra Indoor Golf Centre, underground complex in Dataran Merdeka, golfers can **Golf**
select from 7 prestigious international courses from a computerized menu, T4432541.
Kelab Golf Negara, Subang (near Subang International Airport), two 18-hole courses,
green fees RM200, T7760388. *Royal Selangor Golf Club*, Jln Kelab Golf, off Jln Tun Razak,
exclusive championship course (including two 18-hole courses and a nine-hole), one of
the oldest in the country, non-members can only play on weekdays, green fees RM210
(without membership introduction), T9848433. *Saujana Golf & Country Resort*, Subang
(near Subang International Airport), two 18-hole championship courses, green fees
RM170 weekdays, RM290 weekends, T7461466. *Sentul Golf Club*, 84 Jln Strachan,
Sentul, built in 1928, recently refurbished and a swimming pool added, green fees
RM30 weekdays, RM50 weekends, T4435571. *Templer Park Country Club*, 21 km north
of KL, fully floodlit course for 24 hr golf, frequented by Japanese golf package tourists,
developed and part-owned by Japanese company, the more environmentally minded
have complained that the course has ruined the north end of Templer Park, jungled
lime *Kelana Jaya Sports Complex*, Lot 1772, Taman Tasek Subang, Kelana Jaya; *YMCA*,
95 Jln Padan Belia, Brickfields.

Fitness International, Parkroyal Hotel, Jln Sultan Ismail. *Good Friend Health Centre*, **Health centres**
33 Jln Tun Sambathan 5. *Recreation Health Centre*, 4th Flr, Furama Hotel, Komleks
Selangor, Jln Sultan Ismail.

Fun World Roller Disco, 1st Flr Asiajaya Shopping Complex, Petaling Jaya. **Roller skating**

Jade Snooker Centre, GBC Plaza, Jln Ampang, T4570345. *Snooker Paradise*, **Snooker**
Kompleks Kotaraya.

Cricket, rugby and hockey are played on the Padang, in the centre of KL, most week- **Spectator**
ends. Football and badminton are Malaysia's most popular sports. Inter-state Malay- **sports**
sia Cup football matches are played at the Merdeka Stadium and the Stadium on Jln
Stadium, off Jln Maharajalela. The (rather more successful) Selangor team play at the
new Shah Alam Stadium; Sat and Tue 2030 kick-off. RM10 entrance fee. A colourful
(and safe) experience. One-way taxi RM15-20, need to ask taxi driver to wait for you as
it is difficult getting back into town.

Bangsar Sports Complex, Jln Terasek Tiga, Bangsar Baru, T2546065. **Squash**

All international-class hotels have their own pools for guests. Public pools charge a **Swimming**
nominal fee. *Bangsar Sports Complex*, Jln Terasek Tiga, Bangsar Baru, T2546065.
Open Mon-Sat 0800-1300, closed Sun; *Weld Swimming Pool*, Jln Raja Chulan. *Public
pool*, next to Chinwoo Stadium, off Jln Hang Jebat.

Kelana Jaya Sports Complex, Lot 1772, Taman Tasek Subang, Kelana Jaya; *YMCA*, 95 **Tennis**
Jln Padan Belia, Brickfields.

Sunway Lagoon and Adventure Park, T7356000. A theme park, with plenty of enter- **Watersports**
tainment both in and out of the water, admission RM15 (RM10 for children), open
1200-2030 Mon, Wed, Thu, 1200-2200 Fri, 1000-2000 Sat, Sun and public holidays.
Getting there: from Klang bus station, Sri Jaya Bus 252B USJ or Klang Bus 51. *The Mines*,
Sungai Besi Tin Mine (T9487402, admission: weekdays adult RM8, child RM4, weekends

Kuala Lumpur

adult RM12, child RM6), 20 mins drive from KL, before the toll booths on highway to Seremban, exit on left (at Taman Sri Petaling), turn right at T-junction, over the railway line and past Shell and Esso stations towards Serdang and Kajang, signposted to the left, located in what was the biggest tin mine in the world, in clean, turquoise water and beneath dramatic rocky cliffs. The 200 acre recreational park boasts a snow house where the temperature is regulated to create all year round snow. Other amusements include a roller coaster, water screen, laser show and a musical fountain.

Tour operators

Most of the big hotels have their own in-house travel agents and ticketing agencies. For domestic flights it can be cheaper to buy tickets through ticketing agencies rather than going to MAS headquarters on Jln Sultan Ismail. If you are staying in a hotel, many ticketing agencies will deliver the tickets to your room. There are plenty of travel agents in the Angkasaraya Building on the corner of Jln Ampang and Jln Ramlee. For slightly different mid-range tours, try *Dee Travel*, Central Market, T2019699. For student/cheap outbound tickets, *MSL* is recommended near the *Grand Central Hotel*, T4424722 or *STA*, 5th Flr, Magnum Plaza, Jln Pudu, T2489800. *Ecstasy Travel*, 754 Jln Sentul, T4425688. Organizes country and city tours for about RM25 for a 3 hr trip. *Thomas Cook*, Level 18, Menara Lion, Jln Ampang (near *Nikko Hotel*), T2649252. MATIC (see below in tourist offices section) provide a telephone booking service for Taman Negara Resort, on T2643929, ext 113.

Transport

Distances from KL Butterworth 383 km, Cameron Highlands 219 km, Ipoh 217 km, Melaka 148 km, Johor Bahru 365 km, Singapore 393 km, Kuantan 274 km, Kuala Terengganu 491 km, Kota Bharu 657 km.

Local
See also Ins & outs, page 72
Bus An *Intrakota* bus map should be available gratis from City Hall, but when we visited KL they were reprinting and the tourist board didn't know the new bus system. Intrakota has taken over most routes now but it's not a particularly easy system to grasp. For enquiries, T7172727. Prices are RM0.60-0.90.

LRT (Light Rail Transit) Before long KL will have no fewer than three metro lines which all go under the heading LRT or Light Rail Transit but which are, in fact, operated by three separate companies. The **STAR line** is an elevated railway and the first to be completed in 1998. The **PUTRA line** is part-elevated and fully automated. In mid-1999 only the northern branch was open although the southern branch should be operational by the time this book is published. The **PRT Monrail line** should have been ready by now but because of the economic downturn has been making slow progress. It will probably not be operational until 2001. The trains operate between 0600 and 2300 with a frequency of train every 3-5 mins during peak hours and every 8-15 mins during off-peak hours. Fares range from RM0.75 (up to two stops) to RM2.95; stored value tickets to the value of RM20 or RM50 are also available saving hassle for those using the system regularly. To travel from Ampang to Sultan Ismail takes around 20 mins; from Ampang to Miharja, 12 mins.

Commuter trains The alternative to the LRT for north-south travel in the city is to hop on a commuter train. The three city stops are Putra, near the World Trade Centre, Bang Negara, and the Railway Station. Trains leave every 15-30 mins (RM1)

Car hire *Apex, Budget, Hertz, Mayflower, National, SMAS, Thrifty, Tomo Express, Toyota* and *U-Drive* all have desks at Subang Airport. *Avis*, T2417144, F2429650.

Economy Car Rental (ECR), T2925427, F2927888. *Hakikat*, T2448404. *Hawk*, T2646455, F2646466. *Hertz*, T2486433. F2428481, enquiry@hertz-malaysia. com *Mayflower*, T6221888, F6279282. *Mansfield*, T2433333, F2426036, 225 Jln Bukit Bintang; *National*, T2480522, F2482823. *Orix*, T2423009, F2423609. *Sintat*, T2457988, F2456057. *SMAS*, T2307788, F2320077. *Thrifty*, T2488877, T7469778 (Airport), F2424907. For breakdown problems the *Automobile Association of Malaysia (AAM)* is on T2625777 or T2625358.

Taxi KL is one of the cheaper cities in Southeast Asia for taxis and there are taxi stands all over town. Most are a/c and metered: RM2 for the 1 km and 10 cents for every 200m thereon. Extra charges between 2400 and 0600 (50% surcharge), and for each extra passenger in excess of two, RM1 for luggage placed in boot. Waiting charges are now RM2 for the first 2 mins and RM0.10 for every subsequent 45 secs. Taxis should not be hailed from the street; there are designated places to queue for one. Try and insist the driver uses the meter. For complaints, T2539044.

NB During rush hours, shift change (around 1500) or it's raining, it can be very difficult to persuade taxis to travel to the centre of town. The answer is to negotiate a price (locals claim that waving a RM10 bill helps) or jump into the cab and feign ignorance; it is illegal for them not to accept a fare within the city limits.

For 24 hour taxi service: *Comfort*, T7330507. *Koteksi*, T7815352. *Sakti*, T4420848. *Selangor*, T2936211. *Telecab*, T2110211. *KL Taxi Drivers' Association*, T2215252. *Mesra*, T4421019. A RM1 surcharge is made for a phone booking. If you are desperate for a taxi go to the nearest hotel and rent a limousine. The cost varies from RM35 to RM60.

Kuala Lumpur's Light Rail Transit (LRT)

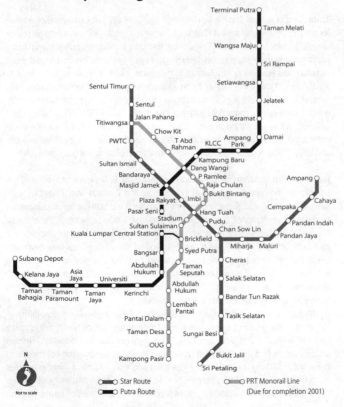

Long distance
See also Ins & outs, page 72

Air KL's new international airport is open at Sepang 72 km from the city. MAS flights to other Malaysian destinations include regular connections with Alor Star, Ipoh, Johor Bahru, Kota Bharu, Kota Kinabalu, Kuala Terengganu, Kuantan, Kuching, Labuan, Lahad Datu, Langkawi, Miri, Penang, Tawau. Note that some domestic flights leave from KL's old airport at Subang, about 25 km southwest of the city centre.

For airport hotels, see page 97

Transport to town: the KLIA coaches provide an efficient and comparatively reasonable service into the city centre for single travellers or couples (for groups of 3-4 it can be cheaper to take a taxi). Bargain hard for a taxi to the city, RM110 is about the minimum. For a taxi from the city to KL Airport expect to pay around RM65. Hotels can arrange a good fare in the RM65-90 range. **NB** make sure the taxi fare includes the motorway toll for either direction. Major car hire firms have desks at the airport terminal. Hotel pick-up service must be arranged in advance or at the office just outside the terminal exit. A railway line, KL Sentral KLIA, is being built between KL and the airport.

Selected Ekspres Nasional bus fares from KL

From KL	(RM)
Alor Star	21.20
Butterworth	17.10
Batu Pahat	10.90
Ipoh	9.40
Johor Bahru	23.70
Kangar	23.40
Kemaman	13.50
Kota Bahru	25.00
Kuantan	12.10
K Terengganu	21.60
Kuala Perlis	23.40
Muar	8.50
Penang	23.50
Singapore	17.80
Taiping/KK	13.20

For more information T2757267, or refer to the timetables & fare charts on pages 645-647

Train Central Railway Station, Jln Hishamuddin, T2747435. Left luggage office on Platform 4 and information desk at Platform 1. The desk is helpful and can advise on schedules. KL is on the main line from Singapore to the south and Butterworth (Penang) to the north; some of these trains go on through to Bangkok (see page 29). To get on the east coastline you have to go to Gemas, the junction south of KL or to Kuala Lipis or Mentakab 150 km to the west of KL. Regular connections with Alor Star, Butterworth, Taiping, Ipoh, Tapah Rd (for Cameron Highlands), Tampin, Gemas, Johor Bahru and Singapore. Tourists, on production of their passport, can buy a KTM rail pass which offers unlimited rail travel, although it is not valid on the Thai system. Outside the western entrance of the station is a restaurant with a colonial style décor, a small Malay menu and Laksa. If you need to wait for a train, this is a good place to hang out for a while.

Bus KL's main bus terminal is **Puduraya** on Jln Pudu. Buses leave here for destinations across the Peninsula as well as to Singapore and Thailand. Most large bus companies have their offices inside the terminal, above the departure hall, including the biggest, *Ekspres Nasional. Ekspres Nasional* also have a ticket counter at the Malaysia Tourist Infomation Centre on Jln Ampang and many hotels and guesthouses will arrange tickets too, which saves on a journey to Puduraya. There are also quite a number of bus offices opposite the terminal along Jln Pudu and, due to overcrowding within, quite a few buses drop off and pick up along that strip of road. It is best to book tickets the day before leaving (although same day departure is usually possible) and during peak holiday periods several days in advance.

NB Avoid buying tickets from touts; only go to the counters. There is an information desk at the terminal, along with a Post Office, tourist police booth, left luggage office (open 0800-2200 Mon-Sun, RM1.50 per item per day) and foodstalls. Though most travellers find that Puduraya serves their travelling needs – the key exception being those wishing to visit Taman Negara National Park – KL has a number of other bus terminals. The **Pekeliling Station**, T4421256 is in the north of the city, off Jln Tun Razak. Buses to Pahang State leave from here including Jerantut (for Taman Negara) and Kuala Lipis which do not depart from Puduraya. Other destinations include Kuantan and the Genting Highlands. The **Putra Station**, T4429530, facing the Putra World Trade Centre, serves the East Coast and there are connections with destinations in Kelantan, Terengganu and Pahang including Kuantan, Kuala Terengganu and Kota Bharu. Buses to Penang, Ipoh and Johor Bahru leave from **Medan Mara**. Regular connections with Singapore, Johor Bahru, Melaka, Butterworth (and Penang, 5 hrs), Ipoh, Kuantan, Kota Bharu. Finally the small **Klang Station** in Chinatown, on Jln Hang Kasturi, serves Port Klang and the suburb of Shah Alam.

Outstation taxis: leave from Jln Pudu, outside the Puduraya bus station. Share taxis run to most large towns on the Peninsula and fares are about double those of equivalent bus journeys. As there are no scheduled departures it is a case of turning up and seeing which taxis have space and where they are going.

Directory

Aeroflot, Ground Floor, Wisma Tong Ah, 1 Jln Perak, T2613331. *Air India*, Bangunan Ankasa Raya, 123 Jln Ampang, T2420323. *Air Lanka*, UG4 Bangunan Perangasang Segemai, Jln Kampung Attap, T2323633. *Alitalia*, Plaza See Hoy Chan, Jln Raja Chulan, T2380366. *America West Airlines*, UBN Tower, 10 Jln P Ramlee, T2387057. *American Airlines*, Bangunan Angkasa Raya, 123 Jln Ampang, T2480644. *Bangladesh Biman*, Subang International Airport, T7461118. *British Airways*, 8th Flr West Wing Rohas Perkasa, 8 Jln Perak, T2676188. *Cathay Pacific*, UBN Tower, 10 Jln P Ramlee, T2383377. *China Airlines*, Level 3, Bangunan Amoda, 22 Jln Imbi, T2427344. *Czechoslavak Airlines*, 12th Flr, Plaza Atrium, 10 Lorong P Ramlee, T2380176. *Delta Airlines*, UBN Tower, Jln P Ramlee, T2324700. *Garuda*, Suite 3.01, Level 3, Menara Lion, Jln Ampang, T2622811. Opposite Ampang Park Shopping Mall. *Japan Airlines*, 1st Flr, Pernas International, Lot 1157, Jln Sultan Ismail, T2611728. *KLM*, Shop 7, Ground Floor, President House, Jln Sultan Ismail, T2427011. *Korean Air*, 17th Flr, MUI Plaza, Jln P Ramlee, T7465700. *Lufthansa*, 3rd Flr, Pernas International Bldg, Jln Sultan Ismail, T2614646/2614666. *MAS*, UMBC Bldg, Jln Sulaiman, T2610555. MAS Bldg, 33rd Flr, Jln Sultan Ismail, T7463000. Dayabumi Complex, T2748734. The Mall, World Trade Centre, Level 3 T4426759. *Northwest Airlines*, UBN Tower, Jln P Ramlee, T2433542. *Pelangi Airways*, 18th floor, Technology Resources Tower, 161B Jln Ampang, T2624446, F2624515. *Philippine Airlines*, 104-107 Wisma Stephens, Jln Raja Chulan, T2429040. *PIA*, Ground Floor, Angkasa Raya Bldg, 123 Jln Ampang, T2425444. *Qantas*, 8th Floor West Wing Rohas Perkasa, 8 Jln Perak, T2676188. *Royal Brunei*, 1st Flr, Wisma Merlin, Jln Sultan Ismail, T2307166. *Royal Jordanian*, 8th Flr, Mui Plaza, Jln P Ramlee, T2487500. *Sabena*, 1st Flr, Wisma Stephens, Jln Raja Chulan, T2425820. *Saudi*, c/o Safuan Travel & Tours, 7 Jln Raja Abdullah, T2984566. *Scandinavian Airlines*, Bangunan Angkasa Raya, 123 Jln Ampang, T2426044. *Singapore Airlines*, Wisma SIA, 2 Jln Sang Wangi, T2923122. *Thai International*, Kuwasa Bldg, 5 Jln Raja Laut, T2937100. *Turkish Airlines*, *Hotel Equatorial*, 20 Jln Sultan Ismail, T2614055. *United Airlines*, Bangunan MAS, Jln Sultan Ismail, T2611433. *UTA French Airlines*, Plaza See Hoy Chan, Jln Raja Chulan, T2324179. *Virgin Atlantic*, 77 Jln Bukit Bintang (2nd Flr), T2430322/3.

Airline offices

There are money changers in all the big shopping centres and along the main shopping streets. Most branches of the leading Malaysian and foreign banks have foreign exchange desks, although some (eg Bank Bumiputra) impose limits on charge card cash advances. The following addresses are for bank headquarters: *Bank Bumiputra*, Menara Bumiputra, Jln Melaka, T2988011; *Bank of America*, 1st Flr, Wisma Stephens, Jln Raja Chulan, T2021133. *Chase Manhattan*, 1st Flr, Bangunan Pernas International, Jln Sultan Ismail; *Hongkong & Shanghai Banking Corporation*, 2 Leboh Ampang (off Jln Gereja), T2300744. *Maybank*, 100 Jln Tun Perak, T2308833. *Public Bank*, Bangunan Public Bank, 6 Jln Sultan Sulaiman (off Jln Syed Putra), T2741788. *Standard Chartered Bank*, 2 Jln Ampang, T2326555. *United Malayan Banking Corporation*, Bangunan UMBC, Jln Sultan Sulaiman (off Jln Syed Putra), T2309866.

Banks

General Post Office: Dayabumi Complex, Jln Sultan Hishamuddin (Poste Restante). **Overseas telephone service:** Kedai Telekom at the airport. *Kaunter Telegraf STM*, Wisma Jothi, Jln Gereja; Ground Floor, *Syarikat Telekom Malaysia*, Bukit Mahkamah. **Internet**: there are two internet places on Jln Raja Laut, Chow Kit; one on the corner of Jln Haji Taib and the other is opposite the junction with Jln Sri Amar. Both charge RM6 per hr.

Communications

Kuala Lumpur

Embassies & consulates
Australia, 6 Jln Yap Kwan Sweng, T2423122. *Austria*, 7th Flr, MUI Plaza, Jln P Ramlee, T2484277. *Belgium*, 4th Flr, Wisma DNP, 12 Lorong Yap Kwan Seng, T2485733. *Brunei Darussalam*, 8th Flr, Wisma Sin Heap Lee (next to the *Crown Princess Hotel*), Jln Tun Razak, T2612800. *Canada*, 7th Flr, Plaza MBS, 172 Jln Ampang, T2612000. *China*, 229 Jln Ampang, T2428495. *Czech Republic*, 32 Jln Mesra (off Jln Damai), T2427185. *Denmark*, 22nd Flr, Bangunan Angkasa Raya, 123 Jln Ampang, T2022101. *Finland*, 15th Flr, MBF Plaza, Jln Ampang, T2611088. *France*, 196 Jln Ampang, T2484318. *Germany*, 3 Jln U Thant, T2429666. *India*, 2 Jln Taman Duta, off Jln Duta, visas take 3-4 days. *Indonesia*, 233 Jln Tun Razak, T9842011. *Italy*, 99 Jln U Thant, T4565122. *Japan*, 11 Persiaran Stonor, off Jln Tun Razak, T2427044. *Laos*, 108 Jln Damai, off Jln Ampang, T2483895. *Myanmar* (Burma), 5 Jln Taman U Thant Satu, T2423863. *Netherlands*, 4 Jln Mesra (off Jln Damai), T2485151. *New Zealand*, 193 Jln Tun Razak, T2382533. *Norway*, 11th Flr, Bangunan Angkasa Raya, Jln Ampang, T2420144. *Pakistan*, Jln Ampang, in front of Tourist Centre. *Papua New Guinea High Commission*, 1 Lorong Ru Kedua (off Jln Ampang), T2455145. *Philippines*, 1 Chnagkat Kia Peng, T2484233. *Poland*, 495, 4½ mile, Jln Ampang, T4576733. *Romania*, 114 Jln Damai, T2423172. *Singapore*, 209 Jln Tun Razak, T2616277. *Spain*, 200 Jln Ampang, T2484868. *Sweden*, 6th Flr, Angkasa Raya Bldg, 123 Jln Ampang, T2485433. *Switzerland*, 16 Persiaran Madge, T2480622. *Thailand*, 206 Jln Ampang, T2488333. *Turkey*, Bangunan Citi 1, Jln Perumahan Gurney, T2986455. *UK*, 185 Jln Ampang, T2482122. *USA*, 376 Jln Tun Razak, T2489011. *USSR*, 263 Jln Ampang, T4560009. *Vietnam*, Vietnam House, 4 Persiaran Stonor, T2484036.

Language courses
Available at many places (see Yellow Pages), but not cheap. *Time Spoken Language Centre*, 226-227 2nd Flr, Campbell Complex, T2921595. Recommended but not especially based on 'travelling bahasa', flexible schedules.

Libraries
National Library, Jln Tun Razak, T2923144. *British Council Library*, Jln Bukit Aman, T2987555. *Lincoln Resource Centre*, 376 Jln Tun Razak, T2420291.

Medical facilities
Hospitals: All have casualty wards open 24 hrs. *Assunta Hospital*, Petaling Jaya, T7923433. *City Medical Centre*, 415-427 Jln Pudu, T2211255. *Damai Service Hospital*, 115-119 Jln Ipoh, T4434900. *Pudu Specialist Centre*, Jln Baba, T2429146. *Tung Shin Hospital*, 102 Jln Pudu, T2321655.

Places of worship
Churches: Times of English-language Sun services: *Baptist Church*, 70 Cangkat Bukit Bintang, 0830, 0945. *St Andrews International Church*, 31 Jln Raja Chulan, 0900, 1100. *St John's Cathedral* (Roman Catholic), 5 Jln Bukit Nanas, 0800, 1030, 1800. *St Mary's (Anglican) Church*, Jln Raja, 0700, 0800, 0930 (family Eucharist), 1800. *Wesley Methodist Church*, 2 Jln Wesley, 0815, 1030, 1800.

Tourist offices
Tourism Malaysia, Information Centre, Level 2, Putra World Trade Centre, 45 Jln Tun Ismail, T4411295, T2935188, F2935884. *Tourist Information Desks*, Terminals 1 & 2, Subang International Airport, T7465707. As well as the *Information Counter* at the Railway Station, T2746063. *KL Visitors Centre*, 3 Jln Sultan Hishamuddin, T2301369 (next to the National Art Gallery). A non-governmental tourist association, not particularly conveniently located and their most useful publication is an A3 map of the city, which is available from the Tourism Malaysia offices in any case; www.tourism.gov.my. *Malaysian Tourist Information Centre (MATIC)*, 109 Jln Ampang, T2643929, F2621149. Located in an opulent mansion formerly belonging to a Malaysian planter and tin miner, information on all 13 states, cultural performances and demonstrations of traditional handicrafts, it also provides money-changing facilities.

Useful information
American Express, 18th Flr, *The Weld* (near KL Tower), Jln Raja Chulan, T2130000. **Assisted International Calls:** T108. **Directory Enquiries:** T103. **Fire:** T994. **Immigration:** Jln Pantai Bharu, T7578155. **KL Tourist Police:** T2496593. **Police/ambulance:** T999. **Telegram Services:** T104. **Trunk Calls Assistance:** T101. **Weather Report:** T1052. **Wildlife and National Parks Department:**, Km 10, Jln Cheras, T9052872, F9052873.

Northern Peninsula

4

Northern Peninsula

The north-south highway, Malaysia's equivalent of the autobahn, which runs from KL to the Thai border, doesn't give the traveller much of a sense of excitement about this northern quarter of the Peninsula. But there is much more here than asphalt and Protons. North of KL are the cool hill resorts and tea plantations of the Cameron Highlands and Fraser's Hill. The former tin-rush town of Ipoh offer Straits Chinese architecture and some superb food. Offshore there is the 25 km-long island of Penang with its fine captial Georgetown and an array of beachside hotels. Less developed than Penang is Pulau Pangkor to the south and Pulau Langkawi to the north, the latter closer to Thailand than to mainland Malaysia.

Barisan Titiwangsa and the Hill Stations

On the road north, Peninsular Malaysia's mountainous jungled backbone lies to the east. It is called the Barisan Titiwangsa or Main Range. It is largely unsettled apart from the old British hill stations, Fraser's Hill, Cameron Highlands and Maxwell Hill, and scattered Orang Asli aboriginal villages. During the Malayan Emergency in the late 1940s and early 1950s, the Communist guerrillas operated from jungle camps in the mountains and later used the network of aboriginal trails to infiltrate the peninsula from their bases in southern Thailand.

Genting Highlands

Phone code: 03
Colour map 2, grid A2

The Genting Highlands, just 51 km northeast of KL, is the city's closest hill resort and a popular source of entertainment, Las Vegas-cum-Disneyland style. They were first developed as a resort in the 1960s by a prominent Malaysian businessman, Tan Sri Lim Goh Tong. At the time, investing in construction at an altitude of 2,000m above sea level was considered a hairbrained idea. Building the tortuous and impossibly steep road through the dense, jungle-covered hills took seven years alone. However, the idea took off, and the government conceded to allow Malaysia's only casino to operate here.

The resort's main attraction is the Casino de Genting which is one of the largest in the world, with endless rows of slot machines, games tables and even a computerized racetrack where it is possible to bet on Royal Ascot. The décor is glitzy; red plush and glittering chandeliers abound. Occasional grand sweeps are made: an Indonesian recently put a RM4 keno token into a machine and came away with 1.5 million ringgit. The casino attracts an estimated 30,000 clients a day and provides the main source of revenue in the Highlands. Other attractions in the resort include a theme park, which is rated amongst the best in Malaysia. The park comprises an outdoor theme park which is being constantly expanded, and an indoor theme park and leisure zone to cater for wet-weather days, which are frequent in the Highlands, particularly at the end of the year. It takes at least a day to get around all the venues – and at least as long to work out how to get around. With this bonanza of entertainment on offer, not surprisingly, weekends and public holidays are very busy; Chinese New Year and Hari Raya are two of the peak holidays.

Sleeping   The accommodation at Genting Highlands comes under the umbrella of the *Genting Highlands Resorts*. Weekends and holidays have the disadvantage of having to queue at check in and out times, it is best to visit on a weekday if possible.

A *Awana Golf & Country Resort*, T2113015, F2113555. The 30-storey octagonal tower dominates the resort, which is 10 km below the main resort peak, and overlooks an 18-hole golf course. All rooms have fans (a/c not needed at this altitude), bath, TV and balconies offering panoramic views, facilities including a heated pool, tennis, gymnasium, sauna, children's library, coffee house, restaurant, cocktail lounge and golf (see Sport below). Recommended. **A** *Genting Hotel*, T2111118, F2111888. Located in the heart of the action, deluxe Genting Club rooms, a heated pool and jacuzzi, restaurant, coffee house and easy access to all the resort facilities. **A** *Highlands Hotel*, T2112812, F2113535. Massive (900 rooms), quite new and very smart; it calls its décor London-style. **A** *Kayangan Apartments*, units designed to accommodate extensive families, the smallest unit has 3 rooms and sleeps 6, the 4-room unit sleeps 8. Splitting the costs between a group, rates per head are in the **B-C** category. **A** *Resort Hotel*, T2111118, F2113535. Mainly caters for tour groups and is rated as a 3-star outlet. **A** *Ria Apartments*, a 2-room unit sleeps 4 and in low season is priced at the lower end of the **A** range, a 3-room unit is even more economical and sleeps 6, either unit can take an additional 2 beds at a charge of RM20 each. **B** *Theme Park Hotel*, T2111118, F2113535. The first hotel to be built at the resort, but recently refurbished, and as its name suggests, the rooms overlook the outdoor theme park.

Awana Golf and Country Resort 4 *Japanese Restaurant*. Recommended for sushi. 4 *Sails Grill*, second floor, successfully achieves the romantic, candle-lit look combined with dark wood and ethnic masks, excellent quality, international cuisine, 5-star service. Recommended. 3 *Genting Theatre Restaurant*, second floor, tables arranged around the stage, eat while watching a show. 3 *Korean Restaurant*. 3-2 *Rajawali Coffee House*. 2 *Restaurant Kampung*, lobby floor, traditional Malay fare, good value buffet and set lunch. 2 *Sidewalk Café*, lobby floor, a 24-hour coffee shop.

Highlands Hotel 3 *The Bistro*, continental food, pizza. 3-2 *Good Friends Restaurant*, Chinese food.

Indoor Theme Park Over 20 fast food outlets, including 2 *KFC*, 2 *McDonalds* and 2 *Theme Park Noodle House*.

Resort Hotel 2 *Resort Café*, all-day à la carte and buffet breakfast, lunch and dinner.

Theme Park Hotel 2 *Happy Valley Restaurant*, large and very popular Chinese restaurant.

Eating
Eating places are all within the resort which caters for most tastes & budgets

Casino de Genting, *Genting Hotel*: formal dress, tie for men or hire a batik shirt at the door, blackjack, baccarat, roulette, Tai-Sai amongst the table games, slot machines, computerized racing, the International Room, for card-holders only, caters for more serious players. *Indoor Theme Park*, the usual video games as well as a Virtual Reality Dungeon, 3D Experience and Space Odyssey 2020 – their most recent simulator addition, a World Train Ride for the less techno-minded, and plenty of rides for tots. *Leisure Zone*, 32-lane computerized bowling alley – the second largest in Malaysia, table tennis, snooker. *Outdoor Theme Park*, the most recent additions are the Corkscrew Roller Coaster and the Rolling Thunder Mine Train, a monorail makes a circuit of the park and offers good views on a clear day, a cable car runs across the park – also good for views. *Big Rock Disco Café*, the main disco at the resort.

Entertainment

Golf *Awana Golf & Country Resort*, Km 13, T2113015, F2113535. An 18-hole, international class course featuring bunkers, ponds and streams, putting green, three-tiered driving range, open daily 0730-1730, green fees RM100 weekdays, not open to public at weekends, driving range. **Horse riding** *Awana Horse Ranch*, T2112026. Open daily 0800-1800, pony rides for children, jumps, horse trekking.

Sports

Northern Peninsula

Transport
51 km to KL
131 km to Kuantan

Bus The resort operates an a/c express bus service between the KL Puduraya bus station and Genting Highlands. The service runs every 30 mins at peak times and hourly at other times from 0800 to 1800 with an extended service on Sun and public holidays to 1900. The journey takes 1 hr and costs RM5, inclusive of the cable car which runs from near the *Awana Hotel* to the resort at the peak. The ticketing office at Puduraya is at counter 43, and buses leave from platform 13. For advance reservations T032326863. A free shuttle service operates every 2 hrs between the *Awana* and the *Resort Hotel*. An hourly, 24-hr, free shuttle service connects the *Resort Hotel*, *Genting Hotel* and *Ria Apartments*.

Cable car The 'flying carpet cable car' operates between the resort at the peak and a station near *Awana*. It runs every 20 mins between 1200 and 2030 on Mon, 0830 and 2030 Tue to Fri, and 0830 to 2130 weekends and public holidays. Travelling time is 12 mins and the one way fare is RM3. For enquiries T032111118, ext 7751. There are plans to build a cable car from Batu caves, just outside KL, to the cable car station at the *Highlands Hotel*, which will cut travelling time considerably.

Directory
Banks *Maybank, Genting Hotel.* **Communications** Area code: 03. **General Post Office:** *Genting Hotel.*

Fraser's Hill

Phone code: 09
Altitude: 1,524m
Colour map 2, grid A2

Fraser's Hill is named after Englishman Louis James Fraser, who ran a gambling den, traded in tin and opium and operated a mule train in these hills at the end of the 19th century. He went on to manage a transport service between Kuala Kubu and Raub. Before Mr Fraser lent his name to it, the seven hills were known as Ulu Tras. The development of the hill station began in the early 1920s.

It was along the road from Kuala Bubu Bharu that Sir Henry Gurney, the British High Commissioner, was ambushed and killed by Communist insurgents during the Malayan Emergency in 1951 (see page 392). A few years earlier British soldiers were involved in the massacre of suspected Communist sympathizers near Kuala Kubu. They shot dead a number of rubber tappers from a local village. There are a number of Orang Asli villages along rivers and tracks leading from the twisting road up the hill.

Fraser's Hill is close enough to KL to be a favoured weekend resort. Because it was easily accessible by train from Kuala Kubu Road, it was a popular weekend retreat long before the Cameron Highlands. Most of colonial Malaya's big companies, such as Sime Darby, Guthries' and Harrisons and Crosfield, built holiday bungalows among the hills. More and more luxury bungalows are now being built here to cater for wealthy Malaysians, but it is still more tranquil and attractive than Genting. Although it is not as varied as the Cameron Highlands by way of attractions, there is one trail (a three hour walk) which starts just to the south of the tennis courts and ends at the *Corona Nursery Youth Hostel*, good opportunities for birdwatchers and wild flower enthusiasts, a golf course, tennis courts and gardens. Swimming at Jeriau waterfalls is limited as the concrete pool has all but silted up so that the water is only knee deep, but standing under the powerful waterfall is very refreshing.

Sleeping
Many of the hotels have recreation facilities such as tennis, squash, riding, snooker

AL *Ye Olde Smokehouse Hotel*, T3622226, F3622035. Small 13-room hotel in the Olde English style of the *Smokehouse*, Cameron Highlands; with breakfast, a/c, TV, minibar, bath, in-house movie, tea and coffee-making facilities, restaurant, pool. Rooms are spacious, clean, with bathroom and some balconies overlooking the golf course – excellent views. Price includes breakfast, which makes it good value. **A** *Silverpark Holiday Resort*, Jln Lady Maxwell, T3622888, F3622185, reservations

T2916633. Apartments only, no cooking facilities, associated with De Club golf course, pool, restaurant, children's playground. **B** *Fraser's Hill Development Corporation*, T3622311, F3622273. The organization manages the *Puncak Inn*, next to the bus stop, a nondescript 27-room hotel, and a series of 3 to 4 bedroom bungalows, including the **C** *Temerloh*, unusual circular but rather tatty chalets divided into 2 large rooms. Very basic with shared bathroom. *Raub*; *Pekan*. *Jelai* and *Rompin*, rates are charged per room and an additional fixed rate is available for 3 daily meals, hiking and birdwatching tours are arranged. **C** *Gap Resthouse*, 8 km before Fraser's Hill. Restaurant serving good Chinese food, poor Western and Malay-Indian food, recently renovated large rooms but still excellent value and a very characterful place to stay. Recommended. **C** *Seri Berkat Rest House*, T038041026, book through district office at Kuala Kubu Bharu. Another colonial building with high ceilings and big rooms. **C** *Fraser Hill Travel Lodge* (YHA), MC G/5 Taman Setia (Sg. Hijua), Fraser Hill, T3622443. Run by Mike Chan who will bend over backwards to help you and is very informative. Definitely the best budget option in town. Bedroom apartment with shared kitchen and bathroom with hot water. Around 15 mins walk from town or a 5 min shuttle bus ride.

Eating

Chinese **3** *Kheng Yuen Lee Eating Shop*, sports club. **3** *Spices*, Jalan Genting, 49000 Bukit Fraser, T3622510. Serves Guinness and has a small but interesting menu (Indian, Chinese and Western food). The place has a 1950s feel to it. Recommended. **3** *Satay's Corner*, Chinese, up the hill from the main town, next to the mosque. Serves a good breakfast. **International** **3** *Old Smokehouse*, similar to Cameron Highlands establishment, serving English style dishes such as Beef Wellington and Devonshire cream teas. Recommended. **3** *Restoran Puncak*, below *Puncak Inn*. **3** *Temerloh Steak House*, Temerloh Bungalow.

Bars

Ye Olde Tavern, above the *Puncak Inn*, Fraser's answer to an English inn, with log fire. *Spices*, see above.

Sports

Golf *De Club at Fraser's*, 18-hole course for members, 9-hole course for public, green fees RM30 weekdays, RM40 weekends, RM15 for club hire, T382777. **Horse riding, paddle boats** For hire on Allan's Water.

Transport
104 km to KL

Bicycle hire From Fraser's Hill Development Corporation Office, RM4 per hour. **Bus** Regular connections from KL – the 66 bus from platform 21 of KL's Pudu Raya station (buy ticket on bus) gets in to Kuala Kubu Bharu. Change here to Fraser's Hill. Bus only runs at 0800 and 1200 from Kuala Bubu Bharu to Fraser's Hill and returns at 1000 and 1400. **Car** One way traffic system operates from 0630-1900, 8 km from Fraser's Hill: uphill traffic gets right-of-way on the odd hours, downhill traffic on the even hours. **Taxi** Shared taxis go direct to Fraser's Hill. KL (RM10 from Kubu Bharu, or RM40 for the whole cab).

Directory

Banks It is possible to change money at *Maybank*, *Merlin Hotel*, also *Malaysia Bank*, along from *Merlin Hotel* entrance in the same complex of shops. **Communications** Area code: 09. **Tourist offices** *Fraser's Hill Development Corporation Office* between golf club and the *Merlin Hotel*, maps and general information available.

Northern Peninsula

Cameron Highlands

Phone code: 05
Colour map 1, grid C3

The biggest and best known of Malaysia's hill stations lies on the northwest corner of Pahang, bounded by Perak, to the west, and Kelantan to the north. On the jungley 1,500m plateau the weather is reassuringly British, unpredictable, often wet and decidedly cool, but when the sun blazes out of an azure-blue sky, the Camerons are hard to beat.

Daytime temperatures average around 23°C, and in the evening, when it drops to 10°C and the hills are enveloped in swirling cloud, known as 'the white witch', pine log fires are lit in the hilltop holiday bungalows. The weather has become more unpredictable in the last fifity years: torrential downpours and landslides are no longer confined to the monsoon months of November and December. But the mountain air is still bracing enough to entice thousands of holiday makers to the Camerons from the steamy plains. Today coach loads of Singaporeans wind their way up the mountain roads and, together with well-heeled KL businessfolk, fork out extortionate sums for weekends in timeshare apartments and endless rounds of golf.

History

In the colonial era the mountain resort was a haven for homesick, overheated planters and administrators. Its temperate climate induced an eccentric collection of them to settle and retire in their Surrey-style mansions where they could prune their roses, tend their strawberries, sip G and Ts on the lawn, stroll down to the golf course or nip over to Mr Foster's mock-Tudor Smokehouse for a Devonshire cream tea. The British Army also had a large presence in Tanah Rata until 1971 – their imposing former military hospital (now reverted to being a Roman Catholic convent) still stands on the hill overlooking the main street. To the left of the road leading into Tanah Rata from Ringlet are a few remaining Nissen huts from the original British army camp.

While most of the old timers - the likes of Stanley Foster, Captain Bloxham (who nursed racehorses at his bougainvillaea-fringed 'spelling station' at Ringlet) and Miss Gwenny Griffith-Jones (founder of Singapore's Tanglin School) – have now gone to rest, they bequeathed an ambience which the Camerons has yet to shake off. Miss 'Griff' had been one of the original pioneers, trudging up through the jungle from Tapah on an oxcart, when they first cut the hair-pinned road in the 1930s.

Fifty years elapsed between the discovery of the highland plateau and the arrival of the first settlers. William Cameron, a government surveyor, first claimed to have stumbled across "a fine plateau .. shut in by lofty mountains" while on a mapping expedition in 1885. In a letter in which he gave an account of this trip, he wrote: "[I saw] a sort of vortex in the mountains, while for a wide area we have gentle slopes and plateau land". The irony was that Cameron's name was bestowed on a place he never set eyes on. He

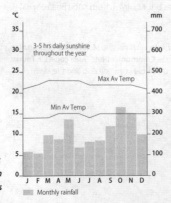

Climate:
Cameron
Highlands

Northern Peninsula

Cameron Highlands tea plantations

The Cameron Highlands provide an ideal climate for tea growing. There are several large and well-established tea estates, including the Bharat and Gold Dollar tea estates, located in the lower Highlands between Ringlet and Tanah Rata, and the Blue Valley tea estate in the upper Highlands. The largest and best known estate in the Highlands is the Boh Plantation. Boh tea is the standard household brand in most Malaysian homes. It has 1,200 hectares of mature tea plantations. Both the Fairlie (lower Highlands) and the Sungei Palas (upper Highlands) operate free guided tours of their factories, every hour or so, daily except Monday; the factories have no tea to process on a Monday, as no tea gets plucked on a Sunday. The Sungei Palas is probably the more attractive of the two, perched high on the steep, green hills above Brinchang, and is less inundated with visitors; see page 133 to get there.

Like all Cameronian tea estates, Boh Plantations (lower Highland) employ a hardcore of tea pluckers whose forebears originally came from South India. Many of the workers are third or fourth generation having been brought here in the late 1920s to start the first plantations. The workers live in self-contained quarters on the estates, most of which have their own shops and school. The original tea plants also came from India, mainly Darjeeling stocks, many of which are still productive. Now bonsai specimens, they can be recognized by their thick trunks and dark green leaves. Bushes planted from the 1960s onwards are mainly cloned varieties and have much lighter coloured leaves.

During the 1920s, the Cameron Highlands were under the control of a British Governor. The founder of the Boh Plantations, John Archibald Russell (known to his friends as Archie), was the son of a British government official. In conjunction with Mr AB Milne, an old tea planter from Ceylon, in 1927, JA Russell applied for and was granted a concession of land in the Cameron Highlands. This became the Boh Estate, which was carved out of virgin jungle, an extraordinary feat considering that the work was carried out without machinery and only with the assistance of mules.

In the 1920s, tea plucking and processing was also an all-manual process. Nowadays, machinery is used, although it is still manually intensive, with an average of 6-10 people required to look after each acre of plantation. Part of the reason for the intensity of manual labour is that the tea bushes are grown on slopes that in places are so precipitous that machinery is almost impossible to use: 45° slopes are commonplace. However, on the whole, the workers use a plucking machine, a hefty gadget requiring two men to hold it, while double blades slice off the top-most shoots which are blown into a bag, otherwise hand shears are used. Plucking takes place year round every 15-25 days, depending on growth which tends to be slower during the rainy season. Maintenance is a year round task too. The bushes need to be regularly fertilized and weeded, while pruning takes place every three years.

The green tea leaf is weighed (the pluckers are paid per kilogram) before being taken to the factory to be processed where every 5 kg of green leaf produces around 1 kg of tea. The first process in the factory is to wither the leaves under artificial blowers, for 12-16 hours, depending on the moisture content. The leaves are then rolled, or broken up using a rotary blade, and graded before being put into trays for fermentation. Finally the tea is fired in an oven, the timing of which is critical, before being graded for a second time. The tea is mostly packaged in KL, from where it is distributed, mainly to local destinations as the quantity is limited.

Northern Peninsula

probably came across the smaller plateau area farthest from Tanah Rata, known as Blue Valley. The highland plateau itself was discovered years later by a Malay warrior named Kulop Riau who accompanied Cameron on his mapping expeditions. Cameron's report engendered much excitement. Sir Hugh Low, who, 34 years earlier, had made the first attempt at Sabah's Gunung Kinabalu, was by then the Resident of Perak. He wanted to develop the newly reported highland area as "a sanitorium, health resort and open farmland". Twenty years elapsed before the first pioneers made their way up to the so-called 'Cameron's Land'.

Cameron Highlands

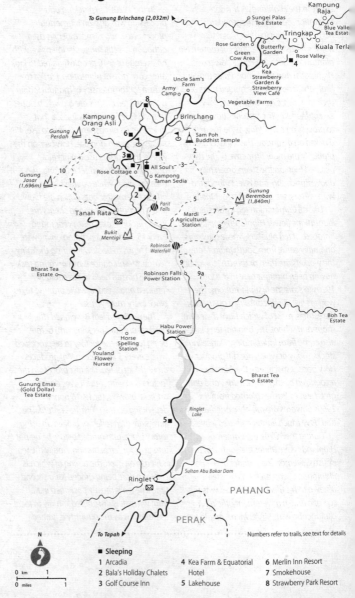

Numbers refer to trails, see text for details

N

| 0 km | 1 |
| 0 miles | 1 |

■ **Sleeping**

1 Arcadia
2 Bala's Holiday Chalets
3 Golf Course Inn
4 Kea Farm & Equatorial Hotel
5 Lakehouse
6 Merlin Inn Resort
7 Smokehouse
8 Strawberry Park Resort

Hot on the heels of the elderly gin and Jaguar settlers (most of them insisted on solid British cars for the mountain roads) came the tea planters and vegetable farmers. The cool mountain climate was perfect for both. The forested hillsides were shaved to make way for more tea bushes and cabbages and the deforestation appears to have affected the climate. The local meteorological station reports that the average temperature has risen 2°C in the past 50 years.

The Camerons' most talked-about visitor arrived in March 1967 for a quiet sojourn in Moonlight bungalow, perched on a hilltop above the golf course. The disappearance of the US-born Thai silk emperor, art collector and military intelligence agent Jim Thompson from a lonely Cameronian backroad, propelled the hill resort into the headlines. Teams of Orang Asli trackers combed the jungle in vain while detectives, journalists and film makers toyed with credible explanations: he had been given a new identity by the CIA; he had been kidnapped and smuggled from the highlands in the boot of a Thai taxi; he had been eaten by a tiger. The fate of Thompson, the Lord Lucan of Southeast Asia, is still a mystery.

Sights

Most of the tourist attractions in the Cameron Highlands are on and around the plateau but there are a handful of sights on the road from Tapah. These are listed in order from the bottom of the mountain up. There are three main townships in the Highlands: Ringlet, Tanah Rata – literally 'flat land' – and Brinchang. The latter two are in the plateau area, either side of the golf course.

Unfortunately, the Cameron Highlands is no longer a peaceful bolt-hole in the sky. Frenetic development is turning the area, in critics' eyes, into a building site where forest is fast making way for golf courses and luxury tourist developments. When Prime Minister Dr Mahathir's plan for a new road from Ipoh to the Cameron Highlands is put underway, further expansion can be expected. At present the road from Tapah is the only way up and down; this road runs through Perak until it reaches Ringlet, and the Perak state authorities are unlikely to spend much money upgrading it as Pahang state accrues all the financial returns of Cameron Highlands' tourism.

Tapah This is a centre for making the large bamboo baskets that are used to collect the tea. The town itself is very small, a single street of dilapidated shophouses with a couple of basic hotels including the **E** *Bunga Raya* (T4011436) and **E** *Hotel Utara* (T4012299), and a few eating places, including *KFC*. The bus station in Tapah is on Jalan Raja, just off the main road. There are hourly connections with Tanah Rata as well as occasional departures for KL and Penang. Most long distance bus departures from Tapah (including KL, Melaka, Penang, Kuantan, and Lumut as well as connections with Hat Yai in southern Thailand) are from the *Caspian Restaurant* on the main highway. The Tapah Road Railway Station is about 10 km from town.

Kuala Woh, a jungle park with a swimming pool, fishing and natural hot pools, is only 13 km from Tapah, on the road to the Camerons and has a basic camping area.

Lata Iskandar Waterfall, 22½ km from Tapah, is a beautiful jungle waterfall, right by the roadside, which has been ruined by commercial ventures capitalizing on the picnic spot. However, it is a good place to pick up the local terracotta pottery, crafted Kampung Kerayung. The **19th Mile**, further up the hill, is a more pleasant spot for a stop-off. To the right of the little shop, a path leads along the side of the river, up into the jungle, past Orang Asli villages, waterfalls and jungle pools. Good for birdwatching and butterflies.

Jungle walks: Cameron Highlands

The Cameron Highlands is great walking country, although many of the longer trails were closed in the 1970s when the army found secret food dumps for the Communist Party of Malaya, which used the Main Range as its insurgency route from its bases near Betong in South Thailand. Despite the CPM calling a halt to hostilities in 1990, the trails have not reopened. There are however a handful of not-so-strenuous mountains to climb and a number of jungle walks. Cameronian trails are a great place for people unfamiliar with jungle walks. They are also very beautiful.

Basic sketch maps of trails, with numbered routes, are available at the Tourist Information kiosk in Tanah Rata and from most hotels. Walkers are advised to take plenty of water with them as well as a whistle, a lighter and something warm. It is very easy to lose your way in jungle – and the district officer has had to call out Orang Asli trackers on many occasions over the years to hunt down disoriented hikers. Always make sure someone knows roughly where you are going and approximately what time you are expecting to get back.

There is a centuries-old Orang Asli trail leading from Tanjung Rambutan, near Ipoh, up the Kinta River into the Main Range. One branch of this trail goes north to the summit of Gunung Korbu (2,183m), 16 km away. When William Cameron and his warrior companion Kulop Riau left on their elephant-back expedition into the mountains, they followed the Kinta River to its source, and from the summit of nearby Gunung Calli, saw Blue Valley 'plateau'. Cameron's view of the plateau that would later bear his name was obscured by two big mountains, Irau (the roller-coaster-shaped one) and Brinchang.

At 2,032m, Gunung Brinchang is the Highlands' highest peak and the highest point in Malaysia accessible by road. The area around the communications centre on the summit affords a great panorama of the plateau, although it spends most of its life shrouded in cloud. The road up the mountain veers left in the middle of Boh's Sungei Palas tea estate past Km 73. From the top of Brinchang it is possible to see straight down into the Kinta valley, on the other side. Ipoh is only 15 km away, as the hornbill flies. There is an old and rarely used trail up Gunung Brinchang from the back of the old airstrip (behind the army flats) at the top end of Brinchang town.

Gunung Beremban (1,840m) makes a pleasant hike, although its trails are well

Ringlet This is the first township on the road to the Cameron Highlands, just inside Pahang state. It was relocated to its present site in the 1960s when the original village was flooded to make way for the Sultan Abu Bakar hydroelectric scheme. *Ringlet* is the Semai aboriginal word for a jungle tree. The town itself is basically unattractive, the apartment blocks erected here in the 1960s now looking very shabby. The *Lakehouse Hotel* is located here (see **Sleeping** below), and there are a couple of basic hotels – the *Hotel Cathay* and the *Hotel da Restoran Sha* – which have rooms in the **D** category. There is also a cluster of hawker stalls in the town centre and a well-used temple.

After Ringlet, the road follows a wide river to a large murky brown lake, connected to a hydroelectric dam. The lake is overlooked by the famous *Lakehouse*, a Tudor-style country house, formerly the home of Colonel Stanley Foster and now a cosy 18-room hotel. The lake is also overlooked by a row of food and souvenir stalls. At the Habu power station, a road leads right to two of the tea growing estates of the Boh Plantations. The original Boh Estate is 6 km from the junction and the Fairlie Estate is 12 km. ■ *Free guided tours of the factory given almost every hour at the Fairlie Estate, Tue-Sun.*

Youland Nursery is on the road to Gold Dollar tea estate, left off the main road to Tanah Rata from Ringlet (milestone 32). At the same turn-off there is a

Northern Peninsula

worn. It can be reached from Tanah Rata (trail No 7 goes up through the experimental tea in the MARDI station past the padang off Jalan Persiaran Dayang Endah), Brinchang (trail No 2 leads up from behind the Sam Poh Buddhist temple – a more arduous route), or the golf course (follow trail No 3 past the Arcadia bungalow where the road stops) – this is the easiest. Allow about four hours to get up and down. There is a good view down Tanah Rata's main street from the top. It is also possible to climb Gunung Beremban from Robinson Falls (trail No 8 leads off trail No 9). The trail heading for the latter is from the very bottom of the road leading past MARDI from Tanah Rata.

Gunung Jasar (1,696m), between the golf course and Tanah Rata, is a pleasant – but gentler – walk of about three hours (trail No 10). The trail goes from halfway along the old back road to Tanah Rata near the meteorological station (the road – Jalan Titiwangsa – leaves Tanah Rata from behind a hotel (south of town) and emerges at the golf course, on the corner next to the Golf Course Hotel). The Jasar trail also forks off to Bukit Perdah (trail No 12, which branches off the Jasar trail) two to three hours to the top and back. The path down from the summit comes out on a road leading back into the top end of Tanah Rata.

The trails to Robinson Falls (trail No 9, an hour's walk) and Parit Falls (trail No 4, 30 minutes' walk) are more frequently trampled. The trail branches off to No 9a which leads down to the Boh tea estate road near Ringlet Lake. The walk to the Boh tea estate is a long one, but it is possible to hitch along the road or catch a bus with great views when you get there. There are tours every hour. The estate is closed on Monday, and closed at 1700 on other days; the last bus leaves the factory at 1730. The short trail to Parit Falls starts behind the Garden Hotel and mosque on the far side of Tanah Rata's padang and ends up below the Slim army camp. Parit Falls is a small waterfall in between the two, with what was once a beautiful jungle pool before it became cluttered with daytrippers and their rubbish.

There are hundreds of other trails through the Camerons, traversing ridges and leading up almost every hill and mountain. Most are Orang Asli paths, some date from the Japanese occupation in the Second World War (these are marked by barbed wire) and some aren't really trails at all – beware.

racehorse spelling station, formerly owned by Cameronian pioneer Captain Bloxham. Before reaching Tanah Rata, on the right is a waterfall and picnic spot, on the left is the *Cameron Bharat* tea shop which has a fine view over the Bharat tea estate.

Tanah Rata

A further 5 km up the mountain is Tanah Rata, the biggest of the three Cameronian towns. Having said this, it is still not very large, comprising a row of shophouses straddled along the main road where there are two or three restaurants, imitating British cafés with fish and chips on most menus. It is a friendly little town, with a resort atmosphere rather like an English seaside town. There are also several souvenir shops, including the *Yung Seng Souvenir Shop* which is more upmarket than the others and has an interesting selection of well-priced asli crafts, ranging from blowpipes to woodcarvings. It is also worth looking in local shops for teas from surrounding estates.

Well-priced half day tours of the area are organized by *Bala's Holiday Chalets* (see **Sleeping** below) which saves on trying to negotiate the highlands by public transport.

Phone code: 05
Altitude: 1,440m
Colour map 1, grid C3

Sleeping
■ *on maps, below*
& page 124
Price codes:
see inside front cover

NB It should be noted that normally during public holidays, accommodation gets fully booked and prices rise by 30-50%. However, because of the present economic downturn, this is currently not the case. It is also busy at peak school holiday periods: Apr, Aug and Dec. The most economic form of accommodation is to share a bungalow between a group of people. Most bungalows have gardens, logfires and are away from the towns.

A *Heritage*, T4913888, F4915666, located just west of Tanah Rata next to the Convent School. This place has a rather bland international look, out of keeping with its surroundings. It has 170 spacious rooms, bath, TV, in-house video, mini-bar, tea and coffee-making facilities, Chinese restaurant, coffee house, sauna (currently closed), health centre, squash, tennis. Price includes breakfast. **A** *Lakehouse*, T4956152, F4956213, www.cameron.concorde.net. This is located a few kilometres outside Tanah Rata but has fantastic views. It is a Tudor-style country house, the final brain-child of Colonel Stanley Foster, with 18 rooms of antique furnishings, four-poster beds and en suite bathrooms, overlooking lake, restaurant serving English food, Cameron Bar and Highlander Lounge both have English country pub atmosphere, a great place to stay and reasonable value considering. **A** *Smokehouse Hotel*, T4911215, F4911214. This place is modelled on its namesake, the *Smokehouse* in Mildenhall (UK) and it preserves its home counties ethos and 'ye olde English' style of old-time resident Colonel Stanley Foster. Its rooms are first class, there is an original red British telephone box in the garden, restaurant serves expensive English food.

B *Merlin Inn Resort*, T4911211/4911205, F4911178. Excellent position overlooking the golf course, north of Tanah Rata, 100 rooms extension completed in early 1997, there are other more atmospheric places to stay at this price. **B** *Strawberry Park Resort*, T4911166, F4911949. Magnificent setting above Tanah Rata, dominating a hilltop with its 8 blocks of walk-up rooms and apartments, built in Tudor/Swiss-chalet style. Interior is starting to look dated, rooms are designed to hold maximum capacity, even the smallest studio rooms and 1 room apartments can sleep 4 people. All rooms with bath (inadequate water heaters), TV, in-house video, fridge, tea and coffee-making facilities. Resort facilities include indoor pool (the only one in the Cameron Highlands), tennis, squash, sauna, indoor games rooms, mini-putting

Tanah Rata

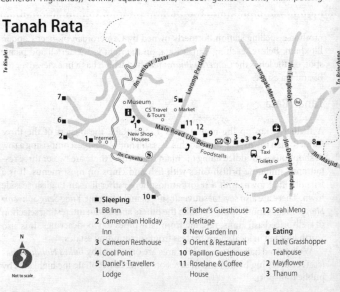

■ Sleeping
1 BB Inn
2 Cameronian Holiday Inn
3 Cameron Resthouse
4 Cool Point
5 Daniel's Travellers Lodge
6 Father's Guesthouse
7 Heritage
8 New Garden Inn
9 Orient & Restaurant
10 Papillon Guesthouse
11 Roselane & Coffee House
12 Seah Meng

● Eating
1 Little Grasshopper Teahouse
2 Mayflower
3 Thanum

Not to scale

green, children's play area, 7 km jogging track, *Monroe's Pub* (with the only disco in the Cameron Highlands and karaoke rooms), coffee house, *Tudor Grill* steakhouse, Chinese restaurant. Recommended.

C *Cool Point*, Jln Dayang Indah, T4914914, F4914070. A tacky interpretation of the Tudor style and rather dated décor, but comfortable, TV, tea and coffee-making facilities, own bathroom, restaurant. Half price rooms at present, good value. **C** *New Garden Inn*, Jln Masjid, T4915170, F4915169. Forty seven rooms in 3 separate buildings, of which the Old Scottish House is the only one with any character, generally outdated décor, facilities include a cinema in the former Dalat School; with bathroom. **C** *Roselane*, 44 Jln Besar, T4912377. Above the *Roselane* coffee shop, large comfortable rooms. **C** *Rumah Rehat*, Jln Dayang Endah, T4911254. Exceptionally nice little resthouse, tends to get overbooked by government employees so it pays to book in advance, tennis court. Recommended.

D *Bala's Holiday Chalets*, T4911660, F4914500. Located 1 km outside Tanah Rata on road to Brinchang (RM3 taxi ride). Not chalets at all, but a rambling colonial house (one of the oldest in the area, formerly a British school) with character and a pleasant garden, rooms a little dank and run down, private bathrooms with hot water (sporadically available) shower, great view, private cable TV. Bala knows the Camerons well, there is a pinboard with information on jungle walks and the latest news from travellers, common sitting-rooms, log fires, good atmosphere but relying on reputation, reasonably priced restaurant. **D** *Cameron Highlands Resthouse*, T4911066. Restaurant, must book first, well run. **D** *Cameronian Holiday Inn*, 16 Jln Mentigi, T4911327, F4914966, nasan@pc.jaring.com. Restaurant, garden, TV, games, sitting area, hot showers in more expensive rooms, this is one of the better mid-budget places in town with a large lawn and a suitably relaxing atmosphere, dorm bed also available (**F**). Quiet and back from the main road, popular. Bike and car hire arranged. Recommended. **D-E** *Daniel's Travellers Lodge*, 9 Lorong Perdah, T4915823, F4915828. Clean and friendly place to stay, although rooms are small and it can be noisy. More expensive rooms have own bathrooms. Lots of useful information available and a good place to eat, dorm beds (**F**). Video library and a daily walk organized around the Highlands. Enthusiastic staff. **D-E** *Father's Guesthouse*, Jln Gereja, T4912484. Near the convent, up a long flight of steps. A popular backpacker's haunt. Although the rooms are basic, the guesthouse has a very friendly atmosphere and a great communal area with grand views. There is also access to cable TV and a number of videos are available to watch. Tours to the tea plantations and butterfly garden go daily (RM15). *Father's* also offers internet access. Dorms beds available (**E**). **D** *Hotel BB Inn*, 79a Pesiaran Camelia 4, Tanah Rata, 39000, Cameron Highlands, T4914551, F4914552, timurcan@tm.net.my. Bathroom, TV in room, good value and very friendly. **D** *Orient*, 38 Jln Besar, T4911633. Located above *The Orient* Chinese restaurant. Recommended. Price includes own bathroom and breakfast. If you want to avoid the hostels, it's a great budget choice. **D** *Papillon Guesthouse*, Jln Mentigi, T4914069. Close to the *Twin Pines Chalet*, good-sized rooms (more expensive with own bathrooms) and dorm beds available, friendly and enthusiastic management. Set back from the main road amongst surrounding huts and houses, this is the non-tourist option. **D** *Seah Meng*, 39 Jln Besar, T4911618. On the main street but quiet. Fairly typical Chinese hotel with little atmosphere but the large rooms are kept spotless. Attentive staff. More expensive rooms have showers. Recommended. **D-E** *Twin Pines Chalet*, 2 Jln Mentigi, T4912169, furhill@tm.net.my. Popular guesthouse at top end of town. Small clean rooms and dorm, more expensive rooms have own hot showers. Reasonable value. Bus tickets and tours bookable here, good source of information (good on transport around Malaysia). Its once peaceful outlook has been marred by a shopping centre development.

Northern Peninsula

Bungalows Rates are for whole bungalow, per night unless stated; most prices include resident cook. Rates may vary according to season – discounts on request. Most are dotted around the town, in the countryside, with their own gardens. There are a great many to choose from, the following gives an idea of the type of range available: **AL** *Fair Haven*; **AL** *Golf View Villa*; **A** *Highlands Villa*; **B** *Gunder Singh*; **B** *Lutheran Bungalow*; **D** *Rumah Tetamu Sri Pahang*.

Eating **Chinese** **3-2** *Mayflower*, 22 Jln Besar, specialize in Highland steamboat, seafood, popular with locals. **3-2** *Little Grasshopper Tea House*, Perisan Camellia 3 (opposite *CS Tours*), specializes in Steamboat and Chinese tea ceremony where the proprietor talks you through the ins and outs of the ceremony. Popular. **2** *The Orient*, 38 Jln Besar, steamboat and soups are popular, good value set lunch. **2** *The Oriental Melody*, 44 Jln Besar, popular.

Indian **2-1** *Thanum*, 25 Jln Besar, claypot and Hainam chicken rice recommended, excellent breakfast rotis and murtabak, chairs and tables outside. **1** *Kumar*, good value banana leaf, popular breakfast spot. **1** *Restoran No 14*, on the main road, very popular place doing good thalis and dosas at good prices.

International **4** *Lakehouse*, traditional English food, typical Sun lunch fare and cream teas. **4** *Smokehouse*, similar to *Lakehouse*, favourites include: beef Wellington, roast beef, Yorkshire pudding, steak and kidney pie, and Devonshire cream teas. **3** *Merlin*, international menu, and pleasant atmosphere but not very good value. **2** *Bala's*, in *Bala's Holiday Chalets* (see above), good breakfasts and vegetarian dinners, also a popular stop for cream teas. **2** *Roselane Coffee House*, Western and local food, set meals are good value.

Foodstalls **2-1** Next to the bus station, opposite the main row of shops on Jln Besar, serve good selection of Malay, Indian and Chinese food.

Entertainment The only nightlife as such takes place in the *Strawberry Park Resort* where there is the only disco in town, karaoke, and a bar. The hotel bars at the *Lakehouse* and *Smokehouse* are also popular venues for their country pub atmosphere and air of exclusivity.

Sports **Golf** *Cameron Highlands Golf Club*, T4911126. Located north of Tanah Rata, connected by a pleasant footpath, founded in 1885 by the British surveyor William Cameron, the 18-hole course is magnificently appointed, occupying pride of place in the centre of the plateau, surrounded by jungled hills. It is a favourite haunt of Malaysian royalty, green fees: RM40 weekdays, RM60 weekends and public holidays, RM18 caddy fee, T4911126. Note that players are expected to wear appropriate clothing, which rules out singlets and revealing shorts. RM10 for shoe hire, RM30 for clubs. **Tennis** Courts across the road from golf clubhouse, rackets and balls on hire at clubhouse shop.

Tour operators *CS Travel & Tours*, 47 Jln Besar, T4911200, F4912390. Local tours, air/train/bus tickets, accommodation reservations.

Transport **NB** Those who suffer from travel sickness are advised to take some anti-nausea medication before setting out on the mountain road. A new road to the west was under construction in 1999.

214 km to KL
121 km to Ipoh

Local **Bus/taxis**: nearly all the buses from Tapah (last bus 1600) go through Ringlet, Tanah Rata and on to Brinchang and it is easy enough to climb aboard one of the buses that do this route through the day. *Rex* buses go from Tanah Rata to the farthest outpost on the mountain. Taxis are available for local travel – they can be chartered for about RM15 per hour. It is also possible just to take a seat in a taxi, going from Tanah Rata to Brinchang, for example. Taxi and local bus station (T4911485) on either side of the Shell station in Tanah Rata. To order a taxi: T4911234/4912355.

Car hire: because visitors pose a serious insurance problem on the mountain roads, the car rental business is not well developed in the Camerons. The only one available is semi-official: contact Ravi at *Rainbow Garden Centre* (between *The Smokehouse* and Tanah Rata), T491782. If you are driving, remember to sound your horn at bends and beware the lorries that hurtle along. If you are wondering why there are lorries on the road it is because there is a large replantation project underway as well as construction work.

Long distance Train: the nearest station to the Camerons is Tapah Rd in Tapah, 67 km from Tanah Rata. Regular connections with Ipoh, KL, Butterworth 5 a day, 6 hrs.

Bus: a daily bus leaves KL's Puduraya terminal, for the Cameron Highlands, at 0830, 5 hrs , but it gets heavily booked. The *Bintang Mas* bus service operate direct a/c buses from **KL** to Tanah Rata (leaving from Jln Pudu, at the foot of the pedestrian bridge to the Puduraya bus station), departing 0900 and 1530 daily (T2324285). Most other buses for the Cameron Highlands leave from **Tapah**, 67 km from Tanah Rata in the Camerons, regular hourly connections with Brinchang and Tanah Rata and with Sungai Palas and Kampung Raja (in the north of the Camerons). Tickets for the return journey can be booked at travel agents or at the bus station in Tanah Rata. There are 2 daily express buses from the Camerons to KL, leaving at 0830 and 1530, and one express bus to **Georgetown**, Penang, 0930. Regular connections from Tapah with Ipoh, KL, Butterworth, Kuantan, Melaka (5 hrs), Singapore. Can reserve tickets at *CS Travel & Tours*, Tanah Rata. **NB** Buses coming down from the Camerons tend to be more expensive. Express buses now go from Tanah Rata to Penang, via Ipoh at 0830 and 1430 (6 hrs).

Banks All the banks are on Jln Besar. They include: *Arab-Malaysian Finance*, *Hong Kong Shanghai Bank*, *Maybank*, *Sampanian National* and *Visa Finance Berhad*. It is also possible to change money at *CS Travel & Tours*, next to *Roselane Hotel* and *Coffee House* on Jln Besar. **Communications Area code**: 05. **General Post Office**: next to the *Orient Hotel & Restaurant*, Jln Besar. **Internet cafés** Two cafés on Jln Camelia, RM5 per hr. **Medical facilities Hospitals**: opposite gardens at north end of town, on Jln Besar, T4911966. **Places of worship** Anglican: *All Souls' Church*, between Kampung Taman Sedia and golf course. Converted army Nissen hut with lych-gate in memory of Miss Griffith-Jones. Services 1030 Sun. **Tourist offices** *Tourist Information Centre*, on the right as you come into Tanah Rata, poor source of information. Open: 0800-1615 Mon-Thu, 0800-1215 and 1445-1615 Fri, 0800-1245 Sat. There is a small museum attached to the tourist office. The *Orang Asli* exhibit is worth a browse. Book lending scheme available at office. **NB** Closed during our last visit but the intention is to open at some unspecified date. **Useful addresses District office**: T4911455, alert this office if someone you know is long overdue after a jungle walk. **Police**: T4911222, opposite gardens at north end of town.

Directory

Brinchang

In recent years Brinchang, 7 km beyond Tanah Rata, on the far side of the golf course, has grown fast: since the mid-1980s several new hotels have sprung up, mainly catering for mass-market Malaysian Chinese and Singaporean package tourists. It is not a very beautiful little town, although the central square with craft centre has a certain character.

*Phone code: 05
Colour map1, grid C3*

Sam Poh Buddhist Temple, a popular sight with Chinese visitors who arrive by the coach load, is located just outside Brinchang, along Jalan Pecah Batu, overlooking the golf course. It is backed by the Gunung Beremban hills and comprises both a temple and monastery which were built here in 1971. Emphasis is on size and grandeur, with monumental double gates with dragons at either side leading into the complex. The inner chamber with its six red-tiled pillars holds a vast golden effigy of a Buddha.

Northern Peninsula

Sleeping

For budget travellers Tanah Rata has a better selection of accommodation Price codes: see inside front cover

NB It should be noted that during public holidays, accommodation gets fully booked and prices rise by 30-50%. It is also busy at peak school holiday periods – Apr, Aug and Dec. The most economic form of accommodation is to share a bungalow between a group of people. Most bungalows have gardens, log fires and are away from the towns.

A-B *Jasmine Holiday Apartments*, 40 Jln Besar, T4912408, overlooking the main square. Attractive furnished flats of varying cost and size with cooking facilities, barbecue and rooftop garden. Recommended. **A** *Rosa Passadena*, T4912288, F4912688. Large mock-Tudor block, dominates Brinchang town centre, 120 rooms, bath, TV, in-house video, mini-bar, safe, restaurant, karaoke lounge. Rooms offer superb views of the surrounding Highlands. Restaurant serves everything from steaks to Chinese steamboats.

B *Country Lodge*, T4913071, F4911396. Located on hillside above Brinchang, typical black and white Tudor-style, décor rather on the severe side, parquet floors and rattan furniture, spacious standard and deluxe rooms as well as suites, restaurant, karaoke lounge. Price is for either hotel room or apartment; great value. **B** *Iris Hotel* 56, Jln Kuari, T4911818, F4912828. No restaurant, but new and otherwise good value. TV and banqueting facilities. **B** *Parkland Hotel*, T4911299, F4911399. Modern 30-room hotel at edge of town, bath, TV, café, restaurant, reasonable value for money. **B** (twin with bathroom) *Rainbow Garden Hotel*, Lot 25, T4914628, F4914668. Brand spanking new, 36 good value comfortable rooms all with TVs and minibar. Good views on one side. Recommended, although there is no restaurant.

C *Brinchang Hotel*, 36 Jln Besar, T4911755, F4911246. Hot showers, TV. Enthusiastic Indian owner; but rooms are scruffy, and some are windowless. **C** *Hill Garden Lodge*, 15-16 Jln Besar, T4912988, F4912226. Bath, TV, clean. Rooms facing street noisy, discounts available in off-peak season. Nothing to get excited about. **C** *Hotel New Plastro*, 19 Jln Besar, T4911009, mediocre. **C** *Kowloon Hotel*, 34-35 Jln Besar, T4911366, F4911803. Above popular Chinese restaurant, nice rooms with shower, good value for money.

D *Pines and Roses*, T4912203. Good value family rooms with TV and water heater although basic furnishings, dorm also available, very clean. **E** *Silverstar Hotel*, T4911387. Shower, basic but good value. Restaurant on the ground floor.

Eating

Price codes: see inside front cover

Chinese 2 *Brinchang*, below hotel of same name on Jln Besar, popular for its steamboat, good selection of vegetable dishes. Recommended. **2** *Kowloon*, busy restaurant, red tablecloths and clean tiled floors, menu priced according to size of portion, lemon chicken and steamboat are popular. Recommended. **2** *Kwan Kee*, next door to *Hotel Lido*, good steamboat. **2** *Silverstar*, on the other side of *Hotel Lido*, not special. **Indian 2** *Shal's Curry House*, 25 Jln Besar, upmarket coffee shop serving top quality Indian cuisine, excellent South Indian claypot dishes, sweet and savoury thosai, peanut, honey or banana roti good for breakfast, run by former manager of the *Smokehouse*, attractive

Brinchang

To Tringkap, Kuala Terla & Kampung Raja

To Tanah Rata

N
Not to scale

Sleeping
1 Brinchang & Restaurant
2 Country Lodge
3 Garden Lodge
4 Iris Hotel
5 Kowloon & Restaurant
6 Pines & Roses
7 Rainbow Garden
8 Rosa Passadena
9 Silverstar & Restaurant

Eating
1 Kwan Kee
2 Shal's Curry House

presentation on real banana leaf, some tables and chairs outside, overlooking square. Recommended. **International 3** *Parkland*, Grill restaurant in *Parkland Hotel*, steaks, breakfast menu (**2**). **3** *Ferns Restaurant*, *Rosa Passadena Hotel*, Western and oriental, good value buffet. **Foodstalls** Hawker stalls in the central square, open after 1600, good for satay and roti.

Apart from a couple of karaoke bars that have recently sprung up in the town, any nightlife that exists takes place in the *Rosa Passadena Hotel*. **Entertainment**

Golf *Cameron Highlands Golf Club*, see Tanah Rata, page 130. **Sports**

Jade Holidays, 37a and b Jln Bandar, T4912318, F4912071, local tours, air/bus tickets, accommodation bookings, jungle trekking; *Titiwangsa Tours & Travel*, 36 Jln Besar, T4912122, F4911246, similar services to *Jade Holidays*. **Tour operators** *See Tanah Rata, page 130*

Local Taxis are available for local travel and can be chartered for about RM15 per hour. For travel between Tanah Rata, Brinchang and Tapah it is easy enough to climb aboard one of the buses that do this route through the day. **Transport** *See Tanah Rata, page 130*

Banks *Public Bank*, next to *Hill Garden Lodge*. **Communications** Area code: 05. General Post Office: opposite the Petronas petrol station at the north end of the town. **Medical facilities** See Tanah Rata, page 131. **Useful addresses** Police: in central square, next to children's playground. **Directory**

Around Brinchang

Up the hill from Brinchang the Cameron Highlands becomes one big market garden and the terrain becomes increasingly steep and hilly. One of the first market gardens outside Brinchang, just after the army camp on the left, is *Uncle Sam's Farm*. The farm specializes in the cultivation of the Kaffir Lily, as well as strawberries, oranges, apples and a selection of cacti. Beyond Uncle Sam's, 4 km up the road from Brinchang, there is a large market selling local produce to eager customers from the plains below.

The Cameronian climate is particularly suited to the cultivation of vegetables more usually associated with temperate climates. Cabbages, cauliflowers, carrots and tomatoes, as well as fruit such as strawberries and passion fruit, are taken by truck from the Camerons to the supermarkets of Kuala Lumpur and Singapore. **Kea Farm**, with its neatly terraced hillsides, is down the first right turn after the market area. At the Kea turning, on the main road, Kea Farm has a small shop and café and restaurant called the *Strawberry View*. Here, perched on the hillside is the *Equatorial Hill Resort* (**AL**), T4961777, F4961333. This is a monstrosity of 500 plus rooms, very mock Tudor in style, with all the facilities of a four-star hotel: a heated pool, tennis, squash, bowling alley, Cineplex; not exactly an intimate little place.

The **Butterfly garden** is past the Kea Farm turning. There is a large shop attached to the garden, where everything from framed dead butterflies to Cameronian souvenirs (beetles embedded in key rings) is on sale. Outside there are fruit and vegetable stalls – all very popular with Chinese visitors. ■ *0800-1700 Mon-Sun, about RM2.50.*

The **rose garden** is 2 km further up the mountain. To get there, take the first left turn after the butterfly farm, on Jalan Gunung Brinchang, at what is known as the Green Cow area; a village there was burned to the ground by the Communists during the insurgency. A few kilometres beyond the Rose Garden, continue up Jalan Gunung Besar, which is a very picturesque narrow road, on the right is a turning for one of the Boh tea plantations – the Sungai Palas.

Northern Peninsula

There are guided tours of the Sungai Palas tea processing factory every 10 minutes from Tuesday-Sunday. The newly built visitors' centre has a video about tea cultivation and a shop, as well as a charming terrace where you can order a pot of tea and enjoy the dramatic view across the steeply terraced tea plantations.

Back at the Green Cow area, the main road, the C7, continues into the mountains, finally ending at the Blue Valley Tea Estate, 13 km from the junction with Jalan Gunung Brinchang. Midway along the C7, at the village of Trinkap, a right turn leads to a large rose-growing establishment, Rose Valley. It boasts 450 varieties of rose including the thornless rose, the black rose, and the green rose, said to be the ugliest of the rose family. It also has a cactus plantation where some of the plants are 40 years old and lays claim to having the largest flower vase in Malaysia. ■ *0800-1800 daily, adults RM3, children RM1.50.*

Ipoh

Population: 500,000
Phone code: 05
Colour map 1, grid C3

The northern state of Perak is known for its tin ore (mainly in the Kinta Valley) and Ipoh, its capital, is Malaysia's third city. The city is situated in the Kinta Valley, between the Main Range and the Keledang Mountains, to the west.

Ipoh is named after the abundance of the huge, elusive ipoh (or upas) trees that once grew there; the Orang Asli tribes procured the poison for their blowpipe darts from its fabled lethal sap. It was known as the deadliest poison in the world. The city also has an abundance of imposing limestone outcrops. These jungle-topped hills, with their precipitous white cliffs, are riddled with passages and caves, many of which have been made into cave temples.

In its early days, Ipoh's citizens became wealthy on the back of the tin mining industry. In 1884 the Kinta Valley tin rush brought an influx of Chinese immigrants to Ipoh; many made their fortunes and built opulent town houses. Chinese immigrants have bequeathed what is now one of Malaysia's best-preserved Chinatowns (the 'Old Town'). In the 1880s Ipoh vied with Kuala Lumpur to be the capital of the Federated States of Malaya, and long after KL took the title, Ipoh remained the commercial 'hub of Malaya'. The city has long had an active 'flesh trade': there are frequent round-ups of Thai and Burmese prostitutes who are smuggled across Malaysia's north border.

Few tourists spend long in Ipoh – most are *en route* to Penang, KL or Pulau Pangkor. Those who do stay rarely regret it: there are excellent Chinese restaurants (a speciality is the rice noodle dish, *Sar Hor Fun* which literally means 'melts in your mouth'), Buddhist temples and examples of Straits Chinese architecture. It is also a good place to pick up Chinese imported goods, such as baskets and chinaware. The shophouses on and around Jalan Yau Tet Shin make for good browsing. Ipoh also has a handful of very well-established bakers. On Jalan Raja Eleram the two bakeries here have been in the business for well over 50 years. They specialize in French bread, buns and cakes.

Sights

The Kinta River, spanned by the Hugh Low Bridge, separates the old and new parts of town. The **Old Town** is centred along the river between Jalan Sultan Idris Shah and Jalan Sultan Iskander Shah and is known for its old Chinese and British colonial architecture particularly on Jalan Sultan Yusuf, Jalan Leech and Jalan Treacher.

Perak: the silver state that grew rich on tin

Perak is nicknamed the Silver State because perak is the Malay for silver. This was, according to one account, a misnomer, as the locals mistook their plentiful tin ore for silver. All the way through the Kinta and Perak river valleys, huge areas of sand lie bleached and desolate after the tin dredges have passed over them. A more likely derivation of Perak's name is from the word bharat, *meaning west. In maps prior to 1561 the area is marked as Perat; historians speculate this may be a corruption of Bharat. The state became 'the senior state of the federation' in colonial Malaya, before its governmental role passed to Kuala Lumpur at the end of the 19th century.*

Perak's ancient name was Gangga-Negara, a Sanskrit word, meaning 'City on the Ganges'; in this case referring to an ancient kingdom centred on the estuary of the Perak River, where the village of Bruas is today. Gangga-Negara was the capital of this powerful kingkom, referred to by an Arab chronicler as far back as 644 AD. It is said that many Buddha statues have been found in the area. Gangga-Negara was the site chosen by the Bendahara rulers of old Melaka who founded the Perak dynasty. The settlement was finally sacked by Rajendra Chola, the son of the first Hindu ruler of Kedah, who also destroyed Temasek, which in later life re-emerged as Singapore.

Prominent landmarks include the **Birch Memorial**, a clock tower erected in memory of the first British resident of Perak, JWW Birch. His murder in 1875 was one of colonial Malaya's first anti-British incidents and the three perpetrators, after being hanged, promptly became local heroes, which they remain. The four panels decorating the base of the tower depict the development of civilization; the upper part of the tower holds a bust of JWW Birch who was, local history relates, not well liked in the area. The Moorish-style **railway station** (off Jalan Kelab), built in 1917, bears close resemblance to its Kuala Lumpur counterpart, and is known as the 'Taj Mahal' of Ipoh. The *Station Hotel* has recently reopened and is a colonial classic worth noticing. **Ipoh Town Hall**, with its Palladian façade, stands opposite. A solitary ipoh (or *upas*) tree, after which the city is named, stands in the centre of **Taman DR Seenivasagam** (a park north of the centre). The park also contains an artificial lake and a children's playground. There are also **Japanese Gardens**, complete with a typical Japanese carp pond, nearby on Jalan Tambun. ■ *1600-2000 Mon-Fri, 0900-2000 Sat-Sun*. The **Geological Museum**, on Lorong Hariman, out of town centre, was set up in 1957. It is known for its exhibition of tin ore and collection of fossils and precious stones as well as over 600 samples of minerals. ■ *0800-1615 Mon-Fri, 0800-1245 Sat. Free, but entry permission from the information counter is necessary*. On Jalan SP Seenivasagam there is an old colonial mission **school** with an impressive white stone façade and an Indian **mosque** next door.

Heading out of town, past St Michael's School, on Jalan Panglima Bukit Gantang Wahab, after about 500m on the right is an elegant, white colonial building which houses the **Perak Darul Ridzuan Museum**. The building which is over 100 years old, once the home of Malay dignitaries of Kinta, now houses a collection that illustrates the history of Ipoh, and mining and forestry within the state. ■ *0900-1600 Sat-Wed, 0900-1200 Thur*.

Excursions

Kellie's Castle Down the road to Batu Gajah, just to the south of Ipoh (about a 30 minute drive), is the eccentric edifice of Scotsman William Kellie Smith, a rubber tycoon in the late 19th century. He shipped in Tamil workers from South India to build his fanciful Moorish-style mansion, and after an outbreak of fever, he allowed them to build the Sri Maha Mariamman Hindu temple in the grounds, about 500m before the castle. Another story has it that Mr Smith built the temple in 1902 after his prayers for a son and heir were answered after six years of marriage. An image of Smith is among the sculpted Hindu pantheon on the temple roof.

The castle was never completed as Smith left in the middle of its construction and died in Portugal on a business trip (local rumour has it, after inhaling the smoke of a poisoned cigar). During the war the grounds of the castle were used by the Japanese as an execution area; locals say that the tall trees were used as makeshift gallows. No wonder the place is presumed to be haunted: although the wine cellar is open, the rest of the subterranean rooms are closed to visitors. A white bridge leading to the castle was completed in 1994. ■ *0830-1930, Mon-Sun, RM0.50.*

Ipoh

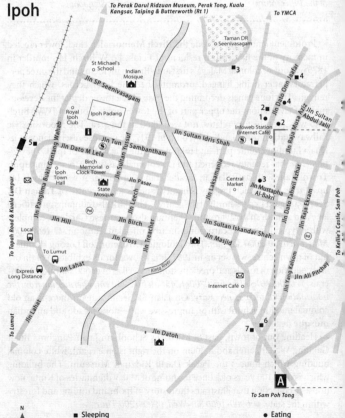

To Perak Darul Ridzuan Museum, Perak Tong, Kuala Kangsar, Taiping & Butterworth (Rt 1)

To YMCA

Taman DR Seenivasagam

St Michael's School
Indian Mosque
Jln SP Seenivasagam
Royal Ipoh Club
Ipoh Padang
Jln Dato Onn Jaafar
Jln Raja Musa Aziz
Jln Sultan Abdul Jalil
Infoweb Station (Internet Café)
Jln Tun Yussuf
Jln Dato M Lela
Jln Sultan Idris Shah
Jln Dato Tahwil Azhar
Jln Raja Ekram
Jln Sultan Yussuf
Birch Memorial Clock Tower
Ipoh Town Hall
State Mosque
Jln Pasar
Jln Leech
Central Market
Jln Mustapha Al-Bakri
Jln Panglima Bukit Gantang Wahab
Jln Laksamania
To Tapah Road & Kuala Lumpur
Jln Hill
Jln Birch
Jln Cross
Jln Treacher
Jln Sultan Iskandar Shah
Jln Masjid
To Kellie's Castle, Sam Poh
Local
To Lumut
Express Long Distance
Jln Lahat
Kinto River
Internet Café
Jln Yang Kalsom
Jln Ali Pitchay
To Lumut
Jln Lahat
Jln Datoh
To Sam Poh Tong
A

N
0 metres 100
0 yards 100

Related map
A Ipoh detail, page 138

■ **Sleeping**
1 Eastern
2 French
3 Grandview & Restaurant
4 Lotte
5 Majestic (or Station)
6 New Hollywood
7 Ritz Garden

● **Eating**
1 Blue Window Café
2 KFC
3 McDonalds
4 Pizza Hut

At Gunung Rapat, 5 km south of Ipoh, is the largest of the cave temples in the area. There are Buddha statues among the stalactites and stalagmites. The temple was founded 100 years ago by a monk who lived and meditated in the cave for 20 years and it has been inhabited by monks ever since. The only break was during the Japanese occupation when the cave was turned into a Japanese ammunition and fuel dump. There is a pond at the entrance where locals release turtles to gain merit while young boys sell turtle food to earn money. Various statues of Buddha sit among the stalactites. ■ *0730-1800, Mon-Sun. Getting there: Kampar bus 66.* **Sam Poh Tong**

One of the largest Chinese temples in Malaysia is 6½ km north of Ipoh on Jalan Kuala Kangsar. Built in 1926 by a Buddhist priest from China, the temple houses over 40 Buddha statues and mystical traditional Chinese-style murals depicting legends. It is visited by thousands of pilgrims every year and is the most ornately decorated of the many cave temples at the base of the 122m limestone hill. A path beyond the altar leads into the cave's interior and up a brick stairway to an opening 100m above ground with a view of the surrounding countryside. Another climb leads to a painting of Kuan Yin, Goddess of Mercy, who looks out from the face of the limestone cliff. A 15m-high reinforced concrete statue of the Buddha stands in the compound. ■ *0900-1600 Mon-Sun. Getting there: Kuala Kangsar bus or city bus no 3.* **Perak Tong**

Traces of a 10,000 years-old civilization were discovered at these caves, 3 km from Ipoh near Tambun, in the 1930s. The ochre drawings on the cave walls and the limestone cliffs depict the life of prehistoric man, especially interesting is the 'Degong' fish, a drawing of a large fish which feeds on meat, rather like a piranha. Tambun Hot Springs nestle at the foot of this limestone hill. The Japanese were responsible for their initial development during the occupation. Two swimming pools have been built – one filled with lukewarm water and one with hot. Saunas also. ■ *Caves: 0900-1600 Mon-Sun, RM5. Hot springs: 1500-2400 Mon-Sun. Getting there: Tambun bus, a 15 min drive from Ipoh.* **Gua Tambun (Tambun Cave)**

Essentials

A *Casuarina*, 18 Jln Gopeng, out of town, T2505555, F2508177. Over 200 rooms, a/c, restaurant, pool, Ipoh's finest but not central. **A** *Central*, 26 Jln Ali Pitchay, T2424777, F2424555. A/c, recently upgraded. Oriental atmosphere. **A** *Syuen*, 88 Jln Sultan Abdul Jalil, T2538889, F2640580, syuenht@tm.net.my. A/c, 10 food and beverage outlets, central new hotel with real style, 300 rooms, overlooking the bougainvillea park, a/c, TV, minibar, comfortable and well-furbished rooms, discotheque, the *Car Disco*, one of Malaysia's new night spots, pool, business centre, sauna, tennis. Recommended. **Sleeping** ■ *on maps, pages 136 & 138 Price codes: see inside front cover*

B *A-House Ipoh Station Hotel* aka *Majestic Hotel*, Bangunan Stesyen Keretapi, Jln Panglima Bukit Gantang Wahab, T2555605, F2553393. A/c, restaurant, 100 rooms, managed by the Singapore-based A-House group of hotels. Old colonial-style décor has been retained, good range of facilities from in-house movies to a health service, well run and priced. **B** *Eastern*, 118 Jln Sultan Idris Shah, T2543936, F2501468. Small and rather grim 1970s building, a/c, restaurant and in-house videos. **B** *Excelsior*, 43 Jln Sultan Abdul Jalil, T2536666, F2536912. A/c, restaurants, new tower block, one of the tallest buildings in Ipoh, added in 1994, the hotel now has over 150 rooms. Hotel organizes golf trips to local courses. **B** *Grandview Hotel* 36 Jln Horley, T2431488, F2431811. Opened June 1999, shower, ac, TV, restaurant. Although lacking in character, the clean and tasteful furnishings, along with the friendly and efficient service, make this one of the best value options in town. **B** *Tambun Inn*, 91 Jln Tambun,

T577211. Located 4 km from city centre, most rooms are deluxe double which are priced at upper end of **B** category but offer good value, TV, a/c, in-house video, health centre, karaoke lounge.

C *Cathay*, 90-94 Jln CM Yussuf, south of town, T2413322. Some a/c and private bathrooms, noisy and rather grubby, plenty of furniture, security poor. **C** *Fair Park*, 85 Jln Kamaruddin Isa, T2547129. The newest budget hotel in Ipoh, near DBI Sports Centre. Recommended. **C** *Fairmont* 10 Jln Kampar, T2559999, F2556352. Bath, car park and a good value restaurant. **C** *French*, 60-62 Jln Dato Onn Jaafar, T2533111, F2552975. Another uninspiring small concrete block, a/c, restaurant. Real 1970s atmosphere – out of date in every way. **C** *Lotte*, 97 Jln Dato Onn Jaafar, T2542215, F2551160. Its well maintained exterior is hugely deceptive. Rooms are basic. Shower, a/c. **C** *Merloon*, 92-98 Jln Mustapha al-Bakri, T2541351, F2536755. Recently undergone an inspirational name change from Merlin. A/c, shower, restaurant. Clean but basic for the price – many better options. **C** *New Hollywood*, 72-76 Jln Yussuf, T2415404. Restaurant, kept clean and the room rates are reasonable but there is little to mark this place out in any way. **C** *Ritz Garden*, 78 Jln C M Yussuf, T2547777, F2545222. A/c, bath, TV, in-house video, mini-bar, coffee house, health centre, sauna, not exactly oozing character but the rooms are well priced. Restaurant recently closed. **C** *Ritz Kowloon*, 92-96 Jln Yang Kalsom, T2547778, F2533800. Run by a charming camp Indian; a/c, TV, in-house video, safe, tastefully furnished rooms. Recommended. **C** *Robin*, 106-110 Jln Mustapha al-Bakri, T2413755, F2541818. A/c, TVs, mini-bars in all rooms. Attatched to a restaurant and health club. **C** *YMCA*, 211 Jln Raja Musa Aziz, take a small path along the river to get here, T2540809. Tennis courts, dorm (**E**) beds available, this place is good value and the grounds as well as the rooms are spacious, but the location is inconvenient.

D *Golden Inn*, 17 Jln Che Tak, T2530866, a/c, efficiently run. Recommended. **D** *New Winner*, 32-38 Jln Ali Pitchay, T2415177. Some a/c, a bit archaic but good value and very clean. The disco directly below can be a bit noisy. **D** *Shanghai*, 85 Jln Mustapha al-Bakri. Fan only, shower, restaurant, clean and central. Although in need of modernizing this is the best budget option in town.

Eating
● *on map, page 136*
Price codes:
see inside front cover

Ipoh is well known for its Chinese food, especially Ipoh chicken rice and *kway teow* – liquid and fried versions. The pomelo and the seedless guava are both grown in the state of Perak, and the state is also known for its delicious groundnuts.

Malay 3 *Perwira*, Medan Gopeng, 3 km south of town centre, before Sam Poh Tong. **3** *Sabar Menanti*, Jln Raja Musa Aziz. **3** *Semenanjung*, Jln Sultan Idris Shah.

Chinese 3 *Central*, 51-53 Cowan St. **2** *Foh San*, Jln Osbourne, *dim sum*. **2** *Kawan*, Jln Sultan Iskandar Shah, also Malay and Indian dishes. **2** *Kok Kee*, 272 Jln Sultan Iskandar Shah. **2** *Ming Court*,

Ipoh detail

Jln Abdul
Jln Leong Sin Nam
Jln Sultan Idris Shah
Jln Dato Tahwil Azari
Jln Raja Ekram
Jln Jubilee
Children's Playground
Heris Express Travel Agency
Jln Yang Kalsom
Jln Ali Pitchay
Jln Sultan Iskandar Shah
Restoran Impressive Foodstalls
Jln Lim Seng Chew
Jln Chung Thye Phin
Jln Gopeng
Jln Pasir Putih
Jln CM Yusuf
Jln CM Yusuf
Jln Ulu
Hawkers Market
Medical Centre
Jln Tokong
Jln Kampar
Shell

N

0 metres 100
0 yards 100

■ **Sleeping**
1 Casuarina
2 Cathy
3 Central
4 Excelsior
5 Fairmont
6 Merloon
7 New Winner
8 Ritz Kowloon
9 Shanghai
10 Syuen

36 Jln Leong Sin Nam, *dim sum*. **2** *Mung Cheong*, 511 Jln Pasir Putih, Cantonese. **2** *Nam Thim Tong*, Mile 3.5 Gopeng Rd, Chinese, vegetarian, serve ersatz meat dishes made of soya bean. **1** *Chuan Fong*, 175 Jln Sultan Iskandar, speciality: curry laksa. **1** *Foh San*, 2 Osbourne St, popular for Hong Kong *dim sum*, served 0600-1200. **1** *Woh Heng Coffee Shop*, Osbourne St, good rice and noodles.

Indian **3** *Comfy Corner*, 61 Jln Pasar. **3** *Gopal Corner*, Buntong. **3** *Guru's Chapati*, *Cheong Seng Restaurant Complex*, Lebuh Raya Ipoh, Punjabi. Recommended. **3** *Krishna Bhawan*, 8 Jln Lahat. **2** *Majeedia*, Jln Dendahara/Jln Leong Boon Swee. **2** *Shal's Curry House*, 4 Jln Dato Maharaja Lela, a/c, excellent South Indian food and good vegetarian dishes. Recommended. **1** *Mohamad Ibrahim*, 786 Jln Yang Kalsom, speciality: *mee rebus*.

International **4** *Royal Casuarina Coffee House*, and *Il Ritrove*, Italian restaurant specializing in nouvelle cuisine, 18 Jln Gopeng. **3** *Blue Window Café*, 56 Jln Dato Onn Jaafar, Western food, aspires to 'romantic' atmosphere. **3** *Station Hotel Coffee House*, Jln Kelab. **2** *Excelsior Hotel Coffee House*, 43 Jln Clarke. **2** *Ever Fresh Juice Station*, 21 Jln Mustapha al Bakri, good fresh juice bar. **2** *Nam Shan Thai SeaFood Restaurant*, 29 Jln Yau Tet Shin. A very friendly and helpful manager, with great command of the English language. Excellent value Thai and Chinese food.

Foodstalls Jln Clarke, Jln Dewan, Ipoh Garden, Jln Sultan Idris Shah, mainly Chinese stalls. *Railway Station*, Jln Kelab. Recommended. *Wooley Food Centre*, Canning Gardens. On Jln Ali Pitchay is *Restoran Impressive Foodstalls*; cheap (RM10), clean and new. Recommended.

Fast food *McDonalds* and *KFC* on Jln Dato Onn Jaafar.

Sports

Golf *Royal Perak Golf Club*, Jln Sultan Azlan Shah, 3 km from town centre, 18-hole course laid out on 172 acres, only open to visitors on weekdays, members only at weekends and holidays, green fees RM150, caddy fee RM20, clubhouse facilities include bowling alley, cards and billiards room, bar. **Racing** Races held every Sat and Sun at *Perak Turf Club*. **Swimming** *DBI Sports Complex*, Perak Sports Centre, Lebuh Raya Thivy, T5460651. Largest swimming complex in Southeast Asia. Other facilities include: tennis, indoor badminton, table tennis, volleyball, basketball, a velodrome rugby pitch, stadium. Admission RM1 weekdays, RM2 weekends. Open 0900-2100 Mon-Sun.

Tour operators

Fiyen Travels, 1-3 Jln Che Tak, T2533455, F2506709, sightseeing tours, hotel reservations, domestic and international air ticketing; *Reliance*, Lot 1-12 1st Flr, Bangunan Sri Kinta, Jln Sultan Idris Shah, T2518711, F2538458, ticketing, travel shop, travel insurance; *HWA Yik Tour & Travel*, 23 Jln Che Tak, T2504060, F2530118, tours, hotel reservation, domestic and international air ticketing, mini-bus rental; *K & C Travel & Tours*, 250 Jln Sultan Iskandar, T2506999, F2502154, airline ticketing, hotel reservation, travel insurance, foreign exchange; *Deluxe Tours*, 58 Jln Dato Tahwil Azhar (Jln Osbourne), T2537260 F2558969, air ticketing, tours, hotel reservations. *Heris Express Travel Agency*, T2416999.

Transport
250 km to KL
161 km to Butterworth

Local Car hire: *Avis*, Sultan Azian Shah Airport, T206586; *Hertz, Royal Casuarina Hotel*, 18 Jln Gopeng, T2505533, and Sultan Azlan Shah Airport, T3127109. **Taxi**: if you want to order a taxi try the Nam Taxi Company, 15 Jln Raja Mus Aziz, T2412189. Taxi to Ipoh airport (RM10). Radiocab T2540241.

Long distance Air: Sultan Azlan Shah Airport, T3122459, approximately 15 km south of town, RM10 taxi ride. Regular connections with Johor Bahru (55 mins), Kota Bharu, Kota Kinabalu, KL (30 mins), Penang (25 mins) and Kuching on *MAS* and with Johor Bahru on *Pelangi Air*. 24-hr reservation T7463000. *MAS* provides quite a few international connections from Ipoh. Daily connections on *Pelangi Air* with Medan, Sumatra.

Northern Peninsula

Train: Ipoh is on the main north-south line. Five daily connections with **Butterworth** and **KL**, T2540481. One train daily to **Singapore** (1100), and **Hat Yai** (0845). See page 35 for timetable.

Bus: Ipoh is on the main north-south road and is well connected. The bus terminal is at the intersection of Jln Kelab, Kidd and Silbin (known as Medan Kidd), a short taxi trip from the town centre. Buses to **Taiping** (RM3), and **Kuala Kangsar** leave from the local bus terminal. Regular connections with **Butterworth** (RM7), **KL** (3 hrs , RM8.50), **Alor Star** (RM11.90), **Kuantan**, **Sungai Petani** (RM8.80), **Johor Bahru** (RM25.80), **Kangar** (RM14.00), **Kuala Perlis** (RM14.00), **Taiping**, **Lumut** and **Tapah** (90 mins). There are also services to **Kota Bharu** (RM18) and **Grik/Gerik** (RM5). An express coach company has a booking office at 2 Jln Bendahara, T535367. They operate a daily service to Singapore, Johor Bahru, KL, Butterworth, Penang, Lumut, Alor Star and Kuala Kangsar. **Taxi**: shared taxis leave from beside the bus station. KL, Butterworth, Taiping, Alor Star, Tapah.

Connections with Hat Yai in southern **Thailand** and **Singapore** (0900, 1400, 1900, 2100, RM25) T2412182.

Directory **Airline offices** *MAS*, Lot 108 Bangunan Seri Kinta, Jln Sultan Idris Shah, T2414155; *Pelangi Air*, Sultan Azian Shah Airport, T3124770, F3132725. Airport T3122459. **Banks** *Bank Bumiputra*, *Malayan Banking*, *Hock Hua Bank*, and *Maybank* are all on Jalan Sultan Idris Shah; *UMBC*, *Oriental Bank* and *Public Bank*, are on Jln Yang Kalsom; in the new town, along Jln Sultan Yussuf there is a *Southern Bank*, *Hong Kong Bank*, *Standard Chartered*, and *Bank of Commerce*. *K & C Travel* (see below) also have foreign exchange facilities. **Communications** Area code: 05. **General Post Office**: next to the railway station on Jln Panglima Bukit Gantang Wahab. There is another Post Office on Jln Dato Onn Jaafar. **Internet cafés**: *Infoweb Station*, Jln Dato Onn Jaafar, near Jln Sultan Idris Shah. There is another café on Jln Dato Onn Jaafar next to the Post Office, RM2. Avoid early afternoon, when it's full of school children. **Tourist offices** None of Ipoh's three tourist offices offer much in the way of help and assistance, bar a map. *Ipoh City Council Tourist Office*, Jln Abdul Adil, open: 0800-1245 and 1400-1615 Mon-Thu, 0800-1212 and 1400-1615 Fri, 0800-1245 Sat. *Perak Tourist Information Centre*, State Economic Planning Unit, Pejabat Setiausaha Kerajaan, Jln Panglima Bukit Gantang Wahab, open 0800-1245, 1400-1615 Mon-Thu, 0800-1215, 1445-1615 Fri, 0800-1245 Sat, closed Sun, T2412957, F2418173; *Tourist Information*, *Casuarina Hotel*, 18 Jln Gopeng, T2532008.

Lumut

Colour map 1, grid C2 Lumut is primarily a base for the Royal Malaysian Navy which has a population of around 25,000, compared to the populace of 1,000 in Lumut itself. Lumut is also a transit point for Pulau Pangkor, and in recent years it has also begun tentatively to develop as a holiday destination in its own right. The *Orient Star*, a new international class hotel, looms large on the coast where the former government resthouse used to stand, apartment blocks are rearing their ugly heads on Bukit Engku Busu, the hill backing the town, and Lumut has most definitely forsaken its sleepy fishing village identity for a busy seaside town. The town is at its zenith during the *Pesta Laut*, a sea festival, which takes place every August at nearby Teluk Batik.

The naval base houses the **Royal Malaysian Navy Museum**, which really speaks for itself. ■ *Closed Fri.* **Teluk Batik**, 7 km south of Lumut, is a popular beach spot (often used by the naval base), with chalets, food stalls and changing rooms backing the sweeping, sandy bay. There is another good sandy beach at **Teluk Rubiah** which is a further 6 km south. It is near the Teluk Rubia Royal Golf Club (T2619555) which has a pool and tennis courts in addition to the golf course.

A *Orient Star*, Lot 203 and 366, Jln Iskandar Shah, T6834199, F6834223, tosrlso@po.jaring.my. A hotel with 150 a/c rooms, TV, in-house video, mini fridge, free-form pool with swim-up bar, paddling pool, gymnasium, jet-ski hire, bicycle hire, coffee house, bar, palatial in size and décor, pleasantly furnished rooms with balconies and sea views but no beach. **AL** *Swiss-Garden Resort*, T6183333. RM208, 101-107 Jln Titi Panjang. New, clinical feel, but has good facilities. **A** *Blue Bay Resort*, T6836939, F6835396. Breakfast included. TV, tea and coffee-making facilities, complimentary newspaper, late check-out (1500), pool, a/c. Jungle and fishing treks organized, also Island cruises. Great value.

B *Hotel Manjun Permai*, Lot 211-213, Jln Iskandar Shah, T6834934, F6834937. A/c, comfortable, but décor on the tacky side. **B** *Lumut Country Resort*, Jln Titi Panjang, T6835109, F6835396. A hotel with 44 a/c rooms, swimming pool, paddling pool, tennis courts, does not stand up to the *Orient Star*, but has some attractive features such as hand-printed batik bed covers and wooden floors. Disco, function room. Very good value; best deal in town.

C *Harbour View Hotel*, Lot 13 and 14, Jln Titi Panjang, T6837888, F6837088. Small, quiet hotel on main road along sea front, a/c, TV, mini fridge, tea and coffee-making facilities, bathroom. Recommended. **C** *Hotel Indah*, 208 Jln Iskandar Shah, T6835064, F6834220. One of the newest budget hotels on the main road along the coast, a/c, TV, hot shower, adjoining coffee house, simply furbished and clean with pleasant views over the esplanade. **C-D** *Lumut Villa Inn*, Batu 1, Jln Sitiawan, T6835982, F6836563. Inconveniently located outside the town if you do not have your own transport, but good value for money, rooms without a/c in **D** category.

D *Phin Lum Hooi*, 93 Jln Titi Panjang, T6835641. The cheapest place around, rooms are clean and the management friendly, not far from the jetty. Popular with local navy, so can be noisy in the restaurant downstairs, best budget option.

Sleeping
Price codes: see inside front cover

Lumut

Sleeping
1 Blue Bay Resort
2 Harbour View
3 Lumut Country Resort
4 Orient Star
5 Swiss Garden Resort

Eating
1 Makanan Laut Ocean
2 Ocean Seafood
3 Phin Lum Hooi

Chinese **3** *Ocean Seafood Restaurant*, 115 Jln Tit Panjang, a/c, specializes in seafood. **3-2** *Sin Pinamhui*, 93-95 Jln Titi Panjang, traditional Chinese food. **2** *Phin Lum Hooi*, next to Chinese Temple on Jln Titi Panjang, cheap Chinese coffee shop fare. **Indian 2** *Restoran Samudera Raya*, 39 Jln Sultan Idris Shah, Indian and Malay food. **International** *Kentucky Fried Chicken*, Jln Sultan Abdullah. *Makanan Laut Ocean Restaurant*, Jln Titi Panjang, fresh fish dishes available.

Eating
Price codes: see inside front cover

Bus The bus station is in the centre of town, a few minutes' walk from the jetty. Regular connections with Ipoh, KL and Butterworth and less regular connections with Melaka and Tapah (for the Cameron Highlands). Bus every 30 mins from Ipoh, duration 1 hr 45 mins, RM3.80. Buses also run between Lumut and Singapore.

Transport
183 km to KL
170 km to Butterworth
83 km to Ipoh

Taxi Services available to Ipoh, KL and Butterworth.

Ferry Regular crossings, at least every 30 mins from 0645 to 2000 from Lumut Jetty to Pangkor village on Pangkor Island. Return fare is RM4 for adult and RM2 for child, crossing takes under an hour. Crossings every 2 hrs from 0845 to 1830 to Pan Pacific Resort at north end of Pangkor Island. Return fare is RM6 for adult and RM3 for child. For further information contact *Lumut Ferry Station*, T935541, or *White Yellow Black Ferry*, Kompleks Kraftangan and Pusat Pemandu Pelancong, T934062. Half-hourly crossings from the jetty are available from the companies combined.

International connections with Sumatra: *Kuala Perlis Langkawi Ferry Service (KPLFS)*, T6854258, run a service between Lumut and Belawan, Medan's port in Sumatra, Indonesia. The service leaves Lumut at 1000 on Thur and returns from Belawan on Wed at 1100, 3½ hrs. *Indomas Express* also operates boats on this route. Fare for both companies is RM90 one way, RM160 return and both include bus connections between Belawan and Medan. In Medan tickets for *Indomas* can also be booked through *Tobali Tour and Travel*, Jln Juanda Baru 52 and for *KPLFS* through *Indoma Citra Agung*, Jln Katamso 33D.

Directory **Communications** Area code: 05. **Tourist offices** *Lumut Tourist Information Centre*, Jln Titi Panjang (near petrol station), T6834057, not open on a regular basis.

Pulau Pangkor

Population: 25,000
Phone code: 05
Colour map 1, grid C2

Just 7 km across the straits from Lumut is Pangkor, one of the most easily accessible islands in Malaysia. It was on board a British ship anchored off the island that the historic Treaty of Pangkor was signed in 1874, granting the British entry into the Malay States for the first time. Before the Second World War the island was used as a leper colony.

Pangkor is one of the largest fish suppliers in Peninsular Malaysia. Old Pangkor has the fishing villages of Sungai Pinang Kecil, Sungai Pinang Besar and Pangkor (main village). Modern Pangkor to the north has a modern luxury resort. To the southwest is the tiny island of Pankgor Laut. The main island is pretty but gets very busy, particularly at weekends and during school holidays, as it is one of the few places on the west coast with good beaches. However, it is disappointing compared with some of the peninsula's east coast islands.

Some of the best beaches and coral can be found on nearby islands, such as **Emerald Bay** on Pangkor Laut, a private island only open to guests of the resort there (see **Sleeping** below). Emerald Bay is the spot where F Spencer Chapman escaped from Malaya after three years fighting the Japanese behind enemy lines, all recounted in his book *The Jungle is Neutral*. There are some hidden beaches on the main island: north of **Pasir Bogak**, the most developed beach, turtles lay their eggs right on **Teluk Ketapang** beach, mainly during May, June and July. North of this are two of the best beaches **Coral Bay** (Teluk Nipah) and **Golden Sands** (Teluk Belanga). The most popular beach is at Pasir Bogak. Visitors can also take boats to Pulau Mentangor and Pulau Sembilan.

For such a small place, circumnavigating the island is surprisingly entertaining

There are good walks round the island; it takes nearly a day to walk all the way round; by bicycle, half a day, and by motorcycle two to three hours. The west coast is comparatively secluded with stretches of quiet beach and the odd fishing settlement, while the east coast hums with commercial activity, like boat building and fish processing, and because the population is so ethnically diverse, there is a lot of variety.

There is a South Indian temple, **Sri Pathirakaliaman**, at Sungai Pinang Kecil and the **Foo Lin Kong Temple** at the foot of Sungai Pinang Besar, with a miniature Great Wall of China in the garden. To the south at Teluk Gedung there are ruins of a Dutch fort, **Kota Belanda**. It was built by the Dutch East India Company in 1680 to protect Dutch interests, especially the rich tin traders, from attack by Malay pirates. It was heavily fortified and apparently its cannon could protect the whole Strait of Dinding also known as the Manjung Straits. The Dutch were forced to leave the fort after an assault by the Malays although they reoccupied it from 1745-1748. Little more than a shell of the former building now remains. Pangkor village is also attractive. Its main street is lined with stores selling dried fish packaged in pink plastic bags. There are also souvenir shops, mostly selling T-shirts, and a handicraft centre. One or two of the coffee houses along the street still have their original marble topped tables and Straits wooden chairs.

Excursions

Pulau Sembilan lies 27 km south of Pulau Pangkor. There are a group of nine small islands and outcrops here, which offer good diving and marine life.

Pulau Pangkor

■ **Sleeping**

1 Beach Hut
2 Coral Bay Resort
3 Coral Beach Camp
4 Hornbill Resort
5 Khoo's Holiday Resort
6 Nazri Nipah Camp
  & Joe Fisherman Village
7 Nipah Bay Villa
8 Pan Pacific Resort
9 Pangkor Bay View
  Resort
10 Pangkor Laut Resort
11 Pangkor Village Beach
  Resort
12 Seaview
13 Sri Bayu Beach Resort
14 Suria Beach Resort

Sleeping

■ on map, page 143
Price codes:
see inside front cover
Room rates are
discounted during the
week – especially the
more expensive hotels

Most of the mid and upper range accommodation is at Pasir Bogak and can be reached from Pangkor village by taxi. Many of the budget places are at Teluk Nipah on the west coast which require a rather longer taxi ride in one of the vehicles belonging to Pangkor's taxi mafia.

Pasir Bogak **A** *Coral Bay Resort*, T6855111, F6855666, coralbay@tm.net.my. TV, a/c, pool, health club, disco/karaoke. Two restaurants, and watersports are organized. Great value. **A** *Sri Bayu Beach Resort*, T6851929, F6851050. Chalet accommodation only, oriental style décor, a/c, TV, bath, coffee-making facilities, pool, tennis, karaoke, restaurant, children's club, rather overpriced but the best place to stay on Pasir Bogak. Breakfast included.

B *Khoo's Holiday Resort*, T6852190. Restaurant, chalets on the hill and rooms in a block, with or without a/c, sea tours arranged. Breakfast included. **B-E** *Pangkor Village Beach Resort*, T6852227, F6853787. A/c chalet (**B**) inclusive breakfast and dinner, A-frames (**D**), longhouse (**E**) (max 10 people), all inclusive of breakfast, near the main cluster of food stalls in Pasir Bogak, can be noisy and the tents are hot during the day. Basic, but close to sea. Not very good value. **B** *Seaview*, T6851605. A/c, restaurant, watersports, fishing, boat trips, breakfast included in room rate. **C** *Beach Hut*, T6851159. A/c, restaurant, watersports, one of the older hotels here and the years are beginning to show, set in a garden close to the beach.

Teluk Nipah **B** *Hornbill Resort*, T6852005, F6852006. All rooms with sea views, a/c, TV, hot shower, seafood restaurant, popular bar with local and imported brews, and recommended at sunset. **B** *Nipah Bay Villa*, T6852198. A/c, shower, attractive wooden cottages, well equipped. Access to video library, also has a restaurant. **B** *Palma Beach Resort*, T6853693, F6854431. Fourteen chalets, a/c, restaurant, free bicycles and rowing boats. Breakfast included. **B** *Pangkor Bay View Resort*, Lot 4449, Teluk Nipah. T6853540, F6851308. Wood panelled decent rooms. A good option. **B-D** *Coral Beach Camp*, T6852711. A-frame huts (**D**), with additional cost for bathroom, family rooms split between 5 (**D**), organize watersport, motorbike hire. **D** *Suria Beach Resort*, Lot 4441, Teluk Nipah, T6853922 F6853921. A/c, shower. Jungle treks organized. Restaurant serves Thai and Chinese food. **D** *Joe Fisherman Village*, T6852389. One of the most popular budget places to stay with simple 'A' frame chalets with 2 mattresses on the floor and a fan, bicycles for hire, meals available. **D** *Nazri Nipah Camp*, T6852014. Pretty similar to *Joe Fisherman's* and as they are virtually next door it is easy enough to check them both out.

Pangkor Laut **L** *Pangkor Laut Resort*, Pangkor Laut Island, T6991100, F6991200. Malaysia's top resort, officially opened in 1994 by Luciano Pavarotti who is quoted as saying: "I almost cried when I saw how beautiful God had made this paradise." Alan Whicker put the event on film, calling it 'Pavarotti in Paradise', and the Prime Minister of Malaysia chose to spend his birthday here, all this acclaim is no exaggeration, the *Pangkor Laut Resort* is idyllic. The chalets, a blend of Malay and Balinese architecture, are magnificently set, either over the sea (linked by wooden walkways) or on the jungled hillside, each is beautifully furbished, with carved wood and rattan work. Luxurious bathrooms with recessed tubs and orchids floating on the water's surface greet you upon arrival. A/c, mini-bar (ice buckets regularly delivered), tea/coffee-making facilities, CD player (TV in lounge only), immaculate kimonos, fresh fruit. Other facilities include well-stocked library (books and CDs), 3 swimming pools, squash, watersports, health club, gymnasium, sauna, spa, jacuzzi. A steep hike, or a short shuttle ride, takes you to Emerald Bay, one of the most perfect sandy bays in Malaysia. Eating at the resort is also a delight, top quality seafood at the *Fisherman's Cove*, steamboat at *Uncle Lim's*, or Western fare at the *Sumudra* where chimes blow in the breeze. The wildlife on Pangkor Laut is also remarkably abundant and diverse – from hornbills to macaques – and the jungle treks are recommended. If you can afford it, Pangkor Laut is not to be missed. Recommended.

Other places AL *Pan Pacific Resort*, Teluk Belanga, T6851091, F6851852, resv@pprp.po.my. Heavily discounted at present. A/c, restaurants, two pools, limited golf course, tennis courts, watersports, limited business facilities. More expensive rooms have sea views, cheaper ones look onto the garden. Excellent location on wide sandy bay, 250 rooms of varying standard and price, to get there take a ferry to the Pan Pacific Jetty from where a hotel minibus takes you the short journey to the resort.

Most hotels and chalets have their own restaurants and most guests end up eating where they are staying. Seafood is always on the menu.
    Chinese 2 *Fook Heng*, Pangkor village, simple coffee shop but excellent quality Chinese food, seafood prices are high. **2** *Guan Guan*, Pangkor village, specializes in seafood. **2** *Wah Mooi*, Sungai Pinang Kecil, steamed carp recommended by locals. **Seafood** *Ye Lin Seafood Garden*, 200 Jln Pasir Bogak, popular outdoor restaurant, prides itself on its low prices. **Foodstalls** On Pasir Bogak and Teluk Nipah.

Eating
Price codes: see inside front cover

Golf *Pan Pacific Resort*, T6851091, Teluk Belanga, Golden Sands, 9-hole, on the coast, green fees RM50; *Pangkor Yacht Club*, Teluk Gedong, T6853478, F6853480, watersports facilities, including jet skis, sailing and snorkelling, also organize fishing trips and round island tours.

Sports

Local Bus/taxi: there are taxis, most of which are actually minibuses (Kereta Isewa), from Pangkor village to accommodation at Pasir Bogak as well as to Teluk Nipah and the *Pan Pacific Resort*. There is also a local bus service but this is not regular and locals usually take all the seats. For information contact the bus office in Pangkor village: Syarikat Kenderan Sri Pangkor, T6851178, which is near the jetty.
    Motorbike/bicycle hire: it is possible to hire motorbikes from Pangkor village for RM20-30 per day. Soon Seng Motor is one of several companies in the village that hire out motorbikes. They are at 12 Main Rd (near jetty), T6851269, and also have a branch at Standard Camp, Pantai Pasir Bogak, T6851878. Bicycles are available from many of the chalet operations, RM10 per day.

Transport
90 km SW of Ipoh

Long distance Air: the airport is now fully operational. *Pelangi Air* makes daily flights to KL. Currently this is the only destination that is served. The flight takes 45 mins. T6854516.
    Boat: ferries leave from Lumut jetty. Connections every 30 mins to Pangkor jetty (RM4 return), also regular connections with *Pan Pacific Resort* jetty close to Golden Sands (RM6 return). The first boat to Pangkor is at 0645 and the last at 1930. From Pangkor, the first boat leaves at 0630 and the last 1830. For further information contact the *Pan Silver Ferry*, 1a Jln Besar, Pangkor, T6851046, F6851782. **Ferry**: there are inter-island ferries or it is possible to hire fishing boats from the main villages. Large hotels will organize trips to the islands.

Banks Large hotels will change money and there's a *Maybank* in Pangkor village. **Communications** Area code: 05.

Directory

Northern Peninsula

Kuala Kangsar

Phone code: 05
Colour map 1, grid B2

Half way between Ipoh and Taiping is this royal town. It lies on the Kangsar River, a tributary of the Perak River. On the east bank of the Kangsar River lies the home of the Sultan of Perak. To get there, find the main roundabout in the town which has a distinctive clock tower at its centre, and head southeast towards the gates marking the start of the road to the palace estate. The road twists alongside the Perak River where there is also a back walkway for those on foot. The first monument that you come to is the **Ubudiah Mosque**, built on the slopes of Bukit Chandan. Completed in 1917, it is one of the most beautiful mosques in the country with its golden domes and elegant minarets. Next to it are the graves of the Perak royal family.

Present members of the Perak royal family are resident in the beautiful **Istana Iskandariah** (and south bank of the Perak), which was built in 1930 sits on the summit of Bukit Chandan, overlooking the Perak River and Ubudiah Mosque. It is a massive marble structure with a series of towers, topped by golden onion domes set among trees and rolling lawns. It is not open to the public, but the former palace, Istana Kenangan (next door to the current Istana), is now the **Museum di Raja** and exhibits royal regalia. It is a fine example of Malay architecture and was built by Sultan Idris of Perak between 1913 and 1917 without recourse to any architectural plans or a single nail. ■ *0930-1900 Sat-Wed, 0930-1245 Thur, closed Fri.*

In the vicinity of the palaces are several **traditional grand wooden Malay homes**, which used to house court officials. There is also another **former palace** (not open to public) near the Ubudiah Mosque. This grand white building was erected in 1903 for the 28th Sultan of Perak, and is now used as a school. Besides these grand buildings, in the grounds of the district office near the Agricultural Department, is one of the first three rubber trees planted in Malaysia. HN Ridley, also known as 'Crazy Ridley' was responsible for developing Kuala Kangsar as a rubber planting district. He obtained rubber seeds from London's Kew Gardens and brought them, first to Singapore, and then to Kuala Kangsar where the seeds were sown in 1877, when Sir Hugh Low was British President in Perak. The sole tree to remain is now marked with a memorial plaque to Ridley. Across the road from Kuala Kangsar's famed rubber tree is a charming pavilion, built in 1930 as a viewing gallery from which

Kuala Kangsar

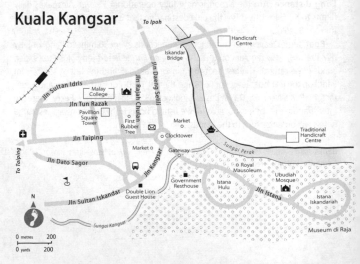

the sultan could watch polo on the padang. The padang is also overlooked by the red roofed building of the Malay college. Considered the Eton of Malaysia, the school was built in 1905 for the children of the Perak royal family. During the Japanese occupation in the Second World War, the college was turned into administration offices for the Japanese Imperial Army who interrogated and subsequently beheaded anyone found to be a traitor. A school once again in the 1950s, it attracted a celebrated crowd – Anthony Burgess taught here (see **Further reading** on page 63 for a listing of his novels with a Malaysian theme).

Across the Perak River (20 sen ferry ride) there is a village where **traditional pottery-making** goes on, mostly within the Handicraft Centre there. The pottery is earthenware and fired in padi husk which gives it a rich black colour. The traditional product of the potteries is the labu sayong, a water pitcher, in the shape of a gourd.

There are very few places to stay in Kuala Kangsar; none is particularly desirable apart from the *Rest House*, and all are small – the largest hotel has 14 rooms.

B *Rest House (Rumah Rehat Kuala Kangsar)*, Bukit Candan, T7763872. Pleasant position just inside the gates to the palace road, old colonial mansion, poor value restaurant but excellent views. **D** *Mei Lai*, 7f Jln Raja Chulan, T7761729. **D** *Tin Heong*, 34 Jln Raja Chulan, T7762066. **D-E** *Double Lion*, 74 Jln Kasa, T7761010, some a/c, an alternative to the *Rest House* and a pleasant enough place to stay with large rooms, some overlooking the river.

Sleeping
Although Kuala Kangsar is not a popular stopover spot, due to the limited number of rooms, it is best to book in advance

Canoeing Three-day canoe safaris depart from Kuala Kangsar and follow the Perak for almost its entire length to the Cherendoh dam. For further information contact, No 3 MDKK, Jln Tebing, T7769717.

Sports

Train The station is out of town to the northeast, on Jln Sultan Idris. Trains every 2 hrs from Ipoh and trains on the KL-Butterworth route also stop here. **Bus** The bus terminal is in the centre of town on Jln Raja Bendahara. Regular connections with Ipoh, Butterworth, KL, Lumut and Taiping. There is also one morning departure a day for Kota Bharu on the east coast. **Taxi** These leave from close to the bus station for destinations including Butterworth, KL, Ipoh and Taiping.

Transport
50 km NW of Ipoh
123 km S of Butterworth
270 km to KL

Communications Area code: 05. **General Post Office:** Jln Taiping, near the clock tower.

Directory

Taiping

With a backdrop of the Bintang Mountains, Taiping is the old capital of Perak and one of the oldest towns in Malaysia. Around 1840, Chinese immigrants started mining tin in the area, and the town, as its name suggests, is predominantly Chinese. In the 1860s and 1870s the Larut district of Taiping, then known as Kelian Pauh, was the scene of the Perak War, caused by bloody feuding between two rival Chinese secret societies, the Hai San and Ghee Hin, over rights to the rich tin deposits. The fighting between these Hakka and Hokkien groups resulted in British armed intervention and when it subsided, the town was renamed *thai-peng*, or 'everlasting peace'. It is the only big Malaysian town with a Chinese name.

Phone code: 05
Colour map 1, grid B2

In the *Straits Times* in 1933, colonial administrator G L Peet wrote: "What a pleasant town Taiping is! I first saw it some years ago on a rainy, cool evening, when the air was laden with the scent of flowering angsana trees and golden light bathed the slopes of the *ijau* [green] range. Taiping has the feeling of being lived in for a long time. It was a thriving and well-appointed town when Ipoh was still a Chinese village, when Seremban was in the same state and when

Kuala Lumpur was just beginning to take on some semblance of permanence and solidity."

The Japanese built a prison in Taiping during the war (next to the Lake Garden), which was then converted into a rehabilitation centre for captured Communist Terrorists during the Emergency. Some of the executions carried out under Malaysia's draconian drugs legislation now take place in Taiping jail (see page 32).

Today the town has a rundown feel about it and many new buildings have replaced the former shophouses which are laid out on a monotonous grid plan. The streets are wide and the traffic noisy; probably one of the main reasons for coming here is to visit Maxwell Hill (see below). Nonetheless there is more colonial-era architecture here than in many of Malaysia's towns. Jalan Iskandar has some fine examples of Chinese shophouse architecture and there are also some attractive colonial-era buildings including the former District Office on Jalan Kota.

Sights As early as 1890 the **Lake Garden** or **Taman Tasik** was set up on the site of an abandoned tin mine. It is very lush due to the high rainfall and is the pride of the town. Covering 66 hectares, the park lies at the foot of Bukit Larut (Maxwell Hill). At one end of the park is **Taiping Zoo**, which is one of the oldest in Malaysia and boasts over 800 animals, including Malaysian elephants, tigers and hornbills. ■ *1000-1800 daily, RM1.* In the early morning locals use the park for their tai chi exercises. Rowing boats for hire on lake. Built in 1883, the lovely colonial **Perak Museum** on the Butterworth Road, opposite the prison is the oldest museum in Malaysia. It contains a collection of ancient weapons, aboriginal implements, stuffed animals and archaeological finds. ■ *0930-1700 Sat-Thur, 0900-1215, 1445-1700 Fri, free.* Near the museum is **All Saints' Church**. Built of wood in 1889, it is the oldest Anglican church in Malaysia. The graveyard contains graves of early settlers and those who died in

Taiping

Ling Nam Temple
Perak
Museum
Jln Taming Sari
Prison
● 9 ■ 10
All Saints
Jln Air Terjun
Jln Taming Sari
Jln Istana Larut
Jln Kelab Lama
Jln Muzium Hulu
Taiping Zoo
Jln Circular
Jln Sultan Mansor
Museum
King
Edwards
School
1 ✉
Lake Gardens
(Taman Tasik)
4 ■
Jln Stesyen
3 ■
Jln Barrack
Esso $
Clock Tower $
Jln Sultan Abdullah
Lake Gardens
(Taman Tasik)
To Bukit Larut (Maxwell Hill) & War Cemetery
Jln Taming Jati
Jln Tupai
Jln Pasar
Central
Market
7 ■
Old Shophouses
Jln Peng Loong
2 ■
Jln Iskandar
Jln Kota
Jln Mesjid
Hawker
Food Centre
Jln Panggung Wayang
8 ■
5 ■
Pasar Malam
(Night Market)
Jln Stephens
6 ■

N

0 metres 75
0 yards 75

■ Sleeping	4 Lake View	8 Peace
1 Fuliyean	5 Legend Inn	9 Rumah Rehat Baru
2 Furama	6 Meridien	10 Seri Malaysia
3 Government Resthouse	7 Panorama	

the Japanese prisoner-of-war camp nearby. The **Ling Nam Temple** on Station Street is worth a visit for the Chinese antiques inside and is said to be the oldest Chinese temple in Perak state. The **railway station** on Jalan Steysen, now a school, is the oldest in Malaysia and holds a museum.

Excursions

Kuala Sepetang lies 16 km west of Taiping and contains a Mangrove Forest Museum, the first of its kind in Malaysia. The site lies in 40,700 hectares of mangrove swamp, which is more than half the swamp area in Peninsular Malaysia. The museum aims to highlight forestry operations in Malaysia.

Malaysia's oldest hill station

The foot of **Bukit Larut**, formerly known as **Maxwell Hill**, is just 12 km or so east of Lake Gardens and most people climb the hill, whether on foot or by Land Rover, as a day excursion from Taiping. At an elevation of 1,034m it is the wettest place in Malaysia, receiving an average of 5,029 mm of rain a year, and was once a tea plantation. Bukit Larut is a small resort with limited facilities compared to the peninsula's other hill stations. The road up was built by prisoners of war during the Japanese occupation in the Second World War. It is in such bad repair that it is virtually inaccessible in anything other than a four-wheel drive vehicle, in any case private transport is not permitted.

On the way up you pass a **Commonwealth War Cemetery**. Many of the gravestones here are marked December 1941, which was the date a single company from the Argyle Regiment tried to hold back the Imperial Japanese 42nd Infantry on the road north of Kuala Kangsar. Another stop are the **Tea Gardens** at the Batu 3.5 mark – or what is left of them. The administration office is at the Batu 6 marker and about 1 km on from here is the end of the road – at the *Gunung Hijau Rest House*. From here travel is on foot. On clear days, from the top, it is possible to see for miles along the coast. The walk to the summit takes about 30 minutes. Jungle walks near the top of the hill (but leeches are bad). To walk all the way down takes around two to three hours. ■ *T827243 for information.*

Sleeping and eating For bungalows it is essential to book in advance (between 0900-1200), T8077241 or write to Officer in charge, *Bukit Larut Hill Resort*, Taiping. **B** *Cendana*. **B** *Tempinis* all between the 6th and 7th milestones. **D** *Beringin*. **E** *Bukit Larut*, large bathroom, excellent value. **E** *Gunung Hijau*. There is a campsite (**F**).

Food is available at **3** *Gunung Hijau* or *Bukit Larut* guesthouses. At the bungalows, meals can be arranged with the caretaker.

Transport The steep walk from Taiping Lake Gardens takes about 2½-3½ hrs. The road is restricted and private cars are not permitted. A Land Rover service runs from the foot of the hill just above the Lake Garden in Taiping, every hour from 0700-1800 (RM2.50 one way to the administration office, RM2.50 to the Gunung Hijau Rest Stop), T827243.

Sleeping

Price codes: see inside front cover

B *Fuliyean*, 14 Jln Barrack, T8068648. A/c, TV, bath, quite new and good value, rooms kept very clean. **B** *Legend Inn*, 2 Jln Long Jaafar, T8060000, F8066666. A hotel block with 88 rooms, bath, TV, video channel, coffee house, plushest place in town with well-equipped rooms. **B** *Meridien*, 2 Jln Simpang, T8081133. A/c, TV, shower, coffee house, restaurant. **B** *Panorama*, 61-79 Jln Kota, T834111. A/c, TV, in-house video, bath, mini fridge, coffee-making facilities, joined to a 3-storey supermarket, the *Fajar*, restaurant. **B** *Seri Malaysia*, 4 Jln Sultan Mansor, T8069502. One of the new chain of budget hotels, located outside the town, near the Lake Gardens, spotlessly clean to the point of being sterile.

C *Furama*, 30 Jln Peng Loong, T821077. A/c, restaurant. Recommended. **C-D** *New Resthouse (Rumah Rehat Baru)*, 1 Jln Sultan Mansor, Taman Tasek, T8072044. Fan or a/c, restaurant, situated a little out of town and the new block is hardly attractive but the rooms are large, with attached bathrooms, it overlooks the Lake Gardens and is good value. Recommended.

D *Ann Chuan*, 25 Jln Kota, T8075322. A/c or fan, restaurant. **D** *Government Resthouse*, Jln Residensi (opposite King Edwards School), T822044. Restaurant. Recommended. **D** *Lake View*, opposite Lake Gardens, 1a Jln Circular, T8074941. A/c, very noisy karaoke but cheap and clean. **D** *Merlin*, 73 Jln Halaman Pasar, T8075833. Restaurant. **D** *Nanyung*, 129-131 Jln Pasar, T8074488. A/c or fan. **D** *Peace*, 32 Jln Iskandar, T8073379. Lots of character, basic and noisy, good value. **D** *Town*, 320 Jln Kota, T8071166, basic.

Eating **Chinese** **3** *Dragon Phoenix*, Jln Kota. **3** *Malaysia Restoran*, 36 Jln Eastern. **2** *Kum Loong*, 45-47 Jln Kota, good *dim sum* 0500-0800. **2** *Prima Restaurant*, 21-23 Jln Kota. **1** *Kedai Kopi Sentosa*, Jln Kelab Cina, good Teow Chiew noodles. **Indian** Number of places along Jln Pasar and Jln Panggung Wayang selling the usual array of biryani dishes and roti. **International 3** *Nagaria Steak House*, 61 Jln Pasar, dark interior, popular for beer drinking. **3** *Panorama*, 61-79 Jln Kota, mediocre Western food and steakhouse. **Foodstalls** Large night market on Jln Panggung Wayang. *Hawker Centre* in Metro Arcade (Shopping Centre), 54 Medan Simpang (5 km from town centre, on road to Kuala Kangsar). *Malay hawker stalls* on Jln Tupai. Burger, rice and fried chicken stalls near foot of Bukit Larut (Maxwell Hill).

Sport **Golf** *Bukit Jana Golf & Country Club*, Jln Bukit Jana, T8837500, green fees RM50 weekdays, RM80 weekends. Clubhouse has pool, paddling pool, tennis, squash, kids' playground, card room, restaurant.

Tour operators *Poly Travels*, 53 Jln Mesjid, T820155, ticketing, currency exchange, hotel reservation, tours; *Trans Asia Pacific*, 112 Jln Barrack, T828451, ticketing, hotel reservation, car hire, package tours; *Fulham Tours*, 25 Jln Kelab Cina, T823069, ticketing, hotel reservation, licensed money changers.

Transport **Train** Station is on the east side of town. Lying on the north-south railway line, there
304 km N of KL are regular connections with Ipoh, KL and Butterworth. See page 35 for timetable.
88 km to Butterworth

Bus The main long-distance bus station is 7 km out of town and getting there means either catching a town bus or a taxi. Regular connections with Butterworth, Ipoh, Sungai Petani and KL. There is also a morning bus to Kuantan on the east coast. For other connections, change at Ipoh. Local buses for Ipoh, Grik and Kuala Kangsar leave from the local bus station which is much more conveniently located in the centre of town at the intersection of Jln Mesjid and Jln Iskandar.

Directory **Banks** *Bank Bumiputra* and *UMBC* on Jln Kota; *Standard Chartered* at crossroads of Jln Kota and Jln Sultan Abdullah. *Poly Travels*, 53 Jln Mesjid and *Fulham Tours*, 25 Jln Kelab Cina, have foreign exchange facilities. **Communications** Area code: 05. General Post Office: Jln Barrack.

Butterworth

Phone code: 04 This industrial and harbour town and base for the Royal Australian Air Force
Colour map 1, grid B2 was billeted here under the terms of the Five Powers Pact. It is the main port for ferries to Penang, and most tourists head straight for the island; Butterworth is not a recommended stopping point.

B *Beach Garden Hotel* 4835 Jln Pantai T3322845. No sign of the beach or a garden in this dull hotel. Located very close to the bus stop/ferry terminal, unlike all the other hotels. TV, a/c and shower, basic. **B** *Berlin*, 4802 Jln Bagan Luar, T3321701 F3323388. A/c, TV. Next to *Sayang Coffee House*, which serves meals. The best option, if you are unfortunate enough to require accommodation in Butterworth. **B** *Travel Lodge*, 1 Lorong Bagan Luar, T3333399 F3323599. A/c, TV, restaurant, shower. **C** *Hotel Ambassadress*, 4425 Jln Bagan Luar, T3327788. A/c, bathroom. Pretty basic, and not particularly good value. **D** *Capital*, 3838 Jln Bagan Luar, T331882. To be avoided. Dark and dirty, although it is very cheap.

Sleeping
Nearly all the hotels are located a good 20 min walk from the bus terminal, so a taxi ride is advisable

Butterworth is the main transport hub for Penang and buses and trains operate into Thailand and down to KL and Singapore. **Train** The railway station is beside the Penang ferry terminal. Regular connections with Alor Star, Taiping, Ipoh, KL and JB. See page 35 for timetable. To Bangkok, Thailand (19 hrs) and to Singapore (14 hrs). Butterworth is one of the main stopovers on the Eastern and Orient Express, which travels in style from Singapore to Bangkok. Passengers disembark here to make the 3 hour trip by ferry and rickshaw to Georgetown.

Bus Bus station next to the ferry terminal. Regular connections with **KL** (RM17.10), **Taiping**, **Kuala Kangsar** (RM5.60), **Melaka**, **JB** (RM33.50), **Kota Bharu** (RM16.50), **Kuala Terengganu**, **Kuantan** and **Ipoh**, 2 hrs. Buses leave every 30 mins from Butterworth for **Kuala Perlis** (Langkawi ferry). There are also buses to **Keroh**, on the border with Thailand, from where it is possible to get Thai taxis to Betong.

Taxi These leave from next to the ferry terminal. If you take a taxi across to Penang you must pay the taxi fare plus the toll for the bridge.

Ferry These are for pedestrians and cars and leave for Georgetown every 15-20 minutes.

Transport
369 km to KL
386 km to Kota Bharu

Banks *Maybank*, *UMBC* and *HSBC* on Jln Bagan Luar. **Communications** Internet Café: *Genesys*, 4922 Jln Bagan Luar, T3243710. RM6 per hour.

Directory

Penang

Population: 1.2 million
Phone code: 04
Colour map 1, grid B1

Penang – or more properly, Pulau Pinang – is the northern gateway to Malaysia and is the country's oldest British settlement. It has been sold to generations of tourists as 'the Pearl of the Orient' but in shape Penang looks more like a frog than a pearl.

Penang state includes a strip of land on the mainland opposite, Province Wellesley – named after Colonel Arthur Wellesley, later to become the Duke of Wellington, who went on to defeat Napoleon at Waterloo. The 738 km² Province Wellesley is also known by its Malay name, Seberang Perai. Georgetown's founder, Captain Francis Light, originally christened Penang 'Prince of Wales Island'. In Malay, *pinang* is the word for the areca nut palm, an essential ingredient of betel nut (see page 517). The palm was incorporated into the state crest in the days of the Straits Settlements during the 19th century. Today Pulau Pinang is translated as 'betel nut island'. Light called Georgetown after George, the Prince of Wales, who later became King George IV as it was acquired on his birthday; most Malaysians know the town by its nickname: *Tanjung*, as it is situated on a sandy headland called Tanjung Penaga.

Ins and outs

Getting there
See also Transport, page 171

Penang airport is 20 km north of Georgetown and there are regular connections with Kuala Lumpur and several other domestic destinations, as well as international links with a handful of regional capitals. With the completion of the 13 km-long Penang Bridge to Butterworth there are direct bus connections with KL and many other Peninsula towns as well as international services to destinations in Thailand and to Singapore. Those wishing to take the train need to alight at Butterworth and make their way across the bridge from there (or take the ferry). Ferries leave from Georgetown for Belawan, on Sumatra, Indonesia and for Langkawi and from there to Thailand.

Getting around

There are bus services around the island and in the tourist areas there are many taxis. It is also possible to hire self-drive cars and motorbikes from local and international firms. In Georgetown there are city buses and taxis as well as a smattering of trishaws. It is also possible to rent bicycles.

History

Before the arrival of Francis Light, who captained a ship for a British trading company, in 1786, Penang was ruled by the Sultan of Kedah. The sultanate had suffered repeated invasions by the Thais from the north and

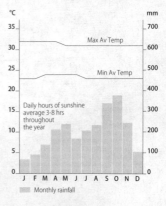

Climate: Penang

Penang highlights

Museums and historical sights Fort Cornwallis, on the site of Francis Light's original stockade (page 157); Penang Museum and Art Gallery, located in Penang's former English public school, founded in 1816 (page 157); Khoo Kongsi, a magnificent and well-preserved Chinese clan association house (page 160).

Temples and mosques Goddess of Mercy Temple (Kuan Yin Teng), built by Chinese settlers at the beginning of the 19th century (page 159); Kek Lok Si (Monastery of Supreme Bliss) which took 20 years to build and is modelled on a monastery in China (page 163); Snake Temple (Temple of the Azure Cloud), built in 1850 and populated by Pit Vipers (page 164); Sri Mariamann (Hindu) Temple, built by Georgetown's South Indian community in 1883 (page 160); Kapitan Kling Mosque, built in 1800 (page 160); Wat Chayamangkalaram (Wat Buppharam) Thai Buddhist temple with Burmese temple opposite (page 161).

Other sights Chinatown, one of the liveliest and best-preserved in the region; Clan Piers, a Chinese water village, linked to Pengkalan Weld (Weld Quay) by jetties named after different clans (page 160); Penang Hill, overlooking Georgetown, with a funicular railway to the top (page 162); Butterfly Farm, claiming to be the largest tropical butterfly farm in the world, with over 120 Malaysian species (page 174).

Beaches Batu Ferringhi, the most famous beach in Malaysia, now a hotel strip (page 172); Muka Head, on the northwest tip of the island, with a series of secluded coves around a rocky headland (page 173).

Shopping Antiques, basketware, handicrafts and batik (page 176).

Sports Golf, swimming, watersports and sailing – including yacht cruises around the islands of the Langkawi group (page 177).

Penang Website
http://penang.Insights.com.my/

Orang Bugis pirates from the sea. Sultan Muhammad Jawa Mu'Azzam Shah II was also beset by a secession crisis and when this turned into a civil war he requested help from Francis Light, then based at Acheen in Sumatra, whom he met in 1771. Light was in search of a trading base on the north shore of the Strait of Melaka which could be used by his firm, Jordain, Sulivan and De Souza, and the British East India Company. In 1771, Light sent a letter to one of his bosses, De Souza, in which he first described Penang's advantages:

"Withinside of Pulo Pinang is a fine clear channel of seven and 14 fathoms which a ship can work anytime. There is plenty of wood, water and provisions there (the European ships), may be supplied with tin, pepper, beetelnut, rattans and birdsnests, and all other vessels passing through the Straits may be as easily supplied as at Malacca."

But before De Souza made up his mind, Light struck a private deal with the Sultan of Kedah. The Sultan installed Light in the fort at Kuala Kedah and gave him the title of Deva Rajah, ceding to him control of the Kedah coast as far south as Penang. In turn, Light promised to protect the Sultan from his many enemies.

A frisson between Sultan Muhammad and the East India Company brought developments to a standstill in 1772. Light left Kedah and sailed to Ujung Salang, which English sailors called Junk Ceylon and is now known as Phuket, where he built up a trading network. Eleven years later he finally repaired relations with Kedah and the newly installed Sultan Abdullah agreed to lease Penang to the British; again, in return for military protection. On 11 August 1786, Light formally took possession of Penang. The island was covered in dense jungle and was uninhabited, apart from a handful of Malay fishermen and a few Bugis pirates.

Northern Peninsula

A small township grew up around the camp by the harbour. A wooden stockade was built to defend the island on the site of the original camp and the cantonment was called Fort Cornwallis, after Marquis Cornwallis, then the Governor-General of India. Light declared Prince of Wales Island a free port to attract trade away from the Dutch, and this helped woo many immigrant traders to Penang. Penang's status as a free port was only withdrawn in 1969. Settlers were allowed to claim whatever land they could clear. The island quickly became a cultural melting pot with an eclectic mix of races and religions. By 1789, Georgetown had a population of 5,000 and by the end of the next decade, this had more than doubled.

The Sultan of Kedah was upset that the East India Company had not signed a written contract setting out the terms of Penang's lease. When the Company began to haggle with him over the price and the military protection he had been promised, Sultan Abdullah believed the British were backing out of their agreement. In alliance with the Illanun pirates, the Sultan blockaded Penang in 1790 and tried to force the Company's hand. Light went on the offensive and quickly defeated the Sultan's forces. The vanquished Sultan Abdullah agreed

Penang

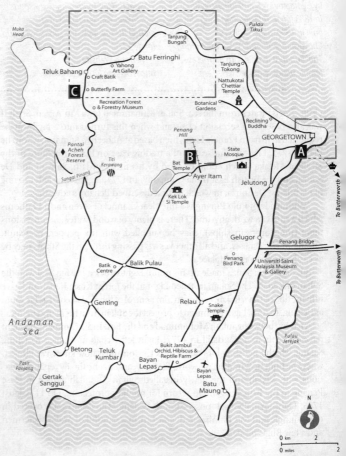

to an annual fee of 6,000 Spanish dollars for Penang. Francis Light remained the island's superintendent until his death, from malaria, in 1794. The disease, which struck down many early settlers, earned Penang the epithet of 'the White Man's Grave'.

Despite Georgetown's cosmopolitan atmosphere, there remained a strong British influence: the British judicial system was introduced in 1801 with the appointment of the first magistrate and judge, an uncle of novelist Charles Dickens. The previous year, Colonel Arthur Wellesley had signed a new Treaty of Peace, Friendship and Alliance with Kedah's new Sultan Diyauddin, which superseded Light's 1791 agreement and allowed for Penang's annexation of Province Wellesley, on the coast of the peninsula, in return for an annual payment of 10,000 Spanish dollars.

In 1805 Penang's colonial status was raised to that of a Residency. A young administrative secretary, Stamford Raffles, arrived to work for the governor. Georgetown became the capital of the newly established Straits Settlements, which included Melaka and Singapore (see page 492). But the glory was shortlived. With the rise of Singapore, following Raffles' founding of the settlement in 1819, Georgetown was quickly eclipsed by the upstart at the southern tip of the peninsula and by the 1830s had been reduced to a colonial backwater. From an architectural perspective, this proved a saving grace: unlike Singapore, Penang retains many of its original colonial buildings and rich cultural heritage.

In the early 19th century Penang was used as a staging post for the opium trade between India and China. The East India Company auctioned off licences to gambling dens, brothels and opium traders; the latter accounted for about 60 percent of colonial Penang's revenue. Vice gangs carved out territories for themselves in Georgetown and secret society feuds finally erupted on the streets in the Penang Riots of 1876. The nine days of fighting started when a member of the White Flag society (a Malay gang) threw a rambutan skin at a Toh-Peh-Kong society member whom he caught peering through his front door. Open warfare ensued and bullet holes can still be seen in the walls of the shophouses in Cannon Square. The riots were finally put down when troop reinforcements arrived from Singapore. The societies were fined RM5,000 each, which funded the construction of four new police stations in the different parts of town where the societies operated.

Colonial Penang prospered, through tin booms and rubber booms, until the outbreak of the Second World War. When the Japanese raced down the peninsula on stolen bicycles, Penang was cut off, without being formally taken. The British residents were evacuated to Singapore within days, leaving the undefended island in the hands of a State Committee, which, after three days, put down the riots which followed the British withdrawal. The Japanese administration lasted from December 1941 to July 1945; remarkably, Georgetown's buildings were virtually unscathed, despite Allied bombing attacks.

Chinese make up just over half of Penang's population, while 35 percent are **Modern Penang** Malay and 11 percent Indian. Penang, along with the other two Straits settlements of Melaka and Singapore, was a centre of Peranakan culture. Peranakans, also known as Babas or Straits Chinese, evolved their own unique blend of Malay and Chinese cultures (see page 534). The Babas of Penang, however, have almost disappeared as a distinctive group – although various shops and restaurants play to the Peranakan theme.

Georgetown, the capital of Penang state, is on the northeast point of the island, nearest the mainland; Bayan Lepas Airport is on the southeast tip. The 13 km Penang Bridge, linking the island to Butterworth, is halfway down the east coast, just south of Georgetown. Batu Ferringhi, now a strip of luxury hotels, is Penang's most famous beach and is on the north coast. It is hard to believe but in 1970 just 39,454 foreign visitors were recorded as landing on the island. By 1981 this figure had risen to 249,118, and in 1990 – during Visit Malaysia Year – over 630,000 arrived. In 1998 5.2 million people visited Peninsula Malaysia and it is thought that around a million chose to drop in on Penang. Nonetheless there are still a handful of small secluded coves with good beaches on the northwest tip of the island. The west of the island is a mixture of jungle-covered hills, rubber plantations and a few fishing kampungs. There are more beaches and fishing villages on the south coast. A short steep mountain range forms a central spine, which includes Penang Hill, overlooking Georgetown, at 850m above sea level.

Although Penang is best known as a beach resort, there is much more here than just sand and (rather dirty) sea. To dwell briefly on the 'dirt' aspect, an interesting headline in the *New Straits Times* in August 1999 read: 'Penang must rid itself of refuse dump image'. The island is also a cultural and architectural gem with Chinese, Malay and Indian influences. Georgetown has the largest collection of pre-war houses in all Southeast Asia. The Penang Heritage Trust has been established by concerned residents in the face of commercial pressures on Penang's unique heritage. Those interested in Georgetown's architectural heritage should try to get hold of Khoo Su Nin's *Streets of Georgetown, Penang*.

Georgetown

Penang's Chinatown is one of the liveliest in Malaysia; its atmosphere & most of its original architecture remain intact

The first four streets of Georgetown – Beach (now known as Lebuh Pantai), Lebuh Light, Jalan Kapitan Kling Mosque (previously Jalan Pitt) and Lebuh Chulia – still form the main thoroughfares of modern Georgetown. Lebuh Chulia was formerly the Cantonese heartland of the Ghee Hin triad, one of the secret societies involved in the 1867 Penang Riots. The older part of town to the west of Weld Quay, in the shadow of Kapitan Kling Mosque, is predominantly Indian.

Georgetown is, however, mainly Chinese; the main Chinatown area is contained by Jalan Kapitan Kling Mosque, Lebuh Chulia, Jalan Penang and Jalan Magazine. The shophouses were built by craftsmen from China: the rituals, burial customs, clan associations, temples and restaurants make up a self-contained Chinese community. Despite the traffic and a skyline pierced by the KOMTAR (Kompleks Tun Abdul Razak) skyscraper, the crowded streets still have plenty of charm. There are an estimated 12,000 pre-war houses still standing in Georgetown, making the town an architectural gem in Southeast Asian terms.

How Penang has managed to preserve at least some of its heritage while that in other Malaysian towns has been torn down, is linked to a rent control cut – on the statute books for years – which has frozen rents and therefore made redevelopment unprofitable. The houses may be mouldering, but at least they aren't (usually) being demolished. But developers are bringing pressure on the federal government to abolish the Rent Control Act. To alleviate the immediate need for alternative housing and to facilitate adjustments by tenants to payment of rental at market rates, a transitional period has been introduced whereby tenants will have to pay rentals based on a formula provided by the Government. The rates are still lower than the market rates. At the end of the transition period on 31 December 1999, owners became entitled to recover vacant possession of the premises (*The Star*, 1 September 1997).

Not all of the island is worthy of 'gem' status however. Pollution and litter have spoiled parts of Penang in recent years. Some beaches are dirty and very few people swim in the sea. The coral which used to line the shore at Batu Feringghi has all gone, mainly due to the silt washed around the headland during the construction of the Penang Bridge. But the sea is not as dirty as in some of the region's other big resorts, as testified by the presence of otters on the beach at Batu Feringghi in the early morning. It has also been reported that an island-wide clean-up campaign has had some success.

Sights

NB Street names in Georgetown are confusing as many are now being rechristened with Malay names; streets are known by both their Malay and English names (eg Jalan Penang/Penang Road – not to be muddled with Lebuh Penang/Penang Street). Of particular note: Lebuh Pitt (Pitt Street) has been renamed Jalan Kapitan Kling Mosque; Beach Street is now Lebuh Pantai.

Tours The three main tours offered by companies are: the city tour, the Penang Hill and temple tour and the round-the-island tour. All cost RM20-30 and most run every hour.

At the junction of Lebuh Light and Lebuh Pantai is the Penang Clock Tower, which was presented to Georgetown by a Chinese millionaire, Chen Eok, in 1897 during Queen Victoria's Diamond Jubilee celebrations. The tower is 60 foot (20m) tall: a foot for every year she had been on the throne.

Clock Tower & Fort Cornwallis

Opposite the clock tower is Fort Cornwallis, on the north tip of the island. It stands on the site of Francis Light's wooden stockade and was built by convict labour between 1808 and 1810; only its outer walls remain. Named after Marquis Cornwallis, a Governor-General of India, the fort has had an insignificant history. Its only taste of military action came during an Allied air-strike in the Second World War. The main cannon, *Serai Rambai*, which was cast in the early 17th century, is popularly regarded as a fertility symbol; offerings of flowers and joss sticks are often left at its base. It was presented to the Sultan of Johor by the Dutch in 1606 and ended up in Penang. The modern amphitheatre hosts concerts and shows. There is an example of a wooden Malay kampung house near the entrance. ■ *0830-1900 Mon-Sun*. There are many colonial buildings on Lebuh Farquhar like the high court, mariners' club and the town hall.

Behind the high court is the museum and gallery, on the junction of Lebuh Light and Lebuh Farquhar. The building was the first English language public school in the east, established in 1816. A statue of Francis Light, cast for the 150th anniversary of the founding of Penang, stands in front of the building. As no photograph of Georgetown's founding father was available, his features were cast from a portrait of his son, Colonel William Light, founder of Adelaide in Australia. The statue was removed by the Japanese during the Second World War and later returned, minus the sword. The museum contains another sculpture: a 19th century bust of Germany's Kaiser Wilhelm II, which turned up in Wellesley primary school. How it came to be there in the first place is a mystery.

Penang Museum & Art Gallery

The small museum has a fine collection of old photographs, maps and historical records charting the growth of Penang from the days of Francis Light. There are some fascinating accounts in the History Room of the Penang Riots in August 1876, see **History** above. Downstairs there is a replica of the main hall of a Chinese trader's home and upstairs, a Straits Chinese exhibition with a marriage chamber and a room of traditional ornamental gowns. The art gallery, also upstairs, has a series of temporary exhibitions. ■ *0900-1700, closed Fri, RM1.*

St George's Church, next door to the museum on Lebuh Farquhar, was the first Anglican church in Southeast Asia. It was built in 1817 with convict labour. The building was designed by Captain Robert Smith (some of his paintings are in the State Museum). ■ *Bus 1,4,7,10*.

Other sights in the centre

Nearby, also on **Lebuh Farquhar**, is the twin-spired **Cathedral of Assumption**. This Roman Catholic church houses the only pipe-organ in Penang. The Convent of the Holy Infant Jesus – slightly further east, is the site of Francis Light's original house. Light was Adelaide's architect and planner. His grave can be found on Jalan Sultan Ahmad Shah.

Georgetown

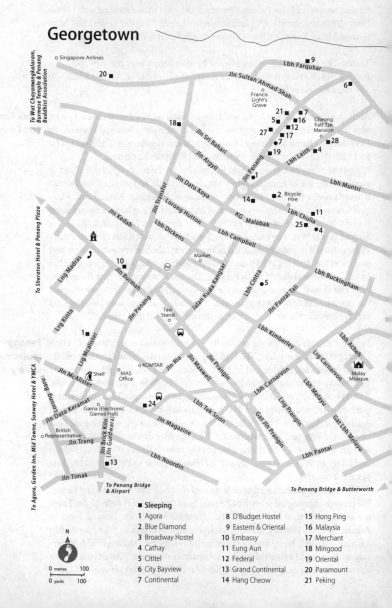

■ **Sleeping**

1 Agora	8 D'Budget Hostel
2 Blue Diamond	9 Eastern & Oriental
3 Broadway Hostel	10 Embassy
4 Cathay	11 Eung Aun
5 Cititel	12 Federal
6 City Bayview	13 Grand Continental
7 Continental	14 Hang Cheow

15 Hong Ping
16 Malaysia
17 Merchant
18 Mingood
19 Oriental
20 Paramount
21 Peking

Northern Peninsula

The **Goddess of Mercy Temple**, also known as Kuan Yin Teng, on Jalan Kapitan Kling Mosque/Lorong Steward is a short walk from St George's, in the heart of Georgetown. It was built at the beginning of the 1800s by the island's early Chinese immigrants. Kuan Yin is probably the most worshipped of all the Chinese deities, and is revered by Buddhists, Taoists and Confucians. The goddess is a Bodhisattva, one who rejected entry into nirvana as long as there was injustice in the world. The goddess is associated with peace, good fortune and fertility, which accounts for her popularity. Kuan Yin is portrayed as a serene goddess with 18 arms; two arms are considered inadequate to rid the world of suffering. The roof tops are carved to represent waves, on which stand two guardian dragons. Shops in the area sell temple-related goods: lanterns, provisions for the after life (such as paper Mercedes'), joss sticks and figurines.

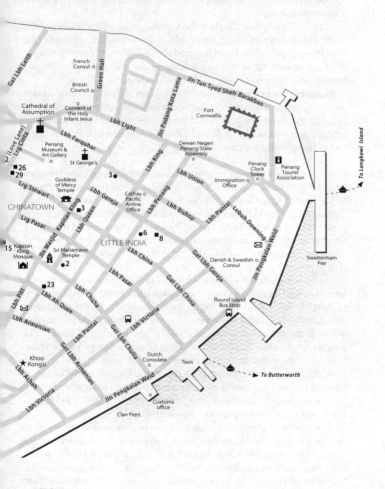

Although Georgetown is mainly Chinese, it has always had a large population of Indians, living in the city centre. The Hindu **Sri Mariamann Temple**, on Lebuh Queen/Lebuh Chulia, was built in 1883. It is richly decorated and dedicated to the Hindu god Lord Subramaniam. The main statue is strung with gold, silver, diamond and emerald jewellery. It is normally used to lead a chariot procession to the Waterfall Temple during Thaipusam (see page 50). The symbols of the nine planets and the signs of the zodiac are carved into the ceiling. The surrounding area is largely Indian, with money changers and jewellery shops, as well as restaurants and tea-stalls.

There is also a Muslim community in Georgetown and the Indo-Moorish **Kapitan Kling Mosque** (on Jalan Kapitan Kling Mosque) was built by the island's first Indian Muslim settlers around 1800. It was named after the 'kapitan' or headman of the Kling – the South Indian community. As a sight it is rather disappointing.

Straight down Lebuh Chulia is the Chinese water village off Pengkalan Weld. The entrance is through the temple on the quayside. It is known as the **Clan Piers**, as each of the jetties is named after a different Chinese clan. None of the families pays tax as they are not living on land. Rows of junks belonging to the resident traders are moored at the end of the piers.

Armenian Street is worth a wander as this area of the city is being remodelled and conserved because of its historical value; you can see the house of the rich Arab merchant who constructed the mosque opposite the park and a bit further down the road the traditional Chinese house where Dr Sun Yat Sen is said to have planned the Canton uprising.

Khoo Kongsi Located on Jalan Acheh, off Lebuh Pitt, Khoo Kongsi is approached through an archway to Cannon Square, and is one of the most interesting sights in Georgetown. A *kongsi* is a Chinese clan house which doubles as a temple and a meeting place. Clan institutions originated in China as associations for people with the same surname. Today they are benevolent organizations which look after the welfare of clan members and safeguard ancestral shrines. Most of the kongsis in Penang were established in the 19th century when clashes between rival clans were commonplace.

The Khoo Kongsi is the most lavishly decorated of the kongsis in Penang, with its ornate Dragon Mountain Hall. It was built in 1898 by the descendants of Hokkien-born Khoo Chian Eng. A fire broke out in it the day it was completed, destroying its roof. It was rebuilt by craftsmen from China and was renovated in the 1950s; the present tiled roof is said to weigh 25 tonnes. The kongsi contains many fine pieces of Chinese art and sculpture, including two huge carved stone guardians which ensure the wealth, longevity and happiness of all who came under the protection of the kongsi. The interior hall houses an image of Tua Sai Yeah, the Khoo clan's patron saint, who was a general during the Ch'in Dynasty in the second century BC. ■ *0900-1700 Mon-Fri, 0900-1300 Sat, admission pass from adjoining office.*

There are other kongsis in Georgetown, although none is as impressive as the Khoo Kongsi. The Chung Keng Kwee Kongsi is on Lebuh Gereja and the Tua Peh Kong Kongsi on Lebuh Armenian. The Khaw Kongsi and the modern Lee Kongsi are both on Jalan Burmah; Yap Kongsi on Lebuh Armenian and the combined kongsi of the Chuah, Sin and Quah clans at the junction of Jalan Burmah and Codrington Avenue. Every kongsi has ancestral tablets as well as a hall of fame to honour its 'sons' or clansmen who have achieved fame in various spheres of life. Today women are honoured in these halls of fame too.

Near the Khoo Kongsi, on Jalan Acheh, is the **Malay Mosque**. Its most noteworthy feature is the Egyptian-style minaret – most in Malaysia are

Moorish. In the past it was better known as the meeting place for the notorious White Flag Malays, who sided with the Hokkien Chinese in street battles against the Cantonese (Red Flags) in the Penang Riots of 1867. The hole half-way up the minaret is said to have been made by a cannonball fired from Khoo Kongsi during the clan riots. The mosque is one of the oldest buildings in Georgetown, built in 1808.

Apart from the RM850m **Penang Bridge** and several new hotels, one of the few visible architectural monuments of the 20th century is **Kompleks Tun Abdul Razak (KOMTAR)** on Jalan Penang. This cylindrical skyscraper, which houses the state government offices and a shopping centre, dominates Georgetown. There should be spectacular views of the island and across the straits to the mainland from the 58th floor, but unfortunately the windows are filthy and even if they were clean the smog usually prevents a clear view. There is also a souvenir centre here where the cost of your ticket to ascend the tower (RM5) is offset against any purchase. The viewing gallery encircles the souvenir centre and has coin-operated telescopes. There is also a licensed money changer here. ■ *1000-2200. All buses stop at Komtar.*

20th century landmarks
At 13.5 km, Penang bridge is the longest in Asia & the third longest in the world

On Jalan Burmah is **Wat Chayamangkalaram**, also known as Wat Buppharam, the largest Thai temple in Penang. It houses a 32m-long reclining Buddha, Pra Chaiya Mongkol. There is a nine-storey pagoda behind the temple. The Thais and the Burmese practise Theravada Buddhism as opposed to the Mahayana school of the Chinese. Queen Victoria gave this site to Penang's Thai community in 1845. Opposite Wat Chayamang-kalaram is Penang's only **Burmese temple**. It has ornate carvings and two huge white stone elephants at its gates. The original 1805 pagoda (to the right of the entrance) has been enshrined in a more modern structure. ■ *Getting there: city bus 2 from Lebuh Victoria terminal.*

Outside the town centre

The **Penang Buddhist Association** is at 182 Jalan Burmah. The Buddha statues are carved from Carrara marble from Italy, the glass chandeliers were made in what was Czechoslovakia and there are paintings depicting the many stages of the Buddha's path to enlightenment. Next door at No 184 is a 1960s Art Deco style building which is a clan hall for the Lee family. Both buildings lie opposite the Chinese recreational club, which is presided over by a statue of Queen Victoria. ■ *Getting there: city bus 202 from Lebuh Victoria terminal.*

Cheong Fatt Tze Mansion, on Lebuh Leith, is now a state monument. Built by Thio Thiaw Siat, a Kwangtung (Guandong) businessman who imported craftsmen from China, this stately home is one of only three surviving Chinese mansions in this style; the others are in Manila and Medan. It has become famous as 'Penang's most foremost restoration project'. ■ *Fully guided restoration tours every Mon, Wed, Fri, Sat at 1100. RM10. T4751227.*

Other sights in & around Georgetown

Jalan Sultan Ahmed Shah (previously Northam Road Mansions) became known as millionaires' row as it was home to many wealthy rubber planters in the wake of the boom of 1911-20. Many of the palatial mansions were built by Straits Chinese in a sort of colonial baroque style, complete with turrets and castellations. Many of them have now gone to seed as they are too expensive to keep up; a few have been lavishly done up by today's generation of rich Chinese businessmen. The largest houses are the Yeap family mansion, known as the White House, and the Sultan of Kedah's palace.

Excursions

Around the Island From Georgetown, the round-island trip is a 70 km circuit. It is recommended as a day trip as there is little or no accommodation available outside Georgetown apart from the north coast beaches.

Batu Ferringhi and **Teluk Bahang** see page 172. The **Butterfly Farm** is close enough to Georgetown to visit in one day using public transport. See page 174.

The **Nattukotai Chettiar Temple** on Waterfall Road was built by members of the Indian Chettiar money-lending fraternity and is the biggest Hindu temple on the island. It is a centre of pilgrimage during the Thaipusam festival (see page 50). ■ *Getting there: city bus 7 from Lebuh Victoria terminal; get off at the stop before the Botanical Gardens.*

The Botanical Gardens, also on Waterfall Road, are situated in a valley surrounded by hills 8 km from Georgetown. The gardens are well landscaped and contain many indigenous and exotic plant species. They were established in 1844. The more interesting plants are kept under lock and key and are open to visitors 0700-1900 Monday-Friday. A path leads from the Gardens' Moon Gate up Penang Hill; the 8 km hike takes about 1½ hours. ■ *Daylight hours Mon-Sun. Getting there: city bus 7 from Lebuh Victoria terminal.*

The absence of a paved road up Penang Hill means that its essential qualities of seclusion & peace have been preserved on an island otherwise battered by the forces of commercialism

Penang Hill A short distance from Kek Lok Si is the funicular railway, which started operating in 1922. It climbs 850m up Penang Hill and leaves every 30 minutes 0630-2330. A vintage steam engine is on display at the Penang Museum. The railway was originally completed in 1899, but on its inauguration by the governor it didn't work and had to be dismantled. Penang Hill is about 5°C cooler than Georgetown and was a favoured expatriate refuge before the advent of air conditioning. Indeed, it was the first colonial hill station developed on Peninsular Malaysia. The ridge on top of Penang Hill is known as Strawberry Hill after Francis Light's strawberry patch. On a clear day it is possible to see the mountains of Langkawi and North Kedah from the top.

Penang Hill

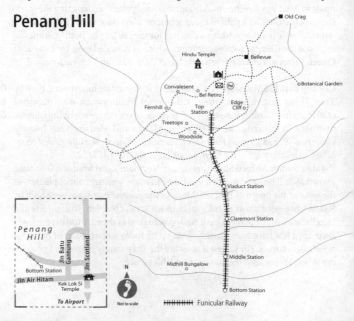

Bel Retiro, designed as a get-away for the governor, was the first bungalow to be built on the hill. There is a small hotel (**B** *Bellevue*, T8299500, F8292052, spectacular views), some pleasant gardens, a temple, a mosque and a post office and police station on the top. There are also a few restaurants and a small hawker centre. The hill gets very crowded on weekends and public holidays. A well marked 8 km path leads down to the Moon Gate at the Botanical Gardens (about an hour's walk) from between the post office and the police station; a steep but delightful descent, with plenty of places to sit along the way. The hill supports the last relic patch of tropical rainforest on Penang and as such is deemed of considerable natural value. The flora and fauna here have been protected since 1960.

In September 1990 a memorandum of understanding was signed between the Penang State Government and the company *Bukit Pinang Leisure* which proposed to build a waterworld, two large hotels, an adventure park and 'Summit Acropolis'. Although the more extreme elements of the proposal were later dropped following sharply negative public reaction, there remain fears that future development could radically transform Penang Hill. ■ *Getting there: city bus 130,101 (from Lebuh Victoria terminal), to Kek Lok Si, then bus 8 to the railway. Funicular is RM4 return.*

State Mosque, Jalan Ayer Itam/Jalan Masjid Negeri, is the largest and newest mosque in Penang and can accommodate 5,000. It was designed by a Filipino architect. There are good views from the top of the 57m-high minaret. ■ *Getting there: city bus 1 from Lebuh Victoria terminal.*

Bat Temple at Ayer Itam, is a sanctuary for fruit bats, which hang from the cave roof. The sacred bats are zealously protected by Buddhist monks. About 60 years ago the wealthy Madam Lim Chooi Yuen, built the bat temple to protect the bats. ■ *Getting there: city bus 1 from Lebuh Victoria terminal.*

Ayer Itam Dam is a pleasant place to relax just above the town. There are several trails around the lake, originally shortcuts to other parts of the island. ■ *Getting there: city bus 1 (from Lebuh Victoria terminal) then change to 8.*

Kek Lok Si Temple (or Monastery of Supreme Bliss), south of Ayer Itam, can be seen from some distance away. It took Burmese, Chinese and Thai artisans, who were shipped in specially, two decades to build it. The abbot of the Goddess of Mercy Temple on Lebuh Pitt came from China in 1885 and the landscape around Ayer Itam reminded him of his homeland. He collected money from rich Chinese merchants to fund the construction of the huge temple, modelled on Fok San Monastery in Fuchow, China. On the way up the 'ascending plane' is a pond for turtles, which are a symbol of eternity.

The temple sprawls across 12 hectares and is divided into three main sections: the Hall of Bodhisattvas, the Hall of Devas and the sacred Hall of the Buddha. The seven-tier pagoda, or Ban Po, the Pagoda of a Thousand Buddhas, is built in three different styles: the lower follows a Chinese design honouring the Goddess of Mercy, Kuan Yin; the middle is Thai-Buddhist and commemorates Bee Lay Hood (the Laughing Buddha) and the upper Burmese levels are dedicated to the Gautama or historic Buddha with thousands of gilded statues. The topmost tier contains a relic of the Buddha, a statue of pure gold and other treasures, but it is closed to visitors. All pretty tacky stuff and more than half the complex has been turned into a shopping centre. ■ *0900-1800, free, voluntary contribution to climb the 30m-high tower. Getting there: city bus 1 from Lebuh Victoria terminal, bus numbers 1, 91, 101, 85, minibus 84, 21.*

Penang Bird Park, on Jalan Todak, Seberang Jaya (7 km from the Penang Bridge), includes a rusty walk-in aviary. Very run down, disappointing. ■ *0900-1900 daily, adult RM4, child RM2, T3991899. Getting there: yellow bus 65 from Pengkalan Weld (Weld Quay).*

Universiti Sains Malaysia Museum and Gallery is at Minden near the Penang Bridge interchange. It has a large ethnographic and performing arts sections with a special exhibition on *wayang kulit* (shadow puppets – see page 548). There is also an art gallery with works by Malaysian artists and visiting temporary exhibitions. ■ *0900-1700 Mon-Sun. Getting there: yellow bus 65 from Pengkalan Weld (Weld Quay).*

Snake Temple, also known as Temple of the Azure Cloud, was built in 1850 at Bayan Lepas 12 km from Georgetown. Snakes were kept in the temple as they were believed to be the disciples of the deity Chor Soo Kong, to whom the temple is dedicated. The temple was built as the result of a donation from a Scotsman, David Brown, after he was cured by a local priest of an 'incurable disease', using local medicines. Nowadays the reptilian disciples (almost exclusively Wagler's pit vipers) are a bit thin on the ground. The number of snakes in the temple varies from day to day – there are usually more around during festivals. The incense smoke keeps them in a drugged stupor, and most of them have had their fangs extracted. Photographs with (defanged) snakes can be posed for in a new annex next door to the temple (RM4). ■ *0700-1900, RM1. Getting there: yellow bus 66, minibus 32 from Pengkalan Weld (Weld Quay).*

Batu Maung is a Chinese fishing village near Bayan Lepas and is known for its 'floating' seafood restaurant, built out over the water. To get there, take a yellow 69 bus. Around the south coast, there are a few beaches and a couple of unremarkable fishing kampungs. The southern beaches are more secluded than the ones along the north coast; the drawbacks are the absence of accommodation and the litter. Veering north towards the centre of the island, however, beyond Barat, is **Balik Pulau**, a good *makan* stop with a number of restaurants and cafés. Around the town, which is known as the Durian capital of Penang, there are a number of picturesque Malay kampungs. Further up the west side of the island is the **Pantai Acheh Forest Reserve**, which also has well marked trails into the jungle and to the bays further round; for example, Pantai Keracut (one hour). After the Pantai Acheh junction, and on up a twisting, forested section of road, there is a waterfall with a pleasant pool, suitable for swimming, just off the road (twentieth milestone), called **Titi Kerawang**. ■ *Getting there: yellow buses 11 or 66 go from Pengkalan Weld (Weld Quay) or Jalan Maxwell in Georgetown to the south of the island. Change at Balik Pulau to bus 76 for Teluk Bahang. From there blue bus 93 to Georgetown.*

Longer fare stages cost anything up to RM1.50. As the island buses are infrequent, it is advisable to check departure times at each place to avoid being stranded. It is much easier to explore the kampungs and beaches around the south and west coasts – most of which are off the main road – if you have private transport. Most of them are off the main road.

The Bukit Jambul Orchid and Hibiscus and Reptile Garden is found along Persiaran Bukit Jambul, close to the *Hotel Equatorial* and five minutes' drive from the airport. As its name suggests, it specializes in orchids and hibiscus. There is also a reptile house here. ■ *0930-1830 daily. Snake show on Sat, Sun, public holidays at 1130 and 1530. RM4 for adults, RM1 for children.*

Essentials

AL *Berjaya Georgetown Hotel*, T2277111, F2267111. One of the newest luxury hotels in Georgetown, 330 rooms, part of one-stop Midland Park Complex. All the usual amenities: swimming pool, health centre, several restaurants, business centre. **AL** *Shangri-La*, Jln Magazine, T2622622, F2626526. A/c, restaurant, pool, small fitness centre, mostly used by business people rather than tourists, next to KOMTAR. Late check-out (1800), good conference facilities. **AL-A** *Sheraton*, 3 Jln Larut, T2267888, F2266615. Five-star hotel with 280 rooms. Special facilities in rooms include direct fax line, electronic safe, iron, newly opened. For those who get really hungry there is a 24-hr restaurant.

Sleeping
■ *on map, page 158*
Price codes:
see inside front cover
In Georgetown, most
upmarket hotels are
concentrated in the Jln
Penang area. Most
cheaper hotels are
around Lebuh Chulia &
Lebuh Leith

A-B *Agora*, 202a Lorong Mcalister, T2266060, F2265959. Formerly *Ming Court*, 2 restaurants, two karaoke lounges, pool. Very good deal. **A** *City Bayview Hotel*, 25a Lebuh Farquhar, T2633161, F2634124. A/c, restaurant, pool, revolving restaurant and bar on 14th floor, shabby rooms with uncomfortable beds. Price includes breakfast. **A** *Eastern & Oriental (E&O)*, 10 Farquhar St, T2630630, F2634833. A/c, restaurant, pool, built in 1885 by the Armenian Sarkies brothers, who operated Singapore's *Raffles Hotel* (see page 583) and the *Strand Hotel* in Rangoon (Yangon), Noel Coward and Somerset Maugham figured on former guest lists. Friendly but tatty and not at all up to the standard of the *Raffles Hotel*. **A** *Equatorial International*, 1 Jln Bukit Jambal, T6438111, F6448000, info@pen.equatorial.com. A/c, restaurant, between the airport and town, on a hill with a view over the Penang Bridge, mostly used by visiting business people as it is conveniently located for Penang's duty-free industrial zone, which lies between it and the airport. A monstrous block of 400 plus rooms with good sports facilities and adjacent 18-hole golf course. **A-B** *Garden Inn*, 41 Jln Anson, T2263655. A/c, restaurant, good hawker centre on the doorstep. **A-B** *Grand Continental*, 68 Brick Kiln Rd (Jln Gurdwara), T2636688, F2630299. A/c, restaurant, pool, health club, coffee lounge, massage centre, karaoke lounge. Good value. **A** *Malaysia*, 7 Jln Penang, T2633311, F2631621. A/c, restaurant, dated high-rise hotel, plush décor with coffee house, disco, health centre. **A-B** *Sunway*, 33 New Lane, T2299988, F2292033, allson@po.jaring.my. Pleasant décor, good facilities in rooms, a/c, TV, pulsating shower, in-house video, iron, fridge, complimentary tea/coffee, pool, jacuzzi, restaurant, tea-house, pub, tennis and squash arranged. Breakfast included, not much character but great value for money.

B *Bellevue*, Penang Hill, T8299600. A/c, restaurant, colonial-style house, cool retreat up on the hill. **B** *Cathay*, 15 Lebuh Leith, T2626271. A/c, large old Chinese house, scrupulously maintained, organizes minibuses to Hat Yai and Phuket (Thailand), coffee shop, not particularly good value. Their 'Health Care' annex is a euphemism for their (Chinese) brothel. **B** *Cititel*, 66 Jln Penang, T3701188, F3702288, email@ cititel-pen.com.my. Breakfast included, 24 hr café, Chinese and Japanese restaurants, sports bar with electronic darts and video games. Recommended. **B** *Continental*, 5 Jln Penang, T2636388, F2638718. A/c, restaurant, 18 storeys with great views from higher rooms. Very comfortable. **B-C** *Merchant*, 55 Jln Penang, T2632828, F2625511. A/c, restaurant, handsomely decorated, smart marble lobby, a/c, TV, in-house video, mini bar, coffee house, trishaws for hire RM15 per hour. Good value. **B** *Mid Towne*, 101 Jln Mcalister, T2269999, F2295146. New hotel, not very central but good value, actually situated out of town, does not stand out. **B** *Mingood*, 164 Argyle Rd, T2299922, F2292210. A/c, restaurant, not good value for money. **B** *Oriental*, 105 Jln Penang, T2634211/6. A/c, restaurant, dated décor, big rooms and good value, welcoming staff, well located with good views from the upper floors. Recommended. **B** *Seri Malaysia*, off Jln Mayang Pasir I, Bandar Bayan Baru, T6429452, F6429461. Chain budget hotel.

Northern Peninsula

C *Embassy*, 12 Jln Burmah, T2267515. A/c, restaurant. Some hot water showers. Spacious rooms with old décor. **C** *Federal*, 39 Jln Penang, T2634170. Good location, near some excellent restaurants, recently revamped, although style is still 1920s, nothing special. **C** *Paramount*, 48F Jln Sultan Ahmad Shah, T2273649. A/c, restaurant, big rooms in run-down colonial house, right on the sea, but not central. Recommended. **C** *Peking*, 50a Jln Penang, T2636191. Once a luxury hotel, now very run-down, a/c, bath, TV. Antiquated, but large rooms. **C** *Towne House*, 70 Jln Penang, T2638621. Chocolate brown and cream block, features an automatic massage chair in lobby, 50 sen, a/c, restaurant, TV, fridge, dingy but good value for money. **C** *Waldorf*, 13 Leith St, T2626140. A/c, bath, dated décor but good value. **C** *YMCA*, 211 Jln Macalister, T2288211. A/c, fan only rooms (**D**).

D *Blue Diamond*, 422 Lebuh Chulia, T2611089. Restaurant, fan, Chinese nationalist General Chiang Kai Shek once took refuge here, spacious rooms, bar and cheap restaurant downstairs. RM30 with shower, RM25 without. **D** *Broadway Hostel*, 35f Jln Masjid Kapitan Kling, T2628550, F2619525. Clean and basic, some a/c (**D**), dorm (**F**), one of the best budget options. **D** *D'Budget Hostel*, 9 Lebuh Gereja, T2634794. Some a/c, roof terrace, laundry, money changer, tea-making, TV, hot water shower, near Medan ferry, clean but sterile, soulless place, quiet, friendly and helpful management, dorm (**E**). **D** *Eung Aun*, 380 Lebuh Chulia, T2612333. Fan, restaurant, old house set back from the road, basic but popular with clean rooms and friendly service. **D-E** *New Asia*, 110 Jln Pintal Tali, T2613599. A/c, bar, family run. Recommended. **D** *Oasis Hotel*, 23 Love Lane, T2616778. Reasonable value – better than most on Lebuh Chulia in a less frenetic corner of town, shared bathrooms, fan and basin in room, dilapidated. Popular with backpackers, dorm bed (**F**) available. **D** *Pin Seng*, 82 Love Lane, T2619004. Original tiled floors and iron beds, fan only, run-down. Good information on local and national buses, very basic. **D** *Plaza Hostel*, 32 Lebuh Ah Quee, T2630570. Popular, clean and friendly, lockers, ticketing service (**F** dorm), small rooms, cheap laundry service available. Good budget option. **D** *Swiss*, 431 Lebuh Chulia, T2620133. A better bet than some of the others in this area, clean and quiet with friendly management, cheap breakfast, next door are motorbikes for hire – (quite cheap at RM15 per day), and good selection of books to rent or buy. Not recommended by residents. **D** *Wan Hai*, 35 Love Lane, T2616853. Fan, restaurant, run-of-the-mill budget hotel, motorcycles for hire, visa applications for Thailand and bus tickets to Thailand organized, dorm (**F**), terrace.

E-F *Eastern Hotel*, 509 Chutra Street, T2614597. Fan, small rooms, reasonable budget option. **E** *Hang Cheow*, 51 Lebuh Chulia, T2610810. Restaurant. Recommended by travellers. **E** *Hong Ping*, 273B, Lebuh Chulia, above *Coco Island* restaurant, T2625234. A/c, private bath, TV, bare but quiet rooms. **E** *Nam Wah*, 381 Lebuh Chulia, T2610557, old building with character but very basic. **E** *Yeng Keng*, 362 Lebuh Chulia, T2610610. Central but basic, good-sized rooms but hotel is very run down.

Eating
● *on map, page 158*
Price codes:
see inside front cover

Penang's specialities include *assam laksa* (a hot-and-sour fish soup), *nasi kandar* (a curry), *mee yoke* (prawns in chilli-noodle soup) and *inche kabin* (chicken marinated in spices and then fried).

Best from the stalls

Malay 3 *Eliza*, 14th Flr, *City Bayview Hotel*, 25a Lorong Farquhar, sumptuous menu eaten in traditional style, seated on pandan mats, good views over the town and coast. **2** *Nazir*, 4th level, KOMTAR. **2** *Hot Wok*, Desa Tanjung, 125D Jln Tanjung Tokong, Nyonya and local cuisine in a recreated shop house. Recommended. **1** *Spice Café*, 55 Jln Penang (next to *Merchant Hotel*), excellent choice of local food, with Malay, Chinese, Thai and some international.

Chinese 4 *Shang Palace*, *Shangri La Hotel*, Hong Kong *dim sum* brunch, Cantonese dishes. 3 *Dragon King*, 99 Leboh Bishop, recommended by travellers. 3 *Goh Huat Seng*, 59A Lebuh Kimberley, Teochew cuisine, best known for its steamboats. 3 *Tower Palace*, level 58-60 KOMTAR, good value *dim sum*. 2 *Ang Hoay Loh*, 60 Jln Brick Kiln, Hokkien food: specialities include glass noodles and pork and prawn soups. 2 *Lum Fong*, 108 Muntri St, lively coffee shop with an arcaded front, old wooden tables and chairs, good noodles. 2 *May Garden*, 70 Penang Rd, good food and very popular. 2 *Sin Kheng Hooi Hong*, 350 Lebuh Pantai, Hainanese cuisine, *lor bak* (crispy deep-fried seafood rolls, with sweet-and-sour plum sauce) recommended. 2 *Tropics*, *Sunway Hotel*, 33 New Lane, good value steamboat buffet. 1 *Loke Thye Kee*, 2B Jln Burmah, Hainanese cuisine, good place to try *inche kabin* – stewed marinated chicken. 1 *Potbless*, Hutton Lane, *nasi lemale*, banana leaf, steamboat.

Nyonya 2 *Dragon King*, 99 Lebuh Bishop, family-run business, probably the best Nyonya food in any of the old Straits Settlements, specializes in fish-head curry, good satay, *otak-otak*, curry Kapitan and *kiam chye boey* – a meat casserole. Recommended. 2 *Nyonya Corner*, 15 Jln Pahang, excellent *otak-otak* (fish marinated in lime and wrapped in banana leaf).

Penang & Melaka are the culinary centres of Nyonya cuisine (see page 47)

Indian Penang's 'Little India' is bounded by Lebuh Bishop, Lebuh Pasar and Lebuh King, close to the quay. There is a string of good Indian restaurants along Lebuh Penang, in this area, notably: *Murugan Vilas*, *Nava India*, *Susila* and *Veloo Vilas*. They are renowned for their banana-leaf curries. 3 *Kashmir*, base of *Oriental Hotel*, 105 Jln Penang (**NB** Not Lebuh Penang), North Indian food – usually very busy. Recommended. 3 *Madras New Woodlands Vegetarian Restaurant*, 60 Penang St, North and South Indian food, newly opened and bristling clean. 2 *Dawood*, 63 Lebuh Queen (across from Sri Mariamman Temple), Indian Muslim restaurant known for its curries, original 60s décor, Kari Kapitan (chicken curry), and duck are popular. Recommended. 2 *Kaliaman's*, 43 Lebuh Penang, one of Penang's best Indian restaurants, South Indian food at lunch, Northern Indian food in the evening, not very clean. 2 *The Tandoori House*, Lorong Hutton, nicer décor than *Kashmir* (above), evergreen North Indian specialities. 1 *Hameediyah*, 164A Lebuh Campbell, Indian Muslim food, murtabak, rotis, large portions. 1 *Kassim Mustafa*, 12 Lebuh Chulia, basic coffee shop which prides itself in cooking a handful of dishes very well, most trade done between 0500 and 1200, specialities are nasi dalcha (rice cooked with ghee and cinnamon), ayam negro and mutton kurma. Recommended. 1 *Kassim Nasi Kandar*, 2-1 Jln Brick Kiln, hot Indian Muslim food, open 24 hrs, recommended by locals. 1 *Kedai Kopi Yasmeen*, 177 Jln Penang, simple open-fronted Indian coffee shop, murtabak, roti etc. Recommended. 1 *Banana Leaf*, Lebuh Penang, about two blocks south of Lebuh Gereja. Serves excellent southern Indian food notably thali and lassi.

Indonesian 2 *Tambuah Mas*, Level 4 Komtar Tower. 1 *Nasi Padang*, 511 Lebuh Chulia.

Japanese *The City Bayview* and the *Bellevue* hotels all have Japanese restaurants. The latter serves a good steamboat (last orders 2000). 4 *Kurumaya*, 269 Burma Rd, top quality sushi and sashmi. 3 *Kong Lung*, 11c Leith St, immaculate traditional décor, teppenyaki and set lunches. Recommended. 3 *Miyabi*, 216 Jln McAlister, well established Japanese restaurant. 3 *Shin Miyako*, 105 Jln Penang (next to the *Oriental Hotel*), smart-looking restaurant, and reasonably priced for Japanese food.

3 *Annalakshmi*, Basington Avenue, T2288575, 1800-2130, serves a great vegetarian curry. 2-3 *Kashmir*, Penang road, 1200-1430, 1900-2230.

Northern Peninsula

Thai 2 *Café D'Chiangmai*, 11 Burmah Cross, serves an interesting mixture of Thai and local dishes, renowned for its fish-head curry, popular in the evenings. 2 *Thai Food Restaurant*, below *New Pathe Hotel*, Lebuh Light. 2 *Yellow Light*, 1C Jln Fettis. 3 *Coca Restaurant*, Island Plaza, 1130-2200, particularly good Thai steamboat.

International 3 *Beetle Nuts Fun Café*, 9-11 Leith St, in same old block as 20 Leith St, theme is American, tex-mex, trendy. 3 *Bella Casa*, 105a Penang Road, Georgetown. T2642030, a large choice of Italian menu. Lasagne di carne recommended. 2 *Brasserie*, *Shangri La Hotel*, Californian cuisine. 2 *Café Tower Lounge*, 59th Flr, KOMTAR, buffet lunch, good view over the city and afterwards free entrance to viewing gallery. 2 *Rainforest Restaurant*, 294a Chulia St, new sister company of *Green Planet*, popular with budget travellers, interesting scrapbooks of travellers' experiences, wide selection of food: nachos, sandwiches, steak, pizza, apple crumble (recommended), all home-cooked and no preservatives. 2 *Coco Island Café*, Lebuh Chulia, good food, popular. 2 *Eden Steak House*, Jln Hutton. 1 *Green Planet*, 63 Lebuh Cintra, a backpackers' joint serving classic travellers food. Also provides information, ticketing services, motorbike rental, hot showers, excellent food and helpful owner. *English Thai Café*, 41/b Lebuh Chulia. *Magnolia Snack Bar*, Jln Penang. *The Ship Steakhouse*. *OG Bakery*, Jln Penang. *Tye Ann Hotel*, Lebuh Chulia, recommended for breakfast.

Seafood 4 *Eden*, 11B Lorong Hutton, popular chain of restaurants, seafood and grills. 3 *Grand Garden Seafood*, 164 Jln Penang, seafood market restaurant, outside eating. 2 *Lam Kee Seafood*, next to stalls on Esplanade (Padang Kota Lama). 2 *Maple*, 106 Jln Penang (near *Oriental Hotel*), same management as *May Garden* and food is in the same league. 2 *May Garden*, 70 Penang Rd (next to *Towne House*), reckoned to be among the best seafood restaurants in Georgetown, with an aquarium full of fish and shellfish to choose from. The crab is excellent and *May Garden's* speciality is frogs' legs, fried with chilli and ginger or just crispy. Recommended. 2 *Ocean-Green*, 48F Jln Sultan Ahmad Shah (in quiet alleyway in front of *Paramount Hotel*), specialities include lobster and crab thermidor, drunken prawns and fresh frogs' legs ('paddy chicken'), lovely location, overlooking fishing boats. Recommended. 2 *Sea Palace*, 50 Jln Penang (next to *Peking Hotel*), huge menu, popular, a/c, Chinese tableware, good value. Recommended.

Coffee shops Most Chinese coffee shops are along Jln Burmah and Jln Penang, also some in the financial district along Lebuh Bishop, Lebuh Cina and Lebuh Union. *Khuan Kew* and *Sin Kuan Hwa*, both in Love Lane are particularly popular – the latter is well known for its Hainan chicken rice. The *Maxim Cakehouse and Bakery* on Penang Rd is also a popular stop. The oldest in Georgetown is the *Kek Seng* (382 Jln Penang), founded in 1906 and still serving *kway teow* soup and colourful *ais-kacangs*.

Penang's hawker stalls are renowned in Malaysia & serve some of the best food on the island. We have received reports though, that many have closed due to a public health drive

Foodstalls *Datuk Keramat Hawker Centre* (also called *Padang Brown*), junction of Anson and Perak roads, this is one of the venues for Georgetown's roving night market – possible to check if it's on by calling tourist information centre, T2614461. Recommended. *Food Court*, base of KOMTAR. *Kota Selera Hawker Centre*, next to Fort Cornwallis, off Lebuh Light. Recommended. *Lebuh Keng Kwee*, famed locally for its *cendol* stalls – cocktails of shaved ice, palm sugar and jelly topped with *gula melaka* and coconut milk. *Lebuh Kimberley* (called noodle-maker street by the Chinese), good variety of hawker food at night. *Lorong Selamat Hawker Stalls*, highly recommended by locals. *Padang Kota Lama/Jalan Tun Syed Sheh Barakbah* (Esplanade), busy in the evenings. Recommended. *Pesiaran Gurney Seawall* (Gurney Drive), long row of hawkers opposite the coffee shops, good range of Malay, Chinese and Indian food, very popular in the evenings. Recommended. There are also popular stalls along Jln Burmah, Love Lane and at Ayer Itam. Good *roti-canai* opposite *Plaza Hostel*, Lebuh Ah Quee.

Carmen's Inn, 15th Flr, *City Bayview Hotel*, 25a Farquhar St, views over the town and coast, starts turning 1700. *20 Leith St* (next to *Waldorf Hotel*), pleasant bar, building is 150 years old and many original features have been retained, pitchers of Carlsberg, satay and prawn and other light snacks. *George's*, *Sunway Hotel*, 33 New Lane, quintessentially English, live music.

Bars

Discos *Celebrity*, 48H Jln Sultan Ahmad Shah; *Hotlips Disco*, next to *Continental Hotel*; *Penny Lane*, bottom of *City Bayview Hotel*; *Xanadu Disco*, next to *Malaysia Hotel*; *Rockworld*, 1 Drury Lane (off Campbell St), high tech lighting and laser show; *Street One*, *Shangri La Hotel*, popular with air-hostesses; *Sol Fun Disco*, 6 Weld Quay, ex-warehouse, techno disco, live band, karaoke, pool, virtual reality games, bar.

Entertainment
Most of the big hotels have in-house nightclubs & discos. Expect to pay cover charges if you are not a guest

Cinemas *Cathay Cinema* on Jln Penang (between Jln Hutton and Jln Dato Koyah). *Rex Cinema*, junction of Jln Burmah and Transfer. Komtar cinema in the Komtar centre.

May *Penang Bridge Run* (end of month) open to all visitors.

Festivals

June *Penang International Dragon Boat Race*, near Penang Bridge; teams compete from around the region and beyond. *International Beach Volleyball Championship* (end); held on Kital Beach, Batu Ferringhi, next to *Bayview Beach Hotel*.

July *Penang on Parade*, with three major annual events; details from Tourist Information Centre. *Floral Festival* at KOMTAR. *City parades* by Malays (at Fort Cornwallis), Chinese (at Khoo Kongsi) and Indians (at Market Street).

September *Penang Lantern Festival* (end), parade with lanterns.

November *Deepavali Open House*, festivities in Little India.

This requires a lot of wandering around the narrow streets & alleyways off Jln Penang. Main areas are Jln Penang, Jln Burmah and Lebuh Campbell.

Shopping

Antiques An export licence is still required for non-imported goods. Shops on and around Jln Penang with the best ones at the top end opposite *Eastern and Oriental Hotel*, such as the *Oriental Arts Co*, 3f Penang Rd. Also antique shops along Rope Walk (Jln Pintal Tali). Most stock antiques from Burma, Thailand, Indonesia, Malaysia, Sabah and Sarawak, as well as a few local bargains. *Eastern Curios*, 35 Lebuh Bishop. *Kuan Antique*, 7A Aboo Sitee Lane. *Penang Antique House*, 27 Jln Patani, showcase of Peranakan (Straits Chinese) artefacts – porcelain, rosewood with mother-of-pearl inlay, Chinese embroideries and antique jewellery. *Saw Joo Aun*, 139 Rope Walk (Jln Pintal Tali), the best in a row of similar shops.

Art galleries Georgetown has a College of Art and Music, housed in a grand colonial building on Leith St. Exhibitions are occasionally on view in the College Gallery (7 Leith St, T2618087). Other galleries in Georgetown include *The Art Gallery*, 36B Burmah Rd, T2298219; *Galerie Mai*, 54 Tung Hing Building, Jln Burmah, T377504. *Yahong Art Gallery*, Batu Ferrenghi, T8811093, 0930-2100, which has a variety of batik exhibits.

Basketry There are several shops along Jln Penang, around junction with Jln Burmah.

Batik *Asia Co*, 314 Jln Penang. *Maphilindo Baru*, 217 Penang Rd, excellent range of batiks and sarongs (including songket) from Malaysia, Sumatra and Java. *Sam's Batik House*, 159 Jln Penang. *Yuyi Batik House*, Level 3, Kompleks Tun Abdul Razak (KOMTAR), Jln Penang. Factory outlet in Teluk Bahang and souvenir shops in Batu Ferringhi.

Books There are several bookshops in Lebuh Chulia near *Swiss Hotel* which sell second-hand books. *Yasin Bookshop*, 417a Lebuh Chulia. *Parvez Book Store*, 419 Lebuh

Chulia (as well as dealing in books they arrange Thai visas and trips, and car/motor-bike hire). *HS Sam Bookstore*, 144 Lebuh Chulia, prides itself on being well organized and runs a side-line in travel services: Thai visas, bus ticketing, car/bike rental and has a luggage storage. *MPH Bookstore*, Island Plaza, Jln Tanjong Tokong. *Times Bookshop*, Penang Plaza, 1st Flr, 126 Burmah Rd. *Popular Bookshop*, Arked Ria 2, KOMTAR Tower and at Midland Park Complex, Jln Burmah; reasonable selection in Yaohan Department Store in KOMTAR.

Camping gear *Tye Yee Seng Canvas*, 162 Chulia St, good stock of tents, rucksacks, sleeping bags and beach umbrellas.

Cassettes, electrical and photographic equipment Jln Campbell, Jln Penang.

CD Roms Fakes available from *Midland Park Complex*, 6th Flr, Jln Burmah.

Curios and unusual bargains *Lebuh Chulia*, Bishop and Rope Walk (Jln Pintal Tali). Many of the curios are imported from China and are very well priced. There is a good selection at *Tan Embroidery Co*, 20 Lebuh Pantai.

Food shops There are a number of outlets, mostly Chinese-run in Georgetown selling locally produced specialities. Dragon Ball biscuits, pastry balls filled with a mung bean paste are made by *Wee Ling*, 132 Chulia St. Similar products, including *pong pneah* (pastry filled with molasses or caramel) are made at *Him Heang*, 162 Jln Burmah. For a selection of unusual pre-packaged products, such as dried mango, jackfruit, nutmeg oil and coconut cookies go to one of the large, a/c outlets of *Cap Jempol Tropiks*, either at 17 Leith St (next to *Cathay Hotel*), or 50c Penang Rd (next to *Peking Hotel*). Chinese teas and ginseng in a variety of forms are the speciality of *Eu Yan Sang*, 156 Chulia St, who offer herb-boiling service in a cauldron that bubbles inside the doorway.

Handicrafts Jln Penang is a good place to start with *Peking Arts & Crafts* at 3b, *Federation Arts & Crafts* at 3c, and *China Handicraft Co* at 3d. *See Koon Hoe*, 315 Lebuh Chulia sells Chinese opera masks, jade seals and paper umbrellas; *The Mah Jong Factory* in Love Lane sells high-quality Mah Jong sets. *Arts and Culture Information Centre*, T2642273, 1200-1400 Thu to Sat.

Jewellery Lebuh Campbell and Lebuh Kapitan Klang.

Markets Penang's night market (1900-2300) changes locations every fortnight. To check venue, call Tourist Information Centre (T2614461) or refer to the Penang Diary column in the daily newspapers.

Shopping complexes *Midland Park*, Jln Burmah, opposite Adventist Hospital, amusement arcades, roller skating, bowling alley, several fast-food outlets, hawker food. *Popular Bookshop* and CD Rom shops. *Island Plaza*, Jln Tanjung Tokong, on road to Batu Ferringhi, upmarket shops – *East India Company, Guess, Fila, Coca Restaurant*, the *Forum*, a Food Court and a new cinema. *Bukit Jambul Shopping Complex*, close to the airport, good range of shops, food outlets and an ice-rink. *KOMTAR*, hundreds of boutiques, two department stores, fast-food restaurants, amusement arcade.

Supermarkets *Gama*, behind the KOMTAR Tower is excellent for stocking up on basics.

Watches Reasonable quality fakes from by the Snake Temple (see page 164).

Bowling alley *Midland Park Complex*, Jln Burmah. **Golf** *Airforce Golf Club*, Butterworth, T3322632, 9-hole course, green fees weekdays RM20, weekends RM30. *Bukit Jambul Golf & Country Club*, Jln Bukit Jambul, T6442255, hilly course, green fees weekdays RM100, weekends RM150. *Indoor Golf Club*, Level 56, KOMTAR building. *Penang Turf Club*, Golf Section, Jln Batu Gantong, T2266701, 18-hole, RM84 weekdays, RM126 weekends. *Kristal Golf Resort*, Jln Valdor, Seberang Perai Selatan, T5822280, green fees weekdays RM105, weekends RM150. *Penang Golf Resort*, Lot 2462, Mk6, Jln Bertram, 13200 Kepala Bates. T5782002, F5750226. **Horse racing** *Penang Turf Club*, Jln Batu Gantung, every 2 months. **Ice rink** *Bukit Jambul Shopping Complex*, close to the airport, RM12 for 2 hrs (skate rental extra). **Roller skating** *Midland Park Complex*, Jln Burmah. **Swimming** *Chinese Swimming Club*, between Tanung Bunga and Georgetown (about 8 km from the city). Admission RM2. Open 0900-2045 Mon-Sun. *Swimwell*, 192 Jln Burmah, T2291932.

Everrise Tours & Travel, Lot 323, 2nd Flr, Wisma Central, 202 Jln, T2264329; *Georgetown Tourist Service*, Jln I, T2295788 city island tours; *MSL Travel*, Ming Court Inn Lobby, Jln Macalister, T2272655 or 340 Lebuh Chulia, T2616154, student and youth travel bureau; *MS Star Travel Agencies*, 475 Lebuh Chulia, T2622906. For all your travelling needs. *Tour and Incentive Travel*, 76 7th Flr Menara BHL, T2274522.

Sports

Tour operators
Most of the budget travel agents are along Lebuh Chulia

NB Butterworth is the railway stop for Georgetown and Penang; taxis also tend to terminate there, with local taxis making the run across the bridge to the island; long distance taxis will however cross the bridge for an extra charge.

Transport
See also Ins & outs, page 152

Local Bicycle hire: rental from the *Eng Ann Hotel* or *Swiss Hotel*, both on Lebuh Chulia, RM20 per day.

Bus: city buses leave from Lebuh Victoria near the Butterworth ferry terminal and serve Georgetown and the surrounding districts. Green, yellow and blue buses leave for various points around the island from Pengkalan Weld (Weld Quay) – next to the ferry terminal or Jln Maxwell. No. 83 will take you the airport; nos. 101 or 130 towards Penang Hill but you will need to change to No. 8 near your arrival. No 78 will take you to the Snake Temple; and No. 93 to the northern beaches. Blue buses go west along the north coast to Tanjung Bungah, Batu Ferringhi and Teluk Bahang. Green buses head towards the centre of the island to Ayer Itam area. Yellow buses go south (including Snake Temple and Bayan Lepas Airport), and then up the west side to Teluk Bahang. Prices from RM0.60 to RM0.90.

Car hire: *Avis*, Bayan Lepas Airport, T6439633, *Rasa Sayang Hotel* Lobby, T8811522; *Budget*, 28 Jln Penang, T6436025 and Bayan Lepas Airport; *Hawk Rent-a-car* T8813886. *Hertz*, 38 Lebuh Farquhar, T2635914 and Bayan Lepas Airport; *National Car Rental*, 17 Lebuh Leith, T2629404; *Orix*, City Bayview Hotel, 25A Lebuh Farquhar, T2618608; *Ruhanmas*, 76 Batu Ferringhi, T8811023; *SMAS*, Bayan Lepas Airport, T6452288; *Thrifty*, Bayan Lepas Airport, T6430958; *Tomo*, 386A, 1st Flr Wayton Court, Jln Burmah, T22665636.

Motorcycle hire: in Georgetown there are several motorbike rental shops, many of them along Lebuh Chulia. Cost: from about RM20 per day depending on size; most are Honda 70s.

Taxi: taxi stands on Jln Dr Lim Chwee Leong, Pengkalan Weld and Jln Magazine. Fares are not calculated by meter, so agree a price before you set off; short distances within the city cost RM3-6. A trip to the airport costs RM10-12. Radio taxis: T2625721 (at ferry terminal); *C T Radio Taxi Service*, T2299467/ 2262441. **Trishaw**: bicycle rickshaws that carry 2 people are one of the most practical and enjoyable ways to explore Georgetown. Cost RM1 per half mile or RM15 per hour; if taking an hour's trip around town, agree on the route first, bargain and set the price in advance.

Transport to Penang: for details on transport to Penang, see page 177.

Directory **Airline offices** *Cathay Pacific*, AIA Building, Lebuh Farquhar, T2260411. *MAS*, Kompleks Tun Abdul Razak (KOMTAR), Jln Penang, T2620011 (the ticket office is on the ground floor, at the southern side of KOMTAR, and can only be entered from outside the complex) or at the airport T6430811. *Pelangi Airways*, unit 249, 2nd floor, Penang Plaza, 126 Jln Burma, T2277311, F2274897. *Singapore Airlines*, Wisma Penang Gardens, 42 Jln Sultan Ahmad Shah, T2263201. *Thai International*, Wisma Central, 202 Jln Macalister, T2296250, *Air Asia* T2629882, *Cathay Pacific* T2260411, *Emirates* T2631100, *United* T2636020.

Banks Most banks in Georgetown are around the GPO area and Lebuh Pantai. Most money changers are in the banking area and Jln Masjid Kapitan Keling and Lebuh Pantai, close to the Immigration Office. *Bank Bumiputra*, 37 Lebuh Pantai; *Citibank*, 42 Jln Sultan Ahmad Shah; *Hong Kong Bank*, Lebuh Pantai; *Maybank*, 9 Lebuh Union; *Standard Chartered*, 2 Lebuh Pantai. *Hong Kong Bank* issues Thomas Cook TCs and gives cash advances against Visa cards.

Communications Area code: 04. **General Post Office:** Lebuh Pitt, efficient poste restante, also provides a parcel-wrapping service. T2618973. **Telecoms office (international calls; fax and telex facilities):** Jln Burmah.

Embassies & consulates *Denmark*, Bernam Agencies, Hong Kong Bank Chambers, Lebuh Downing, T2624886; *France*, 82 Bishop St, Wisma Rajab, T2629707; *Germany*, Bayan Lepas Free Trade Zone, T6415707; *Indonesia*, 467 Jln Burmah, T2274686; *Japan*, 2 Jln Biggs, T2268222; *Netherlands*, Algemen Bank Nederland, 9 Lebuh Pantai, T2616471; *Thailand*, 1 Jln Ayer Raja, T2268029 (visas arranged in 2 days); *UK*, Birch House, 73 Jln Datuk Keramat, T2625333.

Libraries *Penang Public Library*, Dewan Sri Pinang, Lebuh Light, T2622255. *The British Council*, T2630330.

Medical facilities Hospitals: *General Hospital* (government), Jln Residensi, T2293333; *Lam Wah Ee Hospital* (private), 141 Jln Batu Lancang, T6571888.

Places of worship *St George's Church*, Lebuh Farquhar, services in English 0830 and 1830 every Sun.

Tourist offices *Penang Tourist Centre*, Penang Port Commission Building, Jln Tun Syed Sheikh Barakbah (off Victoria Clocktower roundabout, opposite Fort Cornwallis), T2616663; Open weekdays 0830-1630 (closed 1300-1400), Sat 0830-1300. Closed Sun. *Tourism Malaysia Northern Regional Office*, 10 Jln Tun Syed Sheh Barakbah, round the corner from the Penang Tourist Association (above), T2620066; *Tourist Information Centre*, 3rd Flr, KOMTAR Tower, Jln Penang, T2614461, also branch at Batu Ferringhi, outside *Eden Seafood Village* and at Bayan Lepas Airport (T6430501), the information centre has a list of tour companies in Georgetown. Open 0900-1700 daily.

Useful addresses Immigration Office: on the corner of Lebuh Light and Lebuh Pantai, T2615122.

Batu Ferringhi and Teluk Bahang

Colour map 1, grid B1 The main beach, Batu Ferringhi, whose hot white sands were once the nirvana of Western hippies, has been transformed into an upmarket tropical version of the Costa Brava. There are now at least 10 hotels along the beach strip and graf-fiti are splashed across the famous Foreigner's Rock. *Ferringhi* – which is related to the Thai word *farang*, or foreigner – actually means 'Portuguese' in Malay. Portuguese Admiral Albuquerque, who captured Melaka in 1511, stopped off at Batu Ferringhi for fresh water on his way down the Straits. St Francis Xavier is said to have visited Batu Ferringhi in 1545. Towards the end of the 16th century, Captain James Lancaster, who later founded the East India Company in 1600, also came ashore at the beach.

To the majority of today's tourists, Batu Ferringhi *is* Penang. The beach is just over 3 km long but it has been extended to the fishing village of Teluk Bahang at the west end. Most holidaymakers and honeymooners prefer to stick to their hotel swimming pools rather than risk bathing in the sea. Pollution, siltation, and an influx of jellyfish have affected water quality, but of late, the hotels have taken much more care of the beach itself. Despite the explosion of development, Batu Ferringhi still meets most visitors' expectations. With its palms and casuarina trees and its (almost) turquoise water, it retains at least some of its picture-postcard beauty. The hotels offer many different activities: windsurfing, water skiing, diving, sailing and fishing as well as jungle walks and sightseeing tours of the island.

Apart from the string of plush modern hotels, the Batu Ferringhi area also has many excellent restaurants, hawker stalls and handicraft shops. The **Yahong Art Gallery**, 58d Batu Ferringhi Road, T8811251, F8811093, displays batik paintings by the Teng (born in China in 1914) family. The elder Teng is regarded as the father of Malaysian batik painting.

Teluk Bahang

This small fishing kampung is situated at the west end of this north stretch of beach. It is where the Malabar fishermen used to live and has now been dramatically changed by the *Penang Mutiara Beach Resort*. Beyond Teluk Bahang, around **Muka Head**, the coast is broken into a series of small secluded coves separated by rocky headlands; there are several tiny secluded beaches. Some of these are only accessible by boat, which can be hired either from the beach hotels, or from fishermen in Teluk Bahang, which is much cheaper. Trails also lead over the headland from the fishing kampung. One goes along the coast past the Universiti Malaya Marine Research Station to Mermaid Beach and Muka Head lighthouse (1½ hours); another leads straight over the headland to Pantai Keracut (two hours).

Northern Peninsula

Penang's beaches

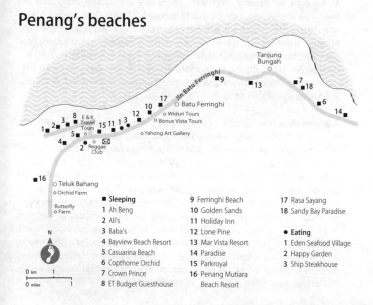

Sleeping
1 Ah Beng
2 Ali's
3 Baba's
4 Bayview Beach Resort
5 Casuarina Beach
6 Copthorne Orchid
7 Crown Prince
8 ET Budget Guesthouse
9 Ferringhi Beach
10 Golden Sands
11 Holiday Inn
12 Lone Pine
13 Mar Vista Resort
14 Paradise
15 Parkroyal
16 Penang Mutiara Beach Resort
17 Rasa Sayang
18 Sandy Bay Paradise

● Eating
1 Eden Seafood Village
2 Happy Garden
3 Ship Steakhouse

The **Teluk Bahang Recreation Forest** has several well marked trails and a **Forestry Museum**. ■ *0900-1300, 1400-1700 Tue-Thur, Sat-Sun; 0900-1200, 1445-1700 Friday*. **The Butterfly Farm**, a kilometre up the road from the Teluk Bahang junction, claims to be the largest tropical butterfly farm in the world. It has around 4,000 butterflies at any one time, representing over 120 species of Malaysian butterflies. The best time to visit the farm is in the late morning or early afternoon when the butterflies are most active. There is a small but excellent reptile and insect museum next door. The farm is also an important research centre and breeding station. ■ *0900-1700 Mon-Fri, 0900-1800 Saturday-Sun, RM5*. There are two **batik factories** along the road near the butterfly farm; visitors welcome. **Craft Bank** is just beyond the Teluk Bahang junction, before the butterfly farm. Batik cloth is sold by the metre in the showroom starting at RM22, while finished garments cost RM45 upwards. Demonstrations of batik block designing, stamp waxing and dyeing.

Sleeping
■ *on map, page 173*
Price codes:
see inside front cover

The big international hotels all have excellent facilities, including tennis, watersports, sailing and sightseeing tours. They also offer free shuttle services at least once a day to Georgetown. A room glut in the early 1990s, due mainly to the knock-on from recession in the West, has meant several hotels have been offering very competitive deals. With fewer European customers, many turned their attention to the incentive travel business and the Asian market, targeting Singaporeans in particular. Hotels are still going up though. While middle-to-upmarket tourists are spoilt for choice, budget travellers' options on the north coast are rather more limited.

Batu Ferringhi AL-A *Bayview Beach*, T8812123, F8812140. A/c, 2 restaurants, pool, over 400 rooms, pleasant location, away from others on the strip. Kids play area, bike hire, marble reception with hanging ivy and recorded bird noises. An amusing attempt at a tropical atmosphere. **AL-A** *Casuarina Beach*, T8811711, F8812155. Elegant rooms, a/c, restaurant, pool, named after the trees which line Batu Ferringhi beach, particularly nice grounds and a good beach, a variety of watersports arranged, theme parties. **AL** *Golden Sands*, T8811911, F8811880. A/c, restaurant, pool, popular and central on the beach, arguably the best swimming pool, a *Shangri La* outfit. **AL-A** *Holiday Inn Penang*, T8811601, F8811389. A/c, restaurant, good pool and beach area, tennis courts. Extending on to the beach side of the road. Not much character; other better options are available. Choice of sea view (**AL**) or garden view (**A**). **AL** *Rasa Sayang* T8811811, F8811984, www.shangri-la.com. A/c, restaurants, pool, one of the *Shangri La* group, winner of Tourism Malaysia 1995 Award for Excellence in Hotel Services. Over 500 rooms, probably the most popular along the beach strip, modern interpretation of Minangkabau-style, horse-shoe design around central pool and garden area. Recommended.

A-B *Ferringhi Beach*, T8905999, F8905100. A/c, restaurant, pool, 350 rooms, a/c, minibar, TV, in-house video, overhead bridge to beach, offers golf packages, caters mainly for tour groups. **A** *Lone Pine*, T8811511. A/c, restaurant, one of the oldest hotels along Batu Ferringhi (opened in 1948), a/c, TV, minibar, pool, reasonably priced, but not up to the standards of its neighbours. Wouldn't win a beauty contest but has 4 acres of landscape garden. Nightly live band, set back from beach slightly. **A** *Mar Vista Resort*, T8903388, F8903886. All 120 suites have kitchenette (utensils extra charge), sea views, a/c, TV. Dated décor, pool, paddling pool, jacuzzi, health club, restaurant. Apartment rental ranges from weekly to yearly. Resort has all the facilities one would expect. **A** *Parkroyal*, T8811133, F8812233. A/c, 4 restaurants, attractive pool, gym, tennis court, large 300-room 5-star hotel, with excellent facilities especially for families, including children's play area, special children's programmes and baby-sitting. Beautiful garden area and large airy rooms with sea views. Recommended.

C-D *Ah Beng*, 54c Batu Ferringhi, right on beach, T8811036. A/c, clean. At the end of the budget hotel road, rooms with a/c (**C**) or fan (**D**). **C-D** *Ali's*, 53b, T8811316. Alongside *Ah Beng's* (53 & 54b Batu Ferringhi), clean and good value. Full of character, some rooms with a/c and shower, bar, restaurant. One of the best budget options. **C-D** *Baba's*, 52 Batu Ferringhi, T8811686. Clean, homely and relaxed. Some rooms have a/c and shower. **C-D** *ET Budget Guest House*, 47 Batu Ferringhi, T8811553. Good tour and bus information, laundry service.

Teluk Bahang L *Penang Mutiara Beach Resort*, Jln Teluk Bahang, T8852828, F8852829. A/c, restaurant, pool, over 400 rooms, the last outpost of 5-star luxury along the beach, and a member of the 'Leading Hotels of the World' group. The *Mutiara* (Malay for 'pearl') has landscaped garden, great pool with a bar and every conceivable facility including a children's wonderland, a drink at the *Mutiara* bar costs the same as a huge meal in some nearby restaurants. Recommended. **E** *Madame Loh*, near the mosque (left at the roundabout), clean, good atmosphere. **E-F** *Rama's*, 365 Mukim 2, T811179. Homestay-type accommodation, dorm or rooms.

Tanjung Bungah A *Copthorne Orchid Penang*, T8903333, F8903303. A/c, 2 restaurants, pool, good business facilities. A very formal atmosphere. **A** *Crown Prince*, Tanjung Bungah, T8904111, F8904777. Over 280 rooms, not as good as *Paradise* hotels but sometimes offers good value promotions. **A** *Sandy Bay Paradise*, 527 Jln Tanjung Bungah, T8999999, F8990000, Sandbay@po.jaring.my, www.paradisehotel.com. Over 300 rooms, all of which are suites of varying size with kitchenette, balconies, sea views, TV, in-house video, mini-bar, complimentary coffee/tea, a/c and bath. The décor is tasteful and facilities are good, free-form pool, paddling pool, watersports, tennis, squash and gym, 24-hr coffee house and lounge overlooking sea, set around grand open lobby. Recommended. **B** *Paradise*, T8908808, F8908333. www.paradisehotel.com, beach@po.jaring.my. Another large hotel in the new *Paradise* chain, over 200 rooms, slightly downmarket to the *Sandy Bay Paradise*, less spacious rooms but lower room rates, a/c, bath, TV, fridge, restaurant – good value buffets.

Many of the big Batu Ferringhi hotels have excellent restaurants. They have to be good as there is plenty of good quality competition from roadside restaurants.

Malay 3 *Shores*, Paradise Hotel, Jln Tanjung Bungah, *nasi kandar* and *mee rebus* set lunches. **2** *Papa Din's Bamboo*, 124-B Batu Ferringhi (turn left after police station and *Eden Restaurant*, 200m up the kampung road by *Happy Garden Restaurant*), home-cooked Malay fish curries made by loveable bumoh who prides himself on being able to say 'thank you' in 30 languages, Papa Din Salat is also a renowned masseur.

Eating
● on map, page 173
Price codes:
see inside front cover
Virtually every cuisine is
represented along
this stretch

Seafood 3 *Eden Seafood Village*, 69a Batu Ferringhi, if it swims, *Eden* cooks it – priced according to weight – not cheap, nightly cultural shows, *Eden* has now expanded to include two other big, clean red restaurants, adjacent and opposite the original, the *Ferringhi Village* at 157b and *Penang Village*. **3** *Pearl Garden*, 78 Batu Ferringhi, affiliated to *Eden*, similar set-up, open courtyard or a/c interior. **3** *The Catch*, Jln Teluk Bahang, next to *Mutiara Hotel*, Malay, Chinese, Thai and international seafood dishes, huge fish tanks for fresh fish, prawns, crabs, lobster etc, hour-long cultural show daily, pleasant setting, one of the best seafood restaurants on the island. Recommended. **2** *End of the World*, end of Teluk Bahang beach, huge quantities of fresh seafood, its chilli crabs are superb and its lobster is the best value for money on the island (about RM25 each), pleasant setting on beach, not too many tourists. Recommended. **2** *Happy Garden*, Batu Ferringhi, left after police station and *Eden* restaurant, pretty garden, Chinese and Western dishes. **2** *Hollywood*, Tanjung Bungah, Batu Ferringhi, great views over the beach, serves *inche kabin* chicken stews and good selection of seafood.

Northern Peninsula

Chinese 4 *House of Four Seasons*, *Mutiara Beach Resort*, Jln Teluk Bahang, closed Tue, good old-fashioned opulence, black marble, silk and carpets, interesting menu, Cantonese and Szechuan dishes. Recommended. 4 *Marco Polo*, *Bayview Beach Resort*, Batu Ferringhi, wide selection of Cantonese dishes, shark's fin is popular, bright lighting and typical Chinese décor with tables set around a courtyard. 3 *Fok Lok Sow*, *Mar Vista Resort*, Batu Ferringhi, good value buffet (RM22) and 7-course set dinner. 3 *Shang San*, *Paradise Hotel*, Tanjung Bungah, good value Chinese food, *dim sum* brunch. 2 *Sin Hai Keng*, 551 Tanjung Tokong, overlooks the sea and serves everything from noodles to pork chops, excellent satay.

International 4 *Feringgi Grill*, *Rasa Sayang Resort*, Batu Ferringhi, popular restaurant, aims to imitate an English club, 3-piece band, specialities include prime US rib of beef served with Yorkshire pudding, expensive but memorable. 4 *La Farfalla*, *Mutiara Beach Resort*, 1 Jln Teluk Bahang, closed Mon, romantic setting overlooking pool, live string band play in background, authentic Italian chef, specialities include beef carpaccio, scallops and lobster. 4 *The Ship*, Batu Ferringhi (next to *Eden*), purpose-built wooden ship with steakhouse inside. 4 *Tiffins*, *Parkroyal Hotel*, Batu Ferringhi, very popular with locals, especially business people wishing to impress clients, Nyonya décor, wood carvings and antique furniture, eclectic cooking style, many interesting items, set meal good value (RM37 for 3 courses). 3 *Guan Guan Café*, Batu Ferringhi (opposite Yahong Art Gallery), where backpackers hang out, good value snacks; 3 *Kokomo*, 1c Jln Sungai Kelian, Tanjung Bungah (opposite *Novotel Hotel*), hip meeting place, light meals and snacks, happy hour 1800-2100. 3 *Wunderbar*, 37f Jln Cantonment (near Gurney Drive), authentic German restaurant.

Japanese 4 *Honjin*, *Bayview Beach Resort*, Batu Ferringhi, peaceful Japanese-style setting with a garden at centre of restaurant, good quality food, set meals are best value. 4 *Japanese Restaurant*, *Rasa Sayang Resort*, Batu Ferringhi, typically spartan Japanese décor, two main areas on menu: sushi and sashimi, and teppanyaki.

Thai 3 *Dusit Thai*, 92 Batu Ferringhi (next to *Lone Pine Hotel*). 2 *Thai Spices*, 62 Cantonement Rd (near Gurney Drive), good value set lunch, good Thai chefs.

Bars *Beers*, *Parkroyal*, Batu Ferringhi, good selection of beers, some draught, low prices, darts and snooker nights; *Sapphire*, *Ferringhi Beach Hotel*, Batu Ferringhi, 2400-0100, 30% discount on pouring brands and draught beer, Ladies' Night Tue. *Swing Pub*, *Bayview Beach Resort*, Batu Ferringhi, cross between a pub and a disco.

Entertainment **Cultural shows** *Eden Seafood Village*, Batu Ferringhi; *Penang Cultural Centre*, near the *Mutiara*, Teluk Bahang, daily Malay Cultural Tour lasting the marathon length of 2½ hrs, with Silat demonstration, handicrafts, traditional game demonstrations, a visit to a Longhouse, the Heritage Gallery and, last but not least, a 45 min Cultural Show. T8851175, F8842449. Theme dinners can be booked at the *Istana-Malay Theatre Restaurant*, there also facilities for business events. Most of the larger hotels also have cultural shows in evening. **Discos** *Borsalino*, *Parkroyal*, Batu Ferringhi, 2100-0200; *Cinta*, *Rasa Sayang Resort*, Batu Ferringhi, 2100-0200; *Ozone*, *Mar Vista Resort*, Batu Ferringhi, 2100-0200, also karaoke and live band area; *Shock!*, *Novotel*, Batu Ferringhi, 2100-0200, videotheque, live band, and one of the largest dance floors in Penang.

Shopping **Batik** *Craft Batik*, Mukim 2, Teluk Bahang, batik cloth sold by metre starting at RM22 and as ready-made garments RM45 upwards, demonstrations can be seen to rear of showroom; *Deepee's Silk Shop*, offering reasonable tailoring service; *Sim Seng Lee Batik and Handicrafts*, 391 Batu Ferringhi.

Sailing The most popular route is to sail north towards the islands around Langkawi and Turatao. *Pelangi Cruises*, *Mutiara Beach Resort*, Jln Teluk Bahang, T8812828/8811305, F8812829/8811498. Twelve yachts, with or without skipper, RM50 per person for 3 hrs, RM100 per person for 6 hrs, also runs overnight cruises, buying fresh fish from fishermen *en route*. It takes 8-10 hrs to Langkawi. **Traditional massage** *Papa Din*, 124B Batu Ferringhi (see directions under Malay, Eating, above). Health clubs, such as the *Do-Club* in the *Mar Vista Resort*, Batu Ferringhi, in all major hotels offer massage. | **Sports**

Bonus Vista Tours, Jln Batu Ferringhi, next to *Widuri Tours*. *E & K Travel Tours*, Jln Batu Ferringhi, Next to *Casuarina Beach* hotel, T8811629. Car hire. *Widuri Tours*, T8811558, F8811419. Golf, car hire. | **Tour operators**

Local Boat: trips can be arranged through fishermen at Teluk Bahang. Negotiate the price in advance. **Car hire**: *Avis*, *Rasa Sayang Hotel*, Batu Ferringhi; *Hertz*, *Casuarina Beach Hotel*, Batu Ferringhi; *Kasina Baru*, 651 Mukim 2, Teluk Bahang (opposite *Mutiara Beach Resort*), T8811988; *Mayflower*, *Casuarina Beach Hotel*, Batu Ferringhi; *Ruhanmas*, 157B Batu Ferringhi, T8811576; *Sintat Rent-a-Car*, *Lone Pine Hotel*, Batu Ferringhi. **Motorbike hire**: quite a few places along Batu Ferringhi all of them clearly signposted on the road. **Bus**: blue bus 93 goes to Batu Ferringhi/Teluk Bahang from Pengkalan Weld (Weld Quay) or Jln Maxwell in Georgetown. **Taxi**: stands on Batu Ferringhi (eg opposite *Golden Sands Hotel*). The big hotels along the strip are well served by taxis. | **Transport**

Long distance Air: Bayan Lepas Airport is an international airport, 20 km south of Georgetown and 36 km from Batu Ferringhi, T6434411. Transport to town: taxis operate on a coupon system from the airport (30 mins to Georgetown, RM16) or take yellow bus 83 for either Teluk Bahang (up the west coast) or Georgetown (up the east coast). Regular connections with Johor Bahru, KL, Kota Bharu, Kota Kinabalu, Kuala Terengganu, Kuching, Langkawi and Miri. Worldwide international connections on *MAS*, most via Kuala Lumpur. Regular connections to Singapore and Medan, Sumatra.

Train: station is by the Butterworth ferry terminal, T2610290/2617125. Advance bookings for onward rail journeys can be made at the station or at the ferry terminal, Pengkalan Weld, Georgetown. From Butterworth regular connections with Alor Star, Taiping, Ipoh, KL 6 hrs, Johor Bahru, see page 35 for timetable. See also Butterworth, page 151.

Bus: terminal is beside the ferry terminal at Butterworth. Booking offices along Lebuh Chulia. Some coaches operate from Pengkalan Weld direct to major towns on the peninsula (see Butterworth, page 150). *Masa Mara Travel* (54/4 Jln Burmah) is an agent for direct express buses from Penang to **Kota Bharu** and **KL** (5 hrs, RM18.50). Minibus companies now organize an early morning pick-up from your hotel, to **Hat Yai** (RM26), from where there are connections north to Thailand. There are also regular bus connections to **Bangkok**, **Phuket** and **Surat Thani**. Also some hotels eg *New Asia* and *Cathay* organize minibuses to destinations in Thailand. Bus and ferry to Koh Samui, Krabi and Phuket. There is an overnight bus to **Singapore**. **Taxi**: direct taxis from Penang to Thailand: overnight to Hat Yai; Surat Thani for Koh Samui, Krabi (for Phuket).

Car: the recent completion of the north-south expressway makes the journey from Penang to KL reasonably painless, 4½ hrs and a total toll cost of RM25. RM7 toll to drive across the Penang Bridge onto Penang. No payment required for the outward journey.

Taxi: long-distance taxis to all destinations on peninsula operate from the depot beside the Butterworth ferry on Pengkalan Weld.

Boat: boats from Georgetown for **Langkawi** Mon-Sun, depart 0800 and return from Langkawi at 1815, 3 hrs (RM35 one way, RM60 return). Tickets can be bought from travel agents all over town. Boats leave from Swettenham Pier. Possible to take motorcycle or bicycle (RM10). There is also a weekly overnight service to Langkawi (fortnightly during the monsoon season) from Swettenham Pier. Leaves Georgetown at 2300 and arrives Langkawi at 0700 the next morning. For schedules contact Sanren Delta Marine at *E & O Shopping Complex*, 10 Lebuh Farquhar or Kuala Perlis Ferry Service, PPC Shopping Complex, Pesara King Edward, T2625630. **Ferry**: passenger and car ferries operate from adjacent terminals, Pengkalan Raja Tun Uda, T3315780. 24-hours ferry service between Georgetown and **Butterworth**. Ferries leave every 20 mins 0600-2400. RM0.40 return. *Selasa Express Ferry Company* has its office by the Penang Clock Tower, next to the Penang Tourist Office, T2625630. There is now a regular ferry service from Georgetown to Langkawi and on to **Phuket**; check details at Kuala Perlis Ferry service (see below).

A number of companies operate ferries to Belawan (Medan's port), **Sumatra**, from Swettenham Pier. *Ekspres Bahagia* leave Penang for Medan on Mon and Tue at 0900 and on Wed and Fri at 1000. They depart Medan/Belawan for Penang on Mon and Tue at 1330 and on Thu and Sat at 1000. The fare is RM90/95,000Rp one way, RM160/160,000Rp return, journey time 4½ hrs. Note that the Sat departure is often full, so book a ticket beforehand if possible. Their address in Penang is *Ekspres Bahagia*, Ground Floor, Penang Port, Commission Shopping Complex, Jln Pesara King Edward, T2631943/2635255. Their agent in Medan is *Eka Sukma Wisata Tour and Travel*, Jln Sisingamangaraja 92A. *Perdana Express* is another outfit that runs high speed ferries on the Penang-Medan route. From Penang boats leave on Tue, Thu and Sat at 0900, journey time 4 hrs; from Medan they depart on Wed, Fri and Sun at 1000. The fares are the same as *Ekspres Bahagia*. In Penang the *Perdana Express* offices are on the Ground Floor, Penang Port, Commission Shopping Complex, Jln Pesara King Edward; and in Medan, they have their offices at Jln Brig Jend Katamso 35C. *Selasa Express* is yet another company operating ferries between Belawan and Penang. Their office is by the Penang Clock Tower, next to the Penang Tourist Office, T2625630 and their agent in Medan is *Tobali Tour and Travel*, Jln Juanda Baru 52. All the companies offer free transfer between Belawan and Medan.

Alor Star

Phone code: 04
Colour map 1, grid A2

Alor Star is the capital of Kedah state on the road north to the Thai border. It is the home town of Prime Minister Dr Mahathir Mohamad and is the commercial centre for Northwest Malaysia. Its name, which has been corrupted from Alor Setar, means 'grove of setar trees' (which produce a sour fruit). Kedah is now Malaysia's most important rice-growing state; together with neighbouring Perlis, it produces 44 percent of the country's rice, and is known as jelapang padi *or 'rice barn country'.*

Kedah is the site of some of the oldest settlements on the peninsula and the state's royal family can trace its line back several centuries. The ancient Indian names for the state are Kadaram and Kathah, and archaeologists believe the site of the fifth century kingdom of Langkasuka was just to the southeast of Kedah Peak (Gunung Jerai), in the Bujang River valley, halfway between Butterworth and Alor Star (see below).

Sights

Alor Star has some interesting buildings, most of which are clustered round the central Padang Besar (Jalan Pekan Melayu/Jalan Raja); apart from them, the town is unremarkable. The most interesting is the state mosque, the Moorish-style **Masjid Zahir**, completed in 1912. Almost directly opposite is the Thai-inspired **Balai Besar**, or audience hall, built in 1898, which is still used by the Sultan of Kedah on ceremonial occasions; it houses the royal throne. It is not open to the public. Close to the mosque is the **Balai Seni Negeri**, or State Art Gallery, which contains a collection of historical paintings and antiques. ■ *1000-1800, Sat-Thur, 1000-1200, 1430-1800 Fri.* Further down Jalan Raja is the 400-year-old **Balai Nobat**, an octagonal building topped by an onion dome. This building houses Kedah's royal percussion orchestra or *nobat*; it is said to date back to the 15th century. Again, it is not open to the public.

    Royal Museum Kedah, or Muzium Di Raja, is next to the Baslai Besar and gives an insight into the heritage and traditions of the Sultans of Kedah. ■ *Sat-Thur 1000-1800, Fri 1000-1200 and 1430-1800, free.*

    The **State Museum**, or Muzium Negeri, situated north of the centre, is styled on the Balai Besar and was built in 1936. The museum houses exhibits on local farming and fishing practices, a collection of early Sung Dynasty porcelain and some finds from the archaeological excavations in the Bujang Valley (see below). ■ *1000-1800 Sat-Thur, 0900-1200, 1500-1800 on Fri.* The **Pekan Rabu**, or Wednesday market (which is now held all week long) is a good place to buy local handicrafts and try some of the traditional food of Kedah.

    Two other places of interest are the **Royal Boat House**, near the Sungai Anak Bukit, west of the clocktower. It houses boats belonging to former rulers of Kedah. For Prime Minister-watchers, the house where Dr Mahathir Mohamad was born has been opened as a museum, giving an insight into his early days. It is to be found at 18 Lorong Kilang Ais, off Jalan Pegawai. ■ *0900-1800 Sat-Thur, 0900-1200, 1500-1800 Fri.*

Excursions

Situated near the small town of **Sungai Petani** to the southeast of Kedah Peak (Gunung Jerai), is this site of some of Malaysia's most exciting archaeological discoveries: finds there have prompted the establishment of the Bujung Valley Historical Park, under the management of the National Museum. The name Bujang is derived from a Sanskrit word, *bhujanga* meaning serpent. It is thought to be the site of the capital of the fifth century Hindu kingdom of Langkasuka, the hearthstone of Malay fairytale romance. While the architectural remains are a far cry from those of Cambodia's Angkor Wat, they are of enormous historical significance.

    The city is thought to represent one of the very earliest Hindu settlements in Southeast Asia, several centuries before Angkor, and at least 200 years before the founding of the first Hindu city in Java. The capital of Langkasuka is thought to have been abandoned in the sixth century, probably following a pirate raid. There have been some remarkable finds at the site, including brick and marble temple and palace complexes – of both Hindu and Buddhist origin – coins, statues, Sanskrit inscriptions, weapons and jewellery. In 1925 archaeologists stumbled across "a magnificent little granite temple near a beautiful waterfall" on a hillside above the ancient city. One of them, Dr Quarith Wales, the director of the Greater-India Research Committee wrote of the temple: "It had never been robbed, except of images, although the bronze trident of Shiva was found. In each of the stone post-holes were silver caskets containing rubies

Bujang Valley

Northern Peninsula

and sapphires." More than 50 temples have now been unearthed in the Bujang area, most of them buried in soft mud along the river bank.

For several centuries, Indian traders used the city as an entrepôt in their dealings with China. Rather than sail through the pirate-infested Melaka Strait, the traders stopped at the natural harbour at Kuala Merbok and had their goods portered across the isthmus to be collected by ships on the east side. There is speculation that the area of the Sungai Bujang was later used as a major port of the Srivijaya Empire, whose capital was at Palembang, Sumatra. But recent findings by Malaysian archaeologists have begun to contradict some of the earlier theories that Hinduism was the earliest of the great religions to be established on the Malay peninsula. Recently excavated artefacts suggest that Buddhism was introduced to the area before Hinduism. The local archaeologists maintain the Buddhist and Hindu phases of Bujang Valley's history are distinct, with the Hindu period following on much later, in the 10th-14th centuries. This is at odds with previous assertions by archaeologists that the remains of the temples' "laterite sanctuary towers are of the earliest type and not yet suggestive of pre-Angkorian architecture".

Many of the finds can be seen in the museum at Bukit Batu Pahat near Bedong; alongside the museum is a reconstruction of the most significant temple unearthed so far, **Candi Bukit Batu Pahat**, Temple of the Hill of Chiselled Stone. Eight sanctuaries have been restored and a museum displays statues and other finds. ■ *0900-1600 Mon-Thu, 1445-1600 Fri, 0900-1215 Sat-Sun.* There are a number of hotels in the nearest town, Sungai Petani. The plushest is the **B** *Sungai Petani Inn*, Jalan Kolam Air, T044213411, with air conditioning and pool. Among the budget places is the **D** *Hotel Duta*, 7 Jalan Petri. To get there, change buses at Bedong; it is easier to take a taxi from Alor Star.

Gunung Jerai
Altitude: 1,206m

Otherwise known as Kedah Peak, Gunung Jerai is the highest mountain in the northwest and is part of the **Sungai Teroi Forest Recreation Park**. The peak has been used as a navigational aid for ships heading down the Strait of Melaka for centuries. It is between the main road and the coast, north of Sungai Petani. In 1884 the remains of a sixth century Hindu shrine were discovered on the summit. It had been hidden under a metre-thick layer of peat, which caught fire, revealing the brick and stone construction, thought to be linked with the kingdom of Langkasuka (see above). Archaeologists speculate that the remains may originally have been a series of fire altars. But they are destined to remain a mystery as a radio station has now been built on top. About 3 km north of Gurun, between Sungai Petani and Alor Star, a narrow road goes off to the left and leads to the top of the mountain (11 km). There is even a small hotel just below the summit and the Museum of Forestry on top. There are good views out over Kedah's paddy fields and the coast. In mid-1994 the Kedah State Government scrapped plans for a huge Disney-style theme park on the coast below the mountain. Work on the prestigious US$7bn Jerai International Park was to have begun in June that year. It was to have been bigger than the Disney parks in California and France. State officials pulled the plug on the project following vociferous protests from local rice farmers and fishermen.

Sleeping **B** *Gunung Jerai Resort*, T04414311. A 1920s resthouse, rooms and chalets, garden, chalets. **B** *Peranginan Gunung Jerai*, Sungai Teroi Forest Recreation Park, T044223345. A/c, restaurant, attached bathrooms with hot water showers, a little worn but reasonable.

Transport Gunung Jerai is about 4 km north of Garun. Jeeps from Gurun to the resort run 0900-1700. Gurun is 33 km south of Alor Star and 60 km north of Butterworth.

Essentials

A *Grand Continental*, Lot 134-141, Jln Sultan Badlishah, T7313333, F7316368. A/c, 138 rooms, bath, TV, in-house movies, coffee house, business centre, car rental, central location and great value discounts from the rack rate usually available.

B *Grand Crystal*, 40 Jln Kampung Perak, T7313333, F7316368. A/c, TV, bath, pool, coffee house – like the *Grand Continental*, discounts often on offer, includes breakfast. **B** *Samila*, 27 Jln Lebuhraya Darulaman, T7318888, F7339934. A/c, restaurant, nightclub, a step down from the *Grand Crystal* in terms of price. Very dated, early 1970s décor. **B** *Seri Malaysia*, Mukim Alor Malai, Daerah Kota Setar, Jln Stadium, T7308738, F7307594. A 100-room hotel, one of the 'amazingly affordable' chain, a/c, TV, shower, tea/coffee-making facility, in-house video, café, clean, functional and good value, located between stadium and public swimming pool at north end of town.

C *Flora Inn*, 8 Kompleks Medan Raja, Jln Pengkalan Kapal, T7324235, F7337846. Overlooking the Kedah River, a/c, TV, food court. Apartments available, TV, coffee-making facilities, Rather tired décor but spacious. Not the best value option in town.

Sleeping
■ *on map*
Price codes:
see inside front cover

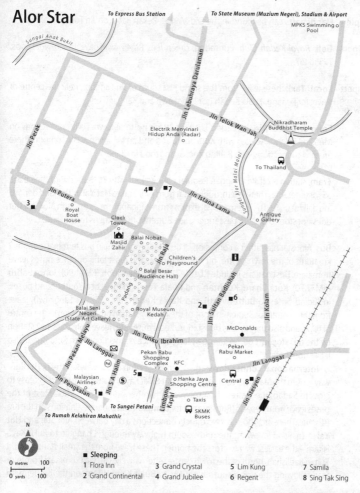

Alor Star

To Express Bus Station   *To State Museum (Muzium Negeri), Stadium & Airport*

MPKS Swimming Pool

Sungai Anak Bukit

Jln Lebuhraya Darulaman

Jln Telok Wan Jah

Nikradharam Buddhist Temple

Jln Perak

Electrik Menyinari Hidup Anda (Radar)

To Thailand

Sungai Alor Malai Malai

Jln Putera

4 **7**

Jln Istana Lama

3

Royal Boat House

Clock Tower

Balai Nobat

Antique Gallery

Masjid Zahir

Jln Raja

Children's Playground

Balai Besar (Audience Hall)

Padang

Jln Sultan Badlishah

Jln Kolam

2 **6**

Balai Seni Negeri (State Art Gallery)

Royal Museum Kedah

Jln Tunku Ibrahim

McDonalds

Pekan Rabu Market

Jln Pekan Melayu

Jln Langgar

Pekan Rabu Shopping Complex

KFC

Jln S A Halim

Jln Langgar

5

Malaysian Airlines

Limbong Kapal

Hanka Jaya Shopping Centre

Central

8 Jln Stesyen

Jln Pengkalan

1

Taxis

To Sungei Petani

SKMK Buses

To Rumah Kelahiran Mahathir

N

0 metres 100
0 yards 100

■ **Sleeping**
1 Flora Inn
2 Grand Continental
3 Grand Crystal
4 Grand Jubilee
5 Lim Kung
6 Regent
7 Samila
8 Sing Tak Sing

C-D *Grand Jubilee Hotel*, 429 Jln Kancut, T7330055. Clean, organized. Rooms with shower, some with a/c. **C** *Regent*, 1536 Jln Sultan Badlishah, T7311900, F7311291. All 25 rooms with a/c rooms, great value for money. Recommended. **C** *Rumah Rehat* (*Government Resthouse*), 75 Pumpong, T722422. Some a/c, book beforehand as it tends to fill up with government people.

D *Sing Tak Sing*, 2nd Flr, Jln Stesyen, T7325482. Fan only, large, dirty rooms, not a great option but cheap. **E** *Lim Kung*, 36A Jln Langgar, T722459. Fan only, good value. Recommended.

Eating   **Chinese** **3** *Samila Hotel*, 27 Jln Kancut. Recommended. **2** *Sri Pumpong*, Jln Pumpong, speciality: barbecued fish. **Indian** **2** *Bunga Tanjong*, Jln Seberang, Indian Muslim food, seafood curries. **Thai** **2** *Café de Siam*, Jln Kota, lashings of Thai-style seafood. *Kway Teow Jonid*, Jln Stadium (next to the police station), fried *kway teow*, washed down with *teh tarik*. **Foodstalls** *"Garden" Hawker Centre*, Jln Stadium, good range of cuisines, next to stadium, Jln Langgar (in front of cinema); *Old Market* (*Pekan Rabu*), Jln Tunku Ibrahim. **Fast food** *McDonalds*, Jln Tunku Ibrahim; *Kentucky Fried Chicken*, Jln Langgar.

Shopping   **Handicrafts** can be found in the Old Market, Pekan Rabu, on Jln Tunku Ibrahim.

Sport   **Golf** *Royal Kedah Club*, Pumpong, green fees RM45 weekdays, RM60 weekends, T7330467.

Transport   **Local Taxi**: these leave from the stand just south of Jln Langgur, near the centre of

93 km N of Butterworth   town, for Penang, Kuala Kedah (for Langkawi) and Kangar (Perlis).

462 km N of KL

409 km to Kota Bharu   **Long distance Air**: the airport is about 10 km north of town. Daily connections on MAS and Pelangi Airways with Kota Bharu and and on MAS with Kuala Lumpur. There are also connections with Beijing and Guangzhou in China.

Train: station is off Jln Langgar. Regular connections with KL, Butterworth, see page 35 for timetable. There is a through-train from Alor Star to **Hat Yai** in Thailand departing daily at 0619. The international express from Singapore goes through Alor Star but does not stop to pick up passengers. See Butterworth for trains to Thailand.

Bus: Alor Star has rather a confusion of bus stations. The main bus terminal is about 2 km north of the town centre, off Jln Bakar Bata, and most long distance buses leave from here. Destinations include **KL** (RM21.20), **Melaka**, **Ipoh** (RM11.90), **Johor Bahru** (RM37.70), **Kota Bharu**, **Kuantan** and **Kuala Terengganu**. Local southbound buses, including buses to **Butterworth** and **Kuala Kedah** (RM1.20) (for Langkawi), leave from the central bus station in front of the railway station on Jln Stesyen in the centre of town and also the express bus station. Local buses also leave from the small station by the taxi stop just off Jln Langgar; long distance connections with Kota Bharu also leave from here.

International connections: the northern section of the new north-south Highway runs to the Malaysian border crossing at Bukit Kayu Hitam, from where it is easy to cross to **Sadao**, the nearest Thai town on the other side of the border. Most of the buses leave from Penang/Butterworth for **Bangkok** and other destinations on the Kra Isthmus. There are, though, two direct connections a day between Alor Star and **Hat Yai** in Thailand following the north-south highway through Changlun to Bukit Kayu Hitam – the easiest way to cross the border. These leave from the small station on Jln Sultan Badlishah, north of the town centre. Alternatively, catch a bus or taxi from Alor Star, following the north-south highway, to **Bukit Kayu Hitam**, on the border with

Thailand. It is then a shortish walk past the paraphernalia of border-dom to the bus and taxi stop where there are connections with the Thai town of Sadao (a few kilometres on) and Hat Yai. A less popular alternative is to travel to Padang Besar (accessible from Kangar in Perlis), where the railway line crosses the border. From here it is an easy walk to the bus or train station for connections to Hat Yai. The other option is to take a taxi from Sungai Petani to Keroh and cross the border into Thailand's red-light outpost at Betong.

There are also bus connections with **Singapore** from the main long distance terminal, or Express Bus Station, 1 km north of town, RM5 in a taxi. A shuttle bus (RM0.60) also goes here, from Jln Langar in the centre.

Airline offices *MAS*, 180 Kompleks Alor Star, Lebuhraya Darulaman, T711106; also next to *Flora Inn*, Jln Pengkalan. *Pelangi Airways*, c/o MAS, T7311106. **Banks** *Bank Bumiputra*, Jln Tunku Ibrahim; *Chartered Bank*, *Overseas Union Bank* and *UMBC* are all on Jln Raja. **Communications** Area code: 04. **General Post Office:** Jln Langgar, opposite the Police Station. **Tourist offices** *Kedah State Tourist Office*, 2nd Flr, State Secretariat Building, Jln Sultan Badlishah. Limited selection of brochures, not much information on Alor Star or Kedah.

Directory

Historically the town has been an important port for trade with India and there are the ruins of an old fort, built between 1771 and 1780. The fort was built for defence of the state capital from pirate attacks. It fell into the hands of the Siamese army, under the leadership of Raja Ligor in 1821 and was occupied by Siam until 1842, after which it was abandoned. Kuala Kedah is renowned for its seafood stalls. It is also a departure point for Langkawi (see below).

Kuala Kedah

Transport Bus: buses leave every 30 mins from Alor Star to Kuala Kedah (RM0.80). **Taxi**: from Alor Star (RM1.50). **Boat**: regular connections with Langkawi. Langkawi ferry leaves 0800, 0930, 1130, 1200, 1330, 1430 and 1600 (RM13).

12 km W of Alor Star

The state of Perlis, the smallest in Malaysia, is a very picturesque area with limestone outcrops surrounded by paddy. The capital of Perlis is Kangar, a small and unremarkable town with a lively *Pasar Tani*, a farmers' market every Saturday. There is also a *Pasar Malam*, a night market, which sets up at 1700 every Wednesday. The town is otherwise of little interest, with a few blocks of shabby, modern shophouses and a large concrete shopping centre being

Kangar

Kangar

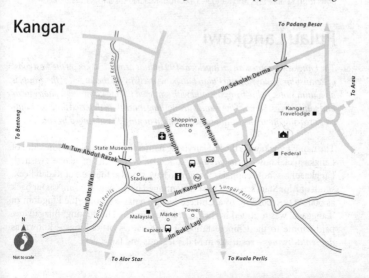

developed at its centre. The historical monuments of Perlis, the state mosque and palace, are located 12 km outside the town, in **Arau**, where a Pasar Malam takes place on a Friday.

Sleeping A *Kangar Travelodge*, 135 Jln Kangar, T9767755, F9761049. All 146 rooms have a/c, bath, TV. Also restaurant, business centre, pool. **C** *Federal*, 104b Jln Kangar, T9766288, F9766224. Some of the 46 rooms have a/c; shower, TV, restaurant. **D** *Malaysia*, 67 Jln Jubli Perak, T9761366. A/c, seen better days. **D-E** *Ban Cheong*, 79a Jln Besar, T9761184. Cheapest place in town, basic but serviceable.

45 km to Alor Star
138 km to Butterworth

Transport Bus: the bus terminal is on Jln Hospital, near the centre of town. Regular connections with Butterworth, Alor Star, KL (RM23.40), Ipoh (RM14.00), Johor Bahru, Kuantan. Local bus no 56 to Kuala Perlis, no. 59 to Padang Besar. **Taxi**: Alor Star (RM16), Kuala Perlis (RM8), Butterworth (RM50).

Kuala Perlis This small fishing port at the delta of the Sungai Perlis is mainly a jumping-off point for Pulau Langkawi and Phuket (in Thailand). Food stalls by the jetty. It is noted for its local fast food *laksa*. If you miss the boat to Langkawi, the *Soon Hin Hotel* (**E**) is across from the taxi rank or *Pens Hotel* F9854131 (**B**), Jalan Kuala Perlis, T049854122. Night Market every Tuesday. The *Putra Golf Club* is an 18 hole, par 72 course in Sungai Batu Pahat; 12 km from Kangar.

14 km to Kangar

Transport Bus and taxi: both leave from the ferry terminal. Regular connections by bus and taxi with **Butterworth**, less regular links with **Alor Star**, **KL** and **Padang Besar** (for connections with Thailand, see below) and local buses to **Kangar**. **High-speed ferry**: departs from Kuala Perlis jetty approximately every hour between 0900 and 1415, the journey takes 45 mins. *Kuala Perlis Langkawi Ferry Service*, Kuala Perlis, T9854406. Last ferry back to Kuala Perlis leaves at 1600.

Padang Besar This is a border town. The railway station platform is very long as half is managed by Thai officials and half by Malaysians. *Pekan Siam*, opposite the railway station, is full of Thai goods and a popular shopping spot for Malaysians.

50 km to Kangar

Transport Bus: the station is about 1 km from the border crossing. Regular connections from Kuala Perlis and Kangar. **Taxi**: from Kuala Perlis and Kangar.

Pulau Langkawi

Phone code: 04
Colour map 1, grid A1

The Langkawi group is an archipelago of 99 islands around 30 km off the west coast of Peninsular Malaysia, and Pulau Langkawi itself, by far the largest of the group, is a mountainous, palm-fringed island with scattered fishing kampungs, paddy fields and sandy coves. Some of the islands are nothing more than deserted limestone outcrops rearing out of the turquoise sea, cloaked in jungle, and ringed by coral.

The name Langkawi is the last surviving namesake of the ancient kingdom of Langkasuka, known as *negari alang-kah suka*, or 'the land of all one's wishes'. Langkasuka, whose capital is thought to have stood at the base of Kedah Peak, south of Alor Star (see page 180) is mentioned in Chinese accounts as far back as 500 AD. According to a Chinese Liang Dynasty record, the kingdom of 'Langgasu' was founded in the first century and its Hindu king, Bhagadatta, paid tribute to the Chinese Emperor. The names of its kings – known as *daprenta-hyangs* – resurface in Malay legends and fairytales.

In January 1987 the Malaysian government conferred duty-free status on Langkawi to promote tourism on the island. The small airport was upgraded, and the ferry service from Penang was instructed to run regularly. These efforts to turn Langkawi into one of Malaysia's big tourism money-spinners are bearing fruit as the island is attracting increasing numbers of visitors. The promotion campaign and improved transport links to the mainland means the islands can no longer be touted as 'Malaysia's best kept secret'. New hotels, shopping centres and restaurants have sprouted with typical Southeast Asian speed and, for some former visitors at least, the Langkawi of old is just a memory. But development has been concentrated in a handful of places, so much of the island remains relatively unspoilt. Budget accommodation is still available and the construction of up-market hotels and resorts means that a broader spectrum of tourists is being attracted. Nearby islands are just starting to develop.

Every so often, Langkawi's beautiful beaches are threatened by oil spills in the nearby Strait of Melaka. Langkawi had a close call in January 1993 when the *Maersk Navigator*, a Danish-owned supertanker carrying two million barrels of crude oil to Japan, was in collision with another vessel. One of its tanks was ruptured, the ship burst into flames and oil began gushing into the sea just north of Sumatra. The slick fortunately drifted off into the Indian Ocean where it was broken down with chemical dispersants. But Malaysia's environment minister, Law Hieng Ding, predicted that unless there was more rigid policing of the busy waterway, and adequate pollution-prevention measures were enforced, it would only be a matter of time before Malaysia was struck by a pollution disaster.

It is easy to get round the island at a fairly leisurely pace within a day

Northern Peninsula

Pulau Langkawi

Kuah The main town is strung out along the seafront, and is the landing point for ferries from Satun (Thailand), Kuala Perlis and Kuala Kedah. The town is growing fast and developers have reclaimed land along the shoreline to cope with the expansion. One of the largest developments on the new shores of Kuah is the *Tiara Hotel* with its pink towers and turrets which incorporates a large shopping centre. There is also a new and rather stark park area overlooked by a giant effigy of an eagle on Dataran Lang (Eagle Square), symbol of the island's flight to prosperity. The park area itself, Chogm Park, was built to commemorate the Commonwealth Heads of Government Meeting (CHOGM) in 1989. The old part of Kuah has several restaurants, a few grotty hotels, banks, plenty of coffee shops and a string of duty-free shops, which do a roaring trade in cheap liquor, cigarettes and electronics. There is also an attractive but historically and architecturally unimportant mosque.

The town's name 'Gravy' (*Kuah*), is said to derive from a legend about a fight that broke out between two families which fell out over the breaking of a betrothal. Kitchen pots and pans were thrown around and a cooking pot smashed onto *Belanga Pecah* ('broken pot'); its contents splashed all over Kuah. A saucepan of boiling water landed at *Telaga Air Hangat* (the motley hot springs on the north of the island).

Makam Mahsuri The road west to the golf course goes to Makam Mahsuri, the tomb of the legendary Princess Mahsuri, in the village of Mawat 12 km from Kuah. The beautiful Mahsuri was condemned to death for alleged adultery in 1355. She protested her innocence and several attempts to execute her failed. According to the legend, the sentence was finally carried out using her own *tombak* (lance) and her severed head bled white blood, thus confirming her innocence. Before Mahsuri died she cursed the island, saying it would remain barren for seven generations. Shortly afterwards, the Thais attacked, killing, plundering, looting and razing all the settlements to the ground. At the time of the Thai attacks, villagers buried their entire rice harvest on Padang Matsirat in Kampung Raja, but the Thais found it and set fire to it too, giving rise to the name Beras Terbakar, the 'field of burnt rice', nearby. The legend is more interesting than the field. ■ *0800-1700, RM1.*

Pantai Cenang & Pantai Tengah

Pantai Cenang is still one of the nicest beaches on the island & there is accommodation to suit all budgets

Southwest of Mahsuri's tomb, past some beautiful paddy fields and coconut groves, are the two main beaches, Pantai Cenang and Pantai Tengah. Pantai Cenang is a strip about 2 km long, with budget and mid-range chalet operations, most of which have only a limited length of beachfront, and a few upmarket places, such as the *Pelangi Beach Resort* at the top end. At low tide between November and January a sandbar appears, and it is possible to walk across to the nearby **Pulau Rebak Kecil**. It is also possible to hire boats to the other islands off Pantai Cenang from the beach. Pantai Cenang also has a range of watersport facilities on offer and boasts the *Langkawi Underwater World*, one of the largest aquariums in Asia. It comprises over 100 tanks with over 5,000 types of marine life. The highlight of the aquarium is the 15m long walk-through tunnel tank. ■ *1000-1930 daily, RM10 (RM6 for children), T9556100.*

Most of the new beach chalet development is along the 3 km stretch of coast from Pantai Cenang to Pantai Tengah, which is at the far southern end, around a small promontory. Pantai Tengah is less developed and quieter than Pantai Cenang. The beaches can get crowded at weekends and during school and public holidays.

The road west leads, past the airport, to Pantai Kok, once a magnificent unspoilt bay with a dramatic backdrop of the forested Gunung Mat Cincang. However, recent years have seen considerable development all along the west coast; the backpackers have been pushed out to make way for the more favoured well-heeled travellers and accommodation has been built to house them all. There are several isolated beaches along the bay, accessible by boat from either Pantai Kok itself, Pantai Cenang (12 km away) or Kampung Kuala Teriang, a small fishing village *en route*. On the west headland, a 2 km walk from Pantai Kok, the **Telaga Tujuh** waterfalls used to be the island's so-called 'most wonderful natural attraction'. It can no longer claim to be that, as the area has been bought by *Berjaya Leisure Berhad*, 'mother' of the *Berjaya Hotels Group*. A pipeline running next to the pools, and the waterfall, goes all the way to the *Berjaya Beach and Spa Resort* on nearby Burau Bay, so water no longer cascades down a steep hillside, between huge rocks and through a series of seven (*tujuh*) pools (*telaga*); so much for development.

Pantai Kok

Right on the northwest tip of Langkawi is **Datai Bay**, which has a beautifully landscaped golf course and one of the most sophisticated resorts in Malaysia. Guests also enjoy exclusive access to one of the island's best beaches. It is accessible via a new road, which cuts up through the hills to the coast from the Pantai Kok-Pasir Hitam road. There is a **Crocodile Farm** just beyond the junction, housing more than 1,000 crocodiles. ■ *0900-1800, RM6 (RM4 for children), daily shows at 1115 and 1445, T9552559*. **Pasir Hitam** is at the centre of the north coast, past the Kedah Cement Plant (the island's only industrial monster). As its name suggests, Pasir Hitam is streaked with black sand; but that is about the only thing worth noting about it.

North coast

Pantai Rhu (also known as Casuarina Beach) is a beautiful white-sand cove, enclosed by a jungled promontory with **Gua Cerita**, or the 'Cave of Legends', at the end of it. Within the cave, Koranic verse has been written on the walls. Beneath the sheer limestone cliff faces, there are a couple of small beaches accessible by boat. The Thai island Koh Turatao is just 4 km north. Past the *Mutiara Hotel*, there is a collection of foodstalls and small shops next to the beach. It is possible to hire boats and canoes from the beach, which is backed by a small lagoon. **Telaga Air Hangat** is another recently completed tourist attraction, centred around some hot springs. Activities include displays of traditional crafts, elephant and snake 'displays', performances of traditional dance, an 18m long hand-carved river stone mural etc. There is a restaurant and a shop here. ■ *1000-1800, RM4, T9591357*. At the ninth milestone, a 3 km-long path branches off to the **Durian Perangin** waterfall, on the slopes of Gunung Raya which rises to 911m.

Excursions to neighbouring islands

This island, whose name means 'Island of the Pregnant Maiden', is the second largest island in the archipelago, and lies just south of Langkawi. Separated from the sea by only a few metres of limestone, is a freshwater lake renowned for its powers to enhance the fertility of women; unfortunately it is also said to be inhabited by a big white crocodile, although there are no recent reports of white croc attacks and most people swim there unmolested. The myth surrounding this lake involves a beautiful girl named Telani, who became pregnant by the king's son. This indiscretion so angered the god Sang Kelembai that he brought a drought upon the land and turned the new-born baby into a white crocodile. Telani was turned into a rock and the king's son was transformed into an island. To the north of the lake is the intriguingly named **Gua**

Pulau Dayang Bunting

Langsir, or 'Cave of the Banshee'. The cave is high on a limestone cliff and is home to a large population of bats. Other nearby islands include **Pulau Bunbun**, **Pulau Beras Besar** and **Pulau Singa Besar**; there is some coral between the last two. Pulau Singa Besar is now a wildlife sanctuary, with about 90 resident bird species, wild boar and a huge population of mouse deer. A network of paths and trails will be built around the island.

Transport Boat trips are organized to Pulau Dayang Bunting by many of the larger hotels and travel agents; or boats can be chartered privately from Pantai Cenang. Most trips also include a chance to snorkel off Pantai Singa Besar. Note that visibility is poor between July and Sept and that the sea can be rough.

Pulau Paya
Just to the south of Payar there is a good coral reef, reckoned to be the best off Malaysia's west coast

This tiny island, 2 km long and 250m wide, about an hour southeast of Langkawi, is part of a marine park. The other islands are **Segantan**, **Kala** and **Lembu**. A reef platform has been built with an underwater observation chamber and diving facilities (tank and weights RM50, full diving gear RM70, introductory dive RM100), bar and restaurant, souvenir shop. There are basic facilities on the island for day visitors, but those intending to camp on the island require the permission of the Fisheries Management and Protection Office, Wisma Tani, Jalan Mahameru, KL, T2982011 or Wisma Persekutuan, Jalan Kampung Baru, Alor Star, T725573. Trips to the islands can be arranged through many of the hotels or tour companies listed below. Several hotels and companies run day trips to Pulau Payar. These islands are also within reach of Kuala Kedah, on the mainland.

Best time to visit The wet season on Langkawi usually spans the months between April to October. Water clarity is poor between July and September, the months of the monsoon, and the sea can be rough.

Essentials

Sleeping
Price codes: see inside front cover

Langkawi is no longer a haven for backpackers. Even budget accommodation is at the top end of the budget bracket. There are numerous mid- and upper-range places to stay, although people who have sampled accommodation elsewhere in Malaysia claim that prices are high. The island is particularly popular during the months Nov-Feb, and during school holidays. Outside these periods, room rates are often cut.

Most of the hotels in Kuah itself tend to be rather seedy & poor value for money. Tourists are advised to head straight for the beach resorts

Kuah A *Tiara Langkawi*, Pusat Dagangan Kelana Mas, T9662566, F9662600. Brand new waterfront hotel, 200 well furbished rooms, French-style architecture – reputedly modelled on a castle. Rooms have a/c, shower, TV. There are also restaurants and a disco. **A-B** *The Gates*, Jln Persiaran Putra, T9668466, F9668443. TV, a/c, showers, beautiful

Kuah

Sleeping
1 Asia
2 Central
3 Grand Continental
4 Langkawi
5 Tiara Langkawi
6 Twin Peaks Island Resort

wooden chalets located in tropical gardens situated about 5 mins from the jetty. Has tennis courts and a pool, as well as two restaurants. Organizes tours, and car rental. Hugely different prices in high or low season. Recommended.

B *City Bayview*, Jln Pandak Mayah, T9661818, F9663888. New block dominating Kuah village, 280 rooms with 4-star facilities, including a pool and health centre. In a central location. **B** *Grand Continental*, Lot 398, Mk Kuah, T9660333, F9660288. A/c, TV, in-house movies, tea/coffee-making facilities, restaurant, pool, gymnasium and health club. Although it is slightly out of the centre of town, it has good views over surrounding islands. **B** *Hotel Central*, 33 Jln Persiaran Putera, T9668604, F9667385. Over 100 rooms, a/c, comfortable, discounts sometimes available. Breakfast included. **B-D** *Malaysia*, 30 Pusat Mas, T4895301. A/c, attached bathrooms, rooms also have a fridge. Dorm beds also available. Basic.

C *Asia*, 1 Jln Persiaran Putra, T9666216. A/c, reasonable place with attached bathrooms, 15 mins' walk from the jetty. Clean and quiet in a good location. Recommended. **C** *Nagoya City Hotel*, Pusat Mas, T9660700, F9660479. Located next to the *Malaysia*, this hotel offers a significant step up in quality. TV, a/c, bath, sea views available. **C** *Seri Pulau Motel*, 42c Jln Penarak, T9667185. Large clean ac rooms, with shower. **C-D** *Langkawi*, 6-8 Jln Persiaran, T9666248, F9632874. Some a/c, basic place, small and airless fan rooms without windows. **D** *Island Motel*, 18 Dundong, T9667143. A/c and fan, small rooms, bathroom outside (see Tours), hires cars and motorcycles.

Outside Kuah **L** *Sheraton Perdana*, Jln Pantai Dato' Syed Omar, T9662020, F9666414. A/c, restaurant, pool, formerly the *Langkawi Island Resort*, has its own private beach with watersports facilities, and all the comforts you would expect of a *Sheraton*. **AL** *Sheraton*, Teluk Nibong, T9551901, F9551968. Pool overlooking the islands, restaurants, children's centre, health club, watersports activities, rooms arranged in individual Malay-style chalets serviced by resort bus. Total of 6 lounges and bars to choose from. Beautiful hotel, but its beach is a disappointment. **A** *Beringin Beach Resort*, round the corner from the *Sheraton Perdana*, T9666966, F9667770. A/c, restaurant, own private beach. Recommended. **A** *Twin Peaks Island Resort*, Jln Kelibang, T9668255, F9667458, new wooden chalets surrounding shadeless pool, children's playground, island tours.

Pantai Cenang On Pulau Rebak Besar (dubbed Fantasy Island), opposite Pantai Cenang, there is a new resort with 150 chalets, and berthing docks for 200 leisure boats. **AL** *Pelangi Beach Resort*, T9551001, F9551122. A/c, restaurant, pool, chalet-styled 5-star resort – guests and their baggage are whisked around in electric cars, holiday camp atmosphere, with daily activities, dirty beach. **A** *Beach Garden Resort*, T9551363, F9551221. A/c, restaurant, pool, apart from the *Pelangi* this is the nicest hotel along this stretch, with thatched roofs, a tiny swimming pool and a wonderful restaurant on the beach. Good value and to be recommended. **B** *Semarak Langkawi Beach Resort*, T9551377. A/c, good restaurant, simple but attractive rooms and recently renovated chalets. **B** *Sandy Beach*, T9551308. A/c and fan, restaurant, simple A-frame chalets with more upmarket a/c rooms, good restaurant and bar on the beach, and friendly staff. Newly furnished chalets. **C** *AB Motel*, T9551300, F9551466. Rooms with fan or a/c, and showers. Organizes island hopping and sightseeing tours. Also has a restaurant. **C** *Cenang Resthouse*, cramped terraced rooms, with ac and shower. Pretty rundown. Has two computers with internet access open to anyone at RM 4 per hour. **C** *Suria Beach Motel*, T9551776. You get what you pay for. Also organizes a bland looking tour. **D** *Beach View* T9551449. Best backpackers place in the bay. Although it is not right on the beach, it has a nice setting, and decent communal area with satellite TV. Very friendly owner who does good Western breakfasts. Small wooden chalet, with shower and a/c. Recommended.

The most popular of the 3 main beaches, with plenty of hotels & chalets to choose from; some are cramped a little too closely together. Despite the development, it is a picturesque beach

Northern Peninsula

Next beach adjoining Pantai Cenang but not as nice

Pantai Tengah **A** *Lanai*, T9653401, F9653410. Situated at the end of the beach, with a spacious set up. Two pools (one for kids) and a games room. Rooms have a/c, TV. Hotel organizes island tours. Good value. **A** *Langkawi Holiday Villa*, T9551701, F9551504. Over 250 rooms, 2 pools, squash, tennis, restaurants and all the amenities you would expect of a first-class resort, including a health centre, and squash courts. **A** *Langkawi Village Resort*, Jln Teluk Baru, T9551511, F9551531, www. langkawivillageresort.com. A resort with 100 bunglows with seaviews. A/c, bath and shower, cable TV and fridge. Tennis courts and a pool, and from 2200 onwards there is the 'Coco Jam' disco. Recommended. **B** *Aseania Resort*, Jln Pantai Tengah, T9552020, F9532136. This large pink and white building resembles a strawberry gateau, but with a 154m pool complete with waterfalls it is a good option for those looking to relax. Rooms with TV, a/c, shower and fridge. Two restaurants and a business centre. Watersports organized, and bikes can be hired. Breakfast included. **B** *Charlie's*, T9551200, F9551316. A/c and fan, restaurant, chalets, at the end of Pantai Tengah, so has a more private stretch of beach, one of the more established places here and often booked up, only 15 rooms. Recommended. **B** *Green Hill Beach Motel*, T9551935. Fan or a/c, restaurant. Comfortable and quiet, although a bit run down. **B** *Sunset Beach Motel*, T9551751. A/c, restaurant, some time-share apartments and 24 rooms, good restaurant and bar. Recommended. **C-D** *Tanjung Mali Beach Resort*, T9551891. A/c, TV, restaurant, pretty standard but organizes vacuum-packed island tours by what its brochure calls 'hoover craft'.

Pantai Datai **L** *Andaman*, www.theandaman.com. Sister hotel to the *Datai*, with less snooty clientele. This excellent hotel has a beautiful pool set amongst mature trees in plenty of shade (unlike *Datai*). Very friendly and helpful staff. Resident naturalist takes guests on nature walks and jungle treks. Free transport between the two (or 10 mins' walk along the beach). **L** *Datai*, T9592500, F9592600. Two pools, health club, 40 individual 'villas' each with private sun-bathing terrace, spacious marble bathroom, a/c, bar, minimalist décor offset by Jim Thompson silks from Bangkok, connected by walkways set in 400 ha of primary jungle where hornbills and flying squirrels remain undisturbed. There are a further 60 rooms, designed with panache, large rooms with sitting areas and cool wooden floors, own balcony with jungle (and some sea) views, private beach, fine white sand, a wealth of watersports. *Beach Restaurant* serves top quality buffet in the evening, idyllic setting under atap-roofed structure, supported on trunks of original trees that were cleared to make way for resort. *Pavilion Restaurant* on stilts amongst treetops serves Thai food, *Dining Room*, a/c serves Malay and Western food, 18 hole golf course adjacent, attractive, very luxurious resort. Recommended.

A smaller resort than Datai, but with a more secluded beach. Has undergone a radical change since 1997

Pantai Kok Having once been the most popular place for those on a lower budget to stay it is now largely an exclusive resort with a few top class hotels located in absolute seclusion. All other accommodation has disappeared to make way for a planned golf course. **AL** *Berjaya Langkawi Beach Resort*, Burau Bay, T9591888, F9591886, lgk@hr.berjaya.com.my, www.berjayaresorts.com.my. Malaysian-style chalets spread over 70 acres of tropical rainforest, some on stilts over water, some on jungled hillside, all serviced by minibuses. Each chalet has a/c, TV, CNN, in-house movies, minibar, balcony, massage shower and is very comfortably furbished with oriental carpets and classical furniture. Excellent facilities include pool, jacuzzi, Japanese restaurant, tennis, watersports, daily organized activities, white sand beach, beach restaurant, Chinese restaurant (a/c) and good value buffet served in Dayang café, inside vast main lobby overlooking sea, surprisingly this 400-room resort manages to feel friendly and not impersonal, moderate value. Recommended. **AL** *Mahsuri Beach Resort*, Bukit Tekoh, Jln Pantai Kok, Km 6, T9552977. Has its own small beach. Private chalets have ac, shower, TV. **A** *Burau Bay Resort*, Jln Teluk Burau, T9591061, F9591172, sales-mktg.

pbl@meritus-hotels.com. A/c, restaurant, at the far end of Pantai Kok, with Gunung Mat Cincang behind it, away from other chalets, twinned with *Pelangi* (but much more attractive), so offers same facilities, excellent value for money, quieter, cleaner beach. Recommended.

Kuala Muda A few new resorts have sprung up along and around this rather disappointing beach which does not offer any of the more spectacular views that can be found in other areas of the island. These resorts are positioned close to the airport.

A *De Lima Resort*, Kuala Muda, T9551801, F9551802. Restaurants, pool, large hawker centre, shopping mall, 1,200 rooms in chalet-style accommodation. **B** *Langkasuka Resort*, T9556888, F9555888. Large hotel with 214 rooms aimed primarily at the Japanese and Korean tourist market. Rooms with a/c, shower, TV. Hotel has pool and several restaurants. Little to offer. **B** *Singgahsana Kub*, Jln Kuala Muda, T9556262, F9555787. Small hotel with just 73 rooms. A 5 min walk from the beach. Pool, restaurant, disco. Rooms with a/c, shower, TV. Popular with Malays.

Pantai Rhu L *Radisson Tanjung Rhu Resort*, Mukim Air Hangat, T9591033, F9591899, radtr@tm.net.my, www.tanjungrhu.com.my. Exquisitely laid out resort of only 100 rooms with understated décor, beautifully presented, dining on the beach, luxurious facilities, a honeymooners' paradise. **A** *Mutiara Beach Hotel*, T9556488. A/c, restaurant, pool, smaller of the two hotels here.

The bay has a great view of Thailand's Koh Turatao & other islands. Only 2 hotels & not as popular as the other beaches

Mee Gulong is Langkawi's speciality: fried noodles cooked with shredded prawns, slices of beef, chicken, carrots, cauliflower are rolled into a pancake, served with a thick potato gravy. Langkawi is also known for its Thai cuisine. Being close to the Thai border, Thai influences even creep into the Malay dishes with the use of hot and spicy ingredients. Thai-styled seafood is also fairly commonplace. Virtually all of the beach hotels have their own restaurants, some of which are excellent; seafood is an obvious choice on Langkawi.

Eating
Price codes:
see inside front cover

Kuah There are several Chinese seafood restaurants along the main street in Kuah, all quite good and reasonable value for money. **2** *Fortuna*, Dekan Kuah. Recommended. by locals. **2** *Golden Dream Café*, Jln Persiaran Putra (near *Asia Hotel*), good seafood. **2** *Orchid*, 3 Dundong Kuah, Chinese. *Naga Emas Restaurant*, 31 Pusat Bandar, Jln Pandak Mayah, Thai seafood and steamboat. **2** *Noble House*, Lot 23 and 24 Pusat Mas, popular with Thai seafood. **2** *Sangkar Ikan*, Jln Pantai Penarak, seafood restaurant and fish farm where you can hire rods (RM4) and catch fish for your own dinner. **2** *Sari Seafood*, Kompleks Pasar Lama, built out on stilts over the sea – which is now being reclaimed – vast selection of seafood.

Foodstalls Roadside foodstalls in Kuah, down from *Langkasuka Hotel*. Recommended. There is also a collection of stalls behind *Langkawi Duty Free*.

Pantai Cenang and Pantai Tengah Of particular note among hotel restaurants are the 2 first-class international restaurants at **4** *Pelangi Beach Resort* and the **3** *Beach Garden Restaurant* next door, which offers a good international selection, beautifully prepared. The latter is right on the beach and is highly recommended. Both are on Pantai Cenang. **3** *Orkid*, great Thai seafood restaurant on Pantai Cenang. Great variety and good value. **3** *Champor Champor*, T9551449. International food in fantastically decorated restaurant with strong African theme. **3** *Bon Ton*, a seafront bungalow, near the *Pelangi Beach Resort*, Nyonya and Western cuisine, different menus for lunch, afternoon tea and dinner, good homemade cakes and ice cream at tea time, Bali prawns and Nyonya noodles at lunch and Nyonya chicken pie at dinner, good value.

Northern Peninsula

Pantai Datai **4** *Pavillion*, *The Datai*, Datai Bay, stunning setting on a high terrace in jungle tree tops, top class Thai chefs, papaya salad, excellent seafood. **4** *The Dining Room*, *The Datai*, Datai Bay, quintessentially tasteful in the style of the resort, over-looking turquoise pool and spotlit jungle, French chef combines Malay and Western cuisine, interesting menu.

Pantai Kok **4** *Oriental Pearl*, *Berjaya Langkawi Beach Resort*, Buran Bay, upmarket Chinese restaurant, simple a/c restaurant with ocean views, steamboat recommended.

Elsewhere **3** *Barn Thai*, Kampung Belanga Pecah, Mukim Kisap, T9666699, 9 km from Kuah on road to Padang Lalang, unique restaurant set in mangrove swamp, reached by 450m wooden walkway, fine wooden building blends with natural surroundings, excellent Thai food, jazz music.

Nightlife Nightlife in Langkawi is mainly centred in the larger hotels which offer bars, discos, karaoke and live music. Otherwise there are a few discos including *Top Ten*, in Kuah, *Beach Disco*, Kelibang, and *Dallas*, Jln Penarak, outside Kuah. On Pantai Cenang there is the *Reggae Bar* which serves until 2am-ish. In Pantai Tengah there is the *Coco Jam Disco* at the Langkawi Village Resort.

Shopping Duty free shops line the main street in Kuah, alcohol is especially good value. There is a duty free shopping complex at the jetty. The only shop selling alcohol here, *Sime Duty Free*, is on the first floor. Although Langkawi enjoys duty free status there is not much reason to come here for the shopping. At least on a cursory appraisal, the range seems to be limited and the prices hardly bargain basement. There is also Cenang Duty Free next to Underwater World, and the new Langkawi Fair Shopping Centre, Persiaran Putra, Kuah near the jetty. **Fishing tackle** shop opposite the *Langasuka Hotel* in Kuah. **Handicrafts** Many small shops in Kuah selling textiles. The best-stocked handicraft shop is in front of the *Sari Restaurant* in Kuah, *Batik Jawa Store*, 58 Pekan Pokok Asam.

Sports **Golf** *Langkawi Golf Club*, Jln Bukit Malut. T9667195. *Datai Bay Golf Club*, Teluk Datai, T9592620, F9592216, green fees RM140, 18-hole course, magnificent fairways, sea views. **Watersports** The big resorts and hotels all offer watersports facilities. *Langkawi Marine Sports* in the centre of Pantai Cenang.

Tour operators Organized tours around Langkawi and neighbouring islands can be booked through the larger hotels like the *Pelangi Beach Resort* and *Sheraton Perdana*. *Langkawi Coral* operate a regular Catamaran trip from Kuah (dep 1030) to Pulau Payar (dep 1530). The journey takes 45 mins and the package costs RM180 adult, RM120 child, T9667318, F9667308; *Indra Travel & Tours*, 17 Jln Psn Mutiara, T9660163, organizes island tours, car and motorbike hire; *Le Bumbon Island Resort*, T3332797, organizes a variety of tours including island hopping (3 days, 2 nights, RM258, day trip RM45). Many hotels run boat trips and fishing trips round the islands. *Sheraton Perdana* runs fishing trips (RM39-180, depending on duration) and diving trips to Pulau Payar (RM220). *Suaska Kristal*, 5 Telok Baru, Pantai Tengah, T9555295. Island hopping and tours available. *Mahamas Tours*, Jetty Point, Kuah, T9667797, F9666189, Car, van, motorcycle rental, hotel reservations, island hopping and tours. *Rangsajaya Holidays*, 83 Jln Teluk Baru, Pantai Tengah. T9555598, F9557594. Watersports tours, scuba diving and snorkelling.

Transport
112 km N of Penang
30 km to Kuala Perlis
Local **Bicycle hire**: on the main beaches, RM10-15 per day. **Boats**: it is well worth hiring a boat if you can get a large group of people together, otherwise it tends to be expensive – approximately RM150 per day. Many of the beach hotels run boat trips to the islands as well as one or two places in Kuah (see **Tour operators** above). Trips to Fantasy Island (opposite Pantai Cenang) leave from the beach next to *Pelangi Resort*

(signposted from the road). *Langkawi Marine Sports* in the middle of Pantai Cenang organizes island trips. **Bus**: Tourist information advise that there are no local buses. **Car hire**: *Mayflower Acme*, *Pelangi Beach Resort*, Pantai Cenang, T911001; *Tomo Express*, 14 Jln Pandak Maya 4, Pekan Kuah, T9669252; *Langkawi Island Resort* (see above) and *Island Motel* in Kuah (also see above). Expect to pay about RM80 per day. **Motorcycle hire**: motorbikes, usually Honda 70s, are reasonably cheap to hire (RM35 per day) and are far-and-away the best way to scoot around the island. Rental shops in Kuah and on all the main beaches. Kuah: *Island Motel*, 18 Dundong, T9669143. Pantai Cenang: *MBO*, opposite Semarak Langkawi. Pantai Tengah: *ASK*, opposite *Green Hill Beach Motel*. Pantai Kok: *Mila Beach Motel*, T9551049. *Tropica Beach Motel*, T9551049. **Taxi**: fares around the island are very reasonable eg jetty-Kuah RM2, Kuah-Pantai Cenang RM14, jetty to Datai Bay RM25-30, the problem is getting hold of one – especially at the jetty. T9551800.

Long distance Air: the international airport is the other side of Pantai Cenang, about 30 km from Kuah. Transport to town: a taxi to Kuah is RM12 and around RM10 to Pantai Kok. Prices are fixed – coupons on sale in the airport building. Daily connections with Johor Bahru, Kota Kinabalu, KL, Kuching, and Penang on *MAS*. The runway is currently being extended to cater for 747s in the future. *MAS* and *Silk Air* operate daily connections with Singapore and there are various other irregular international connections. Germany's *LTU International Airways* now operates a direct, 14-hr, weekly (Thur) flight from Munich.

Train (and boat): take a train to Alor Star (see page 35 for timetable), T7314025, from there a bus to Kuala Perlis and then the boat to Langkawi.

Road (and boat): it is a 7-8 hour drive or journey from KL to Kuala Perlis; from there catch the boat to Langkawi (see below).

Boat: from Kuah jetty. Timetables subject to seasonal change (fewer boats during the monsoon months, Apr-Sep); *Lada Ferry Service*, Kuah jetty, T9668820; *Kuala Perlis-Langkawi Ferry Service*, Kuah jetty, T9666950. Regular connections with Kuala Perlis every hour from 0600-1800 (RM15), 45 mins. From Kuala Kedah there are boats every 90 mins or so, 0800-1830, 1 hr. Cheaper for the slow boats. The Kuala Perlis-Langkawi Ferry Service operates daily boats to Penang, leaving at 1730, 2½-3 hrs. From Penang, the boat leaves at 0800. *Nautica Ferries*, T9666929 (Penang), T9666950 (Kuala Kedah & Kuala Perlis). Regular express boat connections with Pak Bara (port 8 km from Satun, Thailand); departures 0930, 1200, 1600, 1700, Mon-Sun. Boats leave Satun at 0900, 1300 and 1600. Private yachts also make the journey during the high season.

Airline offices *MAS*, Ground Floor, Langkawi Fair Shopping Mall, Persiaran Putra, Kuah. **Directory** T9666622; *Silk Air*, c/o MAS, T9666622, F9667535. **Banks** *Maybank* and *United Malayan Banking Corporation* are just off the main street in Kuah in the modern shophouse block. Note that banks are open all day Mon-Thu and Sun, but only in the morning on Fri and Sat. Several money changers along the main street, mainly in textile shops. There is also a money changer at Pantai Cenang (across the road from *Sandy Beach* and 100m north), open all day Mon-Thu, Sat and Sun, 1500-2100. **Communications Area code:** 04. **General Post Office:** at the jetty end of the main street in Kuah. **Tourist offices** *Langkawi Tourist Information Centre*, Jln Pesiaran Putra, Kuah, T9667789, F9667889. There is also an information booth at the jetty. Office and booth are open: 0900-1300, 1400-1800, daily. **Useful addresses Customs office** T9666227, **Immigration Office** T9694005.

Northern Peninsula

Southern Peninsula

5

Southern Peninsula

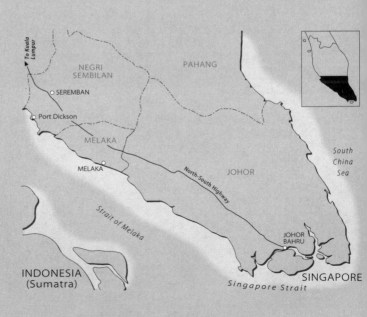

The drive south from KL through Seremban to Melaka runs on the first-to-be-completed stretch of the much-vaunted north-south Highway and is an easy, pleasant drive through rubber and oil palm plantations. Like the route north from KL, the towns are predominantly Chinese, while the rural kampungs are almost exclusively Malay. Negri Sembilan, a confederacy of nine small states, is renowned for its Minangkabau-style architecture. This is characterized by buffalo-horn shaped roof peaks, reflecting the influence of the state's first inhabitants who came from Sumatra.

On the coast, southwest of Seremban, off the main highway, is the seaside resort town of Port Dickson (PD), which serves as a popular weekend retreat from KL. The drive southeast from PD to Melaka (Malacca) is much more interesting along the coastal backroads which run through open countryside and Malay kampungs. Melaka is one of the Malaysian tourism industry's trump cards, thanks to its Portuguese, Dutch and British colonial history, its rich Peranakan (Straits Chinese) cultural heritage and its picturesque hinterland of rural Malay kampongs. The route south from Melaka is a pleasant but unremarkable drive through plantation country to Johor Bahru (JB), on the southernmost tip of the peninsula. It is a short hop across the causeway from JB to Singapore, and Malaysia's east coast islands and resorts are within easy reach.

Seremban

Seremban is the capital of the state of Negri Sembilan, which translates from Bahasa as 'nine states', and was historically a loose federation of districts, lorded over by four territorial chiefs. The town can easily be visited in a day from either KL or Melaka.

History

Seremban (formerly known as Sungei Ujong) started life as another rough and ready tin-mining centre with a large population of Chinese. Tin mining flourished in the early years of the 19th century – one of the reasons Melaka continued as a thriving trading port. The control of the river, Sungei Linggi, which was the route Sungei Ujong's tin took to the sea, became a great source of contention between the 1820s and 1860s. The *Dato Klana*, or territorial chief of the Sungei Ujong district, frequenty clashed with other members of the council of chiefs over the highly profitable river taxes and port dues. All wanted a share of the river tolls and erected illegal forts along the river to levy tolls from the Chinese merchants from Melaka and the Chinese miners. In 1857 the British sent an expedition up the river to destroy these fortified toll booths, but in no time they were back in business. In 1860 the confrontation came to a head when the tin miners in Sungei Ujong rebelled against the chiefs; hundreds were killed in the subsequent riots. One of the Chinese ring-leaders was a ruthless young Hakka ruffian name **Yap Ah Loy**. who went on to become headman of a new tin boomtown called Kuala Lumpur in 1862.

Sights

Along the fringe of the outstanding **Taman Bunga** (Lake Gardens) is the **State Mosque**, with its nine pillars representing the nine old mine-states of Negri Sembilan. the **Teman Seni Budaya** (Cultural Complex) is on a site of four hectares at the junction of Jalan Sungai Ujong and the KL-Seremban road, 2 km from the centre of town. The main building is the **Terak Perpatih**, originally constructed as the pavilion for an international Koran-reading competition in 1984 and now a museum. On the ground floor are handicraft displays and upstairs there is an exhibition of historical artefacts. Also within the complex is a beautifully carved traditional Minangkabau wooden house, **Rumah Contoh Minangkabau**, built in 1898 (originally at Kampung Air Garam).

In 1924 it was shipped to England and exhibited as an example of Malay architecture. On its return it was reassembled near the Lake Gardens in Seremban before being moved to Taman Seni Budaya. The **State Museum** is also part of the complex and is itself a good example of Minangkabau architecture; it is a reconstructed 19th-century palace (Istana Ampang Tinggi), a high stilt building with an atap roof. The museum houses a small collection of ceremonial weapons and tableaux depicting a royal wedding and some photographs and other memorabilia from the Emergency. ■ *1000-1800 Tue-Wed, 0815-1300 Thu, 1000-1215, 1445-1800 Fri, 1000-1800 Sat-Sun, closed Mon.*

Excursions **Sri Menanti**, the old Minangkabau capital of Negri Sembilan, is 30 km east of Seremban, about 10 km before Kuala Pilah. This area is the Minangkabau heartland. *Sri* is the Minangkabau word for 'ripe paddy', and *Menanti* means 'awaiting' – although it is colloquially translated as 'beautiful resting place'. It was also common for early kings to add the Sanskrit honorific Sri to their titles

Minangkabau: the 'buffalo-horn' people from across the water

Negri Sembilan's early inhabitants were immigrants from Minangkabau in Sumatra. They started to settle in the hinterland of Melaka and around Sungai Ujong (modern Seremban) during the 16th and 17th centuries and were skilled irrigated paddy farmers. Minangkabau roughly translates as 'buffalo horns' and the traditional houses of rural Negri Sembilan and Melaka have magnificent roofs that sweep up from the centre into two peaks. The Minangkabau architectural style has been the inspiration behind many modern Malaysian buildings, notably the Muzium Negara (National Museum) and the Putra World Trade Centre in Kuala Lumpur.

The Minangkabau introduced Islam, a sophisticated legal system and their matrilineal society to the interior of the Malay peninsula. In 1773 they appealed to the Minangkabau court at Pagar Ruyong in Sumatra to appoint a ruler over them and a Sumatran prince – Raja Melewar – was installed as the first king, or Yang di-Pertuan Besar of the confederacy of mini-states, with his capital at Sri Menanti. But Negri Sembilan's four undang, or territorial chiefs, saw to it that he wielded no real power. In all there were four kings from Sumatra, all of them ineffectual, and the link with Sumatra finally ended in 1824 with the establishment of an indigenous hereditary royal family. The current Sultan of Seremban, educated at Oxford, continues to reside in his palace outside the town.

and palaces. The former royal capital is on the upper reaches of Sungai Muar, which meanders through the valley which was known as Londar Naga, or the tail of the dragon. The Istana Lama Sri Menanti is a beautifully carved wooden palace built in Minangkabau style in 1908. It has 99 pillars depicting the 99 warriors of the various *luak-luak* (clans). It was, until 1931, the official residence of the Yang di-Pertuan Besar, the state ruler. On the fourth floor is a display of royal treasures. It is not officially a museum but is open to visitors. ■ *1000-1800 Sat-Wed, 0815-1300 Thu, closed Fri.* This royal town also has a large mosque. Most people come here on a day trip from Seremban, but there is a reasonable resort hotel next to the Istana Lama, the **B** *Sri Menanti Resort*, T4976200, with air conditioning, pool and restaurant and good, well equipped rooms. *United Bus* goes to Kuala Pilah every 15 minutes.

Essentials

Seremban has only a handful of hotels, one of which is amongst the best of Malaysia's resort hotels, the *Allson Klana*. There are 3 mid-range hotels; the rest are basic, Chinese-run establishments which are of an almost uniformly poor quality.

Sleeping
■ *on map, page 200*
Price codes:
see inside front cover

AL *Allson Klana Resort*, PT4388 Jln Penghulu Cantik, Taman Tasik Seremban, T7629600, F7639218. Once the new KL airport is built at Sepang, the *Allson* will be a good alternative to staying in KL, the airport being only 20 mins from the new site, set in 18 acres of landscaped gardens the *Allson Klana* is a luxurious and well-established resort hotel, it overlooks one of the largest lagoon shaped pools in Malaysia and has over 200 very comfortable and spacious rooms with a/c, in-house video, shower and bath, mini-bar, other facilities include tennis, health club, sauna, business centre, delicatessen and boutique, outstanding food outlets include *Yuri Japanese Restaurant*, *Blossom Court Chinese Restaurant* as well as a coffee house.

B *Carlton Star*, 47 Jln Dato Sheikh Ahmad, T7625336, F7620040. Good central position, a/c, coffee house, fitness centre, karaoke lounge, recently refurbished but with a lack of flair and an excess of kitsch. **B** *Seri Malaysia*, Jln Sungai Ugung, T7644181,

Southern Peninsula

Brand-name Satay from the source

Kajang, about 20 km south of KL on the Seremban road, is named after the palm-leaf canopy of a bullock cart, once ubiquitous and still occasionally seen in Negri Sembilan. At hawker centres all over

Malaysia, there are stalls called 'Satay Kajang': the town long ago gained the reputation for the best satay in the country. There are many satay stalls in Kajang today. Selamat makan!

F7644179. One of the 'ey polivalue for money' chain, good and new but not central. **B** *Tasik*, Jln Tetamu, T7630994, F7635355. Located next to the Lake Gardens, a/c, TV, shower, restaurant, pool, business centre, seen better days but has a good central position and outlook over the Lake Gardens.

D *Happy*, 35 Jln Tunku Hassan, T7630172. Probably the best of the budget places to stay, although that is not saying much, the rooms may be dark but at least they are reasonably clean. **D** *Golden Hill*, 42 Jln Tuan Sheikh, T7613760. Basic. **D** *New International*, 126 Jln Tan Sri Manickavasagam, T7634957. Fan only. **D** *Oriental*, 11 Jln Lemon, T7630119. Restaurant, just about tolerable. **D-E** *Nam Yong*, 5 Jln Tuanku Munawir, T7620155. Restaurant, grotty hotel, the only plus being the price of the rooms. **D-E** *Century*, 25-29 Jln Tuanku Munawir, T7626261.

Eating
Price codes: see inside front cover

Malay *Anira*, Kompleks Negeri Sembilan; *Bilal*, 100 Jln Dato Bandar Tunggal; *Fatimah*, 419 Jln Tuanku Manawir; *Flamingo Inn*, 1a Jln Za'aba.

Chinese 4 *Blossom Court*, *Allson Klann Resort*, classy Chinese restaurant, expensive-looking décor, popular for extensive range of *dim sum*, good Peking duck and

Seremban

■ **Sleeping**

1 Carlton Star	4 Nam Yong	7 Tasik
2 Century	5 Oriental	
3 Golden Hill	6 Seri Malaysia	

Southern Peninsula

Cantonese dishes. *Happy*, 1 Jln Dato Bandar Tunggal. *Regent*, 2391-2 Taman Bukit Labu. *Seafood*, 2017-8 Blossom Heights, Jln Tok Ungku; *Suntori*, 10-11 Jln Dato Sheikh Ahmad.
Indian 1 *Samy*, 120 Jln Yam Tuan, banana leaf. *Anura*, 97 Jln Tuanku Antah.
Japanese 4 *Yuri*, *Allson Klana Resort*, excellent quality, traditional Japanese good, private Tatami rooms, sushi bar, Teppanyaki counter, good value set meals (**3**).
Foodstalls *Jalan Tuanku Antah*, near the post office; *Jalan Dr Murugesu*, opposite Masjid Janek mosque.

Train Connections every 2 hrs with KL, express service to Singapore, see page 35 for timetable. **Bus** New, brightly coloured station on Jln Sungai Ujong. Connections with JB, Melaka, KL, Kota Bharu and Port Dixon. **Taxi** Port Dickson, KL, Melaka, T7610764. **Transport** *62 km S of KL* *83 km N of Melaka*

Banks *Bumiputra*, Wisma Dewan Permagaa Melayu; *Maybank*, 10-11 Jln Dato Abdul Rahman; *OCBC*, 63-65 Jln Dato Bandar Tunggal; *Public Bank*, 46 Jln Dato Lee Fong Yee; *Standard & Chartered*, 128 Jln Dato Bandar Tunggal; *UMBC*, 39 Jln Tuanku Munawir. **Communications** Area code: 06. **Post Office:** Jln Tuanka Antah. **Tourist offices** *State Economic Planning Unit*, 5th Flr Wisma Negeri, T7622311. **Directory**

Southern Peninsula

Port Dickson

Port Dickson, typically shortened to PD, is 32 km from Seremban and is one of the most popular seaside resorts in Malaysia, as testified by all the modern condominium developments. The pace of development has given the little fishing port a pollution problem in recent years and many people regard the sea as so toxic that it is best not to swim at all. This is a narrow point of the Melaka Strait and large ships use the deep-water channel which cuts close to the Malaysian coast. Rarely a month goes by during which the Malaysian authorities aren't giving chase to tankers which have an increasingly alarming tendency to dump thousands of tonnes of sludge, oil and effluent into the strait. Although for KL's residents it may be a convenient destination for a day trip or weekend, it is, frankly, hard to imagine why those with more time on their hands would wish to come here. *Phone code: 02* *Colour map 2, grid B2*

The port town, originally called Tanjung Kamuning, was renamed after Sir Frederick Dickson, British Colonial Secretary and acting Governor in 1890. Port Dickson itself is quiet and undistinguished but to the south is a long sandy beach, stretching 18 km down to the **Cape Rachado** lighthouse, although there are cleaner places to swim in Malaysia. Built by the British on the site of a 16th-century Portuguese lighthouse, Cape Rachado has panoramic views along the coast (it is necessary to acquire permission from the Marine Department in Melaka to climb to the top). At **Kota Lukut**, 7 km from Port Dickson, is Raja Jamaat fort, built in 1847 to control the tin trade in the area.

Port Dickson

■ **Sleeping**
1 Bayu Beach Resort
2 Delta Paradise
  Lagoon Resort
3 Regency
4 Seri Malaysia
5 Tanjung Tuan Resort
6 Travers

● **Eating**
1 Haw Wah Seafood
2 Kemang Seafood
3 Pantai Ria
4 Santan Belada

Sleeping

■ on map, page 201
Price codes:
see inside front cover

Because PD is a favourite family getaway for KL's weekenders, beach hotels are often quite full – and rates are comparatively high. During the week, discounts are often on offer. There is not much selection for the budget-minded traveller, who may be wise to give Port Dickson a miss.

AL *Ilham Resort* Tanjung Biru, T6626800 F6625646. Resort comprising of 59 apartments. All rooms have a/c, and phones. Facilities include a pool, tennis court, squash court and spa on site. A babysitting service is available. **A** *Bayu Beach Resort*, Batu 4½, Jln Pantai, T6473703, F6474362. Pool, luxury 300-room beach resort, good watersports facilities, all rooms with a/c, kitchenette, TV, minibar, Chinese restaurant, coffee house, karaoke lounge. **A** *Delta Paradise Lagoon*, 3½ km Jln Pantai, T6477600, F6477630. New luxury hotel, the best on the strip, over 200 rooms, all with ocean views, bath, TV, in-house video, mini bar, tea/coffee-making facilities, other amenities include pool, children's playground, tennis, squash, watersports, business centre, coffee house. **A** *Regency*, Batu 5, T6474090, F6474792. Minangkabau-style architecture, tennis, squash, children's pool, two restaurants, business centre. **A** *Tanjung Tuan Beach Resort*, Batu 5, Jln Pantai, T662013. A/c, restaurant, pool, good sports facilities and weekday discounts.

B *Seri Malaysia*, Batu 4 Jln Pantai, T6476070, F6476028. One of newer additions to this budget chain of hotels, good views across beach and good value. Recommended. **B** *Travers Hotel*, Batu 9, T6625273. Quiet location facing the sea, charges include breakfast, clean and fairly new. **B-C** *Golden Resort*, Batu 10 Jln Pantai, T6625176. Rooms have a/c, mini-fridge and TV. Facilities include restaurant, pool.

C *Beach Point Motel*, Batu 9, Jln Pantai, T6625889. Located down a track off main road, a/c, shower, basic but spotlessly clean. **C** *Lido*, Batu 8, Jln Pantai, T6625273. Restaurant, quiet location, set in large grounds. **D** *Kong Meng*, Batu 8, Teluk Kemang, T6625683. restaurant, on the beachfront, reasonable for the price. **E** *Port Dickson Youth Hostel*, Km 6 Jln Pantai, T6472188. YHA card holders only (although some non-members seem to land a room), separate dorm for men and women, dining/cooking area, large compound, camping facilities.

Eating

● on map, page 201
Price codes:
see inside front cover

Malay **2** *Santan Berlada*, Batu 1, Jln Pantai. **Chinese** **2** *Pantai Ria*, Batu 7½, Jln Pantai, seafood. **Seafood** **3** *Blue Lagoon*, Cape Rachado (on the way to the lighthouse). **2** *Haw Wah Seafood*, Teluk Kamang, simple but clean coffee shop at end of row of modern shophouses on main road, good seafood. **2** *Kemang Seafood*, Batu 7, Malay seafood, crab sold by weight (1 kg RM25). **Western** *Kentucky Fried Chicken*, PD centre. **Foodstalls** Scattered around town and along Jln Pantai.

Transport
94 km to KL
32 km to Seremban
90 km to Melaka

Bus Station on Jln Pantai, just outside the main centre but buses will normally stop on request anywhere along the beach. Regular connections with KL (RM5) and Melaka. **Taxi** T7610764, shared taxis to Melaka, KL and Seremban.

Directory

Banks *Bumiputra*, 745 Jln Bharu; *Public*, 866 Jln Pantai; *Standard Chartered*, 61 Jln Bharu. **Communications** Area code: 06. General Post Office: opposite bus station in PD. **Medical facilities** Hospital: on the waterfront by the bus station, Jln Pantai.

Southern Peninsula

Melaka (Malacca)

Thanks to its strategic location on the strait which bears its name, Melaka was a rich, cosmopolitan port city long before it fell victim to successive colonial invasions. Its wealth and influence are now a thing of the past, and the old city's colourful history is itself a major money-spinner for Malaysia's modern tourism industry.

Phone code: 06
Colour map 2, grid B3

Ins and outs

There is an airport 10 km from town but few people arrive here by air. It is a comparatively painless overland journey either south from KL (150 km) or north from Singapore (250 km). There are numerous express buses plying the KL-Melaka and Singapore-Melaka routes and there are also connections with numerous other towns on the Peninsula including Seremban, Port Dickson, Ipoh, Lumut, Klang, Penang, Butterworth, Alor Star, JB, Muar, Kuantan, Kuala Terengganu and Kota Bahru. The railway line does not run through Melaka – the nearest stops is at Tampin some 40 km north of town. There are daily express international ferry connections with Dumai on Sumatra.

Getting there
See also Transport, page 222

While Melaka is a largish town it is still possible to enjoy many of the sights on foot; bicycles are also available for hire from some of the guesthouses and shops in town. There is a town bus service but it is unlikely to be of much use to visitors; metered taxis are plentiful. While trishaws are available for rent these are not part of Melaka's public transport system: they survive by providing a service to tourists who are willing to shell out of the enjoyment of being pedalled around town.

Getting around

History

The city was founded by Parameswara, a fugitive prince from Palembang in Sumatra. According to the 16th century *Sejara Melayu* (the Malay Annals), he was a descendant of the royal house of Srivijaya, whose lineage could be traced back to Alexander the Great. Historians, however, suspect that he was really a Javanese refugee who, during the 1390s, invaded and took Temasek (Singapore) before he himself was ousted by the invading Siamese. He fled up the west coast of the peninsula and, with a few followers, settled in a fishing kampung.

The Malay Annals relate how Parameswara was out hunting one day, and while resting in the shade of a tree watched a tiny mouse deer turn and kick one of his hunting dogs and drive it into the sea. He liked its style and named his nearby settlement after the *malaka* tree he was sitting under. Sadly it seems more likely that the name Melaka is derived from the Arabic word *malakat* – or market – and from its earliest days the settlement, with its sheltered harbour, was an entrepôt. Melaka was sheltered from the monsoons by the island of Sumatra, and perfectly located for merchants to take advantage of the trade winds. Because the Strait's deep-water channel lay close to the Malayan coast, Melaka had command over shipping passing through it.

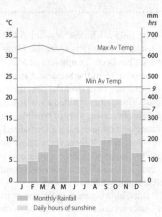

Climate: Melaka

☞ *The Flor de la Mar: sunken treasure beyond measure*

From the early years of the first millennium, Chinese junks were plying the Nanyang, or the South Seas, and by the 1400s a sophisticated trade network had built up, linking Asia to India, the Middle East and Europe. For three centuries, Melaka was at the fulcrum of the China trade route and even before the Europeans arrived, hundreds of merchants came each year from Arabia, Persia, India, China, Champa, Cambodia, Siam, Java, Sumatra and the eastern Isles. By the early 1500s, more than 100 large ships were anchoring at Melaka every year. It was known as the emporium of the east.

But this trade was not without its casualties and the sunken wrecks littering the coastal waters of the South China Sea and the Strait of Melaka have today given rise to a new, highly profitable industry: treasure hunting. Divers, in league with marine archaeologists and maritime historians, have flocked to the region in recent years. The most publicized find was the 1987 salvage of a cargo of Chinese porcelain from a vessel which sank off the Riau Islands in 1752; the booty was auctioned by Christie's in Amsterdam two years later for US$16m. But treasure hunting carries with it political sensitivities over the ownership of wrecks. Salvage operators have been jailed in Indonesia and salvaged antiquities have been confiscated in Thailand.

But the ultimate sunken treasure trove lies in what remains of the wreck of the Flor

de la Mar, at the bottom of the Strait of Melaka. The Portuguese vessel, commanded by Admiral Alfonso d'Albuquerque, is thought to be the richest ship ever lost. Having left Lisbon in 1503, Albuquerque plundered his way from Mozambique, the Red Sea and India to the coastal regions of Burma and Thailand. By July 1511, when he anchored off Melaka he had amassed untold riches. After capturing the city, he plundered it.

In his book The Search for Sunken Treasure, *the treasure hunter Robert F Marx writes: "The spoils the Portuguese took from Malacca stagger the imagination." They included more than 60 tonnes of gold booty in the form of solid gold statues of elephants, tigers, birds and monkeys, all studded with gemstones. There was gilded furniture, gold ingots, gold coins, gold-plated royal litters, chests full of diamonds, rubies and sapphires and several tonnes of Chinese and Arabic coins. And this was just the loot from Sultan Ahmad's palace. Most of it, writes Marx, was loaded onto the Flor de la Mar where "it took up so much space that the crew had trouble stowing additional gem-filled chests". In London, Sotheby's auction house tentatively valued the treasure at US$9bn, making it by far the world's richest wreck. Albuquerque stole so much gold that Melaka was left without any coinage. Tin coins were minted instead, for the first time.*

Two days after setting off for Portugal, his fleet of four ships ran into a storm at the

In 1405 a Chinese Muslim Admiral, the eunuch Cheng Ho, arrived in Melaka bearing gifts from the Ming Emperor (including a yellow parasol, which has been the emblem of Malay royalty ever since) and the promise of protection from the Siamese. Cheng Ho (Zheng Ho) made seven voyages to the Indian Ocean over the next three decades and used Melaka as his supply base. The Chinese gained a vassal state and Melaka gained a sense of security: Parameswara was wary of possible Siamese encroachment. Court rituals, ceremony and etiquette were formalized and an exclusive royal court language evolved. In 1411, three years before his death, Parameswara sailed with Cheng Ho to China with a large retinue and was received by the third Ming Emperor, Chu Ti. Melaka's next two rulers continued this tradition, making at least two visits each to China.

But China began to withdraw its patronage in the 1430s, and to make sure Melaka retained at least one powerful friend, the third ruler, Sri Maharaja,

northeastern tip of Sumatra. Two ships went down, then the Flor de la Mar itself hit a reef. Albuquerque survived the shipwreck and managed to salvage a gold sword, a jewel-encrusted crown, a ruby bracelet and a ring which today are on display in a Lisbon museum. The rest was lost in 37m of water. The admiral returned to Portugal on his one remaining ship. With his pilot, who also survived, he drew up a chart indicating where the ship went down – 8 km off Tanjung Jambu Air in Aceh.

It lay there, forgotten, for nearly 500 years. In 1988 an Italian specialist in underwater wrecks and an Australian marine historian claimed to have located the Flor de la Mar, hidden under several metres of mud, using satellite imaging. The Indonesian government – in whose territorial waters the wreck lay – then awarded a salvage contract to PT Jayatama Istikacipta, a company linked to the family of President Suharto, which sub-contracted the diving operation to an Australian, arrested in Indonesia the previous year for illegal treasure-hunting. He hired former divers from the British Navy's Special Boat Squadron to join the search. In 1989 they found a couple of wrecked Chinese junks but no Flor de la Mar and, in frustration, the operation was called off.

The same year, the Indonesians granted a search permit to a Singapore salvage firm. After a year's fruitless exploration, they hired Robert Marx, who, with the aid of a facsimile of Albuquerque's chart, located the reef which the ship had struck. Numerous artifacts were recovered, but, he writes, "a thorough sonar and magnetometer survey revealed that the main section of the wreck lies in an area the size of five football fields at a depth of 37m under 15m of concrete-like mud."

The discovery sparked a political row. Malaysia and Portugal contested Indonesia's claim to the booty and the matter was passed to the International Court in The Hague for adjudication. Meanwhile, an endless stream of conspiracy stories – none of them confirmed – surrounds the fate of the Flor de la Mar. In 1991, it was reported that "powerful interests linked to President Suharto" had harassed other treasure-hunters researching the location of the wreck and had privately tried to force them to help mount a covert salvage operation. In late-1991, following further reports that Indonesian Navy divers had tried again, Jakarta and Kuala Lumpur reportedly entered a joint-venture agreement. Under it, Malaysia agreed to bear the entire cost of the operation and split the booty 50/50. If any salvage work is currently going on, it is being kept very quiet. There are constant rumours about secret salvage operations circulating among Singapore's commercial diving community, but the matter is so sensitive and the stakes potentially so high that lips are firmly sealed.

married the daughter of the sultan of the flourishing maritime state of Samudra-Pasai in Sumatra. Historian Mary Turnbull says "he embraced Islam and hitched Melaka's fortunes to the rising star of the Muslim trading fraternity". He adopted the name Mohamed Shah, but retained the court's long-standing Hindu rituals and ceremonies. He died without a child from his marriage to the Pasai princess and a succession crisis followed. The rightful royal heir, the young Rajah Ibrahim was murdered in a palace coup after a year on the throne and Kasim, one of Mohamed's sons by a non-royal marriage declared himself Sultan Muzaffar Shah. Melaka's first proper sultan made Islam the state religion and beat off two Siamese invasions during his reign. Islam was also spreading through the merchant community. In the latter half of the 15th century the faith was taken from Melaka to other states on the peninsula as well as to Brunei and Javanese port cities which were breaking away from the Hindu kingdom of Majapahit.

In the late 15th century, Malay power reached its pinnacle. Muzaffar's successor, Sultan Mansur Shah, extended Melaka's sway over Pahang, Johor and Perak, the Riau archipelago and Sumatra. Contemporary European maps label the entire peninsula 'Malacca'. According to the Malay Annals, the sultan married a Chinese princess in 1460. This marriage and the arrival of the princess and her followers marked the formal beginning of the unique and prosperous Straits Chinese *Peranakan* culture (see page 210).

Another cultural blend that had its roots in medieval Melaka was the Chitty Indian community, the result of Indian merchants inter-marrying with local women, including the Malay nobility. Because foreign traders had to wait several months before the winds changed to allow them to return home, many put down roots and Melaka, 'the city where the winds met', had hundreds of permanent foreign residents. There were no taboos concerning cross-cultural marriage: the polygamous Muslim Sultan Mansur Shah even visited the crumbling Majapahit court in East Java where he cemented relations by his second royal marriage, to the Hindu ruler's daughter.

By the beginning of the 16th century Melaka was the most important port in the region. Foreign merchants traded in Indian and Persian textiles, spices from the Moluccas (Maluku), silk and porcelain from China as well as gold, pepper, camphor, sandalwood and tin. The Malay language became the *lingua franca* throughout the region.

Tales of luxuriance and prosperity attracted the Portuguese. They came in search of trading opportunities and with the aim of breaking the Arab merchants' stranglehold on trade between Europe and Asia. Spices from the Moluccas came through the Strait and whoever controlled the waterway determined the price of cloves in Europe. The Portuguese – known to Melakans as 'the white Bengalis' – combined their quest for riches with a fervent anti-Muslim crusade, spurred by their hatred of their former Moorish overlords on the Iberian peninsula. They arrived in 1509, received a royal welcome and then fled for their lives when Gujerati (Indian) traders turned the Sultan against them. Alfonso d'Albuquerque, the viceroy of Portuguese India, returned two years later with 18 ships and 1,400 men. After an initial attempt at reconciliation, he too was beaten off. D'Albuquerque then stormed and conquered the city in July 1511, the year after he seized Goa on India's west coast. The Melakan court fled to Johor where Sultan Ahmad re-established his kingdom.

The foreign merchants quickly adapted to the new rulers and under the Portuguese the city continued to thrive. Tomé Pires, a Portuguese apothecary who arrived with d'Albuquerque's fleet and stayed two years, wrote in his account, *Suma Oriental*: "Whoever is lord of Melaka has his hand on the throat of Venice," adding that "the trade and commerce between different nations for a thousand leagues on every hand must come to Melaka". The port became known as the 'Babylon of the Orient'. Despite the two-year sojourn of Spanish Jesuit priest St Francis Xavier, Christianity had little impact on the Muslim Malays or the hedonistic merchant community. A large Eurasian population grew up, adding to Melaka's cosmopolitan character; there are still many Pereiras, D'Cruzes, de Silvas, da Costas, Martinezes and Fernandezes in the Melaka phone book.

Back in Lisbon in the early 17th century, the Portuguese monarchy was on the decline, the government in serious debt and successive expeditions failed to acquire anything more than a tenuous hold over the Spice Islands, to the east. The Portuguese never managed to subdue the Sumatran pirates, the real rulers of the Strait of Melaka. As Dutch influence increased in Indonesia, Batavia (Jakarta) developed as the principal port of the region and Melaka declined. The Dutch entered an alliance with the Sultanate of Johor and foreign traders began

Southern Peninsula

to move there. This paved the way for a Dutch blockade of Melaka and in 1641, after a six month seige of the city, Dutch forces, together with troops from Johor, forced the surrender of the last Portuguese governor.

Over the next 150 years the Dutch carried out an extensive building programme; some of these still stand in Dutch Square. Melaka was the collecting point for Dutch produce from Sumatra and the Malay peninsula, where the new administration attempted to enforce a monopoly on the tin trade. They built forts on Pulau Pangkor and at Kuala Selangor, north of Klang, to block Acehnese efforts to muscle in on the trade, but the Dutch, like the Portuguese before them, were more interested in trade than territory. Apart from their buildings, the Dutch impact on Melaka was minimal. Their tenure of the town was periodically threatened by the rise of the Bugis, Minangkabaus and Makassarese who migrated to the Malay peninsula having been displaced by the activities of the Dutch East India Company in Sulawesi and Sumatra. In 1784 Melaka was only saved from a joint Bugis and Minangkabau invasion by the arrival of the Dutch fleet from Europe.

Melaka

■ Sleeping	8 Kancil	15 Robin's Nest
1 Baba House	9 Majestic	16 Sunny's Inn
2 City Bayview	10 Melaka Town Holiday	
3 Eastern Heritage	Lodge	🚌 Bus Stations
4 Emperor	11 Melaka Youth Hostel	1 Express
5 Equatorial	12 Ng Fook	2 Meden Portugis
6 Grand Continental	13 Palace	3 Melaka
7 Heeren House	14 Ramada Renaissance	

Related map
A Melaka detail,
page 209

By the late 18th century, the Dutch hold on the China trade route was bothering the English East India Company. In 1795 France conquered the Netherlands and the British made an agreement with the exiled Dutch government allowing them to become the caretaker of Dutch colonies. Four years later the Dutch East India Company went bankrupt, but just to make sure that they would not be tempted to make a comeback in Melaka, the British started to demolish the fortress in 1807. The timely arrival of Stamford Raffles, the founder of modern Singapore, prevented the destruction from going further, and in 1824, under the Treaty of London, Melaka was surrendered to the British in exchange for the Sumatran port of Bencoolen (Bengkulu).

In 1826 Melaka became a part of the British Straits Settlements, along with Penang and Singapore. But by then, its harbour had silted up and it was a town of little commercial importance. In 1826 it had a population of 31,000 and was the biggest of the settlements; by 1860, although its population had doubled, it was the smallest and least significant of the three. In 1866, a correspondent for the *Illustrated London News* described Melaka (which the British spelled *Malacca*) as "a land where it is 'always afternoon' – hot, still, dreamy. Existence stagnates. Trade pursues its operations invisibly. It has no politics, little crime, rarely gets even two lines in an English newspaper and does nothing towards making contemporary history". In 1867 the Straits Settlements were transferred to direct colonial rule and Melaka faded into obscurity, Strangely, it was the town's infertile agricultural hinterland which helped re-envigorate the local economy at the turn of the century. The first rubber estate in Malaya was started by Melakan planter Tan Chay Yan, who accepted some seedlings from 'Mad' Henry Ridley, director of Singapore's Botanic Gardens and planted out 1,200 hectares in 1896. The idea caught on among other Chinese and European planters and Melaka soon became one of the country's leading rubber producers.

Sights

Arriving in Melaka by road it is not immediately apparent that the city is Malaysia's historical treasure-trove

Jalan Munshi Abdullah, which runs through the middle of the more recent commercial district, is like any Malaysian main street. The taxi station and express bus terminal are away from the central core of old Melaka, and while the old city is quite compact, the town itself is neither as small or medieval-looking as visitors are led to suppose. The historical sights from the Portuguese and Dutch periods are interesting because they are in Malaysia – not because they are stunning architectural wonders. That said, the old red Dutch buildings on the east bank of the river and the magnificent Peranakan architecture and stuccoed shophouses on the west side, lend Melaka an atmosphere unlike any other Malaysian town. It also lays claim to many of the country's oldest Buddhist and Hindu temples, mosques and churches.

Exploring historical Melaka

NB It is possible to walk around Melaka's historical sights. There is now an interesting 'trail' – called the **Jerak Warisan Heritage Trail**, which starts at the Tourist Office (details available here); by following this trail the visitor gets to see all the major cultural sights of interest (see map on opposite page). The route crosses the bridge, to the Baba Nyonya Heritage Museum, takes in all the temples on Jonkers Street and then back across the bridge to Stadthuys, St Paul's Church, St Paul's Hill and the Porta de Santiago Independence Monument. For a 'handout' on the trail, ask at the Tourist Office. A more leisurely way to get around is by trishaw. There are also many places around town which rent bicycles.

There are boat tours (see below) down the river through the original port area and past some of the old Dutch houses. On the west bank is **Kampung Morten**, a village of traditional Melakan houses. It was named after a man who built Melaka's wet market and donated the land to the Malays. The main attraction here is Kassim Mahmood's hand-crafted house.

The most interesting parts of the old town are close to the waterfront

The Dutch colonial architecture in the **town square** is the most striking feature of the riverfront. The buildings are painted a bright terracotta red and are characterized by their massive walls, chunky doors with wrought iron hinges and louvred windows. The most prominent of these is the imposing **Stadthuys**. Completed in 1660, it is said to be the oldest-surviving Dutch building in the East, and served as the official residence of the Dutch governors. The recently renovated building now houses a good **history museum** detailing in maps, prints and photographs the history and development of Malacca/Melaka. Also here are a cultural museum and a literature museum which are of less obvious interest to the average visitor. ■ *0900-1800 Sat-Thu 0900-1215, 1445-1800 Fri, RM2.* Just southwest from Stadthuys, on the river is a half-size replica of the galley that the viceroy of Portuguese India arrived in. The **Tang Beng Swee Clock Tower** looks Dutch but was built by a wealthy Straits Chinese family in 1886. **Christ Church** was built between 1741 and 1753 to replace an earlier Portuguese church, which was by then a ruin (church records date back to 1641). Its red bricks were shipped out from Zeeland in Holland. It is Malaysia's oldest Protestant church and the floor is still studded with Dutch tombstones. The original pews are intact – as are its ceiling beams,

Southern Peninsula

Melaka detail

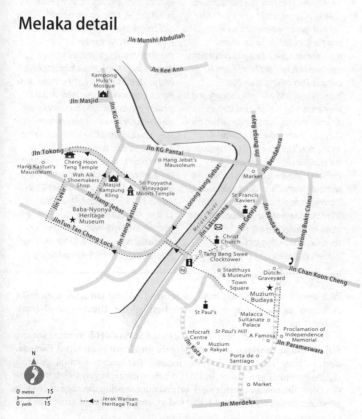

The Nyonyas and the Babas

Chinese traders in the Nanyang, or South Seas, visited Melaka from its earliest days and by the early 1400s the town was one of the most important ports of call for Chinese trade missions. They arrived between November and March on the northeast monsoon winds and left again in late June on the southwest monsoon. This gave them plenty of time to settle down and start families. Melaka's early sultans made several visits to China, paying obeisance to the Ming emperors to ensure Chinese imperial protection for the sultanate. When Sultan Mansur Shah married the Ming Chinese princess Hang Li Poh in 1460, she brought with her a retinue of 500 'youths of noble birth' and handmaidens who settled around Bukit Cina – or Chinese Hill.

Subsequent generations of Straits Chinese came to be known as Peranakans – the term comes from the Bahasa word anak, or offspring and means 'born here'. Peranakan women were called Nyonyas and the men, Babas. Sultan Mansur's marriage set a precedent and Peranakans combined the best of Chinese and Malay cultures. They created a unique, sophisticated and influential society and were known for their shrewd business acumen and opulent lifestyles. When the Dutch colonists moved out in the early 1800s, more Chinese moved in, continuing the tradition of intermarriage while clinging to the ancient customs brought with them from China. Jonas Vaughan, a Victorian colonial administrator wrote: "One may see in Malacca Babas who can claim no connection with China for centuries, clad in long jackets, loose drawers, and black skull caps, the very counterparts of Chinese to be seen any day at Amoy, Chusan, or under the walls of Nanking."

Peranakan culture reached its zenith in the 19th century. Although Melaka was the Peranakan hearthstone, there were also large Straits Chinese communities in Penang and Singapore too. The Nyonyas adopted Malay dress – they wore Malay-style jackets and sarongs and were known for their fastidiousness when it came to clothes. The women were renowned for their intricate jewellery and glass beadwork – which are now prized antiques. The Nyonyas imported colourful porcelain from China for ceremonial occasions which became known as Nyonya-ware and was typically emblazoned with phoenix and peony-flower motifs. They also imported craftsmen from China to make their intricate silver jewellery including elaborate belts, hairpins, and pillow end plates.

Peranakan weddings were elaborate affairs; couples were paired off by marriage-brokers, contracted by the groom's parents to consult horoscopes and judge the suitability of the match. If a match proved auspicious, there was a lengthy present-exchanging ritual for the young couple who were not permitted to see each other until they finally got to the nuptial chamber. Wedding rituals often went on for 12 days and ended in a lavish feast before the couple went upstairs and the heavily veiled bride first showed her face to her new husband. As was the custom, he would then say: "Lady, I have perforce to be rude with you", whether he liked what he saw or not, for the marriage had to be consummated immediately.

each hewn from a single tree trunk more than 15m long. On the altar there is a collection of sacramental silverware bearing the Dutch coat-of-arms. ■ *Thu-Tue*.

On Jalan Kota, which runs in a curve round **St Paul's Hill** from the square, is the **Porta de Santiago**, the remains of the great Portuguese fort **A Famosa**, said to have been built in four months flat under Admiral Alfonso d'Albuquerque's supervision in 1511. What remains is largely a Dutch reconstruction, the result of repair work carried out following the siege in 1641; it prominently displays the Dutch East India Company's coat-of-arms. The fort

Peranakan architecture is exemplified in the Chinese Palladian townhouses – the best examples of which are in Melaka – with their open courtyards and lavish interiors, dominated by heavy dark furniture, inlaid with marble and mother-of-pearl. Aside from their magnificent homes, one of the Peranakans' most enduring endowments is their cuisine, which is the result of the melding of cultures. The food is spicy but uses lots of coconut milk and is painstakingly prepared – one reason that Nyonya-Baba restaurants are difficult business propositions. Traditionally, would-be brides would have to impress their future mother-in-laws with their kitchen-competence, particularly in their fine-slicing of ingredients. Typical meals, served with rice and sambal (crushed chilli fried in oil), include otak-otak and ayam pongteh and desserts such as iced chendol, and gula melaka (for details on particular dishes, see page 47).

The cliquey Peranakan upper-class assimilated easily into British colonial society, following the formation of the Straits Settlements in 1826. The billiard-playing, brandy-swilling Babas, in their Mandarin dresses, conical hats, pigtails and thick-soled shoes successfully penetrated the commercial sector and entered public office. Many became professionals: lawyers, doctors and teachers, although they were barred from entering government above the clerical level. "Strange to say," wrote Vaughan, "that although the Babas adhere so loyally to the customs of their progenitors they despise the real Chinamen and are exclusive fellows indeed; [there is] nothing they rejoice in more than being British subjects... They have social clubs of their own to which they will admit no native of China." In Penang they were dubbed 'the Queen's Chinese'. Over the years they evolved their own Malay patois, and, in the 19th century, English was also thrown into their linguistic cocktail. They even devised a secret form of slang by speaking Baba Malay backwards.

Although they chose not to mix with immigrant Chinese, they retained a strong interest in events in China. The Straits Settlements provided a refuge for exiled reformers from the motherland – most notably Dr Sun Yat-sen, who lived in both Singapore and Penang in the early 1900s and became the first president of the Republic of China in 1911.

The Baba community's most famous son was Tan Cheng Lock, who was born into a distinguished Melakan Baba family in 1883. He lent his name to the Peranakans' architectural treasure, Jalan Tun Tan Chen Lock (formerly Heeren Street) in Melaka's Chinatown. Tan served in local government in colonial Melaka from 1912-1935 and vociferously fought British discrimination against the Straits and Malayan Chinese. He charged that the British had done nothing to "foster and strengthen their spirit of patriotism and natural love for the country of their birth and adoption". Tan was the spokesman for Malaya's Chinese community and fought for equality among the races; he founded the Overseas Chinese Association and became a prominent reformist politician in the years leading up to Malaysian independence.

Southern Peninsula

originally sprawled across the whole hill and housed the entire Portuguese administration, including their hospitals and five churches. It was flattened by the British between 1806 and 1808 when they occupied Melaka during the Napoleonic Wars. They wanted to ensure that the fort was not reclaimed by the Dutch. Stamford Raffles arrived for a holiday in Melaka just in time to forestall the destruction of its last remaining edifice.

From behind the gate, a path leads up to the ruins of **St Paul's Church**, built on the site of the last Melakan sultan's istana. The small chapel was originally built by the Portuguese in 1521 and called *Nossa Senhora da Annunciada*, Our

Lady of the Annunciation. The body of St Francis Xavier (the 16th century Jesuit missionary who translated the catechism into Malay and visited the church regularly), was temporarily interred in the church vault following his death off the coast of China in 1552. His remains were later sent to Portuguese Goa on the west coast of India. An armless marble statue, erected in 1953, now commemorates Malaysia's best known missionary. The Portuguese added gun turrets and a tower to the church and it became a fortress between 1567 and 1596. During the Dutch seige of Melaka in 1641, it was badly damaged but the invaders repaired it and renamed it St Paul's. It became a Protestant church and remained so until Christ Church was completed in 1753. St Paul's ended its life as a cemetery; it was used as a special burial ground for Dutch nobles, whose tombs line the walls.

A wooden replica of Sultan Mansur Shah's 15th century istana now houses the **Muzium Budaya** (Melaka Cultural Museum) below St Paul's. The palace has been painstakingly reconstructed from a description in the 16th century *Serjarah Melayu* (Malay Annals) and built in 1985 using traditional construction techniques and materials. Mansur – who came to the throne in 1459 – inherited what was reputed to be the finest royal palace in the world, with a roof of copper and zinc in seven tiers, supported by wooden carved pillars. According to the Annals, his magnificent istana was destroyed by fire after being struck by lightning the year after his accession. Exhibits in the museum focus on Melakan culture including clothes, games, weapons, musical instruments, stone inscriptions and photographs. It also features a diorama of the Sultan's court. ■ *0900-1800, closed Tue, closed Fri 1215-1445, RM1.50.*

The **Proclamation of Independence Memorial**, opposite the Cultural Museum, was built in 1912 and formerly housed the Malacca Club. The old Dutch colonial building was the social centre of British colonial Melaka. It now contains a collection of photographs and exhibits depicting the run-up to Malaysian independence in 1957. ■ *0900-1800 Tue-Thu, Sat-Sun, 0900-1200 Fri, closed Mon, free.*

A concrete bridge from the south end of Dutch Square leads to **Chinatown**, the old trading section of Melaka. **Jalan Hang Jebat**, formerly known as **Jonkers Street**, is famous for its antique shops: Nyonya porcelain, Melakan-style 'red and gold' carved furniture, wooden opium beds, Victorian mirrors, antique fans and Peranakan blackwood furniture inlaid with mother-of-pearl. There are some good examples of Peranakan architecture along the street – notably the renowned Jonkers Melaka Restoran. But none of these Peranakan houses compare with the picturesque **Jalan Tun Tan Cheng Lock**. Named after a leading Melakan Baba, instrumental in pre-independence politics (see box, page 210), it is lined with the Straits Chinese community's ancestral homes and is Melaka's 'Millionaires Row'. Many of the houses have intricately carved doors that were often specially built by immigrant craftsmen from China. Today tour buses exacerbate the local traffic problem which clogs the narrow one-way street, but many of its Peranakan mansions are still lived in by the same families that built them in the 19th century.

One of the most opulent of these houses has been converted into the **Baba-Nyonya Heritage Museum**, 48-50 Jalan Tun Tan Cheng Lock. It is in a well preserved traditional Peranakan town house, built in 1896 by millionaire rubber planter Chan Cheng Siew. Today it is owned by William Chan and his family, who conduct tours of their ancestral home. The interior is that of a typical 19th-century residence and all the rooms left as they would have been 100 years ago. The house contains family heirlooms and antiques, including Nyonyaware porcelain and blackwood furniture with marble or mother-of-pearl inlay, and silverware. There is also a collection of traditional wedding costumes, photographs and kitchen utensils. The kitchen sink has the name of William Chan's great grandfather carved on it. The information-packed tours are run regularly throughout the day. ■ *0900-1800, closed Tue all day, closed Fri 1215-1445, RM7.*

For two generations the Yeo family at **Wah Aik Shoemaker Shop**, 92 Jonkers Street (Jalan Hang Jebat), have been the only cobblers catering for the country's dwindling population of ageing Chinese women with bound feet. The practice, which was considered *de rigeur* for women of noble stock during the Ch'ing Dynasty (1644-1912), was rekindled among the families of nouveau riche Chinese tin towkays during the days of the British Straits Settlements. The process involved binding the feet firmly with bandages before they were fully formed; it was supposed to add to a woman's sensuality, but in reality it just caused a lot of pain. In China, the practice was outlawed in 1912. There are only a handful of women in Malaysia with bound feet, most of them in Melaka and all of them in their 80s or 90s. Mr Yeo Sing Guat makes these *san choon chin lian* (three-inch golden lotus feet) shoes – with brocade on authentic Shanghai Hang Chong silk – for them and as tourist souvenirs; he also makes the Peranakan *kasut manik* 'pearl shoes', sewn with miniature pearl beads.

Malaysia's most unusual shoe shop

The **Cheng Hoon Teng Temple**, on Jalan Tokong, was built in 1645, although there were later additions in 1704 and 1804. The name literally means 'Temple of the Evergreen Clouds' and was founded by Melaka's Kapitan Cina, Lee Wi King from Amoy, a political refugee who fled from China. All the materials used in the original building were imported from China as were the craftsmen who built it in typical South Chinese style. The elaborate tiled roofs are decorated with mythological figures, flowers and birds, and inside there are woodcarvings and lacquer work. The main altar houses an image of Kuan Yin, the Goddess of Mercy (cast in solid bronze and bought from India in the last century), who is associated with peace, good fortune and fertility. On her left sits Ma Cho Po, the guardian of fishermen and on her right, Kuan Ti, the god of war, literature and justice. The halls to the rear of the main temple are dedicated to Confucius and contain ancestral tablets.

The oldest Chinese temple in Malaysia

Nearby, on Jalan Tukang Emas, is the **Sri Poyyatha Vinayagar Moorthi Temple**, built in 1781 and the oldest Hindu temple in use in Malaysia. It is dedicated to the elephant-headed god Vinayagar (more usually known as Ganesh). Near to this Hindu temple on Jalan Tukang Emas is the **Masjid Kampung Kling**, a mosque built in 1748 in Sumatran style, with a square base surmounted by a three-tiered roof and pagoda-like minaret. Another 18th-century mosque in the same style is the **Masjid Tranquerah**, 2 km out of town on the road to Port Dickson. Next door is an unusual free-standing octagonal minaret with Chinese-style embellishments, in marked contrast to Malaysia's traditional Moorish-style mosques. In the graveyard is the tomb of Sultan Hussein Shah of Johor who, in 1819, signed the cession of Singapore to Stamford Raffles.

St Peter's Church on Jalan Taun Sri Lanang was built in 1710 by descendants of the early Portuguese settlers when the Dutch became more tolerant of different faiths. Iberian design is incorporated in the interior where Corinthian pillars support a curved ceiling above the aisle, similar to churches in Goa and Macau. It is the centre of the Catholic church in Malaysia. Easter candlelit processions to St Peter's seem strangely out of context in Malaysia. ■ *Until 1900 Mon-Sun.*

In 1460 when Sultan Mansur Shah married Li Poh, a Ming princess, she took up residence on Melaka's highest hill, **Bukit Cina**, which became the Chinese quarter. The Malay Annals do not record what became of the Princess's palace but the hill, off Jalan Munshi Abdullah/Jalan Laksamana Cheng Ho, remained in the possession of the Chinese community and because of its good *feng shui* – its harmony with the supernatural forces and the elements - it was made into a graveyard. The cemetery now sprawls across the adjoining hills of Bukit Gedona and Bukit Tempurong and is the largest traditional Chinese burial ground outside China, containing more than 12,000 graves. Chinese graveyards are often built on hillsides because the hill is said to protect the graves from evil winds; this hill has the added advantage of overlooking water and the ancestral spirits are said to enjoy the panoramic view over the city and across the Strait of Melaka. Some of the graves date back to the Ming Dynasty but most of these are overgrown or disintegrating.

The hill was ceded in perpetuity to the Chinese by successive colonial governments, but in mid-1991 the city burghers, backed by the Lands and Mining Department, demanded RM10m in rent arrears, going back 500 years, from the general manager of Cheng Hoon Teng temple, who is responsible for the upkeep of Bukit Cina. Unless the Chinese community paid up in full, the city threatened to repossess the 42 hectares of prime-site real estate it sits on. An impasse ensued which was still unresolved at the time of writing.

At the foot of the hill is an old Chinese temple called **Sam Poh Kong**, built in 1795 and dedicated to the famous Chinese seafarer, Admiral Cheng Ho (see page 204). It was originally built to cater for those whose relatives were buried on Bukit Cina. Next to the temple is the **Sultan's Well** (*Perigi Rajah*), also called the **Hang Li Poh Well**, said to have been sunk in the 15th century. It is believed that drinking from this well ensures a visitor's return to Melaka – but anyone foolhardy to try this today is liable to contract dysentery and instead stay rather longer than they anticipated.

The ruined **Fort St John**, another relic of the Dutch occupation, is to the west of Bukit Cina on Jalan Bendahara (Air Keroh road, off Jalan Munshi Abdullah at *Renaissance Melaka*). Its hill top location affords some excellent views although its aspect has been spoiled by the water treatment plant and high rise apartment block on either side of it.

The **Maritime Museum** is housed in a full scale reconstruction of the Portuguese trading vessel *Flor de la Mar*, on the riverbank, 200m downstream from the River Boat embarkation point. Of all the museums in Melaka, this is one of the better ones – many of the other museums are rather repetitive, but as Melaka's history is the history of sea-trade, this is a more interesting option. It has a collection of models of foreign ships that docked at Melaka during its maritime supremacy from the 14th century to the Portuguese era. The *Flor de la Mar* itself ended its days on the sea bed just off-shore, laden with treasure that was bound for Portugal (see box on page 204). ■ *0900-1800, closed Tue all day, closed Fri 1215-1445, RM2*. Entry to the Maritime Museum also gives access to the **Royal Malaysian Navy Museum**, across the road, which displays the salvaged remains of 19th century vessels that have foundered or been sunk in the Melaka Strait as well as more contemporary bits and pieces.

Portuguese Settlement About 3 km from the town centre, is the Portuguese Settlement (Medan Portugis) at Ujong Pasir, where the descendants of the Portuguese occupiers settled. A Portuguese community (of sorts) has managed to survive here for nearly five centuries; unlike the subsequent Dutch and British colonial régimes, the Portuguese garrison was encouraged to intermarry and generally treat the Malays as social equals. Today these Malaysians of Portuguese descent number around 4,500 (although other estimates are much lower). In the country as a whole, there are thought to be some 20,000. The process of integration was so successful that when the Dutch, after capturing the city in 1641, offered Portuguese settlers a choice between amnesty and deportation to their nearest colony, many chose to stay. In the 1920s, as their distinctive culture was threatened with extinction, the leaders of the community pleaded with the British to allot them a piece of land on which they could settle. A small area of swampland was duly allocated and the neat and well-planned settlement visible today was built, its street named after Portuguese heroes largely unrecognized in Malaysia. The main square, built only in 1985, is a concrete replica of a square in Lisbon – and is visibly ersatz. The descendants of the original settlers still speak a medieval Portuguese dialect called *Cristao* (pronounced 'Cristang'), spoken nowhere else in the world.

Today there are just a few tourist-oriented restaurants and shops in the modern Portuguese Square, and cultural shows are staged on Saturday nights (see **Eating** below). Other than tourism, the residents of the Portuguese settlement earn their livelihoods by fishing and through a small number of cottage industries including shrimp paste production. The central role that the sea plays in the community's coherence and identity is threatened by a land reclamation project which will cut off its access to the sea. This will destroy the settlement's fishing industry, its fish-based cottage industries and also undermine its attraction to tourists. As Gerard Fernandis remarked in August 1995, "Our history, our culture, songs, dances and food are all linked to the sea", adding that without the sea the "settlement will become an island in a sea of concrete." To get there, take a bus 17 (RM 0.45).

Tours

Tickets for the river boat can be purchased from the tourist office (45 minutes, RM6) to see the old Dutch trading houses; predictably this area is known as Melaka's 'Little Venice', which does not live up to the description. However, guides are informative, pointing out settlements and wildlife. There are views of the giant lizards on the banks and plenty of rubbish floating downstream.

Boat tours of Melaka's docks, go-downs, wharves and seafront markets run from the quay close to the *Tourism Malaysia* office. Boats leave when full and usually there is a departure every hour or so between 1000 and 1400 (RM6; RM3 for children).

Excursions

Tanjung Kling

About 9 km northwest of Melaka is Tanjung Kling, a much more relaxing place to stay than in Melaka itself. It is a pleasant drive past beachside kampungs. But because passing tankers have a habit of swilling out their tanks, the sea is muddy and the beach dirty. This does not seem to affect the taste of the seafood and there are several restaurants and hawker stalls along the roadside at **Pantai Kundor**, where there are a number of hotels. Kampung Kling is thought to have got its name from Tamils who originally settled there, having come from Kalingapatam, north of Madras.

Sleeping A *Klebang Beach Resort*, 92-1, km 9, Batang Tiga, Tanjung Kling, T3155888, F3151713. New, small hotel, clean and comfortable, but unimaginative décor, small free-form pool, paddling pool, children's playground, 2 restaurants. **A** *Mutiara Malacca Beach Resort*, Pantai Kundur, Tanjung Kling, T3517419, F3517517. Over 218 all-suite units, a/c, TV, mini-bar, kitchenette, spacious but not stylish, 2 restaurants (limited menu), Bubbles Fun Pub, tennis, pool, mountain bikes, watersports, sauna, gymnasium, 20 mins' taxi ride from the centre of Melaka, with views over the Straits and the oil refinery, awful beach and a spartan resort but friendly staff. **A** *Riviera Bay Resort*, 10 km Jln Tanjung Kling, T3151111, F3153333. Opened late 1995, classical architecture on a palatial scale, takes the form of a U-shaped building on 14 floors with 450 spacious suites, tastefully decorated in shades of green and all sea-facing, with a/c, TV, in-house movies, tea and coffee-making facilities, mini-bar,

There is now little budget accommodation due to a fall in demand

Southern Peninsula

other amenities include 3 restaurants under a top Swiss chef, the Buccaneer pub, hair salon, children's playground, watersports, tennis, pool with swim-up bar, paddling pool. Recent reports have been of rather slap-dash service and levels of cleanliness. **B** *Shah's Beach Resort*, 9 km, Tanjung Kling, T3152120. A/c, restaurant, pool, 1950s front with two lines of a/c chalets behind, tennis court and pool can be used by non-guests for a fee. Breakfast included. **C** *Motel Tanjung Kling*, 5855C Pantai Pangkalan Perigi, Tanjung Kling, T515749. A/c, restaurant. **C** *Straits View Lodge*, C-7886, Pantai Kundur, Batu 9, Tanjung Kling, T514627, F325788. Simple chalets, friendly atmosphere, boat, bike and fishing equipment for hire.

Eating **1** *Roti John*, Pantai Kundor, on the seafront, Melaka's Roti John specialist. **2** *Yashika Traveller Hostel*, Batu 8, Pantai Kundor, beach restaurant, international.

Transport *Patt Hup* buses 51, 18, 42 and 47 buses can be caught from Jln Tengkera (at the north end of Jln Tun Tan Cheng Lock, in Melaka); there are also taxis.

Tanjung Bidara Further up the road towards Port Dickson, about 20 km northwest of Melaka, is Tanjung Bidara. It has a long beach and plenty of hawker stalls but the sea is generally rather dirty. There is the upmarket chalet-style **A** *Tanjung Bidara Beach Resort*, T3842990, with air conditioning, a restaurant and pool. Take a *Patt Hup* bus to get there, see **Transport**, above.

Ayer Keroh Situated just off the highway to KL, 11 km northeast of Melaka, Ayer Keroh has a lake, jungle, a golf course and a country club. It is also the site of **Melaka Zoo** (RM3, RM1 for children), **reptile park** (RM3, children RM1) and **Mini-Malaysia Complex**, where the various states of Malaysia are represented by 13 traditional houses containing works of art and culture (similar to the Karyaneka Handicraft Centre in KL) as well as an Orang Asli village. All the houses look remarkably alike, except the Borneo one. It also stages cultural shows. It is, however, overstaffed and badly managed. Mini-ASEAN is next door and is more varied (and included in the ticket price). ■ *All the above sights are open 0900-1800, Mon-Sun, RM4, children RM2*. The Ayer Keroh Golf and Country Club is the longest golf course in Malaysia, with green fees at RM70 for weekdays and RM100 for weekends, T320822, handicap cards must be produced. To get there, take bus 19 (known as Townbus 19), every 30 minutes.

Sleeping **A** *Malacca Village Paradise Resort*, T2323600, F2325955. Formerly the *Park Plaza*, this is a recent addition to the Paradise chain, popular with Singaporeans at weekends, but reduced rates often available during week, over 500 rooms in imposing Malaccan-red buildings, 2 swimming pools, 2 tennis courts, gymnasium, 2 squash courts, recreation centre, health club (good value shiatsu massage), beauty salon, jogging track, children's playground and sand pit, 2 restaurants, all rooms with a/c, bath, mini-bar, tea and coffee-making facilities, TV, in-house video. Breakfast included, great

Ayer Keroh

value. Recommended. **B-C** *Air Keroh Country Resort*, T2325211, F2320422. Motel-like atmosphere, a/c, restaurant, pool. **Camping** Only at Ayer Keroh Recreational Forest and at Durian Tunggal Recreational Lake (on the way to Selandar).

Contrary to its name, Pulau Besar is a small, quiet island, about 8 km southeast of Melaka, which is popular at weekends. According to local legend, a princess became pregnant to a Melakan commoner and was banished to the island to die. There is a shrine on the island dedicated to an early Muslim missionary, who is said to have come to Melaka in the 1400s. The island has good beaches (although the sea is not clean and most of the coral is dead) and there are jungle walks. Located on 22 hectares of the 133-hectare island is the **B** *Panda Nusa Resort*, at 37 Jalan Chan Koon Cheng, T2818007, a deluxe beach resort designed to look like a traditional Melakan village. It has air conditioning, a restaurant, RM1.2m pool complex complete with open-air jacuzzi.

Pulau Besar

This is one of the peninsula's best known mountains, otherwise known as Mount Ophir, located on the east side of the north-south Highway, equidistant from Melaka and Muar and just inside Johor state. It is isolated from the mountains of the Main Range and is sacred to the Orang Asli of Melaka. A Straits Chinese and Malay rumour has it that the mountain is the domain of a beautiful fairy endowed with the local version of the Midas Touch: she has a habit of turning Gunung Ledang's plant-life into gold. The mountain is said to be guarded by a sacred tiger which is possessed by the fairy.

Gunung Ledang
Altitude: 1,276m

Gunung Ledang is a strenuous climb involving some very steep scrambles, particularly towards the top. In 1884 an expedition reached the summit while trying to demarcate the boundary between Johor and Melaka. Most climbers choose to camp overnight on the summit, although, at a push, it can be done in a day, from dawn to dusk. The mountain is surrounded by and covered in virgin jungle, and rises through mossy forest (where there are several varieties of pitcher plant, see page 526) to the rocky summit. Climbers are strongly advised to stick closely to the trails: since 1987, two separate parties of Singaporeans have become lost for several days after straying off the trail. The trail is complex in places and the climb should be carefully planned: would-be climbers are strongly recommended to refer to the detailed trail-guide in John Briggs' *Mountains of Malaysia*, which is available in Singapore and KL bookshops. There are two main trails up the mountain; the best route starts 15 km from Tangkak, just beyond Sagil. Waterfalls (*Air Terjun*) are signposted off the road which leads to Air Penas, an over-popular local picnic spot. The trail begins just beyond the rubber factory. Those attempting the climb without a trail-guide can hire a local guide from Tangkak.

Sleeping A *Gunung Ledang Resort*, 91-a, Jln Sutera, Taman Sentosa, T3347061, F3344270 (Sales office: 28, Jln Segamat, 84020 Sagil, T9772888, ledang@tm.net.my, www.ledang.com/index21.html. This place has 60 chalets and 30 jungle huts set in the jungle, facilities and activities include a swimming pool, gym, health centre, restaurant and convention centre. The resort is about 2 hours' drive on the North-South Express through Tangkak Town to Sagil; from there drive up the mountain.

Essentials

There's plenty of choice in Melaka but the cheaper hotels tend to be further out of town. There are several good hotels around Tanjung Kling (see **Excursions**, above). There are several good budget hotels at Taman Melaka Raya.

Sleeping
■ *on map, page 207*
Price codes:
see inside front cover

Southern Peninsula

AL *Pan Pacific Legacy Malacca*, 146 Jln Hang Tuah, T2816868, F2819898, pplhm@plegacy.po.my. New and sophisticated hotel with 250 plus rooms, business facilities, gymnasium, pool and more. Well designed and popular with business visitors. **A** *Century Mahkota*, Jln Merdeka, T2812828, F2812323. On the waterfront next to the Mahkota Parade Shopping and Entertainment Complex. Two pools, health centre, tennis court, two squash courts, mini golf, children's playground, spread out over several towers, the 617 'rooms' are actually suites and apartments, with the usual facilities plus kitchen, good introductory offers may have ceased by the time this book goes to press. **A** *City Bayview*, Jln Bendahara, T2839888, F2836699, cbviewmk@tm.net.my. A/c, restaurant, pool, the rooms visitors are shown are not like the ones they will end up with, the large construction in front of the hotel does not help its image. The most hideous crystal chandelier greets you as you enter the hotel. This poor taste is in keeping with much of the hotel. **A** *Equatorial*, Jln Bandar Hilir, T2828333, F3089333, info@mel.equatorial.com. A monstrous new 500-room block, pools, gym, several restaurants including Chinese, Nyonya and Japanese. Conference facilities. Towers over the south side of town, includes 'Churchill's cigar and wine bar', good value. **A** *Ramada Renaissance*, Jln Bendahara, T2848888, F2849269, enquiries@renaissance-melaka.com, www.renaissance-melaka.com. The only 5-star hotel in Melaka, 24-storeys high, it is the tallest building in the town, with 300 rooms all of which are spacious and elegantly appointed with Malaccan wood furniture, a/c, mini-fridge, TV, in-house video and grand views either over the town or to the sea, other amenities include coffee shop, restaurants, fitness centre, pool on the ninth floor. Recommended. **A-B** *Heeren House*, 1 Jln Tun Tan Cheng Lock, T2814241, F2814239. A/c, restaurant, rates include breakfast, 5 a/c nicely furnished rooms in colonial and Peranakan style, with canopied 4-poster beds (booking recommended) co-owned by a British lecturer from Singapore and his Chinese partner, good afternoon tea, pleasant position in front of the river. Timber floors and 4-poster beds add to the charm of this riverside hotel. Expensive for what you get (rooms are small). Breakfast included. Recommended.

B *Accordian Hotel*, 114 Jln Bendahara, T2821911, F2821333. A/c, shower, TV. Rooms in this rather gloomy hotel are a bit cramped. Price includes breakfast. **B** *Emperor*, 123 Jln Munshi Abdullah, T2840777, F2838989. A/c, restaurant, pool, good sea view, reasonably clean. Great sea views and excellent value at present prices. Breakfast included. Recommended. **B** *Grand Continental*, 20 Jln Tun Sri Lanang, T2840088, F2848125. A/c, restaurant, large rooms, good service, buffet for all meals, at a good price. Recommended. Breakfast included. **B** *Hotel Orkid*, 138 Jln Bendahara, T2825555, F2827777. Smart hotel at an affordable price. A/c, shower, TV. Facilities include a spa, restaurant and bar. Primarily a business visitor's stopover but offers value to tourists. Quite a distance from the centre of town. **B** *Lucky Inn*, 116 Jln Bendahara, T2810070, F2810071. New hotel. Rooms carpeted and newly furnished with TV and shower. **B** *Mimosa Hotel*, 108 Jln Buya Raya T2821113, F2819122. New hotel located in Chinatown – decent fully carpeted rooms with ac, TV and shower. Its restaurant is curiously only open between 0700-1400. **B** *Palace*, 201 Jln Munshi Abdullah, T2825355, F2848833. A/c restaurant, rooms are rather lacklustre and on the small size. Steer clear. **B** *Straits Meridian*, 1 Jln Malinja, Taman Malinja, towards Ayer Keroh, T2841166, F2830030. All suite accommodation. **B-C** *Baba House*, 125-127 Jln Tun Tan Cheng Lock, T2811216, F2811217. In the centre of Chinatown, a/c, no restaurant, TV, attractive traditional Baba house, beautiful design, rooms quite plain and some overly small but clean, mostly without windows.

C *Lotus Inn*, 2846 Jln Semabok, T2837211, F2837213. A/c, restaurant, east of town and inconveniently situated. **C** *Majestic*, 188 Jln Bunga Raya, T2822367/2822455. A/c, shower, restaurant, in a big colonial-style house, with high-ceilinged rooms, plenty of atmosphere and good downtown location. Close to the river.

D *Chong Hoe*, Jln Tukang Emas, T2826102. A/c, good location near all the central sights and temples and reasonable value. **D** *Eastern Heritage*, 8 Jln Bukit Cina, T233026. Great old Chinese building with carved wood and gold inlay, spacious rooms on second floor, dorm on third floor, small pool on first floor, batik lessons available, closer to the heart of the city than other low budget places. Extremely popular with an authentic feel. **D** *Kancil*, 177 Jln Parameswara (Bandar Hillir), T2814044, kancil@machuita.com.sg. Cool and quiet, quiet backyard/garden, bicycles for hire. Inconveniently situated on a narrow main road with no pavement. Basic rooms, some without windows, reasonable. **D** *Melaka Town Holiday Lodge*, 148b Taman Melaka Raya, T2848830. Limited breakfast included, hot showers, bikes for hire, laundry service, clean and well looked after, dormitory or rooms, friendly. Recommended. City tours and postal service available. **D** *Ng Fook*, 154 Jln Bunga Raya, T2828055. Some a/c, clean but simple rooms. **D** *Robin's Nest 2*, 202 Jln Taman Melaka Raya, T6026022. This new addition to Robin's expanding empire is located next door to the original. Virtually identical although (unsurprisingly) it has a newer feel to it and a/c is available. Shared shower/toilet. Very friendly owners. **D** *Sunny's Inn*, 253B Jln Taman Melaka Raya, T2275446. A couple of single and double rooms and a dorm (**F**), kitchen, bikes for hire, nightly video, good information, friendly staff, bus tickets. Very similar to most budget hotels in this area. **D** *Travellers Guest House*, 151 Jln Bunga Raya, T2824962. With a/c but without windows. Rabbit hutches with basin and shower head in room, together with drain (and the smells from all the other rooms and toilets). Overpriced.

E *Melaka Youth Hostel*, 341 Taman Melaka Raya, T2827915. Clean and well run with dorm beds (including an a/c dorm). **E-F** *Robin's Nest*, 205B Jln Taman Melaka Raya, T2829142. Clean and comfortable, helpful proprietor, dorm and fan rooms. Nightly video, shared washing facilities.

Malay 2 *Anda*, 8b Jln Hang Tuah, popular modern coffee shop, specialities include *ikan bakar* (grilled fish), *sayur masak lemak* (deep-fried marinated prawns) and *rendang*. 1 *Mini*, 35 Jln Merdeka, good for *ikan panggang* (grilled fish with spicy sauce), also *nasi campur*. 1 *Sederhana*, 18A Jln Hang Tuah, near the bus station, good selection of Malay dishes. 1 *Taman*, 10 Jln Merdeka, on the sea front, known for its *ikan assam pedas* – hot (chilli-hot) fish curry.

Eating
Price codes: see inside front cover

Chinese 3 *Good New World Restoran*, Taman Melaka Raya, 12842528, large and modern, specializes in Cantonese dishes. 2 *Dragon Village Restaurant*, 1 Jln Kubu Melaka, T2815678, in charming old building, popular, although out of the hub of things at the edge of Chinatown. 2 *Chop Teo Soon Leng*, 55 Jln Hang Tuah, Teochew cuisine. 2 *Keng Dom*, 148 Taman Melaka Raya, T2826409, renowned for its steamboats. 1 *Bee Bee Hiong*, City Park, Jln Bunga Raya, for fish-ball fans. 1 *Hoe Kee Chicken Rice*, Jln Hang Jebat, Hainanese chicken rice in Chinatown coffee shop, incredibly popular with workers at lunchtime. Recommended. 1 *Kim Swee Huat*, 38 Jln Laksamana, big menu with staple Western fillers (include travellers' food) as well as local food. 1 *New Oriental Satay and Mee*, 82 Jln Tengkera (road to Tanjung Kling), being a Chinese stall, serves pork satay and other variations such as cuttlefish (*sotong*) satay, also well known for its *yee kiow mee*. 1 *UE Teahouse*, 20 Lorong Bukit Cina, *dim sum* from early morning until 1200. Recommended.

Nyonya 3 *Jonkers*, 17 Jln Hang Jebat, old Nyonya house, with restaurant in the old ancestral hall. Good atmosphere and excellent food – Nyonya and International, set menu good value at RM20 (changes regularly), worth a visit for the house alone but the food is also excellent. Recommended. 3 *Nam Hoe Villa* (Restoran Peranakan), 317c Klebang Besar (6 km towards Port Dickson), T3154436, open 1100-1500, 1830-2300. Cultural show at 2000 (except Sat), originally the house of a Chinese rubber tycoon, now a restaurant and Peranakan showpiece, all the best known Nyonya dishes are served, buffet. **3 Restoran Peranakan Town House**, 107 Jln Tun Tan Cheng Lock, T245001, same management and concept as *Nam Hoe Villa*. **3 Ole Sayang**, 1988199 Taman Melaka Raya, T2831966, serves all the favourites, including chicken *pongteh* (in sweet and sour spicy sauce). Recommended. **3 Restoran Manis Sayang**, 617-618 Taman Melaka Raya, T2813393, traditional Nyonya chicken and fish dishes. **2 Nyonya Makko**, 124 Taman Melaka Raya, T2840737, located near the bottom of St Paul's Hill, good selection, cheap and friendly. Recommended. **2 Heeren House**, 1 Jln Tun Tan Cheng Lock, good value set lunch, cakes, appeals to Western tastes, some Peranakan and Portuguese dishes, a/c, attractive Peranakan furniture.

Indian **2 Mitchell Raaju Nivaas**, Jln Laksamana, aside from its good curries, this restaurant also offers cooking lessons, RM2, for those who want to make Indian breads and basic curries. **2 Veni**, 34 Jln Temenggong, banana leaf restaurant with good selection of meat curries and vegetarian dishes, roti canai breakfasts. **1 Banana Leaf**, 42 Jln Munshi Abdullah, South Indian meat curries and vegetarian dishes, biriyani specials on Wed and Sat evenings. **1 Kerala**, Jln Melaka Raya, good value. **1 Sri Lakshmi Villas**, intersection of Bendahara and Temenggong, fabulous *dosai masalas* and other good value Indian dishes.

Thai **3 My Place**, 357 Jln Melaka, also some Malay, Chinese and Indian dishes.

Portuguese Most restaurants in the *Medan Portugis* are expensive tourist traps but some of the spicy seafood dishes are worth trying. **3 Restaurante d'Nolasco**, 18b Medan Portugis, specializes in Portuguese cuisine. **3 Restoran de Lisbon**, Portuguese Square, run by Senhor Alcantra this places comes recommended with its dishes that blend Malaysian and Portuguese cuisines – including devil chicken curry and sea bass roasted in a banana leaf, all washed down with ice cold Portuguese lager or wines, cultural shows Sat evenings. **3 San Pedro**, Portuguese Settlement (just off the square), family run and probably the best at the Portuguese settlement, specialities include spicy baked fish, wrapped in banana leaf.

International **4 Taming Sari Grill**, *Renaissance Melaka Hotel*, Jln Bendahara, T2848888, seafood and meat cooked on marble with a little olive oil, served with bread, baked potato and salad. **2 Pandan**, Jln Kota, T2836858 (behind tourist information office), Western and local dishes, claypot noodle a speciality, pleasant location by roadside, friendly staff but over-salted food. Good for juices. **2 Café Sixties**, 12 Jln Melaka Raya 23, Taman Melaka Raya, T2819507, rock 'n' roll interior, fish 'n' chips, steak, curry and others.

Seafood *Pengkalan Pernu* (Pernu Jetty), 10 km south on the way to Muar, has several fish restaurants and stalls where you can pick your own fish and have it grilled. North of Melaka, towards Tanjung Kling there are a few Chinese seafood restaurants along the beach. **4 Bunga Raya Restaurant**, 39-40 Jln Taman, T2836456, crab, prawn and lobster are house specialities.

Fast food *Kentucky Fried Chicken*, Jln Taming Sari and Melaka Plaza, Jln Hang Tuah. *McDonalds*, Soon Seng Plaza, Jln Tun Ali.

Foodstalls *Satay celup* is a Melakan variation on a Malaysian theme: an assortment of skewered meats, fishballs, quails' eggs, crab, prawns, mussels, mushrooms and yams with traditional peanut sauce. *Glutton's Corner*, along the old esplanade on Jln Merdeka/Jln Taman: excellent choice of food although the stalls now face a painted wall rather than the sea, thanks to a land reclamation project. *Prince Satay Celup* at No 16.

Recommended. *Jalan Bendahara*, several noodle stalls and a Mamak man (Indian Muslim) who serves *sup kambing* (mutton soup) and the bits – for marrow suckers (opposite the *Capitol*), Chinese food. *Jalan Bukit Baru*, just off the main road past the state mosque, mostly Chinese food. *Jalan Bunga Raya*, stalls (next to Rex Cinema), sea-food recommended. *Jalan Semabok* (after Bukit Cina on road to JB), Malay-run fish-head curry stall which is a local favourite. *Klebang Beach*, off Jln Klebang Besar, Tanjung Kling – stalls, with several *ikan panggang* (grilled fish) specialists.

Bakery and softee ice-cream In basement of *Parkson Grand Department Store & Supermarket*, two more outlets in *Mahkota Parade Shopping Mall*; *Renaissance Melaka Hotel* has a good bakery shop in lobby.

Entertainment

Cinemas Jln Bunga Raya for English language films. **Cultural shows** At the Portu-guese Settlement every Sat at 2030. Songs and dances including the famous *beranyo*, an excuse for a sing-along and knees-up. *Nam Hoe Villa* (Restoran Peranakan), 317c Klebang Besar (6 km towards Port Dickson), T3154436, 2000 Sun-Fri, *Taman Mini Malaysia*, Ayer Keroh, 1120 and 1430 Sat, Sun and public hols. **Son et Lumière** *Melaka Light and Sound Show*, on the Padang, opposite St Paul's Hill, T011-664166, chronological history of Melaka, an hour-long show with a distinctly Malay nationalist perspective, 5 mins mention of European rule and no mention of the contribution by the Chinese and Indian ethnic communities, not expertly pre-sented. Mon-Sun, 2000 (Malay), 2130 (English), RM 10.

Festivals

March/April *Easter Procession* (movable), on Good Friday and Easter Sunday, starts from St Peter's Church.
May *Saint Sohan Singh's Prayer Anniversary* (movable) thousands of Sikhs from all over Malaysia and Singapore congregate at the Melaka Sikh temple, Jalan Temenggong, to join in the memorial prayers.
June *Pesta San Pedro (Feast of St Peter)* (movable) celebrated at the Portuguese Settlement by fishermen. The brightly decorated fishing boats are blessed and prayers offered for a good season. *Mandi Safar* (movable) bathing festival at Tanjung Kling. *Kite Festival* (movable) on the sea front.

Shopping

Melaka is best known for its antique shops, which mainly sell European & Chinese items

Antiques *Jalan Hang Jebat* (formerly Jonker St) is the best place for antiques. **Books** *Boon Hoong Sports and Bookstore*, 13 Jln Bunga Raya; *Times Bookshop*, Jaya Jusco Stores, Mukim Bukit Baru. **Book exchange** Jln Taman Melaka Raya for a good number of English language books. **Clothing** Artist Charles Cham sells very original T-shirts from his shop the *Orang Utan House*, 59 Lorong Hang Jebat. His place is hard to miss – a huge orange orang utan is painted on the outside of his shop. **Food** *Tan Kim Hock Product Centre*, 153 Jln Laksamana Cheng Ho, T2835322, distinguishable by its colour (pink), this shop is near the *Ramada Renaissance Hotel*, and is a delight for the eye and stomach: cookies and sweets in a great many varieties. Just ask for the 'Dodol Man'; everybody knows who he (Tan Kim Hock) is, a self-made man who became a billionaire with his business. A hotel in town has been named after him.

General Main shopping centres on Jln Hang Tuah and Jln Munshi Abdullah. *Mahkota Parade Shopping and Entertainment Complex*, including *Parkson Grand Department Store and Supermarket*, 1 Jln Merdeka, just south of the river mouth, a good choice of shops – the centre won an award for the best shopping centre in the country. **Handicrafts** *Karyaneka* (handicraft) centres at *1 Jalan Laksamana* and *Mini Malaysia Complex*, Ayer Keroh. Also *Crystal D'beaute*, 18 Medan Portugis. **Paintings** *The Orang Utan House*, 59 Lorong Hang Jebat, paintings by local artist Charles Cham. **Shoes** *Wah Aik Shoemaker Shop*, 92 Jln Hang Jebat. Shoes are still made here for Chinese grannies with bound feet (see page 213) and tourists.

Woodwork *Malacca Woodwork*, 312c Klebang Besar, T3154468, specialist in authentic reproduction antique furniture including camphor wood chests.

Sports **Golf** *Ayer Keroh Golf & Country Club*, 14 km from Melaka, green fees RM70 weekdays; RM100 weekends T2320822; *"A" Famosa Golf Resort*, Jln Kemus, Pulan Sebang, T5520888, near the Alor Gajah interchange of the north-south expressway, 18-hole course, green fees weekdays RM100, weekends RM150, buggy RM40, caddy RM20.

Tour operators *Annah (Melaka) Tours & Travel*, 27 Jln Laksamana, T2835626; *AR Tours*, 302a Jln Tun Ali, T2831977; *Satik Tour & Travel*, 143 Jln Bendahara, T2835712.

Transport **Local** **Bicycle hire**: many of the cheaper hotels/hostels rent out bikes, as do one or
See also Ins & outs, two shops in town, RM5-8 per day. **Buses**: local buses leave from Jln Hang Tuah, right
page 203 next to the long distance bus station. Less than RM1 round town. There is also an his-
149 km to KL torical shuttle bus which takes tourists through the main historical areas and out to
90 km to Port Dickson Ayer Keroh. A day pass costs RM5 and this allows three journeys. Hourly departures,
216 km to Johor Bahru 0930-1630. **Car hire**: *Avis*, 124 Jln Bendahara, T2846710. *Hawk* T2837878 *Sintat*, *Renaissance Melaka Hotel*, Jln Bendahara, T2848888; *Thrifty*, G-5 Pasar Pelancong, Jln Tun Sri Lanang, T2849471. **Taxi**: all taxis now have meters. There are stands outside major hotels and shopping centres, or T2823630. Between 0100 and 0600, there is a 50% surcharge. **Trishaws**: mostly for the tourist trade, they congregate at several points in town (there are usually a number near the the tourist information centre on the town square) – RM2 for single destination or RM10-15 per hour.

It is necessary to secure **Long distance** **Air**: airport is at Batu Berendam, 10 km out of town. Town bus 65 runs
a visa from the to the airport from the local bus station. Service on Wed, Fri and Sun with *Pelangi Air-*
Indonesian Embassy in *ways* to Pekanbaru in Sumatra. Airport flight information: T2822648 (*Pelangi* T3851175).
KL (see page 172) before **Train**: nearest station is at Tampin, 40 km north; Tampin railway station, T411034.
departing for Sumatra See page 35 for timetable.
from Melaka **Bus**: long distance buses leave from the terminal on Jln Hang Tuah. Regular con-
nections with KL, Seremban, Port Dickson, Ipoh, Butterworth, Lumut (Pulau Pangkor), Kuantan, Kuala Terengganu, Kota Bharu, Johor Bahru and Singapore (direct, 4 hrs).
Taxi: station opposite the local bus terminal on Jln Gaha Maju, just off Jln Hang Tuah. Vehicles leave for KL, Seremban, Penang, Mersing, Johor Bahru. Passengers for Singapore must change taxis at the long-distance terminal in JB.
Ferry: express ferries to Dumai (Sumatra), leave daily from the public jetty on Melaka River, 2 hrs (RM80). Tickets from *Atlas Travel Service*, Jln Hang Jebat, T2820777; *Madai Shipping*, Jln Tun Ali T2840671 – service leaves Malacca at 0900, one-way adult fare RM 80; Return RM 150. Other ferry companies include: *Tunas Rupat Utama Express*, 17A Jln Merdeka, T2832506; *Maharani*, (Ferry Malaysia Sdn Bhd) T-472, Jetty Quayside, T2844344.

Directory **Airline offices** *MAS*, 1st Flr, Hotel Shopping Arcade, *City Bayview Hotel*, Jln Bendahara, T2835722 (confirmations), T2829597 (enquiries). *Pelangi Airways*, Bangunan Terminal, Batu Berendam Airport, T3174175, F3173763. **Banks** *Bumiputra*, Jln Kota. *Hong Kong & Shanghai*, Jln Kota. Several banks on Jln Hang Tuah near the bus station and Jln Munshi Abdullah. *Spak Sdn*, 29 Jln Laksamana, T282674, authorized money changer. *Islah Enterprise*, G 79 Spice Route 27, Mahkota Parade, Jln Merdeka, T2811488, authorized money changers. **Communications** Area Code: 06. **General Post Office**: Just off Jln Kota next to Christ Church. In addition to stamps the PO sells a range of cards. **Medical facilities** Hospitals: *Straits Hospital*, 37 Jln Parameswara, T2835336. **Tourist offices** *Tourism Malaysia*, Jln Kota (opposite *Christ Church*), T2846622, F2849022. Open 0845-1700 Sat-Thu, 0845-1215 and 1445-1700 Fri. Also tourist information desk at Ayer Keroh, T3125811. **Useful addresses** Central Police Station: Jln Kota, T2825522. **Immigration office**: Bangunan Persekutuan, Jln Hang Tuah, T2824958/2824955 (for visa extensions). **Tourist Police**: Jln Kota, T2703238 (close to the Tourism Malaysia office).

Johor Bahru

Modern Johor Bahru – more commonly called JB – is not a pretty town. It lies on the southernmost tip of the peninsula and is the gateway to Malaysia from Singapore. JB is short on tourist attractions but has for many years served as a tacky red-light reprieve for Singaporeans. But Johor's paucity of cultural features belies its pivotal role in Malay history.

Phone code: 07
Colour map 2, grid C5

Ins and outs

JB has grown in size and stature over the last 5 years or so and is now a very important industrial centre. Senai airport is 20 km from town and there are connections with KL and several other destinations in East and Peninsular Malaysia. There are international air links with several destinations in Indonesia. A shuttle bus service runs from the airport to town. There is a regular bus service between Singapore and KL and links with most other towns on the Peninsula. Outstation taxis provide a service to KL, Melaka, Kuantan and Kota Bharu. The KL-Singapore railway line runs through JB and there are trains to both destinations including commuter trains to Singapore. There is a FerryLink service between Changi Point in Singapore and Tanjung Belungkor as well as ferries from JB's new jetty to Mersing on the East Coast.

Getting there
See also Transport, page 230

Cheap metered taxis provide the main form of transport for most visitors. There is also a comprehensive town bus service. For those who want to explore out of town there is a good range of local and international car hire firms to choose from. Note that hiring cars in JB is considerably cheaper than in Singapore.

Getting around

During the 1980s JB became an industrial adjunct to Singapore, attracting land and labour-intensive manufacturing industries. Johor's manufacturing boom has brought a measure of prosperity to the state capital and its dingy streets have begun to get a much-needed face-lift. Foreign investors have embarked on property buying sprees and new hotels, shopping plazas and office complexes have been springing up. The state government's intention is to emulate the development process of neighbouring Singapore.

At weekends JB is jammed with Singaporeans here, it would seem, largely for the sex and/or the shopping – and, perhaps, the chance to escape for a few hours from the stultifying atmosphere of their own clean and green country. During 1997 JB became the subject of a bitter spat between Malaysia and Singapore. In March, Singapore's Senior Minister Lee Kuan Yew suggested that the city was "notorious for shootings, muggings and car-jackings". The Malaysian press and some politicians reacted with fury – The Youth head of the ruling United Malays National Party (UMNO) going so far as to accuse Lee of being 'senile and uncouth'. Lee later apologized 'unreservedly'.

The old causeway across the *Selat Tebrau* (Strait of Johor), built in 1924, is still the only land-link to Singapore. It is overburdened with road traffic and also carries the railway and water pipelines: Singapore relies on Johor for most of its water supply. A

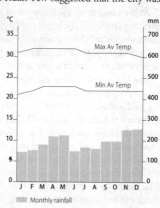

Climate:
Johor Bahru

Monthly rainfall

Southern Peninsula

☞ *Modern Johor: riding on the merlion's tail*

Johor is still a predominantly agricultural state, and is Malaysia's leading producer of palm oil, rubber, cocoa and coconuts. But in recent years, Singapore's prosperity has spilled across the 1.2 km causeway linking the island republic with JB. An explosion in foreign manufacturing investment led by Singapore has turned Johor into an industrial oasis.

The state planners are as startled as anyone at the suddenness of the transformation: in the past few years Johor has attracted about a quarter of total foreign investment in Malaysia. The industrial estates surrounding JB produce everything from typewriters and televisions to condoms and Kentucky Fried Chicken. Almost everything is immediately exported from JB's Pasir Gudang port. Recently, big Japanese and Taiwanese

petrochemicals plants have set up in the state too, one of them near Johor Lama, the site of the old royal capital.

Johor is now the northern point of the so-called 'Growth Triangle' which also incorporates Singapore and parts of Indonesia's Riau Archipelago. The state government, now facing a labour shortage, wants its industries to be increasingly hi-tech, and the Chief Minister has repeatedly stated that he aims to turn his state into a Singapore-clone by the year 2000. Tourism is big in Johor too, mainly because Singaporeans flood across the causeway to get a break from city life. Nearly three-quarters of all tourists visiting Malaysia come from Singapore: each day about 50,000 people cross the causeway to JB.

new link between JB and Singapore has finally been completed and is known, perhaps inevitably, as the Second Link. But it is not very popular. It is situated 30 km out of town to the west at Gelang Patah and the toll is actually higher than the causeway.

History

Following his trouncing by the Portuguese invaders in 1511, Melaka's young Sultan Ahmad fled south with what remained of the royal court, eventually arriving at Bintan in the Riau Archipelago. Ahmad was promptly executed by his father, Mahmud, for gross ineptitude and there then followed 15 years of attrition between the Portuguese and Mahmud, before the Portuguese destroyed his capital at Bintan in 1526. Mahmud died two years later and his remaining son became the first Sultan of Perak while his stepson established the Sultanate of Johor near Kota Tinggi, to the east of modern JB.

At the same time, the Sultanate of Aceh, on the north tip of Sumatra, was enjoying a meteoric rise to prominence. Rivalry between Johor and Aceh over-shadowed either's hatred of the Portuguese and the Acehnese terrorized Johor for another 60 years, frequently sacking the capital and twice carrying the royal family back to Sumatra as prisoners.

The Johor court was re-established on the Johor River in 1641 and the sultanate grew powerful again as an entrepôt, until the capital was destroyed by the rival Sumatran kingdom of Jambi in 1673. The sultanate moved to Bintan, then back to Kota Tinggi in 1685. But Sultan Mahmud was a tyrant who frightened off foreign traders; he was also a murderer and sexual pervert and was finally assassinated by his own people, thus ending the centuries-old Melaka Dynasty. Switching its capitals between the Johor River and Riau, the sultanate declined and remained weak throughout the 18th century; the Malay rulers, wracked by in-fighting, were by then firmly under the thumb of the ascendant Buginese and constantly squabbling over trade issues with the Dutch.

In 1818, with the Dutch temporarily absent due to the Napoleonic Wars, the British resident of Melaka, Colonel William Farquhar, signed a trade pact with the sultan in Riau. Thomas Stamford Raffles was meanwhile looking to set up a British trading post on the south end of the peninsula and after casting around the Riau Archipelago, settled on Singapore. There, in 1819, he signed a deal with Temenggong Abdur Rahman, the sultan's minister on the island, and later with one of two blue-blooded Malays claiming to be Sultan of Johor, allowing the English East India Company to establish a trading post in Singapore.

The 1824 Treaty of London between the British and the Dutch put an end to the Johor-Riau Empire, partitioning it between the two European powers. The Riau side became known as the Sultanate of Lingga, while the Temenggong was left to wield Malay power. Abu Bakar, the grandson of Singapore's Temenggong Abdur Rahman, moved his headquarters to the small settlement of Tanjong Putri in Johor, which he renamed Johor Bahru in 1866. The Anglophile Abu Bakar was known as the Maharajah of Johor until 1877, and in 1885, was recognized as Sultan by Queen Victoria. He developed the state's agricultural economy and, in the early 20th century, Johor attracted many European rubber planters. Sultan Abu Bakar is known as the father of modern Johor, which became the last state to join the colonial Malay Federation, in 1914.

Sights

One of the most prominent buildings in JB is the recently renovated **Istana Besar**, the Sultan's former residence on Jalan Tun Dr Ismail (built by Sultan Abu Bakar in 1866). It is now a royal museum, the **Royal Abu Bakar Museum**. Today the Sultan lives in the Istana Bukit Serene, which is on the west outskirts of town (it is not open to the public). The Istana Besar is a slice of Victorian England set in beautiful gardens, overlooking the strait. In the north wing is the throne room and museum containing a superb collection of royal treasures, including hunting trophies, as well as Chinese and Japanese ceramics. ■ *0900-1800 Mon-Sun, US$7 (ringgit equivalent), children under 12 US$3*.

The Royal Museum is one of Malaysia's best museums & makes a stay in otherwise unexciting JB worthwhile

Not far away, on Jalan Abu Bakar, is the **Sultan Abu Bakar Mosque**, which faces the Strait of Johor. It was finished in 1900 and clearly reflects the Victorian climate of the period. The mosque can accommodate 2,500 worshippers.

The 32m-high tower of the 1930s **Istana Bukit Serene** on Jalan Skudai – the home of the Sultan of Johore and not open to the public – is only outdone by the 64m tower of the State Secretariat, on Bukit Timbalan, which dominates the town.

Excursions

On the Straits of Melaka 40 km southwest of Johor is a small Chinese fishing kampung renowned throughout the country – and in Singapore – for its seafood, especially prawns and chilli crab. Most of the restaurants, known as *kelong*, are built on stilts over the water. The kampung has become so popular with Singaporeans that coach tours are laid on, and some of the restaurants – notably *Restoran Kukup* – are geared to cater for big groups. Weekend visits are not recommended for this reason. The kampung is also now dominated by a 36-hole golf course, the *Kukup Golf Resort*, Pekan Penorok, T6960952, F6960961, green fees weekdays RM120, weekends RM165. Next to the resort is a new dolphin learning centre where dolphin shows are held. To get there, take bus 3 to Pontian Kecil; from there to Kukup by taxi, or take a taxi the whole way. A pier has been built at Kukup and direct ferry connections with Tuas in Singapore are likely.

Kukup

Lombong At Lombong, 56 km northeast of JB below Gunung Muntahak, a series of waterfalls have cut natural swimming pools. Lombong is 13 km from **Kota Tinggi**, a former royal capital of Johor. Many of the mausoleums of the former sultans of Johor – including that of Mahmud Shah, the last sultan of the Melaka Dynasty – are nearby. The mausoleum of Sultan Mahmud, the feared ruler who was finally assassinated by one of his courtesans (see page 224) is at Kampung Makam (turn right 1 km north of Kota Tinggi, before Desaru sign).

The site of the old royal capital of **Johor Lama** ('Old Johor' – as opposed to Johor Bahru, or 'New Johor') is on the east bank of the Johor River, south of Kota Tinggi. Because it was twice burned to the ground there are no impressive ruins. The site is, however, clearly signposted off the Kota Tinggi-Desaru road (12 km). Just before Telok Sengat, turn right down a laterite track through an oil palm estate. Johor Lama, most of which lies under a rubber tappers' kampung, is 6 km down the track. There is no public transport to the site or to Telok Sengat so it is necessary to charter a taxi.

Sleeping and eating C *Waterfall Chalet*, Kota Tinggi Waterfall, T8331146 (must be booked in advance). A/c, reasonably well maintained. C *Sri Bayn Resort*, near Telok Sengat (5 km up laterite track through oil palm estate opposite turn-off to Johor Lama), only accessible for those with own transport. This is possibly the most tranquil and certainly the most remote chalet resort on the peninsula, set on steep hillside overlooking Johor estuary among coconut palms in neat gardens, chalets have balconies and fantastic views. **Kota Tinggi**: there are a number of places to stay including the D *Sin May Chun Hotel*, 36 Jln Tambatan, T8333573. Spacious, good value rooms. C *Nasha Hotel*, 40 Jln Tambatan, T078338000.

Seafood restaurant and coffee shops in nearby Telok Sengat. Recommended.

Transport From JB take bus 41 to Kota Tinggi (many departures), and from Kota Tinggi bus 43 to the waterfall. Or a taxi the whole way.

Desaru This holiday resort, set on a 20 km-long beach at Tanjung Penawar, 90 km east of JB, has been aggressively marketed in Singapore and as a result it gets invaded on weekends and public holidays. By the mid-1990s around half a million tourists were visiting the area each year. Although the beach is picturesque, the sea can get very rough, and there is a strong undertow; most holiday-makers stick to their hotel pools. The most popular pursuit here is golf on its beautifully landscaped seaside course. In 1991, in a fit of dollar-driven madness, a consortium of American and Japanese investors proposed transforming Desaru into a resort of obscene proportions at a projected cost of US$1.4bn. Incredibly, they even planned to build a Winter Wonderland complete with snow. Fortunately, it died soon after birth. However, in 1995 a new investor proposed a slightly more modest plan, worth just US$200m, to build hotels, more golf courses, a shopping complex et al. So change is in the air.

Designed with golf-crazed Singaporeans in mind, although on weekdays, chalet accommodation is reasonable. Budget travellers are better advised to head for Mersing & the offshore islands

Sleeping AL *Desaru Golf Inn*, T8221106, F8221408. A/c, restaurant, pool. **A** *Desaru View* (PO Box 71, Kota Tinggi), Tanjung Penawar, T8238221. A/c, restaurant, pool. **A-C** *Desaru Golden Beach Resort*, PO Box 50, Tanjung Penawar, T8221101, F8221480. A/c, restaurant, pool, former *Merlin Inn* with standard 4-star facilities, fills up with golfers on weekends, chalets next door are part of same resort (guests can use hotel pool) and are good value during the week. **C** *Tanjung Balau Fishing Village*, T8221201, F8221600. Dormitory-only accommodation in fishing village just outside Desaru, for those wanting to experience a fisherman's life.

Transport Bus 41; regular connections with JB via Kota Tinggi; taxi from JB. Two daily shuttles from most major hotels in Singapore. Regular boats connect Desaru with Changi Point, Singapore to Tanjung Pengileh, where taxis are available to Desaru.

Those taking the road north from Kota Tinggi may be tempted by countless roadside signs to *Jason's Bay Beach Resort* at Teluk Mahkota (25 km off main east coast road from turning 15 km northeast of Kota Tinggi). Despite its privacy, it is not really worth the bother. The once-lovely beach is muddy and disappointing; the resort is grimy and rooms smell musty. To get there, take bus 300 from Kota Tinggi.

Teluk Mahkota

Essentials

JB's top hotels cater for visiting businesspeople and have all the 5-star facilities. JB's expansion over the last few years has led to the opening of a number of new business hotels. Middle-market and cheaper hotels are as tacky as ever though: the 'hostess girl industry' is big business in JB. Many hotels rent out rooms by the hour. As such facilities are usually prominently advertised, patrons should know what to expect. Though many of these hotels are brothels to locals, for a tourist they are reasonably priced hotels in an otherwise expensive city. Room rates also increase on Fri and weekends. Because most budget travellers don't bother to stop in JB there really isn't much to choose from at the bottom end, except for an array of seedy short-stay hotels.

Sleeping
■ *on map, page 228*
Price codes:
see inside front cover

A *Holiday Inn Crowne Plaza*, Jln Dato Sulaiman, Century Garden, T3323800, F318884, Admin@holinn.po.my. A/c, restaurant, pool, 24 hr coffee house, unhelpfully located on suburban one-way system, frequented by the rich and the royal because of its Szechuan restaurant recently renovated. **A** *Hyatt Regency*, Jln Sungai Chat, T2221234, F2232718. Over 2 km west of town centre, all the comforts you would expect of the *Hyatt* chain including pool, tennis and an internet room. **A** *Merlin Inn*, 10 Jln Bukit Meldrum, T2237400, F2248919. A/c, restaurant, pool, comfortable hotel that looks like a truncated Toblerone, with a new wing recently added, good value but cut off from centre of town by railway and flyovers. **A** *Puteri Pan Pacific*, Jln Trus, T2233333, F2236622, general@panpjjb.po.my. A/c, 3 restaurants, pool, sauna, fitness and business centres, good city centre location for those on business, 500 rooms, tennis and squash courts, babysitting arranged, room rate includes airport transfer, fruit basket and welcome drink. Recommended.

B *Causeway Inn*, 6b Jln Meldrum, T2248811, F2248820. A/c, unlike neighbouring premises, this is a clean, quiet, well-run hotel that looks smart and does not overcharge with TV, excellent bathroom (bath). Check the room though because some have no view. Recommended. **B** *Crystal Crown*, 117 Jln Harimau, 117 Jln Tebrau, T3334422, F3343582, www.asia.online.com/crystalcrown, cchpj@crystalcrown.com.my. A/c, restaurants, TV, tea and coffee-making facilities, minibar, pool, organizes car hire. Breakfast included. **B** *Grand Continental*, 799 Jln Tebrau, T3323999, F3321999. Part of the *Grand Continental Chain*, rates include breakfast, rooms with a/c, TV, minibar and tea and coffee-making facilities, pool, health centre and business centre. Breakfast included. **B** *Rasa Sayang Baru*, 10 Jln Dato Dalam, T2248600. A/c, restaurant, inconveniently situated on the outskirts of town, discounts available in off-peak season. **B** *Straits View*, 1d Jln Scudai, T2241400, F2242698. A/c, restaurant (next door to *Jaws 5*), not much of a Straits view from downstairs rooms but the hotel is clean and the management friendly. **B** *Surf Pacific Hotel*, Jln Pelanduk, Century Garden, T3333300, F3333385. Three-star boutique hotel, 80 comfortable rooms with a/c, TV, in-house video, mini-fridge, tea and coffee-making facilities. Breakfast included. **B** *Top Hotel*, 12 Jln Meldrum, T2244755. Much better value than most of the mid-range hotels in this area. Large rooms with huge beds. Bathrooms of a very good standard. Recommended. **B** *Tropical Inn*, 15 Jln Gereja, T2247888, F2241544. A/c, restaurant, pool. Slightly reminiscent of an airport lounge but this offers very good value for JB. Breakfast included.

C *Gateway Hotel*, 61 Jln Meldrum, T2235029, F2235248. Colourful hotel exterior, a/c, shower, TV, central location. Good value. **C** *Hawaii*, 23 Jln Meldrum, T2240633, F2240631. Average Chinese-run hotel; much better value on weekdays when rates

Johor Bahru

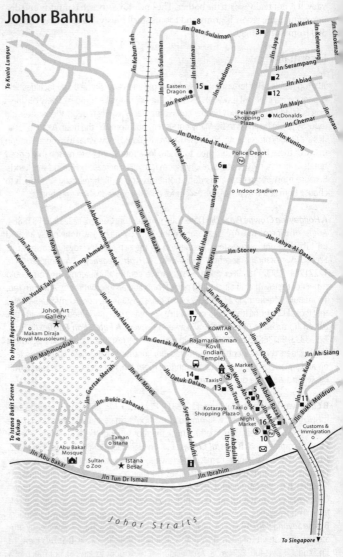

■ **Sleeping**	7 Hawaii	14 Rasa Sayang Baru
1 Causeway Inn	8 Holiday Inn Crowne Plaza	15 Surf Pacific
2 Cosy Inn	9 JB	16 Top
3 Crystal Crown	10 Le Tian	17 Tropical Inn
4 Footloose Homestay	11 Merlin Inn	18 Wadi Hassan Traveller's
5 Gateway	12 Meyah	Home
6 Grand Continental	13 Puteri Pan Pacific	

are slashed. Cheaper than most but by no means outstanding. **C** *JB Hotel*, 80a Jln Wong Ah Fook, T2234788. Some a/c, clean, reasonably spacious rooms and at this price. **C** *Le Tian*, 2, A-D Jln Sin Nam (just off Jln Meldrum), T2248151. Beyond the absolutely terrifying Chinese receptionist, the rooms are run down and the bathrooms resemble a public convenience; a/c. Better options are available elsewhere. **C** *Meyah Hotel*, 22 Jln Jaya, T3328789, F3325789. Clean, well managed, quiet place. Simple rooms with TV, a/c, shower. Inconvenient location for this mid-range hotel.

D *Cosy Inn*, 38a Jln Jaya, T3353388. Poorly maintained Chinese hotel with very basic amenities, avoid. **E** *Footloose Homestay*, 4H Jln Ismail, T2242881. In a quiet area of town outside the city centre, just 1 double room along with some dorm beds, friendly and well maintained, room rate includes breakfast. Recommended. **E** *Wadi Hassan Traveller's Home*, 52E Jln Wadi Hassan. Restaurant, dorm rooms, family rooms with fan, breakfast included, laundry service, tours organized, good local information. Recommended.

JB is best known for its seafood which is considerably cheaper than Singapore, leading scores of Singaporeans to cross the causeway at the weekend to throng the restaurants along the seafront road, Jln Ibrahim, running west from the town centre.

Eating
Price codes:
see inside front cover

Malay **3** *Dapur Rembia*, 1A-2 Jln Mohd Amin (close to *Jaws 5 restaurant*), old bungalow with tables outside. **2** *Sedap Corner*, 11 Jln Abdul Samad, Chinese as well as Malay dishes, a good line in fish-head curries. **1** *Wadi Hassan Travellers Home*, good traditional food.

Chinese **4** *Grand Court Restaurant*, *Hotel Grand Continental*, 3rd flr, T3345578, good selection including some Cantonese and Nyonya dishes. **3** *Eastern Dragon Restoran*, 49851 Jln Serigala, Century Garden, T3319600. Very popular. **3** *Ming Dragon*, G12-14 *Holiday Plaza*. Recommended. **2** *Teoyuan*, 21 Jln Maju, T331278. A/c, very clean.

Indian There are some good Indian restaurants in town including the **2** *Restoran Nilla* at 3 Jln Ungku Puan.

Thai **4** *Manhattan Grill*, Plaza Kotaraya, Jln Trus (opposite Pan Pac), haunt of JB's rich and relatively famous, new grill room with excellent food at half the price of the equivalents across the causeway. **4** *Meisan*, *Holiday Inn JB*, Jln Dato Sulaiman, Century Garden, superb but expensive spicy Szechuan restaurant. **4** *Selashi*, *Puteri Pan Pacific*, The Kotaraya, top quality Malay cuisine in tastefully decorated, expensive restaurant. **3** *134 Jalan Serampang*, Taman Pelangi, tables in the garden. **3** *Jaws 5 Seafood*, 1d Jln Skudai, very popular, next to *Straits View Hotel* and Machinta strip club, the food is very good, but not cheap, specialities include drunken prawns, frogs' legs and chilli crabs, diners may find flashing neons and revolving stage unsettling. Recommended. **3** *Newsroom Café*, Puteri Pan Pacific, The Kotaraya, offering reasonably priced local/continental dishes (enclosed brasserie area called *Editor's Corner*). **2** *Medina*, corner of Jln Meldrum and Jln Siew Niam, cheap and delicious murtabak, rotis, fish-head curries etc, open 24 hrs.

Foodstalls *Tepian Tebrau*, Jln Skudai (facing the sea beside the *General Hospital*) good for Malay food – satay and grilled fish. There is also good stall food at the long-distance bus terminal and outside the railway station. There is a sprawling outdoor hawker centre right in the centre of town, adjacent to the Plaza Kotaraya on Jln Trus. *Pantai Lido* is another well known hawker centre and there is a 'food court' in the *Kompleks Tun Abdul Razak* Jln Wong Ah Fook as well as the *Plaza Kotaraya* on Jln Trus. The night market on Jln Wong Ah Fook is also a great place to sample the full array of stall dishes.

Southern Peninsula

Entertainment **Discos** *Caesar's Palace*, *Holiday Plaza*; *Millennium*, *Holiday Inn*, Jln Dato Sulaiman.

Shopping **Books** *Johore Central Store*, Plaza Kota Raya, Jln Abdullah Ibrahim; *MPH Bookstore*, Holiday Plaza, Jln Dato Sulaiman; *Times Bookshop*, Plaza Pelangi, 4th Flr, in Kerry's Department Store, 2 Jln Kuning.

General Large shopping complexes include *Holiday Plaza*, Jln Datuk Sulaiman; *Kompleks Tun Abdul Razak* (KOMTAR), Jln Wong Ah Fook; *Plaza Pelangi*, Jln Tebrau; *Sentosa Complex*, Jln Sutera; *Kotaraya*, off Jln Trus, a pink building situated in the centre of the city, opposite the night market – possibly the best place to shop with a hawker centre upstairs.

Handicrafts *Craftown Handicraft Centre*, Jln Skudai; *Jaro*, Jln Sungai Chat; *Johorcraft*, Kompleks Kotaraya and Kompleks Tun Abdul Razak, Jln Trus; *Karyaneka Centre* at Kompleks Mawar, 562 Jln Sungeai Chat; *Mawar*, Jln Sultanah Rogayah, Istana Besar. There is also a big new *Johorcraft* complex 1 km before Kota Tinggi on the road from JB selling rather downmarket arts and crafts from all over Malaysia. It is aimed at big coach tours from Singapore, has a large restaurant and provides demonstrations of pottery, batik and songkhet production. Open Mon-Sun 0800-1800.

Sports **Bowling** *Holiday Bowl*, 2nd Flr Holiday Plaza, Jln Dato Sulaiman. **Golf** *Royal Johor Country Club*, Jln Larkin, T2233322, green fees RM100 weekdays, RM200 weekends. *Palm Resort Golf and Country Club*, Jln Persiaran Golf, Off Jln Jumbo (near airport), Senai, T5996222, F5996001, course is part of a 5-star resort which includes tennis, squash, bowls, pool, fitness centre, sauna, Japanese baths and luxury hotel and bungalows, green fees weekdays RM135, weekends RM250, caddy fee RM25, buggy RM20.

Transport
See also Ins & outs, page 223
134 km to Mersing
224 km to Melaka

Local **Bus**: local buses leave from the main bus terminal on Jln Wong Ah Fook; there is no shortage of local taxis (no meters). **Car hire**: it is much cheaper to hire a car in JB than it is in neighbouring Singapore but check whether the car hire company allows the car to go to Singapore. *Avis*, *Tropical Inn Hotel*, 15 Jln Gereja, T2244824; *Budget*, Suite 216, 2nd Flr Orchid Plaza, T2243951; *Calio*, *Tropical Inn*, Jln Gereja, T2233325; *Halaju Selatan*, 4M-1 Larkin Complex, Jln Larkin; *Hertz*, Room 646, Puteri Pan Pacific Hotel, Jln Salim, T2237520; *National*, 50-B Ground Floor Bangunan Felda, Jln Sengget, T2230503 (and at the airport); *Thrifty*, *Holiday Inn*, Jln Dato Sulaiman, T3332313; *Sintat*, 2nd Flr, Tun Abdul Razak Kompleks (KOMTAR), Jln Wong Ah Fook, T2227110. **Taxi**: popular and quite cheap.

Long distance **Air**: *MAS* and *Pelangi* fly into Senai, JB's airport, 20 km north of the city. Transport to town: buses every hour and taxis. For passengers flying *MAS* to Singapore, there is a shuttle service from the airport to *Novotel Orchid Inn*, Singapore with express immigration clearance. *MAS* operates an a/c shuttle bus from *Puteri Pan Pacific Hotel* to the airport. Regular connections on *MAS* with Ipoh, Kota Kinabalu, KL, Kuala Terengganu, Kuantan, Kuching, Labuan, Lahad Datu, Miri, Penang and Tawau. *Pelangi Airways* flys to Ipoh and KL.

MAS also operates international connections with Denpasar (Bali), Jakarta, Surabaya, Sandakan and Ujung Pandang, all in Indonesia as well as other worldwide destinations. *Pelangi Airways* flies daily to Medan and 4 times a week to Padang and Palembang, allin Sumatra, Indonesia.

Train: the station is on Jln Campbell, near the causeway, off Jln Tun Abdul Razak. Regular connections with **KL** and all destinations on the west coast, see page 35 for timetable. Malaysian and Singapore immigration desks are actually in the Singapore railway station, so for those wanting to avoid delays on the causeway, this is a quick way to get across the border; there are regular commuter trains across to the island, see page 35 for details of timetable.

Bus: the Larkin bus terminal is inconveniently located 4 km north of the town centre. Book opposite railway station on Jln Tun Abdul Razak. Regular connections with **Melaka**, **KL** (RM20), **Lumut**, **Ipoh** (RM25.80), **Butterworth** (RM33.50), **Mersing**, **Kuantan**, **Kuala Terengganu**, **Alor Star** (RM37.70), **Kota Bharu**.

The *Singapore Bus Service* between **Singapore** and JB runs every 10 mins from 0630 to 2400. The Ban San Terminal in Singapore is between Queen St and Rochor Canal Rd. From Singapore, it costs twice as much as from JB, and from JB the Singapore Bus Service takes almost double the time to do the journey. The 170 Singapore bus and the SBS Johor/Singapore Express only leave from the JB Larkin terminal. To save time at the border, get entry forms for Singapore at the terminal.

Taxi: the main long-distance taxi station is attached to the Larkin bus terminal 4 km north of town. However the old terminal, on Jln Wong Ah Fook, is also still operating and much more convenient. Taxis from here to destinations including KL, Melaka, Mersing and Kuantan.

Malaysian taxis leave for **Singapore** from the taxi rank on the first floor of the car park near the KOMTAR building on Jln Wong Ah Fook. They leave when full and go to the JB taxi rank on Rochor Canal Rd in Singapore. Drivers provide immigration forms and take care of formalities making this a painless way of crossing the causeway. Touts also hang around JB's taxi rank offering the trip to Singapore in a private car. They will take you directly to your address in Singapore, although their geography of the island is not always expert. This is also a fairly cost-effective way to travel and is reliable.

Road: the causeway between JB and Singapore can get jammed, particularly at rush hours although a Special Priority Lane is now open for speedier clearance of tourists.

Avoid the causeway at all costs during public holidays

Sea: JB's ferry terminal to the east of the causeway is operating ferry services to **Mersing** and **Tanjung Belungkor**. Bumboats leave from various points along Johor's ragged coastline for **Singapore**; most go to Changi Point (Changi Village), on the northeast of the island where there is an immigration and customs post. The bumboat routes from Tanjung Surat and Tanjung Pengileh to Changi Point make sense for those coming from the east coast, Teluk Makhota (Jason's Bay) or Desaru (taxis to the jetty from Desaru cost RM28). The boats run from 0700-1600 and depart when full (12 passengers). There is now a vehicle ferry from Tanjung Belungkor (JB) to Changi Point 3 times a day, T653236088. JB's ferry terminal east of the causeway ferry connnections with Changi Point and the World Trade Centre in Singapore, and Batam in Indonesia.

Airline offices *MAS*, 1st Flr Plaza Pelangi, Menara Pelangi, Jln Kuning, Taman Pelangi, T3341003/3341001 – a little over 2 km from the town centre. *Pelangi Airways*, c/o MAS, Menara Pelangi, Jln Kuning, Taman Pelangi, T3341001, F3340043. **Banks** *Bumiputra, Hong Kong and Shanghai* and *United Asia* are on Bukit Timbalan. Other big banks are on Jln Wong Ah Fook, several money changers in the big shopping centres and on/around Jln Ibrahim/Jln Meldrum. **Communications** Area Code: 07. Post Office: Jln Tun Dr Ismail. **Telephone office:** Jln Trus (opposite the *Puteri Pan Pacific Hotel*). **Medical facilities** Hospitals: *Sultanah Aminah General Hospital*, Jln Skudai. **Tourist offices** *Johor Tourist Information Centre (JOTIC)*, T2249960, and *Malaysian Tourism Promotion Board*, T2223591, both located at 2 Jln Air Molek. Open: 0900-1700 Mon-Sat, 1000-1600 Sun. *Southern Region Tourism Office*, 4th Flr, KOMTAR, T2223591. **Useful addresses** Immigration office: 1st Floor, Block B, Wisma Persektuan, Jln Air Molek, T2244253.

Directory

Southern Peninsula

Southern Peninsula

East Coast Peninsula

6

East Coast Peninsula

It might just be on the other side of the peninsula, but Malaysia's east coast could as well be on a different planet than the populous, hectic and industrialized west coast. Its coastline, made up of the states of Johor, Pahang, Terengganu and Kelantan, is lined with coconut palms, dotted with sleepy fishing kampungs and interspersed with rubber and oil palm plantations, paddy fields, beaches and mangroves.

With its jungle, beaches and islands and its strong Malay cultural traditions, it holds many attractions for tourists. The only problem is that during the Western world's winter holiday period, the east coast is awash with monsoon flood water, which confines the tourist season to between March and October. Many beach resorts completely close down during these monsoon months as do the offshore islands. The best known tourist attraction on the east coast is the grimy village of Rantau Abang in Terengganu, where leatherback turtles lumber up the beach to lay their eggs between May and October.

Background

For centuries, the narrow coastal plain between the jungled mountains and the sea was largely bypassed by trade and commerce and its 60-odd coral-fringed (and largely uninhabited) offshore islands were known only to local fishermen. The mountainous interior effectively cut the east coast off from the west coast, physically, commercially and culturally. The east coast did not have the tin deposits which attracted Chinese speculators and miners to the towns on the other side of the Main Range in the 19th century; and in more recent decades it was left behind as Malaysia joined the development race. The rural parts have been buffered from Western influence; traditional kampung lifestyles have been tempered only by the arrival of the electric lightbulb, the outboard motor and the Honda 70. The east coast's fishermen and paddy farmers are Malaysia's most conservative Muslims. In the 1990 general election, the people of Kelantan voted a hardline Islamic opposition party into power. In the 1995 general election they made the same choice once more. Parti Islam now runs the state government and represents its Kelantan constituencies in federal parliament. The rural Malays of the east coast have not enjoyed much in the way of 'trickledown' from Malaysia's new-found economic prosperity. Although they are *bumiputras* – or 'sons of the soil' (see page 510) – few have reaped the benefits of more than two decades of pro-Malay policies.

During the Second World War, the Japanese Imperial Army landed at Kota Bharu and sped the length of the peninsula within six weeks on stolen bicycles (see page 496). The east coast did not figure prominently during the war, except in the realm of literary fiction, where it starred in Neville Shute's *A Town Like Alice*.

Before and after the war, rubber and oil palm plantations sprang up – particularly in the south state of Johor – which changed the shape of the agricultural economy. But the most dramatic change followed the discovery of large quantities of high-grade crude oil and natural gas off the northeast coast in the 1970s. By the mid-1980s, huge storage depots, gas processing plants and refineries had been built in Terengganu, and the battered old coast road was upgraded to cater for Esso and Petronas tankers. The town of Kerteh, halfway between Kuantan and Kuala Terengganu, is a refinery town, built along one of the best beaches on the peninsula. The construction boom and the rig work helped boost the local economy and provide employment, but the east coast states (bar Johor, which straddles the entire south tip of the peninsula) have singularly failed to attract much industrial investment in the way their west coast neighbours have. Oil money has, however, helped transform the fortunes of Terengganu.

On the whole, the east coast has been less sullied by industrial pollution; the South China Sea is a lot cleaner than the Strait of Melaka. Despite the oil the east coast is still the rural backwater of the peninsula (95 percent of state revenues from oil go straight into federal coffers in KL).

Getting there   The east coast can be reached from various points on the west coast. Routes from Butterworth (Penang) and Kuala Kangsar in the north, lead across to Kota Bharu on the northeast coast. The highway from KL goes to Kuantan (halfway down the east coast) and the railway cuts north from Gemas (south of KL) to Kota Bharu. There are also road routes from KL to the southeast coast. Another common route is to follow the trunk road north from Johor Bahru which hits the east coast at Mersing, the launch-pad for Pulau Tioman and the islands of the Seribuat group.

Islam on the east coast: fundamental pointers

Because the east coast states are a bastion of Islamic conservatism, which was reinforced by the victory of Parti Islam in Kelantan in the 1995 general election, visitors should be particularly sensitive to the strictures of Islam. Those determined to get an all-over tan should not attempt to acquire it on the east coast's beaches, and women should dress 'respectfully' in public. Many Malay women choose to wear the tudung, the veil which signifies adherence to the puritanical lifestyle of the fervently Islamic dakwah movement. The east coast stands in contrast to other parts of the peninsula, where this garb is more often a fashion accessory than representative of a lifestyle. In 1988 cultural purists on the east coast began voicing concern about the 'cultural and moral pollution' that tourism brought in its wake. But any resentment that the arrival of Western tourists may have sparked seems to have evaporated in the face of the economic opportunities generated.

Malaysia's Islamic powerhouse in the states of Kelantan and Terengganu poses one possible occupational hazard for tourists, particularly if they travel north-to-south. In these two states, the weekend starts on Thursday lunchtime and everyone drifts back to work on Saturday. By and large, even the Chinese businesses observe the Muslim weekend. This means

banks are shut and those unfortunate to mistime their travels can find themselves arriving in Kuantan just in time for the banks there to close down too. Pahang state observes the Saturday/Sunday weekend. Be warned. In common with other strict Islamic states, there have also been moves in Kelantan to restrict the sale of alcohol, although at present it is still available in Chinese-run shops. Malay-run establishments in Terengganu and Kelantan are barred from serving alcohol. The bars and discos which contribute to a lively nightlife scene on the west coast are conspicuously absent on the east coast. In Kota Bharu even the large hotels do not serve alcohol, and recently there was a petition to form separate queues in supermarkets for men and women. In 1997 the state government in Kelantan went so far as to issue an edict that cinemas keep their lights on when showing films – just in case movie-goers have any amorous intentions. During Ramadan, which is strictly observed, Malay food and beverage outlets remain closed until Muslims break puasa (fast) after sundown. Although this means that it is impossible to find a good rendang or satay until the evening, travellers can feast on the amazing variety of colourful kueh – or cakes – which are sold at roadside stalls.

Mersing

This small fishing port is a pleasant but undistinguished little town. Most people are in a hurry to get to the islands and spend as little time as possible in the town, but as fishing boats can only make it out into the sea at high tide, some people will inevitably get stuck here for the night. In the past couple of years a number of good little restaurants have sprung up and Mersing is not an unpleasant place to spend a day or two. The town is evidently prospering, thanks to the through flow of tourists to the islands.

Phone code: 07
Colour map 2, grid B5

A big new plaza opened in 1992 and now accommodates the plethora of tour and ticketing agencies. The riverside jetty just out of town to the east is the jumping-off point for Pulau Tioman, the best known of the east coast's offshore islands. There are, however, 64 islands in total; others that can be reached from Mersing include Pulau Rawa, Pulau Sibu, Pulau Tinggi, Pulau Tengah, Pulau Aur and Pulau Pemanggil (see below).

Nine kilometres north of Mersing on the road to Endau, there is a reasonably good beach, **Pantai Air Papan**, signposted off the road. Formerly, the most popular beach was **Sri Pantai**, but it is now stony and unpleasant.

Excursions

For details of Endau Rompin National Park, see page 253.

Pantai Air Papan, 9 km north of Mersing, is the best mainland beach in the area. It is 5 km off the main road north and the beach is about 2 km long, between two headlands. The beach is quite exposed but is backed by lines of casuarina and coconut palms. There is a liberal scattering of rubbish among the trees. There are a number of places at the end of the road offering budget accommodation within the **C-E** range. These include *Teluk Godek Chalet (Lani's Place)*, T7994469 which looks the newest and best; *Mersing Chalet and Restaurant (Seri Mersing)*, T7994194; *Air Papan Chalets*, T7992384. More secluded is *Nusantara Chalet*, 1½ km north through the kampung which stretches along the beach. There are a few beach shelters dotted along the beach.

Transport Bus: Mersing-Endau bus (No 5) to Simpang Air Papan (turn-off); there is no bus service connecting with the beach, although it is possible to hitchhike. **Taxi**: chartered taxi available. Arrangements can be made for pick-ups later in the day.

Essentials

Sleeping **B** *Mersing Inn*, 38 Jln Ismail, T7991919. Fairly new, so discounts are available (overpriced at full price), clean and bright, but bathrooms are very small and there's no restaurant. **B** *Seri Malaysia*, Jln Ismail, T7991876, F7991886. A/c, tea and coffee-making facilities, pool, restaurant, just out of the centre. **B** *Timotel*, 839 Jln Endau, T79995898, F7995333. Looks like a set of offices from the outside but offers huge, luxurious rooms. Just out of the centre of town.

C *Country Hotel*, 11 Jln Sulaiman, T7991799/7179564. A/c or fan, formerly the *Mandarin Hotel*, very overpriced but has a convenient location near the market and the bus and taxi stands. **C-D** *Embassy*, 2 Jln Ismail, T7993545/7991301. Some a/c, restaurant, very well-kept hotel – scrupulously clean, rooms without TVs considerably cheaper. Recommended. **C** *Kali's Guesthouse*, No 12E Kampung Sri Lalang, T7993613. Fan only, restaurant, arguably the best-kept, friendliest and most relaxed place to stay in Mersing area, rooms range from longhouse dorm to 'A'-frames and bungalows, atap-roofed bar and small Italian restaurant in garden next to beach, managed by Kali (a qualified diving instructor) and two Italians. Highly recommended. *Getting there*: Mersing-Endau bus or taxi. **D** *Golden City*, 23 Jln Abu Bakar, T7995028, F7991723. Bathroom (shower), near the bus station, clean but a bit run-down. Rooms with fan cheaper than a/c. **D** *Mersing Hotel*, 1 Jln Dato Mohammed Ali, T7991004. A/c, restaurant, spartan rooms now a bit tatty, clean enough but *Embassy* a better bet. Some a/c. **D** *Omar Backpackers' Dorm*, Jln Abu Bakar, T7995096, F7744268. Clean and well looked-after but only 10 beds, excellent information on Sibu and other less visited islands, treks and river

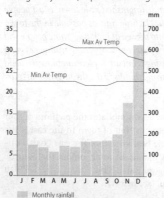

Climate: Mersing ▬ Monthly rainfall

cruises. Relaxed place where the owner seems to let the guests run things. Very basic rooms. Recommended.

E *East Coast Hotel*, 43a Jln Abu Bakar, T7991337. Rooms here are spacious and clean. Fan, shared bathroom. **E** *Syuan Koong*, 44A Jln Abu Bakar, T7991498. Fan only, some rooms with attached bath, clean but dated. **F** *Sheikh Guesthouse*, 1B Jln Abu Bakar, T7993767. Dorms only, clean and friendly, efficient tourist agency attached with information on all the islands, the *Sheikh Tourist Agency* downstairs offers ticketing, tours, accommodation booking and up-to-date information on Tioman and other islands. Ask here for details on other accommodation up the coast. **F** *Tioman Lodging*, 2 Jln Ismail (above *Malayan Muslim Seafood Restaurant*), dorms and rooms run by young Malay couple from Tioman, clean, with information about islands, ticketing.

Malay 1 *Malayan Muslim Seafood*, 2 Jln Ismail, very cheap and unusual Malay restaurant with coconut seafood dishes, special Indonesian fish-head curry. Recommended. **1** *Malaysia*, opposite the bus stop, open all night. **1** *Restoran Al-Arif*, 44 Jln Ismail (opposite *Parkson* supermarket), cheap Muslim restaurant with good rotis and curries. **1** *Sofair*, 25 Jln Ismail, Indian coffee shop serving rotis and murtabak. **1** *Sri Mersing Café*, opposite *Restoran Malaysia*. **1** *Zam-Zam*, 51 Jln Abu Bakar, more Muslim food with dosai, prata and Mersing's best murtabaks.

Chinese 3 *New I came also*, 181 Jln Jemalang, excellent Chinese food, very friendly service. **2** *Embassy Hotel Restaurant*, 2 Jln Ismail, big Chinese seafood menu, reasonably priced, chilli crabs, drunken prawns, wild boar and kang-kong belacan. Recommended. **2** *Mersing* (Ground Floor, *Mersing Hotel*), Jln Dato Mohammed Ali, excellent seafood. **2** *Mersing Seafood*, 56 Jln Ismail, a/c restaurant with spicy Szechuan or Cantonese seafood dishes, try squid with salted egg yoke, spicy coconut butter prawns, big menu, reasonable prices. **2** *Sin Nam Kee Seafood*, 387 Jln Jemaluang (1 km out of town on Kota Tinggi road), huge seafood menu and reckoned by locals to be the best restaurant in Mersing, occasional karaoke nights can be noisy. **1** *Yung Chuan Seafood*, 51 Jln Ismail, big open coffee shop with vast selection, speciality: seafood steamboat.

Indian 1 *Taj Mahal*, Jln Abu Bakar.

Foodstalls There are a number of upmarket stalls and coffee shops in the new *Plaza R & R* next to the river.

Eating
Restaurants seem to close quite early here

Internet café *Mersing Café*, Jln Endau, below the *Timotel Hotel*, T7995888, open 1800 – 0000, MTV, live football, internet.

Cafés

Arts Souvenir, 1, Gerai MDM, Jln Tun Dr Ismail, next to Malay restaurants on the corner after *R & R Plaza*. Artist Sulaiman Aziz specializes in colourful t-shirts, shorts and beachware and hand-painted batiks. There are some knick-knack souvenir shops in the *R & R Plaza*.

Shopping

There are ticketing and travel agents all over town dealing with travel to and from the islands and accommodation. They are much of a muchness and visitors are unlikely to be ripped off. Many agents are now located in the new *Plaza R & R* on Jln Tun Dr Ismail, next to the river. Competition is intense at peak season and tourists can be hassled for custom. Many agents also promote specific chalet resorts on the islands to which they offer package deals; sometimes these can be good value, but buying a boat ticket puts you under no obligation to stay at a particular place. Among the better agents are: *Golden Mal Tours*, 9 Jln Sulaiman, T7991463; *Omar's*, opposite the Post Office, T7995096; *Island Connection*, 19 R & R Plaza (owns *Mukut Village Chalets* on Tioman), T7992535; *Sheikh Tourist Agency*, 1B Jln Abu Bakar, T7994990. *Kebina*, Jln Abu Bakar, T7993123, F7995118.

Tour operators

East Coast Peninsula

Transport

133 km N of Johor Bahru
189 km S of Kuantan
353 km to KL

Local Bus: the local bus station is on Jln Sulaiman opposite the *Country Hotel*.

Long distance Bus: long-distance buses leave from two locations: the roundabout by the *Restoran Malaysia* and Jln Abu Bakar, not far from the jetty. Regular connections with **KL** (1200, 2200; RM16.50), **JB** (1230 express; RM11, 0815 and 1400 local; RM5.10), **Kuala Terengganu** (1200, 2300; RM19), **Kuantan** (1200, 1300; RM10.35), **Ipoh** (1200, 2200; RM26), **Penang** (1700; RM35), **Melaka** (1100, 1600; RM11.20), and **Singapore** (1300, 1600; RM11.10), **KB** (2130; RM25.10). Passengers have reported having their bags stolen *en route* between Mersing and Singapore while stored in the luggage compartment of the coach; eg on buses of the *Johora Express*.

Taxi: taxis leave from Jln Sulaiman opposite the *Country Hotel*, next to the local bus station; **KL**, **JB** (RM80) (for Singapore, change at JB), **Melaka** (RM25), **Kuala Terengganu** and **Kuantan**.

Boat: the jetty is a 5-min walk from the bus stop. Most of the ticket offices are by the jetty but boat tickets are also sold from booths near the bus stop. (See transport to individual islands.) **NB** The boat trip to the islands from Mersing can be extremely rough during the monsoon season; boats will sometimes leave Mersing in the late afternoon, on the high tide, but rough seas can delay the voyage considerably. During peak monsoon all ferry services are cancelled and the ferry companies move to the west coast to find work there. It is advisable only to travel during daylight hours. Mersing Island Ferry Information, Jln Abu Bakar, T7993606/0107734496.

Directory

Banks *Maybank*, Jln Ismail; *UMBC*, Jln Ismail, no exchange on Sat. Money changer on Jln Abu Bakar and *Giamso Safari*, 23 Jln Abu Bakar also changes TCs. **Communications** Area code: 07. **Post Office**: Jln Abu Bakar. **Internet**: See **Cafés**, above. **Medical facilities** Dentists: Dr Logesh, Klinik Pergigian, 28 Jln Mohd, Ali, T7993135. **Doctors**: Dr Lai Chin Lai, Klinik Grace, 48 Jln Abu Bakar, T7992399. **Tourist offices** *Mersing Tourist Information Centre*, Jln Abu Bakar (about 1 km from the jetty walking into town), T7995212. Friendly and useful source of information.

Pulau Tioman

Phone code: 07
Colour map 2, grid B6

Tioman, 56 km off Mersing, is the largest island in the volcanic Seribuat Archipelago at 20 km by 12 km. The island is dominated by several jagged peaks, notably the twin peaks of Nenek Semukut and Bau Sirau towards the southern end of the island, and in Malay legend its distinctive profile is the back of a dragon whose feet got stuck in the coral. It is densely forested and is fringed by white coral-sand beaches; with kampungs around the coast.

The highest peak is Gunung Kajang (1,049m) or Palm Frond Mountain. It has been used as a navigational aid for centuries and is mentioned in early Arab and Chinese sailing charts. In the mid-1970s, 12th-century Sung Dynasty porcelain was unearthed on the island.

Despite the growth in hotels and guesthouses, Tioman, once rated as one of the world's 10 best 'desert island escapes' by *Time* magazine, remains a beautiful island. In the 1950s it was discovered by Hollywood and selected as the location for the musical *South Pacific* where it starred as the mythical island of Bali Hai. All this attention put Tioman on the map; tourism accelerated during the 1970s and 1980s as facilities were expanded. However, during the 1990s business has not been quite so brisk and prices, which for some establishments during the 1980s were absurdly high, given the level of amenities on offer, have now levelled out. Indeed most hotels have not increased their rates for five years or so. Even so there are various new hotels under construction and guest-houses still seem to be building new chalets or upgrading existing ones.

The cheaper beach-hut accommodation is mostly to be found on the north-west side of the panhandle, and despite a growth in the number of places to stay, these little kampungs have retained their charm and are still very laid back, making them an idyllic retreat for anyone who is looking for a deserted beach, a touch of snorkelling or diving and some great seafood. Thankfully, as yet, there are no nightclubs or fast-food restaurants and the tourist trinket shops are very low key. But the emergence of a condotel – even the name must be one of the ugliest in the English language – to the south of the *Berjaya Tioman Beach Resort* (and owned by them) is, perhaps, a sign of things to come. The Tioman website, www4.jaring.my/spsj/island/tioman/tio_main.htm, has lots of local information and pictures of many guesthouses and resorts.

Getting around the island

There are very few trails around the island and only one road, a 2 km stretch from the airstrip at Tekek to the *Berjaya Tioman Beach Resort*. Plans are afoot to build a road across to the less-developed east side of the island, presently connected by a beautiful jungle trail (see trekking, below), but there has been talk of this for a number of years. To get from one kampung to another, the best way is to go by boat and a 'sea bus' service works its way around the island (see **Transport**, below).

The **cross-island trail**, from the mosque in Kampung Tekek to Kampung Juara, on the east coast, is a two to three hour hike (around 4 km), which is quite steep in places. The trail is reasonably well marked: follow the path past the airport and then turn inland towards the mosque. From Juara, the trail begins opposite the pier. It is a great walk, although for those planning to stay at Juara, it is a tough climb with a full pack. The section from Tekek is part natural path, part concrete steps. Three-quarters of the way up from Tekek there is a small waterfall, really just a jumble of rocks and water, just off the path to the right. It can be wonderfully refreshing after the arduous climb, but check for leeches when you emerge. Shortly after the waterfall the route levels out and works it way through an upland plateau. This is the most enchanting part of the walk: massive trees and dense forest, strangling figs – a real taste of jungle. It is not unusual to see squirrels, monkeys and various tropical insects. Some enterprising Livingstones have even carved 'Jane' and 'Tarzan' on one of the trees. Just as the path begins to descend towards Juara there is a small drinks stop, the *Rest Cross*, incongruously located amongst the giant trees. This marks the beginning of the concrete trail which winds down to Juara. A

Treks
See cross section below

East Coast Peninsula

Tekek to Juara

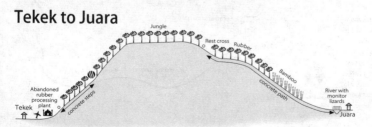

Tekek - Juara: 4 km
Tekek - Rest Cross: 1.5 hrs
Rest Cross - Juara: 1 hr

motorcycle taxi service is available for the truly exhausted as well as fruit juices and soft drinks. The section down to Juara is less dramatic and more cultivated with rubber trees and banana groves, but even here it is common to see some wildlife, including monkeys and squirrels. To return to the west coast, there is a daily sea bus service from Juara leaving at 1500.

There are also many easier jungle and coastal walks along the west coast: south from Tekek, past the resort to kampungs Paya and Genting and north to Salang. Mount Kajang can be climbed from the east or west sides of the island; an unmarked trail leads from the Tioman Island golf course (advisable to take a guide). It is also possible to trek to Bukit Nenek Semukut (Twin Peaks) and Bukit Seperok. The trail up Semukut starts from Pasir Burong, the beach at Kampung Pasir. Guides available from *Berjaya Tioman Beach Resort* and *Happy Café*, Juara and *Zaha's Information Service* (near the jetty at Tekek) and Kampung Tekek. The trail from Kampung Juara, on the east coast, is longer and more arduous.

Pulau Tioman

Related maps
A *Kampung Salang,*
page 247
B *Kampung Ayer*
Batang, page 246
C *Kampung Tekek,*
page 245
D *Kampung Juara,*
page 249

N

0 km   1
0 miles   1

Diving

Tioman's coral reefs are mainly on the western side of the island, although sadly large areas have been killed off. This is in part due to fishing boats dragging anchor, partly through nimble-fingered snorkellers pilfering coral stalks (this kills neighbouring corals), partly because all the boat activity kicks up sand and retards the growth or kills the coral, and partly because of the crown-of-thorns starfish (see page 280). Wholesale coral 'harvesting' has also been going on, to feed the increasingly lucrative trade in salt-water aquaria. Live coral specimens are loaded into water-filled bags, having been hacked off reefs with pick axes. This practice has more or less ended around Tioman now, but is still reported to be going on off other east coast islands. Pollution is also said to be a coral-killer. Both sewerage and effluent from building sites can alter water salinity levels, killing coral and resulting in the proliferation of harmful algae.

There are still some magnificent coral beds within easy reach of the island. Pulau Renggis, just off the *Berjaya Tioman Beach Resort*, is the most easily accessible coral from the shore, with a depth of up to 12m and a good place for new divers to find their flippers. For more adventurous dives, the islands off the northwest coast are a better bet. There is cave diving off Pulau Chebeh, 20 minutes from the *Berjaya* (up to 25m), and varied marine life off the cliff-like rocks of Golden Reef (25 minutes from the *Berjaya* and up to 20m) and nearby Tiger Reef (20 minutes from *Berjaya* and up to 50m). Off the northeastern tip of the island is Magicienne Rock (30 minutes from *Berjaya* and 25m dives) – where bigger fish have been sighted. Off the southwestern coast is Bahara Rock (30 minutes from *Berjaya* and 20m), considered one of the best spots on the island. Best time to dive: mid-March to May, when visibility is at its best, but it is possible to dive through to the end of October. There are dive shops based in most of the kampung: at Salang, Tekek, Genting, Paya, Ayer Batang and at the *Berjaya Tioman Beach Resort* (see the listings under each kampung entry).

Best time to visit

Many guesthouses and resorts close down between November and February when it is wet and can be windy and rough. Chinese New Year seems to be a popular time for places to open, cashing in on the Singapore market, but as Chinese New Year is a moveable feast the date can vary considerably from year to year. Transport from Mersing also becomes more difficult during the off season; ferries will only leave if there is sufficient demand to make it worth their while.

Boat tours

Boats leave from Kampung Tekek: to Pulau Tulai (or Coral Island) Turtle Island; to a waterfall at Mukut, or an around-island trip. All boats must be full otherwise prices increase. Boat trips can also be arranged to other nearby islands. Boats can be booked through *Zaha's Information Service*, near the jetty, Kampung Tekek and from many of the guesthouses.

East Coast Peninsula

Essentials

Sleeping
Sandflies can be a problem on Tioman & mosquito coils are recommended

The *Berjaya Tioman Beach Resort* and most of the cheaper places to stay are scattered along the west coast (the island is virtually uninhabited on the southeast and southwest sides and north of Juara Beach on the east coast, apart from a few fishing kampungs). Most of the accommodation on the island is simple: atap or tin-roofed chalets/huts (**C-E** categories), 'A'-frames (**E-F**) or dorms (**F**). Chalets with attached bathrooms fall into our **C-D** categories and upwards. Not all have electricity. Rooms are fairly spartan; expect to pay more for mosquito nets and electricity. Inevitably, beachfront chalets cost more. Due to stiff competition, many prices are negotiable depending on the season.

Kampung Lalang is not really a kampung at all but a beach devoted solely to the *Berjaya Tioman Beach Resort* and its sister condotel. **AL** *Berjaya Tioman Beach Resort*, Lalang, T4145445, F4145718. A hotel with 400 rooms set in 200 acres of land, built on the site of the old Kampung Lalang. Bought by Tan Sri Vincent Tan in 1993, when it was dramatically expanded, this tourist class hotel is by far the biggest and most expensive resort on Tioman, with a good range of facilities and a lovely stretch of beach. This is not the place to come if you are hoping for a quiet retreat; during holiday periods, the whole place is heaving with activity. Rooms are adequately equipped but furnishings are a little dated. Choice of rooms; the cheapest have garden views and are the older one storey chalets. The deluxe and superior two storey chalets are bigger and are more suitable for families, some overlook the sea (if you crane your neck). All rooms have wooden floors and balconies, a/c, TV and mini-bar. Rather shabby bathrooms, with hot water shower only (bath tubs in deluxe rooms only). The suites are very forgettable. Several restaurants (see **Eating** below). Rather cramped area for the freeform pool with children's slides and jacuzzi. Watersports centre (including scuba diving facilities, RM800 for a 6-7 day PADI certification course) with boats for diving and snorkelling parties to nearby islands (it is possible to snorkel 100m out from the northern end of the bay and at the very southern end, near the beach), jet skis, windsurfers, 18-hole golf course (see **Sports** below), gym – with good range of (underused) equipment, donkey and horse riding, tennis courts. The *Condotel* is a very ugly 4 storey block perched on a rocky promontory to the south of the *Berjaya*, which opened in March 1997. All the rooms are suites, with a sitting area looking onto balconies. The drawback here is that there are no eating outlets (just a small shop with ready to eat food and pantries in all the suites). A shuttle bus service runs to the hotel at meal times. There is a large lengths pool with no shade. The best rooms face south. The *Condotel* is largely a time share affair but will also be used as an overflow place for the *Berjaya*.

Sleeping
*■ on map, page 245
Price codes:
see inside front cover*

Kampung Tekek is the kampung-capital of Tioman and, frankly, is nothing special. However because boats from Mersing first call at Tekek's large concrete jetty, and the airport is also here, many visitors decide to stay put rather than face another journey. Others find they have to stay a night here 'in transit'. Tekek has the longest beach on the island, but for a large stretch north of the jetty it is rather dirty and with an ugly concrete breakwater. Almost all the coral is dead and broken, the river is polluted and there are rusting oil drums and other paraphernalia littering the town. There are many places to stay at Tekek, mostly south of the jetty or towards the northern end of the bay. However, much of the accommodation is run down and the place doesn't have much of a tropical island resort atmosphere. It feels like a small service centre, which is what it is. Tekek has a small post office, a police post, a clinic, a couple of money changers, the administrative HQ for the island, a few mini-marts, and an immigration post. There are two main areas of accommodation. One group of guesthouses is south of the jetty within 5-10 mins' walk of the jetty and airport. A second group begins 500m north of the jetty and airport and stretches towards the National Park office at the far end of the bay. These are quieter, cheaper, but in general do not seem to be so well run. The 'road' here is just a 1m-wide concrete path.

A-C *Babura Sea View*, T011767502. Some a/c, restaurant, the last place at the south end of the beach with 23 varied rooms. It consists of 3 separately owned businesses – the resort, a good Chinese restaurant, and *Tioman Reef Divers*, a PADI/NAUI dive shop. The rooms are clean and well maintained although some can be dark; the best are in the new block on the beach front. Recommended. **B** *Persona Island Resort*, T/F4146213 (in Kuantan T093155566, F095130510). Some a/c, restaurant, turn right at jetty and this place is a 10 min walk. It is the flashest place to stay in Tekek with 24 clean and functional rooms in 2-storey buildings but it is not on the beach. Large restaurant. **B-D** *Coral Reef Holidays*, T011766326. Some a/c, restaurant, a group of chalets all looking rather jaded and dusty, some facing onto the sea, others set back and facing one another. **B-C** *Peladang*, T094146249, F094146249. Some a/c, a well-kept little place with clean and comfortable chalets. Its big drawback is that it is on the opposite side of the road some distance from the beach so it is neither possible to watch the sun go down over the horizon nor dash headlong from your chalet into the water. **B-D** *Sri Tioman Beach Resort*, T094145189. Some a/c, restaurant, a popular place and one of the better places to stay in this price range in Tekek. Sea-facing chalets shaded beneath casuarina trees, good restaurant with prawn, squid and fish dishes as well as the usual range of pancakes etc. **C** *Mastura*, T011715283. Restaurant (American breakfast included in room rate) on the beach and run by Zuki. Much the same as *Tekek Inn* and *Sri Tioman Beach Resort* (the three actually share guests when they are full) although *Mastura* suffers from being next to what looks like an oil storage depot. **D** *Seroja Inn II*, T7995209. Restaurant, 24 undistinguished chalets in front of beach, bicycles for hire. The following are all around RM25 and there is little to mark them out from one another: *Faira*, *Ramli's House*, and *Tioman Sea View*. **D** *Tekek Inn*, T011358395. This is perhaps the best of the cheaper places to stay. It is on the beach, rooms are OK with attached showers, the management is

Kampung Tekek

Not to scale

■ **Sleeping**
1 Babura Sea View, Chinese Restaurant & Dive Shop
2 Coral Reef Holidays
3 Faira
4 Mastura
5 Peladang
6 Persona Island Resort
7 Rai Leh Villa
8 Ramli's House
9 Seroja Inn II
10 Sri Tioman Beach Resort
11 Tekek Inn
12 Tioman Enterprise
13 Tioman Seaview

East Coast Peninsula

suitably relaxed and there are snorkels and canoes for hire. No restaurant here, just a drinks station. Recommended. **D** *Tioman Enterprise*, T011952856. Lovingly cared for but very small chalets – more like Wendy Houses. The guesthouse is right at the end of the runway.

Kampung Penuba C-D *Penuba Paradise Inn*, situated just to the north of Kampung Ayer Batang, on the next promontory, and has its own jetty. Attractively laid out chalets built on stilts on the hillside, many with seaviews. Rocky beach, snorkelling in front of resort, restaurant, rather idyllic being so secluded, homely atmosphere, **F** for dorms.

Sleeping
■ *on map*
Price codes:
see inside front cover
On the whole,
accommodation at Ayer
Batang is better
than at Tekek

Kampung Ayer Batang This lies just north of Tekek. Accommodation here is spread out around the bay and is generally quite good. The beach is rocky at low tide and the sandy area quite small. There are said to be some monitor lizards here and the tall coconut palms are home to scores of bickering fruit bats during the day. Mini market next to *Sri Nelayan's* for basic supplies and souvenirs.

B-C *Johan's House*, big plot with small chalets on the beach and some newer and bigger rooms with a/c on the hill. Extensive travellers' food menu, snorkelling equipment for hire, library, speedboat available. **B-D** *Nazri's*, the most southerly of the guesthouses in Ayer Batang This has a range of accommodation. The complex is set around a mangrove swamp (so bring your mosquito coils), reputedly home to large monitor lizards. Some rooms in rows with a running verandah (5 with a seaview), some simple 'A' frames at the back of the plot, amongst the mango trees. Spartan but clean rooms, restaurant on seafront, friendly management, good discounts available during low season. Recommended. **C** *Nazri 11* (also called *Air Batang Beach Cabanas*), the most expensive on this beach and by far the nicest, with decent, clean and not too cramped rooms with wooden floors and seaviews. A raised restaurant provides a spectacular view of the bay. Laundry service, jet ski, fishing and snorkelling available. Recommended. **C-E** *Mokhtar's*, huts look onto an attractive little garden, fan and mosquito nets provided, basic restaurant, unfriendly owner. **D-E** *South Pacific*, 19 basic but adequate and clean rooms with fans and mosquito nets in choice of setting, some have seaview, 2 restaurants with good fish, notably the owner's fresh water catfish which he rears in ponds behind the guesthouse. Plenty of fruit available from trees on plot in the right season. Friendly owner from Kuantan will happily negotiate a good price for room. Recommended. **D-E** *TC*, 12 'A' frames, very basic, mosquito nets provided, no food here.

E *ABC*, last place to stay at northern end of beach, good beach here, small 'A'-frames, attractive rather intimate little plot with family atmosphere, good cheap food, hammocks, volleyball, friendly service. Recommended. **E** *Double Ace*, small rooms in 'A'-frames on a cramped plot. **E** *Mawar*, basic rather gloomy 'A' frames all with balconies right on the beach. Restaurant with lots of seafood, hammocks.

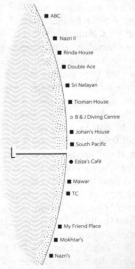

Kampung Ayer Batang

- ABC
- Nazri II
- Rinda House
- Double Ace
- Sri Nelayan
- Tioman House
- ○ B & J Diving Centre
- Johan's House
- South Pacific
- ● Eziza's Café
- Mawar
- TC
- My Friend Place
- Mokhtar's
- Nazri's

N

Not to scale

East Coast Peninsula

E *My Friend Place*, very small rooms, fan and mosquito net. **E** *Rinda House*, small rooms with mosquito nets set around a very attractive little garden with outside café. **E** *Sri Nelayan*, row of 10 small chalets. **E** *Tioman House*, 20 small huts built at right angles to the beach, a bit cramped, basic with fans. Seaside restaurant.

Kampung Salang The northernmost development on the island and is set in a sheltered cove with a beautiful beach. The mangrove swamp to the south of the jetty, though dirty, still holds plenty of monitor lizards which cruise around like primeval monsters. Some are getting on for 2m in length. There are minimarts at *Salang Indah* and at *Khalid's Place* for basic supplies such as drinks, toilet paper, nibbles, fruit etc. A 150-room resort, the unattractively named *Nadia Inn Comfort*, has been under construction for at least 2½ years at the south end of the Bay, past *Zaid's Place*, despite a supposed ban on new developments. When it is finally completed Salang's laid back atmosphere may become part of history.

Sleeping
■ *on map*
Price codes:
see inside front cover
Development here is
quite ramshackle, with a
scattering of beachside
restaurants & a relaxed
atmosphere

B-D *Salang Beach Resort*, Chinese restaurant, spacious chalets with verandahs set in well-kept grounds, some with a/c. This is the northernmost development so it is quiet and the beach is virtually a private one. The management can be brusque. **C** *Zaid's Place*, a popular place, with fairly switched-on management. There's a choice of rooms, some with seaview, others which face onto a little garden, all are clean and have fans. Money changer, library, good restaurant. Recommended. **B-D** *Salang Indah*, T793155. Large, rather garish, restaurant with some delicious seafood specialities. Variety of chalets in all price brackets, some with attached bathrooms right on the sea, others with a/c and private stairs down to the sea, plus the original rather drab rooms in a U-shaped barrack of a building. The guesthouse is owned by the Orang Kayah and expansion is still underway with a number of new Minang-style chalets built in 1997, provides a minimart and various other services. It is hard to avoid the

East Coast Peninsula

Kampung Salang

South China Sea

Salang Beach Resort
Dive Asia
Salang Beach Minimart
Salang Indah
Sunset Boulevard
Salang Indah Minimart
Fishermen Dive Centre
Ben's Diving Centre
Salang Dreams
Amin's Café
Pier
Khalid's Place
Paklong
Zaid's Place
Pier
New Development

N
Not to scale

conclusion that it has over-expanded. **B-D** *Khalid's Place*, 36 rooms in relatively new compound, a pleasant garden setting with fairly basic rooms. Family room available. If Khalid's girth is anything to go by, the restaurant must be good. **D** *Paklong*, 5 rooms with fan, no sea view, but friendly family management, rather fetid swamp close by.

A quiet place with a small surau (prayer hall) & a couple of restaurants

Kampung Paya is south of Tekek. The jetty here has now been upgraded and the ferries from Mersing stop here. The beach is attractive enough but at low tide a belt of dead and broken coral makes swimming difficult.

A *Paya Resort* (booking office Jln Sulaiman 11, Mersing, T077991432. Or in Singapore at 101 Upper Cross St, 01-36 People's Park Centre, T5341010), T01762534. Restaurant, small resort with 30 a/c rooms, which is clean and well looked-after but perhaps a little overpriced given the standard of the rooms. There is a PADI dive school attached to the hotel, the resort is owned by the director of *Giamso Safari* tour agency in Mersing. The resort is closed Nov-Jan. **B-D** *Sri Paya Tioman Enterprise*, T011-765744, T02(Singapore)3656974. Ten a/c bungalows with twin double beds so that four can share and attached bathrooms, 8 small fan rooms. Clean but not a place to induce that tropical island paradise feeling. **D** *Sri Paya Holiday*, 26 small bungalows in the middle of the village by the pier, little character.

Kampung Genting lies to the south of Kampung Paya and is the second largest village on the island. However it is not as popular as some of the other kampungs and has the feeling of a locals' resort. The extensive jetty gives an impression that the village had hoped for greater things. The beach here is poor; rocks are exposed at low tide and the coral is largely broken and dead. There is, though, an incredibly modest sight: the graves of Tun Mohamad bin Tun Adbul Majid, the sixth Bendahara of Pahang, and his wife, also of royal blood being the daughter of Sultan Mahmud of Johore-Riau-Lingga-Pahang. In 1803 the Bendahara (who had assumed the position the year before) and his wife were at sea between Tioman and the mainland when their boat foundered in a thunderstorm. With their cabin locked the couple were unable to escape and both drowned. Their bodies, though, were recovered and buried here after having been washed in fresh water from the local river – which is now known as the Sungai Air Rajah. Another version has it that the bodies were never found and the graves are purely symbolic. There is a *surau*, or prayer hall, by the jetty.

B *Tropical Coral Inn*, T011713465. This place is owned by *Sany Travel and Tour*, 545 Orchard Rd (Far East Shopping Centre), Singapore, T4661360, F7328137 and 70% of guests come from Singapore on package deals. The chalets are adequate, there is a/c, a good restaurant and *Sharkey's Dive Shop* is attached. **D** *Bayu*, at the north end of the beach, quiet and secluded. **D** *Damai*, bookable in Mersing at Jln Abu Bakar, T07793048. About 80 rather grotty looking double chalets with balconies, restaurant, minimarket and 24-hour electricity, speedboat to Mersing. **D** *Island Reef Resort*, set back on hillside behind jetty, with chalets side on to beach, so no views except in the restaurant. **D** *Sun Beach Resort*, about 50 rambling bungalows built too close together, some on the seafront, others piled up the hill behind. Monstrous restaurant on stilts.

Kampung Nipah (south of Kampung Genting). **B-D** *Desa Nipah*, beachside chalets with attached bathrooms. Because this is the only accommodation available, Kampung Nipah is one of the most secluded and tranquil spots on the island.

Kampung Mukut on south side of island. **C** *Mukut Village Chalets*, restaurant, backed by coconut palms, traditional-style atap-roofed chalets with balconies, secluded, beautiful location with magnificent backdrop of the 'Twin Peaks', owned by *Island Connection* ticketing agency, 19 Plaza R & R, Mersing. **D** *Asah Resort* and **D** *Mukut Waterfall Backpacker Resort*.

East Coast Peninsula

Kampung Juara This is the only kampung on the east coast with accommodation. It has beautiful long white beaches which sometimes have good breakers. The snorkelling though, is poor. Being on the seaward side, Juara has a completely different atmosphere from the west coast kampungs; it is quieter, friendlier, more laid-back and bucolic, thanks mainly to its seclusion. There is a path from Kampung Tekek, through the jungle, to Juara (see **Treks** above). Alternatively, it is possible to take a boat from Tekek. Accommodation is cheaper at Juara. The Sungai Baru which flows into the sea here is home to some monitor lizards. **Getting to Kampung Juara**: being on the east side of the island, the ferries from Mersing rarely call here and it is necessary to catch one of the sea buses that circle the island, RM18 from Tekek to Juara, 2 hrs. To walk from Tekek to Juara is a tough 2 hour walk.

D *Juara Bay Resort*, restaurant, rather ugly series of new hillside chalets at the southern end of the main beach. This is the most sophisticated place to stay and there have even been murmurings of a/c. Though it is quiet and the chalets have attractive views over the bay they do not have the beach front position of the other places. **D** *Saujana Bay Resort*, the last place to stay at the southern end of the bay. It is quite a walk from the jetty over the headland. **D-E** *Juara Mutiara*, organizes diving trips or island tours, booking office in Mersing, 6 Jln Abu Bakar, near *Plaza R & R*. The more expensive rooms sleep 4, all have attached showers, clean and popular, some chalets right on the beach, can be noisy (for Juara) as there are other chalet operations on both sides. **E** *Bushman*, near the southern end of the beach, simple 'A'-frame huts. **E** *Paradise Point*, restaurant with extensive menu, one of only two places to stay on the northern side of the beach. Simple rooms, attached showers, the chalets siding onto the beach get the breeze, a quiet place with a relaxed atmosphere. Recommended. **E-F** *Atan's Place*, T7992309. Same management as *Juara Mutiara*, restaurant (*Turtle Café* – but you don't go there for the food), 'A'-frames and chalets with small verandahs. **E-F** *Busong*, same ownership as *Paradise Point* and close to the northern end of the beach, near a mangrove fringed lagoon which, after heavy rain, discharges into the sea. There are some simple 'A'-frame huts as well as more recently built chalets. Very quiet and right on the beach. **E-F** *Musni Chalet*, over the headland at the southern end of the beach, isolated and quiet. **E-F** *Sunrise*, restaurant, simple and small 'A' frame huts that become airless and stuffy on still days. Good water activities: canoes, windsurfers and boats for hire.

Sleeping
■ *on map*
Price codes:
see inside front cover

East Coast Peninsula

Kampung Juara

N

Not to scale

■ **Sleeping**
1 Atan's Place
2 Bushman
3 Busong
4 Juara Bay Resort
5 Juara Mutiara
6 Musni Chalet
7 Paradise Point
8 Saujana Bay Resort
9 Sunrise

● **Eating**
1 Beach Café
2 Mini Café

Eating

Most restaurants are small family-run kitchens attached to groups of beach huts. All provide Western staples such as omelettes and French toast, as well as Malay dishes. On the whole, the food is of a high standard. Understandably it makes most sense to eat seafood: superb barbecued shark, barracuda, squid, stingray and other fish.

Eating
Not all restaurants sell beer

Kampung Lalang *Berjaya Tioman Beach Resort Restaurant* offers a choice of restaurants, none of which are outstanding. The best bet is the buffet meal, which is quite good value and a huge spread is on offer. The other restaurants offer barbecue and steamboat. Service for à la carte meals is painfully slow and pretty inefficient. The golf club offers a snack bar with good pizzas and sandwiches.

Kampung Tekek This has a good range of restaurants. The *Babura Sea View Chinese Restaurant* (separate ownership from the guesthouse) is recommended and so too is the *Liza Restaurant*, which is the most sophisticated place to have a meal and serves delicious Malay food. Of the guesthouse restaurants the one at the *Sri Tioman Beach Resort* is worth trying, especially the squid and chilli prawns, while the small *Malay No Name Restaurant* north of the *Babura* and before the bridge is also recommended, as are the food stalls just north of the pier. There are a number of minimarts in the Kampung; *Pak Ali Nasir's* stall is the best place for fruit; and there is a very small market area next to the *Peladang Restaurant*.

Kampung Ayer Batang *Eziza's Café* near the jetty offer simple dishes.

Kampung Salang This is a sizeable hamlet, so there are a number of restaurants independent of the guesthouses. *Sunset Boulevard* is built over the sea north of the *Salang Indah*. Good seafood and the best spot for a cold beer. Among the best of the warungs is the place just north of the *Sunset Boulevard* – simple dishes, breakfast served. Another good option is *Amin's Café* right by the jetty; it provides breakfast, lunch and dinner, simple, low key place. *Salang Dreams* next to the *Salang Indah Minimart* has good Malay food and a good evening seafood barbecue.

Kampung Paya The *Mekong Restaurant* at the south end of the bay produces good Chinese seafood dishes.

Kampung Juara All the guesthouses serve roughy the same dishes: curries, noodle and rice dishes, pancakes, fish, omelettes etc. There are also a couple of independent restaurants – the *Mini Café* and the *Beach Café*, both near the pier. Inevitably fish is good: chilli fish, sweet and sour, or simply grilled.

Shopping **Souvenirs** Tioman is not a place to come shopping. However, there are a handful of souvenir shops in Tekek selling the usual range of sea-derived knick-knacks including shells fashioned into improbable scenes and jewellery which most people discard immediately upon their return home.

Sports **Diving** Most beaches have dive centres attached to at least one guesthouse. PADI, NAUI and SSI (Scuba Schools International) certification available.

Kampung Tekek: the best dive shop is reputedly *Tioman Reef Divers* attached to *Babura Sea View*. It offers PADI and NAUI certification courses. Other dive shops include *Scuba Point* (PADI) next to *Coral Reef Holidays*, and a new dive shop (PADI) attached to the *Tekek Inn*.

Kampung Ayer Batang: *B&J Diving Centre* next to *Johan's House* has a small pool for diving practice and can provide PADI certification.

Kampung Salang: Salang is sold as a snorkellers' haven but, sadly, that is history – the coral is disappointing. It does, however, get better further out, and where the coral cliff drops off to deeper water, there is a more interesting variety of marine life including the odd reef shark. *Ben's Diving Centre*, next to *Salang Indah* hires out equipment and can organize PADI certification and diving trips to nearby islands. A 4-day PADI course costs RM625, two dives RM110, which include equipment and boat. *Dive Asia* by the *Salang Beach Resort* also offers PADI certification; one dive with a full set is costed at RM70, night dives also arranged. *Fishermen Dive Centre* near the *Salang Indah* offer SSI (Scuba Schools International) certification, a full course costs RM750, a full day's diving, RM140. There is also *B&J* another PADI outfit, T011717014, F011954247. Snorkels and fins can be hired just about everywhere, about RM7-10 per day.

Kampung Paya: dive shop at the *Paya Resort* with PADI certification courses.

Kampung Genting: *Sharkeys*, the *Tropical Coral Inn*, runs SSI certificated courses.

Kampung Juara: snorkelling and fishing gear can be hired from most guesthouses.

Golf *Tioman Island Golf Club*, T445445, F445716, most club-members are weekend trippers from KL and Singapore, beautiful 18-hole course, green fees RM80 weekdays, RM100 weekends. Equipment including clubs (full set RM50), golf shoes (RM10), and buggy (RM40 weekdays, RM50 weekends) all available for hire.

Zaha's, Tekek Pier, sells boat tickets to Mersing and round-the-island excursions.

Tour operators

Local Boat: beaches and kampungs are connected by an erratic sea-bus service, which runs roughly every hour or so from 0800 to 1800. The early-morning sea-bus goes right round the island; otherwise it is necessary to charter a boat to get to the waterfalls (on the south coast) and Kampung Juara. All the boats from Mersing take passengers to the kampungs on the west side; the first port of call is Kampung Tekek. Sea-bus fares (per person, children half price) from Kampung Tekek to: Kampung Ayer Batang/ABC (RM4), Penuba (RM6), Salang (RM9), Lalang (*Berjaya Tioman Beach Resort*) (RM6), Juara (RM20). Note that there is a slightly different schedule on Fri. The east coast is accessible by (very slow) boat or by the jungle trail.

Transport
60 km to Mersing

Long distance Air: the airport is in the centre of Tekek. The runway is being extended to take larger aircraft. The *Berjaya* sends a bus to meet each plane and various touts approach likely looking passengers. The jetty is just 100m or so away. Daily connections with KL's Subang Airport and Kuantan on *Pelangi Air*, and with Subang alone on *Berjaya Air*. Multiple daily connections with Johor Bahru on *Tiram Air* and daily with Mersing.

Baggage allowance is 10 kg

Several connections a day with Seletar Airport (on north side of Singapore Island, see page 564) on *Pelangi Air* (RM191 one way) and *SilkAir*. A bus from the *Berjaya Tioman Resort* meets each arrival and transports guests to the hotel. Alternatively walk to the pier and catch one of the sea-buses to the other beaches.

Boat: most people arrive on Tioman by ferry from Mersing. The jetty at Mersing is 5 mins' walk out of Mersing next to the blue-roofed *R & R Plaza*. It is best to buy a one way ticket; the ferry timetable is only drawn up a month in advance because it depends on tides. Fast boats leave at hourly intervals when the tide is high. A/c fast boats (eg *Seagull Express*, T7994297, and *Damai Express* T793048): RM25 (one way, child RM15), 1½-2 hrs; moderate speed boats taking about 45 passengers: RM20 (one way), 3 hrs; fishing boats can be chartered by groups of 12 or more people for RM180 (for the boat), 4-5 hrs. During the monsoon season (Nov-Feb) the sea can get quite rough and it is inadvisable to leave Mersing after 1500. During these months departures can be erratic; boats may not run if there are insufficient passengers. It can be difficult to find accommodation after nightfall and most restaurants close early. All boats land on the west coast of Tioman and call at each of the main kampungs; occasionally they may cross to the east side of the island and call at Juara, but it is usually necessary to catch one of the 'sea-buses' that circle the island. If intending to stay at Juara leave enough time to catch a sea-bus; it takes around 2 hrs from Kampung Tekek to Juara. There are also boats twice a day from Tanjung Gemok (Endau), just north of Mersing, to Tioman during the busy season (Mar-Oct) run by *Kuala Perlis Langkawi Ferry Service*, RM25 (one way, RM13 children), 1½ hrs.

The *Auto Tioman* leaves from Tanah Merah, Singapore 0830 and returns 1430, 4½ hrs (S$85 one way, children S$55). Reservations at *Auto Batam*, 1 Maritime Square, World Trade Centre, Singapore T2714866, www.sembcorp.com.sg/autobatam.

East Coast Peninsula

Directory   **Airline offices** *Silk Air and Pelangi*, both operate out of *Berjaya Resort*, T4145445, F4145718.
Banks There are 2 money changers at Tioman Airport in the new blue-roofed shopping plaza.
Some shops in Salang will also change money. TCs can be changed at the *Berjaya Tioman Beach
Resort* (large surcharge). Recently, some smaller resorts have begun to accept them.
Communications Public phones in all villages, IDD calling from *Berjaya* and some guesthouses.
Phones to be installed in guesthouses sometime in the near future. **Area code:** 07. **Post Office:**
mini-post office in Kampung Tekek. **Card phones:** in Tekek next to the Mini Pos (cards
available at Post Office). **Medical facilities** There is a small clinic in Tekek.

Other islands

There are a total of 64 islands off Mersing; many are inaccessible and uninhab-
ited. There is accommodation available and boats to Pulau Rawa, Pulau Babi
Besar (Big Pig Island), Pulau Tinggi, Pulau (Babi) Tengah, Pulau Sibu, Pulau
Aur (Bamboo Island) and Pulau Pemanggil.

A small island 16 km off Mersing, **Pulau Rawa** is owned by a nephew of the
Sultan of Johor and is highly rated by lots of travellers. The island has a fantastic beach and for those in need of a desert island break, Rawa is perfect, for
there is absolutely nothing to do except mellow out. Unfortunately the coral
reef is disappointing, but more active visitors can windsurf, canoe, and fish.
The island gets busy at weekends as it is close enough for day visitors; it is also a
popular getaway for Singaporeans.

Pulau Babi Besar is larger and closer to the mainland than Rawa. It is a very
peaceful island and is particularly well known for its beaches and coral. **Pulau
Tinggi** is probably the most dramatic-looking island in the Seribuat group,
with its 650m volcanic peak. **Pulau Tengah**, formerly a refugee camp for Vietnamese boat people, is an hour away from Mersing. The government has
declared it a marine park because of its reef and the fact that giant leatherback
turtles (see page 279) lay their eggs there between June and August. **Pulau
Sibu**, otherwise known as the Island of Perilous Passage because it used to be a
pirate haunt, has been recommended by many travellers for its beaches and
watersports. Sibu is frequented more by Singaporeans and expatriates than by
Western tourists. It is popular for fishing and diving and because it is larger
than the other islands there is more of a sense of space and there are also some
good walks. The best beaches on **Pulau Pemanggil** are at kampungs Buan and
Pa Kaleh, which is fortunately where the accommodation is sited.

In addition to these more established islands, there are also other places
being developed. It is worth asking around in Mersing for more information
and enquiring from people on the jetty who have just returned. Islands currently under development include **Pulau Hujung** and **Pulau Aur**. The latter is
the most remote.

Websites   There are a few pictures of Pulau Rawa and updated information on resort
rates at www4.jaring.my/spsj/island/rawa/rawa.htm. Information on the
Johor islands is at www4.jaring.my/spsj/island/.

Essentials

Sleeping &   All resorts have their own restaurants. Most of the accommodation on these islands
eating   is run by small operators, who organize packages from Mersing. Resort bookings
Price codes: see inside
front cover   must be made in either Mersing or Johor Bahru.

Pulau Rawa **A-B** *Rawa Safaris Island Resort*, Tourist Centre, Jln Abu Bakar, Mersing T7991204. Some a/c, restaurant (Malay and international dishes), bungalows, chalets and 'A'-frames, watersports, Sahid mixes some powerful cocktails in the bar; drink more than two Rawa specials and you'll be on the island for good.

Rawa has no kampungs on it and, as yet, only one resort

Pulau (Babi) Besar **A** *Harlequin*, (aka *D'Coconut Island Resort*), built on the land of an old coconut plantation, with chalets, a large restaurant, pool and watersports. **A** *Radin Island Resort*, 9 Tourist Information Centre, Jln Abu Bakar, Mersing, T7994152. Restaurant (some a/c) stylish traditional chalets with jungle hillside backdrop. **A-C** *Nirwana Beach Resort*, choice of chalets, some with a/c, restaurant attached, dorms available. **A-C** *White Sand Beach Resort*, 98 Jln Harimau Tarum, Century Garden, Johor Bahru, T077994995. Runs diving packages, 4 days for 2 people. **B** *Besar Marina Resort*, 10 Tourist Information Centre, Jln Abu Bakar, Mersing, T7993606. **B** *Hillside Beach Resort*, 5B Jln Abu Bakar, Mersing or book through Suite 125, 1st Flr, Johor Tower, 15 Jln Gereja, Johor Bahru, T077994831, F2244329. Restaurant, very attractively designed Kampung-style resort, nestling on jungled slopes above beach, watersports. **C** *Besar Beach Chalet*, new resort with government-style chalets backed by Irish jungle. **C** *Perfect Life Resort*, range of rooms from chalets to honeymoon suites. **C-E** *Batu Kembar*, 18 large chalets on a hillside, for 4 people each in bunks, a/c, hot showers and balconies. **E** *Atlantis Bay*, basic with outdoor showers, non-a/c. **E** *Bluewater Resort*, chalet or longhouse accommodation in this place in Aur village.

Pulau Tinggi **A** *Nadia Comfort Inn*, c/o 17 Tingkat 2, Tun Abdul Razak, Kompleks (KOMTAR), Jln Wong Ah Fook, Johor Bahru, T072231694. Booking office in Mersing opposite *Plaza R & R*, Jln Abu Bakar, restaurant, pool, luxurious Malay-style wooden chalets. Also 'A'-frames (**F**), chalets (**D**) and bungalows (**C**) on the island; **A-B** *Tinggi Island Resort*, bookings from *Sheikh Tourist Agency*, 1B Jln Abu Bakar, Mersing, T7993767/7994451. Attractive chalets balanced precariously on steep hillside and next to beach, excellent range of indoor and outdoor facilities, boat trips arranged to nearby islands (Pulau Lima and Pulau Simbang) for diving.

Pulau (Babi) Tengah More accommodation is planned on the island. **B** *Pirate Bay Island Resort*, restaurant, spacious cottages built in traditional style with full selection of amenities, watersports.

Pulau Sibu Besar **A** *Twin Beach Resort*, 40 chalets, no a/c or hot water but good sports facilities. **A-D** *Sibu Island Cabanas* (c/o G105 *Holiday Plaza*, Century Garden JB), T073317216. Restaurant, chalets and deluxe bungalows. **C-D** *O & H Kampung Huts* (c/o 9 Tourist Information Centre, Jln Abu Bakar, Mersing), T7993124/7993125. Good restaurant, chalets, some with attached bathrooms, clean and friendly, trekking and snorkelling. Recommended. **C-D** *Sea Gypsy Village Resort*, 9 Tourist Information Centre, Jln Abu Bakar, Mersing, T7993124. Restaurant, chalets and bungalows. Recommended.

Pulau Sibu Tengah **C** *Sibu Island Resorts*, Suite 2, 14th Flr, KOMTAR, Jln Wong Ah Fook, Johor Bahru, T072231188. Restaurant, bungalows only, watersports.

Pulau Aur **F** *Longhouse* provides basic accommodation.

Pulau Pemanggil Package deals for *Wira Chalets and longhouse* (also has dive shop). There is a small agent at the very front of Mersing's *Plaza R & R* dealing exclusively with Pemanggil travel and accommodation. **C-E** *Dagang Chalets and Longhouse*, Kampung Buau (1 longhouse room sleeps 8 at RM10 per person), restaurant serving local food, *Mara Chalet* at Kampung Pa Kaleh, on southwest side. Contact *Tioman Accommodation & Boat Services*, 3 Jln Abu Bakar, Mersing, T7993048.

East Coast Peninsula

Transport **Sea Boats**: to the islands leave daily from Mersing, usually around 1100 and return 1530 (all slow boats): Rawa (1½ hrs, RM25 return), Tengah (RM18 return), Babi Besar (RM30 return), Sibu (RM25 return), Tinggi (RM50 return). No regular boats to Pulau Aur or Pulau Pemanggil – though this may change as the islands develop. Getting to Pulau Aur takes 4 hrs or more. Also boats to Sibu from Tanjung Sedili Besar at Teluk Mahkota (23 km off the Kota Tinggi-Mersing road), south of Mersing (RM22 return).

Endau Rompin National Park

Phone code: 09
Colour map 2, grid B5

This park straddles the border of Johor and Pahang states and is one of the biggest remaining tracts of virgin rainforest on the peninsula; about 80,000 hectares.

In the late 1980s it was upgraded to the status of a national park to protect the area from the logging companies. Within the park, it may be possible to see Sumatran rhino, tigers, wild boars, tapir, elephant, deer and mousedeer. Birdlife includes hornbills and the argus pheasant. Amongst the flora there are fan palms (*Endau ensis*), walking stick palm (*Phychorapis singaporensis*) and climbing bamboo (*Rhopa loblaste*), pitcher plants and orchids.

Access to the park will become easier and cheaper during the next few years and accommodation is planned for upriver. At present transport and accommodation facilities are limited. Unlike Taman Negara National Park, trips to Endau require careful planning and are best organized by tour agents who usually end up cheaper than trying to arrange it independently, see below. There has been talk for a number of years about Endau Rompin becoming more accessible but this has still to materialize (which is perhaps why the park remains such an adventure). As a result anyone thinking of visiting the park should allot four days and three nights.

It is possible to hire boats from Endau, on the coast road, up Sungai Endau. The first 10 km to Kampung Punan is navigable by larger motor boats; from there, smaller boats head on upstream to Orang Asli villages. The junction of the Endau and Jasin rivers (nine hours from Endau) is a good campsite and base for trekking and fishing expeditions. Boats go further upstream, but it is advisable to take a guide. They can be hired from Endau or from the Orang Asli kampungs for RM20-30 per day. At present it is necessary to take all provisions and camping equipment with you. It is inadvisable to travel during the monsoon season from November to March. Following the drowning of a Singaporean student in rapids in 1992, it has become much more difficult to visit Endau Rompin independently and it is essential to secure a permit. Permits are considered necessary because the area still falls under the Internal Security Act; in the days before the surrender of the Communist Party of Malaya in 1990, the Endau-Rompin jungle used to be part of the guerrillas' supply route through the peninsula. Visitors are strongly recommended to go to Endau with a travel agency, which can obtain permits on a visitor's behalf (see below).

Most package trips involve a 70 km jeep trip from Mersing to Kampung Peta followed by a 1½ hour longboat ride to first campsite. The rest of the trip involves trekking around the Asli trails and visiting spectacular waterfalls, the biggest of which is the Buaya Sangkut waterfall on Sungai Jasin. Fishing trips are best organized between February and August.

Permits & From National Parks Johor Corporation, JKR 475 Bukit Timbalan, Johor Bahru,
information T2237471, F2237472. Applications for permits must be made at least two weeks in advance, in writing, with passport details, two passport photographs, and

Pahang: the land of the sacred tree

A Malay legend tells of a huge, majestic Mahang (softwood) tree that once stood on the bank of the Pahang River, not far from Pekan, towering over everything else in the jungle. The tree was said to resemble the thigh of a giant and considered sacred by the Orang Asli and the Jakun tribespeople. The Malays adopted the name, which, in time, became Pahang. Perhaps not coincidentally, pahang also happens to be the Khmer word for 'tin'; there are ancient tin workings at Sungai Lembing near Kuantan, where traces of early human habitation have been found.

Until the end of the 19th century, Pahang, the peninsula's largest but least populous state, had always been a vassal. It paid tribute to Siam, Melaka and then Johor. In 1607 the Dutch set up a trading post in Pahang, but the state found itself caught in the middle of protracted rivalries between Johor and Aceh, the Dutch and the Portuguese. Pekan was sacked repeatedly by Johor and Aceh in the early

17th century, before coming under the direct rule of the Sultan of Johor in 1641; it stayed that way for two centuries.

In 1858, the death of the chief minister of Pahang, resulted in a five-year civil war. The dispute between his two sons was finally settled when the younger, Wan Ahmad, declared himself Chief Minister and then became the Pahang's first sultan in 1863. Sultan Wan Ahmad was autocratic and unpopular, so the British entered the fray, declaring the state a protectorate in 1887. An anti-British revolt ensued, supported by the sultan, but Wan Ahmad's power was whittled away. In 1895 the state's administrative capital was moved from Pekan to Kuala Lipis, 300 km up the Pahang River and later to Kuantan. Pahang became part of the federated Malay states in 1896. It was completely cut off from the west coast states, except for a couple of jungle trails, until a road was built from Kuala Lumpur to Kuantan in 1901. Pahang remains a predominantly Malay state.

proposed length of trip. The travel agencies listed below can secure permits within five days, but it is advisable to leave more time if possible.

Two websites with information on the park are www.kwikxs.com.my/NPC/index2.html and www.johortourism.com.my/html/eco/e.end.fac.html.

Park essentials

Kuala Rompin A *Lanjut Golden Beach Resort*, 20 km north of Kuala Rompin. A golf resort with a/c, 2 restaurants, pool, rooms and bungalows. **B** *Seri Malaysia Rompin*, Tg Gemok, T7944724, F7944732. Located 55 km from the national park, organizes tours, clean and comfortable rooms in new government chain hotel. **B-D** *Hotel Sri Rompin*, T4146236. A gem of a place, built 1998, clean and very comfortable, 2 mins from the bus station. **C** *Government Resthouse*, clean-looking. **C** *Rumah Rehat* (*Rest House*), 122.5 Milestone, T565245. Restaurant, 2-storey resthouse, all rooms with attached bathroom. **D-E** *Watering Hole Bungalows* (closed during wet season), 3 km south of Kuala Rompin and then 2 km or so towards the coast, T011411894. Quiet and clean, price including breakfast and dinner, we have had reports the Swiss-Malaysian couple who run this place could be friendlier and more welcoming but it is still a relaxing hideaway and well run.

Camping At the moment the only facilities for overnight stays in Endau Rompin are campsites at Kuala Jasin, Batu Hampar, Upih Guling and Kuala Marong, which have a combined capacity of 250-300 visitors. The long-awaited chalets, dorms, barbecue pits, restaurants and sanitation facilities are under construction but not expected to be completed until 2002.

Sleeping
Price codes: see inside front cover
There is no accommodation available in the park; camping only

East Coast Peninsula

Tour operators Organized expeditions, in which prices are inclusive of return vehicle and boat transfer, camping equipment, cooking utensils and permits, can be booked through: *Eureka Travel*, 277A Holland Ave, Holland Village, Singapore, T654625077, F4622853. Offers ecologically orientated tours to Endau Rompin National Park. Recommended. *Giamso Travel*, 23 Jln Abu Bakar, Mersing, T077992253. Approximately RM190 per person for 3 days/2 nights, RM210 per person for 4 days, 3 nights. The company can supply camping equipment, or through *Shah Alam Tours*, 138 Mezz Flr, Jln Tun Sambanthan, Kuala Lumpur T032307161, F032745739. *Sheikh Tourist Agency*, 1B Jln Abu Bakar, Mersing, T793767. Trips of 4 days/3 nights RM380 per person, all in RM100 deposit payable on booking; *Wilderness Experience*, 6B Jln SS 21/39, Damansara Utama, Petaling Jaya, T037178221. Hotels and guesthouses in Kuala Rompin also usually organize trips into the park.

Transport **Bus** Connections with JB, Terengganu and Kuantan. Buses from Johor Bahru and
130 km S of Kuantan Kuantan stop on demand at Endau, or regular local buses from Mersing to Endau.
37 km N of Mersing There is a 56 km jungle road from Kahang town to Kampung Peta where there is a visitors' centre and the entry point to the park. **Taxi**: from Mersing. **Boat** Speed boats to first Orang Asli village (Kampung Punan). This can cost anything from RM200-400 for a 2 day trip. It is possible to charter longboats (carrying up to 6 passengers) from Kampung Punan to go further upstream.

Pekan

Colour map 2, grid A5 The old royal capital of Pahang, Pekan has a languid feel to it. It has a reasonably picturesque row of older wooden shophouses on the busy street along the river, but is otherwise not a particularly photogenic town. Aside from its mosques, Pekan's most distinguishing feature is its bridge, which straddles the Pahang River, the longest river on the peninsula.

Pekan means 'town' in Malay. It used to be known as Pekan Pahang, the town of Pahang. Even before the Melakan sultanate was established in the late 14th century, it was known by the Sanskrit name for town: *Pura*. It is divided into Old Pekan (Pekan Lama) and New Pekan (Pekan Bharu); the former was the exclusive abode of the Malay nobility for centuries.

There are two mosques in the centre of Pekan: the **Abdullah Mosque**, Jalan Sultan Ahmad (beyond the museum), and the more modern **Abu Bakar Mosque** next door. On the north outskirts of the town is the **Istana Abu Bakar**, the royal palace, just off Jalan Istana Abu Bakar. Its opulent trimmings are visible from the road, but it is closed to the public. The small but interesting **Sultan Abu Bakar Museum**, on Jalan Sultan Ahmad, is housed in a splendid colonial building and has a jet-fighter mounted Airfix-style in the front garden. The museum includes a collection of brass and copperware, royal regalia, porcelain from a wrecked Chinese junk and an exhibition of local arts and crafts. In the back garden there is a depressing mini-zoo which rarely gets visited. It is home to Malayan honey bears, a tapir, a collection of monkeys, a black panther and a fish eagle, all squeezed into tiny cages. A good map of Pekan is provided. ■ *0930-1700 Tue-Thur, Sat-Sun; 0930-1215, 1445-1700 Fri, RM1.*

Sleeping **D** *Pekan*, 60 Jln Tengku Ariff Bendahara, T71378. A/c, restaurant, badly run, but quite
There is a poor selection friendly people. **D** *Rumah Rehat* (rest house), beside the football field (*padang*), off Jln
of hotels in Pekan; the Sultan Abu Bakar, T421240. A big, low-slung colonial building in need of a lick of paint
government rest house with a cool, spacious interior and big, clean rooms, restaurant. It is advisable to try to
is the best bet book accommodation in advance if visiting during the Sultan's birthday celebrations.

East Coast Peninsula

2 *Pekan Hotel Restaurant*, 60 Jln Tengku Ariff Bendahara, nothing special. There are a   **Eating**
couple of reasonable coffee shops in the new town. The foodstalls on Jln Sultan
Ahmad, near the bus/taxi stands, are the best Pekan has to offer.

October *Sultan's Birthday* (24th: state holiday) celebrated with processions, danc-   **Festivals**
ing and an international polo championship which the sultan hosts on his manicured
polo ground at the istana.

Polo Matches are held in season; Prince Charles is said to have played here. The polo   **Sports**
field is surrounded by traditional Malay houses.

Bus Bus stop on Jln Sultan Ahmad in the centre of town. Regular connections with   **Transport**
Kuantan and from there onward although there are direct buses to Mersing.   *47 km S of Kuantan*
Taxi Taxis for Kuantan and elsewhere stand between Jln Sultan Ahmad and the
waterfront, opposite the indoor market.

Banks *Bumiputra*, 117 Jln Engku Muda Mansur. **Communications** Post Office: in the middle   **Directory**
of town.

Kuantan

The modern capital of Pahang has a population of around 100,000 and is a bus-   *Phone code: 09*
tling, largely Chinese, town at the mouth of the Kuantan River. Kuantan is the   *Colour map 2, grid A5*
main transport and business hub for the east coast; most visitors spend at least a
night here.

Ins and outs

Kuantan's airport is 20 km from town. There are connections with KL, Kota Bahru and   **Getting there**
Kuala Terengganu as well as with Tioman. There are bus connections with all towns
up and down the east coast as well as with key destinations on the west, including KL.
Outstation taxis travel to Kuala Terengganu, KL and Mersing.

Kuantan is not a large town. City buses provide a regular service to the beach and   **Getting around**
hotels at Teluk Cempedak and there are also a number of car hire firms in town.

Kuantan's short on sights, but the brand new **Sultan Ahmad Shah** mosque, in
the centre of town, is worth wandering around. It is an impressive building,
freshly decorated in blue and white with a cool marbled interior. It has blue
and yellow stained glass windows and the morning sun projects their coloured
patterns on the interior walls. Kuantan has several streets of old shophouses
which date from the 1920s. Most of the oldest buildings are opposite the
padang on **Jalan Makhota**. The **Kuantan River** might also qualify as a sight,
such is the dearth of obvious things to see. The 300 km stretch of coast between
Kuantan and Kota Bharu is comprised of long beaches, interspersed with fishing kampungs and the occasional natural gas processing plant and oil refinery.

Excursions

Just 4 km east of Kuantan is Teluk Cempedak, see page 263. There are regular   **Teluk**
connections on bus no 39 from the local bus station. A short walk north of   **Cempedak**
Teluk Cempedak are Methodist Bay and Teluk Pelindong, which are beyond
the range of most picknickers.

East Coast Peninsula

Tasek Cini This is an amalgam of 13 freshwater lakes about 100 km southwest of Kuantan, see page 264. Getting there is not easy on public transport. See page 264 for details.

Tasek Bera
The biggest natural lake in Malaysia

Temerloh is one of the best access points for Tasek Bera, or the lake of changing colours. There are several Jakun, so-called proto-Malays, and Semelai aboriginal kampungs (including the largest Kota Iskandar) around the lake, once a major centre for the export of jelutong resin, used as a sealant on boats and as jungle chewing gum. Similar to Tasek Cini (see page 35), Tasek Bera is a maze of shallow channels connecting smaller lakes, in all about 5 km wide and 27 km long. During the dry season it is little more than a swamp, but in the wet it becomes an interconnected array of shallow lakes. The Semelai traditionally exploited the expansion and contraction of the lake(s), fishing during the wet season and collecting non-timber forest products during the dry. When the waters reached their peak, and wild pigs became stranded on the many islands that dot the lake, the Semelai would hunt. One of the lake's resident species is the rare fish-eating 'false' gharial crocodile (*Tomistoma schlegeli*). Asli boatmen on the lake can be hired for about RM10 per day.

Do not attempt this trip without taking adequate supplies & provisions, including basic cooking utensils

Transport There is no scheduled public transport to the lake. It is possible to take a bus or share taxi to Triang, due south of Temerloh, and then charter a taxi to the lake. Or take a taxi from Temerloh, an expensive option which may make sense in a group. Alternatively, bus from Kemayan to Bahau, 45 mins; bus from Bahau to Ladang Geddes, 30 mins; hitch or taxi to Kota Iskandar on the south side of the lake (where there are bungalows with cooking facilities, bookable through the Department of Aboriginal Affairs in Temerloh). Kota Iskandar is one of the best places on the peninsula to visit Orang Asli villages. Boats can be hired to explore the lake but requires enthusiastic negotiation.

Caras Caves These lie 25 km northwest of town; take a right fork at the 24 km mark. In 1954, the Sultan of Pahang gave a Thai Buddhist monk permission to build a temple in a limestone cave at Pancing, known as the 'yawning skull' cave. A steep climb up 200 stone steps leads into the cave which contains shrines and religious icons cut into the rock. The collection is dominated by a 9m-long reclining Buddha, set among the limestone formations. There is always a monk in residence in the cave. ■ *RM2, catch bus 48 running towards Sungai Lembing from the local bus station and get off at Panching, from here it is 5 km to the caves, although it may be possible to catch a lift on the back of a motorbike.*

Beyond the caves is **Sungai Lembing**, an old tin mine and the site of some of the oldest tin workings on the peninsula. It claims to be the deepest tin mine in the world. It has now opened to visitors. To get there, take bus 48, every hour.

Gunung Tapis Park This is a new state park, 49 km from Kuantan, offering rafting, fishing and trekking. Arrangements have to be made through the Tourist Information Centre or the local Outward Bound Society. It is only accessible by jeep via Sungai Lembing; from here accessible via a 12 km track.

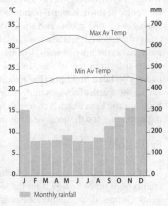

Climate: Kuantan

Dateline Kuantan: Churchill's Malayan nightmare

"In all the war, I never received a more direct shock," wrote former British wartime Prime Minister Winston Churchill in his memoirs. *"As I turned and twisted in bed, the full horror of the news sank in upon me."* On 10 December 1941 Churchill got the news that a Japanese air strike force operating from Saigon (South Vietnam) had destroyed and sunk two of the most powerful warships in the Royal Navy. HMS Prince of Wales, *a 35,000-ton battleship,* and HMS Repulse, *a 32,000-ton battle cruiser, sank within an hour of each other, with the loss of 1,196 lives, 95 km off Kuantan.*

A few days earlier the ships had arrived in Singapore, then the biggest naval operations base in the world, to underscore Britain's commitment to protecting its colonies in the East. They were soon speeding north in an effort to pre-empt and disrupt Japan's amphibious invasion of Malaya, but the flotilla, which had no air cover, was spotted by a Japanese submarine. The first wave of Japanese fighter-bombers arrived at 1100; by 1233, the Repulse, *its thick armour-plated hull holed by five torpedoes, was sunk. The Prince of Wales went down 47 minutes later in about 60m of water. Accompanying destroyers rescued 1,900 men from the two vessels before retreating to Singapore, which fell to the Japanese Imperial Army eight weeks later. The wrecks of the two ships were declared war graves and in 1991, on the 50th anniversary of the Japanese attack, a team of British Navy divers laid white ensign flags on both ships to commemorate the dead.* ❦

Once a picturesque fishing kampung, 10 km north of Kuantan, Beserah has now become a rather touristy suburb of the town. But like Teluk Cempedak to the south it does provide a slightly quieter place to stay. To get there, take bus nos 27, 28, 30 from the main bus terminal in Kuantan, which all run through Beserah. Departures are every 30 minutes.

Beserah

Essentials

The upmarket hotels are mostly at Teluk Cempedak (4 km north of Kuantan, see page 263). There are plenty of cheap Chinese hotels in Kuantan itself, mostly on and around Jln Teluk Sisek and Jln Besar. Several smart new hotels have sprung up in the **B-C** range which offer excellent value for money.

Sleeping
■ *on map, page 260*
Price codes.
see inside front cover

AL *Golden Tulip Swiss Garden Resort*, Lot 2656 & 2657, Mukim Sungai Karang, Berserah, T5447333, F5449555. An international class hotel on the beach with over 300 rooms, gardens and a good pool, business facilities, health club and sauna, and much more. Situated 8 km from town. **A** *MS Garden Hotel*, Jln Lorong Garnbut T5555899, F5554558. This hotel is being converted to a Holiday Inn in 2000. You can almost lose yourself in this enormous hotel, which is very elegant in appearance on the inside, at the business end of town. Restaurant and coffee garden. Includes breakfast. **A-B** *Samudra River View*, Jln Besar, T5555333, F5130618. A/c, restaurant has recently closed down, next to Kuantan Swimming Centre, was Kuantan's best and with a good position on the river, but new mid-market hotels are smarter and better value, carpets shabby, doubles are small, twins bigger with sitting area.

B *Cityview Hotel*, Jln Haji Abdul, T5553888, F5552999, cityview@pd.jaring.my Quite bare, with few extras but comfortable rooms. Good value. Breafast included. **B** *Hotel Grand Continental*, Jln Gambut, T5158888, F5159999, hgcktm@pd.jaring.my, www.grandcentral.com.sg. New addition to the *Grand Continental* chain, not much character but comfortable and smart, over 200 rooms all with a/c, TV, in-house movie, tea and coffee-making facility, other facilities include pool, coffee house, Chinese restaurant, health centre, business centre. The present rate is a promotional one. **B** *Le Village Beach Resort*, Lot 1260 Sungai Karang, T5447900, F5447899, fal@tm.net.my. Indian management, a pleasant enough place with a pool and tennis, getting popular with tour groups. **B-C** *Bersatu*, 2-4 Jln Darat Makbar (off Jln Wong Ah Jang), T5142328. A/c, TV, shower very clean, aimed at Malaysian executives although it is run down.

C *Shahzan Inn*, Lot 240 Jln Bukit Ubi, T5136688, F5135588. A/c, shower, TV. Hotel also has a pool, bar and restaurant in opulent environment. Complimentary paper and breakfast included. **C** *Classic*, 7 Bangunan LKNP, Jln Besar, T5554599, F5134141. A/c, extremely clean, big rooms and spacious attached bathrooms, certainly represents good value – conveniently located next to Kuantan Swimming Centre, behind the *Samudra River View* next door. Recommended. **C** *Pacific*, 60-62 Jln Bukit Ubi, T5141980. A/c, restaurant, one step down from the *Samudra*, the sixth floor has recently been renovated and upgraded, tasteful and recommended, good hotel in central location. But better value can be found elsewhere. **C** *Suraya*, 55-57 Jln Haji Abdul Aziz, T5154266, F5126728. A/c, coffee area, simple, well-appointed rooms, attached bathrooms, video, catering mainly for business people and domestic tourist market, good value. **C-D** *Hotel Makmur* Lorong Pasar Baru 1, T5141363. A/c, clean and cheap. Decent size rooms, although not all have windows. More expensive rooms have bathrooms attached.

D *Chusan*, 37-39 Jln Dato Wong Ah Jang, T5134422. Friendly staff who deliver an English language paper to your room in the morning. However, the place is dirty and noisy. **D** *Deluxe*, 1st Flr, 53 Jln Wong Ah Jang (next to *Chusan Hotel*), T5131410. A/c, above all-night restaurant, small rooms but clean, although the whole place has not seen any renovations in about the last 20 years and certainly does not live up to its

Kuantan

To Beserah & Kuala Terengganu

Jln Teluk Sisek

17

Jln Tanjung Api

To Sungai Lembing & Caras Caves

To Airport & Kuala Lumpur

Jln Bukit Sekilau

Jln Tun Ismail

Jln Beserah

12

8

4

Jln Gambut

Jln Bukit Ubi

Jln Stadium

1

10

19   Immigration

Jln Meldeka

13

7

Market

MAS Office

Sultan Ahmad Shah Mosque

Tiki's

15

Jln H J Abdul Aziz

Jln Besar

2

Food stalls

6

3

Jln Haji Abdul Rahman

14

Jln Makhota

Foodstalls

5

Jetty

Tanjung Api Mosque

Jln Penjara

oTaxi Foodstalls

16

2

18

Kuantan River

Jln Mat Kilau

N

0   km   1

0   miles   1

■ **Sleeping**
1 Annex Rest House
2 Bersatu
3 Chusan

4 Cityview
5 Classic
6 Deluxe
7 Embassy & Suraya

8 Grand Continental
9 Kuantan
10 Makmur
11 Merlin Inn

name. **D** *Embassy*, 60 Jln Teluk Sisek, T5127486. Ac, well looked after, all rooms have attached bathroom, good value, above *Tanjung Ria* coffee shop, some rooms rather noisy because of main road. **D** *Hotel Top One*, 8-10 Jln Pasar Baru, T5139573. Some a/c, bathroom with hot water but dark and slightly dirty. **D** *New Meriah*, 142 Jln Telok Sisek, T5125433. A/c, TV, some rooms with attached bathrooms and hot water, very large rooms but run down. **D** *Oriental Evergreen*, 157 Jln Haji Abdul Rahman, T5130168. A/c, Chinese restaurant, prominently advertised hotel. The décor leaves a bit to be desired, but it is clean and comfortable, great value. Recommended.

E *Sin Nam Fong*, 44 Jln Teluk Sisek, T5121561. Restaurant, friendly management but when the traffic is heavy you might as well be camped on the central reservation. **E** *Tong Nam Ah*, 98 Jln Besar, T5144204. Fan, conveniently located for bus station and hawker stalls. Rooms are very basic (with a fan and basin), but it is what you would expect from the cheapest place in town.

3 *Cheun Kee*, Jln Mahkota, large open-air Chinese restaurant, good selection of sea- **Eating** food. **2** *BKT* (also known as *Restoran Malam*), 53 Jln Wong Ah Jang, open cof- fee-shop/restaurant under *Hotel Deluxe*, best known for chicken rice and fish-head curries and for being open until 0400. **2** *Cantina*, 16 Lorong Tun Ismail 1 (off Jln Bukit Ubi), smart a/c restaurant with waiters in batik bajus, Indonesian-style seafood and curries. Recommended by locals. **2** *Kuantan Seafood*, Jln Wong Ah Jong, opposite *BKT* (*Restoran Malam*), hawker-style stalls in big open restaurant, very popular. **1** *Choo Kong*, Jln Mahkota, Chinese noodles, cold beer, marble top tables, basic but good. Recommended. **1** *Kheng Hup*, 17 Jln Makhota (on corner), opposite *Taman Salera Hawker Centre*, big old coffee shop with marble-top tables, raised voices and good *nasi lemak* and *nasi daggang* in the mornings, unchanged for 50 years. **1** *Salme*, 10 Jln

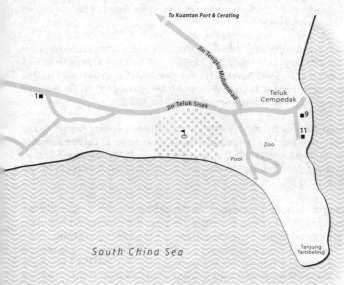

Besar, cheap Malay dishes – *ikan bakar* (grilled fish) and *nasi campur* (pick-your-own curries). 1 *Sri Patani*, 79 Bangunan Udarulaman, Jln Tun Ismail, excellent Malay/South Thai food. Recommended. 1 *Tanjung Ria Coffee Shop*, 60 Jln Teluk Sisek (below *Embassy Hotel*), good breakfasts (especially *nasi lemak*), bright and sunny and friendly. 1 *Tiki's*, Jln Mahkota (opposite Maybank), cheap Western fare and local dishes, good for Western-style breakfast. *Zul Satay*, junction of Jln Teluk Sisek and Jln Beserah (known as Kuantan Garden, between Kuantan and Teluk Cempedak), upmarket satay joint with all the usual plus rabbit, liver and offal. Recommended.

Foodstalls Malay cafés and foodstalls along the river bank, behind the long distance bus station, busy and popular. Recommended, especially for seafood. There are more hawker stalls on junction of Jln Mahkota and Jln Masjid (Taman Salera), next to local bus station. *Kuantan Garden*, junction of Jln Teluk Sisek and Jln Beserah (between Kuantan and Teluk Cempedak), large number of Chinese stalls.

Bars *The Sampan Bar*, on the *Hyatt Hotel* beachfront, is in the atap-roofed shell of a junk which beached in 1978 with 162 Vietnamese refugees aboard. The bar capitalizes on this slightly perverse novelty by charging more. *Boom Boom Bar* Jln Besar. Pool, bands and restaurant.

The best bars & nightlife are along the beachfront at Teluk Cempedak

Shopping **Books** *Hamid Brothers*, 23 Jln Mahkota; *Syarikat Ganesh*, 18C Jln Besar; *Teruntum Enterprise*, Wakil Dewan Bahasa, Jln Mahkota. Several craft shops along Jln Besar, expensive and touristy.

Sports **Golf** *Royal Pahang Golf Club*, green fees RM100 weekdays, RM1500 weekends. **Swimming** *Kuantan Swimming Centre* (behind *Classic* and *Samudra View* hotels on Jln Besar) is a public pool next to the river, RM5 per day, restaurant next to river, very clean and good value.

Tour operators Tours including trips around the Kuantan area, river tours and trips to Lake Kenyir (see page 285). *Kenyir Lake Tourist*, 01-83 Jln Tun Ismail, T5105687; *Reliance*, 66 Jln Teluk Sisek, T5102566. *SMAS Travels*, 1st Flr, Kompleks Teruntum, Jln Mahkota, T5113888. *Syarikat Perusahaan*, 38, 2nd Flr, Bangunan DPMP, Jln Wong Ah Jang. *Taz Ben Travel & Tours*, 2nd Flr, Kompleks Teruntum, Jln Mahkota, T5102255.

Transport **Local Bus**: local bus station is on junction of Jln Haji and Jln Abdul Rahman. Regular connections with Teluk Cempedak; for Cherating take bus no. 27. **Car hire**: *Budget*, 59 Jln Haji Abdul Aziz, T5126370 or *Coral Beach Resort*, 152 Sungai Karang, Beserah, T5447544. *Hertz*, *Samudra River View Hotel*, Jln Besar, T5122688. *National*, 49 Jln Teluk Sisek, T5127303.

219 km to Kuala Terengganu 229 km to KL 325 km to Johor Bahru

Long distance **Air**: Sultan Ahmad Shah Airport is 20 km south of town. Regular connections with Johor Bahru, KL and Kuala Terengganu. It is also possible to fly direct from Kuantan to Pulau Tioman daily on Pelangi Airways. Taxi to town RM10.

Bus: there is a new long distance bus station on Jln Stadium and companies have their offices on the second floor. Regular connections with KL (RM21.10), Mersing, JB, Singapore, Melaka, Penang, Kuala Terengganu and Kota Bharu. To get to Cherating take bus no. 27 from the local bus station on Jln Haji.

Taxi: taxi station on Jln Besar, near intersection with Jln Abdul Rahman. KL, Mersing (RM100-150 for 4 people) and Kuala Terengganu.

Boat: *Cruise Muhibbah* (*Feri Malaysia*) starts in Kuantan and goes to Kota Kinabalu, Kuching, Singapore and Port Klang. To KK, Kuching and Singapore. The well-appointed ferry leaves Kuantan Sat 1800. Schedules subject to change: enquire at tourist information centre.

Airline offices *MAS*, Ground Floor, Wisma Bolasepak Pahang, Jln Gambut, T5157055, F5157870; *Pelangi Airways*, Sultan Ahmad Shah Airport, T5381177, F5381713; *Silk Air*, c/o MAS, T5157055, F5157870. **Banks** Along Jln Mahkota and Jln Besar, between GPO and bus station. **Communications** Area Code: 09. General Post Office: Jln Mahkota (east end). **Medical facilities** Hospitals: Jln Mat Kilau. **Tourist offices** *LKNP Tourist Information Centre*, 15th Flr, Kompleks Teruntum, Jln Mahkota, T5133026; *Tourist Information Centre*, Tingkat Bawah Bangunan, Jln Haji Abdul Aziz. **Useful addresses** Immigration Office: Wisma Persekutuan, Jln Gambut, T5142155.

Directory

Teluk Cempedak

Phone code: 09
Colour map 2, grid A5

This beach resort is just 4 km east of Kuantan and marks the beginning of the beaches. The Pahang state government has reserved the 30 km stretch of coast from Teluk Cempedak beach north to the Terengganu state border exclusively for tourism-related projects, so there is likely to be much more development in the next few years. Teluk Cempedak was once the site of a quiet kampung, and is now a beach strip with a range of hotels, a string of bars and restaurants. There is a government-run handicraft shop (*Kedai Kraf*) beside the beach, specializing in batik.

AL *Hyatt Regency Kuantan*, T5661234. A/c, several restaurants and bars, 2 pools, low-rise hotel in landscaped gardens and a beautiful setting on the beach, good sports (including watersports) facilities, well-stocked craft shop, well-managed with good views, Sampan Bar (formerly a Vietnamese refugee boat), the hotel has recently been extended to include apartments. Recommended. **A** *Merlin Inn*, adjacent to *Hyatt*, T5141388. Not as good facilities as the *Hyatt*. **B** *Samudra Beach Resort*, T5135933. A/c, restaurant, rooms look like municipal toilets from the outside, but they have big French windows overlooking spacious gardens and the bay, nice place. **B-C** *Annex Rest House*, Jln Teluk Sisek, 2 km before Teluk Cempedak. Restaurant (rather inadequate), newly renovated, though we have had reports of bad service and broken down facilities, spacious grassy grounds. **B-C** *Kuantan*, opposite *Hyatt*, T5680026. A/c, restaurant, very clean, cheaper rooms fan only but all have attached bathroom, noisy television lounge, very pleasant terrace for sundowners, although it now faces the new Hyatt extension. Recommended. **C** *Hill View*, a/c, restaurant in block of karaoke lounges, bars and restaurants, not good value for money. **D** *Sri Pantai Bungalows*, some a/c, situated close to the *Hillview Hotel* this is one of the better cheaper places to stay, rooms are clean and reasonable for this price.

Sleeping
Teluk Cempedak provides a more relaxed alternative to the noisier hotels in Kuantan

3 *Nisha's Curry House*, 13 Teluk Cempedak, North Indian cuisine plus fish-head curry. **2** *Cempedak Seafood*, A-1122, Jln Teluk Sisek, big Chinese restaurant at the crossroads on the way to Teluk Cempedak, specialities: chilli crab and freshwater fish. **2** *Pattaya*, on the beach front, good views of the beach, serves crab priced by weight, good food and good value. **2** *Tan's*, 29 Teluk Cempedak, Malay/Chinese. Recommended, fish-head curry. **Foodstalls**: group of gerai makan in new brick kiosks, next to beach alongside Handicraft centre.

Eating

There are a number of bars along the seashore. One pub which comes recommended is the *Country Ranch* not far from the *Hilton Hotel*.

Bars

East Coast Holidays, 33 Teluk Cempedak, T5105228, helpful staff; *Mayflower Acme Tours*, *Hyatt Kuantan*, Teluk Cempedak, T5121469; *Morahols Travel*, 11 Teluk Cempedak, T5100851.

Tour operators

Transport
4 km E of Kuantan

Car hire *Avis*, *Hyatt Hotel*, Teluk Cempedak, T5661234, and Ground Floor, Loo Bros Bldg, 59 Jln Haji Abdul Aziz, T5123666; *Mayflower*, *Hyatt Kuantan*, Teluk Cempedak, T5131234; *Sinat*, Lot 3, *Merlin Inn*, Teluk Cempedak, T5141388; *Thrifty*. **Bus** Regular connections from Kuantan: bus 39 from the its local bus station. A short walk north of Teluk Cempedak are Methodist Bay and Teluk Pelindong, which are beyond the range of most picknickers.

Tasek Cini

Phone code: 09
Colour map 2, grid A4

Tasek Cini is an amalgam of 13 freshwater lakes, whose fingers reach deep into the surrounding forested hills, 100 km southwest of Kuantan. The lake and the adjoining mountain are sacred to the Malays; legend has it that Lake Cini is the home of a huge white crocodile. The Jakun proto-Malay aboriginals, who live around Tasek Cini, believe a naga, or serpent, personifying the spirit of the lake, inhabits and guards its depths. Some commentators think that as tourism picks up there, Tasek Cini will acquire the status of Scotland's Loch Ness, although Lake Cini's monster has not been spotted now for 12 years. Locals call their monster 'Chinnie'.

More intriguing still are tales that the lake covers a 12th-14th century Khmer walled city. The rather unlikely story maintains that a series of aquaducts were used as the city's defence and that when under attack, the city would be submerged. In late-1992, however, the *Far Eastern Economic Review* reported that recent archaeological expeditions had uncovered submerged stones a few metres underwater at various points around the lake. But the Orang Asli fishermen do not need archaeologists to support their convictions that the lost city exists. Between June and September the lake is carpeted with red and white lotus flowers.

Tours

There are a few tour companies which run package tours to the lake. Recommended is *Malaysian Overland Adventures*, Lot 1.23, 1st Flr, Bangunan Angkasaraya, Jalan Ampang, Kuala Lumpur, T03-2413569.

Sleeping

C *Lake Cini Resort*, T4086308/4567897. Ten chalets, some with attached bathrooms, camping (**F**), small restaurant attached to the resort serving simple dishes. **E** *Rajan Jones Guest House*, this is the cheapest place to stay situated 30 mins walk from the *Lake Cini Resort*, room rate includes all meals but the accommodation is very basic, no running water or electricity, tours and treks arranged.

Transport

Getting to Tasek Cini is difficult by public transport; by far the easiest way to visit the lake is on an organized tour (RM60). Contact the Tourist Information Centre, 15th Flr, Kompleks Teruntum, Jln Mahkota, T505566, Kuantan. **Bus and boat** Take the KL highway (Rt 2) from Kuantan towards Maran; 56 km down the road, Tasek Cini is signposted to the left. From here there used to be buses to Kampung Belimbing, a trip of 12 km, but there are reports that this service has been suspended. If so, hitch or walk to Belimbing. At Belimbing it is possible to hire a boat across the Pahang River and onto the waterways of Tasek Cini (RM40-50). It is also possible to be dropped off at the resort and picked up at an arranged time (RM80). An alternative way to get to Tasek Cini is by catching a bus from Kuantan or Pekan for Kampung Cini (12 km from the resort). From here there is a sealed road to the resort but, again, no public transport – although people have managed to persuade local motorcyclists to take them pillion.

Beserah

Once a picturesque fishing kampung, 10 km north of Kuantan, Beserah now sprawls and is not much more than a suburb of Kuantan. Beserah is a friendly place but aesthetically it bears little comparison with villages further north. There is, however, a local handicraft industry still; there is a batik factory to the north of the village. The village's speciality is *ikan bilis*, or anchovies, which are boiled, dried and chillied on the beach and end up on Malaysian breakfast tables, gracing *nasi lemak*. Beserah's fishermen use water buffalo to cart their catch directly from their boats to the kampung, across the middle of the shallow lagoon. The kampung has become rather touristy in recent years, but there is a good beach, just to the north, at Batu Hitam.

Phone code: 09
Colour map 2, grid A5

Kampung Sungai Ular (Snake River Village), 31 km north of Kuantan, is a typical laid-back and very photogenic Malay fishing village. There is a small island, Pulau Ular, just offshore. The beach is usually deserted, is backed by coconut palms and has fine white sand. The Kampung is signposted to the right, just off the main road. Catch a bus running up the east coast road and asked to be dropped off at Kampung Sungai Ular.

Excursions

Sleeping A-B *Ombak Beach Resort*, Mukim Sungai Karang (35 km north of Kuantan), T6095819166, F6095819433. Thirty a/c rooms in 3 acres of land, all with own terrace and parking space so this is clearly directed mainly at people with their own transport. Right on the beach, swimming pool, limited conference facilities.

A *Coral Beach Resort* (formerly *Ramada*), 152 Sungai Karang (about 6 km north of Beserah), T5447544, F5447543. A/c, restaurants, pool, paddling pool, playground, good range of facilities including tennis, squash, badminton, gymnasium, jacuzzi and watersports. Adjacent to fine white-sand beach, popular stop-over for cruises, hence its amphitheatre which can seat 800 people for cultural shows, all rooms spacious, a/c, TV, in-house video, mini-bar, tea and coffee-making facilities, non-smoking rooms available; *Reliance tour agency* in arcade. **A-B** *Le Village Beach Resort*, Sungai Karang, T5447900, F5447899. Restaurants, pool, beach front with watersport facilities, tennis, playground and paddling pool, neatly landscaped grounds with well-spaced chalets and a new 66-room extension, good atmosphere and attractive décor. **B** *Blue Horizon Beach Resort*, Kampung Balok (5 km north of Beserah), T5448119, F5448117. North of Beserah on good beach, pool, clean and spruce with big wooden chalet rooms, built around central area, garden a bit of a wilderness, discounts often available. **B** *Gloria Maris Resort* (1 km north of Beserah), T5447788, F5447619. A/c, restaurant, watersports, very small pool, sandwiched between road and Pasir Hitam (not such a good stretch of beach), small chalets and friendly management. **B** *Tiara Beserah Beach Resort*, 812 Jln Beserah, T5448101, F5141979. Thirty two rooms in new atap-roofed chalets, a/c, TV, pool, café. **E** *La Chaumiere*, T5447662. This is the most popular of the budget places to stay, under French management it is well run and pleasant, to get here ask to be let off at Kampung Pantai Beserah and walk towards Kampung Pelidong and the sea, about 1 km. **E-F** *Jaffar's Place*, very rudimentary kampung accommodation, room rate includes all meals, away from the beach.

Sleeping
Most of the resort hotels are around Sungai Karang, 3-6 km N of Beserah village itself

3 *Pak Su Seafood Restaurant*, popular Chinese restaurant on terrace next to the beach. Recommended. **3** *Beserah Seafood*, Malay/Chinese, speciality: buttered prawns. **3** *Gloria Maris Golden Cowrie Restaurant*, near the chalets, Malay/Indian/Thai and traditional Sun lunch at fixed price, seafood salad by weight.

Eating

East Coast Peninsula

Transport **Bus** Bus nos 27, 28 and 30 from Kuantan's main bus terminal all pass through Beserah, departures every 30 mins.

Temerloh
Phone code: 09

Situated on the Pahang River, Temerloh is the halfway point on the KL-Kuantan road and a popular makan stop. The Karak Highway tunnels through the Genting Pass, to the northeast of KL and the road then runs east through Mentakab (where there is a railway station) to Temerloh. From Temerloh it is possible to take a river trip to **Pekan**, the old royal capital of Pahang (see page 256) and to **Tasek Bera** (page 258). Frankly, there's not much to bring people to Temerloh, although it is emerging as an important administrative and service centre.

The accommodation in
Temerloh is basic

Sleeping **B** *Hotel Green Park*, Lot 373, Jln Serendit, T2963055, F2962517. A/c, complimentary tea/coffee, TV, newly opened and smartly furbished. Recommended. **B** *Seri Malaysia Temerloh*, Lot 370/6/92, Jln Mazmah, T2965776. One of the new budget chain, a/c, TV, coffee/tea-making facilities, money changer, restaurant, good value. Recommended. **C** *Kam San*, C-67 Jln Datuk Ngau Ken Lock, T2965606. **C** *Rumah Rehat* (*Rest House*), Jln Datuk Hamzah, T2961254/2963254. Some a/c, restaurant, great position on the river, large rooms. Recommended. **C-D** *Ban Hin*, 40 Jln Tangku, T2962331. Some a/c, better rooms with attached bathrooms, reasonable. **D** *Kwai Pan*, 66 Jln Datuk Ngau Ken Lock, T2961431. **D-E** *Isbis*, 12 Jln Tengku Babar, T2963126/2963136. Some a/c, the best of the cheaper places to stay, more expensive rooms with attached bathrooms.

Transport **Train** The nearest railway station is at Mentakab, 12 km west of Temerloh. Connections south with Singapore and north to Kota Bharu, see page 35 for details of timetabling. **Bus and taxi** The bus terminal is close to the centre of town. Daily connections with KL's Pekeliling terminal, Melaka, Penang, Kota Bharu and Kuantan. Taxis run to KL, Kuantan, Mentakab and Jerantut.

Taman Negara National Park

Phone code: 09
Colour map 1, grid C5

Once known as King George V Park, Taman Negara was gazetted as a national park in 1938 when the Sultans of Pahang, Terengganu and Kelantan agreed to set aside a 43,000 hectare tract of virgin jungle where all three states meet. Taman Negara is in a mountainous area (it includes Gunung Tahan, the highest mountain on the peninsula) and lays claim to some of the oldest rainforest in the world. This area was left untouched by successive ice ages and has been covered in jungle for about 130 million years which makes it older than the rainforests in the Congo or Amazon basins.

Altitude: 2,187m

Gunung Tahan is the highest of three peaks on the east side of the park, and marks the Pahang-Kelantan border. Its name means 'the forbidden mountain': according to local Asli folklore the summit is the domain of a giant monkey, who guards two pots of magic stones. The first expeditions to Gunung Tahan were despatched by the Sultan of Pahang in 1863 but were defeated by the near-vertical-sided Teku Gorge, the most obvious approach to the mountain, from the Tahan River. The 1,000m-high gorge ended in a series of waterfalls which came crashing 600m down the mountain. Several other ill-fated European-led expeditions followed, before the summit was finally reached by four Malays on another British expedition in 1905.

Until the park was set up, **Kampung Kuala Tahan**, now the site of the park headquarters, was one of the most remote Orang Asli villages in North Pahang, at the confluence of the Tembeling and Tahan rivers. This area of the peninsula remained unmapped and mostly unexplored well into the 20th century. These days, Kuala Tahan is sometimes over-run with visitors; park accommodation has expanded rapidly under private sector management. But most visitors do not venture more than a day or two's walk from headquarters, and huge swaths of jungle in the north and east sections of the park remain virtually untouched and unvisited. Taman Negara now has scores of trails, requiring varying amounts of physical exertion; the toughest walk is the nine day Gunung Tahan summit trek.

The range of vegetation in the park includes riverine species and lowland forest to upland dwarf forest on the summit of Gunung Tahan. Over 250 species of bird have been recorded in Taman Negara, and wildlife includes wild ox, sambar, barking deer, tapir, civet cat, wild boar and even the occasional tiger and elephant herd. However, the more exotic mammals rarely put in an appearance, particularly in the areas closer to Kuala Tahan.

Hides

Some hides or *bumbun* are close to the park headquarters, as close as a five minute walk, and nearly all are within a day's walk or boat ride. Visitors can stay overnight, but there are no facilities other than a sleeping space (sheets can be borrowed from Kuala Tahan for RM5 per night) and a pit latrine. Take a powerful torch to spotlight any animals that visit the salt-licks. You are more likely to see wildlife at the hides further from the park HQ, as the numbers of people now visiting Taman Negara have begun to frighten the animals away. Rats are not frightened: food bags must be tied securely at night. During popular periods and on weekends it is best to book your spot at a salt-lick.

Permits

The Department of Wildlife has a bureau at the Kuala Tembeling jetty (see below) and issues permits and licences. Park permit RM1; fishing licence RM10; camera licence RM5.

Fishing

Fishing is better further from Kuala Tahan; there are game-fishing lodges near the confluence of the Tenor and Tahan rivers, at Kuala Terenggan (up the Tembeling from Kuala Tahan) and at Kuala Kenyam, at the confluence of the Kenyam and the Tembeling. The best months to fish are February-March and July-August; during the monsoon season. The rivers Tahan, Kenyam and the more remote Sepia (all tributaries of the Tembeling) are reckoned to be the best waters. There are more than 200 species of fish in the park's rivers including the *kelasa* which is a renowned sport fish. A permit costs RM10, rods for hire (see also Booking, Equipment and Sleeping, below).

River trips

Boat trips can be arranged from park HQ to the Lata Berkoh rapids on Sungai Tahan (near Kuala Tahan), Kuala Terenggan (several sets of rapids to be negotiated), and to Kuala Kenyam (from where a trail leads to the top of a limestone outcrop). A trip to the rapids, misleadingly called a waterfall, by park authorities, on a boat that accommodates four passengers will cost RM80. Although this is a comparatively expensive way to see the park it is probably the most enchanting and when split between a number of people (boats carrying up to 12 people can be booked) is worthwhile.

East Coast Peninsula

Treks

Trails are signposted from park HQ. Tours are conducted twice daily by park officials and these include night walks (RM15 per person), cave treks (RM35) and other treks and walks. Because most visitors tend to stick to the trails immediately around the park HQ, even a modest day's outing will take you away from the crowds. A full listing and details on various routes can be obtained at park HQ. Independent day treks/walks can be taken to caves, swimming holes, waterfalls, along rivers (again with swimming areas), to salt-licks and hides, and, of course, through forest. Longer overnight treks are also possible although guides must be taken on all these longer forays. The most demanding is climbing Gunung Tahan.

Gunung Tahan
Altitude: 2,187m

This is a nine day trek to the summit and back. It is best climbed in February and March, the driest months. **Day 1**: Kuala Tahan to Kuala Melantai (four to five hours). **Day 2**: Kuala Melantai to Kuala Puteh (eight hours). No streams *en route*; succession of tough climbs along the ridge, final one is Gunung Rajah; 1½ hours descent to campsite by Sungai Tahan. **Day 3**: Kuala Puteh to Kuala Teku (2½-4½ hours). Route follows Sungai Tahan, which must be crossed several times. The campsite is at the Sungai Teku confluence and was the base camp for the first successful Gunung Tahan expedition in 1905. **Day 4**: Kuala Teku to Gunung Tangga Lima Belas (seven hours). Long uphill slog

Taman Negara

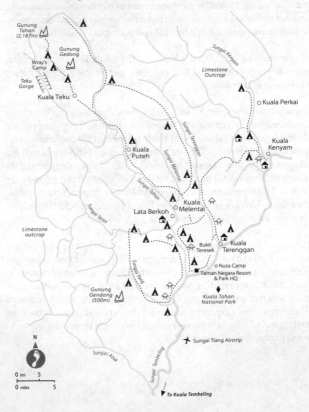

(4½ hours) to Wray's Camp (named after 1905 expedition member). This is a good campsite; alternatively climb through mossy forest to Gunung Tangga Lima Belas campsite, which has magnificent views, but is very exposed. **Day 5**: Gunung Tangga Lima Belas to summit, returning to the Padang. After a scramble up the side of a rockface on Gunung Gedong, the trail leads to the Padang – a plateau area (three to four hours). Set up tents and leave equipment at campsite; route to summit follows ridge and takes 2½ hours. Essential to take raincoat; summit often shrouded in mist. Begin descent to the Padang by 1600. **Days 6-9**: Padang to Kuala Tahan, following the same route. **Hiring a guide** A guide is necessary for this climb (RM400 per week, RM50 for each additional day); maximum of 12 people with one guide. **NB** A sleeping bag and a tent are vital, all of the camps have water and firewood.

Another mountain in Taman Negara that is less frequently climbed is **Gunung Gagau** (1,377m), far to the northeast of Kuala Tahan. It is a six to seven day trek of which one day is spent travelling up river on Sungai Sat. This area of the park is rarely visited and it is advisable to take a guide.

The new **Canopy Walk**, half an hour from headquarters, is worth a visit. The walkway is suspended about 30m above the forest floor and stretches for over 400m. ■ *1100-1500 Mon-Thur and Sat-Sun, RM5.*

Equipment

For trekking it is worth having walking boots for even the shortest of excursions as rain turns mud paths into skid patches, a thick pair of socks and long (loose) trousers. Leeches are common in the park after rain, spraying clothes and boots with insect repellent helps. Having said this, minimal clothing is needed, as it's hot work. A good torch is essential equipment for those going to hides and a water bottle is also essential on longer walks and treks. A raincover may be useful. Visitors are not permitted to carry glass into the park. The shop at Park HQ hires out torches, tents, water bottles, cooking equipment and fishing tackle - even jungle boots. Camera permit $5.

Booking

Visits to the national park can be arranged individually or be pre-arranged at *River Park Sdn Bhd*, 260 h, 2nd Mile Jalan Ipoh, KL, T032915299 or *Malaysian Tourist Information Centre* (MATIC), Jalan Ampang, KL, T032643929 ext 25. Visitors are required to pay a RM30 deposit to confirm bookings for the park boat and accommodation at Kuala Tahan (park HQ). The boat to headquarters costs RM15 per person (one way). Those who risk turning up at the Kuala Tembeling jetty without booking may be turned away if boats are full.

Best time to visit

Between March and September, during the dry season. The park may be closed during the height of the monsoon season from the beginning of November to the end of December, when the rivers are in flood, although this isn't always the case.

Park headquarters

At Kuala Tahan, on the south boundary of the park, accessible by boat from Kuala Tembeling, a two to three hour beautiful journey. At Kuala Tahan all visitors are required to check in at the reception desk. ■ *0800-2200, Mon-Sun. Park headquarters provide a range of facilities, although prices tend to be steep, including shop, restaurant, money changing facilities (poor rates), telephone service, equipment hire, etc.*

East Coast Peninsula

Tours

Various companies run tours to Taman Negara. It is a more expensive way to visit the park, but permits, itineraries etc are well organized in advance. Many visitors, particularly those unfamiliar with travelling in Malaysia, have recommended tours for their logistical advantages. Since the park has been run privately, however, it has become much more user-friendly and it is easy to visit independently. The disadvantage of independent travel is that tour groups tend to book up the hides. *Asia Overland Services*, 35M Jalan Dewan Sultan Sulaiman Satu (off Jalan Tunku Abdul Rahman), Kuala Lumpur, T2925622, three-day safari US$245. *Malaysia Overland Adventures*, Lot 1.23, 1st Flr, Bangunan Angkasaraya, Jalan Ampang, Kuala Lumpur, T032413659. *NKS Hotel & Travel SDN BHD*, in Sri Emas Hotel, Jln Besar, Jerantut, T2664499. *Overland Discovery Tours*, Unit 5, 1st Podium Flr, *Shangri-La Hotel*, 11 Jalan Sultan Ismail, Kuala Lumpur, T2302942. *Scenic Holidays and Travel*, Lot SO64, 2nd Flr Sungai Wang Plaza, Jalan Sultan Ismail, Kuala Lumpur, T2424522. *SPKG Tours*, 16th Flr LKNP Building, Bandar Baru, Jerantut, T262369. *Tuah Travel & Tours*, 12 Jalan Lipis, Kuala Lipis, T312144. *Camp Nasa*, 16 LKNP Building, New Town Jerantut, T262369, F264369. Packages can also be organized by Kuala Tahan Office, Taman Negara Resort, Kuala Tahan, T263500, F261500.

Park essentials

Sleeping **Kuala Tahan and Kampung Kuala Tahan** The management of *Taman Negara* was handed over to the private sector in 1990. All accommodation for the Taman Negara Resort must be booked in advance, either direct to **Taman Negara Resort**, Kuala Tahan, 27000 Jerantut, Pahang T09-2663500, F092661500 or through the sales office: 2nd Floor, *Hotel Istana*, no. 73 Jln Raja Chulan, T032455585, F032455430. The resort encompasses a range of rooms and types of accommodation (some with self-catering facilities): starting at the bottom of the range are bunk beds in the hostel (8 people per dorm) with communal facilities at RM40 per person including breakfast. Moving up, rooms in the original accommodation centre cost RM110. Self-contained chalets and bungalows range from the standard wooden chalet at RM216, to RM300 for the deluxe chalet, to RM600 for 2-bedroom suite bungalows. Note that it is also possible to camp (see below).

An alternative to the park is to stay in **Kampung Kuala Tahan**, on the other side of the river (which can be crossed by a small boat for 50c throughout the day – last boat 2300), where accommodation is much cheaper – albeit slightly less convenient. **B** *Teresek View*, T011911530, range of places to stay including dorm beds, basic chalets and more sophisticated bungalows with attached bathrooms. **E** *Argoh Chalets*, basic doubles with fan and shower RM 35, dorm beds also available. **E** *Liang Hostel*, basic with 4 beds per room. **E-F** *Tembeling Hostel*, much like *Liang* in price and standard, but 2 beds per room. Upriver from Kampung Kuala Tahan is **D-F** *Nusa Camp*, restaurant, across the river from Park HQ and then 15 mins upriver, bookable in KL at MATIC, T032643929 ext 25 or T092662369, spkg@tm.net.my. Offers a range of accommodation including dorms with two bunk beds per room, bungalows with attached bathrooms, and also tents for hire, the owner 'Byoing' is keen to help and will organize trips to the rapids (not particularly exciting), various hikes and trips to an Orang Asli village. To get to *Nusa Camp* take one of the longboats from Park HQ (there is a shuttle boat every 2 hrs); they also run a direct service from Kuala Tembeling with boats leaving at 0900 and 1400 every day (Fri 1430).

Accommodation elsewhere in the Park In addition, there are a number of fishing lodges in the park, in which beds and mattresses are provided; there is no bedding or cooking equipment however. These can be booked at Kuala Tahan HQ (RM8 per night). Visitor Lodges (**B**) for hides at **Kuala Terenggan** and **Kuala Kenyam** can also be booked from Kuala Tahan HQ. These are right away from the crowds but are surprisingly comfortable with attached bathrooms and restaurant. There is no charge for staying in the hides themselves.

Camping The newly landscaped campsite can accommodate up to 200, but fortunately never does. *Taman Negara Resort* rents out tents (2/3/4-person) for RM6-12 per night. There is an additional RM1 fee for use of the campsite. Tents, once hired, can be taken with you on treks. There are communal toilet facilities and lockers are available.

Eating
Because of the cost of food at the resort, many tourists prefer to bring their own

The resort operates two restaurants and a bar – the rotan and bamboo *Tembeling Lounge* which even gets daily newspapers, it is open 1100-2400, Mon-Sun. The *Tahan Restaurant* and *Teresek Cafeteria* serve both local and Western cuisine; the former is more expensive, both are open 0700-2300 Mon-Sun.

On the other side of the river at **Kampung Kuala Tahan** are a number of floating restaurants which serve unremarkable food but at prices considerably lower than those in the park complex. Beer, though, tends to be expensive.

Useful services The *Taman Negara Resort* include an overpriced mini-market (selling provisions for trekking and camping, open 0800-2230), a clinic (open 0800-1615 Mon-Sun; hospital attendant on call 24 hrs, for emergencies), a mini-post office, a library and a Pelangi Air reservations and ticketing counter. There is also a jungle laundry service. In the 'Interpretative Room', there is a thrice daily film and slide-show on the park's flora and fauna (2045 Mon-Sun).

Transport
All access to Taman Negara – other than for those who fly in – is by longboat from Kuala Tembeling

Air *Pelangi Air* used to run a service between Taman Negara's Sungai Tiang airstrip (30 mins boat ride from Kuala Tahan) and KL and Kerteh in Terengganu. However as of mid-1997 this service had been discontinued.

Train Tembeling Halt, the nearest stop for Kuala Tembeling, is accessible from Kuala Lumpur, Kota Bharu and Singapore. It is necessary to inform the guard/conductor if you want to alight at Tembeling Halt, as it is still an unscheduled stop. From there it is a 30 min walk to the jetty at Kuala Tembeling. From Kota Bharu: to Tembeling Halt; departures from Wakaf Bharu station (outside KB) at 1150 on Sun, Tue, Wed and Fri. From KL: trains to Tembeling Halt, via Gemas (on KL-Singapore line). The overnight sleeper departs 2200, arrives Tembeling Halt 0630. From Singapore: change at Gemas; connections to Tembeling Halt at 0530 Mon-Sunday. Note that trains rarely pick up at Tembeling Halt and the nearest regular station is at Mela, a short bus journey away from the jetty.

Bus/taxi The easiest way into the park is to catch one of the direct tourist minibuses from KL to Kuala Tembeling, where the jetty for boats to the park is situated. Most guesthouses in KL can arrange tickets and also some tour companies. The nearest town to Kuala Tembeling is Jerantut where there is a range of accommodation. For those who want to use regular public transport or who are travelling from elsewhere, there are regular connections from KL via Temerloh (see Jerantut entry below for details). There is now a road all the way from Jerantut to Kampung KualaTahan but it is rough and requires 4WD – transport is provided by guesthouses in Jerantut but it means missing out on the river journey.

East Coast Peninsula

Boat It is a 59 km journey from Kuala Tembeling jetty, up the Sungai Tembeling to Kuala Tahan (Park HQ), 2½ hrs, depending on river level; departures at 0900 and 1400 (1430 on Fri). The return trip takes 2 hrs; departures at 0900 and 1400. *Nusa Camp* also operates a boat service from Kuala Tembeling to their own resort (see **Sleeping**, above). Although it is now possible to go by road all the way to Kampung Kuala Tahan the boat journey is far more interesting and enjoyable.

Jerantut
Phone code: 09

The nearest town to Kuala Tembeling, the most popular entry point into Taman Negara, is Jerantut some 16 km away; a trip that costs RM15 by taxi. For those travelling to the park on public transport it may be necessary to spend a night here and there is a range of accommodation on offer.

Sleeping and eating **B** *Sri Emas Hotel*, T2664499, F2664801, howann@tm.Net.my. Some a/c, shower, the most sophisticated hotel in town, excellent source of information on the park, free transport to and from bus/rail station. *NKS Tour* who run the hotel will also organize trips to the park and will book your accommodation there, dorm beds available – as well as a storeroom to leave your luggage while you are in the park. (**F**). **C-D** *Jerantut Resthouse*, T2664488, nkstour@hotmail.com (also run by *NKS*). Some a/c, restaurant, popular place with range of options including a/c rooms with attached bathrooms, simple fan rooms, and dorm beds (**F**), they organize daily trips to the park. **E** *Chett Fatts*, adequate. **E** *Hotel Jerantut*, T2665568. Not recommended. **E** *Hotel Piccadilly*, 312 Sungai Jan.

There are a number of Malay-style coffee shops in town as well as the usual stalls in the market area.

Transport
16 km to Kuala Tembeling

Train Jerantut is accessible from KL, Kota Bharu and Singapore. From Kota Bharu: to Jerantut; departures from Wakaf Bharu station (outside KB). There are two options: the slow, but scenic jungle train leaving at 0615 and arriving in Jerantut at 1630 (RM12); or the express train that leaves Wakaf Bharu at 2020 arriving in Jerantut at 1340 (2nd class RM21, 3rd class RM17). From KL: trains to Jerantut, via Gemas (on KL-Singapore line) including the overnight sleeper. From Singapore: change at Gemas for connections to Jerantut.

Bus and taxi The bus and taxi station in Jerantut is in the centre of town. Regular connections from KL's Pekeliling terminal via Temerloh. Taxis direct to Jerantut from KL leave from the Puduraya bus terminal. From the east coast, there are hourly buses from Kuantan to Jerantut as well as taxis. For Kuala Tembeling (and Taman Negara) there are buses and taxis; some of the guesthouses also lay on minibuses. There is now a road all the way from Jerantut to Kampung Kuala Tahan but it is rough and requires 4WD. Transport is provided by guesthouses in Jerantut but it means missing out on the river journey.

Kuala Lipis and the Kenong Rimba National Park

Phone code: 09
Colour map 1, grid C4

This is a pleasant and relaxed town on the Jelai and Lipis rivers. Unlike other towns it has not been thoughtlessly redeveloped and many of the colonial buildings still survive. This is probably because Malaysia's development has passed Kuala Lipis by. At the end of the 19th century it grew to prominence as a gold mining town and, for a short period, was the administrative capital of the area. However gold fever has passed (although the mines have recently been re-opened) and the town's administrative role passed on to Kuantan in 1955. Today, as well as being a good base from which to trek to Kenong Rimba, it also has its own not inconsiderable charms.

Kenong Rimba Park is 1½ hours east of Kuala Lipis by boat down the Jelai River to Kampung Kuala Kenong. The park, which encompasses the Kenong River valley and encompasses some 120 km², is the home of the *Batik Orang Asli* tribe, who are shifting cultivators. There is a network of Asli trails around the park and several caves and waterfalls. There are two campsites along the river; the first, *Kesong Campsite*, has three atap huts which serve as basic accommodation. There are also some simple huts, the *Persona Chalets*, at Gunung Kesong. The park is a good alternative to Taman Negara. Though it may not have the same variety of animal life (and especially large mammals) it is less touristed and trekking here is cheaper. Note that a registered guide is required. For tours and treks to Kenong Rimba, see **Tours** below. Entrance to the park is to Batu Sembilan (accessible on the jungle train), and from there by boat to Jeti Tanjung Kiara. **Excursions**

Mr Appu Annandaraja who runs the *Kuala Lipis Hotel* (see **Sleeping** below) comes highly recommended as a trek organizer. He organizes a four day trek including food and boat transport in and out of Kenong Rimba for approximately US$65. Another guesthouse which organizes trips to the park for much the same price is the *Gin Loke Hotel*, 64 Jalan Besar. Organized treks into Kenong Rimba are also run by *Tuah Travel & Tours*, 12 Jalan Lipis, Kuala Lipis, T312144. There are other registered freelance guides who can be hired from Kuala Lipis. **NB** Travellers have warned us of one guide called 'Johnny' who is alleged to have drugged and raped several women. **Tours**

B *Taipan*, Jln Lipis Bentar, T3122555. A/c, new hotel on the outskirts of town and the most expensive place to stay. **C-D** *Rumah Rehat* (*Rest House*), T3122599. Some a/c, this place was formerly the home of the British Resident in Pahang, large rooms with attached bathrooms, certainly the most atmospheric of places to stay in Kuala Lipis, outside town on a hill. **D** *Hotel Kuala Lipis* (aka *Appu's Guesthouse*), 63 Jln Besar, T3121388. Some a/c, shared bathrooms run by Mr Appu who runs highly recommended tours to Kenong Rimba (see tours), good source of information. Recommended. **D** *Hotel Sri Pahang*, T3122445, some a/c, clean and well-run place. **D** *Hotel Jelai*, 44 Jln Jelai, T3121562. Near the Jelai River, clean rooms and reasonable value. **E** *Gin Loke*, 64 Jln Besar, T3121388. Simple rooms, shared facilities, organizes treks into Kenong Rimba. **E** *Hotel Tongkok*, Jln Besar, T3121027. Clean, good value. **Sleeping**

Train The Golden Blowpipe train, travels from Kuala Lumpur through Kuala Lipis. There are also slow jungle trains and connections with Kota Bharu and Jerantut/Tembeling Halt (for Taman Negara). Connections with Singapore, either direct or via Gemas. **Bus** Regular bus connections with Kuala Lumpur leave from the Pekeliling bus terminal in KL. Daily connections from Kuala Lipis with Kota Bharu and Kuantan. There are also connections with Fraser's Hill. **Transport**

Kampung Cherating

A quiet seaside village, set among coconut palms, a short walk from the beach, Kampung Cherating has become a haven for those who want to sample kampung life or just hang out in a simple chalet-style budget resort.

Phone code: 09
Colour map 1, grid C6

Cherating never was much of a kampung until the tourists arrived – there was a small charcoal 'factory', using *bakau* mangrove wood, but the local economy is now entirely dependent on sarong-clad Westerners and, more recently, growing numbers of Malaysian and Singaporean tourists. The beach at Cherating is big, but not brilliant for swimming because the sea is so shallow; it is also quite dirty. Cherating is named after the sand-crabs which are very common along the beach. They may look like heavily armoured tanks, but they are not dangerous. There are a couple of very private and beautiful little beaches tucked into the rocky headland dividing Cherating beach and the *Club Med* next door. These are more easily accessible from the sea (boats can be hired from the kampung) than from the steep trail leading over the promontory. This path goes right over to the *Club Med* Beach which is private. Bathers and sun-bathers should be prepared for periodic low-level fly-pasts by the Royal Malaysian Army whose helicopters swoop over the beaches.

Cherating has grown explosively in recent years. Big, modern resort complexes have sprung up 3 km south of the original kampung; it is known as Cherating Bharu, or New Cherating. The old roadside village (together with the string of atap-roofed chalet resorts) is called Cherating Lama, or Old Cherating. Although the old kampung atmosphere has been irreversibly tempered by the arrival of Anchor Beer and the population explosion, Cherating is still a peaceful haunt with some excellent places to stay and one or two of the best bars in Malaysia. Cherating's Malay residents have taken the boom stoically – although their obvious prosperity has helped them tolerate the 'cultural pollution'.

It is possible to hire boats to paddle through the mangroves of the Cherating River, to the south side of the kampung, where there is a good variety of birdlife as well as monkeys, monitor lizards and otters. For a price there are also demonstrations of silat, the Malay martial art, top-spinning, kite-flying and batik-printing in the village. There are some monkeys in the kampung which are trained to pluck coconuts. A couple of kilometres up the road, on Cendor Beach, green turtles come ashore to lay their eggs; they are much smaller than the leatherbacks which lay their eggs at Rantau Abang, further north. Cherating is also a good base to visit some of the sights in this part of the east coast including Tasek Cini (see page 264) and the Caras Caves (see page 258), for example.

Boat trips These are organized from Checkpoint Cherating (see below) and by several beach hotels/chalets, six people are needed to fill a boat, with a full boat approximately RM8 per person, depending on distance up river.

Essentials

Sleeping Many new bungalows and chalets have sprung up along the beach in the past decade; larger developments including the *Impiana* resort which has gone up about 2 km north of Cherating Lama. There is a good range of accommodation available, from simple kampung-style stilt-houses and 'A'-frame huts to upmarket chalets. Some of the accommodation in the kampung proper is family run; 'A'-frame and chalet accommodation is along the beach. The smarter, plusher hotels 3 km down the road at Cherating Bharu are much closer to the sea –and have a much nicer stretch of beach. 'A'-frame huts start at about RM10-15 while the more salubrious chalets cost from RM15-20. Note that the mid- and upper-range places whose guests are predominantly Malaysians and Singaporeans on weekend breaks, usually offer discounts during the week.

L-A *Cerating Holiday Villa*, Lot 1303, Mukim Sungai Karang, T5819500. A/c, restaurant, disco (boasts to be largest in town), pool, 2 rooms and 13 Malaysian chalets – corny but nice inside. Recommended. **AL** *Impiana Resort Cherating*, Km 32, Jln Kuantan, T5819000, F5819090. A hotel with 250 rooms in spacious buildings elegantly decorated with wood and rattan, good range facilities including pool, kid's pool, outdoor jacuzzi, tennis, children's playground and playhouse with caretaker. Two restaurants, pub with happy hour, all rooms have balconies facing sea, a/c, fan, TV, in-house movies, CNN, minibar, tea/coffee-making facilities, four-poster wooden beds with nets. Recommended. **AL** *Legend*, Lot 1290, Mukim Sungai Karang (Cherating Bharu), T5819818. A/c, Italian and Thai restaurant, huge pool, villas near the beach with smartly appointed rooms, sports centre, tennis courts, watersports facilities, disco, rooms, which overlook big garden and beach, are pleasant and bright. Recommended.

A *Canoona Beach Resort* (just north of *Holiday Villa*, Cherating Bharu), pleasant hotel with chalet blocks in grounds next to beach. **A** *Club Med* (round the headland from Kampung Cherating), T439131/591131. A/c, restaurant, totally self contained resort designed to resemble a Malay village – private beach, watersports facilities, body-building classes and evening entertainment, minimum stay: two nights. Closed November-January. The 'Circus Village' teaches children and adults to juggle, walk a tightrope or fly a trapeze – will be familiar to those who know Club Meds elsewhere. **A-B** *Ombak Beach Resort*, Lot 2466 Mukim Sungai Karang, T5819166, F5819433. Friendly 30-room hotel, surrounding pool, short distance from sandy beach, restaurant, simple tiled rooms, a/c, TV, fridge, tea/coffee-making facilities, discounts offered in off-peak season making it exceptionally good value for money, managed by the *Berjaya* chain with professionalism. **A-B** *Cherating Bay Resort* Opening January 2000. Large place with pool and children's play area, all rooms a/c. Five minute walk from the beach.

B *Cerating Bayview Resort*, Cherating Lama, T5819248, F5819415. Modern chalets on beach front, some with a/c and TV, restaurant, a good mid-range place to stay. Slightly overpriced for the fan, shower and breakfast included. **B** *Residence Inn Cerating*, on the same lane as *The Moon*, at the northern end of the village, between the main road and the 'village street', T5819333, F5819252. Pool, kid's pool, jacuzzi, restaurant, disco, karaoke, comfortable rooms with a/c, minibar, TV, tea/coffee-making facilities. Breakfast included.

Kampung Cherating

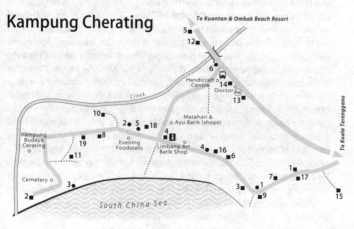

3 Cherating Beach Mini Motel	**10** Green Leaves Inn	**19** Tanjung Inn
4 Cherating Cottage	**11** Kampung Inn Guesthouse	
5 Cherating Holiday Villa	**12** Legend	● **Eating**
6 Cherating Inn	**13** Mak De's House	**1** B&R
7 Cherating Palm Resort	**14** Mak Long Teh's Homestay	**2** Blue Lagoon
8 Coconut Inn	**15** The Moon	**3** Driftwood
9 Duyong Beach Resort & Restaurant	**16** Ranting Resort	**4** Mimi's
	17 Residence Inn	**5** Payung Café
	18 Riverside Beach Hut	**6** Sunrise Seafood

■ **Sleeping**
1 Cherating Bay Resort
2 Cherating Bayview Resort

East Coast Peninsula

C *Cherating Palm Resort*, T5819378 F5819328. New place with clean modern chalets with TV, ac, bathroom all set in an immaculately maintained garden. Good value. **C** *Duyong Beach Resort*, Batu 28, T5819189 (left at end of lane from main road, at far end). Modern chalets at the end of the beach next to jungled hillside, mainly attracts Malaysian and Singaporean tourists, some rooms with a/c and TV. **C** *Kampung Inn*, right at end of lane from main road, at far end on left, T5819344. Fan, shower – nothing too special with very average chalet accommodation and 'A'-frames and not much atmosphere, but advantageously located near *Boathouse Bar* and close to beach. Hugely overpriced. **C** *Ranting Resort*, T5819068 (turn left at bottom of lane from main road bridge). Popular restaurant (Western and local dishes), extra for a/c and 2-room chalets on stilts, no TV, quite smart.

D *Cherating Cottage*, T5819273. A range of accommodation, from dorms to large a/c chalets all set in spacious gardens. Good value and in a central location, although the restaurant is slightly expensive. Recommended. **D** *Cherating Inn* T5819266. Fan, shower – Shabby looking chalets in poorly maintained garden. **D** *Cherating Beach Mini Motel*, T5819335. Under same management as neighbouring *Duyong Beach Resort*. Decent chalets on the beach, which is a pretty unique set up in Cherating, rooms have fan and bathroom. **D** *Green Leaves Inn*, right at end of lane from main road, on right, T3378242. Tucked in among the riverside mangroves. *Green Leaves* looks like a Vietcong jungle camp, albeit with decent 'A'-frames, sheltered and shaded, close to sea and cheap, with breakfast thrown in, very clean. **D** *Mak De's House*, in the old village, next to police station, T5819316. *Mak De* has been offering kampung accommodation since the late-1970s and has an equally long-standing reputation for hospitality and good food, quiet chalets in good condition. Recommended. **D** *Mak Long Teh Guesthouse*, T503290. Restaurant, like *Mak De*, this family-run operation was up-and-running long before Cherating was discovered by main-stream tourists, friendly, with excellent Malay home cooking – again, and like *Mak De's*, it can be noisy. Unfortunately the garden is messy and full of rubbish and the place is increasingly run-down. **D** *Matahari Chalets*, T5819835. On the southern of the two lanes from the main Juantan-Kemaman road, no phone. Two rows of attractive bungalows facing each other, with a lawn of about 30m in between. Some bungalows (with spacious verandahs) have fridges. One of the more pleasant places to stay here. Recommended. **D** *Moon*, T5819186 or T0109877564 (the northernmost chalet resort on the loop off the main road). Fan and bathroom, attractive, more rustic chalets in spacious leafy grounds, up a hillside, excellent bar (see below) and restaurant, chalets and longhouse (**E**), much more tranquil surroundings than chalet resorts along the beach. Recommended. **D** *Riverside*, some a/c, popular place with some more sophisticated rooms. The owners are not particularly helpful. **D** *Tanjung Inn*, turn right at bottom of lane down from main road, after *Coconut Inn*, T5819081. Attractive choice of accommodation ranging from first class big bungalows for families to budget chalets (with communal shower and toilet), restaurant, set in carefully tended and landscaped grounds with palms and two ponds, has a good restaurant which serves excellent breakfasts. This is a charming place to stay and has won the second prize for best-kept accommodation in the state of Pahang. Recommended.

E *Coconut Inn*, T5819299. Run by Ilal, one of the kampung's best-known characters, and his Dutch wife. 'A'-frames with rusting roofs, badly in need of some maintenance, but very cheap.

Eating
There are plenty of foodstalls

A few new restaurants have sprung up along the main road but because most chalet hotels have attached restaurants there's not much demand for outside food outlets.

3 *Sunrise Seafood Restaurant*, one of the new restaurants on main road, pleasant terrace set back from road, Western and local dishes. **2** *Blue Lagoon* (right at end of land from main road, after *Moonlight Lagoon* restaurant), another big neon-lit establishment offering wide selection of Chinese, Malay and Western dishes, good on seafood, friendly atmosphere. **2** *B & R*, north end of Cherating beach road (next to *Duyong*), travellers' fare and some local dishes. **2** *Payung Inn 'n' Café*, next to river, opposite *Coconut Inn*, pleasant little open coffee shop, but forget the 'inn' bit. **2** *Restoran Dragon*, simple atap-roofed terrace at side of road in Cherating Lama, good claypot and buttered crab. **2** *Restoran Duyong*, T5819578 (inside the *Duyong Beach Resort*), lovely setting on raised wooden terrace at edge of beach, lobster and prawns sold by weight, good selection of Western and local dishes. **2** *The Deadly Nightshade* (part of *The Moon* chalet resort at northwest end of loop off main road), also known as 'the restaurant at the end of the universe', enchantingly vague menu, mainly Western with some concessions to local tastes, great atmosphere. *Mimi's Restaurant, Services and Tours* (left at end of lane from main road, on left), restaurant inefficient, and tours par for the course, but *Mimi's* offers useful laundry service.

Bars *The Moon* (part of chalet resort of same name at northwest end of loop off main road), great bar amid atap and leafy foliage, second only to the *Boathouse*. Recommended. *The Driftwood*, at southern end of beach, very laid back, serves Western food; *Nan's Beach Bar*, behind *Coconut Inn*, the most popular beach bar, with Dire Straits and Celine Dion as favourites on the CD player.

Entertainment *Kampung Budaya Cerating (Cerating Cultural Centre)*, western end of the village street, before the *Cerating BayView Resort*, pavilion-style attraction, in landscaped garden with a big rather uncosy restaurant, where shows take place. Batik painting, top spinning, songkhet weaving and other typical east coast activities can be seen.The work of artist Ayam is particularly worth a look.

Shopping **Batik** There are 3 batik shops in Cherating; all the artists offer classes; prices (which include tuition) t-shirt RM20-25, sarong RM25, singlet RM18. *Limbang Art* (left at bottom of lane down from main road bridge), mainly shirts, t-shirts painted by *Munif Ayu Art* (on lane down from main road bridge); *Cerating Collection* (in old village, next to main road and *Mak De's*), designs more colourful and abstract than its two local competitors; *Matahari Chalets* local artist Ayu sells his batik t-shirts here and does batik painting classes.

Sports **Golf** *Kelab Golf Desa Dungun*, T8441041, Dungun, 18 holes, green fees RM40. **AL** *Awana Kijal Beach and Golf Resort*, Kijal, just south of Kerteh Airport, opened in 1996, same management as Genting Highlands, 5-star resort and 18-hole golf course, T603262 3555, F603261 6611, rather monstrous design, with extensive facilities, surrounded by golf course and the beach. **Watersports** *Cerating Beach Recreation Centre*, arranges water skiing and windsurfing, RM10 hire, RM15 lesson; *Club Med*, watersports facilities and body-building classes open to non-guests 0900-1100 and 1400-1600 Mon-Sun (RM60 for half day).

Transport
50 km to Kuantan
See Checkpoint Cherating, under **Useful addresses**, below. **Air** Kerteh Airport is about 40 km north of Cherating. *Pelangi Airways* operates regular connections with KL. **Bus** Regular buses from Kuantan (Kemaman bus). Bus stops at both ends of the kampung. Regular connections with Rantau Abang, Kuala Terengganu, Marang, Kota Bharu. Minibuses leave Checkpoint Cherating for Kuantan at 0730 Mon-Sun and to Kemaman, to change to northbound express buses. **Taxi** Rantau Abang, Kuantan, Kuantan airport.

East Coast Peninsula

Directory **Airline offices** *Pelangi Airways*, Kerteh Airport, T8261187, F8263972. **Banks** See *Checkpoint Cerating*, under **Useful addresses**, below. The nearest bank is at Kemaman, 12 km north. **Communications** Area code: 09. Internet: See *Checkpoint Cerating* below. **Useful addresses** *Badgerlines Information Services* (about 20m down on left from lane leading from main road bridge), an additional source of local info, which is independently run. Open 0900-1700 and 2000-2200. *Checkpoint Cherating* (about 100m down on left from lane leading from main road bridge), ticketing (buses, taxis, minibuses), vehicle hire: car, motorbike, mountain bike, boats, foreign exchange (including TCs, poor rate), mobile phone, book rental, newspapers and tourist information; also organizes tours to Tasek Cini, Terengganu National Park and batik factories. Only place in Cherating to offer internet access.

Kemasik On the road north from Cherating there are several stretches of beach, among the best of which is Kemasik. It is off the main road to the right (85 km north of Kuantan, 28 km north of Cherating), just before the oil and gas belt of Kerteh. Ask buses to stop shortly after windy stretch through hills. At Kemasik, the beach is deserted; there is a lagoon, some rocky headlands and safe bathing. There are no facilities.

Kuala Abang *Phone code: 09* Turtles also come ashore at Kuala Abang, a few kilometres north of Dungun, which is much quieter than Rantau Abang, although there are still a few hotels. There are also several places to stay, although not right on the beach, at the small port of **Kuala Dungun**, famed for its *kuini*, a local mango. There is a weekly night market (*pasar malam*) in Dungun on Thursdays. From there it is possible to hire a boat to Pulau Tenggol, 29 km out, popular with snorkellers.

Sleeping **B** *Merantau Inn*, T8441131. At the south end of the turtle beach, some a/c, restaurant, big, clean chalets above old fish ponds, past its prime, but 3 decent chalets on the beach. Not outstanding but reasonable value. **C-D** *Kasanya*, 225-227 Jln Tambun, T9841704. A/c. **C-D** *Sri Dungun*, K135 Jln Tambun, T9841881. A/c, restaurant. **D** *Mido*, 145-6 Jln Tambun, a/c, T9841246. **D** *Sri Gate*, 5025 Jln Sura Gate, a/c. **D** *Sun Chew*, 10 Jln Besar Sura Gate, T9841412. A/c, restaurant.

Tanjung Jara: **AL-A** *Tanjung Jara Beach Hotel*, 6 km north of Dungun, T8441801, F8442653. A/c, restaurant, pool, the best known 5-star beach resort on the east coast, its Malay-inspired design won it the Aga Khan award for outstanding Islamic architecture, tour excursions, windsurfing, golf and tennis facilities, also offers local tours.

Transport **Bus**: express buses leave for Kuantan, Mersing, KL and JB/Singapore. **Taxi**: Kuala Terrenganu, Kota Bharu, Dungun, and Kuantan.

Rantau Abang

Phone code: 09
Colour map 1, grid B6

This strung-out beachside settlement owes its existence to turtles. Every year between May and September, five different species of turtle (penyuin Malay) come to this long stretch of beach to lay their eggs, including the endangered giant leatherbacks.

Every year, tens of thousands of tourists also make the pilgrimage. During the peak egg-laying season, in August (which coincides with Malaysia's school holidays), the beach gets very crowded. Up until the mid-1980s the egg-laying 'industry' was poorly controlled; tourists and locals played guitars around bonfires on the beach and scrambled onto turtles' backs for photographs as they laid. Conservationists became increasingly concerned about the declining number of giant leatherbacks that chose to nest on the beach and began to press for stricter policing and management.

Parts of the beach have now been set aside by the government, and access is prohibited; there are also sections of beach with restricted access, where a small

The giant leatherback turtle (Dermochelys coriacea)

The symbol of the old Malaysian Tourist Development Corporation, the giant leatherback turtle is so-called for its leathery carapace, or shell. It is the biggest sea turtle and one of the biggest reptiles in the world. The largest grow to 3m in length and most of the females who lumber up Rantau Abang's beach to lay their eggs are over 1½m long. On average they weigh more than 350 kg, but are sometimes more than double that. Giant leatherbacks are also said to live for hundreds of years. They spend most of their lives in the mid-Pacific Ocean, although they have been sighted as far afield as the Atlantic, and return to this stretch of beach around Rantau Abang each year to lay their eggs, in the way salmon return to the same river. The beach shelves steeply into deeper water, allowing turtles to reach the beach easily.

They are not well designed for the land. It requires huge effort to struggle up the beach, to above the high-tide mark. After selecting a nesting site, the turtle first digs a dummy hole before carefully scooping out the actual nest pit, in which she lays up to 150 soft white eggs between the size of a golf ball and a tennis ball. The digging and egg-laying procedure, punctuated by much groaning and heaving and several rest-stops, takes up to two hours, after which she covers the hole and returns to the sea. During the egg-laying period, the turtle's eyes secrete a lubricant to protect them from the sand, making it appear as if it is crying. In the course of the egg-laying season (from May to September) this exhausting slog up the beach might be repeated up to nine times.

The gestation period for the eggs is 52-70 days. During this period the eggs are in danger from predators, so the Fisheries Department collects up to 50,000 eggs each season for controlled hatching in fenced-off sections of beach. The eggs are also believed to be an aphrodisiac and can be bought in wet markets along the east coast for about RM1 each (a small quota is set aside for public consumption). Young hatchlings are regularly released into the sea from the government hatchery. Many are picked off by predators, such as gulls and fish, and few reach adulthood. The turtles have been endangered by drift-net fishing and pollution. It is also prized for its shell which is thought to have the most beautiful markings of any sea turtle. In nature it is used to camouflage, it is thought, the turtle against a dappled coral background. The 'tortoiseshell' is fashioned into combs and cigarette boxes. In 1990 the Malaysian government announced it would start fitting radio transmitters to leatherbacks to enable satellites to monitor their movements in international waters. French satellite information is providing a stronger database on turtle populations and movements allowing the formulation of a more effective conservation strategy.

Even so, the leatherback turtle appears to be fighting a losing battle against extinction. There are just five main places in the world where these behemoths lay their eggs: South Africa's east coast, Surinam, Costa Rica, the Pacific coast of Mexico, and Rantau Abang. In the mid-1950s 10,000 turtles were arriving at Rantau Abang alone; in 1996 it was a mere 68. When one considers the odds against an egg turning into a mature adult leatherback – around one in a 1,000 (some say, 10,000) – and couple that with all the new threats that the leatherback has to contend with from drift nets to pollution, it is small wonder that some marine biologists believe this magnificent creature could, by the end of the millennium, be on the verge of extinction.

Green turtles come ashore to lay their eggs later in the season. For more details on these, see page 459.

East Coast Peninsula

East Coast Peninsula

The crown-of-thorns – the terminator on the reef

The crown-of-thorns starfish (Acanthaster planci) – a ruthlessly efficient, cold-blooded killing machine – launched an invasion of the Pulau Redang Marine Park in the early 1990s. The destructive starfish, which did serious damage to Australia's Great Barrier Reef in the 1980s, can regenerate and multiply rapidly leading to sudden infestations on coral reefs. The crown-of-thorns grazes on staghorn coral (Acropora) in particular and if population explosions are left unchecked, the starfish can reduce rich coral colonies into blanched skeletal debris. One crown-of-thorns can suck the living tissues from a coral in a matter of hours and, if present in large numbers, they can eat their way across a reef, devastating it in a matter of weeks or months.

The crown-of-thorns is aptly named. It measures about 50 cm across and is covered in thousands of poisonous spines, each 3-5 cm long. The spines are extremely sharp and toxic – if they puncture human skin, they cause a severe reaction, including nausea, vomiting and swelling. These short spines grow on the starfish's legs, of which it has more than

20. But marine conservationists, concerned about the threat to the coral and fish breeding grounds, face a daunting task in ridding reefs of the unwelcome echinoderms. Because of their amoeba-like regenerative abilities, the crown-of-thorns cannot simply be chopped in half in situ, because this would create two of them. Instead, each one has to be prised off the coral, taken to the surface and buried on land.

The Malaysian Fisheries Department, with private sector backing, mounted a reef-rescue expedition to Redang in 1992 to do exactly this. The department's marine biologists were unsure as to what had triggered the infestation of crown-of-thorns starfish; it could be that they invade in natural cycles or human interference could have something to do with it. The last major infestation was in the early 1970s. Following their difficult task of picking the starfish off the reef, the divers buried them on shore, as instructed. Perhaps they should have driven wooden stakes through their hearts too: the starfish can go for as long as nine months without food.

---

admission charge is levied by guides. The Fisheries Department does not charge. Local guides, who trawl the beach at night for leatherbacks coming ashore, charge tourists RM2 a head for a wake-up call. Turtle-watching is free along the stretch around the Turtle Information Centre. The Fisheries Department also runs three hatcheries to protect the eggs from predators and egg-hunters: they are a local delicacy. The closest is five minutes' walk from *Awang's*. Officers from the department patrol the beach in three-wheeler beach buggies.

NB Do not interfere with the turtles while they are laying. There is now a ban on flash photography and unruly behaviour is punishable by a RM1,000 fine or six months' imprisonment. Camp fires, loud music, excessive noise and littering are all illegal, although the latter is not well enforced.

Rantau Abang Turtle Information Centre, 13th Mile Jalan Dungun, T8441533, F8442653, opposite the big new *Plaza R & R*, has an excellent exhibition and film presentation about sea turtles, focusing on the giant leatherback. A slide-show also opened in 1993. The Fisheries Department at the centre is very helpful and friendly. ■ *Sat-Thur 0900-1300, 1400-1900, 2000-2300, Fri 0900-1200, 1500-2300 (Jun-Aug); 0800-1245, 1400-1600 Sat-Wed, 0800-1245 Thur, closed Fri (Sept-April).*

Excursions **Kuala Abang**, south of Rantau Abang, is easily accessible. See page 278.

Rantau Abang's accommodation is strung-out along the main road; there are many **Sleeping**
overpriced, unpleasant little hovels. New places are opening and old ones closing all
the time. Security is a problem here: it is inadvisable to leave valuables in rooms. The
only upmarket place to stay near here (unless new outfits have opened) is the beautiful *Tanjung Jara Beach Hotel* which is roughly halfway between Rantau Abang and
Kuala Dungun, see Kuala Abang above for details.

B-E *Ismail's*, T8441054. Next to *Awang's*, good restaurant (only open in peak season),
south of the Visitor's Centre, average beach-side set-up, similar to *Awang's*.
C-D *Awang's*, T8443500. Restaurant, some a/c, some rooms are very poor, the best are
only average. Not good value for money. **C-D** *Dahimah's*, T8452483. One kilometre
south of Visitor's Centre, restaurant, clean rooms in Malay wooden chalets. Some a/c.

Most hotels have their own restaurants, but there are stalls along the roadside and **Eating**
several coffee shops around the bus stop.
    2 *Awang's*, right on the beach, Awang was formerly the chef at the *Tanjung Jara
Beach Hotel*. *Ismail's* also has a restaurant and there are some stalls in the *Plaza R & R*;
Mikinias, just down from *Awang's*. Big menu but service is slow if it gets busy.

22 km north of Kuala Dungun, 58 km south of Kuala Terengganu, 160 km north of **Transport**
Kuantan. **Bus** Regular connections with Kuala Terengganu and Kuala Dungun from
opposite *Turtle Information Centre*. From Kuala Dungun connections with Kuantan
and other destinations.

Marang

This is a colourful Malay fishing kampung at the mouth of the Marang River, *Phone code: 09*
although it is not as idyllic as the tourist literature suggests. To get into the *Colour map 1, grid B6*
town from the main road, follow signs to LKIM Komplex from the north end
of the bridge. The recent rush to put up budget accommodation has placed it
firmly on the tourist map. Since then it has begun to acquire a bit of a
run-down look. It is still a very lovely village though, with its shallow lagoon
full of fishing boats. The best beach is opposite Pulau Kepas at Kampung Ru
Muda. It was the centre of a mini-gold-rush in 1988 when gold was found 6 km
up the road at Rusila. On the road north of Marang there are a number of batik
workshops, all of which welcome visitors.

Pulau Kapas is 6 km (30 minutes) off the coast, with some good beaches. **Excursions**
Those wanting a quiet beach holiday should avoid weekends and public holidays when it is packed. The coral here has been degraded somewhat and there
is much better snorkelling at **Pulau Raja**, just off Kapas, which has been
declared a marine park. All the guesthouses organize snorkelling and the
Kapas Garden Resort also has scuba equipment. Many hotels in Marang offer
day trips to the islands and it is easy enough to grab a ride. The *Abdul Tourist
Boat Service* is helpful and will pick up even at low tide. They have fast boats.

Sleeping A *Primula Kapas Island Village Resort*, T/F6236110. Malay-style chalets,
pool. Since a change of management this place seems to have gone downhill: service
is poor, the beach dirty, bathrooms poorly maintained, food ghastly and therefore significantly overpriced. **B-C** *Tenggol Aqua Resort*, Pulau Tenggol, T9861807. The only
accommodation on the island. **C** *Tuty Purri Island Resort*, T0192151938. **C** *Kapas
Garden Resort*, T0109841686. Fourteen rooms. **C-D** *Makcik Gemok Chalet*,
T6181221. Largest outfit on the island with a range of rooms from simple huts with
shared facilities through to larger chalets with attached bathrooms. **C** *Pulau Kapas*

Resort, T6236110. Restaurant, snorkelling, forest tours, fishing trips (RM150 per day). **D** *Cadten Lighthouse*, T0102155338. **D** *Kapas Garden Resort*, T0119871305. Friendly place with well maintained rooms, some with attached bathrooms. **D-E** *Zaki Beach Resort*, T6120258. Restaurant, chalets.

River and island tours Half-day river tours organized by *Rapas Travel and Tours (Primula Hotel)*, T6235915. The same people also offer efficiently run tours to nearby islands; most hotels in town can arrange trips to Pulau Kapas.

Sleeping
■ *on map,*
Price codes:
see inside front cover
There are hotels &
guesthouses in Marang
itself & in Kampung Rhu
Muda, about 2 km
before the bridge over
the Marang River

A *Marang Resort and Safaris*, 1 Jln Dungan, T6182588, F6182334. A/c, 60 rooms, one of the few upmarket options in the area. **B** *Seri Malaysia Marang*, Lot 3964 Kampung Paya, T6182889, F6181289. One of the *Seri Malaysia* chain, opened in 1995, good value, views of Pulau Kapas, a/c, TV, coffee/tea-making facility, restaurant, launderette, organize island trips, the best option along this row of accommodation although not extravagant, breakfast included. Good value. **B-D** *Anguillia Beach House*, 12¼ milestone, Kampung Rhu Muda, T6181322, F6181322. Some a/c, restaurant (with good set meal), extremely friendly, family-run chalet resort on lovely stretch of beach opposite Pulau Kapas (therefore sheltered), leafy, well-kept grounds and very clean chalets (no alcohol served), some visitors reckon it is overpriced. Recommended.

C *Island View*, opposite the lagoon, T6182006. Some a/c, free bicycles, chalets with attached bathrooms and some simpler rooms, popular. Very attractive setting with a central bougainvilia garden to relax in. **C** *Rumah Rehat Semarak* (*Rest House*), Taman Rehat Semarak, Km 17, Jln Kuala Terengganu (4 km south of Marang), T6227631. Chalets on the beach, formerly government-owned, past its prime, but pleasant rooms with balconies, the best ones facing the sea, small restaurant and stalls next door. **C-E** *Mare Nostrum Holiday Resort*, Kampung Rhu Muda, T6182417. A/c, restaurant, clean and hospitable, boat trips, pleasant little resort next door to *Anguillia*, well-kept compound (if a little cramped) and clean chalets. Recommended.

Marang

To Kuala Terengganu

Pulau Kapas

South China Sea

Footbridges

Children's Playground
Market

Jetty

Marang River

Mare Nostrum Holiday Resort ■
Anguillia Beach House ■
Zakaria Guesthouse ■

N

0 metres 500
0 yards 500

To Rantau Abang

Related map
A Northwest Marang,
page 283

E *Green Mango Inn*, A-71 Bandar Marang, T6182040. Fan, small, bare A-frame chalets but cheap. Dorm rooms available. **E** *Marang Inn & Garden Café*, 132 Bandar Marang, T6182132. Restaurant, in decorated blue-and-orange shophouse overlooking lagoon, helpful, organizes tours around Terengganu and trips to islands. **E** *Zakaria Guest-house*, Kampung Rhu Muda, T6182328. Basic and further out of the village, dorm or rooms. **E-F** *Kamal's*, T6182181. Opposite the lagoon, very popular, dormitory and chalets, now very rundown but still popular with friendly staff. Tours and activities organized. **E-F** *Marang Inn*, Batu 22 Rhu Muda, T6182288. Dorm and chalets.

Most hotels have good restaurants serving Malay and international dishes. There are cheap food stalls along the waterfront next to the market. Stalls at Taman Selera, Kampung Rhu Muda, along the roadside are well known, particularly by long-distance bus and taxi drivers, for their Malay and Thai-style seafood (closed Fri). **Eating**

Handicrafts Market in Marang has a craft market upstairs and there are several handicraft shops along the main street. *Balai Ukiran Terengganu* (Terengganu Woodcarving Centre), Kampung Rhu Rendang, near Marang, master-carver Abdul Malek Ariffin runs the east coast's best-known woodcarving workshop, makes wide range of intricately carved furniture from cengal wood, carved with traditional floral geometric and Islamic calligraphic patterns, the varnished cengal wood is not to everyone's taste, but everything from mirrors to beds can be ordered for export, because most pieces are made to order there is little on show in Abdul's chaotic workshop, but carvers can be seen at work during the day. Good **batik** in Marang. **Shopping**

Bus Bus stop on the main road up the hill from Marang. Tickets can be bought from the kiosk nearby on Jln Tg Sulong Musa, however, this runs very unpredictable hours so book in advance. Connections with Kuala Terengganu every hour, and with Kuala Dungun via Kuala Abang. **Transport**
18 km to Kuala Terengganu

East Coast Peninsula

Northwest Marang

To Kuala Terengganu

Carving Hall

Marang Handicrafts

Kg Paya

Jln Paya Hulu Banang

Jln Kastam Lama

3
5
2   Lookout Point

Children's Playground

Food Stalls

Market   Small Jetty

Jln Hakaf Tapai   Jln Tg Sulong Musa

Jln Tanah Lot

Jln Kumia Jaya

1   Bandar Marang   To Pulau Kapas

4

Large Jetty

To Kuantan & Rantau Abang

Not to scale

N

■ **Sleeping**
1 Green Mango Inn
2 Island View
3 Kamal's
4 Marang Inn & Garden Café
5 Seri Malaysia Marang

Kuala Terengganu

Phone code: 09
Colour map 1, grid B6

The royal capital of Terengganu state was a small fishing port (the state accounts for about a quarter of all Malaysia's fishermen) until oil and gas money started pumping into development projects in the 1980s. The town has long been a centre for arts and crafts, and is known for its kain songket, batik, brass and silverware.

Like neighbouring Pahang, Terengg- anu state was settled at least as far back as the 14th century, and over the years has paid tribute to Siam and, in the 15th century, to the sultanate of Melaka. When the Portuguese forced the Melaka royal house to flee to Johor, Terengganu became a vassal of the new sultanate. In the 18th century, Terengganu is recorded as having a thriving textile indus-try; it also traded in pepper and gold with Siam, Cambodia, Brunei and China. A Chinese merchant community grew up in Kuala Terengganu. In 1724, the youngest brother of a former sultan of Johor, Zainal Abidin, established Terengganu as an independent state and declared himself its first sultan. Today's sultan is a direct descendant. The state has always been known for its ultra-conservative Islamic traditions.

Sights

The **Pasar Besar Kedai Payang**, the main market place on Jalan Sultan Zainal Abidin, is the busiest spot in town – particularly in the early morning, when the fishing fleet comes in. The market sells batik, brocade, songket, brassware, and basketware as well as fruit and vegetables. **Jalan Bandar**, leading off from the market, is a street of old Chinese shophouses and there is also a busy and colour-fully painted Chinese temple. Nearby is the imposing **Zainal Abdin Mosque**. Not far from the mosque (on the other side of Jalan Kota) is the apricot-coloured **Istana Maziah**, the old home of Terengganu's royal family, built in French style. It is now only used on ceremonial occasions and is not open to the public.

Some of Kuala Terengganu's older buildings have fine examples of tradi-tional Malay carvings. One of these has been moved from the centre of town to the southern outskirts, along the seafront on Pantai Batu Buruk, and houses the **Pengkalan Budaya** (Cultural Centre) (see **Entertainment** page 289). Another of these traditional houses was taken apart and reassembled in Kuala Lumpur in the grounds of the National Museum as an example of classical Malay architecture.

The **State Museum** has recently moved to Losong, a town a few kilo-metres southwest of the city. It is situ-ated at the end of Jalan Losong Feri, facing Pulau Sekati. The museum exhibits rare Islamic porcelain, silver jewellery, musical instruments and weaponry – including a fine selection of *parangs* and *krises*. It is an eclectic collection, erratically labelled. ■ *0900-1700 all week (closed Fri 1200-1400). Take bus no. 10.* **Bukit Puteri**, near the Istana, has fortress remains on it and provides excellent views of the town.

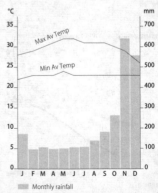

Climate: Kuala Terengganu

Excursions

There is a thriving cottage industry in and around Kuala Terengganu and many of Malaysia's best-known handicrafts are made locally. Surrounding kampungs practise silverwork, batik-printing, songket- weaving and *wau* kite-building, but the best way to see these under one roof is in the Cendering handicraft centres (see below).

A number of tour agents offer tours to the offshore islands & trekking tours to the Kenyir Lake area (see page 289)

Pulau Duyung Besar This is the largest island in the Terengganu Estuary and famed for its boat-building. It mainly survives by custom-building yachts. Take minibus no. 20, and then a boat (50c).

Sleeping F *Awi's Yellow House*, T6231741. Built out over the river on stilts, this hotel is very popular with budget travellers, dorm and atap-roofed huts, some with balconies over river, pleasant location with cool breezes, there are some stalls at the bus stop near the bridge, but most travellers bring their own food from KT and have use of kitchen facilities, *Awi's Yellow House* is not yellow and can be hard to find but is well enough known to sniff out.

Transport Boat from jetty on Jln Bandar – last boat around 2200 – or by road, via the new *Sultan Mahmud* bridge (taxis or bus from KT). The river is navigable for quite a distance upstream and it is possible to hire boats from the jetty for river trips.

Floating Mosque This is situated on the estuary of the Ibai River. Its name is a slight misnomer; it has been built in such a way that it gives the illusion of floating. Located 6 km from town; take bus either 13 or 13c (60c).

Kampung Pulau Rusa This songket-weaving and batik centre, 6 km upriver, is known for its traditional Petani-Terengganu wooden houses. Take a boat from the jetty on Jalan Bandar. The village can also be reached by bus from the bus station on Jalan Syed Hussin.

Cendering Home to several handicraft centres, Cendering lies 7 km south of Kuala Terengganu. *Kraftangan Malaysia*, with a beautifully displayed selection of silver, woodwork, silk, batik, brass and basketware as well as handicrafts from elsewhere in Malaysia, is very classy compared with *Rusila* (below). To get there, take Marang-bound buses from Jalan Syed Hussin – 13, or 13c. The turning is clearly signposted off the main road. ■ *0830-1700 Sat-Wed, 0830-1200 Thur.* Next door to *Kraftangan Malaysia* is the huge *Nor Arfa Batik Factory*, producing modern and traditional designs and readymades. Behind *Kraftangan Malaysia* is the *Sutera Semai* silk factory.

Planetarium The Planetarium, at Kompleks Planetarium Megeri, Padang Hiliran, T6248934, has an impressive array of information including shows in the afternoon at 1630 and 1730 (throughout the day on Saturday). Take minibus 20 or 16 (60c). ■ *RM3.*

Kenyir Lake This man-made 370 km² lake, 55 km south of Kuala Terengganu, is Kuala Terangganu's latest holiday destination. Having completed the Kenyir Dam in 1985, the state economic development board has built a 2½ km access road, a jetty and a tourist information centre at a place called Pengkalan Gawi. There are facilities for fishing, canoeing and boating. Major hotel and resort developments have gone up over the last few years, as well as luxury chalets – some of them 'floating chalets', built over the lake – and the inevitable 18-hole golf course. Most are centred on Pengkalan Gawi or at Pengkalan Utama, 5 km away.

See also the very informative website http://tourism.gov.my/terengganu/kenyir.html

East Coast Peninsula

The lake is surrounded by jungled hills although the lake edge itself is still rather bare and devastated. There are plans to use Kenyir Lake as a back-door to the remote east side of Taman Negara. The lake itself has more than 300 islands. In parts swimming can be as hazardous as navigation thanks to the millions of submerged and semi-submerged trees. It has been stocked with fish and tour operators from Kuala Terengganu, some of which have house-boats on the lake, offer fishing tackle, canoeing and water-skiing as part of the package. The **Sekayu waterfalls**, with natural water-cut pools for swimming, are also 15 km from Kuala Berang.

Mosquitoes are a problem around the lake

Sleeping There are plans to provide camping facilities in the area although currently there is no budget accommodation. **A-B** *Primula Kenyir Lake Resort*, Poh Island, T095146002/T011950609. Restaurant, 73 rooms, children's play area, pool, Malay-style chalets (and 8 floating chalets), no a/c, mosquito nets at windows, tiny shower room, no fridge or tea/coffee-making facilities, organizes activities on the lake. Other developments about 30 mins by boat from Pengkalan Gawi are the **AL-A** *Musang Kenyir Resort,* Sungai Tembat, T6231888. **AL-A** *Tasik Lenir Golf Resort,* T6668888, F6668316. **AL-B** *Tasik Kenyir Golf Resort,* Pengkalan Gawi, T6249150. **AL-C** *Hundred Island Lake Resort,* Pulau Muping, T6811348. **A** *Abdillah Aris Resort* T6813288, F6813711. **B** *Muping Island Resort* (T096812197) and **A** *Uncle John's Resort,* T096229596, 12 rooms. **C** *Nature Lodge,* Lata Terap, T9840876. **C** *Pulau Anggur Besar,* T6813288. **C** *Rumah Rehat Kerajaan Persekutuan,* Pulau Sah Besar, T2952266.

Transport Bus to Kuala Berang, off the inland road south at Ajil, and then taxi to the lake, or by taxi from Kuala Terengganu. From KL (RM22), buses depart at 0900 and 2100 from Putra Station. Many tour companies in Kuala Terengganu run inclusive packages to the lake.

Beaches & islands

Batu Buruk beach, running down the northeast side of KT, is not safe for swimming. But there are some good beaches near Kuala Terengganu: Merang 30 km (see page 290) and Batu Rakit 20 km north. There is a (**D**) guesthouse at the latter. There are regular buses to both beaches from Jalan Syed Hussin.

Numerous **islands** lie off shore from Kuala Terengganu including **Pulau Redang** (see page 291) and **Pulau Perhentian** (see page 291). Boats leave for the islands from Merang and from the Jalan Bandar jetty in Kuala Terengganu, from which there are now scheduled departures.

Essentials

Sleeping There are only a couple of hotels at the top end of the market but there are several cheaper hotels scattered round town, mainly at the jetty end of Jln Sultan Ismail and on Jln Banggol, but the selection is not great. For budget travellers it is worth considering staying at *Awi's Yellow House* on Pulau Duyung (see **Excursions**, above).

A *Park Inn*, Jln Sultan Mahmud, T6222122, F6222121. A/c, gym, pool, spacious rooms, restaurant, in a pleasant resort setting just outside town. **A** *Permai Park Inn*, Jln Sultan Mahmud, T6222122, F6222121. Good quality hotel offering value for money, just under 150 rooms, friendly staff, very comfortable, carpeted rooms with a/c, TV, in-house movies, mini fridge, tea/coffee-making facilities, pleasant pool and children's pool, restaurant, *SI Travel Services* organize local packages, eg Lake Kenyir. Breakfast included. Recommended.

B *Kenangan*, 65 Jln Sultan Ismail, T6222688, F6233688. A/c, restaurant, bathroom. Slightly cheaper than the *KT Mutiara* next door and not nearly as nice. **B** *KT Mutiara,*

67 Jln Sultan Ismail, T6222655, F6236895. A/c, shower (hot water), TV, recently redecorated and extremely good value. Recommended. **B** *KT Travellers Inn*, 201, 1st Flr, Jln Sultan Zainal Abidin, T6223666, F6232692. Convenient location downtown, a/c, TV, clean rooms. Quite expensive for what you get. **B** *Midtown*, Jln Tok Lam, T6235288, F6234399. A/c, laundry, business centre, tea/coffee-making facilities, fridge, restaurant. In the centre of town with good facilities and a variety of information on transport and sights. **B** *Seri Malaysia*, Lot 1640, Jln Hiliran, T6236454, F6238344. A/c, restaurant (good, inexpensive), another in the well-run modern *Seri Malaysian* chain, a/c, TV, minibar, light airy rooms overlooking the river. Recommended.

C *Batu Burok Chalet*, 906-A, Pantai Batu Burok, T6221410, F6232904. Some a/c, restaurant, the only chalet-style accommodation in town, not bad, but a bit over-priced, pleasant open restaurant overlooking beach (which is dangerous for swimming). **C** *Bunga Raya*, 105-111 Jln Banggol, T6221911, F6223084. Bit run-down and noisy, on road. **C** *Motel Desa*, Bukit Pak Api, T6223033, F6223863. A/c, TV, in-house video, minibar, restaurant, pool, set in gardens on a small hill overlooking the town, a possibility for those with own transport. **C** *Primula Parkroyal*, Jln Persinggahan, T6222100, F6233360. A new name, but not a new look unfortunately, a/c, restaurant (good Malay-food buffet for RM25), good pool, highrise hotel with all mod-cons but rooms are shabby and not soundproofed, they do have a sea view though, also organizes island excursions. Great value for money. **C** *Qurata Riverside*, Lot 175K Kuala Ibai, T6175500, F6175511. Small and friendly hotel, 7 km south of Kuala Terengganu, 21 rooms in individual wooden chalets on stilts near the Kuala Ibai River. Designed by a nephew of the local royal family to resemble a Malay village, set in meticulous garden, only marred by proximity of main road, comfortable rooms with wood floors, a/c,

Kuala Terengganu

■ Sleeping

1 Almanda	4 Midtown
2 Kenangan & KT	5 Primula Parkroyal
Mutiara	6 Ping Anchorage
3 KT Travellers' Inn	7 Rex

8 Seaview
9 Seri Hoover
10 Seri Malaysia
11 Terengganu

East Coast Peninsula

ceiling fans, TV and shower room. At low tide it is possible to walk across the river mouth to nearby sand beach. Recommended. **C** *Seaview Hotel*, 18a Jln Masjid Abidin, T6221911, F6223084. Slightly overpriced but near the jetty with clean, comfortable rooms, a/c, centrally located opposite Istana Maziah, good mid-range place to stay. **C** *Seri Hoover*, 49 Jln Sultan Ismail, T6233823, F6233863. A/c, restaurant, big, clean rooms, bathroom with hot water, although slightly musty smell. **C-D** *Alamanda*, 28 Jln Tok Lam, T6228888, F6238899. A/c, shower (hot water), TV. Quite good value although the bathrooms are matchbox size and not all rooms have windows. **C-D** *Terengganu*, 12 Jln Sultan Ismail, T/F6222900. A/c (with fan **D**), plush new foyer, rooms could do with lick of paint but clean and reasonable value. Recommended.

D *Rex*, 112 Jln Sultan Ismail, T6221540. Clean Chinese hotel, fan only, some rooms with attached bathroom. Run down but a good position and cheap. **E** *Ping Anchorage*, 77A Jln Dato' Isaac, T6220851. Roof-top café, free breakfast, helpful with travel information, organizes trekking trips to Kenyir Lake area and offshore islands, dorm beds available. Extremely bare rooms and thin cardboard walls so noise can be a problem but competitive prices.

Eating *Nasi dagang* – known as 'fishermen's breakfast' – is a speciality of the area. It is made with aromatic or glutinous rice, served with *gulai ikan tongkol* (tuna fish with tamarind and coconut gravy). *Keropok* – or prawn crackers – are another Terengganu speciality.

Malay **3** *Rhusila Coffee House*, *Primula Beach Resort*. **3** *Permai Park Inn*, Jln Sultan Mahmud, good value buffet. **2** *Keluarga IQ*, 74 Jln Banggol, good place for *nasi dagang* breakfast, also excellent *nasi campur* (curry buffet), open 0630-0300, closed Fri. **1** *Mali*, 77 Jln Banggol, near the bus station, popular, cheap coffee shop – *nasi lemak*, *nasi campur*, satay and good rotis. **1** *Nik*, 104 Jln Sultan Ismail, standard curries. **1** *Zainuddin*, Jln Tok Lam; *Sri Intan*, 14 Taman Sri Intan, Jln Sultan Omar, well-appointed restaurant serving standard Malay dishes.

Chinese **4** *KT Wok*, 1081 Block W, Jln Sultan Sulaiman, T6243825, ultra modern décor, black and pink colour scheme, specialize in *dim sum*. **2** *Awana*, near public swimming pool, Jln Pantai Batu Buruk. Recommended by locals. **2** *Golden Dragon Restaurant*, 198 Jln Bandar, good pork, interesting vegetable dishes, some tables on street. Recommended. **2** *One-Two-Six*, 102 Jln Kampung Tiong 2 (off Jln Sultan Ismail), big open-air restaurant with hawker stalls, good seafood menu, special: fire chicken wings (comes to table in flames). Recommended. *Restaurants Good Luck, Kui Ping and Lee Kee* all along Jln Engku Sar, standard Chinese fare.

Indian *Taufik*, 18 Jln Masjid Abidin (opposite Istana Maziah), North and South Indian dishes, well-known for its rotis; *Kari Asha*, 1-H Jln Air Jermh, good range of curries (including fish heads, dosai and rotis).

International *Husni*, 954 Jln Sultan Mohammed, Thai, Malay and Western dishes, vast menu. *Midtown Café*, Jln Tok Lam, a broad selection of Western and Eastern cuisine, should suit all tastes. RM5 – RM30.

Seafood *Nil*, Jln Pantai Batu Buruk (near the *Pantai Primula Hotel*), view of the beach, good selection of seafood and renowned for its butter crabs in batter; *Taz*, Jln Sultan Zainal Abidin (below *Seri Pantai Hotel*).

Foodstalls *Gerai Makanan* (foodstalls) opposite the bus station; Malay; *Kampung Tiong* (off Jln Bandar), excellent hawker centre with Malay food on one side, Chinese and Indian on the other, open 8 till late; *Jalan Batu Buruk*, near the Cultural Centre, some excellent Malay food and seafood stalls. Recommended. Also *Warung Pak Maidin*, nearby on Jln Haji Busu, which is good on seafood; *Kompleks Taman Selera Tanjung* (1st Flr), huge area of stalls with good variety of dishes, open-air terrace; *Majlis Perbandaran* stalls, Jln Tok Lam; *Pasar Besar Kedai Payang* (Central Market), 1st Flr, Malay snacks, good views over the river. There are also some stalls next to *Stadium Negeri*.

Cultural shows *Pengkalan Budaya* (Cultural Centre), Pantai Batu Buruk. Displays of **Entertainment** *silat* (Malay art of self-defence), traditional dances, top-spinning and sometimes *wayang kulit* (shadow puppets), 1700-1900 and 2100-2300 Fri and Sat.

Batik Some of the best batik in Malaysia can be found in the central market (*Pasar* **Shopping** *Besar Kedai Payang*). *Wan Ismail Tembaga & Batik*, near turtle roundabout, off Jln Sultan Zainal Abidin – a small, old-fashioned batik factory. There are a number of small craft and batik factories in Kampung Ladang – the area around Jln Sultan Zainal Abidin; *Desa Craft*, 73 Jln Sultan Ismail, in the centre of town, has a good selection of silk and batik readymades and sarongs. The Central Market sells batik, silk, songket etc. Other shops selling batik can be found on Jln Bandor, including the *Bank Gallery* at number 194 and *Yuleza* at number 208.

Handicrafts The **Central Market** is touristy, but offers a range of handicrafts, textiles, brassware etc. *Desa Craft*, on Jln Sultan Ismail, is another good centre. Out of town, there are centres in Cendering (see **Excursions**, page 285).

Diving *Merlin Enterprise*, 1-E, 1st Flr, Wisma Guru, Jln Hiliran, T636200, manager **Sports** David Chua has a reputation as one of the country's leading divers and is well known for his scuba expeditions. **Golf** *Badariah Golf Club*, south of town, 9 holes, requires special permission from the Sultan's private secretary's office, T632456. *Berjaya Redang Golf Club*, T6233369.

Hedaco Travel, Ground Floor, Terengganu Foundation Bldg, Jln Sultan Ismail, **Tour operators** T631744; *The Little Traveller*, PO Box 117, T673218, F671527, trips to islands, equipped with comfortable houseboats on Lake Kenyir; *WLO Travel & Air Cargo*, Ground Floor, *Hotel Pantai Primula*, Jln Persinggahan, T635844. *Hubungan Travel and Tours*, Terminal Feri Shah Bandar, Jln Sultan Zainal Abidin, T6263501, F6263502.

Local Bus: from the main bus terminal on Jln Masjid. **Car hire**: *South China Sea*, **Transport** *Permai Park Inn*, T6224903. **Taxi**: T621581. **Trishaw**: RM2-3 for short trips around town. *455 km to KL*
168 km to Kota Bharu
209 km to Kuantan

Long distance Air: the Sultan Mahmud airport lies 18 km northwest of town, T6664204 for information. Regular connections with KL, Kuantan, Penang and Johor Bahru. Transport to town: RM15 by taxi. *MAS* T6221415.

  Bus: Kuala Terengganu has two bus stations. The express, long distance bus terminal is at Medan Selera, on the northern edge of the city centre. Local and intra-provincial buses leave from the MPKT station on Jln Syed Hussin which runs off Jln Masjid. Connections every 2 hrs to **KL** (RM21.70), **JB** (RM32.70), **Kota Bharu** (RM7.50), **Kuantan** (RM9), **Rantau Abang**, **Mersing**, **Singapore**, **Melaka**, **Butterworth** (RM23.50), **Alor Star** and **Marang**.

  Taxi: taxis operate from next to the bus station on Jln Masjid and from the waterfront. Destinations include Kota Bharu, Rantau Abang, Marang, Kuantan, KL, JB and Penang.

Airline offices *MAS*, 13 Jln Sultan Omar, T6222266/6221415; *Pelangi Airways*, No 29-D, Jln **Directory** Sultan Ismail, T6247071, F6047072. **Banks** There are several banks along Jln Sultan Ismail.

East Coast Peninsula

Bumiputra, UMNO Jln Masjid Zainal Abidin; *Hong Kong Bank*, 57 Jln Sultan Ismail; *Maybank*, 69 Jln Paya Bunga; *Public*, 1 Jln Balas Baru; *Standard Chartered*, 31 Jln Sultan Ismail; *UMBC*, 59 Jln Sultan Ismail. There are virtually no money changers in Kuala Terengganu. **Communications** Area code: 09. **General Post Office:** Jln Sultan Zainal Abidin. **Telekom:** Jln Sultan Ismail. **Medical facilities** Hospitals: Jln Peranginan (just off Jln Sultan Mahmud). **Tourist offices** *Tourism Malaysia*, 2243 Ground Floor, Wisma MCIS, Jln Sultan Zainal Abidin, T6221433/ 6221893, F6221791. *State Tourist Information Centre* (TIC), Jln Sultan Zainal Abidin, near the Istana Meziah on the jetty, T6221553. Impressive looking place bursting with information.

Merang

Phone code: 09
Colour map 1, grid B6

Merang is a small fishing kampung with a long white sandy beach; it is also the departure point for the many offshore islands, the biggest and best-known of which is Pulau Redang. Recently, Pulau Bidong has opened to tourists (Bidong's coral is said to be superb); throughout the 1980s it served as a Vietnamese refugee camp. The only island with accommodation is Pulau Redang.

Excursions A number of islands are accessible from Merang, notably **Pulau Redang** (see below). Other islands, most of which are uninhabited and all of which are endowed with good coral, include Pulau Pinang, Pulau Lima, Pulau Lang Tengah, Pulau Tenggol and Pulau Ekor Tebu; fishing boats are usually happy to stop off on request. Tenggol is notable for its diving opportunities, with a sandy bay on the west coast, and good diving on the east. Tours can be organized to this island and surrounding islands.

Sleeping **L-AL** *Aryani Resort*, Jln Rhu Tapai-Merang, Pantai Peranginan Merang, 21010 Setiu, T6241111, F6248007. The original heritage timber suites have private courtyards with outdoor bath (but are in the **L** price bracket), elevated restaurant, pool, luxurious. **A-B** *Sutra Beach Resort*, Kampung Rhu Tapai, T6696200/6233718, F669410. A/c, restaurants, pool, 124 chalets, good sports facilities, 20 mins from Kuala Terengganu's airport. **C** *Stingray Beach Chalet*, built in 1997, directly on the beach, fan, bathroom, immaculately run and offers a dive service. Recommended. **D** *Mare Nostrum Beach Resort*, 1 km out of town on road to *Penarik*, restaurant, rooms and 'A'-frames on beautiful stretch of beach. **D** *Kembara Resort*, 474 Pantai Peranginan Merang, 21010 Setiu, T6238771, F6238201. Situated on an endless palm-fringed deserted white beach, running south from the jetty, set in a beautiful garden compound, relaxed atmosphere, just 8 bungalows and 8 rooms all with attached shower and toilet, and fans. Cheap dorm accommodation. No restaurant but there's a large kitchen in the court which is well equiped and can be used freely, a little-known paradise. Recommended. **E** *Sugi Man's Homestay*, 500m beyond junction, on road to Penarek (signposted from the road). Restaurant, basic kampung farm house, quite a walk from the beach, cooking lessons and kite making, including meals. **E-F** *Naughty Dragon's Green Planet Homestay*, popular place in the village, dorm rooms available, simple but relaxed and welcoming.

Transport **Bus** Two buses a day from Kuala Terengganu to Merang (RM1.70), and then on to Penarek. Minibus connections also available from Kuala Terengganu, from Jln Masjid.
38 km N of KT, on the coast road **Taxi** Taxis from Merang to Penarek.

Pulau Redang

Twenty-seven kilometres off Merang is this archipelago, a marine park of nine islands with some of Malaysia's best reefs, making it one of the most desirable locations for divers. In the months after the monsoon, visibility increases to at least 20m but during the monsoon the island is usually inaccessible. Line-fishing is permitted and squid fishing, using bright lights, is popular between June and September; the fishermen use a special hook called a *candat sotong*. The lamps light the surrounding waters, attracting the squid. *Scuba Quest* (T/F032636032) organize diving trips to the islands.

Phone code: 09
Colour map 1, grid B6

Resorts on Redang offer competitive and flexible package deals – check with *Tourism Malaysia*. **A** *Berjaya Redang Golf and Country Resort*, T6971111, F6971100. A hotel with 152 rooms with a/c, TV, minibar, pool, restaurants, health spa, gym, 18-hole golf course, popular destination for business visitors wishing to combine work and golf (limited business facilities), dive centre, gym, tennis courts, health spa. Not popular with locals or environmentalists. **A** *Redang Beach Resort*, T6222599 (contact office: 36E, 1st Flr, Jln Dato' Isaac). Full range of facilities, package deals available. **A** *Redang Pelangi Resort*, T6223158, F6235202. **D** *Pulau Redang Resort*, book in Kuala Terengganu, T6227050. Bungalows, 'A'-frames slightly cheaper.

Sleeping

Boat These leave for the islands from Merang as well as from the jetty in Kuala Terengganu. It has, however, become very expensive to charter boats from Merang. *Tourism Malaysia* in Kuala Terengganu recommends that tourists take advantage of the package deals offered by the island's resorts; further details can be obtained from the *Tourism Malaysia* office. There are now scheduled departures to Redang from Kuala Terengganu. From Merang: RM70 return for boat (takes 8 people) or slow fishing boat for RM30 return (takes 12 people). A typical 2 days/2 nights trip costs around RM230 per person; all food, camping and snorkelling equipment included. As always, if you value a measure of privacy and seclusion, avoid weekends and public holidays. For further information contact *Coral Redang*, Wisma Awang Chick, Sultan Mahmud, T6236200.

Transport

Pulau Perhentian

Two more beautiful east coast islands, Pulau Perhentian Besar (big) and Pulau Perhentian Kecil (small), just over 20 km off the coast are separated by a narrow sound with a strong current. Despite considerable development in recent years, with more hotels, restaurants, bars, diving outfits and much more noise, the Perhentian islands still remain a paradise, with excellent diving and snorkelling, magnificent beaches and some of the best places for swimming on the east coast. There is a fishing village and a turtle hatchery in the middle of Long Beach (Pasir Panjang) on Perhentian Kecil. There are jungle trails across Perhentian Besar; all are well marked.

Colour map 1, grid A5

Best time to visit Travellers should be wary of risking the boat trip too close to the beginning or end of the December-February monsoon season.

NB All the resorts and chalets now have their own generators; and all have fresh water from wells. Competition for accommodation is fierce due to the ever increasing popularity of the Perhentians. Indeed this must be one of the few places in the world where demand regularly outstrips the number of beds available – strict planning laws ensure development is restricted. As the islands are not on the main phone system many of the phone numbers provided are mobile numbers which are liable to change at short notice and some places have no phone. Bookings are therefore difficult to

Sleeping

East Coast Peninsula

make, and many places are reluctant to take any. The exceptions are the more upmarket resorts which have booking agents on the mainland. In an attempt to beat this problem it is advisable to take the earliest boat possible to the islands (particularly Kecil) and accept the first offer of accommodation. It is not uncommon for some travellers to end up sleeping on restaurant floors on their first night.

Perhentian Besar There are a number of bays with accommodation on the larger island. The majority of it is located on the west coast, which is divided into 3 small beaches by outcrops of rock. There is more accommodation in the secluded bay of Telok Dalam. **A** *Coral View Island Resort*, T096910943 or sales and reservations 89A Depan Stesen Bas, Kuala Besut T096918271. A/c, shower. Quite an exlusive resort with 72 chalets at northern end of beach, rooms close together, bathroom attached. Sea views more expensive. **A** *Perhentian Island Resort* (bookings c/o 25 Menara Promet, Jln Sultan Ismail, KL, T03 2448530, F2434984), T096910946 or T0109010100, pir@po.jaring.my, www.jaring.my/perhentian. Some of the 103 rooms have a/c, licensed but expensive restaurant, some watersports facilities, tennis, swimming pool, diving equipment and courses available. **B-D** *Flora Bay Chalet*, Telok Dalam, T011977266. Provides a range of accommodation in the south of the island. **C** *ABC*, T096972085. Eight cheap and basic huts, on the beach. **C** *Coco Hut Chalets*, restaurant, unspecial 'A'-frames, although new ones with showers are being constructed. **C** *Cozy Chalet*, T0193285572 or T0123715234. Located at the end of the main beach on Besar. Chalets are perched elegantly on rocks over the sea. *Fauna Beach Chalets*, also on Telok Dalam. Reasonable chalets. **C** *Mama's* T0109840232 or T0109813359. Fan, shower. Selection of chalets for families or couples. Like every other hostel a daily snorkelling trip

Perhentian Islands

South China Sea

Teluk Kerma

Pulau Perhentian Kecil

Coral Bay

Pasir Panjang

Rock Garden

Perhentian Village

Pasir Petani

Teluk Dalam

N

Not to scale

■ **Sleeping**

1 ABC	6 Cozy Chalet	11 Mama's Chalet
2 Abdul's	7 D'Lagoon	12 Matahari
3 Coco Hut Chalets	8 D'Lahar	13 Mohsin
4 Cempaka	9 Flora Bay Chalet	14 Moonlight Chalets
5 Coral View Island Resort	10 Ibi's Chalet	15 Panorama

is organized. **C** *Perhentian Paradise Resort*, T0199813359. Family or doubles available. Nice location set slightly back from the beach. Electricity from 1900-0700. **C-E** *Abdul's*, T0109837303. Decent looking chalets on the beach, fan and shower, with popular restaurant. **C-D** *Ibi's Chalet*, T0109106294. Fan, shower. Run down chalets on the beach, **D** with seaview. **E** *Seahorse Chalets*, T0109841181. Affiliated to a dive centre, also offers internet access. Run-down 'A'-frames; cheap.

Camping: RM5 at *Perhentian Island Resort*; camping is not restricted on the island. Restaurant and dive shop floors go for RM10; anybody found sleeping on the beach will be moved on.

Perhentian Kecil There is more budget accommodation on Kecil and it is a quieter island to Besar, particularly popular among backpackers. Accommodation is split, with some huts on the beautiful white sandy beach of Pasir Panjang, on the east side of the island, and some on Coral Bay, on the west. There are a couple of places at the southern tip, not far from Perhentian village and an isolated spot at Teluk Kerma.

Long Beach: **A-B** *D'Lahar*, T0109853589. Significantly more expensive than any other accommodation on Long Beach although not noticeably better than some, a/c, **B** with fan. **B** *Matahari*, excellent restaurant, the best place to stay on the island, often full, proof of its popularity. Set back slightly from the beach but central. **C** *Mohsin*, T0103338897. Elevated position behind *Cempaka*, steep stairs to get to the restaurant where there are great views. Thirty rooms, mostly in rows. Considered one of the best places on the island, with attached bathrooms and 24 hr electricity. Good restaurant and daily snorkelling tour. One of the only places on the island to take bookings.

*Pulau
Perhentian
Besar*

C *Panorama*, attractive chalets with attached showers and toilets, fans and mosquito nets, a reasonable option. **D** *Cempaka*, southern end, pleasantly uncramped site with sea views for all the 10 chalets, no electricity, but lamps are provided, charcoal for cooking is provided, shared bathroom. Run down but functional. **D** *East West*, below Mohsin's, shared bathroom, very basic, but cheap. **D** *Simfony*, simple chalets with common showers and toilets, with fan and 24 hr electricity, no bathroom. **D** *Moonlight Chalets*, no fan, shared bathroom and reports of rats, frogs and lizards in the rooms. To be avoided at all costs.

Coral Bay: **B** *Sunset View Chalets*, Coral Bay, elevated restaurant with good sea views, with 24 hr electricity. **C** *Aur Beach*, and nicer than DJ's next door. Cheaper rooms available without bathroom. **C** *Butterfly Chalets*, built on the rocks at the end of the beach. Fan. **C** *Coral Bay*, modern, clean chalets and good restaurant. **D** *Rajiwali's*, at the end of the bay with elevated views, dirty and old, but extremely friendly and helpful staff. **D** *DJ's*, another reasonable option on the beach. Separate bathroom, fan.

East Coast Peninsula

Other: C *D'Lagoon*, Teluk Kerma, T09970105. Very remote position at the northern end of the island, some rooms in a longhouse, chalets have attached bathrooms, restaurant, a secluded, quiet spot with excellent snorkelling. **C** *Pasir Petani Resort*, at the southern end of the island, chalets with fans and attached bathrooms. **D** *Mira Beach Chalets*, Mira beach, south of Coral Bay (accessible on foot). Cheap chalets on this small but beautiful beach.

Eating There are a couple of restaurants on Perhentian Besar serving simple food – banana pancakes etc. Particularly popular are the restaurants attatched to *Coral View Island Resort*, *Coco Hut Chalets* and *Abdul's*. There are also coffee shops in the kampung on Perhentian Kecil and almost all the chalets here have restaurants at very similar prices (RM8). Milkshakes, fruit juices and pancakes are particularly recommended. On Coral Bay *Barracuda's* is good.

Sports **Diving and snorkelling** The coral around the Perhentian islands is some of the best off the east coast. Most guesthouses arrange snorkelling trips and provide masks, snorkels and fins. There are also dive shops (PADI) on Pulau Perhentian Besar which run courses and arrange dives for beginners to old hands, including night dives. *Turtle Bay Divers* (Long Beach, Perhentian Kecil) T0103319624. It is advisable to shop around for the best deal, and seek other tourists' advice to get an idea about the quality of the instructors who tend to vary from season to season.

Transport *20 km offshore* **Bus** From Kuala Terengganu (Jln Masjid): Kota Bharu-bound bus to Jerteh. Regular connections between Jerteh and Kuala Besut. From Kota Bharu: Bus 3, south-bound to Pasir Puteh (36 km south). Regular connections between Pasir Puteh and Kuala Besut. From Kuala Lumpur: *Rangkalan Mewah* bus company leaves at 0900 and 2130, T4432805. Boats leave from here to Perhentian.

Taxi Kuala Terengganu; Kota Bharu. Taxis from Pasir Puteh or Jerteh to Kuala Besut. Boats leave from here to Perhentian.

Boat Fast boats leave Kuala Besut at 0930,1030, 1430, and take 30 mins, RM60 return, boats carry 8-10 people. The same boats leave Pulau Perhentian for Kuala Besut between 1130-1200 and 1530-1600. Slow boats leave Kuala Besut at approximately 0900 and 1630, take 1½-2 hrs and carry 12 people, RM40 return. They return from the islands at 0800, 1200 and 1600. For further information, call *Perhentian Ferry Travel & Tours*, T6919679. Those staying at the more remote *Pasir Petani Resort* on Perhentian Kecil should pre-arrange a pick-up time. Travellers should be wary of risking the boat trip too close to the beginning or end of the Dec-Feb monsoon season. The fishing boats are not best equipped for rough seas and life jackets are rarely available. In Mar 1994, 2 passengers in a boat carrying 30 tourists died when the vessel capsized after being hit by huge waves.

Directory **Communications** Internet cafés: there are only two cafés on the islands, both located on Besar. They are very expensive compared to the mainland: 30 mins will set you back around RM12. The locations are: *Checkpoint*, which doubles as a shop and tour organizer, and the *Seahorse Dive Centre and Chalets*.

Kota Bharu

Kota Bharu is the royal capital of Kelantan, 'the land of lightning', and is situated near the mouth of the Kelantan River. The city is one of Malaysia's Malay strong-holds, despite its proximity to the Thai border. This was reinforced during the latest general elections when the opposition PAS once again managed to secure KB and Kelantan. While some people react against the state government's enthusiastic support for an Islamic interpretation of public (and private) morals, KB is one of Malaysia's more culturally interesting and colourful towns.

Phone code: 09
Colour map 1, grid A5

The state's south and west regions include some of the most mountainous country on the peninsula, but the fertile alluvial soils of the Kelantan River valley and the coastal plain have supported mixed farming and a thriving peasant economy for centuries.

Ins and outs

KB's airport is 8 km from town. There are links on Pelangi and MAS with KL, Penang and Ipoh. Unusually, the train station is 5 km from town at Wakaf Bharu. The line runs south to KL and Singapore. There is a confusion of 3 bus terminals in KB but the majority of express buses depart from the most central. There are connections with all major destinations on the Peninsula. Buses also run to Rantau Panjang and Pengkalan Kubor, both on the Thai border. Outstation taxis also offer a service to many larger towns.

Getting there

The trishaw used to be the backbone of the town's public transport system, but taxis have just about elbowed them out of the scene. There is also a city bus service and a number of local and international car hire firms.

Getting around

East Coast Peninsula

History

Kelantan may have been part of the second century kingdom of Langkasuka (see page 179), but from early in the first millennium AD, it was an established agricultural state which adopted the farming practices of the kingdom of Funan on the lower Mekong River. Because it was effectively cut off from the west coast states of the peninsula, Kelantan always looked north: it traded with Funan, the Khmer Empire and the Siamese kingdom of Ayutthaya.

By the 14th century, Kelantan was under Siamese suzerainty, although at that time it also fell under the influence of the Javanese Majapahit Empire. For a while, during the 15th and 16th centuries, Kelantan joined other peninsular states in sending tribute to the Sultanate of Melaka, and its successor, Johor. By then the state had splintered into a number of small chiefdoms; one local chief, Long Mohammed, proclaimed himself Kelantan's first sultan in 1800.

When a succession dispute erupted on the death of the heirless Sultan Mohammed, Siam supported his nephew, Senik the 'Red-Mouth' who reigned for 40 peaceful years. On

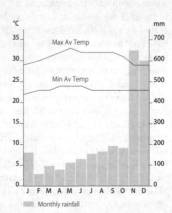

Climate: Kota Bharu

East Coast Peninsula

The Pergau Dam affair – aid-for-arms

The Pergau Dam affair marred Anglo-Malaysian relations for a year from early 1994. The dam in Kelantan was funded to the tune of £234m from Britain's overseas aid budget and the aid, as it turned out, was linked to a £1.3bn arms deal. The British government, led by former prime minister Margaret Thatcher, had managed to secure the quid pro quo deal as it tried to claw its way back into the lucrative Malaysian market. When the UK Sunday Times alleged that backhanders were paid by British companies to prominent Malaysian politicians, Malaysia's Prime Minister Mahathir hit back. He imposed a ban on public sector contracts going to British companies and lambasted the West in general and Britain in particular as morally bankrupt, hypocritical and neo-colonialist in attitude.

In London, investigations showed that the aid-for-arms link was an abuse of the aid programme. In agreeing to the deal, ministers ignored two years of technical advice which showed that the dam was poor value for money and Sir Tim Lankester, permanent secretary of the Overseas Development Administration, went so far as to write a 'memorandum of dissent' to show that he had not approved the project. Just to add insult to injury, the World Development Movement, a UK-based pressure group, won a case in the High Court in London when it argued that funding the dam was an illegal use of taxpayers' money. The government was forced to make up the shortfall in the aid budget elsewhere and emerged from the affair as tawdry and dishonest.

the next succession crisis, in 1900, Bangkok installed its own nominee as sultan. But in 1909, a treaty between Siam and Britain pushed Bangkok to cede its suzerainty over Kelantan to the British. This severed the state from its Islamic neighbour, the former sultanate of Petani, in Southeast Thailand. British interference caused much resentment and provoked a brief revolt in 1912. After using Kota Bharu as one of their beachheads for the invasion of Malaya in December 1941, the Japanese Imperial Army won support for restoring Kelantan to Thailand. In October 1945 however, Kelantan reluctantly joined the Malayan Union, under the British colonial administration.

Modern Kelantan Today Kelantan is Malaysia's most conservative and traditional state and since October 1990 it has been ruled by the hard-line Parti Islam – or *PAS*, its Malay acronym. In 1993 the PAS-led state government voted to introduce strict Islamic – or Syariat – law. Non-Muslims in the state – mainly in Kota Bharu, where one-third of the population is Chinese or Indian – were alarmed by the prospect of the '*hudud*' criminal code being implemented. It dictates that for crimes such as theft, fornication, intoxication and apostasy, 'criminals' should have their hands and/or legs severed or should be lashed until death if unrepentant. When Islamic officials broke up a rowdy Chinese New Year party in Kota Bharu in 1994, the local Chinese community thought their fears had been realized and that this was a taste of things to come.

Hudud can't become law until it's passed by a two-thirds majority in Federal Parliament, but the whole matter has become a conundrum for Muslim politicians in KL. Dr Mahathir's government does not want to be seen as un-Islamic by opposing Kelantan's move, so the Prime Minister has been busily polishing his own Islamic credentials by building new mosques and sponsoring Koran-reading competitions. For Dr Mahathir, the idea of having a mini-Iran as part of his Malaysian Federation is anathema. It totally conflicts with the vision of Islamic moderates and modernists. The battle between Kelantan and the government in KL continues. In the most recent general elections the opposition

PAS once again managed to hold onto Kelantan despite the most fervent efforts by UMNO to secure a victory here and the promise of massive development funds. The state is a hotbed of opposition politics. PAS's newspaper is effectively the country's only opposition publication (or it was until its publishing license was withdrawn at the beginning of 2000). Tunku Razaleigh Hamzah, a prince of the Kelantan royal family, is a long term thorn in Mahathir's side. In March 2000 there were reports that he would stand for the position of UMNO deputy president in the elections in May - effectively pitting his popularity against the wishes of Prime Minister Mahathir. As Mahathir has declared that this will be his last term as PM, and as the deputy president is the de facto heir apparent of UMNO, and as the president of UMNO just about automatically becomes the PM of Malaysia, the reasons why this is a critical battle are pretty clear. A few years back, when Razaleigh again faced up against Mahathir by trying to establish a breakaway mainstream Malay party (in which he failed), he said: "We don't have the problems that exist elsewhere. In Malaysia's quest for industrialization, those in power accept any development, whatever the cost to the environment. In Kelantan we resist."

This highly charged political and religious atmosphere contrasts with the Kelantanese people's laid-back, gentle manner. Tourists visiting the state should be particularly aware of Islamic sensitivities (see page 237), but the trappings of Islam rarely impinge on the enjoyment of the state's rich cultural heritage. But don't expect to find much in the way of funfairs: it was reported at the end of 1995 that the state government had banned bumper cars and Ferris wheels on the pretext that they allow teenagers too much body contact.

The crafts for which Kelantan is renowned – such as silverware, weaving and metal-working – were in part the result of the state's close relations with the Siamese kingdom of Ayutthaya in the 17th century. The *makyung*, a traditional Malay court dance, is still performed in Kelantan and *wayang kulit* (shadow puppet plays) still provide entertainment on special occasions in the kampungs. Kota Bharu is the centre for Malay arts and crafts, although batik printing, woodcarving, songket-weaving and silver working are more often confined to the villages.

Sights

The heart of Kota Bharu is the **central market** off Jalan Temenggong, which is one of the most vibrant and colourful wet markets in the country. It is housed in a three-storey octagonal concrete complex painted green which has a glass roof and, because it's so bright, is a photographer's paradise. In the modern Buluh Kubu complex across the road on Jalan Tengku Petra Semerak, there are many shops selling Kelantanese batik and other handicrafts. Nearby is the **Istana Balai Besar**, the 'palace with the big audience hall', built in Patani-style in 1844 by Sultan Mohammed II. The istana, with its decorative panels and wood-carvings is still used on ceremonial occasions. The palace contains the throne-room and the elaborate royal barge, which the sultan only ever used once for a joy ride on the Kelantan River in 1900. It is not usually open to the public but visitors can obtain permission to visit from the palace caretaker. Beside the old istana is the single-storey **Istana Jahar**, constructed in 1889 by Sultan Mohammed IV; it is now the 'centre for royal customs' and is part of the new cultural complex (see below). It exemplifies the skilled craftsmanship of the Kelantanese woodcarvers in its intricately carved beams and panels. There is a small craft collection including songket and silverware. ■ *0830-1645 except Fri, RM3.*

Kampung Kraftangan or Handicraft Village is close to the central market. It aims to give visitors a taste of Kelantan's arts and crafts all under one roof.

The large enclosure, in which *merbuk* birds (doves) sing in their bamboo cages, contains four buildings, all wooden and built in traditional Malay style. They are part of the Kelantan cultural zone area which will include several museums, including the Istana Jahar. The complex is quite impressive, but visitors appear few and far between, giving the sprawling place a slightly empty, lackadaisical feel. The Handicraft Museum contains exhibits and dioramas of traditional Kelantanese crafts and customs. There is also a batik workshop and demonstration centre where local artists produce hand-painted batiks. There are several stalls, stocked with handicrafts such as batik, silverware and songket, for sale. At ground level there is a pleasant restaurant serving Kelantanese delicacies. ■ *Kampung Kraftangan free; Handicraft Museum RM1.* Opposite the new complex is the **Istana Batu**, the sky-blue Stone Palace, which was built in 1939 and was one of the first concrete buildings in the state. The former royal palace was presented to the state by the Sultan for use as a royal museum and contains many personal possessions of the royal family.

A little north of the commercial centre is **Padang Merdeka**, built after the First World War as a memorial. Merdeka Square is also where the British hanged Tok Janggut, 'Father Long-beard', who led the short-lived revolt against British land taxes in 1915. Opposite, on Jalan Sultan Zainab, is the **State Mosque**, which was completed in 1926. Next door is the State Religious Council building, dating from 1914. Next to the mosque on Jalan Merdeka is a magnificent two-storey green-and-white mansion with traditional Islamic latticework carving on eaves, which houses the **Islamic Museum**. The building itself is more noteworthy than its eclectic contents. ■ *0830-1645 Sat-Thur; donations only.* The **War Museum** next to the Islamic Museum gives visitors an informative account of the Second World War in Southeast Asia. Beginning with Pearl Harbor, it tells the story of the Japanese invasion of Kelantan in December 1941 and the subsequent conquest of Malaya. It includes many pictures and items from the period. ■ *0830-1645 except Fri, RM2 adult, RM1 child.*

Directly west of the mosque, running north-south along the riverbank is **Jalan Pasar Lama**, off Jalan Post Office Lama. This is an interesting area for a gentle stroll; there are many beautiful but rapidly decaying old Chinese shophouses (there's a large Chinese community in this part of town). Most of the buildings date to the early 1900s. Some have been rendered completely uninhabitable because vast trees have taken root inside them.

At the **Gelanggang Seni** (Cultural Centre), on Jalan Mahmud, opposite the stadium and close to *Perdana Hotel*, many traditional arts are regularly performed. The centre tends to get rather touristy but it is the best place to see a variety of cultural performances in one place. For more detail on each of these traditional forms of entertainment, see page 552. These include:

Demonstrations of *silat* (the Malay art of self-defence).

Drumming competitions (Wednesday afternoons) using the *rebana ubi* Kelantan drums, made from hollowed-out logs.

Wayang kulit (shadow-puppet) performances (Wednesday nights).

Kite-flying competitions (Saturday afternoons) with the famous paper-and-bamboo *wau bulan* – or Kelantan moon-kites, the symbol of MAS. This has been a Kelantanese sport for centuries; the aim is to fly your kite higher than anyone else's and, once up there, to defend your superiority by being as aggressive as possible towards other competitors' kites. Kite-flying, according to the Malay Annals, was a favourite hobby in the heyday of the Melaka sultanate in the 15th century. *Top-spinning* competitions (Wednesday and Saturday afternoons).

Other cultural performances include traditional dance routines such as the royal *Mak Yong* dance and the *Menora*, both of which relate local legends. A set programme of shows, available from the Tourist Promotion Board, usually starts at 1530-1730 Monday; 1530-1730 and 2130-0000 Wednesday and Saturday, March-October. **NB** No shows during Ramadan.

The **State Museum** is situated on Jalan Sultan Ibrahim near the clock tower and next to the Tourism Malaysia office. Its proudest boast is its big collection of krisses. There is also an assemblage of Chinese porcelain. ■ *0830-1645, Sat-Thur, T7482266. RM2.*

Excursions

Also known as Tin Heng Keong, this Chinese temple is 1 km out of town, on the road to PCB (see below). It is about 100 years old and is particularly colourful; best time to visit is 0900-1000 each day when the temple is particularly lively. There is another smaller temple with a grotesque laughing Buddha and a grotto on the riverbank, closer to town. From KB follow road to PCB; after 500m, on sharp right bend, turn left at vegetable market; go down dirt track and turn right through Chinese gateway at bottom.

Kong Mek

This is KB's most famous beach, now renamed **Pantai Cahaya Bulan**, but still known as **PCB**, 10 km north of the city. It is really only famous for its name, meaning the 'Beach of Passionate Love'. In 1994 the Islamic state government, which takes a dim view of passionate love, rechristened it the Beach of the Shining Moon, which conveniently retains the old acronym, PCB. In comparison with some other east coast beaches, it is an unromantic dump. In Malay, the word *berahi* is, according to one scholar, "loaded with sexual dynamite ... a love madness". Local Malays, alluding to this heated innuendo, used to euphemistically call it *pantai semut api* – the beach of the fire ants. Today, young Malay lovers do not even dare to hold hands on the beach, for fear of being caught by the religious police and charged with *khalwat*, the crime of 'close proximity', under *Syariat* Islamic law. The origin of the name *cinta berahi* is lost. One theory is that it was used as a code word by Malay and British commandos during the Japanese wartime occupation: the site of the Imperial Army's invasion, in 1941, is nearby, on Pantai Dasar Sabak (see page 299). Despite being rather over-rated, there are several resorts along the beach. It gets crowded on weekends and room rates rise accordingly. To get there take a minibus 10, which leaves every 20 minutes from Bazaar Buluh Kubu, off Jalan Tengku Chik or from Jalan Padang Garong, or take a taxi.

Pantai Cinta Berahi

Sleeping A *Perdana Resort* (also known as *PCB Resort*), Jln Kuala Pa'Amat, T7744000, F7744980. A/c, restaurant, pool, watersports, pleasanter stretch of beach, dotted with white chalets colour schemed blue, green and pink according to room type, not very well maintained, popular with business conventions and meetings. **C-D** *Long House Beach Motel*, T7731090. Some a/c, restaurant (Thai food), not bad value really but it doesn't have a great deal of charm. **D-E** *HB Village*, T7734993. Very clean, very friendly and very big crocodiles in attached farm.

Pantai Dalam Rhu, also known as Pantai Bisikan Bayu, or the Beach of the Whispering Breeze, lies 40 km southeast of KB: There is **E** *Dalam Rhu Homestay*, which has simple kampung-style accommodation and is well looked after. Take a bus 3, southbound, and change at Pasir Puteh. **Pantai Irama**, the 'Beach of Melody', 25 km south of KB, is the best of the nearby beaches for swimming. The **B-C** *Motel Irama Bachok*, Bachok, T7788462, is clean and reasonable value. To get there, take a bus 2A or 2B to Bachok, which leaves every 30 minutes. **Pantai Dasar Sabak**, 13 km northeast of KB, is where the Japanese troops landed on 7

Other beaches

East Coast Peninsula

December 1941, 90 minutes before they bombed Pearl Harbor. Nearby Kampung Sabak is a good place to watch fishing boats come in in the morning. To get there, take a bus 8 or 9 from old market terminal.

Other excursions

Waterfalls In the area round Pasir Puteh there are several waterfalls: Jeram Pasu, Jeram Tapeh and Cherang Tuli. **Jeram Pasu** is the most popular, 35 km from Kota Bharu. It is most easily accessible by taxi or bus 3 to Padang Pak Amat (RM1.70) and taxi to the waterfalls.

Tumpat Around Tumpat, next to the border, are small Thai communities where there are a few Thai-style buildings and wats; they do not, however, compare with the Thai architecture on the other side of the border. **Wat Phothivian** at Kampung Berok 12 km east of KB, on the Malaysian side of Sungai Golok, has a 41m reclining Buddha statue, built in 1973 by chief abbot Phra Kruprasapia Chakorn, which attracts thousands of Thai pilgrims every year. Take bus 27 or 19 to Chabang Empat and then a taxi the last 3-4 km to Kampung Jambu. This last part of the journey also makes for a pleasant enough rural stroll.

Masjid Kampung Laut at Kampung Nilam Puri, 10 km south of KB, was built 300 years ago by Javanese Muslims as an offering of thanks for being saved from pirates. Having been damaged once too often by monsoon floods, it was dismantled and moved inland to Kampung Nilam Puri, which is an Islamic scholastic centre. It was built entirely of cengal, a prized hardwood, and constructed without the use of nails. It vies with Masjid Kampung Kling (in Melaka) for the title of Malaysia's oldest mosque. Bus 44 or express bus 5 leaves every 30 minutes.

River trips From Kuala Kerai (a 1½-hour bus trip south from Kota Bharu, bus 5) departs 0745 Monday-Sunday, it is possible to take a boat upriver to Dabong, a small kampung nestled among the jungled foothills of the Main Range (two hours, departs 1000 but not on Friday), where there is a resthouse and restaurant. Dabong, in the centre of Kelantan state, is on the north-south railway, so it is possible to catch the train back to Wakaf Bharu (across the river from KB), the journey takes two hours 45 minutes (third class only). Alternatively, take a taxi.

Tours

KTIC (Kolantan State Tourist Information Centre) organizes a number of tours – river and jungle-safari trips, staying in kampungs and learning local crafts. They also organize three-day 'Kampung Experience' tours which are not as contrived as their name suggests. Full board and lodging provided by host families which can be selected from list including potters, fishermen, batik-makers, kite-makers, silversmiths, dance instructors, top-makers and shadow puppet-makers. Cost from RM160 (all in); minimum two people. They also run short Kelantanese cooking courses.

Essentials

Sleeping
None of the hotels except for the Murni serves alcohol so minibars are usually a bleak sight

Budget travellers are spoilt for choice in KB; there are some very pleasant cheaper hostels and guesthouses (most of them in secluded alleyways with gardens) and they are locked in fearsome competition. As a result, new ones start up all the time as old ones fold; the State Tourist Information Centre has a list of budget accommodation and is happy to make recommendations. Until recently, the selection of top-bracket and mid-range hotels was poor – however, a number of new **A-B** bracket hotels have recently opened.

A *Perdana*, Jln Mahmud, T7485000, F7447621. A/c, restaurant, pool, tennis and squash courts, bowling alley, best in town, central location, babysitting, gym, sauna, traditional massage. Broad spectrum of tour information available and also a travel agent on site. **A-B** *Mawar*, Jln Parit Dalam, T7448888, F7476666. New and well located. **A-B** *Murni*, Jln Datuk Pati, T7482399. A/c, restaurant, the original 'luxury' hotel in KB but now appears rather dark and dingy, location is its only advantage.

B *Ansar*, Jln Maju, T7474000, F7461150. New, clean hotel, conveniently located near the night market, it is an Islamic hotel, so no shoes, prayers in the hallways and signs mentioning Allah in the elevators, basic breakfast included, overpriced. Very comfortable with decent rooms and business centre. **B** *Dynasty Inn*, 2865 D and E Jln Sultan Zainab, T7473000, F7473111, dynasty@hotmail.com. A hotel with 47 rooms, a/c, TV,

Kota Bharu

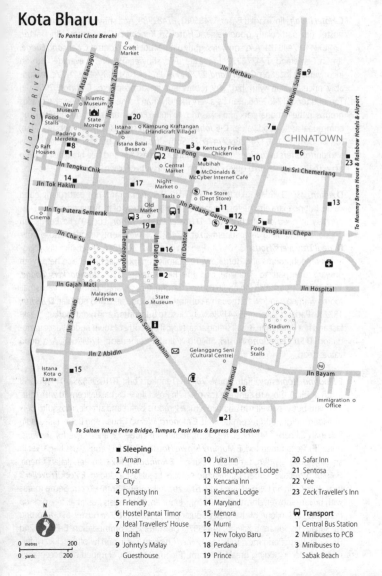

East Coast Peninsula

■ Sleeping

1 Aman	10 Juita Inn	20 Safar Inn
2 Ansar	11 KB Backpackers Lodge	21 Sentosa
3 City	12 Kencana Inn	22 Yee
4 Dynasty Inn	13 Kencana Lodge	23 Zeck Traveller's Inn
5 Friendly	14 Maryland	
6 Hostel Pantai Timor	15 Menora	**🚌 Transport**
7 Ideal Travellers' House	16 Murni	1 Central Bus Station
8 Indah	17 New Tokyo Baru	2 Minibuses to PCB
9 Johnty's Malay	18 Perdana	3 Minibuses to
Guesthouse	19 Prince	Sabak Beach

hot shower, good views, rooftop coffee house, Chinese seafood restaurant. Extra bed available for RM18. **B** *Juita Inn*, Jln Pintu Pong, T7446888, F7445777, Hotel@tm.net.my. Attractive hotel with 70 rooms, a/c, TV, minibar, restaurant, room rates include breakfast. Rooms are small but clean and well furnished – note that the superior rooms have no windows, not particularly good value. **B** *Kencana Inn*, Jln Padang Garong, T7447944. A/c, restaurant, reasonable value for money; do not confuse with sister hotel, *Hotel Sri Kencana*. **B** *Safar Inn*, Jln Hilir Kota, T7478000, F7479000. A hotel with 31 rooms, a/c, TV, carefully furnished rooms with wall-to-wall carpets. Good location, in the heart of town. **B** *Sentosa*, 3180-A Jln Sultan Ibrahim, T7443200. A/c, restaurant (formerly *Irama Baru & Apollo Hotel*), all spruced up, very clean and car rental organized. Great value. **B-C** *New Tokyo Baru*, 3945 Jln Tok Hakim, T7449488. A/c, well-maintained place, friendly. Recommended.

C *Hotel Indah*, Jln Tengku Besar, T7485081, F7482788. A/c, shower. Another average hostel, not particularly good value. **C** *Hotel Sri Kencana* (City Centre), Jln Doktor, T7440944, F7440181. A/c, shower, slightly dingier but large rooms. **C** *Kencana Lodge*, Jln Sn Cemerang, T74772222, F7477111. A/c, shower, TV. Pretty average with an inconvenient location. **C** *Maryland*, 2726-2727 Jln Tok I Iakim, T7482811. A/c, reasonably priced, clean with big, airy rooms but no atmosphere. **C** *Prince*, 2953 Jln Temenggong, T7482066. Run by a very friendly man named Fendi (who also guides groups in the national park and takes trips to Pulau Perhentian), a/c, clean, with large communal area, good value. **C-E** *Johnty's Malay Guesthouse*, 822 Jln Kebun Sultan, (off Jln Dusun Raja), T7448866/7478677. Some a/c, popular but past its peak, rooms and dorm, offers excursions, bike hire, traditional massage and free breakfast to keep up with the Joneses, in a quiet corner on the outskirts of town.

D *Aman*, 23C/D Jln Tengku Besar, T7443049. A/c, restaurant, not particularly good value, but no extra charge for regular alarm calls courtesy of mosque next door. Desperately in need of refurbishment. **D** *Hostel Pantai Timor*, Lot 391 Jln Pengkalan Chepa, behind Safra Jaya supermarket, T7483753. Well kept, friendly, also dorms. **D** *Ideal Travellers' House*, 5504a Jln Padang Garong, T7442246. Quiet, friendly, pleasant verandah, rooms and dormitory. This family-run, popular hostel also helps with onward transport to Thailand and the Perhentians. **D** *KB Backpackers Lodge*, T7432125. Opposite *KB Inn* on Jln Padang Garong, fan, separate bathroom, very small rooms with no windows although a comfortable lounge area and popular. **D** *KB Inn*, 1872 Jln Padang Garong, T7441786. Very close to bus station and night market, breakfast and hot drinks free, small sitting area, typical of centre of town budget accommodation. **D** *Sri Cemerlang Hostel*, 5640 U-X Jln Sri Cemerlang, T7449648. A/c, good value, clean.

E *Floating Homestay*, Raft House 70, Jln Tengku Chik, T010-906252/011-977252 (both mobile). Close to centre of town, off Jln Post Office Lama; unlicensed with tourist board but very well run and river cruises, rooms clean and simple, mosquito nets provided; unique and recommended. **E** *Menora*, Wisma Chua Tong Boon, (1st Flr) Jln Sultanah Zainab, T7481669. Well kept, facilities include TV and powerful showers, dorm (**F**). Recommended. **E** *Mummy Brown House*, 4398 Jln Pengkalan Chepa. Set in an old house, garden, breakfast included. **E** *Rainbow*, 4423 Jln Pengkalan Chepa. Helpful, attractive garden but near noisy road, breakfast included. **E** *Zeck Traveller's Inn*, 7088-G Jln Sri Cemerlang, T7431613, ztraveller_Inn@hotmail.com. Some rooms with private shower, dorm rooms (RM6), verandah, light meals available, free pick-up from bus station, one of the most popular places to stay. **E** *Zee Hostel*, 696-a Lorong Hj. Sufian, Jln Sultanah Zainab, T7445376. Dormitory accommodation. **E-F** *City*, 2nd Flr, 35 Jln Pintu Pong (next to *Kentucky Fried Chicken*), clean and helpful on local information, price including breakfast, dorm (**F**), email facility, cramped but acceptable.

E-F *Friendly*, 4278D Jln Kebun Sultan, T7442246. Dorm and rooms, garden. **E-F** *Town*, 4959B (1st Flr) Jln Pengkalan Chepa, T7485192. Roof restaurant, friendly and clean, close to the bus terminal, travel services, dorm and rooms. **E-F** *Wann's*, Jln Sultanah Zainab, T7485381 (behind silversmith). Clean, good value. Recommended. **E-F** *Yee*, Jln Padang Garong, 2nd Flr, T7441944. Everything you need: laundry, breakfast, showers, travel information, bicycles for hire, dorm (**F**), unfortunately, the rooms are dirty.

F *DE999*, next to *Rebana*, Jln Sultanah Zainab, T7481955. Cheap and clean rooms, close to the Cultural Centre, price including breakfast, free bicycles, dorm and rooms.

The Kelantan speciality is *ayam percik* – roast chicken, marinated in spices and served with a coconut-milk gravy. *Nasi tumpang* is a typical Kelantanese breakfast; banana-leaf funnel of rice layers interspersed with prawn and fish curries and salad. *Kuchino Italiano*, 147 Jln Pengkalau Chepa, on main road between city centre and the airport, family run restaurant, a poor attempt at Italian cuisine; *Ambassador*, 7003 Jln Kebun Sultan, big Chinese coffee shop next to *Kow Lun* (below), Chinese dishes including pork satay and other iniquitous substances – like beer; *Azam*, Jln Padang Garong, North Indian tandoori, with fresh oven-baked naan, good rotis and curry; *Kow Lun*, 7005 and 7006 Jln Kebun Sultan, good lively Chinese coffee shop with large variety of dishes and lots of beer; *Malaysia*, 2527 Jln Kebun Sultan, Chinese cuisine, speciality: steamboat, this is the place to sample turtle eggs – legally; *Meena Curry House*, 3377 Jln Gajah Mati, Indian curry house, banana leaf restaurant. Recommended. *Neelavathy*, Jln Tengku Maharani (behind *Kencana Inn*), South Indian banana-leaf curries. Recommended. *Qing Liang*, Jln Zainal Abidin, excellent Chinese vegetarian, also Malay and Western dishes. Recommended. *Satay Taman Indraputra*, Jln Pekeliling/Jln Hospital garden; *Syam*, Jln Hospital, Thai-influenced.

Eating
Beer & other alcoholic beverages are only available in certain Chinese coffee shops, notably along Jln Kebun Sultan

Indian Food can be found on Jln Gajah Mati. **Chinese** food is available on Jln Kebun Sultan. **Fastfood** *McDonalds* at the bus station.

Foodstalls *Night market* (in car park opposite local bus station, in front of Central Market), exclusively Malay food, satays and exquisite array of curries; colour-coded tables – if you eat from a certain stall and sit at a blue table, you are obliged to buy your drink from stall in blue area; excellent fruit juices, no alcohol. Recommended. *Nasi Padang Osman Larin* (otherwise known as *Nasi Hoover* as it is outside *Hotel Hoover*) is a stall on Jln Datuk Pati (between the Tourist Information Centre and the bus station) famed locally for its curries. By the stadium in Jln Muhamud.

Bakery *Mubihah Vegetarian Restaurant and Cake House*, opposite *Kentucky Fried Chicken*, 157 Jln Pintu Pong. Eat in or takeaway; excellent breads, pastries, cakes etc – one of the best '*kek and roti*' shops in Malaysia.

Cultural shows Regular cultural shows at the *Gelanggang Seni* (cultural centre), Jln Mahmud (see above).

Entertainment

May/June: *Malaysia International Kite Festival*, Pantai Seri Tujuh (Beach of the Seven Lagoons), Turnport (adjacent to Thai border), 7 km from KB. *Getting there*: bus 43.
July: *Drum festival* (movable) a traditional east coast pastime. *Sultan's birthday celebrations* (10th-12th).
August: *Bird Singing Contest* (movable) when the prized *merbuk* (doves) or *burong ketitir* birds compete on top of 8m-high poles. Bird singing contests are also held on Friday mornings around Kota Bharu.
September: *Top-spinning contest* (movable) another traditional east coast sport which is taken very seriously.

Festivals

East Coast Peninsula

Shopping **Antiques** *Lam's*, Jln Post Office Lama (in contrast to the modern town walk there are several old bamboo raft houses along this street).

Batik *Astaka Fesyer*, 782K (3rd Flr). Recommended. *Bazaar Buluh Kubu*, Jln Tengku Petra Semerak, just across the road from the Central Market, houses scores of batik boutiques; also in the building are tailors' shops which can turn out very cheap shirts, blouses and dresses within 24 hrs.

Handicrafts The Central Market is cheapest for handicrafts. There are numerous handicraft stalls, silver-workers, kite-makers and wood-carvers scattered along the road north to Pantai Cinta Berahi. At Kampung Penambang, on this road, just outside KB, there is a batik and songket centre.

Silverware On Jln Sultanah Zainab (near *Rabana Guest House*), before junction with Jln Hamzah, there are 3 shops selling Kelantan silver including *KB Permai*, a family business which works the silver on the premises. The new *Kampung Kraftangan* (Handicraft Village) contains many stalls with a huge range of batik sarongs and ready-mades, silverware, songket, basketry and various Kelantanese knick-knacks.

Sports **Golf** *Royal Kelantan Golf Club*, 5488 Jln Hospital, green fees weekdays RM80, weekends RM120, 18-hole course.

Tour operators *Batuta Travel & Tour*, 1st Flr, Bangunan PKDK, Jln Dato' Pati, T7442652; *Boustead Travel*, 2833 Jln Temenggong, T7449952; *Kelmark Travel*, Kelmark House, 5220 Jln Telipot, T7444211; *Pelancongan Bumi Mars*, Tingkat Bawah, Kompleks Yakin, Jln Gajah Mati, T7431189. The Tourist Information Centre also arrange tours as do several of the guesthouses in town.

Transport
474 km to KL
168 km to Terengganu
371 km to Kuantan

Local **Bus**: city buses and many long-distance express buses leave from the Central Bus Station, Jln Hilir Pasar, so there is no need to go to the inconveniently located long distance bus stations in the south of the city. Regional buses to places like Gua Musang and Pasir Puteh also depart from this station. **Car hire**: *Avis*, *Hotel Perdana*, Jln Sultan Mahmud, T7484457, South China Sea, airport, T7744288, F7736288; from *Perdana Hotel*. *Pacific*, T7447610. **Trishaw**: short journeys RM2; RM10-12 per hour; recommended way of touring town but they are gradually disappearing as salaries rise and people opt for motorized transport.

Long distance **Air**: airport is 8 km from town; RM12 per taxi. Regular connections with Ipoh, KL, Penang on *MAS* and KL on *Pelangi Airways*. Transport to town: by taxi RM10 per person or town bus No 9.

Train: Wakaf Bharu station is 5 km out of town, across the Kelantan River. Bus 19 or 27 (RM1). Daily connections with Singapore and KL via Gua Musang, Kuala Lipis, Jerantut and Gemas. The jungle railway is slow but the scenery makes the journey worthwhile. *Golden Blowpipe* departs Wakaf Bharu in the early afternoon and arrives Gemas at around midnight (connections arrive Singapore/KL early next morning). Second class a/c connections with Jerantut-Taman Negara, KL and Singapore.

Bus: KB has 3 long-distance bus stations although many express buses leave from the central terminal on Jln Hilir Pasar, saving on a trip to one of the two out of town stations. The main intercity express bus company is the state-owned SKMK and its buses leave both from the central station on Jln Hilir Pasar and from the Langgar bus station south of town on Jln Pasir Puteh. The second out of town bus terminal is also south of town on Jln Hamzah and all bus companies other than SKMK operate vehicles from here. Regular connections with: Grik, Kuala Terengganu, Jerantut, Kuantan, KL (RM25), JB, Penang, Alor Star, Kuala Lipis, Butterworth, Melaka, Mersing, Temerloh, and many other destinations. Buses from Kuala Lumpur leave at 0900 and 2100 from Putra Station (*Mutiara*

Express, T4433655, *PPMP*, T4445699, *Naela Express*, T4439155). **Taxi**: taxi station next to the Central Bus Station, Jln Hilir Pasar. Destinations include Kuala Terengganu, Kuantan, KL, JB, Butterworth, Grik. Also taxis to Rantau Panjang (for Sungai Golok, Thailand).

International connections The Thai border is at the Malaysian town of Rantau Panjang; on the other side is the Thai settlement of Sungai Golok. Bus no. 29 for Rantau Panjang leaves on the hour through the day from the central bus station, off Jln Hilir Pasar (1½ hrs). From here it is a shortish 1 km walk across the border to Sungai Golok's train and bus stations where there are connections to other destinations in Thailand including Hat Yai, Surat Thani (for Koh Samui) and Bangkok. Trishaws and motorbike taxis wait to assist people making the crossing. Another route into Thailand is via Pengkalan Kubor, a quieter and much more interesting crossing to Ta Ba (Tak Bai). Bus nos. 27, 27a and 43 go to Pengkalan Kubor. Small boats cross the river regularly and there is also a car ferry. Long-tails cater for the clientele of the cross-border prostitution industry only. There are also regular bus connections with Singapore.

Directory

Airline offices *MAS*, Ground Floor, Komplek Yakin, Jln Gajah Mati (opposite the clock tower), T7447000 and T7440557 at the airport; *Pelangi Airways*, c/o MAS, T7447000, F7440557. **Banks** Money changers in main shopping area. *Bumiputra*, Jln Maju; *D & C*, Jln Gajah Mati; *Hongkong & Shanghai*, Jln Sultan. **Communications** Area code: 09. **General Post Office:** Jln Sultan Ibrahim. **Telegraph Office:** Jln Doktor. **Embassies & consulates** *Royal Thai Consulate*, Jln Pengkalan Chepa, T7440867 (open 0900-1200, 1330-1530, Mon-Thu and Sat). **Medical facilities** Hospitals: Jln Hospital. T7485533. **Tourist offices** *Tourist Information Centre*, Jln Sultan Ibrahim, T7485534, F7482120. A helpful office, which will arrange taxis and ferries to the islands, as well as booking accommodation on the islands. **Useful addresses** Immigration Office: 3rd Flr, Federal Bldg, Jln Bayam. T7482120.

Gua Musang

Gua Musang is the largest town on Route 8, the road through the interior, and lies in Kelantan state close to the border with Pahang. It began life as little more than a logging camp but has now expanded into a thriving administrative centre. The jungle is studded with limestone outcrops in this area of the Peninsula and a particularly impressive one overshadows Gua Musang. There have been reports of large mammals including wild elephants, tigers and tapirs along the roads near here and this is about as wild as Peninsular Malaysia gets outside the national parks and wildlife reserves.

Sleeping C *Kesedar Inn*, T099121229. On the edge of town, attractive lawn, clean rooms, friendly. **E** *Rest House*, rather run down but an attractive place to stay, shared facilities.

Transport Bus: daily buses from Kuala Lipis to Gua Musang (0800 and 1300) and Kuala Krai (1430) with onward connections to Kota Bharu.

Grik

Also spelt Gerik, Grik was once a remote logging town just a few kilometres south of the Thai border. It is now on an important junction, and the beginning of the east-west highway. Few people stay the night there, but it is a good staging post and midday *makan* stop. The huge Temenggor and Lenering man-made reservoirs are nearby.

Grik can be reached from Kuala Kangsar in Perak (see page 146) or from Butterworth via either Kulim (directly east of the town) or Sungai Petani (35 km north of town) which lead first to Keroh, on the Thai border, then on to Grik. The Kuala Kangsar route is a particularly scenic drive along a 111 km road which winds its way up the Perak River valley, enclosed by the Bintang mountains to

East Coast Peninsula

the west and the Main Range to the east. *En route*, the road passes Tasek Chenderoh, a beautiful reservoir, surrounded by jungled hills. At **Kota Tampan**, just north of the lake, archaeologists have unearthed the remains of a Stone Age workshop, with roughly chiselled stone tools dating back 35,000 years. The road cuts through the jungle and there are some spectacular viewpoints. There are landslides along this stretch of road during the wet season.

Because Grik is not on the main tourist track, accommodation is basic

Sleeping **A** *Banding Island Resort*, PO Box 69, Banding, T7912273. Restaurant situated on an island on Lake Temengor and 15 years old. It went through a bad patch but has recently been renovated and expanded with new facilites and bungalows. The only shame is that the previously beautiful views of the inlet and headland have been reportedly partially obscured. Popular with tour groups. **D** *Diamond*, 40A Jln Sultan Iskander, T892388. **D** *Kong Seng*, 32 Jln Sultan Iskander, T892180. **D** *Rumah Rehat Grik*, Jln Meor Yahaya, T891211. **D-E** *Bee Hoon*, Jln Tan Sabah, T892201.

Transport **Bus**: Connections with Butterworth, KL, Taiping and Ipoh. For Kota Bharu change at Tanah Merah. It is possible to cross the border into Thailand from Keroh, 50 km north of Grik. There are regular taxis from Keroh to the border post and Thai taxis and *saamlors* (trishaws) on the other side. There are Thai taxis to Betong which is 8 km from the border.

Coast to coast

The East-West highway makes for a memorable journey. It runs from Kota Bharu to Penang, straight across the forested backbone of the peninsula and was one of the biggest civil engineering projects ever undertaken in Malaysia. During its 11 year construction, contractors had to push their way through densely jungled mountains, coping with frequent landslides and even hit-and-run attacks by Communist insurgents.

To the east of **Grik**, the highway runs close to the former bases of the Communist Party of Malaya, which, until 1989, operated out of their jungle headquarters near Betong, just across the Thai border. The area was known as 'Target One' by the Malaysian security forces. The construction of the road opened the previously inaccessible area up to timber companies; there has been much illegal logging – and cross-border drug-smuggling – in this 'cowboy country' of North Perak and Kelantan. The 200 km-long highway opened in 1982, and for the first few years was closed to traffic after 1600 because of the security threat posed by Communist insurgents; this threat has now ended. However, road maintenance is something of a hazard, and the journey is slow going with a whole series of road works and places where the road has subsided.

The *Golden Blowpipe* trundles along the railway line which cuts a diagonal through the peninsula, running due north from Gemas (south of KL on the KL-Singapore line) to **Kota Bharu**. Much of the route is through the jungle, and the track skirts the west boundary of **Taman Negara**, the national park (see page 266). Those heading into Taman Negara must disembark at **Tembeling Halt**, to the southeast of **Kuala Lipis**, or at **Jerantut**. The train is slow, but it is an interesting journey. From **Gemas** the line goes through Jeranut, Kuala Lipis, **Gua Musang**, **Kuala Krai** and on to Kota Bharu. It is possible to catch the train at **Mentakab** (along the Karak Highway, east of KL) or at Kuala Lipis, which can be reached by road via **Fraser's Hill** and **Raub**. It is also possible to drive from Kuala Lipis via Gua Musang to Kota Bharu. There are buses from Kuala Lipis to Gua Musang and Kuala Krai.

Sarawak

7

Sarawak

Sarawak, 'the land of the hornbill', is the largest state in Malaysia, covering an area of nearly 125,000 km² in Northwest Borneo. In the mid-19th century, Charles Darwin described Sarawak as "one great wild, untidy, luxuriant hothouse, made by nature for herself." Despite the state's rapacious logging industry, which has drawn world attention to Sarawak in recent years, more than two-thirds of its land area, roughly equivalent to that of England and Scotland combined, is still covered in jungle, much though, degraded and a far cry from 'virgin' rainforest. Some of it is still as the Victorian naturalist, Alfred Russel Wallace, whose theories influenced Darwin, saw it in 1855. "For hundreds of miles in every direction," he wrote, "a magnificent forest extended over plain and mountain, rock and morass." Sarawak has swampy coastal plain, a hinterland of undulating foothills and an interior of steep-sided, jungle-covered mountains. The lowlands and plain are dissected by a network of broad rivers which are the main arteries of communication; Sarawak has a population of just over two million, most of which is settled along the rivers.

Kuching

Population: 70,000
Phone code: 082
Colour map 3, grid C1

Because of Kuching's relative isolation and the fact that it was not bombed during the Second World War it has retained much of its 19th-century charm; despite the increasing number of modern high-rise buildings. Chinese shophouses still line many of the narrow streets. Covered sampans, or perahu tambang, paddle back and forth across the river from the riverfront esplanade to the kampongs and the Astana on the north bank.

Sarawak's capital is divided by the Sarawak River; the south is a commercial and residential area, dominated by Chinese while the north shore is predominantly Malay in character with the old kampong houses lining the river. The Astana, Fort Margherita and the Petra Jaya area, with its modern government offices, are also on the north side of the river. The two parts of the city are very different in character and even have separate mayors. Kuching's cosmopolitan make-up is immediately evident from its religious architecture: Chinese and Hindu temples, the imposing state mosque and Protestant and Roman Catholic churches.

Of all the cities in Malaysia, Kuching was worst affected by the smog associated with the fires that engulfed Indonesian Borneo (Kalimantan) in mid-1997 (see page 528). At the peak of the 'emergency' in late September – for that is what it became – the city came to a stop. It was too dangerous to drive and, seemingly, too dangerous to breathe. People were urged to remain indoors. Schools, government offices and factories closed. The port and aiport were also closed. Tourism traffic dropped to virtually zero and for 10 days the city stopped. At one point there was even discussion of evacuating the population of the State of Sarawak. People began to buy up necessities and the prices of some commodities rose 500 percent.

Ins and outs

Getting there
See also Transport
page 326

There are daily connections with KL and also regular flights to other destinations in Peninsular and East Malaysia. International connections are limited to Bandar Seri Begawan (Brunei), Singapore, Hong Kong, Taipei, Manila, Seoul, Tokyo and Pontianak (Kalimantan, Indonesia). There are several out-of-town bus companies and they provide services to destinations along the main coastal road north to Miri, close to the border with Brunei, and south to Sematan. Interior towns are sometimes difficult to access by road. There is also a bus service to Pontianak in Kalimantan (Indonesia) and to Brunei, via Miri. Express boats serve Sibu and Sarikei.

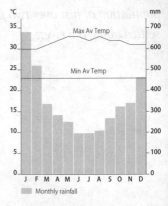

Climate: Kuching

A town called Cat

There are a number of explanations as to how Sarawak's capital acquired the name 'Cat'. (Kuching means 'cat' in Malay – although today it is more commonly spelt kucing as in modern Bahasa, 'c' is pronounced 'ch'.) Local legend has it that James Brooke, pointing towards the settlement across the river, inquired what it was called. Whoever he asked, mistakenly thought he was pointing at a passing cat. If that seems a little far-fetched, the Sarawak museum offers a few more plausible alternatives. Kuching may have been named after the wild cats (kucing hutan) which, in the 19th century, were commonly seen along jungled banks of the Sarawak River. Another theory is that it was called after the fruit buah mata kucing ('cat's eyes'), which grows locally. Most likely however, is the theory that the town may originally have been known as Cochin – or port – a word commonly used across India and Indochina.

There are 2 city bus companies that provide a cheap and fairly efficient service. Taxis are found outside many of the larger hotels and at designated taxi stands. There are also several international as well as local self-drive car hire firms in Sarawak. Sampans, known locally as tambangs, provide cross-river transport and operate as river taxis. **Getting around**

History

Shortly after dawn on 15 August 1839 James Brooke sailed round a bend in the Sarawak River and, from the deck of his schooner, *The Royalist*, had his first view of Kuching. According to the historian Robert Payne, he saw "...a very small town of brown huts and longhouses made of wood or the hard stems of the nipah palm, sitting in brown squalor on the edge of mudflats." The settlement, 32 km upriver from the sea, had been established less than a decade earlier by Brunei chiefs who had come to oversee the mining of antimony in the Sarawak River valley. The antimony – used as an alloy to harden other metals, particularly pewter – was exported to Singapore where the tin-plate industry was developing.

By the time James Brooke had become Rajah in 1841, the town had a population of local Malays and Dayaks and Cantonese, Hokkien and Teochew traders. Chinatown dominated the south side of the river while the Malay kampongs were strung out along the riverbanks to the west. A few Indian traders also set up in the bazaar, among the Chinese shophouses. Under Charles Brooke, the second of the White Rajahs, Kuching began to flourish; he commissioned most of the town's main public buildings. Brooke's wife, Ranee Margaret, wrote: "The little town looked so neat and fresh and prosperous under the careful jurisdiction of the Rajah and his officers, that it reminded me of a box of painted toys kept scrupulously clean by a child."

Sights

Kuching's biggest attraction is this internationally renowned museum, situated on both sides of Jalan Tun Haji Openg. The old building to the east of the main road is a copy of a Normandy town hall, designed by Charles Brooke's French valet. The Rajah was encouraged to build the museum by the naturalist Alfred Russel Wallace, who spent over two years in Sarawak, where he wrote his first paper on natural selection. The museum was opened in 1891, extended in 1911, and the new wing built in 1983. Its best known curators have been naturalist Eric Mjoberg, who made the first ascent of Sarawak's highest **Sarawak Museum** peak - Gunung Murud - (see page 365) – in 1922, and ethnologist and explorer Tom Harrisson, whose archaeological work at Niah made world headlines in 1957. The museum overlooks pleasant botanical gardens and the Heroes Memorial, built to commemorate the dead of the Second World War, the Communist insurgency and the confrontation with Indonesia. Across the road, and linked by an overhead bridge, is the Dewan Tun Abdul Razak building, a newer extension of the museum.

The museum has a strong ethnographic section, although some of its displays have been superseded by the Cultural Village (see below), Sarawak's 'living museum'. The old museum's ethnographic section includes a full-scale model of an Iban longhouse, a reproduction of a Penan hut and a selection of Kayan and Kenyah woodcarvings. There is also an impressive collection of Iban war totems (*kenyalang*) and carved Melanau sickness images (*blum*), used in healing ceremonies. The museum's assortment of traditional daggers (or *kris*, see page 491) is the best in Malaysia. The Chinese and Islamic ceramics include 17th-20th century Chinese jars, which are treasured heirlooms in Sarawak (see page 314).

The natural science collection, covering the flora and fauna of Sarawak, is also noteworthy. The new Tun Abdul Razak ethnological and historical collection includes prehistoric artefacts from the Niah caves (see page 359); there is even a replica of Niah's Painted Cave – without the smell of guano.

Kuching

■ **Sleeping**
1 Anglican Guesthouse
2 B&B Inn
3 Borneo
4 Crown Plaza Riverside
5 Fata
6 Hilton
7 Holiday Inn
8 Longhouse
9 Mandarin & Orchid Inn
10 Merdeka Palace
11 Metropole Inn
12 Supreme & Hua Hock Inn
13 Telang Usan

There is a library attached to the museum as well as a giftshop, the Curio Shoppe, all proceeds of which go to charity and a bookshop. Permits to visit the Niah's Painted Cave can be obtained, free of charge, from the curator's office. ■ *Daily 0900-1800. Audio-visual showings: 1015, 1215, 1430, 1445, 1530. Museum open 0800-1800 Tue-Sun, free.*

Sarawak Islamic Museum

Not far from the Sarawak Museum is this museum, located on Jalan P Ramlee in the restored Maderasah Melayu Building, an elegant, single storey colonial edifice. As its name suggests, the museum is devoted to Islamic artefacts from all the ASEAN countries, with the collection of manuscripts, costumes, jewellery, weaponry, furniture, coinage, textiles and ceramics spread over seven galleries, each with a different theme, and set around a central courtyard. ■ *Sat-Thur 0900-1800.*

Astana

Apart from the Sarawak Museum, the White Rajahs bequeathed several other architectural monuments to Kuching. The Astana, a variant of the usual spelling *istana*, or palace, was built in 1870, two years after Charles Brooke took over from his uncle. It stands on the north bank of the river almost opposite the market on Jalan Gambier. The Astana was hurriedly completed for the arrival of Charles' new bride (and cousin), Margaret. It was originally three colonial-style bungalows, with wooden shingle roofs, the largest being the central bungalow with the reception room, dining and drawing rooms. "How I delighted in those many hours spent on the broad verandah of our house, watching the life going on in the little town on the other side of the river," Ranee Margaret later reminisced in her book *My Life in Sarawak*. The crenellated tower on the east end was added in the 1880s at her request. Charles Brooke is said to have cultivated betel nut in a small plantation behind the Astana, so that he could offer fresh betel nut to visiting Dayak chiefs. Today it is the official residence of the governor, Yang Di Pertuan Negeri, of Sarawak and is only open to the public on Hari Raya Puasa, at the end of Ramadan. To the west of the Astana, in the traditionally Malay area, are many old wooden kampong houses.

Sarawak

Map labels:
- ■ 7
- Rahman
- ● 5
- MAS Office ○
- ○ Royal Brunei Airlines
- ■ Kuching Cat Statue ○
- Sarawak Plaza ○ ● 4
- 8
- Jln Petanak
- Market & ○ Hawker Centre
- 8 ■ Jln Abell
- Jln Padungan
- (P)
- Jln Song Thian Cheok
- Turf Club
- Jln Central Timur
- To Express Wharf (boats to Sibu)
- To Kingwood Inn

Fort Margherita

Not far away (and also on the north shore) is this fort, now the Police Museum, on Jalan Sapi. It was also built by Rajah Charles Brooke in 1879 and named after Ranee Margaret, although there was a fort on the site from 1841 when James Brooke became Rajah. It commanded the river approach to Kuching, but was never used defensively, although its

● **Eating**
1 Beijing
2 Green Vegetarian
3 Green Hill Corner
4 KTS Seafood Canteen
5 McDonalds
6 San Francisco Grill
7 See Good
8 Suan Chicken Rice & Pizza Hut
9 Thompson's Corner
10 Top Spot Food Court

A ceramic inheritance

Family wealth and status in Sarawak was traditionally measured in ceramics. In the tribal longhouses upriver, treasured heirlooms include ancient glass beads, brass gongs and cannons and Chinese ceramic pots and beads (such as those displayed in the Sarawak Museum). They were often used as currency and dowries. Spencer St John, the British consul in Brunei, mentions using beads as currency on his 1858 expedition to Gunung Mulu. Jars, or pesaka, had more practical applications; they were (and still are) used for storing rice, brewing tuak (rice wine) or for keeping medicines. Their value was dependent on their rarity: brown jars, emblazoned with dragon motifs, are more recent and quite common while olive-glazed dusun jars, dating from the 15th-17th centuries are rare. The Kelabit people, who live in the highlands around Bario, treasure the dragon jars in particular. Although some of the more valuable antique jars have found their way to the Sarawak Museum, many magnificent jars remain in the Iban and other tribal longhouses along the Skrang,

Rejang and Baram rivers. Many are covered by decoratively carved wooden lids.

Chinese contact and trade with the north coast of Borneo has gone on for at least a millennium, possibly two. Chinese Han pottery fragments and coins have been discovered near the estuary of the Sarawak River and from the 7th century, China is known to have been importing birds' nests and jungle produce from Brunei (which then encompassed all of North Borneo), in exchange for ceramic wares. Chinese traders arrived in the Nanyang (South Seas) in force from the 11th century, particularly during the Sung and Yuan dynasties. Some Chinese pottery and porcelain even bore Arabic and Koranic inscriptions – the earliest such dish is thought to have been produced in the mid-14th century. In the 1500s, as China's trade with the Middle East grew, many such Islamic wares were traded and the Chinese emperors presented them as gifts to seal friendships with the Muslim world, including Malay and Indonesian kingdoms.

construction was prompted by a near-disastrous river-borne attack on Kuching by the Ibans of the Rejang in 1878. Even so, until the Second World War a sentry was always stationed on the lookout post on top of the fort; his job was to pace up and down all night and shout "All's well" on the hour every hour until 0800. The news that nothing was awry was heard at the Astana and the government offices.

After 1946, Fort Margherita was first occupied by the Sarawak Rangers and was finally converted into a police museum in 1971, which is a lot more interesting than it sounds. There is a large collection of armour and weaponry on the ground floor, including weapons captured during the Indonesian *konfrontasi* from 1963-65 (see page 388). Up the spiral staircase, on the second floor, there is a display of police uniforms and communications equipment used by jungle patrols. The third floor houses an exhibition on drugs, counterfeit currency and documents, supplies and weapons captured from Communist insurgents in the 1960s and 1970s. From the top, there are good views across the city and up and down the Sarawak River. *En route* to the courtyard at the bottom, former prison cells have been set up to recreate an opium den – complete with emaciated dummy – and to reinforce the dangers of *dadah*, the courtyard itself contains the old town gallows complete with hanging dummy. During the rule of the White Rajahs, however, death sentences were carried out by a slash of the *kris* through the heart. ■ *1000-1800 Tue-Sun, closed public holidays, free. Getting there: sampan across the river from the Pangkalan Batu next to Square Tower on Main Bazaar to the Istana and Fort (RM30 one way; the boats can be hired quite cheaply, and on an hourly rate).*

The **Malay kampungs** along the riverside next to Fort Margherita are seldom visited by tourists – however, they have some beautiful examples of traditional and modern Malay architecture.

Around Main Bazaar are some other important buildings dating from the Brooke era; most of them are closed to the public. The **Supreme Court** on Main Bazaar was built in 1871 as an administrative centre. State council meetings were held here from the 1870s until 1973, when it was converted to law courts. In front of the grand entrance is a memorial to Rajah Charles Brooke (1924) and on each corner, there is a bronze relief representing the four main ethnic groups in Sarawak – Iban, Orang Ulu, Malay and Chinese. The clock tower was built in 1883. The **Square Tower**, also on Main Bazaar, was built as an annex to Fort Margherita in 1879 and was used as a prison. Later in the Brooke era it was used as a ballroom and is now a one-stop information centre for tourists, with a video wall and an interactive video on Sarawak past and present and a Waterfront Information Counter, providing details of forthcoming events. The square tower marks one end of Kuching's new waterfront esplanade which runs alongside the river for almost 900m to the *Hilton*. ■ *Daily 1000-1400, 1600-2130.*

South side of the river

The **Waterfront** has recently been transformed into a landscaped esplanade through restoration and a land reclamation project. It has become a popular meeting place, with foodstalls, restaurants and entertainment facilities including an open-air theatre. There is a restored Chinese pavilion, an observation tower, a tea terrace and musical fountains, as well as a number of modern sculptures. During the day, the waterfront offers excellent views of the Astana, Fort Margherita and the Malay kampungs which line the north bank of the river. At night, the area comes alive as younger members of Kuching's growing middle class make their way down here to relax.

The **General Post Office**, with its majestic Corinthian columns, stands in the centre of town, on Jalan Tun Haji Openg. It was built in 1931 and was one of the few buildings built by Vyner Brooke, the last Rajah.

The **Court House** complex was built in 1871 as the seat of Sarawak's government and was used as such until 1973. It remains one of Kuching's grandest structures. The buildings have belian (ironwood) roofs and beautiful detailing inside and out, reflecting local art forms. The colonial-baroque **clock tower** was added in 1883 and the **Charles Brooke Memorial** in 1924. The complex also includes the **Pavilion Building** which was built in 1907 as a hospital. During the Japanese occupation it was used as an information and propaganda centre and it is now the Education Department headquarters. The **Round Tower** on Jalan Tun Abang Haji Openg (formerly Rock Road) was originally planned as a fort (1886) but was never fully completed. The whole area is undergoing restoration for future art galleries and cultural exhibits. The **Steamship Building** was built in 1930 and was previously the offices and warehouse of the Sarawak Steamship Company. It has been extensively restored and now houses a restaurant, souvenir stalls, a handicrafts gallery and an exhibition area.

The **Bishop's House**, off Jalan McDougall, near the Anglican cathedral, is the oldest surviving residence in Sarawak. It was built in 1849, entirely of wood, for the first Anglican Bishop of Borneo, Dr McDougall. The first mission school was started in the attic – developed into St Thomas's and St Mary's School, which is now across the road on Jalan McDougall.

Kuching's Chinese population, part of the town's community since its foundation, live in the shophouses lining the narrow streets around **Main Bazaar**. This street, opposite the waterfront, is the oldest in the city. The

Sarawak

Chinese families who live here still pursue traditional occupations such as tin smithing and woodworking. Kuching's highest concentration of antique and handicraft shops is to be found here. **Jalan Carpenter**, parallel to Main Bazaar, has a similar selection of small traders and coffee shops, as well as foodstalls and two small Chinese temples. Off **Leboh China** (Upper China Street), there is a row of perfectly preserved 19th century Chinese houses. The oldest Chinese temple in Kuching, **Tua Pek Kong** (also known as Siew San Teng), in the shadow of the *Hilton* on Jalan Tunku Abdul Rahman, was built in 1876, although it is now much modernized. There is evidence that the site has been in use since 1740 and a Chinese temple was certainly here as early as 1770. The first structure was erected by a group of Chinese immigrants thankful for their safe journey across the hazardous South China Sea. New immigrants still come here to give thanks for their safe arrival. The Wang Kang festival to commemorate the dead is also held here.

The **Chinese History Museum** stands on the Waterfront, opposite Tua Pek Kong Temple. The building itself is of interest: it was completed in 1912 and became the court for the Chinese population of Kuching. The Third Rajah was keen that the Chinese, like other ethnic groups, should settle disputes within their community in their own way and he encouraged its establishment. From 1912 until 1921, when the Chinese court was dissolved, all cases pertaining to the Chinese were heard here in front of six judges elected from the local Chinese population. The building itself is a simple cella with a flat roof and shows English colonial influences. In 1993 it was handed over to the Sarawak Museum and was turned into the Chinese History Museum. The museum documents the history of the Chinese in Sarawak, from the early traders of the 10th century to the waves of Chinese immigration in the 19th century. The museum building was constructed in the early 20th century as the Chinese court, officially established in 1911 by Rajah Charles Brooke. ■ *Sat-Thur 0900-1800, T231520.* **Hian Tien Shian Tee** (Hong San) temple, at the junction of Jalan Carpenter and Jalan Wayang, was built in 1897. The **Indian mosque**, on Lebuh India, originally had an atap roof and *kajang* (thatch) walls; in 1876 belian-wood walls were erected. The mosque was built by South Indians and is in the middle of an Indian quarter where spices are sold along the main bazaar. When the mosque was first built only Muslims from South India were permitted to worship here; even Indian Muslims from other areas of the subcontinent were excluded. In time, as Kuching's Muslim population expanded and grew more diversified, so this rigid system was relaxed. It is hard to get to the mosque as it is surrounded by buildings. However a narrow passage leads from Lubuh India.

The Moorish, gilt-domed **Masjid Bandaraya** (old state mosque) is near the market, on the east side of town; it was built in 1968 on the site of an old wooden mosque dating from 1852.

Petra Jaya   The new **State Mosque**, which is currently being extended, is situated across the river at Petra Jaya. Its interior is of Italian marble.

Kuching's architectural heritage did not end with the White Rajahs; the town's modern buildings are often based on local styles. The new administration centre is in Petra Jaya, on the north side of the river. The **Bapak** (father) **Malaysia** building is named after the first Prime Minister of Malaysia and houses government offices; the **Dewan Undangan Negeri**, next door, is based on the Minangkabau style. Kuching's latest building is the ostentatious **Masjid Jamek**. Also in Petra Jaya, like a space launch overlooking the road to Damai Peninsula, is the **Cat Museum** which houses everything you ever wanted to know about cats. ■ *Tue-Sun 0900-1700. Getting there: Petra Jaya Transport No 2B or 2C.*

The **Timber Museum** nearby, on Wisma Sumber Alam (next to the stadium), is meant to look like a log. It was built in the mid-1980s to try to engender a bit more understanding about Sarawak's timber industry (see page 374). The museum, which has many excellent exhibits and displays, toes the official line about forest management and presents facts and figures on the timber trade, along with a detailed history of its development in Sarawak. The exhibition provides an insight into all the different forest types. It has background information on and examples of important commercial tree species, jungle produce as well as many traditional wooden implements. The final touch is an air-conditioned forest and wildlife diorama, complete with leaf-litter; all the trees come from the Rejang River area. While the museum sidesteps the more delicate moral issues involved in the modern logging business, its detractors might do worse than to brush up on some of the less emotive aspects of Sarawak's most important industry. The museum has a research library attached to it. ■ *Mon-Thur 0830-1600, Fri 0830-1130, 1430-1630, Sat 0830-1230, closed Sun.*

On the south side of the river the extraordinary-looking **Civic Centre** on Jalan Taman Budaya, is Kuching's stab at the avant garde. It has a viewing platform for panoramas of Kuching. ■ *0800-0930, 1030-1200, 1400-1530, 1630-1800.* The Civic Centre complex houses an art gallery with temporary exhibits, mainly of Sarawakian art, there is also a restaurant and a pub-cum-karaoke bar one floor down, together with a public library. ■ *Mon-Thur 0915-1730, Sat and Sun 0915-1800.* Malaysia's first planetarium is also within the complex: **Sultan Iskandar Planetarium**. It opened in 1989 and has a 15m dome and a 170-seat auditorium. ■ *Shows at: 1500 Mon-Sun plus 1930 Tue and Thur. On public holidays there are afternoon and evening shows. Admission RM2. Getting there: bus from Lebuh Market, south along Jalan Tun Haji Openg.*

Civic centre & Planetarium

Excursions

Permits for national parks and the orang utan sanctuary are available from the Sarawak Tourist Information Centre on Padang Merdeka, T248088 or the National Parks office in Petra Jaya, Wisma Sumber Alam, T442180.

Semenggoh, 32 km from Kuching, on the road to Serian, became the first forest reserve in Sarawak when the 800 hectares of jungle was set aside by Rajah Vyner Brooke in 1920. It was turned into a wildlife rehabilitation centre for monkeys, orang utans, honey bears and hornbills in 1975. All were either orphaned as a result of logging or were confiscated having been kept illegally as pets. The aim is to reintroduce as many of the animals as possible to their natural habitat. The centre is not set up as a tourist attraction but visitors are most welcome. The feeding platform is a five minute walk from the park office, which is about 1 km walk from the main gates along a tarmac road. Feeding times are 0830-0900 and 1430-1530 Monday-Sunday. The star attraction is the 19-year-old orang utan called Bullet, who earned his name after being shot in the head by hunters. There are a few trails around the park including a plankwalk and a botanical research centre, dedicated to jungle plants with medicinal applications. As an orang utan rehabilitation centre, however, it does not compare with Sepilok in Sabah (see page 460), which is an altogether more sophisticated affair; that said, Semonggoh gets few visitors and is a good place to watch orang utans close up. Visitors need a permit (free) to visit the sanctuary, available from Visitors' Information Centre on Padang Merdeka. **NB** There are plans to transfer the animals at Semenggoh to the Matang Wildlife Centre in the near future; check with the Visitors' Information Centre before making your way out here. ■ *Mon-Sun*

Semenggoh Orang Utan Sanctuary

Sarawak

0800-1615. Getting there: Sarawak Transport Co bus 6 from Ban Hock Wharf, Jawa Street. From there, hitch a lift to the centre which is another 3 km away.

Jong's Crocodile Farm, Mile 18.5 Kuching (29 km from Kuching), Jalan Endap, off the Serian Highway, has several types of crocodile – albino, saltwater, and the freshwater Malayan gharial (*Tomistoma schlegeli*) – all bred for their skins. These are 'harvested' at about 10 years of age and 2 cm² of skin fetches about RM60; younger crocodiles are also killed for their valuable tender belly skin. In the entrance area, there is a ghoulish collection of photographs of people who have been mauled by crocodile and one depicting the contents of a maneater's stomach – not for the faint-hearted. There have been eight fatal attacks from crocodiles in Sarawak since the mid-1970s; thus far none of these has been at Jong's which is a rather squalid affair and does not inspire much confidence as far as security goes. Feeding times every Sunday at 1000. ■ *Daily 0900-1700, RM8 adult, RM2 child. Take bus 3, 3A, 9A, 9B from STC bus station.*

Taman Nor Badia Wildlife & Reptile Park Apart from crocodiles there are also numerous species of birds and animals only found in Borneo at this park: monkeys, leopard-cats, sunbears, bearcats, pheasants, civets, barking deer, sambar deer, turtles, fruit bats, monitor lizards, pythons and hornbills. ■ *Daily 1000-1800, RM5 adults, RM2 children. Getting there: Sarawak Transport Co. bus 3, 3A and 9A and 9B from Ban Hock Wharf, every 15 mins.*

Gunung Penrissen
Altitude: 1,329m
This is the highest peak in the mountain range south of Kuching running along the Kalimantan border. The mountain was visited by naturalist Alfred Wallace in 1855. Just over 100 years later the mountain assumed a strategic role in Malaysia's *konfrontasi* with Indonesia (see page 388) – there is a Malaysian military post on the summit. Gunung Penrissen is accessible from Kampong

Around Kuching

N

0 km 5
0 miles 5

■ Sleeping
1 Camp Permai
2 Holiday Inn Resort Damai Beach
3 Holiday Inn Resort Damai Lagoon
4 Santubong Kuching Resort

Padawan on the road to Serian, to the southeast of Kuching. It is a difficult mountain to climb requiring two long days, but affords views over Kalimantan to the south and Kuching and the South China Sea to the north. Guides – most of whom were former border scouts during *konfrontasi* – can be hired through the headman at Kampung Padawan; prospective climbers are advised to consult the detailed trail-guide in John Briggs' *Mountains of Malaysia*. The book is usually obtainable in the Sarawak museum bookshop.

Gunung Gading National Park was constituted in 1983 and covers 41,1060 hectares either side of Sungai Lundu. There are some marked trails, the shortest of which takes about two hours and leads to a series of waterfalls on the Sungai Lundu. Gunung Gading and Gunung Perigi summit treks take seven to eight hours; it is possible to camp at the summit. The park is made up of a complex of mountains with several dominant peaks including Gunung Gading (906m). The Rafflesia, the largest flower in the world, is found in the park but if you are keen to see one in bloom, it might be worth phoning the park headquarters first, since it has a very short flowering period. ■ *T735714.*

Park essentials Upon arrival in the park, visitors must register at the headquarters, which is small, consisting of an information centre, toilet blocks, and accommodation. Park fees are RM3 for adults, RM1 for children, with additional fees for cameras and videos. There are 2 2-room chalets (**B**), washrooms, toilets, electricity and a *Hostel* (**D**), with 4 beds per room, bookable through the Visitors' Information Centre in Kuching. Gunung Gading National Park is between Lundu and Semantan, with regular bus connections with Kuching (see below).

Bau About 60 km from Kuching is Bau, which used to be a small-scale mining town. Nowadays, it is a market town and administrative centre. There are several caves close by; the **Wind Cave** is a popular picnic spot. The **Fairy Cave**, about 10 km from Bau, is larger and more impressive, with a small Chinese shrine in the main chamber and varied vegetation at the entrance. A torch is essential. ■ *Tour companies organize trips, or take a taxi.*

Lundu & Semantan These villages have beautiful, lonely beaches and there is a collection of deserted islands off Sematan. One of the islands, **Talang Talang**, is a turtle sanctuary and permission to visit it must be obtained from the local district officer. In Lundu are *Lundu Gadung Hotel*, Lot 174 Lundu Town District, T735199, and *Cheng Hat Boarding House*, 1094 Lundu Bazaar, T735018. In the centre of Sematan is *Sematan Hotel* (**C-D**), T731162, with some air conditioning. Sarawak Transport Co bus 2B goes to Lundu via Bau (two hours); from there take a Pandan bus and ask to be dropped off at the park.

Kubah National Park This is a mainly sandstone, siltstone and shale area, 20 km west of Kuching, covering some 2,230 hectares with three mountains: Gunung Serapi, Gunung Selang and Gunung Sendok; there are at least seven waterfalls and bathing pools. Flora include mixed dipterocarp and *kerangas* (heath) forest; the park is also rich in palms (93 species) and wild orchids. Wildlife includes bearded pig, mouse deer and hornbills and numerous species of amphibians and reptiles. Unfortunately for visitors, Kubah's wildlife tends to stay deep in the forest; it is not really a park for 'wildlife encounters'. There are four marked trails, ranging from 30 minutes to three hours, one of which, the Rayu Trail, passes through rainforest that contains a number of bintangor trees (trees which are believed to contain two chemicals which have showed some evidence of being effective against AIDS). Visitors may be able to see some trees which have been tapped for this potential rainforest remedy.

Sarawak

Park essentials Permits can be obtained through the National Parks Booking Office, Kuching; day visitors can pay and register at the park headquarters (T225003) or at the gate of the Matang Wildlife Centre, RM3/RM1. There are 5 huge double storey bunga-lows at the park HQ at RM180 per night with full kitchen facilities, 4 beds (2 rooms), a/c, hot water, TV and verandah. Book through the Visitors' Information Centre in Kuching or through the National Parks Booking Office, T082248088. To get to the park, take the Matang Transport Company bus No 11 or 18 that departs from outside the Saujana Car Park. Travel agents arrange tours to the park.

The **Matang Wildlife Centre** (T225012) is part of the Kubah National Park. It is still in the process of being developed but will eventually house endangered wildlife in spacious enclosures which are purposefully placed in the rainforest. There will also be an Information Centre and education programmes, which will enable visitors to learn more about the conservation of Sarawak's wildlife. There are chalets at RM120 and an eight-room hostel block (**F**). Matang Transport Company bus No 11 or 18 departs from outside the Saujana car park. Travel agents arrange tours to the park.

Tanjung Datu National Park
This is the newest and smallest park in the state of Sarawak, first gazetted in 1994, at the westernmost tip. The land is covered with mixed dipterocarp for-est, rich flora and fauna, and beautiful beaches with crystal clear seas and coral reefs. Facilities for visitors are currently being developed and it may be worth checking with the tourist office in Kuching whether it is open to visitors. Take a bus to Sematan and boat to the park.

Tours

Most tour companies offer city tours as well as trips around Sarawak: to Semenggoh, Bako, Niah, Lambir Hills, Miri, Mulu and Bario. There are also competitively priced packages to longhouses (mostly up the Skrang River – see page 337). It is cheaper and easier to take organized tours to Mulu, but these should be arranged in Miri (see page 363) as they are much more expensive if arranged from Kuching. Other areas are easy enough to get to independently.

Essentials

Sleeping
■ *on map, page 312*
Price codes:
see inside front cover
It is possible to negotiate
over room rates & many
of the hotels seem to
have special deals

There is a good choice of international standard hotels in Kuching. Most of them are along Jln Tunku Abdul Rahman with views of the river and the Astana and Fort Margherita on the opposite bank. The choice at the lower end of the market is limited, except for the *Anglican Guesthouse*; the cheaper hotels and lodging houses are con-centrated around Jln Green Hill, near the Tua Pek Kong temple. Some newer, mid-range accommodation has grown up in the area around Jln Ban Hock.

L-AL *Crowne Plaza Riverside*, Jln Tunku Abdul Rahman, PO Box 2928, T247777, F425858, hickh@po.jaring.my. Five-star, high-rise glitz hotel now owned by *Holiday Inn*, with an adjoining, 5-storey shopping complex complete with bowling alley and cineplex. All 250 have a/c, mini-bar, tea and coffee-making facilities, personal safe, TV, in-house movies, en suite bathroom with marble vanity and good shower, plush car-pets, wood furnishings carved with Sarawak designs. Facilities include pool, fitness centre, squash court, pâtisserie, 3 restaurants including the *Sri Sarawak* on the 18th floor which has panoramic views and serves Malay and international food, regular shuttle (RM10) to sister hotel, *Damai Lagoon*, on the Damai Peninsula. Recom-mended. **L-AL** *Hilton*, Jln Tunku Abdul Rahman, PO Box 2396, T248200, F428984. White modern block commanding superb views of river and town. Lives up to its name in providing quality and exclusive atmosphere. All 322 rooms have a/c, TV, in-room movies, mini-bar, tea and coffee making facilities. Very pleasant pool with swim-up bar, shaded by palms, and separate children's pool and playground, tennis, fitness centre. Four restaurants including good steak house (air-freighted meat from Australia), boutique, hair salon, travel agent. Recommended. **AL-A** *Holiday Inn*, Jln Tunku Abdul Rahman, PO Box 2362, T423111, F426169, www.holidayinn-sarawak. com, hikch@po.jaring.my. The first international hotel to open in Kuching and the only one right on the river front. Popular with families, plenty of organized activities, 305 rooms with a/c, tea and coffee-making facilities, TV with movies and satellite channels, mini-bar, pool, fitness centre, 3 restaurants, souvenir and bookshop.

A *Kingwood Inn*, Jln Padungan, T330888, F332888, kingwd@po.jaring.my. Rooms have TV. Facilities include a pool, coffee house and bar. Late checkout available. Out of town but pleasant. **A** *Merdeka Palace* Jln Tun Abang Haji Openg, T258000, F425400, mpalace@po.jaring.my, www.jaring.my/mpalace. New place with central location. Pool, health-club and business facilities. Rooms have mini-bar, satellite TV and coffee/tea-making facilities. Six bars, restaurants on site. Great value. Recommended.

B *Borneo*, 30 Jln Tabuan, T244122, F254848. Chinese atmosphere in this hotel located about a 10 min walk from the centre of town. Rooms with a/c and bath. Good value restaurant, breakfast included. **B** *Grand Continental*, Lot 42, Section 46, Jln Ban Hock, T230399, F230339. Pool and business centre. **B** *Metropole Inn*, 22-23 Jln Green Hill, PO Box 2202, T412561. A/c, poor quality and expensive. **B** *Rajah Court*, Jln Tun Razak, T484799, F482750, rajcourt@tm.net.my. Budget hotel with good facilities for conferences, slightly out of town but pleasant place with variety of rooms, chalets and apartments, pool, squash court, good atmosphere. **B** *Supreme*, Jln Ban Hock, T255155, F252522. Seventy-four rooms in brand-new block, a/c, en suite bath or shower, mini-bar, TV with in-house videos, with evening entertainment in the form of bands or karaoke. A little run down. **B** *Telang Usan*, Jln Ban Hock (next to *Supreme*), T415588, F425316, tusan@po.jaring. The best of these 2 hotels located in an untidy area of town. A/C, TV, bath, restaurant, in-house travel agent, orang ulu owned and managed hotel, friendly with traditional kenyah décor, karaoke and bar, conference rooms, smart and comfortable, quiet location, excellent value.

C *Fata*, Jln McDougall, T248111, F428987. Clean hotel with a 1970s feel. A/c, restaurant, rooms in the older part of the hotel are cheaper and better value for money. **C** *Goodwood Inn*, 16-17 Jln Green Hill, T244862 F235690. A/c, TV, very similar to the other hotels around it. Little to make it stand out. **C** *Longhouse*, Jln Abell, T419333, F421563. A/c, restaurant, good value but a bit out of town (past the *Holiday Inn*). **C** *Mandarin* , 6 Jln Green Hill, T418269, F410139. The best and cleanest of the groups of hotels located in the Jln Green Hill area. Rooms have a/c, TVs, and are fairly small, but with good bathrooms and reasonably well furnished. **C** *New Furama House*, 4 Jln Green Hill, T413561. A/c, TV, smelly and slightly damp, has bath but no shower. Run down. **C** *Orchid Inn*, 2 Jln Green Hill, T411417, F241635. A/c. Very similar to the *Mandarin*, but a little more run down. **C** *Riverview Inn*, 22-23 Jln Green Hill, T412551 F256302. A/c, TV. Large rooms but quite tatty. Friendly management although more expensive than most of its range.

D *Anglican Guesthouse*, back of St Thomas' Cathedral (path from Jln Carpenter), T414027. Fan, old building set in beautiful gardens on top of the hill, spacious, pleasantly furnished rooms, with basic facilities, far and away the best of the cheaper accommodation in town. Family rooms are big with sitting room and attached bathroom, recent visitors warn, however, of a spate of thefts from the guesthouse, so take precautions. Recommended. **D** *B&B Inn*, Tabuan Rd, T237366, F239189. Although popular, not particularly cheap for what is offered. Helps organize tours. **D** *Kuching*, Lebuh Temple, T413985. Adequate Chinese-run hotel, reasonable rates for rooms with fan and wash-hand basin, shared bathrooms.

Eating
● *on map, page 312*
Price codes:
see inside front cover
Local dishes worth looking out for include Umai – a spicy salad of raw marinated fish with limes & shallots

Kuching, with all its old buildings and godowns along the river, seems made for open-air restaurants and cafés – but good ones are notably absent. However, the town is not short of hawker centres.

Malay Malay food here seems to be less spicy than on the Peninsula. *Rex Café*, Main Bazaar, good mixed rice, rojak and laksa. *National Islamic Café*, Jln Carpenter. *Sri Sarawak*, Riverside Majestic Hotel, gourmet food, good views. *Glutton's Corner*, Lorong Rubber 12, wide selection, closed 1900 and on Sunday. *Home Cook*, Jln Song Thian Cheok, clean and good value, speciality Assam fish. *Suan Chicken Rice*, Jln Tunku Abdul Rahman, next to Sarawak Plaza, steamed or curried chicken. There are a handful of Malay/Indian coffee shops on India Street including *Madinah Café*, *Jubilee* and *Malaysia Restaurant*.

All the major hotels have Chinese restaurants; most open for lunch & dinner, closing in between

Chinese **2** *Hot and Spicy House*, Lot 303, Section 10, Rubber Rd, T250873. Closed Tuesday, Chinese cooking with West Malaysian influence. Speciality is Ipoh-style *yong tau hoo* (vegetables stuffed with beancurd), just outside the city centre. *Lok Thian*, 1st Flr, Bangunan Beesan, Jln Padungan, T331310. Good food, pleasant surroundings and excellent service, booking advisable, especially at the weekends. *Marie Café*, Jln Ban Hock (near *Liwah Hotel*), Chinese food Sarawak-style, open for breakfast and lunch only. *Minsion Canteen*, end of Jln Chan Chin Ann, on right, speciality is *daud special* (thick noodles in herbal soup with chunks of chicken). *Tsui Hua Lau*, Lot 321-324, Jln Ban Hock, T414560. Shanghai-style dishes. **3** *City Tower*, top of Civic Centre, T234396. Wonderful views and gourmet food. **3** *River Palace*, Riverside Majestic Hotel, first-class Chinese restaurant, offers regular food promotions. **3** *Hornbill Corner Café*, 85 Jln Ban Hock. All-you-can-eat steamboat and barbecue, popular. *Red Eastern Café*, Jln Ban Hock, specializes in steamboat **2** *Meisan*, Holiday Inn, Jln Tunku Abdul Rahman, *dim sum*, RM12.50 set lunch; Sunday eat-as-much-as-you-can *dim sum* special (RM13), also Sechuan cuisine. Recommended. *Lan Ya Keng*, Jln Carpenter, opposite old temple, specializes in pepperfish steak. **2** *Beijing Riverbank*, enjoys good location on riverfront, opposite *Riverside Majestic*, in a circular pavilion style building, serves Chinese Muslim food and coffee-shop fare. Recommended. **2** *Min Kong Kee*, 157 Jln Pandungan. A good selection of dishes with authentic Chinese and Malay breakfasts.

Indonesian *Minangkabau Nasi Padang*, 168 Chan Chin Ann Rd, spicy Padang food including such classics as beef rendang, lunch time only.

There are several cheap Indian Muslim restaurants along Lebuh India

Indian *Bismillah*, Leboh Khoo Hun Reang (near Central Police Station), North Indian Muslim food, good tandoori chicken. *Green Vegetarian Restaurant*, 16 Main Bazaar, open all day, good choice of Southern Indian food, vegetarian, non-vegetarian, rajak, murtabak, roti canai etc. *LL Banana Leaf*, 7G Lorong Rubber 1, T239404. Open all day, specializes in Indian banana leaf meals, reasonable prices. *Pots 'n' Buns*, Taman Sri Sarawak Mall, opposite rear store entrance, good roti canai, murtabak, plus usual hawker stall food. *Rahamath Café*, 19 Jln Padungan, good roti canai. **3** *Lyn's Restaurant*, Lot 62, 10G Lg. 4, Jln Nanas, a taxi-ride from the centre but worth the trip – genuine North Indian tandoori cuisine, excellent naan, locals recommend it, closed Sunday evenings. **3** *Serapi*, Holiday Inn, specializes in North Indian tandoori, good vegetable dishes, naan, also serves air-freighted steak and other Western dishes. Recommended.

Japanese **4** *Robata Yaki*, 493G Jln Rambutan, T251021. Although décor is not as fancy as *Kikyo-Tei*, this is highly recommended by locals, take a taxi to get there.

4 *Ten-Ichi*, Bangunan Bee San, Jln Pandungan, T331310. Elegant surroundings. **3** *Kikyo-Tei*, Jln Crookshank, in front of Government Resthouse, also some Chinese and Western dishes, large main room with separate Teppanyaki and Tatami rooms. Recommended by locals. **3** *Minoru*, Lot 493, Section 10, Rubber Rd, T251021. Set lunch and dinner as well as an extensive menu and good service.

Thai 3 *Steamship Restaurant*, Kuching Waterfront, wide selection of Thai-Chinese and Singaporean dishes in former building of the Steamship Company, trendy. **2** *Bangkok Thai Restaurant*, Jln Pending, maybe not up to Bangkok standards, but not bad for Sarawak, pleasant surroundings, good service, advisable to book. Recommended by locals.

Seafood *Benson Seafood*, Lot 122/3, Section 49, Jln Abell, T255262. Full range of Sarawak seafood. *Ah Leong*, Lot 72, Jln Pandungan, near *Kingwood Inn*, good choice of seafood. *KTS Seafood Canteen*, 157, Jln Chan Chin Ann, excellent butter prawns and grilled stingray. *Pending Seafood Centre*, behind Kuching Port, in industrial area, good range of stalls selling fabulous choice of seafood, if you go by taxi, arrange a pick-up time to avoid getting stranded. *See Good*, Jln Bukit Mata Kuching, behind MAS office, extensive range of seafood and friendly owners. Recommended by locals. Strong flavoured sauces and lots of herbs, extensive and exotic menu, unlimited free bananas, closed 4th and 18th of every month. On Kampung Buntal are several seafood restaurants built on stilts over the sea, 25 km north of Kuching, very popular with Kuchingites.

Excellent seafood is to be found in Kuching

International 4-3 *Serapi*, *Holiday Inn*, imported steaks, excellent selection of grills and seafood, North Indian tandoori, elegant surroundings, open lunch and dinner but not between times. **3** *Orchid Garden*, *Holiday Inn*, Jln Tunku Abdul Rahman, good breakfast and evening buffets, international and local cuisine. Recommended. **3** *San Francisco Grill*, 76 Jln Ban Hock, steak house, cosy atmosphere, live piano, largely Chinese clientele which means steak is seasoned with five spices, meat is air-freighted, chips mediocre but nice atmosphere. **2** *Dulit Coffee House*, *Telang Usan Hotel*, Jln Ban Hock, pleasant terrace café, mix of Western and Eastern food, specializes in French oxtail stew and the only genuine chicken kebabs in Kuching. **2** *Hani's Bistro*, Jln Chan Chin Ann (near *Holiday Inn*), reasonably priced café, good mix of Eastern and Western cuisine, generous helpings, tasty haricot oxtail, good background music. Recommended. **2** *Majestic Café*, *Riverside Majestic Hotel* (also accessible from Riverside Shopping Complex), Western and Malay food, good value buffet. **2** *Trumps*, 2nd Flr, Civic Centre, Jln Taman Budaya, Malay dishes more reasonable than Western and Chinese, good view. **3** *Waterfront*, Hilton Hotel, Jln Tunku Abdul Rahman, reasonably priced for the venue, the best pizzas and a family brunch buffet on Sunday which is very popular.

Sarawak

Coffee shops *Fook Hoi*, Jln Padungan, old-fashioned coffee shop, famous for its *sio bee* and *ha kau* (pork dumpling). **1** *Life Café*, 108 Ewe Hai St (near Carpenter St, behind Main Bazaar), T411954. Closed Tuesday, attractive café serving mostly vegetarian food plus a good range of teas and coffees (including Sarawak tea), friendly staff and pleasant atmosphere. *Borneo Deli*, *Borneo Hotel*, Jln Tabuan, selection of coffees, teas, cakes and pastries in a relaxing atmosphere. *Chang Choon Café*, opposite *City Inn* Jln Abell. *Choon Hui Café*, Jln Ban Hock. *Green Hill Corner*, Lebuh Temple; *Tiger Garden*, opposite Rex Cinema, Lebuh Temple. *Wonderful Café*, opposite Miramar Theatre, Jln Palm.

Many good Chinese coffee shops, serving excellent laksa (breakfast) of curried coconut milk soup with noodles, prawns, shredded omelette, chicken, bean sprouts, coriander & a side plate of sambal belacan (chillied prawn paste)

Fast food *McDonalds*, Jln Tunku Abdul Rahman, opposite *Sarawak Plaza*. *Pizza Hut*, Jln Tunku Abdul Rahman, opposite side to *McDonalds*, a little further down. *KFC*, branches in *Sarawak Plaza* and *Riverside Shopping Centre*. *Hertz Chicken*, *Sarawak Plaza*. *Sugar Bun*, in *Riverside Shopping Centre* with other branches throughout town.

Some of the best food centres are located in the suburbs; a taxi is essential

Foodstalls and food centres *Hock Hong Garden*, Jln Ban Hock, opposite *Grand Continental*, finest hawker stall food in Kuching, little English spoken. *Chinese Food Centre*, Jln Carpenter (opposite temple), Chinese foodstalls. *King's Centre*, Jln Simpang Tiga (bus no 11 to get there), large range of foodstalls, busy and not many tourists. *Kubah Ria Hawker stalls*, Jln Tunku Abdul Rahman (on the road out of town towards Damai Beach, next to Satok Suspension Bridge), specialities *sop kambling* (mutton soup). *Petanak Central Market*, Jln Petanak, above Kuching's early morning wet market, light snacks, full seafood selection, good atmosphere, especially early in the morning. *Satok Bridge*, under the suspension bridge, very good barbecued chicken and seafood. *Saujana Food Centre*, 5th floor of the car park near the mosque (take the lift), mostly Malay food but also seafood. *Song Thieng Hai Food Centre*, between Jln Padungan and Jln Ban Hock, every type of noodle available. *Third Mile (Central Park)*, opposite Timberland Medical Centre, difficult to get to, mainly hawker stalls. **2** *Permata Food Centre*, behind Malaysian Airways office, purpose-built alternative to the central market, prices are higher but the choice is better, bird-singing contests (mainly Red-Whiskered Bulbuls and White-Rumped Sharmas) every Sunday morning, excellent range of fresh seafood. Recommended. *Batu Lintang Open-Air Market*, Jln Rock (to the south of town, past the hospital). *Capital Cinema Hawker Centre*, Jln Padungan. *Jln Palm Open-Air Market*. *Lau Ya Keng*, Jln Carpenter, opposite temple, specializes in Chinese dishes. *Rex Cinema Hawker Centre*, Jln Wayang/Jln Temple, squashed down an alleyway, satay. Recommended. *Thompson's Corner*, Jln Palm/Jln Nanas. *Top Spot Food Court*, Jln Bukit Mata Kuching, top floor of a car park, wide range of stalls, popular. *Tower Market*, Lebuh Market.

Bars

Most bars close around 0100-0200

Casablanca Lounge, *Riverside Majestic Hotel*, cocktail lounge and karaoke. *Cat City*, Jln Chan Chin Ann (turn left at *Pizza Hut*), happy hour 2030-2215, followed by live bands (usually Filipino) playing a mixture of Western rock covers and Malay and Chinese ballads, open late. *The Club*, *Riverside Majestic Hotel*, large video screen and private karaoke rooms. *De Tavern*, Taman Sri Sarawak Mall (facing *Hilton* car park), friendly kayan-run corner pub, serves good rice wine, open 1630-0130, happy hour until 2030. *Dulit Terrace and Tuak Bar*, *Telang Usan Hotel*. *The Fisherman's Pub*, 1st Flr, Taman Sri Sarawak Mall, karaoke, friendly staff and a pleasant crowd of regulars. *Hornbill's Corner Café*, Jln Ban Hock, breezy open air pub. *Margerita Lounge*, *Hilton Hotel*, the best cocktails and live music. *Rejang Lobby Lounge*, *Holiday Inn*, small but popular. *Tribes*, downstairs at *Holiday Inn*, ethnic food, tribal décor and a variety of live music, open 1600-0100.

Entertainment

Cinemas *Riverside Cineplex*, Riverside Complex, T427061, check local press for details of programme. *Miramar*, on the corner of Jln Satok and Jln Tun Ahmad Zaidi Adruce (Palm Rd), T411488, highest tech of the cinemas, with a ground floor karaoke lounge, a food court and a rooftop beer garden. *Laserdisc centres*, all around town, where you can watch a scheduled film in a small cinema or rent a private room to see the film of your choice.

Cultural shows *Cultural Village*, Damai Beach, cultural shows, with stylized and expertly choreographed tribal dance routines, 1130 and 1630, Monday-Sunday. **Discos** *Peppers*, *Hilton Hotel* (downstairs), top 40 hits and pool table, very busy on ladies nights (Wednesday and Friday). *Marina Fun Pub and Disco*, Jln Ban Hock, live band until 0200, then a DJ until 0330, crowded at weekends. *Tropical Pub & Bar*, Jln Abell. The place to go for a lively local disco (Malaysian music).

Exhibitions The **Society Atelier** holds regular exhibitions at various venues in the city. Its HQ is an old government house near to the Civic Centre, 10 mins' walk from Main Bazaar. Phone for details of current and forthcoming events, Jln Taman Budaya, T243222.

Karaoke Karaoke lounges abound, with songs in Chinese, English, Iban, Malay, Japanese and Korean. *City Tower*, top of the Civic Centre, good views and well priced drinks. *Palm Super Lounge*, Jln Tun Ahmad Zaidi Adruce (Palm Rd), in Miramar Cinema Building. Some private rooms, smart bar and wide range of songs, good service. *Dai Ichi Karaoke*, Jln Tunku Abdul Rahman (above *Pizza Hut*), for connoisseurs, large choice of songs, friendly and good service.

When it comes to choice, Kuching is the best place in Malaysia to buy tribal handicrafts, textiles and other artifacts, but they are not cheap. In some of Sarawak's smaller coastal and upriver towns, you are more likely to find a better bargain, although the selection is not as good. If buying several items, it is a good idea to find one shop which sells the lot, as good discounts can be negotiated. It is essential to shop around: the best-stocked handicraft and antique shops in and near the big hotels are usually the most expensive. It is possible to bargain everywhere. **NB** It is illegal to export any antiquity without a licence from the curator of the Sarawak Museum. An antiquity is defined as any object made before 1850. Most things sold as antiquities are not: some very convincing weathering and ageing processes are employed.

Shopping

Antiques and curios Most of these shops are scattered along Main Bazaar, with a few in the Padungan area. **Artwork** *Galleri M*, *Hilton* Lobby, paintings from a wide range of Sarawakian artists. **Birds' nests** Mostly exported to China. *Teo Hoe Hin Enterprise* (next to *McDonalds*) is worth visiting to view the delicacies.

Books and maps *Berita Book Centre*, Jln Haji Taha, has a good selection English-language books. *HN Mohd Yahia & Son*, *Holiday Inn*, Jln Tunku Abdul Rahman, and in the basement of the Sarawak Shopping Plaza, sells a 1:500,000 map of Sarawak. It is also possible to get good maps from the State Government offices (2nd Flr) near the end of Jln Simpang Tiga. It is necessary to obtain police clearance for the purchase of more detailed sectional maps. *Times Books*, 1st Flr, Riverside Shopping Complex, Jln Tunku Abdul Rahman, best and biggest bookshop for foreign language books. *Pasara Bookstore*, Jln Haji Taha.

Handicrafts Most handicraft and antique shops are along Main Bazaar, Lebuh Temple and Lebuh Wayang. *Telang Usan Hotel*, some Orang Ulu and Penan crafts, including good modern beadwork and traditional headgear. *Sarakraf*, 14 Main Bazaar, wide range of souvenirs and handicrafts with outlets in major hotels in Kuching, Damai, Sarawak Cultural Village and Miri airport (chain set up by the Sarawak Economic Development Corporation). *Gallerie M*, *Hilton* Lobby, exclusive jewellery, bead necklaces and antiques, best available Iban hornbill carvings. *Bong & Co*, 78 Main Bazaar. *Borneo Art Gallery*, Sarawak Plaza, Jln Tunku Abdul Rahman. *Borneo Arts & Crafts*, 56 Main Bazaar. *The Curio Shoppe* is attached to the Sarawak Museum, prices are high but profits go to charity. There is a Sunday market on Jln Satok, to the southwest of town, with a few handicraft stalls. *Eeze Trading*, Lot 250, Section 49, Ground Flr, Jln Tunku Abdul Rahman. *Karyaneka (handicrafts) Centre* at Cawangan Kuching, Lot 324 Bangunan Bina, Jln Satok. *Loo Pan Arts*, 83 Jln Ban Hock. *Native Arts*, 94 Main Bazaar. *Sarawak Batik Art Shop*, 1 Lebuh Temple. *Sarawak House*, 67 Main Bazaar (more expensive). *Syarikat Pemasarah Karyaneka*, Lot 87, Jln Rubber. *Tan & Sons*, 54 Jln Padungan. *Thian Seng*, 48 Main Bazaar (good for *pua kumbu*); *Art Gallery*, 5 Wayang St, designer T-shirts with Sarawak motifs amongst other crafts. *Fabriko*, Main Bazaar in beautifully restored Chinese shophouse, interesting souvenirs and gallery.

Most shops are closed Sun

Markets The *Vegetable* and *Wet market* are on the riverside on Jln Gambier; further up is the *Ban Hock Wharf market*, now full of cheap imported clothes. The *Sunday Market* on Jln Satok sells jungle produce, fruit and vegetables (there are a few handicraft stalls) and all sorts of intriguing merchandise; it starts on Saturday night and runs through Sunday morning and is well worth visiting. There is a jungle produce market, Pasar Tani, on Friday and Saturday at Kampong Pinang Jawa in Petra Jaya.

Sarawak

Postcards *Adventure Images showroom*, 55 Main Bazaar, good range of both colour and black and white postcards, also sell greetings cards and posters. **Pottery** Rows of pottery stalls along Jln Penrissen, out of town, take a bus (STC 3, 3A, 9A or 9B) or taxi to Ng Hua Seng Pottery bus stop. Antique shops sell this pottery too. **Shopping complexes**: *Sarawak Plaza*, next to the *Holiday Inn*, Jln Tunku Abdul Rahman; *Riverside Shopping Complex*, next to *Riverside Majestic Hotel*, best complex in Kuching, has Parkson Department Store and good supermarket in basement.

Sports **Bowling** Riverside Complex, Jln Tunku Abdul Rahman, 24-lane bowling alley. **Fishing** Offshore from Santubong or deep sea game fishing at Tanjung Datu (near Indonesian border), contact Mr Johnson, Fui Lip Marketing, 15 Ground Flr, Wisma Phoenix, Jln Song Thian Cheok. **Golf** *Damai Golf Course* , Jln Santubong, T846088, F846044. Green fees RM150 weekdays, RM180 weekends. Due to its popularity bookings should be made 3 days in advance, designed by Arnold Palmer, right on the sea, 18 holes, swimming, tennis and squash courts are among the other facilities available here. *Kelab Golf Course*, Petra Jaya, 18 holes, green fee RM84 (weekdays), RM126 (weekends), T440966. *Prison Golf Club*, Jln Penrissen, T613544, 9-hole, green fees RM30. *Sarawak Golf and Country Club*, Petra Jaya, T440966, green fees RM100 weekdays, RM150 weekends. **Hash house harriers** Men only harriers on Tuesday at 1730, ladies harriettes on Weds at 1730, mixed city hash on Sats at 1630. Contact Tom Leng (T010888436) or Jennifer Yap (T411694, F413700). **Jogging** Track at Reservoir Park. **Mountain biking** Good trails from Kamppung Singgai, about 30 mins from Kuching (across the Batu Kawa bridge). Beginners to intermediate – good trail near Kampung Apar. Advanced trail – Batang Ai. *Borneo Adventure* (T245175) on Main Bazaar rent mountain bikes and can arrange specialized tours. Alternatively, hire a bike from Kuching and tour the Malay villages adjacent to the Astana and Fort Margherita. Cross the Sarawak River by sampan (RM1 for you and your bike) and then follow the small road that runs parallel to the river. **Outward bound** *Camp Permai Sarawak*, PO Box 891, Satok Post Office, T321497, F321500. **Spectator sports** Malaysia Cup football matches held in the *Stadium Negeri Sarawak*, Petra Jaya. The *Turf Club* on Serian Rd is the biggest in Borneo (see newspapers for details of meetings). **Swimming** *Kuching Municipal Swimming Pool*, next to Kuching Turf Club, Serian Rd, admission RM1, open mornings only. Another public pool is on Jln Pandungan, just past the Kuching City South Council office complex. **Watersports** Damai Beach.

Tour operators Borneo Adventure, No 55 Main Bazaar, T245175, F422626, bakch@po.jaring.my. Known for its environmentally friendly approach to tourism. Offers tours all over Sarawak. Recommended. *Ibanika Expeditions*, Lot 435, Ground Flr, Jln Ang Cheng Ho, T424022, F424021, ibanika@po.jaring.my. Long established company offering longhouse and more general tours, also offers French and German-speaking guides. *Tropical Adventure*, 1st Flr, 17 Main Bazaar, T413088, F413104. *Saga Travel*, Level 1, Taman Sri Sarawak Mall, Jln Tunku Abdur Rahman, T418705, F426299. *Pan Asia Travel*, 2nd Flr, Unit 217-218, Sarawak Plaza, Jln Tunku Abdul Rahman, T419754, half day excursions from Kuching. *Harrisons Travel*, 28 Jln Green Hill, T240977, F244542. Advice on tours as well as air, bus and boat tickets.

Transport **Local** **Boat**: sampans cross the Sarawak River from next to the Square Tower on Main Bazaar to Fort Margherita and the Astana on the north bank (RM0.30). Small boats and some express boats connect with outlying kampungs on the river. Sampans can also be hired by the hour (RM15-20) for a tour up and down the river. The Waterfront Development Office plan to take boat hire under their control so that tourists will have to purchase coupons from the Waterfront office.

See also Ins & outs, page 310

Sarawak

Bus: there are 2 bus companies around town: Blue and white *Chin Lian Long* buses serve the city and its suburbs. Major bus stops are at Jln Mosque, the Post Office and Gambier St. The green and yellow *Sarawak Transport Company* (STC) buses leave from the end of Lebuh Jawa, next to Ban Hock Wharf and the market. *STC* buses operate on regional routes; bus 12A (RM0.80) goes to the airport, service starts at 0630 and departs every 40 mins until 1915. *Chin Lian Long* blue buses 19 or 17 go to the jetty, the Bintawa Express Wharf, for boats to Sibu (RM0.40).

Car hire: *Pronto Car Rental*, 1st Flr, 98 Jln Padungan, T/F236889, also at Kuching International Airport; *Mayflower Car Rental*, Lot 4.24A, 4th Flr, Bangunan Satok, Jln Satok, T410110, F575233, Kuching International Airport booth, T575233.

Taxi: local taxis congregate at the taxi stand on Jln Market, or outside the big hotels, they do not use meters, so agree a price before setting off. 24-hr radio taxi service T343343/342255. Short distances around town should cost RM5. 'Midnight' surcharge of RM50 2400-0600.

Long distance Air: the airport is 10 km south of Kuching. Regular connections with KL, JB, KK, Bintulu, Miri, Sibu, Penang, Labuan, Mukah, Bandar Seri Begawan, Brunei (RM288). **NB** *MAS* has advance purchase fares and 50% group discounts on certain flights (bookable only in Malaysia). *MAS* offers connections between Kuching and Kuala Lumpur, Johor Baru and Kota Kinabalu, as well as many interior towns in East Malaysia. *Air Asia* has daily flights to Kuala Lumpur's old Subang airport while SAEAGA Airlines fly to Sibu, KK and the Mulu National Park. *Saenga Airlines* flies to Sibu. Green bus *Sarawak Transport Co*, 12A (RM0.90) from Lebuh Jawa or taxi to town (RM16).

   MAS has flights to Bandar Seri Begawan (Brunei), Singapore, Hong Kong, Taipei, Manila, Seoul, Tokyo and Pontianak (Indonesia). *SIA* offers daily connections with Singapore (RM267), *Royal Brunei Airlines* with Bandar Sri Begawan, and *Dragon Air* a twice weekly direct service to Hong Kong.

Bus: there are several different bus companies serving varying destinations. The *Sarawak Transport Company* (T242967) operates green and yellow buses and leave from Lebuh Jawa, next to Ban Hock Wharf. They serve the Kuching area and southwest Sarawak. *Petra Jaya Transport* (T429418) serves Bako, Damai and Santubong. Their buses (yellow with black and red stripes) depart from the open air market near Electra House. *Matang Transport Company's* yellow and orange buses depart from outside the Saujana Car Park and go to Matang and Kubah. Long distance buses depart from the Regional Express Bus Terminal on Jln Penrissen. The most convenient place to buy tickets is at the *Biaramas Express* office on Jln Khoo Hun Yeang (near Electra House), T429418. *Biaramas* also has a 24-hr office at the terminal (T452139). Buses to Sibu, Bintulu and Miri often involve a change of bus in Sarikei.

   International connections: regular express buses go to **Pontianak** in Kalimantan, Indonesia, 10 hrs (depart 0700-1230, RM34.50). It is necessary to have a valid Indonesian visa (see **Embassies & consulates** below). Buses leave from Khoo Hun Yeang St. Booking office: Mile 3.5, Penrissen Rd, T454548/454668 or through Kedai Jam Ban Poh, 130 Jln Padungan or *Borneo Interland Travel*, 63 Main Bazaar. There are now several bus companies, providing a/c, reclining seats, wc. *SJS Executive Bus Co*, leaves from 3½ mile Bus Terminal, Jln Penrissen – daily service to Pontianak, morning departure, 10 hrs (so long as there is no delay at the border). Other companies include *Biaramas* and *Tebakong*. For a more adventurous route, it is possible to take *Sarawak Transport Company* buses 3 or 3A to Serian, 1 hr; *Mara Transport Company* bus from Serian to Tebedu, 1½ hrs, and from Tebedu it is possible to trek across the border to Balai Kerangan in Kalimantan.

See box on page 328 for details of fares & destinations

Sarawak

Bus fares and destinations, Kuching

Destination	Bus No/ Company	Duration	Departure	Fare
Kuching Airport	STC 12A	30 minutes	every 50 minutes 0630-1900	RM0.90-1.00
Bako	Petra Jaya 6	45 minutes	0640-1800	RM2.10
	(minibuses also leave Electra House for Kampung Bako, RM3)			
Bau	STC 2	1 hour	every 40 minutes 0600-1800	RM3 (a/c)
Bintulu	(see Sarikei)			RM52
Buntal	Petra Jaya 2B	35 minutes		RM2
Damai/ Cultural Village		50 minutes	0900 and 1230	RM2.70
	Shuttle bus from Holiday Inn, Riverside Majestic, Borneo Hotel, Santubong Inn, 2 pickups daily, T846411			
Kubah	Matang 11	50 minutes	0600-1640	RM1.65
Lubok Antu	Biaramas	4 hours	departs 1300	RM20 (a/c)
Lundu (for G Gading)	STC 2B	2 hour	0800-1600	RM6.80-7.80
Miri	(see Sarikei)			RM70
Penrissen Bus Terminal	STC		0630-2100	RM0.50
Pontiana (Indonesia)		10 hours	0700-1230	RM34.50
Santubong Village	Petra Jaya 2B	40 minutes	0645-1800	RM2.30
Sarikei Biaramas/ Borneo Express		5-6 hours	0630-2200	RM28
Sematan	STC 2B to Lundu, then connecting Lundu-Sematan bus			
Semenggoh	STC 6		every hour	RM1.50
Serian	STC 3 or 3A	1 hour	every 35 minutes 0630-1750	RM4.60-5
Sibu	(see Sarikei)	7 hours		RM32
Sri Aman	Biaramas, STC	3 hours	0730-1930	RM15(a/c)

NB 1999 prices quoted

Boat: express boats leave from the Marine Base, Jln Pending, 4 km east of town. Blue bus 19 or 17 from Lebuh Jawa; taxi from Lebuh Market. Tickets for the Kuching-**Sibu** express boats can be bought in advance at the *Metropole Inn Hotel*, 196 Jln Padungan or *Borneo Interland Travel*, 63 Main Bazaar. Regular connections with Sibu (involving a change to a river express boat at Sarikei); 4 hrs. There are also cargo boats going to Sibu and Miri 18 hrs: further information from Sarawak Tourist Association.

Directory **Airline offices** *British Airways*, 92 Jln Green Hill, T242367. *Hornbill Skyways*, North Pan Hangar, International Airport, PO Box 1387, T455737, F455736. *MAS*, Lot 215, Jln Song Thian Cheok, T246622, F244563. *Merpati* ticket agent, *Sin Hwa Travel Service*, 8 Lebuh Temple, T246688. *Singapore Airlines*, Jln Tunku Abdul Rahman, T240266, F238487. *Royal Brunei*, 1st Flr, Rugayah Building, Jln Song Thian Cheok, T243344, F244563. *Dragonair*, 1st Flr, Wisma Bukit Mata Kuching, Jln Tunku Abdul Rahman, T233322, F238819. *Saega Airlines*, Level 16, Wisma Ting Pek Khing, 1 Jln Pandungan, T236905, F236922. *Qantas*, 41 Jln P Ramli, T231832.

Banks Money changers in the main shopping complexes usually give a much better rate for cash than the banks – although if changing TCs the rates are much the same. *Standard Chartered*, opposite *Holiday Inn*, Jln Tunku Abdul Rahman. *Hongkong*, 2-4 Jln Tun Haji Openg (Main Bazaar end). *American Express*, 3rd Flr MAS Building, Jln Song Thian Cheok (assistance with Amex traveller's cheques) T252600. *Majid & Sons Money Changer*, 45 Jln India. *Mohamed Yahia & Sons* (money changer), Lower Ground Flr, Sarawak Plaza. *Bank of Commerce* 23 Jln Khoo Hun Yeang.

Sarawak

Communications Area code: 082. **General Post Office:** Jln Tun Haji Openg, open Mon-Sat 0800-1800, Sun 1000-1300. **Internet:** *Cyber City*, Taman Sri Sarawak (opposite the *Hilton*), T419016, , open 1000-2200 (RM10 per hr). *Net@Café* T234008, Lot 352, Lorong 12, Rubber Rd 0900-2100 (RM6 per hr). **Telekom:** (for international telephone calls) Jln Batu Lintang (open 0800-1800 Mon-Fri; 0800-1200 Sat and Sun). International calls can also be made from most public cardphones. Major hotels all have cardphones in their lobbies.

Embassies & consulates *Indonesian Consulate*, 5a Jln Pisang, T241734, RM10 for visa, only if travelling overland. *Getting there*: blue bus 5A or 6 from State Mosque. *Australian Honorary Consul*, T245661. *British Consulate*, Rugayah Building, Jln Song Thian Cheok, T231320. *Canadian Consulate*, 1 Jln Padungan, T233000. *Chinese Consulate*, Lorong 5, Jln Tan Pint Timur, T453344. *French Consul*, c/o *Telong Usan Hotel*, T415588. *New Zealand Consulate*, T482177.

Medical facilities Dentist: Taman Sri Sarawak (behind *De Tavern*). **Hospitals:** *Kuching General Hospital*, Jln Tan Sri Ong Kee Hui, off Jln Tun Haji Openg, T257555. *Normah Medical Centre*, across the river on Jln Tun Datuk Patinggi Hj. Abdul Rahman Yakub, T440055, private hospital with good reputation. *Doctor's Clinic*, Main Bazaar, opposite Chinese History Museum (RM20 for consultation). *Poliklinik*, 11 Jln P Ramlee, T240741. *Timberland Medical Centre*, Rock Rd, T234991. Recommended. **Pharmacies:** *Apex Pharmacy*, 125 1st Flr, Sarawak Plaza, open 1000-2100; *YK Farmasi*, 22 Main Bazaar, open 0830-1700; *UMH*, Ban Hock Rd, open 0900-2030, Sat 0900-1800.

Places of worship Christian churches conduct services in a number of languages. The Muslim Council of Sarawak provides details of Muslim prayer times throughout the state, T429811. **Anglican:** St Thomas' Cathedral, Jln McDougall, T240187 for times of services. **Baptist:** Sarawak Baptist Church, Setampak, Stampin, T413462. **Evangelical services:** Lot 1863 Block 10, 26 Iris Gardens, T425212. **Methodist:** Trinity Methodist Church, 57 Jln Ellis, T411044. **Roman Catholic:** St Joseph's Cathedral, Jln Tun Abang Hj, T423424.

Tourist offices The state and national tourism organizations are both well informed and helpful; they can offer advice on itineraries, travel agents and up-to-date information on facilities in national parks. *National Parks and Wildlife Office*, Wisma Sumber Alam, Jln Stadium, Petra Jaya (T442180, F441377) for information on national parks and advance bookings (note that the office is inconveniently located and it is easier to use the National Park Booking Office in the Sarawak Tourist Information Centre). Visitors' Information Centre, 31 Jln Masjid, Padang Merdeka, T410944, F256301, stb@po.jaring.my (beside the new wing of the Sarawak Museum). It is possible to book national park accommodation and obtain permits for Bako at this office. Historical exhibitions on Sarawak, open 0800-1615 Mon-Thur, 0800-1645 Fri, 0800-1245 Sat and the centre holds 2 shows daily (at 1000 and 1500) on the variety of attractions in the state. *Sarawak Tourism Centre*, waterfront, Main Bazaar, T240620, F427151 or Kuching International Airport, T456266, good for information on bus routes, approved travel agents and itineraries. *Sarawak Tourism Board*, 3.44, Level 3, Wisma Satok, Jln Satok, 93400 Kuching, T423600, F416700, sarawak@po.jaring.my, www.sarawaktourism.com. It is possible to call the STB toll-free from Kuala Lumpur (T8009291) or from Singapore (T8006011043) from 0800-1245, 1400-1615 Mon-Fri and 0800-1245 Sat. *Tourism Malaysia*, Bangunan Rugayah, Jln Song Thian Cheok, T246775, information on Sarawak and rest of Malaysia – good stock of brochures.

Useful addresses Immigration: 1st Flr, Bangunan Sultan Iskandar (Federal Complex) Jln Simpang Tiga, T245661. **Police:** T241222. Office located opposite Padang Merdeka. **Resident's Office:** T243301.

Sarawak

Damai Peninsula

Colour map 3, grid C1

The peninsula, 35 km north of Kuching, is located at the west mouth of the Sarawak River and extends northwards as far as Mount Santubong, a majestic peak of 810m. Its attractions include the Sarawak Cultural Village, trekking up Mount Santubong, sandy beaches, a golf course, adventure camp and three resorts which are particularly good value off season when promotional rates are available. It has been developed over recent years by the Sarawak Economic Development Corporation, partly to create local employment and partly to open up the area to tourism.

Santubong & Buntal

The village of **Santubong** itself, located at the mouth of the Sarawak River, is small and quiet. Formerly a fishing village, most of the villagers now work in one of the nearby resorts. However, some fishing still goes on, and the daily catch is still sold every morning at the quayside. Near the quayside are two or three Chinese-run grocery stores and a simple coffee shop. The rest of the village is made up of small houses strung out along the road, built in the Malay tradition on stilts – many are wooden and painted in bright colours. The only other village on the peninsula is **Buntal** which lies just off the Kuching-Santubong road. Popular with local Kuchingites who come here at the weekends for the seafood restaurants, the resort that was built here never really took off and it is planned to be turned into a hotel training centre.

Sarawak Cultural Village

The Sarawak Cultural Village (Kampong Budaya Sarawak) was the brainchild of the Sarawak Development Corporation which built Sarawak's 'living museum' at a cost of RM9.5m to promote and preserve Sarawak's cultural heritage. With increasing numbers of young tribal people being tempted from their longhouses into the modern sectors of the economy, many of Sarawak's

Sarawak Cultural Village

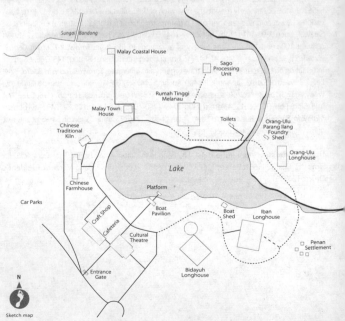

The Penan – museum pieces for the 21st century?

Economic progress has altered many Sarawakians' lifestyles in recent years; the oil and natural gas sector now offers many employment prospects and upriver tribespeople have been drawn into the logging industry (see page 374). But it is logging that has directly threatened the 9,000-strong Penan tribe's traditional way of life. Sarawak's nomadic hunter-gatherers have emerged as 'the noble savages' of the late 20th century, as their blockades of logging roads drew world attention to their plight. In 1990, Britain's Prince Charles' remarks about Malaysia's "collective genocide" against the Penan prompted an angry letter of protest from Prime Minister Dr Mahathir Mohamad. He is particularly irked by Western environmentalists – especially Bruno Manser, who lived with the Penan in the late 1980s. "We don't need any more Europeans who think they have a white man's burden to shoulder," Dr Mahathir said.

Malaysia wants to integrate the Penan into mainstream society, on the grounds that it is morally wrong to condemn them to a life expectancy of 40 years, when the average Malaysian lives to well over 60. "There is nothing romantic about these helpless, half-starved, disease-ridden people," the Prime Minister said. The government has launched resettlement programmes to transform the Penan from hunters into fishermen and farmers. One of these new longhouses can be visited in Mulu (see page 370); it has failed to engender much enthusiasm from the Penan, although 4,000-5,000 Penan have now been resettled. Environmentalists countered that the Penan should be given the choice, but, the government asks, what choice do they have if they have only lived in the jungle?

The Cultural Village, opened by Dr Mahathir in 1990, offered a compromise of sorts – but the Penan had the last laugh. One tribal elder, called Apau Madang, and his grandson were paid to parade in loincloths and make blowpipes at the Penan hut while tourists took their snapshots. The arrangement did not last long as they did not like posing as artefacts in Sarawak's 'living museum'. They soon complained of boredom and within months had wandered back to the jungle where they could at least wear jeans and T-shirts. Today, the Penan hut is staffed by other Orang Ulu. There are thought to be only 400 Penan still following their traditional nomadic way of life.

traditional crafts have begun to die out. The Cultural Village set out to teach the old arts and crafts to new generations. For the state development corporation, the concept had the added appeal of creating a money-spinning 'Instant Sarawak' for the benefit of tourists lacking the time or inclination to head into the jungle. As with any such artificial scheme, it is rather contrived, but the Cultural Village has been a resounding success and contains some superb examples of traditional architecture. It should be on the sightseeing agenda of every visitor to Kuching, if only to provide an introduction to the cultural traditions of all the main ethnic groups in Sarawak.

Each tribal group is represented by craftsmen and women who produce handicrafts and practise traditional skills in houses built to carefully researched design specifications. Many authentic everyday articles have been collected from longhouses all over Sarawak. In one case the Village has served to preserve a culture that is already effectively dead: today the Melanau people all live in Malay-style kampongs, but a magnificent traditional wooden Melanau house has been built at the Cultural Village and is now the only such building in Sarawak. Alongside it there is a demonstration of traditional sago processing. A resident Melanau craftsman makes sickness images (*blum*) – each representing the spirit of an illness, which were floated downriver in tiny boats as part of the healing ritual.

There are also Bidayuh, Iban and Orang Ulu longhouses, depicting the lifestyles of each group. In each there are textile or basket-weavers, wood-carvers or sword-makers. There are exhibits of beadwork, bark clothing, and *tuak* (rice wine) brewing. At the Penan hut there is a demonstration of blowpipe making and visitors are invited to test their hunting skills. There is a Malay house and even a Chinese farmhouse with a pepper garden alongside. The tour of all the houses, seven in all (you can collect a stamp from each one for your passport!) is capped by an Andrew Lloyd Webber-style cultural show which is expertly choreographed, if rather ersatz. It is held in the on-site theatre which is fully air conditioned.

The Cultural Village employs 140 people, including dancers, who earn around RM300 a month and take home the profits from handicraft and tuak sales. Special application must be made to attend heritage centre workshops where courses can be requested in various crafts such as wood-carving, mat-weaving, batik-painting; also intensive day and three to four day courses. There is a restaurant and craft shop, *Sarakraf*. ■ *Mon-Sun 0900-1715, cultural show 1130-1215 and 1630-1715, adult RM45, child (6-12 years) RM22.50, including cultural show, Scv@visitsarawak.com, T846411, F846988.*

Excursions

Gunung Santubong
Altitude: 810m

Situated on the Santubong Peninsula, Gunung Santubong's precipitous southern side provides a moody backdrop to Damai Beach. The distinctive – and very steep – mountain is most accessible from the east side, where there is a clear ridge trail to the top. There are two trails to the summit, one of which begins opposite the *Palm Beach Seafood Restaurant and Resort*, about 2½ km before the *Holiday Inn Damai Beach*. The conical peak – from which there are spectacular views – can be reached in seven to nine hours (the last stretch is a tough scramble), guides are not necessary (but can be provided), check with the hotel recreation counters or at the Santubong Mountain Trek Canteen. ■ *T846153.* The official *Damai Guide* provides a more detailed description of the trek. Take supplies of food and water. There is a bus to Damai Beach or (more regularly) to Santubong.

Pulau Satang Besar

North of Kampung Telaga Air, Pulau Satang Besar has been designated as a Turtle Sanctuary to protect the green turtles which come ashore here to lay their eggs. Inquire at the Visitor Information Centre in Kuching for departures from Santubong or Kampung Telaga Air.

Salak River

Trips up the Salak River depart from the terminal at Santubong village, a 10 minute drive from the resort hotels. River tours last about three hours. The journey ventures into smaller rivers and a creek and it is a good introduction to the mangrove forest ecosystem. Contact hotel recreation counters or tour operators for details.

Malay villages in Damai & Santubong

These can be visited from the resort hotels – on recommended excursions. These include Kampung Santubong, Buntal, Pasir Panjong or Pasir Pandak. You will need your own transport.

Essentials

Sleeping
■ *on map, page 318*
Price codes:
see inside front cover

L-AL *Holiday Inn Resort Damai Lagoon*, Teluk Penyuk, Santubong, PO Box 3159, T846991, F846901. Managed by *A&A Hotels*, it is the sister of the *River Majestic* in Kuching. Superbly located at the foot of Mount Santubong, on a small, well-kept, sandy beach, its 256 rooms and 30 chalets are in stylish buildings with steep, wood-shingled roofs. There are polished wood floors and decorative woodcarving throughout; a monumental, timber-roofed lobby open to the sea, and pleasant gardens dotted with tribal wooden effigies surrounding a lagoon-style pool (the largest in Sarawak) which has a sandy slope for kids at one end and a man-made cave, complete with cascade and stage for shows, at the other. The lagoon also has a circular, swim-up bar, shaded by colonial, wood-shingled roof, all rooms have a/c, TV, in-house movies, mini-bar, tea and coffee-making facilities, balcony and personal safe. Other facilities include restaurant, tea-house (excellent for sunset views), bar, health club (with spa), tennis, boutique, bicycle hire, canoe hire, watersports and children's playground. Sterling competition for the *Holiday Inn* and definitely better in terms of access to beach and general tranquillity. Recommended.

A *Holiday Inn Resort Damai Beach*, Teluk Bandung, Santubong, PO Box 2870, T846200, F846777, hirdb02@po.jaring.my. Taken over from the *Sheraton* in 1987, the resort calls itself the 'Crown Jewel of Sarawak', although the real jewel in the crown is the large, private, wooden mansion at the top of the resort which belongs to the Sultan of Brunei. The new hill-top extension, directly below the Sultan's mansion, has chalets modelled on ethnic designs, such as the circular Bidayuh buildings which make this a better than average *Holiday Inn*. The beach is bigger than that at *Damai Lagoon Resort*, but less accessible if you are staying at the hill-top site. All 302 rooms, including 179 chalets, have a/c, colour TV, in-house movie, coffee and tea-making facilities. Other facilities including 2 pools, tennis, spa pool, watersports, kiddies' club, bicycle/scooter hire, games room, restaurant (good value buffet), PV Fun Pub (a popular night spot for Kuchingites), children's playground and lobby shops.

A-B *Damai Rainforest Resort (Camp Permai)*, Pantai Damai, Santubong, PO Box B91, Satok Post Office, T321498, F321500. Located at the foot of Mount Santubong, near the *Damai Lagoon Resort*, this is an outward bound centre which offers a number of courses including adventure training and leadership development. Other facilities include artificial climbing wall, obstacle course, abseiling, sailing, canoeing, paintball competitions. Sleeping in 10 a/c tree houses or log cabins, cafeteria, tents and camping equipment for hire. **B** *Santubong Kuching Resort*, Jln Santubong, PO Box 2364, T846888, F846666. Surrounded by the *Damai Golf Course*, 380 rooms all with a/c, restaurant, large pool, chalets with jacuzzis, tennis, basketball, volleyball, gym, mountain biking etc. Nestling beneath Mount Santubong, a low-rise resort popular with golfers, it also has the largest conference and banquet facilities in Sarawak. Price includes breakfast.

Eating *Santubong Mountain Trek Canteen*, 5 mins' walk from hotels, rice and noodle dishes, in nearby *Buntal village* there are excellent seafood restaurants.

Bars *PV The Fun Pub* at *Holiday Inn Damai Beach* is Damai's main night spot and very popular – an open air pub with pool and karaoke and live bands.

Entertainment **Cultural shows** *Cultural Village, Damai Beach*, cultural shows, with stylized and expertly choreographed tribal dance routines, 1130 and 1630, Monday-Sunday.

Sports **Golf** *Damai Golf Course*, Jln Santubong, PO Box 400, T846088, F846044, international standard, 18-hole golf course designed by Arnold Palmer, laid out over approximately 6½ km, 10-bay driving range, green fees weekdays (RM150), weekends (RM180). Caddies, clubs and shoes for hire, spacious club house, restaurant, bar, pro shop, tennis, squash, pool.

Transport **Bus** There are shuttle buses from the *Holiday Inn* and *Riverside Majestic* or take the public bus, operated by Petra Jaya Transport (yellow buses with black and red stripes)

Sarawak

at a fraction of the price from the market place at the end of Jln Gambier. Tour companies offer packages for US$60, for transport on shuttle bus, entrance to the Sarawak Cultural Village and lunch. **Taxi** From Kuching costs RM30, from the airport RM46.50.

Bako National Park

Established in 1957, Bako was Sarawak's first national park. It is a very small park (2,742 hectares) but it has an exceptional variety of flora, and contains almost every type of vegetation in Borneo.

Very soon the park will be privatized, which will guarantee its conservation and tourism will be more actively promoted. Bako is situated on the beautiful Muara Tebas peninsula, a former river delta which has been thrust above sea level. Its sandstone cliffs, which are patterned and streaked with iron deposits, have been eroded to produce a dramatic coastline with secluded coves and beaches and rocky headlands. Millions of years of erosion by the sea has resulted in the formation of wave-cut platforms, 'honeycomb' weathering, solution pans, arches and sea stacks. Bako's most distinctive feature is the westernmost headland – Tanjung Sapi – a 100m high sandstone plateau, which is unique in Borneo.

Flora & fauna There are seven separate types of vegetation in Bako. These include mangroves (*bakau* is the most common stilt-rooted mangrove species), swamp forest and heath forest – known as *kerangas*, an Iban word meaning 'land on which rice cannot grow'. Pitcher plants (*Nepenthes ampullaria*) do however grow in profusion on the sandy soil (see page 526). There is also mixed dipterocarp rainforest (the most widespread forest type in Sarawak, characterized by its 30-40m-high canopy), beach forest, and *padang* vegetation, comprised of scrub and bare rock from which there are magnificent views of the coast. The rare *daun payang* (umbrella palm) is found in Bako park; it is a litter-trapping plant as its large fronds catch falling leaves from the trees above and funnel them downwards where they eventually form a thick organic mulch enabling the plant to survive on otherwise infertile soil. There are also wild durian trees in the forest, which can take up to 60 years to bear fruit.

Bako is one of the few areas in Sarawak inhabited by the proboscis monkey (*Nasalis larvatus*), known by Malays as 'Orang Belanda', or Dutchmen, or even 'Pinocchio of the jungle', because of their long noses (see page 522). Bako is home to approximately 150 rare proboscis monkeys. They are most often seen in the early morning or at dusk in the Teluk Assam, Teluk Paku and Teluk Delima areas (at the far west side of the park, closest to the headquarters) or around Teluk Paku, a 45 minute walk from the park headquarters. The park also has resident populations of squirrels, mousedeer, sambar deer, wild pigs, long-tailed macaques, flying lemur, silver leaf monkeys and palm civet cats. Teluk Assam, in the area around the park headquarters is one of the best places for birdwatching: over 150 species have been recorded in the park, including pied and black hornbills. Large numbers of migratory birds come to Bako between September and November. The blue fiddler crab, which has one big claw, and is forever challenging others to a fight, can also be seen in the park and mudskippers, evolutionary throw-backs (half-fish, half-frog), are common in mangrove areas. Also in the park there are two species of otter: the oriental small-clawed otter and the hairy-nosed otter (the best area to see them is at Teluk Assam). The Bornean bearded pig is the largest mammal found at the park and is usually seen snuffling around the park headquarters. There are many lizards, with the water monitor being the largest and often found near the accommodation. The only poisonous snake occasionally seen is the Wagler's pit viper. Nocturnal animals include flying lemur, pangolin, mouse-deer, bats, tarsier, slow loris and palm civet (the beach by the park headquarters is a great place for a night time stroll).

Treks There are a good range of well marked trails throughout the park – over 30 km in total; all paths are colour coded, corresponding with the map available from park headquarters. The shortest trek is the steep climb to the top of Tanjong Sapi, overlooking Teluk Assam, which affords good views of Gunung Santubong, on the opposite peninsula, across Tanjong Sipang, to the west. Some trails are temporarily closed – check with park headquarters. Full day treks and overnight camping expeditions can be arranged. There are plank walkways with shelters at intervals to provide quiet watching spots particularly required for viewing the proboscis monkey in the early morning.

Beaches The best swimming beach is at Teluk Pandan Kecil, about 1½ hours' walk, northeast from the park headquarters. It is also possible to swim at Teluk Assam and Teluk Paku. Enquire about jellyfish at the park headquarters before swimming in the sea; it is advisable not to swim in March and April.

Park essentials **Transport** It is possible to hire boats around the park: speed boats RM85 (can accommodate 5-6).

Permits These are available from the National Parks Booking Office, Sarawak Tourist Information Centre on Padang Merdeka, T248088, F256301. Daytrippers can pick up a day permit at the Bako boat jetty in Kampung Bako. On arrival visitors are required to register at the park headquarters.

Sarawak

Bako National Park trails

1 Tanjung Sapi	7 Lintang	14 Telok Sibur
2 Telok Paku	8 Tajor	15 Telok Limau
3 Ulu Assam	9 Tanjung Rhu	16 Telok Keruing
4 Telok Delima	10 Bukit Keruing	17 Pulau Lakei
5 Serait	11 Paya Jelutong	18 Wildlife Observation Post
6 Telok Pandan Besar &	12 Bukit Gondol	
Telok Pandan Kecil	13 Ulu Serait	

N

0 km   1
0 miles   1

Information Centre This is next to park HQ, with a small exhibition on geology, flora and fauna within the park. Visitors can request to see an introductory video to Bako National Park, duration 42 minutes. Open 0800-1245 (0800-1100 on Friday) 1400-1615 Monday-Sunday.

Entrance to Park RM3 per adult, RM1 per child or student. Photography permit RM5, video camera RM10, professional camera RM200.

Sleeping All bookings to be made at the National Parks and Wildlife Booking Office, c/o Visitors' Information Centre, Lot 31, Jln Masjid, Kuching, T248088, F256301. The hostels are equipped with mattresses, kerosene stoves and cutlery. Resthouses have refrigerators and electricity until 2400. Unless a researcher, the recommended length of stay is 2 days/1 night. Resthouses and the hostel have fans, *Lodge*, RM40 per room. *Hostel* RM40 per room, RM10 per bed, check-out time 1200.

Camping For those not intending to trek to the other side of the park, it is not worth camping as monkeys steal anything left lying around and macaques can be aggressive. In addition, the smallest amount of rain turns the campsite into a swimming pool. It is however necessary to camp if you go to the beaches on the Northeast peninsula. Tents can be hired for RM8 (sleeps 4); campsite RM4.

Eating The canteen is open 0700-2100. It serves local food at reasonable prices and sells tinned foods and drinks. No need to take food, there is a shop available and a good seafood restaurant near the jetty.

Transport
37 km to Kuching

Bus and boat Petra Jaya (yellow/red/black stripes) bus 6 or bus company *Chin Lian Long*, *Regas Transport* or *Sarawak Transport* every 15 mins from Electra House on Lebuh Market to Kampong Bako, 45 mins (RM3.50) every hr; also minibuses from Lebuh Market. From Kampong Bako, charter a private boat to Sungai Assam (30 mins) which is a short walk from park HQ, RM30 per boat each way – ask price before boarding (up to 6 people). **NB** In the monsoon season, between Nov and Feb, the sea can be rough. Local tour operators also organize trips and boats to the park are operated by villagers who live nearby.

Bandar Sri Aman

Colour map 3, grid C2 *Previously called Simmanggang, Bandar Sri Aman lies on the Batang Lupar and is the administrative capital of the Second Division. The river is famous for its tidal bore and divides into several tributaries: the Skrang River is one of these (see below). The Batang Lupar provided Somerset Maugham with the inspiration for his short story Yellow Streak in Borneo Tales. It was one of the few stories he wrote from personal experience: he nearly drowned after being caught by the bore in 1929.*

Fort Alice is the only building of note and was constructed in 1864. It has small turrets, a central courtyard, a medieval-looking drawbridge, and is surrounded by a fence of iron spikes. Rajah Charles Brooke lived in the Batang Lupar district for about 10 years, using this fort – and another downriver at Lingga – as bases for his punitive expeditions against pirates and Ibans in the interior. The fort is the only one of its type in Sarawak and was built commanding this stretch of the Batang Lupar River as protection against Iban raids. The original fort here was built in 1849 and named Fort James; the current fort was constructed using much of the original materal. It was renamed Alice in honour of Ranee Margaret Brooke (it was her second name). It is said that every evening at 2000 until the practice was ended in 1964 a policeman would call from the fort (in Iban): "Oh ha! Oh ha! The time is now 2000. The steps have been drawn up. The door is closed. People from upriver, people from downriver are not allowed to come to the fort anymore." (It probably sounded better in Iban.)

Most tourists do not stop in Bandar but pass through on day trips up the Skrang River from Kuching. The route to Bandar goes through pepper plantations and many 'new' villages. During Communist guerrilla activity in the 1960s (see page 388), whole settlements were uprooted in this area and placed in guarded camps.

Excursions

The Skrang River, the second longest river in Sarawak, was one of the first areas settled by Iban immigrants in the 16th-18th centuries. The slash-and-burn agriculturalists originally came from the Kapual River basin in Kalimantan. They later joined forces with Malay chiefs in the coastal areas and terrorized the Borneo coasts; the first Europeans to encounter these pirates called them 'Sea Dayaks' (see page 392). They took many heads. Blackened skulls – which local headmen say date back to those days – hang in some of the Skrang longhouses. In 1849, more than 800 Iban pirates from the Batang Lupar and Skrang River were massacred by Rajah James Brooke's forces in the notorious Battle of Beting Marau. Four years later the Sultan of Brunei agreed to cede these troublesome districts to Brooke; they became the Second Division of Sarawak.

Skrang longhouses

There are many traditional Iban longhouses along the Skrang River, although those closer to Pias and Lamanak (the embarkation points on the Skrang) tend to be very touristy – they are visited by tour groups almost every day. Long Mujang, the first Iban longhouse, is an hour upriver. Pias and Lamanak are within five hours' drive of Kuching. Jungle trekking is available (approximately two hours), RM20. The guide provides an educational tour of the flora and fauna.

Sleeping All longhouses along the Skrang River are controlled by the Ministry of Tourism so all rates are the same – RM40 inclusive of all meals. Resthouses at most of the longhouses can accommodate 20-40 people, mattresses and mosquito nets are provided in a communal sleeping area with few partitions, basic conditions, with flush toilet, shower, local food (visitors are sometimes allowed to sleep on the

Interior of a Sea Dyak Longhouse, from William T Hornaday's (1885) Two years in the jungle: the experience of a hunter and naturalist in India, Ceylon, The Malay Peninsula and Borneo

Sarawak

communal area), phone available and clinic nearby. If the stay is three days/two nights, on the second night it is possible to camp in the jungle and then get a return boatride to the longhouse.

Transport Bus 14 and 19 to Pias and bus 9 to Lemanak. Self-drive car rental (return) or minibus (8-10 people, return) from Kuching to Entaban. From these points it is necessary to charter a boat to reach the nearest longhouses. Many of the Kuching-based tour agencies offer cut-price deals for 1-2 day excursions to Skrang. Unless you are already part of a small group, these tours work out cheaper because of the boat costs.

Batang Ai The Batang Ai River, a tributary of the Batang Lupar, has been dammed to form Sarawak's first hydro-electric plant which came into service in 1985; it provides 60 percent of Sarawak's electricity supply, transmitting as far as Limbang. The area was slowly flooded over a period of six months to give animals and wildlife a chance to escape, but it has affected no less than 29 longhouses, 10 of which are now completely submerged. The re-housing of the longhouse community has been the topic of controversial debate over the last 10 years. The communities were moved into modern longhouses and given work opportunities in local palmeries. However, it now seems that the housing loans that were initially given are not commensurate with local wages and will be very difficult for the longhouse communities ever to pay off. In addition, the modern longhouses were not provided with farmland, so many local people have returned to settle on the banks of the reservoir. Near the dam there is a freshwater fish nursery. These fish are exported to Korea, Japan and Europe. Those families displaced by the flooding of the dam largely work here and many of the longhouses surrounding the dam depend upon this fishery for their own fish supply.

The Batang Ai dam has created a vast and very picturesque manmade lake which covers an area of some 90 km², stretching up the Engkari and Ai rivers. Beyond the lake, more than an hour's boat ride upriver from the dam, it is possible to see beautiful lowland mixed dipterocarp forest. The **Batang Ai National Park** covers an area of over 24,040 hectares and was inaugurated in 1991. It protects the much endangered orang utan, and is home to a wide variety of other wildlife, including hornbills and gibbons. As yet there are no visitor facilities, but four walking trails have been created, one of which takes in an ancient burial ground. Trips to one of the 29 longhouses surrounding the dam and to Batang Ai National Park are organized by *Borneo Adventure Travel Company* who are based in Kuching (55 Main Bazaar, T410569, F422626) and have a counter in the *Hilton Batang Ai Longhouse Resort*. Many of the restaurant staff in the resort are locals and discreet enquiries may get you a trip to a longhouse and/or Batang Ai National Park for considerably less than the *Borneo Adventure Travel Company* charge. The park is 250 km from Kuching and takes two hours from the jetty by boat.

Sleeping A *Hilton International Batang Ai Longhouse Resort*, c/o *Kuching Hilton International*, T248200, F428984. On the eastern shore of the lake, the *Hilton* have built a luxury longhouse resort. Opened in 1995, the resort is made up of 11 longhouses, built of the local belian (ironwood) to traditional designs. Unfortunately this means that despite its lakeside location there are no views, except from the walkways, as longhouses are built, for purposes of defence, to face landwards – in this case over the buggy track. However, compromises to modern comforts have been made with the result that the rooms are somewhat cluttered with furniture and TV sets. One hundred rooms all with a/c, fan, TV, shower room, tea and coffee-making facilities, mini-bar, other facilities include a pool and paddling pool, restaurant, 18 km jogging track,

Visiting longhouses: house rules

There are more than 1,500 longhouses in Sarawak, and as the state's varied tribal culture is one of its biggest attractions, trips to longhouses are on most visitors' itineraries. Longhouses are usually situated along the big rivers and their tributaries, notably the Skrang (the most easily accessible to Kuching, see page 337), the Rejang (see page 347) and the Baram (see page 365). The Iban, who are characteristically extrovert and hospitable to visitors, live on the lower reaches of the rivers. The Orang Ulu tribes – mainly Kayan and Kenyah – live further upriver, and are generally less outgoing than the Iban. The Bidayuh (formerly known as the Land Dayaks) live mainly around Bau and Serian, near Kuching. Their longhouses are usually more modern than those of the Iban and Orang Ulu, and are less often visited for that reason. The Kelabit people live in the remote plateau country near the Kalimantan border around Bareo (see page 379).

The most important ground rule is not to visit a longhouse without an invitation. People who arrive unannounced may get an embarrassingly frosty reception. Tour companies offer the only exception to this rule, as most have tribal connections. Upriver, particularly at Kapit, on the Rejang (see page 347), such 'invitations' are not hard to come by; it is good to ensure that your host actually comes from the longhouse he is inviting you to. The best time to visit Iban longhouses is during the gawai harvest festival at the beginning of June, when communities throw an open house and everyone is invited to join the drinking, storytelling and dancing sessions, which continue for several days.

On arrival, visitors should pay an immediate courtesy call on the headman (known as the tuai rumah in Iban longhouses). It is normal to bring him gifts; those staying overnight should offer the headman between M$10 and M$20/head. The money is kept in a central fund and saved for use by the whole community during festivals. Small gifts such as beer, coffee, tea, biscuits, whisky, batik and food (especially rice or chicken) go down well. It is best to arrive at a longhouse during late afternoon after people have returned from the fields. Visitors who have time to stay the night generally have a much more enjoyable experience than those who pay fleeting visits. They can share the evening meal and have time to talk and drink. Visitors should note the following:

On entering a longhouse, take off your shoes.

It is usual to accept food and drink with both hands. If you do not want to eat or drink, the accepted custom is to touch the brim of the glass or the plate and then touch your lips as a symbolic gesture; sit cross-legged when eating.

When washing in the river, women should wear a sarong and men, shorts.

Ask permission to take photographs. It is not uncommon to be asked for a small fee.

Do not enter a longhouse during pantang (taboo), a period of misfortune – usually following a death. There is normally a white (leaf) flag hanging near the longhouse as a warning to visitors. During this period (normally one week) there is no singing, dancing or music, and no jewellery is worn.

Bow your head when walking past people older than you. It is rude to stride confidently past with head held high.

Try not to shout or be loud and noisy.

Trips upriver are not cheap. If you go beyond the limits of the express boats, it is necessary to charter a longboat. Petrol costs M$2-4/litre, depending on how far upriver you are. Guides charge M$40-80 a day and sometimes it is necessary to hire a boatman or front-man as well. Prices increase in the dry season when boats have to be lifted over shallow rapids. Permits are required for most upriver areas; these can be obtained at the resident's or district office in the nearest town.

Sarawak

shuttle from *Kuching Hilton International*, tour desk. If the *Hilton* is not your style (or your pocket cannot stretch to it), there is, unfortunately, not much else. The park does not supply any rooms. However, there are some private tour companies which provide accommodation in the longhouses here, in a much more central location within the park than the *Hilton* (which is not very close to the longhouses).

Bukit Saban Resort This is located on the rarely visited Paku River, just north of the Skrang and Lemnak rivers, about 4½ hours from Kuching. Sales office T232351, F245551. Fifty rooms in longhouse style with traditional sago palm thatch, RM92, restaurant, air conditioning, TV, hot water, seminar facilities.

Essentials

Sleeping & eating
There is only a limited selection of hotels

B-C *Alison*, 4 Jln Council, T322578/9. **B-C** *Hoover*, Tiong Hua Building, 139 Jln Club, T321985-8. **B-C** *Taiwan*, 1 Jln Council, T322493. A/c. **C** *Sum Sun*, 62 Jln Club, T322191, a/c.

1 *Alison Café & Restaurant*, 4 Jln Council, Chinese cuisine. *Chuan Hong*, 1 Jln Council, Chinese coffee shop, also serves Muslim food. *Melody*, 432 Jln Hospital, Chinese and Muslim food.

Transport 135 km to Kuching. **Bus** Regular connections with Kuching (RM12) and Sibu (via Sarikei).

Directory **Useful addresses** Resident's Office: T322004.

The Rejang River and Sibu

The Batang Rejang is an important thoroughfare and Malaysia's longest river at 563 km (it is, however, 12 times shorter than the Nile). Tours to upriver longhouses can be organized from Sibu, or more cheaply from Kapit and Belaga. The second largest town in Sarawak, Sibu is sited at the confluence of the Rejang and the Igan rivers 60 km upstream from the sea. It is the starting point for trips up the Rejang to the towns of Kapit and Belaga.

Population: 150,000
Phone code: 084
Colour map 3, grid B3

Thanks to the discovery of the Kuala Paloh channel in 1961, Sibu is accessible to boats with a sizeable draft. Sibu is a busy Chinese trading town – the majority of the population came originally from China's Foochow Province – and is the main port on the Batang Rejang (also spelt 'Rajang'). In 1899, Rajah Charles Brooke agreed with Wong Nai Siong, a Chinese scholar from Fukien, to allow settlers to Sibu. Brooke had reportedly been impressed with the industriousness of the Chinese: he saw the women toiling in the paddy fields from dawn to dusk and commented to an aide: "If the women work like that, what on earth must the men be like?"

The Kuching administration provided these early agricultural pioneers with temporary housing on arrival, a steamer between Sibu and Kuching, rice rations for the first year and tuition in Malay and Iban. The town grew quickly (its rapid early expansion is documented in a photographic exhibition in the Civic Centre), but was razed to the ground in 'the great fire' of 1828. The first shophouses to be constructed after the fire are the three-storey ones still standing on Jalan Channel. In the first few years of the 20th century, Sibu became the springboard for Foochow migration to the rest of Sarawak. Today it is an industrial and trading centre for timber, pepper and rubber. It is home to some of Sarawak's wealthiest families – nearly all of them timber towkays.

The Rajahs' fortresses – war and peace in the Rejang

The lower reaches of the Batang Rejang are inhabited by the Iban and the upper reaches by the Kenyah and Kayan tribes, the traditional enemies of the Iban (for details on tribes, see page 390). During the days of the White Rajahs, a number of forts were built along the river in an effort to keep the peace and prevent head-hunting (see page 346). All the forts in Sarawak had chambers where confiscated heads were stored, each with a tag detailing the name of the tribe which took it and the name of the victim. Head-hunting proved a difficult practice to stamp out. In 1904, when Vyner Brooke was based at Kapit Fort as Resident of the Third Division (before he succeeded Charles as Rajah) he reported an attack on one longhouse in which head-hunters severed the heads of 80 women and children while their men were working in the fields. Tribal head-hunting raids were regular occurrences until 1924, when wild boars were exchanged between the Iban and Orang Ulu tribes at a peace-making ceremony in Kapit, presided over by the Rajah. (There are photographs of this ceremony in the Kapit Museum.)

The river fortresses were also used as bases for punitive raids against tribal rebels in the interior. One of the first stops on the route upriver from Sibu is Kanowit,

where Charles Brooke built Fort Emma. In 1859 the Rejang Resident and the fort commander were murdered there by local tribespeople. Charles Brooke swore to bathe his hands in the blood of the murderers. With 15,000 'friendly' Ibans, he went upriver in 1862, and led his expedition past the Pelagus Rapids and Belaga to the Kayan and Kenyah strongholds. Brooke then led the Ibans into a lengthy pitched battle in which hundreds died that finally broke the power of the Orang Ulu.

While the Brookes successfully forged alliances with the Rejang's Ibans, some individual groups rebelled from time to time. In her book My Life in Sarawak, *Ranee Margaret (Charles Brooke's wife) relates the story of one Iban chief's dawn attack on the Rajah's fort at Sibu. Inside were several other 'friendly' Dayak chiefs. "The manner in which the friendly Dyak chiefs behaved during the skirmish amused me very much," she wrote, "for they did nothing but peer through the lattice-work, and shout Dyak insults at the attacking party, most of whom they knew very well. They made unpleasant remarks about the enemy's mothers, and inquired whether the men themselves belonged to the female sex, as their efforts were so feeble."*

Sights

The old trading port has now been graced with a pagoda, a couple of big hotels and a smart **esplanade**, completed in 1987. The 1929 shophouses along the river are virtually all that remains of the old town. The seven-storey **pagoda**, adjacent to Tua Pek Kong Temple, cost RM1.5m to build; there are good views over the town from the top. In the **Sibu Civic Centre**, 2½ km out of town on Jalan Tun Abang Haji Openg, there is an exhibition of old photographs of Sibu and a mediocre tribal display. This serves as Sibu's municipal museum. Five aerial photographs of the town, taken every five years or so between 1947 and 1987, chart the town's explosive growth. ■ *1500-2000 Tue-Sat, 0900-1200, 1400-2000 Sun.*

Most companies run city tours plus tours of longhouses, Mulu National Park and Niah Caves. It is cheaper to organize upriver trips from Kapit or Belaga (see below) than from Sibu. **Tours**

Essentials

Sleeping
■ *on map*
Price codes:
see inside front cover

Hotels are scattered all over Sibu; cheaper ones tend to be around the nightmarket in Chinatown. A couple of the top hotels are good, but those at the lower end of the market are very mediocre.

A *Kingwood*, 12 Lorong Lanang 4, PO Box 1201, T335888, F334559. Largest hotel in Sibu with 168 rooms, more expensive ones have views of Rejang River. All rooms with a/c, TV, mini-bar, *Riverfront Cage*, Chinese Restaurant, pool, health centre. **A** *Premier*, Jln Kampung Nyabor, T323222, F323399. Restaurant, clean rooms with a/c, TV, own bath, bar. Some rooms with river view, clean. Helpful staff, adjoins the *Sarawak House Shopping Centre*, discounts often available. Recommended. **A** *Tanahmas*, Jln Kampung Nyabor, T333188, F333288. A/c, restaurant, run to a very high standard, very well-appointed modern hotel with swimming pool and conference facilities. Recommended.

B *Bahagia*, 11 Jln Central, T320303. A/c, restaurant, reasonable value for money. **B** *Capitol 88*, 19 Jln Wong Nai Siong, T336444, F311706. A/c, restaurant, rooms are clean and reasonable value. **B** *Garden*, 1 Jln Hua Ping, T317888, F330999. A/c, restaurant, well-kept and efficiently run. **B** *LiHua* Long Bridge Commercial Centre, T324000, F326272. Slightly out of town, but located along the river. TV, a/c, restaurant, coffee house and roof-top swimming pool. Good value.

Sibu

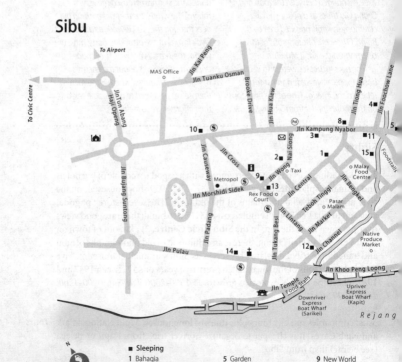

■ Sleeping

1 Bahagia	5 Garden	9 New World
2 Capitol 88	6 Kingwood	10 Phoenix
3 Centre Point Inn	7 LiHua	11 Premier & Sarawak
4 Emas	8 Mandarin	House Shopping Centre

Sarawak

C *Centre Point Inn*, Jing Hwa Building, off Jln Central, T320222, F320496. A/c, often offers sizeable discounts. **C** *Phoenix*, 1 & 3 Jln Kai Peng (off Jln Kampung Nyabor), T313877, F320392. TV, a/c. A very well run hotel with spacious rooms and decent bathrooms. **C** *Sarawak*, 34 Cross Rd, T333455, F320536. A/c, attached bathroom, TV. Centrally located and a well furnished place, good value. **C** *Sentosa Inn*, 12 Jln Pulau, T349875, F311706. A/c, TV, simple but good value. **C** *Wen Ya*, 1st Flr, 39 High St (Teboh Tinggi), T321288/321290. Big rooms, one of the better in this price bracket, with clean rooms. Good option.

D *Mandarin*, 183 Jln Kampung Nyabor, T339177, F333425. A/c, popular with travellers, great value. **D** *New World*, 1 Jln Wong Nai Siong, T310311. A/c, clean rooms with attached bathrooms. **D** *Ria* 21 Jln Channel, T326622. A/c, reasonable value. **D** *Emas*, 3A Foochow Lane, T310877, F320848. Some a/c, clean. **D** *Rejang*, 40 Jln Blacksmith (opposite *Standard Chartered Bank*), T315590. Some a/c, some rooms have attached bathrooms.

Malay 2 *Sheraton*, Delta Estate (out of town), Malay (and some Chinese), fish head curries recommended by locals. **1** *Metropol*, 1st Flr, 20 Jln Morshidi Sidek, also serves Melanau curries.

Eating
Price codes: see inside front cover

Chinese 3 *Jhong Kuo*, 13 Jln Wong Nai Siong, Foochow. **2** *Blue Splendour*, 1st Flr, 60-62 Jln Kampung Nyabor (opposite *Premier Hotel*), recommended by locals. **2** *Golden Palace*, *Tanahmas Hotel*, Jln Kampung Nyabor, Cantonese and Schezuan. **2** *Hock Chu Leu*, 28 Jln Blacksmith, Foochow dishes only.

Sarawak

To Sunday Market

Jln Pedada

Sibu Superbowl

Jln Bukit Assek

✝ Catholic
■ Church

Jln Mission

Jln Lanang

Jln Tan Sri

Lorong Lanang 4

🚌

Jln Maju   ■7

■6

Rejang Esplanade

River

12 Ria
13 Sarawak
14 Sentosa Inn
15 Tanahmas

International *Peppers Café*, *Tanahmas Hotel*, Jln Kampung Nyabor, Western and local food, curries particularly recommended, popular. *Villa by the Grand*, Grand Meridien Building, 2nd Flr, 131 Jln Kampung Nyabor, run by a group of Canadian graduates. *McDonalds*, Sarawak House Shopping Complex, Jln Kampung Nyabor.

Foodstalls There is a hawker centre on Jln Market, in the centre of town. *Rex Food Court*, 28 Jln Cross, is new and clean, one correspondent recommends it, saying it serves an excellent selection of foods.

Handicrafts Stalls along express boat wharves at Jln Channel, mainly selling basketware. One shop on Jln Central for a variety of handicrafts. **Markets** Pasar Malam, along High St, Jln Market and Lembangan Lane (Chinatown). Native market (Lembangan market), on Lembangan River between Jln Mission and Jln Channel, sells jungle produce. **Pottery** Two potteries at Km 7 and 12 Ulu Oya Rd. **Supermarket** Sarawak House Shopping Complex, Jln Kg Nyabor, has Premier Department Store.

Shopping

Sarawak's river express boats – smoke on the water

Sarawak's Ekspres boats, powered by turbo-charged V-12 engines, are the closest most upriver tribespeople come to experiencing supersonic flight. They look like floating aircraft fuselages, are piloted from a cockpit and have aircraft-style cabins below, complete with reclining seats and head rests. Journeying downriver, these sleek Chinese-run bullet-boats reach speeds of 70 km/hour, and in their wake, longhouse landing rafts are left rocking in metre-high swell. On straighter stretches of river, pilots like to race each other, while the 'front-man', perched on the bows, keeps a lookout for semi-submerged logs – or 'floaters' – which regularly damage propellers. Incapsulated in the air-conditioned cabins, passengers (everyone from Chinese businessmen to tattooed Orang Ulu) are oblivious to the hazards. Most of them remain gripped, throughout the trip, by the deafening kung-fu films continuously screened on video.

Express boats are used on most of the major rivers in Sarawak; ocean-going versions also ply the coastal waters. They have reduced travelling time dramatically: when Ranee Margaret Brooke made the most exciting trip of her life, from Kapit to Belaga and back in the 1880s, the journey upriver took six days. Today it can be done in five hours. But navigating the coffee-coloured waters of the Rejang and Baram rivers is a dangerous occupation. Free-floating logs pose an ever-present threat. Log rafts, huge chevrons of timber, up to 500m long, which are towed downstream by tugs, swing wide on meanders, leaving narrow gaps for the express boats. But a pilot can only claim to have cut his teeth once he has shot the Rejang's famous Pelagus Rapids, 45 minutes upriver from Kapit.

Over this 2½ km-long stretch of white water, he has to contend with logs, rocks, whirlpools and cataracts while keeping a look-out for express boats from the opposite direction. When Ranee Margaret Brooke shot these rapids over a century ago, she wrote: "As I stood looking at the whirlpool, Hovering Hawk [her Iban steersman], who was standing near me, pointed with his thumb to the swirling water, all flecked with foam. 'See there,' he said, 'who knows how many eyes lie buried beneath that foam!'" More eyes have been buried beneath the foam in recent years with the loss of 10 lives in June 1991 when an express boat capsized.

But accidents happen even without the rapids. In 1990, two express boats collided head-on in early morning fog just downriver from Kapit. One boat rolled and sank within seconds. Older boats have just one emergency exit, at the back, which is said to be impossible to open underwater as it opens outwards; windows are sealed. Newer boats have more exits, fitted under a more rigid safety code introduced in 1990. On the older boats it is possible to ride the gauntlet on the roof-top (tourists are strongly advised to take adequate precautions against sunburn). Other points to bear in mind when contemplating travel by express boat: first, given the number of express boat trips made daily, the actual accident rate is low; and second, flying from Kapit to Belaga is only marginally more expensive.

Sports   **Golf** *Sibu Golf Club*, Km 17 Ulu Oya Rd, green fees RM15. **Bowling** *Sibu Superbowl*, 2 Lorong Perpati (off Jln Wong King Huo), T331111, F318980. Open Monday-Saturday 1000-0000, Sunday 0900-0000.

Tour operators   Hornbill, 1, 1st Flr, Jln Bengkel, T321005, F318987. *Equatorial Tour & Travel Centre*, 11 Raminway, T331599, F330250. *Golden Horse Travel*, 20B-21B Sarawak House Complex, T323288, F310600. *Hornbill Holiday*, No 1, 1st Flr, Jln Bengkel, Lorong 1, T321005, F318987. *Hunda Holiday Tours*, 11 Tingkat Bawah, Lorong 1, Brooke Drive, T326869, F310396. *Kiew Kwong Travel*, 175B Jln Kampung Nyabor, T315994, F318236. *Metropolitan Travel*, 72-4 Jln Pasar, T322251, F310831; ylwong8@tm.net.my. *R H Tours & Travel*,

32 Blacksmith Rd, T316767, F316185. *Sazhong Trading & Travel*, 4 Jln Central, T336017, F338031, very efficient and courteous. Recommended. *Sibu Golden Tours*, 15 1st Flr, Jln Workshop, T316861, F318680. *Sitt Travel*, 146 Ground Flr, Jln Kampung Nyabor, T320168. *Travel Consortium*, 14 Jln Central, T334455, F330589. *WTK Travel*, Ground Flr, Bangunan Hung Ann, T319393, F319933.

Air The airport is 25 km north of town, bus 1 or taxi. Regular connections with **Transport** Kuching, Bintulu, Miri, Marudi, Kapit and Belaga. There are also some connections with Kota Kinabalu. Sibu airport information centre, T307072.

Bus These leave from Jln Khoo Peng Loong. Regular connections with **Bintulu**, 3 hrs   *The express bus station* (RM16.50) and **Miri** (RM34) along a surfaced road. Best to purchase tickets the day   *is a 10 min drive* before departure. The early morning buses to Bintulu connect with the buses direct to   *out of town* Batu Niah (see Bintulu). There are also connections with **Kapit** and **Kuching** via Sarikei (2 hrs to Sarikei, 5-6 hrs Sarikei to Kuching, RM32).

Boat These leave from the wharf in front of the pagoda. Ticket agents Sibu-Kuching: Ekspress Bahagia 20 Jln Tukang Besi and *Capitol Hotel 88*; 1 Bank Rd and 14 Jln Khoo Peng Loong. There are 3 express boats a day between Sibu and Kuching. These boats stop off at Sarekei. It is necessary to change to an ocean-going boat at Sarekei for Sibu. Boats to Kapit leave from the Kapit wharf, a little further upriver. Regular express boats to Kapit 2-3 hrs and in the wet season, when the river is high enough, they continue to Belaga, 5-6 hrs. If travelling from Sibu through Kapit to Belaga, take one of the early morning boats (the first leaves at 0545), as they connect all the way through. The last Sibu-Kapit boat departs at around 1300. In the dry season passengers must change on to smaller launches to get up-river to Belaga (see below). The Sibu-Kapit boats also stop off at Kanowit and Song on their journey up-river.

Airline offices *MAS*, 61 Jln Tunku Osman, T326166. *Singapore Airlines*, T332203.   **Directory** **Banks** *Standard Chartered*, Jln Cross. Hong Kong 17 Jln Wong Nai Siong Hock Hua, Jln Pulau. **Communications** Area code: 084. General Post Office: Jln Kampung Nyabor. **Tourist offices** *Visitors' Information Centre*, Ground Flr, 32 Cross Rd, T340980, F341280, stbsibu@tm.net.my. **Useful addresses** Police: Jln Kampung Nyabor, T322222. **Resident's Office:** T321963.

Kapit

Kapit is the 'capital' of Sarawak's Seventh Division, through which flows the   *Population: 70,000* Batang Rejang and its main tributaries, the Batang Balleh, Batang Katibas,   *Phone code: 084* Batang Balui and Sungai Belaga. In a treaty with the Sultan of Brunei, Rajah   *Colour map 3, grid C4* James Brooke acquired the Rejang Basin for Sarawak in 1853. Kapit is the last 'big' town on the Rejang and styles itself as the gateway to 'the heart of Borneo' – after Redmond O'Hanlon's book (*Into the Heart of Borneo*) which describes his adventure up the Batang Balleh in the 1980s. Kapit is full of people who claim to be characters in this book. Like O'Hanlon and his journalist compan-ion James Fenton, most visitors coming to Belaga venture into the interior to explore the upper Rejang and its tributaries, where there are many Iban and Orang Ulu longhouses.

There are only 20 km of metalled road in and around Kapit, but the little town has a disproportionate number of cars. It is a trading centre for the tribespeople upriver and has grown enormously in recent years with the expansion of the logging industry upstream (see page 374). Logs come in two varieties – 'floaters' and 'sinkers'. Floaters are pulled downstream by tugs in

Sarawak

huge chevron formations. Sinkers – like belian (ironwood) – are transported in the Chinese-owned dry bulk carriers which line up along the wharves at Kapit. When the river is high these timber ships are able to go upstream, past the Pelagus Rapids. The Batang Rejang at Kapit is normally 500m wide and in the dry season, the riverbank slopes steeply down to the water. When it floods, however, the water level rises more than 10m, as is testified by the high water marks on Fort Sylvia. The highest recorded level was in 1983 when the water reached halfway up the fort's walls.

Sights

Fort Sylvia was built of belian (ironwood) by Rajah Charles Brooke in 1880, and is now occupied by government offices – it is near the wharves. It was originally called Kapit Fort but was renamed in 1925 after Rajah Vyner Brooke's wife. Most of the forts built during this time were designed to prevent the Orang Ulu going downriver; Fort Sylvia was built to stop the belligerent Iban head-hunters from attacking Kenyah and Kayan settlements upstream.

The other main sight is the **Kapit Museum**, recently enlarged and moved to Fort Sylvia. It exhibits on Rejang tribes and the local economy. It was set up by the Sarawak Museum in Kuching and includes a section of an Iban longhouse and several Iban artifacts including a wooden hornbill (see page 525). The Orang Ulu section has a reconstruction of a longhouse and mural, painted by local tribespeople. An Orang Ulu *salong* (burial hut), totem pole and other wood-carvings are also on display. The museum also has representative exhibits from the small Malay community and the Chinese. Hokkien traders settled at Kapit and Belaga and traded salt, sugar and ceramics for pepper, rotan and rubber; they were followed by Foochow traders. Appropriately, the Chinese exhibit is a shop. There are also displays on the natural history of the upper Rejang and modern industries such as mining, logging and tourism. All exhibits are labelled in English. The museum's energetic and erudite curator, Wilfred Billy Panyau, is very knowledgeable on the area. ■ *0900-1200, 1400-1600 Mon-Fri, 0900-1200 Sat and Sun. The museum often seems closed during opening hours and it may be necessary to actively search for the curator to open it.*

Kapit has a particularly colourful daily **market** in the centre of town. Tribeswomen bring in fruit, vegetables and animals to sell; it is quite normal to see everything from turtles, frogs, birds and catfish to monkeys, wild boar and even pangolin and pythons.

Excursions

Pelagus Rapids These are 45 minutes upstream from Kapit on the Batang Rejang. The 2½ km long series of cataracts and whirlpools are the result of a sudden drop in the riverbed, caused by a geological fault-line. Express boats can make it up the Pelagus to Belaga in the wet season (September-April), but the rapids are still regarded with some trepidation by the pilots (see page 344). When the water is low (May-August), the rapids can only be negotiated by the smallest longboats. There are seven rapids in total, each with local names such as 'The Python', 'The Knife' and one, more ominously, called 'The Grave'.

Sleeping A *Pelagus Resort*, set on the banks of the Rejang overlooking the rapids, T/F084796050, T082238033, F238050. Forty longhouse style rooms, with restaurant, pool, bar and sun-deck, deluxe rooms have a/c, otherwise there are fans. Trips organized from resort to longhouses, nature treks and river safaris, white water rafting on the rapids. Regular express boats pass through the rapids upstream.

The longhouse – prime-site apartments with river view

Most longhouses are built on stilts, high on the riverbank, on prime real estate. They are 'prestigious properties' with 'lots of character', and with their 'commanding views of the river', they are the condominiums of the jungle. They are long-rise rather than high-rise however, and the average longhouse has 20-25 'doors' (although there can be as many as 60). Each represents one family. The word long in a settlement's name – as in Long Liput or Long Terawan – means 'confluence' (the equivalent of kuala in Malay), and does not refer to the length of the longhouse.

Behind each of the doors – which even today, are rarely locked – is a bilik, or apartment, which includes the family living room and a loft, where paddy and tools are stored. In Kenyah and Kayan longhouses, paddy (which can be stored for years until it is milled) is kept in elaborate barns, built on

stilts away from the longhouse, in case of fire. In traditional longhouses, the living rooms are simple atap roofed, bamboo-floored rooms; in modern longhouses – which are designed on exactly the same principles – the living rooms are commonly furnished with sofas, lino floors, a television and an en suite bathroom. At the front of the bilik is the dapur, where the cooking takes place. All biliks face out onto the ruai, or gallery, which is the focus of communal life, and is where visitors are usually entertained. The width of the wall which faces onto the ruai indicates the status of that family. Attached to the ruai there is usually a tanju – an open verandah, running the full length of the house – where rice and other agricultural products are dried. Long ladders – notched hardwood trunks – lead up to the tanju; these can get very slippery and do not always come with handrails.

Some longhouses are accessible by road and several others are within an hour's longboat ride from town. In Kapit you are likely to be invited to visit one of these. Some hotels will help organize trips, or inquire at the Police Station. There are guides in Kapit who charge too much for very unsatisfactory tours. Visitors are strongly advised not to visit a longhouse without an invitation, ideally from someone who lives in it. As a general rule, the further from town a longhouse is, the more likely it is to conform with the image of what a traditional longhouse should be like. That said, there are some beautiful traditional longhouses nearby, mainly Iban. One of the most accessible, for example, is **Rumah Seligi**, about 30 minutes' drive from Kapit. Cars or vans can be hired by the half-day; RM10.

Longhouses around Kapit
Those planning to visit longhouses should refer to the guidelines on visiting them, see page 339

Sarawak

Only a handful of longhouses are more than 500m from the riverbanks of the Rejang and its tributaries. Most longhouses still practise shifting cultivation (see page 390); rice is the main crop but under government aid programmes many are now growing cash crops such as cocoa. **NB** Longhouses are also referred to as *Uma* (Sumah) and the name of the headman, ie Long Segaham is known locally as Uma Lasah, Lasah being the chief.

Longhouse tours To go upriver beyond Kapit it is necessary to get a permit (no charge) from the offices in the State Government Complex. The permit is valid for travel up the Rejang as far as Belaga and for an unspecified distance up the Balleh. **NB** On our last visit, Belaga was temporarily closed. For upriver trips beyond Belaga another permit must be obtained there; however, these trips tend to be expensive and dangerous.

The vast majority of the population, about 72 percent, in Sarawak's Seventh Division is Iban. They inhabit the Rejang up to, and a little beyond, Kapit as well as the lower reaches of the Balleh and its tributaries. The Iban people are traditionally the most hospitable to visitors, but as a result, their longhouses are the most frequently visited by tourists. Malays and Chinese account for five percent and three percent of the population respectively. The Orang Ulu live further upriver; the main tribes are the Kayan and the Kenyah (12 percent) and a long list of sub-groups such as the Kejaman, Beketan, Sekapan, Lahanan, Seping, and Tanjong. In addition there are the nomadic and semi-nomadic Penan, Punan and Ukit. Many tribal people are employed in the logging industry, and with their paid jobs, have brought the trappings of modernity to even the remotest longhouses.

Longhouses between Kapit and Belaga are accessible by the normal passenger boats but these boats only go as far as Sungai Bena on the Balleh River (2½ hours). To go further upriver it is necessary to take a tour or organize your own guides and boatmen. The sort of trip taken by Redmond O'Hanlon and James Fenton (as described in O'Hanlon's book *Into the Heart of Borneo*) would cost more than RM1,500 a head. Longhouse tours along the Rejang and Balleh rivers can be organized by the following: *Ark Hill Inn*, Lot 451, Shop Lot 10, Jalan Airport, T794168, F796337, manager David Tan (who is very helpful) can organize upriver trips and tours of longhouses around Kapit. If contacted in advance, they can arrange full itinerary from Kuching or Sibu; *Dinnel Nuing*, PBDS office, Kapit, T796494; *Rejang Hotel*, 28 New Bazaar, T796709. Recommended. *Tan Seng Hi*, Jln Tan Sit Leong. The *Resident's office* also has some official tourist guides on its books. **Warning** Readers have alerted us to Donald Ak Ding and his associate Ajim Anyie of *Hornbill Adventures* – they are said not to speak Kayan or Kenyah, they overcharge for petrol and may disappear at any moment!

Exterior of a Sea Dyak Longhouse, *from William T Hornaday's (1885)* Two years in the jungle: the experience of a hunter and naturalist in India, Ceylon, The Malay Peninsula and Borneo

Rumah Tuan Lepong Balleh Only enter this longhouse with the local policeman called Selvat Anu who lives there; ask for him at Kapit Police Station. During the day Selvat and some members of the longhouse can take visitors on various adventure tours: river trips, visiting longhouses, jungle treks, fishing, pig-hunting, camping in the jungle, trips up to logging areas, swimming in rivers, mountain trekking. Selvat is very knowledgeable and has good relations with the longhouse communities. Visitors can eat with the family and occasionally have the chance to experience a traditional Iban ceremony. You can stay in his longhouse, RM20-25, inclusive of meals, generator until 2300, basic. It is about one hour's drive from Kapit; take a minibus and ask for 'Selvat and Friends Traditional Hostel and Longhouse'.

Essentials

B *Greenland Inn*, 463 Jln Teo Chow Beng, T796388, F797989. A/c, well maintained small hotel with good rooms. Recommended. Although it charges an inflated rate for what is offered, it is comfortably the smartest hotel in town. **B-C** *New Rejang Hotel*, clean rooms in a modern mid-range hotel. Rooms with a/c, bathroom with fantastic showers, desk and satellite TV. **C** *Meligai*, 334 Jln Airport, T796817/796611. Full range of accommodation from VIP suite to dingy standard rooms, has some of the accoutrements of a city hotel but the rooms are generally poor. Also home to a cheap restaurant and the Meligai pub. **C** *Orchard Inn*, 64 Jln Airport, T796325. A/c, restaurant, clean rooms and helpful staff, although communication with some of the Chinese management can be problematic. Deluxe rooms with a/c, TV, bath to economy rooms (cheapest rooms have no window).

D *Ark Hill Inn*, 451 Jln Airport, T796168, F796337. A/c, bathroom, friendly, clean rooms. It is also situated on the river and there are great views from some of the rooms. Recommended. **D** *Dragon Inn*, Lot 467, Jln Teo Chow Beng, T796105. Central, near Express wharves, clean and well kept. **D** *Dung Fang Hotel*, 116 Jln Temenggong. T797779. A/c, own bathroom, fully carpeted. Great value. **D** *Hiap Chong*, 33 Jln Temenggong Jugah, T796314. Some a/c, no attached bath, top floor best bet. **D** *Rejang*, 28 New Bazaar, T796709. Some a/c, basic but clean - if you can afford the

Sleeping
■ *on map*
Price codes:
see inside front cover
All hotels are within
walking distance of
the wharves

Sarawak

Kapit

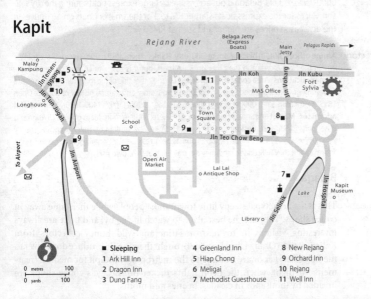

■ Sleeping	4 Greenland Inn	8 New Rejang
1 Ark Hill Inn	5 Hiap Chong	9 Orchard Inn
2 Dragon Inn	6 Meligai	10 Rejang
3 Dung Fang	7 Methodist Guesthouse	11 Well Inn

extra cash its new sister hotel is a better option. **D** *Well Inn*, 40 Jln Court, T796009. A/c, variable rooms but ask to look at the range. **E** *Methodist Guesthouse*. Sometimes budget rooms available here.

Eating

Price codes: see inside front cover Kapit's cuisine is predominantly Chinese

Malay *MI*, Jln Pedral, Malay Muslim food.

Chinese 1 *Hua Hua*, Jln Airport/Jln Court, Chinese food. **1** *Lily Pond*, in the middle of the lily pond, off Jln Hospital, pleasant setting, plenty of mosquitoes and an unimaginative menu. **1** *S'ng Ee Ho Restaurant*, next to Metox supermarket, happy to cook anything you ask for. *Jade Garden*, Jln Pedral, local and Chinese food, smart. *99*, Jln Pedral, fresh air, clean local and Chinese food. *Seafood Restaurant*, Jln Pedral.

International 3 *Orchard Inn*, 64 Jln Airport, T796325. The most upmarket restaurant in Kapit, food well presented but the coffee shops taste just as good, disco from 2200-0100.

Fast food 1 *Frosty Boy*, Jln Teo Chow Beng (below *Greenland Inn*), fast food: pizzas, burgers, ice cream. *American Fried Chicken*, Jln Pedral.

Bakeries and breakfast 1 *Ung Tong Bakery*, opposite the market, bakery and café, good continental style breakfasts – big selection of rolls and good coffee, fresh bread baked twice daily (0600 and 1100). Recommended. *Chuong Hin*, opposite the Sibu wharf, best stocked coffee shop in town. *Sugar Bun*, near Main Square.

Foodstalls Stalls at the top end of the road opposite the market (dead-end road; brightly painted on the outside). Good satay stall on Jln Hospital, next to the lily pond.

Shopping

Handicrafts *Lai Lai Antique shop*, next road along on the right from the *Putena Jaya* (see below), small selection of woven rugs/sarongs, prices are high but they are similar to the starting prices at the longhouses. *Din Chu Café*, next to *Methodist Resthouse*, sells antiques and handicrafts.

Transport

160 km to Sibu

Air The airport is 4 km south of town. There is a weekly connection with **Sibu** and **Belaga** leaving on a Sunday morning. Book in advance. Low cloud at Kapit often prevents landing and the plane goes straight to Belaga.

Boat All 3 wharves are close together. Regular connections with **Sibu** from 0600-1530, 2-3 hrs. **Belaga** is not accessible by large express boats during the dry season. Prices for the express boats start at RM15. For the smaller boats going upriver in the dry season prices are higher and start at RM60.

Directory

Airline offices *MAS* in block opposite Sibu jetty. **Banks** There are 2 banks which will accept TCs, one in the New Bazaar and the other on Jln Airport, but it is easier to change money in Sibu. **Communications** Area code: 084. **Libraries** On the other side of the road from first floor State Government Complex. Good selection of books on history and natural history of Borneo. Open 1615-2030 Mon-Sat, 0900-1115, 1400-1630 Sat, 0900-1100, 1400-1830 Sun. **Useful addresses** Maps: Land Survey Department, Jln Beletik on Jln Airport. Maps of Kapit Division and other parts of Sarawak. **Resident's Office:** 1st Flr State Government Complex (opposite the lily pond), T796963. Permits for upriver trips. Tourists going to Baleh or Upper Rejang areas must sign a form saying they fully understand they are travelling at their own risk.

Belaga

Phone code: 084
Colour map 3, grid B5

This is the archetypal sleepy little town; most people while their time away in coffee shops. They are the best place to watch life go by, and there are always interesting visitors in town, from itinerant wild honey-collectors from Kalimantan to Orang Ulu who have brought their jungle produce downriver to the Belaga bazaar or are heading to the metropolis of Kapit for medical treatment. At night, when the neon lights flicker on, Belaga's coffee shops are invaded by thousands of cicadas, beetles and moths.

A few Chinese traders set up shop in Belaga in the early 1900s, and traded with the tribespeople upriver, supplying essentials such as kerosene, cooking oil and shotgun cartridges. The Orang Ulu brought their beadwork and mats as well as jungle produce such as beeswax, ebony, gutta-percha (rubbery tree gum) and, most prized of all, bezoar stones. These are gall-stones found in certain monkeys (the *wah-wahs*, *jelu-merahs* and *jelu-jankits*) and porcupines. To the Chinese, they have much the same properties as rhinoceros horn (mainly aphrodisiacal) and even today, they are exported from Sarawak to Singapore where they fetch S$300 per kg.

Belaga serves as a small government administration centre for the remoter parts of the Seventh Division. There is a very pretty **Malay kampung** (Kampung Bharu) along the esplanade downriver from the Belaga Bazaar. The Kejaman burial pole on display outside the Sarawak Museum in Kuching was brought from the Belaga area in 1902.

To go upriver beyond Belaga it is necessary to obtain a permit from the Resident's office and permission from the police station. When the river is high, express boats go upstream as far as **Rumah Belor** on the Batang Balui, but for the purpose of visiting longhouses in the Belaga area, it is best to hire a boat in Belaga. Many of the longhouses around Belaga are quite modern, although several of the Kenyah and Kayan settlements have beautifully carved wooden tombstones, or *salongs*, nearby. All the longhouses beyond Belaga are Orang Ulu. Even longhouses which, on the map, appear very remote (such as Long

Excursions

Sarawak

Upper Rejang

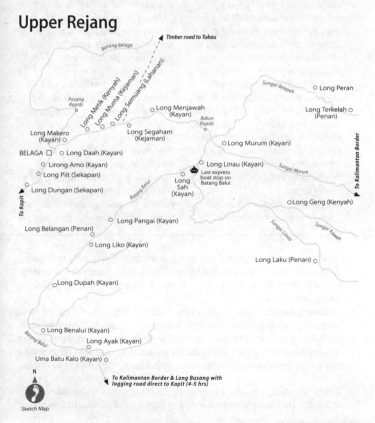

The Bakun hydroelectric project: dam time bomb

The Malaysian Prime Minister, Dr Mahathir Mohamad, is not known as someone prone to changing his mind. But in January 1993 he made a US$6bn U-turn by giving the green light to Southeast Asia's biggest infrastructure project. The Bakun Dam, upriver from Belaga on the Upper Rejang and 400 km east of Kuching, will flood a tract of virgin rainforest that supports 43 species of endangered mammals and birds. It will also displace around 8,000 tribespeople living in at least 14 longhouses. These displaced tribespeople will, largely, become plantation workers. Just three years previously the Prime Minister announced that the project had been scrapped for environmental reasons.

It's not clear why Mahathir changed his mind, but the contract was awarded – without tender – to the swashbuckling Sarawakian entrepreneur Ting Pek Khiing and his company Ekran. He had made a name for himself with the PM through a series of instant-resort developments in Sarawak and Langkawi. His company, which is widely believed to be backed by Malaysia's powerful former finance minister Daim Zainnudin, has no experience in managing projects the size of Bakun. The dam is going to be twice the height of the Aswan Dam in Egypt and will flood an area of 69,000 hectares – bigger than Singapore. Mahathir has described it as "a project whose time has come". Environmentalists say it will be an ecological time bomb in the heart of Borneo.

It is hoped that Bakun will generate 2,400 MW of electricity by the early 21st century. Most of the power will be exported to Peninsular Malaysia to feed its industries, first by 670 km of overhead cables and then by 650 km of cables under the South China Sea. Experts say subaqua transmission on this scale has never before been attempted anywhere. The project will require the construction of roads through dense jungle to bring building materials and engineering equipment to the remote site, above the Bakun Rapids (see map, page 351). Malaysian lobby groups such as the Environmental Protection Society predict that the project will cause severe soil erosion in an area already suffering from the effects of logging. Ten years ago the riverwater was clear and fish abundant; now the river is a muddy brown and water levels fluctuate wildly. Nor is the project a long-term one: even the government admits its productive life is likely to be in the region of 25 years before it silts up.

Two of Ekran's main shareholders are the sons of Sarawak's Chief Minister, Abdul Taib Mahmud, who is widely believed to own a third of the state's timber concessions through nominees and political allies. Another leading shareholder is James Wong, Sarawak's environment minister who doubles as a big timber concessionnaire in Limbang (the district adjacent to Mulu). In May 1994 a group of longhouse dwellers from the Long Murum area were prevented from delivering a petition opposing the Bakun project to the Sarawak state parliament. They allege that members of the government-appointed committee on

Busang), are now connected by logging roads from Kapit, only four hours' drive away. To get well off the beaten track, into Penan country, it is possible to organize treks from Belaga towards the Kalimantan border, staying in longhouses *en route*.

Pasang Rapids About 2 km up the Batang Belaga from Belaga are these spectacular rapids, which are certainly the biggest in Sarawak. It appears that no one has purposely tried to shoot them as they are too dangerous. Boats can get reasonably close, however, and in the dry season, it is possible to climb up to a picnic area, overlooking the white water. To get there, hire a boat from Belaga.

Tours The *Belaga Hotel* will contact guides for upriver trips and the District Office can also recommend a handful of experienced guides. In this part of

Bakun do not defend their interests because, like Wong and Taib's sons, they are the very people responsible for selling tribal land they don't own to loggers.

Over recent years, 17 technical studies – including environmental impact analyses – have been carried out on Bakun. Most, though, have not been released to the public. In 1995 one study carried out by a team from Sarawak University concluded that severe environmental effects were unavoidable. Friends of the Earth Malaysia says: "This project is going to have a tremendous effect on the lives of natives, plants and animals and bio-diversity of the pristine forests where it is going to be built". The local tribespeople, whose ancestors battled for decades against the White Rajahs, have, it seems, finally met their match, in Malaysia's relentless thrust towards modernity.

At the beginning of 1995 the Environment Ministry approved the first stage of the project – allowing logging of the forest to be flooded to begin. But notwithstanding the powerful economic and political forces backing the Bakun project, new delays and difficulties crop up just as soon as old ones are ironed out. In mid-1997 a conflict between the main contractor, the Swiss-Swedish firm ABB, and Ekran, the Malayasian firm which manages the project, emerged. ABB insisted that all subcontract work be put out to competitive tender; while Ting Pek Khiing, who dominates Ekran, had earlier stated that his firms would get the lion's share of the work.

While these conflicts held progress on the dam up, it seemed that there was little to stop this Mahathir-backed project from going ahead. But the dam's supporters had not counted on the Asian economic crisis to mess up their plans. In late 1997 Prime Minister Mahathir, desperate to save money as his country sunk into recession, announced that plans for the dam would be 'shelved'. On the same day, Ekran announced that it was terminating its contract with ABB. Environmentalists hope that the breathing space offered by the economic crisis will allow ministers to reconsider the economic benefits and environmental costs of the project and decide to keep it on the shelf without losing face. But projects like these have their own momentum. In 1998 3,000 local people were relocated from the dam site, and in 1999 another 10,000 were due to have been moved. Reports are that the dam will go ahead but on a scaled-down basis.

For web links see:

www.irn.org/index.html - Homepage of the International Rivers Network, with a Bakun related page and map.

vcn.bc.ca/spc/bakun.html - Sarawak's peoples' campaign. Activist site fighting for the rights of tribal peoples and the forest against the Malaysian government and commercial interests.

www.edf.org/programs/International/D ams/AsiaOceania/a_Bakun.html - home page of Environmental Defense, another global site with a Bakun entry.

www.forest.gov.my/ - for the Sarawak Forestry Department's (rose tinted) view of it all.

Sarawak

Sarawak, guides are particularly expensive – sometimes up to RM80 a day, mainly because there are not enough tourists to justify full-time work. It is necessary to hire experienced boatmen too, because of the numerous rapids. The best guide for longer trips (to jungle areas northeast of Belaga and to Penan areas along the Kalimantan border) is Ronald Bete. Such trips require at least five or six days. Prices for trips to longhouses upriver vary according to distance and the water level, but are similar to those in Kapit. As a rough guideline, a litre of petrol costs about RM10-15; a 40 hp boat uses nearly 20 litres to go 10 km. English is not widely spoken upriver, basic *Bahasa* comes in handy. (See page 44.)

The massacre at Long Nawang

The Japanese Imperial Army invaded the country 100 years and three months after James Brooke was proclaimed Rajah of Sarawak. On Christmas Day 1941, when Rajah Vyner Brooke was visiting Australia, they took Kuching; a few days earlier they had occupied the Miri oilfields. Japanese troops, dressed for jungle warfare, headed upriver. They did not expect to encounter such stiff resistance from the tribespeople. The Allies had the brainwave of rekindling an old tribal pastime – head-hunting, which successive Brooke administrations had tried to stamp out. Iban and Orang Ulu warriors were offered 'ten-bob-a-knob' for Japanese heads, and many of the skulls still hanging in longhouses are said to date from this time. The years of occupation were marked by terrible brutality, and many people fled across the border into Dutch Borneo – now Kalimantan. The most notorious massacre in occupied Sarawak involved refugees from Kapit.

Just a month after the Japanese invasion, a forestry officer stationed on the Rejang heard that a group of women and children from Kapit were planning to escape across the Iran Range into Dutch territory. He organized the evacuation, and led the refugees up the rivers and over the mountains to the Dutch military outpost at Long Nawang. The forester returned to Kapit to help organize resistance to the Japanese. But when the invading forces heard of the escape they dispatched a raiding party upriver, captured the Dutch fort, lined up the fifty women and ordered the children to climb into nearby trees. According to historian Robert Payne: "They machine-gunned the women and amused themselves by picking off the children one by one... Of all those who had taken part in the expedition only two Europeans survived."

Sleeping **D** *Bakun Puri Hotel*, Lot 57 Belaga Bazaar, T461371. Fan only, marginally overpriced in comparison to its two competitors. **D** *Bee Lian Hotel*, 11 Belaga Bazaar, T461439. A/c, rooms are fine. **D** *Belaga Hotel*, 14 Belaga Bazaar, T461244. Some a/c, restaurant, no hot water, particularly friendly proprietor, good coffee shop downstairs, in-house video and cicadas. Best option.

Eating Several small, cheap coffee shops along Belaga Bazaar and Main Bazaar, the menus are all pretty similar.

Shopping **Handicrafts** *Chop Teck Hua*, Belaga Bazaar has an intriguing selection of tribal jewellery, old coins, beads, feathers, woodcarvings, blowpipes, parangs, tattoo boards and other curios buried under cobwebs and gekko droppings at the back of the shop, although the owner is noticeably uninformed about the objects he sells.

Transport At the moment Belaga is comparatively isolated and overland links are poor. It is possible to travel by road and river to Bintulu (see below), but it is drawn out and expensive. However it is likely, especially if the Bakun Dam project goes ahead (in late 1997 it was delayed/shelved due to Malaysia's financial difficulties), that road links will improve.

Air Connections on Sunday with **Kapit** and on to **Sibu**. **Boat** There is a daily boat from **Kapit** leaving early in the morning, which costs RM60, for a trip that takes approximately 6 hrs depending on the season. In the dry season passengers disembark at the rapids and walk this distance, while the pilot picks a route through these potentially dangerous obstacles. When the river is very low the only option is to fly to Belaga.

To **Tabau** and on to **Bintulu**: it is possible to hire a boat from Belaga to Kestima Kem (logging camp) near Rumah Lahanan Laseh (RM60 per person in a group or RM260 for 2-3 people); from there logging trucks go to Tabau on the Kemena River. **NB** Logging trucks leave irregularly and you can get stuck in logging camps. It is a 3 hr drive to Tabau; this trip is not possible in the wet season. There are regular express boats from Tabau to Bintulu (RM20). This is the fastest and cheapest route to Bintulu, but not the most reliable. It is necessary to obtain permission from the Resident's office and the police station in Belaga to take this route.

To **Kalimantan**: it is not legal to cross the border by way of Kapit, Belaga and up the Batang Balui to Long Nawang, although it has been done. You may be turned back.

Airline offices *MAS* c/o Lau Chun Kiat, Main Bazaar. **Communications** Area code: 084. **Post Office:** In the District Office building. **Useful addresses** District Office: (for upriver permits) on the far side of the basketball courts.

Directory

Bintulu & Similaju National Park

Bintulu

The word Bintulu is thought to be a corruption of *Mentu Ulau*, which translates as 'the place for gathering heads'. Bintulu, on the Kemena River, is in the heart of Melinau country and was traditionally a fishing and farming centre until the largest natural gas reserve in Malaysia was discovered just offshore in the late 1970s, turning Bintulu into a boomtown overnight. Shell, Petronas and Mitsubishi moved to the town in force. In 1978 the town's population was 14,000; it is now over 50,000. More than RM11bn was invested in Bintulu's development between 1980 and 1990.

Population: 50,000
Phone code: 086
Colour map 3, grid B4

Few tourists stay long in Bintulu, although it is the jump-off point to the Similajau National Park (which opened in 1991) and Niah Caves. The longhouses on the Kemena River are accessible, but tend not to be as interesting as those further up the Rejang and Baram rivers. The Penan and Kayan tribes are very hospitable and eager to show off their longhouses and traditions to tourists.

The remnants of the old fishing village at Kampong Jepak are on the opposite bank of the Kemena River. During the Brooke era the town was a small administrative centre. The **clock tower** commemorates the meeting of five representatives from the Brooke government and 16 local chieftains, the birth of Council Negeri, the state legislative body.

The first project to break ground in Bintulu was the RM100m crude oil terminal at Tanjong Kidurong from which 45,000 barrels of petroleum are exported daily. A deep-water port was built and the liquefied natural gas (LNG) plant started operating in 1982. It is one of the Malaysian government's biggest investment projects. The abundant supply of natural gas also created investment in related downstream projects. The main industrial area at Tanjong Kidurong is 20 km from Bintulu. The **viewing tower** at Tanjong Kidurong gives a panoramic view of the new-look Bintulu, out to the timber ships on the horizon. They anchor 15 km offshore to avoid port duties and the timber is taken out on barges.

Bintulu has a modern **Moorish-style mosque**, completed in 1988, called the **Masjid Assyakirin**; visitors may be allowed in when it is not prayer time. There is a new colourful centrally located Chinese temple called **Tua Pek Kong**. **Pasar Bintulu** is also an impressive new building in the centre of town, built to house the local jungle produce market, foodstalls and limited handicrafts stalls. A landscaped **Wildlife Park** has been developed on the outskirts of town, on the way to Tanjong Batu. It is a local recreational area and contains a small zoo and a botanic garden (the only one in Sarawak). ■ *0800-1900 Mon-Sun, RM2.*

Sarawak

Excursions **Similajau National Park**, see below. **Niah Caves and National Park**, see page 359. The Niah Caves are just off the Miri-Bintulu road and are easily accessible from both towns. Trips to Similajau National Park and longhouses on the Kemena River (rarely visited) can be organized from Bintulu. **Upriver** More than 20 Kemena River longhouses can be reached by road or river within 30 minutes of Bintulu. Iban longhouses are the closest; further upriver are the more traditional Kayan and Kenyah longhouses. Overpriced tours are organized by *Similajau Adventure Tours* (see tour companies) or hire a boat from the wharf. A two-hour river cruise, five-hour Iban longhouse tour, four-hour Iban longhouse tour (by boat), two-hour longhouse tour (by boat).

Essentials

Sleeping **B** *Hoover*, 92 Jln Keppel, T337166. Restaurant, cable TV, coffee house, smallish rooms, but well kept place. A great deal better than the slightly cheaper hotels nearby. **B** *Plaza*, Jln Abang Galau, 116 Taman Sri Dagang, T335111, F332742. A/c, restaurant, pool, very smart hotel, and, compared with other upmarket hotels in Sarawak, excellent value for money. Recommended. Very popular, so definitely worth booking. **B** *Regent*, Kemena Commercial Complex, Jln Tanjong Batu, T335511, F333770. Forty-seven rooms with a/c, TV, mini-bar, restaurant, coffee house. **B** *River Front Inn*, 256 Jln Sri Dagang, T333111, F339577. Smart place with good restaurant. Set slightly back from the main road, overlooking the river. **B** *Royal Inn*, 10-12 Jln Pedada, T315888, F334028. Overpriced.

C *Fata Inn*, 113 Taman Sri Dagang, Jln Masjid, T332998. A/c, TV, bathroom. Reasonable. **C** *Kemena*, 78 Jln Keppel, T331533. A/c, refurbished and on a quiet street, good quality room with TV, fridge. Recommended. **C** *King's Inn*, 162 Taman Sri Dagang, Jln Masjid, T337337, F332570. **C** *National*, 2nd Flr, 5 Jln Temple, T337222, F334304. A/c, clean and well kept. Recommended. **C** *Queen's Inn*, 238 Taman Sri Dagang, T338922. This hotel and its sister, the King's Inn, are carbon copies from the receptions to the rooms. Both charge a reasonable rate and have small, clean, carpeted a/c rooms with cramped bathroom. OK for a night. **C** *Sea View*, 254 Jln Masjid, Taman Sri Dagang, T339118. A/c, shower, TV, spacious rooms with views over the river. Good value for Bintulu. **C** *Sunlight Inn*, 7 Jln Pedada, T332577, F334075. A/c, TV.

D *AA Inn*, 1st Flr, 167 Taman Sri Dagang, T335733. One of the cheapest options in town but dirty and run down.

Bintulu
To Tanjung Kideron Mosque & Wildlife Park, Miri
Clock Tower
Pasar Bintulu
Jln Tun Razak
Pasar Malam Market
To Airport
Wet Market & Foodstalls
Jln Law Gek Soon
Kemena River
Jln Somerville
Jln Reservoir
Taxi
Jln Market Foodstalls
Market
Jln Temple
Taxi
Main Bazaar
Jln Pedada
Market
MAS
Jetty
Jln Sri Dagang
Food Stalls
Jln Masjid
Jln Abang Galau
Sleeping
1 AA Inn
2 Dragon Inn
3 Kemena
4 King's Inn
5 National
6 Plaza
7 Queen's Inn
8 River Front Inn
9 Royal Inn
10 Sea View
11 Sunlight
0 metres 50
0 yards 50

Sarawak

Watch out for the cockroaches. **D** *Dragon Inn*, Jln Abang Galau. Some a/c, a reasonable place to stay and the a/c rooms are good value.

There are several cheap options (RM20) on Jln Sri Dagang. However, they are extremely run down and dirty with a few dodgy characters hanging around. Only if you're desperate.

Umai, raw fish pickled with lime or the fruit of wild palms (*assam*) and mixed with **Eating** salted vegetables, onions and chillies is a Melanau speciality. Bintulu is famed for its *belacan* – prawn paste – and in the local dialect, prawns are *urang*, not *udang*. Locals quip that they are 'man-eaters' because they *makan urang*.

3 *Marco Polo*, on the waterfront on the edge of town, locals recommend pepper steak. **2** *Fook Lu Shou*, *Plaza Hotel*, Jln Abang Galau, Taman Sri Dagang, seafood and Chinese cuisine, including birds' nest soup, boiled in rock sugar (RM45). **2** *River Inn*, opposite wharf, Western and local food.

1 *Popular Corner*, opposite Hospital, Chinese. **1** *Kemena Coffee House*, Western, Malay and Chinese, open 24 hrs. **1** *Sarawak*, 160 Taman Sri Dagang (near *Plaza Hotel*), cheap Malay food.

Foodstalls **2** *Pantai Ria*, near Tanjong Batu, mainly seafood, only open in the evenings. Recommended. **1** *Chinese stalls* behind the Chinese temple on Jln Temple. Stalls at both markets.

Handicrafts *Dyang Enterprise* Lobby Flr, *Plaza Hotel*, Jln Abang Dalau, Taman Sri **Shopping** Dagang. The latter is rather overpriced because of the Plaza's more upmarket clientele; the best handicrafts are to be found at *Li Hua Plaza*, near the *Plaza Hotel*, in a 4 storey building.

Golf *Tanjong Kidurong*, new 18-hole course, north of Bintulu, by the sea (regular **Sports** buses from town centre), green fees RM15. **Sports Complex** Swimming pool (RM2), tennis, football. To get there, fork right from the Miri road at the Chinese temple, about 1 km from town centre.

Deluxe Travel, 30 Jln Law Gek Soon, T331293, F334995; *Similajau Travel and Tours*, **Tour operators** *Plaza Hotel*, Jln Abang Dalau offers tours around the city, to the Niah caves, longhouses and Similajau National Park. *Hunda Travel Services*, 8 Jln Somerville, T331339, F330445. There are half a dozen other agents in town.

Air The airport is in the centre of town. Regular connections with Kuching (RM122), **Transport** Miri (RM74), Sibu (RM69). There are also some connections with Kota Kinabalu.

Bus There are two stations in town. The terminal for local buses is in the centre of town. The long-distance Medan Jaya station is 10 mins by taxi from the centre (RM8). Regular connections with **Miri** (RM18), **Sarikei** (RM32), **Batu**, **Niah** (RM10) and **Sibu** (RM16). There are several bus companies but the main one is the *Syarikat Bas Suria* T334914.

Taxi For **Miri** and **Sibu**, taxis leave from Jln Masjid. Because of the regular bus services and the poor state of the roads, most taxis are for local use only and chartering them is expensive.

Boat Regular connections with **Tabau**, 2½-3 hrs, last boat at 1400 (RM18). Connections with **Belaga**, via logging road, see page 354; this route is popular with people in Belaga as it is much cheaper than going from Sibu. Direct boat connections with Sibu, Miri, Kuching, Song, Kapit and Belaga (enquire at the wharf for times and prices).

Airline offices *MAS*, Jln Masjid, T331554. **Banks** *Bank Bumiputra* and *Bank Utama* on Jln **Directory** Somerville; *Standard Chartered*, Jln Keppel. **Communications** Area code: 086. **General Post Office:** Far side of the airport near the Resident's office, 2 km from town centre – called Pos Laju. **Useful addresses** National Parks Booking Office: T331117, ext 50, F331923.

Sarawak

Similajau National Park

Sarawak's most unusually shaped national park is more than 32 km long and only 1.5 km wide. Similajau was demarcated in 1978, but has only really been open to tourists since the construction of decent facilities in 1991. Lying 20 km northeast of Bintulu, Similajau is a coastal park with sandy beaches, broken by rocky headlands. **Pasir Mas**, or Golden Sands, is a beautiful 3½ km long stretch of coarse beach, to the north of the Likau River, where green turtles (see page 459) come ashore to lay their eggs between July and September. A few kilometres from the park headquarters at **Kuala Likau** is a small coral reef, known as Batu Mandi. The area is renowned for birdwatching. Because it is so new, and because Bintulu is not on the main tourist track, the park is very quiet. Its seclusion makes it a perfect escape.

The beaches are backed by primary rainforest: peat swamp, *kerangas* (heath forest), mixed dipterocarp and mangrove (along Sungai Likau and Sungai Sebubong). There are small rapids on the Sebulong River. The rivers, particularly the beautiful **Sungai Likau**, have sadly been polluted by indiscriminate logging activities upstream.

Flora & fauna One of the first things a visitor notices on arrival at Kuala Likau is the prominent sign advising against swimming in the river, and to watch your feet in the headquarters' area: Similajau is well known for its saltwater crocodiles (*Crocodylus perosus*). Similajau also has 24 resident species of mammals (including gibbons, Hose's langurs, banded langurs, long-tailed macaques, civets, wild boar, porcupines, squirrels) and 185 species of birds, including many migratory species. Marine life includes dolphins, porpoises and turtles; there are some good coral reefs to the north. Pitcher plants grow in the *kerangas* forest and along the beach.

Treks Several trails have been cut by park rangers from the park headquarters. One path follows undulating terrain, parallel to the coast. It is possible to cut to the left, through the jungle, to the coast, and walk back to Kuala Likau along the beach. The main trail to Golden Beach is a five to six hour walk, crossing several streams and rivers where estuarine crocodiles are reputed to lurk. Most of these crossings are on 'bridges', which are usually just felled trees with no attempt made to assist walkers (some 'bridges' have drops of around 5m) – a good sense of balance is required.

Park essentials Permits are available from the Bintulu Development Authority. The information centre at is at park headquarters, T085737450, F085737454, at the mouth of Sungai Likau, across the river from the park. A boat is needed to cross the 5m of crocodile-infested river. **NB** Because the facilities to the park are actually outside the park, visitors do not need a permit to stay there. This has led to the 'park' becoming very popular with Bintulites at the weekend.

Sleeping C Two chalets, 2 hostels and a 'mega' hostel – with 27 4-bed rooms. The latter has attractive polished hardwood décor. It can get block-booked. There is 24-hr electricity. The canteen at park headquarters serves basic food. Picnic shelters at park HQ.

Transport A new road from Bintulu has been completed. Taxis travel the route (30 mins). Boats are available from the wharf or arrange through *Similajau Tours* in Bintulu.

Niah National Park

Niah's famous caves, tucked into a limestone massif called Gunung Sabis, made world headlines in 1959, when they were confirmed as the most important archaeological site in Asia. The park is one of the most popular tourist attractions in Sarawak and attracts more than 15,000 visitors every year. The caves were declared a national historic monument in 1958, but it was not until 1974 that the 3,000 hectares of jungle surrounding the caves were turned into a national park to protect the area from logging.

Colour map 3, grid A5

About 40,000 years ago, when the Gulf of Thailand and the Sunda Shelf were still dry ground, and a land-bridge connected the Philippines and Borneo, Niah was home to *Homo sapiens*. It was the most exciting archaeological discovery since Java man (*Homo erectus*).

Scientist and explorer A Hart Everett led expeditions to Niah Caves in 1873 and 1879, after which he pronounced that they justified no further work. Seventy nine years later, Tom Harrisson, ethnologist, explorer and conservationist and curator of the Sarawak Museum, confirmed the most important archaeological find in Southeast Asia at Niah. He unearthed fragments of a 37,000-year-old human skull – the earliest evidence of *Homo sapiens* in the region – at the west mouth of the Niah Great Cave itself. The skull was buried under 2.4m of guano. His find debunked and prompted a radical reappraisal of popular theories about where modern man's ancestors had sprung from. A wide range of Palaeolithic and Neolithic tools, pottery, ornaments and beads were also found at the site. Anthropologists believe Niah's caves may have been permanently inhabited until around 1400 AD. Harrisson's excavation site, office and house have been left intact in the mouth of the Great Cave. A total of 166 burial sites have been excavated, 38 of which are Mesolithic (up to 20,000 years before present) and the remainder Neolithic (4,000 years before present). Some of the finds are now in the Sarawak Museum in Kuching.

To reach the caves, take a longboat across the river from park headquarters at Palangkalan Lubang to the start of the 4 km belian (ironwood) plankwalk to the entrance of the **Great Cave**. Take the right fork 1 km from the entrance.

Sarawak

Niah National Park

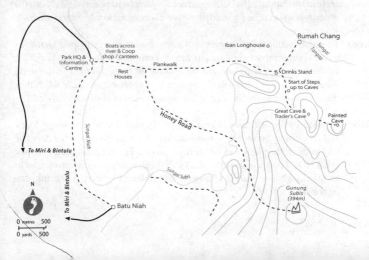

Niah's guano collectors: scraping the bottom

Eight bat species live in the Niah Caves, some of them more common ones such as the horseshoe bat and fruit bats. Other more exotic varieties include the bearded tomb bat, Cantor's roundleaf horseshoe bat and the lesser bent-winged bat. The ammonia-stench of bat guano permeates the humid air. People began collecting guano in 1929 – it is used as a fertilizer and to prevent pepper vines from rotting. Guano collectors pay a licence fee for the privilege of sweeping up tahi sapu *(fresh guano)* and digging up tahi timbang *(mature guano)* which they sell to the Bat Guano Co-operative at the end of the plankwalk.

The remains of a small kampong, formerly inhabited by birds' nest collectors (see below) and guano collectors, is just before the entrance, in the shelter of overhanging rocks. It is known as **Traders' Cave**. Beware of voracious insects; wear long trousers and plenty of repellent. There are no lights in the Great Cave (see **NB** below), so torches are needed.

The **Painted Cave** is beyond the Great Cave, and has been closed for preservation work since 1992. Prehistoric wall paintings – the only ones in Borneo – stretch for about 32m along the cave wall. Most of the drawings are of dancing human figures and boats, thought to be associated with a death ritual. On the floor of the cave, several 'death-ships' were found with some Chinese stoneware, shell ornaments and ancient glass beads. These death-ships served as coffins and have been carbon-dated to between 1 and 780 AD. By around 700 AD there is thought to have been a flourishing community based in the caves, trading hornbill ivory and birds' nests with the Chinese in exchange for porcelain and beads. But then it seems the caves were suddenly deserted in about 1400. In Penan folklore there are references to 'the ancestors who lived in the big caves' and tribal elders are said to be able to recall funeral rites using death boats similar to those found at Niah.

NB In February 1994 the generators that light the Niah Caves for visitors were destroyed by a fire and the caves closed. It is believed that the Berawan tribal group sabotaged the generators to thwart attempts to develop the Baram River as a tourist attraction. The caves themselves are regarded as sacred by a number of tribes and their development for tourism is resented by some members. Supporters of tourism development, for their part, maintain that the tribal peoples are being manipulated by outside parties. Six years on it appears unlikely that the generators will ever be replaced, therefore it is essential to take a good torch.

Flora & fauna The Niah National Park is primarily comprised of alluvial or peat swamp as well as some mixed dipterocarp forest. Long-tailed macaques, hornbills, squirrels, flying lizards and crocodiles have all been recorded in the park. There are also bat hawks which present an impressive spectacle when they home in on one of the millions of bats which pour out of the caves at dusk.

Treks A lowland trail called Jalan Madu (Honey Rd), traverses the peat swamp forest and up Gunung Subis; it is not well marked. Return trips need a full day. The trail leads off the plankwalk to the right, about 1 km from Pangkalan Lubang (Park HQ). The left fork on the plankwalk, before the gate to the caves, goes to an Iban longhouse, Rumah Chang (40 minutes' walk), where cold drinks can be bought.

Sarawak

How to make a swift buck

The Malay name for Niah's Painted Cave is Kain Hitam – or 'black cloth' – because the profitable rights to the birds' nests were traditionally exchanged for bolts of black cloth. The Chinese have had a taste for swiftlets' nests for well over 1,000 years, and the business of collecting them from 60m up in the cavernous chamber of the Great Cave is as lucrative - and as hazardous - a profession now as it was then. The nests are used to prepare birds' nest soup - blended with chicken stock and rock salt - which is a famous Chinese delicacy, prized as an aphrodisiac and for its supposed remedial properties for asthma and rheumatism. Birds' nests are one of the most expensive foods in the world: they sell for up to US$500/kilo in Hong Kong, where about 100 tonnes of them (worth US$40m) are consumed annually. The Chinese communities of North America import 30 tonnes of birds' nests a year. Locally, they fetch RM150-600/kg, depending on the grade.

Hundreds of thousands – possibly millions – of swiftlets (of the Collocalia swift family) live in the caves. Unlike other parts of Southeast Asia, where collectors use rotan ladders to reach the nests (see Gomontong Caves, Sabah, page 453), Niah's collectors scale belian (ironwood) poles to heights of more than 60m. They use bamboo sticks with a scraper attached to one end (called penyulok) to pick the nests off the cave-roof. The nests are harvested three times each season (which run from August to December and January to March). On the first two occasions, the nests are removed before the eggs are laid and a third left until the nestlings are fledged. Nest collectors are now all supposed to have licences, but in reality, no one does. Although the birds' nests are supposed to be protected by the national park in the off-season, wardens turn a blind eye to illegal harvesting – the collectors also know many secret entrances to the caves. Officially, people caught harvesting out of season can be fined RM2,000 or sent to jail for a year, but no one's ever caught. Despite the fact that it is a dangerous operation (there are usually several fatal accidents at Niah each year), collecting has become such a popular pursuit that harvesters have to reserve their spot with a lamp. Nest collecting is run on a first-come, first-served basis.

Nests of the white nest swiftlets and the black nest swiftlets are collected – the nests of the mossy-nest and white-bellied swiftlets require too much effort to clean. The nests are built by the male swiftlets using a glutinous substance produced by the salivary glands under the tongue which is regurgitated in long threads; the saliva sets like cement producing a rounded cup which sticks to the cave wall. In the swifts' nest market, price is dictated by colour: the best are the white nests which are without any plant material or feathers. Most of the uncleaned nests are bought up by middlemen, agents of traders in Kuching, but locals at Batu Niah also do some of the cleaning. The nests are first soaked in water for about three hours, and when softened, feathers and dirt are laboriously removed with tweezers. The resulting 'cakes' of nests are left to dry overnight: if they are dried in the sun they turn yellow.

On 1 December 1993, a two year ban on the collection of nests in Niah's Great Cave was introduced. The authorities were swayed by evidence that the number of birds nesting there had declined to fewer than 100,000 from the estimated four million in 1962. Environmentalists say the aerodramus species is now endangered. Reports from the ground suggested, however, that illegal collecting continued during the ban. The authorities blamed Indonesian immigrants.

Sarawak

Park
Information
Centre

At the park headquarters is this centre, with displays on birds' nests and flora and fauna. The exhibition includes the 37,000-year-old human skull which drew world attention to Niah in 1958. Also on display are 35,000-year-old oyster shells, as well as palaeolithic pig bones, monkey bones, turtle-shells and crabs which were found littering the cave floor. There are also burial vessels dating from 1600 BC and carved seashell jewellery from around 400 BC. ■ *0800-1230, 1400-1615 Mon-Fri; 0800-1245 Sat; 0800-1200 Sun.*

Park essentials

The park headquarters are at Pangkalan Lubang next to Sungai Subis. You must apply for an entry permit here before proceeding into the park. You will need your passport and pay an RM3 entry fee for each person and RM5 for camera, RM10 for video and RM200 for professional photography. The park and caves are open daily, the park 0800-1700, with the caves closing 30 mins earlier. A guide is not essential but they provide information and can relate legends about the paintings. But even with a guide, visitors cannot cross the barrier 3m in front of the cave wall. A guide will cost RM35 for groups of up to 20 and can be hired from the park headquarters.

Transport around the Park From park headquarters, longboats can be hired for upriver trips (maximum of eight people per boat).

Equipment Visitors are advised to bring a powerful torch for the caves. Walking boots are advisable during the wet season as the plankwalk can get very slippery.

For more information on the park, contact Deputy Park Warden, Niah National Park, PO Box 81, Miri Post Office, Batu Niah, T085 737450, F085 737918.

Sleeping
Call Miri, at the Old Forestry Building, Jln Angkasa, T085436637. All accommodation has 24-hr electricity & treated water

Family Chalet similar to hostel but cooker and a/c are planned for the future, 2 rooms with 4 beds in each, RM65 per room. *5 Hostels*, each with 4 rooms of 4 beds each, all rooms have private bathrooms, clean and Western style with shower, toilet, electric fans, fridges, large sitting area and kitchen. No cooking facilities but kettle, crockery and cutlery can be provided upon request. Booking advisable during holiday season (Jun, Aug, Dec), RM42 for 1 room of 4 beds, or RM10.50 for 1 bed. *VIP Resthouse*, RM250 per room, a/c, TV, hi-fi.

Batu Niah There are also 4 small hotels in Batu Niah (4 km from park headquarters). **C** *Park View Hotel*, T085737023. Range of comfortable rooms with TV, a/c, bath but no shower. Some rooms face inwards, discounts often available. **C** *Niah Caves Inn*, T(085) 737333, F737332. A/c, shower, spacious, fully carpeted rooms. Reasonable value. **D** *Niah Caves Hotel*, T085737726, Some a/c, shared facilities, 6 rooms (singles, doubles and triples available). Basic, but light and clean, next to the river. A fair budget option.

Camping Tents can be hired from park headquarters (RM8) or from the site (RM4).

Eating
Emergency rations recommended

The Guano Collectors' Co-operative shop at the beginning of the plankwalk sells basic food and cold drinks and camera film. There is another basic shop/restaurant just outside the park gates. There is a canteen at park headquarters, which serves good local food and full Western breakfast, good value, barbecue site provided, the canteen is supposed to be open from 0700-2300, but is a little erratic.

Transport
109 km from Miri to Batu Niah

Bus Hourly connections with Miri, 2 hrs, 7 buses a day to Bintulu, 2 hrs and Sibu via Bintulu to Batu Niah. **Taxi** From Miri to park headquarters, will only leave when there are 4 passengers. From Bintulu to Batu Niah (RM30). RM10 to park headquarters, however the river boat is far more scenic. **Boat** From Batu Niah (near the market) to park headquarters at Pengkalan Lubang, Niah National Park (RM10 per person or if more than 5 people, RM2 per person) or 45 mins walk to park headquarters.

Sarawak

Miri and the Baram River

Miri

Miri is the starting point for adventurous trips up the Barani River to Marudi, Bario and the Kelabit Highlands. Also accessible from Miri and Marudi is the incomparable Gunung Mulu National Park with the biggest limestone cave system in the world and one of the richest assemblages of plants and animals.

Phone code: 085
Colour map 3, grid A5

The capital of Sarawak's Fourth Division is a busy, prosperous town, with more than half its population Chinese. Many new buildings have gone up over the last few years, including two big new hotels, the *Mega* and the *Grand Palace* each of which has an adjoining shopping mall. One of the newest projects is a waterfront development with a marina – there is a pleasant walk on the peninsula here across the Miri River, and some good fishing. Another project recently completed is the *Bintang Plaza*, a large shopping complex on the edge of town on the road to the Baram River which contains *Parkson*, one of Malaysia'a largest department store chains.

History

In the latter years of the 19th century, a small trading company set up in Sarawak, to import kerosene and export polished shells and pepper. In 1910, when 'earth oil' was first struck on the hill overlooking Miri, the little trading company took the plunge and diversified into the new commodity – making, in the process, Sarawak's first oil town. The company's name was Shell. Together with the Malaysian national oil company, Petronas, Shell has been responsible for discovering, producing and refining Sarawak's offshore oil deposits. Oil is a key contributor to Malaysia's export earnings and Miri has been a beneficiary of the boom. There is a big refinery at Lutong to the north, which is connected by pipeline with Seria in Brunei. Lutong is the next town on the Miri River and the main headquarters for Shell.

The oil boom in this area began on Canada Hill, behind the town (where, incidentally, this limestone ridge provides excellent views of the town). **Oil Well No 1** was built by Shell and was the first oil well in Malaysia, spudded on 10 August 1910. The well was still yielding oil 62 years later, but its productivity began to slump. It is estimated that a total of 600,000 barrels were extracted from Well No 1 during its operational life. It was shut off in 1972. There are now 624 oil wells in the Miri Field, producing 80 million barrels of oil a year.

Sights

Juxtaposed against Miri's modern boom-town image is **Tamu Muhibba** (the native jungle produce market, open 24 hours), opposite the *Park Hotel* in a purpose-built concrete structure with pointed roofs on the roundabout connecting Jalan Malay and Jalan Padang. Orang Ulu come downriver to sell their produce, and a walk round the market provides an illuminating lesson in jungle nutrition. Colourful characters run impromptu 'stalls' from rattan mats, selling yellow cucumbers that look like mangoes, mangoes that look like turnips, huge crimson durians, tiny loofah sponges, sackfuls of fragrant Bario rice (brown and white), every shape, size and hue of banana, *tuak* (rice wine) in old Heineken bottles and a menagerie of jungle fauna – including mousedeer, falcons, pangolins and the apparently delicious long-snouted *tupai*, or jungle squirrel. There is a large selection of dried and fresh seafood – fish and *bubok* (tiny prawns), and big buckets boiling with catfish or stacked with turtles, there are also some handicrafts.

Taman Bulatan is a scenic centrally located park with foodstalls and boats for hire on the manmade lake.

Sarawak

Excursions

Miri is the main centre for organizing tours up the Baram River, to Mulu National Park

Permits are required to go anywhere upriver. Apply at the Resident's office, Jalan Kwantung, T433205 – with passport photocopy. Permits are also available from Marudi. After acquiring a permit, the Police Station will need to stamp it. If travelling with a tour company it will take care of the bureaucracy.

Niah Caves & National Park, see page 359. **Gunung Mulu National Park**, see page 370. **Hawaii Beach** is a pristine palm fringed beach, popular for picnics and barbecues. There are chalets to stay in. It is 15 minutes' taxi ride from Miri.

Lambir Hills The park mainly consists of a chain of sandstone hills bounded by rugged cliffs, 19 km south of Miri and just visible from the town; the park's main attraction is its beautiful waterfalls. *Kerangas* (heath forest) covers the higher ridges and hills while the lowland areas are mixed dipterocarp forest. Bornean gibbons, bearded pigs, barking deer and over 100 species of bird have been recorded in the park. There is only one path across a rickety suspension bridge at present, but there are numerous waterfalls and tree towers for birdwatching. The park attracts hordes of daytrippers from Miri at weekends. ■ *Park entrance: RM3, photography RM5, video camera RM10, professional camera RM100. The park headquarters is close to the Miri-Niah road, there is an audio visual room with seating for 30 here. Getting there: from Park Hotel take Bintulu or Bakong bus.*

Sleeping and eating Five chalets, one with 2 rooms, 3 beds, 4 units with 2 rooms, 2 beds, RM40 per room or RM80 per house; a/c chalet, 2 rooms with 3 beds, RM60 per room or RM120 per house. **Campsite** Rental RM4. A canteen is provided, no cooking allowed in chalet, you can cook at campsite or take food into canteen.

Miri

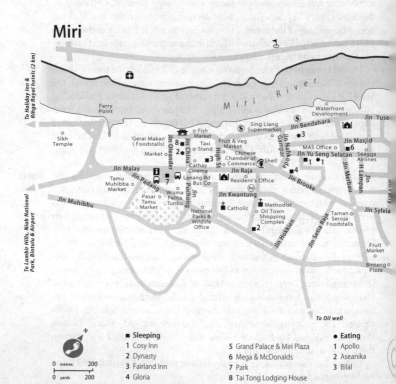

■ **Sleeping**
1 Cosy Inn
2 Dynasty
3 Fairland Inn
4 Gloria
5 Grand Palace & Miri Plaza
6 Mega & McDonalds
7 Park
8 Tai Tong Lodging House

● **Eating**
1 Apollo
2 Aseanika
3 Bilal

Loagan Bunut National Park is located in the upper reaches of the Sungai Bunut and contains Sarawak's largest natural lake. At approximately 650 hectares, Loagan Bunut may not be large but it is no ordinary lake since the water level in the lake is totally dependent on the water level of the rivers Bunut, Tinjar and Baram. The level is at its lowest in the months of February, May and June and sometimes, for a period of about two to three weeks, the lake becomes an expanse of dry cracked mud. The main cultural attraction at the lake is the traditional method of fishing (*selambau*), which has been retained by the Berawan fishermen. The surrounding area is covered with peat swamp forest. The common larger birds found here are the darters, egrets, herons, bittern, hornbill and kites. Gibbons are also common. At present, there are no visitor facilities.

Luconia Island is surrounded by a pristine coral reef. Trips can be organized through tour operators in Miri.

Tours

Although most tour companies specialize in trips up the Baram River to Mulu National Park, some are much better than others – in terms of facilities and services offered. The best agents are *Alo Doda* and *Tropical Adventure* which have private accommodation in the park and run an interesting selection of more off-beat treks to remote destinations; they are also the most expensive. *Alo Doda*, for example, organizes treks to the Penan areas and Kenyah longhouses of Ulu Baram – on the upper stretches of the river. Every agency in Miri has a Mulu National Park itinerary covering the caves, pinnacles, and summits. It is also possible to trek to Bario and Mount Murud, as well as to Limbang from Mulu. Most of the agencies employ experienced guides who will be able to advise on longer, more ambitious treks. The Mulu National Park is one destination where it is usually cheaper to go through a tour company than to try to do it independently. Costs vary considerably according to the number of people in a group. For the three day Mulu trip, a single tourist can expect to pay RM500; this drops to RM400 a head for a group of four and about RM350 each for a group of 10, all accommodation, food, travel and guide costs included. An eight day tour of Ulu Baram longhouses would cost RM1,800 for one person and RM1,200 per person in a group of 10. A 20-day trek will cost two people (minimum number) around RM2,000 each, and a group of 6-10, RM1,300 a head. For those who want to visit remote longhouses, tour companies present by far the best option. Tour fees cover 'gifts' and all payments to longhouse headmen for food, accommodation and entertainment.

Sleeping
■ *on map*
Price codes:
see inside front cover

Most people going to Mulu will have to spend at least a night in Miri. The town has a growing selection of mid-to-upmarket hotels; many offer discounts of

Sarawak

30-40% off quoted prices as a matter of course. Many of the mid-range hotels are around Jln Yu Seng Selatan. But being an oil town and close to Brunei Miri has a booming prostitution industry. Many of the cheaper lodging houses, particularly those around Jln China, are sleazy brothels. The cheaper accommodation listed below represents the more respectable end of the market, but there is not much for anyone hoping to stay somewhere that's cheap and not a brothel.

A *Dynasty*, Lot 683, Block 9, Jln Pujut-Lutong, T421111, F422222, dyhlmyy@po.jaring.my. A/c, restaurants, pool, health centre, next to Oil Town Shopping Complex. **A** *Grand Palace*, 2 km Jln Miri-Pujut, Pelita Commercial Centre, T428888, F427777, jrobson@pc.jaring.my. Imposing peach and pastel building on town outskirts next to Miri Plaza Shopping Centre, 125 comfortable, carpeted rooms with a/c, TV, bathroom, mini-bar, tea and coffee-making facilities, pool, fitness centre, karaoke, restuarant. **A** *Holiday Inn*, Jln Temenggong Datuk Oyong Lawai, T418888, F419999, himiri@po.jaring.my. Situated 2 km from town centre, at mouth of the Miri River, this 5-storey, modern, white block curves around the South China Sea, very popular with families at weekends (check for special weekend rates (**B**) price category), 168 rooms all with a/c, TV (no less than 11 channels), bathroom, tea and coffee-making facilities, mini-bar, balcony, thick carpets and comfy beds, sunsets over sea, colourful but noisy river traffic, free-form pool, pleasantly surrounded by plants and palms with swim-up bar in form of traditional boat (popular with kids), jacuzzi and baby pool, sandy area for kids to play, beach too near town to be clean and sea not safe for swimming but pleasant for sunset strolls, coffee house, Chinese restaurant, bar and bakery/delicatessen, fitness centre, sauna. Recommended. **A** *Mega*, Lot 907, Jln Merbau, T432432, F433433, megahot@po.jaring.my, www.megahotel.net. The tallest and largest hotel in Miri town centre, 228 rooms with a/c, TV, bathroom, Chinese restaurant, coffee house, pool with jacuzzi, health centre, business centre, internet facilities, shopping mall attached. **A** *Rihga Royal*, Lot 799, Jln Temenggong Datuk Oyong Lawai, T421121, F421099. Japanese-managed hotel on coast south of Miri, 5-star comforts, 225 rooms, all rooms with a/c, mini-bar, TV, tea and coffee-making facilities, Japanese restaurant (the only one in Miri), Chinese restaurant and coffee house, pool, tennis, health centre.

B *Gloria*, 27 Jln Brooke, T416699, F418866. A/c, restaurant, 42 rooms, better than it looks from outside, although the economy rooms are windowless, comparatively expensive. **B** *Kingwood Inn*, Jln Yu Seng Utara, T415888, F415009. A/c, restaurant, one of the smaller mid-range places to stay.

C *Cosy Inn*, 545-547 Jln Yu Seng Selatan, T415522, F415155. A/c, restaurant. Looks better from the outside than it is, nevertheless better than others in its class. **C** *Milton Inn*, 6 South Yuseng Rd, T415077, F415085. A/c, TV, shower. The external appearance belies what is found within. Rundown, cramped overpriced rooms. **C** *Park*, Jln Raja, T414555, F414488. A/c, Chinese restaurant. Until the *Holiday Inn* opened, the *Park* was the best hotel in town. Ranked at about a 3-star hotel, although now rather run down, it is good value for money and convenient location for bus station. People, though, seem to have rather mixed experiences – some report things being pilfered from their rooms, other have been propositioned, but still more recommend it without reservation. **C** *Rasa Sayang*, Lot 566 Lee Tak St, T413880. A/c, TV, slightly away from the main road. A cheap hotel with nothing but price to recommend it. **C-D** *Tai Tong Lodging House*, 26 Jln China, T411498. Some a/c, Chinese guesthouse-cum-hotel with range of rooms from a/c with attached bathrooms to fan-cooled with shared facilities, dorm beds also available (**F**), although possessions left here are reputedly not very secure. **D** *Fairland Inn*, Jln Raja, T413981. A/c, small, dirty rooms, bathroom with minuscule toilet but the best of a bad bunch of budget hotels in Miri.

Malay 2 *Aseanika*, Jln China, also serves good Indian and Indonesian food. **1** *Nabila's*, 1st Flr, 441 DUBS Building, Jln Bendahara, also serves Indonesian and Oriental, curries, good rendang.

Chinese 3 *Kok Chee*, 1st Flr *Park Hotel*, Jln Kingsway. **2** *Apollo*, Lot 394 Jln Yu Seng Selatan (close to *Gloria Hotel*), good seafood, popular. **2** *Sea View Café*, Jln China.

Indian 2 *Bilal*, Jln Persiaran Kabor, excellent curries and rotis, coffee house.

International 3 *Golden Steak Garden*, *Gloria Hotel*, 27 Jln Brooke, steak. **3** *Park View Restaurant* (coffee house of *Park Hotel*), Jln Malay, most sophisticated menu in town, jellyfish, good selection of seafood and grill. **2** *McDonalds*, next to *Mega Hotel*. **2** *Bonzer Garden Steak House*, Jln Yu Seng Utara, local dishes much cheaper than burgers. **1** *Sugar Bun*, Ground Flr, Wisma Pelita Tunku, burgers, pastries, cakes etc. *Cosy Garden* (and in *Mega Hotel* block), pleasant restaurant, but the a/c inhibits any cosiness, limited menu but reasonable prices, steak.

Bakeries *Appletree*, Ground Flr, Wisma Pelita Tunku. *Deli Corner*, *Holiday Inn*.

Foodstalls 1 *Taman Seroja*, Jln Brooke, Malay food, best in the evenings. *Tamu Muhibba* (Native Market), opposite *Park Hotel* on roundabout connecting Jln Malay and Jln Padang, best during the day. *Tanjong Seafood stalls*, Tanjung Lobung (south of Miri), best in evening. *Gerai Makan*, near Chinese temple at end of Jln Oleander, Malay food.

Eating
● *on map, page 364*
Price codes:
see inside front cover

Miri has scores of karaoke lounges and discos, mostly along Jln Yu Seng. Check local paper for information on films and cultural events. The *Holiday Inn* stages regular performances of Western music and theatre. *Rig* disco in *Regal Hotel*, very popular.

Entertainment

Books *Pelita Book Centre*, 1st Flr, Wisma Pelita Tunku; *Parksons Department Store*, Bintang Plaza.

Handicrafts *Longhouse*, 2nd Flr, Imperial Mall, the best in town. *Kong Hong*, Wisma Pelita, 1st Flr. *Sarawak Handicrafts*, 2nd Flr, Soon Hup Centre. *Joy art and fashion House*, M Flr, Wisma Pelita Tunju. *Syarikat Unique arts and handicrafts centre*, Lot 2994. *Morsjaya Commercial Centre*, Jln Miri. *Royal Selangor*, 28F, High St. *Swet Love Gift Shop*, Lot 219, 2nd Flr, Wisma Pelita Tunku. Roadside stalls at Nakat, 18 km down the southbound road to Niah (1 km before Lambir Hills National Park) also sell baskets.

Shopping malls *Bintang Plaza* Jln Miri. *Imperial Mall*, Jln Parry. *Soon Hup Tower*, next to *Mega Hotel* with Parkwell's supermarket and department store. *Wisma Pelita Tunku*, near bus station, department store. *Miri Plaza*, next to *Grand Palace Hotel* – mediocre supermarket – not worth the trek out here.

Supermarket *Pelita*, Ground Flr, Wisma Pelita Tunku, useful for supplies for upriver expeditions; *Sing Liang Supermarket* on Jln Nakhoda Gampar – Chinese store; *Parkson Grand*, Bintang Plaza; *Ngiukee*, moving from Pelita to Imperial Mall.

Shopping

Golf *Miri Golf Club*, Jln Datuk Patinggi, T416787, F417848, by the sea, green fees RM80-120. **Swimming** Public pool off Jln Bintang, close to the Civic Centre, RM1. **Fitness centres** *Holiday Inn* and *Rihga Hotels* both have centres where non-residents can become short-term members.

Sports

Borneo Adventure, *Pacific Orient Hotel*, 49 Jln Brooke, T414935, F419543, has been recommended over the years by a number of readers; they may be expensive by comparison with other outfits, but it appears to be worth it. *Borneo Leisure*, Lot 227, Ground Flr, Jln Maju, Beautiful Jade Centre, T413011. *Borneo Overland*, 37 Ground Flr, Bangunan Raghavan, Jln Brooke, T4302255, F416424. *East-West*, 792 Jln Bintang, T410717, F411297. *Hornbill Travel*, G26 Park Arcade, Jln Raja, T417385, F412751. *JJ Tour Service*, Lot 231 Jln Maju Taman, Jade Centre, T418690, F413308. *JJM Tours & Travel*, Lot 3002, Ground Flr, Morsjaya Commercial Centre, 2.5 Miles, Miri-Bintulu Rd, T416051, F414390, young company with some very experienced guides. Recommended. *KKM Travel &*

Tour operators

Sarawak

Tours, 236 Jln Maju, T417899, F414629. *Malang Sisters Agency*, 248 Jln Bendahara, T417770, F417123. *Robert Ding*, Lot 556, 1st Flr, Royal Snooker Centre, Jln Permaisuri, T416051, F414390, recommended by National Parks Office. *Seridan Mulu*, Lot 351, 2nd Flr, Jln Brooke, T422277, F415277, private accommodation within park, recommended by National Parks Office. *Transworld Travel Service*, 9th Flr Wisma Pelita Tunku, T422226, F410057, simtw@pc.jaring.my. *Tropical Adventure*, Ground Flr, *Mega Hotel*, Jln Merbau, Soon Hup Tower, PO Box 2197, T419337, F414503, hthee@pc.jaring.my, private accommodation within Mulu Park. Recommended.

Transport **Local Car hire**: *Mega*, No 3, Lorong 1, Sungai Krokop, T431885. Fleet of Proton Sagas available. RM120-150 per day. *Kimoto*, T411007. *Jasara Service*, T870980.

Ferry: operates every 15 mins from 0630-2000. **Taxi**: T432277.

Long distance Air: regular connections on MAS with Kuching, Sibu, Marudi, Bario via Marudi, Bintulu, Limbang, Lawas, Mulu and Labuan. Also connections with Kota Kinabalu. For transport information, T33433. Fare by taxi to town from Padang Kirbua Terminal is RM20, or RM12 to the old bus station. Bus no 7 runs between town and the airport from early morning to early evening. Royal Brunei operate twice daily flights to BSB (RM111 including tax).

Bus: a new bus terminal has opened at Pujuk Padang Kerbau, Jln Padang. Regular connections from early morning to early/mid-afternoon with **Batu Niah** 2-3 hrs, **Bintulu** 3 hrs, **Sibu** 6 hrs, and **Kuching**. Tickets can be booked at following agents: *Lanang Road Bus Co*, next to *Park Hotel*, T435336, *Syarikat Bas Express*, next to *Park Hotel*, T439325. Express buses to **Marudi**, depart from Kuala Baram, the port area, 2 hrs, RM18.

To **Kuala Baram** and the express boat upriver to **Marudi** Regular bus connections with Kuala Baram; there are also taxis to Kuala Baram, either private or shared. Express boats upriver to Marudi from Kuala Baram, 3 hrs. Roughly 1 boat every hr from 0715. Last boat 1430. This is the first leg of the journey to Mulu and the interior.

Regular connections (Miri-Belait Transport Company, T419129) with Kuala Belait in **Brunei**, 1½ hrs, RM12. Travelling by your own means of transport from Miri it is necessary to take the car ferry across the Baram River, then pass through immigration, before another ferry across the Belait River. At weekends and public holidays there are long queues for the ferries as well as at immigration – so be prepared for a long, hot wait. Be warned also that the ferry across the Belait River takes an unscheduled 1 hr break for lunch. Distance itself is nothing – the ferry crossings take no more than 10 mins each and Miri to Kuala Belait is just 27 km. Bus passengers bypass the queues because they board the ferry as foot passengers and then hop on another bus the other side of the river. From Kuala Belait regular connections with Seria, 1 hr and from Seria regular connections with Bandar Seri Begawan ($1 Brunei), 1-2 hrs. It takes minimum 5 hrs to reach Bandar Seri Begawan.

Directory **Airline offices** *MAS*, 239 Halaman Kabor, off Jln Yu Seng Selatan, T414144. *Royal Brunei*, Lot 263, South Yu Send Rd (Halaman Kabor), T426322. *Seagga*, Jln Sim Cheng Kay, near mosque, T439954. **Banks** All major banks are represented in Miri. **Communications** Area code: 085. **General Post Office**: just off Jln Gartak. **Telecom Office**: Jln Gartak, open Mon-Sun 0730-2200. **Medical facilities** Hospital: opposite Ferry Point, T420033. **Tourist offices** *Tourist Information Centre*: Lot 452, Jln Malay (next to bus station), T434181, F434179. Permits and accommodation bookings for Niah, Mulu and Lambir. Stb@po.jaring.my. Accommodation booking, T434184. **Useful addresses** Immigration Office: Jln Unus, T442100. **National Parks and Wildlife Office**: Jln Puchong, T436637, F431975. **Police Station**: Jln Kingsway, T432533. **Resident's Office**: Jln Kwantung, T43320

Marudi

Four major tribal groups – Iban, Kelabit, Kayan and Penan – come to Marudi *Phone code: 085*
to do business with the Chinese, Indian and Malay merchants. Marudi is the *Colour map 3, grid A5*
furthest upriver trading post on the Baram and services all the longhouses in
the Tutoh, Tinjar and Baram river basins. Most tourists only stop long enough
in Marudi to down a cold drink before catching the next express boat upriver;
as the trip to Mulu National Park can now be done in a day, not many have to
spend the night here. Because it is a major trading post, however, there are a lot
of hotels, and the standards are reasonably good.

Fort Hose was built in 1901, when Marudi was still called Claudetown, and has **Sights**
good views of the river. It is named after the last of the Rajah's residents, the
anthropologist, geographer and natural historian Dr Charles Hose. The fort is
now used as administrative offices. Also of note is the intricately carved **Thaw
Peh Kong Chinese Temple** (diagonally opposite the express boat jetty), also
known as Siew San Teen. It was shipped from China and erected in Sarawak in
the early 1900s, although it was probably already 100 years old by the time the
temple began life in its new location.

Gunung Mulu National Park, see below. **Brunei** The Marudi-Kampong **Excursions**
Teraja log walk is normally done from the Brunei end, as the return trek, across *Permits are necessary to*
the Sarawak/Brunei border takes a full day, dawn to dusk. It is, however, possible *go upriver from Marudi.*
to reach an Iban longhouse inside Brunei without going the full distance to *Permits for Mulu & Bario*
Kampong Teraja. The longhouse is on the Sungai Ridan, about 2½ hours down *are issued by the district*
the jungle trail. The trail starts 3 km from Marudi, on the airport road. A local *officer in Fort Hose*
Chinese man, who runs an unofficial taxi service to and from the trail head, may
spot you before you find the trail (ask at the houses along the road). There is no
customs post on the border; the trail is not an official route into Brunei. Trekkers
are advised to take their passports in the unlikely event of being stopped by
police, who will probably turn a blind eye. Kampong Teraja in Brunei is the furthest accessible point which can be reached by road from Labi.

    Longhouses Three longhouses, *Long Seleban*, *Long Moh* and *Leo Mato*,
are accessible by four-wheel drive vehicle from Marudi.

A-C *Grand*, Lot 350 Backlane, T755711, F775293. Some a/c, large but good hotel, res- **Sleeping**
taurant, 30 clean rooms with cable TV, close to jetty and plenty of information on
upriver trips. **B** *Mount Mulu Hotel*, Lot 80 & Lot 90, Marudi Town District, T756671,
F756670 A/c; discounts are available making this place very good value. **C** *Victoria*,
Lot 961-963 Jln Merdeka, T756067, T7556864. All 21 rooms have cable TV; there's also
a business centre. **D** *Mayland*, 347 Mayland Building, T755106, F755333. A/c, 41
rooms, slightly rundown but a good range of accommodation.

There are several coffee shops dotted around town. The **1** *Rose Garden*, opposite **Eating**
Alisan Hotel is an a/c coffee shop serving mainly Chinese dishes.

Air The airport is 5 km from town. Connections with Miri (RM29) Bario (RM55), Sibu **Transport**
(RM100). **Boat** These leave from opposite the Chinese temple. Connections with
Kuala Baram; 8 boats a day from 0700-1430 (RM18), **Tutoh** (for longboats to Long
Terawan and Mulu National Park, 1 boat at 1200) (RM20), **Long Lama** (for longboats
to Bario) 1 boat every hr 0730-1400.

Banks There are 2 local banks with foreign exchange facilities. **Communications** Area code: **Directory**
085. **Post Office**: Airport Rd. **Useful addresses** **Police station**: On Airport Rd.

Gunung Mulu National Park

Colour map 3, grid A6

Tucked in behind Brunei, this 52,866 hectare park lays claim to Gunung Mulu, which at 2,376m is the second highest mountain in Sarawak, and the biggest limestone cave system in the world. In short, Mulu is essentially a huge hollow mountain range, sitting on top of 180-million-year-old rainforest. Its primary jungle contains astonishing biological diversity.

In Robin Hanbury-Tenison's book *The Rain Forest*, he says of Mulu: "All sense of time and direction is lost." Every scientific expedition that has visited Mulu's forests has encountered plant and animal species unknown to science. In 1990, five years after it was officially opened to the public, the park was handling an average 400 visitors a month. Numbers have increased markedly since then – the area is now attracting about 12,000 tourists a year – and as the eco-tourism industry has extended its foothold, local tribespeople have been drawn into confrontation with the authorities. A series of sabotage incidents in 1993 have been blamed on the Berawan tribe, who claim the caves and the surrounding jungle are a sacred site.

In 1974, three years after Mulu was gazetted as a National Park, the first of a succession of joint expeditions led by the British Royal Geographical Society (RGS) and the Sarawak government began to make the discoveries that put Mulu on the map. In 1980 a cave passage over 50 km long was surveyed for the first time. Since then, a further 137 km of passages have been discovered. Altogether 27 major caves have now been found – speleologists believe they probably represent a tiny fraction of what is actually there. The world's biggest cave, the **Sarawak Chamber**, was not discovered until 1984.

The first attempt on Gunung Mulu was made by Spencer St John, the British consul in Brunei, in 1856 (see also his attempts on Gunung Kinabalu, Sabah, page 439). His efforts were thwarted by "limestone cliffs, dense jungle and sharp pinnacles of rock". Dr Charles Hose, Resident of Marudi, led a 25 day expedition to Gunung Mulu in 1893, but also found his path blocked by 600m high cliffs. Nearly 50 years later, in 1932, a Berawan rhinoceros hunter called Tama Nilong guided Edward Shackleton's Oxford University expedition to the summit. One of the young Oxford undergraduates on that expedition was Tom Harrisson, who later made the Niah archaeological discoveries, see page 359. Tama Nilong, the hunter from Long Terawan, had previously reached the main southwest ridge of Mulu while tracking a rhinoceros.

The cliffs of the Melinau Gorge rise a sheer 600m, & are the highest limestone rockfaces between North Thailand & Papua New Guinea

The limestone massifs of Gunung Api and Gunung Benarat were originally at the same elevation as Gunung Mulu, but their limestone outcrops were more prone to erosion than the Mulu's sandstone. Northwest of the gorge lies a large, undisturbed alluvial plain which is rich in flora and fauna. Penan tribespeople (see page 331) are allowed to maintain their lifestyle of fishing, hunting and gathering in the park. At no small expense, the Malaysian government has encouraged them to settle at a purpose-built longhouse at **Batu Bungan**, just a few minutes upriver from the park headquarters, but its efforts have met with limited success. Penan shelters can often be found by river banks.

Reeling from international criticism, the Sarawak state government announced in 1994 that it had set aside 66,000 hectares of rainforest as what it called 'biosphere', a reserve where indigenous people could practise their traditional lifestyle. Part of this lies in the park. In Baram and Limbang districts, the remaining 300 Penan will have a reserve in which they can continue their nomadic way of life. A further 23,000 hectares has reportedly been set aside for 'semi-nomadic' Penan. In 1994 Malaysian officials said that 16 non-governmental organizations around the world had raised US$250,000 on behalf of the Penan.

Flora & fauna

In the 1960s and 1970s, botanical expeditions were beginning to shed more light on the Mulu area's flora and fauna: 100 new plant species were discovered between 1960 and 1973 alone. Mulu park encompasses an area of diverse altitudes and soil types – it includes all the forest types found in Borneo except mangrove. About 20,000 animal species have been recorded in Mulu Park, as well as 3,500 plant species and 8,000 varieties of fungi (more than 100 of these

Gunung Mulu National Park

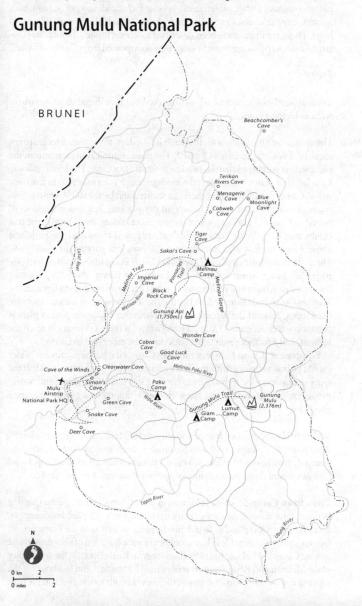

BRUNEI

Beachcomber's Cave

Terikan Rivers Cave

Menagerie Cave

Blue Moonlight Cave

Cobweb Cave

Tiger Cave

Sakai's Cave

Melinau Camp

Melinau Trail

Pinnacles Trail

Imperial Cave

Black Rock Cave

Melinau Gorge

Gunung Api (1,750m)

Wonder Cave

Lutut River

Melinau River

Cobra Cave

Good Luck Cave

Clearwater Cave

Melinau Paku River

Cave of the Winds

Simon's Cave

Mulu Airstrip

National Park HQ

Green Cave

Paku Camp

Nipo River

Gunung Mulu Trail

Lumut Camp

Gunung Mulu (2,376m)

Snake Cave

Giam Camp

Deer Cave

Tapin River

Ulung River

N

0 km   2
0 miles 2

Sarawak

are endemic to the Mulu area). Mulu's ecological statistics are astounding: it is home to 1,500 species of flowering plant, 170 species of orchid and 109 varieties of palm. More than 280 butterfly species have been recorded. Within the park boundaries, 262 species of birds (including all eight varieties of hornbill), 67 mammalian species, 50 species of reptile and 75 amphibian species have been recorded.

Mulu's caves contain an unusual array of flora and fauna too. There are three species of swiftlet, 12 species of bat, and nine species of fish, including the cave flying fish (*Nemaaramis everetti*) and blind catfish (*Silurus furnessi*). Cave scorpions (*Chaerilus chapmani*) – which are poisonous but not deadly – are not uncommon. Other subterranean species include albino crabs, huntsman spiders, cave crickets, centipedes and snakes (which dine on swiftlets and bats). These creatures have been described as "living fossils...[which are] isolated survivors of ancient groups long since disappeared from Southeast Asia."

Treks

Trails around headquarters are well marked but it is illegal to go anywhere without hiring a guide.

Gunung Mulu
The views from the summit are best during April & May

The minimum time to allow for the climb is four days, three nights; tents are not required if you stay at Camps 1 and 2. The main summit route starts from the plankwalk at park headquarters heading towards Deer Cave. The Mulu walkway forks left after about 1 km. From the headquarters it is an easy four to five hour trek to Camp 1 at 150m, where there is a shelter, built by the RGS/Sarawak government expedition in 1978. The second day is a long uphill slog (eight to 10 hours) to Camp 4 (1,800m), where there is also a shelter. Past Camp 3, the trail climbs steeply up Bukit Tumau, which affords good views over the park, and above which the last wild rhinoceros in Sarawak was shot in the mid-1940s. There are many pitcher plants (*Nepenthes lowii*) along this stretch of trail (see page 526). From Camp 4, known as 'The Summit Camp', the path passes the helicopter pad, from where there are magnificent views of Gunung Benarat, the Melinau Gorge and Gunung Api. The final haul to the summit is steep; there are fixed ropes. Around the summit area, the *Nepenthes muluensis* pitcher plant is common – it is endemic to Mulu. From Camp 4 it takes 1½ hours to reach the summit, and a further seven hours back down the mountain to Camp 1.

Equipment Camp 1 has water, as does Camp 4 if it has been raining. Water should be boiled before drinking. It is necessary to bring your own food; in the rainy season it is wise to bring a gas cooking stove. A sleeping bag and waterproofs are also necessary and spare clothes, wrapped in a plastic bag, are a good idea.

Mulu can also be climbed from the south ridge of Melinau Gorge (see below) – three hours to Camp 1, five hours to Camp 3, steep four to five hour climb to Camp 4, two hours to the top. Forest changes from alluvial/swamp forest through mixed dipterocarp to mossy sub-montane and summit scrub.

Treks from Camp 5, which is located in the Melinau Gorge, facing Gunung Benarat, take about four to six hours upstream from the park headquarters. From the camp it is possible to trek up the gorge as well as to the Pinnacles, on Gunung Api. It is advisable to hire a longboat for the duration of your time at and around Camp 5. The boat has to be abandoned at Kuala Berar, at the confluence of the Melinau and Berar rivers. It is only used for the first and last hours of the trip, but in the event of an emergency, there are no trails leading back to the park headquarters and there are grim stories of fever-stricken people being stranded in the jungle. For a three-day trip, a longboat will cost about RM350 (bargain hard) to hire – as opposed to RM350 if you just arrange to be collected three days later. It takes two to three hours, depending on the river level, from park headquarters to Kuala Berar; it is then a two to three hour trek (8 km) to Camp 5. Visitors to the Camp 5 area are also advised to plan their itinerary carefully as it is necessary to calculate how much food will be required and to carry it up there.

Sleeping There is a basic shelter (built by the RGS/Sarawak government expedition in 1978), which can house about 30 people. The camp is next to the Melinau River; river water should be boiled before drinking.

Melinau Gorge Camp 5 nestles at the south end of the gorge, across a fast-flowing section of the Melinau River and opposite the unclimbed 1,580m Gunung Benarat's stark, sheer limestone cliffs. The steep limestone ridges, that lead eventually to Gunung Api, comprise the east wall of the gorge. Heading north from Camp 5, the trail fizzles out after a few minutes. It takes an arduous two to three hours of endless river crossings and scrambles to reach a narrow chute of white water, under which is a large, deep and clear jungle pool with a convenient sandbank and plenty of large boulders to perch on. Alfred Russel Wallace's *Troides brookiana* – the majestic Rajah Brooke's birdwing – is particularly common at this little oasis, deep in undisturbed jungle. The walk involves criss-crossing through waist-deep, fast-flowing water and over stones that have been smoothed to a high polish over centuries: strong shoes are recommended – as is a walking stick. Only occasionally in the walk upstream is it possible to glimpse the towering 600m cliffs.

The Pinnacles are a forest of sharp limestone needles three-quarters of the way up Gunung Api. Some of the pinnacles rise above tree-tops to heights of 45m. The trail leaves from Camp 5, at the base of the Melinau Gorge. It is a very steep climb all the way and a maximum time of three to four hours is allowed to reach the pinnacles (1200m); otherwise you must return. There is no source of water *en route*. It is not possible to reach Gunung Api from the pinnacles. It is strongly recommended that climbers wear gloves as well as long-sleeved shirts, trousers and strong boots to protect themselves against cuts from the razor-sharp rocks. Explorers on Spenser St John's expedition to Mulu in 1856 were cut to shreds on the pinnacles: "three of our men had already been sent back with severe wounds, whilst several of those left were much injured," he wrote, concluding that it was "the world's most nightmarish surface to travel over".

Gunung Api (Fire Mountain) The vegetation is so dry at the summit that it is often set ablaze by lightning in the dry season. The story goes that the fires were so big that locals once thought the mountains were volcanoes. Some of the fires could be seen as far away as the Brunei coast. The summit trek takes a minimum of three days. At 1,710m, it is the tallest limestone outcrop in Borneo and, other than Gunung Benarat (on the other side of the gorge), is probably the most difficult mountain to climb in Borneo. Many attempts to climb it ended in failure; two Berawans from Long Terawan finally made it to the top in 1978, one of them the grandson of Tama Nilong, the rhinoceros-hunter who had climbed Gunung Mulu in 1932. It is impossible to proceed upwards beyond the Pinnacles.

Kerangas forest From Camp 5, cross the Melinau River and head down the Limbang trail towards Lubang Cina. Less than 30 minutes down the trail, fork left along a new trail which leads along a ridge to the south of Gunung Benarat. Climbing higher, after about 40 minutes, the trail passes into an area

A land where money grows on trees

Ever since Sarawak's riverbanks were first settled, the Iban and Orang Ulu tribespeople have practised shifting cultivation, growing crops in their clearings. Today, most of the clearing is done by commercial loggers and the cash-crop is the jungle itself. No one can travel up the Baram without feeling alarmed at the volume of logs, stockpiled like giant matchsticks, on either side of the river for mile after mile. In July 1991 members of two European environmental protest groups chained themselves to logs at Kuala Baram; they were promptly arrested and deported. In March 1992, James Barclay, author of A stroll through Borneo, *a book about logging on the Baram, was also deported from Sarawak after a month in jail. The government says environmentalists are ill-informed and are presenting a false picture to the world. Sarawak's forests, it maintains, will be there in perpetuity.*

The Borneo Company first tried logging on the Baram in the early 1900s, and built Sarawak's first timber mill at Kuala Baram in 1904 but early logging operations were not successful as the timber was attacked by pests. Commercial logging only really began in the 1950s with the arrival of the tractor and the chainsaw. During the 1980s and early 1990s, Sarawak's 130 million-year-old forests were being felled at an unprecedented rate. In the first eight months of 1999 Sarawak exported 3.6 million m³ of logs or a total of more than 6 million m³ of wood products - with a value of RM4bn. While logging has slowed down considerably over the last five years

or so, this is partly, it seems, because the more accessible and valuable forests have been logged out.

Who derives the benefits from the lucrative logging industry is a sensitive political issue – in Sarawak, politics is timber. Logging licences are tickets to get rich quick and the state's chief minister can award timber concessions to whoever they want. In 1987 a rival politician disclosed that the Chief Minister and his allies held about a third of the state's logging concessions alone. The previous Chief Minister had held nearly as much. Sarawak's Minister for Tourism and the Environment, James Wong, is himself a partner in a 180,000-hectare logging concession in Limbang. Environmentalists say these politicians, together with Chinese timber tycoons, are amassing fortunes at the expense of forest tribes. The rush to extract what they can before environmental pressure puts them out of business has fuelled allegations of political manoeuvring, corruption and malpractice.

Although logging companies have provided jobs for upriver tribespeople (a total of 150,000 people are employed in Sarawak's timber industry), logging has wreaked ecological havoc and impinged on tribal lands. The traditional lifestyles of the Penan hunter-gatherers and other Orang Ulu tribes have been threatened as loggers push deeper into the jungle. In the past, Kayan tribesmen would simply have decapitated anyone caught trespassing on their tribal lands; these days the Orang Ulu protest against the encroachment by blockading logging access roads. Many

of leached sandy soils called *kerangas* (heath) forest. This little patch of thinner jungle is a tangle of many varieties of pitcher plants.

Limbang   It is possible to trek from Camp 5 to Limbang, although it is easier to do it the other way. (See page 380.)

Caves

In 1961 geologist Dr G Wilford first surveyed Deer Cave and parts of the Cave of the Winds. But Mulu's biggest subterranean secrets were not revealed until the 1980s.

have been jailed for such protests. The government argues that the jungle tribes are a sideshow and says they have been hijacked by Western environmental groups in a bid to give their campaigns a human face. Environmentalist groups counter that the livelihoods of the forest tribes are as important in the sustainability stakes as the trees themselves.

Since the early 1980s, the water in Sarawak's main rivers has turned brown due to the sediment which is washed into it from the timber camps upstream. Water supplies have been contaminated by chemical pollutants and fish stocks have been depleted – few can survive in the turgid waters. In Belaga, on the upper Rejang, the price of fish has risen 10-fold in a decade. In Orang Ulu longhouses, tribespeople complain that logging operations have chased their game away, turning hunting trips for wild boar into major expeditions.

The state government is eager to allay fears that it is logging without regard to the forest ecology and the indigenous tribes. But while the state's forestry policy looks good on paper, the Enforcement Division of the Forest Department cannot cope with the vast territory it has to police; it is now using satellites to detect areas where illegal logging has occurred. The government dismisses warnings that Sarawak's logging rates (which are the highest in the world) cannot be sustained as scaremongering. But in 1991, the Japan-based International Tropical Timber Organization said that if logging rates were not halved, the state could be 'logged-out' within the decade.

While so-called sustainable logging is now being practised (many environmentalists scoff at the idea), the state remains dependent on the revenue it derives from logging concessions and taxes. The great bulk of income from oil and gas is diverted to federal coffers in Kuala Lumpur. Without logging Sarawak would be left high and dry. To ensure the survival of the industry, wood-processing industries are being promoted, because furniture and sawn timber exports will yield more money from fewer logs. For environmentalists the announcement in 1992 of the creation of the 187,000 hectare Lonjak Entimau forest reserve on the border with Kalimantan was a faint ray of light in an otherwise rather gloomy situation.

Useful websites www.forest.gov.my/ - as one would expect from the Forestry Department's site, very pro-logging, but to their credit in the links page they include Greenpeace, the Sierra club and more!

www.ran.org/ - the Rainforest Action Network's very professional site; some Malaysia information but generally Latin America focused.

www.wcmc.org.uk/forest/data/ - World Conservation Monitoring Centre

vcn.bc.ca/spc/ - Sarawak People's Campaign website, an activist group which represents the interests (as they see it) of the Penan.

www.spotimage.fr/home/appli/forest/ borneo/welcome.htm - a rather technical site which shows how Sarawak's timber reserves are being estimated using SPOT satellite imagery. Some nice pictures.

This part of the Clearwater System, on a small tributary of the Melinau River, is 107 km long. The cave passage – 75 km of which has been explored – links Clearwater Cave (Gua Ayer Jernih) with the **Cave of the Winds** (*Lubang Angin*), to the south. It was discovered in 1988. Clearwater is named after the jungle pool at the foot of the steps leading up to the cave mouth, where the longboats moor. Two species of monophytes – single-leafed plants – grow in the sunlight at the mouth of the cave. They only grow on limestone. A lighting system has been installed down the path to Young Lady's Cave, which ends in a 60m-deep pot hole.

Clearwater Cave
The longest underground cavity in SE Asia & the 7th longest in the world

On the cave walls are some helictites – coral-like lateral formations – and, even more dramatic, are the photokarsts, tiny needles of rock, all pointing towards the light. These are formed in much the same way as their monstrous cousins, the pinnacles (see above), by vegetation, in this case algae, eating into and eroding the softer rock, leaving sharp points of harder rock which 'grow' at about half a mm a year. Inside Clearwater it is possible to hire a rowing boat for RM10 – the river can be followed for about 1½ km upstream, although the current is strong. It is illegal to fish at Clearwater, although it is possible to fish anywhere else in park waters with a hook and line. Clearwater can be reached by a 30-minute longboat ride from the park headquarters. Individual travellers must charter a boat for a return trip. Tour agents build the cost of this trip into their package, which works out considerably cheaper.

Deer Cave This is another of Mulu's record-breakers: it has the world's biggest cave mouth and the biggest cave passage, which is 2.2 km long and 220m high at its highest point. Before its inclusion in the park, the cave had been a well known hunting ground for deer attracted to the pools of salty water running off the guano. The silhouettes of some of the cave's limestone formations have been creatively interpreted; notably the profile of Abraham Lincoln. Adam's and Eve's Showers, at the east end of the cave, are hollow stalactites; water pressure increases when it rains. This darker section at the east end of Deer Cave is the preferred habitat of the naked bat. Albino earwigs live on the bats' oily skin and regularly drop off. The cave's east entrance opens onto 'The Garden of Eden' – a luxuriant patch of jungle, which was once part of the cave system until the roof collapsed. This separated Deer Cave and Green Cave, which lies adjacent to the east mouth; it is open only to caving expeditions.

The west end of the cave is home to several million wrinkle-lipped and horseshoe bats. Hundreds of thousands of these bats pour out of the cave at dusk. Bat hawks can often be seen swooping in for spectacular kills. The helipad, about 500m south of the cave mouth, provides excellent vantage points. VIPs' helicopters, arriving for the show, are said to have disturbed the bats in recent years. From the analysis of the three tonnes of saline guano the bats excrete every day, scientists conclude that they make an 80 km dash to the coast for meals of insects washed down with seawater. Cave cockroaches eat the guano, ensuring that the cavern does not become choked with what locals call 'black snow'. ■ *Getting there: an hour's trek along a plank walk from park headquarters.*

Lang's Cave Part of the same hollow mountain as Deer Cave, Lang's Cave is less well known but its formations are more beautiful, and contains impressive curtain stalactites and intricate coral-like helictites. The cave is well illuminated and protected by bus-stop-style plastic tunnels.

The Sarawak Chamber
The largest natural chamber in the world

Discovered in 1984, this chamber is 600m long, 450m wide and 100m high – big enough, it is said, to accommodate 40 jumbo jets wing-tip to wing-tip and eight nose-to-tail. Unfortunately it is not open to the public as it is considered too dangerous.

For cavers wishing to explore caves not open to the public, there are designated 'adventure caves' within an hour of park headquarters. Experienced cave guides can be organized from headquarters. The most accessible of these is the one hour trek following the river course through Clearwater Cave. Cavers should bring their own equipment.

Rapids Just outside the national park boundary on the Tutoh River there are rapids which are possible to shoot; this can be arranged through tour agencies.

Park essentials

See also the following 2 websites: tourism.gov.my/nationalpark/mulu.html; members.tripod.com/~lipscombe/index-2.html. The latter covers the Mulu Caves.

Entrance fee & permits
It is best to avoid visiting the park during school & public holidays.
In Dec the park is closed to locals, but remains open to tourists

Admission is RM3, RM5 for camera, RM10 for video, RM200 for professional filming. Permits can be obtained from the National Parks and Wildlife Office, Old Forestry Building, Jln Angkasa, Miri, T436637/431975, also from Visitors' Information Centre, Lot 452, Jln Melayu, Miri, T434184, F434179. Open Mon-Thur 0800-1245 and 1400-1645, Fri 0800-1130 and 1430-1645, Sat 0800-1245. It is necessary to book and pay a deposit for accommodation at the same time. Permits can also be picked up from the National Parks and Wildlife Office, 1st Flr, Wisma Sumber Alam, Kuching, T248088. Accommodation can be booked through Kuching too. It is also necessary to get a permit from the police and the Miri or Marudi Residents. In Marudi, both the resident's office (Fort Hose) and the police station are on the airport road. This bureaucratic mess can be avoided if travel arrangements are left to a Miri travel agent. For further information, email sarawak@po.jaring.my or visit the website, www.sarawaktourism.com.

There is a small store at the park headquarters that sells basic necessities; there is also a small shop just outside the park boundary, at Long Pala. A sleeping bag is essential for Gunung Mulu trips; other essential equipment includes good insect repellent, wet weather gear and a powerful torch.

Equipment

No visitors are permitted to travel in the park without an authorized guide which can be arranged from park headquarters or booked in advance from the National Parks office in Miri (see above). Most of the Mulu Park guides are very well informed about flora and fauna, geology and tribal customs. Tour agencies organize guides as part of their fee. **Guide fees**: RM20 per cave (or per day) and an extra RM10 per night. Mulu summit trips: minimum of RM264 for 4 days, 3 nights; Melinau Gorge and Pinnacles: minimum RM110 (3 days, 2 nights). Ornithological guides cost an additional RM10 a day. Porterage: max 10 kg and RM30 per day. RM1 for each extra kilo. Mulu summit: minimum RM90; Melinau Gorge (Camp 5): minimum RM65.

Guides
It is usual to tip guides & porters

Sleeping in the park must be booked in advance at the National Parks and Wildlife Office Forest Department in Miri or Kuching. Booking fee is RM20 per party and the maximum party size is 10 people. Bookings must be confirmed 5 days before visit. Two Miri-based travel agents have private accommodation in the park: *Seridan Mulu Tour* (RM10 per night) and *Tropical Adventure* (RM10 per night).

Sleeping

Park headquarters *Annexe* (hostel) (1 room, 10 per room) RM10 per person; *Annexe* (8 rooms, 5 per room) RM75 per room; *Chalet class 3* (4 rooms, 4 per room) RM63 per room; *Chalet class 2* (2 rooms, 3 per room) RM94 per room or RM180 per house; *VIP Chalet* (3 per room), RM200, *Rumah Rehat Jenis 2*, RM210 per room; *Rumah Rehat Jenis 3*, RM157 per room. For accommodation bookings contact the National Parks and Wildlife Office. There is also a privately owned hostel, the *Melinau Canteen*, T011291641 or T085657884, with dorm beds about 5 mins' walk downstream from the park headquarters, on the other bank of the river, RM10 per person.
   Long Pala AL *Royal Mulu Resort*, Sungai Melinau, Muku, Miri, T085421122, F085421088. A/c, restaurants, owned by Japan's Royal Hotel Group Rihga the resort currently has 50 chalets and plans more, also proposes to carve an 18-hole golf-course out of rainforest adjacent to parks, 35 mins from Miri, has sparked much resentment among local tribespeople. In August 1993, Berawan tour guides, boat-operators and labourers in the park went on strike for 2 weeks because they say the resort was built on land which is theirs by customary right. A 20 min (RM5) boat

Sarawak

ride downstream from park headquarters. Two hostels, run and owned by tour companies but with rooms available for drop-ins if not already booked, kitchen and bathrooms, crockery and bed linen provided. Private guesthouses are run by tour companies (RM10-15 plus meals). Tour agents offer private accommodation of a high standard, just outside the national park boundary. There is 12-hr electricity supply; the water supply is treated but it is advised to boil the water before drinking.

Camping You can only use tents provided, RM8.

Eating There are stoves and cooking utensils available and the small store at park headquarters also sells basic supplies. There is a small canteen at park headquarters but the menu is limited and the food rather boring. As an alternative, cross the suspension bridge and walk alongside the road to the first house on the left; down the bank from here is the *Mulu Canteen*, which fronts onto the river (so there is no sign on the road). There is also the *Melinau Canteen*, just downriver from the park headquarters. There is a small shop with basic supplies at Long Pala. All tour companies with their own accommodation offer food.

Transport Visitors are recommended to go through one of the Miri-based travel agents (see page 367). The average cost of a Mulu package (per person) is RM350-400 (4 days/3 nights) or RM500 (6 days/5 nights).

Around the park Independent travellers will find it more expensive arranging the trip on their own. Longboats can be chartered privately from park headquarters, if required (maximum 10 people per boat). The cost is calculated on a rather complicated system which includes a rate for the boat, a charge for the engine based on its horsepower, a separate payment for the driver and front-man, and then fuel on top of that. The total cost can be RM100+. How far these boats can actually get upriver depends on the season. They often have to be hauled over rapids, whatever the time of year.

Air Daily flights from Miri to Marudi, 15 mins. A new airstrip has been constructed just downriver from park headquarters and is now able to accommodate larger 50 seater planes. Currently 3 flights per day from Miri, and 2 daily from Marudi and Limbang. The price of a flight is only marginally more expensive than taking the bus and boat from Miri.

Bus/taxi/boat Bus or taxi from Miri to Marudi express boat jetty near Kuala Baram at mouth of river Baram (see page 368). Regular express boats from Kuala Baram to Marudi, 3 hrs (RM15) from early morning until about 1500. One express boat per day (leaves around noon) from Marudi to Long Tarawan on the Tutoh River (tributary of the Baram), via Long Apoh. During the dry season express boats cannot reach Long Terawan and terminate at Long Panai, on the Tutoh River, where longboats continue to Long Terawan (RM20). Longboats leave Long Tarawan for Mulu park headquarters: this used to be regular and comparatively cheap; now that most people travel to Mulu by air, longboats are less frequent and sometimes need to be privately chartered – an expensive business. Mulu Park HQ is 1½ hrs up the Melinau River (a tributary of the Tutoh) (RM35). As you approach the park from Long Tarawan the Tutoh River narrows and becomes shallower; there are 14 rapids before the Melinau River, which forms the park boundary. When the water is low, the trip can be very slow and involve pulling the boat over the shallows, this accounts for high charter rates. For a group of 9 or 10 it is cheaper to charter a boat (RM250 one-way). The first jetty on the Melinau River is Long Pala, where most of the tour companies have accommodation. The park headquarters is another 15 mins upriver. Longboats returning to Long Terawan leave the headquarters at dawn each day, calling at jetties *en route*.

Bario and the Kelabit Highlands

Bario (Bareo) lies in the Kelabit Highlands, a plateau 1,000m above sea level   *Colour map 4, grid C2*
close to the Kalimantan border. The highlands are Sarawak's answer to the hill
stations on the peninsula. The undulating Bario valley is surrounded by moun-
tains and fed by countless small streams which in turn feed into a maze of irriga-
tion canals.

The local Kelabits' skill in harnessing water has allowed them to practise wet
rice cultivation rather than the more common slash-and-burn hill rice techniques. Fragrant Bario rice is prized in Sarawak and commands a premium in
the coastal markets. The Kelabit Highlands' more temperate climate also
allows the cultivation of a wide range of fruit and vegetables.

The plateau's near-impregnable ring of mountains effectively cut the
Kelabit off from the outside world: it is the only area in Borneo which was
never penetrated by Islam. In 1911 the Resident of Baram mounted an expedition which ventured into the mountains to ask the Kelabit to stop raiding the
Brooke Government's subjects. It took the expedition 17 days to cross the
Tamu Abu mountain range, to the west of Bario. The Kelabit were then
brought under the control of the Sarawak government.

The most impressive mountain in the Bario area is the distinctive twin peak
of the sheer-faced 2,043m **Bukit Batu Lawi** to the northwest of Bario. The
Kelabit traditionally believed the mountain had an evil spirit and so never went
near it. Today such superstitions are a thing of the past since locals are mostly
evangelical Christians.

In 1945, the plateau was selected as the only possible parachute drop zone in
North Borneo not captured by the Japanese. The Allied Special Forces which
parachuted into Bario were led by Tom Harrisson, who later became curator
of the Sarawak Museum and made the famous archaeological discoveries at
Niah Caves (see page 359). His expedition formed an irregular tribal army
against the Japanese, which gained control over large areas of North Borneo in
the following months.

Because of the rugged terrain surrounding the plateau, the area mainly attracts   **Treks around**
serious mountaineers. There are many trails to the longhouses around the pla-   **Bario**
teau area, however. Treks to Bario can be organized through travel agents in   *It is necessary to have a*
Miri, see page 365. Guides can also be hired in Bario and surrounding   *permit to visit the Bario*
longhouses for RM30-40 per day. It is best to go through the Penghulu, Ngiap   *area, obtainable from*
Ayu, the Kelabit chief. He goes round visiting many of the longhouses in the   *the Resident's offices in*
area once a month. It is recommended that visitors to Bario come equipped   *Miri or Marudi*
with sleeping bags and camping equipment. There are no formal facilities for
tourists and provisions should be brought from Miri or Marudi. The best time
to visit Bario is between March and October. **NB** There are no banks or money
changers in Bario.

Several of the surrounding mountains can be climbed from Bario, but they
are, without exception, difficult climbs. Even on walks just around the Bario
area, guides are essential as trails are poorly marked. The lower ('female') peak
of **Bukit Batu Lawi** can be climbed without equipment, but the sheer sided
'male' peak requires proper rock-climbing equipment – it was first scaled in
1986. **Gunung Murudi** (2,423m) is the highest mountain in Sarawak; it is a
very tough climb.

Sleeping Bario Lodging House, above the shop, or with the Penghulu in his kampong house, at Bario Bharu, 10 mins from the airstrip. There is also another recommended place to stay, ***Tarawe's*** (**D**), which is a good source of information and well run. Most visitors camp.

Transport **Air** Bario's airstrip is very small and because of its position, flights are often cancelled because of mist and clouds. During school holidays flights are also often booked up. Connections with Miri and Marudi. **Foot** It is a 7-day trek from Marudi to Bario, sleeping in longhouses *en route*. This trip should be organized through a Miri travel agent (see page 365). *Alo Doda* is recommended.

Limbang

Very few tourists reach Limbang or Lawas but they are good stopping-off points for more adventurous routes to Sabah and Brunei. Limbang is the finger of Sarawak territory which splits Brunei in two.

Colour map 4, grid B2

Limbang is the administrative centre for the Fifth Division, and was ceded to the Brooke government by the Sultan of Brunei in 1890. The Trusan Valley, to the east of the wedge of Brunei, had been ceded to Sarawak in 1884.

Limbang's **Old Fort** was built in 1897, renovated 1966, and was used as the administrative centre. During the Brooke era half the ground floor was used as a jail. It is now a centre of religious instruction, *Majlis Islam*. Limbang is famous for its **Pasar Tamu** every Friday, where jungle and native produce is sold. Limbang also has an attractive small museum, **Muzium Wilayah**, 400m south of the centre along Jalan Kubu. Housed in a wooden villa, painted beige and white, the museum has a collection of ethnic artefacts from the region, including basketry, musical instruments and weapons. ■ *0900-1800, Tue-Sun*. To the right of the museum, a small road climbs the hill to a park with a man-made lake.

Sarawak

Excursions

Sitt Travel specializes in treks in this area & is the ticketing agent for Miri tour operators

Trek to Gunung Mulu National Park Take a car south to Medamit; from there hire a longboat upriver to Mulu Madang, an Iban longhouse (three hours, depending on water level). Alternatively, go further upriver to Kuala Terikan (six to seven hours at low-water, four hours at high-water) where there is a simple zinc-roofed camp. From there take a longboat one hour up the Terikan River to Lubang China, which is the start of a two-hour trek along a well used trail to Camp 5. There is a park rangers' camp about 20 minutes out of Kuala Terikan where it is possible to obtain permits and arrange for a guide to meet you at Camp 5. The longboats are cheaper to hire in the wet season.

Essentials

Sleeping Limbang has become a sex stop for Bruneians whose government takes a more hardline attitude to such moral transgressions and consequently many hotels and guesthouses have a fair share of short-time guests.

B *Centre Point Hotel*, T212922. Newish place with a/c and restaurant which tops Limbang's limited bill of hotels. **B-C** ***Muhibbah***, Lot T790, Bank St, T213705, F212153. Located in town centre, has seen better days, but rooms are fairly clean with a/c, TV and bathroom. **B-C** ***Metro***, Lot 781, Jln Bangkita, T211133, F211051. A fairly new addition to Limbang's mid-range accommodation, under 30 rooms, all with a/c, TV, fridge, tea and coffee-making facilities, good quality beds, small but clean rooms. Recommended. **B-C** ***National Inn***, 62a Jln Buangsiol, T212922, F212282. Probably the best of the 3 hotels along the river here, comfortable a/c rooms with TV, mini-bar, tea and coffee-making facilities, higher rates for river view.

3 *Tong Lok* a/c Chinese restaurant next to *National Inn*, gruesome pink table cloths **Eating** and fluorescent lighting, but good quality Chinese food.
2 *Maggie's Café* on the riverside near *National Inn*, Chinese coffee shop, pleasant location, tables outside next to river in evening – braziers set up in evening too for good grilled fish on banana leaf. Recommended.
1 *Hai Hong*, 1 block south of *Maggie's*, a simple coffee shop – good for breakfast with fried egg and chips on the menu.

May The movable *Buffalo Racing* festival marks the end of the harvesting season. **Festivals**

Air Daily connections with Miri, Mulu and Lawas; weekly flights to Labuan; and twice **Transport** weekly connections with KK. The airport is about 5 km from town and taxis ferry passengers in. **Boat** Regular connections with Lawas, departs early in the morning (2 hrs, RM15). There is also an early morning express departure to Labuan. **International connections with Brunei** Regular boat connections with Bandar Seri Begawan, Brunei (30 mins, RM15).

Useful addresses Resident's Office: T21960. **Directory**

Lawas

Lawas District was ceded to Sarawak in 1905. The Limbang River, which cuts through the town, is the main transport route. It is possible to travel from Miri to Bandar Seri Begawan (Brunei) by road, then on to Limbang and Lawas. From Lawas there are direct buses to Kota Kinabalu in Sabah.

A-B *Country Park Hotel*, Lot 235, Jln Trusan, T85522 A/c, restaurant. **C** *Lawas Federal*, **Sleeping** 8 Jln Masjid Baru, T85115. A/c, restaurant. **D** *Hup Guan Lodging House*, T85362. Some a/c, above a pool hall so can be noisy but the rooms are clean and spacious and reasonable value for money.

Air Connections with Miri, Limbang, Kuching, Labuan and Kota Kinabalu. **Bus** Con- **Transport** nections with Merapok on the Sarawak/Sabah border (RM5). From here there are connections to Beaufort in Sabah. Twice-daily connections with Kota Kinabalu, 4 hrs (RM20). **Boat** Regular connections to Limbang, 2 hrs. Daily morning boat departures for Brunei.

Sarawak

Background

For general background on Borneo, see page 489. For information on Sarawak's geography, climate, flora & fauna, page 516

About a third of the population is made up of Iban tribespeople – who used to be known as the 'Sea Dayaks' – former headhunters, who live in longhouses on the lower reaches of the rivers. Chinese immigrants, whose forebears arrived during the 19th century, make up another third. A fifth of the population is Malay; most are native Sarawakians, but some came from the peninsula after the state joined the Malaysian Federation in 1963. The rest of Sarawak's inhabitants are indigenous tribal groups, of which the main ones are the Melanau, the Bidayuh and upriver Orang Ulu such as the Kenyah, Kayan and Kelabits; the Penan are among Southeast Asia's few remaining hunter-gatherers.

For over 150 years, Sarawak was under the rule of the 'White Rajahs' who tried to keep the peace between warring tribes of headhunters. The Brooke family ran Sarawak as their private country and their most obvious legacies are the public buildings in Kuching, the state capital, and the forts along the rivers. Outside Kuching, the towns have little to offer; most are predominantly Chinese and are mainly modern, without much grace or character. One or two are boom-towns, having grown rich on the back of the logging and oil and gas industries. From a tourist's point of view, the towns are just launching-pads for the longhouses and jungle upriver.

History

Sarawak earned its place in the archaeological textbooks when a 40,000-year-old human skull belonging to a boy of about 15 was unearthed in the Niah Caves in 1958 (see page 359), predating the earliest relics found on the Malay peninsula by about 30,000 years. The caves were continuously inhabited for tens of thousands of years and many shards of Palaeolithic and Neolithic pottery, tools and jewellery as well as carved burial boats have been excavated at the site. There are also prehistoric cave paintings. In the first millennium AD, the Niah Caves were home to a prosperous community, which traded birds' nests, hornbill ivory, bezoar stones, rhinoceros horns and other jungle produce with Chinese traders in exchange for porcelain and beads.

Some of Sarawak's tribes may be descended from these cave people, although others, notably the Iban shifting cultivators, migrated from Kalimantan's Kapuas River valley from the 16th-19th centuries. Malay *Orang Laut*, sea people, migrated to Sarawak's coasts and made a living from fishing, trading and piracy. At the height of Sumatra's Srivijayan Empire in the 11th and 12th centuries, many Sumatran Malays migrated to North Borneo. Chinese traders were active along the Sarawak coast from as early as the seventh century: Chinese coins and Han pottery have been discovered at the mouth of the Sarawak River. Most of the coins and ceramics, however, date from the Chinese Song and Yuan periods in the 11th-14th centuries.

From the 14th century right up to the 20th century, Sarawak's history was inextricably intertwined with that of the neighbouring Sultanate of Brunei, which, until the arrival of the White Rajahs of Sarawak, held sway over the coastal areas of North Borneo. For a more detailed account of how Sarawak's White Rajahs came to whittle away the sultan's territory and expand into the vacuum of his receding empire.

Enter James Brooke

As the Sultanate of Brunei began to decline around the beginning of the 18th century, the Malays of coastal Sarawak attempted to break free from their tributary overlord. They claimed an independent ancestry from Brunei and exercised firm control over the Dayak tribes inland and upriver. But in the early 19th century Brunei started to reassert its power over them, dispatching Pangiran Mahkota from the Brunei court to govern Sarawak in 1827 and supervise the mining of high-grade antimony ore, which was exported to Singapore to be used in medicine and as an alloy. The name 'Sarawak' comes from the Malay word *serawak*, meaning 'antimony'.

Mahkota founded Kuching, but relations with the local Malays became strained and Mahkota's problems were compounded by the marauding Ibans of the Saribas and Skrang rivers who raided coastal communities. In 1836 the local Malay chiefs, led by Datu Patinggi Ali, rebelled against Governor Mahkota, prompting the Sultan of Brunei to send his uncle, Rajah Muda Hashim to suppress the uprising. But Hashim failed to quell the disturbances and the situation deteriorated when the rebels approached the Sultan of Sambas, now in Northwest Kalimantan, for help from the Dutch. Then, in 1839, James Brooke sailed up the Sarawak River to Kuching.

Hashim was desperate to regain control and Brooke, in the knowledge that the British would support any action that countered the threat of Dutch influence, struck a deal with him. He pressed Hashim to grant him the governorship of Sarawak in exchange for suppressing the rebellion, which he duly did. In 1842 Brooke became Rajah of Sarawak. Pangiran Mahkota – the now disenfranchised former governor of Sarawak – formed an alliance with an Iban pirate chief on the Skrang River, while another Brunei prince, Pangiran Usop, joined Illanun pirates. Malaysian historian J Kathirithamby-Wells writes: "… piracy and politics became irrevocably linked and Brooke's battle against his political opponents became advertised as a morally justified war against the pirate communities of the coast."

The suppression of piracy in the 19th century became a full-time occupation for the rulers of Sarawak and Brunei – although the court of Brunei was well known to have derived a substantial chunk of its income from piracy. Rajah James Brooke believed that as long as pirates remained free to pillage the coasts, commerce would not pick up and his kingdom would never develop; ridding Sarawak's estuaries of pirates – both Iban ('Sea Dayaks') and Illanun – became an act of political survival. In his history of the White Rajahs, Robert Payne writes:

"Nearly every day people came to Kuching with tales about the pirates: how they had landed in a small creek, spread out, made their way to a village, looted everything in sight, murdered everyone they could lay their hands on, and then vanished as swiftly as they came. The Sultan of Brunei was begging for help against them."

Anti-piracy missions afforded James Brooke an excuse to extend his kingdom, as he worked his way up the coasts, 'pacifying' the Sea Dayak pirates. Brooke declared war on them and with the help of Royal Naval Captain Henry Keppel (of latter-day Singapore's Keppel Shipyard fame), he led a number of punitive raids against the Iban 'Sea Dayaks' in 1833, 1834 and 1849. "The assaults", writes DJM Tate in *Rajah Brooke's Borneo*, "largely achieved their purpose, and were applauded in the Straits, but the appalling loss of life incurred upset many drawing-room humanitarians in Britain." There were an estimated 25,000 pirates living along the North Borneo coast when Brooke became Rajah. He led many punitive expeditions against them, culminating in his notorious battle against the Saribas pirate fleet in 1849.

In that incident, Brooke ambushed and killed hundreds of Saribas Dayaks at Batang Maru. The barbarity of the ambush (which was reported in the *Illustrated London News*) outraged public opinion in Britain and in Singapore – a commission of inquiry in Singapore acquitted Brooke, but badly damaged his prestige. In the British parliament, he was cast as a 'mad despot' who had to be prevented from committing further massacres. But the action led the Sultan of Brunei to grant him the Saribas and Skrang districts (now Sarawak's Second Division) in 1853, marking the beginning of the Brookes' relentless expansionist drive. Eight years later, James Brooke persuaded the sultan to give him what became Sarawak's Third Division, after he drove out the Illanun pirates who had disrupted the sago trade from Mukah and Oya, around Bintulu.

James Brooke: the white knight errant

James Brooke lived the life of a Boy's Own comic-book hero. To the socialites of London, many of whom idolized him, he was the king of an exotic far-away country, on a mysterious jungled island, inhabited by roving tribes of headhunters. It was a romantic image, but while it was also a tough life, it was not far from the truth. The Brookes were a family of benevolent despots, characterized by historian Robert Payne as "tempestuous and dedicated men, who sometimes quarrelled violently among themselves, but closed ranks whenever the fortunes of their people were at stake. They were proud and possessive, but also humble." There were three White Rajahs, who ruled for over a century, but it was James Brooke, with his forceful personality, violent temper, vengeful instincts but compassion for his people, that set the tone and created the legend.

James was born in India in 1803, the son of a High Court judge in Benares. He joined the Indian army, and fought in the First Anglo-Burmese War as a cavalry officer, where he was mentioned in dispatches for "most conspicuous gallantry." But in 1825 he was hit in the chest by a bullet and almost left for dead on the battlefield. He was forced to return to England where any military ambitions he might have had were dashed by the severity of his injury. He recovered enough

to make two trips to the East in the 1830s, on one of which he visited Penang and Singapore where he became an admirer of Sir Thomas Stamford Raffles, Singapore's founding father. Back in England, he bought a schooner, The Royalist, and drew up plans to sail to Maurdu Bay (North Sabah), to explore the fabled lake at Kini Ballu (see page 435). His trip did not work out as planned.

The Royalist arrived in Singapore in 1839 and the governor asked Brooke to deliver a letter of thanks to Rajah Muda Hashim, the ruler in Kuching, who had rescued some shipwrecked British sailors. He called in briefly, as promised, was intrigued with what he found, but sailed on. When he returned a year later, the Rajah Muda was still struggling to contain the rebellion of local Malay chiefs. Hashim said that if Brooke helped suppress the rebellion, he could have the Sarawak River area as his and the title of Rajah. Brooke took him up on the offer, quelled the revolt and after leaning heavily on Hashim to keep his word, became acting Rajah of Sarawak on 24 September 1841. His title was confirmed by the Sultan of Brunei the following year.

The style of Brooke's government – which also characterized that of his successors – is described by historian Mary Turnbull as "a paternal, informal government based upon consultation

In 1857, James Brooke ran into more trouble. Chinese Hakka goldminers, who had been in Bau (further up the Sarawak River) longer than he had been in Kuching, had grown resentful of his attempts to stamp out the opium trade and their secret societies. They attacked Kuching, set the Malay kampongs ablaze and killed several European officials; Brooke escaped by swimming across the river from his *astana*. His nephew, Charles, led a group of Skrang Dayaks to chase after the Hakka invaders, who fled across the border into Dutch Borneo; about 1,000 were killed by the Ibans on the way; 2,500 survived. Historian Robert Payne writes: "The fighting lasted for more than a month. From time to time Dayaks would return with strings of heads, which they cleaned and smoked over slow fires, especially happy when they could do this in full view of the Chinese in the bazaars who sometimes recognized people they had known." Payne says Brooke was plagued by guilt over how he handled the Chinese rebellion, for so many deaths could not easily be explained away. Neither James nor Charles ever fully trusted the Chinese again, although the Teochew, Cantonese and Hokkien merchants in Kuching never caused them any trouble.

with local community chiefs". Brooke realized the importance of maintaining tribal laws and observing local customs; he also recognized that without his protection, the people of Sarawak would be open to exploitation by Europeans and Chinese. He determined to keep such influences out. In 1842, shortly after he was confirmed as Rajah, he wrote: "I hate the idea of a Utopian government, with laws cut and dried ready for the natives... I am going on slowly and surely basing everything on their own laws, consulting all the headmen at every stage, instilling what I think is right – separating the abuses from the customs." Like his successors, James Brooke had great respect for the Dayaks and the Malays, whom he treated as equals. In the 1840s he wrote: "Sarawak belongs to the Malays, Sea Dayaks, Land Dayaks, Kenyahs, Milanos, Muruts, Kadayans, Bisayahs, and other tribes, and not to us. It is for them we labour, not for ourselves."

Unlike most colonial adventurers of the time, Brooke was not in it for the money. He had a hopeless head for figures and his country was constantly in debt; it would have gone bankrupt if it were not for an eccentric English spinster, Angela Burdett-Coutts, who lent him large amounts of money. In his history of The White Rajahs of Sarawak, Robert Payne wrote that "he was incapable of drawing up a balance sheet [and] could never concentrate upon details. He had the large view always and large views incline dangerously towards absolute power, and he had seized power with all the strength and cunning that was in him. He possessed the Elizabethan love for power, believing that some Englishmen are granted a special dispensation by God to wield power to the uttermost."

By pacifying pirate-infested coastal districts, Brooke persuaded the Sultan of Brunei to cede him more and more territory, so that towards the end of his reign, Sarawak was a sizeable country. An attack of smallpox, combined with the emotional traumas of a Chinese rebellion in 1857 and the public inquiry into his punitive ambush on the Saribas pirates, seems to have broken his spirit, however. His illness aged him, although an old Malay man, who knew him well, said his eyes remained "fierce like those of a crocodile". Rajah Sir James Brooke (he was knighted by Queen Victoria) visited Sarawak for the last time in 1863 following a succession dispute in which he disinherited his heir, Brooke Johnson. He retired to Dorset in England a disillusioned and embittered man. On Christmas Eve 1867 he had a stroke, and died six months later. When news of his death reached Sarawak, guns sounded a thunderous salute across the Sarawak River.

Charles Johnson (who changed his name to Brooke after his elder brother, Brooke Johnson, had been disinherited by James for insubordination) became the second Rajah of Sarawak in 1863. He ruled for nearly 50 years. Charles did not have James Brooke's forceful personality, and was much more reclusive – probably as a result of working in remote jungle outposts for 10 years in government service. Historian Robert Payne notes that "in James Brooke there was something of the knight errant at the mercy of his dream. Charles was the pure professional, a stern soldier who thought dreaming was the occupation of fools. There was no nonsense about him." He engendered great loyalty, however, in his administrators, who he worked hard for little reward.

The second generation: Rajah Charles Brooke

Charles maintained his uncle's consultative system of government and formed a Council Negeri, or national council, comprised of his top government officials, Malay leaders and tribal headmen, which met every couple of years to hammer out policy changes. His frugal financial management meant that by 1877 Sarawak was no longer in debt and the economy gradually expanded. The country was not a wealthy one, however, and had very few natural resources – its soils proved

Sarawak

Piracy: the resurgence of an ancient scourge

The straits of Melaka and the many islands in this, one of the world's busiest waterways, have always had a murderous reputation. In the first three months of 1999 there were 66 pirate attacks on shipping around the world; 38 occurred in this small corner of the globe's seas, according to the International Maritime Bureau. Some ships just suffer hit-and-run attacks; other pirates hijack entire vessels, whose cargo is removed and the ship resold under another name. In the autumn of 1998 the Japanese-owned Tenyu, carrying a cargo worth US$2m, left an Indonesian port – and a day later, radio contact was lost. In December 1998 the ship, renamed and with a new crew, was discovered in a Chinese port, the original crew presumed murdered and thrown overboard. The original owners of the vessels had to pay the equivalent of nearly US$200,000 to get their ship back.

Many modern pirates use high-speed boats to escape into international waters and avoid capture by racing from one country's waters into another's. Co-operative international action offers the only way to successfully patrol the shipping lanes. Following the IMB conference, a Regional Piracy Centre was set up in Kuala Lumpur.

But while modern shipping companies might consider the rise in piracy a new and dangerous threat, there is nothing new about piracy in Southeast Asian waters. For centuries, pirates have murdered and pillaged their way along the region's coasts, taking hundreds of slaves as part of their booty. As far back as the 6th century, pirates are thought to have been responsible for the destruction and abandonment of the ancient Hindu capital of Langkasuka, in the northwest Malaysian state of Kedah. Piracy grew as trade flourished: the Strait of Melaka and the South China Sea were perfect haunts, being on the busy trade routes between China, India, the Middle East and Europe. Most of the pirates were the Malay Orang Laut (sea gypsies) and Bugis who lived in the Riau Archipelago, the Acehnese of North Sumatra, the Ibans of the Sarawak estuaries and – most feared of all – the Illanun and Balinini pirates of Sulu and Mindanao in the Philippines. The Illanuns were particularly ferocious pirates, sailing in huge perahus with up to 150 slaves as oarsmen, in as many as three tiers. The name lanun means pirate in Malay.

unsuitable for agriculture. In the 1880s, Charles' faith in the Chinese community was sufficiently restored to allow Chinese immigration, and the government subsidized the new settlers. By using 'friendly' downriver Dayak groups to subdue belligerent tribes upriver, Charles managed to pacify the interior by 1880.

When Charles took over from his ailing uncle in 1863, he found himself in charge of a large country; but he proved to be even more of an expansionist. In 1868 he tried to take control of the Baram River valley, but London did not approve secession of the territory until 1882. It became the Fourth Division; in 1884, Charles acquired the Trusan Valley from the Sultan of Brunei, and in 1890, he annexed Limbang ending a six-year rebellion by local chiefs against the sultan. The two territories were united to form the Fifth Division, after which Sarawak completely surrounded Brunei. In 1905, the British North Borneo Chartered Company gave up the Lawas Valley to Sarawak too. "By 1890," writes Robert Payne, "Charles was ruling over a country as large as England and Scotland with the help of about 20 European officers." When the First World War broke out in 1914, Charles was in England and he ruled Sarawak from Cirencester.

At the age of 86, Charles handed the reins to his eldest son, Charles Vyner Brooke, in 1916 and died the following year. Vyner was 42 when he became Rajah and had already served his father's government for nearly 20 years. "Vyner was a man of peace, who took no delight in bloodshed and ruled with humanity and compassion," writes Robert Payne. He was a delegator by nature, and under him the old paternalistic style of government gave way to a more professional bureaucracy. On the centenary of the Brooke administration in September 1941, Vyner promulgated a written constitution, and renounced his autocratic powers in favour of working in co-operation with a Supreme Council. This was opposed by his nephew and heir, Anthony Brooke, who saw it as a move to undermine his succession. To protest against this, and his uncle's decision to appoint a mentally deranged Muslim Englishman as his Chief Secretary, Anthony left for Singapore. The Rajah dismissed him from the service in September 1941. Three months later the Japanese Imperial Army invaded; Vyner Brooke was in Australia at the time, and his younger brother, Bertram, was ill in London.

Japanese troops took Kuching on Christmas Day 1941 having captured the Miri oilfield a few days earlier. European administrators were interned and many later died. A Kuching-born Chinese, Albert Kwok, led an armed resistance against the Japanese in neighbouring British North Borneo (Sabah) – see page 476 – but in Sarawak, there was no organized guerrilla movement. Iban tribespeople instilled fear into the occupying forces, however, by roaming the jungle taking Japanese heads, which were proudly added to much older longhouse head galleries. Despite the Brooke régime's century-long effort to stamp out head-hunting, the practice was encouraged by Tom Harrisson (one of Sarawak's most famous 'adopted' sons) who parachuted into the Kelabit Highlands towards the end of the Second World War and put together an irregular army of upriver tribesmen to fight the Japanese. He offered them 'ten-bob-a-nob' for Japanese heads. Australian forces liberated Kuching on 11 September 1945 and Sarawak was placed under Australian Military Administration for seven months.

After the war, the Colonial Office in London decided the time had come to bring Sarawak into the modern era, replacing the anachronous White Rajahs, introducing an education system and building a rudimentary infrastructure. The Brookes had become an embarrassment to the British government as they continued to squabble among themselves. Anthony Brooke desperately wanted to claim what he felt was his, while the Colonial Office wanted Sarawak to become a crown colony or revert to Malay rule. No one was sure whether Sarawak wanted the Brookes back or not.

In February 1946 the ageing Vyner shocked his brother Bertram and his nephew Anthony, the Rajah Muda (or heir apparent), by issuing a proclamation urging the people of Sarawak to accept the King of England as their ruler. In doing so he effectively handed the country over to Britain. Vyner thought the continued existence of Sarawak as the private domain of the Brooke family an anachronism; but Anthony thought it a betrayal. The British government sent a commission to Sarawak to ascertain what the people wanted. In May 1946, the Council Negri agreed – by a 19-16 majority – to transfer power to Britain, provoking protests and demonstrations and resulting in the assassination of the British governor by a Malay in Sibu in 1949. He and three other anti-cessionists were sentenced to death. Two years later, Anthony Brooke, who remained deeply resentful about the demise of the Brooke Dynasty, abandoned his claim and urged his supporters to end their campaign.

As a British colony, Sarawak's economy expanded and oil and timber production increased which funded the much-needed expansion of education and health services. As with British North Borneo (Sabah), Britain was keen to give Sarawak political independence and, following Malaysian independence in 1957, saw the best means to this end as being through the proposal of Malaysian Prime Minister Tunku Abdul Rahman, who suggested the formation of a federation to include Singapore,

The third generation: Charles Vyner Brooke

The end of empire

Sarawak

Konfrontasi

The birth of the Federation of Malaysia on 31 August 1963 was not helped by the presence of heckling spectators. The Philippines was opposed to British North Borneo (Sabah) joining the federation because the territory had been a dependency of the Sultan of Sulu for over 170 years until he had agreed to lease it to the North Borneo Chartered Company in 1877. But Indonesia's objection to the formation of the federation was even more vociferous. In Jakarta, crowds were chanting 'Crush Malaysia!' at President Sukarno's bidding. He launched an undeclared war against Malaysia, which became known as konfrontasi, or confrontation.

Indonesian armed forces made numerous incursions across the jungled frontier between Kalimantan and the two new East Malaysian states; it also landed commandos on the Malaysian peninsula and despatched 300 saboteurs who infiltrated Singapore and launched a bombing campaign. Sarawakian Communists fought alongside Indonesians in the Konfrontasi and there were countless skirmishes with Malaysian and British counter-terrorist forces in which many were killed. Sukarno even managed to secure Soviet weapons, dispatched by Moscow "to help Indonesia crush Malaysia". Konfrontasi fizzled out in 1965 following the Communist-inspired coup attempt in Indonesia, which finally dislodged Sukarno from power.

Sarawak, Sabah and Brunei as well as the peninsula. In the end, Brunei opted out, Singapore left after two years, but Sarawak and Sabah joined the federation, having accepted the recommendations of the British government. Indonesia's President Sukarno denounced the move, claiming it was all part of a neo-colonialist conspiracy. He declared a policy of confrontation – *Konfrontasi*. A United Nations commission which was sent to ensure that the people of Sabah and Sarawak wanted to be part of Malaysia reported that Indonesia's objections were unfounded.

Communists had been active in Sarawak since the 1930s. The *Konfrontasi* afforded the Sarawak Communist Organization (SCO) Jakarta's support against the Malaysian government. The SCO joined forces with the North Kalimantan Communist Party (NKCO) and were trained and equipped by Indonesia's President Sukarno. But following Jakarta's brutal suppression of the Indonesian Communists, the Partai Komunis Indonesia (PKI), in the wake of the attempted coup in 1965, Sarawak's Communists fled back across the Indonesian border, along with their Kalimantan comrades. There they continued to wage guerrilla war against the Malaysian government throughout the 1970s. The Sarawak state government offered amnesties to guerrillas wanting to come out of hiding. In 1973 the NKCP leader surrendered along with 482 other guerrillas. A handful remained in the jungle, most of them in the hills around Kuching. The last surrendered in 1990.

Politics and modern Malaysia

Politics   In 1957 Kuala Lumpur was keen to have Sarawak and Sabah in the Federation of Malaysia and offered the two states a degree of autonomy, allowing their local governments control over state finances, agriculture and forestry. Sarawak's racial mix was reflected in its chaotic state politics. The Ibans dominated the Sarawak National Party (SNAP), which provided the first Chief Minister, Datuk Stephen Kalong Ningkan. He raised a storm over Kuala Lumpur's introduction of Bahasa Malaysia in schools and complained bitterly about the federal government's policy of filling the Sarawakian civil service with Malays from the peninsula. An 'us' and 'them' mentality developed: in Sarawak, the Malay word *semenanjung* – peninsula – was used to label the newcomers. To many, semenanjung was Malaysia, Sarawak was Sarawak.

In 1966 the federal government ousted the SNAP, and a new Muslim-dominated government led by the Sarawak Alliance took over in Kuching. But there was still strong political opposition to federal encroachment. Throughout the 1970s, as in Sabah, Sarawak's strongly Muslim government drew the state closer and closer to the peninsula: it supported *Rukunegara* – the policy of Islamization – and promoted the use of Bahasa Malaysia. Muslims make up less than one-third of the population of Sarawak. The Malays, Melanaus and Chinese communities grew rich from the timber industry; the Ibans and the Orang Ulu (the upriver tribespeople) saw little in the way of development. They did not reap the benefits of the expansion of education and social services, they were unable to get public sector jobs and to make matters worse, logging firms were encroaching on their native lands and threatening their traditional lifestyles.

It has only been in more recent years that the tribespeoples' political voice has been heard at all. In 1983, Iban members of SNAP – which was a part of Prime Minister Dr Mahathir Mohamad's ruling Barisan Nasional (National Front) coalition – split to form the Party Bansa Dayak Sarawak (PBDS), which, although it initially remained in the coalition, became more outspoken on native affairs. At about the same time, international outrage was sparked over the exploitation of Sarawak's tribespeople by politicians and businessmen involved in the logging industry. The plight of the Penan hunter-gatherers came to world attention due to their blockades of logging roads (see page 374) and the resulting publicity highlighted the rampant corruption and greed that characterized modern Sarawak's political economy.

The National Front remain firmly in control in Sarawak. But unlike neighbouring Sabah, or indeed any other state in the country with the exception of PAS-ruled Kelantan, Sarawak's politicians are not dominated by the centre. The chief minister of Sarawak is Taib Mahmud, a Melanau, and his Parti Pesaka Bumiputra Bersatu is a member of the UMNO-dominated National Front. But in Sarawak itself UMNO wields little power.

While the Anwar case dominated political debate on the Peninsula in the months leading up to the recent elections and led many voters – especially the young – to vote against UMNO, this was not the case in Sarawak which, even in political terms, can sometimes seem a world apart. Furthermore, Sarawak survived the economic crisis relatively unscathed, so even this did not carry much influence in the campaign. The ruling National Front won the election in Sarawak with much to spare, successfully playing on voters' local concerns and grievances. The opposition DAP, which in the last election won just one seat, was hamstrung by a long-running and acrimonious dispute between the DAP national leader, Lim Kit Siang, and local strongman Sim Kwang Yang which led the latter to join the Parti Keadilan Nasional. The problem for the opposition was that local people think that it is the state legislature which can make a difference, not the federal parliament in KL which seems distant and ineffective. For this reason, UMNO does not have a presence and it is the Parti Pesaka Bumiputra Bersatu which represents Sarawak in the National Front. One source of concern, which the opposition did not effectively exploit, was the feeling that Sarawak's Chief Minister Tan Sri Abdul Taib Mahmud has been in post for far too long.

The challenge of getting the voters out in some of the most remote areas of the country was clearly illustrated in Long Lidom. There it cost the government RM65,000 to provide a helicopter to poll just seven Punan Busang in a longhouse on the Upper Kajang, close to the border with Indonesia. Datuk Omar of the election Commission said that mounting the general election in Sarawak, with its 28 parliamentary seats, was a "logistical nightmare." Along with a small air force of helicopters, the Commission used 1,032 long boats, 15 speed boats and 3,054 land cruisers. The Commission's workforce numbered a cool 13,788 workers in a state with a population of just two million.

Sarawak

Sarawak

Shifting cultivation – how to grow hill rice

Winding upriver on Sarawak's express boats, it is hard not to notice that the hillsides on either bank have been shaved of their jungle: evidence of shifting cultivation (see page 519). The Iban, who live in the middle reaches of Sarawak's big rivers, have always been shifting cultivators; the deep peat soils meant it was impossible to farm wet-rice. Any secondary forest (belukar) seen growing on the riverside slopes is really just fallow land, and in 8-15 years' time, it will be cut again and the ladang will be replanted. The Malaysian government claims there are three million hectares of land like this in Sarawak, left idle, through slash-and-burn cultivation. In defence of its environmental record, it says shifting cultivators are more destructive than logging firms and cause
serious soil erosion.

What the government tends to overlook, however, is that the rivers were clear before the loggers arrived and that the swidden farmers, in labour terms, managed highly productive agricultural systems. As long as the land is allowed to lie fallow for long enough, the Iban can produce rice with far less effort than lowland wet rice farmers. The Iban clear their designated hillsides in the middle of the year and burn them off in August. In September, planting starts: holes are made in the soot-blackened soil with sharp-pointed dibble-sticks called tugal. Women drop a few grains into each hole and the rice is interplanted with maize. Harvesting is done by the women, who use special knives called ketap.

Today there are many in Sarawak as well as in Sabah, who wish their governments had opted out of the Federation like Brunei. Sarawak is of great economic importance to Malaysia, thanks to its oil, gas and timber. The state now accounts for more than one-third of Malaysia's petroleum production (worth more than US$800m per year) and more than half of its natural gas. As with neighbouring Sabah however, 95 percent of Sarawak's oil and gas revenues go directly into federal coffers.

A famous cartoon in a Sarawak newspaper once depicted a cow grazing in Sarawak and being milked on the peninsula. While Sarawak has traditionally been closer to federal government than Sabah (there has never been any hint of a secessionist movement), discontent surfaces from time to time. In late 1989, all it took was a quarrel over a football match between Sarawak and Selangor state to touch off deep-seated resentments in Kuching.

Culture

People

For those intending to visit any of Sarawak's tribal peoples, see page 339

About 30 percent of Sarawak's population is Iban, another 30 percent Chinese, 20 percent is Malay and the remaining 20 percent is divided into other tribal groups. The people of the interior are classified as Proto-Malays and Deutero-Malays and are divided into at least 12 distinct tribal groups including Iban, Murut (see page 481), Melanau, Bidayuh, Kenyah, Kayan, Kelabit and Penan. In upriver Dayak communities, both men and women traditionally distend their earlobes with brass weights – long earlobes are considered a beauty feature – and practise extensive body tattooing. For the longhouse communities, the staple diet is hill rice, which is cultivated with slash-and-burn farming techniques.

Malay About half of Sarawak's 300,000-strong Malay community lives around the state capital; most of the other half lives in the Limbang Division, near Brunei. The Malays traditionally live near the coast, although today there are small communities far upriver. There are some old wooden Malay houses, with carved façades, in the kampongs along the banks of the Sarawak River in Kuching; other traditional Malay houses still stand on Ha Datus in Kuching. In all Malay communities, the mosque is

Tribal tattoos

Tattooing is practised by many indigenous groups in Borneo, but the most intricate designs are those of the upriver Orang Ulu tribes. Designs vary from group to group and for different parts of the body. Circular designs are mostly used for the shoulder, chest or wrists, while stylized dragon-dogs (aso), scorpions and dragons are used on the thigh and, for the Iban, on the throat. Tattoos can mean different things; for the man it is a symbol of bravery and for women, a good tattoo is a beauty feature. More elaborate designs often denote high social status in Orang Ulu communities – the Kayans, for example, reserved the aso design for the upper classes and slaves were barred from tattooing themselves at all. In these Orang Ulu groups, the women have the most impressive tattoos; the headman's daughter has her hands, arms and legs completely covered in a finely patterned tattoo. Designs are first carved on a block of wood, which is then smeared with ink. The design is printed on the body and then punctured into the skin with needles dipped in ink, usually made from a mixture of sugar, water and soot. Rice is smeared over the inflamed area to prevent infection, but it usually swells up for some time.

Tattooed Kenowit, with pendulous earlobes, Illustrated London News, 10 November 1849

the centre of the village, but while their faith is important to them, the strictures of Islam are generally less rigorously enforced in Sarawak than on the peninsula. Of all the Malays in Malaysia, the Sarawak Malays are probably the most easy-going. During the days of the White Rajahs, the Malays were recruited into government service, as they were on the Malay peninsula. They were renowned as good administrators and the men were mostly literate in Jawi script. Over the years there has been much intermarriage between the Malay and Melanau communities. Traditionally, the Malays were fishermen and farmers.

Chinese Hakka goldminers had already settled at Bau, upriver from Kuching, long before James Brooke arrived in 1839. Cantonese, Teochew and Hokkien merchants also set up in Kuching, but the Brookes did not warm to the Chinese community, believing the traders would exploit the Dayak communities if they were allowed to venture upriver. In the 1880s, however, Rajah Charles Brooke allowed the immigration of large numbers of Chinese – mainly Foochow – who settled in coastal towns like Sibu (see page 340). Many became farmers and ran rubber smallholdings. The Sarawak government subsidized the immigrants for the first year. During the Brooke era, the only government-funded schools were for Malays and few tribal people ever received a formal education. The Chinese, however, set up and funded their own private schools and many attended Christian missionary schools, so they formed a relatively prosperous, educated élite. Now the Chinese comprise nearly a third of the state's population and are almost as numerous as the Iban; they are the middlemen, traders, shopkeepers, timber towkays (magnates) and express-boat owners. At the last census on 30 June 1990, the Chinese population numbered 483,301 with similar numbers of Foochow and Hakka (each representing 32 percent of the total), being the largest groups. Hokkien constitute 13 percent of the Chinese population, and Teochew, nine percent.

👉 *The palang – the stimulant that makes a vas diferens*

One of the more exotic features of upriver sexuality is the palang, or penis pin, which is the versatile jungle version of the French tickler. Traditionally, women suffer heavy weights being attached to their earlobes to enhance their sex appeal. In turn, men are expected to enhance their physical attributes and entertain their womenfolk by drilling a hole in their organs, into which they insert a range of items, aimed at heightening their partner's pleasure on the rattan mat. Tom Harrisson, a former curator of the Sarawak Museum, was intrigued by the palang; some suspect his authority on the subject stemmed from

first-hand experience. He wrote: "When the device is put into use, the owner adds whatever he prefers to elaborate and accentuate its intention. A lively range of objects can so be employed – from pigs' bristles and bamboo shavings to pieces of metal, seeds, beads and broken glass. The effect, of course, is to enlarge the diameter of the male organ inside the female." It is said that many Dayak men, even today, have the tattoo man come and drill a hole in them as they stand in the river. As the practice has gone on for centuries, one can only assume that its continued popularity proves it is worth the agony.

See also box, page 390 **Iban** Sarawak's best known erstwhile head-hunters make up nearly a third of the state's population and while some have moved to coastal towns for work, many remain in their traditional longhouses. But with Iban men now earning good money in the timber and oil industries, it is increasingly common to see longhouses bristling with television aerials, equipped with fridges, self-cleaning ovens and flush-toilets, and with Land Cruisers in the car park. Even modern longhouses retain the traditional features of gallery, verandah and doors. The Iban are an outgoing people and usually extend a warm welcome to visitors. Iban women are skilled weavers; even today a girl is not considered eligible until she has proven her skills at the loom by weaving a ceremonial textile, the *pua kumbu* (see page 398). The Ibans love to party, and during the Gawai harvest festival in June, visitors are particularly welcome to drink copious amounts of *tuak* (rice wine) and dance through the night.

The Iban are shifting cultivators who originated in the Kapuas River basin of West Kalimantan and migrated into Sarawak's Second Division in the early 16th century, settling along the Batang Lupar, Skrang and Saribas rivers. By the early 19th century, they had begun to spill into the Rejang River valley. It was this growing pressure on land as more and more migrants settled in the river valleys that led to fighting and headhunting (see page 394). Probably because they were shifting cultivators, the Iban remained in closely bonded family groups and were a classless society. Historian Mary Turnbull says "they retained their pioneer social organization of nuclear family groups living together in longhouses and did not evolve more sophisticated political institutions. Long-settled families acquired prestige, but the Ibans did not merge into tribes and had neither chiefs, *rakyat* class, nor slaves."

The Ibans joined local Malay chiefs and turned to piracy – which is how Europeans first came into contact with them. They were dubbed Sea Dayaks as a result – which is really a misnomer as they are an inland people. The name stuck, however, and in the eyes of Westerners, it distinguished them from Land Dayaks, who were the Bidayuh people from the Sarawak River area (see page 395). While Rajah James Brooke only won the Ibans' loyalty after he had crushed them in battle (see page 383), he had great admiration for them, and they bore no bitterness towards him. He once described them as "good-looking a set of men, or devils, as one could cast eye on. Their wiry and supple limbs might have been compared to the troops of wild horses that followed Mazeppa in his perilous flight." The Iban have a very easygoing attitude to love and sex, which is best explained in Redmond O'Hanlon's book *Into the Heart of Borneo*. Free love is the general rule among Iban

Green pen pals: Mahathir versus Manser

Few people infuriate Prime Minister Datuk Seri Mahathir Mohamad more than Bruno Manser, green activist and self-styled defender of the tribal peoples of Borneo, and particularly the Penan. The Swiss Manser spent six years living with the Penan and now fights for their rights. Mahathir's views on Manser, 'green imperialism' in general, and the 'plight' of the tribals comes through nowhere clearer than in a letter he wrote to Manser in March 1992:

Herr Manser,
If any Penan or policeman gets killed or wounded in the course of restoring law and order in Sarawak, you will have to take the blame. It is you and your kind who instigated the Penans to take the law into their own hands and to use poison darts, bows, arrows and parangs to fight against the Government.

As a Swiss living in the laps of luxury with the world's highest standard of living, it is the height of arrogance for you to advocate that the Penans live on maggots and monkeys in their miserable huts, subjected to all kinds of diseases. It is fine for you to spend a short holiday tasting the Penan way of life and then returning to the heated comfort of your Swiss chalet. But do you really expect the Penans to subsist on monkeys until the year 2500 or 3000 or forever? Have they no right to a better way of life? What right have you to condemn them to a primitive life forever?

Your Swiss ancestors were hunters also. But you are now one of the most 'advanced' people living in beautiful Alpine villages, with plenty of leisure and very high income. But you want to deny even a slight rise in the standard of living for the Penans and other Malaysians.

The Penans may tell you that their primitive life is what they like. That is because they are not given a chance to live a better life like the other tribes in Sarawak. Those of the Penans who have left the jungle are educated and are earning a better living have no wish to return to their primitive ways. You are trying to deny them their chance for a better life so that you can enjoy studying primitive peoples the way you study animals. Penans are people and they should be respected as people. If you had a chance to be educated and live a better life, they too deserve that chance.

Stop being arrogant and thinking that it is the white man's burden to decide the fate of the peoples in this world. Malaysians, the Penans included, are an independent people and are quite capable of looking after themselves. Swiss imperialism is as disgusting as other European imperialism. It is about time that you stop your arrogance and your intolerable European superiority. You are no better than the Penans. If you have a right to decide for yourself, why can't you leave the Penans to decide for themselves after they have been given a chance to improve their living standards.
Dr Mahathir Mohamad
Reproduced in Far Eastern Economic Review, 27 August 1992

communities which have not become evangelical Christians, although once married, the Iban divorce rate is low and they are monogamous.

Melanau The Melanau are a relaxed and humorous people. Rajah James Brooke, like generations of men before and after him, thought the Melanau girls particularly pretty. He said that they had "agreeable countenances, with the dark, rolling, open eye of the Italians, and nearly as fair as most of that race". The Melanau live along the coast between the Baram and Rejang rivers; originally they lived in magnificent communal houses built high off the ground, like the one that has been reconstructed at the Cultural Village in Kuching, but these have long since disappeared. The houses were designed to afford protection from incessant pirate raids (see page 383), for the Melanau were easy pickings, being coastal people. Their stilt-houses were often up to

Skulls in the longhouse: heads you win

Although head-hunting has been largely stamped out in Borneo, there is still the odd reported case, once every few years. But until the early 20th century, head hunting was commonplace among many Dayak tribes and the Iban were the most fearsome of all. Following a head-hunting expedition, the freshly taken heads were skinned, placed in rattan nets and smoked over a fire, or sometimes boiled. The skulls were then hung from the rafters of the longhouse and they possessed the most powerful form of magic.

The skulls were considered trophies of manhood (they increased a young bachelor's eligibility), symbols of bravery and they testified to the unity of a longhouse. The longhouse had to hold festivals – or gawai – to appease the spirits of the skulls. Once placated, the heads were believed to bring great blessing – they could ward off evil spirits, save villages from epidemics, produce rain and increase the yield of rice harvests. Heads that were insulted or ignored were capable of wreaking havoc in the form of bad dreams, plagues, floods and fires. To keep the spirits of the skulls happy, they would be offered food and cigarettes and made to feel welcome in their new home. Because the magical powers of a skull faded with time, fresh heads were always in demand. Tribes without heads were considered spiritually weak.

Today, young Dayak men no longer have to take heads to gain respect. They are, however, expected to go on long journeys (the equivalent of the Australian aborigines' Walkabout), or bejalai in Iban. The one unspoken rule is that they should come back with plenty of good stories, and, these days, as most bejalai expeditions translate into stints at timber camps or on oil rigs, they are expected to come home bearing video recorders, TV sets and motorbikes. Many Dayak tribes continue to celebrate their head-hunting ceremonies. In Kalimantan, for example, the Adat Ngayau ceremony uses coconut shells, wrapped in leaves, as substitutes for freshly cut heads.

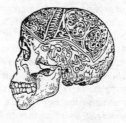

Dayak decorated human skull
Adapted from Hersey, Irwin (1991) Indonesian
Primitive Art, OUP: Singapore

12m off the ground. Today most Melanau live in Malay-style pile-houses facing the river. Hedda Morrison, in her classic 1957 book *Sarawak*, says: "As a result of living along the rivers in swamp country, the Melanaus are an exceptionally amphibious people. The children learn to swim almost before they can walk. Nearly all progress is by canoe, sometimes even to visit the house next door."

The traditional Melanau fishing boat is called a *barong*. Melanau fishermen employed a unique fishing technique. They would anchor palm leaves at sea as they discovered that shoals of fish would seek refuge under them. After rowing out to the leaves, one fisherman would dive off his barong and chase the fish into the nets which his colleague hung over the side. The Melanaus were also noted for their sago production – which they ate instead of rice. At Kuching's Cultural Village there is a demonstration of traditional sago production, showing how the starch-bearing pith is removed, mashed, dried and ground into flour. Most Melanau are now Muslim and have assimilated with the Malays through intermarriage. Originally, however, they were animists (animist Melanau are called *Likaus*) and were particularly famed for their elaborately carved 'sickness images', which represented the form of spirits which caused specific illnesses (see page 400).

Bidayuh In the 19th century, Sarawak's European community called the Bidayuh Land Dayaks, mainly to distinguish them from the Iban Sea Dayak pirates. The Bidayuh make up 8.4 percent of the population and are concentrated to the west of the Kuching area, towards the Kalimantan border. There are also related groups living in West Kalimantan. They were virtually saved from extinction by the White Rajahs. Because the Bidayuh were quiet, mild-mannered people, they were at the mercy of the Iban head-hunters and the Brunei Malays who taxed and enslaved them. The Brookes afforded them protection from both groups.

Most live in modern longhouses and are dry rice farmers. Their traditional longhouses are exactly like Iban ones, but without the *tanju* verandah. The Bidayuh tribe comprises five sub-groups: the Jagoi, Biatah, Bukar-Sadong, Selakau and Lara, all of whom live in far West Sarawak. They are the state's best traditional plumbers, and are known for their ingenious gravity-fed bamboo water-supply systems. They are bamboo-specialists, making everything from cooking pots and utensils to finely carved musical instruments (see page 398) from it. Among other tribal groups, the Bidayuh are renowned for their rice wine and sugar cane toddy. Henry Keppel, who with Rajah James Brooke fought the Bidayuhs' dreaded enemies, the Sea Dayaks, described an evening spent with the Land Dayaks thus: "They ate and drank, and asked for everything, but stole nothing."

Orang Ulu The jungle, or upriver, people encompass a swathe of different small tribal groups. Orang Ulu longhouses are usually made of belian (ironwood) and are built to last. They are well known swordsmiths, forging lethal *parangs* from any piece of scrap metal they can lay their hands on. They are also very artistic people, are skilled carvers and painters and are famed for their beadwork – taking great care decorating even simple household utensils. Most Orang Ulu are plastered with traditional tattoos (see box, page 391).

Kenyah and Kayan These two closely related groups were the traditional rivals of the Ibans and were notorious for their warlike ways. Historian Robert Payne, in his history *The White Rajahs of Sarawak* described the Kayans of the upper Rejang as "a treacherous tribe, [who] like nothing better than putting out the eyes and cutting the throats of prisoners, or burning them alive". They probably originally migrated into Sarawak from the Apo Kayan district in East Kalimantan. Kenyah and Kayan raids on downriver people were greatly feared, but their power was broken by Charles Brooke, just before he became the second White Rajah, in 1863. The Kayans had retreated upstream above the Pelagus Rapids on the Rejang River (see page 346), to an area they considered out of reach from their Iban enemies. In 1862 they killed two government officers at Kanowit and went on a killing spree. Charles Brooke led 15,000 Ibans past the Pelagus Rapids, beyond Belaga and attacked the Kayans in their heartland. Many hundreds were killed. In November 1924, Rajah Vyner Brooke presided over a peace-making ceremony between the Orang Ulu and the Iban in Kapit (there is a photograph of the ceremony on display in the Kapit Museum).

The Kenyahs and Kayans in Sarawak live in pleasant upriver valleys and are settled rice farmers. They are very different from other tribal groups, have a completely different language (which has ancient Malayo-Polynesian roots) and are class-conscious, with a well-defined social hierarchy. Traditionally their society was composed of aristocrats, noblemen, commoners and slaves (who were snatched during raids on other tribes). One of the few things the Kayan and Kenyah have in common with other Dayak groups is the fact that they live in longhouses, although even these are of a different design, and are much more carefully constructed, in ironwood. Subgroups include the Kejamans, Skapans, Berawans and Sebops. Many have now been converted to Christianity.

In contrast to their belligerent history, the Kenyahs and Kayans are much more introverted than the Ibans; they are slow and deliberate in their ways, and are very artistic and musical. They are also renowned for their parties; visitors recovering from drinking *borak* rice beer have their faces covered in soot before being thrown in the river. This is to test the strength of the newly forged friendship with visitors, who are ill-advised to lose their sense of humour on such occasions.

Penan Perhaps Southeast Asia's only remaining true hunter-gatherers live mainly in the upper Rejang area and Limbang. They are nomads and are related, linguistically at least, to the Punan, former nomadic forest-dwellers who are now settled in longhouses along the upper Rejang. The Malaysian government has long wanted the Penan to sedentarise too, but has had limited success in attracting them to expensive new longhouses. Groups of Penan hunter-gatherers still wander through the forest in groups to hunt wild pigs, birds and monkeys and search for sago palms from which they make their staple food, sago flour. The Penan are considered to be the jungle experts by all the other inland tribes. Because they live in the shade of the forest, their skin is relatively fair. They have a great affection for the coolness of the forest and until the 1960s were rarely seen by the outside world. For them sunlight is extremely unpleasant. They are broad and much more stocky than other river people and are extremely shy, having had little contact with the outside world. Most of their trade is conducted with remote Kayan, Kenyah and Kelabit longhouse communities on the edge of the forest.

In the eyes of the West, the Penan have emerged as the 'noble savages' of the late 20th century for their spirited defence of their lands against encroachment by logging companies. But it is not just recently that they have been cheated: they have long been the victims of other upriver tribes. A Penan, bringing baskets full of rotan to a Kenyah or Kayan longhouse to sell may end up exchanging his produce for one bullet or shotgun cartridge. In his way of thinking, a bullet will kill one wild boar which will last his family 10 days. In turn, the buyer knows he can sell the same rotan downstream for RM50-100. Penan still use the blowpipe for small game, but shotguns for wild pig. If they buy the shotgun cartridges for themselves, they have to exchange empties first. Some of their shotguns date back to the Second World War, when the British supplied them to upriver tribespeople to fight the Japanese. During the Brooke era, a large annual market would be held which both Chinese traders and Orang Ulu (including Penan) used to attend; the district officer would have to act as judge to ensure the Penan did not get cheated.

Those wishing to learn more about the Penan should refer to Denis Lau's *The Vanishing Nomads of Borneo* (Interstate Publishing, 1987). Lau has lived among the Penan and has photographed them for many years; some of his recent photographs appear in the photographic collection entitled *Malaysia – Heart of Southeast Asia* (published by Archipelago Press, 1991).

Kelabit The Kelabits, who live in the highlands at the headwaters of the Baram River, are closely related to the Murut (see page 481) and the Lun Dayeh of Kalimantan. It was into Kelabit territory that Tom Harrisson parachuted with Allied Special Forces towards the end of the Second World War. The Kelabit Highlands around Bario were chosen because they were so remote. Of all the tribes in Sarawak, the Kelabits have the sturdiest, strongest builds, which is usually ascribed to the cool and invigorating mountain climate. They are skilled hill-rice farmers and their fragrant Bario rice is prized throughout Sarawak. The highland climate also allows them to cultivate vegetables. Kelabit parties are also famed as boisterous occasions, and large quantities of *borak* rice beer are consumed – despite the fact that the majority of Kelabits have converted to Christianity. They are regarded as among the most hospitable people in Borneo. For information on religion, see page 543.

Dance, drama and music

Dayak tribes are renowned for their singing and dancing, and the most famous is the hornbill dance. In her book *Sarawak*, Hedda Morrison writes: "The Kayans are probably the originators of the stylized war dance which is now common among the Ibans but the girls are also extremely talented and graceful dancers. One of their most delightful dances is the hornbill dance, when they tie hornbill feathers to the ends of their fingers which accentuate their slow and graceful movements. For party purposes everyone in the longhouse joins in and parades up and down the communal room led by one or two musicians and a group of girls who sing." On these occasions, drink flows freely. With the Ibans, it is *tuak* (rice wine), with the Kayan and Kenyah it is *borak*, a bitter rice beer. After being entertained by dancers, a visitor is under compunction to drink a large glassful, before bursting into song and doing a dance routine themselves. The best guideline for visitors on how to handle such occasions is provided by Redmond O'Hanlon in his book *Into the Heart of Borneo*. The general rule of thumb is to be prepared to make an absolute fool of yourself, throwing all inhibition to the wind. This will immediately endear you to your hosts.

The most common dances in Sarawak are: *Kanjet Ngeleput* (Orang Ulu) dance performed in full warrior regalia, traditionally celebrating the return of a hunter or head-hunters. *Mengarang Menyak* (Melanau) dance depicting the processing of sago from the cutting of the tree to the production of the sago pearls or pellets. *Ngajat Bebunuh* (Iban) war dance, performed in full battle dress and armed with sword and shield. *Ngajat Induk* (Iban) performed as a welcome dance for those visiting longhouses. *Ngajat Lesong* (Iban) dance of the *lesong* or mortar, performed during gawai. *Tarian Kris* (Malay) dance of the *kris*, the Malay dagger, which symbolizes power, courage and strength. *Tarian Rajang Beuh* (Bidayuh) dance performed after the harvesting season as entertainment for guests to the longhouse. *Tarian Saga Lupa* (Orang Ulu) performed by women to welcome guests to the longhouse, accompanied by the *sape* (see below). *Ule Nugan* (Orang Ulu) dance to the sound of the *kerebo bulo*, or bamboo slates. The music is designed to inspire the spirit of the paddy seeds to flourish. The male dancers hold a dibbling stick used in the planting of hill rice.

Gongs range from the single large gong, the tawak, to the engkerumong, a set of small gongs, arranged on a horizontal rack, with five players. An engkerumong ensemble usually involves between five and seven drums, which include two suspended gongs (tawak and bendai) and five hour-glass drums (ketebong). They are used to celebrate victory in battle or to welcome home a successful head-hunting expedition. Sarawak's Bidayuh also make a bamboo gong called a pirunchong. The jatang uton is a wooden xylophone which can be rolled up like a rope ladder; the keys are struck with hardwood sticks.

The Bidayuh, Sarawak's bamboo-specialists, make two main stringed instruments: a three-stringed cylindrical bamboo harp called a tinton and the rabup, a rotan-stringed fiddle with a bamboo cup. The Orang Ulu (Kenyah and Kayan tribes) play a four-stringed guitar called a sape, which is also common on the Kalimantan side of the border. It is the most common and popular lute-type instrument, whose body, neck and board are cut from one piece of softwood. It is used in Orang Ulu dances and by witch doctors. It is usually played by two musicians, one keeping the rhythm, the other the melody. Traditional sapes had rotan strings, today they use wire guitar strings and electric pick-ups. Another stringed instrument, more usually found in Kalimantan, or deep in Sarawak's interior, is the *satang*, a bamboo tube with strings around the outside, cut from the bamboo and tightened with pegs.

One of the best known instruments in Sarawak is the engkerurai (or *keluri*), the bagpipes of Borneo, which is usually associated with the Kenyahs and Kayans, but is also found in Sabah (where it is called a *sompoton*). It is a hand-held organ in which

Sarawak

four vertical bamboo pan-pipes of different lengths are fixed to a gourd, which acts as the wind chamber. Simple engkerurai can only manage one chord; more sophisticated ones allow the player to use two pipes for the melody, while the others provide an harmonic drone. The Bidayuh are specialists in bamboo instruments and make flutes of various sizes; big thick ones are called branchi, long ones with five holes are kroto and small ones are called nchiyo.

Crafts

Textiles The weaving of cotton *pua kumbu* is one of the oldest Iban traditions, and literally means 'blanket' or 'cover'. Iban legend recounts that 24 generations ago the God of War, Singalang Burong, taught his son how to weave the most precious of all *pua*, the *lebor api*. Dyed deep red, this cloth was traditionally used to wrap heads taken in battle.

The weaving of *pua kumbu* is done by the women and is a vital skill for a would-be bride to acquire. There are two main methods employed in making and decorating pua kumbu: the more common is the *ikat* tie-dyeing technique, known as *ngebat* by the Iban. The other method is the *pileh*, or floating weft. The Ibans use a warp-beam loom which is tied to two posts, to which the threads are attached. There is a breast-beam at the weaving end, secured by a back strap to the weaver. A pedal, beneath the threads, lowers and raises the alternate threads which are separated by rods. The woven material is tightly packed by a beater. The material is tie-dyed in the warp.

Because the pua kumbu is made by the warp-tie-dyeing method, the number of colours is limited. The most common are a rich browny-brick-red colour and black, as well as the undyed white sections; blues and greens are used in more modern materials. Traditionally, pua kumbu were hung in longhouses during ceremonies and were used to cover images during rituals. The designs and patterns are representations of deities which figure in Iban myths and are believed to protect individuals from harm; they are passed down from generation to generation. Such designs, with deep spiritual significance, can only be woven by wives and daughters of chiefs. Other designs and patterns are representations of birds and animals, including hornbills, crocodiles, monitor lizards and shrimps, which are either associated with worship or are sources of food. Symbolic representations of trees, plants and fruits are also included in the designs as well as the events of everyday life. A typical example is the zigzag pattern which represents the act of crossing a river – the zigzag course is explained by the canoe's attempts to avoid strong currents. Many of the symbolic representations are highly stylized and can be difficult to pick out.

Malay women in Sarawak are traditionally renowned for their *kain songket*, sarongs woven with silver and gold thread.

Woodcarvings Many of Sarawak's tribal groups are skilled carvers, producing everything from huge burial poles (like the Kejaman pole outside the Sarawak museum in Kuching) to small statues, masks and other decorative items and utensils. The Kenyah's traditional masks, which are used during festivals, are

Mask
From Henry Ling Roth's The Natives of Sarawak and British North Borneo (1896)

elaborately carved and often have large protruding eyes. Eyes are always emphasized, as they are to frighten the enemy. Other typical items carved by tribal groups include spoons, stools, doors, walking sticks, *sapes* (guitars), ceremonial shields, tops of water containers, tattoo plaques, and the hilts of *parang ilang* (ceremonial knives). The most popular Iban motif is the hornbill, which holds an honoured place in Iban folklore (see page 524), being the messenger for the sacred Brahminy kite, the ancestor of the Iban. Another famous Iban carving is the sacred measuring stick called the *tuntun peti*, used to trap deer and wild boar; it is carved to represent a forest spirit. The Kayan and Kenyahs' most common motif is the *aso*, a dragon-like dog with a long snout. It also has religious and mythical significance. The Kenyah and Kayan carve huge burial structures, or *salong*, as well as small ear pendants made of hornbill ivory. The elaborately carved masks used for their harvest ceremony are unique.

Bamboo carving

The Bidayuh ('Land Dayaks') are best known for their bamboo carving. The bamboo is usually carved in shallow relief and then stained with dye, which leaves a pattern in the areas which have been scraped out. The Bidayuh carve utilitarian objects as well as ceremonial shields, musical instruments and spirit images used to guard the longhouse. The Cultural Village (Kampong Budaya) in Kuching is one of the best places to see demonstrations of Bidayuh carving.

Blowpipes

Blowpipes are made by several Orang Ulu tribes in Sarawak and are usually carved from hardwood – normally belian (ironwood). The first step is to make a rough cylinder about 10 cm wide and 2.5m long. This rod is tied to a platform, from which a hole is bored through the rod. The bore is skilfully chiselled by an iron rod with a pointed end. The rod is then sanded down to about 5cm in diameter. Traditionally, the sanding was done using the rough underside of *macaranga* leaves. The darts are made from the *nibong* and wild sago palms and the poison itself is the sap of the *upas* (Ipoh) tree (*Antiaris toxicari*) into which the point is dipped.

Beadwork

Among many Kenyah, Kayan, Bidayuh, and Kelabit groups, beads have long been symbols of status and wealth; necklaces, skull caps and girdles are handed down from generation to generation. Smaller glass or plastic beads, usually imported from Europe, are used to decorate baby carriers, baskets, headbands, jackets, hats, sheaths for knives, tobacco boxes and handbags. Beaded baby carriers are mainly used by the Kelabit, Kenyah and Kayan and often have shells and animals' teeth attached which make a rattling sound to frighten away evil spirits. Rounded patterns require more skill than geometric patterns, the quality of the pattern used to reflect the status of the owner. Only upper-classes are permitted to have beadwork depicting 'high-class' motifs such as human faces or figures. Early beads were made from clay, metal, glass, bone or shell (the earliest have been found in the Niah Caves). Later on, many of the beads that found their way upriver were from Venice, Greece, India and China – even Roman and Alexandrian beads have made their way into Borneo's jungle. Orang Ulu traded them for jungle produce. Tribes attach different values to particular types of beads.

Mask
From Henry Ling Roth's
The Natives of Sarawak
and British North
Borneo *(1896)*

Sarawak

Sickness images The coastal Melanau, who have now converted to Islam, but used to be animists, have a tradition of carving sickness images (*blum*). They are usually carved from sago or other soft woods. The image is believed to take the form of the evil spirit causing a specific illness. They are carved in different forms according to the ailment. The Melanau developed elaborate healing ceremonies; if someone was struck down by a serious illness, the spirit medium would perform the *berayun* ceremony, using the blum to extract the illness from the victim's body. Usually, the image is in a half-seated position, with the hands crossed across the part of the body which was affected. During the ceremony, the medium attempts to draw the spirit out of the sick person and into the image, after which it is set adrift on a river in a tiny purpose-made boat or it is hidden in the jungle. These images are roughly carved and can, from time to time, be found in antique shops.

Basketry A wide variety of household items are woven from rotan, bamboo, bemban reed as well as nipah and pandanus palms. Malaysia supplies 30 percent of the world's demand for *manau rotan* (rattan). Basketry is practised by nearly all the ethnic groups in Sarawak and they are among the most popular handicrafts in the state. A variety of baskets are made for harvesting, storing and winnowing paddy as well as for collecting and storing other items. The Penan are reputed to produce the finest rattan sleeping mats – closely plaited and pliable – as well as the *ajat* and *ambong* baskets (all-purpose jungle rucksacks, also produced by the Kayan and Kenyah). Many of the native patterns used in basketry are derived from Chinese patterns and take the form of geometrical shapes and stylized birds. The Bidayuh also make baskets from either rotan or sago bark strips. The most common Bidayuh basket is the *tambok*, which is simply patterned and has bands of colour; it also has thin wooden supports on each side.

Hats The Melanau people living around Bintulu make a big colourful conical hat from nipah leaves called a *terindak*. Orang Ulu hats are wide-brimmed and are often decorated with beadwork or cloth *appliqué*. Kelabit and Lun Bawan women wear skull-caps made entirely of beads, which are heavy and extremely valuable.

Pottery Malaysia's most distinctive ceramic designs are found in Sarawak where Iban potters reproduce shapes and patterns of Chinese porcelain which was originally brought to Borneo by traders centuries ago (see page 314). Copies of these old Chinese jars are mostly used for brewing *tuak* rice wine.

Sabah

8

Sabah

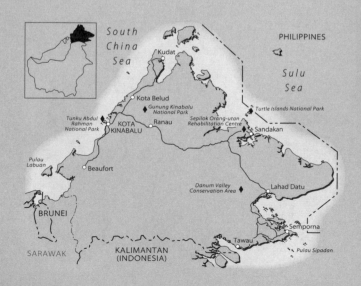

Sabah may not have the colourful history of neighbouring Sarawak, but there is a good deal here. It is second largest Malaysian state after Sarawak, covering 72,500 km^2, making it about the size of Ireland. Occupying the northeast corner of Borneo it is shaped like a dog's head, the jaws reaching out in the Sulu and Celebes seas, and the back of the head facing onto the South China Sea. The highlights of Sabah are natural and cultural, from caves, reefs, forests and mountains to tribal peoples. The Gunung Kinabalu National Park is named after Sabah's (and Malaysia's) highest peak and is one of the state's most popular destinations. Also popular is the Sepilok Orang-utan Rehabilitation Sanctuary outside Sandakan. Marine sights include the Turtle Islands National Park and Sipadan Island, one of Asia's finest dive sites. While Sabah's indigenous tribes were not cossetted in the way that they were in Sarwak by the White Rajahs, areas around towns like Kudat, Tenom, Keningau and Kota Belud still provide memorable insights in the peoples of the area.

Kota Kinabalu

Population: 180,000
Phone code: 088
Colour map 4, grid B3

KK is most people's introduction to Sabah for the simple reason that it is the only town with extensive air links to other parts of the country as well as with a handful of regional destinations. KK is a modern state capital with little that can be dated back more than 50 years. Highlights include the state museum and the town's markets. Out of town, within a day's excursion, are good beaches like Tanjung Aru Beach and those near Tuaran as well as a number of Kadazan and Bajau districts with their distinctive markets. While it is necessary to go rather further afield to get a real glimpse of tribal life, this is better than nothing.

The city is strung out along the coast, with jungle-clad hills as a backdrop. Two-thirds of the town is built on land reclaimed from the shallow Gaya Bay; during the spring tides it is possible to walk across to the island. The modern town lacks the colonial charm of Sarawak's state capital Kuching.

Only light fishing boats and passenger vessels can dock at KK's wharves; heavy cargo is unloaded at Likas Bay, to the north. Jalan Pantai, or Beach Rd, is now in the centre of town. Successive land reclamation projects have meant that many of the original stilt villages, such as Kampung Ayer, have been cut off from the sea and some now stand in stinking, stagnant lagoons. The government plans to clean up and reclaim these areas in the next few years and the inhabitants of the water villages are being rehoused.

Ins and outs

Getting there KK's airport is 5 km from town. There are connections with other towns in East Malaysia and the Peninsula as well as with various destinations in the Asian region. There is a limited railway line with trains to Beaufort and Tenom and a rather more extensive array of bus, minibus and taxi links to destinations in Sabah. Ferries leave several times daily for Labuan.

Getting around City buses and minibuses provide a service around town and to destinations in the vincinity of KK. Taxis are unmetered. There is a good number of international and local car hire firms.

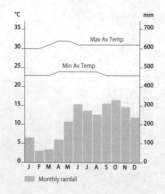

Climate:
Kota Kinabalu

Monthly rainfall

History

Kota Kinabalu started life as a trading post in 1881; not on the mainland, but on Gaya Island, opposite the present town, where a Filipino shanty town is today. On 9 July 1897 rebel leader Mat Salleh, who engaged in a series of hit-and-run raids against the North Borneo Chartered Company's administration, landed on Pulau Gaya. His men looted and sacked the settlement and Gaya township was abandoned.

Two years later the Europeans established another township but this time located on the mainland, opposite Pulau Gaya, adjacent to a Bajau stilt village. The kampung was called '*Api Api*' – meaning 'Fire! Fire!' – because it had been repeatedly torched by pirates over the years. After the Gaya experience, it was an inauspicious name. The Chartered Company rechristened it Jesselton, after Sir Charles Jessel, one of the company directors. But for years, only the Europeans called it Jesselton; locals preferred the old name, and even today Sabahans sometimes refer to their state capital as 'Api'.

Jesselton owed its raison d'être to a plan that backfired. William C Cowie, formerly a gun-runner for the Sultan of Sulu, became managing director of the Chartered Company in 1894. He wanted to build a trans-Borneo railway (see page 426) and the narrow strip of land just north of Tanjung Aru and opposite Pulau Gaya, with its sheltered anchorage, was selected as a terminus.

Photographs in the Sabah State Museum chart the town's development from 1899, when work on the North Borneo Railway terminus began in earnest. By 1905, Jesselton was linked to Beaufort by a 92 km narrow-gauge track. By 1911 it had a population of 2,686, half of whom were Chinese and the remainder Kadazans and Dusuns; there were 33 European residents. Jesselton was of little importance in comparison to Sandakan, the capital of North Borneo.

When the Japanese Imperial Army invaded Borneo in 1942, Jesselton's harbour gave the town strategic significance and it was consequently completely flattened by the Allies during the Second World War. Jesselton followed Kudat and Sandakan as the administrative centre of North Borneo, at the end of the Second World War. In September 1967 Jesselton was renamed Kota Kinabalu after the mountain; its name is usually shortened to KK.

Sights

Only three buildings – the old **General Post Office** on Gaya St, **Atkinson's Clock Tower** (built in 1905 and named after Jesselton's first district officer) and the old red-roofed **Lands and Surveys building** remain of the old town. The renovated post office now houses the Sabah Tourist Promotion Corporation.

For tours in & around KK see under Excursions below

The golden dome of **Masjid Sabah**, on Jalan Tunku Abdul Rahman, is visible from most areas of town although it is actually about 3 km out of town. Regular minibuses connect it with the town centre. Completed in 1975, it is the second biggest mosque in Malaysia and, like the Federal Mosque in Kuala Lumpur, is a fine example of contemporary Islamic architecture. It can accommodate 5,000 worshippers.

Masjid Sabah & Sabah State Museum

Perched on a small hill overlooking the mosque is the **Sabah State Museum** (and State Archives) on Jalan Mat Salleh/Bukit Istana Lama. The museum is designed to look like a longhouse. It has a fascinating ethnographic section which includes an excellent exhibition on the uses of bamboo. Tribal brassware, silverware, musical instruments, basketry and pottery are also on display. On the same floor is a collection of costumes and artifacts from Sabah tribes like the Kadazan/Dusun, Bajau, Murut and Rungus.

One of the most interesting items in this collection is a *sininggazanak* – a sort of totem pole. If a Kadazan man died without an heir, it was the custom to erect a sininggazanak – a wooden statue supposedly resembling the deceased – on his land. There is also a collection of human skulls – called a *bangkaran* – which before the tribe's wholesale conversion to Christianity, would have been suspended from the rafters of Kadazan longhouses. Every five years a *magang* feast was held to appease the spirits of the skulls.

The museum's archaeological section contains a magnificently carved coffin found in a limestone cave in the Madai area. Upstairs, the natural history section, provides a good introduction to Sabah's flora and fauna. Next door is a collection of jars, called *pusaka*, which are tribal heirlooms. They were originally exchanged by the Chinese for jungle produce, such as beeswax, camphor and birds' nests.

Next door is the **Science Museum**, containing an exhibition on Shell's offshore activities. The **Art Gallery and Multivision Theatre**, within the same complex, are also worth a browse. The art gallery is small and mainly exhibits works by local artists; among the more interesting works on display are those of Suzie Mojikol, a Kadazan artist, Bakri Dani, who adapts Bajau designs and Philip Biji who specializes in burning Murut designs onto chunks of wood with a soldering iron. The ethnobotanical gardens are on the hillside below the museum complex. There is a cafeteria at the base of the main building. ■ *1000-1800 Mon-Thur, 0900-1800 Sat-Sun.*

Sabah has a large Christian population and the **Sacred Heart Cathedral** has a striking pyramidal roof which is clearly visible from the Sabah State Museum complex.

Viewpoints Further into town and nearer the coast are a series of water villages, including **Kampung Ayer**, although its size has shrunk in recent years. **Signal Hill** (Bukit Bendera), just southeast of the central area, gives a panoramic view of the town and islands. In the past, the hill was used as a vantage point for signalling to ships approaching the harbour. There is an even better view of the coastline from the top of the **Sabah Foundation (Yayasan Sabah) Complex**, 4 km out of town, overlooking Likas Bay. This surreal glass sculpture has circular floors suspended on high-tensile steel rods and houses the Chief Minister's office. The Sabah Foundation was set up in 1966 to help improve Sabahans' quality of life. The foundation has a 972,800 hectare timber concession, which it claims to manage on a sustainable-yield basis. Two-thirds of this concession has already been logged. Profits from the timber go towards loans and scholarships for Sabahan students, funding the construction of hospitals and schools and supplying milk, textbooks and uniforms to school children. The Foundation also operates a 24-hour flying ambulance service to remote parts of the interior. See also www.ysnet.org.my.

The fact that between the Yayasan Sabah and the core of the city is one of Borneo's largest squatter communities visibly demonstrates that not everyone is sharing equally in the timber boom.

Markets **Gaya street market** is held every Sunday from 0800, selling a vast range of goods from jungle produce and handicrafts to pots and pans. The market almost opposite the main minibus station on Jalan Tun Fuad Stephens is known as the **Filipino market**, as most of the stalls are run by Filipino immigrants. A variety of Filipino and local handicrafts are sold in the hundreds of cramped stalls, along winding alleyways which are strung with low-slung curtains of shells, baskets and bags. The Filipino market is a good place to buy cultured pearls (about RM5 each) and has everything from fake gemstones to camagong-wood salad bowls, fibre shirts and traditional Indonesian medicines. Further into town, on the waterfront, is the **central market** selling mainly fish, fruit and vegetables. The daily fishing catch is unloaded on the wharf near the market.

Excursions

Most companies run city tours. Other tours that are widely available include: Kota Belud tamu (Sunday market), Mount Kinabalu Park (including Poring Hot Springs), Sandakan's Sepilok Orang-utan Rehabilitation Centre, train trips to Tenom through the Padas Gorge and tours of the islands in the Tunku Abdul Rahman National Park. Several companies specialize in scuba-diving tours, see page 415.

Tours
For Tunku Abdul Rahman Park, see page 418

This is the best beach near KK, after those in Tunku Abdul Rahman National Park, and is close to *Tanjung Aru Resort*, 5 km south of KK (see **Sleeping** and **Eating** below). It is particularly popular at weekends and there is a good hawker centre. Minibuses leave from the terminus in front of the market, Jalan Tun Fuad Stephens; red and white buses to Tanjung Aru leave from outside the MPKK building, next to the State Library, or take a red bus marked 'beach' from Jalan Tunku Abdul Rahman.

Tanjung Aru Beach

This Kadazan district is 13 km from KK. The old town of Donggongon was demolished in the early 1980s and the new township built in 1982. The population is mainly Kadazan or Sino-Kadazan and about 90 percent Christian. The oldest church in Sabah, **St Michael's** Roman Catholic church, is on a steep hill on the far side of the new town. Turn left just before bridge – and after turn-off to the new town – through kampung and turn left again after school. It was

Penampang

Around Kota Kinabalu

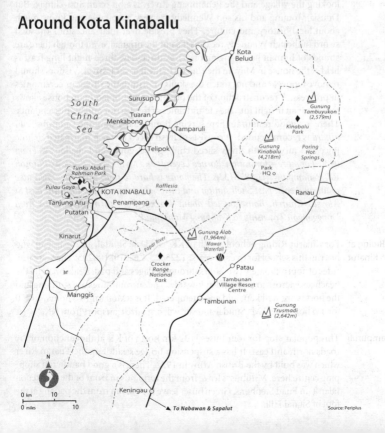

Source: Periplus

originally built in 1897 but is not dramatic to look at and has been much reno-vated over the years. Services are conducted in Kadazan but are fascinating to attend and visitors are warmly welcomed; hymns are sung in Kadazan and Malay. The social focus of the week is the **market** every Sunday.

There are many **megaliths** in the Penampang area which are thought to be associated with property claims, particularly when a landowner died without a direct heir. Some solitary stones, which can be seen standing in the middle of paddy fields, are more than 2m tall. The age of the megaliths has not been determined. Wooden figures, called *sininggazanak* can also be seen in the ricefields (see page 405). *Yun Chuan* (**2**), Penampang New Town (also known as Donggongon Township), specializes in Kadazan dishes, such as *hinava* – or raw fish, the Kadazan equivalent of sushi. Tapai chicken is also recommended. See page 47 for details on Kadazan cuisine. To get there, take a green and white Union Transport bus from in front of the MPKK building next to the State Library.

House of Skulls This is in Kampung Monsopiad (named after a fearsome Kadazan war-rior-cum-headhunter – Siou do Mohoing, the so-called Hercules of Sabah) just outside Penampang. There are 42 fragile human skulls in the collection, some of which are said to be 300 years old and possess spiritual powers. They are laced together with leaves of the *hisad* palm, which represents the hair of the victims. For those who have already visited longhouses in Sarawak, this collection of skulls, in the rafters of an ordinary little kampung house over-looking the village and the Penampang River, is a bit of an anti-climax. But Dousia Moujing and his son Wennedy are very hospitable and know much about local history and culture. They preside over their ancestor's dreaded sword (although Wennedy reckons it's not the original, even though there are strands of human hair hanging off it). A three-day, three-night long feast is held at the house in May, in the run-up to the harvest festival. Visitors should remove footwear and not touch the skulls or disturb the rituals or ceremonies in progress. A reconstruction of the original Monsopiad main house allows the visitor an insight into the life and times of the warrior and his descendants. There is a good restaurant here serving traditional dishes; the *kadazandusun hinara* is recommended. It consists of fresh sliced raw fish marinated in lime juice and mixed with finely sliced chilli, garlic, gourd and shallots. ■ *From 0930. For more information, Borneo Legends and Myths, 5 km Ramaya/Putaton Rd, Penampang, T088761336. The house is hard to find; from new town take main road east, past Shell station and turn right at sign to Jabatan Air; past St Aloysus Church, house on left about 1½ km from turn-off; minibus from Donggongon Township to Kampung Monsopaid.*

Riding at Kinarut For Kinarut Riding School, south of KK, call Dale Sinidal, an Australian who has run this school for over 10 years, T225525, Cell0108100233. There are trail rides of approximately two hours through villages and padi fields or along the beach and across to an island at low tide. The surroundings are stunning and the horses are well kept and good tempered. It is RM60 for two hours, RM50 for 1½ hours. Call Ms Sinidal and she will organize transport from KK.

Tampuruli This popular stop for tour buses is 32 km north of KK at the junction of the roads north and east. It has a suspension bridge straddling the Tuaran River which was built by the British Army in 1922. There is a good handicraft shop-ping centre here. Minibuses leave from the terminus in front of the market on Jalan Tun Fuad Stephens. Green buses leave for Tuaran from the padang at the foot of Signal Hill.

This Bajau, or sea gypsy, fishing stilt village is within easy reach of KK (see page 404) and is likened to an Asian Venice. The village is particularly photogenic in the early morning, before Mount Kinabalu, which serves as a dramatic backdrop, is obscured by cloud. The fishermen leave Mengkabong at high tide and arrive back with their catch at the next high tide. They use sampan canoes, hollowed out of a single tree-trunk, which are crafted in huts around the village. Some of the waterways and fields around Menkabong are choked by water hyacinth, an ornamental plant that was originally introduced by Chinese farmers as pig-fodder from South America. To get there, take a minibus to Tuaran, from where there are taxis to Menkabong.

Mengkabong Water Village

For visitors wanting to escape the popular beaches close to KK, **Tuaran**, offers a quieter alternative. It lies 45 minutes north of KK and is a good access point for several different tourist destinations including Mengkabong.

Sleeping **AL** *Rasa Ria Resort*, Pantai Dalit Beach, PO Box 600, T792888, F792777, rrr@po.jaring.my. Top-class *Shangri-La* resort with 330 rooms, free-form pool, watersports, 18-hole golf course, driving range, spacious gardens, conference facilities, cultural events, several restaurants including an Italian and a seafood beach front restaurant, unique torch lighting ceremony, 30ha of forest nature reserve nearby means that orang-utans are visitors to the resort. To get there, take a local bus to Tuaran. Recommended.

The nearby **Karam Bunai Beach** has a good picnic area, clean beach and sea. Close by is **Mimpian Jadi**, where there is the *Mimpian Jadi Resort* (**A-B**), No 1 Kuala Matinggi, Kampung Pulau, Simpangan, T787799, F787775. It has chalets, private beach, watersports, fishing, mini zoo, karaoke bar, horseriding, volleyball, children's playground, Malay/Chinese and Western food. **Surusup** is another 10-15 minutes beyond Tuaran. Ask at the store in Surusup for Haji Abdul Saman, who will take visitors by boat to the lesser known Bajau fishing village, **Kampung Penambawan**, also likened to an Asian Venice, on the north bank of the river. Nearby there is a suspension bridge and rapids where it is possible to swim. There is the *Pantai Palit Resthouse*. To get there, take a boat from Surusup.

Essentials

The scenic Karambunai peninsula 30 km north of KK has been transformed by a sprawling multi-million dollar golf and beach resort complex. The *Nexus Golf Resort Karambunai*, PO Box 270, 88450 Menggatal, T411222, F411020, nexushtl@tm.net.my, www.borneo-online.com.my/nexus/mf001.htm. The complex is built on 45 acres of land and has 490 rooms with views of the ocean along with all the usual facilities including a new golf course, convention centre etc. South of KK, the *Borneo Golf and Beach Resort*, including two 18-hole courses – one designed by Jack Nicklaus, the other by his son – is up-and-running. The *Shangri-La* group, which now owns the *Tanjung Aru*, has built the *Rasa Ria Resort* at Pantai Dalit, near Tuaran (see excursions above). Well-heeled tourists will seek the more refined out-of-town resorts; but in KK itself, mid-range hotels have improved immeasurably in recent years. The best bets, offering good value for money, are those catering for itinerant Malaysian businessmen, such as the *Mandarin Palace* and *Shangri-La*.

Sleeping
■ *on map, page 410*
Price codes:
see inside front cover

AL *Shangri-La Tanjung Aru Resort*, Tanjung Aru, T225800, F244871/217155, www.shangri-la.com, star@po.jaring.my. A/c, 500 rooms, pool, one of the best hotels in Sabah, although it is now in competition with its new sister hotel the *Rasa Ria*. Tanjung Aru is a public beach, frequented by kite-flyers, swimmers, joggers, and

Sabah

lovers, the hotel is noticeably on the European honeymoon circuit. Recommended. **A** *Berjaya Palace*, 1 Jln Tangki, Karamunsing, T211911, F211600. A/c, restaurant, 160 rooms, pool, conference rooms, gym, proprietor James Sheng has a small resort, with chalets, on Pulau Gaya, at Maluham Bay, east of Police Bay, enquire at hotel. **A** *Beverly Hills 'Vanria Holiday' Apartment*, Lot A6-3, Block A, 3rd Flr, Beverly Hills, T8212098. Ten kilometres from city centre, suitable for family groups with 2 bedroom apartments and dorms (**E**) with breakfast included in the room rate. The apartment has fan rooms and cooking facilities. Van rentals and tours organized, swimming pool. **A** *Jesselton*, 69 Jln Gaya, T223333, F240401. A/c, restaurant, the first hotel to be opened in KK, dates from 1954, remains a classic with just 32 rooms. Old establishment with everything from a London taxi to shoe-shining at your service. **A** *Langkah Syabas Beach Resort*, PO Box 451, Tanjung Aru, 88858, T752000, F752111, lsr@po.jaring.my. A resort with 14 chalets, a/c, fans, TVs and pool. **A** *Promenade*, 4 Lorong Api-Api 3, Api-Api Centre, T265555, F253980, acnv@pc.jaring.my. Several restaurants, business facilities, gym with good range of equipment, pool.

B *Borneo Resthouse*, Mile 3.5 Jln Penampang, Taman Fraser, T718855, F718955. A/c, 2 star hotel with 50 rooms, restaurant, pool, garden. **B** *Capital*, 23 Jln Haji Saman, T231999, F237222. A/c, TV, 102 rooms, coffee shop, central position. **B** *Century*, Lot 12 Jln Masjid Lama, T242222, F242929. A/c, 54 rooms, good seafood restaurant. **B** *Holiday* Lot 1 & 2, Block F, Segama Shopping Complex, off Jln Tun Razak, T213116. A/c, quite good with central location, but overpriced. **B** *Holiday Home (B&B)*, No 6, Block 1, Taman Likas Haya, Jln Teluk Likas, Lorong Kenari, T/F 423993. Close proximity to city centre, beach and sports complex within easy reach, tour and travel information

Kota Kinabalu

■ **Sleeping**	4 City Inn	8 Hyatt Kinabalu
1 Ang's	5 Diamond	9 Jesselton
2 Berjaya Palace	6 High Street Inn	10 Mandarin
3 Capital	7 Holiday	11 New Sabah

provided, dorms (**E**) beds available. **B** *Hotel Shangri-La*, 75 Bandaran Berjaya, T212800, F212078, kkshang@po.jaring.my. A/c, restaurant, not in the international *Shangri-La* group; reasonable hotel though and the haunt of business visitors. **B** *Hyatt Kinabalu International*, Jln Datuk Saleh Sulong, T221234, F252455. A/c, 288 rooms, 3 restaurants, pool and children's small pool, good central location, rooms vary in standard, business centre, live entertainment (*Shananigan's* Irish pub). Tours and treks organized. Good value. **B** *Kinabalu Daya*, Lot 3 & 4, Jln Pantai, T240000, F263909. Sixty eight rooms, a/c, the top floor restaurant serves Asian and Western food, video in bedrooms, seminar room. Breakfast included in the price. **B** *Mandarin*, 138 Jln Gaya, T225222, F225481. A/c, restaurant, very swish, marble floors, well-fitted rooms, excellent central location, friendly staff, sixth floor rooms with good view over town; deluxe and super-deluxe particularly spacious. Recommended.

C *Ang's*, 28 Jln Bakau, T234999, F217867. A/c, 35 rather threadbare rooms. **C** *City Inn*, 41 Jln Pantai, T218933, F218937. A/c, bathroom and TV; good for the price, often full. **C** *Diamond*, Jln Haji Yaakub, T261222, F231198. Very adequate 32 rooms. **C** *Golden Inn*, Sinsuran Complex, T211510. **C** *High Street Inn*, 38 Jln Pantai, T218111, F219111. A/c, TV, in-house films, hot water, small but comfortable rooms – very typical of the characterless hotels in this price range. **C** *New Sabah*, Block A, No 9-11 Jln Padas, Lot 394 Segama Complex, T224648, F235875. A/c, TV, bathroom, average hotel, very noisy. **C** *Pantai Inn*, 57 Jln Pantai, T219221, F216839. A/c, good central location, well-appointed rooms, small but very clean. **C** *Rosel*, 2nd Flr, Block B, Lot 1 & 2 Segama Complex, T256709, F263220, chapsel@pc.jaring.my. A/c, above the Indian Muslim restaurant *Bilal*, this centrally located hotel, although basic, is spotless and bright with friendly management, rooms have hot water showers and TV, tourist information. Recommended. **C** *Ruby*, Jln Laiman Diki, Kampung Ayer T213222, F231198. Total of 90 rooms, in a rather drab block. Better off elsewhere. **C** *Suang Hee*, Block F, 7 Segama Shopping Centre, T254168, F217234. A/c, restaurant, 24 rooms, clean Chinese hotel, reasonable value for money, a/c, TV and bathroom. **C** *Town Inn*, 31-33 Jln Pantai, T225823, F217762. A/c, 24 rooms, clean with excellent facilities, central location, good for the price. Recommended. **C** *Wah May*, 36 Jln Haji Saman, T266118, F266122. Modern Chinese hotel, 36 clean rooms kitted out with a/c, TV, fridge. Tight security with CCTV in operation. **C** *Winner*, 9 & 10 Jln Pasar Baru, Kampung Ayer, T243222, F217345. A/c, 36 rooms, restaurant, pleasant hotel in a central location with friendly staff and a good restaurant.

D *Islamic Hotel*, Kampung Ayer, cheap accommodation with fan only rooms and separate mandis. Excellent restaurant downstairs sells very good roti. **D** *Jack's B&B*, 17, 1st Flr, Block B, Karamunsing Warehouse, Jln Karamunsing, T232367, bbjack@tm.net.my. A/c, including

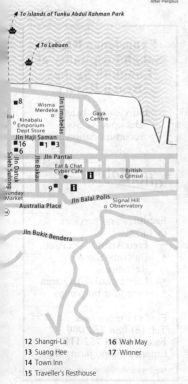

12 Shangri-La
13 Suang Hee
14 Town Inn
15 Traveller's Resthouse
16 Wah May
17 Winner

breakfast, clean and friendly, jungle tours organized. Recommended. **D** *Travellers' Rest Hostel*, Block L, 3rd Flr, Lot 5 & 6, Sinsuran Complex, Bangunan Pelancungan, T224720. Some a/c, no attached bath, some rooms don't have a window, friendly, lots of travel information, cooking and laundry facilities, tours around Sabah arranged here. Very clean, well organized and efficient place; a good bet for those on a budget. Price includes breakfast. **D** *Trekkers Lodge*, 46 Jln Pantai, T252263, Trekkerslodge@ hotmail.com. Price is per person, in a/c dorm style rooms. Breakfast is included. Recently opened, centrally located, managed by USA-trained Alex Yee, who is extremely helpful. All the staff have been well trained and the place is spotlessly clean. Laundry and storage facilities available. Recommended.

E *Backpacker Lodge*, Australia Pl, 25 Lorong Dewan T261495, lucychong@backpackers.com, www.sabahnet.com.my/backpacker. Friendly, clean dorms with a good breakfast included in the room rate. **E-F** *Borneo Wildlife Youth Hostel*, Lot 4, Block L, Sinsuran Complex, T213668, F219089. A newish place almost next door to the *Travellers' Resthouse* and above the *Borneo Wildlife Adventure Tour Company*, basic but clean with both dorm beds and individual rooms – all shared facilities.

Home away from Home, 413 Jln Saga, Mile 4½, Likas, T428733, F424998 echohome@ tm.net.my, www.sabahnet.com.my/home-away. Kampung accommodation organized for all parts of Sabah; contact Ms Faridah Abdul Rahman, director.

Eating   Malay 2 *Copelia*, Jln Gaya, *nasi lemak* for breakfast, also does takeaway. **1** *Restoran Ali*, Segama Complex, opposite *Hyatt Hotel*, best in a string of coffee shops, all of which are good value for money.

Chinese 3 *Hyatt Poolside Hawker Centre*, *Hyatt*, Jln Datuk Saleh Sulong, steamboat (minimum 2 people). **2** *Avasi Cafeteria & Garden Restaurant*, EG 11 Kompleks Kuwasa, steamboat and seafood. **2** *Nan Xing*, opposite the *Hyatt* and emporium, *dim sum* and Cantonese specialities. **2** *Phoenix Court*, *Hyatt*, Jln Datuk Saleh Sulong, *dim sum* 0700-1400. **2** *Tioman*, Lot 56 Bandaran Berjaya, good claypot and lemon chicken. **1** *Chuan Hin*, Jln Kolam (next to the Cottage Pub), excellent *ikan panggang*. **1** *Friendly*, Tuaran Rd, Mile 2, Likas, cheap.

Nyonya 2 *Sri Melaka Restoran*, 9 Jln Laiman Diki, Kampung Ayer (Sedco Complex, near *Shiraz*).

Other Asian cuisine 3 *Azuma*, 3rd Flr, Wisma Merdeka, Japanese. **3** *Jaws*, 4th Flr, Gaya Centre, Jln Tun Fuad Stephens, Thai/Chinese cuisine, such as *tom yam* steamboat. **3** *Nishiki*, Gaya St (opposite Wing On Life Building), Japanese. **2** *Korean*, Jln Bandaran Berjaya, next to *Asia Hotel*, large selection, barbecues speciality. **2** *Shiraz*, Lot 5, Block B, Sedco

Square, Kampung Ayer, Indian. Recommended. **1** *Bilal*, Block B, Lot 1 Segama Complex, Indian Muslim food, rotis, chapatis, curries. Recommended. **1** *Islamic Restoran*, Kampung Ayer, the best roti in town. *Sri Sakthi*, Mile 4.5 Jln Penampeng (opposite Towering Heights Industrial Estate), South Indian banana-leaf – good value. *Jothy's Curry Restaurant*, Api Api Centre.

International 3 *Gardenia*, *Jesselton Hotel*, 69 Jln Gaya. **3** *Peppino*, *Tanjung Aru Beach Resort*, tasty but expensive, Italian, good Filipino cover band. **2** *Sri Kapitol*, Ground Floor, *Hotel Capital*, 23 Jln Haji Saman, T219688, European breakfasts. **1** *Fat Cat*, Jln Haji Saman, cheap slap-up breakfasts. *MacDonalds*, Api Api Centre. *Pizza Hut*, Centre Point, Gaya St. *Sugarbun*, Centre Point, Gaya St. *KFC*, in half a dozen locations around town including Centre Point, Gaya St, Tuaran, Tanjung Aru. *Burger King*, Segama, Centre Point, Gaya St.

Seafood 3 *Garden Restaurant*, *Tanjung Aru Beach Resort*, tables outside. **3** *Merdeka*, 11th Flr, Wisma Merdeka, reasonably good seafood, but the view is better in this restaurant which offers 'karaoke at no extra charge'. **3** *Seafood Market*, Tanjung Aru Beach, T238313, pick your own fresh seafood and get advice on how to have it cooked. **2** *Golf Field Seafood*, 0858 Jln Ranca-Ranca (better known by taxi-drivers as *Ahban's Place*), excellent marine cuisine, local favourite. Recommended. **1** *Port View*, Jln Haji Saman (opposite old customs wharf), huge selection of fresh seafood and delicious chilli crab, open until 0200 weekdays and 0300 on Sat, very popular with locals. *Golf View*, Jln Swamp (near Sabah Golf and Country Club), recommended by locals.

This is seasonally prone to red tide. Locals will know when it's prevalent. Avoid all shellfish if there is any suspicion

Coffee shops Found in most areas of KK, hot and cold drinks are served as well as a variety of local noodle and rice dishes.

Bakeries KK bakers abound and are particularly good.

Foodstalls 2 Stalls above central market. **2** *Sedco Square*, Kampung Ayer, large square filled with stalls, great atmosphere in the evenings, ubiquitous *ikan panggang* and satay. Night market on Jln Tugu, on the waterfront at the Sinsuran Food Centre and at the *Merdeka Foodstall Centre*, Wisma Merdeka. *Tanjung Aru Beach*, mainly seafood – recommended for *ikan panggang* – and satay stalls: very busy at weekends, but on weekdays it is rather quiet, with only a few stalls to choose from.

Bars *Hard Rock Café*, Sutera Harbour. *The Cottage*, Jln Bukit Padang.

Entertainment

Cinemas Poring and Capital cinemas, near Sedco Complex. **Cultural shows** *Kadazan-Dusun Cultural Centre* (Hongkod Koisaan), KDCA Building, Mile 4.5, Jln Penampang, restaurant open year-round, but at the end of May, during the harvest festival, the cultural association comes into its own, with dances, feasts and shows and lots of *tapai* (RM15). *Tanjung Aru Beach Hotel* on Wed and Sat, 2000. **Discos** *Shennanigan's*, Hyatt Hotel, the smartest in town. *Next Door*, Tanjung Aru Beach Hotel. *Tiffiny*, Tanjung Aru, opposite Sacred Heart Church. *LA Rock*, along the left side of Tong Hing Supermarket. *Rockies*, Promenade Hotel. **Karaoke** very popular in KK; found in Damai, Foh Sang and KK centre. **MTV** *Popeye's MTV* in Bandaran.

Festivals

May *Magavau* (see page 51), a post-harvest celebration, carried out at Hongkod Koisaan (cultural centre). Mile 4.5, Jalan Penampang. To get there, take a green and white bus from the MPKK Building, next to state library.

Sabah

Shopping
For markets see page 406

Antiques Good antiques shop at the bottom of the Chun Eng Building on Jln Tun Razak, a couple also on Gaya St. It is necessary to have an export licence from the Sabah State Museum if you intend to export rare antiques.

Books *Arena Book Centre*, Lot 2, Ground Floor, Block 1, Sinsuran Kompleks. *Rahmant Bookstore*, *Hyatt Hotel*, Jln Datuk Salleh Sulong. *Iwase Bookshop*, Ground Floor, Wisma Merdeka, T233757, selection of English language books and magazines.

Clothes *The House of Borneo Vou'tique* Lot 12A, First Floor, Lorong Bernam 3, Taman Saon Kiong, Jln Kolam, T268398, F263398, for that ethnic, exotic and exclusive look for men and women – corporate uniforms, souvenir items, tablecloths, cushion covers etc.

Handicrafts Mainly baskets, mats, tribal clothing, beadwork and pottery. *Borneo Gifts*, Ground Floor, Wisma Sabah. *Borneo Handicraft*, 1st Flr, Wisma Merdeka, local pottery and material made up into clothes. *Elegance Souvenir*, 1st Flr, Wisma Merdeka, lots of beads of local interest (another branch on Ground Floor of Centre Point). *Malaysian Handicraft*, Cawangan Sabah, No 1, Lorong 14, Kg Sembulau, T234471, F223444, open Mon-Sat 0815-1230 and Fri 0815-1600. *The Crafts*, Lot AG10, Ground Floor, Wisma Merdeka, T252413. *Filipino Market*, Jln Tun Fuad Stephens (see page 406). *Kaandaman Handicraft Centre* below *Seafood Market Restaurant*, Tanjung Aru Beach. *Kampung Air Night Market*, mainly Filipino handicrafts. *Sabah Art and Handicraft Centre*, 1st Flr, Block B, Segama Complex (opposite *New Sabah Hotel*). *Sabah Handicraft Centre*, Lot 49 Bandaran Berjaya (next to *Shangri-La*) good selection (also has branches at the museum and the airport). There are also several handicraft shops in the arcade at the *Tanjung Aru Beach Hotel* and one at the airport. *Api Tours*, Lot 49, Bandaran Berjaya also has a small selection of handicrafts.

Jewellery Most shops in Wisma Merdeka.

Shopping complexes *Segama* on Jln Tun Fuad Stephens and *Sinsuran*. **NB** Beware of pick pocketing during the day and more particularly at night, when KK's transvestite population is at large. *Kinabalu Emporium*, Wisma Yakim, Jln Daruk Salleh Sulong is the main department store. *Likas Square* Likas, pink monstrosity with two floors of shopping malls, foodstalls and restaurants. Cultural shows in central lobby.

Supermarkets: *Kemayan* Likas. *Tong Hing* KK and Damai. *Home and Garden*, *Merdeka*, KK. *Milemewah*, KK.

Sports
The sports complex at Likas is open to the general public. It provides volleyball, tennis, basketball, a gym, badminton, squash, aerobics and a swimming pool. To get there take a Likas-bound minibus from town. *Likas Square*, the monstrous pink shopping complex north of Likas Sports Complex, has a Recreation Club within it providing tennis, squash, jogging, golf, driving range, a pool and a children's playground.

Bowling *Merdeka Bowl*, 11th Flr, Wisma Merdeka. **Diving** Snorkelling and scuba-diving in Tunku Abdul Rahman National Park. Tour operators specializing in dive trips also organize dives all over Sabah. See also box opposite. **Golf** Green fees are considerably higher over the weekend – as much as double the weekday rate. Fees range from a low of about RM50 during the week at the cheaper courses, to as much as RM200 or more over the weekend at flasher clubs. Courses at Tanjung Aru and the *Sabah Golf and Country Club* at Bukit Padang, T247533, an 18-hole championship course, which affords magnificent views of Mount Kinabalu on clear days, green fees RM150 (weekdays), RM200 (weekends). *Kinabalu Golf Club*, T234904,

Layang-Layang Atoll: OK coral

Malaysia is just one of five claimants to the countless reefs and atolls in the Spratly group. While Vietnam and China are more interested in the prospective riches from what are thought to be oil-bearing strata beneath the seabed, Malaysia is the only country to have cashed in on tourism on the reefs themselves. Layang-Layang (or 'Kite') atoll is about 250 km northwest of Kota Kinabalu – a 16 hour boat ride – and has recently been added to other coral reefs such as Sipadan Island, off Sabah's east coast (see page 468) as part of the state's growing list of fabulous dive sites. Layang-Layang – formerly known as

Swallow Reef – is 7 km long and 5 km wide, with a lagoon in the middle. There is a Malaysian navy base at one end and basic tourist accommodation (in concrete and breeze block houses) next to it. The island attracts migratory birds, but is best-known as a scuba paradise. Divers visiting Layang-Layang usually stay aboard the MV Coral Topaz and make trips to other nearby reefs. There are reportedly several wrecks in the area, but most diving focuses on the coral walls on the outer edges of the reefs which drop sheer to the seabed 2,000m below. This area also has some of Southeast Asia's finest game fishing.

Tanjung Aru Beach. **Hashing** There are three hashes in KK. **1**: *K2 H4* (KK Hash House Harriers) – men only, T428535, Mon, 1715. **2** *K2 H2* (KK Hash House Bunnies) – women (but not exclusively), T244333, ext 389. **3** *K2 H4* (KK Hash House Harriers and Harriets) – mixed, T217541, Fri, 1715. **Roller blading** Centre Point, 3rd Floor, Gaya St. **Sailing** Yacht club at Tanjung Aru, next to the hotel. **Watersports** *Tanjung Aru Marina*, snorkelling RM10 per day, water skiing RM120 per hour, fishing RM12-25 per day, sailing RM20-40 per hour, water scooter RM60 per hour. Snorkelling equipment for rent at good prices from the *Travellers Resthouse*. **White water rafting** Papar River (Grades I & II), Kadamaian River (Grades II & III), Padas River (Grade IV). Usually requires a minimum of 3 people. Main operators including *Api Tours*, *Borneo Expeditions* and *Discovery Tours* (see page 407).

Api Tours (Borneo), No 13 Jln Punai Dekut, Mile 5, Jln Tuaran, PO Box 12851, T421963, F424174, apitour@po.jaring.my, www.jaring.my/apitours. Offers a wide variety of tours, including some more unusual ones such as overnight stays in longhouses. Recommended. *Borneo Divers*, 9th Floor, Menara Jubit, 53 Jln Gaya, T222226, F221550, bdivers@po.jaring.my, www.jaring.my/bdivers (there is another branch in the *Tanjung Aru Beach Hotel*), operates exotic scuba diving trips and runs a dive station on Pulau Sipadan (see page 468), *Borneo Divers* also runs an excellent dive store and operates 5-days training courses with classes tailored for beginners or advanced divers (RM875-575 depending on group size), the company also has an office in Tawau T089761214, F089761691, and in Labuan T087 415867, F087 413454 (see page 428) which organizes 2-days dives to shipwrecks off the island, trips are seamlessly organized, but very expensive. *Borneo Eco Tours*, Lot 12A, 2nd Floor, Lorong Bernam 3, T234009, F233688, betsb1@po.jaring.my, www.jaring.my/bet, adventure and culture tours, ecotourist specialists – their *Sukau Rainforest Lodge* on the Kinabatangan River is highly recommended. *Borneo Sea Adventures*, 1st Flr, 8a Karamunsing Warehouse, T230000, F221106, bornsea@pop1.jaring.my, also conducts scuba diving courses and runs diving and fishing trips all around Sabah. It specializes in the 'Wall Dive' off Pulau Sipadan (see page 468). *Borneo Wildlife Adventures*, Lot 4, Block L, Ground, 2nd and 3rd Floors, Sinsuran Complex, T213668, F219089, bwa@tm.net.my, one of the newer eco-tour companies, specializing in nature tours, wildlife and cultural activities. *Coral Island Cruises*, 10th Floor, Wisma Merdeka, T223490, F223404, miao@po.jaring.my Specializes in boat cruises, mostly around Tunku Abdul Rahman National Park, and offers night fishing trips. *Coral Island*

Tour operators

The Sabah Tourism Promotion Corporation has a full list of tour & travel agents operating in the state

Sabah

Cruises has teamed up with the Labuan-based dive company *Ocean Sports* to run 6-days scuba-diving trips to Layang Layang, an atoll in the disputed Spratly group, 6-16 days dive packages, costing RM1,000+, leave 2-3 times a month in peak season (Jun-Aug) (see box, page 415). Also operates dive voyages aboard *MV Coral Topaz* to Sipadan/Ligitan islands (see page 469). Recommended. *Discovery Tours*, Lot G28, Wisma Sabah, Jln Haji Saman, T221244, F221600, distour@po.jaring.my. Run by experienced tour operator Terry Lim. Recommended. *Exotic Borneo Holidays*, Lot 24, 1st Flr, Suite B, Likas Industrial Centre, Tuaran Rd, T429224, F429024, exotic@po.jaring.my ,organize well-run theme tours including culture, adventure and nature, at a price. *North Borneo Tours*, 65 Lorong Angsa 1, off Jln Kolam, Luyang, Kota Kinabalu. T268339, F268893, nbtt@tm.net.my. Specializes in arranging golf days and tours. *Pan Borneo Tours & Travel*, 1st Floor, Room 127, Wisma Sabah, T221221, F219233, panborn@po.jaring.my. Sightseeing, diving, wildlife tours. *Sabah Air*, Sabah Air Building, Old Airport Rd, T256733, F235195, sabair@tm.net.my, organizes aerial sightseeing flights and air charter. *Sipadan Dive Centre*, 10th Flr, Wisma Merdeka, Jln Tun Razak, T240584, F240415, sipadan@po.jaring.my, www.jaring.my/sipadan. PADI dive courses taught and accommodation on Sipadan organized. Diving at Tunku Abdul Rahman Park also arranged. *Tanjung Aru Tours*, The Marina, *Tanjung Aru Beach Hotel*, T214215/240966, F240966, tattsb@tm.net.my. Fishing and island tours – particularly to Tunku Abdul Rahman National Park. *Transworld*, 2nd Flr, Bangunan Dewan Perniagaan, Bumiputera Sabah, Jln Gaya, T/F 240866 (also an office at *Tanjung Aru Beach Resort*). Glass-bottom boat trips to Tunku Abdul Rahman National Park.

Transport

77 km to Kota Belud
128 km to Keningau
386 km to Sandakan

Local Buses: city buses leave from area between Jln Tun Razak and Jln Tugu. Buses from behind the Centre Point Shopping Complex go to Kapayan, Queen Elizabeth Hospital, Sembulan, Putatan, Jln Baru and Penampang. Red and white buses go to Penampang and Tanjung Aru and leave from the bus station in front of the MPKK Building, next to the state library. Green buses go to areas north of KK (Tuaran, Likas etc) and leave from the padang at the bottom of Signal Hill. *Luen Thong* white a/c buses go from in front of the *Shangri-La Hotel*, they go to Tuaran, Telipok, Dayavila and Kampung Likas. From MPKK building, *Luen Thong* a/c buses go to Tanjung Aru and Kapayan.

Car hire: not all roads in the interior of Sabah are paved and a 4WD vehicle is advisable. However, car hire is expensive and starts at around RM300-400 per day. Rates often increase for use outside a 50 km radius of KK. All vehicles have to be returned to KK as there are no agency offices outside KK, although local car-hire is usually available. *Adaras Rent-a-Car*, Lot G03, Ground Floor, Wisma Sabah, T211866, F216010. *Avis*, *Hyatt Kinabalu Hotel*, Jln Datuk Salleh Sullong, T428577. *Borneo Car Rental*, Lot 24, 1st Flr, Suite A, Likas Industrial Centre, Tuaran Rd, T429224. *Extra Rent-a-Car*, 3rd Floor, Karamunsing Hotel, Jln Kemajuan. *E & C Limousine Services*, 2nd Floor Karamunsing Kompleks, T239996, F221466. *Hertz*, Block B, Sedco Complex, T221635. *Kinabalu Rent-a-Car*, Lot 3.61, 3rd Flr, Kompleks Karamunsing, T232602.

Minibuses: all minibuses have their destinations on the windscreen, most rides in town are RM0.40-0.60 and they will leave when full. You can get off wherever you like.

Most taxis are not metered

Taxis: there are taxi stands outside most of the bigger hotels and outside the General Post Office, the Segama complex, the Sunsuran complex, next to the MPKK building, the Milemewah supermarket, the Capitol cinema and in front of the clocktower (for taxis to Ranau, Keningau and Kudat). Approximate fares from town: RM8 to *Tanjung Aru Beach Resort*, RM10 Sabah Foundation, RM10 to the museum, RM17 airport.

Long distance Air: the airport is 6 km from town. Taxi RM17 to town centre; coupon can be purchased in advance from the booths outside the arrivals hall. Regular connections with KL, cheaper flights if in a group of 3 or more, late-night flights, or book 14 days in advance (RM311, 2 hrs 30 mins). There are also connections from KK with Bintulu, Johor Bharu, Kuching (RM233, 1 hour 20 mins), Kudat, Lahad Datu, Labuan, Miri (RM100, 40 mins), Penang, Sandakan (RM88, 40 mins), Sibu and Tawau (RM101, 45 mins). International connections are with Singapore, Brunei, Hong Kong, Manila, Seoul, Jakarta,Taipei and Tokyo.

Train The station is 5 km out of town in Tanjung Aru. Diesel trains run three times daily to Beaufort, 4 hrs and on to Tenom, a further 3 hrs. Departure times are subject to change, T52536/54611. *Transport to town*: long distance buses stop near the station.

Bus: buses around the state are cheaper than minibuses but not as regular or efficient. The large buses go mainly to destinations in and around KK itself. **Minibus and taxi**: there is no central bus station in KK. Taxis and minibuses bound north for Kota Belud, Tamparuli and Kudat and those going south to Papar, Beaufort, Keningau and Tenom leave from Bandar Berjaya opposite the Padang and clocktower. Taxis and minibuses going west to Kinabalu National Park, Ranau and Sandakan leave from Jln Tunku Abdul Rahman, next to the Padang and opposite the State Library. Tamparuli, a few kilometres east of Tuaran, serves as a mini-terminus for minibuses heading to Kinabalu National Park. Minibuses leave when full and those for long-distance destinations leave in the early morning. Long-distance taxis also leave when full from in front of the clocktower on Jln Tunku Abdul Rahman. Minibus services from KK to Tuaran 45 mins, Kota Belud 2 hrs, Kudat 4-5 hrs, Beaufort 2-3 hrs, Keningau 2-3 hrs, Tenom 4 hrs, Kinabalu National Park 1½ hrs, Ranau 2 hrs, Sandakan 8-10 hrs.

Boat: 3 boats a day leave for Labuan, 2½ hrs (RM30). Boats leave from the jetty behind the *Hyatt Hotel*. Reservations can be made at *Rezeki Murmi Sdn Bhd*, Lot 3, 1st Flr, Block D, Segama Shopping Complex, T236834/5, F237390.

Airline offices *British Airways*, Jln Haji Saman, T428057/428292. *Cathay Pacific*, Ground Floor, Block C, Lot CG, Kompleks Kuwasa, 49 Jln Karamunsing, T428733. *Garuda Airways*, Wisma Sabah. *MAS*, 10th Flr, Karamunsing Kompleks (off Jln Tunku Abdul Rahman, south of Kampung Ayer), Jln Kemajuan, T203500, F240135, also have an office at the airport. *Philippine Airlines*, 2nd Flr, Karamunsing Complex, Jln Kemajuan, T239600. *Royal Brunei Airlines*, T242193, Ground Flr, Kompleks Kowasa. *Sabah Air*, KK Airport, T428733/428326. *Singapore Airlines*, 12-13 Ground Flr, Block C, Kompleks Kowasa, T255448. *Thai Airways*, T232896, Lot CG14, Block C, Ground Flr, Kompleks Kowasa. *Qantas*, T216998.

Directory

Banks There are money changers in main shopping complexes. *Hong Kong & Shanghai*, 56 Jln Gaya. *Sabah Bank*, Wisma Tun Fuad Stephens, Jln Tuaran. *Standard Chartered*, 20 Jln Haji Saman. *Maybank*, Jln Kemajuan/ Jln Pantai.

Communications Area code: 088. **General Post Office:** Jln Tun Razak, Segama Quarter (poste restante facilities). **Telekom:** Block C, Kompleks Kuwaus, Jln Tunku Abdul Rahman, international calls as well as local, fax service. **Internet cafés:** *Cybercafé*, Lot 95, Jln Gaya, T231089. Open 1000-0100. *Cybermaster*, Ground and 1st Flr, Api-Api Centre, T239868. Open 0900-0100.

Embassies & consulates *British Consul*, Hong Kong Bank Building, 56 Jln Gaya. *Indonesian Consulate*, Jln Karamunsing, T428100. *Japanese Consulate*, Wisma Yakim, T428169.

Medical facilities **Health Care:** one of the better private clinics is the Damai Specialist Centre.

Parks offices *Forestry Division*, Sabah Foundation, Sabah Foundation Building, Likas, T34596. *Innoprise Corporation Building*, Sadong Jaya, T243251 for the Danum Valley Field Centre (see page 465). *Sabah National Parks Office Headquarters*, 1st Flr, Lot 1-3, Block K, Sinsuran Kompleks, Jln Tun Fuad Stephens, T211652, F211585, necessary to book accommodation for the national

Sabah

parks (T211881), particularly Mount Kinabalu National Park or Poring Hot Springs. Also has general information on the parks, the office has a good library with reports on wildlife in the parks and natural history surveys which can be used with the permission of the office, open 0800-1600 Mon-Fri, 0830-1230 Sat.

Places of worship English: *St Simon's Catholic Church*, Likas, Sun 1700. *Stella Maris* (Tanjung Aru) Sun 0700. *SIB*, Likas (Baptist), Sun 0800.

Tourist offices *Sabah Tourist Promotion Corporation*, 51 Jln Gaya, T212121, F212075, www.jaring.my/sabah, sabah@po.jaring.my. *Tourism Malaysia Sabah*, Ground Flr, Wing On Life Building, Jln Sagunting, T248698, mtpbki@tourism.gov.my. Both offices have a wealth of information although the Tourism Malaysia office is of little use for Sabah. The *Sabah Tourist Promotion Corporation* is excellent and very helpful.

Useful addresses British Council: Wing On Life Building, Jln Sagunting, 1st Flr, not very helpful. **Business centres:** at the *Hyatt Hotel* and *Shangri-La Tanjung Aru Resort* and *Shangri-La Rasa Ria*. **Immigration:** 4th Flr Government Building,' Jln Haji Yaakub. Visas can be renewed at this office, without having to leave the country.

Tunku Abdul Rahman Park

Colour map 4, grid A3 *The five islands in Gaya Bay which make up Tunku Abdul Rahman Park lie 3-8 km offshore. They became Sabah's first national park in 1923 and were gazetted in an effort to protect their coral reefs and sandy beaches. Geologically, the islands are part of the Crocker Range formation, but as sea levels rose after the last ice age, they became isolated from the massif. Coral reefs fringe all the islands in the park. The best reefs are between Pulau Sapi and Pulau Gaya, although there is also reasonable coral around Manukan, Mamutik and Sulug. The islands can be visited all year round.*

Flora and fauna

Some of the only undisturbed coastal dipterocarp forest left in Sabah is on Pulau Gaya. On the other islands most of the original vegetation has been destroyed and established secondary vegetation predominates, such as ferns, orchids, palms, casuarina, coconut trees and tropical fruit trees. Mangrove forests can be found at two locations on Pulau Gaya. Animal and bird life includes long-tailed macaques, bearded pig and pangolin (on Pulau Gaya), white-bellied sea eagle, pied hornbill, green heron, sandpipers, flycatchers and sunbirds.

There is a magnificent range of marine life because of the variety of the reefs surrounding the islands. The coral reefs are teeming with fish-tank exotica such as butterfly fish, Moorish idols, parrot fish, bat fish, razor fish, lion fish and stone fish, in stark contrast to the areas which have been depth-charged by Gaya's notorious dynamite fishermen.

The islands

Four of the five islands have excellent snorkelling and diving as well as jungle trails. The largest island, **Pulau Gaya**, was the site of the first British North Borneo Chartered Company settlement in the area in 1882. The settlement lasted only 15 years before being destroyed in a pirate attack. There is still a large settlement on the island on the promontory facing KK – but today it is a shanty town, populated mainly by Filipino immigrants (see page 483). On Pulau Gaya there are 20 km of marked trails including a plank-walk across a mangrove swamp. Police Bay has a beautiful shaded beach.

Sleeping A *Gayana Resort Bay*, Lot 16, Ground Floor, Wisma Sabah, Jln Tun Razak, T245158, F245168. For more information, east coast of the island, a/c chalets, restaurant (serves Asian and Western food), barbecue site, private beach, activities include diving, snorkelling, windsurfing, trekking in the jungle, fishing, yachting.

Pulau Sapi, the most popular of the island group for weekenders, also has good beaches and trails. It is connected to Pulau Gaya by a sandbar. A glass-bottomed boat is available here for hire for those who wish to view the coral and marine life; there are good day-use facilities. **Pulau Mamutik** is the smallest island but closer to the mainland and has a well-preserved reef off the northeast tip. **Pulau Manukan** is the site of the park headquarters and most of the park accommodation. It has good snorkelling to the south and east and a particularly good beach on the east tip. It is probably the best of all the islands but is heavily frequented by day trippers and rubbish is sometimes a problem. Marine sports facilities stretch to the hire of mask, snorkel and fins (RM15 plus RM50 deposit for the day), no sub-aqua gear available, swimming pool. The best reefs are off **Pulau Sulang**, which is less developed being a little bit further away. Unfortunately the beach here is full of rubbish and the island has a neglected air.

Park essentials

NB It is necessary to hire snorkel, mask and fins from boatmen at the KK jetty beforehand. Fishing with a hook and line is permitted but the use of spearguns and nets is prohibited. Permits are not necessary.

Park headquarters On Pulau Manukan; ranger stations on Gaya, Sapi and Mamutik.

Chalets and resthouses on Pulau Mamutik and Pulau Manukan. **AL** (weekends)–**A** (weekdays) *Resthouse*, Pulau Mamutik, under refurbishment, but will be open by the time this book goes to press and now managed by *Borneo Divers* of KK. **A** (weekends)–**B** (weekdays) *Chalets*, Pulau Manukan, restaurant, pool, facilities including tennis and squash courts, football field, 1,500m jogging track and a diving centre. *Chalets at Maluham Bay*, east of Police Bay, Pulau Gaya. Enquire at *Palace Hotel*, KK. **Camping** It is possible to camp on any of the islands (obtain permission from the Sabah Parks Office in KK). Basic facilities on Pulau Mamutik.

Sleeping
Rooms are significantly discounted during the week

Excellent restaurant on Pulau Manukan. Pulau Mamutik and Pulau Sapi each have a small shop selling a limited range of very expensive food and drink. Cooked food on Pulau Sapi is sometimes in short supply. For Pulau Sulang, Sapi and Mamutik take all the water you need – there is no drinkable water supply here, shower and toilet water is only provided if there has been sufficient rain.

Eating

Boat: most boats leave from the jetty opposite the *Hyatt Hotel*. Regular ferry services leave from the Jetty Taman Sabah (near the *Hyatt*) for Manukan at 0900, 1100, 1200, 1300 and return to KK 1500, 1600, 1700 (RM20 adult, RM12 child). If you want to visit more than one island, a boat needs to be chartered, at a cost of about RM280 for a three island tour or RM360 for a five island tour, taking 12 passengers. Contact Sutima Express, 1st Flr, Lot 5, Sinsuran Complex. It is possible to negotiate trips with local fishermen. Boats also leave from *Tanjung Aru Beach Hotel*.

Transport
3-8 km offshore

Useful addresses For reservations and more information on the park, contact *Coral Island Cruises*, Ground Flr, Wisma Sabah, PO Box 14527, KK, T223490, F223404. *Sea Quest Tours and Travel*, Wisma Merdeka, Phase 2, 2nd Flr, Lot B207, T230943, or *Tanjung Aru Tours*, Tanjung Aru Beach Hotel, T214215, F217155.

Directory

Sabah

South of Kota Kinabalu

Travelling south from KK, the route crosses the Crocker Range to Tambunan. Continuing south the road passes through the logging town of Keningan and on to Tenom, where it is possible to take the North Borneo railway, which snakes down the Padas Gorge to Beaufort. The Padas River is the best place to go white-water rafting in Sabah. Few towns are worth staying in for long on this route but it is a scenic journey.

Tambunan

Colour map 4, grid B3 The twisting mountain road that cuts across the **Crocker Range National Park** (see page 422) and over the Sinsuran Pass at 1,649m is very beautiful. There are dramatic views down over Kota Kinabalu and the islands beyond and glimpses of Mount Kinabalu to the northeast. The road itself, from KK to Tambunan, was the old bridle way that linked the west coast to the interior. Inland communities traded their tobacco, rattan and other jungle produce for salt and iron at the coastal markets. The road passes through Penampang. Scattered farming communities raise hill rice, pineapples, bananas, mushrooms and other vegetables which are sold at road-side stalls, where wild and cultivated orchids can also be found. After descending from the hills the road enters the sprawling flood plain of Tambunan – the Pegalam River runs through the plain – which, at the height of the paddy season, is a magnificent patchwork of greens.

The Tambunan area is largely Kadazan/Dusun and the whole area explodes into life each May during the harvest festival when copious quantities of *lihing*, the famed local rice wine, are consumed and the Bobolians or high priestesses are still called upon to conduct various rituals. There is a Lihing brewery inside the *Tambunan Village Resort Centre*. The Tambunan District covers an area of 134,540 hectares and has a population of about 24,000. At an altitude of 650m to 900m, it enjoys a spring-like climate during much of the year.

Tambunan, or 'Valley of the Bamboo', as there are at least 12 varieties of bamboo to be found here, also lays claim to the Kitingan family. Joseph was Sabah's first Christian Chief Minister until deposed in March 1994. His brother, Jeffrey, was formerly head of the Sabah Foundation. He entered politics in 1994 on his release from detention on the peninsula. He had been charged under Malaysia's Internal Security Act of being a secessionist conspirator.

A modest plaque just outside Tambunan, among the ricefields and surrounded by peaceful kampung houses, commemorates the site of **Mat Salleh's fort**. Mat Salleh, now a nationalist folk-hero, led a rebellion for six years against the Chartered Company administration until he was killed in 1900 (see box). There is not much left of his fort for visitors to inspect.

The Rafflesia Information Centre (T087774691), located at the roadside on the edge of a Forest Reserve that has been set aside to conserve this remarkable flower (see box). The Information Centre has a comprehensive and attractive display on the Rafflesia and its habitat and provides information on

Mat Salleh – fort-builder and folk hero

Mat Salleh was a Bajau, and son of a Sulu Chief, born in the court of the Sultan of Sulu. He was the only native leader to stand up against the increasingly autocratic whims of the North Borneo government as it sequestrated land traditionally belonging to tribal chiefs. Under the Chartered Company and the subsequent colonial administration, generations of school children were taught that Mat Salleh was a deplorable rabble-rouser and trouble-maker. Now Sabahans regard him as a nationalist hero.

In the British North Borneo Herald of 16 February 1899, it was reported that when he spoke, flames leapt from his mouth; lightening flashed with each stroke of his parang and when he scattered rice, the grains became wasps. He was said to have been endowed with 'special knowledge' by the spirits of his ancestors and was also reported to have been able to throw a buffalo by its horns.

In 1897 Mat Salleh raided and set fire to the first British settlement on Pulau Gaya (off modern-day Kota Kinabalu). For this, and other acts of sabotage, he was declared an outlaw by the Governor. A price tag of 700 Straits dollars was put on his head and an administrative officer, Raffles Flint, was assigned the unenviable task of tracking him down. Flint failed to catch him and Mat Salleh gained a reputation as a military genius.

Finally, the managing director of the Chartered Company, Scottish adventurer and former gun-runner William C Cowie, struck a deal with Mat Salleh and promised that his people would be allowed to settle peacefully in Tambunan, which at that time was not under Chartered Company control. After the negotiations Cowie wrote: "His manner and appearance made me aware that I was face to face with the Rob Roy of British North Borneo, the notorious Mat Salleh, whom I at once saluted with a takek [a greeting from an inferior]."

Half the North Borneo administration resigned as they considered Cowie's concessions outrageous. With it looking less and less likely that the terms of his agreement with Cowie would be respected, Mat Salleh retreated to Tambunan where he started building his fort; he had already gained a fearsome reputation for these stockades. West Coast Resident G Hewett described it as "the most extraordinary place and without [our] guns it would have been absolutely impregnable". Rifle fire could not penetrate it and Hewett blasted 200 shells into the fort with no noticeable effect. The stone walls were 2.5m thick and were surrounded by three bamboo fences, the ground in front of which was studded with row upon row of sharpened bamboo spikes. Hewett wrote: "...had we been able to form any idea of the external strength of the place we should never have attempted to rush in as we did." His party retreated having suffered four dead and nine wounded.

Mat Salleh had built similar forts all over Sabah, and the hearts of the protectorate's administrators must have sunk when they heard he was building one at Tambunan. A government expedition arrived in the Tambunan Valley on the last day of 1899. There was intensive fighting throughout Jan, with the government taking village after village, until at last, the North Borneo Constabulary came within 50m of Mat Salleh's fort. Its water supply had been cut off and the fort had been shelled incessantly for 10 days. Mat Salleh was trapped. On 31 January 1900 he was killed by a stray bullet which hit him in the left temple.

flowers in bloom. If trail maps are temporarily unavailable, ask the ranger to point out the site where blooms can be seen on the large relief model of the Forest Reserve at the back of the Information Centre. The blooming period of the flower is very short so to avoid disappointment, it may be worth phoning the Centre first. ■ *Mon-Fri 0845-1245, 1400-1700, Sat-Sun 0800-1700.*

Rafflesia: the largest flower in the world

The rafflesia (Rafflesia arnoldi), named after Stamford Raffles, is the largest flower in the world. The Swedish naturalist Eric Mjoberg wrote in 1930 on seeing the flower: "The whole phenomenon seems so amazing, so unfamiliar, so fantastic, that we are tempted to explain: such flowers cannot be real!". Stamford Raffles, who discovered the flower for Western science one hundred years earlier during his first sojourn at Bengkulu on the west coast of Sumatra, noted that it was "a full yard across, weighs 15 pounds, and contains in the nectary no less than eight pints [of nectar]...". The problem is that the rafflesia does not flower for very long – only for a couple of weeks, usually between August and December. Out of these months there is usually nothing to see. The plant is in fact parasitic, so appropriately its scent is more akin to rotting meat than any perfume. Its natural habitat is moist, shaded areas.

Sleeping C *Gunung Emas Highlands Resort*, Km 52 (about 7 km from the Rafflesia Centre) some dorm rooms (**E**), some very basic tree houses, a fresh climate and good views. Mini zoo and restaurant serving local food. To get there take the Rabunan or the Keningau minibus and then another bus from Tambunan.

Ahir Terjan Sensuron is a waterfall 4 km from Rafflesia Information Centre on the Tambunan-KK road (heading towards KK). From the road, it is a 45 minute walk to the waterfall. A large **market** is held here every Thursday morning – on sale are tobacco, local musical instruments, clothing, strange edible jungle ferns and yeast used to make fermented rice wine. There are also bundles of a fragrant herb known as *tuhau*, a member of the ginger family that is made into a spicy condiment or sambal redolent of the jungle. A smaller market is held every Sunday in Kampung Toboh, north of Tambunan.

Excursions **Crocker Range National Park** incorporates 139,919 hectares of hill and montane forest, which includes many species endemic to Borneo. It is the largest single totally protected area in Sabah. No visitors' facilities have yet been developed. But private development is taking place along the narrow strips of land each side of the KK-Tambunan road, which were unfortunately overlooked when the park was gazetted. A decrepit motel – complete with a horrifying menagerie – has sprung up at Sinsuran Pass and an outward bound school also has its headquarters here. To get there, see **Transport** below, as for Tambunan. The **Mawah Waterfall** is reached by following the road north towards Ranau to Kampung Patau, where a sign beside the school on the left indicates a gravel road leading almost to the waterfall (*Mawah Airterjun*). It is 15 minutes down road by car and 5-10 minutes' walk along the trail.

Altitude: 2,642m **Gunung Trusmadi**, 70 km southeast of KK, is the second highest mountain in Malaysia, but very few people climb it. There are two main routes to the top: the north route, which takes four days to the summit (and three days down) and the south route, which is harder but shorter; two days to the summit. Trusmadi is famous for its huge, and very rare, pitcher plant *Nepethes trusmadiensis*, which is only found on one spot on the summit ridge (see page 526). It is also known for its fantastic view north, towards Gunung Kinabalu, which rises above the Tambunan valley. There is a wide variety of vegetation on the mountain as it rises from dipterocarp primary jungle through oak montane forest with mossy forest near the summit and heath-like vegetation on top. The best time to climb is in March and it is advisable to take guides and porters for the tough climb (ask the District Officer in Tambunan). An

Sabah

expedition to Trusmadi requires careful planning – it should not be undertaken casually. A more detailed account of the two routes can be found in *Mountains of Malaysia – A Practical Guide and Manual*, by John Briggs.

C *Tambunan Village Resort Centre (TVRC)*, signposted off the main road before the town located on both sides of the Pegalam River, collection of chalets and a 'longhouse' dormitory made of split bamboo. Restaurant, motel and entertainment centre (with karaoke and slot machines), hall and sports field. There are also a couple of retreat centres located about 10 mins' walk away. **C-D** *Government Resthouse*, T774339.

Sleeping & eating
Both hotels are out of town

The area is renowned for its rice wine (*lihing*). Visitors can watch it being brewed at the factory within the *TVRC (Tambunan Village Resort Centre)*.

Handicrafts *Handicraft Centre* just before the Shell petrol station, for traditional weaving and basketry from the area. **Market** *Tamu* on Thur.

Shopping

Minibus: minibuses for Tambunan leave from the corner of Australia Pl/Jln Tunku Abdul Rahman in KK. Those leaving Tambunan go from the centre of town by the mosque. Regular connections to KK, 1½ hrs (RM10) and Ranau (RM10).

Transport
90 km to KK

Keningau

The Japanese built fortifications around their base in Keningau during the Second World War. It is now rather a depressing, shabby lumber town, smothered in smoke from the sawmills. The timber business in this area turned Keningau into a boom town in the 1980s and the population virtually doubled within a decade. The felling continues, but there is not much primary forest left these days. There are huge logging camps all around the town and the hills to the west. Logging roads lead into these hills off the Keningau-Tenom road which are accessible by four-wheel drive vehicles. It is just possible to drive across them to Papar, which is a magnificent route. **NB** Anyone attempting the drive should be warned to steer well clear of log-laden trucks as they make their way down the mountain.

Colour map 4, grid B3

Sabah

Murut villages Sapulut is deep in Murut country and is accessible from Keningau by a rough road via Kampung Nabawan. At Sapulut, follow the river of the same name east through Bigor and Kampung Labang to Kampung Batu Punggul at the confluence of Sungai Palangan. **Batu Punggul** is a limestone outcrop protruding 200m above the surrounding forest, 30 minutes' walk from the kampung, it can be climbed without any equipment, but with care. It is quite a dangerous climb but the view of the surrounding forest from the top is spectacular. Both the forest and the caves in and around Batu Punggul are worth exploring. Nearby is the recently discovered, but less impressive limestone outcrop, **Batu Tinahas**, which has huge caves with many unexplored passages. It is currently being surveyed and it is believed to have at least three levels of caves and tunnels.

Excursions

From Sapulut, it is a fairly painless exercise to cross the border into Kalimantan. A short stretch of road leads from Sapulut to Agis which is just a four-hour boat ride from the border. There is even an immigration checkpoint at Pegalungan, a settlement *en route*. One particular longhouse is **Kampung Selungai**, only 30 minutes from Pegalungan. Here it is possible to see traditional boat builders at work, as well as weaving, mat making and beadwork. There are many rivers and longhouses in the area worth exploring. Given the luxury of time, it is a fascinating area where traditional lifestyles have not been much eroded. It is possible to charter a minibus along the Nabawan road to

Sapulut, where you can hire boats upriver. At Sapulut, ask for Lantir (the headman, or *kepala*). He will arrange the boat trip upriver, which could take up to two days depending on the river, and accommodation in Murut longhouses, through the gloriously named *Sapulut Adventurism Tourism Travel Company*, run by Lantir and his mate. As in neighbouring Sarawak, these long upriver trips can be prohibitively expensive unless you are in a decent-sized group.

Sleeping & eating

B *HillView Garden Resort*, PO Box 210, Keningau, T333678 F331757, hilview@ tm.net.my, www.idis.com/alfons/hill.html. New place with 25 rooms. Good option. **B** *Perkasa*, Jln Kampung Keningau, T331045, F334800. On the edge of town, a/c, Chinese restaurant, coffee house, health centre, comfortable rooms. **C** *Kristal Hotel*, Pegalan Shopping Complex, T338888. Reasonable place, void of any real character, but a relatively cheap option in a town short on decent cheap accommodation. **D-E** *Government Rest House*, T331525, dorms (**F**), book through Rural Development Corporation, T088428910.

Seri Wah Coffee Shop, on the corner of the central square. Selection of foodstalls.

Transport
40 km to Tenom
128 km to KK

Air Connections with KK. **Minibus** Minibuses leave from centre of town, by the market. Regular connections with KK and Tenom.

Tenom

Colour map 4, grid B3

Situated at the end of the North Borneo Railway, Tenom is a hilly inland town, with a population of about 4,000, predominantly Chinese. Although it was the centre of an administrative district under the Chartered Company from the turn of the century, most of the modern town was built during the Japanese occupation in the Second World War. It is in the heart of Murut country, but do not expect to see longhouses and Murut in traditional costume. Many Murut have moved into individual houses except in the remoter parts of the interior, and their modernized bamboo houses are often well equipped.

The surrounding area is very fertile and the main crops here are soya beans, maize and a variety of vegetables. Cocoa is also widely grown. The cocoa trees are often obscured under shade trees called *pokok belindujan*, which have bright pink flowers. The durians from Tenom (and Beaufort) are reckoned to be the best in Sabah. *Tamu* (market) on Sunday.

Excursions

Murut villages There are many Murut villages surrounding Tenom all with their own churches. In some villages there is also an over-sized mosque or *surau*. The federal government has viewed the spread of Christianity in Sabah with some displeasure and there are financial incentives for anyone converting back to Islam. The best local longhouses are along the Padas River towards Sarawak at Kampung Marais and Kampung Kalibatang where blowpipes are still made. At Kemabong, about 25 km south of Tenom, the Murut community has a *lansaran* dancing trampoline. The wooden platform is sprung with bamboo and can support about 10 Murut doing a jig. There are irregular minibuses to the Murut villages.

Lagud Sebren Cocoa Research Station, 10 km northeast of Tenom, is in fact better known for its orchids, although it was originally a research centre for cocoa and rubber. Much of the work has been done by British botanist Tony Lamb who has turned the station into an important breeding centre for orchids. The flowering season is mainly between October and February. The centre also conducts research on tropical fruits and coffee. ■ *0800-1300, Mon-Fri. Rumah Rehat Lagud Sebren* (Orchid Research Station Resthouse, **E**) is 5 km from the centre and has air conditioning. Take a minibus from the main road and if driving, take the road over the railway tracks next to the station and head down the valley.

Batu Bunatikan Lumuyu (rock carvings) are at Kuala Tomani near Kampung Tomani, 40 km south of Tenom. A huge boulder, now protected from the elements by a corrugated tin roof, is carved with mysterious, distorted faces. Swirling lines, etched into the rock, depict various facial features as well as feet, a bird and a snake. The rock was discovered by villagers clearing land for agriculture around the river Lumuyu in April 1971. The Sabah State Museum in KK has no idea what the patterns represent or how old they are. The local explanation is an absurd story about seven brothers, one of whom is killed, the other six doodle on a rock in their bereaved depression as they head into the mountains to bury him. Disappointing. You need a four-wheel drive vehicle to get there: from Tenom, head south, crossing the Padas River at Tomani. After two km, turn right, follow this track for 20 km, through Kampung Kungkular to Kampung Ulu Tomani. Outside Kampung Ulu Tomani, turn right just before the river. Follow the track for 1½ km. At the point where a stream crosses the track, take the footpath to the rock carvings (20 minutes). An HEP station was built on the Tenom River about 15 years ago. The power it generates supplies Tenom and all the surrounding districts.

Sleeping

AL-B *Perkasa*, top of the hill above the town (RM3 taxi ride), PO Box 225, T735811, F736134. A/c, restaurant, the *Tenom Perkasa* (one of a chain of three – the others are at Keningau and Kundasang) is a large, modern hotel, 7 storeys high, commanding superb views over Tenom and surrounding countryside. Rooms are spacious, carpeted, attractively furnished, with a/c, en suite bathroom, TV. As guests are few and far between, the restaurant has a limited but well-priced selection of Chinese and Western dishes. Staff are friendly and helpful in organizing local sightseeing. Recommended. **C** *Orchid Hotel*, Block K, Jln Tun Mustapha, Tenom, T737600, F736600, excelng@tm.net.my. Small but friendly with clean, well maintained rooms. **D** *Hotel Sri Jaya*, PO Box 47, T736000. The cheapest option, with 12 a/c rooms, shared bathroom, basic but clean and recently tiled.

Orchid Hotel & Sri Jaya Hotel are both within walking distance of the bus stop

Sabah

Tenom

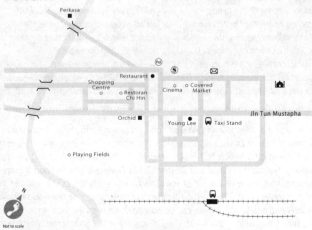

👉 ## The railway which ran out of steam

In the last years of the 19th century, William Cowie, the managing director of the North Borneo Chartered Company, had a vision. With Governor Beaufort, he outlined his ambitious plans for a Trans-Borneo Railway, cutting through 200 km of dense jungle, from Brunei Bay to Sandakan, straight through the interior of North Borneo. Work started at Weston on Brunei Bay in 1896 and two years later, the stretch of line linking the new township and Beaufort triumphantly opened.

But AJ West, the railway engineer who humbly named the new town after himself, somehow overlooked the fact that Weston was surrounded by an impenetrable mangrove swamp, not an ideal location for a railway terminus or port. Two alternative sites were toyed with before the stretch of narrow land opposite Pulau Gaya was finally selected as the site for the new terminus in 1899. It was thought to be a promising site for a town as it had a sheltered harbour. They called it Jesselton.

But Cowie's visionary railway project, and the innovative telegraph line that was to run alongside the track, was to be a costly undertaking. The administration, headed by Governor Beaufort, levied a new tax on rice to pay for it: a move which proved disastrously unpopular. Chinese retailers and tribal chiefs petitioned London to intervene, but to no avail. Historians believe the North Borneo Railway indirectly sparked the six-year Mat Salleh rebellion (see page 421).

The 92 km line between Jesselton and Beaufort started operating in 1905. The track was pushed into the interior at the same time, and on 5 April 1905 the first train steamed into Tenom. The line went on to the railhead at Melalap, 16 km further up the valley. But that was as far as the 186 km 'trans-Borneo railway' ever got – it seems that after struggling up the Padas Gorge from Beaufort, the prospect of building another 200 km of track was too much to bear. The idea was abandoned. The towns of Papar, Beaufort and Tenom however, became totally dependent on the railway. The Chartered Company administration refused to build roads in an effort to force people to use it.

Oscar Cook, a former District Officer in the North Borneo Civil Service, served in Tenom in 1912, and recorded his journey from Beaufort in his 1923 book, Borneo: the Stealer of Hearts. "Normally the journey of about 30 miles took three hours, but one always considered it lucky to reach one's destination only an hour late. The route twisted and turned to such an extent, as the line followed its precarious course along the river bank, that passengers in the front portion could almost put their hands out of the windows and shake those of passengers in the rear. On wet days up certain grades passengers have even been known to descend and help push the train over the most slippery and steepest gradients, while at one watering place chocks of wood were invariably put under the engine wheels to prevent the train from slowly slipping backwards!"

The train, now pulled by a diesel engine, still creeps along the 45 km narrow-gauge track, and the 2½ hour trip is well worth it.

Eating

Foodstalls are at Gerai Makanan, above the market

2 *Jolly*, near the station, serves Western food (including lamb chops) and karaoke. **2** *Restaurant Curry Emas*, which specializes in monitor lizard claypot curries, dog meat and wild cat. **2** *Sabah*, Jln Datuk Yaseen, Muslim Indian food, clean and friendly. **2** *Sapong*, Perkasa Hotel, local and Western. **2** *Y&L (Young & Lovely) Food & Entertainment*, Jln Sapong (2 km out of town), noisy but easily the best restaurant in Tenom. It serves mainly Chinese food: freshwater fish (steamed *sun hok* – also known as *ikan hantu*) and venison, these can be washed down with the local version of *air limau* (or *kitchai*) which comes with dried plums, there is a giant screen which is shipped in to allow Tenomese to enjoy the 1990 Football World Cup. Recommended. **1** *Yong Lee Restaurant*, coffee shop serving cheap Chinese fare in town centre. **1** *Restoran Chi Hin*, another Chinese coffee shop.

Train Leaves 4 times a day and takes about 3 hrs to Beaufort and another 2½ hrs to Tanjung Aru. **Minibus** Minibuses leave from centre of town by the market. Regular connections with Keningau and KK 4 hrs. Minibuses to Keningau leave from rail station after a train has arrived.

Transport
140 km to KK
45 km to Beaufort

Sipitang, located on the coast, is a sleepy town with little to offer the traveller apart from a supermarket and the *Shangsan Hotel*, T821800, **B-C**, which has fairly comfortable rooms with air conditioning and TV. Cheaper, but dirtier rooms are available in the *Hotel Lian Hin*, a few doors along. There is the ubiquitous coffee shop in the same street and a line of minibuses and taxis along the waterfront. The jetty for ferries to Labuan is a 10 minute walk from the centre.

Beaufort

This small sleepy, unexciting town is named after British Governor P Beaufort of the North Borneo Company, who was a lawyer and was appointed to the post despite having no experience of the East or of administration. He was savaged by Sabahan historian KG Tregonning as "the most impotent Governor North Borneo ever acquired and who, in the manner of nonentities, had a town named after him." Beaufort is a quaint town, with riverside houses built on stilts to escape the constant flooding of the Padas River. Tamu on Saturday.

Phone code: 087
Colour map 4, grid B3

C *Beaufort Hotel*, Lot 19-20 Lochung Park, T211911 F212590. Centre of town, a/c, 25 rooms. **D** *Mandarin*, Lot 38, Jln Beaufort Jaya, T212800. A/c. **D** *Padas*, riverfront by the bridge (opposite the fish market), T211441. A/c, restaurant, not as nice as the Beaufort.

2 *Jin Jin Restaurant*, behind *Beaufort Hotel*, Chinese, popular with locals. *Beaufort Bakery*, behind *Beaufort Hotel*, "freshness with every bite". **1** *Ching Chin Restaurant*, Chinese coffee shop in town centre.

Sleeping & eating
A poor selection of hotels, all roughly the same & slightly overpriced. Rooms are a/c & have bathrooms

Sabah

Train The KK-Tenom line passes through Beaufort: Tenom, 2½ hrs, KK, 3 hrs. **Minibus** Minibuses meet the train, otherwise leave from centre of town. Regular connections with KK, 2 hrs.

Transport
90 km to KK

Banks *Hongkong Bank & Standard Chartered* in centre of town. **Communications** Area code: 087. **General Post Office & Telekom:** next to Hongkong Bank.

Directory

Beaufort
To KK
To Sipitang
Sungai Padas
Covered Market
Cinema
Market
Ching Chin
Beaufort
Taxi Stand
Supermarket Block
Playing Field
N
Not to scale
Pol

To Sarawak Sipitang is south of Beaufort and the closest town in Sabah to the Sarawak border. It is possible to take minibuses from Beaufort to Sipitang. The road has reportedly been rebuilt, with a new stretch being added to Weston, take minibus or taxi with air conditioning if roadworks are still underway as it is too dusty to travel with windows open, and from there on to Merapok in Sarawak, one hour. There is an immigration checkpoint at Sipitang. From Sipitang there are also regular boats to Labuan, for reservations T087822350/422124.

Pulau Labuan

Population: 30,000
Phone code: 087
Colour map 4, grid B2

Labuan is one of the historically stranger pieces of the Malaysian jigsaw, and it remains such. Originally part of the Sultanate of Brunei, the island, 8 km off the coast of Sabah, was ceded to the British in 1846 - who were enticed to take it on because of the discovery of rich coal deposits. It joined the Malaysian Federation in 1963, along with Sabah and Sarawak. In 1984 it was declared a tax free haven - or an International Offshore Financial Centre - and hence this small tropical island with just 40,000-odd inhabitants has a plethora of name plate banks and investment companies. For the casual visitor - rather than someone wanting to salt away their million but in somewhere other than Switzerland - it offers some attractions, but not many. There are good hotels, lots of duty free shopping, a golf course, sport fishing and diving plus a handful of historic and cultural sights.

History

The Sultan of Brunei ceded this 92 km² island to the British crown in 1846. The island had a superb deep water harbour. Labuan promised an excellent location from which the British could engage the pirates which were terrorizing the Northwest Borneo coast. Labuan also had coal, which could be used to service steamships. Sarawak's Rajah James Brooke became the island's first governor in 1846. Two years later it was declared a free port. It also became a penal colony: long-sentence convicts from Hong Kong were put to work on the coal face and in the jungle, clearing roads. The island was little more than a malarial swamp and its inept colonial administration was perpetually plagued by fever and liver disorders. Its nine drunken civil servants provided a gold mine of eccentricity for the novelists Joseph Conrad and Somerset Maugham.

Bandar Labuan

■ Sleeping	3 Global	6 Oriental	9 Pulau Labuan Inn
1 Federal	4 Labuan	7 Pantai View	10 Sheraton
2 Federal Inn	5 Mariner	8 Pulau Labuan	11 Victoria

By the 1880s ships were already bypassing the island and the tiny colony began to disintegrate. In 1881 William Hood Treacher moved the capital of the new territory of British North Borneo from Labuan to Kudat. And eight years later, the Chartered Company was asked to take over the administration of the island. In 1907 it became part of the Straits Settlements, along with Singapore, Malacca (Melaka) and Penang.

In 1946 Labuan became a part of British North Borneo and was later incorporated into Sabah as part of the Federation of Malaysia in 1963. Datuk Harris is thought to own half the island (including the *Hotel Labuan*). As Chief Minister, he offered the island as a gift to the federal government in 1984 in exchange for a government undertaking to bail out his industrial projects and build up the island's flagging economy. The election of a Christian government in Sabah in 1986 proved an embarrassment to Malaysian Prime Minister Dr Mahathir Mohamad: making it Malaysia's only non-Muslim-ruled state. As a result, Labuan has assumed strategic importance as a Federal Territory, wedged between Sabah and Sarawak. It is used as a staging post for large garrisons of the Malaysian army, navy and air force.

Modern Labuan

In declaring Labuan a tax haven – or, more properly, an International Off-shore Financial Centre – the Malaysian government set out its vision of Labuan becoming the Bermuda of the Asia-Pacific for the 21st century. More than 250 off-shore banks, insurance firms and trust companies had set up operations on the island by mid-1994. The island has attracted loans and deposits of more than US\$1.6bn. Critics and sceptics have long pointed to the fact that the standard trimmings of a tax haven are still hundreds of millions of dollars away, but a new financial park complex with four 16-floor office towers has recently been completed. This, together with new hotels including the *Sheraton* and the *Waterfront* which overlooks a brand new marina, springing up too, makes it seem that Labuan's days of being a sleepy rural backwater are over.

Sabah

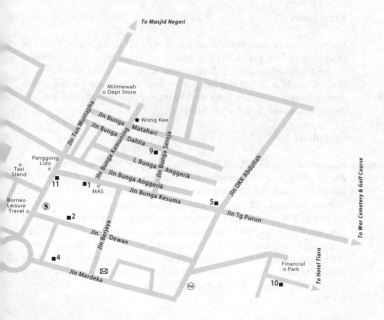

In addition to the island's population of about 30,000 are 10,000 Filipino refugees, with about 21 different ethnic groups. The island is the centre of a booming 'barter' trade with the South Philippines; the island is home to a clutch of so-called string vest millionaires, who have grown rich on the trade. In Labuan, 'barter' is the name given to smuggling. The Filipino traders leaving the Philippines simply over-declare their exports (usually copra, hardwood, rotan and San Miguel beer) and under-declare the imports (Shogun jeeps, Japanese hi-fi and motorbikes), all ordered through duty-free Labuan. With such valuable cargoes, the traders are at the mercy of pirates in the South China Sea. To get round this, they arm themselves with M-16s, bazookas and shoulder-launched missiles. This ammunition is confiscated on their arrival in Labuan, stored in a marine police warehouse, and given back to them for the return trip.

Sights

Away from the bustling barter jetty, Labuan Town, a name largely superseded by its name of Port Victoria, is a dozy, unremarkable Chinese-Malaysian mix of shophouses, coffee shops and karaoke bars. There is a new US$11m mosque, and a manicured golf course. Illegal cockfights are staged every Sunday afternoon. There is an old brick coal chimney at Tanjung Kubong, or coal point, with a good view of the east coast. It was built in 1847 by the British who needed fuel for their steamships on the Far Eastern trade route. On the west coast there are pleasant beaches, mostly lined with kampungs. There is a large Japanese war memorial on the east coast and a vast, and well tended, Allied war cemetery between the town and the airport with over 3,000 graves, most of which are unknown soldiers. In 1995 a commemoration service was held at the cemetery to mark the 50th anniversary of Allied Forces landing in Labuan. It was attended by veterans from the US, Australia and Britain.

Excursions

Boat trips can be made to the small islands around Labuan, although only by chartering a fishing vessel. The main islands are Pulau Papan (a boring island between Labuan and the mainland), Pulau Kuraman, Pulau Rusukan Kecil (known locally as '*the floating lady*' for obvious reasons) and Pulau Rusukan Besar ('*floating man*'). The latter three have good beaches and coral reefs (see *Diving*, below) but none has any facilities.

Essentials

Sleeping
■ *on map, page 428*
Price codes:
see inside front cover

AL *Sheraton Labuan*, Lot TL 462, Jln Merdeka, T422000, F422222, www.sheraton.com. Another new block, cream with green roofs, built opposite the Financial Park complex, this deluxe city hotel has 183 rooms all with spacious bathrooms, a/c, TV, in-house films channel, mini-bar, tea and coffee-making facilities, iron and ironing board. Other facilities include pool with whirlpool and swim-up bar, business centre (in-room personal computer and faxes also available). Décor has all the opulence of a Sheraton with a vast lobby, clad in marble and dripping with chandeliers, which resounds to live pianoforte in the afternoons, and classy food outlets including Victoria's Brasserie for European fare and The Emperor Chinese Restaurant which specializes in Cantonese food. Staff are professional and offer top service with a smile. Recommended.

A *Labuan*, Jln Merdeka, T412502, F415355. A/c, restaurant, large concrete block on edge of town, grand lobby with an arcade of shops, rooms have seen better days but have a/c, in-house video and attached bathroom, Chinese and Japanese restaurants, coffee house and the Rock Café Fun Pub, pool. **A** *Manikar Beach Resort*, Jln Batu Manikar, T418700, F418732. On the northwest tip of Labuan, 20 mins from town centre (complimentary shuttle), although local ex-pats like to comment that things have slipped since it was taken over by the *Sheraton*, it is a stylish resort built with polished wood (the owner is a timber tycoon), set in 15 hectares of gardens, dotted with tall palms which reach down to the beach. The 235 rooms, all sea-facing with generous balconies, are very spacious, paved with stone, tastefully furnished, complete with a/c, mini-bar, TV, in-house video, tea and coffee-making facilities. Large pool set at sea level with swim-up bar, separate children's pool, fitness centre, tennis, play-room, business centre, duty-free shop. The beach is regularly cleaned and sprayed so sandflies are not a problem, but the sea is not recommended for swimming due to jellyfish. Restaurant with indoor and outdoor dining areas, excellent quality food, good value theme buffet nights. Enquire about discounts offered on room rates – 50% discount for bookings and payment 14 days in advance. **A** *Tiara Labuan*, Jln Tanjung Batu, PO Box 80537, T414300, F410195. On the west coast next to the golf course, 5-min taxi ride from town centre, beautiful hotel and serviced apartments surrounding a large lotus pond and deep blue pool complete with jacuzzi. Built onto Adnan Kashoggi's old mansion, the property has an Italian feel with terracotta tiles, putty pink stone, a glorious gilt fountain, and long shady arcades. The original mansion now holds the reception, restaurant (food mediocre), and acres of opulent lounge including an Arab lounge which has low sofas, hubbly-bubbly pipes and a marble fountain. All 25 rooms, and also the 48 serviced apartments (1 or 2 bedroom) are complete with a/c, TV, mini-bar, ring electric hob, cooker hood and sink, and a living room. The Tanjung Batu beach, just across the road, is rather muddy, but good for walks when the tide is out. The *Labuan Beach Restaurant* is here too. On the whole, holiday-makers opt for the larger hotels, especially families, as the *Tiara* has no organized activities nor kiddy pool, but this is partly what makes it a haven of tranquillity. Recommended. **A** *Waterfront Labuan Financial Hotel*, 1 Jln Wawasan, T418111, F413468. This property, overlooking the new yacht marina (and also an industrial seascape) has cultivated a marina-look combined with the atmosphere of being on a luxury cruise. It has over 200 rooms, all with a/c, mini-bar, TV, tea and coffee-making facilities and opulent fittings. The main restaurant, in seafaring spirit, called the Clipper, serves Western and local food, there is also a bar, the Anchorage, which has live entertainment every evening except Mon. Other facilities include pool, tennis and health centre. The hotel also manages the marina with its total of 50 berthing spaces each of which has internationally rated facilities. The Harbour Master not only oversees the running of the Marina but also organizes yacht charters and luxury cruises. Recommended.

B *Mariner*, Jln Tg Purun (on crossroads opposite police HQ), T418822, F418811. A/c, restaurant, rooms well-equipped (including mini fridge, a/c, TV, in-house video and attached bathroom), good coffee house. Generous discounts available on request. **B** *Federal Inn*, Jln Dewan, T417811, F417996. Smart hotel, clean and reasonable, 39 rooms with a/c, attached bathroom, TV, in-house video and mini-bar. **B** *Oriental*, U0123-4, Lot 33 and 34, Jln Bunga Mawar, T419019, F419408. Reception on first floor, clean, tiled rooms with a/c, TV, private bathroom. **B** *Pulau Labuan*, 27-28 Jln Muhibbah, T416288, F416255. A/c, restaurant (*Golden Palace Restaurant* downstairs). **B** *Global*, U0017, Jln OKK Awang Besar (near market), T425201, F425180. Best value for money in town, a/c, mini-bar, tea and coffee, TV, in-house video, complimentary shuttle to ferry and airport. Recommended.

C *Federal Hotel*, Jln Bunga Kesuma, T411711, F411337. A/c, restaurant, all rooms have a/c, TV, in-house video, mini-bar fridge, complimentary tea and coffee maker, pink and pastels colour scheme, Chinese-run catering mainly for business people, clean, good value, run by same management as *Federal Inn*. **B-C** *Pantai View*, Lot 119 and 120, Jln OKK Awang Besar, T411339, F419408. A/c, basic, not very clean and not much of a view of the *pantai*. **B-C** *Pulau Labuan Inn*, Lot 8, Jln Bunga Dahlia, T416833, F441750. The downmarket sister of the *Pulau Labuan*, spotlessly clean but small a/c rooms.

C *Kelab Golf*, Jln Tanjung Batu, a/c, restaurant, 6 simple but pleasant rooms in the club-house, 3 have a view down the manicured fairways. C *Pertama*, Hujong Pasir, Jln OKK Awang Besar (next to fish market), T413311. A/c. C *Victoria Hotel*, Jln Tun Mustapha, T218511, F218077. 17 Jln Sentosa one of the oldest hotels in Labuan, pale pink exterior with white stucco decorated lobby, 46 rooms, a/c, private bath. Recommended.

Eating
Price codes:
see inside front cover

Malay 2 *Restoran Zainab*, Jln Merdeka (opposite duty-free shop), Indian/Muslim. *Seri Malindo*, next to *Federal Inn*, mixture of Malay and Western food.

Chinese 4 *The Emperor Chinese Restaurant*, Sheraton Labuan, top-class Chinese cuisine, Cantonese specialities, fresh seafood, special *dim sum* on Sun and public holidays. Recommended. 3 *Golden Palace*, 27 Jln Muhibbah. 3 *Wong Kee*, Lot 5 and 6, Jln Kemuning, large, brightly lit restaurant with a/c, good steamboat. Recommended. 1 *Café Imperial*, Chinese coffee shop behind *Federal Hotel*, better than average coffee shop fare.

International 3 *Country Deli Restaurant and Wine Bar*, Lot 25, Block D, Jati Commercial Centre, T410410. Malaysian pizza, take-aways possible. 3 *Labuan Beach*, Jln Tanjung Batu, T415611. International and local cuisine, breezy location on sea shore, food not special but ambience makes up for it, as does very well chilled draft Carlesberg. Recommended. *Victoria's Brasserie*, *Sheraton Labuan*, European brasserie-style, good theme buffets as well as á la carte, prides itself on its 'show kitchen concept'. Recommended. *The Clipper*, *Waterfront Labuan Financial Hotel*, 24-hour up-market coffee shop with local and Western cuisine. Recommended.

Seafood 3 *Restaurant Pulau Labuan*, Lot 27-28, Jln Muhibbah, smart interior complete with chandeliers, a/c, fresh fish sold by weight – good tiger prawns). Recommended. 3 *Sung Hwa Restaurant*, 2nd Flr, Ujong Pasir, Jln OKK Awang Besar (across from fish market and above Kedai Kopi South Sea. Recommended. 2 *New Sung Hwa Seafood*, Jln Ujong Pasir, PCK Building, amongst best value seafood restaurants in Malaysia, chilli prawns, grilled stingray steak recommended, no menu. Recommended.

Foodstalls Above wet market and at the other end of town, along the beach next to the *Island Club*. There is an area of stalls on Jln Muhibbah opposite the end of Jln Bahasa, next to the cinema and there are a few hawker stalls behind *Hotel Labuan*.

Shopping

Labuan Duty-free, Bangunan Terminal, Jln Merdeka, T411573. This opened in Oct 1990, 142 years after Rajah James Brooke first declared Labuan a free port. The island's original duty-free concession did not include alcohol or cigarettes, but the new shop was given special dispensation to sell them. Two months later the government extended the privilege to all shops on the island, which explains the absurd existence of a duty-free shop on a duty-free island. The shop claims to be the cheapest duty-free in the world, however, you will find competitively priced shops in town too, including Monegain. It can undercut most other outlets on the island due to the volume of merchandise it turns over: more than RM1m a month. The shop owes its success to Filipino 'barter traders' who place bulk purchase orders for VCRs or hundreds of thousands of dollars' worth of Champion cigarettes. These are smuggled back to Zamboanga and Jolo and find their way onto Manila's streets within a week. Brunei's alcohol-free citizens also keep the shop in business – they brought nearly RM2m worth of liquor from Labuan into Brunei within the first 3 months of the shop opening. **NB** If you plan to take duty-free goods into Sabah or Sarawak, you have to stay on Labuan for a minimum of 72 hrs. Behind Jln Merdeka and before the fish market, there is a congregation of corrugated tin-roofed shacks which houses a small *Filipino textile and handicraft market* and an interesting *Wet market*.

Supermarkets *Milimewah*, Lot 22-27 Lazenda Commercial Centre, Phase II, Jln Tun Mustapha, department store with supermarket on ground floor. *Financial Park*, Jln Merdeka, shopping complex with Milimewah supermarket. *Thye Ann Supermarket*, central position below *Federal Inn*. *Labuan Supermarket*, Jln Bunga Kenanga, centre of town.

Diving *Borneo Divers*, Lot 28, Lazenda Commercial Centre, Phase II (next to water- **Sports** front), T415867, F413454. Specializes in 2 day packages diving on shipwrecks off Labuan for certified scuba divers, there are four wrecks in total, each wreck costs about RM100, 2 day packages with accommodation at the Manikar are possible. *Ocean Sports*, 134 Jln OKK Awang Besar, T415389, F411911/415844. Offers 5-days full-time scuba courses for RM700 and reef dives on the nearby islands of Pulau Kuraman, Pulau Rusukan Kecil and Pulau Rusukan Besar. These islands have good beaches but no facilities. Diving around Pulau Papan is not very exciting and the water is often cloudy because of river silt. The reefs around Labuan suffer from the after-effects of the Allied bombing during the Second World War and from Filipino dynamite fishermen. *Ocean Sports*, in association with Coral Island Cruises in KK takes groups of divers 18 hrs into the South China Sea to Terumba Layang Layang, an atoll on the edge of the disputed Spratly group, reputed to be "even better than Sipadan" (see also page 415). **Golf** *Kelab Golf*, Jln Tanjung Batu. Magnificent 9-hole golf course. Visitors may be asked to see proof of handicap or a membership card from your own club. Non-members pay RM30 a round on weekdays, RM50 on weekends. There are also tennis courts at the golf club and a swimming pool which can be used by visitors for a modest fee.

Local Bus: local buses around the island leave from Jln Bunga Raya. **Taxi**: old Singa- **Transport** pore NTUC cabs are not in abundant supply, but easy enough to get at the airport and *70 km to mainland* from outside *Hotel Labuan*. It is impossible to get a taxi after 1900. **Car hire**: *Adaras Rent-a-Car*, T422630. *Travel Rent-a-Car*, T423600.

Long distance Air: airport 5 km from town. Regular connections with KK, Miri. The MAS office is in the *Federal Hotel* block, T412263.

Boat: from the Bangunan Terminal Feri Penumpang (T411573) next to the duty-free shop on Jln Merdeka. Regular connections with Memumbuk every 45 mins. Speedboats leave every few minutes. There are 2 speedboats every day to Limbang (Sarawak), enquiries T22908. Three boats a day to Kota Kinabalu, 2½ hrs. One express boat daily to Sipitang (Sabah mainland, see page 427).

To Brunei: on weekends and public holidays in Brunei the ferries are packed out and it is a scramble to get a ticket. It is possible to reserve tickets to Brunei at the following agents: *Victoria Agency House* (T412332) (next to the *Federal Hotel* in Wisma Kee Chia), *Borneo Leisure Travel*, T410251, F419989 (opposite Standard Chartered) and the booking office at the back of the Sports Toto on Jln Merdeka all deal with advanced bookings to Brunei. *Broadwin Agency*, also on Jln Merdeka, takes bookings for ferries to Malaysian destinations. Five express boats leave Labuan for Brunei (Bandar Seri Begawan). They depart at 0800, 1300, 1400, 1500 Mon-Sat, 0800, 1000 and 1200, Sun, 1½ hrs.

Sabah

Directory **Airline offices** *MAS*, Wisma Kee Chia, Jln Kesuma, T412263. **Banks** *Hongkong*, Jln Merdeka. *Standard Chartered*, Jln Tanjung Kubang (next to *Victoria Hotel*). *Syarikat K Abdul Kader*, money changer. **Communications** Area code: 087. **General Post Office:** Jln Merdeka. **Tourist offices** Tourist Information, Lot 4260 Jln Dewan/Jln Berjaya T423455 mtpblbu@tourism.gov.my. **Useful information** A useful background website is http://tourism.gov.my. A search of Labuan sites reveals a whole host relating to its tax-free status.

Papar

Colour map 4, grid B3 Formerly a sleepy Kadazan village, about 40 km south of KK, Papar is developing fast. In *bandar lama* (the old town) there are several rows of quaint wooden shophouses, painted blue and laid out along spacious boulevards lined with travellers' palms. There is a large market in the centre of town, Tamu on Sundays. The Papar area is famous for its fruit and there is a good *tamu* every Sunday.

There is a scenic drive between Papar and KK, with paddy fields and jungle lining the roadside. The nearby beach at Pantai Manis is good for swimming and can be reached easily from Papar. It is also possible to make boat trips up the Papar River, which offers gentle rapids for less-energetic white-water-rafters. Whitewater rafting trips can be organized through tour agents in KK (see page 407).

Excursions **Pulau Tiga National Park** is 48 km south of KK. Declared a forest reserve in 1933, the 15,864 hectare park is made up of three islands: Pulau Tiga, Kalampunian Damit and Kalampunian Besar. Pulau Tiga's three low hills were all formed by mud volcanoes. The last big eruption was in 1941, which was heard 160 km away and covered the island in a layer of boiling mud. The dipterocarp forest on the islands is virtually untouched and they contain species not found on other west coast islands, such as a poisonous amphibious sea snake (*Laticauda colubrina*), which comes ashore on Pulau Kalampunian Damit to lay its eggs. Rare birds such as the pied hornbill (*Anthracoceros convexus*) and the megapode (*Megapodus freycinet*) are found here, as well as flying foxes, monitor lizards, wild fruit trees and mangrove forest. A network of trails, marked at 50m intervals leads to various points of interest. The best time to visit is between February and April, when it is slightly drier and the seas are calmer.

The park headquarters, on the south side of Pulau Tiga, is mainly used as a botanical and marine research centre and tourism is not vigorously promoted, as a result there are no special facilities for tourists. Boats run from Kuala Penyu fishing village at the tip of the Klias Peninsula, 45 minutes.

Sleeping Two cabins (2 people per cabin) at RM60 per cabin. There is also a hostel that can accommodate 32 people. Accommodation must be booked in advance through the Sabah Parks Office in KK; no food is provided. It is possible to camp.

Pantai Manis, just outside Papar, is a 3 km long stretch of golden sand, with a deep lagoon.

Sleeping **B** *Beringgis Beach Resort*, Km 26, Jln Papar, Kampung Beringgis, Kinarut, T752333, F752999. A/c, hot baths, car rental, conference halls, private beach, pool, watersports, tours and sports facilities. **A** *KRK 'Mai Amam Country Rest House*, KM 35, off Old Papar Rd, Kg. Gana. T088-912580, F256717, verus@pc.jaring.my. Six room country resthouse and 12 room bush hostel. Luxurious place, with fishing on site in spacious grounds that house an orchard. **B-E** *Sea Side Travellers Inn*, Km 20 Papar Highway, Kinarut, T088-750555, F088-750479. Located about 10 km from Papar. A/c (**B**) or fan

(**D**), restaurant, range of accommodation from dorm (**E**) to detached bungalows, breakfasts included, pleasant location off the beach. Tennis court, pool. Horse-riding and tours can be organized.

There are several run-of-the-mill coffee shops and restaurants in the old town. **1** *Seri Takis*, Papar New Town (below the lodging house), Padang food; *Sugar Buns Bakery*, old town.

Eating

Minibus: leave from Bandar Lama area. Regular connections with KK, 1 hr and Beaufort, 1 hr.

Transport
40 km S of KK

North of Kota Kinabalu

From KK, the route heads north to the sleepy Bajau town of Kota Belud which wakes up on Sunday for its colourful tamu *market. Near the northernmost tip of the state is Kudat, the former state capital. The region north of KK is a more interesting area with Gunung Kinabalu always in sight. From Kota Belud, the mountain looks completely different. It is possible to see its tail, sweeping away to the east and its western flanks, which rise out of the rolling coastal lowlands.*

Sabah

Kota Belud

This town is in a beautiful location, nestling in the foothills of Mount Kinabalu *Colour map 4, grid A3* on the banks of the Tempasuk River. It is the heart of Bajau country – the so-called 'cowboys of the East'. It is a busy little town, but of little obvious interest to most tourists.

The first Bajau to migrate to Sabah were pushed into the interior, around Kota Belud. They were originally a seafaring people but then settled as farmers in this area. The famed Bajau horsemen wear jewelled costumes, carry spears and ride bareback on ceremonial occasions. The ceremonial headdresses worn by the horsemen, called *dastars*, are woven on backstrap looms by the womenfolk of Kota Belud. Each piece takes four to six weeks to complete. Traditionally, the points of the headdress were stiffened using wax; these days, strips of cardboard are inserted into the points.

The largest *tamu*, or traditional open air market, in Sabah is held every Sunday in Kota Belud behind the mosque, starting at 0600. Visitors are strongly recommended to get there early. A mix of races, Bajau, Kadazan/Dusun, Rungus, Chinese, Indian and Malay, come to sell their goods and it is a social occasion as much as it is a market. Aside from the wide variety of food and fresh produce on sale, there is a weekly water buffalo auction at the entrance to the *tamu*.

This is the account of a civil servant, posted to the KB district office in 1915: "The tamu itself is a babel and buzz of excitement; in little groups the natives sit and spread their wares out on the ground before them; bananas, langsats, pines and bread-fruit; and, in season, that much beloved but foul-smelling fruit the Durian. Mats and straw-hats and ropes; fowls, ducks, goats and

Tamus in Kota Belud District

Tuesday: Pandasan (along the Kota Belud to Kudat road).
Wednesday: Keelawat (along the Kota Belud to KK road).
Thursday: Pekan Nabalu (along the Kota Belud to Ranau road).

Friday: Taginambur (along the Kota Belud to Ranau road, 16 km from Kota Belud).
Monday and Saturday: Kota Belud.
Market time: 0600-1200. All tamus provide many places to eat.

buffaloes; pepper, *gambia sirih* and vegetables; rice (padi), sweet potatoes, *ubi kayu* and indian-corn; dastars and handkerchiefs, silver and brassware. In little booths, made of wood, with open sides and floors of split bamboos and roofs of atap (sago palm-leaf) squat the Chinese traders along one side of the Tamu. For cash or barter they will sell; and many a wrangle, haggle and bargain is driven and fought ere the goods change hands, or money parted with."

Excursions **Tempasuk** has a wide variety of migrating birds and is a proposed conservation area. More than 127 species of birds have been recorded along this area of the coastal plain and over half a million birds flock to the area every year, many migrating from north latitudes in winter. These include 300,000 swallows, 50,000 yellow longtails and 5,000 water birds. The best period for birdwatching is from October to March.

Between Kota Belud and the sea, there are mangrove swamps with colonies of proboscis monkeys. It is possible to hire small fishing boats in the town to go down the Tempasuk River (RM10 per hour).

Sleeping **C** *Kota Belud*, 21 Lebuh Francis (just off the central square), T976576. A/c, noisy. **C** *Tai Seng*, also on Central Square, some a/c, minimalist but adequate. **D** *Impian Siu Motel*, Kg Sempirai, Jln Kuala Abai, T976617. Just 5 rooms in this reasonable place. You get what you pay for. **E** *Government Resthouse*, Jln Ranau (on hill north of town, signed from the main road), T967532. Some a/c, often full of officials.

Homestay programme in Kota Belud village: there is no limit to your length of stay. Live with and be treated as part of the family, getting invited to celebrations such as weddings etc. Activities include buffalo riding, jungle trekking, river swimming, cultural dancing, visits to local *tamus*, padi planting. The basic price is RM10 per week. Arrange through *Borneo Expedition and Exotic Borneo*, for more information contact Terisah Yapin, PO Box 13337, T242433, F223443. Very affordable for young travellers and an excellent way to learn the language and gain an in-depth knowledge of the culture.

Eating There are several Indian coffee shops around the main square. **2** *Bismillah Restoran*, 35 Jln Keruak (main square), excellent *roti telur*. *Indonesia Restoran*, next to the car park behind the *Kota Belud Hotel*.

Entertainment The annual *Tamu Besar* includes a parade and equestrian games by the Bajau Horsemen, a very colourful event.

Shopping Market in main square every day, fish market to the south of the main market. Large *tamu* every Sun and an annual Tamu Besar, with a wide variety of local handicrafts on offer. **Handicraft Centre** Just outside town.

Transport 77 km to KK. **Minibus** Leave from main square. Regular connections with KK, Kudat and Ranau.

Directory

Banks *Public Bank Berhad*, Jln Kota Kinabalu. *Sabah Finance*, Jln Ranau. *Bank Pertanian*, Jln Kudat. **Places of worship** There are no English churches but people are happy to interpret. *Catholic Church*, Jln Ranau, *Basel Christian Church of Malaysia*, off Jln Kota Kinabalu, *SIB* (Evangelical Church of Borneo), off Jln Ranau, SIB Taginambur, Jln Ranau (20 mins' drive from Kota Belud and the centre of a religious revival).

Kudat

Kudat town, surrounded by coconut groves, is right on the northern tip of Sabah, 160 km from KK. The local people here are the Rungus, members of the Kadazan tribe. The gentle, warm and friendly Rungus have clung to their traditions more than other Sabahan tribes and some still live in longhouses, although many are now building their own houses. Rungus longhouses are built in a distinctive style with outward-leaning walls; the Sabah State Museum incorporates many of the design features of a Rungus longhouse. The Rungus used to wear coils of copper and brass round their arms and legs and today the older generation still dress in black. They are renowned for their fine beadwork and weaving. A handful of Rungus longhouses are dotted around the peninsula, away from Kudat town.

Colour map 4, grid A4

The East India Company first realized the potential of the Kudat Peninsula and set up a trading station on Balambanganan Island, to the north of Kudat. The settlement was finally abandoned after countless pirate raids. Kudat became the first administrative capital of Sabah in 1881, when it was founded by a Briton, AH Everett. William Hood Fletcher, the protectorate's first governor, first tried to administer the territory from Labuan, which proved impossible, so he moved to the newly founded town of Kudat which was nothing more than a handful of atap houses built out into the sea on stilts. It was a promising location, however, situated on an inlet of Marudu Bay, and it had a good harbour. Kudat's glory years were shortlived: it was displaced as the capital of North Borneo by Sandakan in 1883.

Today it is a busy town dominated by Chinese and Filipino traders (legal and illegal) on the coast, and prostitutes trading downtown. Kudat was one of the main centres of Chinese and European migration at the end of the 19th century. Most of the Chinese who came to Kudat were Christian Hakka vegetable farmers: 96 of them arrived in April 1883, and they were followed by others, given free passages by the Chartered Company. More Europeans, especially the British, began to arrive on Kudat's shores with the discovery of oil in 1880. Frequent pirate attacks and an inadequate supply of drinking water forced the British to move their main administrative offices to Sandakan in 1883.

Kudat is dotted with numerous family farms cultivating coconut trees, maize, ground nuts and keeping bees. Being surrounded by the sea, seafood is also an important element in the diet and fisheries an important industry. Kudat is inhabited by many other ethnic groups: Bonggi, Bajau, Bugis, Kadazandusun, Obian, Orang Sungei and Suluk. *Tamu* is on Mondays.

Sabah

Beaches There are some beautiful and extensive unspoilt white sand beaches north of town, the best known is **Bak-Bak**, 11 km from Kudat. This beach, however, can get crowded at weekends and there are plans to transform it into a resort. It is signposted off the Kota Belud-Kudat road. You can get there by minibus.

Excursions

Sikuati is 23 km west of Kudat, with a good beach. Every Sunday (0800) the Rungus come to the *tamu* in this village, on the northwest side of the Kudat peninsula. Local handicrafts are sold. You can get there by minibus.

🖙 The Rungus of Kudat

Arts and crafts The Rungus are renowned in Sabah as highly skilled artisans who traditionally make colourful beaded necklaces from local plant seeds and clay. The most notable Rungus beadworks are the pinakol or shoulder bands which are long and broad with multi-strands and worn diagonally across the chest. The beadwork motifs are drawn from traditional designs and usually tell legends from Rungus folklore. Rungus women are also highly skilled in the arts of weaving and basketry. Their traditional attire is made from home-grown, hand spun cotton which is woven on a back strap loom. Their black cotton sarongs are decorated with an intricate and colourful border, created using a type of needle weaving. Again, traditional motifs and designs are employed. All this requires painstaking hours of time and attention.

Rungus men can be easily distinguished by their richly embroidered traditional headgear or sigal tinohian, traditionally worn as part of their daily attire. The sigal plays an important part in social life, distinguishing between ranks at festivals and other celebrations. The traditional colour of the Rungus is black. Aside from the different patterns and designs of their beadwork and headgear, Rungus women also used to adorn their necks, arms and legs with heavy brass coils. This tradition is likely soon to disappear as many young girls today opt not to wear these coils and the skills needed to make them are dying out.

Beliefs, rites and rituals Despite conversion to Islam and Christianity, the Rungus have maintained their cultural and traditional beliefs through the practice of traditional Rungus rites and rituals, mainly performed through ritual specialists known as Bobolizan. For example, when selecting a site for a longhouse, the Rungus will invite a male Bobolizan to initiate a ritual known as the mamabat. Prayers (moguhok) are chanted and a four-string puzzle known as a mongumbang is used to protect the longhouse residents from evil spirits. Other rituals involve the use of paddy grains, clam shells and prayers recited in ancient Rungus. To contact spiritual beings, the kamagi, a special beaded necklace, is worn and the Bobolizan shakes a rattle or gonding at the start of the ritual to summon the 'good' spirits. These rituals may last anything from a day to a week.

Part of the female Bobolizan's task is healing the sick by fighting off 'angry' spirits. The ritual specialists also take the role of the local 'doctor' and have an intimate knowledge of medicinal herbs and other forest remedies. Certain ceremonies also include traditional ritualistic dances, which are sometimes also performed at special festivities.

The longhouse The Rungus align their longhouses west-east, facing Mount Kinabalu, in the belief that a cool, airy atmosphere is attained for ideal living and good health. Rungus builders choose only trees that bring good luck; brittle plants and those with red sap (which signifies blood) are considered to bring bad luck and are avoided.

Between Kota Belud and Kudat there is a marsh and coastal area with an abundance of birds. Costumed Bajau horsemen can sometimes be seen here.

Look at Longhouse rules for advice on visiting longhouses (see page 339)

The **'Longhouse Experience'** is possibly the most memorable thing to do in Kudat. A stay at a longhouse enables visitors to observe, enjoy and take part in the Rungus' unique lifestyle. There are two Baranggaxo longhouses with 10 units. Nearby there are the village's only modern amenities, toilets and showers. During the day, the longhouse corridor is busy with Rungus womenfolk at work stringing elaborate beadworks, weaving baskets and their traditional cloth. Visitors can experience and participate in these activities. Longhouse meals are homegrown, fish and seafood come from nearby fishing villages, drinks consist of young coconuts and local rice wine. Evening festivities consist of the playing of gongs with dancers dressed in traditional Rungus costume. Tour companies organize trips.

For those wanting a less touristy visit to a longhouse, **Matunggong** is an area found on the road south of Kudat best known for its longhouses.

At **Kampung Gombizau**, visitors get to see bee-keeping and the process of harvesting beeswax, honey and royal jelly; while **Kampung Sumangkap**, an enterprising little village, offers visitors traditional gong-making and handi-craft-making by the villagers.

C *Greenland*, Lot 9/10, Block E, Sedco Shophouse (new town), T613211, F611854. A/c, standard rooms, shared bath. **C** *Kinabalu*, Kudat Old Town, T613888. A/c, clean enough, average value. **C** *Sunrise*, 21 Jln Lo Thien Hock, T611517. A/c, restaurant (*Silver Inn*). **D** *Southern Hotel*, Kudat Old Town, T613133. Only 10 rooms, but quite cheap and represents reasonable value in comparison to its competitors. **E** *Government Resthouse*, T61304. *Oriental*, Jln Lo Thien Chock, T61677/61045. A/c, big, clean rooms, some shared bathrooms.

    Malay 1 *Restoran Rakyat*, Jln Lo Thien Hock. *Cahaya Timur*, Jln Lo Thien Hock (next to *Kudat Hotel*). **Chinese 2** *Silver Inn*, Jln Lo Thien Hock (below *Sunrise*).

Sleeping & eating
The Sunrise & Oriental hotels are within walking distance of the bus stop

Air Connections with KK, Sandakan. **Minibus** Minibuses leave from Jln Lo Thien Hock. Regular connections with KK, 4 hrs.

Transport
122 km N of KK

Banks *Standard Chartered*, Jln Lo Thien Hock.

Directory

Gunung Kinabalu Park

Gunung Kinabalu is the pride of Sabah, the focal point of the national park and probably the most magnificent sight in Borneo. Although Mount Kinabalu has foothills, its dramatic rockfaces, with cloud swirling around them, loom starkly out of the jungle. The view from the top is unsurpassed and on a clear day you can see the shadow of the mountain in the South China Sea, over 50 km away.

Colour map 4, grid A3

In the first written mention of the mountain, in 1769, Captain Alexander Dalrymple of the East India Company, observing the mountain from his ship in the South China Sea, wrote: "Though perhaps not the highest mountain in the world, it is of *immense* height." During the Second World War Kinabalu was used as a navigational aid by Allied bombers – one of whom was quoted as saying "That thing must be near as high as Mount Everest". It's not, but at 4,101m, Gunung Kinabalu is the highest peak between the Himalayas and New Guinea. It is not, though, the highest mountain in Southeast Asia: peaks in Northern Burma and the Indonesian province of Irian Jaya are higher.

    There are a number of theories about the derivation of its name. The most convincing is the corruption of the Kadazan *Aki Nabulu* – 'the revered place of the spirits'. For the Kadazan, the mountain is sacred as they consider it to be the last resting place of the dead, and the summit was believed to be inhabited by their ghosts. In the past the Kadazan are said to have carried out human sacrifices on Mount Kinabalu, carrying their captives to the summit in bamboo cages, where they would be speared to death. The Kadazan guides still perform an annual sacrifice to appease the spirits. Today they make do with chickens, eggs, cigars, betel nuts and rice, on the rock plateau below the Panar Laban Rockface.

Sabah

The Chinese also lay claim to a theory. According to this legend, a Chinese prince arrived on the shores of Northern Borneo and went in search of a huge pearl on the top of the mountain, which was guarded by a dragon. He duly slew the dragon, grabbed the pearl and married a beautiful Kadazan girl. After a while he grew homesick, and took the boat back to China, promising his wife that he would return. She climbed the mountain every day for years on end to watch for her husband's boat. He never came in and in desperation and depression, she lay down and died and was turned to stone. The mountain was then christened *China Balu* – or Chinaman's widow.

In 1851, Sir Hugh Low, the British colonial secretary in Labuan made the first unsuccessful attempt at the summit. Seven years later he returned with Spencer St John, the British Consul in Brunei. Low's feet were in bad shape after the long walk to the base of the mountain, so St John went on without him, with a handful of reluctant Kadazan porters. He made it to the top of the conical southern peak, but was "mortified to find that the most westerly [peak] and another to the east appeared higher than where I sat." He retreated, and returned three months later with Low, but again failed to reach the summit, now called Low's Peak. It remained unconquered for another 30 years. The first to reach the summit was John Whitehead, a zoologist, in 1888. Whitehead spent several months on the mountain collecting birds and mammals and many of the more spectacular species bear either Low's or Whitehead's name. More scientists followed and then a trickle of tourists but it was not until 1964, when Kinabalu Park was gazetted, that the 8½ km trail to the summit was opened. Today the mountain lures around 200,000 visitors a year. Although the majority are day visitors who do not climb the peak, the number of climbers is steadily increasing, with around 30,000 making the attempt each year.

In plan, the top of the mountain is U-shaped, with bare rock plateaux. Several peaks stand proud of these plateaux, around the edge of the U; the space between the western and eastern arms is the spectacular gully known as Low's Gully. No one has ever scaled its precipitous walls, nor has anyone climbed the Northern Ridge (an extension of the eastern arm) from the back of the mountain. From Low's Peak, the eastern peaks, just 1½ km away, look within easy reach. As John Briggs points out in his book *Mountains of Malaysia*, "It seems so close, yet it is one of the most difficult places to get to in the whole of Borneo."

The 754 km² Gunung Kinabalu Park was established in 1964 to protect the mountain and its remarkably diverse flora and fauna. Gunung Kinabalu is an important watershed: eight major rivers originate on the mountain.

Flora and fauna

It has one of the richest assemblages of flora in the world, with over 2,000 species of flowering plants

The range of climatic zones on the mountain has led to the incredible diversity of plant and animal life. Kinabalu Park is the meeting point of plants from Asia and Australasia. There are thought to be over 1,200 species of orchid alone, and this does not include the innumerable mosses, ferns and fungi. These flowering plants of Kinabalu are said to represent more than half the families of flowering plants in the world. Within the space of 3 km, the vegetation changes from lowland tropical rainforest to alpine meadow and cloud forest. The jungle reaches up to 1,300m; above that, to a height of 1,800m, is the lower montane zone, dominated by 60 species of oak and chestnut; above 2,000m is the upper montane zone with true cloud forest, orchids, rhododendrons and pitcher plants. Above 2,600m, growing among the crags and crevices of the summit rock plateau are gnarled tea trees (*Leptospermums*) and stunted rhododendrons. Above 3,300m, the soil disappears, leaving only club mosses, sedges and Low's buttercups (*Ranunculus lowii*), which are alpine meadow flowers.

Mountain rescue: five soldiers and seven white chickens

Anyone who has peered from Kinabalu's summit into the seemingly bottomless depths of Low's Gully will appreciate the special sort of lunacy exhibited by two groups of British and Hong Kong soldiers who decided to abseil down it. One group emerged traumatised and exhausted a week later than they said they would. The other team got lost in the jungle below and were not found for three weeks. The dramatic jungle mountain rescue story, which took place in March 1994, catapulted the name Kinabalu into the British media, where it was mispronounced with gay abandon.

For the five soldiers who tackled the precipitous walls of the Gully which plunge a sheer 1,600m from Kinabalu's summit, Sabah's much-touted "paradise" turned into a living hell. Having abseiled down the rock faces (which have yet to be scaled) they disappeared. More than 300 troops, rangers and mountain rescue specialists were involved in the search. When they were finally discovered, it emerged that they had been unable to move from their little jungle encampment

at the foot of the gully; the terrain was too hostile even for them. Although their rations had run out, the soldiers recovered quickly after spending a night in hospital in Kota Kinabalu.

They were lucky men. Irene Charuruks, the head of Sabah's Tourism Promotion Corporation, was quick to point out that "Aki Nabalu means the resting place of the dead in Kadazan". She said that because the five soldiers had been entering an area of the mountain never trodden before, they would have been well advised to have sacrificed seven white chickens so as to avoid offending the spirits of the mountain. Whether or not the spirits were involved, the men owe their lives to a Malaysian helicopter rescue team. The rescue effort was a successful story of co-operation between Malaysia and Britain, who at the time were still embroiled in an acrimonious trade dispute over British press allegations that Malaysian politicians are corrupt. Sadly the happy ending at the resting place of the dead was not enough to prompt the resurrection of Anglo-Malaysian relations.

Among the most unusual of Kinabalu's flora is the world's largest flower, the rust-coloured Rafflesia (see box on page 422). They can usually only be found in the section of the park closest to Poring Hot Springs. Rafflesia are hard to find as they only flower for a couple of days; the main flowering season is from May to July.

Kinabalu is also famous for the carnivorous pitcher plants, which grow to varying sizes on the mountain. A detailed guide to the pitcher plants of Kinabalu can be bought in the shop at park headquarters. Nine different species have been recorded on Kinabalu. The largest is the giant Rajah Brooke's pitcher plant; Spencer St John claimed to have found one of these containing a drowned rat floating in four litres of water. Insects are attracted by the scent and when they settle on the lip of the plant, they cannot maintain a foothold on the waxy, ribbed surface. At the base of the pitcher is an enzymic fluid which digests the 'catch' (see box, page 526).

Rhododendrons line the trail throughout the mossy forest (there are 27 species in the park), especially above the Paka Cave area. One of the most beautiful is the copper leafed rhododendron, with orange flowers and leaves with coppery scales underneath.

It is difficult to see wildlife on the climb to the summit as the trail is well used, although tree shrews and squirrels are common on the lower trails. There are, however, more than 100 species of mammal living in the park. The Kinabalu summit rats, which are always on cue to welcome climbers to Low's Peak at dawn, and nocturnal ferret badgers are the only true montane mammals in

Sabah

Sabah. As the trees thin with altitude, it is often possible to see tree-shrews and squirrels, of which there are over 28 species in the park. Large mammals, such as flying lemurs, redleaf monkeys, wild pigs, orang-utan and deer, are lowland forest dwellers. Nocturnal species include the slow loris (*Nycticebus coucang*) and the mischievous-looking bug-eyed tarsier (*Tarsius bancanus*).

Over half of Borneo's 518 species of birds have also been recorded in Kinabalu Park, but the variety of species decreases with height. Two of the species living above 2,500m are endemic to the mountain: the Kinabalu friendly warbler and the Kinabalu mountain blackbird.

More than 75 species of frogs and toads and 100 species of reptile live in the park. Perhaps the most interesting frog in residence is the horned frog, which is virtually impossible to spot thanks to its mastery of the art of camouflage. The giant toad is common at lower altitudes; he is covered with warts, which are

Gunung Kinabalu Trail

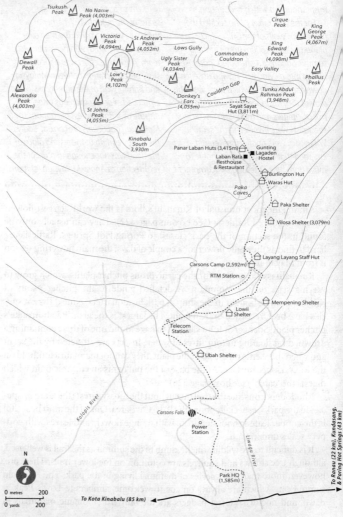

poisonous glands. When disturbed, these squirt a stinking, toxic liquid. Other frogs found in the park include the big-headed leaf-litter frog, whose head is bigger than the rest of its body, and the green stream shrub frog, who has a magnificent metallic green body, but is deadly if swallowed by any predator.

The famous flying tree snake (the subject of an early film by the British nature documentary-maker David Attenborough) has been seen in the park. It spreads its skin flaps, which act as a parachute when the snake leaps blindly from one tree to another.

There are nearly 30 species of fish in the park's rivers, including the unusual Borneo sucker fish (*Gastomyzon borneensis*), which attaches itself to rocks in fast-flowing streams. One Sabah Parks publication likens them to 'underwater cows', grazing on algae as they move slowly over the rocks.

Walkers and climbers are more likely to come across the park's abundant insect life than anything else. Examples include pill millipedes, rhinoceros beetles, the emerald green and turquoise jewel beetles, stick insects, 'flying peapods', cicadas, and a vast array of moths (including the giant atlas moth) and butterflies (including the magnificent emerald green and black Rajah Brooke's birdwing).

The climb

The climb to the summit and back should take two days; four to six hours from park HQ at 2,580m to the *Laban Rata Resthouse* (3,550m) on the first day and then three hours to the summit for dawn, returning to the park headquarters at around 1300 hours on the second day. Gurkha soldiers and others have made it to the summit and back in well under three hours. For the really keen, or the really foolhardy, depending on one's perspective and inclination, there is also the annual Kinabalu Climbathon which is held in early October. In 1997 the race was hampered by the fires which ravaged Indonesian Borneo and created such dangerous atmospheric conditions in Sabah and Sarawak.

Mount Kinabalu is a tough, steep climb but requires no special skills or equipment

A jeep for 12 people can take groups from headquarters to the power station at 1,829m where the trail starts (RM10-20). A minibus also makes the 5½ km run to the power station from park headquarters on a regular basis (RM2). It is a 25 minute walk from the power station to the first shelter, Pondok Lowi. The trail splits in two soon afterwards, the left goes to the radio station and the helipad and the right towards the summit. The next stop is Layang Layang staff headquarters (drinking water, cooking facilities, accommodation) – also known as *Carson's Camp* (2,621m), named after the first warden of the park. There is one more shelter, Ponkok Villosa (2,942m, and about 45 minutes from Carson's Camp) before the stop at the path to Paka Caves – really an overhanging rock on the side of a stream. Paka is a 10-minute detour to the left, where Low and St John made their camps.

From the cave/fifth shelter the vegetation thins out and it is a steep climb to Panar Laban huts – which includes the well equipped *Laban Rata Resthouse*, affording magnificent views at sunset and in the early morning. The name *Panar Laban* is derived from Kadazan words meaning 'place of sacrifice': early explorers had to make a sacrifice here to appease the spirits and this ritual is still performed by the Kadazan once a year. Sayat Sayat (3,810m) hut – named after the ubiquitous shrubby tea tree – is an hour further on, above the Panar Laban Rockface. Most climbers reach Panar Laban (or the other huts) in the early afternoon in order to rest up for a 0300 start the next morning in order to reach the summit by sunrise. The trail is well laid out with regular half mile resting points. Ladders, hand-rails and ropes are provided for the steeper parts. The first two hours after dawn are the most likely to be cloud-free. For

Sabah

enthusiasts interested in alternative routes to the summit, John Briggs's *Mountains of Malaysia* provides a detailed guide to the climb.

Equipment   A thick jacket is recommended, but at the very least you should have a light waterproof or windcheater to beat the windchill on the summit. Remarkably, no one appears to have set up rental facilities; contrary to rumour, it is not possible to hire jackets or windcheaters from park HQ. It is also necessary to bring a sweater or some thick shirts. Walking boots are recommended, but not essential – many people climb the mountain in trainers. Sleeping bags are provided free of charge in both the Laban Rata Resthouse and the Sayat Sayat; they are crucial for a good night's sleep. Carry food and a few sweets as a precaution. Essential items include: torch, toilet paper, water bottle, plasters, headache tablets and suntan lotion. A hat is also a good idea – as protection against the sun and the cold. Gloves, Balaclavas and torches can be bought at the shop at Park HQ, which also sells a range of food and drinks suitable for the climb. Lockers are available, RM1 per item, at the park headquarters reception office. The *Laban Rata Resthouse* has welcome hot water showers, but soap and towels are not provided. The hostel is well heated and bedding is provided.

Guides   Hiring a guide is compulsory: RM60 for the round trip (one to six people). Porters available at a charge of RM6 for every kilogram carried, maximum load 11kg. Guides and porters should be reserved at least a day in advance at the park headquarters or at the parks office in KK. On the morning of your climb, go to the HQ and a guide will be assigned to you. A guide is not compulsory if you want to walk the trail only as far as Laban Rata, below the rockface. A small colour pamphlet, *Mount Kinabalu/A Guide to the Summit Trail* published by Sabah Parks and widely available, serves as a good guide to the wildlife and the trail itself.

Permits   RM50 per person to climb Gunung Kinabalu, an entry permit costing RM3 must be purchased on arrival by all park visitors. Compulsory insurance costs RM3.50.

Treks   There is a map of trails around the park available from Park HQ. Most are well used and are easy walks, but the Liwagu Trail is a good three to four hour trek up to where it joins the summit trail and is very steep and slippery in places; not advised as a solo trip. Guided trail walk 1100 Monday-Sunday from park administration building. This is a gentle walk with a knowledgeable guide, although the number of participants tends to be large.

Park headquarters

A short walk from the main Ranau-KK road and all the accommodation and restaurants are within 15 minutes walk from the main compound. **Souvenir and bookshop**: next to the park headquarters has good books on the mountain and its flora and fauna. **Slide and film shows** are held in the mini-theatre in the Administration Building at 1400 during the week and at 1930 on weekends and public holidays, while naturalists give escorted trail walks every morning.

Mountain Garden   Situated behind park administration building, this landscaped garden has species from all over the mid-levels of the mountain, which have been planted in natural surroundings. Tours leave at 0900, 1200, 1500 and cost RM4 – the Garden is closed at other times.

This is at headquarters with information on local flora and fauna. Beetles "as large as Tom Jones' medallions" and foot-long stick insects. There is also a slide show introducing some of the park's flora and fauna at 1930. **Museum**

Mini-buses to the springs leave park HQ at 0900, 1300, 1600; alternatively flag down a bus/minibus to Ranau on the main road two minutes' walk from HQ and taxi from there to Poring (see page 448). **Poring Hot Springs** *See also page 448*

Best time to visit

The average rainfall is 400 cm a year, with an average temperature of 20°C at park headquarters but at Panar Laban it can drop below freezing at night. With the wind chill factor on the summit, it feels very cold. The best time to climb Gunung Kinabalu is in the dry season between March and April when views are clearest. The worst time has traditionally been November to December during the monsoon, although wet or dry periods can occur at any time of the year. The forest fires of August, September and October 1997 also presented climbers with particular health problems, not to mention rather truncated views. Avoid weekends, school and public holidays if at all possible.

NB The park is occasionally closed to climbers during certain periods. It was shut most of September 1999 before and during a series of competitions held in the month, such as the World Mountain Racing Trophy. It is certainly worth contacting the Parks Office (088 243629) or Kinabalu Gold Resorts (088 243629) to check the mountain is open for climbing at the time of your visit.

Park essentials

(Also see Ranau and Kundasang below.) **NB** Management of the park has recently been privatized. It is currently being managed by a company called *Kinabalu Gold Resorts*. All accommodation in the park must be booked in advance through this company. They can be contacted at: Lot 3.46 & 3.47, 3rd Floor, Block C, Kompleks Karamunsing, Kota Kinabalu. T088257941, F088242861. For direct information from Park Office about any matter T243629/245742. **Sleeping**

Park headquarters Each cabin is provided with a fireplace, kitchen, shower, gas cooker, refrigerator and cooking and eating utensils. Electricity, piped water and firewood are all provided free of charge. The rates quoted below are reduced on weekdays: *Annex suite*, 4 people, RM184 per night. *Double storey deluxe cabin*, 7 people, RM207 per night. *Duplex chalet*, 6 people, RM173 per night. *Kinabalu Lodge*, 8 people, RM200 per night. *Nepenthes Villa*, 4 people, RM207 per night. *New Hostel*, RM12 per night. *Old Hostel*, RM12 per night. *Single storey deluxe cabin*, 5 people, RM150 per night. *Twin bed cabin*, 2 people, RM58 per night.

Gunung Kinabalu *Laban Rata Resthouse*, Panar Laban, 54 rooms (space is often made for extra bodies by laying out matresses on the restaurant floor), a good quality though pricey canteen (but sometimes rather limited food – it all has to be walked up the mountain) and hot water shower facilities plus electricity and heated rooms, bedding provided. RM28 per night per person.

Sayat Sayat Huts: RM12 per person shared rooms with 5 wooden bunks, matresses, and sleeping bags, gas cylinder cooking stoves supplied and limited eating utensils; no heating provided. Climbers may want to bring their own food for cooking, although there is a restaurant just below the Panar Laban Huts. These huts are often used as emergency accommodation when the Laban Rata Huts are fully booked. It is

Sabah

very basic and gets cold – but it is a bed, and does leave you less work on the 2nd day, giving you a 'lie in' until 4am.

NB Booking accommodation and a guide are in theory essential. Most people organize these through a tour company based in KK days in advance. Alternatively they can personally book accommodation through *Kinabalu Gold Resorts* for the night before departure at HQ, and then report to the Park Office at around 0700 on the morning of the ascent, in order to be allocated a guide. A third option for those who are desperate to go, short of time, and have been informed that there is no accommodation available on the mountain in the next few days by tour companies in KK (as can happen all too often at busy periods such as school holidays) is to try your luck and turn up in person! A bus to the park leaves KK at 0800, and will drop you outside park HQ before 1000 – certainly arrive no later if you are hoping to climb the mountain that day. We have had a number of reports that once someone has turned up in person to enquire, beds/matresses up the mountain are often found. You should also be able to pick up a guide if you are there before 1000, although you will be unlikely to find anyone else to share with at this time. Once things are in place you can begin the climb around 1100, which is time enough to reach Laban Rata, or even Sayat Sayat if necessary. This method should be an absolute last resort, and it is by no means guaranteed to work. However, it has proved successful to a number of people who are prepared to accept the risk. If things don't work out, accommodation will probably be available at park HQ, or there are a number of good places within 2 km of the park, which can be used as a base to explore the park.

Sleeping close to Park HQ
Price codes: see inside front cover

The accommodation in the park can occasionally be fully booked, and you may be forced to find somewhere close by. Alternatively you may choose to stay just outside the park, where good quality, well priced accommodation is available.

A *Haleluyah Retreat Centre*, Jln Linouh, Km 61, Tuaran-Ranau Highway, PO Box 13337, T011 817937, F088223443. Reservations at Sinsuran Complex, Block A, Lot 8, Second Floor, KK. This Christian centre is open to all and is located at 1,500m close to the foot of Mount Kinabalu. It makes a good stop off point before climbing the mountain. Set amidst 2 acres of natural jungle and approximately 15 mins' walk from the Park Headquarters, it is isolated but safe, clean, friendly and with a relaxing atmosphere. Cooking and washing facilities, camping area, multi-purpose hall and meeting rooms makes it a suitable venue for seminars, meetings, youth camps or family holidays. Food is available at a reasonable price from a canteen, dorm beds also available. **B** *Kinabalu Rose Cabin*, T899233. Kundasang, a/c, restaurant, 2 km from the park, towards golf course (30% discount to golfers); range of rooms, suites. **B** *Sonny's Village*, T088750555. Six bedrooms with spectacular views. **C** *Rina Ria Lodge*, Batu 36, JlnKK, Ranau, T088889282. About 1 km from the Kinabalu National Park, rooms have attached kitchen and basic bathroom, arm chairs and beautiful views. There is also a shop. Prices increase at weekends. Dorms also available (**E**). **C** *Mountain View Motel*, located 5 km east of the Kinabalu National Park on the Ranau-Tamparuli Highway, T088 875389, bbmtkinabalu@hotmail.com. Price includes breakfast, hot water, restaurant, laundry facilitites, local tours, climbing gear available for rent. The corrugated iron roof can be loud when it rains. **E** *Mountain Resthouse and Restaurant*, T771109. Located just outside the park, this has small 4 person dorms that are cheaper, newer, cleaner and warmer than the park dorms. Also spectacular views. This is arguably preferable to the park accommodation.

Eating

Park headquarters The best places to stay are here although the restaurants are rather spread out requiring a walk between buffet and bed. **2** *Club Canteen*, decent meals. **2** *Steak & Coffee House*. Cooking facilities at *Kinabalu Lodge*, *Double storey*, *Single storey*, *Duplex chalet*, *Nepenthes villa*, *New hostel*, *Old hostel*.

Minibus Regular connections from KK to Ranau, ask to be dropped at the park, 2 hrs. Return minibus must be waved down from the main road. Chartered 28-seater minibus from the National Parks office: RM300. **Bus** Scheduled a/c bus from Kota Kinabalu to Ranau at 0800 and 1230 (RM7), slower than the minibus but more luggage space. **Taxi** At least RM100 per taxi from KK.

Transport
60 km NE of KK

This resort is the newest rainforest resort in Sabah, nestled at the foot of Mount Kinabalu at 2,000m. The main attractions are the cool climate and the superb views up the mountain and across the plains toward Ranau and the sea. It is possible to scale the peaks of the mountain using the resort as a base, providing an alternative route from which to launch any assault on Low's Peak. Taking this new trail, one would join the main trail at Layang Layang. Alternatively there are a number of walks to be made around the reserve, in this secluded location.

Mesilau nature resort

Sleeping A-D There is a range of tasteful wooden chalets that blend neatly into the environment housing groups of up to 6 people. There is also more budget accommodation provided in dorms in the hostel. The nature resort, like the park, is managed by Kinabalu Gold Resorts and all accommodation bookings need to be arranged through them. For further enquiries and bookings contact Kinabalu Gold Resorts, Lot 3.46 & 3.47, 3rd Floor, Block C, Kompleks Karamunsing, Kota Kinabalu T088257941, F088242861.

Other services available include laundry, a gift shop and regular educational talks. The nature reserve is situated conveniently close to the Mt. Kinabalu Golf Club, just a few mins' drive away.

The Kedamaian Restaurant will provide the three main meals. The alternative is the *Malaxi Café*, which has a stunning verandah offering great views of the mountain.

Eating

Ranau and Kundasang

The Ranau plateau, surrounding the Kinabalu massif, is one of the richest farming areas in Sabah and much of the forest not in the park has now been devastated by market gardeners. Even within the national park's boundaries, on the lower slopes of Mount Kinabalu itself, shifting cultivators have clear-felled tracts of jungle and planted their patches. More than 1,000 hectares are now planted out with spinach, cabbage, cauliflower, asparagus, broccoli and tomatoes, supplying much of Borneo.

Colour map 4, grid B4

Kundasang and Ranau are unremarkable towns a few kilometres apart; the latter is bigger. The **war memorial**, behind Kundasang, which unfortunately looks like Colditz, is in memory of those who died in the 'death march' in the Second World War (see page 451). In September 1944, the Japanese marched 2,400 Allied prisoners of war through the jungle from Sandakan to Kundasang. The march took 11 months and only six men survived to tell the tale. The walled gardens represent the national gardens of Borneo, Australia and Britain.

Mentapok and Monkobo are southeast of Ranau. Both are rarely climbed. Mentapok, 1,581m, can be reached in 1½ days from Kampung Mireru, a village at the base of the mountain. A logging track provides easy access halfway up the south side of the mountain. Monkobo is most easily climbed from the northwest, a logging track from Telupid goes up to 900m and from here it is a two-hour trek to the top. It is advisable to take guides, organized from Ranau or one of the nearby villages.

Excursions

Sleeping
Price codes: see inside front cover

B *Kinabalu Pines Resort*, T088889388, F088889288. A/c, great views in this attractive but nevertheless isolated setting, 6 km from the national park. Great value. **B** *Perkasa*, visible on the hill above Kundasang (a further 1 km down the road from *Kinabalu Pines*), T889511, F889101. A/c, restaurant, slightly run down but a good view of the mountain, organizes tours to Kinabalu National Park and surrounding area. **B-C** *Ranau*, on the bottom side of the square, nearest the main road, Lot 9, Block C, Sedco Complex, T875661. Some a/c, TV, more expensive than the *Kinabalu* and nothing to make it stand out. **C** *Hotel Kinabalu*, Lot 3E, Kedai Sedca Baru, Peti Surat 2, T876028. A/c, shower, decent rooms. Next door is the **C-D** *Koktas Inn B&B*, T889117. 1st Flr, Lot 3, Block N, Ranau, fan, TV. Best deal in town with breakfast included. **D** *Ranau Saga*, 1st Flr, Block T, Lot 6, T875864. Situated where the express buses stop, but overpriced and should only be used as a last resort. **D** *Sapati*, top left side of the square, no attached bath.

Eating

Kundasang There are several restaurants along the roads serving simple food, open 0600-2100. **3** *Perkasa Hotel Restaurant*, local and Western dishes, service good and food excellent. **Ranau** **Chinese:** **1** *Five Star Seafood Restaurant*, opposite the market; **1** *Sin Mui Mui*, top side of the square near the market.

Shopping

Cheap sweaters and waterproofs for the climb from *Kedai Kien Hin*, Ranau. A *tamu* is held near Ranau on the first of each month and every Sat. Kundasang *tamu* is held on the 20th of every month and also every Fri.

Sports

Golf *Kundasang Golf Course*, 3 km behind Kundasang in the shadow of the mountain is one of the most beautiful courses in the region. Club hire from the *Perkasa Hotel*, Kundasang, RM25 per round. The *Perkasa* offer golfing packages to include golf fees, accommodation, breakfast and lunch, transfer from hotel to course.

Transport
113 km to KK

Minibus Minibuses leave from the market place. Regular connections to park headquarters, to KK, to Sandakan 8 hrs.

Poring Hot Springs

Colour map 4, grid A4

Poring lies 43 km from Gunung Kinabalu Park Headquarters and is actually part of the national park. The **hot sulphur baths** were installed during the Japanese occupation of the Second World War, for the jungle-weary Japanese troops. There are individual concrete pools with taps which can fit two people, one for the hot spring mineral water and the other for cold; once in your bath you are in complete privacy. The springs are on the other side of the Mamut River, over a suspension bridge, from the entrance. They are a fantastic antidote to tiredness after a tough climb up Gunung Kinabalu. There is also a cold water rock pool. The pools are in a beautiful garden setting of hibiscus and other tropical flowers, trees and thousands of butterflies. There are some quite luxurious private cabin baths available; a standard cabin costs RM15 for the first hour or part thereof, then RM25 for every additional hour. There are also large baths capable of accommodating eight people. The deluxe cabins have lounge areas and jacuzzis and cost RM20 for the first hour then RM30 for each additional hour. The Kadazans named the area Poring after the towering bamboos, of that name, nearby. (These big bamboos were traditionally used as water-carriers and examples can be seen in the museum in KK.) ■ *RM2*. An Information Centre has been built here, plus a rafflesia centre, orchid centre, aviary and tropical garden.

The **jungle canopy walk** at Poring is a rope walkway 35m above the ground, which provides a monkey's eye view of the jungle; springy but quite safe. Guides are available. The entrance is five minutes' walk from the hot springs and the canopy walkway is 15 minutes' walk from the entrance.

Kipungit Falls are only about 10 minutes' walk from Poring and swimming is possible here. Follow the trail further up the hill and after 15 minutes you come to bat caves; a large overhanging boulder povides shelter and a home for the bats.

The **Langanan Waterfall** trail takes 90 minutes one way and is up hill all the way, but it is worth it. There is another hard 90 minute trail to Bat Cave (inhabited, would you believe, by what seems to be a truly stupendous number of bats) and a waterfall. The **Butterfly Farm** was established by a Japanese-backed firm in 1992 and is very educational in the descriptions of butterflies and other insects.

If the weather is clear at Ranau, it is generally safe to assume that the canopy walk will also be clear. The warmer climate at lower altitudes means there is an abundance of wild fruit in the park, which attracts flying lemur, red leaf monkeys; even orang-utans have occasionally been seen here. The bird life is particularly rich and diverse and provides a complete contrast to the montane birds seen round the Park Headquarters. There are also numerous butterflies.

■ *1030-1430 RM2 per person; 1830-2230 RM10 per person; 2230-1030 RM20 per person if in group of 4 or more, otherwise RM30 for 1-3 persons. No admission charge if you have already been to Mount Kinabalu. An inside bath can be rented for RM15-20 per hour. If staying at Poring then there is no admission charge, and the baths can be used all night long. Permits not necessary.*

E *Youth Hostel*, 24 people in a dorm, RM8 adult, RM2 student; *Mamutik Resthouse*, 8 people, RM180 per night; *Manukan Chalet*, 4 people, RM220 per night; *Poring New Cabin*, 4 people, RM95 per night; *Poring Old Cabin*, 6 people, RM115 per night. **Camping** RM5.

2 *Restaurant*, quite good Chinese and Malay food at the springs and other stalls outside the park.

Sleeping & eating
Booking is recommended, see Park essentials, page 445

Minibuses can be shared from Ranau for RM5. **Taxi** Available (RM25).

Transport

The East Coast

From Ranau it is possible to reach Sandakan by road – although the road is not metalled and is a quagmire in the wet season. Several key sights are within reach of Sandakan: the Turtle Islands National Park, 40 km north in the Sulu Sea, Sepilok Orang-utan Rehabilitation Centre and the Kinabatangan Basin, to the southeast. From Sandakan, the route continues south to the wilds of Lahad Datu and Danum Valley and onto Semporna, the jumping off point for Pulau Sipadan. This island has achieved legendary status among snorkellers and scuba divers in recent years.

Sandakan

Sandakan is at the neck of a bay on the northeast coast of Sabah and looks out to the Sulu Sea. It is a post-war town, much of it rebuilt on reclaimed land, and is Malaysia's biggest fishing port; it even exports some of its catch to Singapore.

Phone code: 089
Colour map 4, grid B5

Sandakan is often dubbed 'mini Hong Kong' because of its Cantonese influence; its occupants are well-heeled and there are many prosperous businesses.

It is now also home to a large Filipino community, mostly traders from Mindanao and the Sulu Islands. The Philippines only recently relaxed its posturing in its claim to Sabah; Sandakan is only 28 km from Philippines' territorial waters.

Ins and outs

Getting there
See also Transport, page 457

The airport is around 10 km from town. There are daily connections with KK and several lesser destinations in Sabah. From the long distance bus terminal in town, there are connections with KK, Tawau, Ranau, Lahad Datu and several other destinations.

Getting around

Sandakan is not a large town and it is easy enough to explore the central area on foot - although it does stretch some way along the coast. Minibuses provide links with out-of-town places of interest.

History

For the Sulu traders, the Sandakan area was an important source of beeswax and came under the sway of the Sultans of Sulu. William Clarke Cowie, a Scotsman with a carefully waxed handlebar moustache who ran guns for the Sultan of Sulu across the Spanish blockade of Sulu (and was later to become the managing director of the North Borneo Chartered Company), first set up camp in Sandakan Bay in the early 1870s. He called his camp, which was on Pulau Timbang, 'Sandakan', which had been the Sulu name for the area for about 200 years, but it became known as Kampung German as there were several German traders living there, and early gun-runners tended to be German. The power of the Sulu sultanate was already on the wane when Cowie set up. In its early trading days, there were many nationalities living in Sandakan: Europeans, Africans, Arabs, Chinese, Indians, Javanese, Dusun and Japanese. It was an important gateway to the interior and used to be a trading centre for forest produce like rhinoceros horn, beeswax, and hornbill ivory along with marine products like pearls and sea cucumbers (*tripang*, valued for their medicinal properties). In 1812 an English visitor, John Hunt, estimated that the Sandakan/Kinabatangan area produced an astonishing 37,000kg of wild beeswax and 23,000kg of bird's nests each year.

The modern town of Sandakan was founded by an Englishman, William Pryer, in 1879. Baron von Overbeck, the Austrian consul from Hong Kong who founded the Chartered Company with businessman Alfred Dent, had signed a leasing agreement for the territory with the Sultan of Brunei, only to discover that large tracts on the east side of modern-day Sabah actually belonged to the Sultan of Sulu. Overbeck sailed to Sulu in January 1878 and on obtaining the cession rights from the Sultan, dropped William Pryer off at Kampung German to make the British presence felt. Pryer's wife Ada later described the scene: "He had with him a West Indian black named Anderson, a half-cast Hindoo named Abdul, a couple of China boys. For food they had a barrel of flour and 17 fowls and the artillery was half a dozen sinder rifles." Pryer set about organizing the three existing villages in the area, cultivating friendly relations with the local tribespeople and fending off pirates. He raised the Union Jack on 11 February 1878.

Cowie tried to do a deal with the Sultan of Sulu to wrest control of Sandakan back from Pryer, but Dent and Overbeck finally bought him off. A few months later Cowie's Kampung German burned to the ground, so Pryer went in search of a new site, which he found at Buli Sim Sim. He called his new settlement Elopura, meaning 'beautiful city', but the name did not catch on. By the

The Borneo Death March

The four years of Japanese occupation ended when the Australian ninth division liberated British North Borneo. Sandakan was chosen by the Japanese as a regional centre for holding Allied prisoners. In 1942 the Japanese shipped 2,750 prisoners of war (2,000 of whom were Australian and 750 British) to Sandakan from Changi Prison, Singapore. A further 800 British and 500 Australian POWs arrived in 1944. They were ordered to build an airfield (on the site of the present airport) and were forced to work from dawn to dusk. Many died, but in September 1944 2,400 POWs were force-marched to Ranau, a 240 km trek through the jungle which only six Australians survived. This 'Death March', although not widely reported in Second World War literature, claimed more Australian lives than any other single event during the war in Asia, including the notorious Burma-Siam railway.

mid-1880s it was recalled Sandakan and, in 1884, became the capital of North Borneo when the title was transferred from Kudat. In 1891 the town had 20 Chinese-run brothels and 71 Japanese prostitutes; according to the 1891 census there were three men for every one woman. The town quickly established itself as the source of birds' nests harvested from the caves at Gomontong (see page 453) and shipped directly to Hong Kong, as they are today.

Timber was first exported from this area in 1885 and was used to construct Beijing's Temple of Heaven. Sandakan was, until a few years ago, the main east coast port for timber and it became a very wealthy town. In its heyday, the town is said to have boasted one of the greatest concentrations of millionaires in the world. The timber-boom days are over: the primary jungle has gone, and so has the big money. In the mid-1990s the state government adopted a strict policy restricting the export of raw, unprocessed timber. The hinterland is now dominated by cocoa and oil palm plantations.

Following the Japanese invasion in 1942, Sandakan was devastated by Allied bombing. In 1946 North Borneo became a British colony and the new colonial government moved the capital to Jesselton (later to become Kota Kinabalu).

Sights

Sandakan is strung out along the coast but in the centre of town is the riotous **daily fish market**, which is the biggest and best in Sabah. The best time to visit is at 0600 when the boats unload their catch. The **Central Market** along the waterfront, near the local bus station, sells such things as fruit, vegetables, sarongs, seashells, spices and sticky rice cakes.

The **Australian war memorial**, near the government building at Mile Seven on Labuk Rd, between Sandakan and Sepilok, stands on the site of a Japanese prison camp and commemorates Allied soldiers who lost their lives during the Japanese occupation. To get there, take Labuk bus service nos 19, 30 and 32. The Japanese invaded North Borneo in 1942 and many Japanese also died in the area. In 1989 a new **Japanese war memorial** was built in the Japanese cemetery, on Red Hill (Bukit Berenda), financed by the families of the deceased soldiers.

St Michael's Anglican church is one of the very few stone churches in Sabah and is an attractive building, designed by a New Zealander in 1893. Most of Sandakan's stone churches were levelled in the war and, indeed, St Michael's is one of the few colonial-era buildings still standing. It is just off Jalan Singapura, on the hill at the south end of town. In 1988 a big new **mosque** was built for the burgeoning Muslim population at the mouth of Sandakan Bay. The main Filipino settlements are in this area of town. The mosque is outside Sandakan, on

Sabah

··

 Agnes Keith's house

American authoress Agnes Keith lived with her English husband in Sandakan from 1934 to 1952. He was the Conservator of Forests in North Borneo and she wrote three books about her time in the colony. The Land Below the Wind relates tales of dinner parties and tiffins in pre-war days; Three Came Home is about her three years in a Japanese internment camp during the war on Pulau Berhala, off Sandakan, and in Kuching and was made into a film. White Man Returns tells the story of their time in British North Borneo. The Keiths' rambling wooden house on the hill above the town was destroyed during the war but was rebuilt by the government to exactly the same design when Harry Keith returned to his job after the war. The house, near Sandakan Viewpoint and Ramada Renaissance Hotel, has been unoccupied for a number of years and its garden neglected.

··

Jalan Buli Sim Sim where the town began in 1879, just after the jetty for Turtle Islands National Park and is an imposing landmark. There is also a large water village here, offering a glimpse of traditional culture and life.

Pertubuhan Ugama Buddhist (Puu Jih Shih Buddhist temple), overlooks Tanah Merah town. The US$2m temple was completed in 1987 and stands at the top of the hill, accessible by a twisting road which hairpins its way up the hillside. The temple is very gaudy, contains three large Buddha images and is nothing special, although the 34 teakwood supporting pillars, made in Macau, are quite a feature. There is a good view of Sandakan from the top, with Tanah Merah and the log ponds directly below, in Sandakan Bay. The names of local donors are inscribed on the walls of the walkway.

There are a couple of other notable Chinese temples in Sandakan. The oldest one, the **Goddess of Mercy Temple** is just off Jalan Singapura, on the hillside. Originally built in the early 1880s, it has been expanded over the years. Nearby is **Sam Sing Kung Temple** which becomes a particular focus of devotion during exam periods since one of its deities is reputed to assist those attempting examinations. The **Three Saints Temple**, further down the hill at the end of the padang, was completed in 1887. The three saints are Kwan Woon Cheung, a Kwan clan ancestor, the goddess Tien Hou (or Tin Hou, worshipped by seafarers) and the Min Cheong Emperor.

The only **Crocodile Farm** in Sabah is a commercial licensed enterprise, set up in 1982 when the government made the estuarine crocodile a protected species. The original stock were drawn from a population of wild crocodiles found in the Kinabatangan River. Visitors can see around 2,000 crocs at all stages of maturity waiting in concrete pools for the day when their skins are turned into bags and wallets and their meat is sold to local gourmets. The farm, at Mile 8, Labuk Road, is open to the public and has about 200 residents. Feeding time and the only active time is at 1000. ■ *0800-1700 Mon-Sun, RM2, Labuk Rd bus*. The **Forest Headquarters** (*Ibu Pejabat Jabatan Perkutanan*) is on Labuk Road next to the Sandakan Golf Course and contains an exhibition centre and a well laid out and interesting mini-museum showing past and present forestry practice.

Excursions

Most tour companies operate tours to Turtle Islands, Sepilok, the Gomontong Caves, Sukau and the Kinabatangan River. See **Tour operators**, page 456. **Sepilok Orang-utan Sanctuary**, see page 460. **Turtle Islands National Park**, see page 458. **Kinabatangan River**, see page 462.

Edible nests

The edible nests of black and white swiftlets are collected from the cave chambers, but the trade is now strictly controlled by Wildlife Department wardens. The white nests (of pure saliva) fetch more than US$500 per kilogram in Hong Kong; black nests go for around US$40 per kilogram. The nest-collectors pick about 250kg a day in the lower chamber and about 50kg a day in the upper chamber. They earn about M$25 a day. The collectors use 60m-long rotan ladders. Heavy bundles of wood are lashed to the ladders to minimize swaying – but fatal accidents do occur. On average, a collector is killed once every four or five years in a fall. Bat guano is not collected from the floor of the cave so that it can act as a sponge mattress in the event of a serious fall.

The nests, which are relished as a delicacy by the Chinese (see page 361), are harvested for periods of 10 days, twice a year. The nests are first harvested just after the birds have made them (between February and April). The birds then build new nests, which are left undisturbed until after the eggs have been laid and hatched; these nests are then gathered, sometime between July and September. Harvesting contracts are auctioned to wholesalers who export the nests to Hong Kong, where their impurities are taken out and they are sold at a huge mark-up. Of the profits, about half go to the state government, and more than a third to the contractor. Less than a fifth goes to the collectors. It is possible to buy the birds' nests in Sandakan restaurants, although they are all re-imported from Hong Kong.

These are 32 km south of Sandakan Bay, between the road to Sukau and the **Gomontong** Kinabatangan River, or 110 km overland on the Sandakan-Sukau road. The **Caves** name Gomontong means 'tie it up tightly' in the local language and the caves represent the largest system in Sabah. They are contained within the 3,924 hectare Gomontong Forest Reserve. There are sometimes orang-utan, many deer, mouse deer, wild boar and wild buffalo in the reserve, which was logged in the 1950s. There are several cave chambers. The main limestone cave is called Simud Hitam, or the *Black Cave*. This cave, with its ceiling soaring up to 90m overhead, is just a five-minute walk from the registration centre and pic- nic area. The smaller and more complex *White Cave* (or Simud Putih) is above. It is quite dangerous climbing up as there is no ladder to reach the caves and the rocks are slippery. Over two million bats of two different species are thought to live in the caves: at sunset they swarm out to feed. Sixty four species of bat have been recorded in Sabah, most in these caves are fruit and wrin- kled-lipped bats whose guano is a breeding ground for cockroaches. The squirming larvae make the floor of the cave seethe. The guano can cause an itchy skin irritation. The bats are preyed upon by birds like the bat hawk, pere- grine falcon and buffy fish owl.

There are also an estimated one million swiftlets which swarm into the cave to roost at sunset, the birds of birds' nest soup fame. The swiftlets of Gomontong have been a focus of commercial enterprise for perhaps 400 or 500 years. However it was not until 1870 that harvesting birds' nests became a serious industry here. The caves are divided into five pitches and each is allo- cated to a team of 10-15 people. Harvesting periods last 15 days and there are three each year (February-April, July-September, and December). Collecting the nests from hundreds of feet above the ground is a dangerous business and deaths are not uncommon. Before each harvesting period a chicken or goat is sacrificed to the cave spirit; it is thought that deaths are not the result of human error, but an angry spirit. The birdlife around the caves is particularly rich, with crested serpent eagles, kingfishers, Asian fairy bluebirds, and leadbirds all often sighted. Large groups of richly coloured butterflies are also frequently sighted drinking from pools along the track leading from the forest into the caves. The Niah Caves (see page 359) are on an even larger scale and yet more interesting. At the park headquarters there is an information centre, a small cafeteria where drinks and simple dishes are sold, and a pit latrine. If you arrive independently then one of the nest workers, a person from the information centre, or a ranger will show you around. ■ *0800-1600, Mon-Sun. The bats can be seen exiting from the caves between 1800 and 1830; to request to see this it is necessary to ask at the information centre (Wildlife Department).*

Sleeping *Proboscis Lodge*, Sukau (T240584 or F240415, Kota Kinabalu), 2 hrs by road from Sandakan, wooden stilt cabins set in the heart of the jungle, restaurant. **A** *Gomantong Rainforest Chalet*, this place is owned by *Sabah Travel* and opened in 1997; chalets are clean, with shared bathrooms and guides are provided.

Transport It is easiest on a tour (see page 452). The caves are accessible by an old logging road, which can be reached by bus from the main Sandakan-Sukau road. The timing of the bus is inconvenient for those wishing to visit the caves, although an alternative is to charter a Labuk/Leila bus from Pryer St, opposite the bus station. It is much easier to take the 1100 boat from Sandakan's fish market to Suad Lamba, 1½ hours. From there it is possible to take a minibus to Gomontong (quite cheap, if there are a reasonable number of passengers). Visitors can stay overnight in the resthouse at nearby Sukau (see below). There are plans afoot to build a chalet and restaurant at Gomontong. Minibuses will pick up passengers for the return trip to Suad Lamba by arrangement. The daily boat back to Sandakan leaves Suad Lamba at 0530.

Pulau Berhala This island is ideal for picnicking and swimming. It has 200m rust-coloured sandstone cliffs on the south end of the island, with a beach at the foot, within easy reach by boat. The island was used as a leper colony before the Second World War and as a prisoner of war camp by the Japanese. Agnes Keith (see page 452) was interned on the island during the war. Boats to the island leave from the fish market.

Essentials

Sleeping
■ *on map, page 456*
Price codes:
see inside front cover

A *Sandakan Renaissance* (formerly the *Ramada Renaissance* and before that the *Sabah Hotel*), Mile 1.5, Jln Leila, PO Box 537, T213299, F271171. With a/c, restaurants, attractive pool, Sandakan's top hotel has been refurbished to 5-star standard with 120 rooms, fitness centre, tennis, pool and squash courts. **A** *Hotel Sandakan*, 4th Ave, T221122, F221100, tengis@tm.net.my. A/c, coffee house, 2 restaurants (Japanese and Cantonese), bar with live music, business centre. Centrally located, this is not cheap but provides excellent service.

B *City View*, Lot 1, Block 23, 3rd Ave, Sandakan, T271122, F273115. Restaurant, bath and shower, TV, fridge, a/c. For a little more than the standard guesthouses this is a considerable step up. Recommended. **B** *Hsiang Garden*, Mile 1.5, Jln Leila, Hsiang Garden Estate, Lot 7 & 8, Block C, PO Box 1003, T273122, F273127. A/c, restaurant, all facilities, good bar. **B** *Ramai*, Km 1.5, Jln Leila, Hsiang Gardens, T273222, F271884. A/c, restaurant. Recommended. **B** *Sepilok Inn*, Block 46, Lot 9, Tingkat 1,2,3, Church Rd, T271222, F273831. A/c, clean rooms with attached bathrooms and TVs, good value.

C *En Khin*, 50 Jln Tiga (next to Maybank), T217300. A/c, shower, clean but dark rooms. Reasonable value with discounts available. **C** *Hung Wing*, Lot 4, Block 13, Jln Tiga, T218855, F271240. Some a/c, shower, a wide variety of rooms and prices available.

Rooms are spacious and light. The owner is very helpful and speaks excellent English. Probably the best of the middle-bracket hotels, clean rooms with own bathroom. **C** *London*, Lot D1, Block 10, Jln Empat, T216371, a/c, shower and bath, TV, light rooms although not large. **C** *Malaysia*, 32 Jln Dua, T218322, F271249. A/c, shower, clean and more spacious than *Hung Wing*, rooms have TVs. Reasonable. **C** *Mayfair*, 24 Jln Pryer, a/c, shower, communal TV. The décor leaves something to be desired but there is a very friendly atmosphere and the hotel holds a central location with views of the market and the sea, good value. **C** *New Sabah*, 18 Jln Singapura, T218949/218711, F273725. A/c, TV, hot shower, well kept.

D *Uncle Tan's*, Mile 17.5 (Km 29), Labuk Rd (5 km beyond Sepilok junction), T089 531639, F089 271215. Set in fruit plantation; bicycle hire RM3 per day, all meals included, tours arranged (see **Tour operators** below), very cheap but not very clean and being on the main road, it's noisy from the logging trucks which continue to thunder past all night long. One redeeming feature is Uncle Tan himself who is a great raconteur, the other is Susie, a Filipino who runs the place and provides excellent food. A popular stop for travellers. **D-E** *Travellers Rest Hostel*, 2nd Floor, Apt 2, Block E, Jln Leila, Bandar Ramai-Ramai, some a/c, no attached bathrooms and limited toilet facilities, friendly with lots of travel information. Cooking and washing facilities.

Malay 2 *Jiaman*, 1st Flr, Wisma Khoo Siak Chiew, serves interesting selection of Malay and Bajau dishes, no alcohol. **2** *Perwira*, *Hotel Ramai*, Jln Leila, Malay and Indonesian, good value. Recommended.

Eating
Sandakan is justifiably renowned for its inexpensive & delicious seafood

Chinese Four Chinese seafood restaurants on Trig Hill overlooking the harbour. The seafood is fantastic. **3** *Golden Palace*, Trig Hill (2 km out of town), fresh seafood, specializes in drunken prawns, crab and lobster, and steamboats (owners will provide transport back to Sandakan if there are no taxis available). Recommended. **3** *Ming Restaurant*, *Sandakan Renaissance Hotel*, T213299. Km 1, Jln Utara, Cantonese and Szechuan cuisine, particularly renowned for *dim sum* (breakfast). **3** *Japanese Corner*, *Hotel Hsiang Garden*, Jln Leila, Hsiang Garden Estate, T273122. Lobster and tiger prawns, good value and a popular local lunch venue. *See Lok Yum*, next door to *Sea View Garden*, also very popular with locals.

Coffee shops *New Bangsawan*, next to New Bangsawan cinema, just off Jln Leila, Tanah Merah, no great shakes, but best restaurant in Tanah Merah (where there are stacks of coffee shops). *Silver Star Ice Cream and Café*, Third Ave, popular coffee shop with on-site satay stall in the evenings, particularly friendly and helpful management. Recommended. *Union Coffee Shop*, 2nd Flr Hakka Association Building, Third Ave, budget.

Foodstalls Malay foodstalls next to minibus station, just before the community centre on the road to Ramai Ramai, also at summit of Trig Hill.

Trig Hill This is a collection of semi-outdoor restaurants situated at the top of Trig (Trigonometry) Hill. Great views of Sandakan and also good food, especially seafood and steamboat.

Indian 1 *Restoran Awalia*, Roti and curry.

Korean 3-2 *Korean Restaurant*, Hsiang Garden Estate, 1½ km, Jln Leila, T43891.

International 3 *X O Steak House*, Lot 16, Hsiang Garden Estate (opposite the *Hsiang Garden Hotel*), Mile 1.5, Jln Leila, T44033, lobster and tiger prawns and a good choice

Sabah

of fresh fish as well as Australian steaks, buffet barbecue on Fri nights. Recommended. **2** *Hawaii*, *City View Hotel*, Lot 1, Block 23, Third Ave, Western and local food, set lunch. Recommended. **2** *Sandakan Recreation Club*, just off the Padang. **2** *Seoul Garden*, Hsiang Garden Estate, Mile 1.5, Leila Rd, Korean. **1** *Apple Fast Food*, Lorong Edinburgh, good spot for breakfasts. **1** *Fat Cat*, 206 Wisma Sandakan, 18 Jln Haji Saman, several branches around town, breakfasts recommended.

Vegetarian **2** *Supreme Garden Vegetarian Restaurant*, Block 30, Bandar Ramai Ramai, Jln Leila, T213292.

Fast food **2** *Fairwood Restaurant*, Jln Tiga, an inexpensive, a/c fast-food place with all the local favourites, situated in the centre of town.

Entertainment **Cinemas** *Cathay Cinema*, next to Wisma Sabah and town mosque. **Discos and karaoke** There is a karaoke parlour on just about every street. *Tiffany Discotheatre and Karaoke*, Block C, 7-10, Ground and first floors, Jln Leila, Bandar Ramai-Ramai.

Shopping Almost everything in Sandakan is imported. There are some inexpensive batik shops and some good tailors. *Wisma Sandakan*, next to the town mosque and the *Cathay*, is the trendiest place in town and offers 3 floors of a/c Singapore-style shopping.

Sports **Bowling** *Champion Bowl*, Jln Leila, Bandar Ramai Ramai. **Golf** *Sandakan Golf Club*, 10 km out of town, open to non-members. **Recreation clubs** *Sepilok Recreation Club*, Bandar Ramai Ramai, with snooker, sauna and darts as well as karaoke.

Tour operators *Alexander Ng Sandakan Adventure Tours*, Pejabat Pos Jln Utara, Batu 1.5, T212225, F219959, caters for specialist interests and offers individually tailored tours. *Uncle Tan's*, Mile 17.5 (Km 29), Labuk Rd (5 km beyond Sepilok junction), T216227, F271215, inexpensive tours to his 'Utan Wildlife Camp' on the Kinabatangan (max 20 people),

Sabah

Sandakan

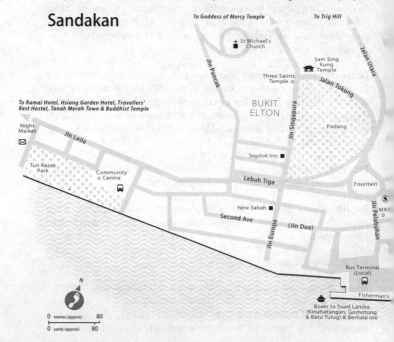

there are guides and a cook at the camp, daily departures during peak season (meals included in price), also runs reasonably priced tours to Turtle Islands and Gomontong Caves, advance bookings can be addressed to PO Box 620, 90007 Sandakan. Recommended. *Unique Tours*, Lot 6, Block 1, Bandar Kim Fung, Batu 4, Jln Utara, T212150. *Wildlife Expeditions*, Room 903, 9th Flr, Wisma Khoo Siak Chiew, Lebuh Tiga, Sim Sim Rd, T219616, F214570 (branches in *Ramada Renaissance Hotel*), the most expensive, but also the most efficient, with the best facilities and the best guides. Recommended. *Discovery Tours*, 1008 10th Flr, Wisma Khoo Siak Chiew, T274106, F274107. *Borneo Ecotours*, c/o *Hotel Hsiang Garden*, Jln Leila, PO Box 82, T220210, F213614. *S.I. Tours*, Lots 1 & 2, 1st Floor, Sandakan Airport Terminal, T0188860449, sitours@po. jaring.my. *Megan Travel Services*, Jln Tiga, T089223377. *Tay Travel Services*, Jln Tiga, T089215584, F271240. Ticketing, tour and hotel services.

Local Local minibuses from the bus stop between the Esso and Shell stations on the sea front on Jln Pryer.

Long distance Air: the airport is 11 km from the town centre (RM10-12 by taxi into town). Early morning flights from KK to Sandakan allow breath-taking close-up views of Mt Kinabalu as the sun rises. Connections with Tomanggong, Miri, Lahad Datu, Kudat, Semporna, Tawau, KK.

Minibus: Sandakan's a/c long distance minibuses leave from the footbridge over Lebuh Tiga or from the minibus station just before the community centre on the Ramai-Ramai road. Be prepared for a long wait before departure, whilst the bus fills up. Regular connections from both stops with most towns in Sabah including Kota Kinabalu, 8 hrs (RM35), Ranau, 3½ hrs (RM25), Lahad Datu (RM15), Tawau (RM25). An a/c coach from KK takes about 7 hrs (RM25).

Transport
See also Ins & outs, page 450
386 km to KK
160 km to Lahad Datu

Airline offices *MAS*, Ground Flr, Sabah Building, Jln Pelabuhan, T273966; *Sabah Air*, Sandakan Airport, T660527, F660545. **Banks** Most around Lebuh Tiga and Jln Pelabuhan. *Hong Kong & Shanghai*, Jln Pelabuhan/Lebuh Tiga. *Standard Chartered*, Jln Pelabuhan. **Communications** Area code: 089. General Post Office: Jln Leila. Parcel post off Lebuh Tiga. **Places of worship** *St Michael's* (Anglican) and *St Mary's* (RC) are on the hill at the south end of Sandakan town. There is also the *True Jesus Church*, *St Joseph's Catholic Church*, the *SIB Baptist Church*, the *All Saints Anglican Church* and the *Basel Church*. **Tourist offices** *National Parks Office*, Jln Leila, T42188. **Useful addresses** Immigration: Federal Building, Jln Leila. Sabah Parks Office: Room 906, 9th Flr, Wisma Khoo, Lebuh Tiga, T273453. Bookings for Turtle Islands National Park (see below). Wildlife Department: 6th Flr, State Secretariat Building, Mile 7 (on road to the airport), T666550, permits for Gomontong caves and Sepilok. Website: www.infosabah.com. my/sabah/city/sandakan.htm, a useful site on the town.

Directory

Sabah

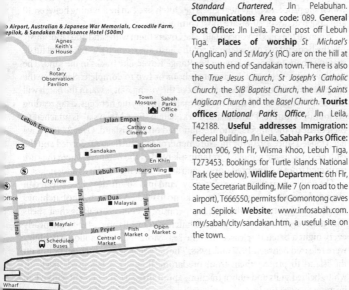

To Airport, Australian & Japanese War Memorials, Crocodile Farm,
epilok, & Sandakan Renaissance Hotel (500m)

Agnes
Keith's
o House

o
Rotary
Observation
Pavilion

Town   Sabah
Mosque Parks
🏛️ Office o

Jalan Empat
Cathay o
Cinema

Lebuh Empat

Sandakan   London

En Khin

Lebuh Tiga   Hung Wing ■

City View ■

Jln Dua
■ Malaysia

Jln Empat
Jln Tiga

■ Mayfair

Jln Pryer   Fish   Open
Central o   Market o Market o
Market

Scheduled
Buses

Jln Lima

Wharf

To Turtle Islands ◥

Turtle Islands National Park

Colour map 4, grid A5 Forty kilometres north of Sandakan, the Turtle Islands are at the south entrance to Labuk Bay. The park is separated from the Philippine island of Bakkungan Kecil by a narrow stretch of water. These eight tiny islands in the Sulu Sea are, together, among the most important turtle breeding spots in all Southeast Asia. The turtle sanctuary is made up of three tiny islands (Pulau Selingaan, Pulau Bakkungan Kecil and Pulau Gulisaan) and also encompasses the surrounding coral reefs and sea, covering 1,700 hectares. On Pulau Bakkungan Kecil there is a small mud volcano.

The islands are famous for their green turtles (*Chelonia mydas*), which account for about four-fifths of the turtles in the park, and hawksbill turtles (*Eretmochelys imbricata*), known locally as *sisik*. Most green turtles lay their eggs on Pulau Selingaan. The green turtles copulate about 50-200m off Pulau Selingaan and can often be seen during the day, their heads popping up like submarine periscopes. Hawksbills prefer to nest on Pulau Gulisaan.

Both species come ashore, year-round, to lay their eggs, although the peak season is between July and October. Even during the off-season between four and 10 turtles come up the beach each night to lay their eggs. Pulau Bakkungan Kecil and Pulau Gulisaan can only be visited during the day but visitors can stay overnight on Pulau Selingaan to watch the green turtles.

The numbers of visitors are restricted to 20 per night in an effort to protect the female turtles, which are easily alarmed by noise and light when laying. Visitors are asked not to build camp fires, shine bright torches or make noise at night on the beach. The turtles should be watched from a distance to avoid upsetting the nesting process. Only the females come ashore; the male waits in the sea nearby for his mate. The females cautiously come ashore to nest after 2000, or with the high tide. The nesting site is above the high tide mark and is cleared by the female's front and hind flippers to make a 'body pit', just under a metre deep. She then digs an egg chamber with her powerful rear flippers after which she proceeds to lay her eggs. The clutch size can be anything between 40 and 200; batches of 50-80 are most common.

When all the eggs have been laid, she covers them with sand and laboriously fills the body pit to conceal the site of the nest, after which the exhausted turtle struggles back to the sea, leaving her Range Rover-like tracks in the sand. The egg-laying process can take about an hour or two to complete. Some say the temperature of the sand effects the sex of the young, if it is warm the batch will be mostly female and if cold, mostly male. After laying her eggs, a tag reading "If found, return to Turtle Island Park, Sabah, East Malaysia" is attached to each turtle by the rangers, who are stationed on each island. Over 27,000 have been tagged since 1970; the measurements of each turtle are recorded and the clutches of eggs are removed and transplanted to the hatchery where they are protected from natural predators – such as monitor lizards, birds and snakes.

The golf ball-sized eggs are placed by hand into 80 cm-deep pits, covered in sand and surrounded by wire. They take up to 60 days to hatch. The hatchlings mostly emerge at night when the temperature is cooler, breaking their shells with their one sharp tooth. There are hatcheries on all three islands and nearly every night a batch is released into the sea. More than 2.6 million hatchlings were released between 1977 and 1988. They are released at different points on the island to protect them from predators: they are a favoured snack for white-bellied gulls and only a fraction, about three to five percent, survive to become teenage turtles.

The tough life of a turtle

Historically, green and hawksbill turtles have been hunted for their meat, shells and their edible eggs (a Chinese delicacy). They were a favourite food of British and Spanish mariners for centuries. Japanese soldiers slaughtered thousands of turtles for food during World War Two. Dynamite fishermen are also thought to have killed off many turtles in both Malaysian and Philippines waters in recent years.

Malaysia, Japan, Hong Kong, Japan and the Philippines, where green turtle meat and eggs are much in demand, are all signatories of the Convention in International Trade in Endangered Species (CITES), and trading in sea turtles has been proscribed under Appendix 1 of the Convention since 1981. However, the eggs are still sold illegally in Sandakan's wet market and can be bought for about RM1 each.

In his book Forest Life and Adventures in the Malay Archipelago, the Swedish adventurer and wildlife enthusiast Eric Mjoberg documents turtle egg-hunting and shell collecting in Sabah and Sarawak in the 1920s. He tells of how the Bajau would lie in wait for hawksbills, grab them and put them on the fire so their horny shields could be removed. "The poor beasts are put straight on the fire so that their shield may be more readily removed, and suffer, in the process, the tortures of the damned. They are then allowed to go alive, or perhaps half-dead into the sea, only to come back again after a few years and undergo the same cruel process." The Bajau, he says, used an 'ingenious

contrivance' to hunt their prey. They would press pieces of common glass against their eyes 'in a watertight fashion' and would lie face-down on a piece of floating wood, dipping their faces into the water, watching for hawksbills feeding on seaweed. They would then dive in, armed with a small harpoon and catch them, knocking them out with a blow to the head.

The British North Borneo Company first introduced conservation measures in 1927 limiting the turtle hunting seasons. In 1964, eight islands in the Selingaan area were constituted as turtle farms; the rights to collect turtle eggs were only granted to contractors, who bid for them at auction. In 1964, the highest bid was RM20,000, which gives some idea of the profitability of the egg-collecting industry. Egg collecting was a hazardous profession: the first (and last) egg collector on Pulau Selingaan was murdered by pirates in 1964. Even today staff at the government hatchery on Pulau Selingaan have to be periodically withdrawn because of the threat posed by pirates. Selingaan always had the richest harvest of about 285,000 eggs a year. Pulau Bakkungan Kecil yielded about 127,000 eggs a year and Pulau Gulisaan, 63,000.

In August 1966 the first turtle hatchery in Malaysia was set up on Pulau Selingaan and in 1971 the three islands now comprising the park were compulsorily acquired by the Sabah state government. See page 279 for a box on the giant leatherback turtle.

Sabah

Permits These are required by all visitors, RM30 from the Sabah Parks Office in Sandakan: Room 906, 9th Floor, Wisma Khoo, Lebuh Tiga (3rd Avenue), T273453. It is necessary to acquire special permits to visit Pulau Bakkungan Kecil and Pulau Gulisaan. Unofficially, however, it is possible to make the five minute boat trip to Pulau Bakkungan Kecil where there is some excellent coral. **NB** Visitors are advised to wait in their chalets for the park ranger, who will tell them when their turtle is laying eggs. Visitors should **not** walk on the beach after dark unaccompanied.

Tours The average cost of a one night tour is RM150-250. Most tour companies (see page 452) operate tours to Turtle Islands and have their own boats, which makes the trip a bit cheaper. An expedition to the islands needs to be well planned;

vagaries such as bad weather, which can prevent you from leaving the islands as planned, can mess up itineraries. Most visitors book their trips in advance.

Best time to visit The driest months and the calmest seas are between March and July. The egg laying season is July-October. Seas are rough between October and February.

Sleeping & eating The number of visitors to the islands is restricted, even at peak season. There are 3 cabins (one with 2 double bedrooms, two with 6 double bedrooms) on Pulau Selingaan (RM150 per night per room). It is necessary to book in advance through the Sabah Parks office, Room 906, 9th Flr, Wisma Khoo, Lebuh Tiga (Third Ave), Sandakan, T273453, F274718. Chalets are equipped with cooking facilities and visitors can bring their own food. Restaurant in the Information Centre building.

Transport *40 km NE of Sandakan* **Ferries** Daily 50-60 seater ferry, 2-3 hrs. The National Parks office in Sandakan can recommend speedboats of licensed tour companies.

Sepilok Orang-utan Sanctuary and Rehabilitation Centre

Colour map 4, grid B5 Sepilok, a reserve of 43 km² of lowland primary rainforest and mangrove was set up in 1964 to protect the orang-utan, *Pongo pygmaeus*, from extinction. It is the first and largest of only three orang-utan sanctuaries in the world and now welcomes around 40,000 visitors a year. Logging has seriously threatened Sabah's population of wild orang-utan, as has their capture for zoos and as pets. The orang-utan (see page 517) lives on the islands of Borneo and Sumatra and there are estimated to be perhaps as few as 10,000 still in the wild. In Sabah there are populations of orang-utan in the Kinabatangan basin region (see page 462) and in the Danum Valley Conservation Area (see page 465) as well as in a few other isolated tracts of jungle.

Sepilok is an old forest reserve, which was gazetted as a forestry experimentation centre as long ago as 1931, and by 1957 logging had been phased out. Orphaned or captured orang-utans which have become too dependent on humans through captivity are rehabilitated and protected under the Fauna Conservation Ordinance and eventually returned to their natural home. Many, for example, may have been captured by the oil palm planters, because they eat the young oil palm trees. Initially, the animals at the Centre and in the surrounding area are fed every day but as they acclimatize, they are sent further and further away or are re-released into the Tabin Wildlife Reserve near Lahad Datu. In 1996, researchers placed microchip collars on the orang-utans enabling them to be tracked over a distance of up to 150 km so that a better understanding of their migratory habits and other behaviour could be acquired.

Sandakan Bay

Small and hairy: the Sumatran rhinoceros

Although not as rare as its Javan brother, the Sumatran, or lesser two-horned rhino (Didermoceros sumatrensis) is severely endangered. It was once widespread through mainland and island Southeast Asia but has now been hunted to the point of extinction; there are probably less than 1,000 in the wild, mostly in Sumatra but with small populations in Borneo, Peninsular Malaysia and Vietnam. Only on Sumatra does it seem to have a chance of surviving. The situation has become so serious that naturalists have established a captive breeding programme as a precaution against extinction in the wild. Unfortunately this has been spectacularly unsuccessful. Around one-third of animals have died during capture or shortly thereafter and, according to Tony and

Jane Whitten, the only recorded birth was in Calcutta – in 1872. The species has suffered from the destruction of its natural habitat, and the price placed on its head by the value that the Chinese attach to its grated horn as a cure-all. Should the Sumatran rhino disappear so too, it is thought, will a number of plants whose seeds will only germinate after passing through the animal's intestines.

The Sumatran rhino is the smallest of all the family, and is a shy, retiring creature, inhabiting thick forest. Tracks have been discovered as high as 3,300m in the Mount Leuser National Park in Sumatra. It lacks the 'armoured' skin of other species and has a soft, hairy hide. It also has an acute sense of smell and hearing, but poor eyesight.

After an initial period of quarantine at Sepilok, newly arrived orang-utans are moved to Platform A and taught necessary survival skills by the rangers. At the age of seven they are moved deeper into the forest to Platform B, about half an hour's walk from Platform A and now not open to the public. At Platform B, they are encouraged to forage for themselves. Other animals brought to Sepilok include Malay sun bears, wild cats and baby elephants. ■ *Feeding times: Platform A, 1000 and 1500.*

Sepilok also has a rare Sumatran rhinoceros, *Didermoceros sumatrensis*, also known as the Asian two-horned rhinoceros, see box above. This enclosure is closed to the public.

The **Mangrove Forest Trail** takes two to three hours one way. The walk takes in transitional forest, pristine lowland rainforest, a boardwalk into a mangrove forest, water holes and a wildlife track. All enquiries at the Visitors' Reception Centre. The **Information Centre**, next to the park headquarters, runs a nature education exhibition with replicas of jungle mammals and educational videos. Video viewing times are at 1130 and 1530. ■ *The park is open from 0900-1130, 1400-1530, RM10, video camera RM10. It is worth getting to the park early.*

The new **Rainforest Interpretation Centre** on the road to Sepilok provides detailed and informative displays about the vegetation in the area. It is run by the Forest Research Centre, which is also found on this road. Great emphasis is given to participation, with questionnaires, games and so on; it offers a wide range of information about all aspects of tropical rainforests and the need for their conservation. The centre is located in the Forest Research Centre's arboretum and in addition to the exhibits there is a 800m rainforest walk around the lake. ■ *Mon-Thur 0815-1215, 1400-1600, Fri 0815-1135, 1400-1600, Sat 0815-1215, free. A free booklet is available. For more information contact the Forest Research Centre, PO Box 14-07, T531522, F531068.*

Excursions

Sabah

Sleeping &
eating
Price codes: see inside
front cover
There is a good
restaurant at the Centre

B *Wildlife Lodge*, Mile 14, Labuk Rd, Sepilok Orang-Utan Sanctuary, PO Box 2082, 100m behind the *Government Resthouse*, T089533031, F089533029. Office in Sandakan: Ground Flr, Lots 1 and 2, Block C, Taman Grandview, Sim Sim Highway, T089273711, F089273010. Some a/c, some dorm beds for RM20, cheaper rooms have shared bathrooms, with hot water showers, cafeteria. The *Lodge* is the realization of a dream for John and Judy Lim, who have gradually purchased all the land on the edge of the forest and over the past 3 years have been landscaping the area surrounding 3 manmade lakes and clearing the fruit orchards they inherited. They have planted lots of flowering and fruiting trees, attracting butterflies and birds in the process. Pleasant restaurant, great setting, clean and comfortable, boats for fishing available. Recommended. **B-C** *Sepilok Jungle Resort* Labuk Rd, Sandakan T089 533031 F533029 sepilokjr@yahoo.com. New wooden chalets, well furnished with a good range of accommodation, price includes breakfast. Some a/c and some cheaper dorm beds. **C** *Orang-Utan Rehabilitation Centre Rest House (Government Resthouse)*, Mile 14 Labuk Rd, T089531180. Basic and characterless The *Sepilok B&B* is preferable. **C** *Sepilok B&B*, Jln Sepilok, of Mile 14, PO Box 155, T089532288, F089217668. Breakfast included. Around 1 km from the Orang-Utan sanctuary. Better than the Centre accommodation and good value although there is no hot water. **Camping** Campsite at *Sepilok Wildife Lodge*.

Transport
23 km to Sandakan

Bus Eight daily public buses from Sandakan, from the central mini-bus terminal in front of *Nak Hotel*. Ask for the Sepilok Batu 14 line. From the airport, the most convenient way to reach Sepilok is by **taxi**. Sepilok is 1.9 km from the main road.

Directory

Useful information Further information about Sepilok can be obtained from: Co-ordinator, Sepilok Orang-Utan Rehabilitation Centre, Sabah Wildlife Department, WDT 200, 95000 Sandakan, T089-531180, F089-531189.

Kinabatangan River

At 560 km, this river is Sabah's longest. Much of the lower basin is gazetted under the Kinabatangan Wildlife Sanctuary and meanders through a flood plain, creating numerous ox-bow lakes and an ideal environment for some of the best wildlife in Malaysia. One of the principal reasons why the Kinabatangan has remained relatively unscathed by Sabah's rapacious logging is because much of the land is permanently waterlogged and the forest contains only a small number of commercially valuable trees. Just some of the animals include: tree snake, crocodile, civet cat, otter, monitor lizard, long-tailed and pig-tailed macaque, silver-, red- and grey-leaf monkey and proboscis monkey. It is the most accessible area in Borneo to see the proboscis monkeys which are best viewed from a boat in the late afternoon, when they converge on tree tops by the river banks to settle for the night. Sumatran rhinoceros have also been spotted (see box) and herds of wild elephant often pass through the park. The birdlife is particularly good and includes oriental darter, egret, storm's stork, osprey, coucal owl, frogmouth, bulbul, spiderhunter, oriole, flowerpecker and several species of hornbill. (For details on Borneo's flora and fauna, see page 517.)

Because of the diversity of its wildlife, the Kinabatangan riverine forest area has been proposed as a forest reserve. In addition, there has been little disturbance from human settlements: the Kinabatangan basin has always been sparsely inhabited because of flooding and the threat posed by pirates. The inhabitants of the Kinabatangan region are mostly Orang Sungai or people of mixed ancestry including Tambanua, Idahan, Dusun, Suluk, Bugis, Brunei and Chinese. The best destination for a jungle river safari is not on the Kinabatangan itself, but on the narrow, winding Sungai Menanggol tributary, about 6 km from Sukau. The Kinabatangan estuary, largely mangrove, is also rich in wildlife, and is a haven for migratory birds. Boats can be chartered from Sandakan to Abai (at the mouth of the river).

Batu Tulug, also known as Batu Putih, or White Stone, on the Kinabatangan River 100 km upstream from Sukau, is a cave containing wooden coffins dating back several hundred years. Some of the better examples have been removed to the Sabah State Museum in KK. The caves are about 1 km north of the Kinabatangan Bridge, on the east side of the Sandakan-Lahad Datu road. Take the Sukau bus from Sandakan, 1400.

Exploring the Kinabatangan Visitors who prefer an in-depth look at the area's wildlife can stay overnight at Sukau, two hours by road from Sandakan, where accommodation is provided by local tour operators. Tour operators take visitors by boat in the late afternoon through the freshwater swamp forest to see proboscis monkeys and other wildlife. There are also walks through the jungle. Because of the lack of public transport to Sukau, the only way to visit the area is with a tour; all tours must be booked in Sandakan or KK.

Sleeping

Most companies running tours to the Kinabatangan put their guests up in Sukau. The one exception is *Borneo Eco Tours* (see below). *Sukau Rainforest Lodge (SRL)*, accessible by boat from Sukau, provides eco-friendly accommodation for 40 visitors, in traditional Malaysian-style chalets, on stilts. All 20 rooms have solar-powered fans, twin beds, mosquito netting, and attached tiled bathroom with hot water. Other facilities include an open dining and lounge area (good restaurant), garden and sundeck overlooking the rainforest, and gift shop. Friendly and efficient service. All in all, a shining example of eco-tourism at its best, highly recommended.

Tour operators

All Sandakan telephone numbers are prefixed with 089

Borneo Eco Tours, c/o *Hotel Hsiang Garden*, Jln Leila, PO Box 82, Sandakan, T220210, F213614. *Discovery Tours*, 1008, 10th Flr, Wisma Khoo Siak Chiew, Sandakan, T274106, F274107. *S.I. Tours*, Lot 3B, 3rd Flr, Yeng Ho Hong Building, Sandakan, T213502, F271513. *Wildlife Expeditions*, Room 903, 9th Flr, Wisma Khoo Siak Chiew, Sandakan and Ground Floor, *Ramada Renaissance Hotel*, Jln Utara, Sandakan, T219616, F214570. *Sukau Rainforest Lodge (SRL)*, owned and managed by *Borneo Eco Tours*, Shoplot 12A, 2nd Flr, Lorong Bernam 3, Taman Soon Kiong, Kota Kinabalu, T234009, F233688, betsbl@po.jaring.my. This last establishment is the most expensive tour operator but is worth it, as it can provide much more than the others and has won several awards for excellence. It is situated at the edge of the sanctuary in a secluded spot on the Kinabatangan River. Qualified guides use wooden boats built by local orang sungai craftsmen, powered by electric engines to minimize noise disturbance to wildlife.

Transport

Road It is possible to charter a minibus to take you from Suad Lamba to Gomontong and on to Sukau. It will pick passengers up again at a set time, by arrangement (RM70-100 return). A bus leaves from Sandakan to Sukau (via Gomontong turn-off) at 1100 and 1400, 115 km 3½ hrs (RM20). The return bus leaves Sukau for Sandakan at 0600.

Boat To Suad Lamba, on the far side of Sandakan Bay leaves from the rear of Sandakan's wet market at 1100 every day, 1½ hrs, RM3. The return boat leaves Suad Lamba at 0530.

Lahad Datu

Lahad Datu is Malaysia's 'wild East' at its wildest, and its recent history testifies to its reputation as the capital of cowboy country. The population is an intriguing mixture of Filipinos, Sulu islanders, migrants from Kalimantan, Orang Bugis, Timorese and a few Malays. Most came to work on the oil palm plantations. Nowadays there are so many migrants few can find employment. There are reckoned to be more illegal Filipino immigrants in Lahad Datu than the whole official population put together. Piracy in the Sulu Sea and the offshore islands in Kennedy Bay is rife; local fishermen live in terror.

The town itself is grubby and uninteresting. During the Second World War, the Japanese made Lahad Datu their naval headquarters for East Borneo. After the war, the timber companies moved in: the British Kennedy Bay Timber Company built Lahad Datu's first plywood mill in the early 1950s. Oil palm plantations grew up in the hinterland after the timber boom finished in the 1970s. As for the town, what it lacks in aesthetic appeal is made up for by its colourful recent history.

Kampung Panji is a water village with a small market at the end of Jalan Teratai, where many of the poorer immigrant families live.

Excursions **Beaches and islands** The only good beaches are on the road to Tungku;
For Danum Valley, see Pantai Perkapi and Pantai Tungku. They can be reached by minibus from
page 465 Lahad Datu or by boat from the old wharf. It is possible to get to the nearby islands from the old wharf behind the *Mido Hotel*, but at the moment it is too dangerous for tourists.

Madai Caves are about 2 km off the Tawau-Lahad Datu road, near Kunak. The caves are an important archaeological site; there is evidence they were inhabited over 15,500 years ago. The birds' nests are harvested three times a year by local Idahan people whose lean-to kampung goes right up to the cave mouth. Your own transport is required for this trip as it doesn't really cater for tourists.

Another 15 km west of Madai is **Baturong**, another limestone massif and cave system in the middle of what was originally Tingkayu Lake. The route is not obvious, so it is advisable to take a local guide. Stone tools, wooden coffins and rock paintings have been found there. Evidence of humans dating from 16,000 years ago, after the lake drained away can be found at the huge rock overhang. Take a torch. It is possible to camp here. To get there, take a minibus from Lahad Datu.

Gunung Silam, 8 km from Lahad Datu on the Tawau road, a track leads up the mountain to a Telekom station at 620m and from there, a jungle trail to the summit. There are good views over the bay, when it isn't misty, and out to the islands beyond. It is advisable to take a guide. There is the *Silam Lodge* (**B**), Silam, T088243245, F088254227, which is owned by the *Borneo Rainforest Lodge* and is mostly used by people in transfer to the Danum Valley. Minibuses run from Lahad Datu.

Sleeping **B** *Executive*, Jln Teratai, T881333, F881777. A smart new 53-room hotel that is easily
Lahad Datu is not a the priciest in town. Rather an uninspiring place and over priced, but nevertheless the
popular tourist spot & safest option if you can afford to spend liberally. **C** *Permaisaba*, Block 1, Lot 3, 1/4 Jln
accommodation is poor Tengah Nipah, T883800, F883681. Five mins' drive from the airport and town, seafood
& expensive. Avoid the restaurant, Malaysian and Indian food, conference hall, free transfers to/from the air-
Perdana & Venus hotels port and town. Big rooms with bathroom attached and hot water, information on the
on Jln Seroja Danum Valley, characterless but convenient. **C** *Mido*, 94 Jln Main, T881800, F881487. A/c, restaurant, the façade (facing the *Standard Chartered Bank*) is pock-marked with M-16 bullet holes, the result of over-curious residents watching the 1986 pirate raid

on the bank; the *Mido* comes with all the sleaze of the 'wild East' and fails miserably to live up to its reputation as the best hotel in town. **C** *Ocean*, Jln Teratai (just past the Esso Station), T881700. A/c, shower. *Government Resthouse*, T81579.

Seafood 3 *Melawar*, 2nd Flr, Block 47, off Jln Teratai (around the corner from the **Eating** *Mido Hotel*), seafood restaurant, popular with locals. **3** *Ping Foong*, 1½ km out of Lahad Datu, on Sandakan Rd, open-air seafood restaurant, highly recommended by locals. **2** *Evergreen Snack Bar and Pub*, on 2nd Flr, Jln Teratai, opposite the Hap Seng Building, a/c, excellent fish and chips and best-known for its tuna steaks. Recommended. **2** *Golden Key*, on stilts over the sea opposite the end of Jln Teratai, it is really just a tumble-down wooden coffee shop, but is well known for its seafood. **2** *Good View*, just over 500m out of town on Tengku Rd. Recommended by locals. **2** *Seng Kee*, Block 39, opposite *Mido Hotel* and next to *Standard Chartered Bank*, cheap and good. *Restoran Ali*, opposite *Hotel New Sabah*, Indian, good roti. **Foodstalls 1** *Pasar Malam* behind *Mido Hotel* on Jln Kastam Lama. Spicy barbecued fish (*ikan panggang*) and skewered chicken wings recommended.

The *Lacin cinema*, which usually screens violent kung-fu movies, is next to the post **Entertainment** office on Jln Kenanga.

There is a new *Central Market* on Jln Bungaraya and a spice market off Jln Teratai **Shopping** where Indonesian smugglers tout Gudang Garam cigarettes and itinerant dentists and bumohs draw large crowds.

Borneo Nature Tours, Block 3, Fajar Centre, T880207, F885051. **Tour operators**

Air connections with Tawau, Sandakan, Semporna, KK and Kudat. **Minibus** Mini- **Transport** buses and what are locally known as wagons (basically seven-seater, 4WD Mitsubishis) leave from the bus station on Jln Bunga Raya (behind Bangunan Hap Seng at the mosque end of Jln Teratai) and from opposite the Shell station. Regular connections with Tawau, 2½ hrs, Semporna (RM10), Sandakan (RM17), Madai. **Boat** Fishing boats take paying passengers from the old wharf (end of Jln Kastam Lama) to the Kennedy Bay islands, Tawau and Semporna, although time-wise (and, more to the point, safety-wise) it makes much more sense to go by road or air.

Airline offices *MAS*, Ground Flr, *Mido Hotel*, Jln Main, T881707. **Banks** *Standard Chartered*, in **Directory** front of *Mido Hotel*. **Communications** Area code: 089. **Post Office:** Jln Kenanga, next to the Lacin cinema. **Useful addresses** *Sabah Foundation* 2nd Flr, Hap Seng Building, Jln Main, T881092. Bookings for Danum Valley. Bookings can also be made at the Sabah Foundation headquarters in Kota Kinabalu (T354496).

Danum Valley Conservation Area

Danum Valley's 438 km² of virgin jungle is the largest expanse of undisturbed *Colour map 4, grid B5* lowland dipterocarp forest in Sabah. The field centre, which is 65 km west of Lahad Datu and 40 km from the nearest habitation was set up by the Sabah Foundation (Yayasan) in 1985 for forest research, nature education and recreation; when we last visited the centre, it was only open to Malaysian school trips. Tourists are allowed to visit **only** through the *Borneo Rainforest Lodge*. The Segama River runs through the conservation area, and past the field centre. The Danum River is a tributary of the Segama joining it 9 km downstream of the Field Centre. Gunung Danum (1,093m) is the highest peak, 13 km southwest of the Field Centre. Within the area is a Yayasan Sabah timber concession, which is tightly controlled.

This area has never really been inhabited, although there is evidence of a burial site which is thought to be for the Dusun people who lived here about 300 years ago. There is also growing evidence of pre-historic cave dwellers in the Segama River area. Not far downstream from the field centre, in a riverside cave, two wooden coffins have been found, together with a copper bracelet and a tapai jar, all of uncertain date. There is evidence of some settlement during the Japanese occupation; townspeople came upstream to escape from the Japanese troops. The area was first recommended as a national park by the World Wide Fund for Nature's Malaysia Expedition in 1975 and designated a conservation area in 1981. The field centre was officially opened in 1986.

The main reason for this large conservation area is to undertake research into the impact of logging on flora and fauna and to try and improve forest management, to understand processes which maintain tropical rainforest and to provide wildlife management and training opportunities for Sabahans. Many are collaborative projects between Malaysian and foreign scientists. The Sabah state tourism promotion board has recently thought to capitalize on this remote tract of jungle though. Following the opening of the Borneo Rainforest Lodge, Danum Valley will be promoted as a high-style expedition centre.

Flora & fauna
For details on Borneo's flora & fauna, see page 517

Because of its size and remoteness, Danum Valley is home to some of Sabah's rarest animals and plants. The dipterocarp forest is some of the oldest, tallest and most diverse in the world, with 200 species of tree per hectare; there are over 300 labelled trees in the conservation area. The conservation area is teeming with wildlife: Sumatran rhinoceroses have been recorded, as have elephants, clouded leopards, orang-utans, proboscis monkeys, crimson langur, pig-tailed macaques, sambar deer, bearded pigs, western tarsier, sunbears and 275 species of bird including hornbills, rufous picolet, flowerpeckers and kingfishers. A species of monkey, which looks like an albino version of the red-leaf monkey, was first seen on the road to Danum in 1988, and appears to be unique to this area. There are guided nature walks on an extensive trail system. Features include a canopy walkway, ancient Dusun burial site, waterfalls and a self-guided trail. ■ *RM30 per person. Leech socks are essential here.*

Sleeping

AL *Danum Valley & Borneo Rainforest Lodge*, c/o Borneo Nature Tours, Block 3, Ground Flr, Fajar Centre, Lahad Datu, T089880207, F089885051. KK office: *Innoprise Jungle Lodge*, Block D, Lot 10, 3rd Flr, Sadong Jaya Complex, T244100, F254227, email ijl@po.jaring.my. One of the finest tourism developments in Sabah. Eighteen bungalows in a magnificent setting beside the Danum River, built on stilts from belian (ironwood) and based on traditional Kadazan design with connecting wooden walkways. There are 28 rooms, each with private bathroom and balcony overlooking the Danum River, good restaurant, jacuzzi (solar-heated water). Based on *Tiger Tops* in Nepal and designed by naturalists, the centre hopes to combine a wildlife experience in a remote primary rainforest with comfort and privacy and provide high quality natural history information. There is a conference hall, excellent guides (including a very good woman called Mizy), who pre-plan their routes so that visitors don't bump into each other while thinking they are latter day Indiana Jones's; day visits to a forest management centre, good library of resource books, after dinner slide shows, a gift shop, rafting is available and night drives can be organized. Mountain bikes, fishing rods and river tubes all available for hire. Electricity available all day; the lodge is being marketed internationally in association with *Tiger Tops*. Expensive but well worth it. Price includes meals and guided jungle excursions. *Forest Cabin* (built by Operation Raleigh), 18 km from field centre. *Hostel*, 30 beds; *Resthouse*, 5 double rooms, often booked up with visiting scientists.

From Lahad Datu, turn left along the logging road at Km 15 on the Lahad Datu-Tawau road to Taliwas and then left again to field centre. The *Borneo Rainforest Lodge* is 97 km from Lahad Datu; they provide a transfer service (2 hrs), telephone the *Lodge* for details. **Air** 2 flights daily with MAS from Kota Kinabalu to Lahad Datu. **Bus** Lahad Datu is 7 hrs from KK, 3 hrs from Sandakan, 3 hrs from Semporna, 2 hrs from Tawau.

Transport
85 km W of Lahad Datu

Semporna

Semporna is a small fishing town at the end of the peninsula and is the main departure point for Sipidan Island, see below. Semporna has a lively and very photogenic market, spilling out onto piers over the water. It is a Bajau town and is known for its seafood. There are scores of small fishing boats, many with outriggers and square sails. There is a regatta of these traditional boats every March. The town is built on an old coral reef, said to be 35,000 years old, that was exposed by the uplift of the sea bed. Many illegal Filipino immigrants pass through Semporna, as it is only two hours from the nearest Philippine island, which gives the place quite a different feel to other Malay towns.

Phone code: 089
Colour map 4, grid B6

The islands off Semporna stand along the edge of the continental shelf, which drops away to a depth of 200m to the south and east of Pulau Ligitan, the outermost island in the group. Darvel Bay, and the adjacent waters, are dotted with small, mainly volcanic islands all part of the 73,000 acre Semporna Marine Park. The bigger ones are Pulau Mabol, Pulau Kapalai, Pulau Si Amil, Pulau Danawan and Pulau Sipadan. The coral reefs surrounding these islands have around 70 genera of coral, placing them, in terms of their diversity, on a par with Australia's Great Barrier Reef. More than 200 species of fish have also been recorded in these waters.

Locals live in traditional boats called *lipa-lipa* or in pilehouses at the water's edge and survive by fishing. In the shallow channels off Semporna, there are three fishing villages, built on stilts: Kampung Potok Satu, Kampung Potok Dua and Kampung Larus. There are many more islands than are marked on the map; most are hilly, uninhabited and have beautiful white sandy beaches.

Reefs in Semporna Marine Park include Bohey Dulang, Sibuan Ulaiga, Tetugan, Mantabuan Bodgaya, Sibuan, Maigu, Selakan and Sebangkat. Pulau Bohey Dulang is a volcanic island with a Japanese-run pearl culture station. Visitors can only visit it if there is a boat from the pearl culture station going out. The Kaya Pearl company leases part of the lagoon and Japanese pearl oysters are artificially implanted with a core material to induce the growth of pearls. The oysters are attached to rafts moored in the lagoon. The pearls are later harvested and exported directly to Japan. The islands can be reached by local fishing boats from the main jetty by the market, including Sibun, Sibankat, Myga and Selakan.

Excursions
For Sipadan, see below

Sabah

B *Dragon Inn*, T781088, F781008. Stands out as the hotel built on stilts over the sea, a/c, restaurant, quite a novel setting but not great value. **C** *Lee's Resthouse and Cafe*, Pekau Baru, Semporna New Town, T784491, F782106, joejack@tm.net.my. Restaurant, a/c, TV, hot shower, recently redone, very helpful staff. Recommended. **C-D** *Seafest Inn*, Jln Kaslam, T782399, F781282. A/c, hot shower, cable TV, overlooking the sea. Owned by a slightly overbearing Australian who has spent time making this the best place in town. Email facilities also available. Cheaper price is for a 3 bed dorm. Recommended.

Sleeping

Eating   **2** *Floating Restoran dan Bar*, attached to *Dragon Inn*, pile house with good seafood, verify prices before ordering. There is an excellent Muslim restaurant at the top end of town, furthest from the market, and a number of coffee shops. **2** *Seafest Restaurant*, next to the *Seafest Inn*, Malay food predominantly with some excellent fish dishes. Good standard for very reasonable prices.

Shopping   Cultured pearls are sold by traders in town. Filipino handicrafts.

Sport   The *Semporna Ocean Tourism Centre* has recently been built, with a marina from where all sea sports can be organized.

Transport   **Air** Regular connections with Sandakan. **Minibus** Minibus station in front of
106 km N of Tawau   USNO headquarters. Regular connections with Tawau and Lahad Datu. **Boat** To charter a boat costs RM200 to Sipadan. There are day trips from Tawau to Sipadan with bigger boats, cutting the price down to RM50 (weekends only); the local papers supply information.

Directory   **Communications** General Post Office: next to minibus station. **Telephone Code:** 089.

Sipadan Island Marine Reserve

Colour map 4, grid C6   The venerable French marine biologist Jacques Cousteau 'discovered' Sipadan in 1989 and after spending three months diving around the island from his research vessel *Calypso* had this to say: "I have seen other places like Sipadan 45 years ago, but now no more. Now we have found an untouched piece of art." Since then Sipadan has become a sub-aqua Shangri-La for serious divers. In September 1990 Australia's *Sport Diving* magazine called the island "one of the most exciting dive spots imaginable an absolutely bewildering underwater experience." The reef is without parallel in Malaysia. But Sipadan Island is not just for scuba divers: it is a magnificent tiny tropical island with pristine beaches and crystal clear water and its coral can be enjoyed by even the most amateur of snorkellers.

Pulau Sipadan is the only oceanic island in Malaysia; it is not attached to the continental shelf, and stands on a limestone and coral stalk, rising 200m from the bed of the Celebes Sea. The limestone pinnacle mushrooms out near the surface, but a few metres offshore drops off in a sheer underwater cliff to the seabed. The reef comes right into the island's small pier, allowing snorkellers to swim along the edge of the coral cliff, while remaining close to the coral-sand beach. The edge is much further out around the rest of the island. The tiny island has a cool forested interior and it is common to see flying foxes and monitor lizards. It is also a stop-over point for migratory birds, and was originally declared a bird sanctuary in 1933. It has been a marine reserve since 1981 and three Wildlife Department officials are permanently stationed on the island. The island is also a breeding ground for the green turtle; August and September are the main egg-laying months (see page 459).

Sipadan is known for its underwater overhangs and caverns, funnels and ledges, all covered in coral. Five metres down from the edge of the precipice there is a coral overhang known as the Hanging Gardens, where coral dangles from the underside of the reef. The cavern is located on the cliff right in front of the island's accommodation area. Its mouth is 24m wide and the cave, which has fine formations of stalactites and stalagmites, goes back almost 100m, sometimes less than 4m below the surface. Visibility blurs where fresh water mixes with sea water. Inside, there are catacombs of underwater passages.

The island is disputed between the Indonesian and Malaysian governments. Indonesia has asked Malaysia to stop developing marine tourism facilities on Sipadan. Malaysia's claim to the island rests on historical documents signed by the British and Dutch colonial administrations. Periodically the two sides get around the negotiating table, but it appears that neither is prepared to make a big issue of Sipadan. Occasionally guests on the island see Indonesian or Malaysian warships just offshore and in 1994 rumours were circulating in Sabah that the Governor of the neighbouring Indonesian province of Kaltim wanted to send settlers to the island. A third party also contests ownership of Sipadan: a Malaysian who claims his grandfather, Abdul Hamid Haji, was given the island by the Sultan of Sulu. He has the customary rights to collect turtles eggs on the island, although the Malaysian government disputes this.

The island's tourist facilities are run by three tour companies, who control everything. They are required to restrict the number of visitors allowed on the island at any one time to about 40 and on arrival visitors have to sign a guarantee that they will do nothing to spoil the island. One of the directors of the Sipadan Dive Centre, a lawyer from Kota Kinabalu, has presented proposals to the state government concerning future environmental safeguards for the island. These have the support of the other resort owners on Sipadan who have agreed to bear the costs together. The proposals recommend that human activity be carefully controlled by further restricting the number of visitors (particularly day-trippers and weekenders), limiting the size and speed of boats using the jetty, the introduction of a bio-digester to dispose of all waste and a scale-down of all diving and snorkelling activities during the height of the northeast and southwest monsoons, to allow the island a recovery period. These proposals have yet to be endorsed by the state government.

Tours Each operator rents out equipment (RM75-100 per day) and provides all food and accommodation. Pre-arranged packages operated by the companies include air transfer to and from Kota Kinabalu. 'Walk-in' rates marginally cheaper. *Borneo Divers*, Rooms 401-412, 4th Flr, Wisma Sabah, Kota Kinabalu, T222226, F221550, bdivers@po.jaring.my. Runs monthly trips, eight to 20 divers for any trip, packages (all in) cost around US$1,065 (five days per four nights). *Pulau Sipadan Resort*, 484, Block P, Bandar Sabindo, T765200, F763575, www.sipadan-resort.com, psrt@po.jaring.my. Organizes dive tours, food and lodging and diving instruction, snorkelling equipment is also available, maximum of 30 divers at any one time; *Sipadan Dive Centre*, A1103, 10th Flr, Wisma Merdeka, Jln Tun Razak, Kota Kinabalu, T240584, F240415, sipadan@po.jaring.my. Packages (all in) approx: US$740 (5D/4N). Recommended. **NB** *Borneo Divers* and *Sipadan Dive Centre* both provide four-day PADI training courses. The PADI Divemaster Scuba courses – conducted off KK's TAR Park islands – cost US$250-US$330. The *Coral Island Cruises tour company* (based in KK see page 415) also operates a small ship, the MV *Coral Topaz*, which makes special diving voyages to the Sipadan/Ligitan island group. The 'live-on-board' dive vessel features a/c accommodation, bars, lounges and buffet meals. Five days/four nights cruises cost US$760 per person (diving equipment included).

Best time to visit The best diving season is from mid-February to mid-December when visibility is greater (20-60m); mostly drift diving; night diving is said to be spectacular.

Sleeping & eating A *Sipadan Longhouse Resort*, fan rooms with shower, buffet Western food, RM390 for 2 days and nights, full board. *Sipadan Lodge*, a/c, hot water, local, Chinese and Western food, private boats available. The island's drinking water is brought in from

Sabah

Lines on the map: sensitive territory

There's a new distraction on the horizon for scuba divers and sun-worshippers on Sipadan Island: warships. Because Sipadan, along with the neighbouring island of Ligitan, is disputed by the Indonesian and Malaysian governments, frigates from the alternate navies regularly make their presence felt by prowling around the turquoise waters like cats sniffing out their territorial boundaries. The issue of the overlapping claims lay dormant for decades but things changed with the discovery of Sipadan's incomparable underwater charms. With Malaysia giving the go-ahead to the construction of resorts on Sipadan, the government in Jakarta has been pressing harder for an urgent diplomatic solution to the dispute.

Under an agreement signed in 1969, Malaysia has been allowed to retain control of the islands until a solution is found. But Indonesia now says that agreement is being flouted. The two sides agreed to halt any developments until the dispute is settled by negotiation, but even the presence of the Indonesian frigates does not appear to have discouraged Malaysian developers. A joint commission has recently been studying the competing claims; both sides have reportedly produced further evidence to substantiate their claims. But a successful resolution of the dispute – which, thanks to good neighbourly relations, is extremely unlikely to escalate – could pave the way to the resolution of other similar disputes in the region.

Another long-standing dispute is the Philippine claim to the whole of Sabah, which Manila has never officially recognized as a legal part of the Malaysian Federation, formed in 1963. The Philippines' historic claim to the territory rests on Sabah's original status as a dependency of the Sultanate of Sulu, in the Philippine islands, southwest of Mindanao. The sultan leased the land to the British North Borneo Chartered Company in 1877 and the British government inherited the lease when Sabah became a crown colony after the Second World War. Manila maintains that London had no right to then cede that lease to Kuala Lumpur and has never relinquished its claim, to the chagrin of Malaysia's federal government.

The very existence of the Association of Southeast Asian Nations (ASEAN) puts the brakes on the escalation of such disputes. Today, trade and investment deals have helped paper over cracks in bilateral relations, formalizing the characteristically non-confrontational Asian way of doing things. But there is one outstanding territorial quarrel which is yet to really raise its ugly head: the Spratly Islands – an archipelago of 250 atolls dispersed over 800,000 km² in the middle of the South China Sea. They are claimed by China, Vietnam, The Philippines, Malaysia and Taiwan; Indonesia and Brunei also stake claims to various islands but have not yet occupied them. Because the atolls straddle shipping lanes to Japan and lie on top of what are thought to be oil and mineral-rich strata, the Spratlys represent Southeast Asia's hottest potential flashpoint.

Semporna. *Sipadan Dive Centre*'s facilities are marginally better; its chalets have attached bathrooms and hot water.

Sport **Deep sea fishing** For tuna, marlin, barracuda and bonito, fishing can be organized from Sipadan. Trawler operated by *Pulau Sipadan Resort* is charged per person and per hour. Early mornings and evenings are best. Because the island and the reef are protected, line fishing from the shore is illegal.

Transport **Boat** Organized by the 2 tour companies from Semporna, including in price of trip.
22 km from Semporna Also boats from Tawau once a week from the main dock (much rougher journey as
in the Celebes Sea have to go more on the open sea). **Speedboat**: hired, 1½ hrs from Semporna.

Located between Semporna and Sipadan, this island of 21 hectares is considerably larger than Sipadan and is partly home to Bajau fishermen who live in traditional palm thatched houses. In contrast to Sipadan's untouched forest, the island is predominantly planted with coconut trees. Diving has been the most recent discovery; an Australian diver claims it is "one of the richest single destinations for exotic small marine life anywhere in the world". It has already become known as the world's best 'muck diving'. The island is surrounded by gentle sloping reefs with depths from 3-35m and a wall housing numerous species of hard corals. Visibility is usually at least 12m.

Mabul Island

Sleeping Mabul was chosen to provide more upmarket accommodation than that found on Sipadan, offering exclusive private chalets. For people diving off Sipadan, Mabul is a convenient place to stay and considerably less crowded. There are two resorts on the island. **AL** *Sipadan Water Village*, for reservation PO Box 62156, T089751777, 089784227, F089752997, swvill@tm.net.my. General sales agent: *Pan Borneo Tours and Travel*, constructed on several wharves in Bajau water village-style on ironwood stilts over the water. Thirty five chalets with private balconies, hot water showers, restaurant serving good range of cuisine, dive shop and centre, deep sea fishing tours available. Budget or student travellers are sometimes given large discounts. Prices range from RM470 for divers, including equipment, to RM370 for non-divers. **L** *Sipadan Mabul Resort*, located at the southern tip of the island, overlooking Sipadan, PO Box 14125, T08823000, F088242003, mabul@po.jaring.my. Twenty five beach chalets with a/c, hot water showers, balcony, pool and jacuzzi, restaurant serving Chinese and Western food in buffet style, all inclusive price, padi diving courses, snorkelling, windsurfing, deep sea fishing, volleyball, private diving boats.

Transport Air and sea: flight to Tawau, met upon arrival and then taken to Semporna (1½ hrs), from where it is a 30 min boat ride to Mabul Island.

Sabah

Tawau

Tawau is a timber port in Sabah's southeastern corner. It is a busy commercial centre and the main channel for the entry of Indonesian workers into Sabah. Kalimantan is visible, just across the bay.

Colour map 4, grid C5

The town was developed in the early 19th century by the British who planted hemp. The British also developed the logging industry in Sabah, using elephants from Burma. The Bombay Burma Timber Company became the North Borneo Timber Company in 1950; a joint British and Sabah government venture.

Tawau is surrounded by plantations and smallholdings of rubber, copra, cocoa and palm oil. The local soils are volcanic and very fertile and palm oil has recently taken over from cocoa as the predominant crop; Malaysian cocoa prices dropped when its quality proved to be 20 percent poorer than cocoa produced in Nigeria and the Ivory Coast. In addition, the cocoa plants became diseased. As a result of the decline, many of the cocoa growers emigrated to the Ivory Coast. KL is now an established research centre for palm oil and recently it has been discovered that palm oil can be used as a fuel.

Now that the Sandakan area has been almost completely logged, Tawau has taken over as the main logging centre on the east coast. The forest is disappearing fast but there are ongoing reforestation programmes. At Kalabakan west of Tawau there is a well established, large-scale reforestation project with experiments on fast-growing trees such as *Albizzia falcataria*, which is said to grow 30m in five years. There are now large plantation areas. The tree is processed into, among other things, paper for paper money.

Excursions **Tawau Hills State Park** lies 24 km northwest of Tawau; it protects Tawau's water catchment area. The Tawau River flows through the middle of the 27,972 hectare park and forms a natural deep water pool, at Table Waterfall, which is good for swimming. There is a trail from there to some hot water springs and another to the top of Bombalai Hill, an extinct volcano. Most of the forest in the park below 500m has been logged. Only the forest on the central hills and ridges is untouched. The park is popular with locals at weekends. **Camping** is possible but bring your own equipment. ■ *RM2, for more information, contact Ranger Office, Tawau Hills Park, T011-810676, F011-884917. Access to the park is via a maze of rough roads through the Borneo Abaca Limited agricultural estates. Probably best to hire a taxi.*

Sleeping **A** *Belmont Marco Polo*, Jln Abaca/Jln Clinic, T777988, F763739. A/c, restaurant, best
Hotels here are not great hotel in Tawau although considerably dearer. **B** *Emas*, Jln Utara, T762000, F763569.
value for money. Avoid A/c, restaurant. **B** *Merdeka*, 3023 Jln Masjid, T776655, F761743. A/c, restaurant.
the cheaper lodging **B** *North Borneo*, 52-53 Dunlop St, T763060, F773066. A/c, TV, hot shower, reasonable
houses around Jln but expensive for Tawau. **B** *Millennium*, 561 Jln Bakau, T771155, F755511. A/c, spa-
Stephen Tan, Jln Chester cious rooms. Considerably cheaper than the Marco Polo and very acceptable.
& Jln Cole Adams **C** *Loong*, Jln Abaca, T765308. A/c, fully carpeted, clean and light. **C** *Pan Sabah*, Jln
Stephen Tan, behind local minibus station, T762488. A/c, TV, attached bathrooms,
clean rooms and very good value compared to other options in town. **C** *Sanctuary*,
Jln Chester, T751155. A/c, a new place that is slightly dull, sterile and characterless. But
it is at least clean and central. **C** *Tawau*, 72-3 Jln Chester, T771100. Cheaper rooms
without attached bathroom and rather smelly and dirty. Best avoided.

Eating **Malay** **2** *Asnur*, 325B, Block 41 Fajar Complex, Thai and Malay, large choice. **2** *Venice Coffee House*, *Marco Polo Hotel*, Jln Abaca/Jln Clinic, 'hawker centre' for late night eating, Malay and Chinese. **2** *Yun Lo*, Jln Abaca (below the *Hotel Loong*), good Malay and Chinese. A popular spot with the locals, this has a good atmosphere. Recommended.

Chinese **2** *Dragon Court*, 1st Flr, Lot 15, Block 37 Jln Haji Karim, Chinese, popular with locals, lots of seafood. **International** **2** *Dreamland*, 541 Jln Haji Karim, also good local selection. **2** *The Hut*, Block 29, Lot 5 Fajar Complex, Town Extension II, Western, Malay and Chinese, large menu. *Kublai Khan*, *Marco Polo Hotel*, Jln Abaca/Jln Clinic. **Seafood** *May Garden*, 1 km outside town on road to Semporna, outside seating. *Maxims*, Block 30, Lot 6 Jln Haji Karim. **Foodstalls** Stalls along the seafront.

Entertainment Cinema is on Jln Stephen Tan, next to central market. There are karaoke bars on every street corner. Several of the hotels have nightclubs and bars.

Shopping General and fish market at the west end of Jln Dunlop, near the Custom's Wharf.

Sport **Diving** *Borneo Divers*, 46 1st Flr, Jln Dunlop, T762259, F761691. **Golf** Nine-hole golf course, modest green fees, even cheaper during the week.

Tour operators *GSU*, T772531, booking agent for Kalimantan; *Pulau Sipadan Resort Tours*, 1st Flr, no 484, Bandar Sabindo, T242262, F213036.

Transport **Air** The airport is 2 km from town centre. Regular connections with KK, Lahad Datu
110 km to Semporna and Sandakan. **Bus** Station on Jln Wing Lock (west end of town). Minibus station on Jln Dunlop (centre of town). It is now possible to take a bus from Tawau to Kota Kinabalu direct, leaving at 0700, 11 hrs, RM45 **4WD** It is possible to drive from Sapulut (south of Keningau, see page 423) across the interior to Tawau on logging roads but a 4WD vehicle is required.

Boat Packed boats leave Tawau's Customs Wharf (behind Pasar Ikan) twice daily at 0800 and 1600 for Pulau Nunukan Timur, in **Kalimantan**, Indonesia, 2 hrs, RM25 per 16,000Rp. It is possible to get a direct boat from Tawau to Tarakan at 0800 (RM45). Tickets available from the offices opposite Pasar Ikan. From there it is possible to get a boat to Tarakan the next day, or a direct boat to Pare Pare (Sulawesi) 48 hrs (45,000Rp). There are no longer direct boats to Tarakan and travellers must stop over at Nunukan (see next entry).

To Tarakan, Indonesia This town is not a visa-free entry point; it is necessary to obtain a 1 month visa in advance (takes 1 day). There is an Indonesian consulate in Tawau and in KK. The cost is RM75 (photograph needed), 2 month tourist visa provided without hassle. It is possible to fly to Tarakan from Tawau; *Indonesian Bouraq* and *MAS* operate flights.

Directory

Airline offices *MAS*, Lot 1A, Wisma SASCO, Fajar Complex, T765533. *Merdeka Travel*, 41 Jln Dunlop, T772534/1, booking agents for Bouraq (Indonesian airline). *Merpati*, 47A Jln Dunlop, 1st Flr, next to Borneo Divers, T752323. *Sabah Air*, Tawau Airport, T774005. **Banks** *Bumiputra*, Jln Nusantor, on seafront. *Hong Kong*, 210 Jln Utara, opposite the padang. *Standard Chartered*, 518 Jln Habib Husein (behind Hongkong Bank). Exchange kiosk at wharf. **Communications** Area code: 089. **Post Office:** off Jln Nusantor, behind the fish market. **Embassies & consulates** Indonesian Consulate, Jln Apas, mile 1.5. **Useful addresses** Immigration: Jln Stephen Tan.

Nunukan
Colour map 4, grid C5

Travellers making the journey between Tawau and Tarakan (in Indonesia) need to stopover in Nunukan as there are no longer any direct boats. Nunukan offers very little for the visitor: there are no beaches and it seems to be impossible to arrange even a canoe trip. On the plus side the people are friendly. There is one bank – *BNI* – on the main square but it gives very poor exchange rates.

Sleeping There are several losmen (guesthouses) in town including: **E** *Losmen Monaco*, 5 mins' walk from the port, clean and reasonable value with shared mandis. **E** *Losmen Arena*, on the main square, a step down from the *Monaco*. **F** *Losmen Nunukan*, on main square, bottom of the range and just about tolerable.

Transport Boat: daily connections by ferries, which are packed, with Tawau in Sabah, Malaysia, 2 hrs. Also daily ferries to Tarakan.

Sabah

Background

The name 'Sabah' probably derives from the Arabic *Zir-e Bad*, meaning 'the land below the wind'. It is an appropriate name for the state as it lies just to the south of the typhoon belt. Officially, the territory has only been called Sabah since 1963, when it joined the Malay federation, but the name appears to have been in use long before that. When Baron Gustav Von Overbeck was awarded the cession rights to North Borneo by the Sultan of Brunei in 1877 (see page 475), one of the titles conferred on him was 'Maharajah of Sabah'. And in the *Handbook of British North Borneo*, published in 1890, it says: "In Darvel Bay there are the remnants of a tribe which seems to have been much more plentiful in bygone days – the Sabahans". From the founding of the Chartered Company until 1963, Sabah was known as British North Borneo.

Sabah has a population of about 1.5 million, about half of whom are illegal immigrants (see page 483). The inhabitants of Sabah can be divided into four main groups: the Murut, the Kadazan, the Bajau and the Chinese, as well as a small Malay population. These main groups are subdivided into several different tribes (see page 478). For information on geography, climate, flora and fauna, see page 514.

History

Prehistoric stone tools have been found in eastern Sabah, suggesting that people were living in limestone caves in the Madai area 17,000-20,000 years ago. The caves were periodically settled from then on; pottery dating from the late Neolithic period has been found, and by the early years of the first millennium AD, Madai's inhabitants were making iron spears and decorated pottery. The Madai and Baturong caves were lived in continuously until about the 16th century, and several carved stone coffins and burial jars have been discovered in the jungle caves, one of which is exhibited in the Sabah State Museum, see page 405. The caves were also known for their birds' nests; Chinese traders were buying the nests from Borneo as far back as 700 AD. In addition, they exported camphor wood, pepper and other forest products to Imperial China.

There are very few archaeological records indicating Sabah's early history, although there is documentary evidence of links between a long-lost kingdom, based somewhere in the area of the Kinabatangan River, and the Sultanate of Brunei, whose suzerainty once extended over most of North Borneo. By the beginning of the 18th century, Brunei's power had begun to wane in the face of European expansionism. To counter the economic decline, the sultan is thought to have increased taxation, which led to civil unrest. In 1704 the Sultan of Brunei had to ask the Sultan of Sulu's help in putting down a rebellion in Sabah, and in return, the Sultan of Sulu received most of what is now Sabah.

The would-be white rajahs of Sabah It was not until 1846 that the British entered into a treaty with the Sultan of Brunei and took possession of the island of Labuan (see page 428); in part to counter the growing influence of the Rajah of Sarawak, James Brooke. The British were also wary of the Americans; the US Navy signed a trade treaty with the Sultan of Brunei in 1845 and in 1860 Claude Lee Moses was appointed American Consul-General in Brunei Town. He was only interested in making a personal fortune and quickly persuaded the sultan to cede him land in Sabah. He sold these rights to two Hong Kong-based American

Sabah

businessmen who formed the American Trading Company of Borneo. They styled themselves as Rajahs and set up a base at Kimanis, just south of Papar. It was a disaster. One of them died of malaria, the Chinese labourers they imported from Hong Kong began to starve and the settlement was abandoned in 1866.

But the idea of a trading colony on the North Borneo coast interested the Austrian consul in Hong Kong, Baron Gustav von Overbeck, who, in turn, sold the concept to Alfred Dent, a wealthy English businessman also based in Hong Kong. With Dent's money, Overbeck bought the Americans' cession from the Sultan of Brunei, and extended the territory to cover most of modern-day Sabah. The deal was clinched on 29 December 1877, and Overbeck agreed to pay the sultan 15,000 Straits dollars a year. A few days later Overbeck discovered that the entire area had already been ceded to the Sultan of Sulu 173 years earlier, so he immediately sailed to Sulu and offered the sultan an annual payment of 5,000 Straits dollars for the territory. On his return, he dropped three Englishmen off along the coast to set up trading posts; one of them was William Pryer, who founded Sandakan (see page 449). Three years later, Queen Victoria granted Dent a royal charter and, to the chagrin of the Dutch, the Spanish and the Americans, the British North Borneo Company was formed. London insisted that it was to be a British-only enterprise however, and Overbeck was forced to sell out. The first managing director of the company was the Scottish adventurer and former gun-runner William C Cowie. He was in charge of the day-to-day running of the territory, while the British government supplied a governor.

The new chartered company, with its headquarters in the City of London, was given sovereignty over Sabah and a free hand to develop it. The British administrators soon began to collect taxes from local people and quickly clashed with members of the Brunei nobility. John Whitehead, a British administrator, wrote: "I must say, it seemed rather hard on these people that they should be allowed to surrender up their goods and chattels to swell even indirectly the revenue of the company". The administration levied poll-tax, boat tax, land tax, fishing tax, rice tax, *tapai* (rice wine) tax and a 10 percent tax on proceeds from the sale of birds' nests. Resentment against these taxes sparked the six-year Mat Salleh rebellion (see page 421) and the Rundum Rebellion, which peaked in 1915, during which hundreds of Muruts were killed by the British.

Relations were not helped by colonial attitudes towards the local Malays and tribal people. One particularly arrogant district officer, Charles Bruce, wrote: "The mind of the average native is equivalent to that of a child of four. So long as one remembers that the native is essentially a child and treats him accordingly he is really tractable." Most recruits to the chartered company administration were fresh-faced graduates from British universities, mainly Oxford and Cambridge. For much of the time there were only 40-50 officials running the country. Besides the government officials, there were planters and businessmen: tobacco, rubber and timber became the most important exports. There were also Anglican and Roman Catholic missionaries. British North Borneo was never much of a money-spinner – the economy suffered badly whenever commodity prices slumped – but it managed to pay for itself for most of the time up until the Second World War.

Sabah became part of *Dai Nippon*, or Greater Japan, on New Year's Day 1942, when the Japanese took Labuan. On the mainland, the Japanese Imperial Army and *Kempetai* (military police) were faced with the might of the North Borneo Armed Constabulary, about 650 men. Jesselton (Kota Kinabalu) was occupied on 9 January and Sandakan, 10 days later. All Europeans were interned and when Singapore fell in 1942, 2,740 prisoners of war were moved to Sandakan, most of whom were Australian, where they were forced to build an airstrip. On its completion, the POWs were ordered to march to Ranau, 240 km through the jungle. This became known as 'The Borneo Death March' and only six men survived (see page 451).

The Japanese interregnum

Sabah

The Japanese were hated in Sabah and the Chinese mounted a resistance movement which was led by the Kuching-born Albert Kwok Hing Nam. He also recruited Bajaus and Sulus to join his guerrilla force which launched the 'Double Tenth Rebellion' (the attacks took place on 10 October 1943). The guerrillas took Tuaran, Jesselton and Kota Belud, killing many Japanese and sending others fleeing into the jungle. But the following day the Japanese bombed the towns and troops quickly retook the towns and captured the rebels. There followed a mass execution in which 175 rebels were decapitated. On 10 June 1945 Australian forces landed at Labuan, under the command of American General MacArthur. Allied planes bombed the main towns and virtually obliterated Jesselton and Sandakan. Sabah was liberated on 9 September, and thousands of the remaining 21,000 Japanese troops were killed in retaliation, many by Muruts.

A British Military Administration governed Sabah in the immediate aftermath of the war, and the cash-strapped chartered company sold the territory to the British crown for £1.4m in mid-1946. The new crown colony was modelled on the chartered company's administration and set about rebuilding the main towns and war-shattered infrastructure. In May 1961, following Malaysian independence, Prime Minister Tunku Abdul Rahman proposed the formation of a federation incorporating Malaya (ie Peninsular Malaysia), Singapore, Brunei, Sabah and Sarawak (see page 500). Later that same year, Tun Fuad Stephens, a timber magnate and newspaper publisher formed Sabah's first-ever political party, the United National Kadazan Organisation (UNKO). Two other parties were founded shortly afterwards – the Sabah Chinese Association and the United Sabah National Organization (USNO). The British were keen to leave the colony and the Sabahan parties thrashed out the pros and cons of joining the proposed federation. Elections were held in late-1962 in which a UNKA-USNO alliance (the Sabah Alliance) swept to power and the following August, Sabah became an independent country...for 16 days. Like Singapore and Sarawak, Sabah opted to join the federation, to the indignation of the Philippines and Indonesia which both had claims on the territory. Jakarta's objections resulted in the *konfrontasi* – an undeclared war with Malaysia (see page 388) which was not settled until 1966.

Modern Sabah

Politics Sabah's political scene has always been lively and never more so than in 1994 when the Malaysian Prime Minister, Dr Mahathir Mohamad, pulled off what commentators described as a democratic *coup d'état*. With great political dexterity, he out-manoeuvered his rebellious rivals and managed to dislodge the opposition state government, despite the fact that it had just won a state election. The reasons why Dr Mahathir was motivated to bulldoze his own party into power there go back 10 years and the roots of Sabah's political instability go back even further.

Following Sabah's first state election in 1967, the Sabah Alliance ruled until 1975 when the newly formed multi-racial party, Berjaya, swept the polls. Berjaya had been set up with the financial backing of the United Malays National Organization (UMNO), the mainstay of the ruling Barisan Nasional (National Front) coalition on the Peninsula. Over the following decade that corrupt administration crumbled and in 1985 the opposition Sabah United Party (PBS), led by the Christian Kadazan Datuk Joseph Pairin Kitingan, won a landslide victory and became the only state government in Malaysia that did not belong to the UMNO-led coalition. It became an obvious embarrassment to Prime Minister Dr Mahathir Mohamad to have a rebel Christian state in his predominantly Muslim federation. Nonetheless, the PBS eventually joined Barisan Nasional, believing its partnership in the coalition would help iron things out. It did not.

When the PBS came to power, the federal government and Sabahan opposition parties openly courted Filipino and Indonesian immigrants in the state, almost all of whom are Muslim, and secured identity cards for many of them, enabling them to vote. Dr Mahathir has made no secret of his preference for a Muslim government in Sabah. Nothing, however, was able to dislodge the PBS, which was resoundingly returned to power in 1990. The federal government had long been suspicious of Sabahan politicians, particularly following the PBS's defection from Dr Mahathir's coalition in the run-up to the 1990 general election, a move which bolstered the opposition alliance. Dr Mahathir described this as "a stab in the back", and referred to Sabah as "a thorn in the flesh of the Malaysian federation". But in the event, the Prime Minister won that national election convincingly without PBS help, prompting fears, in Sabah, of political retaliation. Those fears proved justified in the wake of the election.

Sabah paid a heavy price for its 'disloyalty'; several prominent Sabahans were arrested as secessionist conspirators under Malaysia's Internal Security Act, which provides for indefinite detention without trial. Among them was Jeffrey Kitingan, brother of the Chief Minister head of the influential Yayasan Sabah, or Sabah Foundation (see page 406). At the same time, Joseph Pairin Kitingan himself was charged with corruption. There was a feeling in Sabah that the two Kitingans were bearing the brunt of Dr Mahathir's personal political vendetta.

As the political feud grew more venomous, the federal government added to the fray by failing to promote Sabah to foreign investors. As investment money dried up, so did federal development funds; big road and housing projects were left unfinished for years. Many in Sabah felt that their state was being short-changed by the federal government. The political instability had a detrimental effect on the state economy and the business community began to feel that continued feuding would be economic lunacy. Politicians in the Christian-led PBS, however, continued to claim that Sabah wasn't getting its fair share of Malaysia's economic boom. They said the agreement which enshrined a measure of autonomy for Sabah when it joined the Malaysian federation had been eroded.

The main bone of contention was the state's oil revenues, worth around US$852m a year, of which 95 percent disappeared into federal coffers. There were many other sore points too and as the list of grievances grew longer, the state government exploited them to the full. By 1994, anti-federal feelings were running high. The PBS continued to promote the idea of 'Sabah for Sabahans', a defiant slogan in a country where the federal government was working to centralize power. Because Dr Mahathir likes to be in control, the idea of granting greater autonomy to a distant, opposition-held state was not on his agenda. A showdown was inevitable.

It began in January 1994. As Datuk Pairin's corruption trial drew to a close, he dissolved the state assembly, paving the way for fresh elections. He did this to cover the eventuality of his being disqualified from office through a 'guilty' verdict: he wanted to have his own team in place to take over from him. He was convicted of corruption. But the fine imposed on him was just under the disqualifying threshold, and, to the Prime Minister's fury, he led the PBS into the election. Dr Mahathir put his newly appointed deputy, Anwar Ibrahim, in charge of the National Front alliance campaign.

Datuk Pairin won the election, but by a much narrower margin than before. He alleged vote-buying and ballot rigging. He accused Dr Mahathir's allies of whipping up the issue of religion. He spoke of financial inducements being offered to Sabah's Muslim voters, some of whom are Malay, but most of whom are Bajau tribes people and Filipino immigrants. His swearing-in ceremony was delayed for 36 hours: the governor said he was sick; Datuk Parin said his political enemies were trying to woo defectors from the ranks of the PBS, to overturn his slender majority. He was proved right.

Sabah

Three weeks later, he was forced to resign; his fractious party had virtually collapsed in disarray and a stream of defections robbed him of his majority. Datuk Parin's protestations that his assemblymen had been bribed to switch sides were ignored. The local leader of Dr Mahathir's ruling party, Tan Sri Sakaran Dandai, was swiftly sworn in as the new Chief Minister.

Following this 'constitutional coup', Mahathir might reasonably have hoped that the people of Sabah would come to realize that Datuk Pairin's head was the price they had to pay for political reconciliation with Kuala Lumpur and the financial inducements that would follow. However, in the 1995 general election the PBS did remarkably well, holding onto eight seats and defeating a number of Front candidates who had defected from the PBS the previous year. Sabah was one area, along with the East Coast state of Kelantan, which resisted the Mahathir/BN electoral steamroller.

The March 1999 state elections once again pitted UMNO against Pairin's PBS. And once again the issues were local autonomy, vote rigging, the role of national politics and political parties in state elections, and money. A new element was the role that Anwar Ibrahim's trial might play in the campaign (see page 503) but otherwise it was old wine in mostly old bottles.

The outcome was a convincing win for Mahathir and the ruling National Front who gathered 31 of the 48 state assembly seats - three more than the Prime Minister forecast. Mahathir once again used the lure of development funds from KL to convince local Sabahans where their best interests might lie. Mahathir is a politician who does not mince his words, and is quite happy to pork barrel when needs call: "We are not being unfair" he said. "We are more than fair, but we cannot be generous to the opposition. We can be generous to a National Front government in Sabah. That I can promise." As a *Straits Times* journalist put it: 'Sabahans got the point'. While the elections were marred by allegations of vote buying there can be little doubt that this was an impressive victory for Mahathir and the NF machine.

But worryingly for the National Front, the opposition Parti Bersatu Sabah (PBS) still managed to garner the great bulk of the Kadazan vote and in so doing won 17 seats. That the Kadazan electorate were voting for the party and not for influential local politicians was clear in what happened to those PBS politicians who had crossed over to the National Front in the months leading up to the elections: they lost their seats. In other words, the large Kadazan population still don't believe, whatever Mahathir's rhetoric, that the NF represents their interests. As in Sarawak, the election, in the end, was more about local politics than about the economic crisis and the Anwar trial.

Towards the end of the year it was possible once again to gauge Sabah's enthusiasm for the National Front. And the general elections showed that Mahathir, ultimately, still calls the shots. To begin with, one of the PBS's stalwarts, former Deputy Chief Minister Dr Mark Koding, defected to UMNO a week before the elections creating an opportunity for Mahathir to call on "Kadazandusuns to support and vote for their leaders in Barisan Nasional in next Monday's general election to protect their interests." The election showed that while Mahathir may still dominate the political landscape his opponents have not been entirely vanquished.

Culture

People Sabah's main tribal communities are comprised of the Kadazan, who mostly live on the west coast, the Murut, who inhabit the interior, to the south, and the Bajau, who are mainly settled around Gunung Kinabalu. There are more than 30 tribes, more than 50 different languages and about 100 dialects. Sabah also has a large Chinese population and many illegal Filipino immigrants.

Sabah's ethnic breakdown

	Population	%
Kadazan/Dusun	340,060	19.6
[Kadazan	110,866	6.4]
[Dusun	229,194	13.2]
Murut	50,315	2.9
Bajau	202,995	11.7
Malay	107,570	6.2
Other Muslim	235,960	13.6
Chinese	199,525	11.5
Indonesia	421,605	24.3
Filipino	142,270	8.2
Others	34,700	2.0
Total population	1,735,000	100

Source: 1991 census

Kadazans The Kadazans are the largest ethnic group in Sabah comprising about a third of the population and are a peaceful agrarian people with a strong cultural identity. Until Sabah joined the Malaysian Federation in 1963, they were known as 'Dusuns', meaning 'peasants' or 'orchard people'. This name was given to them by outsiders, and picked up by the British. It became, in effect, a residual category including all those people who were not Muslim or Chinese. Most Kadazans call themselves after their tribal place names. They can be broken into several tribes including the Lotud of Tuaran, the Rungus of the Kudat and Bengkoka Peninsula, the Tempasuk, the Tambanuo, Kimarangan and the Sanayo. Minokok and Tengara Kadazans live in the upper Kinabatangan River basin while those living near other big rivers are just known as *Orang Sungai*, or 'river people'. Most Kadazans used to live in longhouses; these are virtually all gone now. The greatest likelihood of a visitor coming across a longhouse in Sabah is in the Rungus area of the Kudat Peninsula; even there, former longhouse residents are moving into detached, kampung-style houses while one or two remain for the use of tourists.

But Kadazan identity is not that simple. The 1991 census lists both Kadazans (110,866) and Dusuns (229,194). In the 1970 census all were listed as Kadazan, while in the 1960 census they were all Dusun. In 1995 the Malaysian government agreed to add the common language of these people(s) to the national repertoire to be taught in schools. This they named Kadazandusun. The other four are Malay, Chinese, Tamil and Iban.

All the Kadazan groups had similar customs and modes of dress (see below). Up to the Second World War, many Kadazan men wore the *chawat* loin cloth. The Kadazans used to hunt with blowpipes, and in the 19th century, were still head-hunting. Today, however, they are known for their gentleness and honesty; their produce can often be seen sitting unattended at roadside stalls, and passing motorists are expected to pay what they think fair. The Kadazans traditionally traded their agricultural produce at large markets, held at meeting points, called *tamus* (see box). The Kadazan are farmers, and the main rice-producers of Sabah. They used to be animists, and were said to live in great fear of evil spirits; most of their ceremonies were rituals aimed at driving out these spirits. The job of communicating with the spirits of the dead, the *tombiivo*, was done by priestesses, called *bobohizan*. They are the only ones who can speak the ancient Kadazan language, using a completely different vocabulary from modern Kadazan. Most Kadazans converted to Christianity, mainly Roman Catholicism, during the 1930s, although there are also some Muslim Kadazan.

The big cultural event in the Kadazan year is the **Harvest Festival** which takes place in May. The ceremony, known as the *Magavau* ritual, is officiated by a high priestess, or *Bobohizan*. These elderly women, who wear traditional black costumes and colourful headgear with feathers and beads, are now few and far between. The ceremony culminates with offerings to the *Bambaazon*, or rice spirit. After the ceremonies Catholic, Muslim and animist Kadazans all come together to play traditional sports such as wrestling and buffalo racing. This is about the only occasion when visitors are likely to see Kadazan in their traditional costumes. In the Penampang area a woman's costume consists of a fitted, sleeveless tunic and ankle-length skirt of

Tapai – Sabah's rice wine

Tapai, the fiery Sabahan rice wine, is much loved by the Kadazan and the Murut. It was even more popular before the two tribal groups' wholesale conversion to Christianity in the 1930s. Writer Hedda Morrison noted in 1957 that: "The squalor and wretchedness arising from [their] continual drunkenness made the Murut a particularly useful object of missionary endeavour. In the 1930s missionaries succeeded in converting nearly all the Murut to Christianity. The Murut grasped at this new faith much as the drowning man is said to grasp at a straw. From being the most drunken people in Borneo, they became the most sober." In the Sabah State Museum (see page 405) there is a recipe for tapai, also known as buffalos' blood, which was taken down by an administrator during chartered company days:

"Boil 12lbs of the best glutinous rice until well done. In a wide-mouthed jar, lay the rice in layers of no more than two fingers deep, and between layers, place a total of about 20½-oz yeast cakes. Add two cups of water, tinctured with the juice of six beetroots. Cover jar with muslin and leave to ferment. Each day, uncover it and remove dew which forms on the muslin. On the fifth day, stir the mixture vigorously and leave for four weeks. Store for one full year, after which it shall be full of virtue and potence and most smooth upon the palate."

Tapai is drunk from communal jars, which were also used as burial urns, through bamboo straws. The jar is filled nearly to its brim with tapai. Large leaves are placed on the top just under the lower edge of the rim. These leaves are pierced with straws for sucking up the liquid and the intervening space between the leaves and the top of the jar is filled with water.

Etiquette demands that one drinks till the water has been drained off the leaves. They are then flooded again and the process is repeated. There is also the distilled form of tapai, called montaku, which is even more potent. When North Borneo became a British crown colony after the Second World War, the administration was concerned about the scourge of tapai drinking on three counts. First, it was said to consume a large portion of the natives' potential food crop, second, it usually caused a crime wave whenever it was drunk, and thirdly, it was blamed for the high rate of infant mortality as mothers frequently gave their babies a suck at the straw.

Oscar Cook, a former district officer in the North Borneo Civil Service, noted in his 1923 book Borneo: the Stealer of Hearts, that tapai was not to everyone's fancy and certainly not to his. "As an alternative occupation to head-hunting, the Murut possess a fondness for getting drunk, indulged in on every possible occasion. Tapai, or pengasai, as the Murut calls it, is not a nice drink. In fact, to my thinking it is the very reverse, for it is chiefly made from fermented rice... is very potent, and generally sour and possessed of a pungent and nauseating odour. Births, marriages, deaths, sowing, harvesting and any occasion that comes to mind is made the excuse for a debauch. It is customary for Murut to show respect to the white man by producing their very best tapai, and pitting the oldest and ugliest women of the village against him in a drinking competition." Cook admits that all this proved too much for him and when he was transferred to Keningau, he had to employ an 'official drinker'. "The applicants to the post were many," he noted.

black velvet. Belts of silver coins (himpogot) and brass rings are worn round the waist; a colourful sash is also worn. Men dress in a black, long-sleeved jacket over black trousers; they also wear a siga, colourful woven head gear. These costumes have become more decorative in recent years, with colourful embroidery. Villages send the finalists of local beauty contests to the grand final of the Unduk Ngadau harvest festival queen competition in Penampang, near Kota Kinabalu.

Tamus – Sabah's markets and trade fairs

In Sabah, an open trade fair is called a tamu. Locals gather to buy and sell jungle produce, handicrafts and traditional wares. Tamu comes from the Malay word 'tetamu', to meet, and the biggest and most famous is held at Kota Belud, north of Kota Kinabalu in Bajau country (see page 435). Tamus were fostered by the pre-war British North Borneo Chartered Company, when district officers would encourage villagers from miles around to trade among themselves. It was also a convenient opportunity for officials to meet with village headmen. They used to be strictly Kadazan affairs, but today tamu are multiracial events. Sometimes public auction of water buffalo and cattle are held. Some of the biggest tamus around the state are:

Monday:	Tandek
Tuesday:	Kiulu, Topokan
Wednesday:	Tamparuli
Thursday:	Keningau, Tambunan, Sipitang, Telipok, Simpangan
Friday:	Sinsuran, Weston
Saturday:	Penampang, Beaufort, Sindumin, Matunggong, Kinarut
Sunday:	Tambunan, Tenom, Kota Belud, Papar, Gaya Street (KK)

Bajau

The Bajau, the famous 'cowboys' of the 'wild East', came from the South Philippines during the 18th and 19th centuries and settled in the coastal area around Kota Belud, Papar and Kudat, where they made a handsome living from piracy. The Bajau who came to Sabah joined forces with the notorious Illanun and Balinini pirates. They are natural seafarers and were dubbed 'the sea gypsies'; today they form the second largest indigenous group in Sabah and are divided into subgroups, notably the Binadan, Suluk and Obian. They call themselves 'Samah'; it was the Brunei Malays who first called them Bajau. They are strict Muslims and the famous Sabahan folk hero, Mat Salleh, who led a rebellion in the 1890s against British Chartered Company rule, was a Bajau (see page 421). Despite their seafaring credentials, they are also renowned horsemen and (very occasionally) still put in an appearance at Kota Belud's tamu (see page 435). Bajau women are known for their brightly coloured basketry – tudong saji. The Bajau build their atap houses on stilts over the water and these are interconnected by a network of narrow wooden planks. The price of a Bajau bride was traditionally assessed in stilts, shaped from the trunks of bakau mangrove trees. A father erected one under his house on the day a daughter was born and replaced it whenever it wore out. The longer the daughter remained at home, the more stilts he got through and the more water buffalo he demanded from a prospective husband.

Murut

The Murut live around Tenom and Pensiangan in the lowland and hilly parts of the interior, in the southwest of Sabah and in the Trusan Valley of North Sarawak. Some of those living in more remote jungle areas retain their traditional longhouse way of life, but many Murut have now opted for detached kampung-style houses. Murut means 'hill people' and is not the term used by the people themselves. They refer to themselves by their individual tribal names. The Nabai, Bokan and Timogun Murut live in the lowlands and are wet-rice farmers, while the Peluan, Bokan and Tagul Murut live in the hills and are mainly shifting cultivators. They are thought to be related to Sarawak's Kelabit and Kalimantan's Lun Dayeh people, although some of the tribes in the South Philippines have similar characteristics. The Murut staples are rice and tapioca, they are known for their weaving and basketry and have a penchant for drinking tapai (rice wine – see page 480). They are also enthusiastic dancers and devised the lansaran, a sprung dance floor like a trapeze (see page 424). The Murut are a mixture of animists, Christians and Muslims and were the last tribe in Sabah to give up head-hunting, a practice finally stopped by British North Borneo Chartered Company administrators.

Dance

Name of dance	Tribe	District
Sumazau Penampang	Kadan/Dusun	Penampang, west coast
Angalang	Murut	Pensiangan and Tenom interior and south
Mangiluk	Suluk	East coast
Magunatip	Murut and Kwijau Dusun	Interior and south
Adai Adai	Brunei Malay	Sipitang and Membakut, southwest of Sabah
Mongigol Sumundai	Rungus	Kudat and Pitas, north of Sabah
Limbai	Bajau	Kota Belud, west coast
Dansa	Cocos	Lahad Datu, east coast
Bolak Bolak	Bajau	Semporna, east coast
Mongigol Sumayan	Lotud	Tuaran, west coast
Umang-Umang Ting-Ting	Brunei Malay	Bongawan, west coast
Daling-Daling	Suluk	East coast
Sumazau Papar	Kadazan, Dusun	Paper, west coast
Titikas	Orang Sungai	Kinabatangan, east coast
Liliput	Bisaya	Beaufort, west coast
Kuda Pasu	Bajau	Kota Belud, west coast

Chinese The Chinese accounted for nearly a third of Sabah's population in 1960; today they make up just a fifth. Unlike Sarawak, however, where the Chinese were a well-established community in the early 1800s, Sabah's Chinese came as a result of the British North Borneo Chartered Company's immigration policy, designed to ease a labour shortage. About 70 percent of Sabah's Chinese are Christian Hakkas, who first began arriving at the end of the 19th century, under the supervision of the Company. They were given free passage from China and most settled in the

Description

Performed during Annual harvest Pemanpang Festival (Pesta Kaamatan) to honour the rice spirit (Bambaazon). Sumazau means dancing.

A solo warrior dance, accompanied by a group of women dancers (angalong). Originally performed after a victorious battle or head-hunting trip.

Performed at weddings and social events.

These dancers need skill and agility to dance among bamboo poles which are hit together to produce the rhythm of the dance.

Evolved from a song; it tells of the activities of the local fishermen and farmers

Can be performed as part of certain ritual festivals. For instance, Thanksgiving to rice spirit for a bountiful harvest or moving into a new house.

Performed at weddings, characterized by graceful wrist rotations. Accompanying music is called bertitik.

Performed at weddings. It features energetic foot stomping.

Bolak Bolak is Malay for castanets. The dancers hold the castanets and create the rhythm of the music.

Ritual dance performed during Rumaha ceremony to honour spirits of skulls, or the Mangahau ceremony for the spirits of sacred jars.

Celebrates the birth of a newborn child

A 'courting' dance said to be derived from the English 'darling'. Usually accompanied by a love song.

Performed at similar occasions to Sumazau Penampang. Distinctive foot work.

Titikas is based on the Ingki-Ingki game, similar to hopscotch.

Liliput means 'go around'. It is a dance to cast away evil spirits in a possessed person.

Originally performed by horsemen or escort a bridegroom and his entourage to the bride's home. The female dancers hold handkerchieves as a sign of welcome.

Sabah

Jesselton and Kudat areas; today most Hakka are farmers. There are also large Teochew and Hokkien communities in Tawau, Kota Kinabalu and Labuan while Sandakan is mainly Cantonese, who originally came from Hong Kong.

Filipinos

Immigration from the Philippines started in the 1950s and refugees began flooding into Sabah when the separatist war erupted in Mindanao in the 1970s. Today there are believed to be upwards of 700,000 illegal Filipino immigrants in Sabah (although their migration has been undocumented for so long that no one is certain), and the state government fears they could soon outnumber locals. There are many in Kota Kinabalu, the state capital and a large community – mainly women and children – in Labuan, but the bulk of the Filipino population is in Semporna, Lahad Datu, Tawau and Kunak (on the east coast) where they already outnumber locals 3:1. One Sabah government minister, referring to the long-running territorial dispute between Malaysia and the Philippines, was quoted as saying "We do not require a strong military presence at the border any more: the aliens have already landed".

Although the federal government has talked of its intention to deport illegal aliens, it is also mindful of the political reality: the majority of the Filipinos are Muslim, and making them legal Malaysian citizens could ruin Sabah's predominantly Christian, Kadazan-led state government. The Filipino community is also a thorn in Sabah's flesh because of the crime wave associated with their arrival: the Sabah police claims 65 percent of all crimes in the state are committed by Filipinos. The police do not ask many questions when dealing with Filipino criminal suspects; about 40-50 are shot every year. Another local politician was quoted as saying: "The immigrants take away our jobs, cause political instability and pose a health hazard because of the appalling conditions in which some of them live".

There are six different Filipino groups in Sabah: the Visayas and Ilocano are Christian as are the Ilongo (Ilo Ilo), from Zamboanga. The Suluks are Muslim; they come from South Mindanao and have the advantage of speaking a dialect of Bahasa Malaysia. Many Filipinos were born in Sabah and all second generation immigrants are fluent in Bahasa. Migration first accelerated in the 1950s during the logging boom, and continued when the oil palm plantation economy took off; the biggest oil palm plantation is at Tungku, east of Lahad Datu. Many migrants have settled along the roadsides on the way to Danum Valley; it is easy to claim land since all they have to do is simply clear a plot and plant a few fruit trees.

Crafts

Compared with neighbouring Sarawak and Kalimantan, Sabah's handicraft industry is rather impoverished. Sabah's tribal groups were less protected from Western influences than Sarawak's, and traditional skills quickly began to die out as the state modernized and the economy grew. In Kota Kinabalu today, the markets are full of Filipino handicrafts and shell products; local arts and crafts are largely confined to basketry, mats, hats, beadwork, musical instruments and pottery.

The elongated Kadazan backpack baskets found around Mount Kinabalu National Park are called *wakids* and are made from bamboo, rattan and bark. Woven food covers, or *tudong saji*, are often mistaken for hats, and are made by the Bajau of Kota Belud. Hats, made from nipah palm or rattan, and whose shape varies markedly from place to place, are decorated with traditional motifs. One of the most common motifs is the *nantuapan*, or 'meeting', which represents four people all drinking out of the same tapai (rice wine) jar. The Rungus people from the Kudat peninsula also make *linago* basketware from a strong wild grass; it is tightly woven and not decorated (see page 438 for more detail on the Rungus). At *tamus*, Sabah's big open-air markets (see page 481), there are usually some handicrafts for sale. The Kota Belud *tamu* is the best place to find the Bajau horseman's embroidered turban, the *destar* (see page 435). Traditionally, the Rungus people, who live on the Kudat Peninsula, were renowned as fine weavers, and detailed patterns were woven into their ceremonial skirts, or *tinugupan*. These patterns all had different names, but, like the ingredients of the traditional dyes, many have now been forgotten.

Background

9

Background

Introduction

On 31 August 1997 Malaysia turned 40. Over the four decades since independence the country has been transformed from a poor, undeveloped British colony, reliant on the export of primary products like rubber and tin, to a self-confident industrializing nation with a burgeoning middle class and an increasingly sophisticated economy. The figures, as they say, speak for themselves: between 1970 and 1995 per capita income rose ten-fold to RM10,000, the number of children dying before the age of one was cut from 40/1,000 live births to 10 and, most striking of all, the number of people living in poverty in Peninsular Malaysia was reduced from one in two to less than one in 10. Malaysia has become a country where people – and especially the prime minister, Mahathir Mohamad – think big. He has set out a vision which will bring Malaysia developed country status by 2020, and he is forever cajoling his people to join him in the effort.

During 1997 and 1998 many Western pundits – long annoyed by Mahathir's abrasive and anti-Western manner – predicted that the economy was set for a period of slow growth, brought on by the Asian economic crisis (see page 512 for more details). They also speculated that Mahathir himself would fall because his political legitimacy was so closely tied to the country's economic vitality. As it turned out they were wrong on both counts. The economy has since recovered and Mahathir convincingly won a general election at the end of 1999. But they were not completely wrong.

Malaysia is sometimes called 'the lucky country of Asia' because it is so richly endowed with natural resources. It has the world's largest tin deposits, extensive oil and gas reserves and is cloaked in rainforest containing valuable tropical hardwoods. Until very recently, the economy was heavily dependent on these resources and plantation crops such as palm oil, natural rubber, pepper and cocoa. But in the late 1980s and early 1990s, a sudden explosion of industrial growth, spearheaded by a surge in manufacturing, changed the complexion of Malaysia's economy beyond recognition. In 1992, Michael Vatikiotis, Kuala Lumpur correspondent for *The Far Eastern Economic Review*, wrote: "Malaysia in many ways forms the leading edge of social change in Southeast Asia. ... Prime Minister Dr Mahathir Mohamad has captivated his people with a vision of a developed Malaysia by 2020. Deploying this distant vision of the future has allowed Malaysians to think of themselves as becoming a nation of airline pilots and nuclear physicists by 2020."

Malaysia is a young country; until the end of the last century there was just a collection of divided coastal sultanates around the peninsula and three colonial trading settlements. The British grouped the different states into a federation, but Malaysia did not emerge in its present form until 1965, eight years after independence from the British. Today the Federation of Malaysia includes the 11 peninsular states together with Sabah and Sarawak on the island of Borneo (East Malaysia). Singapore left the federation in 1965 after an unsuccessful two year experiment. The politically dominant Malays of the peninsula had felt uncomfortable with the destabilizing effect of Singapore's mainly Chinese population on the country's racial equation and the uncomfortable marriage of convenience came to an end.

A favourite Malaysian dish is *rojak* – a tossed salad with many different ingredients. It is not uncommon to hear the rojak analogy applied to Malaysia's exotic ethnic mix of Malays, Chinese, Indians and indigenous tribes. The country's cultural blend makes Malaysia interesting, but it is also a potentially volatile mixture. Yet only once since independence in 1957 has the communal melting pot boiled over. Today, most Malaysians are too young to remember the 1969 race riots, although they have lived with their consequences ever since. The government's affirmative action policies have attempted to lessen the economic disparities

Biggest = best: Malaysia's race for the skies

Malaysia, one of the world's fastest growing and most self-confident nations, seems intent on dominating the Guinness Book of Records. The country now boasts:

The world's tallest flagpole at 100m in Merdeka Square, Kuala Lumpur.

The Petronas Twin Towers in Kuala Lumpur, rising through 88 storeys to 450m. On their completion in 1996 the towers claimed the title of the tallest building(s) in the world. The Petronas Twin Towers are part of the Kuala Lumpur City Centre project which, when completed, will have no fewer than 22 office blocks.

Asia's tallest tower, the KL Tower, at 421m which opened on 1 October 1996.

The Bakun Hydroelectric Dam in the East Malaysian state of Sarawak. Preparatory work began in 1995 and when it is completed (there is still a chance it won't be) it will be the highest HEP dam in the world and the largest such project in Southeast Asia, generating 2,400 megawatts. The cost? A paltry US$6bn and 10,000 people uprooted.

In 1995 Prime Minister Mahathir laid the foundation stone for Putrajaya, Malaysia's new capital city 35 km south of Kuala Lumpur. It is due for completion in 2005, will support a population of 250,000, and has a price tag of a cool US$8bn. Along with the new international airport and Cyberjaya, both under construction near Putrajaya, the total cost is projected at US$20bn.

Standard Chartered Securities in Kuala Lumpur drew up a list of the 31 largest projects Malaysia had embarked upon or had announced it was undertaking. Totting up the cost, the bill came to RM163bn or US$65bn. **NB** With the weakening of the Malaysian economy during 1997 some of these projects have been delayed or shelved.

---

between the races (see page 510) and have given the Malays – the economic underdogs – a helping hand. Over the years, non-Malays have complained bitterly about discrimination against them by the Malay-led government, but somehow, tensions have been kept below boiling point. Today, there is much more inter-mixing between Malaysians from all ethnic backgrounds; many of them are more interested in cashing in on the economic boom than worrying about race. When Malaysia celebrated 35 years of nationhood in August 1992, Dr Mahathir said that on independence, many had predicted that its multiracial, multicultural and multireligious society would collapse. "Malaysia has proven to the world", he said, "that its multiracial nature has not prevented it from achieving progress and success. We must continue to co-operate and be united."

The tourism industry plays a crucial role in Malaysia's economy. The country is endowed with good beaches, coral reefs, jungle, mountains and hill resorts, islands and, these days, hundreds of golf courses. It also has a handful of urban attractions: notably Penang's beautifully preserved Chinatown and Melaka's architectural heritage. As the world's largest exporter of sawn timber Malaysia's logging industry has earned the country notoriety among environmentalists. The industry is riddled with corruption and the Malaysian government admits to problems enforcing its surprisingly stringent forestry policies. But a substantial part of Malaysia's land area is forested (especially in the states of East Malaysia) and the government has been enthusiastically promoting ecotourism; there are several magnificent national parks, both on the peninsula and in the East Malaysian states of Sarawak and Sabah. In Sarawak there are also many jungle tribes, whose culture has remained remarkably intact.

Background

Putting Malaya on the map

The names of most of Malaysia's states are older than the name Malaya; until the 1870s the scattered coastal sultanates were independent of each other. Many of the Malay areas were colonized by Sumatrans long ago and it is possible that the word 'Melayu' – or 'Malay' – derives from the Sungai Melayu (Melayu River) in Sumatra. The name in turn is derived from the Dravidian (Tamil) word malai, or 'hill'. As the Malays are coastal people, the paradox is explained by their pre-Islamic religion, which is thought to have been based on a cult in which a sacred mountain took pride of place.

The Graeco-Roman geographer Ptolemy called the Malay peninsula Aurea Chersonesus, or the 'The Golden Chersonese': it was the fabled land of gold. By the early 1500s, European maps were already marking Melaka and Pulau Tioman, which were well known to Chinese mariners. During the Portuguese and Dutch colonial periods, the whole peninsula was simply labelled 'Malacca', and the town was the only significant European outpost until the British took possession of Penang in 1786. There was very little mapping of the peninsula until the early 19th century, and the names of states only gradually appeared on maps over the course of the 17th and 18th centuries.

According to cartographic historian RT Fell, the first maps of the interior of the peninsula, beyond the bounds of the British Straits Settlements, did not appear until the late 19th century. In 1885 the Survey Department was founded and charged with mapping the interior – one of the tasks William Cameron was undertaking when he stumbled across the highland plateau named after him that same year. But right into the 20th century, large tracts of mountainous jungle were

Borneo

The East Malaysian states of Sarawak and Sabah, and the Sultanate of Brunei, occupy the northern third of the island of Borneo. Sabah and Sarawak represented the 'other' Malaysia, divided by much more than 500 km of sea from the states of the 'Mainland'. Here, in East Malaysia, 'tribal' Dayaks dominate the human landscape and the local economy is sustained not by manufacturing but by the exploitation of natural resources, particularly timber and oil and gas. Sabah and Sarawak were only integrated into the Federation of Malay States in 1963 and visitors from the mainland are still required to obtain a travel permit to come here and a work permit if they want a job. The states maintain control over immigration, education and language issues because of the fear that without these controls the indigenous peoples of Sabah and Sarawak would be elbowed out by their more sophisticated brethren from across the South China Sea.

The name Borneo is thought to be a European mispronunciation of 'Burni' or Brunei. Early Western books variously spelt Borneo 'Burni', 'Burney', 'Burny', 'Borny', 'Borney', 'Burneo', 'Bornei', 'Bruneo', 'Porne' and 'Borneu'. This was not entirely the Europeans' fault, for as John Crawfurd points out in *A Descriptive Dictionary of the Indian Isles* (1856), the name is "indifferently pronounced by the Malays, according to the dialect they happen to speak – Brune, Brunai, Burne or Burnai". The Chinese, for good measure, referred to the island from the early ninth century as P'o-ni, or P'o-li, or Fo-ni. The sultanate itself became known as 'Borneo Proper', and its capital as Brunei Town. Crawfurd concluded that "the name of the town was not extended to the island by European writers, but by the Mohamedan navigators who conducted the carrying trade of the archipelago before the advent of Europeans". Borneo Proper was first visited by Europeans in the early 16th century, most notably by Antonio Pigafetta, the official chronicler on the Portuguese explorer Ferdinand Magellan's expedition, which called in on the Sultan of Brunei in 1521 (see page 520). The Ibans of Sarawak maintain that the name Borneo derives from the Malay *buah nyior*, meaning 'coconut', while the Malays had another, less well-known name for the island: Kalimantan. This, according to Crawfurd, was the name of a species of wild mango "and the word would simply mean 'Isle of Mangoes'". This was the name chosen by Indonesia for its section of the island; for some reason, it is generally translated as 'River of Diamonds', probably because of the diamond fields near Martapura in the south.

History

Precolonial Malaya

For a historical introduction to Sarawak see page 382 & for Sabah, page 474

With the arrival of successive waves of Malay immigrants about five millennia ago, the earliest settlers – the *Orang Asli* aboriginals (see page 537) – moved into the interior. The Malays established agricultural settlements on the coastal lowlands and in riverine areas and from very early on, were in contact with foreign traders, thanks to the peninsula's strategic location on the sea route between India and China. Although the original tribal inhabitants of Malaya were displaced inland, they were not entirely isolated from the coastal peoples. Trade relations in which 'upriver' tribal groups exchanged forest products for commodities like salt and metal implements with 'downstream' Malays, were widespread (see box on page 514). Malay culture on the peninsula reflected these contacts, embracing Indian cultural traditions, Hinduism among them. In the late 14th century, the centre of power shifted from Sumatra's Srivijayan Empire across the Strait to Melaka (see page 203). In 1430, the third ruler of Melaka embraced Islam, and became the first sultan; the city quickly grew into a flourishing trading port. By the early 1500s, it was the most important entrepôt in the region and its fame brought it to the attention of the Portuguese, who, in 1511, ushered in the colonial epoch. They sacked the town and sent the sultan fleeing to Johor, where a new sultanate was established (see page 224). But because of internal rivalries and continued conflict with the Acehnese and the Portuguese, Johor never gained the prominence of Melaka, and was forced to alternate its capital between Johor and the Riau archipelago (see page 224).

The colonials arrive

The Portuguese were the first of three European colonial powers to arrive on the Malay peninsula. They were followed by the Dutch, who took Melaka in 1641 (see page 203 for a history of Melaka). When Holland was occupied by Napoleon's troops at the end of the 18th century, Britain filled the vacuum, and the British colonial era began. Historian John M Gullick writes: "The main effects of European control were, firstly, to break the sequence of indigenous kingdoms and to disrupt the trade system upon which they had been based; secondly to delimit colonial spheres of influence and thereby to fix the subsequent boundaries of the national states which are heirs to colonial rule; and lastly to promote economic development and establish the infrastructure of government and other services which that development required; mass immigration from India and China was an incidental consequence of economic development."

During the 17th century, the Dutch came into frequent conflict with the Bugis, the fearsome master-seafarers who the Dutch had displaced from their original homeland in South Sulawesi. In 1784, in league with the Minangkabau of West Sumatra, the Bugis nearly succeeded in storming Melaka and were only stymied by the arrival of Dutch warships. The Bugis eventually established the Sultanate of Selangor on the west coast of the peninsula and, in the south, exerted increasing

The kris: martial and mystic masterpiece of the Malay world

The kris occupies an important place in Malay warfare, art and philosophy. It is a short sword – the Malay word keris means dagger – and the blade may be either straight or sinuous (there are over 100 blade shapes), sharpened on both edges. Such was the high reputation of these weapons that they were exported as far afield as India. Krisses are often attributed with peculiar powers; one was reputed to have rattled violently before a family feud. Another, kept at the museum in Taiping, has a particularly bloodthirsty reputation. It would sneak away after dark, kill someone, and then wipe itself clean before miraculously returning to its display cabinet. Because each kris has a power and spirit of its own, they must be compatible with their owners. Nor should they be purchased; a kris should be given or inherited.

The fact that so few kris blades have been unearthed has led some people to assume that the various Malay kingdoms were peaceful and adverse to war. The more likely explanation is that pre-Muslim Malays attributed such magical power to sword blades that they were only very rarely buried. The art historian Jan Fontein writes that "the process of forging the sword from clumps of iron ore and meteorite into a sharp blade of patterned steel is often seen as a parallel to the process of purification to which the soul is subjected after death by the gods".

The earliest confirmed date for a kris is the 14th century; they are depicted in the reliefs of Candi Panataran and possibly also at Candi Sukuh, both on Java. However, in all likelihood they were introduced considerably earlier, possibly during the 10th century.

Krisses are forged by beating nickel or nickeliferous meteoritic material into iron in a complex series of laminations (iron from meteors is particularly prized because of its celestial origin). After forging, ceremonies are performed and offerings made before the blade is tempered. The empu, or swordsmith, was a respected member of society, who was felt to be imbued with mystical powers. After forging the blade, it is then patinated using a mixture of lime juice and arsenicum. Each part of the sword, even each curve of the blade, has a name and the best krisses are elaborately decorated. Inlaid with gold, the cross-pieces carved into floral patterns and animal motifs, grips made of ivory and studded with jewels, they are works of art.

But they were also tools of combat. In the Malay world, a central element of any battle was the amok. Taken from the Malay verb mengamok, the amok was a furious charge by men armed with krisses, designed to spread confusion within the enemy ranks. Amok warriors would be committed to dying in the charge and often dressed in white to indicate self-sacrifice. They were often drugged with opium or cannabis. It was also an honourable way for a man to commit suicide. Alfred Russel Wallace in Malay Archipelago (1869) writes: "He grasps his kris-handle, and the next moment draws out the weapon and stabs a man to the heart. He runs on, with the bloody kris in his hand, stabbing at everyone he meets. 'Amok! Amok!' then resounds through the streets. Spears, krisses, knives and guns are brought out against him. He rushes madly forward, kills all he can – men, women and children – and dies overwhelmed by numbers...". The English expression 'to run amok' is taken from this Malay word.

Recommended reading: Frey, Edward (1986) The Kris: mystic weapon of the Malay world, OUP: Singapore.

Background

influence on the Johor-Riau sultans, until they had reduced them to puppet-rulers. By then however, offshoots of the Johor royal family had established the sultanates of Pahang and Perak. The Minangkabau-dominated states between Melaka and Selangor formed a confederacy of nine states, or Negeri Sembilan (see page 198). To the northeast, the states of Kelantan and Terengganu came under the Siamese sphere of influence.

British Malaya emerges

The British occupied Dutch colonies during the Napoleonic Wars, following France's invasion of the Netherlands in 1794. Dutch King William of Orange, who fled to London, instructed Dutch governors overseas to end their rivalry with the British and to permit the entry of British troops to their colonies in a bid to keep the French out. Historian William R Roff writes: "From being an Indian power interested primarily ... in the free passage of trade through the Malacca Straits and beyond to China, the East India Company suddenly found itself possessor not merely of a proposed naval station on Penang island but of numerous other territorial dominions and responsibilities. Nor were some of the company's servants at all reluctant to assume these responsibilities and, indeed to extend them."

The British had their own colonial designs, having already established a foothold on Penang where Captain Francis Light had set up a trading post in 1786 (see page 152). The Anglo-Dutch Treaty of London, which was signed in 1824, effectively divided maritime Southeast Asia into British and Dutch spheres of influence. Britain retained Penang, Melaka (which it swapped for the Sumatran port of Bengkulu) and Singapore – which had been founded by Stamford Raffles in 1819 (see page) – and these formed the Straits Settlements. The Dutch regained control of their colonial territories in the Indonesian archipelago. Britain promised to stay out of Sumatra and the Dutch promised not to meddle in the affairs of the peninsula, thus separating two parts of the Malay world whose histories had been intertwined for centuries.

The British did very little to interfere with the Malay sultanates and chiefdoms on the peninsula, but the Straits Settlements grew in importance – particularly Singapore, which soon superceded Penang, which in turn, had eclipsed Melaka.

A woodcut depicting Admiral Cornelis Matelieff's 1606 siege of Melaka

Borneo's history

Archaeological evidence from Sarawak shows that Homo sapiens was established on Borneo at least 40,000 years ago (see page 359). The outside world may have been trading with Borneo from Roman times, and there is evidence in Kaltim (East Kalimantan) of Indian cultural influence from as early as the fourth century. Chinese traders began to visit Borneo from about the seventh century, trading beads and porcelain in exchange for jungle produce and birds' nests. By the 14th century, this trade appears to have been flourishing, particularly with the newly formed Sultanate of Brunei. The history of the north coast of Borneo is dominated by the Sultanate of Brunei from the 14th-19th centuries. The Europeans began arriving in the East in the early 1500s, but had little impact on North Borneo until British adventurer James Brooke arrived in Sarawak in 1839. From then on, the Sultan's empire and influence shrank dramatically as he ceded more and more territory to the expansionist White Rajahs (see page 382) and to the British North Borneo Chartered Company to the north (see page 475). Many of the upriver Dayaks were left

Chinese immigrants arrived in all three ports and from there expanded into tin mining which rapidly emerged as the main source of wealth on the peninsula. The extent of the tin rush in the mid-19th century is exemplified in the town of Larut in northwestern Perak. Around 25,000 Chinese speculators arrived in Larut between 1848 and 1872. The Chinese fought over the rights to mine the most lucrative deposits and organized into secret societies and *kongsis*, which by the 1860s were engaged in open warfare. At the same time, the Malay rulers in the states on the peninsula were busily taxing the tin traders while in the Straits Settlements, British investors in the mining industry put increasing pressure on the Colonial Office to intervene in order to stabilize the situation. In late 1873 Britain decided it could not rule the increasingly lawless and anarchic states by remote control any longer and the western-central states were declared a British protectorate. In his account of British intervention, William R Roff quotes a Malay proverb: 'Once the needle is in, the thread is sure to follow'.

In 1874, the Treaty of Pangkor established the Residential system whereby British officers were posted to key districts; it became their job to determine all administrative and policy matters other than those governing Islam and Malay custom. This immediately provoked resentment and sparked uprisings in Perak, Selangor and Negeri Sembilan, as well as a Malay revolt in 1875. The revolts were put down and the system was institutionalized; in 1876 these three states plus Pahang became the Federated Malay States. By 1909 the north states of Kedah, Perlis, Kelantan and Terengganu – which previously came under Siamese suzerainty – finally agreed to accept British advisers and became known as the Unfederated Malay States. Johor remained independent until 1914 (see page 225). The British system of government relied on the political power of the sultans and the Malay aristocracy: residents conferred with the rulers of each state and employed the aristocrats as civil servants. Local headmen (known as *penghulu*) were used as administrators in rural areas.

Meanwhile, the British continued to encourage the immigration of Chinese, who formed a majority of the population in Perak and Selangor by the early 1920s. Apart from the wealthy traders based in the Straits Settlements, the Chinese immigrants were organized (and exploited) by their secret societies, which provided welfare services, organized work gangs and ran local government. In 1889 the societies were officially banned, and while this broke their hold on political power, they simply re-emerged as a criminal underworld. In the Federated Malay States, there was an

Background

Malaysia's monarchs – the public swings against the sultans

Malaysia's nine hereditary rulers, who take it in turn to be king, represent the greatest concentration of monarchs in the world. In 1993 they were at the forefront of the most heated political controversy that Malaysia has seen in years. The battle royal ended in mid-March 1993 with the opposition Democratic Action Party voting with the government to remove the sultans' personal immunity from prosecution. For Prime Minister Dr Mahathir Mohamad, the 1993 Constitutional Amendment Bill was a personal victory. He had long made it known that he regarded the country's nine traditional rulers as a residual anachronism in modern Malaysia. A further constitutional amendment in May 1994 drove that victory home. It makes clear that from now on, the king can only act on the advice of the government. And even if the king does not approve of legislation passed by the government, it becomes law anyway after 30 days.

Malaysia's sultans emerged in the 14th and 15th centuries as the rulers of the small rivermouth states – or negeri – that grew up around the peninsula's coasts. The word 'sultan' is a Turkish term for the Malay Yang di-Pertuan – literally, 'He who is made Lord'. Sultans wielded more than temporal authority (kuasa); they were vested with an aura of sanctity and magical authority, or dualat. Malaya's sultans came through the British colonial period and the Japanese interregnum with their status and powers surprisingly intact. The post-war British government was forced by Malay lobbyists to adhere to the principle set by colonial administrator Sir Hugh Clifford in 1927: "The States were, when the British government was invited by their rulers and chiefs to set their troubled houses in order, Muhammadan monarchies: such they are today, and such they must continue to be".

On independence in 1957, Malaysia became a constitutional monarchy, with the king elected for a five-year term from among the ranks of the sultans. In 1969, following race riots, the government amended the Sedition Act to make it an offence to question the position or prerogatives of traditional rulers. But in 1983, Prime Minister Mahathir provoked a constitutional crisis when he curtailed the power of the king by removing the monarch's right to veto legislation.

Most of Malaysia's rulers have expensive tastes and some live jet-setting playboy lifestyles. Many have used their position to amass prodigious wealth. Several sultans and their wayward offspring fitted snugly into the polo-set and the golfing and yachting elites, frequenting glitzy nightclubs, attended by retinues of security men. Traditional Malays considered such behaviour unacceptable in light of the sultans' traditional position as the upholders of Islamic values. One or two sultans added to their unsavoury reputation by committing acts of violence, safe in the knowledge that they would not be prosecuted. Resentment over such acts could never be articulated without falling foul of the Sedition Act. The activities of some contemporary rulers are not without precedent. In the 17th century, Sultan Mahmud of Johor was notorious for his cruelty, which included shooting men at random to test a new gun. On one occasion he ordered a pregnant woman to be ripped apart because she had eaten a jackfruit from his garden. In the end the woman's husband ran the sultan through with a kris with the full support of palace officials.

Until very recently it has not been possible to print the alleged crimes of Sultan Mahmud's modern successors in the house of Johor. But in early 1993 a government MP referred in parliament to 23 incidents since 1972 involving today's

eight-fold population increase to 1.7 million between 1891 and 1931. Even by 1891 the proportion of Malays had declined to a fraction over a third of the population, with the Chinese making up 41.5 percent and Indians – imported as indentured labourers by the British (see page 536) – comprising 22 percent. To the south, Johor, which in the late 1800s was not even a member of the federation, had a similar ethnic balance.

Sultan Mahmud of Johor and his son, the Rajah Muda Abdul Majid Idris. The most notorious of these concerned the death of a caddie on the Cameron Highlands golf course. Sultan Mahmood allegedly killed him by smashing his head with a club after the caddie sniggered at a duffed shot. On another occasion a man was shot and killed after an argument with the prince in a Johor Bahru nightclub. Abdul Majid was convicted for this but was pardoned by his father.

Other sultans' disregard for various facets of the law of the land was highlighted by His Royal Highness Tuanku Ismail Petra Ibni Al-Marhum Sultan Tahya Petra of Kelantan. He managed to import 30 luxury cars duty free. In March 1992, he eluded customs officials by claiming he was taking his new Lamborghini Diablo for a test drive. Following that incident, the government took full advantage of its ownership of most national newspapers by devoting pages and pages to exposés of the sultans' flamboyant lifestyles. The RM200m it cost Malaysian taxpayers each year to maintain them was broken down in detail. It emerged that entire hospital wards were reserved for their exclusive use. More than RM9m was spent on new cutlery and bedsheets for the King – a sum which the New Straits Times said would have built two new hospitals or 46 rural clinics or 46 primary schools.

Malaysia's defence minister, Najib Razak, added to the stable of royal anecdotes in 1993 when he revealed that a certain unnamed sultan had ordered a Royal Malaysian Navy Commander to jump ship and swim to shore in front of his assembled crew. His sin? To disturb the sultan's windsurfing by churning up too much wake. Coincidentally, the Sultan of Johor is an avid windsurfer.

Dr Mahathir gambled that the unveiling of such royal scams would swing public opinion in favour of constitutional amendments. The Prime Minister had long lost patience with the sultans over their interference in politics and business. He was particularly angered by the Sultan of Kelantan who backed the state's Islamic opposition's campaign against his government in the 1990 general election. In July 1992 his government agreed a 'code of conduct' with the sultans, but they refused to accept constitutional amendments undermining their powers. Mahathir responded by withdrawing royal privileges such as their generous financial stipends. In January 1993, parliament passed amendments removing their legal immunity. Deadlock ensued as Malaysian law said the sultans had to approve legislation affecting their position. Finally, after a tense stand-off, the government and the sultans agreed to a compromise. The sultans secured an undertaking that no ruler would be taken to court without the Attorney General's approval.

Mahathir emerged from the fray with his executive powers strengthened and his no-nonsense reputation enhanced. The sultans' reputation, by contrast, has been severely dented. As one commentator noted, "the palace doors have been thrown open", adding that public prying into royal affairs is unlikely to cease.

This contretemps between the King and the Prime Minister is history because Malaysia must be the only country where a prime minister has outlasted not one king but four - he is now onto his fifth. Malaysia's current monarch is the extravagantly titled the Yang di-Pertuan Agong, Sultan Salahuddin Abdul Aziz Shah, who was named as the country's eleventh constitutional monarch in February 1999. He took on his five-year term from the outgoing Sultan of Negri Sembilan, the urbane, Oxford-educated Ja'afar ibni Abdul Rahman.

For the most part, the Malay population remained in the countryside and were only gradually drawn into the modern economy. But by the 1920s Malay nationalism was on the rise, partly prompted by the Islamic reform movement and partly by intellectuals in secular circles who looked to the creation of a Greater Malaysia (or Greater Indonesia), under the influence of left-wing Indonesian nationalists. These Malay nationalists were as critical of the Malay élite as they were of the British colonialists. The élite itself was becoming increasingly outspoken for different reasons – it felt threatened by the growing demands of Straits-born Chinese and second-generation Indians for equal rights.

The first semi-political nationalist movement was the *Kesatuan Melayu Singapura* (Singapore Malay Union), formed in 1926 (see page). The Union found early support in the Straits Settlements where Malays were outnumbered and there was no sultan. They gradually spread across the peninsula and held a pan-Malayan conference in 1939. These associations were the forerunners of the post-war Malay nationalist movement. In the run-up to the Second World War the left wing split off to form the *Kesatuan Melayu Muda* – the Union of Young Malays, which was strongly anti-British and whose leaders were arrested by the colonial authorities in 1940. The Chinese were more interested in business than politics and any political interests were focused on China. The middle class supported the Chinese nationalist Kuomintang (KMT), although it was eventually banned by the British, as it was becoming an obvious focus of anti-colonial sentiment. The KMT allowed Communists to join the movement until 1927, but in 1930 they split off to form the Malayan Communist Party (MCP) which drew its support from the working class.

Japanese occupation

Under cover of darkness on the night of 8 December 1941, the Japanese army invaded Malaya, landing in South Thailand and pushing into Kedah, and at Kota Bharu in Kelantan (see page 299). The invasion, which took place an hour before the attack on Pearl Harbor, took the Allies in Malaya and 'Fortress' Singapore completely by surprise. The Japanese forces had air, land and sea superiority and quickly overwhelmed the Commonwealth troops on the peninsula. Militarily, it was a brilliant campaign, made speedier by the fact that the Japanese troops stole bicycles in every town they took, thus making it possible for them to outpace all Allied estimates of their likely rate of advance.

By 28 December they had taken Ipoh and all of northern Malaya. Kuantan fell on the 31st, the Japanese having sunk the British warships *Prince of Wales* and *Repulse* (see page) and Kuala Lumpur on 11 January 1942. They advanced down the east coast, centre and west coast simultaneously and by the end of the month had taken Johor Bahru and were massed across the strait from Singapore. By 15 February they had forced the capitulation of the Allies in Singapore (see page). This was a crushing blow, and, according to Malaysian historian Zainal Abidin bin Abudul Wahid, "the speed with which the Japanese managed to achieve victory, however temporary that might have been, shattered the image of the British, and generally the 'whiteman', as a superior people". Right up until the beginning of the Second World War, the British had managed to placate the aristocratic leaders of the Malay community and the wealthy Chinese merchants and there was little real threat to the status quo. The Japanese defeat of the British changed all that by altering the balance between conservatism and change. Because Britain had failed so miserably to defend Malaya, its credentials as a protector were irrevocably tarnished.

For administrative purposes, the Japanese linked the peninsula with Sumatra as part of the Greater East Asia Co-prosperity Sphere. All British officials were interned and the legislative and municipal councils swept aside. But because the Japanese had lost their command of the seas by the end of 1942, nothing could be imported and there was a shortage of food supplies. The 'banana' currency introduced by the Japanese became worthless as inflation soared. Japan merely regarded Malaya as a source of raw materials, yet the rubber and tin industries stagnated and nothing was done to develop the economy.

After initially severing sultans' pensions and reducing their powers, the Japanese realized that their co-operation was necessary if the Malay bureaucracy was to be put to work for the occupation government (see page 494). The Indians were treated well since they were seen as a key to fighting the British colonial régime in India. But Malaya's Chinese, while they were not rounded up and executed as they were in Singapore, were not trusted. The Japanese, however, came to recognize the importance of the Chinese community in oiling the wheels of the economy. The Chinese Dalforce militia (set up by the Allies as the Japanese advanced southwards) joined the Communists and other minor underground dissident groups in forming the Malayan People's Anti-Japanese Army. British army officers and arms were parachuted into the jungle to support the guerrillas. It was during this period that the Malayan Communist Party (MCP) broadened its membership and appeal, under the guise of a nationwide anti-Japanese alliance.

The brutality of the Japanese régime eased with time; as the war began to go against them, they increasingly courted the different communities, giving them more say in the run of things in an effort to undermine any return to colonial rule. But the Japanese's favourable treatment of Malays and their general mistrust of the Chinese did not foster good race relations between the two. A Malay paramilitary police force was put to work to root out Chinese who were anti-Japanese, which exacerbated inter-communal hostility. The Japanese never offered Malaya independence but allowed Malay nationalist sentiments to develop in an effort to deflect attention from the fact they had ceded the North Malay states of Kedah, Perlis, Kelantan and Terengganu to Thailand.

The British return

During the war, the British drew up secret plans for a revised administrative structure in Malaya. The plan was to create a Malayan Union by combining the federated and unfederated states as well as Melaka and Penang, leaving Singapore as a crown colony. Plans were also drawn up to buy North Borneo from the Chartered Company (see page 476) and to replace the anachronous White Rajahs of Sarawak (see page 384) with a view to eventually grouping all the territories together as a federation. As soon as the Japanese surrendered in September 1945, the plan was put into action. Historian Mary Turnbull notes that "Malaya was unique [among Western colonies] because the returning British were initially welcomed with enthusiasm and were themselves unwilling to put the clock back. But they were soon overwhelmed by the reaction against their schemes for streamlining the administration and assimilating the different immigrant communities."

A unitary state was formed on the peninsula and everyone, regardless of race or origin, who called Malaya 'home', was accorded equal status. But the resentment caused by British high-handedness was the catalyst which triggered the foundation of the United Malays National Organization (UMNO) which provided a focus for opposition to the colonial régime and, following independence, formed the ruling party. Opposition to UMNO, led by the Malay ruling class, forced the British to withdraw the Union proposal. The sultans refused to attend the installation of the governor and the Malays boycotted advisory councils. Mary Turnbull notes that the Malayan Union scheme was "conceived as a civil servant's dream but was born to be a politician's nightmare". Vehement Malay opposition prompted negotiations with Malay leaders which hammered out the basis of a Federation of Malaya which was established in February 1948. It was essentially the same as the Union in structure, except that it recognized the sovereignty of the sultans in the 11 states and the so-called 'special position' of the Malays as the indigenous people of Malaya. The federation had a strong central government (headed by a High Commissioner) and a federal executive council.

Background

In this federal system, introduced in 1948, non-Malays could only become Malaysian citizens if they had been resident in Malaya for a minimum of 15 out of the previous 25 years, were prepared to sign a declaration of permanent settlement and were able to speak either Malay or English. This meant only three million of Malaya's five million population qualified as citizens, of whom 78 percent were Malay, 12 percent Chinese and seven percent Indian. Historian Mary Turnbull says that while the British believed they had achieved their objective of common citizenship (even on more restricted terms), they had, in reality "accepted UMNO's concept of a Malay nation into which immigrant groups would have to be integrated, and many difficulties were to develop from this premise".

The rise of Communism

The Chinese and Indian communities were not consulted in these Anglo-Malay negotiations and ethnic and religious tensions between the three main communities were running high, unleashing the forces of racialism which had been lying dormant for years. Because their part in the political process had been ignored, many more Chinese began to identify with the Malaysian Communist Party (MCP) which was still legal. It was not until the Communist victory in China in 1949 that the Chinese began to think of Malaya as home. During the war the MCP had gained legitimacy and prestige as a patriotic resistance movement. The MCP's *de facto* military wing, the MPAJA, had left arms dumps in the jungle, but the Communist leadership was split as to whether negotiation or confrontation was the way forward. Then in 1947 the MCP suffered what many considered to be a disastrous blow: its Vietnamese-born secretary-general, Lai Teck, absconded with all the party's funds having worked as a double agent for both the Japanese and the British. He was suspected of having betrayed the entire MCP central committee to the Japanese in 1942. The new 26 year old MCP leader, former schoolmaster Chin Peng, immediately abandoned Lai's soft approach.

In June 1948 he opted for armed rebellion, and the Malayan Communist Emergency commenced with the murder of three European planters. According to John Gullick, the historian and former member of the Malayan civil service, it was called an 'Emergency' because the Malayan economy was covered by the London insurance market for everything other than war. Premiums covered loss of stock, property and equipment through riot and civil commotion, but not through civil war, so the misnomer continued throughout the 12 year insurrection. Others say it got its name from the Emergency Regulations that were passed in June 1948 which were designed to deny food supplies and weapons to the Communists.

The Emergency was characterized by indiscriminate armed Communist raids on economic targets – often rubber estates and tin mines – and violent ambushes which were aimed at loosening and undermining central government control. Chinese 'squatters' in areas fringing the jungle (many of whom had fled from the cities during the Japanese occupation) provided an information and supply network for the Communists. In 1950 the British administration moved these people into 500 'New Villages', where they could be controlled and protected. This policy, known as 'The Briggs Plan' after the Director of Operations, Lieutenant-General Sir Harold Briggs, was later adopted (rather less successfully) by the Americans in South Vietnam.

In much the same way as they had been caught unprepared by the Japanese invasion in 1941, the British were taken by surprise and in the first few years the MCP (whose guerrillas were labelled 'CTs' – or Communist Terrorists) gained the upper hand. In 1951 British morale all but crumbled when the High Commissioner, Sir Henry Gurney, was ambushed and assassinated on the road to Fraser's Hill (see page 120). His successor, General Sir Gerald Templer, took the initiative, however, with his campaign to 'win the hearts and minds of the people'. Templer's biographer,

John Cloake, gave him Japanese General Tomoyuki Yamashita's old sobriquet 'Tiger of Malaya', and there is little doubt that his tough policies won the war. In his book *Emergency Years*, former mine-manager Leonard Rayner says the chain-smoking Templer "exuded nervous energy like an overcharged human battery". Within two years the Communists were on the retreat. They had also begun to lose popular support due to the climate of fear they introduced, although the Emergency did not officially end until 1960.

Historians believe the Communist rebellion failed because it was too slow to take advantage of the economic hardships in the immediate aftermath of the Second World War and because it was almost exclusively Chinese. It also only really appealed to the Chinese working class and alienated and shunned the Chinese merchant community and Straits-born Chinese.

The road to Merdeka

The British had countered the MCP's claim to be a multi-racial nationalist movement by accelerating moves towards Malayan independence, which Britain promised, once the Emergency was over. The only nationalist party with any political credibility was UMNO. Its founder, Dato' Onn bin Jaafar wanted to allow non-Malays to become members, and when his proposal was rejected, he resigned to form the Independence of Malaya Party. The brother of the Sultan of Kedah, Tunku Abdul Rahman, took over as head of UMNO and to counter Onn's new party, he made an electoral pact with the Malayan Chinese Association (MCA) and the Malayan Indian Congress (MIC). With the MCP out of the picture, the Chinese community had hesitantly grouped itself around the MCA. The Alliance (which trounced Onn's party in the election) is still in place today, in the form of the ruling *Barisan Nasional* (National Front). After sweeping the polls in 1955, the Alliance called immediately for *merdeka*, or independence, which the British guaranteed within two years.

With independence promised by non-violent means, Tunku Abdul Rahman offered an amnesty to the Communists. Together with Singapore's Chief Minister, David Marshall and Straits-Chinese leader Tan Cheng Lock (see page 210), he met Chin Peng in 1956. But they failed to reach agreement and the MCP fled through the jungle into the mountains in southern Thailand around Betong. While the Emergency was declared 'over' in 1960, the MCP only finally agreed to lay down its arms in 1989, in a peace agreement brokered by Thailand. The party had been riven by factionalism and its membership had dwindled to under 1,000. In 1991, the legendary Chin Peng struck a deal with the Malaysian government allowing the former guerrillas to return home.

Historian Mary Turnbull writes: "When Malaya attained independence in 1957 it was a prosperous country with stable political institutions, a sound administrative system and a good infrastructure of education and communications – a country with excellent resources and a thriving economy based on export agriculture and mining." Under the new constitution, a king was to be chosen from one of the nine sultans, and the monarchy was to be rotated every five years. A two-tier parliament was set up, with a *Dewan Rakyat* (People's House) of elected representatives and a *Dewan Negara* (Senate) to represent the state assemblies. Each of the 11 states had its own elected government and a sultan or governor.

Politicians in Singapore made it clear that they also wanted to be part of an independent Malaya, but in Kuala Lumpur, UMNO leaders were opposed to a merger because the island had a Chinese majority. (A straight merger would have resulted in a small Chinese majority in Malaya.) Increasing nationalist militancy in Singapore was of particular concern to UMNO and the radical wing of the People's Action Party, which was swept to power with Lee Kuan Yew at its head in 1959, was

Pityamit one: from guerrilla camp to holiday camp

The Malayan Emergency was one of the few insurgencies which the Communists lost. But their shelling, ambushes, bombings and assassinations cost the lives of more than 10,000 soldiers and civilians over 40 years. The Emergency started just after the Second World War. At its peak, tens of thousands of Commonwealth troops were pitted against an estimated 3,500 Communists, most of whom were Chinese, in the Malayan jungle. Newly independent Malaysia pronounced the Emergency officially over in 1960. They had the Communists on the run. The guerrillas fled across Malaysia's jungled frontier into South Thailand, but once ensconced there, they held out for another 30 years against both the Malaysian and Thai armies.

Most of their secret camps were never found. The Communists had laced the border itself with booby trap devices and regularly launched attacks and ambushes across the border. The people on the frontline of the war were the residents of the Malaysian border town of Pengkalan Hulu (formerly Keroh), which means 'forward base'. Many atrocities were committed in and around the town, which was still under curfew until well into the 1980s. The Communists also made themselves unpopular in Thailand, where they demanded protection money from local businesses around Betong. They never surrendered, but finally, in 1989, they reached what was known as 'an honourable settlement' with the Malaysian and Thai governments, bringing to an end one of the world's longest-running insurgencies. Realizing that most of the former guerrillas would be unwilling to return to their homeland, King Bhumipol of Thailand offered them land around their former camps and built

them houses. One of those camps, Pityamit I, has now opened to the public for the first time. Like others in the vicinity, nobody knew it was there until recently.

Having laid down their Kalashnikovs, former revolutionaries now take tourists round their old jungle stronghold. Some sell herbal medicine and soft drinks to the tourists; others have become vegetable farmers at the Highland Friendship Co-operative (the camp's new name). The trees which once afforded them thick cover from helicopter gunships have been chopped down and the steep hillsides have been planted out. About 1,200 former fighters have now settled into their new lives but few have any regrets about their old ones as members of the Communist Party of Malaya's pro-Moscow splinter group. "Money is important", one of them told a visiting journalist. "Without it you can't do anything." They are happy to regale tourists with tales of the jungle. Some have been living in it since 1948. Although they admit that Communism worldwide appears to have failed, they urge those who are prepared to listen not to jump to hasty conclusions. "The final decisions should be up to our sons and grandsons."

About 100 former Communists have returned to booming modern Malaysia. They are in detention under the country's Internal Security Act in Taiping, where in the words of their comrades across the border, they are being "rehabilitated" and "brain-washed". In Kuala Lumpur, few people stop to think of the Emergency years; they seem like ancient history now because things have moved so fast. But if it's all been partially forgotten, the Communists themselves have not been forgiven as the scars still run deep.

dominated by Communists. Fearing the emergence of 'a second Cuba' on Malaysia's doorstep, Tunku Abdul Rahman proposed that Singapore join a greater Malaysian Federation, in which a racial balance would be maintained by the inclusion of Sarawak, Brunei and British North Borneo (Sabah). Britain supported the move, as did all the states involved. Kuala Lumpur was particularly keen on Brunei joining the Federation on two scores: it had Malays and it had oil. But at the eleventh hour, Brunei's Sultan Omar backed out, mistrustful of Kuala Lumpur's obvious designs on his sultanate's oil revenues and unhappy at the prospect of becoming just another sultan in Malaya's collection of nine monarchs (see page 494).

Prime Minister Tunku Abdul Rahman was disheartened, but the Malaysia Agreement was signed in July 1963 with Singapore, Sarawak and Sabah. Without Brunei, there was a small Chinese majority in the new Malaysia. The Tunku did not have time to dwell on racial arithmetic, however, because almost immediately the new federation was plunged into an undeclared war with Indonesia – which became known as *Konfrontasi*, or Confrontation (see page 388) – due to President Sukarno's objection to the participation of Sabah and Sarawak. Indonesian saboteurs were landed on the peninsula and in Singapore and there were Indonesian military incursions along the borders of Sabah and Sarawak with Kalimantan. Konfrontasi was finally ended in 1966 after Sukarno fell from power. But relations with Singapore – which had been granted a greater measure of autonomy than other states – were far from smooth. Communal riots in Singapore in 1964 and Lee Kuan Yew's efforts to forge a nation-wide opposition alliance which called for 'a democratic Malaysian Malaysia' further opened the rift with Kuala Lumpur. Feeling unnerved by calls for racial equality while the Malays did not form a majority of the population, Tunku Abdul Rahman expelled Singapore from the federation in August 1965 against Lee Kuan Yew's wishes.

Racial politics in the 1960s

The expulsion of Singapore did not solve the racial problem on the peninsula, however. Because the Malay and Chinese communities felt threatened by each other - one wielded political power, the other economic power - racial tensions built up. Resentment focused on the enforcement of Malay as the medium of instruction in all schools and as the national language and on the privileged educational and employment opportunities afforded to Malays. The tensions finally exploded on 13 May 1969, in the wake of the general election.

The UMNO-led Alliance faced opposition from the Democratic Action Party (DAP) which was built from the ashes of Lee Kuan Yew's People's Action Party. The DAP was a radical Chinese-dominated party and called for racial equality. Also in opposition was *Gerakan* (the People's Movement), supported by Chinese and Indians, and the Pan-Malayan Islamic Party, which was exclusively Malay and very conservative. In the election, the opposition parties - which were not in alliance – deprived the Alliance of its two-thirds majority in parliament; it required this margin to amend the constitution unimpeded. Gerakan and DAP celebrations provoked counter-demonstrations from Malays and in the ensuing mayhem hundreds were killed in Kuala Lumpur.

The government suspended the constitution for over a year and declared a **State of Emergency**. A new national ideology was drawn up – the controversial New Economic Policy (see page), which was an ambitious experiment in social and economic engineering aimed at ironing out discrepancies between ethnic communities. The *Rukunegara*, a written national ideology aimed at fostering nation-building, was introduced in August 1970. It demanded loyalty to the king and the constitution, respect for Islam and observance of the law and morally acceptable behaviour. All discussion of the Malays' 'special position' was banned as was discussion about the national language and the sovereignty of the sultans. In the words of historian John Gullick, "Tunku Abdul Rahman, whose anguish at the disaster had impeded his ability to deal with it effectively," resigned the following month and handed over to Tun Abdul Razak. Tun Razak was an able administrator, but lacked the dynamism of his predecessor. He did, however, unify UMNO and patched up the old Alliance, breathing new life into the coalition by incorporating every political party except the DAP and one or two other small parties into the newly named *Barisan Nasional* (BN), or National Front. In 1974 the Barisan won a landslide majority.

Tun Razak shifted Malaysia's foreign policy from a pro-Western stance to non-alignment and established diplomatic relations with both Moscow and Beijing. But within Malaysia, Communist paranoia was rife: as Indochina fell to Communists in the mid-1970s, many Malaysians became increasingly convinced that Malaysia was just another 'domino' waiting to topple. There were even several arrests of prominent Malays (including two newspaper editors and five top UMNO politicians). But when Chin Peng's revolutionaries joined forces with secessionist Muslims in South Thailand, the Thai and Malaysian governments launched a joint clean-out operation in the jungle along the frontier. By the late 1970s the North Kalimantan Communist Party had also been beaten into virtual submission too (see page 388). In 1976 Tun Razak died and was succeeded by his brother-in-law, Dato' Hussein Onn (the son of Umno's founding father). He inherited an economy which was in good shape, thanks to strong commodity prices, and in the general election of 1978, the BN won another comfortable parliamentary majority. Three years later he handed over to Dr Mahathir Mohamad (see profile, page 504) who in April 1995 secured yet another term in office having won a massive majority in Parliament, see below.

Modern Malaysia

Politics

Prime Minister Mahathir & UMNO
On the face of it, Malaysia's political landscape is remarkably unchanging. Dr Mahathir Mohamad, as leader of the United Malays National Organization (UMNO), heads the *Barisan Nasional* (BN), or National Front coalition, and has won every one of five elections since coming to power in 1981. There is no question who leads and dominates the coalition: UMNO. It is notable that Mahathir's hold on power is only really challenged from within UMNO; the other members of the BN would not risk speaking out against the premier and it sometimes seems as though they are only along for the ride.

With the rapid expansion in Malaysia's economy, and notwithstanding the recession associated with the Asian economic crisis of 1997-99, there has emerged a substantial *nouveau riche* middle class. There has, in turn, been the expectation in some quarters that a more open political system might evolve as prosperous, and increasingly well educated, people demand more of a political say. But the government does not readily tolerate dissent and during the premiership of Dr Mahathir power has, in fact, become increasingly concentrated in the hands of the government.

The 1999 general election
The 1999 general election was fought against the background of the trial of former deputy prime minister Anwar Ibrahim (see below) and an economic recession. Both injected elements of uncertainty into the contest. There is no doubt that many Malaysians, and especially younger ones, were appalled at the treatment of Anwar Ibrahim and the apparent vindictiveness of the premier's campaign against his former right-hand man. In addition, Mahathir was fighting against the backdrop of a shrinking economy. In 1998 GDP declined by 7.5 percent as Malaysia battled with the Asian economic crisis. Furthermore there was criticism of the grandiose projects with which the prime minister is closely associated, from the world's tallest buildings to a new federal capital, and with the nepotism that seems to be such a part of the Malaysian political economy. With all this, one might wonder how on earth Mahathir, 74 years old in 1999 and with rumours of ill-health, could win another term of office. But he did; and did so convincingly. The government won

148 seats in the 193-seat parliament. Understanding why Mahathir and UMNO won sheds light on the peculiarities of the Malaysian political system.

To begin with, the media is effectively government-controlled. It is extremely hard for opposition groups to get their voices heard. The only area where the government does not have a stranglehold is the internet and, while Malaysia may view itself as cyber-savvy, there aren't that many people who habitually trawl for news on the web. On 3 May 1999 during World Press Freedom Day the New York-based Committee to Protect Journalists voted Mahathir one of the world's top 10 'enemies of the press'. Even the World Bank classifies the Malaysian press as 'not free'.

There is also no doubt that Mahathir is an extremely astute political operator. He called the election in November so that 680,000 young Malaysians who came onto the electoral role in February 2000 could not vote. Most, he no doubt reasoned, would have voted for the opposition. He is also very adept at playing to his domestic audience. Indeed, it could be argued that most of his anti-Western invective is just for domestic consumption. So when he cautioned, in 1999, his people to watch out for "ethnic Europeans [many of whom] are of the opinion that Muslim people cannot succeed, more so when their skin colour is brown" he was not intending that it should be digested by an overseas audience.

But perhaps most convincing as an explanation as to why Mahathir won the election despite this plethora of problems and concerns is what is termed 'ethnic politics'. The Malays make up a bare majority of the population, about 55 percent. The closely fought general elections of 1969 brought Malay and Chinese into conflict with hundreds of deaths. The fear that this could happen again scares many people into voting for continuity rather than change. This applies mainly to the Chinese who, one might have thought, would naturally vote for a Chinese opposition party. Thus there is a paradox: many people who are disenchanted with Mahathir, UMNO and the BN are also afraid that should the opposition win another bout of communal unrest could follow. So many people would like Mahathir to go, but would not like a defeat which could spark violence.

Finally, and linked to the last reason, there is an enduring sense that the opposition in Malaysia is not a credible one, a view no doubt accentuated by the government's hold over the media. To try and present a united front, in the run-up to the November 1999 elections the opposition parties formed their own alliance, the Alternative Front. This linked the Muslim PAS which is strongly represented in the east coast states of Kelantan and Terengganu, and also in Perlis and Kedah with the Chinese-dominated DAP which usually produces a strong showing in urban centres. These two well-established opposition parties were joined by the multi-ethnic Malaysia People's Party and by the Justice Party (Keadilan), led by Anwar Ibrahim's wife, Wan Azizah Ismail. The four parties agreed on a common platform and also agreed not to challenge one another on their home turfs. (Of Malaysia's 192 constituencies, 134 have a *bumiputra* [Malay] majority, 32 a Chinese majority, while 26 have neither a Chinese nor a *bumi* majority.)

While Mahathir won, and did so handsomely, there were also signs that support was beginning to fall away. The opposition managed to more than double their number of seats, from 16 in the 1995 elections to 42 in 1999, and increase their share of the vote from 35 percent in 1995 to 44 percent in 1999. Furthermore, and significantly, it was mainly Malays who deserted the National Front, not Chinese. It was the PAS and the Justice Party which gained most seats; the DAP (a 'Chinese' party) gained just one. Ironically, it could be argued that it was the Chinese, more than any other group, who won the election for Mahathir.

It may have become commonplace in Malaysia for opposition politicians, free-thinking jurists, environmentalists and other assorted annoyances to be hounded, arrested, tried and jailed, but not mainstream Malay politicians. It is this

Anwar Ibrahim: Malaysia's trial of the century

🖐 ## Mahathir Mohamad – recalcitrance rules OK

He's blunt; he's abrasive and he's headstrong. His detractors regularly accuse him of autocratic tendencies. His supporters talk of a man of conviction. Over the past decade, Prime Minister Dr Mahathir Mohamad has curtailed the power of the judiciary, clamped down on the press, jailed his critics and removed the privileges enjoyed by Malaysia's nine hereditary monarchs. In the international arena, Mahathir has emerged as the self-appointed champion and spokesman for the developing world. He made a name for himself in 1992 by vociferously defending Malaysia's environmental record at the Earth Summit in Rio de Janeiro (see page 529). And Dr M has a virulent dislike of the Western media.

The Malaysian Prime Minister dominated news headlines in Britain in early 1994 when he ordered the cancellation of British contracts in Malaysia worth US$6bn. He had taken offence at London newspaper allegations that senior Malaysian politicians were corrupt. (Ironically, after claiming an apology from the British press, Mahathir himself in 1996 was decrying the corruption in Malaysia's body politic while senior members of his party, UMNO, were resigning for assorted nefarious activities.) The papers may have dubbed him "the Prickliest Premier in the East", but Mahathir has put Malaysia firmly on the world map. "If you can't be famous," he said "then at least be notorious!"

For all the notoriety born of his possibly Machiavellian manoeuvering, the Malaysian premier is also sensitive to criticism. He is a home-grown, made-in-Malaysia product and is quick to seize on any opportunity to lash out at what he sees as the condescending, neo-colonialist attitudes of the West. Today, a slight against him appears to be perceived as a national slur. For Mahathir has become the CEO for Malaysia Inc. He has continued to win elections because with him has come the political stability and prosperity which has kept most Malaysians happy. He's also imbued them with a new self-confidence – particularly the Malays. Britain got its first taste of Mahathir's wrath a decade ago after the British government raised fees for foreign students. His no-nonsense response was to instruct Malaysians to "Buy British Last". In November 1993, the Australian Prime Minister, Paul Keating, tangled with him. He branded Mahathir "recalcitrant" for his refusal to attend a regional summit. That remark nearly provoked a trade war. In the end, Keating was forced to apologize – too much was at stake.

Politics is a game which Mahathir is good at and one in which he has always proved controversial. During Malaysia's race riots of May 1969, he gained notoriety as a rabble-rouser and outspoken critic of Tunku Abdul Rahman, Malaysia's first Prime Minister. He outlined his extreme pro-Malay views in a book, The Malay Dilemma, which was promptly banned. Ironically, Mahathir himself is not fully Malay: his father was an Indian Muslim. But his pro-Malay views struck a

which rocked Malaysia's political establishment when Anwar Ibrahim, former deputy prime minister and Mahathir's successor in waiting, was arrested in late 1998.

Anwar was sacked by Mahathir on 2 September 1998. This was preceded by a series of murky allegations impugning Anwar's morals. In particular, there were whispers that he was bisexual. Not only is this beyond the pale in a largely Muslim country like Malaysia, but homosexuality remains a crime. Anwar's supporters saw this whispering campaign as politically motivated and the result of a widening gulf between Mahathir and his deputy over how to manage the economy.

A few days after he was sacked, Anwar was arrested and charged with five counts of sodomy and five charges of abuse of power. But before his second appearance in court Anwar appeared with bruised arms and a black eye, and accused the police of beating him. Mahathir seemed to imply that the injuries were self-inflicted. Anwar's

chord and through the early 1970s, he fought his way into the upper echelons of the political hierarchy. Mahathir entered the cabinet as education minister and by 1976 had become deputy prime minister. Over the next five years, he gained a reputation as a dynamic Malay leader with a sense of purpose. In 1981 Mahathir was elected President of the politically dominant United Malays National Organization (UMNO); the President automatically becomes Prime Minister.

Unlike his predecessors, Mahathir climbed the political ladder without the help of aristocratic connections. He was the first Malaysian leader not to have been educated in the West – he trained as a medical doctor at the University of Singapore. And he had humble origins; he was born in a small Malay kampung house, next door to an ice factory, on the outskirts of Alor Star in Kedah. In his school days, during the Japanese occupation, the young Mahathir worked as a stallholder at the local market, where he sold ginger drinks and bananas. His first stall was torn down by Japanese soldiers. He revealed all this in 1991, while attempting to convince stallholders in the same market of the wisdom of turning it into a modern shopping complex.

From his first day in office, Mahathir gained respect for his determination to root out corruption, although the rise of money-politics – a consequence of his policy to promote Malay businesses – undermined this. One of his first actions was to loosen Malaysia's ties with the Commonwealth – particularly with Britain, through the 'Buy British Last' campaign, in which he instructed Malaysians to 'Look East' instead to the booming economies of Japan, South Korea and Taiwan. He stressed the importance of self-reliance and one of Mahathir's enduring legacies will be the Proton Saga, the national car (see page 88). It has become the ultimate symbol of the new high-tech 'Made-in-Malaysia' image the Prime Minister has been so keen to promote.

Mahathir has won a string of impressive election victories – most recently in 1999 – and has weathered both economic recession and criticism of his sometimes abrasive and often autocratic style. His health is the one wild card: he suffered a big heart attack in 1989 and in 1997 celebrated his 71st birthday. But so far at least, whenever there has been the merest glimpse of a threat Mahathir has outmanoeuvred his opponent with consummate skill and not a little ruthlessness.

More than anything, Mahathir has changed the way Malaysian's, and especially Malays, think about themselves. When he came to power, Malays were all to ready to put themselves down, to admit defeat to the more assiduous Chinese. Now Malaysians are self-confident and willing not just to compete with the Chinese on a level playing field but to take their new-found confidence into the international arena and to play – and win.

treatment at the hands of the police as well as the crude and one-sided coverage in the government-controlled press angered many Malaysians. They did not believe the charges, and as the trial continued they became less and less credible. Nonetheless, on 14 April 1999, Anwar was convicted of corruption and jailed for six years. More to the point, even when he is released he won't be able to hold political office for a further five years. For Anwar, the verdict, as he put it "stinks to high heaven". At the end of the trial, Anwar read from a prepared statement and said: "I have no hope of justice… The charges are part of a political conspiracy to destroy me and ensure Mahathir Mohamad's continued hold on power at whatever cost". Certainly Mahathir would seem to have succeeded in taking Anwar out of the political equation for at least 11 years.

Calling names

Soros on Mahathir

Mahathir is 'a menace to his own country' and a 'loose cannon'

Mahathir was using Soros 'as a scapegoat to cover up his own failure'

Mahathir on Soros and currency speculators

Currency trading is 'unnecessary, unproductive and immoral'

Foreign investors are 'ferocious beasts'

Soros is 'a moron'

Nonetheless, Anwar's jail sentence may prove – in retrospect – to be a turning point in Malaysia's political fortunes. It brought demonstrators onto the streets of Kuala Lumpur. It created demands for *reformasi*. It led to the creation of a new opposition party, the Justice Party, led by Anwar's wife Wan Azizah. It even brought the US ambassador to remark that Anwar was the world's "newest and most famous political prisoner".

With Anwar sacked and now in jail, Mahathir appointed a new deputy prime minister, Adbullah Badawi. No doubt aware of what happened to Anwar when he got a little bit uppity, Abdullah will, one imagines, be playing the loyal deputy. But with Mahathir in his mid-70s, time is not on the premier's side. Mahathir has publicly said that this will be his last term as prime minister.

Money politics & corruption The entrenched position of UMNO and the BN has, in the eyes of the government's critics, allowed money politics and political patronage to flourish. It is argued that the use of political power to dispense favours and make money has become endemic, so much so that it is accepted as just another part of the political landscape. In 1995 Datuk Rafidah Aziz, the highly respected minister of International Trade and Industry, revealed in court that her son-in-law, a son of Prime Minister Mahathir, and a brother of Anwar Ibrahim had all benefited from share allocations which fell under her largesse. Such allocations are permitted – indeed encouraged – as part of the effort to increase bumiputra representation in the economy. But the scale to which relatives and political supporters benefit is questioned. Mahathir announced a new code of conduct for senior officials and politicians in early 1995 in an attempt to foster greater probity.

Nonetheless, the years since have seen a gradual drip, drip of scandal which has threatened to take the shine off Malaysia's glossy image. This so incensed Prime Minister Mahathir that in an UMNO address in October 1996 he wept as he warned party members that money politics and corruption 'would destroy the country'. Critics have suggested that UMNO's unquestioned political supremacy has created the conditions where corruption and money politics can flourish. In 1996 it was alleged that people in positions of power had managed to manipulate the legal system. The United Nations Centre for Human Rights released a press statement saying: "Complaints are rife that certain highly placed personalities in Malaysia ... are manipulating the Malaysian system of justice and thereby undermining the due administration of independent and impartial justice by courts." The statement referred to a series of allegations that litigants had managed to select judges of their own choice. In an address to the UMNO Supreme Council in May 1997 shortly after two senior UMNO leaders had been sacked in connection with missing funds, Mahathir pointedly said "We will not defend anyone who's corrupt". A few months earlier on 22 December 1996, to the intense embarrassment of the Prime Minister, Muhammad Muhammad Taib, Chief Minister of Selangor, was detained trying to leave Brisbane, Australia with close to US$1m in cash stashed into a suitcase; an offence under Australian law. Muhammad rather feebly explained to a packed and incredulous press conference that the money had been entrusted to him by his brothers to buy property on Australia's Gold Coast. He continued: "I do not feel any sense of wrongdoing in this matter and if it is an offence, it is a technical one ..."

The anti-corruption drive continued through the year and by the middle of 1997 a chief minister (the above Muhammad Muhammad Taib), a deputy minister and a host of government officials and UMNO party stalwarts had been sacked or had resigned. Anwar Ibrahim, the Prime Minister's number two, responded to Mahathir's fears by heading an anti-corruption drive to root out the guilty and announced that the powers of the Anti-Corruption Agency would be strengthened. By all accounts there are more than a few unusually wealthy politicians pacing the deep shag pile of their luxury apartments considering their futures. Although no one considers Mahathir himself to be among the guilty, there are those who suggest that the Prime Minister's style and his emphasis on wealth creation has helped to promote corruption. Chandra Muzaffar, a political scientist at the Science University of Malaysia in Penang, for example, argues that "He's created a culture that places undue emphasis on wealth accumulation for its own sake. The new heroes are all corporate barons."

Another challenge for the government is how to curb the growth of what Prime Minister Mahathir has termed 'social ills'. For a country which has argued that 'Asian values' have permitted it to modernize without the social and moral degradation evident in the West, this is a sensitive subject. Research has revealed a surge in drug taking (particularly recreational drugs like Ecstasy), illegitimate pregnancies, wife abuse, gangsterism and incest. Moreover, this research seems to show that the problem is predominantly concentrated among Malays. Never one to shy away from a problem, however embarrassing, Mahathir has bluntly pointed out: "In terms of population breakdown, the Malays form 55 percent while the Chinese make up about 25 percent and Indians, 10 percent. But when comparing social problems, the Malays account for 67 percent, while Chinese involvement is only 16 percent." State and national government rushed to introduce legislation to control this rash of so-called ills.

Social ills

Since the race riots of 1969 relations between Malaysia's Malay and Chinese populations have dominated political affairs. Now that Malaysia is fast attaining economic maturity a debate is beginning to emerge about whether it is time to consign racial politics, and racial quotas, to the dust heap. Prime Minister Mahathir's Vision 2020 (see page 512), which sets out a path to developed country status by 2020, significantly talks of a 'Malaysian race working in full and equal partnership'. There is no mention here of 'bumiputras' and 'Chinese Malaysians', but of a single Malaysian identity which transcends race.

Racial relations in the New Malaysia

Not everyone agrees with this vision. There are those who note that the communal peace which has descended on the nation since 1969 has been based on a fast-growing economy in which everyone has gained even while the portions of the cake allotted to each group have changed. They worry that a slowing economy could bring racial conflicts to the fore again, although this did not happen to any significant degree during 1998 when the economy contracted by 7.5 percent. Others, like Sarawak's state minister for tourism James Masing, would like to see a plural society where difference is respected and accepted. "To say I'm Iban", Masing explains, "doesn't mean I'm any less Malaysian."

In foreign affairs Malaysia follows a non-aligned stance and is fiercely anti-Communist. This, however, has not stopped its enthusiastic investment in Indochina and Myanmar (Burma). Malaysia is a leading light in the Association of Southeast Asian Nations (ASEAN), and Mahathir has made his mark as an outspoken champion of the developing world. As such, he has frequently clashed with the

Foreign relations

Background

West. Malaysia needs continued foreign investment from industrialized countries, but Dr Mahathir remains deeply suspicious of Western motives and intentions.

Malaysia's most delicate relations are with neighbouring Singapore, a country with which it is connected by history and also by water pipelines and a causeway. For a few years Singapore was part of the Malaysian Federation, until it was ejected in 1965, and Singapore's status as a largely Chinese city state makes for an uneasy relationship with Malay-dominated Malaysia. In 1997 mutual sensitivities were made all too clear in a spat which threatened to escalate into a major diplomatic conflict. The cause? A dispute over whether Johor Bahru was a safe place or not.

Economy

Malaysia has an abundance of natural resources. Today, though, tin mining, rubber and palm oil are declining in importance, and while the country's oil, gas and timber wealth are valuable sources of revenue, the manufacturing sector has become the powerhouse of the economy. At the same time, the service sector is booming, and tourism is now the third largest foreign exchange earner. Over recent years, Malaysia has been one of the fastest-growing economies in the world. The World Bank defines Malaysia as an upper-middle-income country. There is a Malay saying which goes: *ada gula, ada semut* ('where there's sugar, there's ants') and from the late 1980s foreign investors swarmed to Malaysia, thanks to its sugar-coated investment incentives as well as its cheap land and labour, its good infrastructure and political stability.

Until 1997, and despite one banker likening Malaysia's economic policies to 'Noddyomics', the country's economy grew extraordinarily rapidly. It was this, of course, which played a large part in the World Bank including Malaysia in its list of 'Miracle Economies' (rather more prosaically High Performing Asian Economies by the World Bank). But the Asian economic crisis, which began in Thailand in mid-1997 and then spread to Malaysia and other Asian countries, put a spanner in the spokes of Malaysia's fast moving economy.

The evolution of the Malaysian economy

In the late 1800s, as the British colonial government developed the infrastructure of the Federated Malay States, they built a network of roads, railways, telephones and telegraphs which served as the backbone of the export economy. In the 50 years following 1880, export earnings rose 30-fold. Most of the tin mines and plantations were in the hands of British-owned companies and remained foreign-owned until the Malaysian government restructured foreign equity holdings in the 1970s.

On independence in 1957, resource-rich Malaysia's future looked bright and foreign investment was encouraged, the capitalist system maintained and there was no threat to nationalize industry. The first national development plan aimed to expand the agricultural sector and begin to reduce dependence on rubber, which, even then, was beginning to encounter competition from synthetic alternatives. But rubber and tin remained the main economic props. In 1963, when the Federation of Malaysia was formed, only six percent of the workforce was employed in industry and 80 percent of exports were contributed by tin, rubber, oil palm, timber, and oil and gas.

The structure of Malaysia's economy has been radically altered since independence, and particularly since the 1980s. Commodity exports such as rubber and palm oil, which were the mainstay of the post-colonial economy, have declined in significance and, within 30 years, this sector is unlikely to contribute more than six percent of Malaysia's export earnings. A turning point was 1987, when agriculture was overtaken by the manufacturing sector in terms of contribution to GDP. Manufacturing output has almost tripled in 25 years, thanks mainly to the fact that Malaysia has been the darling of foreign investors. The value of manufactured exports is growing even faster; today they are approaching three-quarters of Malaysia's export earnings. The country that used to be the world's biggest producer of rubber and tin is now the world's leading producer of semiconductors and air-conditioning units. In May 1993, another landmark was created in Malaysia's economic history: the *Malaysia Mining Corporation*, one of the country's biggest remaining tin producers, pulled out of tin mining. Tin production costs have increased while the price of tin has slumped. In 1990 there were still 141 tin mines in Malaysia; by 1993 there were only 50.

But the type of products Malaysia manufactures is also undergoing rapid change. One of the main reasons for this is Malaysia's labour squeeze. The main industrial boom zones (the Klang Valley around Kuala Lumpur, Johor and Penang) are already suffering shortages, and while infrastructural developments have just about kept pace with the flood of foreign manufacturing investment, the labour pool is drying up. In 1996 the unemployment rate was, in practical terms, zero and the government was forced to recruit blue-collar migrant labourers from Thailand, Bangladesh, Myanmar (Burma) and Indonesia. But even with this flow of legal migrant labour it was not sufficient to fill the labour void and there has been a much larger flow of illegal migrant labour. It was estimated that there were 1.75 million migrant workers - in a country with a workforce of eight million – of whom just 750,000 were working legally in the country.

The **New Development Policy** (NDP), unveiled in 1991 (see box, page 510) promotes hi-tech industries, higher value-added production, skills development and increased productivity and is the basis of the government's economic development strategy. It is a much more economically and socially liberal document than its predecessor, the New Economic Policy. Through it, the government tacitly concedes that without continued inflows of foreign capital, Malaysia's ambitious targets will not be realized. The NDP envisages a fourfold increase in the value of private-sector investment by 2000 and the private sector – both local and foreign – has been charged with spearheading economic growth and enhancing the country's industrial profile. The Ministry of International Trade and Industry has energetically promoted the concept of 'Malaysia Incorporated' in its effort to foster consultation and dialogue with the private sector and the all-important foreign investors. This has helped cut the red tape. Since Mahathir adopted his 'Look East' policy in the 1980s (instead of relying solely on trade links with the West), most of Malaysia's foreign investment has come from the East.

Evidence of the growing maturity of the Malaysian economy can be seen in the degree to which the country – Malaysia Inc. – is pursuing its industrial ambitions in the global arena. Between 1991 and mid-1996 US$7.1bn was invested in enterprises off-shore. This ranged from the acquisition of Lotus sports cars in Britain, to timber operations in New Zealand, Guyana and Canada, and construction in Albania and Uruguay.

A key element in Malaysia's development strategy is how to manage the transition from a production centre where comparative advantage is based on labour cost to an economy where high levels of education and skills provide the industrial impetus. Malaysia invariably looks across to Singapore as both a role model in this regard and as a competitor.

One of Prime Minister Mahathir's favourite programmes is the so-called MSC or 'Multimedia Super Corridor' – an attempt to build an Oriental Silicon Valley on a 15 km-by-50 km stretch of land south of KL. Like most of Malaysia's plans, the MSC will not come cheap. It will cost US$800m just to provide the optical communications' infrastructure. When you add in the new administrative capital of Putrajaya and associated international airport, along with a technological centre predictably called Cyberjaya, the bill comes to US$20bn. As Daniel Ng of Sun Microsystems was quoted as saying: "It's as if someone said, 'What would be the perfect Silicon Valley?' and then built it."

Transforming the economy

Background

The new economic policy – Malaysia's recipe for racial harmony

Just over two decades ago Malaysia's Malay-led government woke up to the fact that Malays and indigenous groups – collectively called bumiputras, or 'sons of the soil' – made up more than half the country's population but owned just two percent of corporate equity. Their average income was also less than half that of non-Malays. The Malay élite worked in the civil service, but most Malays were poor farmers. Economic power was concentrated in the hands of foreigners and urban Chinese while rural Malays lived on, or under, the breadline. The Chinese virtually ran the economy – they were the bankers, brokers and businessmen. In 1970, in the wake of the bloody race riots in which hundreds died (see page 501), the controversial New Economic Policy, or NEP, was introduced. The NEP aimed to wipe out poverty irrespective of race and completely restructure society by putting the Malay, Chinese and Indian communities on an equal footing. The idea was to abolish racial stereotyping, making it more difficult to associate a person's job with the colour of his or her skin.

The NEP was designed to prevent a recurrence of the bloodletting by keeping multiracial Malaysia intact. It offered Malays, the economic underdogs, a chance to catch up and encouraged them to move to the cities. Racial quotas were introduced to raise their stake in the economy to at least 30 percent. They were granted scholarships and directorships, they were pushed into managerial jobs, subsidized, goaded and given a ticket to get rich quick – which many did. But because the NEP favoured the Malays, it antagonized almost everyone else. For 20 years, the NEP was denounced as racist by its critics and flagrantly abused by many of those it tried to help. The policy was an invitation to bribery and corruption and the hijacking and exploitation of the NEP by wealthy bumiputras alienated non-Malays and fanned resentment.

But the NEP's targets were not met. Although poverty has been markedly reduced since 1970, the bumiputras' stake in the economy was a fraction over 20 percent in 1995 instead of the targeted 30 percent. While the jump from two percent to 20 percent is enormous, only seven percent of that is in the hands of individuals – most is owned by big bumiputra investment companies, institutions and government trust agencies. A sizeable chunk of the remainder is concentrated in the hands

There are critics and sceptics aplenty. There are those who say Malaysia lacks the human resources to justify such grandiose plans. Part of the problem is perceived to be the culture of education in the country. Gary Silverman in the *Far Eastern Economic Review* (1996) writes of a professor of history at the University of Malaya:

"Khoo Kay Kim has a rare complaint: he gets too much respect. Every day at work, Khoo is surrounded by people who hang on his every word, agree with what he says and repeat his statements virtually verbatim months later. It's making him nervous ... he's haunted by the silence in his classroom."

Malaysian students are not expected to challenge or contradict their teachers, but to conform. This is perceived to be unhealthy if Malaysia is to become a thinking economy where people are creative and innovative. More practically, Malaysian graduates are often not sufficiently fluent in English to take full advantage of the IT revolution. This dates back to the 1970s when the government switched from English to Bahasa Malaysia as the medium of instruction in secondary schools. Further, the tertiary level enrolment rate in Malaysia is low: just 7.2 percent of the relevant age group are in higher education.

Tourism Tourism has grown to assume a critical role in Malaysia's economy in the past few years. In 1990, Malaysia launched itself into big league tourism with a bang, joining

of a stratum of bumiputra fat cats who act as 'sleeping partners' in big firms. Today, the government admits that the biggest income disparities in Malaysia are within the bumiputra community itself. There are still relatively few high-calibre Malays with relevant management qualifications and experience to fill the posts available.

In the months before the NEP expired in 1990, many Malays were arguing for the continuation of the policy; they must still be given special treatment, they said, to enable them to catch up. However much the Chinese have been disadvantaged by the policy, their robust business acumen has meant that they are far from being a downtrodden minority. Even the NEP's most outspoken critics accept the need to rectify Malaysia's socio-economic imbalances, but they say the solution does not lie in a programme discriminating along racial lines.

The spectre of a repeat of the 1969 race riots has been constantly raised by the government in an effort to promote racial harmony – but today Malaysians look to the Los Angeles riots of 1992 as an example of unwanted mayhem, rather than 1969. There is little doubt that despite the abuses of political patronage, the bumiputras are now in a better position to compete. A fairly large number of bumiputras have become leading lights in Kuala Lumpur's business and financial community. As a group, Malays are more self-confident and more competitive than they were in 1970; they are also less prone to cast themselves as a disenfranchised majority.

In 1991, the old policy was replaced with the New Development Policy (NDP), which formalized a more liberal strategy. The NDP sets no deadline for the achievement of the 30 percent bumiputra ownership target – although it is still there. The new policy uses incentives instead of quotas – in the words of one commentator, it uses 'more carrot and less stick'. The emphasis now is on ensuring that bumiputras retain and build on the wealth they have accumulated. The government now wants to wean Malays off government hand-outs and patronage but it appears to believe that until the dependency syndrome has completely disappeared, bumiputras should be protected. Most Malaysians have welcomed the change in emphasis, but critics still maintain the NDP is just old wine in a new bottle.

the swelling ranks of Southeast Asian countries to host 'tourism years'. Visit Malaysia Year (VMY) was a big success: 7.4 million tourists arrived – half as many again as in 1989 and receipts rose 61 percent to US$1.5bn. This made tourism Malaysia's third biggest earner after manufacturing and oil – up from sixth position the previous year. Now Prime Minister Dr Mahathir Mohamad calls tourism "Malaysia's goldmine"; he says there should be "no saturation point".

While the vast majority of tourists still come from neighbouring Singapore and Thailand, the government is targeting the big spenders – the 'high-yield markets' like the Japanese, who spend 70 percent more than the average tourist. Smart new hotel and resort complexes are springing up around the country and scores of golf courses are being carved out of the jungle. Until fairly recently, the government paid scant regard to the lower-middle end of the tourism market, favouring sparkling new five-star complexes instead. The government thought VMY 1990 such a success that it decided to do it all over again in 1994. Malaysia was once again aggressively promoted abroad, this time under the slogan 'Visit Malaysia Naturally', with an eye on the eco-market. More colourful extravaganzas filled the calendar as locals shrugged off a feeling of déjà vu. Although VMY 1994 was not quite the success of VMY 1990, 7.2 million visitors arrived in the country during the year, spending RM9bn.

Mapping out the future: Vision 2020

The NDP, unveiled in 1991, is a 10-year policy which forms part of Mahathir's longer term economic blueprint appropriately labelled 'Wawasan 2020' or 'Vision 2020'. This aims to quadruple per-capita income, double the size of the economy and make Malaysia a fully developed industrialized country by the end of the second decade of the century. Vision 2020 is full of lofty ambitions, grand goals and fuzzy rhetoric and it reads more like a corporate mission statement than a well-defined policy. But while it was undeniably ambitious, few people questioned whether Malaysia could not achieve the annual average economic growth rate of seven percent necessary to meet the plan's targets. That, though, was before the economic crisis which saw the economy contract by 7.5 percent in 1998 and grow by just five percent in 1999.

Falling tigers

Malaysia's economic crisis came quick on the heels of Thailand's fall from economic grace in July 1997, which led to the devaluation of the baht and a US$15bn IMF rescue package. Though Thailand's problems were uniquely serious there were enough commonalities to cause concern in KL's financial district: a high current account deficit; a currency linked to the US$; a booming property sector; and a lack of transparency in some aspects of financial management. It was these similarities with Thailand – and perhaps also a sense that the economies of Asean, having boomed together would also fall together – which led currency speculators to attack the ringgit.

Prime Minister Mahathir, predictably, blamed perfidious currency speculators and in particular George Soros, the Hungarian-born billionaire. Mahathir allegedly compared speculators to drug dealers, labelling them anarchists, saboteurs and rogues (*The Economist*, 2 August 1997). In July 1997 at their annual meeting, the nine Asean foreign ministers released a joint communiqué stating that the currency crisis was due to the "well co-ordinated efforts [by speculators] to destabilize ASEAN currencies for self-serving purposes". *The Economist* opined that blaming Soros for Thailand's plight was "rather like condemning an undertaker for burying a suicide".

Unlike the other countries of the region, Mahathir did not stick with the IMF's medicine. Instead he imposed tight currency controls in September 1998. While his actions were widely condemned in the international press, the recovery of the Malaysian economy by mid-1999, in Mahathir's eyes at least, vindicated his actions. Of course, opponents of the controls maintained that the country's economic recovery had little to do with the controls *per se*. Indeed, they say that of all the countries of the region Malaysia was best placed to deal with the crisis and that the currency controls were an irrelevance in the broader economic context. The danger, these critics of Malaysian economic policies maintain, is that because the country was affected least by the crisis it has also done the least to confront the structural problems that created the conditions for the crisis in the first place.

It is perhaps worth reflecting on the results of a survey commissioned by *The Economist* in 1998 to measure people's optimism about their future prosperity. The survey was undertaken in 29 countries around the world and Malaysia came out top – and that despite the fact that it was in the midst of its deepest recession since independence. By early 2000, there was a four-month waiting list for Porsche cars in KL. The grand visions and confidence of the early and mid-1990s are, it seems, back – if they ever went away, that is.

Land and environment

Geography

Malaysia covers a total land area of 329,054 km² and includes Peninsular Malaysia (131,587 km²) and the Borneo states of Sarawak (124,967 km²) and Sabah (72,500 km²). Geologically, both the peninsula and Borneo are part of the Sunda shelf, although the mountains of the peninsula were formed longer ago than those in Borneo. This 'shelf', which during the Pleistocene ice age was exposed forming a land bridge between the two halves of the country, was inundated as the glaciers of the north retreated and sea levels rose.

The Malay peninsula is about 800 km north-south, has a long narrow neck, a tapered tail and a bulging, mountainous, middle. The neck is called the **Kra Isthmus**, which links the peninsula to the Southeast Asian mainland. The isthmus itself is in southern Thailand – Peninsular Malaysia comprises only the lower portion of the peninsula and covers an area larger than England and a little smaller than Florida. Nestled into the southernmost end of the peninsula is the island of Singapore, separated from the peninsula by the narrow Strait of Johor. The thin western coastal plain drains into the Strait of Melaka, which separates the peninsula from Sumatra (Indonesia) and is one of the oldest shipping lanes in the world. The eastern coastal lowlands drain into the South China Sea.

The **Barisan Titiwangsa** (Main Range) comprises the curved jungle-clad spine of Peninsular Malaysia. It is the most prominent of several, roughly parallel ranges running down the peninsula. These subsidiary ranges include the Kedah-Singgora Range in the northwest; the Bintang Range (stretching northeast from Taiping), the Tahan Range (which includes the peninsula's highest mountain, Gunung Tahan, 2,187m). In the northern half of the peninsula, the mountainous belt is very wide, leaving only a narrow coastal strip on either side.

The Main Range – or Barisan Titiwangsa – runs south from the Thai border for nearly 500 km, gradually receding as it approaches the coastal plain, near Melaka. The average elevation is about 1,000m and there are several peaks of more than 2,000m. The southern end of the range is much narrower and the mountains, lower; the most prominent southern 'outlier' is Gunung Ledang (Mount Ophir) in Johor. Until just over a century ago, when William Cameron first ventured into the mountains of the Main Range, this was uncharted territory – British colonial Malaya was, in fact, little more than the west coastal strip. Not only was the west coast adjacent to the important trade routes (and therefore had most of the big towns), its alluvial deposits were also rich in tin. Because roads and railways were built along this western side of the peninsula during the colonial period, it also became the heart of the plantation economy.

In addition to the mountain ranges, the Malay peninsula also has many spectacular limestone outcrops. These distinctive outcrops are mainly in the Kuala Lumpur area, such as Batu Caves and those in and around Templer Park, and in the Kampar Valley near Ipoh, to the north. The erosion of the limestone has produced intricate solution-cave systems, some with dramatic formations. The vegetation on these hills is completely different to the surrounding lowland rainforest.

Malaysia's year-round rainfall has resulted in a dense network of rivers. The peninsula's longest river is the Sungai Pahang, which runs for just over 400 km. Most rivers flood regularly, particularly during the northeast monsoon season, and during the heavy rain the volume of water can more than double in the space of a few hours. It is thought that the flooding of Malaysian rivers has become more pronounced due to logging and mining. Waterfalls are very common features in

River roads

In Borneo, rivers are often the main arteries of communication. Although roads are being built, linking most main towns, many Dayak (tribal) longhouse communities are only accessible by river. Rivers are the mediators that divide forest dwellers from coastal settlers and this is usually expressed in terms of upriver, or hulu and downstream, or hilir. The two terms are not just geographical; they also reflect different lifestyles and economies, different religions and cultures. In Borneo, to be hulu is to set oneself apart from the Malay peoples of the lowlands and coasts.

Contrary to many assumptions, the tribal hulu peoples were never entirely isolated and self reliant. From early times, there was a flourishing trade between the coasts and the interior. Upriver tribal peoples would exchange exotic jungle products like rattan, benzoin, camphor, skins, hornbill 'ivory', precious stones and rare dyes for products that they could not obtain in the forest – like iron, salt, dried fish (now, tinned fish), betel and gambier. They also bartered for prestige objects like brass gongs, large ceramic Chinese pots, and Dutch silver coins. Many of these prestige objects can still be seen in the longhouses of Borneo and have become precious heirlooms or pusaka.

Peninsular Malaysia; these occur where rivers, with their headwaters in the hills, encounter resistant (usually igneous) rocks as they cut their valleys.

Borneo Three countries have territory on Borneo, but only one of them, the once all-powerful and now tiny but oil-rich sultanate of Brunei, is an independent sovereign state in itself. It is flanked to the west by the Malaysian state of Sarawak and to the east by Sabah. Sarawak severs and completely surrounds Brunei. Sabah, formerly British North Borneo, and now a Malaysian state, occupies the northeast portion of Borneo. The huge area to the south is Kalimantan, Indonesian Borneo, which occupies about three-quarters of the island.

Borneo is the third largest island in the world after Greenland and New Guinea covering almost 750,000 km². During the Pleistocene period, Borneo was joined to mainland Southeast Asia, forming a continent which geologists know as Sundaland. The land bridge to mainland Asia meant that many species, both flora and fauna, arrived in what is now Borneo before it was cut off by rising sea levels. Borneo is part of the Sunda shelf. Its interior is rugged and mountainous and is dissected by many large rivers, navigable deep into the interior. The two biggest rivers, the Kapuas and Mahakam, are both in Kalimantan, but there are also extensive river systems in the East Malaysian states of Sabah and Sarawak. About half of Borneo's land area is under 150m, particularly the swampy south coastal region.

Borneo's highest mountain, Gunung Kinabalu in Sabah (4,101m) is often declared the highest mountain in Southeast Asia (see page 439). Despite this claim being repeated so many times that it has taken on the status of a truth, it isn't: there are higher peaks in Indonesia's province of Irian Jaya and in Myanmar (Burma). Kinabalu is a granite mound called a pluton, which was forced up through the sandstone strata during the Pliocene period, about 15 million years ago. The mountain ranges in the west and centre of the island run east-to-west and curve round to the northeast. Borneo's coal, oil and gas-bearing strata are Tertiary deposits which are heavily folded; most of the oil and gas is found off the northwest and east coasts. The island is much more geologically stable than neighbouring Sulawesi or Java – islands in the so-called 'ring of fire'. Borneo only experiences about four mild earthquakes a year compared with 40-50 on other nearby islands. But because there are no active volcanoes, Borneo's soils are not particularly rich.

Climatic variations: yes, we have no monsoons

One of the problems frustrating Peninsular Malaysia's east coast states in their efforts to promote tourism is the weather. Although coconut palms sway gently over sun-splashed sandy beaches most of the year round, the northeast monsoon starts to blow just as the northern hemisphere's Christmas holidays get underway and antipodeans start thinking about their summer getaways. State authorities contend that the November to March monsoon is blown out of all proportion in the minds of Western tourists (and most Malaysians for that matter).

Tourism Malaysia says too much is made of the word 'monsoon' and points the finger at Club Med, which owns an idyllic private beach at Cerating in Pahang, for reinforcing the problem by shutting down during the northeast monsoon season. The tourism committee in Northeast Terengganu state has gone as far as to ban the use of the word altogether because they believe it has created a stigma among tourists and investors. They say 'rainy weather' is a perfectly adequate description. Others might consider this an understatement: more than 600mm of rain has fallen on parts of the east coast within a single day. It also ignores the fact that there are also dry monsoons.

On the other side of the peninsula, however, states occasionally suffer from too little rain. In 1991, for example, there was a water crisis in Melaka – the worst for 30 years – and on behalf of the state government, the Chief Minister contracted an American company, TJC-Atmos Engineers, to help resolve the problem. The company was promised more than RM3m if it created enough rain to fill the local reservoir. But after claiming to have produced rain on 30 separate occasions over a two month period, Kuala Lumpur's Meteorological Services Department (MSD) dismissed the company's techniques as 'unscientific' and said any rain was a natural consequence of the south-west monsoon.

The director of TJC-Atmos claimed to use 'etheric engineering techniques' to attract clouds, by "manipulating the qi [or subtle life-force] in the atmosphere". He had developed the techniques while investigating Unidentified Flying Objects in the 1950s and described himself as 'a hi-tech bomoh' (Malay witch doctor). The director of the MSD took a dim view of his 'metaphysical' techniques however and TJC-Atmos Engineering left Malaysia empty handed.

Background

Climate

The Malay peninsula has an equatorial monsoon climate. Temperatures are uniformly high throughout the year, as is humidity, and rainfall is abundant and well distributed, although it peaks during the northeast monsoon period from November to February.

For more details on the climatic features of Sabah and Sarawak, see page 516

Mean annual temperature on the coastal lowlands is around 26°C. The mean daily minima in the lowlands is between 21.7°C and 24.4°C; the mean daily maxima is between 29.4°C and 32.8°C. The maxima are higher and the minima, lower, towards the interior. In the Cameron Highlands, the mean annual temperature is 18°C. Temperatures dip slightly during the northeast monsoon period. The highest recorded temperature, 39.4°C, was taken on Pulau Langkawi in March 1931. The lowest absolute minimum temperature ever recorded on the peninsula was in the Cameron Highlands in January 1937 when the temperature fell to 2.2°C. The Cameron Highlands also claims the most extreme range in temperature – the absolute maximum recorded there is 26.7°C.

The developed west coast of the peninsula is sheltered from the northeast monsoon which strikes the east coast with full force between November and February. The east coast's climatic vagaries have reinforced its remoteness: it is particularly wet and the area north of Kuantan receives between 3,300mm and 4,300mm a year. About half of this falls in the northeast monsoon period. The northwest coast of the peninsula is also wet and parts receive more than 3,000mm of rain a year. Bukit Larut (Maxwell Hill), next to Taiping has an annual rainfall of more than 5,000mm. The west coast receives its heaviest rainfall in March and April. October and April are the transitional months between the southwest and northeast monsoons.

Thunderstorms provide most of Malaysia's rainfall. In the most torrential downpour ever recorded in Kuala Lumpur 51mm of rain fell in 15 minutes. Heavy rain like this causes serious soil erosion in areas which have been cleared of vegetation.

In the more heavily populated coastal districts of the peninsula, the temperature is ameliorated by sea breezes which set in about 1000 and gather force until early afternoon. In the evenings, a land breeze picks up. These winds are only felt for distances up to 15 km inland. Another typical weather feature on the Malay peninsula is the squall, which is a sudden, violent storm characterized by sharp gusts of wind. These can be very localized in their effect, very unpredictable and, from time to time, very hazardous to light fishing vessels. Squalls are caused by cool air either from sea breezes in the late morning or land breezes in the evening undercutting warmer air; squall lines are marked by stacks of cumulo-nimbus clouds. Most squalls occur between May and August; the ones that develop along the west coast between Port Klang and Singapore during this period are called 'Sumatras' and produce particularly violent cloudbursts. Most Sumatras occur at night or in the early morning, while squalls between November and February usually occur in the afternoon.

Borneo Borneo has a typical equatorial monsoon climate: the weather usually follows predictable patterns, although in recent years it has been less predictable, a phenomenon some environmentalists attribute to deforestation and others to periodic changes to the El Nino Southern Oscillation. Temperatures are fairly uniform, averaging 23-33°C during the day and rarely dropping below 20°C at night, except in the mountains, where they can drop to below 10°C. Most rainfall occurs between November and January during the northeast monsoon; this causes rivers to burst their banks, and there are many short, sharp cloudbursts. The dry season runs from May to September. It is characterized by dry south-easterly winds and is the best time to visit. Rainfall generally increases towards the interior; most of Borneo receives about 2,000-3,000 mm a year, although some upland areas get more than 4,000 mm.

Flora and fauna

Originally 97 percent of Malaysia's land area was covered in closed-canopy forest. According to the government, about 56 percent of Malaysia is still forested – although it is difficult to ascertain exactly how much of this is primary rainforest. Only five percent of the remaining jungle is under conservation restrictions. The Malaysian jungle, which, at about 130 million years old, is believed to be among the oldest forests in the world, supports more than 145,000 species of flowering plant (well over 1,000 of which are already known to have pharmaceutical value), 200 mammal species, 600 bird species and countless thousands of insect species. The rainforest is modified by underlying rock-type (impervious rocks and soils result in swamp forest) and by altitude (lowland rainforest gives way to thinner montane forest on higher slopes). All the main forest types are represented on the peninsula; these include mangrove swamp forest, peat swamp forest, heath forest, lowland and hill mixed *Dipterocarp* forest and montane forest. Where primary forest has been logged, burned or cleared by shifting cultivators or miners, secondary forest grows up quickly. The fields cultivated by shifting cultivators are known as swiddens – a

The universal stimulant – the betel nut

Throughout the countryside in Southeast Asia, and in more remote towns, it is common to meet men and women whose teeth are stained black, and gums red, by continuous chewing of the 'betel nut'. This, though, is a misnomer. The betel 'nut' is not chewed at all: the three crucial ingredients that make up a betel 'wad' are the nut of the areca palm (Areca catechu), the leaf or catkin of the betel vine (Piper betel), and lime. When these three ingredients are combined with saliva they act as a mild stimulant. Other ingredients (people have their own recipes) are tobacco, gambier, various spices and the gum of Acacia catechu. The habit, though also common in South Asia and parts of China, seems to have evolved in Southeast Asia and it is mentioned in the very earliest chronicles. The lacquer betel boxes of Burma and Thailand, and the brass and silver ones of Indonesia and Malaysia, illustrate the importance of chewing betel in social intercourse. Galvao in his journal of 1544 noted: "They use it so continuously that they never take it from their mouths; therefore these people can be said to go around always ruminating". Among Westernized Southeast Asians the habit is frowned upon: the disfigurement and ageing that it causes, and the stained walls and floors that result from the constant spitting, are regarded as distasteful products of an earlier age. But beyond the élite it is still widely practised.

word which is derived from an old English term meaning 'burnt field'. In Malaysia, the secondary regrowth is known as *belukar*. It can take up to 250 years before climax rainforest is re-established. The pioneer plant species colonizing abandoned *ladang* (sites cleared by shifting cultivators) is called *lalang* (elephant grass).

Borneo's ancient rainforests are rich in flora and fauna, including over 9,000-15,000 species of seed plants (of which almost half may be endemic), 200 species of mammals, 570 species of birds, 100 species of snake, 250 species of freshwater fish and 1,000 species of butterfly. The theory of natural selection enunciated by Victorian naturalist Alfred Russel Wallace – while that other great Victorian scientist Charles Darwin was coming to similar conclusions several thousand miles away – was influenced by Wallace's observations in Borneo. He travelled widely in Sarawak between 1854 and 1862.

Despite years of research the gaps in scientists' knowledge of the island's flora and fauna remain yawning and if anything are becoming more so. For a significant proportion of the flora of Borneo, scientists have barely any information on their geographic distribution, let alone details of their ecology. It has been estimated that around one-quarter of plant species are only known from their 'type' specimen (ie the specimen on which the initial identification was based), or from one or two specimens. Even on Gunung Kinabalu, which has been intensively researched for years, there are significant knowledge gaps.

Flora

As late as the middle of the 19th century, the great bulk – perhaps as much as 95 percent – of the land area of Borneo was forested. Alfred Russel Wallace, like other Western travellers, was enchanted by the island's natural wealth and diversity: "ranges of hill and valley everywhere", he wrote, "everywhere covered with interminable forest". But Borneo's jungle is disappearing fast – some naturalists would say that over extensive areas it has disappeared – and since the mid-1980s there has been a mounting international environmental campaign against deforestation. The campaign has been particularly vocal in Sarawak (see page 374) but other parts of the island are also suffering rapid deforestation, notably Sabah and also Indonesia's province of East Kalimantan. Harold Brookfield, Lesley Potter and Byron state in their hard-headed book *In place of the forest* (1995):

Background

Durian: king of fruits

In Southeast Asia, the durian is widely regarded as the most delicious of fruits – to the horror of many foreign visitors. In his book The Malay Archipelago (1869), Alfred Russel Wallace describes it in almost orgiastic terms:

"The consistence and flavour are indescribable. A rich butter-like custard highly flavoured with almonds gives the best general idea of it, but intermingled with it come wafts of flavour that call to mind cream-cheese, onion sauce, brown sherry and other incongruities. Then there is a rich glutinous smoothness in the pulp which nothing else possesses, but which adds to its delicacy. It is neither acid, or sweet, nor juicy, yet one feels the want of none of these qualities, for it is perfect as it is. It produces no nausea or other bad effect, and the more you eat of it the less you feel inclined to stop. In fact to eat Durian is a new sensation, worth a voyage to the East to experience."

Concerning those large areas of forest that have been totally cleared and converted to other uses or that lie waste [in Borneo], we can state only that there is nothing to be gained from bemoaning the past. A great resource has been squandered, and the major part of the habitat of a great range of plant and animal species has been destroyed. Moreover, this has been done with far less than adequate economic return to the two nations [Malaysia and Indonesia] concerned.

How extensive has been the loss of species as a result of the logging of Borneo's forests is a topic of heated debate. Brookfield et al in the volume noted above suggest that there "is very little basis in firm research for the spectacular figures of species loss rates that appear not infrequently in sections of the conservationist literature and that readily attract media attention." But they do admit that the flora and fauna of Borneo is especially diverse with a high degree of endemism and that there has been a significant loss of biodiversity as a result of extensive logging. It has been estimated that 32 percent of terrestrial mammals, 70 percent of leaf beetles, and 50 percent of flowering plants are endemic to Borneo; in other words, they are found nowhere else.

The best known timber trees fall into three categories, all of them hardwoods. Heavy hardwoods include *selangan batu* and *resak*; medium hardwoods include *kapur*, *keruing* and *keruntum*; light hardwoods include *madang tabak*, *ramin* and *meranti*. There are both peat-swamp and hill varieties of meranti, which is one of the most valuable export logs. *Belian*, or Bornean iron wood (*Eusideroxylon zwageri*) is one of the hardest and densest timbers in the world. It is thought that the largest belian may be 1,000 years or more old. They are so tough that when they die they continue to stand for centuries before the wood rots to the extent that the trunk falls. On average, there are about 25 commercial tree species per hectare, but because they are hard to extract, 'selective logging' invariably results in the destruction of many unselected trees.

The main types of forest include: **lowland rainforest** (mixed dipterocarp) predominates up to 600m. Dipterocarp forest is stratified into three main layers, the top one rising to heights of 45m. In the top layer, trees' crowns interlock to form a closed canopy of foliage. The word 'dipterocarp' comes from the Greek and means 'two-winged fruit' or 'two [di]-winged [ptero] seed [carp]'. The leaf-like appendages of the mature dipterocarp fruits have 'wings' which makes them spin as they fall to the ground, like giant sycamore seeds. Some species have more than two wings but are all members of the dipterocarp family. It is the lowland rainforest which comes closest to the Western ideal of a tropical 'jungle'. It is also probably the most species

Fields in the forest – shifting cultivation

Shifting cultivation, also known as slash-and-burn agriculture or swiddening, is one of the characteristic farming systems of Southeast Asia. It is a low-intensity form of agriculture, in which land is cleared from the forest through burning, cultivated for a few years and then left to regenerate over 10-30 years. It takes many forms, but an important distinction can be made between shifting field systems where fields are rotated but the settlement remains permanently sited, and migratory systems where the shifting cultivators shift both field (swidden) and settlement. The land is usually only rudimentarily cleared, tree stumps being left in the ground, and seeds sown in holes made by punching the soil with a dibble stick.

For many years, shifting cultivators were regarded as 'primitives' who followed an essentially primitive form of agriculture, and their methods were contrasted unfavourably with 'advanced' settled rice farmers. There are still many government officials in Southeast Asia who continue to adhere to this mistaken belief, arguing that shifting cultivators are the principal cause of forest loss and soil erosion. They are painted as the villains in the region's environmental crisis, neatly sidestepping the considerably more detrimental impact that commercial logging has had on Southeast Asia's forest resources.

Shifting cultivators have an intimate knowledge of the land, plants and animals on which they depend. One study of a Dayak tribe, the Kantu' of Kalimantan (Borneo), discovered that households were cultivating an average of 17 rice varieties and 21 other food crops each year in a highly complex system. Even more remarkably, Harold Conklin's classic 1957 study of the Hanunóo of the Philippines – a study which is a benchmark for such work even today – found that the Hanunóo identified 40 types and subtypes of rocks and minerals when classifying different soils. The shifting agricultural systems are usually also highly productive in labour terms, allowing far more leisure time than farmers using permanent field systems.

But shifting cultivation contains the seeds of its own extinction. Extensive, and geared to low population densities and abundant land, it is coming under pressure in a region where land is becoming an increasingly scarce resource, where patterns of life are dictated by an urban-based élite, and where populations are pressing on the means of subsistence.

rich forest in Borneo. A recent study of a dipterocarp forest in Malaysia found that an area of just 50 hectares supported no less than 835 species of tree. In Europe or North America a similar area of forest would support less than 100 tree species. The red resin produced by many species of dipterocarp, and which can often be seen staining the trunk, is known as *damar* and was traditionally used as a lamp 'oil'. Another characteristic feature of the trees found in lowland dipterocarp rainforest is buttressing, the flanges of wood that protrude from the base of the trunk. For some time the purpose of these massive buttresses perplexed botanists who arrived at a whole range of ingenious explanations. Now they are thought, sensibly, to provide structural support. Two final characteristics of this type of forest are that it is very dark on the forest floor (explaining why trees take so long to grow) and that it is not the impenetrable jungle of Tarzan fantasy. The first characteristic explains the second. Only when a gap appears in the forest canopy, after a tree falls, do light-loving pioneer plants get the chance to grow. When the gap in the canopy is filled by another tree, these grasses, shrubs and smaller trees die back once more.

Many of the rainforest trees are an important resource for Dayak communities. The jelutong tree, for example, is tapped like a rubber tree for its sap ('jungle chewing gum') which is used to make tar for waterproof sealants – used in boat-building. It also hardens into a tough but brittle black plastic-like substance used for *parang* (machete) handles.

Background

Montane forest occurs at altitudes above 600m, although in some areas it does not replace lowland rainforest until considerably higher than this. Above 1,200m mossy forest predominates. Montane forest is denser than lowland forest with smaller trees of narrower girth. Moreover, dipterocarps are generally not found while flowering shrubs like magnolias and rhododendrons appear. In place of dipterocarps, tropical latitude oaks as well as other trees that are more characteristic of temperate areas, like myrtle and laurel, make an appearance. Other familiar flora of lowland forest, like lianas, also disappear while the distinctive pitcher plant (Nepenthes) become common.

The low-lying river valleys are characterized by **peat swamp** forest, where the peat is up to 9m thick, which makes wet-rice agriculture impossible.

Heath forest or *kerangas* – the Iban word meaning 'land on which rice cannot grow' – is found on poor, sandy soils. Although it mostly occurs near the coast, it is also sometimes found in mountain ranges, but almost always on level ground. Here trees are stunted and only the hardiest of plants can survive. Some trees have struck up symbiotic relationships with animals – like ants – so as to secure essential nutrients. Pitcher plants (Nepenthes) have also successfully colonized heath forest. The absence of bird calls and other animal noises make heath forest rather eerie, and it also indicates their general biological poverty.

Along beaches there are often stretches of **casuarina forest**; the casuarina grows up to 27m, and looks like a conifer, with needle-shaped leaves. **Mangrove** occupies tidal mud flats around sheltered bays and estuaries. The most common mangrove tree is the *bakau* (*Rhizophora*) which grows to heights of about 9m and has stilt roots to trap sediment. Bakau wood is used for pile-house stilts and for charcoal. Further upstream, but still associated with mangrove, is the *nipah* palm (*Nipa fruticans*), whose light-green leaves come from a squat stalk; it was traditionally of great importance as it provided roofing and wickerwork materials.

Mammals The continual development of forested areas has destroyed many habitats in recent years. The biggest mammal in Malaysia and Asia is the Asiatic elephant. Adult elephants weigh up to three to four tonnes; they are rarely seen, although the carnage caused by a passing herd can sometimes be seen in Taman Negara National Park. For more detail on elephants, see page 520. Borneo's wild elephants pose a zoological mystery. They occur only at the far northeast tip of the island, at the furthest possible point from their Sumatran and mainland Southeast Asian relatives. No elephant remains have been found in Sabah, Sarawak or Kalimantan. It is known that some animals were introduced into Sabah – then British North Borneo – by early colonial logging concerns. But it is certain that there were already populations established in the area. Another theory has it that one of the sultans of Sulu released a small number of animals several centuries ago. The difficulty with this explanation is that experts find it difficult to believe that just a handful of elephants could have grown to the 2,000 or so that existed by the end of the last century. Some zoologists speculate that they were originally introduced at the time of the Javan Majapahit Empire, in the 13th and 14th centuries. Antonio Pigafetta, an Italian historian who visited the Sultanate of Brunei as part of Portuguese explorer Ferdinand Magellan's expedition in July 1521, tells of being taken to visit the sultan on two domesticated elephants, which may have been gifts from another ruler.

It is possible, however, that elephants are native to Borneo and migrated from the Southeast Asian mainland during the Pleistocene when sea levels were lower and land-bridges would have existed between Borneo and the mainland. Their concentration in northeast Borneo could be explained by the presence of numerous salt-licks between the Sandakan and Lahad Datu areas of Sabah. This would make the present population a relic of a much larger group of elephants. Borneo's male elephants are up to 2.6m tall; females are usually less than 2.2m. Males' tusks can grow up to 1.7m in length and weigh up to 15 kg each. Mature males are solitary creatures, only joining herds to mate. The most likely places to see elephants in the wild are the Danum Valley Conservation Area (see page 465) and the lower Kinabatangan basin (see page 462), both in Sabah.

Orang utan (*Pongo pygmaeus*): Walt Disney's film of Rudyard Kipling's *Jungle Book* made the orang utan a big-screen celebrity, dubbing him "the king of the swingers" and "the jungle VIP". Borneo's great red-haired ape is also known as 'man of the jungle', after the translation from the Malay: orang (man), utan (jungle). The orang utan is endemic to the tropical forests of Sumatra and Borneo although at the beginning of the historic period it was distributed from tropical China to Java. The Sumatran animals tend to keep the reddish tinge to their fur, while the Bornean ones go darker as they mature. It is Asia's only great ape; it has four hands, rather than feet, bow-legs and has no tail. The orang utan moves slowly and deliberately, sometimes swinging under branches, although it seldom travels far by arm-swinging. Males of over 15 years old stand up to 1.6m tall and their arms span 2.4m. Adult males (which make loud roars) weigh 50-100 kg – about twice that of adult females (whose call sounds like a long, unattractive belch). Orang utans are said to have the strength of seven men but they are not aggressive. They are peaceful, gentle animals, particularly with each other. Orang utans have bluey-grey skin and their eyes are close together, giving them an almost human look. Males develop cheek pouches when they reach maturity, which they fill with several litres of air; this is exhaled noisily when they demarcate territory.

Orang utans mainly inhabit riverine swamp forests or lowland dipterocarp forests. Their presence is easily detected by their nests of bent and broken twigs, which are woven together, in much the same fashion as a sun bear's, in the fork of a tree. They are solitary animals and always sleep alone. Orang utans have a largely vegetarian diet consisting of fruit and young leaves, supplemented by termites, bark and birds' eggs. They are usually solitary but the young remain with their mothers until they are five or six years old. Two adults will occupy an area of about 2 km² and are territorial, protecting their territory against intruders. They can live up to 30 years and a female will have an average of three to four young during her lifetime. Females reach sexual maturity between the ages of seven to nine years and the gestation period is nine months. Female orang utans usually have only one young at a time although twins and even triplets have been recorded. After giving birth, they do not mate for around another seven years.

Estimates of the numbers of orang utan vary considerably. One puts the figure at 10,000-20,000 animals; another at between 70-100,000 in the wild in Borneo and Sumatra. Part of the difficulty is that many are thought to live in inaccessible and little researched areas of peat swamp. But this is just a very rough estimate, based on one ape for each 1½ km² of forest. No one, so far, has attempted an accurate census. What is certain is that the forest is

The 'Oran-ootan' as remembered by an early European visitor.
Source: Beeckman, David (1718) A Voyage to and from the Island of Borneo

Background

disappearing fast, and with it the orang utan's natural habitat. Orang utans' favoured habitat is lowland rainforest and this is particularly under threat from logging. The black market in young apes in countries like Taiwan means that they fetch relatively high returns to local hunters. At the village level an orang utan might command US$100; in local markets, around US$350; and at their international destination, along with all the necessary forged export permits, travel costs and so on, from US$5,000 to as much as US$60,000.

Monkeys: the five species of monkeys found in Malaysia are the long-tailed macaque, pig-tailed macaque, and three species of leaf monkey (langur) – the banded, dusky and silvered varieties. Malaysia's cutest animal is the little slow loris, with its huge sad eyes and lethargic manner; among the most exotic is the flying lemur, whose legs and tail are joined together by a skin membrane. It parachutes and glides from tree to tree, climbing each one to find a new launch-pad.

The proboscis monkey (*Nasalis larvatus*) is an extraordinary-looking animal, endemic to Borneo, which lives in lowland forests and mangrove swamps all around the island. Little research has been done on proboscis monkeys; they are notoriously difficult to study as they are so shy. Their fur is reddish-brown and they have white legs, arms, tail and a ruff on the neck, which gives the appearance of a pyjama-suit. Their facial skin is red and the males have grotesquely enlarged, droopy noses; females' noses are shorter and upturned. The male's nose is the subject of some debate among zoologists: what ever else it does, it apparently increases their sex-appeal. To ward off intruders, the nose is straightened out, "like a party whoopee whistle", according to one description. Recently a theory has been advanced that the nose acts as a thermostat, helping to regulate body temperature. But it also tends to get in the way: old males often have to resort to holding their noses up with one hand while stuffing leaves into their mouths with the other.

Proboscises' penises are almost as obvious as their noses – the proboscis male glories in a permanent erection, which is probably why they are rarely displayed in zoos. The other way the males attract females is by violently shaking branches and making spectacular – and sometimes near-suicidal – leaps into the water, in which they attempt to hit as many dead branches as they can on the way down, so as to make the loudest noise possible. The monkeys organize themselves into harems, with one male and several females and young – there are sometimes up to 20 in a group. Young males leave the harem they are born into when the adult male becomes aggressive towards them and they rove around in bachelor groups until they are in a position to form their own harem.

Proboscis monkeys belong to the leaf monkey family, and have large, pouched stomachs to help digest bulky food – they feed almost entirely on the leaves of one tree – the *Sonneratia*. The proboscis is a diurnal animal, but keeps to the shade during the heat of the day. The best time to see them is very early in the morning or around dusk. They can normally be heard before they are seen: they make loud honks, rather like geese; they also groan, squeal and roar. Proboscis monkeys are good swimmers; they even swim underwater for up to 20m – thanks to their partially webbed feet. Males are about twice the size and weight of females. They are known fairly ubiquitously (in both Malaysian and Indonesian Borneo) as 'Orang Belanda', or Dutchmen – which is not entirely complimentary. In Kalimantan they also have other local names including *Bekantan, Bekara, Kahau, Rasong, Pika* and *Batangan*.

Other monkeys found in Borneo include various species of leaf monkey – including the grey leaf monkey, the white-fronted leaf monkey, and the red leaf monkey. One of the non-timber forest products formerly much prized was bezoar stone which was a valued cure-all. Bezoars are green coloured 'stones' which form in the stomachs of some herbivores, and in particular in the stomachs of leaf monkeys. Fortunately for the leaf monkeys of Southeast Asia though, these stones – unlike rhino horn – are no longer prized for their medicinal properties. One of the most attractive members of the primate family found in Borneo is the tubby slow loris or *kongkang*. And perhaps the most difficult to pronounce – at least in Dusun – is the tarsier which is locally known as the *tindukutrukut*.

The ape family includes the white-handed gibbon (known locally as *wak-wak*), the dark-handed gibbon (which is rarer) and *siamang*, which are found in more mountainous areas.

Rhinoceros: the two-horned Sumatran rhinoceros, also known as the hairy rhinoceros, is the smallest of all rhinos and was once widespread throughout Sumatra and Borneo. The population has been greatly reduced by excessive hunting. The horn is worth more than its weight in gold in Chinese apothecaries, and that of the Sumatran rhino is reputedly the most prized of all. But the ravages of over-hunting have been exacerbated by the destruction of the rhino's habitat. Indeed, until quite recently it was thought to be extinct on Borneo. Most of Borneo's remaining wild population is in Sabah, and the Malaysian government is attempting to capture some of the thinly dispersed animals to breed them in captivity, for they remain in serious danger of extinction (see page 461).

Other mammals: one of the strangest Malayan mammals is the tapir, with its curled snout – or trunk – and white bottom. The starkly contrasting black and white is good camouflage in the jungle, where it is effectively concealed by light and shade. Young tapirs are dark brown with light brown spots, simulating the effect of sun-dappled leaf-litter.

Other large mammals include the common wild pig and the bearded pig, and the *seladang* (or gaur) wild cattle; the latter live in herds in deep jungle. There are two species of deer on the Malay peninsula: the *sambar* (or *rusa*) and the *kijang* (barking deer); the latter gets its English name from its dog-like call. The mouse deer (*kanchil* and *napoh*) are not really deer; they are hoofed animals, standing just 20cm high. The mouse deer has legendary status in Malay lore – for example, the Malay Annals tell of Prince Parameswara's decision to found Melaka on the spot where he saw a mouse deer beat off one of his hunting dogs (see page 203). Despite their reputation for cunning, they are also a favoured source of protein.

Malaysia's most famous carnivore is the tiger – *harimau* in Malay. Tigers still roam the jungle in the centre of the peninsula, and on several occasions have made appearances in the Cameron Highlands, particularly during the dry season, when they move into the mountains to find food. Other members of the cat family are the clouded leopard and four species of wild cat: the leopard cat, the golden cat, the flat-headed cat and the marbled cat. Other jungle animals include the Malayan sun bear (which have a penchant for honey), the *serigala* (wild dog), civet cats (of which there are many different varieties), mongooses, weasels and otters.

Malaysia has several species of fruit bats and insect-eating bats, but the best-known insect-eater is the pangolin (scaly anteater), the animal world's answer to the armoured car. Its scales are formed of matted hair (like rhinoceros horn) and it has a long thin tongue which it flicks into termite nests. More common jungle mammals include rodents, among which are five varieties of giant flying squirrels. Like the flying lemur, these glide spectacularly from tree to tree and can cover up to about 500m in one 'flight'.

Other large mammals include the **banteng**, a wild cattle known as the *tembadau* in Sabah. These are smaller than the *seladang* of Peninsular Malaysia, and are most numerous in lowland areas of eastern Sabah where herds are encountered on country roads. The **bearded pig** is the only member of the pig family found in Borneo and is a major source of meat for many Dayak groups. Of the **deer family**, Borneo supports two species of barking deer or *kijang*, and the Greater (*npau*) and Lesser mouse deer. The latter barely stands 30 cm tall.

Background

Birds In ornithological circles, Malaysia is famed for its varied bird-life. The country is visited by many migratory water birds, and there are several wetland areas where the Malayan Nature Society has set up birdwatching hides; the most accessible to Kuala Lumpur is the Kuala Selangor Nature Park (see page 90). Migratory birds winter on Selangor's mangrove-fringed mudflats from September to May. There are also spectacular birds of prey, the most common of which are the hawk eagles and brahminy kites. Among the most fascinating and beautiful jungle species are the crested firebacks, a kind of pheasant; the kingfisher family, with their brilliantly coloured plumage; the hornbills (see below); greater racquet-tailed drongos – dark blue with long, sweeping tails; and black-naped orioles, saffron-coloured lowland residents. There are also wagtails, mynas, sunbirds, humming birds (flower-peckers), bulbuls, barbets, woodpeckers and weaver-birds. The latter makes incredible, finely woven, hanging tubular nests from strips of grass.

Hornbill There are nine types of hornbill on Borneo, the most striking and biggest of which is the rhinoceros hornbill (*Buceros rhinoceros*) – or *kenyalang*. They can grow up to 1.5m long and are mainly black, with a white belly. The long tail feathers are white too, crossed with a thick black bar near the end. They make a remarkable, resonant "GERONK" call in flight, which can be heard over long distances; they honk when resting. Hornbills are usually seen in pairs – they are believed to be monogamous. After mating, the female imprisons herself in a hole in a tree, building a sturdy wall with her own droppings. The male bird fortifies the wall from the outside, using a mulch of mud, grass, sticks and saliva, leaving only a vertical slit for her beak. She remains incarcerated in her cell for about three months, during which the male supplies her and the nestlings with food – mainly fruit, lizards, snakes and mice. Usually, only one bird is hatched and reared in the hole and when it is old enough to fly, the female breaks out of the nest hole. Both emerge looking fat and dirty.

The 'bill' itself has no known function, but the males have been seen duelling in mid-air during the courting season. They fly straight at each other and collide head-on. The double-storeyed yellow bill has a projection, called a casque, on top, which has a bright red tip. In some species the bill develops wrinkles as the bird matures: one wrinkle for each year of its life. For this reason they are known in Dutch, and in some eastern Indonesian languages as 'year birds'.

Most Dayak groups consider the hornbill to have magical powers and the feathers are worn as symbols of heroism. In tribal mythology the bird is associated with the creation of mankind, and is a symbol of the upper world. The hornbill is also the official state emblem of Sarawak. The best place to see hornbills is near wild fig trees – they love the fruit and play an important role in seed dispersal. The helmeted hornbill's bill is heavy and solid and can be carved, like ivory. These bills were highly valued by the Dayaks, and have been traded for centuries. The third largest hornbill is the wreathed hornbill which makes a yelping call and a loud – almost mechanical – noise when it beats its wings. Others species on Borneo include the wrinkled, black, bushy-crested, white-crowned and pied hornbills.

Reptiles The kings of Malaysia's reptile population are the giant leatherback turtles (see page 279), hawksbill and green turtles (see page 459); there are several other species of turtle and three species of land tortoise. The most notorious reptile is the estuarine crocodile (*Crocodilus porosus*) – which can grow up to 8m long. The largest population of estuarine crocodiles are found in the lower reaches of Borneo's rivers. However, they have been so extensively hunted that they are rarely a threat, although people do very occasionally still get taken. The Malayan gharial (*Tomistoma schlegeli*) is a fish-eating, freshwater crocodile which grows to just under 3m. Lizards include common house geckos (*Hemidactylus frenatus* – or *cikcak* in Malay), green-crested lizards (*Calotes cristatellus*), which change colour like

The Iban Hornbill Festival

One of the main Iban festivals is Gawai
Kenyalang, *or the Hornbill Festival. The*
kenyalang – *a carved wooden hornbill –*
traditionally played an important part in
the ceremony which preceded
head-hunting expeditions, and the often
ornate, brightly painted images also made
appearances at other gawais, or festivals.
The kenyalang is carved from green wood
and the design varies from area to area. A
carved hornbill can be about 2m long and
1m high and is stored until a few days
before the festival, when it is painted,
bringing the carving to life. It is carried in
procession and offered tuak *(rice wine),*
before being mounted on a carved base
on the tanju, *the longhouse's open*
verandah. As the singing gets underway,
the kenyalang is adorned with specially
woven pua kumbu *(see page 398) and*
then raised off the ground to face enemy
territory. Its soul is supposed to attack the
village's enemies, destroying their houses
and crops.

Kenyalang, hornbill image
From Roth, Henry (1896) The Natives of Sarawak and
British North Borneo, *Truslove & Hanson: London*

chameleons, and flying lizards (*Draco*), which have an extendable undercarriage
allowing the lizard to glide from tree to tree. Monitors are the largest of Malaysian
lizards, the most widespread of which is the common water monitor (*Varanus
salvator*), which can grow to about 2½ m.

The Malaysian jungles also have 140 species of frogs and toads, which are
more often heard than seen. Some are dramatically coloured, such as the
appropriately named green-backed frog (*Rana erythraea*) and others have
particular skills, such as Wallace's flying frog (*Rana migropalmatus*) which
parachutes around on its webbed feet.

Of Malaysia's 100-odd land snakes, only 16 are poisonous; all 20 species of sea
snake are poisonous. There are two species of python, the reticulated python
(*Python reticulatus*) – which can grow to nearly 10m in length and has iridescent
black and yellow scales – and the short python (*Python curtus*), which rarely grows
more than 2.5m and has a very thick, rusty-brown body. Most feared are the
venomous snakes, but the constrictors can also pose a threat to humans.

Among the most common non-poisonous snakes is the dark brown house snake
(*Lycodon aulicus*) which likes to eat geckos, and the common Malayan racer (*Elaphe
flavolineata*), which grows to about 2m and is black with a pale underbelly. The most
beautiful non-poisonous snakes are the paradise tree snake (*Chrysopelea paradisi*),
which is black with an iridescent green spot on every scale and the mangrove snake
(*Boiga dendrophilia*) which grows to about 2m long and is black with yellow stripes.
The former is famed for its gliding skills: it can leap from tree-to-tree in a controlled
glide by hollowing its underbelly, trapping a cushion of air below it. In the jungle it is
quite common to see the dull brown river snake which goes by the unfortunate
name of the dog-faced water snake (*Cerberus rhynchops*); it has a healthy appetite
for fish and frogs.

The most feared venomous snake is the king cobra (*Naja hannah*) which grows
to well over 4m long and is olive-green with an orange throat-patch. They are often
confused with non-poisonous rat snakes and racers. The king cobra eats snakes and
lizards – including monitor lizards. Its reputation as an aggressive snake is
unfounded but its venom is deadly. Both the king cobra and the common cobra

Background

Nepenthes – the jungle's poisoned chalice

There are about 30 species of insectivorous pitcher plants in Malaysia; they come in all shapes and sizes – some are bulbous and squat, some are small and elegant, others are huge and fat. All are killers, and are among the handful of insect-eating plants in the world. Pitcher plants grow on poor soils, either in the mountains or in heath (kerangas) forest. The Malay name for the Nepenthes family is periuk kera – or 'monkey cups'. The Chinese call them after the tall wicker baskets used to take pigs to market – shu long cao. The plants remain sealed until they have begun to secrete the fluids which help them supplement their meagre diet. One of these liquids is sweet and sticky and attracts insects; the other, which builds up at the bottom, digests each victim which ventures in. The 'lid' opens invitingly when the plant is ready for business and it is virtually impossible for insects to escape – the pitcher plant's waxed interior offers little traction for the uphill climb and the upper lips, past the overhanging ridge, are serated and very slippery. This plant amazed the first Europeans to visit the Malay archipelago. George Rumphius, the German naturalist, thought it one of nature's freaks when he travelled through the region at the end of the 17th century. Two centuries later, the British naturalist, Frederick Burbridge, wrote that seeing the plants "was a sensation I shall never forget – one of those which we experience but rarely in a whole lifetime".

(*Naja naja*) are hooded; the hood is formed by loose skin around the neck and is pushed outwards on elongated ribs when the snake rears to its strike posture.

Other poisonous snakes are the banded krait (*Bungarus fasciatus*) with its distinctive black and yellow stripes and the Malayan krait (*Bungarus candidus*) with black and white stripes. Kraits are not fast movers and are said to bite only under extreme provocation. Coral snakes (of the genus *Maticora*) have extremely poisonous venom, but because the snake virtually has to chew its victim before the venom can enter the bite (its poison glands are located at the very back of its mouth), there have been no recorded fatalities. Pit vipers have a thermo-sensitive groove between the eye and the nostril which can detect warm-blooded prey even in complete darkness. The bite of the common, bright green Wagler's pit viper (*Trimeresurus wagleri*) is said to be extremely painful, but is never fatal. They have broad, flattened heads; adults have yellow bars and a bright red tip to the tail.

Insects Malaysia has a literally countless population of insect species; new ones are constantly being discovered and named. There are 120 species of butterfly in Malaysia. The king of them is the male Rajah Brooke's birdwing (*Troides brookiana*) – the national butterfly – with its iridescent, emerald zig-zag markings on jet-black velvety wings. It was named by Victorian naturalist Alfred Russel Wallace after his friend James Brooke, the first White Rajah of Sarawak (see page 384). The males can be found along rivers while the much rarer females (which are less spectacularly coloured), remain out of sight among the treetops.

There are more than 100 other magnificently coloured butterflies, including the black and yellow common birdwing, the swallowtails and swordtails, the leaf butterflies (which are camouflaged as leaves when their wings are folded) such as the blue and brown saturn and the rust, white and brown tawny rajah. Among the most beautiful of all is the delicately patterned Malayan lacewing (*Cethosia hypsea*) with its jagged markings of red, orange, brown and white. There are several butterfly farms around the country, including in Kuala Lumpur (see page 91), Penang (see page 174) and the butterfly capital of Malaysia, the Cameron Highlands (see page 133).

Fireflies – flashers in the forest

There are plenty of fireflies (Lampyridae) in Malaysia. But the ones which sit in the trees along the Selangor River, to the west of Kuala Lumpur, are special. They flash in synch – thousands of them go on and off like Christmas-tree lights. Although there are a few reported instances of this happening elsewhere in Southeast Asia, Kampong Kuantan, near Kuala Selangor (see page 90), is the best place to witness the phenomenon, which many visitors suspect is a clever electric hoax. The Lampyrid beetle which exhibits the synchrony is the Pteroptyx malaccae, which grows to about 9mm in length and emits flashes at the rate of just over one per second. In the days before batteries, villagers used to put the fireflies in bottles to serve as torches. Because they stick to the same trees – which are chosen because they are always free of keringga weaving ants (see below) – local fishermen are said to use them as navigational beacons. Only the males are synchronous flashers, and scientists have yet to come up with an explanation for their behaviour. The females, which are the first to settle in the trees, shortly after sunset, emit a dimmer light, and the males, which fly around the water level as it gets dark, join the females which respond to their flashes. The light is produced by cells on the firefly's lower abdomen.

The most spectacular moths are the huge atlas moth (*Attacus atlas*) and the swallow-tailed moth (*Nyctalemon patroclus*); these can be found on exterior walls illuminated by strip-lights late at night, particularly in remoter parts of the country.

The Malaysian beetle population is among the most varied in the world. The best known is the rhinoceros beetle (*Oryctes rhinoceros*), which can grow to nearly 6cm in length and is characterized by its dramatic horns. The empress cicada (*Pomponia imperatoria*) is the biggest species in Malaysia and can have a wingspan of more than 20cm. The male cicada is the noisiest jungle resident. The incredible droning and whining noises are created by the vibration of membranes in the body, the sound of which is amplified in the body cavity.

One of the most famous insects is the praying mantis. In *Malayan animal life*, MWF Tweedie writes: "They owe their name to the deceptively devotional appearance of their characteristic pose, with the fore legs held up as if in prayer. In reality the mantis is, of course, waiting for some unwary insect to stray within reach; if it does, the deadly spined fore limbs will strike and grasp and the mantis will eat its victim alive, daintily, as a lady eats a sandwich." There are several other species of mantis, and the most intriguing is the flower mantis (*Hymenopus coronatus*) which is bright pink and can twist and extend itself to resemble a four-petalled flower, a camouflage which protects it from predators, while attracting meals such as bees.

Of the less attractive insect life, it is advisable to be wary of certain species of wasps and hornets. The most dangerous is the slender banded hornet (*Polistes sagittarius*) which is big (3cm long) and has a black and orange striped abdomen. Its nests are paper-like, and hang from trees and the eaves of houses by a short stalk. They are extremely aggressive and do not need to be provoked before they attack. The golden wasp (*Vespa auraria*) is found in montane jungle – notably the Cameron Highlands, and, like the hornet above, will attack anything coming near its nest. The wasp is a honey-gold colour, it nests in trees and shrubs and its sting is vicious. There are several other wasp species which attack ferociously, and stings can be extremely painful. One of the worst is the night wasp (*Provespa anomala*), which is an orangy-brick colour and commonly flies into houses at night, attracted by lights. Bee stings can also be very serious, and none more so than that of the giant honey bee, which builds pendulous combs on overhanging eaves and trees. It is black with a yellow mark at the front end of the abdomen; multiple stings can be fatal.

Background

Another insect species to be particularly wary of is the fire ant (*Tetraponera rufonigra*). It has a red body and a big black head; it will enthusiastically sting anything it comes into contact with, and the pain is acute. Weaver ants (*Oecophylla smaragdina*) are common but do not sting. Instead, their powerful jaws can be used as jungle sutures to stitch up open wounds. The bites alone are very painful, and the ant (which is also known as the *kerengga*) adds insult to injury by spitting an acidic fluid on the bite. It is difficult to extract the pincers from the skin, and once attached, the ant will not let go. The biggest of all ants, the giant ant (*Camponotus gigas*), can be nearly 3cm in length; (it is also variously known as the elephant ant and the 'big-bum ant'). They are largely nocturnal, however, so tend to cause less trouble in the jungle.

Other jungle residents worth avoiding are the huge, black and hairy *Mygalomorph* spiders, whose bodies alone can be about 5cm long. Their painful bites cause localized swelling. Scorpions are dangerous but not fatal. The biggest scorpion, the wood scorpion (*Hormurus australasiae*) can grow to about 16cm long; it is black, lives under old logs and is mainly nocturnal. In rural areas, the particularly paranoid might shake their shoes for the spotted house-scorpion (*Isometrus maculatus*), which is quite common. Centipedes (*Chilopoda*) have a poisonous bite and can grow up to about 25cm in length. The Malaysian peninsula is malaria-free, although the *Aedes*, tiger mosquito, with its black and white striped body and legs, is a daytime mosquito that carries dengue fever.

The environmental costs of growth As Malaysia has become more wealthy, and the middle class has burgeoned, so environmental concerns have gained greater prominence. In 1993 the Department of the Environment released figures revealing that of Peninsular Malaysia's 116 major rivers, 85 were either 'biologically dead' or 'dying'. Air quality is also a source of concern, especially in the Klang Valley, an agglomeration of industrial activity around Kuala Lumpur. Environmental Impact Assessments (EIAs) are now, in theory, compulsory for every development project, but most companies undertake to do them only grudgingly – if at all – and then place them on a shelf to gather dust. The claim that, as a developing country, Malaysia can ill-afford the 'luxury' of such things is wearing very thin as wealth spreads with each year of eight percent growth. The government recognizes that the environment is fast becoming a political issue, and like any good political party which thinks it has identified a bandwagon with a fair number of votes attached, is trying to climb aboard.

Most accounts of Malaysia's environmental problems – some would characterize it as a 'crisis' – concentrate on the East Malaysian states of Sarawak and Sabah. In a sense the peninsula is a lost cause: deforestation has been so extensive that the only large areas remaining are already gazetted as national parks. In East Malaysia, though, there is a sense that if only logging could be better controlled then the natural wealth of Malaysian Borneo could be preserved.

Scorched earth, bitter winds – the great fires of 1997 The stupendous fires that blazed across the Indonesian island of Sumatra and Indonesian Borneo brought hazardous conditions to Malaysia. In Sarawak the government considered evacuating the entire population of over two million people – but wondered where to put them. The airport in Kuching was closed and residents rushed to stockpile water and basic necessities. Schools, factories and government offices stayed shut as the smog became a threat to health. Fishermen did not venture out on the seas. Visibility became so bad that people stopped using their vehicles – even in the middle of the day. The state government of Sarawak declared a state of emergency and advised people to stay indoors. But even in their own homes people could not escape the acrid smoke and hospitals filled with people suffering from aggravated respiratory and heart complaints. The Air Pollution Index reached 851 at 1300 on 24 September. A figure of 300 is considered 'hazardous' and it was estimated that even a figure of 200-300 is equivalent to

Environment – mud-slinging in the greenhouse

Malaysia is spending US$10m a year on a slick public relations counter offensive to the anti-tropical timber lobby in the West. That's a lot of money, until compared with the US$4.5bn it earns every year from its trees. For the past decade, Malaysia has been the world's biggest exporter of tropical timber.

But the bald figures disguise the fact that the export of raw logs has been reduced by about half in recent years, in line with Malaysia's policy of sustainable forestry management. In 1991 a government minister defended Malaysia's logging policy by saying that "it's not our responsibility to supply the West with oxygen." But things have changed since then and the government has gone green. While continuing to expose Western hypocrisy in environmental matters, Malaysia has done much to clean up its own back yard. Most importantly, it has undertaken to reduce log production to sustainable levels, following apocalyptic warnings of what might happen if it didn't.

Malaysia now claims to be practising selective logging techniques (see page 374), felling a maximum of seven to 12 trees per hectare. Critics have long alleged, however, that Malaysia's forestry laws are being flouted by illegal loggers and corrupt timber concessionaires. The government's answer to these allegations was the introduction in 1993 of tough new laws involving heavy fines and lengthy custodial sentences for poachers and illegal loggers. Concessionaires, whose ranks include sultans and senior politicians, are now liable for the same fines and sentences. Forest rangers will be empowered to arrest and will have the back-up of the police and the army.

The government insists that its stricter policies were not motivated by pressure from the West. It simply says that it would not be so stupid or greedy as to kill the goose that lays the golden egg and it maintains that sustained-yield harvesting means its forests will be there in perpetuity.

The government has long railed against Western nations for their double standards over the environment. Its line is that because industrialized countries have already cleared their forests in the name of development, why shouldn't Malaysia be free to do the same? At the Earth Summit in Rio de Janeiro in June 1992, the Prime Minister, Dr Mahathir Mohamad, noted that poor countries have been told to preserve their forests and other genetic resources for research purposes. He said: "This is the same as telling these countries that they must continue to be poor because their forests and other resources are more precious than the people themselves." In the wake of Rio, hopes that a new global environment fund would help cover the costs of enforcing environmental protection, have been dashed. Dr Mahathir says Western countries have reneged on their undertaking.

There are still holes in Malaysia's forestry policies; adequately policing large tracts of forest against illegal loggers is impossible. Local environmental groups continue to call for greater accountability and a crackdown on corruption. A small élite of extremely wealthy, corrupt and powerful men still control much of the timber trade. But even the government's critics concede that great strides have been made in environmental protection. Until the rest of the world recognizes this, the government has sworn to keep making its point: that the people who created the greenhouse effect should not be throwing stones.

Background

smoking 20 cigarettes a day. In Kuala Lumpur the Air Pollution Index broke through the 300 mark and some foreign embassies and companies began evacuating their staff. Satellite images showed that by late September the smog stretched over 3,000 km from east to west, affecting six countries and afflicting perhaps 70 million people.

Though the fires are concentrated in Indonesia, the Malaysian government has not escaped criticism. The failure of the government to introduce a coherent zoning policy or to control car emissions has been attacked. There seems little doubt that pollution from cars and industry has combined with the smoke from the fires to produce a particularly unpleasant concoction leading to eye irritation, asthma attacks, headaches and breathing difficulties. In 1994 the Malaysian cabinet was presented with a Clean Air Action Plan but it was rejected as potentially undermining the country's industrialization efforts. At the beginning of November the Malaysian government even went so far as to muzzle academics, ordering them not to talk to the press about the ill effects of the smog. This followed one (inaccurate) report that breathing the haze was like smoking 40 cigarettes a day (up from 20 a few weeks earlier!).

Although Singapore was less affected by the fires in Indonesia, even there the air became unpleasant to breathe. Rosemary Richter reporting from the Republic wrote of the experience of breathing the polluted air as 'unbelievably unpleasant' adding that it was like 'inhaling hot cotton wool fibres' and 'living inside a wet blanket redolent of a refuse tip'. Other correspondents reported on the bitter smell, oppressive darkness, watering eyes, the layer of soot that covered everything, the choking sensation, and the itching skin. One Indonesian minister estimated that 20 million Indonesians were suffering from aggravated respiratory problems because of the smog and some environmentalists were even predicting an increase in cancer in two or three decades' time because of the carcinogens that are present in the smoke. To put it bluntly: while a few people will die as a direct result of the smog, many more will die prematurely.

What may be remarkable to many Westerners was the time it took before the politics of blame took hold. Former President Suharto of Indonesia apologized to his fellow Asean nations at an environment conference in September 1997, but criticism from Malaysia and Singapore, the two countries most affected after Indonesia, was astonishingly muted. It was the media in the two countries, chivvied on by an irate public making their feelings known through newspaper letter columns and radio talk shows, that encouraged the governments of Malaysia and Singapore to take a more forthright stance. Warren Fernandez in Singapore's *Straits Times* wrote at the peak of the crisis that it was time to put aside Asean's usual chumminess: "This will entail their being able to set aside traditional inhibitions – diplomatic niceties, worries about national sensitivities, the so-called 'Asean-way' of not interfering in each other's affairs – to take steps to deal with a common problem that transcends national borders." At the beginning of October, President Suharto issued a second apology to his neighbours but once again the problem was described as 'natural' and 'environmental'. The president was not willing to take responsibility for a disaster which most academics and commentators believe has been hugely aggravated by human actions – or inaction. He also seemed to take some action, revoking the licences of 29 timber and plantation companies. But the impression remained among the public in the region that the Indonesian government was driven by more powerful interests than public opinion and, more to the point, was powerless to put out the fires in any case. It is probably appropriate to leave the last words to the Imam of the Central Mosque in the city of Pontianak in Kalimantan, for he probably best articulated what many people in the region felt: 'Allah is giving us a warning'.

2000: the fires return The conflagration of 1997 might have been the most serious (so far), and Suharto and at least some of his cronies may have gone, but that hasn't meant that the fires are a thing of the past. As this book went to press, Malaysia and Singapore were once again suffering from 'the haze' as parts of Sumatra and Kalimantan went up in smoke. Reports from some areas of East Malaysia - including towns like Sibu - were that air quality had sharply deteriorated. Because the haze in 1997 scared so many tourists off, the Malaysian government treats air quality as a state secret and it is not always possible to access reliable information. The Environment Minister, Datuk Law Hieng Ding, asked the local media in mid-March 2000 not to dwell upon the air-quality index because it might keep tourists away. While the Malaysian government may have been in denial, many residents were dusting off their face masks and visibility in the Straits of Melaka was so poor that the Malaysian marine police put out navigation warnings. Plus ça change.

Culture

People

Visitors sometimes get confused over the different races that make up Malaysia's population. All citizens of Malaysia are 'Malaysians'; they are comprised of Malays, Chinese and Indians as well as other 'tribal' groups, most of whom live in the East Malaysian states of Sabah and Sarawak.

Malaysia has a total population approaching 20 million, of whom 83 percent live on the peninsula, eight percent in Sabah and nine percent in Sarawak. Statistics on the ethnic breakdown of Malaysia's multi-racial population tend to differ and because politics is divided along racial lines, they are sensitive figures. For Malaysia as a whole, Malays make up roughly 52 percent of the population, Chinese 29 percent, Indians eight percent and indigenous tribes 11 percent. The Malays and indigenous groups are usually lumped together under the umbrella term *bumiputra* – or 'sons of the soil'. So in the country as a whole, 'bumis' – as they are popularly known – account for 63 percent of the population. On the peninsula the figure is slightly less, with bumis comprising 58 percent of the inhabitants there, while the Chinese make up 31 percent and Indians nine percent.

In theory being a *bumi* bestows certain advantages. The New Economic Policy or NEP (see page 510), introduced after the race riots in 1969, discriminates in favour of the indigenous population – mostly the Malays, but also the non-Malay tribal peoples of East Malaysia and the Orang Asli of the peninsula. They receive preferential treatment when it comes to university places, bumi entrepreneurs have an inside track securing government contracts, and they also benefit from discounts on houses. However there have been stories of non-Malay bumiputras not being accorded the affirmative action rights of Malay bumis. In 1997, for example, it was revealed that an Iban ('tribal' Dayak from East Malaysia) man was refused the five to seven percent discount which bumis are entitled to when he tried to buy a house in Melaka. The federal government was appalled but many commentators were not altogether surprised. What it means to qualify as a bumi has never been adequately defined. It appears that for some people being a bumi not only means being indigenous, it also means being Muslim, and many of the non-Malay bumis are Christian.

Malaysia's population is growing by about 2.5 percent per annum. Since 1970, the bumiputra population has grown fastest, and, on the peninsula, their proportion of the total population has increased from 53 percent. In the same period, the proportion of the Chinese population has declined from 36 percent while the proportion of Indians has remained roughly the same. Mahathir announced at the beginning of the 1990s that for Malaysia to become an industrialized country, it would need a strong domestic market, so he encouraged Malaysians to procreate – his once suggested target was a population of 70 million by 2010, up from 17 million in 1990. The target date has subsequently been revised to 2095. The higher average fertility rate of the Malay compared with the Chinese population means that the delicate racial balance that was such a potential source of instability at independence is becoming less of a worry. It has been estimated that by 2020 the bumiputra population will comprise 70 percent of the total population of the

☞ The new breed: farewell to the old Malaise

In recent years, the easy-going Malay kampung world of old wooden houses, water buffalo and coconut curries has clashed head-on with modern Malaysia and its hi-tech office towers, six-lane highways and polypropylene refineries.

For the past 30 years, the government has done just about everything in its power to coax Malays out of the villages and into the cities in an effort to catapult them into the modern economy. The New Economic Policy formalized this attempt to increase the Malays' stake of national wealth, see page 510. But because life was made easy for them, many massaged the system to their advantage, and arrived on top of the heap having expended comparatively little effort. This engendered much resentment.

The racial quotas introduced by the NEP still have not been met – even with all the scholarships and free directorships, Malays do not comprise a third of the corporate workforce. But today, in Kuala Lumpur's penthouse boardrooms and behind the terminals in dealing rooms, a new breed of Malay professional has begun to appear. At last, they are there not because they are Malay but because they are good.

There is a Malay phase associated with this phenomenon: kurang ajar. It is coarse language – if you accuse someone of being kurang ajar, it means they are extremely rude, ignorant and ill-bred. Not long ago, the phrase was actually banned in the Malaysian parliament after one opposition MP used it to describe a member of the government. But with a little good-humoured antiseptic, the quality of kurang ajar has come to represent the new assertiveness of the 1990s Malay. A Malay who is more critical, more analytical, more willing to stand up for his – or her – rights and a Malay who is more able. Enter bumiputras with attitude: the New Malay. Anwar Ibrahim, the relatively youthful, confident, clean-cut, urbane deputy Prime Minister, has emerged as a role model for the aspiring New Malay.

Although immersed in the wheeling and dealing of modern progressive Malaysia, the boomtown bumiputra has not entirely forsaken his kampung roots. Lat, Malaysia's favourite cartoonist, has a series of books on the theme of the rural Malay struggling to keep pace with the times. His opinion is that every mobile-phone-wielding, Rayban-clad, BMW-driving KL yuppy is really a kampung kid at heart. And to be sure, every weekend and public holiday, the highways and airports become clogged as the new city species – balek kampung – head back to their villages.

country. The fear that the Chinese might represent a political threat to Malay domination is receding as each year passes.

Malays   The Malay people probably first migrated to the peninsula from Sumatra. Anthropologists speculate that the race originally evolved from the blending of a Mongoloid people from Central Asia with an island race living between the Indian and Pacific oceans. They are lowland people and originally settled around the coasts. These 'Coastal Malays' are also known as 'Deutero-Malays'. They are ethnically similar to the Malays of Indonesia and are the result of intermarriage with many other racial groups, including Indians, Chinese, Arabs and Thais. They are a very relaxed, warm-hearted people who had the good fortune to settle in a land where growing food was easy. For centuries they have been renowned for their hospitality and generosity as well as their well-honed sense of humour. When Malays converted to Islam in the early 15th century, the language was written in Sanskrit script which evolved into the Arabic-looking *Jawi*.

Because Malays were traditionally farmers and were tied to rural kampungs, they remained insulated from the expansion of colonial Malaya's export economy. Few of them worked as wage labourers and only the aristocracy, which had been educated in English, were intimately involved in the British system of government, as administrators. "... In return for the right to develop a modern extractive economy within the *negeri* [states] by means of alien immigrant labor," writes historian William R Roff, "the British undertook to maintain intact the position and prestige of the ruling class and to refrain from catapulting the Malay people into the modern world". Rural Malays only began to enter the cash economy when they started to take up rubber cultivation on their smallholdings – but this was not until after 1910. In 1921, less than five percent of Malays lived in towns.

On attaining independence in 1957, the new constitution allowed Malays to be given special rights for 10 years. The idea was that this would allow the Malay community to become as prosperous as the Chinese 'immigrants'. To this end, they were afforded extra help in education and in securing jobs. The first economic development plan focused on the rural economy, with the aim of improving the lot of the rural Malays. It was the Malay community's sense of its own weakness in comparison with the commercial might of the Chinese that led to ethnic tensions erupting onto the streets in May 1969. Following the race riots, the Malays were

Tribes of Borneo

Tribes

1 Banjarese	10 Kenyah/Kayan	18 Modang
2 Bugis	11 Land Dayak	19 Murut
3 Chinese	12 Lun Dayeh	20 Ngaju
4 Desa	13 Limbai	21 Ot Danum
5 Iban	14 Malays	22 Taman
6 Kadazan	15 Maloh	23 Tebidah
7 Kantu	16 Ma'anyan &	24 Tunjung
8 Kedayan	Lawangan	
9 Kelabit	17 Melanau	—— Approx Tribal limits

N

Not to scale

Background

Tikus Rahmat: Malaysian racial relations in rat form

Tikus Rahmat or Blessed Rat written by Hassan Ibrahim and first published in 1963 is the only Malay novel in satire form and it is modelled closely on George Orwell's Animal Farm. The novel is based on relations between various groups of rats in Tikusia Raya (Ratland), each of which is symbolic of the different races in Malaysia. The similarities between the inhabitants of Tikusia Raya and the stereotypical view of the races of Malaysia are clear. The farm rats or tikus ladang symbolize the Chinese: they are the newcomers; they play the role of the middleman; and they are hard-working and diligent. The novelist also writes that they are: "... capable in the art of cheating as it is their way of life, taught by their parents since birth."

The valley rats or tikus lembah are the Malays. They are the poorest rats, whose interests are continually sacrificed in the interests of the rest of the population. But they are also very religious and humble. Needless to say, the other rats view them as lazy good-for-nothings.

The farm rats insist that their own language – cok cak – be used as the lingua franca of Tikusia Raya and in an election the farm rats win a majority. The valley rats rebel against the results of the election and attack and kill the rich white rats (symbolizing white people) and farm rats. The few that survive this epic rat battle agree to settle their differences and follow the Prophet Solomon (Muhammad). Although the novel was written before the 1969 race riots, parts of the story coincidentally mirror the tragic events of that year.

extended special privileges in an effort to increase their participation in the modern economy (see box, page 510). Along with indigenous groups, they were classed as bumiputras, usually shortened to 'bumis' – a label many were able to use as a passport to a better life.

Background

Chinese The Chinese community accounts for about a third of Malaysia's population. In 1794, just eight years after he had founded Georgetown in Penang, Sir Francis Light wrote: "The Chinese constitute the most valuable part of our inhabitants: ... they possess the different trades of carpenters, masons, smiths, traders, shopkeepers and planters; they employ small vessels. They are the only people from whom a revenue may be raised without expense and extraordinary effort by the government. They are a valuable acquisition ..." Chinese immigrants went on to become invaluable members of the British Straits Settlements – from the early 1820s they began to flood into Singapore from China's southern provinces. At the same time they arrived in droves on the Malay peninsula, most of them working as tin prospectors, shopkeepers and small traders.

Although the great bulk of Chinese in Malaysia arrived during the massive immigration between the late 19th and early 20th centuries, there has been a settled community of Chinese in Melaka since the 15th century. Many arrived as members of the retinue of the Chinese princess Li Poh who married Melaka's Sultan Mansur Shah in 1460 (see page 213). Over the centuries their descendants evolved into a wealthy and influential community with its own unique, sophisticated culture (see page 210). These **Straits Chinese** became known as **Peranakans** (which means 'born here'); men were called **Babas** and women, **Nyonyas**. When Peranakans began to be known as such is not known. Baba came into common usage during the 19th century and it is thought that Peranakan was already a well-established label at that time. 'Baba' does not seem to be of Chinese origin but is probably derived from Arabic, or perhaps Turkish, roots. To begin with Baba was used to refer to all local-born foreigners in Malaya, whether they were ethnic Chinese, Indians or Europeans. However, before long it became solely associated with the Straits Chinese.

Running amok

The word amok is one of the few Malay words to have been embraced by the English language, most obviously used in the expression 'to run amuck'. Amok refers to aberrant behaviour which, at least until the early 20th century, was prevalent among the Malay peoples. There are two forms of amok – martial amok, where it is used as an honourable tactic of warfare (martial amok was also common in India), and solitary amok. It is the latter which has attracted the most attention, as it appears to occur suddenly, without warning, and with little apparent reason. The earliest reference to solitary amok occurs in the work of Nicolo Conti dating from the early 15th century. All references agree that it is a frenzied, murderous and usually unselective attack on all and everyone that an amok-runner or pengamok might meet, and that it almost always ended in the death of the attacker, such is the madness of the violence. Some authorities have attributed amok to social alienation (amok-runners are usually new arrivals in an area); others to the disgrace of penury that might force a person into slavery; some to the effects of drugs (this was the usual colonial explanation, as the cause is clear and easily understood); others to some deep-seated grief (for example following the death of a man's wife or child); while still others have maintained that it is religiously motivated. Within the Malay social context, the amok-runner was viewed as a person with a certain honour: the act itself, although it might well lead to the death of innocent bystanders, was seen as an honourable escape from some dire situation.

The British in Malaya tended to view pengamok in Western terms, and to moralize about their crimes. On 8 July 1846, Sunan, a respectable Malay house-builder ran amok in Penang. According to the judicial disposition at his trial:

"... before he [Sunan] was arrested [he] killed an old Hindu woman, a Kling, a Chinese boy, and a Kling girl about three years old in the arms of its father, and wounded two Hindus, three Klings, and two Chinese, of whom only two survived." He had, apparently, been devastated by the death of his wife and only child. Nonetheless, the magistrate sentenced the man with the words:
"The sentence of the Court therefore is, that you, Sunan, be remanded to the place from whence you came, and that on the morning of Wednesday next you be drawn from thence on a hurdle to the place of execution, and there hanged by the neck until you are dead. Your body will then be handed over to the surgeons for dissection, and your mangled limbs, instead of being restored to your friends for decent interment, will be cast into the sea, thrown into a ditch, or scattered on the earth at the discretion of the Sheriff. And may God Almighty have mercy on your miserable soul!"
Source of quote: Spores, John C (1988) Running amok: an historical inquiry, Ohio University Center for International Studies: Athens, Ohio.

The centres of Peranakan Chinese culture were the Straits Settlements of Melaka, Penang and Singapore. There were, however, significant differences between the communities in the three settlements. For example, Nyonya food in Penang shows culinary influences from Thailand, while food in Melaka and Singapore does not.

The Peranakans of Malaysia and Singapore saw their futures being intimately associated with the British. They learnt the English language, established close links with the colonial administration system and colonial businesses, and even their newspapers were written in English rather than Chinese. With the massive infusion of new Chinese blood from the mainland beginning at the end of the 19th century there emerged a two-tier Chinese community. The Peranakans were concentrated in the commercial and professional sectors, and the 'pure' Chinese in the manual sectors. But as the 20th century progressed so the influence of the Peranakans

Background

declined. Competition from non-Baba Chinese became stronger as their businesses expanded and as sheer weight of numbers began to tell. The Straits Chinese British Association (SCBA) was eclipsed by the Malaysian Chinese Association (MCA) as a political force and the Peranakans found themselves marginalized. As this occurred, so the Babas found themselves the object, increasingly, of derision by non-Baba Chinese. They were regarded as having 'sold out' their Chinese roots and become ridiculous in the process. Today the Straits Chinese, in terms of political and economic power, have become – to a large extent – an irrelevance.

Today Peranakan culture is disappearing. Few Baba Chinese identify themselves as Baba; they have become Chinese Malaysians. Only in Melaka (and to some extent in Singapore) does the Baba cultural tradition remain strong. In Penang the numbers of people who see their Baba roots as anything but historical are dwindling. But although Peranakan culture is gradually disappearing, it has left an imprint on mainstream Malaysian culture. For example the custom among Peranakan women of wearing the *sarong* and *kebaya* has become subsumed within Malay tradition and has, in the process, become inter-ethnic. Baba cuisine has also been incorporated within Malay/Chinese cuisine.

The Peranakans may be the most colourful piece in Malaysia's Chinese mosaic, but the vast majority of modern Malaysia's prosperous Chinese population arrived from China rather later, as penniless immigrants. They left China because of poverty, over-population and religious persecution – and were attracted by the lure of gold. In the mid-19th century, these newly arrived immigrants came under the jurisdiction of secret societies and *kongsis* – or clan associations. Some of the most striking examples of the latter are in Penang (see, for example the Khoo Kongsi, page 160). The secret societies sometimes engaged in open warfare with each other as rival groups fought over rights to tin mining areas.

The overseas Chinese have been described as possessing these common traits: the ability to smell profits and make quick business decisions; a penchant for good food (they prefer to sit at round tables to facilitate quicker exchange of information); and a general avoidance of politics in favour of money-making pursuits. Like most stereotypes, these characteristics break down when put to the detailed test but at a certain level of generalization, hold true. It is also true to say – broadly speaking – that the Chinese population felt little loyalty to their host society. At least, that is, until the 1949 Communist take-over in China, which effectively barred their return. Despite the community's political and economic gripes and traumas in the intervening years (see page), Chinese culture has survived intact and the community enjoys religious freedom; Chinese cuisine is enthusiastically devoured by all races and the mahjong tiles are still clacking in upstairs rooms. Today about 80 percent of Chinese schoolchildren attend private Chinese primary schools – although all secondary and tertiary education is in Malay.

Indians Indian traders first arrived on the shores of the Malay peninsula more than 2,000 years ago in search of Suvarnadvipa, the fabled Land of Gold. There was a well established community of Indian traders in Melaka when the first sultanate grew up in the 1400s – there was even Tamil blood in the royal lineage. But most of the 1½ million Indians in modern Malaysia – who make up nearly nine percent of the population – are descendants of indentured Tamil labourers shipped to Malaya from South India by the British in the 19th century. They were nicknamed 'Klings' – a name which today has a deeply derogatory connotation. Most were put to work as coolies on the roads and railways or as rubber tappers.

About 100 years on, four out of five Indians are still manual labourers on plantations or in the cities. This has long been explained as a colonial legacy, but as modern Malaysia has grown more prosperous, the Tamils have remained at the bottom of the heap. Other Indian groups – the Keralans (Malayalis), Gujeratis,

Bengalis, Sikhs and other North Indians, who came to colonial Malaya under their own volition, are now well represented in the professional classes. The South Indian Chettiar money-lending caste, which was once far more numerous than it is today, left the country in droves in the 1930s. Their confidence in British colonial rule was shaken by events in Burma, where anti-Indian riots prompted tens of thousands of Chettiars to return to India. While most of Malaysia's Indian community are Hindus, there are also Indian Muslims, Christians and Sikhs. In Melaka there is a small group of Indians with Portuguese names – known as Chitties.

Today the chanted names of the Hindu pantheon echo around the cool interior of the Sri Mariamman Temple in the heart of Kuala Lumpur as they have since its construction in 1873. But large numbers of Tamils still live in the countryside, where they still make up more than half the plantation workforce. Because the estates are on private land, they fall outside the ambit of national development policies and Malaysia's economic boom has passed them by. The controversial New Economic Policy (see page 510) gave Malays a helping hand, and although it was aimed at eradicating poverty generally, it did not help Indians much – who often, and justifiably, feel that they are the group who have missed out most. They lack the economic clout of the Chinese, and the political might of the Malays, and can, it seems, conveniently be forgotten.

The new policy document which replaced the NEP in 1991 officially recognizes that Indians have lagged behind in the development stakes. Education is seen as the key to broadening the entrepreneurial horizons of Tamils, getting them off the plantations, out of the urban squatter settlements and into decent jobs. But in the privately run Tamil shanty schools on the estates, the drop-out rate is double the national average. Critics accuse the Malaysian Indian Congress (MIC), which is part of the ruling coalition, of perpetuating this system in an effort to garner support. Because Indians are spread throughout the country and do not form the majority in any constituency, the plantations have been the MIC's traditional support base. It is not in the MIC's interests to see them move off the estates.

But things are beginning to change on the plantations – an unprecedented national strike in 1990 guaranteed plantation workers a minimum wage for the first time. Workers are becoming more assertive and aware of their individual and political rights. A new party, the Indian Progressive Front, has drawn its support from working class Indians. It seems that these stirrings of new assertiveness represent rising aspirations on the estates – which will have to continue to rise if the Tamils are ever going to escape from their plantation poverty trap, which one prominent Indian leader refers to as 'the green ghetto'. In 1970 ethnic Indians controlled about 1.1 percent of the country's wealth. By 1992, at the end of the 20-year NEP, this figure had declined to one percent. It has been estimated that two-thirds of Indians still live in poverty and for the Indians the NEP has been largely irrelevant. While Malays have enjoyed cumulative gains from the NEP and the Chinese have seen their slice of the cake grow in size if not in proportion, the Indian community have been left trailing and marginalized – a classic 'excluded' community.

While the Malay population originally settled on the coasts of the peninsula, the mountainous, jungled interior was the domain of the oldest indigenous groups – the aboriginals. They are a sinewy, dark-skinned race, characterized by their curly hair and are probably of Melanesian origin – possibly related to Australian aborigines. During the Pleistocene ice age, when a land-bridge linked the Philippines to Borneo and mainland Southeast Asia, these people spread throughout the continent. Today they are confined to the mountains of the Malay peninsula, Northeast India, North Sumatra, the Andaman Islands and the Philippines. The Negrito aboriginals – who in Malay are known as *Orang Asli*, or 'Indigenous People' – were mainly hunter-gatherers. As the Malays spread inland, the Orang Asli

Orang Asli (Aboriginals)

Background

were pushed further and further into the mountainous interior. Traditionally, the Negritos did not build permanent houses – preferring makeshift shelters – and depend on the jungle and the rivers for their food.

A second group of Orang Asli, the *Senoi* – who are also known as the *Sakai* – arrived later than the Negritos. They practised shifting cultivation to supplement their hunting and gathering and built sturdier houses. The third aboriginal group to come to the peninsula were the Jakuns – or proto-Malays – who were mainly of Mongoloid stock. They were comprised of several subgroups, the main ones being the Mantera and Biduanda of Negeri Sembilan and Melaka and the Orang Ulu, Orang Kanak and Orang Laut ('Sea People') of Johor. Their culture and language became closely linked to that of the coastal Malays, and over the centuries many of them assimilated into Malay society. Most practised shifting cultivation; the Orang Laut were fishermen.

Malaysia's aborigines have increasingly been drawn into the modern economy. Along with the Malays, they are classified as *bumiputras* and as such, became eligible, as with other tribal groups in East Malaysia, for the privileges extended to all bumiputras following the introduction of the New Economic Policy (NEP) in 1970 (see page 510). In reality, however, the NEP offered few tangible benefits to the Orang Asli, and while the government has sought to integrate them – there is a Department of Aboriginal Affairs in Kuala Lumpur – there is no separate mechanism to encourage entrepreneurism among the group.

Religion

Islam   Malays are invariably Muslims and there is also a small population of Indian Muslims in Malaysia. The earliest recorded evidence of Islam on the Malay peninsula is an inscription in Terengganu dating from 1303, which prescribed penalties for those who did not observe the moral codes of the faith. Islam did not really gain a foothold on the peninsula, however, until Sri Maharaja of Melaka – the third ruler – converted in 1430 and changed his name to Mohamed Shah (see page 205). He retained many of the ingrained Hindu traditions of the royal court and did not attempt to enforce Islam as the state religion. The Arab merchant ships which made regular calls at Melaka probably brought Muslim missionaries to the city. Many of them were Sufis – belonging to a mystical order of Islam which was tolerant of local customs and readily synthesized with existing animist and Hindu beliefs. The adoption of this form of Islam is one reason why animism and the Muslim faith still go hand in hand in Malaysia (see below). Mohamad Shah's son, Rajah Kasim, was the first ruler to adopt the title 'Sultan', and he became Sultan Muzaffar; all subsequent rulers have continued to preserve and uphold the Islamic faith. The Portuguese and Dutch colonialists, while making a few local converts to Christianity, were more interested in trade than proselytizing.

The British colonial system of government was more 'progressive' than most colonial régimes in that it barred the British residents from interfering in 'Malay religion and custom'. So-called Councils of Muslim Religion and Malay Custom were set up in each state answerable to the sultans. These emerged as bastions of Malay conservatism and served to make Islam the rallying point of nascent nationalism. The Islamic reform movement was imported from the Middle East at the turn of the 19th century and Malays determined that the unity afforded by Islam transcended any colonial authority and the economic dominance of immigrant groups. The ideas spread as increasing numbers of Malays made the Haj to Mecca, made possible by the advent of regular steamer services. But gradually the sultans and the Malay aristocracy – who had done well out of British rule – began to see the Islamic renaissance as a threat.

On Fridays, the Muslim day of prayer, Malaysian Muslims congregate at mosques in their 'Friday best'. The 'lunch hour' starts at 1130 and runs through to about 1430

The practice of Islam: living by the Prophet

Islam is an Arabic word meaning 'submission to God'. As Muslims often point out, it is not just a religion but a total way of life. The main Islamic scripture is the Koran or Quran, the name being taken from the Arabic al-qur'an or 'the recitation'. The Koran is divided into 114 sura, or 'units'. Most scholars are agreed that the Koran was partially written by the Prophet Mohammad. In addition to the Koran there are the hadiths, from the Arabic word hadith *meaning 'story', which tell of the Prophet's life and works. These represent the second most important body of scriptures.*

The practice of Islam is based upon five central tenets, known as the Pillars of Islam: Shahada (profession of faith), Salat (worship), Zakat (charity), saum (fasting) and Haj (pilgrimage). The mosque is the centre of religious activity. The two most important mosque officials are the imam *– or leader – and the* khatib *or preacher – who delivers the Friday sermon.*

*The **Shahada** is the confession, and lies at the core of any Muslim's faith. It involves reciting, sincerely, two statements: 'There is no god, but God', and 'Mohammad is the Messenger [Prophet] of God'. A Muslim will do this at every **Salat**. This is the daily prayer ritual which is performed five times a day, at sunrise, midday, mid-afternoon, sunset and at night. There is also the important Friday noon worship. The Salat is performed by a Muslim bowing and then prostrating himself in the direction of Mecca (in Malaysian kiblat, in Arabic qibla). In hotel rooms throughout there is nearly always a little arrow, painted on the ceiling – or sometimes inside a wardrobe – indicating the direction of Mecca and labelled kiblat. The faithful are called to worship by a mosque official. Beforehand, a worshipper must wash to ensure ritual purity. The Friday midday service is performed in the mosque and includes a sermon given by the khatib.*

*A third essential element of Islam is **Zakat** – charity or alms-giving. A Muslim is supposed to give up his 'surplus' (according to the Koran); through time this took on the form of a tax levied according to the wealth of the family. In Malaysia there is no official Zakat as there is in Saudi Arabia, but good Muslims are expected to contribute a tithe to the Muslim community.*

*The fourth pillar of Islam is **saum** or fasting. The daytime month-long fast of Ramadan is a time of contemplation, worship and piety – the Islamic equivalent of Lent. Muslims are expected to read one-thirtieth of the Koran each night. Muslims who are ill or on a journey have dispensation from fasting, but otherwise they are only permitted to eat during the night until "so much of the dawn appears that a white thread can be distinguished from a black one".*

*The **Haj** or Pilgrimage to the holy city of Mecca in Saudi Arabia is required of all Muslims once in their lifetime if they can afford to make the journey and are physically able to. It is restricted to a certain time of the year, beginning on the eighth day of the Muslim month of Dhu-l-Hijja. Men who have been on the Haj are given the title Haji, and women hajjah.*

The Koran also advises on a number of other practices and customs, in particular the prohibitions on usury, the eating of pork, the taking of alcohol, and gambling. There is quite a powerful Islamic revival in Malaysia and Brunei. The use of the veil is becoming de rigeur in Brunei and increasingly in Malaysia. The Koran says nothing about the need for women to veil, although it does stress the necessity of women dressing modestly. In Indonesia, the practices and customs are not strictly interpreted.

to allow Muslims to attend the mosque; in big towns and cities, Friday lunchtimes are marked by traffic jams. In the fervently Islamic east coast states, Friday is the start of the weekend. Men traditionally wear *songkoks* – black velvet hats – to the mosque and often wear their best sarung (sometimes *songket*) over their trousers.

Malay magic and the spirits behind the prophet

Despite the fact that all Malays are Muslims, some traditional, pre-Islamic beliefs are still practised by Malays – particularly in the northeast of the peninsula, the conservative Islamic heartland. The bomoh – *witch doctor and magic-man – is alive and well in modern Malaysia. The use of* ilmu *(the malay name for magic), which is akin to voodoo, is still widely practised and bomohs are highly respected and important members of kampong communities. Consulting bomohs is a commonplace event; they are often called in to perform their ancient rituals – sometimes they are contracted to bring rain or to determine the site of a new house; on other occasions to make fields (or married couples) fertile or to heal sickness. The healing ceremony is called the* main puteri: *there are certain illnesses which are believed to be caused by spirits – or* hantu – *who have been offended and must be placated.*

The bomoh's job is to get the protective, friendly spirits on his side, in the belief that they can influence the evil ones. He knows many different spirits by name; some are the spirits of nature, others are spirits of ancestors. Many bomohs are specialists in particular fields. Some, known as pewangs, *traditionally concentrated on performing spells to ensure fruitful harvests or safe fishing expeditions. Bomohs are still consulted and contracted to formulate herbal remedies, charms, love potions and perform traditional massage (*urut*). The* belian – *or shaman – specializes in more extreme forms of magic conducting exorcisms and spirit-raising seances, or berhantu. In Kelantan, a bomoh who acts as a spirit medium is known as a* Tok Peteri *and once a spirit has entered him, during a seance, his assistant, called the* Tok Mindok, *is required to question the spirit, present offerings and address the spirit in a secret language of magic formulae. Seances are always held in public – in front of the whole village – and are held after evening prayers.*

Manipulation of the weather is one area where the magic is still widely used. The government has been known to employ a pewang *to perform rituals designed to keep rain from falling during large public events. In 1991 actors from Kuala Lumpur's Instant Café Theatre Company called on a bomoh to ensure their open-air production of* A Midsummer Night's Dream *was not washed out. The only occasion on which rain interrupted the play was during an extra performance, not covered in the bomoh's contract.*

All natural and inanimate objects are also capable of having spirits and Malays often refer to them using the respectful title Datuk. *Other spirits, like the* pontianak *(the vampire ghost of a woman who dies in childbirth) are greatly feared. Any suspicion of the presence of a pontianak calls for the immediate intervention of a* belian, *who is believed to inherit his powers from a* hantu raya – *great spirit – which attaches itself to a bloodline and is subsequently passed from generation to generation.*

Those who have performed the Haj pilgrimage to Mecca wear a white skullcap. However, at least until recently (see below), Malaysia's Islam has been moderate by Middle Eastern standards. Traditionally, for example, women were not required to wear the head scarf or *tudung*.

But Malaysia has emerged as an outspoken defender of Muslims and Islamic values around the world. While hosting a banquet in honour of the visiting former British Prime Minister, John Major, in late 1993, the Malaysian premier, Dr Mahathir Mohamad, shocked his audience with a blunt full-frontal attack on Western intransigence over the plight of Bosnian Muslims. He urged him to "reconsider Britain's position before the situation in Bosnia-Herzegovina is forever cemented in history as the blackest catastrophe of the modern world." Malaysia has put its money where its mouth is in welcoming Bosnian Muslim refugees and staging conferences

The Ramayana and Mahabharata

Across much of Southeast Asia, the Indian epics of the Ramayana and Mahabharata have been translated and adapted for local consumption. The stories of the **Mahabharata** are the more popular. These centre on a long-standing feud between two family clans: the Pandawas and the Korawas. The feud culminates in an epic battle during which the five Pandawa brothers come face to face with their 100 first cousins from the Korawa clan. After 18 days of fighting, the Pandawas emerge victorious and the eldest brother becomes king. The plays usually focus on one or other of the five Pandawa brothers, each of whom is a hero.

The **Ramayana** was written by the poet Valmiki about 2,000 years ago. The 48,000 line story tells of the abduction of the beautiful Sita by the evil king, Ravana. Sita's husband Rama, King of Ayodhia, sets out on an odyssey to retrieve his wife from Ravana's clutches, finally succeeding with the help of Hanuman the monkey god and his army of monkeys. Today it is rare to see the Ramayana performed; the orchestra needs to be large (and is therefore expensive), and in the case of wayang few puppet masters have a sufficiently large collection of puppets to cover all the characters.

on the Bosnian situation. On other occasions, Dr Mahathir has made outspoken attacks on Western attitudes towards Islam, in which, he says, Muslims are cast as pariahs and bogeymen.

Although not disingenuous, all this was viewed by observers as part of the Prime Minister's efforts to polish his own Islamic credentials. At home, Dr Mahathir's government feels threatened by the rise of fundamentalist sentiments – particularly in the northeastern state of Kelantan, where the Islamic government has approved a bill calling for the introduction of a strict Islamic penal code (see page 296). Hard-line Islam is perceived as a threat to secular society in Malaysia. The deputy Prime Minister, Anwar Ibrahim – once a young Islamic firebrand himself – has become an eloquent proponent of Islamic moderation. He has appealed in articles submitted to international newspapers for less rhetoric in the name of political expediency from Muslim leaders around the world and for greater understanding of Islam in the West.

In 1994, Dr Mahathir was forced to clamp down on a fundamentalist Islamic sect known as **Al Arqam** with 10,000 followers, an estimated 200,000 sympathizers, and assets of RM15mn in businesses ranging from property firms to textile factories. Ashaari Muhammed, the leader of the sect, was arrested after being deported from Thailand and then held in detention under the Internal Security Act. Unlikely liberals leapt to defend Mr Ashaari who taught that women should be kept in their place, and operated his sect almost like a secret society. Why the Prime Minister should have issued an order for Mr Ashaari's arrest was a point of dispute. The Prime Minister's office maintained that the sect's teachings were 'deviationist' – as also argued by the National Fatwah Council – and that he threatened state security. To begin with the government even suggested that the sect had a 313-man 'death squad'. Opponents maintained that his arrest was more to do with domestic politics: Al Arqam was attracting middle class Malays, just the sort of people who are the bedrock of UMNO's support. The arrest was not, in their view, anything to do with religion, but a great deal to do with politics. Nonetheless, the government is very firm over the acceptable limits of Islam. People voicing support for the sect or wearing their garb can be arrested, and their publications are banned. Later the government backtracked on the 'death squad' allegations, but nonetheless were able to get Ashaari Muhammed to renounce his teachings on television, thereby preventing him becoming a martyr.

Background

In Siddhartha's footsteps: a short history of Buddhism

Buddhism was founded by Siddhartha Gautama, a prince of the Sakya tribe of Nepal, who probably lived between 563 and 483 BC. He achieved enlightenment and the word buddha *means 'fully enlightened one', or 'one who has woken up'. Siddhartha Gautama is known by a number of titles. In the West, he is usually referred to as* The Buddha, *ie the historic Buddha (but not just Buddha); more common in Southeast Asia is the title* Sakyamuni, *or Sage of the Sakyas (referring to his tribal origins).*

Over the centuries, the life of the Buddha has become part legend, and the Jataka tales which recount his various lives are colourful and convoluted. But, central to any Buddhist's belief is that he was born under a sal tree (Shorea robusta), that he achieved enlightenment under a bodhi tree (Ficus religiosa) in the Bodh Gaya Gardens, that he preached the First Sermon at Sarnath, and that he died at Kusinagara (all in India or Nepal).

The Budda was born at Lumbini (in present-day Nepal), as Queen Maya was on her way to her parents' home. She had had a very auspicious dream before the child's birth of being impregnated by an elephant, whereupon a sage prophesied that Siddhartha would become either a great king or a great spiritual leader. His father, being keen that the first option of the prophecy be fulfilled, brought him up in all the princely skills (at which Siddhartha excelled) and ensured that he only saw beautiful things, not the harsher elements of life.

Despite his father's efforts Siddhartha saw four things while travelling between palaces – a helpless old man, a very sick man, a corpse being carried by lamenting relatives, and an ascetic, calm and serene as he begged for food. These episodes made an enormous impact on the young prince, and he renounced his princely origins and left home to study under a series of spiritual teachers. He finally discovered the path to enlightenment at the Bodh Gaya Gardens in India. He then proclaimed his thoughts to a small group of disciples at Sarnath, near Benares, and continued to preach and attract followers until he died at the age of 81 at Kusinagara.

It seems that Mahathir is concerned that radical Islam might destabilize Malaysia's delicate racial and religious cocktail. Sects like Al Arqam, and the spread of Shia theology, are closely watched by a government that wishes to maintain its secular credentials and to control what has been termed 'creeping Islamization'. In mid-1997, Mahathir showed his displeasure at the enforcement of a *fatwa* in the state of Selangor banning all beauty contests. In June, three Malay contestants were arrested and handcuffed on stage after they had competed in the Miss Malaysia Petite contest. The prime minister rebuked the religious officials who had exceeded their 'little powers'. Earlier he had set in motion a wide-ranging review of Islamic jurisprudence or *fiqh*. In confronting the clerics and their supporters Mahathir has taken on a powerful conservative group which is closely allied with the opposition PAS. But if there is anyone in Malaysia with the accumulated prestige to challenge the *ulamas* (Muslim theologians) openly, it is Mahathir.

Buddhism While Buddhism is the formal religion of most of Malaysia's Chinese population, many are Taoists, who follow the teachings of the three sages – Confucius, Mencius and Lao Tse. Taoism is characterized by ancestor worship and a plethora of deities. As with Islam, this has been mixed with animist beliefs and spirit worship forms a central part of the faith.

Hinduism Hindu (and Buddhist) religions were established on the Malay peninsula long before Islam arrived. Remains of ancient Hindu-Buddhist temples dating from the kingdom of Langkasuka in the early years of the first millennium have been found in the

In the First Sermon at the deer park in Sarnath, the Buddha preached the Four Truths, which are still considered the root of Buddhist belief and practical experience. These are the 'Noble Truth' that suffering exists, the 'Noble Truth' that there is a cause of suffering, the 'Noble Truth' that suffering can be ended, and the 'Noble Truth' that to end suffering it is necessary to follow the 'Noble Eightfold Path' – namely, right speech, livelihood, action, effort, mindfulness, concentration, opinion and intention.

Soon after the Buddha began preaching, a monastic order – the Sangha – was established. As the monkhood evolved in India, it also began to fragment as different sects developed different interpretations of the life of the Buddha. An important change was the belief that the Buddha was transcendent: he had never been born, nor had he died; he had always existed and his life on earth had been mere illusion. The emergence of these new concepts helped to turn what up until then was an ethical code of conduct, into a religion. It eventually led to the appearance of a new Buddhist movement, Mahayana Buddhism which split from the more traditional Theravada 'sect'.

Despite the division of Buddhism into two sects, the central tenets of the religion are common to both. Specifically, the principles pertaining to the Four Noble Truths, the Noble Eightfold Path, the Dependent Origination, the Law of Karma and nirvana. In addition, the principles of non-violence and tolerance are also embraced by both sects. In essence, the differences between the two are of emphasis and interpretation. Theravada Buddhism is strictly based on the original Pali Canon, while the Mahayana tradition stems from later Sanskrit texts. Mahayana Buddhism also allows a broader and more varied interpretation of the doctrine. Other important differences are that while the Thervada tradition is more 'intellectual' and self-obsessed, with an emphasis upon the attaining of wisdom and insight for oneself, Mahayana Buddhism stresses devotion and compassion towards others.

Bujang Valley, at the foot of Gunung Jerai (Kedah Peak) in Kedah (see page 179). The majority of Malaysia's Indian population is Hindu, although there are also many Indian Muslims.

Borneo

In Sabah and Sarawak, apart from the Malays, Bajaus, Illanuns and Suluks, who accepted Islam, all the inland tribes were originally animists. The religion of all the Dayak tribes in Borneo boiled down to placating spirits, and the purpose of tribal totems, images, icons and statues was to chase bad spirits away and attract good ones, which were believed to be capable of bringing fortune and prosperity. Head-hunting (see page 394) was central to this belief, and most Dayak tribes practised it, in the belief that freshly severed heads would bring blessing to their longhouses. Virtually everything had a spirit, and complex rituals and ceremonies were devised to keep them happy. Motifs associated with the spirit world – such as the hornbill (see page 525) – dominate artwork and textiles and many of the woodcarvings for sale in art and antique shops had religious significance. Islam began to spread to the tribes of the interior from the late 15th century, but mostly it was confined to coastal districts or those areas close to rivers like the Kapuas and Barito where Malays penetrated into the interior to trade. Christian missionaries arrived with the Europeans but did not proselytize seriously until the mid-19th century. The Dutch, particularly, saw missionaries fulfilling an administrative function, drawing the tribal peoples close to the Dutch and, by implication, away from the Muslim Malays of the coast: it was a policy of divide and rule by religious means. Both Christianity and Islam had enormous influence on the animist tribes, and many

Background

converted en masse to one or the other. Despite this, many of the old superstitions and ceremonial traditions, which are deeply ingrained, remain a part of Dayak culture today. (The traditional beliefs of Kalimantan's Dayaks is formalized in the *Kaharingan* faith, which, despite the in-roads made by Christianity and Islam, is still practised by some Mahakam and Barito river groups. The Indonesian government recognizes it as an official religion.)

Art and architecture

Unlike the countries of mainland Southeast Asia and its neighbour, Indonesia, Malaysia is not known for its art and architecture. Arriving at Kuala Lumpur's Sabang International Airport and driving into town, there is apparently scarcely anything worth an aesthetic second glance. Many of Malaysia's artistic treasures have either been torn down to make way for modern buildings with scarcely a concrete ounce of artistic merit, or have simply rotted away through sheer neglect. However, the country is far from being the artistic desert that a cursory glance might suppose. The sadness, though, is that much of what is deemed to be 'worth seeing' (ie a 'sight') is not Malaysian *per se*, but colonial. The most attractive towns – notably Georgetown (Penang) and Melaka – are notable mainly for their Chinese shophouses, and Dutch, Portuguese and English colonial buildings. Vernacular Malay houses must be sought out more carefully; few are preserved, and most are being demolished to make way for structures perceived to be more fitting of a thrusting young country on the verge of developed nation status.

In his book *The Malay House*, architect Lim Jee Yuan writes that traditional houses, which are built without architects, "reflect good housing solutions, as manifested by the display of a good fit to the culture, lifestyle and socio-economic needs of the users; the honest and efficient use of materials; and appropriate climatic design". Classic Malay houses are built of timber and raised on stilts with wooden or bamboo walls and an *atap* roof – made from the leaves of the nipah palm. It should have plenty of windows and good ventilation – the interior is usually airy and bright. It is also built on a prefabricated system and can be expanded to fit the needs of a growing family. Malay houses are usually simple, functional and unostentatious, and even those embellished by woodcarvings blend into their environment. Lim Jee Yuan says "the Malay house cannot be fully appreciated without its setting – the house compound and the kampung". Kampung folk, he says, prefer "community intimacy over personal privacy" which means villages are closely knit communities.

Most Malays on the peninsula traditionally lived in pile houses built on stilts along the rivers. The basic design is called the bumbung panjangi ('long roof'), although there are many variations and hybrids; these are influenced both by the Minangkabau house-forms (of West Sumatra) and by Thai-Khmer designs. The differences in house-styles between regions is mainly in the shape of the roof. The bumbung panjang is the oldest, commonest, simplest and most graceful, with a long gable roof, thatched with atap. There are ventilation grills at either end, allowing a throughflow of air. From the high apex, the eaves slope down steeply, then, towards the bottom, the angle lessens, extending out over the walls. Bumbung

Background

Painted panel from a Dayak coffin
Adapted from: Hersey, Irwin (1991)
Indonesian Primitive
Art, *OUP: Singapore*

The Malay istana – royals on the riverside

The Malay word istana *derives from the Sanskrit for 'sleeping place' – but the Malay sultans adopted it as the term for their royal palaces. Because Malay sultanates were usually focused on the mouths of rivers, the istanas were normally sited on a prominent point on the riverbank, along which the sultan's powerbase extended. This meant they were prone to flooding, however, and over the centuries, a number slipped into the river – notably in Perak. The 16th century* Sejarah Melayu *(Malay Annals) provide a description of Sultan Mansur Shah's palace in Melaka (see page 212). The building has been reconstructed from notes and historical data and now serves as Melaka's Muzium Budaya (Cultural Museum). The original palace was said to have had a seven-tiered roof and 12 halls; it was razed to the ground by the invading Portuguese in 1511.*

Traditionally, istanas included everything from the sultan's private quarters (at the rear) to the state administrative and cultural centre. They also doubled as forts in time of war. The sultan's concubines lived in outhouses, dotted around the compound, which also included the mosque and the rumah wakaf – the lodging house for commoners (such as the Istana Jahar in Kota Bharu, which is now the Kelantan State Museum). There are several other istanas in Kelantan and Terengganu states, all dating from the 19th century. The most impressive of the surviving istanas are the Istana Lama Sri Menanti and the Istana Ampang Tinggi in Negri Sembilan (see page 198), the Istana Balai Besar in Kedah – one of the grandest and best-preserved on the peninsula, and now the state museum – and the Istana Kenangan at Kuala Kangsar in Perak, which is now the Royal Museum (see page 146). There are only 11 wooden palaces remaining in Malaysia, and none of them houses a royal family any longer.

panjang are most commonly found in Melaka, but the design is used widely throughout the peninsula.

These days it is more usual to find the atap replaced with corrugated zinc roofs which require less maintenance and are a measure of status in the community. But zinc turns houses into ovens during the day, makes them cold at night and makes a deafening noise in rainstorms. On the east coast of the peninsula, the use of tiled roofs is more common. Towards the north, Thai and Khmer influences are more pronounced in roof style. As in Thai houses, walls are panelled; there are also fewer windows and elaborate carving is more common. Because Islam proscribes the use of the human figure in art, ornamental woodcarvings depict floral and geometric designs as well as Koranic calligraphy. Most are relief-carvings on wood panels or grilles. In Melaka, colourful ceramic tiles are also commonly used as exterior decoration.

The oldest surviving Malay houses date from only the 19th century. The traditional design is the rumah berpanggung, which is built high off the ground on stilts with an A-shaped roof. The basic features include: *Anjung*: covered porch at the top of entranceway stairs where formal visitors are entertained; *Serambi gantung*: verandah, where most guests are entertained; *Rumah ibu* ('the domain of the mother of the house'): private central core of the house, with raised floor level, where the family talks, sleeps, prays, studies and eats (particularly during festivals); *Dapur*: kitchen, always at the back, and below the level of the rest of the house; most meals are taken here. The dapur is connected to the rumah ibu by the *selang*, a closed walkway. Near the dapur, there is usually a *pelantar*, with a washing area for clothes, a mandi and a toilet.

The best places to see traditional Malay houses are Melaka and Negeri Sembilan, on the west coast, and Terengganu and Kelantan states to the northeast. Minangkabau influence is most pronounced in Negeri Sembilan state, between

Background

World Heritage List potential

Malaysia has proposed six sites for inclusion on the UNESCO World Heritage List. The list currently comprises 582 cultural and natural sites around the world, including such renowned locations as the pyramids of Egypt and the Taj Mahal in India. However, Malaysia is not currently represented. In an attempt to remedy this situation the Government plans to forward six candidates to be considered for inclusion. Sarawak's Gunung Mulu National Park, Sabah's Kinabalu National Park, and Pahang's Taman Negara will be proposed as natural heritage sites, while listing is also being sought for the Niah Caves in Sarawak, Penang's Georgetown and the historic city of Melaka as cultural sites.

The authorities will be hoping that the World Heritage Committee which operates as part of UNESCO will approve its submissions and add the first Malaysian site at one of its annual meetings over the next 10 years. Any of the 157 states that signed the 'Convention Concerning the Protection of the World Cultural and Natural Heritage' that was conceived in 1972 is eligible for inclusion. To date 114 states parties are included on the list and the absence of a country as rich in natural and cultural wonders as Malaysia is surely only temporary. There are clear incentives for the Malaysian authorities to gain inclusion on the list. It would provide a boost to the tourist industry. Statistics have shown a five-fold increase in tourist arrivals once a country gets a site included on the World Heritage List. It would also open the way for possible funding for projects.

But while the government may be trying to get these sites listed as part of the world's heritage it is, at the same time, creating the conditions where some, at least, can have their integrity undermined. In particular, there is serious concern that Melaka and Georgetown are being gradually eroded. Georgetown has more than 10,000 buildings of heritage value showing Malay, Chinese and Indian influences, while Melaka has around 4,000 pre-war buildings which particularly reflect the Dutch colonial influence. UNESCO's regional adviser for culture in Asia and the Pacific, Richard A. Engelhardt, believes that the two towns risk losing their heritage value if efforts are not taken to preserve and revitalize their traditional and commercial aspects. Melaka has recently lost its connection to the sea through a series of insensitive land reclamation projects. There are even more serious concerns about Georgetown's historic enclave which was included in the 1999/2000 edition of the 'World Monuments Watch List of 100 Endangered Sites' published by the New York based World Monuments Fund. It is threatened by severe development pressure, heavy traffic and developers eager to demolish old buildings.

For more information see:
www.unesco.org/whc (website of World Heritage List)
www.worldmonuments.org/ (website of World Monuments Fund).

Kuala Lumpur and Melaka. There, houses have a distinctive, elegant, curved roofline, where the gable sweeps up into 'wings' at each end – the so-called Minangkabau 'buffalo horns'.

Today the traditional Malay house has lost its status in the kampung – now everyone wants to build in concrete and brick. Many planned modern kampungs have been built throughout Malaysia, with little regard for traditional building materials or for the traditional houseforms. Lim Jee Yuan writes that: "Unless there are positive steps taken to uplift the status of the traditional Malay house ... it is bound for extinction in the near future despite its superior design principles and suitability to our environmental, economic and socio-cultural needs." Many like-minded architects despair of the 'vulgarization' of the Malay houseform, which has been used as an inspiration for many modern buildings (notably in Kuala

Lumpur, see page 76). The curved Minangkabau roof, for example, which has been borrowed for everything from modern bank buildings to toll-booths, has merely become a cultural symbol, and has been deprived of its deeper significance.

The Straits Chinese (Peranakan) communities of Melaka, Penang and Singapore developed their own architectural style to match their unique cultural traditions (see page 210). The finest Peranakan houses can be seen along Jalan Tun Tan Cheng Lock in Melaka (see page 212), notably the Baba-Nyonya Heritage Museum. Typical Peranakan houses were long and narrow, and built around a central courtyard. Their interiors are characterized by dark, heavy wood and marble-topped furniture, often highly decorated, and made by Chinese craftsmen who were brought over from China.

Peranakan

Language and literature

Bahasa Melayu (literally, 'Malay Language') – or to give the language its official title, *Bahasa Kebangsaan* ('National Language') – is an Austronesian language which has been the language of trade and commerce throughout the archipelago for centuries. It is the parent language of – and is closely related to – modern Indonesian. In 1972, Indonesia and Malaysia came to an agreement to standardize spelling – although many differences still remain.

Modern Malay has been affected by a succession of external influences – Sanskrit from the seventh century, Arabic from the 14th and English from the 19th century. These influences are reflected in a number of words, most of them of a religious or technical nature. All scientific terminology is directly borrowed from the English or Latin. However, there are many common everyday words borrowed from Arabic or English: *pasar*, for example, comes from the Arabic *bazaar* (market) and there are countless examples of English words used in Malay – particularly when it comes to modern modes of transport – *teksi, bas* and *tren*. Where a Malay term has been devised for a 20th century phenomenon, it is usually a fairly straightforward description. An alternative word for train, for example is *keretapi* (literally 'fire car') and the word for aeroplane is *kapalterbang* (flying ship).

From the seventh century, the Indian Pallava script was in restricted use, although few examples survive. The *Jawi* script, adapted from Arabic, was adopted in the 14th century, with the arrival of Muslim traders and Sufi missionaries in Melaka. To account for sounds in the Malay language which have no equivalent in Arabic, five additional letters had to be invented, giving 33 letters in all. Jawi script was used for almost all Malay writings until the 19th century, and romanized script only began to supplant Jawi after the Second World War. Many older Malays still read and write the script and it is not uncommon to see it along the streets. Some Chinese-owned banks, for example, have transliterated their names into Jawi script so as to make Malays feel a little more at home in them.

Malay literature is thought to date from the 14th century – although surviving manuscripts written in Jawi only date from the beginning of the 15th century. The first printed books in Malay were produced by European missionaries in the 17th century. The best known of Malay literary works are the 16th-century *Sejara Melayu* or Malay Annals; others include the romantic *Hikayat Hang Tuah* and the 19th century *Tuhfat al-Nafis*.

The first of Malaysia's 'modern' authors was the 19th century writer Munshi Abdullah – who has lent his name to a few streets around the country. Although he kept to many of the classical strictures, Abdullah articulated a personal view and challenged many of the traditional assumptions underlying Malay society. His best known work was his autobiography, *Hikayat Abdullah*. However, it was not until the 1920s that Malayan authors began to write modern novels and short stories. Among the best known writers are Ahmad bin Mohd. Rashid Talu, Ishak Hj. Muhammad and

Background

Harun Aminurrashid. Their work laid the foundations for an expansion of Malaysian literature from the 1950s and today there is a prodigious Malay-language publishing industry.

Since independence, the government has promoted Bahasa Melayu at the expense of Chinese dialects and English. However in 1994 Prime Minister Mahathir signalled a switch in strategy when he declared that university courses in the sciences and technology would be taught in English rather than Bahasa. The emphasis on Bahasa is regarded to some extent as yesterday's battle – the battle to build a national, Malaysian identity. Today's battle is to produce an educated workforce conversant and at home in the world of international business – in other words, people who can use English. When comparisons are made between Malaysian and other overseas students, Malaysian students come out poorly. This is one reason why so many wealthy Malays and Chinese send their children to private English language schools – including ministers who in public used to defend the use of Bahasa Melayu in state schools. Now the government appears to have realized the necessity for state schools and universities to reintroduce English. The announcement that a London University campus in Kuala Lumpur would be built is perhaps indicative of this liberalization in education policies. (Not that the process is necessarily one-way: in mid-1997 the government ruled that Islamic civilization would become a mandatory course for all university students – they would need to take and pass it in order to graduate. Needless to say, non-Muslim Malaysians, and some Muslim Malaysians, thought this a step backwards and going against the trend towards a modern, outward-looking, and inclusive Malaysia. Later it was announced that the course would also include study of other Asian civilizations.)

Drama, dance and music

Drama   **Wayang Kulit**   *Wayang* means 'shadow', and the art form is best translated as 'shadow theatre' or 'shadow play'. Shadow plays were the traditional form of entertainment in Malay kampungs. Although film and television have replaced the *wayang* in many people's lives – especially the young – they are still performed in some rural parts of the peninsula's east coast and are regular fixtures at cultural events. Some people believe that the wayang is Indian in origin, pointing to the fact that most of the characters are from Indian epic tales such as the Ramayana and Mahabharata (see page 541).

By the 11th century *wayang* was well-established in Java. A court poet of the Javanese King Airlangga (1020-1049), referred to wayang in *The meditation of King Ardjuna*:

> *There are people who weep, are sad and aroused watching the puppets, though they know they are merely carved pieces of leather manipulated and made to speak. These people are like men, thirsting for sensual pleasures, who live in a world of illusion; they do not realize the magic hallucinations they see are not real.*

It seems that by the 14th century the art form had made the crossing from the Javanese Majapahit Empire to the courts of the Malay Peninsula and from there spread to kampungs across the country.

There are many forms of wayang – and not all of them are, strictly speaking, shadow plays – but the commonest and oldest form is the wayang kulit. Kulits are finely carved and painted leather, two-dimensional puppets, jointed at the elbows and shoulders and manipulated using horn rods. In order to enact the entire repertoire of 179 plays, 200 puppets are needed. A single performance can last as long as nine hours. The plays have various origins. Some are animistic, others are adapted from the epic poems. The latter are known as 'trunk' tales or *pondok* and include the Ramayana.

Making a wayang kulit puppet

Wayang kulit puppets are made of buffalo hide, preferably taken from a female animal of about four years of age. The skin is dried and scraped, and then left to mature for as long as 10 years to achieve the stiffness required for carving. After carving, the puppet is painted in traditional pigments. In carving the puppet, the artist is constrained by convention. The excellence of the puppet is judged according to the fineness of the chisel-work and the subtlety of painting. If the puppet is well made it may have guna – a magical quality which is supposed to make the audience suspend its disbelief during the performance. Puppets accumulate guna with age; this is why old puppets are preferred to new ones.

Each major character has a particular iconography, and even the angle of the head and the slant of the eyes and mouth are important in determining the character. Some puppets may be called on to perform a number of minor parts, but in the main a knowledgeable wayang-goer will be able to recognize each character immediately.

The cempuri or rods used to manipulate the puppet are made of buffalo horn while the studs used to attach the limbs are made of metal, bone or bamboo. Court puppets might even be made of gold, studded with precious stones.

Others have been developed over the years by influential puppet masters. They feature heroic deeds, romantic encounters, court intrigues, bloody battles, and mystical observations, and are known as *carangan* or 'branch' tales.

The gunungan or Tree of Life, is an important element of wayang theatre. It represents all aspects of life, and is always the same in design: shaped like a stupa, the tree has painted red flames on one side and a complex design on the other (this is the side which faces the audience). At the base of the tree are a pair of closed doors, flanked by two fierce demons or *yaksas*. Above the demons are two garudas and within the branches of the tree there are monkeys, snakes and two animals – usually an ox and a tiger. The gunungan is placed in the middle of the screen at the beginning and end of the performance – and sometimes between major scene changes. During the performance it stands at one side, and flutters across the screen to indicate minor scene changes.

Traditionally, performances were requested by individuals to celebrate particular occasions – for example the seventh month of pregnancy (*tingkep*) – or to accompany village festivities. Admission was free, as the individual commissioning the performance would meet the costs. Of course, this has changed now and tourists invariably have to pay an entrance charge.

In the past, the shadows of the puppets were reflected onto a white cotton cloth stretched across a wooden frame using the light from a bronze coconut oil lamp. Today, electric light is more common – a change which, in many people's minds, has meant the unfortunate substitution of the flickering, mysterious shadows of the oil lamp, with the constant harsh light of the electric bulb. There are both day and night wayang performances. The latter, for obvious reasons, are the more dramatic, although the former are regarded as artistically superior.

The audience sits on both sides of the screen. Those sitting with the puppet master see a puppet play; those on the far side, out of view of the puppet master and the accompanying gamelan orchestra, see a shadow play. It is possible that in the past, the audience was segregated according to sex: men on the to'dalang's side of the screen, women on the shadow side.

The puppet-master is known as the *to'dalang*; he narrates each story in lyrical classical Malay – with a great sense of melodrama – and is accompanied by a traditional gamelan orchestra of gongs, drums, *rebab* (violins) and woodwind instruments. He slips in and out of different characters, using many different voices

Background

throughout the performances, which lasts as long as three to four hours. The words *to' dalang* are said to be derived from *galang*, meaning bright or clear, the implication being that the to' dalang makes the sacred texts understandable. He sits on a plinth, an arm's length away from the cloth screen. From this position he manipulates the puppets, while also narrating the story. Although any male can become a to' dalang, it is usual for sons to follow their fathers into the profession. The to' dalang is the key to a successful performance: he must be multi-skilled, have strength and stamina, be able to manipulate numerous puppets simultaneously, narrate the story, and give the lead to the accompanying gamelan orchestra. No wonder that an adept to' dalang is a man with considerable status.

Chinese classical street operas (wayang) date back to the seventh century. They are performed in Malaysia by troupes of roving actors during Chinese festivals, particularly during the seventh lunar month, following the Festival of the Hungry Ghosts. For more details on the wayang, see box, page 549.

Dance **Silat** (or, more properly, *bersilat*) is a traditional Malay martial art, but is so highly stylized that it has become a dance form and is often demonstrated with the backing of a percussion orchestra. *Pencak silat* is the more formal martial art of self-defence; *seni silat* is the graceful aesthetic equivalent. A variety of the latter is commonly performed at ceremonial occasions – such as Malay weddings – it is called *silat pulut*. Silat comprises a fluid combination of movements and is designed to be as much a comprehensive and disciplined form of physical exercise as it is a martial art. It promotes good blood circulation and deep-breathing, which are considered essential for strength and stamina. The fluidity of the body movements require great suppleness, flexibility and poise. Malaysia's best known silat gurus live along the east coast.

The **Mak Yong** was traditionally a Kelantanese court dance-drama, performed only in the presence of the sultan and territorial chiefs. The dance is performed mainly by women (the mak yong being the 'queen' and lead dancer), and is accompanied by an orchestra of gongs, drums and the *rebab* (violin). There are only ever two or three male dancers who provide the comic interludes. The dance is traditionally performed during the Sultan of Kelantan's birthday celebrations. Unlike the wayang kulit shadow puppet theatre (above), the stories are not connected to the Hindu epics; they are thought to be of Malay origin. Other Kelantanese court dances include: the *garong*, a lively up-tempo dance by five pairs of men and women, in a round (a *garong* is a bamboo cow bell). The *payang*, a folk dance, is named after the distinctive east coast fishing boats; traditionally it was danced on the beach while waiting for the kampung fishing fleet to return.

The **joget** dance is another Malay art form which is the result of foreign cultural influence – in this case, Portuguese. It has gone by a variety of other names, notably the *ronggeng* and the *branyo*. It is traditionally accompanied by the gamelan orchestra. In 1878, Frank Swettenham (the first British Resident at Kuala Lumpur, but then, a young colonial officer) witnessed a performance of the joget, which he described in his book *Malay Sketches*. "Gradually raising themselves from a sitting to a kneeling posture, acting in perfect accord in every motion, then rising to their feet, they began a series of figures hardly to be exceeded in grace and difficulty, considering that the movements are essentially slow, the arms, hands and body being the performers, whilst the feet are scarcely noticed and half the time not visible...."

Arab traders were responsible for importing the **zapin** dance and Indonesians introduced the **inang**. Immigrants from Banjarmasin (South Kalimantan), who arrived in Johor in the early 1900s, brought with them the so-called Hobbyhorse Dance – the **Kuda Kepang** – which is performed at weddings and on ceremonial occasions in Johor. The hobbyhorses are made of goat or buffalo skin, stretched over a rotan frame. There are countless other local folk dances around Malaysia, usually associated with festivals – such as the ***wau bulan*** kite dance in Kelantan.

The **Lion Dance** is performed in Chinese communities, particularly around Chinese New Year, and the dances are accompanied by loud drums and cymbals, so are hard to miss. The lion dance actually originated in India, where tame lions were led around public fairs and festivals to provide entertainment along with jugglers. But because lions were in short supply, dancers with lion masks took their place. The dance was introduced to China during the Tang Dynasty. The lion changed its image from that of a clown to a symbol of the Buddha and is now regarded as 'the protector of Buddhism'. The lion dance developed into a ceremony in which demons and evil spirits are expelled (hence the deafening cymbals and drums).

Bharata Natyam (Indian classical dance) is performed by Malaysia's Indian community and is accompanied by Indian instruments such as the *tambura* (which has four strings), the *talam* (cymbals), *mridanga* (double-headed drum), *vina* (single stringed instrument) and flute. In Malaysia, the Temple of Fine Arts in Kuala Lumpur is an Indian cultural organization which promotes Indian dance forms. The Temple organizes an annual Festival of Arts (see page 105).

Music

Traditional Malay music, which accompanies the various traditional dances, offers a taste of all the peninsula's different cultural influences. The most prominent of these were Indian, Arab, Portuguese, Chinese, Siamese and Javanese – and finally, Western musical influence which gave birth to the all-pervasive genre 'Pop Melayu' – typically melancholic heavy rock. Traditional musical instruments reflect similar cultural influences, notably the *gambus* or lute (which has Middle Eastern origins and is used to accompany the *zapin* dance), the Indian harmonium, the Chinese *serunai* (clarinet) and gongs, the *rebana* drums, also of Middle Eastern origin, and the Javanese *gamelan* orchestra. Because Malays have traditionally been so willing to absorb new cultural elements, some of their traditional art forms have been in danger of extinction. Most traditional Malay instruments are percussion instruments; there are very few stringed or wind instruments. There are six main Malay drums, the most common of which is the cylindrical, double-headed *gendang*, which is used to accompany wayang kulit performances and silat. Other drums include the *geduk* and the *gedombak*; all three of these are played in orchestras.

Rebana, another traditional Malay drum, is used on ceremonial occasions as well as being a musical instrument. Traditionally, drumming competitions would be held following the rice-harvesting season (in May) and judges award points for timing, tone and rhythm. The best place to see the rebana in action is during Kelantan's giant drum festivals at the end of June. The drums are made from metre-long hollowed-out logs and are brightly painted. In competitions, drummers from different kampungs compete against each other in teams of up to 12 men. Traditionally the rebana was used as a means of communication between villages, and different rhythms were devised as a sort of morse code to invite distant kampungs to weddings or as warnings of war. *Kertok* are drums made from coconuts whose tops are sliced off and replaced with a block of *nibong* wood (from the sago palm) as a sounding board; these are then struck with padded drumsticks.

There are three main gongs; the biggest and most common, the *tawak* or *tetawak* is used to accompany wayang kulit shadow puppet theatre and Mak Yong dance dramas. The other smaller gongs are called *canang* and also accompany wayang kulit performances. The only Malay stringed instrument is the *rebab*, a violin-type instrument found throughout the region. The main wind instrument is the *serunai*, or oboe, which is of Persian origin and traditionally accompanies wayang kulit and dance performances. Its reed is cut from a palm leaf.

Background

The **Nobat** is the ancient royal orchestra which traditionally plays at the installation of sultans in Kedah, Perak, Selangor, Terangganu and Brunei. It is thought to have been introduced at the royal court of Melaka in the 15th century. The instruments include two types of drums (*negara* and *gendang*), a trumpet (*nafiri*), a flute (*serunai*) and a gong. The Nobat also plays at the coronation of each new king, every five years.

Crafts

The Malay heartland, on the east coast of Peninsular Malaysia, is the centre of the handicraft industry – particularly Kelantan. An extensive variety of traditional handicrafts, as well as batiks, are widely available in this area, although they are also sold throughout the country, notably in Kuala Lumpur and other main towns (see individual town entries). In East Malaysia, Sarawak has an especially active handicraft industry (see page 398).

Kites Kite-making and kite-flying (or *main wau*) are traditional pursuits in the northern Malaysian states of Perlis, Kedah, Kelantan and Terengganu. Malaysia's most famous kite is the crescent-shaped Kelantanese *wau bulan* (moon kite) which has a wingspan of up to 3m and a length of more than 3m; they can.reach altitudes of nearly 500m. Bow-shaped pieces of bamboo are often secured underneath, which make a melodious humming noise (*dengung*) in the wind. Wau come in all shapes and sizes however, and scaled-down versions of wau bulan and other kites can be bought. It is even possible to find batik-covered *wau cantik* or *wau sobek*, which are popular wall-hangings but make for awkward hand-luggage. There are often kite-flying competitions on the east coast, where competitors gain points for height and manoeuvering skills. Kites are also judged for their physical attributes, their ability to stay in the air and their sound. Most kite-flying competitions take place after the rice harvest in May, when kampungs compete against each other. On the east coast, all kites are known as *wau*, a word which, it is said, is derived from the arabic letter of the same sound, which is shaped like a kite. Perhaps the most recognizable one is Terengganu's *wau kucing* (cat kite), which Malaysia Airlines adopted as its logo. There are also *wau daun* (leaf kites) and *wau jala budi* (which literally means 'the net of good deeds kite'). Elsewhere in Malaysia, kites are known as *layang-layang* (literally, 'floating objects').

Tops Top spinning (*main gasing*) is another traditional form of entertainment, still popular in rural Malay kampungs – particularly on the east coast of the peninsula. There are two basic forms of tops. The heart-shaped *gasing jantung* and the flattened top, *gasing uri*. The biggest tops have diameters as big as frisbees and can weigh more than 5 kg; the skill required in launching a top is considerable. To launch the larger tops requires wrapping them in a tightly coiled 4m long rope which is smeared with resin. Once spinning, the top is scooped up on a wooden baton and left to spin on top of a small wooden post – sometimes for as long as two hours. Some tops have added metal or lead, and these are used in top-fighting events. Top-making is a precision-craft, and each one can take up to three days to make; they are carved from the upper roots and stem-bases of merbau and afzelia trees.

Woodcarving Originally craftsmen were commissioned by sultans and the Malay nobility to decorate the interiors, railings, doorways, shutters and stilts of palaces and public buildings. In Malay woodcarving, only floral and animal motifs are used as Islam prohibits depiction of the human form. But most widely acclaimed are the carved statues of malevolent spirits of the Mah Meris, an Orang Asli tribe.

Batik (*Batek*) The word *batik* may be derived from the Malay word *tik*, meaning 'to drip'. It is believed that batik replaced tatooing as a mark of status in the Malay archipelago. (In eastern Indonesia the common word for batik and tattoo are the same.)

Although batik-technology was actually imported from Indonesia several centuries ago, this coloured and patterned cloth is now a mainstay of Malaysian cultural identity. Malaysian batik are very different from their Indonesian counterparts, which are, on the whole, much darker; the best Malaysian batiks come from the east coast states, particularly Kelantan.

Traditionally, the wax was painted onto the woven cloth using a *canting* (pronounced 'janting'), a small copper cup with a spout, mounted on a bamboo handle. The cup is filled with melted wax, which flows from the spout like ink from a fountain pen – although the canting never touches the surface of the cloth. Batik artists have a number of canting with various widths of spout, some even with several spouts, to give varied thicknesses of line and differences of effect.

The canting was probably invented in Java in the 12th century, whereupon it replaced the crude painting stick, enabling far more complex designs to be produced. Inscriptions from this period refer to *tulis warna*, literally 'drawing in colour', which was probably some sort of resist dyeing technique similar, but ancestral, to batik. Cloth produced using a canting should be labelled *tulis* (literally, to write) and one sarong length can take from one to six months to complete. Reflecting the skill and artistry required to produce such batik, waxers used to be called *lukis* or painters. Drawing the design with a canting is a laborious process and has largely been replaced by stamping.

In the mid-19th century the 'modern' batik industry was born with the invention (in Java, but quickly adopted in Malaysia) of the *cap* (pronounced 'jap'). This is a copper, sometimes a wooden stamp which looks something like a domestic iron, except that it has an artistically patterned bottom, usually made from twisted copper and strips of soldered tin. Dripping with molten wax, the jap stamps the same pattern across the length and breadth of the cloth, which is then put into a vat of dye. The waxed areas resist the dye and after drying, the process is repeated several times for the different colours. The cracking effect is produced by crumpling the waxed material, which allows the dye to penetrate the cracks. The cloth is traditionally printed in 12m lengths.

The cap revolutionized batik production. As Wanda Warming and Michael Gaworski say in their book *The world of Indonesian textiles* "... it took a small cottage industry, a fine art, an expression of Javanese sensibilities, and a hobby for aristocratic women, and turned it into a real commercial enterprise". With the invention of the cap, so there evolved a parallel cap-making industry. Old copper stamps have become collectors' pieces. Not only did the cap speed-up production, it also took the artistry out of waxing: waxers merely stamp the design onto the cloth.

Recent years have seen a revival of hand-painted batiks (*batik tulis*), particularly on silk. Price depends on the type of material, design, number of colours used and method employed: factory-printed materials are cheaper than those made by hand. Batik is sold by the *sarung*-length or made up into shirts – and other items of clothing.

Distinguishing hand-drawn from stamped batik It can be hard differentiating drawn (*tulis*) and stamped (*cap*) batik, particularly in the case of the repetitious geometric designs of Central Java. Look for irregular lines and examine repetitive motifs like flowers carefully – stamped batik will show no variation. On poorly-executed stamped cloth, there may be a line at the point where two stamps have been imperfectly aligned. **NB** There is also machine printed cloth with traditional batik designs: this can be identified by the clear design and colour on one side only; batik, whether drawn or printed, will have the design clearly revealed on both sides of the fabric.

Kain songket is Malaysia's 'cloth of gold', although it is also woven in other parts of the region, particularly coastal southern Sumatra. Originally cloth made from a mix of cotton and silk was inter-woven with supplementary gold or silver thread. Today imitation thread is generally used although the metallic thread from old pieces is also removed to provide yarn for new lengths. Some more enterprising weavers have also reportedly used plaited copper wire or yarns thinly coated in metal to achieve the desired effect.

The songket evolved when the Malay sultanates first began trading with China (where the silk came from) and India (where the gold and silver thread derived). Designs are reproduced from Islamic motifs and Arabic calligraphy. It was once exclusive to royalty, but is used today during formal occasions and ceremonies (such as weddings). In Kelantan, Terengganu and Pahang the cloth can be purchased directly from workshops. Prices increase with the intricacy of the design and the number of threads used. Each piece is woven by hand and different weavers specialize in particular patterns – one length of cloth may be the work of several weavers.

Pewterware Pewter-making was introduced from China in the mid-19th century; it was the perfect alloy for Malaysia, which until recently, was the world's largest tin-producer: pewter is 95 percent tin. Straits tin is alloyed with antimony and copper. The high proportion of tin lends to the fineness of the surface. Malaysia's best pewter is made by Selangor Pewter, which has factories in KL and Singapore. It is made mainly into vases, tankards, water jugs, trays and dressing table ornaments. The Selangor Pewter factory on the outskirts of KL (see page 91) employs about 400 craftsmen and has a good showroom. Selangor pewter was started in 1885 by Yong Koon, a Chinese immigrant from Swatow province who came to Malaya by junk. Using the ample supply of tin, he started making items for ancestral worship, such as incense burners and joss-stick holders. The third generation of the Yong family now runs the operation. The dimpling effect is made by tapping the surface with a small hammer. Selangor Pewter is the world's biggest pewter manufacturer.

Wayang kulit (shadow puppets – see box, page 549) are crafted from buffalo-hide and represent figures from the Indian epic tales. They are popular handicrafts as they are light and portable.

Silverware Silverwork is a traditional craft and is now a thriving cottage industry in Kelantan. It is crafted into brooches, pendants, belts, bowls and rings. Design patterns incorporate traditional motifs such as *wayang kulit* (see above) and hibiscus flowers (the national flower). The Iban of Sarawak also use silver for ceremonial headdresses and girdles, and some Iban silvercraft can be found for sale on the peninsula.

Background

Singapore

10

556

Singapore

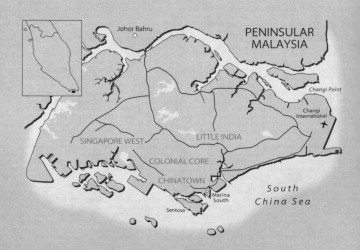

*To some, it has all the ambience of a supermarket
checkout lane. It has even been described as a
Californian resort-town run by Mormons. It has
frequently been dubbed sterile and dull - a report in* The
Economist *judged Singapore to be the most boring city
in the world and for those who fail to venture beyond the
plazas that line Orchard Road, or spend their 3½ days
on coach-trips to the ersatz cultural extravaganzas, this
is not surprising. But there is a cultural and architectural
heritage in Singapore beyond the one which the
government tries so hard to manufacture. Despite its
brash consumerism and toytown mentality, Singapore is
certainly not without its charm.*

*Singapore is difficult to fathom, especially from afar.
Beneath its slick veneer of westernized modernity, many
argue that Singapore's heart and soul are Asian. Behind
the computers, hi-tech industries, marble, steel and
smoked-glass tower blocks, highways and shopping
centres is a society ingrained with conservative
Confucian values.*

*For those stopping over in Singapore for just a few days
- en route, as most of the island's tourists are, to
somewhere else - there are several key sights that should
not be missed. Many who visit, however, consider that it
is far more important to enjoy the food. The island has
an unparalleled variety of restaurants to suit every
palate and wallet. Hawker centres in particular are a
highly recommended part of the Singapore epicurean
experience - they are inexpensive, and many are open
into the early hours.*

Singapore

Essentials

Planning your trip

Best time to visit
For daily weather reports after you have arrived, T5427788

There is no best season to visit Singapore and it is hot right through the year. It gets even stickier before the monsoon breaks in November, while the hottest months are July and August. The wettest months are November, December and January, during the period of the northeast monsoon, when it is also coolest. As one would expect, the hottest time of day is early afternoon when the mean temperature is around 30°C but even during the coolest time of the day, just before dawn, the mean temperature is still nearly 24°C.

Finding out more

The *Singapore Tourist Board* is a useful place to contact. They produce a good free official guide called *New Asia-Singapore*, as well as pamphlets detailing hotels, restaurants and so on. Their website has regularly updated information on hotels, festivals and other tourist-related information: www.newasia-singapore.com, see also box on page 559 for a list of Singapore Tourist Board offices worldwide. See also Tourist information, page 565. Another good site is www.technofind.com.sg, the largest search engine for Singapore websites, updated daily. It covers just about every topic including tourism and is a good place to start hunting.

Other useful websites include: www.sg, the Singapore Infomap site which has website directories covering everything from leisure and entertainment to the economy, and from the National Heritage Board to Singapore's limitless choice of cuisine. Asia Travel's website is http://asiatravel.com/singapore.html. This is a useful site for hotel reservations, weather reports, the very latest travel information and exchange rates and also has a map detailing some places of interest. http://asnic.utexas.edu/asnic.html is the website for the Asian Studies Network Information Center at the University of Texas. This site will give you background information on the history and politics of Singapore.

Before you travel

Getting in
See also box on page 560 for a list of Singapore embassies & consulates worldwide

Visas Visitors must possess a passport valid for at least 6 months, have a confirmed onward/return ticket, sufficient funds to support themselves in Singapore and, where applicable, a visa.

No visa is required for citizens of the Commonwealth, USA or Western Europe. On arrival in Singapore by air, citizens of these countries are granted a month visitor's permit. Tourists entering Singapore via the causeway from Johor Bahru in Malaysia or by sea are allowed to stay for 14 days. Nationals of most other countries (except India, China and the Commonwealth of Independent States) with confirmed onward reservations may stop over in Singapore for up to 14 days without a visa. It is necessary to keep the stub of your immigration card until you leave.

Nationals of the following countries require visas before entering Singapore: Afghanistan, Algeria, Armenia, Azerbaijan, Bangladesh, Belarus, Cambodia, China, Estonia, Georgia, Hong Kong, India, Iraq, Jordan, Kazakhstan, Kyrgyzstan, Lao PDR, Latvia, Lebanon, Libya, Lithuania, Myanmar (Burma), Russia, Syria, Tajikistan, Tunisia, Turkmenistan, Ukraine, Uzbekistan, Vietnam and Yemen.

Singebore Tourist Board Offices

Australia Level 11, AWA Building, 47 York St, Sydney, T612-92902888

Canada Standard Life Centre, 121 King St West, Suite 1000, Toronto, T416-36357552

France Centre d'Affaires Le Louvre, 2 Place du Palais-Royal, Paris, T01-42971616, F01-42971617

Germany Hochstrasse 35-37, Frankfurt, T069-9207700, F069-2978922

Italy c/o Theodore Trancu & Associates, Corso Plebisciti 15, 20129 Milano, Italy, T39-2-70003981, F39-2-7381032

Japan 1st Flr, Yamato Seimei Building, 1 Chome, 1-7 Uchisaiwai-cho, Chiyoda-ku, Tokyo 100, T81-3-35933388, F81-3-35911480; and Osaka City Air Terminal, 4F, 1-4-1, Minato-Machi, Naniwa-ku, Osaka 556, T81-6-6353087, F81-6-6353089

Hong Kong Room 2003, Central Plaza, 18 Harbour Rd, Wanchai, T5989290, F5981040

New Zealand 3rd Flr, 43 High St, Auckland, PO Box 857, T64-9-3581191, F64-9-3581196

Switzerland Löwenstrasse 51, CH-8044, Zurich, T01-2117474, F01-2117422

South Africa 52 3rd Ave, Parktown North 2193, PO Box 81260, T27-11-7880701, F27-11-4427599

Thailand c/o MDK Consultants, Ruamrudi Building, 4th Flr, 566 Ploenchit Rd, Lumpini, Bangkok 10330, T66-2-2524117, F66-2-2524118

UK 1st Flr, Carrington House, 126-130 Regent St, London, W1R 5FE, T020-74370033

USA 2 Prudential Plaza, 180 North Stetson Av, Suite 1450, Chicago, T312-9381888. 8484 Wilshire Boulevard, Suite 510, Beverley Hills, CA90211, T213-8520129. 590 Fifth Av, 12th Flr, New York, NY 10036, T212-3024861.

Visas can be extended for up to 3 months at the Singapore Immigration Head Office, Singapore Immigration Building, 10 Kallang Road, Singapore 208718, T1800-3916400 (toll free information line). Alternatively, it can be just as easy to nip across the causeway to Johor Bahru (in Malaysia) and then re-enter Singapore on a 2 week permit.

Immigration Dept Singapore Immigration Head Office, Singapore Immigration Building, 10 Kallang Road, Singapore 208718, T1800-3916400 (toll free information line).

Currency Local currency is dollars and cents. Bank notes are available in denominations of S$2, 5, 10, 20, 50, 100, 500, 1,000 and 10,000. Coins are in 1, 5, 10, 20 and 50 cent and 1 dollar denominations. In March 2000, the Singapore dollar was valued at S$1.71 to US$1 or S$2.70 to £1. Brunei currency is interchangeable with Singapore currency; the Malaysian Ringgit is not.

Money
Bank opening hours: 0930-1500 Mon-Fri, 0930-1130 Sat

It is possible to change money at banks, licensed money changers and hotels, although a service charge may be added. Licensed money changers often give better rates than banks. It is also possible to withdraw money from cashpoint machines if you have a credit card with a PIN. Singapore is one of the major banking centres of Southeast Asia, so it is relatively easy to get money wired from home. There is no black market.

Credit cards Most of Singapore's hotels, shops, restaurants and banks accept the major international credit cards, and many cash machines allow you to draw cash on Visa or MasterCard. After bargaining, expect to pay at least 3% for credit card transactions; most shops insist on this surcharge although you do not have to pay it.

Notification of credit card loss: American Express, T2998133; Diners Card, T2944222; MasterCard, T5332888; Visa Card, T1-800-3451345

Goods and Services Tax refund scheme Visitors can claim back their 3% Goods and Services Tax from shops displaying the 'Tax Free for Tourists' sign when they spend S$300 or more. A claim form is issued and this is then presented at customs on leaving the country, when visitors are reimbursed. It is also possible to claim by post; the

Singapore

Embassies and consulates

Australia High Commission, 17 Forster Crescent, Yarralumla, Canberra ACT 2600, T6-2733944

Austria c/o Embassy in Bonn; Consulate: Raiffeisen Zentral Bank, Osterreich AG, Am Stadtpark 9, 1030 Vienna, T222-71707-1229

Belgium 198 Ave Franklin Roosevelt, 1050 Brussels, T2-66030908

Canada 1305-999 Hastings St, Vancouver, T604-6695115

China 4 Liangmahe Nanlu, Sanlitun, Beijing 100600, T1-4323926

CIS Per Voyevodina 5, Moscow, T095-2413702

Denmark c/o High Commission in London

Finland c/o Embassy in Moscow

France, 12 Square de l'Ave Foch, 75116 Paris, T45003361

Germany Sudstrasse 133, 5300 Bonn 2, T228-312007

Greece 10-12 Kifissias Ave, 151 25 Maroussi, Athens, T1-6834875

Hong Kong Units 901-2, Admiralty Centre Tower 1, 9th Flr, 18 Harcourt Rd, Hong Kong, T5272212

India High Commission E-6 Chandragupta Marg, Chanakyapuri, New Delhi 110021, T11-604162. Consulates: Bombay T2-2043205; Madras T44-476637

Indonesia Block X/4 KAV No 2, Jl HR Rasuna Said, Kuningan, Jakarta 12950, T21-5201489. Consulate: Medan, North Sumatra, T61-513366

Japan 14th Flr, Osaka, Kokusai Building, 3-13 Azuchimachi 2-Chome, Chuo-Ku, Tokyo T6-2615131

Malaysia 209 Jln Tun Razak, Kuala Lumpur 50400, T03-2616277

Netherlands Rotterdam Plaza, Weena 670 3012 CN, Rotterdam, T20-4042111

New Zealand 17 Kabul St, Khandallah, Wellington, T4-792076

Norway c/o High Commission in London. Consulate: Oslo, T47-2485000

Portugal Lusograin, Rua dos Franqueiros 135-1, 1100 Lisbon, T1-878647

Spain, Huertas 13, Madrid 28012, T1-4293193

Sri Lanka High Commission c/o High Commission in New Delhi

Sweden c/o Embassy in Bonn. Consulate: Stockholm T8-6637488

Switzerland c/o Embassy in Bonn

Thailand 129 South Sathorn Rd, Bangkok, T2-2862111

UK 9 Wilton Crescent, London, SW1X 8SA, T020-72358315

USA 1824 R St NW, Washington DC 20009-1691, T202-6677555. Consulates: Los Angeles T714-7609400; Minneapolis T612-3328063

refund is paid either by bank cheque or to a credit card account. The Singapore Tourist Board publishes a brochure, *Tax Refund for Visitors to Singapore*.

Customs
Singapore is a free port

Currency There is no limit to the amount of Singapore and foreign currency or travellers' cheques you can bring in or take out.

Duty free allowance One litre of liquor, 1 litre of wine or port, 1 litre of beer or stout. Note that because of the government's strict anti-smoking policy there is no duty free allowance for tobacco.

Export restrictions There is no export duty but export permits are required for arms, ammunition, explosives, animals, gold, platinum, precious stones and jewellery, poisons and drugs. No permit is needed for the export of antiques.

Prohibited items

Narcotics are strictly forbidden in Singapore and, as in neighbouring Malaysia, trafficking is a capital offence which is rigorously enforced. In 1992, the Singapore government banned the importation and sale of chewing gum, after the MRT Corporation claimed the substance threatened the efficient running of its underground trains. Chewing tobacco, toy currency, pornographic material and seditious literature are also prohibited items.

Singapore

Getting there

As an international crossroads, Singapore is within easy reach of all key points in the **Air**
region and there are flights from Changi (Singapore's airport) to destinations
throughout Southeast Asia. Over 70 airlines service Singapore, flying to 131 cities in 56
countries. Long-haul prices are not as competitive as London bucket shops, although
they undercut some other Asian capitals. Tickets to Southeast Asian destinations are
subject to minimum selling price restrictions imposed by a cartel of regional airlines. It
is still possible to get special deals to selected destinations from the discount travel
agents (see Singapore *Yellow Pages*) but tickets bought in Bangkok and Penang are
now marginally cheaper.

The Singapore-Kuala Lumpur air shuttle (operated jointly by SIA and MAS) runs
every 50 minutes from Changi Terminal 1. Singapore-KL shuttle tickets can be bought
on a first-come-first-served basis at Changi Airport. For timetables, call SIA on
T2238888 or MAS on T3366777. For return flights to Kuala Lumpur, just buy a single
ticket as it is cheaper to purchase tickets in Malaysia.

Long haul flights from Kuala Lumpur, particularly on MAS, can be considerably
cheaper than outbound flights from Singapore. It is also much cheaper when flying
between Singapore and other points in Malaysia to use Johor Bahru's airport across
the causeway. Johor Bahru is well connected to the Malaysian domestic network.
Chartered express coaches ply between Singapore and JB airport; they leave
Singapore from the *Novotel Orchid Inn* on Dunearn Road but are reserved for MAS
passengers only, S$12 (adult), S$10 (children). The courier ensures express clearance of
Malaysian customs and immigration. Details from MAS office in Singapore: 190
Clemenceau Avenue, T3366777. For those wishing to fly to destinations in Indonesia, it
is cheaper to take the ferry to the Indonesian island of Batam and then catch a
domestic flight from there.

The railway station is on Keppel Road, T2225165, to the south of the city centre. **Train**
Singapore is the last port of call for the Malaysian railway system (Keretapi Tanah
Melayu - KTM). The domed station - apparently inspired by Helsinki's - opened in 1932
and was renovated in 1990. The design, with its rubber-covered walls and their images
of rubber tappers, tin miners and other Malay scenes, was heralded when it opened.
Also notable are the four fine Art Deco images on the front of the station depicting
commerce, agriculture, industry and shipping - suitably industrious for the new, as
well as the old, Singapore. Malaysian immigration and customs clearance for inbound
and outbound passengers is taken care of in the Singapore station (sometimes with
the help of sniffer dogs).

There are two main lines connecting Singapore and Malaysia: one up the west
coast to KL and Butterworth and on to Thailand and another line which goes through
the centre of Peninsular Malaysia and on to Kota Bahru on the northeast coast. Some
travellers use the train to go to Johor Bahru to avoid the long wait going through
customs at the border (S$2.90). There are departures daily at 0845, 1120 and 1805,
journey time 30-40 minutes. Three fully air-conditioned express trains make the trip
daily between Singapore and Kuala Lumpur, 5-7 hours (S$19-60) departing at 0815,
1425 and 2230. The overnight sleeper arrives in Kuala Lumpur at 0655. There is a
cheaper, but slower, mail train which leaves at 2015 each evening and stops at every
station *en route* taking 10 hours to reach Kuala Lumpur at the bargain fare of S$14.80.
There are also daily trains from Singapore to Butterworth, opposite Penang, 13 hours
and an express train 3 times a week to/from Bangkok (Thailand) crossing the
Malaysian/Thai border at Padang Besar. Trains are clean and efficient and overnight
trains have cabins in first class, sleeping berths in second class and restaurants.

Transport to town From the station, bus 10 travels up Robinson Road, past Collyer Quay to Empress Place and the Nicoll Highway; bus 100 goes up Robinson, Fullerton and Beach roads; bus 30 travels west; bus 84 goes to the World Trade Centre; and buses 97 and 131 travel through the centre of town and then up Serangoon Road and through Little India.

Bus The new Express Highway into Malaysia makes for a more efficient bus service and faster travel. Bus 170 goes to Woodlands immigration point and across the causeway to Johor Bahru's Larkin bus terminal as well as the train station. Note that boarding in JB is only permitted at these two stops. Buses leave every 6-10 minutes or so (more frequently during peak hours) from the Ban San Terminal at the northern end of Queen Street (at the junction with Arab Street) and then runs along Rochor Road and Bukit Timah Road to Woodlands Road. The journey to JB takes about an hour, including customs and immigration formalities at the border. There is also the rather more luxurious Singapore-JB Express which departs from the Ban San Terminal every 10 minutes.

Most long distance buses to and from Malaysia operate out of the Lavender Street Terminal at the junction of Lavender Street and Kallang Bahru. Destinations include KL (S$17), Melaka (S$11), Butterworth (S$30), Mersing (S$11), Kota Bahru (S$30), Kuantan (S$17), Ipoh (S$27), and Penang (S$30). Buses to the more distant destinations like Butterworth, Kota Bahru and Ipoh leave in the late afternoon. It is best to book tickets a few days ahead of departure, especially if intending to travel over a holiday period. As well as the Lavender Street services, there is also the Singapore-KL Express which departs from the Ban San Terminal on Lavender Street with buses leaving at 0900, 1300 and 2200 (S$17.30 normal coach, S$25 deluxe). Again, book a couple of days ahead.

Long distance bus companies: *Singapore-Johor Bahru Express*, T2928149; *Kuala Lumpur-Singapore Express*, T2928254; *Malacca-Singapore Express*, T2935915; *A&S Bus Services*, T2816161; *WTS*, T3370337.

Buses to Thailand leave from the Golden Mile Complex on Beach Road: Hat Yai (S$35, S$45 for VIP coach), Bangkok (S$70). There are several agents selling tickets close to the station. Note that it is cheaper to book a ticket to Hat Yai, and then pay for the rest of the journey in Thai baht; or even cheaper still to catch a bus to JB, one from JB to Hat Yai, and then a third from Hat Yai to Bangkok.

Taxis Long distance taxis to Malaysia leave from the Rochor Road terminus. Taxis go as far as Johor Bahru (S$7); from here there are Malaysian taxis on to Melaka (RM80), Kuantan (RM120-150), KL (RM100) and Butterworth (RM180-200).

Boat A small fraction of Singapore's visitors arrive in the world's busiest port by ship, although cruising has become fashionable again and sea arrivals are growing by nearly 50% a year. Passenger lines serve Singapore from Australia, Europe, USA, India and Hong Kong. Ships either dock at the World Trade Centre or anchor in the main harbour with a launch service to shore. Entry formalities as above. *Star Cruises*, T7336988, F7333622, are one of the biggest companies operating in the region. Orient Lines, Pearl Cruises, Seabourn Cruise Lines, Silversea Cruises and Seven Seas Cruise Lines also dock at Singapore.

There are regular high speed ferry connections between **Singapore and Indonesia's Riau islands** of Batam (Sekupang and Batu Ampar) and Bintan (Tanjung Pinang and Loban). Return fares vary from S$27 to Sekupang (40 minutes) to S$58 to Tanjung Pinang (1½ hours). Most leave from the World Trade Centre not far from the city centre, although there are also services from Tanah Merah ferry terminal, east of the city. From the Riau islands it is possible to travel by boat to Sumatra or by air to many other destinations in Indonesia (cheaper than flying direct from Singapore). It is also possible to take a high-speed catamaran from Tanah Merah to Pulau Tioman, off the east coast of Peninsular Malaysia, 4½ hours (S$148-168 return). Ferry operators have their offices at the World Trade Centre and include *Auto Batam*, 1 Maritime Square #02-40/42, World Trade Centre, T2714866, F2733573, autobatam@sembcorp.com.sg, www.sembcorp.com.sg/autobatam/; *Sri Sinjori Ferries Pte Ltd*, T2727540; Dino Shipping, 1 Maritime Square, #03-32 World Trade Centre, T2700311, F2700322.

There is also a ferry from Changi Ferry Terminal to Tanjung Belungkor, east of Johor Bahru in Malaysia. Most people use this service to get to the beach resort of Desaru. Passengers S$19 (S$26 return); cars S$20; 45 minutes. **NB** If travelling from Tanjung Belungkur to Singapore fares are considerably cheaper (payable in ringgit). Ferry times: 0815, 1115, 1415 and 1715, Singapore to Tanjung Belungkur; 0945, 1245, 1545 and 1845, Tanjung Belungkor to Singapore. Contact *Ferrylink Pte*, T5453600/7336744. To get to the terminal take bus 2 to Changi Village and then a taxi.

It is possible to enter Singapore from Malaysia by bumboat from Johor Bahru (S$5), Tanjung Pengileh or Tanjung Surat (S$6) in southern Johor to Changi Point, on the northeast tip of Singapore - a good way of beating the bottleneck at the causeway. First boat 0700, last at 1600. Boats depart as soon as they have 12 passengers.

Touching down

Almost all visitors arrive at Singapore's Changi Airport, which is regularly voted the world's leading or favourite airport. The old British military base at Seletar is used for small plane arrivals and departures, notably flights from/to Pulau Tioman, off the east coast of Malaysia.

Airport information

Changi airport is at the extreme eastern tip of the island, about 20 km from town. The spacious, uncluttered terminals are adorned with cool fountains, luxuriant plants and tropical fish tanks and boast an array of executive leisure facilities, including saunas and squash courts, to help jet-lagged executives unwind. The airport's stress-free terminals belie its status as one of the world's most hectic transit hubs. In 1995 the airport processed 23,196,242 passengers, eight times more than the population of Singapore. About 80% of Singapore's tourists arrive by air and it takes only 20 minutes from touch down to baggage claim, characteristically called "accelerated passenger through-flow". True to form, Singapore's far-sighted government planners have already got a third terminal on the drawing board, which will cater for a further 10 million.

Changi's facilities are excellent and include banks, hotel reservation and Singapore Tourist Board desks, a medical centre, business centre, children's discovery corner, internet centre (open 24 hours), day rooms, restaurants, left-luggage facilities, mail and telecommunications desks, shopping arcades, supermarkets, sports facilities and accommodation, all open 0700-2300. Everything is clearly signposted in English and the two terminals are connected by a monorail. Flight information is available by calling: T5424422 (give flight number). There is an excellent canteen/food centre in Terminal 2, reached via the multi-deck car park. A tourist information pack is available just after Immigration, near the Customs Hall.

Airport tax Payable on departure, S$15 for all flights to all countries. A PSC (Passenger Service Charge) coupon can be purchased at most hotels, travel agencies and airline offices in town before departure, which saves time at the airport.

Free city tours for transit passengers For those who are here in transit and want a snifter of what Singapore has to offer, the Singapore Tourist Board offers free tours of the city. They are run on a first come, first served basis, and for those with time on their hands who do not want to bankrupt themselves wandering the shops of Changi, they offer an excellent interlude. Passengers must show their boarding pass and are then ushered through immigration to a waiting bus. Passports are kept by the officials until they return and no airport departure tax is charged. The tours themselves are rather

Singapore

Touching down

Emergencies Police: T999. Ambulance/Fire brigade: T995.

Business hours Banks 0930-1500 Mon-Fri, 0930-1130 Sat. Some do not offer foreign exchange dealings on Sat although money changers operate throughout the week and for longer hours. Most **shops** in the tourist belt open around 0930 and close at 2100. Around Orchard and Scotts roads, Sun is a normal working day.

Official time 8 hours ahead of GMT.

Voltage 220-240 volts, 50 cycle AC; most hotels can supply adapters.

Weights and measures Metric.

IDD code 65.

Directory enquiries T103.

banal but it is a great idea and works without a hitch, as one might expect. For more details and to book a tour visit one of the Free City Tour desks on arrival. This service operates between 0830 and 1900.

Sleeping at Changi **AL** *Le Meridien Changi*, 1 Netheravon Rd, T5427700, F5425295. Very well run, first class hotel, situated on Changi Beach, just north of the airport. Recommended for efficiency. **A** *Transit Hotel 1*, level 3 Changi Airport Terminal 1, T5430911, F5458365. Short term rate quoted (6 hours). A good place to take a break if you are stuck at Changi for an extended period. **B** *Transit Hotel 2*, departure/transit lounge south, Terminal 2 T5428122, F5426122, airport@pacific.net.sg. Excellent hotel on the airport property, with short stay facility (price quoted is for 6 hours). Booking is recommended as it is so popular. They also provide a 'freshen up' service including use of showers, sauna and gym from S$5.

Transport to town Hotels will only meet guests with a previous arrangement; some charge but others offer the service free. The car pick-up area is outside the arrivals halls of both terminals.

The Airbus was replaced by a 6-seat **shuttle minibus** in 1999. It drops passengers off at all major hotels, S$7 adults, S$5 children, and operates 0900-2300. As a taxi to the city centre costs around S$14, the shuttle minibus only makes sense for couples or people travelling alone. Tickets available from the driver (exact change in S$ only) or in the arrivals area of terminals 1 and 2. T5533880 for information.

A number of **buses** run between the airport and nearby bus interchanges. **Bus 16** runs to Raffles City and then down Orchard Road, takes less than 1 hour and costs S$1.20 (non-a/c) or S$1.50 (a/c). It is easy to catch from Orchard Road. **Bus 36**, which also runs along Orchard Road to Raffles City, is faster but only operates in the morning between 0600 and 0900 when the service operates from the city to airport and from 1700 and 2000 in the evening when it plys between the airport and city. Exact fare needed.

A **MRT** line is currently under construction from the city out to Changi. It is scheduled for completion in 2000-2001 and will provide quick and easy access by train.

Car rental Avis and Hertz desks are in the arrivals hall (open until 1800).

Taxis queue up outside the arrival halls. They are metered plus there is an airport surcharge of S$3. In 1998 the airport introduced a limousine service (London cab or Mercedes) with a flat rate of S$35. This is available from the booking counter in terminal 2 and is soon to be extended to terminal 1, 0730-2330.

Seletar Airport is a military airport but is also used for connections with Pulau Tioman off Malaysia's east coast and for some charter flights. Although the authorities do not allow photographs on the tarmac, checking-in is all very relaxed and informal - very different from the rather brusque efficiency of Changi. There are no public buses to Seletar, most people take taxis, and as at Changi there is a S$3 surcharge. When a scheduled flight is arriving from Tioman the airline usually calls so that the required number of taxis are waiting.

Singapore Tourist Board *Singapore Tourist Board*, Tourism Court, 1 Orchard Spring Lane, Singapore 247729, T7366622; Raffles Hotel Shopping Centre, 02-34 Raffles Hotel Arcade, T3341335/3341336 (open 0830-2000). These are both very helpful, supplying brochures and maps. Complaints can also be registered at these offices. There is a 24 hour Touristline which gives automated information in English, Mandarin, Japanese and German, T1800 8313311 (toll free). See also Finding out more, page 558. **Indonesian Tourist Board**, Ocean Building, 11 Collyer Quay, T5342837. **Malaysian Tourist Board**, Ocean Building, 11 Collyer Quay, T5326351.

Tourist information

Student/Young Person *STA Travel* in the *Orchard Parade Hotel* on Tanglin Road, T7345681, or at the Singapore Polytechnic (next to Canteen 5), Dover Road, T7742270, is Singapore's top student and youth (under 26) travel centre, offering student fares, discounted tours and budget accommodation.

Maps *American Express/Singapore Tourist Board Map of Singapore* and the *Map of Singapore* endorsed by the Singapore Hotel Association are both available gratis from Singapore Tourist Board (STB) offices and many hotels.

Guides *The Singapore Official Guide* and the STB's *Singapore Tour it Yourself* are available from STB offices. The STB are also producing a series of more detailed 'Yours to Explore' guides to selected areas of the city. By mid-1998 they had produced guides to *Chinatown*, *Little India* and the *Singapore River* and have *Kampong Glam* and the *Civic District* in the pipeline. Well worth picking up.

Disabled visitors The Singapore Council of Social Services publishes *Access Singapore*, a guidebook especially for physically disabled visitors, which gives information on easily accessible tourist attractions and facilities for the disabled. Copies can be picked up from the SCSS offices at 11 Penang Lane, T3361544 or by post from National Council for Social Service, Disabled Service Department, 11 Penang Lane, Singapore 238485. Their offices are open 0900-1300, 1400-1800 Monday-Friday.

Clothing Singapore dress is smart but casual. It is rare to find places insisting on jacket and tie, although jeans and T-shirts are taboo at some nightclubs. Flip-flops, singlets and denim cut-offs look out of place in Singapore.

Rules, customs & etiquette

Singapore

Conduct in private homes Most Singaporeans remove their shoes at the door - more out of a keen sense of cleanliness than any deep religious conviction. No host would insist on his or her visitors doing so, but it is the polite way to enter a home.

Eating Chinese meals are eaten with chopsticks and Malays and Indians traditionally eat with their right hands. It is just as acceptable, however, to eat with spoons and forks. In Malay and Indian company, do not use the left hand for eating.

Prohibitions There are several rules and regulations visitors should note: smoking is discouraged and prohibited by law in many public places, such as buses, taxis, lifts, government offices, cinemas, theatres, libraries, department stores, shopping centres and all air-conditioned restaurants. First offenders can be fined up to S$1,000 for lighting up in prohibited places. Many hotels now provide non-smoking floors. Littering may incur a fine of up to S$1,000 for first time offenders and up to S$2,000 for repeat offenders with the added prospect of corrective work of some kind. Although jaywalking is less rigorously enforced than it used to be, crossing the road within 50m of a pedestrian crossing, bridge or underpass could cost you S$500.

Temple manners: a guide to avoiding giving offence

General advice
all temples, mosques and churches are
    places of worship and visitors should
    dress appropriately

Hindu temples
remove shoes on entry and leave them
    outside the gates
walk clockwise around the temple hall
    and circumambulate an odd number
    of times for good luck
menstruating women are considered
    'unclean' and should not enter

Mahayana Buddhist (Taoist) temples
no need to remove shoes here - but don't
    step on the wooden door sills

Theravada Buddhist temples
remove shoes on entry and leave them
    outside the gates
women should avoid personal contact
    with monks

Mosques
remove shoes on entry and leave them
    outside the gates
ensure legs and shoulders are covered
note that only worshippers are allowed to
    enter the prayer hall
it is best not to visit during Friday prayers
    and in the evenings

Safety Singapore is probably the safest big city in Southeast Asia. Women travelling alone need have few worries. It is wise, however, to take the normal precautions and not wander into lonely places after dark.

Tipping Tipping is unusual in Singapore. In cheaper restaurants it is not expected, although in more upmarket places when a service charge is not automatically added to the bill, a tip is usual. Most international hotels and restaurants, however, add 10% service charge and 4% government tax to bills. In general, only tip for special personal services.

Where to stay

See page 617 for a full
listing of
accommodation
by area

Singapore offers an excellent choice of hotels in our upper categories, from luxury to tourist class. Though rooms may be more expensive than equivalent classes of hotels elsewhere in the region, they try to make up for this in terms of service. It is rare to stay in a hotel that does not offer attentive and professional care. Budget hotels are thin on the ground and expensive and budget travellers find that money which may last a week in neighbouring Indonesia or Malaysia disappears in a day or two. However, there are a few cheaper places to stay, see box opposite.

Taxes of 10% (government) plus 3% (goods) plus 1% (services) are added to bills in all but the cheapest of hotels.

**Hotel prices &
facilities**

LL (S$400+) and **L** (S$300-400) Singapore has some of the very best hotels in the world. These offer unrivalled personal service, sumptuous extras, luxury rooms and bathrooms, and just about every amenity that you can think of. Most of the top hotels now provide two in-room phone lines (for modems and calls), 24-hour business facilities, several pools, jacuzzis, health spas, tennis courts, numerous restaurants, and much else besides.

AL (S$200-300) Most of the middle to upper range hotels in this category will provide a business centre (although it is worth checking whether these operate around the clock). Coupled with this, there will be an executive floor or two, with a lounge for private breakfast and evening cocktails, or for entertaining clients. Most of these hotels will also provide a personal safe in each room. There will be a fitness centre and swimming pool and they may have a health centre as well as several restaurants.

Dorm beds

Singapore is not the cheapest of places to stay but there are a number of budget hotels and guesthouses which offer dorm beds, usually with lockers for safe-keeping, for around S$8-15 per night for fan-cooled dorm rooms and S$25 for more salubrious air conditioned dorms. For the full entry on each hotel or guesthouse listed below see Sleeping, page 617.

Colonial core

Willy's Homestay, 494 North Bridge Rd, T3370916, willys@mbox2.singnet.com.sg.
Travellers' Nest, 28C Seah St, T3399095.

Orchard Road

YWCA, Fort Canning Rd, T3384222, F3374222, a/c dorms.

YMCA International House, 1 Orchard Rd, T3366000, F3373140, a/c dorms.

Little India

Hawaii Hostel, 2nd Flr, 171B Bencoolen St, T3384187.
Lee Boarding House, 7th Flr, 52 Peony Mansion, 46-52 Bencoolen St, T3383149, F3365409.

Arab Street

Lee Travellers' Club, 6th Flr of the Fu Yuen apartment block (and next to the Park View Hotel), 75 Beach Rd, T3395490.
Season Homestay, 26A Liang Seah St, T3372400, www.sgweb.com.sg/homestay.
Cozy Corner Lodge (formerly the Backpackers' Cozy Corner), 2a Liang Seah St, T3348761.

A (S$150-200) and **B** (S$100-150) Hotels in this category will range from very comfortable to functional. Rooms in the 'A' category will have most extras – like a minibar, television, and tea and coffee making facilities. They may also have a swimming pool but it is likely to be small. They will have a coffee shop and perhaps a restaurant. Rooms in the 'B' category may be lacking some, or most, of these amenities but should still be clean, comfortable and serviceable.

C (S$50-100) There are not many hotels in this category in Singapore. Rooms may be air conditioned with a hot water shower attached; there might also be a coffee shop. These are no-frills, functional affairs. There are some bargains to be had, but there are also hotels in this category which are pretty sordid.

D (S$25-50) and **E** (less than S$25) Hotels and guesthouses in these two categories (and there aren't many) are basic places, with shared bathroom facilities and box-like rooms. There are a few that are clean and perfectly adequate, and these are the registered establishments; others are squalid. The places on third or fourth floors of apartment buildings usually have no licence and they are often the dirtiest and least well run. Most of these places provide a basic breakfast.

Getting around

In an attempt to discourage Singaporeans from clogging the roads with private cars, the island's public transport system was designed to be cheap and painless. Buses go almost everywhere, and the Mass Rapid Transit (MRT) underground railway provides an efficient subterranean back-up. Smoking is banned on all public transport - transgression is punishable by a large fine. Big Macs and durians are also banned on the MRT.

Since November 1987 Singapore has had one of the most technologically advanced, user-friendly light railway systems in the world; about a third of the system is underground. The designer-stations of marble, glass and chrome are cool, spotless and suicide-free, thanks to the sealed-in, air-conditioned platforms. Nine of the underground stations serve as self-sufficient, blast-proof emergency bunkers for Singaporeans, should they ever need them.

Mass Rapid Transit (MRT)

Singapore

The US$5bn MRT is indeed a rapid way of transiting; it is electrically driven and trains reach 80 km/hour. Within minutes of leaving the bustle of Orchard Road passengers hear the honey-toned welcome to the Raffles City interchange. The MRT's 66 fully automated trains operate every 3-8 minutes, depending on the time of day, between 0600 and 2400. There is a north-south loop and an east-west line with interchanges at Raffles City/City Hall and Jurong East. The lines cover the main tourist belt. A new line is currently under construction from the city out to Changi Airport and is scheduled for completion in 2000-2001. Fare stages are posted in station concourses, and tickets dispensed, with change, from the vending machines. Fares range from 60¢ to S$1.60. Stored value tickets, in various denominations, can be bought at all stations from ticket dispensing machines. (There are note changing machines which will change S$2 notes into coins.) **NB** Children pay the same price as adults.

It is also possible to buy Transitlink cards for the MRT and buses, prices from S$10 to S$50 (including a S$2 refundable deposit) from the Transitlink ticket booths at MRT stations. Buses have 'validator machines'.

Tourist day tickets The tourist day ticket is priced at S$10 and allows passengers to take up to 12 rides a day either on the MRT or on all basic fare bus services.

Bus For anyone visiting Singapore for more than a couple of days, the bus must be the best way of getting around. SBS (Singapore Bus Service) and TIBS (Trans-Island Bus Services) are efficient, convenient and cheap. Routes for all the buses are listed (with a special section on buses to tourist spots) in the pocket-sized and pocket-priced (S$1.40) TransitLink Guide available at news outlets, bookshops and MRT stations, as well as at many hotels. If you intend to do much bus travel, then this guide is well worth buying. The Singapore Tourist Board's *Official Guide* (free at STB offices) also carries a tourist-friendly synopsis of the service. All buses are operated by a driver only, so it is necessary to have the exact fare to hand. Fares range from 60¢ (non a/c) to S$1.50 and buses run from 0600 to 2400 Monday to Sunday. Tickets are available from TransitLink offices found at most MRT stations and at many hotels.

MRT System

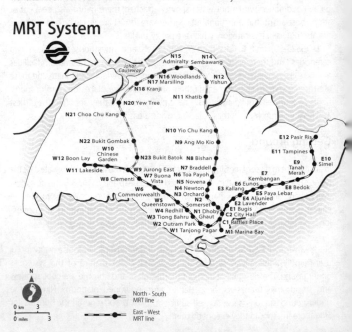

The sightseeing Singapore Trolley is a red 'tram' bus which travels between Orchard Road, the River, Chinatown, Raffles Hotel, Boat Quay, Clarke Quay, Suntec City all day. S$14.90 for adults and S$9.90 for children provides you with unlimited rides throughout the day. For more information call *Singapore Explorer* T3389205/3396833.

Singapore Trolley

This is one of the most expensive ways to get around. It is not worth it unless travelling to Malaysia, as parking is expensive in Singapore (parking coupons can be bought in shops and daily licence booths). If travelling to Malaysia, it is cheaper, in any case, to hire a car in Johor Bahru. Rental agencies require a licence, passport and for the driver to be over 20. Car rental cost is anything from S$60 to S$350 per day, depending on size and comfort, plus mileage. Vans and pickups are much cheaper as they are classified as commercial vehicles and are taxed at a lower rate.

Car hire

Driving is on the left, the speed limit 50 km/hour (80 km/hour on expressways) and wearing a seat belt is compulsory. Avoid bus lanes (unbroken yellow line) during rush hours. Remember that to drive into the restricted zone a licence must be purchased (S$3). In addition to car hire counters at the airport and booking offices in some top hotels, the *Yellow Pages* lists scores of local firms under 'Motorcar Renting and Leasing'.

Taxis are the fastest and easiest way to get around in comfort. More than 15,000 taxis, all of them metered and air conditioned, ply the island's roads. Taxis cannot be hailed anywhere; it's best to go to a taxi stand or about 50m from traffic lights. While there are thousands of taxis, it may be convenient to pre-book if travelling at peak times (see the telephone numbers at the end of this section). The taxis' bells are an alarm warning cabbies once they're over the 80 km per hour expressway speed limit. Fares start at S$2.40 for the first kilometre, and rise 10¢ for every subsequent 240m up to 10 km, after which they rise by 10¢ every 225m. For every 30 seconds waiting time 10¢ is also added. There is a peak period surcharge of S$1 for trips commencing between 0730 and 0930 Monday-Saturday, between 1630 and 1900 Monday-Friday, and from 1130 to 1400 on Saturday. These surcharges do not apply on public holidays. A surcharge of S$1.50 is levied on all trips beginning from the Central Business District (CBD) between 1630 and 1900 on weekdays and between 1130 and 1400 on Saturday (except on public holidays). If this surcharge is levied then the peak period surcharge does not apply. If there are more than two passengers there is a 50¢ surcharge; luggage costs S$1 extra and there's a 50% 'midnight charge' from 2400 to 0600. There is also a S$3 surcharge for journeys starting from (but not going to) Changi International Airport or Seletar Airport, and a S$3.20 flat fee for calling a radio taxi which rises to S$5.20 if booked more than 30 minutes in advance. Trips paid for with credit cards enjoy a 10% surcharge on top of the fare, and taxis hired between 1800 on the evening before a public holiday up to 2400 on the day of the public holiday also get hit with a S$1 surcharge. TIBS taxis now has a fleet of London cabs which may be hired by the hour, and have the advantage of accommodating five passengers. There's a surcharge here too though, of S$1. Even with this veritable extravaganza of surcharges, Singapore's taxis are still excellent value for money and are certainly worth considering if in a group of three or four. Not only do they provide a view of Singapore which is absent from the MRT (at least in the city centre), but taxi drivers, like their brothers (and a few sisters) in most cities, are a great source of information, from political opinion to tourist practicalities. Unlike most of the rest of Asia, language is not a barrier to communication.

Other local transport

The CBD area scheme restricts all cars and taxis from entering the area between 0730-1900 Monday-Friday, 0730-1015 Saturday, unless they purchase an area licence (S$3 cars, $1 for motorbikes). Passengers entering the restricted zone are liable unless the taxi is already displaying a licence. Taxis displaying red destination labels on their dashboards are going home and are only required to take passengers in the direction they are going. Taxis are usually plentiful; there are stands outside most main shopping centres and hotels. Smoking is illegal in taxis. For taxi services ring: *Comfort CabLink* T5521111, *Premier Cabs* T5522828, *City Cab* T5522222, *TIBS* T4811211.

Trishaw, descendants of the rickshaw, have all but left the Singapore street-scene. A few genuine articles can still be found in the depths of Geylang or Chinatown, Serangoon Road, by Bugis Village, off Victoria Street, or outside Raffles City, but most now cater for tourists and charge accordingly, making trishaws the most expensive form of public transport in town. As ever, agree a price before climbing in and expect to pay about S$20 for a moderate length journey. Top hotels offer top dollar trishaw tours. Off-duty trishaw drivers hang out in a large pack at the bottom of Bras Basah Road, near the Singapore Art Museum. The eponymous *Trishaw Tours Pte*, T5456311/8283133, also offers trishaw tours.

Hitchhiking The idea is anathema to most Singaporeans and those trying are unlikely to have much success.

Boat Ferries to the southern islands like Sentosa, Kusu and St John's leave from the World Trade Centre or it is possible to hire a sampan from Jardine Steps on Keppel Road or Clifford Pier. Boats for the northern islands go from Changi Point or Ponggol Point.

Tours of the island For those constrained by time, there is a wide choice of organized tours which cover everything from cultural heritage to island-hopping, eating and shopping. Most city and island tours take about 3½ hours and, depending on admission fees to various sights, cost between S$25 and S$50. For a full day tour expect to pay around S$60-70. Children usually go for slightly more than half-price.

Boat trips **Harbour and Kusu Island** A variety of harbour and island cruises are available from Clifford Pier, but not during the Kusu festival which falls during August or September. The standard cruise takes 2-3 hours and includes a 30 minute stop at Kusu Island where passengers can disembark and see the Malay temple there. Craft vary from bumboats to imperial Chinese vessels (with modern facilities) and luxury cruise boats. Prices range from S$20-29 for the 2-3 hour jaunt with drinks included. Most operate three departures daily: a morning cruise (1030), a 'high tea' excursion (1500) and an 'imperial' evening dinner extravaganza (1830). For starlit dinners prices are higher at S$36-49. Companies that offer these cruises include: *Singapore River Cruises and Leisure*, T2276863 and *WaterTours*, T5339811. Alternatively, it is possible to hire a bumboat yourself, but expect to pay around S$60 per hour.

Tour operators There are many other and varied tours available in Singapore. The Peninsula Plaza, on the corner of Coleman Street and North Bridge Road contains a plentiful supply of travel agents offering discount prices on air tickets. Check in the Singapore Tourist Board's *Official Guide* for what's currently on offer.

Singapore's leading tour operators are: *Holiday Tours*, T7382622; *RMG Tours*, T2201661; *Singapore Sightseeing Tour East*, T3323755; *Singapore Explorer*, T3396833; *Chinatown Tram*, T7346936; *Gray Line Tours*, T3318244; *Malaysia and Singapore Travel Centre*, T7378877; *Sentosa Discovery Tours*, T2779564; and *SH Tours*, T7349923.

Keeping in touch

Language No English-speaking visitor to Singapore need fear that they will not be able to make themselves understood. The official languages are Malay, Chinese (Mandarin), Tamil and English. Interestingly, Malay is the national language and English, the language of administration. Because of the Republic's importance as an international trade centre, there is a high standard of English in business. Many dialects of Chinese are also spoken although the government's 'Speak Mandarin' campaign has begun to change this. Most Singaporeans speak their own lilting and musical version of English, which is dubbed 'Singlish', and is an English patois full of curious Chinese (largely Hokkien and Cantonese) and Malay-inspired idiosyncrasies and phonetic peculiarities.

The main **Post Office** is in Crosby House, Robinson Road and offers a basic service round the clock. **Local postal charges**: start at 22¢, aerograms, 35¢. **International postal charges**: 50¢ (postcard), S$1 (letter, 10g). **Post Office opening hours**: 0830-1700 Monday-Friday, 0830-1300 Saturday. Changi Airport, 0800-2000 Monday-Sunday. **Fax and telex services**: all post offices and almost all hotels have facilities for outgoing messages. The Singapore Post Office provides four sizes of sturdy carton, called Postpacs, for sending parcels abroad. These can be bought cheaply at all post offices. **Poste Restante**: Poste Restante Service, Crosby House, Robinson Road, Singapore. Correspondents should write the family name in capital letters and underline it to avoid confusion.

Postal services

Local In public phones the minimum charge is 10¢ for 3 minutes. Card phones are quite widespread - cards can be bought in all post offices as well as in supermarkets and newsagents and come in units of S$2, S$5, S$10, S$20 and S$50.

Telephone services

Directory enquiries: T103
Local call assistance: T100
Operator-assisted & international calls: T104
Operator-assisted calls to Malaysia: T109

International Singapore's IDD code is 65. For details on country codes dial 162. International calls can be made from public phones with the red 'Worldphone' sign; these phones take 50¢ and S$1 coins or phonecards. International Phone Home Cards are available at all post offices and come in units of S$10 and S$20. Credit card phones are also available. IDD calls made from hotels are free of any surcharge.

Singapore is seriously wired and there are lots of internet cafés. Stamford Road seems to have become a bit of a Mecca in this regard. *Internet city*, 11 Stamford Road, www.internetcity.com.sg. *Chills café*, 39 Stamford Road. *T2* Changi International Airport, 036-120/121 (Level 3), PO Box 1046 Changi Airport, 918156, T5461968, F5461969. *Cybernet Café*, 57 Tanjong Pagar Road, 088478, T3244361, F3244362. *Internet Centre*, Transit North, Changi International Airport, 026-110-01, T5461968, F5461969. *Café@Boat Quay*, 82 Boat Quay, T230014. *Cyberheart Café*, Orchard Road, T7343877.

Internet cafés

Newspapers and magazines The press is privately owned and legally free but is carefully monitored and strictly controlled. It runs on Confucianist principles - respect for one's elders - which translates as unwavering support of the government. In the past, papers that were judged to have overstepped their mark, such as the former *Singapore Herald*, have been shut down. The *Straits Times* has been likened to Beijing's *People's Daily* for the degree to which it is a mouthpiece of the government.

Media

The English language dailies are the *Straits Times* (and the *Sunday Times*), which runs better foreign news pages than any other regional newspaper (available at www.asial.com.sg/straitstimes); the *Business Times* and the *New Paper*, Singapore's very own tabloid. A more recent addition is the *Asian Times* printed in Singapore, Bangkok and Hong Kong. It is an independently run and owned newspaper with high standards of reporting and photography.

Most international news and business magazines can be found in bookshops and on news stands. Many other US, Australian and European general interest glossies are also on sale. Pornographic publications are strictly prohibited under Singapore's Obscene Publications Act. Sometimes this extends to weekly glossies like *Cosmopolitan*. In 1998 the Ministry of Information and the Arts revoked the publishing permit of the British men's magazine *FHM* because it persisted in publishing 'illustrations normally associated with risqué soft porn' magazines.

Singapore

Radio Daily services in English and Chinese from 0600-2400, in Malay from 0445-2400 and Tamil from 0500-2100. There are five local radio stations and two on nearby Batam Island which blast rock music across the Straits of Singapore. The BBC World Service broadcasts 24 hours a day on FM 88.9 thanks to an old British forces transmitter. The *London Calling* programme guide is available from bookshops.

Television Channels 5, 8 and 12 show English, Chinese, Malay and Tamil programmes; most sets also receive Malaysian channels. Many large hotel TV sets receive satellite channels and are also linked with the teletext system, which has information on entertainment, sports, finance, aircraft arrivals and departures and special events from 0700-2400. Programmes for all channels are listed in the daily newspapers.

Food and drink

See box opposite for our restaurant price guide For a full listing of eating places in Singapore, see page 628

Eating is the national pastime in Singapore and has acquired the status of a refined art. The island is a tropical paradise for epicureans of every persuasion and budget. While every country in the region boasts national dishes, none offers such a delectably wide variety as Singapore. Fish-head curry must surely qualify as the national dish but you can sample 10 Chinese cuisines, North and South Indian, Malay and Nonya (Straits Chinese) food, plus Indonesian, Vietnamese, Thai, Japanese, Korean, French, Italian (and other European), Russian, Mexican, Polynesian, and Scottish. There's a very respectable selection of western food at the top end of the market, a few good places in the middle bracket and swelling ranks of cheaper fast food restaurants like *Kentucky Fried Chicken* and *McDonald's* and an explosion of pizza outlets. For young trendy Singaporeans, coffee culture has replaced food court fare and the favoured spots are places like *Delifrance, Spinelli's* and *Starbuck's* which are giving a buzz to thousands.

Do not be put off by characterless, brightly lit restaurants in Singapore: the food can be superb. Eating spots range from high-rise revolving restaurants to neon-lit pavement seafood extravaganzas. A delicious dinner can cost as little as S$3 or more than S$100 and the two may be just yards away from each other. For example, it is possible to have a small beer in one of the bars of the Raffles Hotel for S$8 or more and then stagger 10m across the road and indulge in a huge plate of curry and rice for S$2. For a listing of over 100 more pricey restaurants, *Singapore's Best Restaurants* is worth purchasing; it gives a description of the food and a price guideline and is available from most bookstores for $10.30. It is updated annually. *The Secret Food Map* (available at most bookstores for S$5) is also a good buy.

Hawker centres & food courts The government might have cleared hawkers off the streets, but there are plenty of hawker centres in modern Singapore. Food courts are the modern, air-conditioned, sanitized version of hawker centres. They provide the local equivalent of café culture and the human equivalent of grazing. Large numbers of stalls are packed together under one roof. Hawker centres are found beneath HDB blocks and in some specially allocated areas in the city while food courts are usually in the basement of shopping plazas. The seats and tableware may be basic, but the food is always fresh and diners are spoilt for choice. Customers claim themselves a table, then graze their way down the rows of Chinese, Malay and Indian stalls. It is not necessary to eat from the stall you are sitting next to. Vendors will deliver to your table when the food is ready and payment is on receipt. The food is cheap and prices are non-negotiable.

Coffee shops Mainly family concerns, traditional Singaporean coffee shops or *kopi tiam* are located in the older part of the city, usually in old Chinese shophouses. They serve breakfast, lunch and dinner, as well as beer, at prices only marginally higher than those at hawker centres.

Singapore

Restaurant price guide

5	over S$40
4	S$20-39
3	S$10-19
2	S$5-9
1	below S$5

Drink

Every hawker centre has at least a couple of stalls selling fresh fruit juice, a more wholesome alternative to the ubiquitous bottles of fizzy drink. A big pineapple or papaya juice costs S$2. You can choose any combination of fruits to go in your fruit punch. Freshly squeezed fruit juices are widely available at stalls and in restaurants. Fresh lime juice is served in most restaurants, and is a perfect complement to the banana-leaf curry, tandoori and dosai. Carbonated soft drinks, cartons of fruit juice and air-flown fresh milk can be found in supermarkets. For local flavour, the Malay favourite is *bandung* (a sickly-sweet, bright pink concoction of rose essence and condensed milk), found in most hawker centres, as well as the Chinese thirst quenchers, soya bean milk or chrysanthemum tea. *Red Bull* (*Krating Daeng*), the Thai energy tonic is also widely available and is the toast of Singapore's army of Thai building site labourers.

Tiger and Anchor beers are the local brews and Tsingtao, the Chinese nectar, is also available. Tiger Beer was first brewed at the Malayan Breweries with imported Dutch hops and yeast on Alexandra Road in 1932 and was the product of a joint venture between Singapore's Fraser & Neave and Heineken. Recently, Tiger Beer has produced two new brews: Tiger Classic, a strong bottled beer, and Tiger Light, which is now available on draught in some bars. Anchor was the result of German brewers Beck's setting up the rival Archipelago Brewery. Because of its German roots, Archipelago was bought out by Malayan Breweries in 1941 and is today part of the same empire. Some bars (such as *Charlie's* at Changi) specialize in imported beers but even local beer is expensive (around S$6 a bottle in hawker centres and S$8 a glass in bars and pubs). There is an international selection of drinks at top bars but they're often pricey. Coffee houses, hawker centres and small bars or coffee shops around Serangoon Road, Jalan Besar and Chinatown have the cheapest beer. Expect to pay around S$8-10 for half a pint of beer in most smart bars. Most bars do have a Happy Hour (or hours) though, where bargains can be had.

There is no shortage of wine available in Singapore, but it is expensive; Australian wines are generally a better deal than imported European ones. Supermarkets all have good wines and spirits sections.

The Singapore Sling is the island's best known cocktail. It was invented in the Raffles Hotel in 1915 and contains a blend of gin, cherry brandy, sugar, lemon juice and angostura bitters.

Singapore

Shopping

Singapore is a shopper's paradise. There is an endless variety of consumer goods and gimmicks, with no import duty or sales tax on most items. The choice seems almost unlimited. But don't be deluded that there are bargains galore with rock bottom prices to match the variety. Prices are, in fact, much the same as, say, those in Europe or the US. High wages, soaring rents and a strong dollar have all eaten into the country's price advantage. Singapore's retailers have had to weather several years of stagnant demand. Local shoppers seem to be spending their disposable income in other ways (or themselves go shopping abroad) and tourists no longer come with empty suitcases to stuff full of goodies. Even the people who used to come here from places like Manila, Bangkok and Jakarta can buy just about everything at home. That said, there are some good buys and sales can throw up the odd bargain.

Probably the best area for window shopping is the Scotts and Orchard Road areas, where many of the big complexes and department stores are located (see page 594). This area comes alive after dark and most shops stay open late. The towering Raffles

For a guide to shopping along Orchard Road, see page 594 For the GST (Goods and Service Tax) Tourist Refund Scheme, see page 559

Shopping centres and plazas

Chinatown Point *Eu Tong Sen Street, Chinatown, specializes in small handicrafts.*

Funan Centre *Squeezed in between the Excelsior and Peninsula hotels in the colonial core, with five floors of shops. A good place for electrical equipment - in particular notebooks and software. One of the best and biggest food courts in the area in the basement. Huge screen in central atrium shows cartoons, opera, and pop concerts; makes a good stopping-off spot if the children are tired.*

Liang Court *Opposite Riverside Point, and dominated by a large Diamaru department store, although there is also a big toy shop here - The Toy Place - as well as a good diving equipment shop. The Quayside Food Court in the basement is recommended (with a children's play area). There is a Swensen's on the ground floor. Opposite Liang Court, on the edge of Clarke Quay, there are a couple of great furniture shops.*

Marina Square and Millenia Walk *A huge area of shops with a wide range of exclusive designer labels. There is also an Asian furniture and furnishings area and quite a few carpet shops.*

Suntec City *holds children's stores such as Growing Fun and Oshkosh B'Gosh and designer labels, a wide choice of restaurants and a big food court looking out onto the spectacular fountain (nightly laser shows 2000-2200 at 15 minute intervals).*

Parco Bugis Junction *This trendy air-conditioned shophouse mall is on Victoria Street, north of the colonial core. It is packed with international names, as well as some quirky little shops and cafés. More fun to visit than most shopping centres. There is a mesmerizing fountain in the centre.*

Peninsula Plaza *Next to the Peninsula Hotel this is an old style shopping centre, mostly dedicated to electrical goods - cameras, videos and mobile phones.*

Pidemco Centre *South Bridge Road, Chinatown, good for traditional jewellery.*

Raffles City Complex *Opposite the Raffles Hotel, this huge glitzy, noisy and trendy shopping complex holds all the international (but not designer) labels - including M&S, Max Mara, Body Shop and Knickerbox. Asia's first Lego store is to be found here, third floor of Sogo. There are upmarket foodstalls on the lower level, with another mesmerizing fountain.*

Riverside Point *On the south side of the river, overlooking Clarke Quay. This new dockside development is reminiscent of London's Docklands or San Francisco's Canary Wharf. It is totally un-Asian in design, and quite attractive. Cinema on the top floor, restaurants along the riverfront.*

Sim Lim Tower and Sim Lim Square *Both these shopping centres are on the edge of Little India on Jalan Besar and both sell the same range of electrical equipment - cameras, hi-fi and desktop computers.*

Stamford House *On the corner of Stamford Road and Hill Street is this renovated and ornate colonial building with a range of upmarket shops. These include the Eagle's Art Gallery, an exclusive lighting shop, and the Pennsylvania Country Oven Restaurant and Pennsylvania House on the first floor for all your home décor New England needs. For details of shopping plazas on Orchard Road, see page 594.*

City complex, Parco at Bugis Junction and Marina Square are the other main shopping centres. The East Coast shopping centres are not frequented by tourists. Serangoon Road (or Little India), Arab Street and Chinatown offer a more exotic shopping experience with a range of 'ethnic' merchandise.

Best buys Singapore has all the latest electronic gadgetry and probably as wide a choice as you will find anywhere. It also has a big selection of antiques (although they tend to be over-priced), arts and crafts, jewellery, silks and batiks. For branded goods, Singapore is still marginally cheaper than most other places, but for Asian-produced products it is no longer the cheapest place in the region.

Singapore

This has been set up by the Singapore Tourist Board and has 500 shops on its books. Retailers who belong to this scheme are expected to abide by a code of conduct. The mark of a 'good retailer' is the red and white merlion emblem, and it is valid for the year it displays. The STB produce a booklet listing all their members.

The Good Retailers Scheme

Feel you've been unfairly ripped off? Then contact the Small Claims Tribunal on the fifth floor of the Apollo Centre, T4355937, F4355994. There's a fast track claims mechanism where visitors, after paying a S$10 fee, can have their cases against errant retailers heard, often within 24 hours.

Small Claims Tribunal

Although the government has come down hard on copy-watch touts, tourists can still occasionally be accosted (and ripped off), particularly along Orchard Road.

Touts

Holidays and festivals

Singapore's cultural diversity gives Singaporeans the excuse to celebrate plenty of festivals, most of which visitors can attend. The Singapore Tourist Board produces a brochure every year on festivals, with their precise dates. The dates given here for movable festivals are for 2000-2001. For the latest information, you can check the Singapore Tourist Board's website, www.newasia-singapore.com. *The Monkey King* by Timothy Mo is very descriptive of Chinese customs and festivals, although it is set in Hong Kong.

New Year's Day (1 January – public holiday).

Chinese New Year (movable – public holiday) This 5-day lunar festival celebrated in January or February is the most important event in the entire Chinese calendar. Each new year is given the name of an animal in 12-year rotation and each has a special significance. The seasonal Mandarin catchphrase is *Gong Xi Fa Chai* (Happy New Year).

January-February

Thaipusam (movable - in the Hindu month of Thai) In honour of the Hindu deity Lord Subramaniam, or Murgham, the son of Lord Siva; he represents virtue, bravery, youth and power. Held during the full moon in the month of Thai, it is a festival of penance and thanksgiving. Hindus also believe that wishes made during the 2-day festival will be granted. On the day before the main ceremony, devotees follow a statue of Lord Subramaniam in procession from the Chettiars' Temple (or Sri Thandayuthapani Temple) on Tank Road to the Vinayagar Temple on Keong Saik Road. But the highlight of Thaipusam is the second day, when devotees assemble in their thousands at the Sri Perumal Temple on Serangoon Road. Devotees pay homage to Lord Subramaniam by piercing their bodies, cheeks and tongues with sharp skewers (*vel*) and hooks weighted with oranges and carrying steel structures bearing the image of Lord Subramaniam.

Jade Emperor's Birthday (movable) Crowds converge on the Giok Hong Tian Temple on Havelock Road to celebrate the Jade Emperor's birthday. A Chinese opera is performed in the courtyard of the temple and lanterns are lit in the doorways of houses.

T'se Tien Tai Seng's (the Monkey God's) Birthday (movable – but celebrated twice a year, in February and October) Participants go into a trance and pierce their cheeks and tongues with skewers before handing out paper charms. Celebrated at the Monkey God Temple, Eng Hoon Street near Seng Poh market, Tiong Bahru Road, South Chinatown.

Hari Raya Puasa or Aidil Fitri (movable) Marks the end of Ramadan, the month of fasting for Muslims and is a day of celebration. Once the Muftis have confirmed the new moon of Syawal, the 10th Islamic month, Muslims don traditional clothing and spend the day praying in the mosques and visiting friends and family. During Ramadan, Muslims gather to eat at stalls after dark; Geyland Serai and Bussorah Street (near Arab Street) are favourite makan stops.

Singapore

March-April **Kwan Yin's Birthday** (movable) Chinese visit temples dedicated to the goddess of Mercy (like the one on Waterloo Road). Childless couples come to pray for fertility.

Qing Ming (movable - early April) A Chinese ancestor-worship extravaganza in which family graves are spruced up and offerings of food and wine placed on tombs to appease their forebears' spirits.

Songkran (movable) This Buddhist water festival is celebrated in Thai Buddhist temples. To welcome the New Year, the image of the Buddha is bathed and celebrants are sprinkled with water, as a sign of purification. Offerings of flowers, incense and candles are brought to the temples. The Anada Metyarama Temple on Silat Road is the best place to see this festival.

Tamil New Year (movable April/May) Begins at the start of the Hindu month of Chithirai. Pujas are held at Singapore's main temples to honour Surya, the sun god. An almanac containing the Hindu horoscope is published at this time.

Easter (movable - Good Friday is a public holiday) Services are held in the island's churches. There is a candlelit procession in the grounds of St Joseph's Catholic Church, Victoria Street.

Hari Raya Haji (movable - falls on the 10th day of Zulhijjah, the 12th month of the Muslim calendar). This festival honours Moslems who have made the pilgrimage to Mecca. The feast-day is marked by prayers at mosques and the sacrificial slaughter of goats and buffalo for distribution to the poor as a sign of gratitude to Allah.

May-June **Singapore International Film Festival** (2 week-long festival, movable - April or May). An expanding film festival which shows 150 feature-length and short films. Venues include Capitol Cinema and various Golden Village cinemas.

Labour Day (1st: public holiday).

Vesak Day (movable - usually in May, on the full moon of the fifth lunar month - 18 May 2000) Commemorates the Buddha's birth, death and enlightenment and is celebrated in Buddhist temples everywhere. Kong Meng San Phor Kark See Temple in Bright Hill Drive and the Temple of a Thousand Lights in Race Course Road are particularly lively. In Singapore celebrations begin before dawn, monks chant sutras (prayers) and lanterns and candles are lit to symbolize the Buddha's enlightenment.

Birthday of the Third Prince (movable) Festivities to mark the birthday of this child-god, who carries a magic bracelet in one hand and a spear in the other, while riding wheels of wind and fire. Chinese mediums go into trance, slashing themselves with swords and spikes.

Dragon Boat Festival (movable) Honours the suicide of an ancient Chinese poet-hero, Qu Yuan. He drowned himself in protest against the corrupt government. In an attempt to save him, fishermen played drums and threw rice dumplings to try and distract predators. His death is commemorated with dragon boat races and the eating of rice dumplings. In contemporary Singapore these are international affairs with teams from over 20 countries.

Singapore Festival of Arts (movable, month-long, May-June). A very mini-Edinburgh festival with both mainstream acts and a fringe festival. Invited international groups and artistes.

August- **National Day** (9th August: public holiday) To celebrate the Republic's independence
September in 1965. The highlight of the day is the military parade, air force fly-past and carnival procession on and around the Padang and National Stadium. It is necessary to have tickets to get into the Padang area, but the whole thing is televised live and broadcast again on the weekend. Cheer leaders twirl to a 'Singapore we love you' chant. Political dignitaries and honoured guests look on from the courthouse steps.

Festival of the Hungry Ghosts (*Yu Lan Jie*) (movable - runs for 30 days after the last day of the sixth moon) This is the second most important festival after the lunar new year. Banquets are given by stallholders, lavish feasts are laid out on the streets and there are roving bands of Chinese street opera singers, puppet shows and lotteries. Then there is the ritual burning of huge incense sticks and paper 'hell money' to appease the spirits, who are believed to wander around on earth for a month after the annual opening of the gates of hell.

Mooncake or Lantern Festival (movable - midway through the Chinese eighth moon) This Chinese festival commemorates the overthrow of the Mongul Dynasty in China. Children parade with elaborate candlelit lanterns and eat mooncakes filled with lotus seed paste. According to Chinese legend, secret messages of revolt were carried inside these cakes and led to the uprising which caused the overthrow of their oppressors. A gentler interpretation is that the round cakes represent the full moon, the end of the farming year and an abundant harvest - a bucolic symbolism that must be lost on most city-born Singaporeans.

Pilgrimage to Kusu Island (movable) Around 10,000 Taoist and Muslim pilgrims, over a month, crowd onto ferries to this sacred but ugly little island, half an hour south of Singapore. There they make offerings at the Malay Kramat (shrine) or the Chinese temple dedicated to Ta-po-kung (Tua Pekong), also known as Datok Kung.

Navarathri Festival (movable) Nine days of prayer (*navarathiri* means 'nine lights'), temple music and classical dance honour the consorts of Siva, Vishnu and Brahma (the Hindu trinity of Gods); music and dance performances can be viewed at all Hindu temples from around 1930-2200 each night of the festival. The festival is celebrated notably at the Chettiar Temple on Tank Road, ending with a procession on the 10th day along River Valley Road, Killiney Road, Orchard Road, Clemenceau Avenue and returning to the temple.

Deepavali (movable - usually in October in the Hindu month of Aipasi, 28 October 2000) The Hindu festival of lights commemorates the victory of Lord Krishna over the demon king Narakasura, symbolizing the victory of light over darkness and good over evil. Every Hindu home is brightly lit and decorated for the occasion. Shrines swamped with offerings and altars piled high with flowers. Row upon row of little earthen oil lamps are lit to guide the souls of departed relatives in their journey back to the next world, after their brief annual visit to earth during Deepavali.

October- November

Guru Nanak's Birthday (movable) The first of the 10 gurus of the Sikh faith. The domed Gurdwara in Katong (Wilkinson Road) is buzzing on the Sikh holy day.

Thimithi Festival (movable, in the Hindu month of Aipasi) This Hindu festival in honour of the goddess Draupadi often draws a big crowd to watch devotees fulfill their vows by walking over a 3m long pit of burning coals in the courtyard of the Sri Mariamman Temple on South Bridge Road. Fire walking starts at around 1600 on the arrival of the procession from Perumal Temple on Serangoon Road.

Singapore

Christmas Day (25th: public holiday) Christmas in Singapore is a spectacle of dazzling lights, where the best is along Orchard Road, where the roadside trees are bejewelled with strings of fairy lights. Shopping centres and hotels compete to have the year's most extravagant or creative display. These seasonal exhibitions are often conveniently designed to last through to Chinese New Year. It would not be untypical, for example, to find Santa riding on a man-eater in the year of the tiger. In shopping arcades, sweating tropical Santa Clauses dash through the fake snow. Choirs from Singapore's many churches line the sidewalks and Singaporeans go shopping.

December

Entertainment

Neptune Theatre Restaurant, Collyer Quay. *Studebakers*, Penthouse of Pacific Plaza, Orchard Road. Live performances and dancing. *Boom Boom Room*, 3 New Bugis Street. Cabaret.

Cabaret/music
For a full listing of entertainment in Singapore, see page 641

Cinema With more than 50 cinemas, Singapore gets most of the blockbusters soon after their release in the US. The *Straits Times* Life section publishes listings daily. There are several new cinemas, showing three or four films at any one time. These include the complex at *Riverside Point* opposite Clarke Quay, **Parco Bugis Junction** on Victoria Street, opposite Bugis MRT, the **Lido Cineplex** at the Shaw Centre, Orchard Road and another new complex at *Suntec City*, Marina Square. For arthouse films, **The Picturehouse** next to the *Cathay* on Orchard Road is your best bet.

Health

Vaccinations Certificates of vaccination against cholera and yellow fever are necessary for those coming from endemic areas within the previous 6 days. Otherwise, no certificates are required for Singapore. There is no longer any malarial risk on the island, although sometimes there are outbreaks of dengue fever. Vaccination services are available at the Tan Tock Seng Hospital, Moulmein Road, T3595958 or T3595929 (telephone beforehand).

Water The water in Singapore, most of which is pumped across the causeway from Johor and is treated in Singapore, is clean and safe to drink straight from the tap.

Medical facilities
Ambulance: T995
Hospitals:
Alexandra, T4755222
East Shore, T3447588
Gleneagles, T4737222
Mount Elizabeth, T7372666
National Univeristy, T7795555
Singapore General, T2223322

Singapore's medical facilities are amongst the best in the world. See the *Yellow Pages* for listing of public and private hospitals, doctors (listed under 'Medical Practitioners'), acupuncturists and herbalists. Medical insurance is recommended. Hospitals are experienced in dealing with obscure tropical diseases and serious cases are flown here from all over the region. Most big hotels have their own doctor on 24 hour call. Pharmaceuticals are readily available over the counter. The Singapore Medical Centre (6th Floor, Tanglin Shopping Centre) houses a large community of specialist doctors. Local Chinese cures can be found in traditional clinics in Chinatown where there are medical halls and acupuncture centres.

Sights

Colonial core

Getting there If you are staying outside the immediate area, take the MRT to City Hall which is conveniently located between the Padang and Raffles City. If you are only interested in visiting the Singapore Art Museum, Singapore History Museum or Fort Canning Park, all situated in the north-west corner of this area, then Dhoby Ghaut MRT is marginally more convenient.

Ins & outs
For sleeping & eating, see pages 615 & 628 respectively

Getting around This area is small enough to walk around - just. To walk from the Singapore Art Museum in the far northwest corner of this area to the mouth of the Singapore River shouldn't take more than 30 mins. You may want to take a cab to get to Fort Canning Park if it is a particularly hot and humid day. Several of the newer hotels are in the Marina Bay area at the eastern edge of the Colonial core.

The Colonial core lies to the north of the Singapore River. It is bordered to the northeast by Rochor Road and Rochor Canal Road, to the northwest by Selegie Road and Canning Hill and to the southeast by the sea. Compared with Chinatown or Little India, the Colonial core can seem rather cold. The buildings are grand rather than homely and the roads more like boulevards than lanes. After all, this was where the business of administration was carried out - it was not where people lived.

At the heart of the Colonial core is the Padang, an open, grassed area surrounded by languid rain trees. It is the site of most big sporting and other events in Singapore, including the National Day parades. Many of the great events in Singapore's short history have been played out within sight or sound of the Padang. It was close to here that Stamford Raffles first set foot on the island on the morning of 28 January 1819, where the Japanese surrendered to Lord Louis Mountbatten on 12 September 1945, and where Lee Kuan Yew, the first prime minister of the city state, declared the country independent in 1959.

The area to the north of the Padang has been gradually reclaimed over the years. Until the 1880s, Beach Road was just that - on the beach - while it is now some way inland. The Marina Bay area to the southeast of Nicoll Highway has only been reclaimed and developed since the 1980s and is now a confection of luxury hotels, air-conditioned shopping arcades and conference halls.

Rather more enticing is the area northwest of the Padang where there are several excellent museums, the grand *Raffles Hotel* and the sights of Canning Hill. Many of the early buildings were designed by the Irish architect, George Coleman including the Armenian Church, Caldwell House and Maxwell House. Singapore's other main architect of the period was Alfred John Bidwell, who was responsible for the main wing of *Raffles Hotel*, the *Goodwood Park Hotel*, Stamford House, St Joseph's Church, the Singapore Cricket Club and the Victoria Memorial Hall.

The Padang ('playing field' in Malay) originally fronted on to the sea, but due to land reclamation now stands a kilometre inland. After the founding of Singapore in 1819, English and Indian troops were quartered here and the area was known as the Plain. The name was only later changed to Padang. In 1942, when Singapore fell to the invading Japanese, the European population of the colony were massed on the Padang before the troops were marched away to prisoner-of-war camps, some to camps in Malaya and Siam (where they helped to build the infamous Bridge over the River Kwai), others to Changi (see page 614). The **Cricket Club**, at the end of the Padang, was the focus of British activity. A

The Padang

Singapore general

Singapore

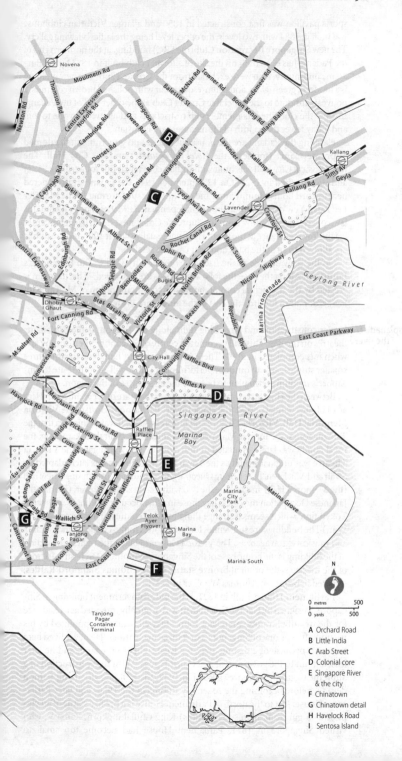

Novena

Moulmein Rd

Thomson Rd

Newton Rd

Central Expressway

Norfolk Rd

Cambridge Rd

Dorset Rd

Owen Rd

Rangoon Rd

Race Course Rd

Balestier St

McNair Rd

Towner Rd

Boon Keng Rd

Bendemeer Rd

Kallang Bahru

Kallang

Kallang Av

B

Lavender St

Serangoon Rd

Kitchener Rd

Sims Av

Geyla

Kallang Rd

Cavanagh Rd

Bukit Timah Rd

Edinburgh Rd

Central Expressway

C

Syed Alwi Rd

Jalan Besar

Albert St

Dhoby Selegie Rd

Bencoolen St

Middle St

Rochor Rd

Ophir Rd

Rochor Canal Rd

Lavender

Crawford St

Jalan Sultan

Geylang River

M Sultan Rd

Clemenceau Av

Dhoby Ghaut

Fort Canning Rd

Bras Basah Rd

Victoria St

North Bridge Rd

Bugis

Beach Rd

Nicoll Highway

Republic Blvd

Marina Promenade

City Hall

Connaught Drive

Raffles Blvd

Raffles Av

D

East Coast Parkway

Havelock Rd

Merchant Rd

North Canal Rd

Raffles Place

Singapore River

Marina Bay

Eu Tong Sen St

New Bridge

Pickering St

Cross St

South Bridge St

Telok Ayer St

Cecil St

Robinson Rd

Raffles Quay

E

Marina City Park

Marina Grove

Keong Saik Rd

Neil Rd

Craig Rd

Tanjong Pagar

Maxwell Rd

Shenton Way

G

Wallich St

Tras St

Tanjong Pagar

Anson Rd

Cantonment Rd

Telok Ayer Flyover

Marina Bay

F

East Coast Parkway

Marina South

Tanjong Pagar Container Terminal

| 0 | metres | 500 |
| 0 | yards | 500 |

N

A Orchard Road
B Little India
C Arab Street
D Colonial core
E Singapore River
   & the city
F Chinatown
G Chinatown detail
H Havelock Road
I Sentosa Island

Singapore

sports pavilion was first constructed in 1850 and a larger Victorian clubhouse was built in 1884 with two levels, the upper level being the ladies' viewing gallery. The new **Singapore Recreation Club** (the SRC) building, at the northern end of the Padang, has been built on the site of a former club built in 1883 by the Eurasian community, who were excluded from the Cricket Club. The new building is a modern, green-glass, aquarium-esque affair with polished brown columns: a nouveau antidote to the venerable Cricket Club at the other end of the Padang. In 1963 the club lifted its membership restrictions and allowed anyone to join and today fewer than a fifth of the members are Eurasian.

Flanking the Padang are the houses of justice and government: the domed **Supreme Court** (formerly the *Hotel de l'Europe*) and the **City Hall**. The neo-classical City Hall was built with Indian convict labour for a trifling S$2m and was finished in 1929. On 12 September 1945 the Japanese surrendered here to Lord Louis Mountbatten and on the same spot, former Prime Minister Lee Kuan Yew declared Singapore's independence in 1959. Today it contains law courts - the overflow from the Supreme Court next door. To get in, enter via the lower entrance at the front. Hearings usually start at 1000 and the public are allowed to sit at the back and hear cases in session.

On the seaward side of the Padang from the City Hall is **Tan Kim Seng's Fountain**. Along the base the following words are inscribed: 'This fountain is erected by the municipal commissioners in commemoration of Mr Tan Kim Seng's donation towards the cost of the Singapore Water Works'.

Esplanade & the river

For a detailed map, see page 589

Under construction and stretching right along the seafront is the Esplanade: theatres on the Bay. This will become the centre of Singapore's performing arts when it is completed in 2001. There will be a concert hall, lyric theatre, three smaller studios, and an outdoor performing space. It will all contribute to Singapore's medium-term plan to become the arts centre of the region.

Between the High Street and Singapore River there are other architectural legacies of the colonial period: the **clock tower**, **Parliament House**, **the Victoria Memorial Hall**, **Victoria Theatre** and Empress Place. It was in this area that the Temenggongs, the former Malay rulers of Singapore, built their kampung; the royal family was later persuaded to move out to Telok Blangah. The **Victoria Theatre** was originally built as the Town Hall in 1856 but was later adapted by Swan and Maclaren, to celebrate Queen Victoria's jubilee, integrating a new hall (the Memorial Hall) and linking the two with a central clock tower. (During the Japanese Occupation the clock, like those in other occupied counties, was set to Tokyo time which seems a strange thing to do even during the Second World War.) The buildings are still venues for Singapore's multi-cultural dance, drama and musical extravaganzas. The Victoria Concert Hall in the right hand section of the building is the home base of the Singapore Symphony Orchestra. In front of the theatre is the original **bronze statue of Sir Thomas Stamford Raffles**, sculpted in bronze by Thomas Woolner in 1887.

Parliament House, built in 1827, is the oldest government building in Singapore. Designed by George Coleman, it was originally intended as a residence for the wealthy Javanese merchant John Maxwell, who was appointed by his friend Raffles as one of Singapore's first three magistrates. He never lived here however, because of a dispute over the legal rights to the land, and he later leased it out to the government as a Court House. With the construction of a Supreme Court in St Andrews Road in 1939, the building stood empty for a decade, before becoming the Assembly Rooms in the 1950s and later Parliament House. Just to the north of Parliament House is a bronze statue of an **elephant** - a gift from Siam's (Thailand's) King Chulalongkorn, Rama V, who visited Singapore in 1871. Parliament House had become too small to accommodate the expanding body of MPs and a new S$80m parliament complex has opened next to the old building.

Empress Place, on the river and near to the old parliament, was one of Singapore's first conservation projects. Built as the East India Company courthouse in 1865 and named after Queen Victoria, Empress of the Empire, it later housed the legislative assembly and then became in turn, part of the immigration department, the offices of other assorted government agencies, and a museum. Now this thoroughly confused building is undergoing yet another reincarnation as the second wing of the Asian Civilisations Museum, which is due to open in 2001 (see page 586).

Running from Raffles Avenue to the river-mouth is Queen Elizabeth Walk, which once ran along the waterfront but is now in danger of being swallowed up by the new opera house/theatre complex, which is under construction here. Further upstream, on the spot where he is believed to have first stepped on to the swampy shore in 1819, is a marble replica of the original **statue of Raffles**, founder of modern Singapore. The plaque on the base of the statue reads: 'On this historic site Sir Thomas Stamford Raffles first landed in Singapore on 28 January 1819 and with genius and perception changed the destiny of Singapore from an obscure fishing village to a great seaport and modern metropole'. The original, sculpted in bronze by Thomas Woolner in 1887, stands in front of the Victoria Theatre (see above). Within a betel spit of the statue is the wharf for cruises of the Singapore River. ■ *30 mins, S$9 adults, S$4 children.*

> **Queen Elizabeth Walk: back to the Padang**

Beyond the Padang is the world's tallest hotel, the *Westin Stamford*, part of the huge **Raffles City Complex** on Stamford Road. Designed by the Chinese-American architect, IM Pei (famous for the glass pyramid in front of the Louvre, and the Bank of China building in Hong Kong), it contains two hotels, offices and a shopping complex.

Just down the road are the four white pillars of the **War Memorial** in Memorial Park on Beach Road, better known as the four chopsticks, symbolizing the four cultures of Singapore: the Chinese, Malays, Indians and 'others'. It was built in memory of the 50,000-odd civilians who died during the Japanese occupation. A memorial service is held at the monument on 15 February each year.

The revamped Raffles Hotel , with its 875 designer-uniformed staff (there is a ratio of two staff to every guest) and 104 suites (each fitted with Persian carpets), eight restaurants (and a Culinary Academy) and five bars, playhouse and custom-built, leather-upholstered cabs, is the jewel in the crown of Singapore's tourist industry. In true Singapore-style it manages to boast a 5,000 m² shopping arcade and there's even a museum of Rafflesian memorabilia on the third floor ■ *1000-2100 Mon-Sun, free.* Next to the museum is the **Jubilee Hall Theatre**, named after the old Jubilee Theatre demolished to make way for the Raffles extension (see below).

> **Raffles Hotel: watering hole or national monument?**

Raffles Hotel's original (but restored) billiard table still stands in the Billiard Room. Palm Court is still there and so is the Tiffin Room, which still serves tiffin. Teams of restoration consultants undertook painstaking research into the original colours of paint, ornate plasterwork and fittings. A replica of the cast-iron portico, known as 'cad's alley' was built to the original 19th century specifications of a Glasgow foundry.

Although just about anyone who's anyone visiting Singapore still makes a pilgrimage to the hotel, there has been a vigorous debate over whether or not in the process of its lavish restoration, Raffles has lost some of its atmosphere and appeal. There is no doubt that it has been done well - architecturally it can hardly be faulted and the lawns and courtyards are lush with foliage. There is also no

Singapore

doubt that it is a very comfortable and well-run hotel. But critics say they've tried a little too hard. The month after it reopened (on former Prime Minister Lee Kuan Yew's birthday, 16 September 1991), *Newsweek* said that in trying to roll a luxury hotel, a shopping mall and a national tourist attraction into one: "The result is synergy run amok ... great if you need a Hermes scarf, sad if you'd like to imagine a tiger beneath the billiard table." Other critics have asked whether the hotel should really be viewed as a national monument. While the hotel was undergoing expansion in 1990-91, the old Jubilee Theatre was torn down to make space for it. The Jubilee Theatre was not only genuinely old - and architecturally just as significant - but it had also played a considerably larger part in the lives of Singaporeans. As local writer Heng put it in 1991, "but it is Raffles and Coward *et al* which are being preserved as heritage and not [the] Jubilee where mothers, aunts and cousins cried their hearts out for actress Ng Kuan Lai and her

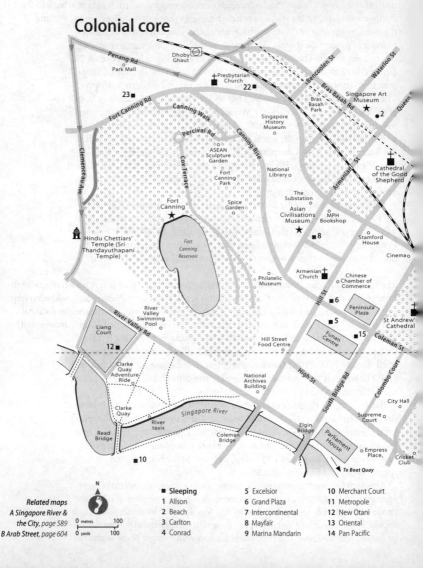

Colonial core

Related maps
A Singapore River & the City, page 589
B Arab Street, page 604

N

| 0 metres | 100 |
| 0 yards | 100 |

■ Sleeping	5 Excelsior	10 Merchant Court
1 Allson	6 Grand Plaza	11 Metropole
2 Beach	7 Intercontinental	12 New Otani
3 Carlton	8 Mayfair	13 Oriental
4 Conrad	9 Marina Mandarin	14 Pan Pacific

Singapore

misfortunes by the banks of the Li-Jiang [referring to one of the Hong Kong actress's best known films, *Blood Debt by the Banks of Lijiang River*]."

South of Raffles lies **St Andrew's Cathedral**, designed by Colonel Ronald MacPherson and built in the 1850s by Indian (Tamil) convict labourers in early neo-gothic style. Its interior walls are coated with a plaster called *Madras chunam*, a decorative innovation devised by the Indian labourers to conceal the deficiencies of the building materials. The recipe for Madras chunam was egg white, egg shell, lime and a coarse sugar (called jaggery), mixed with coconut husks and water into a paste. Once the paste had hardened, it was polished to give a smooth surface, and moulded to give many of the buildings their ornate façades. Note the window commemorating Raffles as the founder of modern Singapore. The cathedral is often packed - 13 percent of Singapore's population

Cathedrals & churches

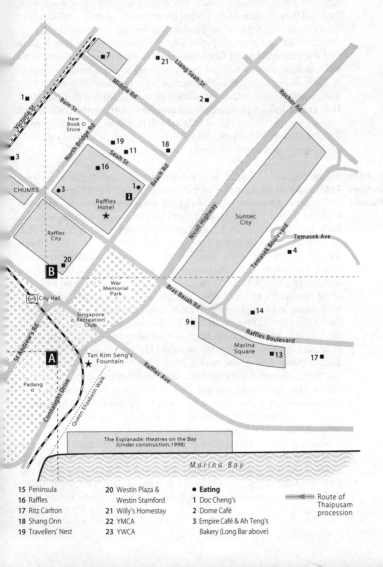

Singapore

15 Peninsula	20 Westin Plaza &	● **Eating**	
16 Raffles	Westin Stamford	1 Doc Cheng's	
17 Ritz Carlton	21 Willy's Homestay	2 Dome Café	
18 Shang Onn	22 YMCA	3 Empire Café & Ah Teng's	Route of Thaipusam procession
19 Travellers' Nest	23 YWCA	Bakery (Long Bar above)	

are Christian - and there are several services a day in different languages (see the notice board in the northwest corner of the plot for times of service).

Built in 1835 (the spire was added in 1850), the **Armenian Church of St Gregory the Illuminator** (the first monk of the Armenian church) on Hill Street is the island's oldest church and was designed by Irish architect George Coleman. This diminutive church seats 50 people at a squeeze. The design is said to have been influenced by London's St Martin-in-the-Fields and Cambridge's Round Church. The construction of the church was largely funded by Singapore's small Armenian community, although a number of non-Christian Asians also contributed. Agnes Joaquim is buried here - she discovered what is now the national flower of Singapore, the Vanda Miss Joaquim orchid. On the other side of the road from the church is a strange pagoda-roofed block, the **Singapore Chinese Chamber of Commerce and Industry** building. This rather unhappy edifice was erected in 1964. Two stone lions imported from mainland China guard the entrance and the murals on either side of the gate are copies of similar murals in Beijing.

One of George Coleman's pupils, Denis McSwiney, designed the **Roman Catholic Cathedral of the Good Shepherd**, on the junction of Queen Street and Bras Basah Road. It was used as an emergency hospital during the Second World War. The building has been gazetted as a national monument, but even so looks as though it could do with a lick of paint. **CHIJMES** or the **Convent of Holy Infant Jesus**, opposite the Cathedral on Victoria Street, is a complex consisting of the convent, chapel and **Caldwell House**, which was designed by George Coleman. It has been redeveloped by a French architect into a sophisticated courtyard of shops, pubs and restaurants.

Asian Civilisations Museum Also on Armenian Street, close to Stamford Road, is a newly restored school. Tao Nan School was built in 1910 and became one of the first Chinese schools in Singapore. It has been taken over by the Singapore Museums Department and in 1997 opened as the Asian Civilisations Museum. As its name suggests, the focus of the museum is Asian culture and civilization, all 5,000 years of it. The emphasis is on civilizations of the East (especially China) and Southeast Asia although the museum's remit extends further west to include the countries of South Asia (India, Pakistan, Bangladesh, Nepal and Sri Lanka) and west Asia (the Middle East). It consists of 10 galleries on three storeys and most of the displays are arranged along thematic lines - for example, symbolism, architecture and city planning, the literati, collecting and connoisseurship. The *Café Les Amis,* a French café, is attached to the museum. A second wing of the museum will be housed in Empress Place when major renovation works there are complete, see page 583. ■ *0900-1730 Tue, Thur-Sun, S$3 adults, S$1.50 children. Free guided tours in English Tue-Fri 1100 and 1400, Sat and Sun 1100, 1400 and 1530. For information on fringe activities at the Asian Civilisations Museum contact suziwati_sarnan@nhb.gov.sg or visit the website, www.museum.org.sg/nhb.* Almost next door to the museum is **The Substation**, 45 Armenian Street, which exhibits contemporary art and there is a rather alternative (for Singapore) coffee shop attached.

Nearby at 23B Coleman Street is the **Singapore Philatelic Museum** or **SPM** which opened to the public in 1995. It is a small but extremely well-run museum and is not just of interest to philatophiles. Children especially will find it a wonderful place to follow up on their stamp collections. ■ *0900-1730 daily, S$2, S$1 for children, 5 mins' walk from the City Hall MRT station.*

Bras Basah Road was so called because wet rice - *bras basah* in Malay - was dried here on the banks of the Sungai Bras Basah (now Stamford Canal). The former Catholic boys school, **St Joseph's Institution**, opposite the RC Cathedral at 71 Bras Basah Road, is another a good example of colonial religious architecture. Built in 1867, it is now home to the **Singapore Art Museum**, where there are several changing exhibitions every few months or so. It can be a welcome break from the heat to wander through the wondrously cool galleries. The Singapore Art Museum's own collection is modest and, understandably, predominantly features Singaporean and Malaysian artists' work. The museum also entertains travelling shows, both modern and classical. ■ *0900-1730 Tue-Sun, S$3 adults, S$1.50 children and senior citizens. Guided tours at 1100 and 1400, daily (1030 in Japanese) and at 1530 on Sat and Sun. For information on fringe activities at the museum contact suziwati_sarnan@ nhb.gov.sg, www.museum.org.sg/nhb.*

Singapore Art Museum

Across the green on Stamford Road is this museum; until a few years ago the only national museum in Singapore. However, now that the contemporary fine art (paintings, sculpture) collection has been shifted across the square to the Singapore Art Museum (see above) and the collection of Asian art has moved to the Asian Civilisations Museum (see page 586) on Armenian Street, the gallery has been left with the task of exhibiting on and educating about Singapore's history. The attached **Children's Discovery Gallery** has changing exhibits every six months. During the week it is closed for two hours every morning and afternoon for school groups. There is plenty of hands-on activity for children. ■ *0900-1730, closed Mon, S$3, children S$1.50. Conducted tours from the information counter at 1100 and 1400, Tue-Fri (1030 in Japanese). Slide shows through the day in the AV Theatre. For information on fringe activities at the museum contact suziwati_sarnan@nhb.gov.sg, www.museum.org.sg/nhb.*

Singapore History Museum

The library is behind the museum, on the other side of Canning Rise. It is a good place to browse, either on one of the many computers or along the bookshelves. The library has recently installed a new computer retrieval system which goes by the acronym VEGAS - the Virtual Exhibition Gallery System. For this the library has digitized part of its archives and visitors can examine old photographs and documents. ■ *Daily until 1700.*

National Library

Behind the museum is Fort Canning Park. The British called it Singapore Hill, but its history stretches back centuries earlier. It is known as Bukit Larangan or Forbidden Hill by the Malays as this was the site of the ancient fortress of the Malay kings and reputedly contains the tomb of the last Malay ruler of the kingdom of Singapura, Sultan Iskandar Shah. Archaeological excavations in the area have uncovered remains from the days of the Majapahit Empire. The name Canning Hill was given to this slight geological protuberance in the 1860s in honour of the first Viceroy of India, Viscount George Canning. Over the last few years Canning Hill has evolved into something a little more ambitious than just a park. The **Battle Box** opened in 1997. It is a museum contained within the bunker where General Percival directed the unsuccessful campaign against the invading Japanese. Visitors are first shown a video recounting, in 15 minutes or so, the events that led up to the capture of Singapore. They are then led into the Malaya Command HQ - the Battle Box - where the events of the final historic day, the 15 February 1942, are re-enacted. There is also a small traditional museum and a souvenir shop. ■ *Tue-Sun 1000-1800, last admission 1700, S$8, S$5 children.*

Fort Canning Park

Singapore

Above the Battle Box are the **ruins of Fort Canning** - the Gothic gateway, derelict guardhouse and earthworks are all that remain of a fort which once covered 3ha. There are now some 40 modern sculptures here. Below the sculpture garden to the southeast is the renovated **Fort Canning Centre** (built 1926) which is the home venue of Theatre Works and the Singapore Dance Theatre. In front of Fort Canning Centre is an old Christian cemetery - **Fort Green** - where the first settlers, including the architect George Coleman, are buried. On one side of Fort Green is a **Spice Garden** which recreates, on a small scale, the garden that Raffles established in 1822. Various spices and aromatic plants, including nutmeg, lemon grass and chilli, are cultivated here. On the other side is the **Asean Sculpture Garden** to which each member of Asean has donated a piece of work (although Asean's most recent signatories - Vietnam, Laos and Myanmar (Burma) - have yet to add their pieces). On the northwestern side of the Hill is the site of **Raffles' first house** which he had built in 1823, while the centre of the hill is given over to a reservoir and is out of bounds.

Chettiar Temple

Below Canning Hill, on Tank Road, is the Hindu Chettiar Temple, also known as the **Sri Thandayuthapani Temple**. The original temple on this site was built by wealthy Chettiar Indians (money lenders). It has been superseded by a modern version, finished in 1984, and is dedicated to Lord Subramaniam. The ceiling has 48 painted glass panels, angled to reflect sunset and sunrise. Its *gopuram*, the five-tiered entrance, aisles, columns and hall all sport rich sculptures depicting Hindu deities carved by sculptors trained in Madras. This Hindu temple is the richest in Singapore - some argue, in all of Southeast Asia. It is here that the spectacular Kavadi procession of the Thaipusam festival culminates (see page 575). ■ *Many Hindu temples close in the heat of the day so are best seen before 1100 and after 1500.*

Marina Square lies to the east of the colonial core on reclaimed land. This is home to Suntec City - Singapore's latest conference centre - a bevvy of five star hotels, an entertainment centre, an exclusive shopping mall, a food court and an arcade of restaurants.

Singapore River and the City

Ins & outs
For sleeping & eating, see pages 619 & 630 respectively

Getting there Raffles Place MRT station is in the heart of the financial district, just south of the Singapore River. Buses 124, 174 and 190 run direct from Orchard Road.

Getting around It is best to explore this area on foot - especially the river. To walk from Cavenagh Bridge near the mouth of the Singapore River to Clarke Quay takes about 20 mins. Bumboat tours of the river leave from Clarke Quay and Raffles Landing while a handful of boats offering an assortment of short cruises to the southern islands depart from Clifford Pier.

The Singapore River separates the high-rise, hi-tech financial district from the colonial heart of town. During the colonial period the contrast between its two banks could hardly have been greater. To the north was the heartland of colonial Singapore, with its grand administrative buildings and promenading Europeans. And to the south were the godowns and shophouses of the Chinese merchant community.

When Major Farquhar landed here with Raffles in 1819 he deemed that the north bank of the river was the only place suitable for European settlement, the south being too marshy. The river itself was the place where Singapore's lifeblood - trade - was transacted and the river was jammed with tongkangs, sampans and twakows. Some of the shophouses have been preserved, most notably those of Boat Quay and Clarke Quay, although today they serve food and drink, not trading interests.

The heart of Singapore's new wealth lies concentrated just south of the Singapore River. From the north bank the godowns and shophouses of Boat Quay, emblematic of Singapore's past vitality, stand framed against the towering corporate headquarters of Singapore's new banks and finance houses. The CBD doesn't offer much for most casual visitors, although some of the modern architecture is praiseworthy and there are one or two remnants of Old Singapore hidden away amidst the glass, steel and concrete.

Standing guard at the mouth of the Singapore River - though rather dwarfed now by a new bridge - is the mythical Merlion, half-lion, half-fish, the grotesque saturnine symbol of Singapore. The statue was sculpted by local artist Lim Nang Seng in 1972 and stands in the miniscule Merlion Park, an unaccountably popular stop for tour groups, where there is a souvenir shop which is sometimes rather ambitiously billed a museum. The merlion is best viewed from the Padang side of the river. It is inspired by the two ancient (Sanskrit) names for the island: *Singa Pura* meaning 'lion city', and *Temasek* meaning 'sea-town'. The confused creature is emblazoned on many a trinket and t-shirt.

Merlion
'Ulysses by the Merlion'
... this lion of the sea
Salt-maned, scaly,
wondrous of tail,
Touched with power,
insistent
on this brief
promontory...
Puzzles.
Edwin Thumboo

Cavenagh Bridge, erected in 1869 by convict labourers (the last big project undertaken by convicts here), was originally called Edinburgh Bridge to commemorate the visit of the Duke of Edinburgh. It was later renamed Cavenagh in honour of Governor WO Cavenagh, the last India-appointed governor of Singapore. The bridge was constructed from steel shipped out from Glasgow (supplied by the same company that furnished the Telok Ayer Market) and was built to provide a link between the government offices on the north side of the river and Commercial Square to the south.

Singapore River & the city

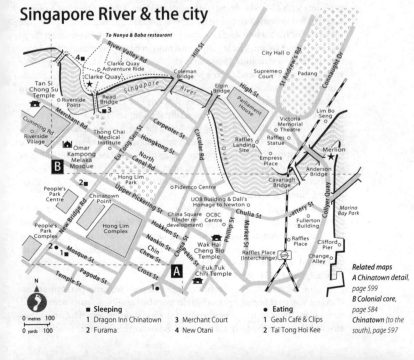

Singapore

Sleeping
1 Dragon Inn Chinatown
2 Furama
3 Merchant Court
4 New Otani

Eating
1 Geah Café & Clips
2 Tai Tong Hoi Kee

Related maps
A Chinatown detail,
page 599
B Colonial core,
page 584
Chinatown (to the
south), page 597

Boat Quay   Along the south bank of the river, facing Empress Place, is Boat Quay; commercially speaking, this is one of the Urban Redevelopment Authority's most successful restoration projects. At the beginning of the 19th century this part of the river was swampland and the original roomah [*rumah* means house] rakits were rickety, stilted affairs built over the mud. However, by the mid-1850s Boat Quay had emerged as the centre of Singapore River's commercial life with three-quarters of the colony's trade being transferred through the godowns here. The opening of the Suez Canal in 1869 increased trade still further but the development of the steamship around the same time threatened the commercial vitality of the area: vessels became too large to dock here. Merchants, worried that shipping companies would move their business to the new port of Tanjong Pagar which opened in 1852, began to use lighters or *tongkangs* to load and unload ships moored outside the river; *tongkangs*, barges and sampans once littered the river, but they were cleared out to Marina Bay, or destroyed and scuttled, as part of the government's river-cleaning programme over a period of 10 years. By the time the URA announced its conservation plans in 1986, Boat Quay had fallen on hard times. The original inhabitants were encouraged to leave, the shophouses and godowns were restored and renovated, and a new set of owners moved in. The strip now provides a great choice of drinking holes and restaurants for Singapore's upwardly mobile young, expats and tourists alike.

   Elgin Bridge marks the upriver end of Boat Quay. The bridge was built in 1929 to link the community of Chinese merchants settled on the south side of the river with the Indian traders of the High Street on the north side and was named after Lord Elgin, Governor-General of India.

Clarke Quay   Further upriver is Clarke Quay, which has also been renovated and redeveloped too. This was once godown country; in colonial days, the streets around the warehouses would have been bustling with coolies. It is now a pleasant pedestrian area with 150-odd shops, restaurants and bars. Clarke Quay has a slightly different feel to Boat Quay; while the latter consists of individual enterprises, the former is controlled by a single company which keeps close tabs on which shops and F&B outlets open. The atmosphere is more ersatz, more managed and controlled, and less vivacious. Unsurprisingly, this is more of a family place, while young, single people tend to congregate downriver at Boat Quay. In the pedestrian lanes, overpriced hawker stalls and touristy knick-knack carts set up from lunchtime onwards selling all manner of goods that people could do without. Despite this, it is still a lot of fun, especially at night, and unlike Boat Quay it is possible to snack from stalls while wandering the alleys of the area. On Sundays there is a flea market here. The big family attraction at Clarke Quay is the **Clarke Quay Adventure Ride**, a Singaporean Pirates of the Caribbean in which visitors take bumboats along an underground river, floating past 80 animated figures, and the noises and sights of Old Singapore. ■ *1100-2230 Mon-Sun, S$5, S$3 for children, family tickets available.*

   A good way of seeing the sights along Singapore River is on a bumboat cruise, which can be taken from Clarke Quay or Boat Quay. A rather banal recorded commentary points out the godowns, shophouses, government buildings and skyscrapers lining the riverbank. ■ *Bumboats operate 0900-2300, S$7, S$3 for children. A river taxi also operates from here, S$1 (morning) and S$3 (afternoon).*

   On the waterfront, a makeshift theatre provides **wayang performances**. Wayang was traditionally performed in tents by travelling artists who would move from town to town, performing for special occasions. The tongkangs moored alongside the quay are now used as floating restaurants. Traditionally they were used as lighters, to transport cargo from larger ships. The eyes were painted on them so that they could see where they were going. ■ *Wed and Fri at 1945-2030. The performers prepare themselves from 1800 onwards and onlookers are welcome to watch the making-up process.*

Spanning the river at Clarke Quay is a pedestrian bridge, **Read Bridge**, erected in the 1880s and named after a famous businessman of the day. Read Bridge leads to Riverside Point, an arcade of upmarket shops and restaurants. Across Merchant Road via an aerial walkway is yet another shopping centre-cum-restaurant complex called **Riverside Village**. At the north-west corner of the complex is the attractive **Tan Si Chong Su Temple** which has successfully resisted attempts at modernization. The temple was built in 1876 as an ancestral temple and assembly hall of the Hokkien Tan clan. The money was donated by Tan Kim Cheng (1829-1892) and Tan Beng Swee (1828-1884), sons of the wealthy philanthropist Tan Tock Seng. The temple faces the Singapore River - as *feng shui* (geomancy) dictates - and it is particularly rich in carvings and other decoration. The series of two courtyards and two altar halls symbolises *li*, the admired characteristic of humbling oneself in deference to others. The dragon-entwined columns, round windows and granite panels are comparatively unusual. Above the main altar table are four Chinese characters which translate as 'Help the world and the people'.

Riverside Point

Shenton Way (Singapore's equivalent of Wall Street), **Raffles Place**, **Robinson Road** and **Cecil Street**, all packed-tight with skyscrapers, form the financial heart of modern Singapore. These streets contain most of the buildings that give the city its distinctive skyline and it is best seen from the Benjamin Sheares Bridge or from the boat coming back from Batam Island. The first foreign institutions to arrive on the island still occupy the prime sites - the *Hong Kong and Shanghai Banking Corporation* and *Standard Chartered Bank*. One of the more striking new buildings on the river is the headquarters of the **United Overseas Bank** (UOB) on Chulia Street, which towers to the maximum permissable height of 280m (to avoid collision with low-flying aircraft). The octagonal tower is said to represent a pile of coins, although this seems simply too crass to believe. Below, in the open under-court area, is a large bronze statue by Salvador Dali entitled *Homage to Newton*, cast in 1985. A short walk away down Philip Street is the small **Wak Hai Cheng Bio Temple** built in 1826, looking particularly diminutive against the buildings around it. The name means Guangdong [Canton] Province Calm Sea Temple and the purpose is pretty clear: to ensure that Chinese immigrants making the voyage through the dangerous South China Seas arrived safely. The two key gods depicted here are Xuan Tien Shang Di (the Heavenly Father) in the right-hand hall and Tien Hou (the Heavenly Mother) in the left. Tien Hou is a particular favourite of sailors. The figures on the roof are extremely vivid and so is some of the carving inside.

Financial centre

See Chinatown map, page 597

Another piece of old Singapore amidst the new is the **Lau Pa Sat Festival Market**, once known as Telok Ayer, between Robinson Road and Raffles Quay. This was the first municipal market in Singapore. The first market here was commissioned by Stamford Raffles in 1822 but the present structure was designed by James MacRitchie and built in cast-iron shipped out from a foundry in Glasgow in 1894. (A little piece of irrelevance: the same foundry cast the iron for Cavenagh Bridge.) It is said to be the last remaining Victorian cast-iron structure in Southeast Asia and was declared a national monument in 1973 but had to be dismantled in 1985 to make way for the MRT, and was then rebuilt. It is now a thriving Food Centre.

Singapore

Orchard Road

Ins & outs
For sleeping & eating,
see pages 620 & 631
respectively

Getting there There are 3 MRT stations on, or close to, Orchard Road. Dhoby Ghaut MRT station lies at the eastern end of Orchard Road, close to the northwest corner of the Colonial core. The Somerset MRT stop is on Somerset Road, which runs parallel to Orchard Road. The Orchard MRT station is at the intersection of Orchard Road and Scotts Road, towards the western end of the strip and close to the main concentration of hotels. A profusion of bus services run along Orchard Road - at last count, some 20 in all.

Getting around To walk Orchard Road from end to end is quite a slog - from Dhoby Ghaut to the north-western end of Orchard Road past Scotts Road is around 2½ km. This is fine, though, if you're taking it slowly, stopping-off for brief respites in one of the many air conditioned shopping arcades. Otherwise consider hopping on a bus or taking the MRT.

Before being cleared for the construction of colonial mansions in the mid-1800s, the Orchard Road area was one vast nutmeg plantation. Choon Keng Tang, a rags-to-riches immigrant from Swatow, bought a plot of land on Orchard Road in 1945 and built CK Tang's Oriental curio store, in Chinese imperial style. In 1982 the old shop was demolished and the new hotel and department store complex went up; the eye-catching pagoda-style *Marriott Hotel* (once the *Dynasty*), with *Tang's* still next to it, is one of the last remaining remnants of Oriental style in an otherwise Occidental street.

Orchard Road is Singapore's catwalk, where the young and beautiful strut and preen, showing off their latest purchases. It is a shopper's paradise and is said to have the highest density of shops in the world, as well as being one of the world's most expensive shopping streets. Most things that the human heart - if

Orchard Road

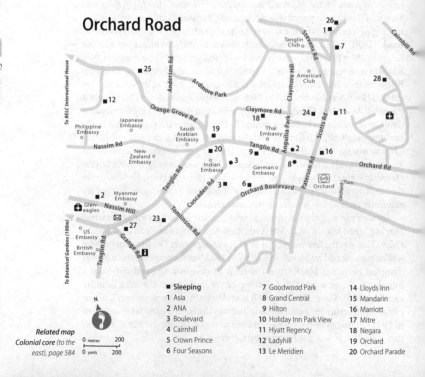

■ Sleeping	7 Goodwood Park	14 Lloyds Inn
1 Asia	8 Grand Central	15 Mandarin
2 ANA	9 Hilton	16 Marriott
3 Boulevard	10 Holiday Inn Park View	17 Mitre
4 Cairnhill	11 Hyatt Regency	18 Negara
5 Crown Prince	12 Ladyhill	19 Orchard
6 Four Seasons	13 Le Meridien	20 Orchard Parade

Related map
Colonial core (to the
east), page 584

0 metres 200
0 yards 200

not the soul - could desire seem to be for sale here: camcorders and CDs, mules and micros, gold and garnet. CK Tang may have been a committed Christian - his Department store is dedicated with the inscription To God be the Glory - but Orchard Road is dedicated to Mammon.

Amidst this shopping extravaganza encased in grandiose high-rise blocks, there are some remnants of Old Singapore which have managed to escape the demolition ball. In particular, there are one or two buildings on Cuppage Road, as well as the pleasant and peaceful Emerald Hill, with its bars and street cafés. The Peranakan (Straits Chinese) shophouses found here - which have been carefully restored to their original condition - were constructed at the beginning of this century and combine European and Chinese architectural elements.

Emerald Hill

This area was laid out by 30 different owners between 1901 and 1925: conforming to the established theme was considered good manners, which has resulted in a charming street of shophouses. The **Peranakan Place Museum** on Emerald Hill gives some idea of what Straits Chinese townhouses were originally like inside, although this recreation is not the best example. ■ *Open on request - contact George on T7326966, F7372411 - and usually only to groups. S$10, S$5 for children.*

Dhoby Ghaut

At the end of Orchard Road is Dhoby Ghaut, which got its name from the Bengali and Madrasi dhobies who used to wash the clothes of local residents in the stream which ran down the side of Orchard Road and dry them on the land now occupied by the *YMCA*. *Ghaut* is a Hindi word meaning landing place or path down to a river. *Dhoby* is from the Sanskrit word *dhona* meaning to wash. The dhobies would walk from house to house collecting their clients' washing, noting each piece down in a little book using a series of marks (they were illiterate).

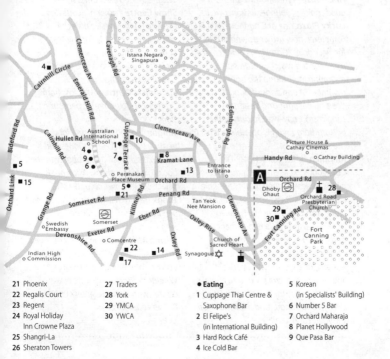

Singapore

21 Phoenix
22 Regalis Court
23 Regent
24 Royal Holiday
   Inn Crowne Plaza
25 Shangri-La
26 Sheraton Towers

27 Traders
28 York
29 YMCA
30 YWCA

● **Eating**
1 Cuppage Thai Centre &
   Saxophone Bar
2 El Felipe's
   (in International Building)
3 Hard Rock Café
4 Ice Cold Bar

5 Korean
   (in Specialists' Building)
6 Number 5 Bar
7 Orchard Maharaja
8 Planet Hollywood
9 Que Pasa Bar

Shopping centres on Orchard Road

Centrepoint, *dominated by* Robinsons *department store,* Mothercare, Lacoste, *large* Times Bookshop *and an* MPH Bookshop, *art Gallery on top floor:* Art Focus.

Far East Plaza, *14 Scotts Road: downmarket shops good for bargains, leather goods, cameras and watches. There are also money changers, tailors, several reasonable restaurants, a small food court, some good electronics shops and cheap CD roms here. Local department store,* Metro, *in the basement, sells clothes, household goods, shoes and accessories. Probably stays open the longest.*

Forum, *predominantly children's clothes* (Guess?, Kids and Baby Guess?) *and a Toys 'R' Us is here.*

Heeren, *has* HMV *music store,* Swatch *watches and* Electric City, *an electronic shop.*

Hilton Shopping Plaza – *connects* Hilton *and* Four Seasons Hotel – *top haute couture designers. Escalators state "Ladies watch your gowns".*

HPL House - Emporio Armani *and a good choice of younger designer wear.*

Lucky Plaza, *one of Singapore's first big complexes, now rather downmarket. OK for electronics* (Gameboys *here), cameras, jewellery and watches, scores of tailors; at ground level, along the front there are a number of opticians offering good deals on Raybans and designer sunglasses. Copy-watch touts at the bottom. Bargaining is possible in most of the stores here.*

Meridien, *by* Meridien Hotel, DFS Collections *in basement for duty free goods, large very good quality furniture store – old and new wooden products.*

Ngee Ann City, *a massive complex housing* Takashimaya *department store, and over 100 speciality stores, mainly fashion boutiques –* Burberrys, Louis Vuitton, Tiffanys, Chanel, Charles Jourdain *and several restaurants.* Sparks, *a disco, is on the top floor. Popular with the rich and famous and a hang out for the young and trendy.*

Orchard Emerald, *Quirky little individual shops – jewellery, unusual boutiques, etc.*

Orchard Point, *large Australian cut-price textiles,* B&N Factory Outlet. *Numerous art galleries and jade shops on the top with an emphasis on Chinese art.*

Pacific Plaza, *dominated by* Tower Records, *also quite a choice of upmarket hairdressers here.*

Palais Renaissance, *hideously trendy design, the best in designer-boutiques and branded goods* (Versace, DKNY, *etc).*

Plaza Singapura, Yaohan *department store and several music shops – both for CDs and for instruments.*

Paragon, *one of the best places for boutique browsers, particularly men's fashions; branded names. Also good for art galleries.*

Park Mall, *Penang Road one of the newer piazzas, full of interior design items: furniture, textiles, lamps. Food in basement.*

Scotts, *6 Scotts Road: department store, 'Picnic' food court in basement, smart female boutiques with contemporary designers. Good electronics shops.*

Shaw Centre, *corner of Scotts Road and Orchard Road: Massive hi-tech block, with a large* Isetan *department store, big bookshop,* Kinokuniya, *with a good range of English books and* Lido Cineplex *on top floors.*

Specialists' Centre, *just across from Centrepoint; downmarket department store.*

Tanglin, *top end of Orchard Road: a treasure trove of Asian antiques and curios, Persian rugs and probably the best bookstore for Southeast Asian books,* Select Books, *closes around 1800.*

Tangs, *next to* Marriott Hotel. *Very smart department store; the Harrods of Singapore.*

Wisma Atria, Isetan *department store, smart fashion boutiques, an* MPH *bookshop, and small food court.*

Wheelock Place, *one of the newer centres, with* Marks & Spencer *and* Borders *bookstore.*

Singapore

At the western end of Orchard Road are the Botanic Gardens, on Cluny Road, not far from Tanglin. The gardens contain almost half a million species of plants and trees from around the world in its 47 hectares of landscaped parkland, primary jungle, lawns and lakes. The Botanic Gardens were founded by an agri-horticultural society in 1859. In the early years they played an important role in fostering agricultural development in Singapore and Malaya as successive directors collected, propagated and distributed plants with economic potential, the most famous of which was rubber. Henry Ridley, director of the gardens from 1888-1912, pioneered the planting of the Brazilian para rubber tree (*Hevea brasiliensis*). In 1877, 11 seedlings brought from Kew Gardens in London were planted in the Singapore gardens. An immediate descendant of one of the 11 originals is still alive in the Botanic Gardens today, near the main entrance. By the lake at the junction of Tyersall and Cluny roads there is a memorial to Ridley on the site where the original trees were planted. Ridley was known as 'Mad Ridley' because of the proselytizing zeal with which he lobbied Malaya's former coffee planters to take up rubber instead. ■ *0500-2400 Mon-Sun.* The Botanic Gardens also houses the **National Orchid Garden** where 700 species and 2,000 hybrids of Singapore's favourite flower are lovingly cultivated. ■ *0830-1900, last ticket sales at 1800, S$2, S$1 children, T4709900. The closest entrance to the Botanics for the Orchid Garden is on Tyersall Avenue. Lots of buses run past the Botanics including SBS nos 7, 77, 105, 106, 123 and 174, alighting at the junction of Cluny and Napier roads, next to Gleneagles Hospital.*

Botanic Gardens

Chinatown

Getting there There is no MRT station within Chinatown proper, but there are two on the fringes. Raffles Place, within the financial district, is a short walk from the eastern edge of Chinatown while Outram Park is right at the western edge. Many bus services run through this area; nos 124, 143, 174 and 190 operate direct from Orchard Road. A new MRT line which is currently under construction will run through Chinatown.

Ins & outs
For sleeping & eating, see pages 623 & 634 respectively

Getting around Chinatown is fairly compact: walking around it is no great sweat. Many of the most interesting streets and alleys are best explored on foot - they are too narrow for buses.

Chinatown is one of the most attractive areas of Singapore to explore. Not only is it visually appealing and comparatively compact; it also has an abundance of cafés, bars and restaurants to retreat to when hunger or the heat become overwhelming.

While much of Old Chinatown has been consumed by Housing Development Board (HDB) blocks and high rise offices, the government recognised just in time that if the process of redevelopment continued unchecked, much of Singapore's urban history would be obliterated. To preserve some of the city's architectural history, the Urban Redevelopment Authority (URA) was established in the 1970s to list old buildings and provide a framework for restoration and conservation.

Immigrants from China settled in Singapore in the latter half of the 19th century, and recreated much of what they had left behind. Clan groups began migrating from the southern provinces of China to the *Nang Yang* or 'Southern Seas' in successive waves from the 17th century. By 1849 the Chinese population had reached 28,000, but the area they inhabited was largely confined to a settlement between Telok Ayer and Amoy streets. The greatest numbers migrated in the 40 years after 1870, mostly coming from the southeastern

Singapore

coastal provinces, with the Hokkiens forming the majority. Each dialect group established their own temple. The Hokkiens founded **Thian Hock Keng** in 1821, the Cantonese established **Fu Tak Chi** on Telok Ayer Street around the same time, as did the Teochews who built **Wak Hai Cheng Bio** on Philip Street. Streets, too, were occupied by different Chinese groups, with clubs and clan houses - or *kongsi* - aiding family or regional ties. The *kongsi* were often affiliated with secret societies, or *tongs* which controlled the gambling and prostitution industries and the drug trade.

Today, Chinatown is overshadowed by the 200m-high skyscrapers of the financial area and indoor markets have replaced the many street stalls and night markets that made the area a favoured tourist spot in days gone by. Many residents have moved out to new, modern flats in the HDB estates scattered around the island. Despite all the refurbishment and 'urban renewal', Chinatown remains one of the most interesting parts of town. The rows of once-derelict shophouses have been bought up, redeveloped and rented out as office space for small design companies, publishing companies, art galleries and so on.

The area known as **Kreta Ayer** encompasses **Smith**, **Temple**, **Pagoda**, **Trengganu** and **Sago streets**. This was the area that Raffles marked out for the Chinese kampong and it became the hub of the Chinese community, deriving its name from the ox-drawn carts that carried water to the area. Renovation by the URA has meant that these streets still retain their characteristic baroque-style shophouses with weathered shutters and ornamentation.

Chinatown architecture
The typical Straits Chinese house accommodated the family business on the ground floor leaving the second and third floors as family living quarters, sometimes accommodating two families (and in later years, as Chinatown became desperately overcrowded, up to five families). A few wealthy Chinese merchants, or *towkays*, built their houses according to traditional Chinese architectural conventions, but almost all of these have long since been demolished. One which has survived is the **Thong Chai Medical Institute** on Eu Tong Sen Street, at the corner of Merchant Road. It was built in southern Chinese palace style with three halls, two inner courts and ornamental gables and was completed in 1892. By the end of the 19th century it had become a centre for traditional medicine, offering its services free to the poor - *thong chai* means 'benefit to all'. In 1911, during a malaria outbreak, it distributed free quinine. The building also became a focal point for the Chinese community, being the headquarters for the Chinese guilds. The Chinese Chamber of Commerce began life here (its headquarters are now on Hill Street, see page 586).

The streets of Chinatown
In **Sago Street** (or 'death house alley' as it was known in Cantonese, after its hospices for the dying), **Temple Street** and **Smith Street**, there are shops making paper houses and cars, designed to improve the quality of the after-life for dead relatives (by burning the models after the funeral, it is believed that one's worldly wealth hurries after you into the next world). Also on these streets, shops sell all the accoutrements needed for a visit to a Chinese temple. At Number 36 Smith Street there is a three storey building that was originally home to a famous Cantonese opera theatre - Lai Chun Yen - and formerly Smith Street was also known as 'Hei Yuen Kai', or Theatre Street. The English probably gave Sago Street its name in the early 19th century as Singapore became a centre of high quality sago production for export to India and Europe. By 1849, there were 15 Chinese and two European sago factories here.

Perhaps because death and health go hand-in-glove, there are also a number of **Chinese medicine shops** in this area - for example, *Kwang Onn Herbal* at 14 Trengganu Street and others on Sago Street. Chinese traditional medicine halls still do a roaring trade, despite the advantages of Medisave schemes and 21st century pharmaceuticals. The **Hong Lim complex** on **Upper Cross Street** has several more such medicine halls. There are also a few skilled Chinese calligraphers still working from shops around Upper Cross Street.

Right next to *Kwang Onn Herbal* at 14b Trengganu Street, up a narrow staircase, is the **Chinaman Scholar's Gallery**, a mini-museum of life in the merchants' and scholars' houses in the 1920s. The gallery is run by Vincent Tan, an antique dealer. Visitors can sip Chinese tea as they wander around the kitchen, bedroom, dining and living areas, and flick through photographs. Mr Tan gives musical interludes with demonstrations of instruments from China, such as the lute, *pipa* (mandolin) and *yang chin* (harp). This is really a private home rather than a museum. ■ *0900-1700 Mon-Sun, but sometimes it's inexplicably closed - knock on the door and hope that someone is in. S$6, S$4 for children.*

As if to illustrate Singapore's reputation as a racial and religious melting-pot, the Hindu Sri Mariamman Temple is situated nearby at 244 South Bridge Road. There was a temple on this site as early as 1827, making it Singapore's oldest Hindu place of worship. Stamford Raffles is said to have granted the land to Narian Pillai, a Tamil who accompanied Raffles to Singapore during his second visit on board the *Indiana*, and set up Singapore's first brickworks. The building is dedicated to Sri Mariamman, a manifestation of Siva's wife Parvati. The temple is the site of the annual Thimithi festival which takes place at the end of October or the beginning of November. Devotees cleanse their spirits by fasting beforehand and then show their purity of heart by walking over hot coals. To the north of the temple, also on South Bridge Road, is the **Jamae Mosque**, built in 1826 by the Chulias from southern India. It harnesses an eclectic mix of Anglo-Indian, Chinese and Malay architecture.

Sri Mariamman Temple

Chinatown

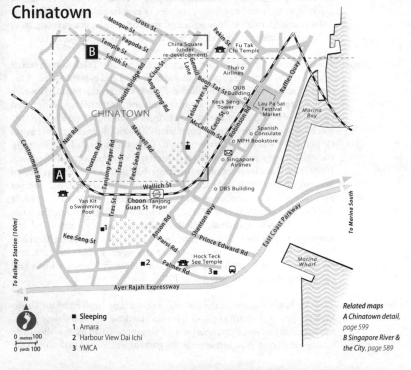

■ **Sleeping**
1 Amara
2 Harbour View Dai Ichi
3 YMCA

Related maps
A *Chinatown detail*,
page 599
B *Singapore River &*
the City, page 589

Singapore

Thian Hock Keng Temple **Telok Ayer Street** is another street full of shophouses and fascinating temples of different religions. This was once one of the most important streets in Singapore, packed with temples, businesses and clan associations. The city's oldest Chinese temple, the Taoist **Thian Hock Keng Temple** or Temple of Heavenly Happiness, is here and is a gem (notwithstanding the naff fibreglass wishing well in one corner). The temple is also very popular; the coaches lined up outside give the game away - but don't let this put you off. Telok Ayer Street was the perfect place for merchants and traders to establish themselves as it was right on the seafront. The temple was funded by a wealthy merchant of the same name and building commenced in 1839. Skilled craftsmen and materials were all imported from China, the cast-iron railings came from Glasgow and the decorative tiles from Holland. The building was modelled on 19th-century southern Chinese architectural traditions, with a grouping of pavilions around open courtyards, designed to comply with the dictates of geomancy (*feng shui*). The main deity of the temple is Tien Hou, the Goddess of Seafarers, and she is worshipped in the central hall. The image here was imported from China in the 1840s and the temple soon became a focal point for newly arrived Hokkien immigrants who would gather to thank Tien Hou for granting them a safe journey. In the left-hand hall there is an image of the Lord of Laws (Fa Zhu Gong) while in the right, the Prince of Prominence, Zai Si Xian He. The ubiquitous Kuan Yin, the Goddess of Mercy, also makes an appearance. A little way north of Thian Hock Keng is another much smaller Chinese temple, the **Fu Tak Chi temple**. This was built in the 1820s and while it is modest - containing just one court and shrine room - it is elegantly proportioned and skilfully decorated. **The Al-Abrar Mosque**, also on Telok Ayer Street, was built between 1850 and 1855 by Indian Muslims, who were also responsible for the fancy turrets of the **Nagore Durgha Shrine** - a little further up the street - which was built in 1829. An intriguing architectural sight is the **Telok Ayer Chinese Methodist Church**, 235 Telok Ayer Street. The church was built in 1924 and combines a mixture of eastern and western influences. There is a flat roof with a Chinese pavilion and a colonnaded ground floor. Its all rather odd. During the Second World War it was used as a refugee camp.

Tanjong Pagar The conservation area of Tanjong Pagar lies southwest of **Telok Ayer Street**. It is bordered by Tanjong Pagar Road and Neil Road and contains some of the best examples of pre-war shophouse architecture on the island. The area around **Kreta Ayer** quickly became a service centre of the red light variety and boatloads of young girls were brought in from China and Hong Kong to provide entertainment for the male population - and with them came their pimps. Or perhaps it was the other way around. Teahouses provided 'singing girls' and opium dens were commonplace (opium smoking was not prohibited until 1964). Fires were frequent since the tinder-box houses were constructed of wood with flimsy cardboard partitions. In 1830 a disastrous fire raged for three days (there were no fire hoses) and in 1917 another fire almost completely destroyed the area. Between 1900 and 1940 Tanjong Pagar became the 'gateway' for Chinese immigrants and clansmen took over almost all the shophouses in the area. Consequently, by the 20th century, Tanjong Pagar had become desperately overcrowded, with houses originally built for one family housing up to five or six. This was also the constituency where Lee Kuan Yew successfully stood in a by-election in 1957.

Redevelopment of Chinatown **Tanjong Pagar** was one of the first major projects undertaken by the Urban Redevelopment Authority (URA). They acquired the area in the early 1980s, realizing that this was a precious piece of Singapore's heritage that should be retained at all cost. And just in time: the government wished to demolish the area as it had become, by then, little more than a slum. Initially, the URA restored and sold off 30 shophouses. Subsequently, they sold the properties unrestored and provided the new owners with guidelines for restoration. The principal stipulation was that façades must remain the same, but new owners were given licence to do almost anything they wanted with the interior, provided that the airwells (an area open to the sky in the middle of the shophouse, which provided light to the back rooms) were retained.

The Tanjong Pagar Heritage Exhibition in the development at 51 Neil Road **Tea Chapter** has a small display of intriguing photographs of old Chinatown, though the accompanying mall and foodcourt, complete with 'authentic' bare brickwork, is a little tacky. More interesting is the **Tea Chapter**, almost next door at 9A-11A, where visitors are introduced to the intricacies of tea-tasting in elegant surroundings. Visitors are invited to remove their shoes (sometimes an aromatic experience in itself) and can choose either to sit in one of their special rooms or upstairs on the floor. Relaxing Chinese plink-plink music, muffled feet, a tiny cup of delicious Supreme Grade Dragon Well, Scarlet Robe or Green Iron Goddess of Mercy at your lips and the cool atmosphere (it's air conditioned upstairs) all contribute towards a soothing experience. As the brochure rather extravagantly puts it, "it is a mythical dream come true for those seeking solace from a harsh and unfeeling existence". This is a popular place for young Singaporeans to visit on a Sunday afternoon. ■ *Mon-Sun, 1100-2300.*

Chinatown detail

Singapore

■ Sleeping	5 The Inn at	● Eating	6 Pasta Brava
1 Air View	Temple St	1 Blue Ginger	7 Siam's Fins
2 Chinatown	6 Keong Saik	2 Chat Point	8 Tea Chapter
3 Damenlou &	7 New Asia	3 Da Paolo's	9 Tiong Shiang
Swee Kee	8 Royal Peacock	4 Geae Café & Bar	
Restaurant	9 Sunshine	& Clips Food & Wine	
4 Duxton	10 Tropical Hotel	5 La Cascade	

Related map
Chinatown,
page 597

N

0 metres 100
0 yards 100

Bird singing On Sunday mornings bird lovers gather at the corner of **Tiong Bahru** and Seng Poh roads for traditional **bird singing competitions**, where row upon row of thrushes, merboks and sharmas sing their hearts out, in antique bamboo cages with ivory and porcelain fittings, hung from lines. The birds are fed on a carefully controlled diet to ensure the quality of their song. Owners place their younger birds next to more experienced songsters to try to improve their voices and pick up new tunes. Birds start twittering at 0730 and are spent by 1000. On the opposite side of the road, there's a shop selling everything you need for your pet bird - including porcelain cage accoutrements. Come here early and combine a visit to hear the birds with breakfast in one of the traditional coffee shops nearby: fresh baked *roti* washed down with sweet black or milky coffee. If you walk on down Seng Poh Road you will come to a fabulous wet **market**; every conceivable vegetable, fruit, fish, meat or beancurd you could ever want to purchase is available here. ■ *Take the MRT to Tiong Bahru or Outram Park or the bus stops right opposite this spot - bus nos 16, 33 and 36.*

Little India

Ins & outs
For sleeping & eating, see pages 625 & 635 respectively

Getting there Bugis is the most convenient MRT stop for Little India, although a 10 min walk is required to get into the heart of the area. Numerous buses run up Serangoon Road including nos 64, 65, 106, 111 and 139 direct from Orchard Road. A new MRT line currently under construction will run along Race Course Road - which runs parallel to Serangoon Road.

Getting around Serangoon Road is Little India's main artery and it stretches some 1½ km from Rochor Canal Road up to Lavender Street - reasonably easily negotiable on foot.

This area remains the heartland of Indian Singapore and on Sundays it can seem as though a significant proportion of the sub-continent's population has miraculously congregated here. Sunday is the day when migrant workers from South Asia come here to eat, chat, shop and worship, revelling in their cultural ties.

Little India encompasses the area straddled by three parallel roads: Serangoon Road, Jalan Besar and Race Course Road. It is largely concentrated to the north of the Rochor Canal and has petered out by the time one reaches Rangoon and Kitchener roads.

Throughout the week, the fragrance of incense and freshly cut jasmine hangs over the area and with the sound-tracks of Tamil epic-musicals blaring from the video shops, the pan salesmen on the sidestreets and colourful milk-sweets behind the glass counters of dosai restaurants, Little India - as the name implies - is the sub-continent in microcosm. Every Indian product imaginable is for sale: lunggyis, dotis, saris and spices, sweetmeats, flower garlands, nostril studs, bidis and stalls with mounds of dried beans, rice and back-copies of *India Today*. Little India can be explored reasonably comfortably in half a day, but it is easy enough to spend a full day here mosying down the attractive side streets and sampling the wealth of Indian dishes available from the simplest coffee houses to sophisticated restaurants.

Markets The lively **Zhujiao** (previously **Kandang Kerbau** or **KK**) **Market** on the corner of Buffalo and Serangoon roads is an entertaining spot to wander. Spices can be ground to your own requirements. Upstairs there is a maze of shops and stalls; the wet market is beyond the hawker centre, travelling west along Buffalo Road. New legislation introduced in 1993, which ruled that no animals could be slaughtered on wet market premises, saw the end of the chicken-plucking machine. It used to do the job in 12.4 seconds.

Little India

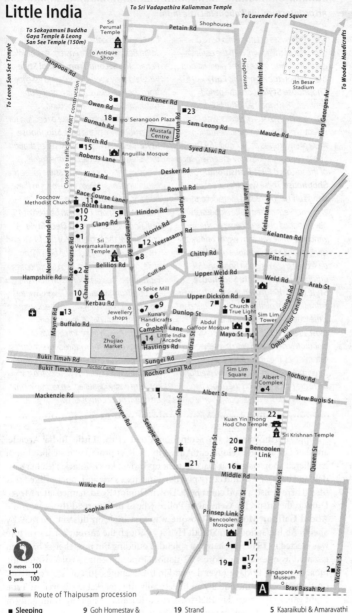

To Sri Vadapathira Kaliamman Temple

To Lavender Food Square

To Sakayamuni Buddha Gaya Temple & Leong San See Temple (150m)

To Leong San See Temple

Sri Perumal Temple

o Antique Shop

Petain Rd   Shophouses

Rangoon Rd

Closed to traffic due to MRT construction

Owen Rd   8■

18■

Burmah Rd   o Serangoon Plaza

Kitchener Rd   ■23

Mustafa Centre

Sam Leong Rd

Verdun Rd

Syed Alwi Rd

Maude Rd

Tyrwhitt Rd

King Georges Av

Jln Besar Stadium

To Wooden Handicrafts

Shophouses

Birch Rd   ■15

Roberts Lane   ♦ Anguillia Mosque

Kinta Rd   Desker Rd

Rowell Rd

Race Course Lane   5●

Foochow Methodist Church   ✝ 11●

Rotan Lane

10●   5■

12●

3●

●1

2●

10   ♦ Kerbau Rd

13■

Buffalo Rd

Mayne Rd

Chander Rd

Northumberland Rd

Race Course Rd

Serangoon Rd

Clang Rd   Hindoo Rd

Norris Rd

12●   Veerasamy Rd

8●

Sri Veeramakaliamman Temple

Belilios Rd

Cuff Rd

o Spice Mill   6●

Kapor Rd

Jalan Besar

Kelantan Lane

Kelantan Rd

Chitty Rd

Upper Weld Rd

Perak Rd

Weld Rd   Pitt St

Arab St

Sungei Rd

Rochor Canal Rd

Jewellery shops   7●   9●

Kuna's Handicrafts   Dunlop St

Campbell Lane   Little India Arcade

14●   Hastings Rd

Madras St   Mayo St

Abdul Gaffoor Mosque

✝ Church of True Light

13●   Sim Lim Tower

14●

Ophir Rd

Upper Dickson Rd   6●   7●

Zhujiao Market

Bukit Timah Rd

Bukit Timah Rd   Rochor Canal   Sungei Rd   Rochor Canal Rd

Sim Lim Square   Albert Complex   ●4   Rochor Rd

Mackenzie Rd   ■1   Albert St   New Bugis St

Niven Rd

Selegie Rd

Short St

Mackenzie Rd

Kuan Yin Thong Hod Cho Temple

22■

Sri Krishnan Temple

Prinsep St   20■

9■   Bencoolen Link

✝   16■   Bencoolen St

■21   Middle Rd

Wilkie Rd

Waterloo St

Queen St

Sophia Rd

Prinsep Link

Bencoolen Mosque

4■   ■11

19■   ■17

■3

Singapore Art Museum

A   Bras Basah Rd

Victoria St

2■

N

0 metres   100

0 yards   100

━━━ Route of Thaipusam procession

Singapore

An architectural walkabout in Little India

The shophouses of Little India have a character of their own, with the earliest examples being some of the plainest and humblest on the island. This **Early Shophouse Style** *spans the period between 1840 and 1900. The buildings were generally 2-storey affairs, with Doric columns and minimal ornamentation; there are examples at 127 and 159 Dunlop Street. The early 1900s saw the emergence of the so-called* **First Transitional Shophouse**. *These were less squat in design and incorporated more decorative elements. Vents, often quite elaborate, were now included above or between the windows, while columns were Corinthian rather than Doric. Examples of this style can be seen at 61 Serangoon Road and 39 Campbell Lane. The* **Late Shophouse Style** *(1900-1940) overlapped with the First Transitional; of all the styles to be found in Little India these are without doubt the most interesting. The entire surface is elaborately decorated with plasterwork and ceramic tiles, the upper floor is divided into three, making a greater window area, and there are balustrades on the upper floor, creating shade for these rooms. Some of the* best examples can be seen at 109-117 Jalan Besar and at the eastern end of Jalan Petain. The* **Second Transitional Style** *was relatively short-lived, dating essentially from the late 1930s. Architects and art historians have seen the Second Transitional as something of a reaction to the exuberance of the* **Late Shophouse Style**. *Designs were much simpler, though they still used ceramic tiles and some ornamentation. It is also possible to see the beginnings of Art Deco influences in these buildings. An example of a Second Transitional shophouse can be seen at 15 Cuff Road. Finally, the* **Art Deco Style** *emerged at the beginning of the 1930s and shophouses continued to be built in this style into the 1960s. Art Deco shophouses represent a logical progression from the Second Transitional style. Designs were simpler still, with proportions being more important than detail. In addition architects began to design groups of buildings rather than individual structures – with particular interest in corner sites. Many of these buildings were dated, so they are easily identified. An example can be found at 22 Campbell Lane.*

Opposite the market on Serangoon Road is the **Little India Arcade**, another Urban Redevelopment Authority (URA) project. This collection of handicraft shops is a great place to pick up Indian knick-knacks: leather sandals and bags, spices and curry powders, incense, saris and other printed textiles. There is also a food court here. Down Dunlop Road, named after Mr AE Dunlop the Inspector General of Police whose private road this was, is the **Abdul Gaffoor Mosque**. A mosque was first built on this site in 1859 by Sheikh Abdul Gaffoor bin Shaikh Hyder although the current brick structure was erected in 1910. It is hardly a splendid building but nonetheless has been gazetted as one of Singapore's 32 national monuments. Avoid visiting the mosque during Friday prayer day and in the evenings. Just off Dunlop Road, on Perak Road, is the equally architecturally unremarkable **Church of True Light** which was erected in 1850 to serve Little India's Anglican community of Hock Chew and Hinghwa descent. ■ *0900-1300 Sat-Sun.*

Walking up Serangoon Road, take a right at Cuff Road to see Little India's last **spice mill** at work in a blue and mustard yellow shophouse - P Govindasamai Pillai's. It's hard to miss the chugging of the mill, let alone the rich smells of the spices. Here spices are ground for use on the day of cooking.

Sri Veeramaka-liamman Temple This temple on Serangoon Road was built for the Bengali community by indentured Bengali labourers in 1881 and is dedicated to Kali, the ferocious incarnation of Siva's wife. The name of the temple means Kali the courageous. It is similar in composition to most other temples of its kind and has three main elements: a shrine for the gods, a hall for worship and a *goporum* (or tower), built so that pilgrims can identify the temple from afar. The gopuram of this temple, with its cascade of gaudy, polychromed gods, goddesses, demons and mythological beasts, is the most recent addition and was only completed in 1987. Worshippers and visitors should walk clockwise around the temple hall, and for good luck an odd number of times. The principal black image of Kali in the temple hall (clasping her club of destruction - not a women to get on the wrong side of) is flanked by her sons, Ganesha and Murugan. ■ *Closed Mon-Sun, 1230-1600.*

Further up Serangoon Road is another Indian temple, **Sri Perumal**, with its high goporum sculptured with five manifestations of Vishnu. The temple was founded in 1855, but much of the decoration is more recent. This carving was finished in 1979 and was paid for by local philanthropist P Govindasamy Pillai, better known as PGP, who made his fortune selling saris. Like other Hindu temples, there is greatest activity on the holy days of Tuesdays and Fridays. For the best experience of all, come here and to the Sri Veeramakaliamman and Hindu Chettiars (see page 602) temples during the two day festival of **Thaipusam**, generally held in January (see page 575), which celebrates the birthday of Murugan, one of Kali's sons. ■ *Mon-Sun, 0630-1200, 1800-2100.*

Further north at 366 Race Course Road (parallel to Serangoon Road) is the Buddhist Sakayamuni Buddha Gaya Temple or Temple of One Thousand Lights dominated by a 15m-high, 300 tonne, rather crude statue of the Buddha surrounded by 987 lights (the lights are turned on if you make a donation). The image is represented in the attitude of subduing Mara - the right hand touches the ground calling the Earth Goddess to witness the historic Buddha's resistance of the attempts by Mara to tempt him with her naked dancing daughters. At the back of the principal image is a smaller reclining Buddha. Devotees come here to worship the branch of the sacred Bodhi tree - under which the Buddha gained enlightenment - and a replica mother-of-pearl footprint of the Buddha showing the 108 auspicious signs of the Enlightened One. ■ *0730-1645 Mon-Sun, remove shoes before entering.*

Sakayamuni Buddha Gaya Temple

Across the road is the Chinese Mahayana Buddhist **Leong San See Temple**, or Dragon Mountain Temple, with its carved entrance, (where you don't have to remove your shoes). It is dedicated to Kuan Yin (the goddess of mercy) who had 18 hands, which are said to symbolize her boundless mercy and compassion. The principal image on the altar shows her modelled, as usual, in white surrounded by a mixed bag of Chinese Mahayana folk gods and Theravada images of the Buddha.

Arab Street

Getting there Bugis MRT station is near the southwestern edge of Arab Street while Lavender is on the northeastern fringe of the area. The only bus to run direct from Orchard Road is no 7.

Ins & outs
For sleeping & eating, see pages 627 & 636

Getting around Arab Street is the smallest of the areas highlighted in this chapter and it is easy to explore on foot.

Originally this area was a thriving Arab village known as Kampong Glam (Glam Village). There is some disagreement over the origins of this name. Some commentators have attributed it to the Gelam tribe of sea-gypsies who once lived in the area. More likely, it refers to the glam tree from which Bugis seafarers extracted resin to caulk their ships.

Singapore

Singapore's Arabs were among the area's earliest settlers, the first being a wealthy merchant called Syed Mohammad bin Harum Al-Junied who arrived in 1819, a couple of months after Stamford Raffles. The Alkaffs were another important local Arab family, who built their ostentatious mansion on Mount Faber (now a restaurant, see page 637). Arab merchants began settling in the area around Arab Street in the mid-19th century. As one would expect, this part of town has the greatest concentration of Muslim restaurants including Indonesian, Malay and Indian. Many of the cheapest - and noisest - are arrayed along busy North Bridge Road. Cut into the Arab quarter and roads like Kandahar, Bussorah and Pahang to find quieter places to eat and drink.

Mosques The focal point of the Arab quarter is the **Sultan Mosque**, with its golden domes, on North Bridge Road. Completed in 1928 and designed by colonial architect Denis Santry of Swan & Maclaren, it is an eclectic mixture of Classical, Moorish and Persian. **NB** Visitors in shorts, short skirts or singlets will not be permitted to enter. ■ *0900-1300, 1400-1600*. Another popular mosque right at the eastern edge of Kampong Glam is the **Hajjah Fatimah Mosque** on Java Road. Unusually, it was financed by a wealthy Melakan-born Malay woman, Hajjah Fatimah (Hajjah is the female equivalent of Haji, meaning someone who has made the pilgrimage to Mecca), married to a Bugis merchant who is said in some sources to have been the Sultan of Gowa in Sulawesi.

Stalls & shops In the maze of side streets around the Sultan Mosque there is a colourful jumble of Malay, Indonesian and Middle Eastern merchandise. Excellent

Arab Street

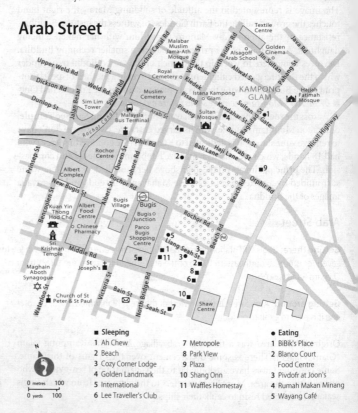

N

0 metres 100
0 yards 100

■ Sleeping		● Eating
1 Ah Chew	7 Metropole	1 BiBik's Place
2 Beach	8 Park View	2 Blanco Court
3 Cozy Corner Lodge	9 Plaza	Food Centre
4 Golden Landmark	10 Shang Onn	3 Pivdofr at Joon's
5 International	11 Waffles Homestay	4 Rumah Makan Minang
6 Lee Traveller's Club		5 Wayang Café

Singapore

selections of batik (which is sold in sarong lengths of just over 2m) jostle for space with, silk and Indian textiles (especially along Arab Street), wickerware, jewellery, perfumes and religious paraphernalia. In the weeks before Hari Raya Puasa, Bussorah Street is lined with stalls selling all kinds of traditional foods - after dark it is a favourite haunt of famished Muslims during Ramadan. Bussorah Street has been gentrified as part of the URA's redevelopment efforts: it is now a pedestrianised, tree-lined street of elegant shophouses. Tombstone-makers are based along Pahang Street. Nearby at the junction of Jalan Sultan and Victoria Street is the **old royal cemetery** which was marked on maps as such from the 1930s. The associated mosque is the **Malabar Muslim Jama-Ath mosque**, which was built in the 1920s. The architect, an Indian named AH Siddique, was unusual in two respects: first he learnt his architectural skills through a correspondence course; and second, it is said he never took a fee for any religious building he designed (Muslim or other).

This street is southwest of Arab Street, right across the road from the Bugis Street MRT station. It is packed with stalls selling cheap T-shirts, copy watches, handicrafts - like a street market you might see in Thailand or Malaysia, but something that seems rather out of place in modern day Singapore. For those who like to see Singapore not just as a giant shopping plaza but also as a real life experiment in ersatz existence, then Bugis Street offers more than key rings and Oriental flim-flam. The whole street has been re-created from a road that was demolished to make way for the MRT in the mid-1980s. On the opposite side of Victoria Street is the new Parco Bugis Centre, a high-tech shopping plaza (in reconstructed air-conditioned shophouses) bustling with life and containing restaurants, shopping malls and yet another of Singapore's fabulous fountains. **Bugis Street**

Waterloo Street, much of which has been pedestrianised, cuts across New Bugis Street and is also worth a modest detour. The **Sri Krishnan Temple** at 152 Waterloo Street dates back to the 1870s when a simple attap hut protected two Hindu images (Krishna didn't arrive until the 1880s). Over the years it has been expanded and refined as the Hindu population of the surrounding area has prospered. Almost next door is a large, modern Mahayana pagoda dedicated to **Kuan Yin** - the **Kuan Yin Thong Hod Cho Temple**. This temple is particularly popular - try visiting around lunchtime (1200-1300) when scores of worshippers come here to pray for good fortune. The central image is of multi-limbed Kuan Yin, while on either side are Ta Ma Tan Shith and Hua Tua. The latter was an important Han Dynasty figure (third century BC) who is now the patron saint of Chinese medics. Perhaps not coincidentally, on the other side of the street in Cheng Yan Court, is a collection of **traditional Chinese pharmacies** selling the usual range of dried fungi, antlers, bones, herbs, roots like ginseng, dessicated sea horses, and other unidentified body parts. **Temples**

Singapore

The World Trade Centre, the Port and Sentosa

Getting there Bus or taxi is the most convenient way to get to the **World Trade Centre**. Bus nos 65, 143 and 167 run direct from Orchard Road; 61, 84, 143, 145, 166 and 167 from Chinatown. The nearest MRT station is at Tanjong Pagar, from which buses 10, 97, 100 and 125 go to the World Trade Centre. A new MRT line currently under construction will terminate at the Centre.

Bus service 'A' operates from the World Trade Centre bus terminal to **Sentosa** from 0700-2000, Mon-Thur, 0700-2300 Fri-Sun. Bus 'C' leaves from the Tiong Bahru MRT station for the ferry terminal and Musical Fountain and operates 0700-2200 Mon-Thur, 0700-2300 Fri-Sun. Service 'E' plies Orchard Road, Bras Basah Road and **Ins & outs**
For sleeping, see page 627. For eating, see page 637

Marina Square, stopping at Lucky Plaza, *Mandarin Hotel*, Peranakan Place, *Meridien Hotel*, Plaza Singapura, Bencoolen Street, POSB Headquarters, Raffles City and *Pan Pacific Hotel*, 1000-2000. Bus services 'A' and 'C' cost S$6 (S$4 for children). Bus service 'E' is S$7 (S$5 for children). These are return fares and include entrance to Sentosa (normally priced at S$5). Taxis are charged a toll of S$3 and can only drop off/pick up at the hotels on Sentosa. An alternative way to reach Sentosa is via the Cable Car. There are 3 stops: Mount Faber (the highest point in Singapore, with scenic views and seafood restaurants - worthwhile), the Cable Car Tower adjacent to the World Trade Centre, and the Cable Car Plaza on Sentosa. Fares: one way S$5.90, return S$6.90. Admission to Sentosa is in addition to these fares. Cable car operates 0830-2100 Mon-Sun. **NB** Taxis are not available at Mt Faber, so if returning by cable car, alight at the World Trade Centre.

Ferries for the southern islands group including Pulau Kusu and St John's leave from the World Trade Centre - as do boats for Sentosa. Tanjong Pagar is the nearest MRT stop to the Tanjong Pagar container terminal. The ferry from the World Trade Centre leaves every 20 mins from 0930-2100, every 15 mins 0830-2100 Sat-Sun. Fare US$1.30 return (with entrance to Sentosa, US$6.30).

The port is not really an area that one 'explores' on foot

Getting around On Sentosa free buses (operating every 10 mins, 0900-2230 Mon-Sun) link the ferry terminal, Underwater World, Fort Siloso, and Images of Singapore. The free night bus (1930-2230 Mon-Sun) runs between the *Beaufort* and *NTUC* hotels and the Musical Fountain and ferry terminal. The monorail, also free, links all the island's attractions and runs at 10-min intervals (0900-2200 Mon-Sun). Bicycles, tandems and trishaws for hire from the ferry terminal. For biking enthusiasts, there is a 6 km cycle track around the island.

The world's busiest port Singapore port is strategically located at the southern end of the Strait of Melaka, halfway between China and India. It is a free port, open to all maritime nations. Largely sheltered from the city, it has seven gateways; the biggest - the container port - is the **Tanjong Pagar terminal**. In 1820 the first resident governor, Colonel William Farquhar, realising the advantages of Keppel Harbour's deep and sheltered water, began to develop it as a port. In 1864 the Tanjong Pagar Dock Company was formed and in 1972 the first container terminal was established.

World Trade Centre To the west of Tanjong Pagar port, on Keppel Road, is the World Trade Centre. Most people visit here either to get to Sentosa, to take the boat to Batam and Bintan islands in Indonesia's Riau Archipelago, or to climb aboard the cable car which connects Sentosa with Mount Faber.

Sentosa The name chosen for the island is hardly appropriate: *Sentosa* means 'peace and tranquillity'. In 1990, Sentosa welcomed a million visitors, about 45 per cent of whom were foreign tourists. It is guaranteed to provide plenty of entertainment for children and adults may be pleasantly surprised with one or two attractions. On weekends, Sentosa can be a nightmare, as crowds converge on the island's attractions.

A second word of warning is that a day at Sentosa tends to be an expensive as well as an entertaining experience. A family of four can easily get through S$200. Basic admission is S$5 (S$3 for children) but there is a charge for each attraction. There are various combination tickets that include admission to Sentosa and to selected attractions. It is slightly cheaper to buy tickets this way at the World Trade Centre or on Mount Faber at the cable car entrance, rather than purchasing tickets at individual attractions after arrival (see each entry for admission charges). The disadvantage of purchasing tickets in this way is that it commits you before seeing what is on offer. Some combination tickets also tie you in to a tour. ■ *0730-2300, Mon-Thur, 0730-2400 Fri-Sun and public holidays. Note that some attractions close before 2300 - many at 1900. T2750388 for additional information.*

Images of Singapore, **Pioneers of Singapore** and the **Surrender Chambers** offer a well-displayed history of Singapore focusing on key figures from the origins of the city state as an entrepôt through to the modern period and also telling the traumatic story of the Second World War. ■ *0900-2100, S$5 (S$3 for children). Monorail station 4, bus nos 2 and A.* **Fort Siloso** is Singapore's only preserved coastal fort, built in the 1880s to guard the narrow west entrance to Keppel Harbour. It has been recently renovated and is a very informative visit, especially if you are interested in the fall of Singapore. ■ *0900-1900, S$3, S$2 for children. Monorail station 3, bus nos 2 and A.*

Only the more important & interesting attractions are listed here

The **Asian Village** is a short walk from the ferry terminal. It opened before it was fully completed in 1993 and has had difficulty attracting patrons. The idea was to construct three theme villages for East Asia, South Asia and Southeast Asia. They're pretty dismal, although some quality souvenirs are for sale. Adventure Asia - a rather half-hearted attempt at an all-Asian kiddies' funfair - was added for good measure. This part of the village is open 1000-1900, and the rides are individually priced from S$2 to S$3, or S$5 for the paddle boats. An all-Asian restaurant and a village theatre, built up a hillside and capable of seating up to 800 people, are other attractions. This is Singapore's attempt at virtual reality: rather than having to travel to these places, the sights are all conveniently brought together on a single site. ■ *1000-2100 Mon-Sun, free but the various shows have an entrance charge. Monorail station 1, bus nos 2 and C.*

Underwater World has a 100m tunnel, with a moving conveyor, which allows a glimpse of some of its 350 underwater species and 5,000 specimens. Giant rays glide overhead while thick-lipped garoupa and spooky moray eels hide in caves and crevices. A new exhibit is the so-called 'creatures of the deep' tank with giant octopus and spider crabs - brace yourself, as they put it, for an

This attraction, with the largest walk-through oceanarium in Asia, is highly recommended

Singapore

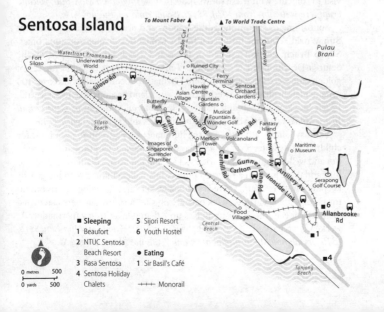

Sentosa Island

To Mount Faber ▲   ▲ To World Trade Centre

Pulau Brani

Fort Siloso

Waterfront Promenade
Underwater World

Cable Car

Causeway

Ruined City

■ 3

Siloso Rd

Ferry Terminal

Hawker Centre

Sentosa Orchard Gardens

■ 2

Asian Village

Butterfly Park

Fountain Gardens

Siloso Beach

Carlton Hill

Siloso Rd

Musical Fountain & Wonder Golf

Fantasy Island

Jetty Rd

Maritime Museum

Images of Singapore/ Surrender Chamber

Merlion Tower

Volcanoland

■ 5

Gateway Av

■ 1

Carnhill Rd

Carlton

Gunner Lane Rd

Ironside Link

Artillery Av

Serapong Golf Course

■ 6

Allanbrooke Rd

Central Beach

Food Village

■ 1

■ 4

Tanjong Beach

N

0 metres 500
0 yards 500

■ **Sleeping**
1 Beaufort
2 NTUC Sentosa Beach Resort
3 Rasa Sentosa
4 Sentosa Holiday Chalets
5 Sijori Resort
6 Youth Hostel

● **Eating**
1 Sir Basil's Café

╫╫╫ Monorail

encounter with the world's ugliest eel and creepy crabs. Other smaller tanks house cuttlefish, turtles, reef fish, sawfish, corals, sea urchins and other marine creatures. ■ *0900-2100. Feeding times are well worth arriving for: 1130, 1430, 1600 and 1630. S$13 for adults, S$7 for children. Monorail station 2, bus nos 2 and A.*

The **Musical fountain** is a disco-lit fountain which gyrates, together with a rather unorchestrated laser light show, to everything from Joan Jett and the Blackhearts to the 1812 overture. The fountain is joined by a 37m high, 12 storey-tall **Merlion** – a stupendous, laser-emitting symbol of Singapore. Combined, they create the *Musical Fountain and Rise of the Merlion Show*. Each performance lasts 30 minutes and they kick off at 1700, 1730, 1930, 2030 and 2130 Monday-Sunday. At other times of day the merlion can be climbed either up to its mouth or its crown for views over Sentosa, the city and port. The shop here (nothing can be built on Sentosa without some merchandising outlet) is themed as a Bugis shipwreck. The Bugis were the feared Malay seafarers who sailed from Sulawesi and controlled the seas of the Malay archipelago before the European period. They have often been likened to the Vikings and, like the Vikings, they were famed for their fearlessness and for their seafaring skills - and for the terror they instilled in the hearts of coastal communities. (The word bogey is said to be derived from bugis, and was first used in 1836 as another term for the devil. Thackeray wrote: The people are all naughty and bogey carries them off. In 1865 the word was bastardized once more into bugbear, a hobgoblin reputed to devour naughty children.) ■ *0900-2200, last admission 2130, S$3, S$2 for children. Monorail station 1 and 4, bus nos 2, A, C.*

Volcanoland, a 'multimedia entertainment park', is another of the newer attractions: it takes you on a subterranean journey into the earth and is supposed to trace the evolution of life - although your children will pass no exams with this rubbish. The main show is entertaining enough, but the rest of the complex is rather disappointing and, as with so much on Sentosa, the visitor exits from the multimedia extravaganza, no doubt filled with grand - but erroneous - thoughts about the origins of life, straight into a shop. There are also occasional Mayan dances, although these are in no sense authentic; time your visit to coincide with these shows if desired. ■ *1000-1900 Mon-Sun, volcano erupts every 30 mins from 1030. S$12, S$6 for children. Bus nos A, C.*

Sunbathing or swimming at the lagoons and nearby '**beach**' is possible at **Sun World**. You can hire pedal boats, windsurfers, canoes or aqua bikes. **Siloso Beach**, at the west end of the island, has been redeveloped by the Sentosa Development Corporation. Tens of thousands of cubic metres of golden sand were shipped in, as were 300 mature coconut palms and over 100 ornamental shrubs and flowering trees. The island has four **beaches**: Central, Beach Monkeys, Siloso and Tanjong. ■ *Monorail station 5 for Central and Beach Monkeys, station 2 for Siloso, bus nos 2, A and M or the Beach Train.*

Fantasy Island, advertised as the 'ultimate water adventure', is a must for children: white water river rapids, play areas in the water and aquatic slides are fun and well-designed. The various slides and chutes are graded from one to four and there is an area reserved purely for smaller children with life guards keeping a wary eye out. There are public lockers and changing rooms but no towels provided. Various snack bars are on site. A sunny day here can turn a pallid European into a lobster in less time than it takes to say thermador. At weekends it is packed. ■ *1000-1830 (closed at 2200 Fri and Sat) Mon-Sun, S$16, S$10 for children. Monorail stations 1 and 7; bus nos 2, A, C, E, and M.*

Singapore West

Getting there The MRT West line runs all the way from the city to Boon Lay, with 9 stops in between. However a number of the main sights in this part of the island are (for Singapore) distant from any MRT station and it is best either to take a bus or taxi. Jurong East Interchange links the MRT West line with the MRT North line.

Getting around This area is spread out and bar a handful of sights which are within walking distance of one another it is usually necessary to catch a train, bus or taxi.

Ins & outs
For eating, see page 637

The western portion of Singapore has been transformed since independence. Not long ago it was an out-of-the-way spot; now it is dotted with new towns and housing developments and is linked to the city via the western line of the MRT, which extends all the way to Boon Lay. Further west still is Singapore's industrial hub - the Jurong Industrial Estate. And right at the western tip of the island is the old fishing settlement of Tuas, now virtually obliterated by the industrial developments that surround it.

This is an area of contrasts. From east to west, there are the hideous Haw Par Villas, better known as the Tiger Balm Gardens, the excellent Jurong Bird Park and its sister Reptile Park, the rather moth-eaten Tang Dynasty Village, the Science Museum and, newest of all, the propogandist Singapore Discovery Centre. Also in this part of the island are glimpses of a Singapore which is largely absent from the city centre. Tree-lined streets like the western end of Jurong Road and its continuation, Upper Jurong Road, laid out like much else of Singapore by that most visionary of colonial city planners, John Turnbull Thomson. Also here is Holland Village with its attractive Mediterranean ambience.

Formerly Tiger Balm Gardens, Haw Par Villa is at 262 Pasir Panjang Road, on the way out to Jurong. Built by Aw Boon Haw and Aw Boon Par, brothers of Tiger Balm fame, it was their family home until they opened it to the public. The delightful estate was finally sequestrated by the Singapore government in 1985 and turned into the island's most revolting theme park, a gaudy adventureland of Chinese folklore - the biggest Chinese mythological theme park in the world. Boon Haw originally designed the gardens for his family's enjoyment. But his gory sculptures have instilled a sense of traditional morality in generations of Singaporeans. ■ *0900-1500 Mon-Sun, S$5, S$3.50 children . NB Do not even think about visiting over Chinese New Year - each year about 12,000 people saunter around it in the space of about 4 days. MRT westbound to Buona Vista, then bus 200; or to Clementi and then bus 10. Direct buses to the Haw Par Villas are 10, 30, 51, 143 (runs from Orchard Road), 176 and 200.*

Haw Par Villa

Holland Village is especially worth visiting at the weekend. This is really a residential area - and was once the home to the British forces barracked in Singapore - but it also developed into one of the trendier parts of suburban Singapore. There are restaurants and bars, small craft and antique shops, and a good wet market - Pasar Holland. The Holland Village Shopping Centre on Holland Avenue is the best stop for Asian arts and crafts and there are ample places to eat and relax while exploring the area. ■ *Take the MRT to Buona Vista and then walk up Commonwealth Avenue to Holland Avenue (about 15 mins) or take buses 106 or 200.*

This park, on Jalan Ahmad Ibrahim, is a beautifully kept 20ha haven for more than 8,000 birds of 600 species from all over the world, including a large

Jurong Bird Park

Singapore

collection of Southeast Asian birds. As it is now difficult to see most of these birds in the wild in Southeast Asia, a trip here is well worthwhile. Highlights include the world's largest collection of Southeast Asian hornbills and South American toucans and an entertaining air-conditioned penguin corner, complete with snow. Another main attraction is one of the largest walk-in aviaries in the world, with a 30m-high manmade waterfall and 1,500 birds. There is also an interesting nocturnal house with owls, herons, frogmouths and kiwis and bird shows throughout the day (the birds of prey show - at 1000 and 1600 - is particularly good). There is a monorail service round the park for those who find the heat too much (S$2.50, S$1 for children). ■ *0900-1800 Mon-Fri, 0800-1800, weekends and public holidays, S$10.30, S$4.12 for children under 12, family tickets available for S$20. T2650022. MRT westbound to Boon Lay then SBS bus 194 or 251 from Boon Lay interchange.*

Jurong Reptile Park, Jalan Ahmad Ibrahim, is next to Jurong Bird Park. This was formerly called the Jurong Crocodile Paradise but after renovation in 1997 has re-emerged under a new name. The name really says it all: 100 reptilian species with an emphasis on poison and danger - cobras, crocodiles, poison arrow frogs, and iguanas (not so scary). ■ *0900-1800 Mon-Sun, S$7, S$3.50 for children under 12. Shows at 1145 and 1400 and at 1600 on weekends and public holidays. MRT westbound to Boon Lay; SBS buses 194 or 251 from Boon Lay Interchange.*

Tang Dynasty City Covering 12ha, Tang Dynasty City on Jalan Ahmad Ibrahim/Yuan Ching Road is a recreation of the ancient Chinese capital of Chang An. Developers worked for three years to build this S$70m theme park. The City includes 100 shophouses and a temple, with carvings by workmen from China, and a

Singapore West

600m-long, 10m-high model of the Great Wall of China, built with bricks imported from Shenzhen. There is also a seven-storey pagoda, housing the monkey god and an impressive artificial waterfall. The main attraction, though, is an 'underground palace', with replicas of the 1,500 terracotta warriors found in the tomb of Shih Huang Ti in Xian, China. Visitors are ushered into a small theatre where a short and bloody film of the emperor's life provides a simple historical background before an entirely irrelevant natural event ends the film show and visitors enter the reconstruction of the tomb to view the arrayed ranks of warriors illuminated by lasers.

The general tenor is one of over-ambition: though S$70m may have been spent on the place, it would have been better to have envisaged something less grandiose and at least have done it well. There is a restaurant on site and a better and cheaper food court across the road in the Jurong Bowl complex. Given these quibbles, the entrance fee is steep for something still half-baked. ■ *1000-1830, Mon-Sun, S$15.45, S$10.30 for children, but advance tickets at slightly reduced rates available from travel agents and other outlets in town. T2611116. MRT to Lakeside and then bus 154, or to Boon Lay and then bus 178.*

The **Chinese and Japanese Gardens** are on Yuan Ching Road, Jurong. These gardens extend over 13ha on two islands in Jurong Lake. The Chinese garden - or Yu-Hwa Yuan - is said to be modelled on an imperial Sung Dynasty garden, and specifically on the classical style of Beijing's Summer Palace. There are artfully scattered boulders, Chinese pavilions, and a brace-and-a-half of pagodas to give it that Oriental flavour but it is hard to believe that the Sung emperors would have been happy with this. Rather more refined is the Penjing Garden (Yun Xiu Yuan - or Garden of Beauty), a walled bonsai garden, which reputedly cost S$6m to develop. The **Double Beauty Bridge** leads to the more peaceful Japanese and

Chinese gardens; the former, said to be one of the largest such gardens outside Japan. **NB** If you want to enjoy the peace it is best to arrive at the gardens when they open at 0900 and there are few people about; avoid weekends when they are crowded. You also stand more chance of seeing the large monitor lizards and turtles that live in the lake. ■ *0900-1900 Mon-Sat, 0830-1900 Sun and public holidays. Last admission 1800. S$4.50, S$2 for children. T2643455. MRT to Chinese Gardens (W10) and then walk the 200m across the open grassed area to the east gate. Alternatively, take bus nos 335 or 180 which also run to the MRT stop and the east gate, or 154 which run past the main west gate.*

Situated on Science Centre Road, **Science Centre** Jurong, the Science Centre might be aimed more at children than adults - it is usually packed with school children enjoying a few hours away from cramming - but there is plenty of fun for grown-ups too. Overall the centre succeeds in its mission to make science

Singapore

come alive, with plenty of gadgets and hands-on exhibits. It makes most sense to come here with children who will be able to spend several hours having fun and maybe even learning something. ■ *1000-1800 Tue-Sun, S$3, S$1.50 for children.*

In the **Omni-theatre** next door, the marvels of science, technology and the universe can be viewed in a 284-seat amphitheatre with a huge hemispherical (3D) screen and a 20,000 watt sound system. Take a seat-of-your-pants thrill ride while learning about the science of roller coasters, climb Everest or experience an exploding volcano (films change periodcally). It has excellent films and is very popular. ■ *Tue-Sun 1000-2100, T5689100 for film schedules, T5603316/5641432. S$10 (S$4 for children) for Omninax movies (screened 1000-2000, Tue-Sun, every hour); S$6 (S$3 for children) for Planetarium show at 1000 and 1100. Take the MRT to Jurong East, and walk the last 300m through the HDB block and across Townhall Road to the museum. Bus nos 66, 198, 335 and TIBS bus No 178 run direct to the the museum. Alternatively get bus nos 51, 78, 97 or 147 to the Jurong East Interchange and then change to a 335 or walk the last 10 mins.*

Singapore Discovery Centre

Singapore's latest attraction, right at the western end of the island, is the **Singapore Discovery Centre**. This is really an epic, S$70m PR exercise for Singapore Inc concocted by the Singapore Defence Forces. A fair number of the attractions are military. There is also a good children's adventure playground, a recreation of significant events from Singapore's history with a walk-through gallery of shophouses and early HDB flats, and a stomach-churningly realistic motion simulator where, for example, you can follow a missile in flight. It is, as one might expect, well done with lots of hands-on interactive computer exhibits. It is also fascinating as an illustration of nation-building. There is also, of course, a food court and retail outlet for those who are empty of stomach or would like to be of pocket. Visit the website at www.asianconnect. com/sdc. ■ *0900-1900 Tue-Fri (last admission, 1800), 0900-2000 Sat-Sun and public holidays (last admission 1900), closed Mon. S$9 (children, S$5), extra charge for motion simulator (S$4) and shooting gallery (S$3). Westbound MRT to Boon Lay (W12) and then connecting SBS bus nos 192 and 193 from the Boon Lay interchange or direct on SBS bus nos 192 and 193.*

East Coast

Ins & outs
For sleeping & eating, see pages 628 & 638 respectively

Getting there The MRT East line runs all the way to Pasir Ris. For Joo Chiat Road, alight at Paya Lebar MRT station. For the coast it is best to take a bus (No 16 from Orchard and Bras Basah roads) or taxi.

Getting around This area is too large, and the sights too spread out, to explore on foot. However some parts, like Joo Chiat Road, are sufficiently compact to walk.

Although the east coast may not be what it was, those who want a change from the order and glitz of Orchard Road could do worse than simply hop on the 16/14 bus which runs along Joo Chiat Road and then onto the East Coast Road. There are good eating places, side streets and interesting shops (antiques, crafts etc), and even a village feel.

The eastern part of the island used to be dotted with small Malay fishing kampungs, most of which have now been demolished and replaced by Housing Development Board tower blocks. Great chunks of land have been reclaimed from the sea and carefully landscaped beaches now line the coast up to Changi. Just off the city end of the East Coast Parkway is the National Sports Stadium.

Katong is an enclave of Peranakan architecture and there are still streets of well-preserved shophouses and terraced houses in their original condition. **Joo Chiat Road** gives a good feel of old Singapore, sandwiched between the upmarket residential districts and government Housing Development Board (HDB) projects. While most of the traditional businesses here have closed down or moved out, there are still some candle makers struggling to make a living and a few other craftsmen. On Koon Seng Road, many of the houses have been carefully restored and it is less touristy than Emerald Hill and Tanjong Pagar. European civil servants and Straits Chinese mandarins had grand houses along the waterfront, a handful of which still stand today among the HDB blocks and condominiums. Restaurants in Katong serve some of the best Peranakan food in Singapore including delicious pastries and sweets. A little further away is **Geylang Serai** on Geylang Road, considered the heart of Malay culture in Singapore; it was once an agricultural area but has been transformed into a modern industrial zone. Geylang market is well-stocked with Malay food and this is a good place to come for Indonesian and Malaysian cuisine. ■ *For Katong take bus 14 or 16 from Orchard Road; for Geylang take the MRT to Paya Lebar.*

Katong & Geylang Serai

The **Malay Cultural Village**, Geylang Serai, is on a 1.7ha site between Geylang Serai, Sims Avenue and Geylang Road. But the Malay answer to the new Tang Dynasty City, with its mock-kampung houses, Malay foodstalls and shops has failed to draw many visitors. The irony of it is not lost on Singapore's Malay community, who have been resettled from their kampungs into HDB flats over the past 20 years. Malay cultural identity is better characterized in the stalls at Geylang market than in the cultural village. In an attempt to claw back visitors from other rival attractions there is a new Lagenda Fantasi presentation which introduces people to legends which could only very loosely be described as Malay - Aladdin, Ali Baba and the like. ■ *0900-1730, Mon-Sun, T7484700, F7411662. Bus, SBS 2, 7; MRT to Paya Lebar, followed by 5 mins' walk.*

East Coast

■ **Sleeping**
1 Amber
2 Chancellor
3 Hotel 81
4 Kim Sun
5 Malacca
6 Paramount
7 Seaview

● **Eating**
1 Bakeries
2 House of Sundanese
  Food & Peranakan

Joo Chiat Road, which runs south down to the sea, is interesting for its unchanged early 20th-century shophouse fronts. The extravagant façades, found both here and on Koon Seng Road are an excellent example of the Singapore Eclectic Style which evolved in the 1920s and 1930s. This whole area was originally a coconut plantation owned by a family of Arab descent - the Alsagoffs. A portion was purchased by a wealthy Chinese, Chew Joo Chiat, after whom a number of the roads are named (not just Joo Chiat Road; also Joo Chiat Lane, Joo Chiat Terrace and Joo Chiat Place). Peter Wee's Katong Antique House at 208 East Coast Road is well worth a visit if you are in the area, with its unsurpassed collection of Peranakan antiques and an owner who is probably the most knowledgeable person in Singapore on the Peranakan culture. ■ *Bus no 16 from Orchard Rd runs down Joo Chiat Road, as does a 33.*

Changi Changi Prison is on Upper Changi Road. The prison, as featured on the 'Go to Jail' square in the Singapore version of *Monopoly*, is where Singapore's hangman dispenses with drug traffickers - with gruesome regularity. It was originally built to house 600 prisoners but during the war more than 3,500 civilians were incarcerated here. In 1944, POWs were moved into the prison, and 12,000 American, Australian and British servicemen were interned in and around it. It is mostly visited by Second World War veterans - there is a small museum with reproductions of WRM Haxworth's paintings and the then 17-year-old trooper George Aspinall's photographs, which record the misery of internment. A replica of the atap-roofed Changi Prison chapel stands in the prison yard. The memorial chapel's original altar cross, whose base was made from a Howitzer shell casing, was returned to the chapel in 1992. James Clavell's novel *King Rat* is more enlightening than a visit to Changi. To view the murals, a weeks' notice is required. ■ *1000-1700 Mon-Sat, T7437885/5430893.* The Chapel holds a service on Sunday evening, 1730. ■ *T5451411.* The Prison Museum has an interesting display. ■ *MTR to Tanah Merah and then bus 2 or bus 2 direct from Orchard Road.*

North of the Island

Ins & outs **Getting there** The MRT North line loops right around this part of the island and has 23 stops. TIBS buses - the Trans-Island Bus Service - are also useful.

Getting around This is the largest of the areas designated in this book and generally the places mentioned are too far apart to walk between. Take a taxi, bus or the MRT.

The north of the island is Singapore's back garden: in between the sprawling new housing estates there are areas of jungled wilderness, mangroves, lakes and landscaped gardens.

Kong Meng San Phor Kark
The complex has been the backdrop for many kung-fu movies & is one of the largest such complexes in Southeast Asia

Kong Meng San Phor Kark See Chinese Temple Complex (Bright Hill Drive) has, since its construction in 1989, grown into a sprawling, million dollar religious centre whose golden roofs spread over 7½ha. Fed up with tastefully mouldering 19th-century Chinese temples? Then this is the place for you. This is Chinese temple garishness on a truly gargantuan scale. Restrained was clearly not a word in the architect's vocabulary. From the main entrance on Sin Ming Avenue pilgrims climb up through a series of halls with images of the historic Buddha and various other gods and goddesses from Chinese Mahayana Buddhism's extensive repertoire. There are halls for prayer and meditation, a pool containing thousands of turtles, a Buddhist library, an old people's home (and, appropriately, a crematorium), as well as a 9m-high marble statue of Kuan Yin, the 15-headed goddess of mercy, carved by Italian sculptors. The walkways are crowded with hawkers selling jade bangles, Buddhist icons and dubious medicinal remedies. Resident geriatrics in the old people's home spend their last days making paper cars and other worldly symbols which are torched after their deaths and, they hope, follow them into the next world.

■ *Take bus 130 from Raffles City or Clifford Pier; alight at the Sin Ming Drive stop which stops opposite the crematorium. Then walk on to the T-junction and turn left down Sin Ming Avenue to the main entrance. Alternatively, take the MRT to Ang Mo Kio, cross the road to the Ang Mo Kio bus interchange and board bus 130. The golden stupa of the temple can be seen from some way off.*

This is one of the world's few open zoos (moats replace bars), making it also one of the most attractive zoos in the world, with animals in environments vaguely reminiscent of their habitats. In its promotional brochure, the 20ha zoo, at 80 Mandai Lake Road, claims that its open-design concept has paid off: "Our reward is happy animals. The proof lies in the zoo's good breeding record: unhappy animals do not make love!". Only the polar bears and the tigers seemed unhappy in their surroundings. It contains over 170 species of animals (about 2,000 actual animals), some of them rare - like the dinosauric Komodo dragons and the golden lion tamarin - as well as many endangered species from Asia, such as the Sumatran tiger and the clouded leopard. The pygmy hippos are relatively recent newcomers; they live in glass-fronted enclosures (as do the polar bears), so visitors can watch their underwater exploits. There are animal shows throughout the day carrying a strong

Singapore Zoological Gardens

North of the island

Singapore

ecological message: primates and reptiles (at 1030 and 1430) and elephants and sealions (at 1130 and 1530). The latest addition to the zoo is a Treetops Trail where visitors can view primates, crocodiles, squirrels and pheasants from a 6m-high boardwalk. There is a children's area too with farm animals, a miniature train and play equipment. There are tram tours for those too weary to walk (S$2.50 and S$1), with recorded commentaries, and several restaurants. Elephant, camel and pony rides are on offer at various times each afternoon. A shop sells environmentally sound t-shirts and cuddly toy animals. Overall, a well-managed and informative zoo; it's well worth the trip out there. Video cameras can be hired (S$10 per hour). ■ *S$10.30, S$4.60 for children 0830-1800 Mon-Sun, T2693411, www.asianconnect.com /zoo/. MRT to Ang Mo Kio and then SBS 138 from the Ang Mo Kio interchange or MRT to Choa Chu Kang and then TIBS 927. Alternatively take bus 171 to Mandai Road and then cross the road to board the SBS 138 to the zoo. On Sun and public holidays Trans-island bus service (TIBS) 926 runs from the Woodlands bus interchange direct to the zoo. Taxis cost about S$10 to the zoo from the Orchard Road area. A bus service runs every 30 mins from 0730 until 2300 from Orchard and Scott roads (ask at your hotel), S$5 one way. Another option is to book a ticket on the a/c Zoo Express which provides guided tours on demand, contact Elpin, T7322133.*

Night Safari
A must for families

The unique Night Safari is situated adjacent to the zoo, covering 40ha of secondary growth tropical forest. The area has been cunningly converted into a series of habitats populated with wildlife from the Indo-Malayan, Indian, Himalayan and African zoogeographical regions. The park supports 1,200 animals belonging to 110 species including the tiger, Indian lion, great Indian rhinoceros, fishing cat, Malayan tapir, Asian elephant, bongo, striped hyaena, Cape buffalo, and giraffe. Visitors can either hop on a tram to be taken on a 40-minute guided safari through the jungle lit by moonglow lighting and informed by a rather earnest commentary, or they can walk along three short trails at their own pace - or they can do both. The whole affair is extremely well conceived and managed, and the experience is rewardingly authentic - possibly because the night-time ambience hides the seams that are usually so evident in orthodox zoos. Children love the safari experience believing that they truly are chancing upon animals in the jungle. At the entrance 'lodge' there is a good noodle bar as well as a *Bongo Burger Bar*. There is also another small café, at the East Lodge. ■ *1830-2400, T2693411, S$15.45, children (3-12 years) S$10.30. Safaris start at 1930 but restaurants are open from 1630. The last tram leaves at 2315. **NB** No flash cameras permitted. Bus take the trans island bus 171 (it stops at Orchard Boulevard and Scotts roads) to Mandai Road and then cross the road and board the SBS 138 which goes direct to the Night Safari. By MRT, either get off at Ang Mo Kio and then board the SBS 138, or alight at Choa Chu Kang and board the TIBS 927. A taxi from the city costs around S$12, 30 mins.*

The Kranji War Memorial & Cemetery

This cemetery, Woodlands Road, on a gentle hillside overlooking the Straits of Johor, is where Allied soldiers killed in Singapore in the Second World War are buried. In the heart of the cemetery is the War Memorial, bearing the names of 24,346 Allied servicemen who died in the Asia-Pacific region during the war. The design of the memorial is symbolic, representing the three arms of the services - the army, navy and airforce. The upright section represents a conning tower, the lateral elements are wings, and the walls symbolize army lines. Flowers are not allowed to be placed on graves, in case tiger mosquitoes breed in the jars. ■ *Bus 170 goes direct from Rochor Road; alight opposite the entrance to the cemetery. On weekends bus 181 also stops here.*

Sungei Buloh Nature Park, Neo Tiew Crescent, is Singapore's first designated wetland nature reserve. It is an important stopover point for birds migrating along the East Asian Flyway. The best time to visit is in November. Carefully constructed hides throughout 87ha provide excellent observation points for visitors to view birds like sea eagles, kites, and blue herons. There is also a mangrove swamp to walk through. ■ *0730-1900 Mon-Fri, 0700-1900 weekends and public holidays, S$1, children S$0.50. T6690377. Binoculars for hire. Audiovisual show 0900, 1100, 1300, 1500 and 1700 Mon-Sat, every hour between 0900 and 1700 on Sat and Sun. Take MRT to Kranji or Woodlands stations. Alternatively take TIBS bus 170 from Queen's Street to the Woodlands interchange. At Kranji or Woodlands, board TIBS bus 925 to Kranji Reservoir. On weekends bus 925 runs all the way to the park entrance but on weekdays it is a further 20-min walk to the park.*

Bukit Timah Nature Reserve, on Hindhede Drive off Upper Bukit Timah Road, nestles in the centre of the island and has a resident population of wild monkeys, pythons and scorpions. It was one of the first Forest Reserves established in 1883 for the purposes of protecting the native flora and fauna. The naturalist Alfred Russel Wallace collected beetles at Bukit Timah in 1854. Jungle trails go through the forested terrain (130 million-year-old tropical rainforest) that once covered the whole island. The artificial lakes supply the city with much of its water. Clearly marked paths (one of them metalled) in the 81ha reserve lead to Singapore's highest point (164m) for scenic views. A visitors' centre includes an informative exhibition on natural history. ■ *0830-1800.* The nature reserve is at its quietest and best in the early mornings. It is a wonderful contrast to the bustle of modern Singapore. ■ *T4709900, take the MRT to Newton Station, then TIBS bus 171 or 182.*

Nature reserves

Essentials

For Sleeping at Changi airport, see page564.

Sleeping

The main shopping area (Orchard Rd) and the CBD are both a short taxi ride away. There is also a group of 5-star hotels in the Marina Bay area at the eastern edge of the Colonial core. This whole zone was reclaimed from the sea a few years back. Three hotels were constructed 10 years ago, but with the arrival of two 5-star hotels, the opening of Suntec City (a high-tech conference centre), 4 new office blocks, hundreds of new shops, over 75 restaurants and an entertainment centre it has become almost a self-contained district which, because of its proximity to the airport, is proving popular with business travellers.

Colonial core
■ *on map, page 584*
Price codes:
see page 566
Most accommodation listed here is well placed for exploring the sights of the colonial city on foot, as well as the restaurants & bars of Clarke and Boat quays

LL *Conrad*, 2 Temasek Boulevard, Marina Bay, T3388830, F3388164. This is the latest 5-star hotel to open in Singapore. It is the closest to Suntec City, and is good for the business traveller. It has 509 beautifully designed contemporary-style rooms with lots of space, big windows and large desks. Superb service, excellent meeting rooms, and an impressive mezzanine level for functions. US$1.3m has been invested in almost 3,000 artworks throughout the hotel. Pool area is still a little bare but should improve, the fitness centre is adequate. Recommended. **LL** *Raffles*, 1 Beach Rd, T3371886, F3397650, raffles@pacific.net.sg. Nine restaurants and a Culinary Academy, 5 bars (see separate entries under Eating and Bars) and surrounded by 70 shops, much has been said about *Raffles* and, despite criticisms, it is still a great place to stay - if you can afford it. The 104 suites have been immaculately refurbished, with wooden floors, high ceilings, stylish

Singapore

colonial furniture and plenty of space. Bathrooms are the ultimate in luxury and the other facilities are excellent - a peaceful rooftop pool with jacuzzis, state of the art fitness centre, both open 24 hours. About half Raffles' guests are business visitors; corporate rates available. Very exclusive and highly recommended. **LL** *Ritz Carlton*, 7 Raffles Ave, Marina Bay, T3378888, F3380001. Both this hotel and the *Conrad* were designed by Hirsch Bedner of the US. Very contemporary furnishings; considerable investment in artworks (notably the Frank Stella and the Dele Chihuly glass balls below the lobby area); rooms are very attractive, with wooden floors and big bathrooms (providing stunning views of the harbour and river). Large pool area with jacuzzi in well landscaped grounds, huge fitness centre. Good business facilities. Recommended.

L *Carlton*, 76 Bras Basah Rd, T3388333, F3396866. A rather drab, tile-encrusted exterior hides a comparatively lavish lobby which, in turn, hides 477 pretty average rooms. Avoid the smoking rooms, which are rank. Buffet lunch (poor) and dinner (OK); functional pool, business facilities, fitness centre with sauna and jacuzzi. Most of the Carlton's guests are corporate visitors from Australia and Japan, good location. **L** *Intercontinental*, 80 Middle Rd, Bugis Junction, T3387600, F3387366. Attractive renovated and extended block of Art Deco shophouses, with a high rise block behind. Over 400 good sized rooms with spacious bathrooms and every luxury provided, attractive rooftop pool with jacuzzi and well-equipped fitness centre. Business centre with small meeting room. The only drawback of the more expensive rooms in the renovated shophouses is the distance of some rooms from the lifts. Beautifully designed to a high standard and one of the best hotels in Singapore. The *Shophouse Room* is the hotel's showpiece and costs an extra S$60 - for which you get original colonial furniture and parquet flooring. **L** *Marina Mandarin*, 6 Raffles Blvd, Marina Sq, T3383388, F3394977, mms888@ singnet.com.sg, www.commerceasia.mandarin. A/c, restaurants, pool, well equipped fitness centre, good business facilities, large rooms. The hotel consists of 3 giant blocks arranged in a triangle enclosing a vast atrium that rises to the very top of the building, filled with cascades of plants and caged birds giving the aural impression of a jungle. **L** *Oriental*, 5 Raffles Ave, Marina Bay, T3380066, F3399537. Another central atrium, this time triangular, with exterior lifts. Its black marble interior and limited natural light makes it all a little sombre in feel. There are 522 bigger than average rooms with attractive bathrooms. Harbour views are more expensive. It has a large pool, a separate children's pool and a fitness centre. Restaurants include the *Chinese Cherry Garden*, Californian cuisine at *Liana's* and an outdoor Italian (*Pronto*) restaurant by the pool. All very efficient with, as one would expect, excellent service, however, the facilities here are not quite as abundant as elsewhere. **L** *Westin Stamford and Westin Plaza*, 2 Stamford Rd, T3396633, F3365117, westin1@singnet.com.sg, www.westin. com.sg. Thirteen restaurants, attractive triple circular pool (great for children), high-tech fitness centre, it was the tallest hotel in the world until recently, this 2-tower complex was designed by Chinese architect IM Pei who also designed the futuristic Bank of China building in Hong Kong. The *Compass Rose Restaurant* on the top floor provides stunning views over three countries - Singapore, Malaysia and Indonesia (haze permitting) – and despite being overpriced, this is a pretty special place to eat. With over 2,000 rooms and a vast echoing lobby it is all a little overwhelming - and too large for that personal touch. However, it has a good reputation in the business world. On our last visit they were too busy to let us see a room.

L-AL *Grand Plaza*, 10 Coleman St, T3363456, F3399311. Two restaurants, attractive but smallish pool and jacuzzi, gym and health spa all on third floor. Large ballroom and 2 smaller meeting rooms, business centre with computers for guests' use. Although the outside of this building is pretty hideous, with its marble cladding, the interior is not so ostentatious and despite its size (340 rooms), it feels quite intimate. Recommended. **L-AL** *Pan-Pacific*, 7 Raffles Blvd, Marina Square, T3368111,

F3391861. Yet another open triangular 36-storey atrium with a rather claustrophobic feel. It has 800 rooms and about 70% of the guests are business travellers. The rooms are large and pleasantly laid out, with three views. Attractive fan-shaped pool, rather overlooked, two tennis courts and a *Clark Hatch* fitness centre. Famous Japanese restaurant *Keyaki*, with a Japanese garden on the fourth floor. *Aromaz* deli – the only 24 hour deli in Singapore – serves delicious pastries, pizzas and coffee. Efficient service, yet lacking in atmosphere.

AL *Allson*, 101 Victoria St, T2260911, F3397019. Chinese in character with heavy furniture, rooms are adequate, average pool but fitness facilities are limited to a running machine. Live band in the bar, quite a friendly place, slightly off the beaten track. **AL** *Excelsior*, 5 Coleman St, T3387733, F3396236. Several restaurants but the hotel coffee shop is in the Excelsior Plaza next door, open 0600-2230. Small pool and no gym, limited business facilities. Guests may use all the facilities of the *Peninsula Hotel* next door, which is under the same management. Rooms are Art Deco in style and are of average size. Personal safe in every room. Cramped lobby and dreary corridors, definitely a tour group place. **AL** *Peninsula*, 3 Coleman St, T3372200, F3393580. Rooms are quite small and frayed at the edges, small pool, with adequate fitness centre, limited business facilities, 24-hour coffee shop, nightclub, cramped lobby area, friendly and in the heart of the colonial core.

B *Metropole*, 41 Seah St, T3363611, F3393610, metropole@metrohotel.com, www.metro-hotel.com. A smallish business hotel with 54 rooms and no frills. **C** *Mayfair City*, 40-44 Armenian St, T3374542, F3371736. An a/c hotel that has so far survived being renovated, it has both advantages and disadvantages. On the plus side it is quite cheap and has a quaint old lift and rooms with improbably tall doors, as if it were designed for a race of giants. On the down side, the rooms are a touch shabby and reveal no tell-tale signs of having come into contact with an interior decorator. **D** *Willy's Homestay*, 494 North Bridge Rd, T3370916, willys@mbox2.singnet.com.sg. Dorms available (**E**), breakfast included, central and clean. **D-E** *Travellers' Nest*, 28C Seah St, T3399095, (hard to spot - it is above the Thin Wah Tong Medical Hall and directly opposite the *Raffles*). This is the cheapest place to stay within spitting distance of the *Raffles Hotel* - here a bed can cost S$8; over the road they start at S$650! But then you do get a little more for your money. Rooms at the *Travellers Nest* are small, they can be rather stuffy, and all have shared showers and toilets. Dorm bunk beds available. The price includes tea, coffee and a simple breakfast. Roof garden for relaxing.

AL *Merchant Court*, 20 Merchant Rd, T3372288, F3340606, mchotel@sing-net. com.sg, www.raffles.com/ril. New 500-room hotel, owned by the *Raffles* group. This is a welcome addition to the mid-range bracket of hotels, many of which are looking rather tired. Attractive freeform pool in rooftop garden setting with slides and a separate Jacuzzi overlooking the river. Excellent fitness centre managed by *Lifestyles*. Great location makes it an appealing choice. **AL** *New Otani*, 177A River Valley Rd, T3383333, F3392854. Right next to Clarke Quay making it a lively place to stay. The rooms are average, there's a good sized pool for lengths and a fitness centre. Not surprisingly, it is popular with Japanese. Location is its strength. **B** *Robertson Quay*, 15 Merbau Rd, T7353333, F7381515, rqhotel@ mbox3.singnet.com.sq, www.robertsonquayhotel.com.sq. A new circular hotel on the river, just upstream from Clarke Quay.

Singapore river & the City
■ *on map, page 589*
Price codes:
see page 566

Singapore

Orchard Road
■ *on map, page 592*
Price codes:
see page 566
You could be forgiven
for mistaking Orchard
Rd for the US for it
retains little that is Asian
in character

There are numerous 4 and 5-star hotels strung out along the road, mostly concentrated towards the western end. There is often little to differentiate between them.

LL *Four Seasons*, 190 Orchard Boulevard, T7341110, F7330682. This intimate hotel of 250 rooms (and 400 staff) provides exceptional personal service; there's no check-in desk and all guests are greeted by name. Rooms are elegantly decorated in traditional European style, with feather pillows, writing desk, multi-disc player, modem/fax hook up and spacious bathrooms. The hotel has a unique Asian art collection, with attractive artwork in all the rooms. There are 2 pools - one is for lengths - and the hotel boasts the only air-conditioned tennis courts in Singapore, a golf simulator, and a well-equipped health and fitness centre, with attendants on hand all day. Restaurants include Cantonese and contemporary American cuisine, with lunch-time buffet. Although this is primarily a business hotel, children are well catered for and a special children's lunch is provided at the weekends. For service and general ambience, this hotel is hard to beat. Recommended. **LL** *Goodwood Park*, 22 Scotts Rd, T7377411, F7328558. Apart from *Raffles*, this is the only other colonial hotel in Singapore. It has had a chequered history, beginning life in 1856 as the German Recreation Club, the Teutonia. During the First World War it was declared enemy property and was seized by the government. In 1929 it was converted into a hotel, but then during Second World War it was occupied by the Japanese. After the war it became a War Crimes Trial Court and did not resume functioning as a hotel until 1947. The exterior is looking a little scruffy and the lobby area isn't very encouraging, but the rooms are exceptional. Of the 235 rooms, there is a choice of colonial or modern style. The former have ceiling fans and windows that can be opened, with very stylish minimalist decor and lots of space. The modern rooms are slightly smaller, but they overlook the Mayfair pool and some rooms on the ground level lead straight out pool side. All rooms are fitted with the latest electronic equipment. Lovely pool area, set in a garden with pagodas, and another larger lengths pool. Several restaurants (see **Eating**, page 631). Recommended. **LL** *Hyatt Regency*, 10-12 Scotts Rd, T7381234, F7321696, sales@hyatt. com.sg, www.travelweb.com/hyatt.htm. Owned by the Sultan of Brunei, unusual lobby area with bird prints on the walls, bustling atmosphere, stunning flower arrangements, bigger than average rooms, all with an alcove sitting area (some with poolside view) and separate showers. Spectacular large fifth floor garden, with roaring waterfall and a very attractive pool area, poolside bar and restaurant. The executive class rooms have their own private Balinese garden (good for families) while those on the fifth floor open out onto a large terrace area. Squash courts, 2 tennis courts, huge fitness centre with aerobics classes, fabulous jacuzzi and sauna. Very popular bar in the basement - *Brannigans*. Its selling point must be its garden and fitness facilities. 85% corporate clients and good discounts available. Recommended.

LL-AL *Melia at Scotts*, 45 Scotts Rd, T7325885, F7321332. This Spanish hotel has an unusual feel, with attractive contemporary art on the walls. The rooms are well appointed and bigger than average with high ceilings (unusual in modern hotels). There is a smallish pool and the only Spanish restaurant in Singapore. The hotel is popular with Japanese. Rather off the main drag but close to Newton MRT and near the huge hawker centre there, hospitable service. Recommended.

L *Hilton*, 581 Orchard Rd, T7372233, F7322917. The first international hotel in Singapore. Its 434 average-sized rooms were recently renovated and despite its age it maintains a good reputation. Particularly popular with business people (with its function rooms constantly in demand) and with Japanese tour groups. *Tradewinds* restaurant serves local and North Indian food in al fresco atmosphere at the poolside, the *Inn of Happiness* serves Chinese food, *Harbour Grill* for French cuisine (different French chefs visit every month), the *Checkers Deli* on the ground floor sells chocolates and desserts and has a reputation for its Philadelphia cheesecake. The *Kaspia Bar* has the largest range of vodkas in Singapore and live jazz. Small, rather dated pool, good facilities in the fitness centre. **L** *Holiday Inn Park View*, 11 Cavenagh/Orchard Rd, T7338333, F7324757. Grand entrance, attractive airy triangular layout of 300 plus rooms around an atrium. Good pool and fitness centre. Rooms provided for handicapped people. Quiet spot just off the main drag. **L** *Le Meridien*, 100 Orchard Rd, T7338855, F7327886. Open-plan lobby with 4 terraces of rooms and garlands of orchids. Good sized rooms (corner rooms are larger), queen sized beds, attractive decor, ask for a room overlooking the pool, as these have a balcony. Good pool for lengths, but barren seating area. Fitness centre with dance floor for classes. **L** *Mandarin*, 333 Orchard Rd, T7374411, F7322361, www.singnet.com.sg Rather disjointed lobby area, with nowhere comfortable to sit. Rooms (1,200) are large and well designed, uninviting pool area but large pool. Revolving *Top of the M* restaurant on the 39th floor. *Chatterbox* coffee shop open 24 hrs, serves rated Hainanese chicken rice. No outstanding features to this hotel, but the service is reportedly good. **L** *Negara*, 10 Claymore Rd, T7370811, F8316617. This 200-room hotel prides itself on an intimate atmosphere. It pampers the business visitor away from home with personalized service (no reception counters here) and a very high standard throughout. There are no 'club' floors; but larger than average and unusual rooms. Spacious bathrooms and separate showers, large pool but rather exposed sitting area. Very sophisticated fitness centre and jacuzzi. Slightly off Orchard Rd, quieter and away from the crowds. Recommended. **L** *Orchard*, 442 Orchard Rd, T7347766, F7335482. Rooms here have been recently renovated - they are decent sized, all with personal safe and the bathrooms have separate showers; a luxury in Singapore. Large pool but no shade, excellent fitness centre and sauna. Its claim to fame is its magnificent ballroom which seats 1,000 for dinner and 1,500 for conferences. For the *Drake Restaurant*, see below. **L** *Regent*, 1 Cuscaden Rd, T7338888, F7328838. Huge ostentatious lobby with bubble lifts and a rather sterile atmosphere reminiscent of tenement blocks. Gloomy corridors and 440 large but quite plain rooms. Excellent fitness centre but boring circular pool and barren sunbathing area. Quiet location at western end of Orchard Rd. Notable for its excellent service and attention to detail. **L** *Shangri-La*, 22 Orange Grove Rd, T7373644, F7373370. One of Singapore's finest hotels set in a beautifully maintained, spacious landscaped gardens extending over 15 acres. It has 300 plus rooms, renovated and upgraded in 1998/99 at a cost of $S100m more to the point, those in the refined and relaxed Valley Wing are best, the service is exceptional. Excellent leisure facilities: spacious pool area, surrounded by greenery and waterfalls, jacuzzi, indoor pool, good fitness centre, squash and tennis courts, and a three hole pitch and putt golf 'course'. Three restaurants - *Shang Palace* for dim sum, *Tanti Bacis* for poolside Italian and a Japanese restaurant. Winner of Singapore Tourism Board's award for best hotel year after year. Recommended. **L** *Sheraton Towers*, 39 Scotts Rd, T7376888, F7371072. Quietly sophisticated lobby, with waterfalls and beautiful flowers everywhere. There are 400 good rooms but the corridors are bare. The more expensive rooms provide an exceptional service, with lots of extras thrown in. The *Cabana* rooms on the rooftop overlook the pool. Attractive pool area with bar. It is popular with US visitors and 80% of its guests are business people. Italian restaurant open evenings only and exclusive Chinese restaurant. The hotel won the Singapore Tourist Board service award 6 years running.

L-AL *ANA*, 16 Nassim Hill, T7321222, F732222, ANAhotel@singnet.com.sg. Restaurants (including excellent Japanese, of course), pool, formerly the *Sheraton*, a short walk from Orchard Rd.

AL *Marriott*, 320 Orchard Rd, T7355800, F7359800. Another 350-room monster, which was once the *Dynasty*. Its distinguishing feature is its rather ridiculous pagoda 'hat' at the top of the tower block. Unusual lobby with 10m-high palm trees and the usual array of facilities. Good fitness centre and large swimming pool with separate whirlpool and *Garden Terrace Café*. Extensive business services, efficient but unwelcoming, very central. **AL** *Novotel Orchid Singapore*, 214 Dunearn Rd, T2503322, F2509292. 446 unexceptional rooms in an unexceptional hotel. The pool is rather old fashioned and right next to a busy road. Added disadvantage of an inconvenient location. **AL** *Orchard Parade*, 1 Tanglin Rd, T7371133, F7330242, www.singnet. com. sg/~webworld/hotels/ orchardp/orchardp.html. Another featureless block but the rooms have an unusual layout and the bathrooms are refreshingly different. Otherwise quite bland. Decent sized pool with a large bare sitting area. Smallish gym under renovation. The hotel is planning an extensive 3-year expansion programme which will probably improve it. **AL** *Royal Crowne Plaza*, 25 Scotts Rd, T7377966, F7376646. 500 rooms in an ugly block, built in 1974. Quite pleasant pool area, big fitness centre. Owned by the Sultan of Brunei, for whom an entire floor of suites is permanently reserved, *surau* provided for Muslims to pray, popular with Japanese and US visitors. **AL** *Traders*, 1A Cuscaden Rd, T7382222, F314314. Lavish pots of orchids at the entrance makes it feel special, but there isn't much to mark this hotel apart from the competition. It has 547 rooms and about three-quarters of its guests are business people. The rooms are average but there is an attractive pool area with a large pool. It has a fitness centre, a business centre and 3 restaurants. No frills. **AL-A** *Asia*, 37 Scotts Rd, T7378388, F7333563. Ugly block with basic rooms, discounts available. **AL-A** *Equatorial*, 429 Bukit Timah Rd, T7320431, F7379426. Very average establishment with a rather public pool and a small coffee house, not a good location either.**AL-A** *Grand Central*, 22 Orchard Rd, T7379944, F7333175. Restaurant and pool, nothing special but its name provides a clue to its key selling point - it's central. **A** *VIP*, 5 Balmoral Crescent, T2354277, F2352824. Restaurant, a/c, pool, situated in quiet area of the city close to *Garden Hotel* and west of the Newton MRT station, good rooms with TV, minibar etc.

B *Lloyd's Inn*, 2 Lloyd Rd, T7377309, F7377847, a/c. Restaurant, scrupulously clean, well-appointed rooms - if a little cramped - quiet location in suburban road near River Valley Rd/Somerset MRT, off Killiney Rd. **B** *Regalis Court*, 64 Lloyd Rd, T7347117, F7361651. Attractive renovated colonial style boutique hotel, originally a school. It provides 43 beautifully appointed rooms, decked out with Indonesian furniture and decor and wooden floorboards. The standard rooms have no windows, but they are well lit. The price is so reasonable because there is no pool or fitness centre. *Peranakan* restaurant on the ground floor and self-service breakfast. Set in a quiet street behind Orchard Rd, it's hard to beat at the price. Highly recommended. **B** *RELC International House*, 30 Orange Grove Rd, T7379044, F7339976. Basic no-nonsense hotel with no extras. An ugly featureless block but quite a good deal for business visitors, conference rooms attached. **B** *YWCA*, Fort Canning Rd, T3384222, F3374222. Large new building with 200 plus rooms, pool, tennis courts, ballroom, exhibition hall. It is not clear why it's called a *YWCA* - it is not what you would expect from your average youth hostel. Dorms **B**.

C *Metropolitan YMCA*, 60 Stevens Rd, T7377755, F2355528. A little out of the way – a 15 minute walk from the end of Orchard Road – but certainly worth considering. All rooms are a/c, a newly renovated no-frills place providing efficient service and clean serviceable rooms. The added bonus is a large swimming pool as well as a gym. Room rate includes buffet breakfast. Very good value. Recommended. **C** *YMCA International House*, 1 Orchard Rd, T3366000, F3373140. The old *YMCA* which stood on Stamford Rd was used by the Japanese during the war as their dreaded interrogation and torture centre. Facilities are well above the usual *YMCA* standards, a/c, restaurant, rooftop pool, squash courts, badminton, billiards and fitness centre. Grotty from the outside, but it is very clean and efficient. Good value for this location, *McDonald's* on the ground floor, S$25 for 4 bed a/c dorm. Recommended. **D** *Mitre*, 145 Killiney Rd (up a side lane, parallel to Lloyd Rd), T7373811. On the verge of extinction, or ripe for redevelopment, the building is best described as 'crumbling colonial', so has heaps of character, but resembles a junk yard and the rooms are very run down. Nicer than the cheap places on Bencoolen St because of its character.

You can find more unusual accommodation here than other areas of town, with several 'boutique' hotels in converted shophouses, a refreshing change from the high-rise anonymity of Orchard Rd or the Colonial core. If you can do without a pool and fitness centre (though some of the new blocks have such facilities), and don't mind having a small room, but appreciate a little more individuality, then try here.

Chinatown
■ on maps,
pages 597 & 599
Price codes:
see page 566

L *Duxton*, 83 Duxton Rd, T2277678, F2271232, duxton@singnet.com.sg, restaurant (*L'Aigle d'Or*, page 634). Intimate, stylish 50-room hotel in row of refurbished shophouses. Deluxe rooms are split level, but even these are small at this price. Guests have use of the large pool at the *Amara Hotel*. Mainly frequented by business people as it's convenient for the financial district. Its ambience and size make it stand out among Singapore's other luxury hotels. Overpriced on the rack rate but good discounts available either from hotel or from travel agents. Recommended.

AL *Amara*, 165 Tanjong Pagar Rd, T2244488, F2243910, reserv@amara.com.sg. Several restaurants (with one of the best Thai restaurants in town - *Thanying* - see **Eating**, page 634) and a coffee shop serving a good buffet spread (**3**), decent sized pool, with café area for steamboat and barbecues. Well maintained with 338 average sized rooms and good extras such as self-service launderette. Four tennis courts, jogging track and a gym. Business centre with conference room and secretaries on hand. Good location for those wishing to explore Chinatown or for business visitors, as it lies on the edge of the CBD. **AL** *Furama*, 60 Eu Tong Sen St, T5333888, F5341489. Grand lobby belies rather scruffy featureless rooms, it needs a facelift. Restaurant and very basic gym. The building itself stands out from the crowd for its unusual but rather ugly and dated design. **AL** *Harbour View Dai Ichi*, 81 Anson Rd, T2241133, F2220749, www. harbourview.com.sg. Good Japanese restaurant, average sized pool and over 400 large but basic rooms in this high-rise block. Request a harbour view as the view of Tanjong Pagar container port is worth an hour or two's quiet attention. Good location for business district and access to Chinatown. Health centre but no gym, personal safes in more expensive rooms. Business centre with limited secretarial assistance. Meeting room available. Popular with Japanese clients.

A *Inn at Temple Street*, 36 Temple Street, T2215333, F2255391. Opened in 1998, this place bills itself as a boutique hotel and the 42 rooms do have a certain charm: they are well appointed with safes, TVs, Peranakan-style furniture (made in Indonesia) and attached shower (in the standard) or bath (in the deluxe) rooms. On the downside the rooms are very small; not even the deluxe rooms have space for a desk (except in the few single rooms), which will put off business travellers. **A-B** *Chinatown*, 12-16 Teck Lim Rd, T2255166, F2253912. Another shophouse renovation with 40 rooms, a/c, no restaurant but breakfast provided. Small shower rooms and rather bland but, like *Keong Saik* and *The Royal Peacock*, it's an intimate place in an attractive street in the heart of Chinatown. It benefits from a small 'business centre' with a meeting room and secretarial assistance.

B *Damenlou*, 12 Ann Siang Rd, T2211900, F2258500. A/c, attached bathroom, TV, minibar, cheaper rooms are very small but neat and clean and well presented. Very friendly management and located in an attractive street of shophouses. Recommended. **B** *Dragon Inn Chinatown*, 18 Mosque St, T2227227, F2226116. New hotel with a/c spreading over 4 shophouses on the second and third floors, making it a bit of a warren of a place. Attractive low rise location, but rooms are small and basic. For rooms onto the street with windows, book in advance. *Homely Kitchen* next door is soon to open, providing complimentary breakfast. **B** *Keong Saik*, 69 Keong Saik Rd, T2230660, F2250660. A/c, opened early 1997, 25 rooms in a sensitively restored shophouse. Attractive all-wood furniture in immaculately presented but small rooms, with little room for anything other than the bed. Standard rooms have no windows or skylights (attic rooms). An intimate little 'business' hotel, let down by its room sizes. **B** *Royal Peacock*, 55 Keong Saik Rd, T2233522, F2211770. A/c, charming little restaurant, *Butterfly Pub* (with Karaoke), 79 rooms spread along 10 shophouses, similar standard to *Keong Saik*, rooms marginally larger, but again standard rooms have no natural light and showers only. Price includes continental breakfast. Avoid rooms over the pub. Recommended for general feel of the hotel but not for room size. **B** *Sunshine*, 51-57 Tras St, T2210330, F2211178. Situated in a renovated salmon pink and green shophouse. The 40 a/c, rather small rooms are immaculately presented although some are without windows. Friendly manager, attractive location and close to MRT - no restaurant but there's one next door and many others nearby.

C *Air View*, 10 Peck Seah St, T2257788, F2256688. Not much to differentiate this from *New Asia*, although it might be marginally cleaner. Outside toilet and unimpressive shower arrangement. **C** *New Asia*, 2 Peck Seah St, T2211861, F2239002. Similar to *Air View* but dingier - a/c, lino floors, smelly rooms, battered furniture. Bleak. **C** *YMCA*, 70 Palmer Rd, T2224666, F2226467. A/c and basic hot water showers in 50 rooms. Out of the way, at the southern end of Chinatown and the business district, but the rate is good and the rooms are spacious if basic (mostly singles with no toilets). At 40 years old, this must be one of the longest running establishments in Singapore. Friendly manageress - the best place in this price range.

West of Chinatown
Price codes: see page 566

Between Chinatown and Orchard Rd, along Havelock Rd, there are five 3-4 star hotels grouped together in an area that some rather optimistic locals call 'Riverside'. All these hotels are undergoing facelifts in a desperate bid to win customers. Unfortunately, location is a bit of a drawback: the area is rather isolated (although it is only a few minutes by taxi or bus to Clarke and Boat quays, Chinatown and Orchard Rd), it is overlooked by some particularly unsightly HDB blocks and there are no shops or restaurants on the doorstep. However, the whole riverside area from here to Clarke Quay is in the process of being 'upgraded' and before long there will be walkways and shopping malls linking these hotels with Clarke Quay.

AL *Apollo*, 405 Havelock Rd, T7332081, F7331588. Built in 1972, this hotel was showing its age in 1997 but has undergone major cosmetic surgery with a new extension of 135 rooms (making it a 400-room hotel), construction of a sizeable pool, tennis court, gym and jacuzzi, the redesign of the lobby area, and renovation of existing rooms. Three restaurants. Good business centre facilities and larger than average rooms (but featureless). **AL** *Concorde*, 317 Outram Rd,

Havelock Road

■ **Sleeping**
1 Apollo
2 Concorde
3 King's
4 Miramar
5 River View

T7330188, F7330989. Three restaurants, pool, tennis court but no gym. The most stunning design of all the hotels in this area, with a huge circular atrium and exterior bubble lifts. Rooms are being gradually renovated - ask for a new one. Popular tour group hotel, especially for Japanese visitors. **AL** *King's*, 403 Havelock Rd, T7330011, F7325764, Kingstel@ singnet.com.sg, www.asianconnect.com/sha/kings.html. A hotel with 300 plus rooms in another ugly high-rise block. Initial impressions are favourable but the rooms are an anticlimax. Deluxe rooms have balconies and all rooms have personal safes. Family rooms available. Barren but large pool. Live band every evening, Japanese and Chinese restaurants, business centre with computer available and meeting rooms. **AL** *Miramar*, 401 Havelock Rd, T7330222, F7334027. Restaurants including a 24-hour coffee shop, big pool and paddling pool. Built in 1971, but renovated in 1995, 340 spacious rooms in tower block overlooking the river. **AL-A** *River View*, 382 Havelock Rd, T7329922, F7321034. A/c, average restaurant, pool, run by Robert Pregarz, a former Italian sailor and ex-manager of the pre-theme park *Raffles*.

Little India is probably a more interesting place to stay but the accommodation in the Arab Street area is a trifle cheaper, see page 627. Cheap accommodation is very limited in Singapore and many of the backpackers' haunts are to be found in apartment blocks and do not have much to recommend them - other than price.

Little India

■ *on map, page 601*
Price codes:
see page 566
Most of Singapore's budget accommodation (such as it is) is to be found in the Little India & Arab Street areas to the north of town. For Arab Street, see page 627

AL-A *Albert Court*, 180 Albert St, T3393939, F3393252, www.fareast.com. sg/hotels. An unusually designed hotel (a mixture of western and Peranakan), lying behind a courtyard of renovated shophouses. This is an intimate place built to high specifications, with attractive extras. Ask for a room with big windows. Restaurant but no other facilities. Right next to a good range of restaurants in Albert Court. Recommended. **A** *Bencoolen*, 47 Bencoolen St, T3360822, F3362250. The hotel that was here in 1997 has been pulled down - and not a toilet flush too soon - and in 1999 was replaced with a much more salubrious establishment with a health centre, in-room internet access and various other facilities. A good deal at this price. **A** *City Bayview*, 30 Bencoolen St, T3372882, F3382880. A/c, restaurant, leafy rooftop pool. Neat little hotel block with business facilities, personal safes in rooms, attentive and friendly service, popular with tour groups. The rooms are smallish but the hotel is competitively priced and well-run.

B *Dickson Court*, 3 Dickson Rd, at Jl Besar end, T2977811, F2977833. Price includes simple buffet breakfast. New, clean and smart, with friendly management. **B** *Summer View*, 173 Bencoolen St, T3381122, F3366346, summerviewhtl@pacific.net.sg, www.summerviewhotel.com.sg. Compact and quite well designed modern block with 80 very small rooms and no restaurant. Popular with regional businessmen. **B-C** *Broadway*, 195 Serangoon Rd, T2924661, F2916414. A/c, restaurant, ugly hotel block stuck on its own, Indian-run and Indian patronized establishment with clean rooms and friendly management, excellent Indian restaurant downstairs (*New Delhi Restaurant*): 'we know the way to your heart is through your stomach'.

C *Kerbau*, 54/63 Kerbau Rd, T2976668, F2976669. A/c, small hotel in modernised shophouse on this quiet dead-end street. The rooms are hardly spacious and nothing special, but they are clean with attached showers and if you get one looking out onto Kerbau Road it is possible to open the shutters in the evening and watch Indian life from above. Good value. Recommended. **C** *Little India Guesthouse*, 3 Veerasamy Rd, T2942866, F2984866. Some a/c, no private bathrooms, but spotless male/female shower areas and immaculate rooms. No food served here, but plenty on the street. Good location if you want to be in the heart of Little India and all in an attractive salmon-pink shophouse. Recommended. **C** *Lucky*, 18 Race Course Rd, T2919122, F2919391. Small rooms, basic but clean. Good price for location. **C** *Mayo Inn*, 9A Jalan Besar, T2956631, F2958218. A/c, this little converted shophouse on

Singapore

the corner of Jalan Besar and Mayo Street opened in 1996. Rooms are small but are clean and have attached bathrooms. **C** *South East Asia Hotel*, 190 Waterloo Street, T3382394, F3383480, seahotel@ mbox2.singnet.com.sg. A/c, rooms here are clean enough, with attached showers, but they are also a trifle musty. The fact that the hotel seems to be tiled from floor to ceiling is presumably a throw back to the Jurassic period in interior decoration. **C** *Strand*, 25 Bencoolen St, T3381866, F3381330. A/c, attractive café and refurbished rather trendy lobby raises expectations which are then dashed by poor rooms; they are big though and it's quite good value. Popular weekend buffet. **C** *Tai Hoe*, 163 Kitchener Rd, T2939122, F2984600. A/c, hot water bath, not visited on our last visit but recommended by a traveller. **C** *Waterloo Hostel*, 4th, 5th and 7th Flr, 55 Waterloo St, T3366555, F3362160. A/c, centrally located, big rooms with TVs and telephones, complimentary tea/coffee and basic breakfast, very pleasant, friendly atmosphere, run by Catholic Welfare Centre. Recommended. If the hostel is full and you are offered rooms in their 'homestay' - avoid, as the rooms are noisy and not recommended.

C-D *Peony Mansion Travellers' Lodge*, 4th Flr, 46-52 Bencoolen St (lift round back of building), T3385638, F3391471. Another place in the same block as the *Lee Boarding House*, marginally better than the *Peony Mansions* across the road. Has the advantage of two good and cheap Muslim restaurants at ground level. **C-D** *San Wah*, 36 Bencoolen St, T3362428, F3344146. Some a/c, public showers, 10 rooms in one of the very few remaining family-run Chinese hotels in Singapore. The lovely villa, more than 50 years old, is set rather incongrously in a largish compound surrounded by new blocks or empy plots. It is run by the elderly Mr Chao Yoke San and his son. While the hotel may not be very clean, and is often noisy, it has a character and ambience that others cannot match. **C-D** *Sun Sun*, 260A-262A&B Middle Road, T3384911. Some a/c, this is a great little hotel, up a flight of stairs at the southern edge of Little India, run by a Chinese gentleman. All rooms have communal facilities but the showers and toilets are very clean. The rooms are large but plain, with a sink in one corner, and an extra few Singapore dollars buys you a/c. Recommended.

D *Goh's Homestay*, 4th Flr (no lift), 169D Bencoolen St, T3396561, F3398606. Tiny rooms with separate showers but an immaculately clean, friendly place with nice snack bar and fax/storage/washing facilities, only 20 rooms so booking is advisable. Recommended. **D** *Hawaii Hostel*, 2nd Flr, 171B Bencoolen St, T3384187. In same block as *Goh*, but not quite as good. 27 small and rather dirty rooms (and an 8 bed dorm for S$18). Simple breakfast included in room rate, washing facilities available, friendly manageress. **D** *Lee Boarding House*, 7th Flr, 52 Peony Mansion, 46-52 Bencoolen St, T3383149, F3365409. Calls itself 'the exclusive club for travellers' but it seems pretty grim. 100 rooms, some a/c, some with bathrooms, complimentary breakfast of sorts, travel information service, **E** for dorm beds. **D-E** *Peony Mansions*, 2nd Flr, 131A Bencoolen St, T3385638, F3391471. Windowless rooms with only beds in them (no space for anything else). Outside cold (broken?) showers. Dirty. For double the money you can have same size room and a/c (of sorts) and a hot shower (also broken?). A plus is the good roti man on street below.

Singapore

In Arab Street budget hotels are centred on, or close to, Liang Seah Street, a narrow street of shophouses that are gradually being gentrified. There is a good range of restaurants here from trendy cafés to cheap Chinese and Muslim restaurants. It lies between the Arab and Indian quarters so is also quite convenient for these two areas of town. It is about a 15 min walk from the Colonial core.

AL *Golden Landmark*, 390 Victoria St, T2972828, F2982038. This 400-room tower block (with Arabic overtones) is looking older than its 1980s birthdate would indicate. It has an Indonesian restaurant, a big pool, corporate floors and a business centre. Caters mainly for tours and corporate clients - not many Europeans stay here. **A-B** *Park View Hotel,* 81 Beach Road, T3388558, F3348558, www.parkview. com.sg. A/c, new medium-sized hotel. There is no pool or gym but the rooms are well appointed - the deluxe rooms are a good size and better value than the slightly cramped standard (no windows) and superior rooms. **B** *Dickson Court*, 3 Dickson Rd, at Jl Besar end, T2977811, F2977833. Price includes simple buffet breakfast. New, clean, smart, with friendly management. **C** *Beach*, 95 Beach Rd (corner of Liang Seah St), T3367712, F3367713. A/c, basic but clean rooms in an ugly block. **C** *Tai Hoe*, 163 Kitchener Rd, T2939122, F2984600. A/c, hot water bath, not checked on our last visit but recommended by a traveller. **C-D** *Ah Chew Hotel*, Liang Seah Street, T3375285. Old hotel in an unrenovated shophouse and the 14 rooms are much as you would expect: old and unrenovated but with some character - cash only.

    D *Shang Onn*, 37 Beach Rd, T3384153. Ten rooms in another ugly apartment block, no breakfast, but efficient service and rooms are adequate (fan only), no dorms, long term visitors encouraged, not very friendly but recommended. **D-E** *Lee Travellers' Club*, 6th Flr of the Fu Yuen apartment block (and next to the *Park View Hotel*), 75 Beach Rd, T3395490. Some a/c, breakfast included, short on bathrooms, but clean rooms, cooking and storage facilities, owner prides himself on security, **E** for dorms. **D-E** *Waffles Homestay*, 2/F, 490 North Bridge Rd. Great little place, friendly management, lovely roof terrace, access through an Indian restaurant - the *Haj*. Recommended. **D** *Season Homestay*, 26A Liang Seah St, T3372400, www.sgweb.com. sg/homestay. Some a/c, this place opened in 1997, rooms are small (or cozy as they bill them) and can be stuffy, but also clean. Breakfast is included in the rate and dorm beds (**E**) are also available. **D-E** *Cozy Corner Lodge* (formerly the *Backpackers Cozy Corner*), 2a Liang Seah St, T3348761. Located above a restaurant, dorm beds available, this is a cheap option, but the rooms are cramped - sardines come to mind. One dorm room doubles up as the reception, remains popular.

Contrary to first impressions, it is possible to escape from Sentosa's hoardes, thanks to the construction of 3 hotels. The hotels are good, and it is easy enough to get to town from here (free shuttle buses are provided) but, as Stan Sesser put it in the title of his *New Yorker* piece on Singapore, it is rather like being a prisoner in a theme park.

L-LL *Beaufort*, Bukit Manis Rd, T2750331, F2750228, Beaufort@ singnet.com.sg. A/c, restaurants, large (33m) pool, gym, tennis courts, archery, volley ball court, squash courts, access to the 18-hole Tanjong golf course, and 27 acres of grounds. The most refined of the hotels on Sentosa, smaller, quieter and more elegant than the *Rasa Sentosa*, with excellent service. **AL** *Rasa Sentosa (Shangri-La)*, 101 Silosa Rd, T2750100, F2750355 (or in the UK on T0181 747 8485). At the southern tip of the island, fronting the beach, a/c, restaurant, freeform pool, sports facilities, creche, clean beach (sterilized sand imported from Indonesia) and the water is OK for swimming. The hotel is built in a curve, behind Fort Siloso, it has first class facilities and an unsurpassed view of the oil refinery just across the water, competitive weekend package deals available - though it can get very busy then. **A** *Sijori Resort*, situated close to the action by the 37m-high Merlion. This hotel/resort opened in early 1997 and is clearly positioned to tempt those people who wish to make full use of Sentosa's attractions.

Arab Street

■ on map, page 604
Price codes:
  see page 566
The Arab Street & Little India areas are the 2 centres of budget accommodation in Singapore; for Little India, see page 625

Sentosa

■ on map, page 607
Price codes:
  see page 566

Singapore

Sentosa Youth Hostel (next to the lagoon), bookings can be made up to 6 months in advance, T2707888 or 2707889. The hostel is really meant for local youth and community groups, but an a/c room accommodating up to 12 costs S$110 a night during the week and S$120 on weekends. Bedding is provided, there are clean and adequate toilet and shower facilities and barbecue pits. *NTUC Sentosa Beach Resort*, 10 a/c chalets housing 6-10 people, with own bathroom and sitting room, also provides 15 camp shelters with attap roofs, for up to 4 per shelter, pool cafe and barbecue area. *Sentosa Holiday Chalets*, to book call Sentosa Information Office at T2707888 or 2707889. Chalets come in 4-, 6- and 12-bed sizes. Minimum stay in the 4-bed chalet is 2 nights (S$70 non-peak, S$100 peak), while the 6- and 12-bed chalets are available for a minimum of 3 nights. The chalets - which are renovated pre-War era officers quarters - contain a/c bedrooms, basic kitchen facilities, toilets and showers. *Sentosa Campsite*, close to Central Beach (monorail station 5) and can accommodate 300 people. To book call Sentosa Information Office at T2707888 or 2707889. 4- (S$12), 6- (S$14.50) and 8-person (S$19) tents are available while camp beds are rented out at S$0.50 a night. BBQ pits and toilet and shower facilities provided.

East Coast
Price codes:
see page 566
There are a handful of
reasonably priced places
to stay in this area of the
city, along Geylang
Road & down Joo Chiat
Road; the Tourist Office
provides a listing

On the whole, the hotels are patronised by Asian business visitors, but if you are looking for an alternative to the bustle of the city, and don't mind having to walk and take the MRT or bus into town, this is an option.

B *Hotel 81*, 305 Joo Chiat Road, T3488181, F3486960, hotel81@pacific.net.sg, www.hotel81.com.sg. Good value place to stay for business visitors on a budget. Attractive shophouse hotel. With reasonable rooms. **B** *Chancellor*, 181 Joo Chiat Road, T7422222, F3488677, intercon@signet.com.sg, www.asiabiz.com/chancellor. Smallish rooms in shophouses, but nice showers and clean and efficient. Pastel shades and a huge TV in each room. Good value but 10 mins' walk from the MRT. **B** *Sea View*, 26 Amber Close, T345222, F3484335. Ugly great block and not particularly friendly. Note that this place is considerably cheaper if booked from the airport hotel desk. **C** *Amber*, 42 Amber Road, T3445255, F3451911. A hotel with 21 comfortable rooms with TV and attached bathrooms, a/c. **C** *Malacca*, 97-99 Still Road, T3457411, F4405121. Another good value business hotel in this area of town, 20 mins' walk from nearest MRT station (Eunos). Rooms are very well appointed at the price with a/c, TV, and attached bathrooms - cash only.

Eating

Colonial core
● *on map, page 584*
Price codes: see box,
page 573

Expensive 4 *Annalakshmi*, 02-10 *Excelsior Hotel* and Shopping Centre, 5 Coleman St, T3399993, (also at Terminal 2, Changi Airport, T5420407). **Indian** vegetarian cuisine, the *Annalakshmi* is run on the same basis as KL's *Annapoorna*, it is staffed by unpaid housewives and profits go to the Kalamandhir Indian cultural group. The health drinks are excellent - especially Mango Tharang (mango juice, honey and ginger) and Annalakshmi Special (fruit juices, yoghurt, honey and ginger) - the restaurant, which sprawls out onto the verandah overlooking the tennis courts, serves North and South Indian vegetarian food. Samy's banana-leaf and fish-head curries are unrivalled, closes at 2130. Recommended.

4 *Bobby Rubinos*, Fountain Court, CHIJMES, 30 Victoria St, T3375477. **International**, good menu of ribs, burgers, chicken, booking recommended.

4 *Doc Cheng's*, *Raffles Shopping Arcade*, Seah St, T3311612. **New Asian**, unusual combinations of flavours but the rather irritating blurb on the menu may put some off. Even so, the food can be excellent.

4 *Grappas*, CHIJMES, 30 Victoria St, T3349928, **Italian**. Large restaurant in this trendy courtyard. Extensive menu, mostly pasta and risotto dishes with some meat entrees, booking advisable, recommended.

5 *Hai Tien Lo*, *Pan Pacific Hotel*, 37th Floor, Marina Square, T4348338. **Cantonese** restaurant in elegant surroundings with stunning views of the city. Sharks' fins, steamed lobster and Kobe beef are specialities. *Dim sum* lunches on Sundays.

4 *Imperial Herbal*, *Metropole Hotel*, 3rd Floor, 41 Seah St, T3370491, **Chinese**. Dr Li, an in-house herbalist, takes your pulse and recommends a meal with the appropriate rejuvenating ingredients to balance your *yin* and *yang*; unusual, delicately flavoured food, booking recommended for dinner.

5 *Lei Gardens*, Ground Floor, CHIJMES, 30 Victoria St, T3393822. Outstanding **Cantonese** food - silver codfish, emperor's chicken and such regulars as dim sum and Peking duck - in fact a menu which is said to comprise 2,000 dishes. Dignatories, royalty and film stars dine here. Tasteful decor and a 2-tier aquarium displaying the day's offerings. Despite seating for 250 you need to book in advance. Worth every penny. Recommended.

5 *Maison de Fontaine*, Ground Flr, CHIJMES, 30 Victoria St, T3347663. Excellent, sophisticated **French** restaurant in an attractive setting. Also sells French deli food in a shop at the back.

5 *Migen*, Ground Floor, CHIJMES, 30 Victoria St, T3323003. Full choice of **Japanese** food in this attractive courtyard. Booking at weekends is recommended.

5 *Raffles Grill*, *Raffles Hotel*, 1 Beach Rd (main building, first floor), T3311611. Elegant colonial surroundings, with silver plate settings, chandeliers and reproduction Chippendale furniture. Serves breakfast, lunch and dinner, excellent **French** cuisine, windows open onto Palm Court.

5 *Ristorante Bologna,* *Marina Mandarin Hotel*, 6 Raffles Blvd, Marina Square, T3383388. Award winning **Italian** restaurant, house specialities include spaghetti alla marinara and baked pigeon, diners lounge amidst sophisticated decor and wandering minstrels strum.

5 *Szechuan Court*, 3rd Flr, *Westin Stamford and Westin Plaza*, 2 Stamford Rd, T4315323, **Sichnanese**. The Raffles City corporate dinner brigade eat here and it is pricey although the 6-course set meal is probably a good bet.

Cheaper **3** *Empire Café*, Ground Flr, *Raffles Hotel*, 1 Beach Rd, **International**. Not bad for pork chops and oxtail stew, prepared by Chinese cooks and served on marble-topped tables, also serves chicken rice, burgers and ice-creams, open 24 hours. *Ah Teng's Bakery* adjoins, selling pricey pastries, pies and biscuits - mostly local favourites.

3 *House of Sundanese Food*, several outlets spread around town, eg Suntec City Marina Square, T5343775. Typical **Sundanese** dishes from West Java include spicy salad (*keredok*), charcoal-grilled seafood (*ikan Sunda*, *ikan mas*) and curries, simply decorated non-a/c restaurant, with a real home-cooked taste.

3 *Han's*, 8 branches around the city including Raffles Link Marina Square. This chain of restaurants is Singapore's answer to the Greasy Spoon - cafes without the acute accent on the 'e', single dish **Chinese** meals, simple (largely fried) breakfasts, some **European** food including such things as steaks, burgers and fries all served in large helpings at very competitive prices.

2 *Komala's Fast Food*, *Peninsula Plaza*, Coleman Street. One of Komala's fast food outlets - good **South Indian** delicacies including thalis, masala dosas and idlis served at competitive prices, a/c (next door is the more upmarket *Ganges Restaurant* which lays on a good lunch time Indian vegetarian buffet spread).

3 *Java Bean*, Liang Seah St (North Bridge Rd end), trendy little café serving a limited **International** menu of sandwiches and salads along with coffee and beers.

3 *Nomad's*, Fountain Court, CHIJMES, 30 Victoria St, T3346466, **Chinese/International**. Mongolian BBQ - choose your raw food (as much as you can eat) and your sauces and then it's cooked for you. Very trendy.

3 *Pennsylvania Country Oven*, Stamford House, Stamford Rd, T3369733. For Americans craving **New England** cooking, with kitsch interior to boot.

3 *Ramayana*, 6 Raffles Boulevard, Marina Square, T3363317. **Indonesian** restaurant big on seafood and an extensive range of milk shakes.

3 *Sanur*, 3rd Flr, 133 New Bridge Rd. Cramped **Malay/Indonesian** restaurant ideally placed for shoppers, specialities include fish-head curries and grilled chicken or fish.

3 *Shrooms*, Ground Flr, CHIJMES, 30 Victoria St, T3362268, **International**, trendy re-vamped restaurant with different menus upstairs and down.

Hawker centres and food courts 2 *Fountain Terrace*, Suntec City, Marina Square. Trendy foodcourt situated under the enormous fountain. **2** *The Marketplace at Water Court*, basement of Raffles City. Sophisticated food court mostly frequented by businesspeople with a penchant for extravagant sandwiches and patisseries - no chicken rice or mutton biryani here. **1** *Funan Centre*, South Bridge Rd. This big shopping plaza contains one of the best food courts in Singapore in its basement, with a huge range of foods to choose from, in particular, an excellent Indian stall. **1** *Hill Street Food Centre,* west side of Hill St. Three floors of hawker stalls, lots of Muslim food and plenty of everything else, very popular and great value.

Tiffin 5 *Tiffin Room*, *Raffles Hotel*, 1 Beach Rd (main building, ground floor). Tiffin curry buffet (plus à la carte menu) in pristine white, over-lit ersatz Victorian grandeur. The food is good but at S$35 for the buffet, you're paying a lot more for the surroundings than for the curry, reservation recommended, no singlets or shorts.

Cafés 3 *Café Les Amis*, Asian Civilisations Museum, Armenian St. New offshoot of *Les Amis*, Shaw Centre, exotic **international** menu. **3** *Dôme*, next door to the Singapore Art Museum on Bras Basah Rd. Delicious foccacia sandwiches, patisseries and some of the best coffee in town, good café atmosphere and a pleasant stop for a midmorning break. **3** *Fat Frog*, The Substation, Armenian St. Attractive leafy courtyard, serving **wholefood** snacks, sandwiches and soups. **3** *Café Aria*, Young Musicians' Society Arts Centre, Waterloo St, popular for a coffee stop.

Tea, cakes and coffee 3 *Compass Rose Lounge*, *Westin Stamford Hotel*, 2 Stamford Rd. Best views in Singapore, strict dress code, expect to queue, available 1130-1730. **3** *Seah Street Deli*, Ground Flr, *Raffles Hotel*, North Bridge Rd. New York-style deli serving everything from corned beef and smoked-salmon to cheese cakes and Turkish pastries. **3** *Ah Teng's Bakery*, Raffles Arcade. Pricey but it has all the goodies you dream about at the end of a long trip away from home. Complimentary second cup of coffee.

Singapore river & City
● *on map, page 589*
Price codes: see box, page 573

Expensive 4 *Bangkok Garden*, Keck Seng Tower, 133 Cecil St (financial district), T2207310. Almost anything **Thai** is available, even if it's not on the menu, speciality fruit juices and crab dishes are very popular.

3 *Blaze Café*, Ground Flr, The Cannery, Clarke Quay, **international**. Pizza, pasta, hotdogs, fish and chips, burgers - a good place to bring the children.

3 *Brewerkz*, Riverside Point, T4382311, a micro brewery with pricey beer and also serving **New Asia** cuisine.

3 *Chilis*, 75 Boat Quay. **American** fare - burgers, grills, sandwiches - a good menu and reasonably priced for this prime location.

4 *Diandin Leluk*, Riverside Point, 30 Merchant Rd, opposite Clarke Quay, T4382890, **Thai**. Special deals and plenty of seafood dishes, attractive location.

3 *Hooters*, Clarke Quay (1st flr), across from the bridge. **American** food, seafood specialities. Good value lunch specials, music in the evenings, lots of merchandising.

5 *Hot Stones Steak and Seafood*, **International**, 53 Boat Quay, T5355188. Speciality: cooking slabs of meat or seafood on baking-hot Serpentine rock at the table.

4 *Paladino di Firenze*, 7 Mohammed Sultan Rd, T7380917. Unusual **Italian** dishes in a restored shophouse setting - the bruschetta is outstanding.

4 *Pasta Fresca da Salvatore*, 30 Boat Quay, **Italian**. Fresh, tasty pizzas and a good range of pasta dishes, open 24 hours.

4 *The Next Level*, Merchant Village, Merchant Road. New, trendy **fusion** restaurant just south of the river.

4 *Riverside Indonesian Restaurant* Riverside Point, 30 Merchant Rd, opposite Clarke Quay, T5350383. Bright functional interior, but some al fresco dining overlooking the river, baked pomfret, chilli crabs, grilled chicken - good menu and attractive location.

3 *Pao Pao Cha Vegetarian Restaurant*, Riverside Point, 30 Merchant Rd, on river, opposite Clarke Quay. Camp little place with a range of teas and **vegetarian** small eats, strange decor.

3 *Sushi Dokoro Yoshida*, 58 Boat Quay, T5341401. Another riverfront restaurant specializing in **Japanese** *izakaya* (barbecued fish) designed around a sushi bar, also a branch in Lucky Plaza, Orchard Rd.

4 *Sukhothai*, 47 Boat Quay, T5382422. Extensive **Thai** menu but the food can be a little hit and miss, booking recommended.

3 *Yu Kong Choon,* Riverside Point, 30 Merchant Rd, opposite Clarke Quay, T4385880. Good location and good **seafood**, open until 0400.

Cheaper 2 *House of Sundanese Food*, 55 Boat Quay. Typical **Sundanese** dishes from West Java include spicy salad (*keredok*), charcoal-grilled seafood (*ikan Sunda*, *ikan mas*) and curries, simply decorated non-a/c restaurant, with a real home-cooked taste.

2 *Nonya and Baba*, 262/264 River Valley Rd, T7341382. Simple place serving excellent **Peranakan** food which blends Chinese and Malay cuisine in a unique fusion. Lots of coconut milk and seafood with dishes such as *otak otak* (spicy pressed fish in coconut milk). The owner is an Elvis fan. The *Next Page Pub*, in a refurbished shophouse, is nearby (see **Bars**, below).

Hawker centres and food courts 2 *Lau Pa Sat Festival Market* (formerly the Telok Ayer Food Centre) at the Raffles Quay end of Shenton Way in the old Victorian market (see page 591). Good range of food on offer: Chinese, Indian, Nonya, Korean, Penang, icecreams, fruit drinks - it's well worth a browse. **2** *Satay Club*, evening stalls in the pedestrian streets of Clarke Quay. The food is good but, being a tourist trap, it's almost double the price of other food courts. **1** *Quayside Food Court*, Basement of Liang Court, next door to Clarke Quay. Good choice of Asian stalls and a *Burger King*, play area for children.

Cafés *Bar Gelateria Bellavista*, Clarke Quay. Delicious Italian ice cream, indoor and outdoor seating. *Polar Café*, B1-04 OUB Centre, Raffles Place (also branch in Lucky Plaza, Orchard Rd). The original home of the curry puff, first created at its former premises on Hill St in 1926, S$0.70 each. Recommended. *Café Boat Quay*, 82 Boat Quay, T2300140. A refurbished shophouse. A dozen computers available for surfing the web, S$10 per hour. Built in NetNanny prevents any sleaze, if you let your children loose here. International 'snack' food, live music some nights. **3** *Dôme*, in the heart of the business district on Cecil St. Delicious foccacia sandwiches, patisseries and some of the best coffee in town, good café atmosphere and a pleasant stop for a midmorning break.

Expensive 4 *Bombay Woodlands*, 19 Tanglin Rd, Tanglin Shopping Centre, Orchard Rd, T2352712. Very reasonably priced for the area, **Indian vegetarian** food.

4 *Bumbu*, Orchard Shopping Centre, Orchard Rd. Trendy new spot offering **Indonesian** cuisine.

5 *Chico's N Charlie's*, 05-01 Liat Towers, 541 Orchard Rd, T7341753. An expat **Mexican** hang-out, good atmosphere, good choice of hacienda food, excellent margaritas and good value.

4 *Esmirada*, No 01-01/02, Peranakan Place, 180 Orchard Rd, T7353476. **Mediterranean**

Orchard Road
● *on map, page 592*
Price codes: see box, page 573

food in Spanish style taverna, good salads, paella, couscous. Always packed, reservations recommended.

4 *Dragon City*, *Novotel Hotel*, 214 Dunearn Rd, T2547070, popular **Szechuan** restaurant with classic ostentatious Chinese decor, renowned for its spicy seafood. The smoked Szechuan duck is a speciality (similar to Peking duck), booking advisable, recommended.

4 *Drake Restaurant*, basement of *Negara Hotel*, 10 Claymore Rd, off Orchard Rd, T8316688, **international**. A theme restaurant taken to extremes, with duck decoys, duck noises, duck prints and an all-duck menu.

4 *El Felipé's*, 360 Orchard Rd 02-09, International Building, T4681520, **Mexican**. *El Felipé's* frozen margaritas are even more delicious than the burritos. Recommended.

5 *Gordon Grill*, Lobby, *Goodwood Park Hotel*, 22 Scotts Rd, T2358637. One of the last Grills in town, Singapore's only **Scottish** restaurant with haggis on the menu ... at 24 hours' advance notice. Plenty of choice cuts of meat to choose from. Superb desserts.

5 *Harbour Grill*, *Hilton Hotel*, 581 Orchard Rd, T7303393, **International**. Contemporary surroundings, oysters are a speciality, but other delicacies include caviar and smoked salmon, impeccable service.

4 *Kintamani*, *Apollo Hotel*, 405 Havelock Rd, T7332081. **Balinese**-style interior, extensive buffet spread available at lunch and dinner.

4 *Korean Restaurant*, Specialists' Centre, Orchard Rd, T2350018. This imaginatively-named restaurant is well known for its *bulgogi* meat barbecues.

5 *Latour*, *Shangri-La Hotel*, 22 Orange Grove Rd, T7373144. Sophisticated - and pricey - **French** restaurant serving classic cuisine, open for lunch and dinner.

5 *Le Chalet*, *Ladyhill Hotel*, 1 Ladyhill Rd (off Orchard Rd), T7372111. Opened in 1968 this Swiss restaurant is still *the* place to eat fondue in Singapore.

3 *Lei Gardens*, Ground Floor, CHIJMES, 30 Victoria St, T3393822, F3342648, also at Orchard Shopping Centre, 321 Orchard Rd, T7343988 and Orchard Plaza, 150 Orchard Rd. Outstanding **Cantonese** food - silver codfish, emperor's chicken and such regulars as *dim sum* and Peking duck - in fact a menu which is said to comprise 2,000 dishes. Dignatories, royalty and film stars dine here. Tasteful decor and a 2-tier aquarium displaying the days offerings. Book in advance. Worth every penny. Recommended.

5 *Maxim's de Paris*, *The Regent*, 1 Cuscaden Rd, T7393091. **French** extravaganza in an art deco setting, booking recommended, excellent food and the most extensive wine list in Singapore, pay through the nose for this spot of sophistication.

4 *Min Jiang*, *Goodwood Park Hotel*, 22 Scotts Rd, T7301704. Large, noisy room, expansive **Szechuan** menu, with excellent reputation - delicious hot and sour soup, and good choice of seafood, 7 private rooms as well, booking recommended.

5 *Nutmegs*, *Hyatt Regency Hotel*, 10-12 Scotts Rd, off Orchard Rd, T7307112. A well established **New Asia** restaurant, guest chefs means that the menu changes regularly. Recommended.

4 *Olio Dome*, Wheelock Place, 501 Orchard Rd, T7377044. *Olio Dome* provides more than just a coffee and a sandwich, range of 'Mediterranean' food, with specials on a blackboard.

4 *Pasta Fresca da Salvatore*, Shaw Centre (convenient for movies upstairs at Shaw Lido Complex), **Italian**. Fresh, tasty pizzas and a good range of pasta, open 24 hours.

4 *Paolo and Ping*, *Royal Crowne Plaza Hotel*, 25 Scotts Rd, T7317985. Popular **New Asian** restaurant.

4 *Saigon*, Cairnhill Place, 15 Cairnhill Rd, off Orchard Rd, T2350626. Spacious and relaxed surroundings, superb **Vietnamese** food, with very helpful waiters to give advice, pan-fried beef recommended and innovative and tasty dishes such as crab in beer.

5 *Seasons*, *Four Seasons Hotel*, 190 Orchard Blvd, T8317250, **International**. Sophisticated surroundings and unusual food combinations makes this a relaxed and pleasurable gastronomic experience, at weekends they cater for children.

5 *Suntory*, 06-01 Delfi Orchard, 402 Orchard Rd, T7325111, **Japanese**. For sushi, tempura, teppanyaki and shabu-shabu-lovers with a serious yen (or two).

Cheaper **2** *Bintang Timur*, 02-08/13 Far East Plaza, 14 Scotts Rd, T2354539. Excellent **Malay** satays and curries, the ambience allows you to forget that you're in a shopping centre.

3 *Chilli Buddy's*, 180 Orchard Rd, Peranakan Place, **International**. Outside dining under umbrellas, informal and relaxed.

3 *Cuppage Thai Food*, 49 Cuppage Terrace, T7341116. Popular **Thai** restaurant with outside tables and photographs of the food to aid decision making, makes for a good evening if combined with a visit to *Saxophone bar*, just a few doors down. Recommended.

3-2 *Han's*, 8 branches around the city including Park Mall (Dhoby Ghaut) and the Far East Plaza (Scotts Road). This chain of restaurants is Singapore's answer to the Greasy Spoon - cafes without the acute accent on the 'e', single dish **Chinese** meals, simple (largely fried) breakfasts, some **European** food including such things as steaks, burgers and fries all served in large helpings at very competitive prices.

3 *Hard Rock Café*, 02-01 HPL House, 50 Cuscaden Rd, **International**. One of the best bets for a decent steak, buffalo wings or a bacon cheeseburger, open until 0200.

2 *Ivin's*, 19/21 Binjai Park, out of town, off Dunearn Rd (north of Orchard Rd). Very good, cheap food in hectic atmosphere, popular restaurant serving all main **Nonya** dishes.

3 *Maharani*, 05-36 Far East Plaza, Scotts Rd, T2358840. Rated as one of the best for **North Indian** cuisine - tandoori chicken and kormas are specialities.

3 *Next Level*, Merchant Village, Merchant Road. New, trendy **fusion** restaurant just south of the river.

3 *Orchard Maharajah*, 25 Cuppage Terrace, T7326331. Excellent **North Indian** food - tandoori and Kashmiri, conveniently located next door to *Saxophone* in converted shophouse, 7 different types of bread to choose from.

3 *Planet Hollywood*, 541 Orchard Rd, **International**. Opened to much showbiz fanfare in 1997, but it isn't up to much. There's a limited menu - pizza, pasta and burgers - young trendies come for the surroundings (leopard and zebra skin walls and carpets) and the merchandise, not for the food. No booking available.

3 *Sanur*, 17/18, 4th Flr, Centrepoint, 176 Orchard Rd, T7342192. Cramped **Malay/Indonesian** restaurant ideally placed for shoppers, specialities including fish-head curries and spicy grilled chicken or fish.

3 *Saxophone*, 23 Cuppage Terrace. Singapore's best live-music joint also has an excellent **French** restaurant: the menu is select, eat at the bar or on the terrace, escargots and chocolate mousse recommended.

3 *Singapore Polo Club*, 80 Mount Pleasant Rd (just off Thomson Rd), **International**. If you're not put off by the polo set or visiting sultans, the Polo Club is a great place to dine (or drink Pimms) on the verandah - especially on match days (Tue, Thur and Sat) when there's plenty to look at. There is a snack menu (steak sandwich, fish and chips etc) for the verandah overlooking the turf and a smarter restaurant inside. Recommended.

3 *Tambuah Mas*, 4th Flr, Tanglin Shopping Centre, T7332220 (another branch at Level 5, Shaw Centre), a/c restaurant. Very popular and cramped **Indonesian** restaurant. What it lacks in ambience, it more than makes up for with the food, specialities include *ayam goreng istimewa* (marinated fried chicken). Recommended.

3 *Tony Romas'*, Orchard Rd Shopping Centre, Orchard Rd, **International**. Good ribjoint.

3 *Papa Joes*, 01-01/02, 180 Orchard Rd, Peranakan Place, T7327012. Under the same ownership as *Chilli Buddy's* and *Esmirada*, serves **Caribbean** food at lunch and from 1800-2230 in the evenings, but is better known for its disco.

3 *Yushiada Ya*, basement of Lucky Plaza, Orchard Rd, **Japanese**. Excellent sushi.

Hawker centres and food courts *Newton Circus*, Scotts Rd, north of Orchard Rd. Despite threats of closure by the government, this huge food centre of over 100 stalls is still surviving and dishing up some of the best food of its kind. **1** *Taman Serasi*, Cluny Rd, opposite entrance to Botanic Gardens, small centre but well known for roti

John and superb satay, mainly Malay stalls, excellent fruit juice. *Cuppage Plaza* and *Orchard Point* both have extensive foodcourts in their basements.

Cafés *Bar Gelateria Bellavista*, Clarke Quay. Delicious Italian ice cream, indoor and outdoor seating. **2** *Cyberheart Café*, basement of Orchard Shopping Centre, Orchard Rd. Pizzas, pasta and sandwiches and lots of fun with the net. **3** *Dôme*, Lane Crawford House, Orchard Rd and The Promenade on Orchard Rd. Delicious foccacia sandwiches, patisseries and some of the best coffee in town, good café atmosphere and a pleasant stop for a midmorning break. **3** *Goodwood Park Hotel*, Scotts Rd. Sophisticated buffet tea, served on the lawn by the pool. **3** *Shangri-La Hotel*, 22 Orange Grove Rd. Said to offer the best tea in town. Recommended.

Chinatown
● *on maps, pages 597 & 599*
Price codes: see box, page 573

Expensive **5** *L'Aigle d'Or*, Duxton Hotel, 83 Duxton Rd, T2277678, **French**. A few Oriental touches and a good vegetarian selection, extensive, expensive menu with wine list to match, sophisticated atmosphere, popular as a business venue at lunch time, booking recommended.

4 *Blue Ginger*, 97 Tanjong Pagar Rd, T2223928. In restored shophouse - good home cooked **Nonya** (Peranakan) food and relaxed atmosphere.

4 *La Cascade*, 7 Ann Siang Rd, T3241808. Attractive and sophisticated little **French** restaurant down a quiet street in Chinatown, serving snails, veal, duck - good menu, recommended.

3 *Chat Point*, Club St. A small restaurant-cum-pub serving **Malay/ Indonesian/Nonya** dishes. Seafood is best: squid, chilli crab, tiger prawns - and live music.

3 *Clips Wine Bar and Restaurant*, Gemmill Lane (at intersection of Cross St and Club St), **International**. This is more of a wine bar than a restaurant, in an attractive Tuscan-coloured shophouse. The wine list (mostly New World) is considerably longer than the food menu, which is nothing out of the ordinary - steaks, fish, mixed grill and chicken. Closed at lunch.

3 *Orchard Garden*, 4th Flr, Lucky Chinatown shopping centre, New Bridge Rd, **Chinese**. *Dim sum* at lunchtime.

4 *Da Paolo*, 66 Tanjong Pagar Rd, T2247081. One of two *Da Paolo's* in Tanjong Pagar, **Italian**. Both are in restored shophouses decorated in contemporary fashion. Popular with expats, home-made pasta, but over-priced.

3 *Pasta Brava*, 11 Craig Rd, Tanjong Pagar. Tastiest **Italian** in town in an equally tasty shophouse conversion, fairly expensive but good choice available. Recommended.

3 *Siam's Fins*, 45 Craig Rd (and at other outlets). Hang Khim is a Bangkok chef and he produces the very best shark's fins - along with an assortment of other **Thai** seafoods.

3 *Swee Kee*, 12 Ann Siang Rd, T2211900. This **Chinese** restaurant has acquired some degree of local reknown due to the owner Tang Kwong Swee - known to his friends as 'Fish-head' - having run the same place for 60 years (although the location has changed). Recommended are the deep fried chicken, Hainanese style, fish head noodle soup and prawns in magi sauce, very popular.

4 *Thanying*, Amara Hotel, T2224688 and at Clarke Quay, T3368146. Provides the best **Thai** food in town, extensive menu and superb food (the 15 female chefs are all said to have trained in the royal household in Bangkok). Specialities include deep fried garoupa, *yam som-o* (spicy pomelo salad), *khao niaw durian* (durian served on a bed of sticky rice - available from May-August) as well as such classics as *tom yam kung* (spicy prawn soup with lemon grass), booking necessary, recommended.

Cheaper **2** *Fratini*, 1 Neil Rd, T3238088. Cheap and cheerful **Italian** pasta joint in a restored shophouse.

3-2 *Geah Café*, Gemmill Lane (at intersection of Cross St and Club St), **International**. Small café/bar with a limited menu of sandwiches, fried chicken wings and corn chips, good location for coffee or beer.

2 *Hillman*, 1st Flr, Block 1 Cantonment Rd, (southern end of Chinatown). Popular good value wholesome **Cantonese** stews served out of earthenware pots.

2 *New Nam Thong*, 8 Smith St, **Cantonese**, including dim sum from 0400 and a lunchtime menu.

3 *Sanur*, 3rd Flr, 133 New Bridge Rd. **Malay/Indonesian** restaurant, one of a chain, specialities include fish-head curry and spicy grilled chicken.

2 *Tai Tong Hoi Kee*, 2 Mosque St, **Cantonese**, dim sum from 0400.

2 *Tiong Shiang*, corner of Keong Saik and New Bridge Rd, very popular **Hainanese** corner café with tables spilling out onto the street.

1 *Ci Yan Vegetarian Health Food*, 2 Smith Street. New restaurant serving pesticide-free vegetarian food, small (seats 25), good and cheap.

Hawker centres and food courts 1 *Amoy Street Food Centre*, just south of Al Abrar Mosque at southern end of Amoy St. Excellent little centre, worth a graze. **1** *Chinatown Complex Hawker Centre*, Block 335, 1st Flr, Smith St. Recommended stall: *Ming Shan* (No 179), for its *kambing* (mutton) soup, famed for decades, though a pretty scruffy food centre. **1** *Maxwell Road Hawker Centre* (corner of Maxwell and South Bridge roads), Tanjong Pagar, mainly Chinese, best known for its two chicken rice stalls.

Tea, cakes and coffee shops *Tea Chapter*, 9A-11A Neil Rd, Chinatown, T2261175. An excellent little place on 3 floors with a choice of seating (on the floor or at tables), a peaceful atmosphere, plenty of choice of teas as well as sweet and savory snacks, games for those who want to tarry, and the director, Lee Peng Shu, and his wife enthusiastically talk you through the tea tasting ceremony (if you wish). Recommended. See page 599 for further details.

Expensive For North Indian cuisine, the best option is to trot down to the southern end of Race Course Rd, where there are 6 good restaurants in a row, all competing for business including the *Banana Leaf Apolo*, *Delhi*, *Nur Jehan* and, most famous of all, *Muthu's*. Some of the best vegetarian restaurants - South Indian particularly - are found on the other side of Serangoon Road, along Upper Dickson Street.

Little India
● *on map, page 601*
Price codes:
see box, page 573
Restaurants here range from sophisticated a/c places to the simplest of banana plate eateries

3 *Amaravathi*, 19/20 Race Course Lane, **Indian**. In the same block as *Kaaraikubi* and also air-conditioned but this place serves Mulli cuisine.

3 *Aziza's*, 02-05 Albert Court, 180 Albert St, T2351130. Renowned for excellent home-cooked **Malay** food. It is said that the Sultan of Brunei eats here when in town.

3 *Banana Leaf Apolo*, 56-58 Race Course Rd, T2938682. **North Indian** food, another popular fish-head curry spot, a/c and more sophisticated than the name might imply - although the food is still served on banana leaves to justify the name.

3 *Delhi*, Race Course Road. **North Indian** food including chicken tikka, various tandooris as well as creamy Kashmiri concoctions.

3 *Kaaraikubi Banana Leaf*, 19/20 Race Course Lane. A/c **Indian** restaurant without much character but with excellent food on this quiet street off Serangoon Road.

3 *Komala Vilas*, 76-78 Serangoon Rd, T2936980. **South Indian** thalis and masala dosas, bustling café, with a little more room upstairs, recommended.

3 *Muthu's Curry*, corner of Rotan and Race Course Rd, T2937029. **North Indian** food, reckoned by connoisseurs to be among the best banana leaf restaurants in town, *Muthu's* fish-heads are famous, recommended.

4 *Taj Jazzaraunt*, Campbell Lane (above the Little India Arcade). This is a slightly different place to eat **Indian** food. Garlic king prawns, tandoori, shashlick and other North Indian delights can be consumed to live jazz. The restaurant stretches along the whole first floor of the shophouse block so it is possible to grab a table on a balcony and watch the Indian life of Serangoon Road.

Singapore

3 *Wing Seong Fatty's Eating House*, 01-33 Albert Complex, T3381087. Established in 1926, excellent steamed garoupa, roast duck and pork, peeled chilli prawns and other **Cantonese** dishes. Recommended.

Cheaper 2-3 *Komala's Fast Food*, Upper Dickson Road. This is the fast food end of the Komala empire - **South Indian** delicacies including thalis, masala dosas and idlis are served in an airconditioned restaurant, very popular and recommended.
2 *Madras Coffee House*, Serangoon Road (opposite the Sri Veeramakaliamman Temple). This is a great little traditional place with marble tables, fans and stainless steel cups and plates as well as excellent sweet and salt lassis, yoghurt rice, dosas and other **South Indian** dishes. Recommended.
2 *Madras New Woodlands*, 12 Upper Dickson Rd (off Serangoon Rd), T2971594. Thalis, masala dosa and **vegetarian** curries, good and cheap, recommended.
2 *New Delhi*, *Broadway Hotel*, 195 Serangoon Rd. Good, cheap vegetarian and non-vegetarian **North Indian** food, specialities are chicken and almond, and seafood curries.
2 *Ponthuk Bawean Restaurant*, Dunlop Street (at Jalan Besar end). Simple, open-air **Malay** restaurant in a wonderfully gaudy shophouse serving such dishes as beef rendang, chilli eggs, and spicy beans.

Hawker centres and food courts 1 *Albert Court*, between Waterloo and Queen Sts. There's a huge area of hawker stalls here. **1** *Lavender Food Square*, Lavender Rd, north of Little India, is one of the best hawker centres in town. **1** *Paradiz Centre Basement Food Centre*, 1 Selegie Rd, recommended stall: *Mr Boo's Teochew Mushroom Minced Meat Mee* (No 34). **1** *Zhujiao or Kandang Kerbau (KK) Food Centre*, in the same complex as the wet market, on the corner of Buffalo and Serangoon roads. Wide range of dishes, and the best place for Indian Muslim food: curries, rotis, dosai and murtabak are hard to beat (beer can be bought from the Chinese stalls on the other side).

Cafés 3 *Café Oriel*, ground flr Selegie Arts Centre, off Prinsep St. Popular for pizzas.

Tea, cakes and coffee shops *Zhong Guo Hua Tuo Guan*, this traditional Chinese tea house has quite a few outlets including an atmospheric one at 52 Queen St (name above the tea house is in Chinese characters), just by the Albert and Waterloo streets roadside market. Sells Hua Tuo's ancient recipes helpful for 'relieving of heatiness' and 'inhibiting the growth of tumor cells,' amongst other things. Very friendly proprietress will introduce you to wild ginseng and showfrog, or longan herbal jelly and tell you why you will feel better (that's if you can get any of the concoctions down!).

Arab Street
● *on map, page 604*
Price codes: see box,
page 573
This is the best area for
Muslim food of all
descriptions - Malay,
Indonesian, Indian
or Arabic

There are some good restaurants around the Sultan Mosque and more on noisy North Bridge Road. Try the Parco Bugis Shopping Centre for non-Muslim restaurants including good Italian and New Bugis Street for simple open-air fare and jugs of cold beer.

3 *Bibik's Place*, Pahang St. Upmarket little place in a renovated shophouse, excellent **Nonya** dishes.
4 *Masakatsu*, 80 Middle Rd, Ground Flr, Parco Bugis Junction, T3348233, **Japanese**. Known for its hotpot. Book at weekends.
4 *Pasta Fresca da Salvatore*, Shaw Centre, **Italian**. Fresh, tasty pizzas and a good range of pasta dishes, open 24 hours.
3 *Pivdofr at Joons*, Liang Seah St, **International**. Another café serving sandwiches and salads although it also has a good set lunch menu.
2 *Rumah Makan Minang*, Kandahar St (facing onto the Istana Kampong Glam). Small restaurant serving cheap Padang (West Sumatran) dishes including beef rendang (dry beef curry), spicy grilled fish and kangkung.

2-3 *Zam Zam Restaurant*, junction of Arab St and North Bridge Rd. **Muslim Malay-Indian** dishes served in busy and chaotic coffee shop. Very popular and recommended for a taste of the other Singapore - spicy meats, char-grilled seafood, creamy curries.

4 *Alkaff Mansion*, Mt Faber Ridge, 10 Telok Blangah Green, T2786979. Built in the 1920s, this huge house has undergone a S$3m refurbishment and makes a magnificent restaurant surrounded by parkland. Go here for the atmosphere, not the food, which is very average. If you do eat, the **continental** cuisine is better than the **Indonesian**.

World Trade Centre & the Port
Price codes: see box, page 573

4 *Long Beach Seafood*, 31 Marina Park, Marina South, T3232222. One of the island's most famous **seafood** restaurants, specializing in pepper and chilli-crabs, drunken prawns and baby squid cooked in honey.

4 *Prima Tower Revolving Restaurant*, 201 Keppel Rd, T2728822. Revolving restaurant atop a huge silo looks out over the harbour and city, established 20 years ago and with the same chef still working here. **Beijing** cuisine, particularly good Peking Duck, book in advance.

1 *Dotty Café*, Bukit Chermin Rd, off Keppel Marina, T2708575 and Telok Blangah Rd, just west of where the cable car goes over the road. Call Dorothy before you go and plan your **seafood** menu to get the best catch of the day. Eat under fairy lights, right on the sea, and admire yachts moored next door, very quiet and peaceful.

Cheaper *Han's*, 8 branches around the city including Harbour Promenade World Trade Centre. This chain of restaurants is Singapore's answer to the Greasy Spoon - cafes without the acute accent on the 'e', single dish **Chinese** meals, simple (largely fried) breakfasts, some **European** food including such things as steaks, burgers and fries all served in large helpings at very competitive prices.

The *Sentosa Food Centre* close to the ferry terminal is a squeaky-clean hawker centre, serving Malay, Chinese, Peranakan, Indian and Western cuisine. The dishes are pricier than elsewhere in Singapore and the food is sometimes disappointing, open 1100-2200. Other restaurants at the ferry terminal include a *Burger King*, ice cream parlour, the *Singapore Riverboat* (a paddlewheel steamer) and the *Camellia Restaurant*. Beside the Merlion is *Sir Basil's Café and Bar* and there are also several burger outlets and snack bars at Siloso, Central and Tanjong beaches as well as those associated with many of the individual attractions. In short, visitors will not starve during their visit. There are more elegant restaurants at the hotels of which the best is *Siggi's* at the *Beaufort*, T2750331. Worth splashing out on the **New Asia** buffet while sitting on the terrace *al fresco*. Every Fri and Sat night it is possible to dine on board the Cable Car, 1830-2030, S$120 for 2, T2779654.

Sentosa
Price codes: see box, page 573
There are fast-food outlets & restaurants dotted around the island

There are really 2 areas in the western portion of the island where more unusual restaurants are concentrated. Pasir Panjang Village, close to the University, and Holland Village, not far to the north. Holland Village is an expat enclave, hugely popular, especially at weekends when it is essential to book. Apart from the 20 or so restaurants on Lorong Mambong where it is possible to eat Japanese, Indian, Italian, Mexican or merely sip coffee at one of the many coffee bars – there is also a strip of restaurants set apart from the village, on the other side of the main road, on Jln Merah Saga.

Singapore West
Price codes: see box, page 573

4-5 *Au Petit Sala*, T4751976. **French** café and patisserie. The least popular on this strip but has some quite good vegetarian options.

4-5 *Da Paolo*, T4761332. Upmarket **Italian** and the most stylish restaurant on the strip.

4-5 *Michelangelo's*, T4759069, fc81@pacific.net.sg. Genuine **Italian** food, wordy menu promises scrumptious treats, but a little disappointing.

4-5 *Original Sin*, T4755605. **Vegetarian**. Excellent and unusual choice.

Singapore

4-5 *Sistina*, T4767782. Genuine pizzeria.

4 *Brazil Churrascaria*, 14-16 6th Ave, T4631923. If carnivore-style is your thing, this **Brazilian** restaurant - with its huge skewers of barbecued (*churrascaria* is portuguese for barbecue) meat - is for you, as much meat as you can eat.

4 *Cha Cha Cha*, 32 Lorong Mambong, Holland Village, T4621650. Small and informal **Mexican** restaurant with some outdoor seating, extensive menu.

4 *El Felipé's* , 34 Lorong Mambong, Holland Village, T4681520, **Mexican**.

4 *Gerry's Fine Foods*, Lorong Mambong, Holland Village. A **steak and ribs** place, great fries, cold beer.

4 *Hazara*, 24 Lorong Mambong, Holland Village, T4674101, **Indian**. Sister restaurant to *Kinara* at Boat Quay, specializing in northwest Frontier cuisine (tandooris etc), particularly good tandoori leg of lamb, splendid decor with genuine frontier feel, slow service.

4 *Restaurant Lucerne*, Pasir Panjang Village, T7761221. Sophisticated **Swiss** restaurant.

5 *Hot Stones Steak and Seafood*, 22 Lorong Mambong, Holland Village, **International**. Another restaurant at 53 Boat Quay (T5355188). Speciality: cooking slabs of meat or seafood on baking-hot Serpentine rock at the table.

5 *Wala-Wala*, 31 Lorong Mambong, Holland Village T4624288, **Mexican**. Buzzy atmosphere and pretty tiles on the tables, good, honest, no pretentions.

East Coast
● on map, page 613
Price codes:
see box, page 573

4 *Chao Phaya Thai Seafood*, Block 730, 2nd Floor, Ang Mo Kio Ave 6, T4560118. Enormous informal restaurant with huge choice of authentic **Thai** dishes including chilli crab, *tom yam kung* and green, yellow or red curried fish. **2** *Charlie's*, Block 2, 01-08, Changi Village, T5420867. Charlie's folks, who were first generation immigrants from China, set up the *Changi Milk Bar* in the 1940s, then *Charlie's Corner* became the favoured watering hole and makan stop for sailors and riggers for decades. His mum still fries up the chips that gave them the reputation as the best chippies east of London's Isle of Dogs, excellent chilli-dogs, spicy chicken wings and 70 beers to choose from, closed weekends, recommended. Bus to Changi Point from Tampines MRT.

There are several **seafood** restaurants on Mount Faber hill, with a good view - they are not that popular and the seafood is far from being the best in town, but it's a pleasant location.

3 *Gold Coast Live Seafood*, T4482020 and **3** *Jumbo Seafood*, T4423435. Serving Singapore specialities like chilli crabs and black pepper crayfish. **3** *House of Sundanese Food*, 218 East Coast Road, T3455020. Typical **Sundanese** dishes from West Java include spicy salad (*keredok*), charcoal-grilled seafood (*ikan sunda*, *ikanemas*) and curries, a/c restaurant with real home-cooked food. There are 10 outlets here and they're all good. In particular - **3** *International Seafood Centre*, also on the ECP, provide trolleys to choose your fish pre-cooking. Not for the squeamish. Recommended. **3** *Kim's Seafood Restaurant*, 477 Changi Road, T7421119. Claypot pepper crabs are the speciality in Mr Tan's cheap and informal seafood restaurant, open to 0130 weekdays and 0230 on Saturday. **3** *Palm Beach Seafood Restaurant*, Palm Beach Leisure Park, 1st and 2nd flrs, 5 Stadium Walk, T3443088. Located near the International Building and the National Stadium, spread over 4 a/c floors, basic decor; tiled flooring and melamine crockery, good shellfish at a fair price - the chilli crab is a speciality. **4** *Forbidden City*, 43/45 East Coast Rd, T3423145. Italian and other European dishes in a 2-storey 'palace'. *UDMC Seafood Centre*, 1000 East Coast Parkway.

Bars

Bar and Billiard Room, *Raffles Hotel*, Beach Rd. Relocated from its original position, the bar is lavishly furnished with teak tables, oriental carpets and two original billiard tables. *Father Flannagan's Irish Pub*, CHIJMES, 30 Victoria St. Ersatz Irish pub with Irish beer on tap and a high density of local businesspeople - some Irish food (stews etc) also available. Several other places within the CHIJMES redevelopment where it is possible to drink al fresco or otherwise with Singapore's chuppies. *Paulaner Brauhaus*, Millenia Walk, micro brewery serving pricey beer to businessfolk. German sausage and other Teutonic delicacies also served. *Somerset's*, *Westin Stamford*, Raffles City. Large and pleasant bar with frieze of the Padang in the days before Raffles City, live jazz music. *The Long Bar*, Raffles Hotel, 1-3 Beach Rd. The home of the Singapore Sling, originally concocted by bar-tender Ngiam Tong Boon in 1915, now on 2 levels and extremely popular with tourists and locals alike, gratuitous tiny dancing mechanical punkawallahs sway out of sync to the cover band. *Writers' Bar*, *Raffles Hotel*, 1 Beach Rd (just off the main lobby). In honour of the likes of Somerset Maugham, Rudyard Kipling, Joseph Conrad, Noel Coward and Herman Hesse who were said either to have wined, dined or stayed at the hotel. Bar research indicates that other literary luminaries from James A Michener to Noel Barber and the great Arthur Hailey are said to have sipped Tigers at the bar - as the bookcases and momentoes suggest. *Lock, Stock and Barrel Pub*, 29 Seah St. Extended Happy Hour from 1600-2000, popular with expats on a budget and backpackers - dark bar/pub with juke box.

There are lots of bars on Boat and Clarke quays; those at the former are wilder and less packaged. It is best just to mosey along and take your fancy. *Crazy Elephant*, Clarke Quay, T3371190, live music (house band), popular place for a drink following a meal. *Brewerkz*, Riverside Point, one of the micro breweries which are all the rage in Asia. Good beer, but pricey. *Escobar*, 36 Boat Quay. A Latin American bar with salsa and cocktails to match. *Espana*, 45 Boat Quay. Margueritas, daiquiris and jugs of Heineken, accompanied by Latin music. *Harry's Quayside*, 28 Boat Quay. Large bar with seating outside overlooking the river, popular with City boys, serves food, pricey, jazz band. *Molly Malone's*, 42 Circular Rd, off Boat Quay, T5345100. Irish pub (complete with stout, Irish folk music etc) with a restaurant upstairs, usually packed. *Next Page Pub*, 15 Jl Mohamed Sultan (River Valley Rd), T2356967. A converted shophouse, great decor - salon style with opium beds, cubby holes and cushions - makes for a good evening if combined with a meal at the nearby *Nonya and Baba* restaurant on River Valley Rd. Recommended. *Riverbank Bar*, 68 Boat Quay. Live music. *The Yard*, 294 River Valley Rd. The Singaporean version of a London pub complete with darts, dominos, fish 'n' chips and Newcastle Brown Ale. *Trader Vics* 5th Floor, *New Otani Hotel*, River Valley Rd. Hawaii 5-0 decor and Chin-Ho's favourite cocktails - try a few goblets of Tikki Puka Puka for something violently different. There is a strip of pubs on Jl Mohamed Sultan (River Valley Rd) - Peranakan-style - *Wong San's* at No 12 (T7383787) and *Zens* at No 10. The building site opposite detracts from the general ambience, but hopefully that is short-term.

Brannigan's (basement of *Hyatt Regency*), 10/12 Scotts Rd. Open until 0100, 0200 on Friday and Saturday, American style, touristy bar with loud live music and video screens, haunt of the infamous SPG (Singapore Party Girl), very popular. *Canopy Bar*, *Hyatt Regency*, 10/12 Scotts Rd. Singapore's only champagne bar for the more sophisticated *bon viveur*. *Hard Rock Café*, Cuscaden Rd, west end of Orchard Rd. Complete with limo in suspended animation and queues to enter. *Ice Cold*, 9 Emerald Hill. If you like a slightly anarchic feel to your bars, with loud music and darts, then this is a good place. In an old shophouse at the top of the pedestrianized section of Emerald Hill, good place for a drink away from Orchard Rd, popular with locals, happy hours 1700-2100. *Jack's Place*, Yen San Building (opposite *Mandarin Hotel*), Orchard Rd. Cellar bar with live music, squashed and not very sophisticated. *Kaspia Bar*, *Hilton Hotel*, Orchard Rd. For the widest selection of vodkas in Singapore and live jazz. *Number 5*, 5 Emerald Hill. Happy hours 1200-2100 Monday-Sat, 1700-2100 Sun, at the top of the pedestrianized section of Emerald Hill, retro-chic restored shophouse bar and restaurant (upstairs), popular with young expats and Chuppies (Chinese yuppies), great music, recommended. *Observation Lounge*, *Mandarin Hotel*, 333 Orchard Rd. Circular cocktail bar on 38th Floor. *Que Pasa*, 7 Emerald Hill. This is a wine bar in a converted shophouse with a small snack menu of tapas, oysters and olives and an extensive wine menu. It is near the top of the pleasant pedestrianised section of Emerald Hill and next door to the slightly wilder *Ice Cold Bar*. *Saxophone*, 23 Cuppage Terrace, T2358385. One of Singapore's most popular bars - particularly with expats, offers good live music (usually rhythm and blues) and pleasant open-air terrace, opens at 1800, recommended. *Woodstock*, Rooftop, 06-02 Far East Plaza, 14 Scotts Rd. Take the bullet lift up the outside of the building, expect to meet long-hairs and hear hard rock, open until 0200.

Chinatown   There are several quiet bars on *Duxton Hill*, Chinatown, in a pleasant area of restored shophouses - a retreat from the hustle and bustle of Boat Quay or the city. *Duxton Road* and *Tanjong Pagar Road* (both in Chinatown) also provide a dozen or so bars in restored shophouses. *JJ Mahoney's*, 55 Duxton Rd, T2256225. Not quite the Irish bar the name might suggest, beer and karaoke. *Elvis Pub*, 1A Duxton Hill, T2201268. Here the name does say it all: nothing but Elvis played all night, Friday is particularly lively. *Beaujolais Winebar*, 1 Ann Siang Hill, T2242227. Very pleasant winebar in restored shophouse, serves reasonably priced wine, candles in wine bottles on the window-sills, atmospheric, good cheese and charcuterie platters. Recommended. *Lone Star Bar*, 54 Tanjong Pagar Rd, run by Mike Brenders, a Texan (ex-US Navy), country and western music, darts, friendly and fun.

WTC & the Port   *Alkaff Mansion*, Mount Faber Ridge, 10 Telok Blangah Green, perfect for sundowner 'stengahs' on the terrace with an excellent view of the harbour.

Singapore west   There are a number of pubs and bars in a row of restored shophouses in Pasir Panjang Village along what is known as *The Pub Row.*

East Coast   1 *Changi Sailing Club*, Changi Village, pleasant and, surprisingly, one of the cheapest places for a quiet beer, overlooking the Strait of Johor. 1 *Charlie's*, Block 2, 01-08, Changi Village. Charlie Han describes his bar as "the pulse of the point", tucked away behind the local hawker centre, he is a teetotaller but serves 70 brands of beer from all over the world, which you can sip as you watch the red-eyes touchdown on runway one, Charlie's is best known for its fish and chips, closed over the weekend (see **Eating** page 638). Recommended.

Clubs

Colonial core   *Rascals*, Pan Pacific Hotel, Marina Square, 6 Raffles Blvd. Open 1800-0300, extended Happy Hour, Sun is gay night. *Scandals*, *Westin Plaza Hotel*, Raffles City Complex, popular hotel disco. *The Reading Room*, *Marina Mandarin Hotel*, Marina Square, is a smart, expensive and pretentious disco which attracts a younger crowd.

Singapore River & the City   *The Warehouse*, 382 Havelock Rd, *River View Hotel*, large dance hall, mainly frequented by teenagers. *Velvet Underground*, Jiak Kim St (off Kim Seng Rd) next door to *Zouk's* bar. Owned by Zouk's, small nightclub, open until 0300, cover S$25, free for women on Wed nights. Recommended. *Zouk's*, 17-21 Jiak Kim St, T7382988, possibly the hippest club-bar in town with great music, a 2000-2100 Happy Hour and open Mon-Sat 1800-0300.

Most big hotels have house discos - they all have a cover charge, usually S$25-30 (which normally includes a drink or two) - and dress is 'smart-casual'. Good hotel discos include: *Boiler*, basement of *Mandarin Hotel*, Orchard Rd; *Ridleys*, *ANA Hotel*, Nassim Hill. *Chinoiserie*, *Hyatt Regency*, 10-12 Scotts Rd, off Orchard Rd. *Xanadu*, *Shangri-La Hotel*, Orange Grove Rd, northwest end of Orchard Rd. *Fabrice's World Music Bar*, Basement, *Singapore Marriott*, 320 Orchard Rd. Run by Fabrice De Barcy, the Belgian of *Saxophone* fame, Arabesque decor with low tables, candles and Persian rugs, live music and dance tracks, open 1700-0300 Mon-Sun, no cover before 2200, S$25 thereafter. Recommended. *Fire*, Orchard Plaza, T2350155. Two levels of music, very popular, admission charges vary. *Rumours*, Level 3, Forum Gallaria, 583 Orchard Rd. Once it was the trendiest spot in town ... now it has gone off the boil. *Sparks*, Ngee Ann City, Orchard Rd. The biggest disco in all of Asia, very glitzy with KTV rooms and jazz bar, packed at weekends, open 1700-0200 (to 0300 on Sat and Sun). Cover: S$15 Mon-Thur, S$20 Fri-Sun. Recommended. *Top Ten Club*, Orchard Towers, 400 Orchard Rd. Huge converted cinema, often has live black-American or Filipino disco bands. Recommended. *Club 392* is also in Orchard Towers.

Orchard Road

Moondance, Tanjong Pagar Rd, Chinatown. S$13 cover charge (S$16 at the weekends), 25% off happy hour from 1900-2100, karaoke from 1900-2200.

Chinatown

Boom Boom Room, 3 New Bugis St, T3398187. Cabaret and stand up comedy shows. Popular with locals; tame by international standards.

Arab Street

Entertainment

Most theatrical and dance performances are held at the *Victoria Hall* and are advertised in newspapers and tourist publications. The latest offering on the thespian and artistic scene is *The Substation*, 45 Armenian St, set up in a former power station. It has an intimate little theatre where it stages plays and shows avante garde films. It also holds drama workshops. Call T3377800 for details of what's on when. *Raffles Jubilee Hall*, 328 North Bridge Rd holds occasional theatrical performances, for information T3311732. *The Esplanade: theatres on the Bay* is under construction next to the Padang (see page 582) and is due for completion in 2001. There will be a concert hall, lyric theatre, three smaller studios, and an outdoor performing space. *Kala Mandhir* is at the *Temple of Fine Arts,* 1st Flr, Excelsior Hotel Shopping Centre, T3390492. Classes available in dance, instrumental music, percussion and singing. Fabulous array of Indian instruments. It might be possible to take a one week course here, although most are longer. Most classical music performances are held at The *Singapore Cultural Theatre* and the *Victoria Hall* - the Singapore Symphony Orchestra gives regular performances and there are often visiting orchestras, quartets and choirs. Check the *Straits Times* for details.

Colonial core

The *Botanic Gardens* at weekends. Chinese classical and folk music organized by the Nanyang Academy of Fine Arts (NAFA), T3376636 for performance details.

Orchard Road

Singapore

Directory

Embassies & consulates

Australia 25 Napier Rd, T7379311. *Austria* Shaw Centre, 1 Scotts Rd, 24-05/06, T2354088. *Belgium* International Plaza, 10 Anson Rd, T2207677. *Brunei* 325 Tanglin Rd, T7339055. *Canada* 15th Storey IBM Towers, 80 Anson Rd, T3253200. *China* People's Republic of, 70-76 Dalvey Rd, T7343080. *Denmark* 13-01 United Sq, 101 Thomson Rd, T2503383. *Finland* 21-03 United Sq, 101 Thomson Rd, T2544042. *France* 5 Gallop Rd, T4664866. *Germany* 14-01 Far East Shopping Centre, 545 Orchard Rd, T7737135. *Greece* 11-25 Anson Centre, 51 Anson Rd, T2208622. *India* 31 Grange Rd, T7376777. *Indonesia* 7 Chatsworth Rd, T7377422. *Ireland* 08-06 Tiong Bahru Plaza, 298 Tiong Bahru Rd, T2768935. *Israel* 58 Dalvey Rd, T2350966. *Italy* 27-02 United Sq, 101 Thomson Rd, T2506022. *Japan* 34th Storey IBM Towers, 80 Anson Rd, T2358855. *Malaysia* 301 Jervois Rd, T2350111. *Myanmar (Burma)* 15 St Martin's Drive, T7350209. *Netherlands* 13-01 Liat Towers, 541 Orchard Rd, T7371155. *New Zealand* 15th Storey, Ngee Ann City, Tower A, 391A Orchard Rd, T2359966. *Norway* 44-01 Hong Leong Building, 16 Raffles Quay, T2207122. *Philippines* 20 Nassim Rd, T7373977. *Poland* 33-11 Shaw Towers, 100 Beach Rd, T2942513. *South Africa* 15-00 Odeon Towers, 331 North Bridge Rd, T3393319. *Spain* 05-08/09 Thong Teck Building, 15 Scotts Rd, T7329788. *Sweden* 05-08 PUB Building, 111 Somerset Rd, T7342771. *Switzerland* 1 Swiss Club Link, T4685788. *Thailand* 370 Orchard Rd, T7372644, open 0915-1215, 1500-1645, applications for visa am only. *UK* 100 Tanglin Rd, T4739333. *USA* 27 Napier Rd, T4769100. *Vietnam* 10 Leedon Park, T4625938.

Footnotes

11

644

Footnotes

645

Air fares

Guide to domestic Mas air fares

Destination	Distance (km)	One-way (RM)	Destination	Distance (km)	One-way (RM)
JB-Kota Kinabalu	1,502	347	Lahad Datu-Tawau	100	48
JB-Kuala Terengganu	-	149	Lawas-Bekelalan	100	46
JB-Kuching	757	169	Lawas-Labuan	54	31
Kota Kinabalu-Kudat	141	50	Lawas-Limbang	44	25
Kota Kinabalu-Lahad Datu	272	106	Lawas-Long Semadoh	74	40
Kota Kinabalu-Labuan	115	52	Long Seridan-Long Lellang	59	35
Kota Kinabalu-Lawas	140	47	Marudi-Bario	135	55
Kota Kinabalu-Miri	294	104	Marudi-Long Lellang	135	46
Kota Kinabalu-Sandakan	226	83	Marudi-Long Seridan	85	42
Kota Kinabalu-Tawau	280	96	Marudi-Sibu	344	100
KL-Alor Star	368	113	Miri-Bario	180	70
KL-Ipoh	178	66	Miri-Bintulu	168	69
KL-JB	354	93	Miri-Labuan	180	66
KL-Kota Bahru	352	104	Miri-Lawas	168	59
KL-Kota Kinabalu	1,678	437	Miri-Limbang	123	45
KL-Kuala Terengganu	318	104	Miri-Marudi	42	29
KL-Kuantan	224	74	Penang-Langkawi	131	51
KL-Kuching	1,035	262	Sandakan-Kudat	177	54
KL-Langkawi	-	135	Sandakan-Lahad Datu	102	40
KL-Penang	283	104	Sandakan-Semporna	170	50
Kuantan-JB	261	93	Sandakan-Tawau	185	74
Kuching-Bintulu	354	117	Sandakan-Tomanggong	85	42
Kuching-Kota Kinabalu	811	228	Sibu-Bintulu	163	64
Kuching-Miri	519	164	Sibu-Kapit	128	48
Kuching-Mukah	250	76	Sibu-Miri	326	112
Kuching-Sibu	191	72			

JB = Johor Bahru   KL = Kuala Lumpur
NB Economy class fares quoted, cheaper fares are available.

Footnotes

Pelangi air fares

Destination	Single (RM)	Destination	Single (RM)
Alor Star-Kota Bharu	71	KL-Tioman	141
Ipoh-KL	66	Kuala Terengganu-KL	125
KL-JB	93	Penang-Kota Bahru	87
KL-Kerteh	125	Singapore-Tioman	S$115
KL-Kota Bharu	104	Tioman-Kuantan	79
KL-Pangkor	120	Tioman-Singapore	157
KL-Penang	104		

JB = Johor Bahru   KL = Kuala Lumpur
NB Return ticket is double price quoted.

Train fares

Express train fares

	Butterworth			Kuala Lumpur			Singapore		
	1	2	3	1	2	3	1	2	3
	RM	RM	RM	RM	RM	RM	$S	$S	$S
Padang Besar	34.00	20.00	11.00	-	-	-	-	-	-
Alor Star	24.00	15.00	8.00	-	-	-	-	-	-
Sungai Petani	15.00	11.00	6.00	-	-	-	-	-	-
Butterworth	-	-	-	67.00	34.00	19.00	127.00	60.00	34.00
Bt Mertajam	10.00	9.00	5.00	65.00	33.00	19.00	125.00	59.00	33.00
Parit Buntar	14.00	11.00	6.00	61.00	31.00	17.00	121.00	57.00	32.00
Taiping	23.00	15.00	8.00	53.00	28.00	16.00	112.00	53.00	30.00
K Kangsar	28.00	17.00	9.00	49.00	26.00	14.00	107.00	51.00	29.00
Ipoh	36.00	21.00	11.00	40.00	22.00	12.00	100.00	48.00	27.00
Batu Gajah	38.00	21.00	12.00	38.00	21.00	12.00	97.00	47.00	26.00
Kampar	41.00	23.00	13.00	34.00	20.00	11.00	94.00	46.00	26.00
Tapah Road	44.00	24.00	13.00	32.00	19.00	10.00	92.00	45.00	25.00
Kuala Lumpur	67.00	34.00	19.00	-	-	-	68.00	34.00	19.00
Seremban	79.00	39.00	22.00	22.00	13.00	7.00	58.00	30.00	17.00
Tampin	85.00	42.00	23.00	27.00	17.00	9.00	50.00	27.00	15.00
Gemas	94.00	46.00	26.00	35.00	20.00	11.00	43.00	23.00	13.00
Segamat	97.00	47.00	26.00	40.00	22.00	12.00	38.00	21.00	12.00
Kluang	110.00	53.00	30.00	52.00	27.00	15.00	26.00	16.00	9.00
Johor Bahru	122.00	58.00	33.00	64.00	33.00	18.00	13.00	10.00	6.00
Singapore	127.00	60.00	34.00	68.00	34.00	19.00	-	-	-

Ordinary train fares

	Butterworth			Kuala Lumpur			Singapore		
	1	2	3	1	2	3	1	2	3
	RM	RM	RM	RM	RM	RM	$S	$S	$S
Padang Besar	25.50	11.10	6.30	81.00	35.10	20.00	139.50	60.50	34.40
Arau	21.80	9.50	5.40	76.50	33.20	18.90	136.50	59.20	33.60
Alor Star	15.30	6.70	3.80	70.50	30.60	17.40	130.50	56.60	32.20
Butterworth	-	-	-	58.50	25.40	14.40	118.50	51.40	29.20
Bt Mertajam	1.80	0.80	0.50	57.00	24.70	14.10	117.00	50.70	28.80
Taiping	14.40	6.30	3.60	45.00	19.50	11.10	103.50	44.90	25.50
K Kangsar	19.50	8.50	4.80	40.50	17.60	10.00	99.00	42.90	24.40
Ipoh	27.80	12.10	6.90	31.50	13.70	7.80	91.50	39.70	22.60
Tapah Road	36.00	15.60	8.90	23.30	10.10	5.80	84.00	36.40	20.70
Kuala Lumpur	58.50	25.40	14.40	-	-	-	60.00	26.00	14.80
Seremban	70.50	30.60	17.40	11.10	4.90	2.80	49.50	21.50	12.20
Tampin	76.50	33.20	18.90	18.80	8.20	4.75	42.00	18.20	10.40
Gemas	85.50	37.10	21.10	27.00	11.70	6.70	34.50	15.00	8.5
Segamat	88.50	38.50	21.80	31.50	13.70	7.80	30.00	13.00	7.40
Kluang	102.00	44.20	25.10	43.50	18.90	10.80	17.30	7.50	4.30
Johor Bahru	114.00	49.40	28.10	55.50	24.10	13.70	4.20	1.90	1.10
Singapore	118.50	51.40	29.90	60.00	26.00	14.80	-	-	-
Hat Yai	34.20	14.90	-	-	-	-	-	-	-
Bangkok	99.20	44.90	-	-	-	-	-	-	-

Train timetables

··

Wau Express (RM)

Timuran Express (RM)

Kuala Lumpur-Tumpat-Kuala Lumpur

Train No	XW/16 Dep	Arr XW/17
Kuala Lumpur	2020	0645
Kajang	2040	0604
Seremban	2118	0518
Tampin	2201	0434
Gemas	2246	0332
Bahau	2343	0256
Mentakab	0057	0042
Jerantut	0148	2355
Kuala Lipis	0243	2303
Gua Musang	0414	2138
Dabong	0513	2036
Krai	0603	1947
Tanah Merah	0634	1916
Pasir Mas	0659	1852
Wakaf Baharu	0713	1840
Tumpat	0735 Dep	Arr 1830

Singapore-Tumpat-Singapore

Train No	XST/14	Arr Dep XST/15
Singapore	2055	0830
Johor Bahru	2155	0720
Kluang	2305	0609
Labis	2350	0524
Segamat	0013	0457
Gemas	0035	0429
Bahau	0114	0353
Triang	0200	0307
Mentakab	0232	0238
Jerantut	0339	0140
Kuala Lipis	0432	0045
Gua Musang	0604	2318
Krai	0800	2127
Tanah Merah	0830	2056
Pasir Mas	0856	2032
Wakaf Bahru	0910	2020
Tumpat	0935 Dep	Arr 2010

··

Bus fares

··

Ekrwres Nasional bus fares (RM)

Destination	Fare	Destination	Fare	Destination	Fare
Alor Star		**Johor Bahru**		Kemaman	13.50
Ipoh	11.90	Alor Star	37.70	Kota Bharu	25.00
Kuala Lumpur	21.20	Butterworth	33.50	Kuantan	12.10
Johor Bahru	37.70	Ipoh	25.80	Kuala Terengganu	21.60
Butterworth		Kuala Lumpur	16.50	Kuala Perlis	23.40
Kuala Lumpur	17.10	**Kangar**		Muar	8.50
Johor Bahru	33.50	Ipoh	14.00	Penang	18.50
Kota Bharu	16.50	Kuala Lumpur	23.40	Singapore	17.80
Kuala Kangsar	5.60	**Kuantan**		Taiping/KK	13.20
Batu Pahat		Kuala Lumpur	21.10	**Muar**	
Kuala Lumpur	10.90	**Kuala Terengganu**		Kuala Lumpur	8.50
Ipoh		Kuala Lumpur	21.60	**Penang**	
Alor Star	11.90	**Kota Bharu**		Kuala Lumpur	18.50
Butterworth	7.10	Kuala Lumpur	25.00	**Singapore**	
Johor Bahru	25.80	**Kuala Lumpur**		Kuala Lumpur	17.80*
Kangar	14.00	Alor Star	21.20	**Taiping**	
Kota Bharu	17.10	Butterworth	17.10	Butterworth	3.80
Kuala Perlis	14.00	Batu Pahat	10.90	Kuala Lumpur	13.20
Kuala Lumpur	9.40	Ipoh	9.40	Sungai Petani	5.50
Sungai Petani	8.80	Johor Bahru	16.50		
		Kangar	23.40		

NB These fares are indicative only.
* Fare in S$

··

Glossary

A

Adat   custom or tradition

Amitabha   the Buddha of the Past (see Avalokitsvara)

Atap   thatch

Avalokitsvara   also known as Amitabha and Lokeshvara, the name literally means 'World Lord'; he is the compassionate male Bodhisattva, the saviour of Mahayana Buddhism and represents the central force of creation in the universe; usually portrayed with a lotus and water flask

B

Bahasa   language, as in Bahasa Malaysia

Barisan Nasional   National Front, Malaysia's ruling coalition comprising UMNO, MCA and MIC along with seven other parties

Batik   a form of resist dyeing common in Malay areas

Becak   three-wheeled bicycle rickshaw

Bodhi   the tree under which the Buddha achieved enlightenment (Ficus religiosa)

Bodhisattva   a future Buddha. In Mahayana Buddhism, someone who has attained enlightenment, but who postpones nirvana in order to help others reach the same state

Brahma   the Creator, one of the gods of the Hindu trinity, usually represented with four faces, and often mounted on a hamsa

Brahmin   a Hindu priest

Budaya   cultural (as in Muzium Budaya)

Bumboat   small wooden lighters, now used for ferrying tourists in Singapore

Bumiputra   literally, 'sons of the soil'; Malays as opposed to other races in Malaysia (see page 510)

C

Cap   batik stamp

Chedi   from the Sanskrit cetiya (Pali, caitya) meaning memorial. Usually a religious monument (often bell-shaped) containing relics of the Buddha or other holy remains. Used interchangeably with stupa

Cutch   see Gambier

D

Dalang   wayang puppet master

DAP   Democratic Action Party, Malaysia's predominantly Chinese opposition party

Dayak/Dyak   collective term for the tribal peoples of Borneo

Dharma   the Buddhist law

Dipterocarp   family of trees (Dipterocarpaceae) characteristic of Southeast Asia's forests

Durga   the female goddess who slays the demon Mahisa, from an Indian epic story

E

Epiphyte   plant which grows on another plant (but usually not parasitic)

F

Feng shui   the Chinese art of geomancy

G

Gambier   also known as cutch, a dye derived from the bark of the bakau mangrove and used in leather tanning

Gamelan   Malay orchestra of percussion instruments

Ganesh   elephant-headed son of Siva

Garuda   mythical divine bird, with predatory beak and claws, and human body; the king of birds, enemy of naga and mount of Vishnu

Gautama   the historic Buddha

Geomancy   or feng shui, the Chinese art and science of proper placement

Goporum   tower in a Hindu temple

Gunung   mountain

H

Hamsa   sacred goose, Brahma's mount; in Buddhism it represents the flight of the doctrine

Hinayana   'Lesser Vehicle', major Buddhist sect in Southeast Asia, usually termed Theravada Buddhism

I

Ikat   tie-dyeing method of patterning cloth

Indra   the Vedic god of the heavens, weather and war; usually mounted on a three headed elephant

J

Jataka(s)   birth stories of the Buddha, of which there are 547; the last 10 are the most important

K

Kajang   thatch

Kala (makara)   literally, 'death' or 'black'; a demon ordered to consume itself; often sculpted over entranceways to act as a door guardian, also known as kirtamukha

Kerangas   from an Iban word meaning 'land on which rice will not grow'

Keraton   see kraton

Kinaree   half-human, half-bird, usually depicted as a heavenly musician

Kongsi   Chinese clan house

Kris   traditional Malay sword (see page 491)

Krishna   an incarnation of Vishnu

Kuti   living quarters of Buddhist monks

L

Laterite   bright red tropical soil/stone sometimes used as a building material

Linga   phallic symbol and one of the forms of Siva. Embedded in a pedestal shaped to allow drainage of lustral water poured over it, the linga typically has a succession of cross sections: from square at the base through octagonal to round. These symbolize, in order, the trinity of Brahma, Vishnu and Siva

Lintel   a load-bearing stone spanning a doorway; often heavily carved

Lokeshvara   see Avalokitsvara

Lunggyi   Indian sarong

M

Mahabharata   a Hindu epic text written about 2,000 years ago (see page 541)

Mahayana   'Greater Vehicle', major Buddhist sect (see page 541)

Mandi   Malay bathroom with water tub and dipper

Maitreya   the future Buddha

Makara   a mythological aquatic reptile, somewhat like a crocodile and sometimes with an elephant's trunk; often found, along with the kala, framing doorways

Mandala   a focus for meditation; a representation of the cosmos

MCA   Malaysian Chinese Association

Meru   the mountain residence of the gods; the centre of the universe, the cosmic mountain

MIC   Malaysian Indian Congress

Mudra   symbolic gesture of the hands of the Buddha

N

Naga   benevolent mythical water serpent, enemy of Garuda

Naga makara   fusion of naga and makara

Nalagiri   the elephant let loose to attack the Buddha, who calmed him

Nandi/Nandin   bull, mount of Siva

NDP   New Development Policy (see page 510)

Negara   kingdom and capital, from the Sanskrit

Negeri   also negri, state

NEP   New Economic Policy (see page 510)

Nirvana   'enlightenment', the Buddhist ideal

O

Orang Asli   indigenous people of Malaysia

P

Paddy/padi unhulled rice

Pantai beach

Pasar market, from the Arabic 'bazaar'

Pasar malam night market

Perahu/prau boat

Peranakan 'half caste', usually applied to part Chinese and part Malay people

Pradaksina pilgrims' clockwise circumambulation of a holy structure

Prang form of stupa built in the Khmer style, shaped rather like a corncob

Prasat residence of a king or of the gods (sanctuary tower), from the Indian prasada

Pribumi indigenous (as opposed to Chinese) businessmen

Pulau island

Pusaka heirloom

R

Raja/rajah ruler

Raksasa temple guardian statues

Ramayana the Indian epic tale (see page 541)

Ruai common gallery of an Iban longhouse, Sarawak

Rumah adat customary or traditional house

S

Sago multi-purpose palm

Sal the Indian sal tree (Shorea robusta), under which the historic Buddha was born

Sakyamuni the historic Buddha

Silat or bersilat, traditional Malay martial art

Singha mythical guardian lion

Siva one of the Hindu triumvirate, the god of destruction and rebirth

Songket Malay textile interwoven with supplementary gold and silver yarn

Sravasti the miracle at Sravasti when the Buddha subdues the heretics in front of a mango tree

Sri Laksmi the goddess of good fortune and Vishnu's wife

Stele inscribed stone panel or slab

Stucco plaster, often heavily moulded

Stupa see chedi

Sungai river

T

tamu market

Tanju open gallery of an Iban longhouse, Sarawak

Tara also known as Cunda; the four-armed consort of the Bodhisattva Avalokitsvara

Tavatimsa heaven of the 33 gods at the summit of Mount Meru

Theravada 'Way of the Elders'; major Buddhism sect also known as Hinayana Buddhism ('Lesser Vehicle')

Tiffin afternoon meal – a word that was absorbed from the British Raj

Timang Iban sacred chants, Sarawak

Tong or towkay, a Chinese merchant

Totok 'full blooded'; usually applied to Chinese of pure blood

Towkay Chinese merchant

Triads Chinese mafia associations

Tunku also Tuanku and Tengku, prince

U

Ulama Muslim priest

Ulu jungle

UMNO United Malays National Organization

Urna the dot or curl on the Buddha's forehead, one of the distinctive physical marks of the Enlightened One

Usnisa the Buddha's top knot or 'wisdom bump', one of the physical marks of the Enlightened One

V

Vishnu the Protector, one of the gods of the Hindu trinity, generally with four arms holding the disc, the conch shell, the ball and the club

W

Waringin banyan tree

Wayang traditional Malay shadow plays

Map index

Footnotes

Index

Note: grid references to the colour maps are shown in italics after place names. So Alor Star *M1A2* will be found on map 1, grid A2.

Footnotes

V

W

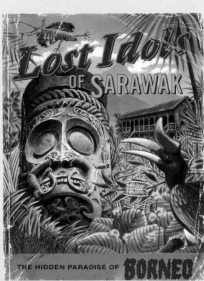

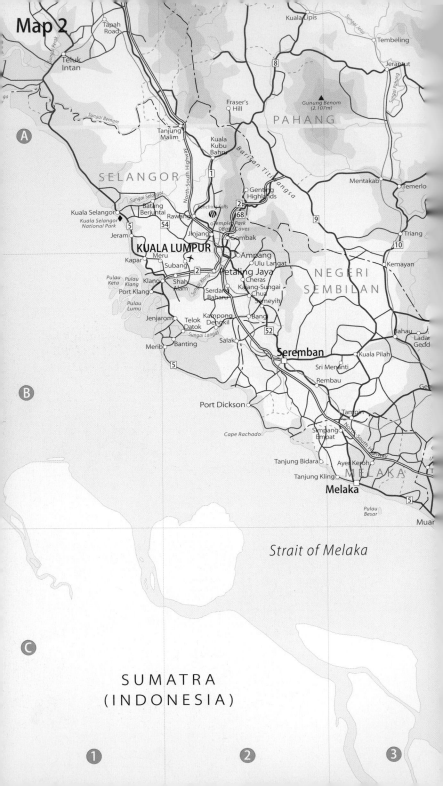

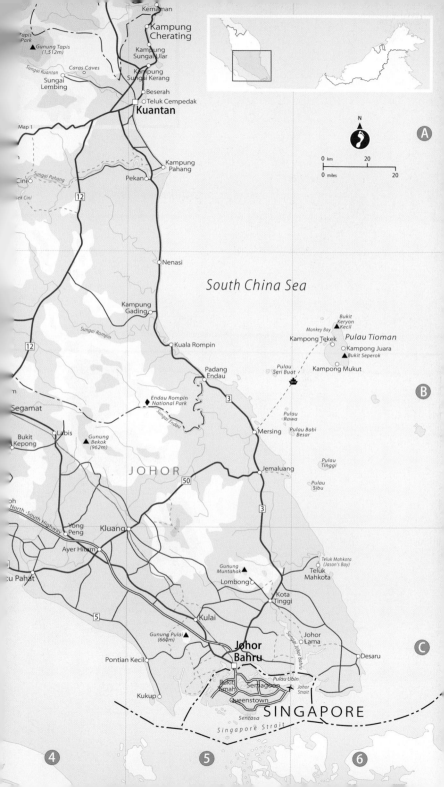

Map 3

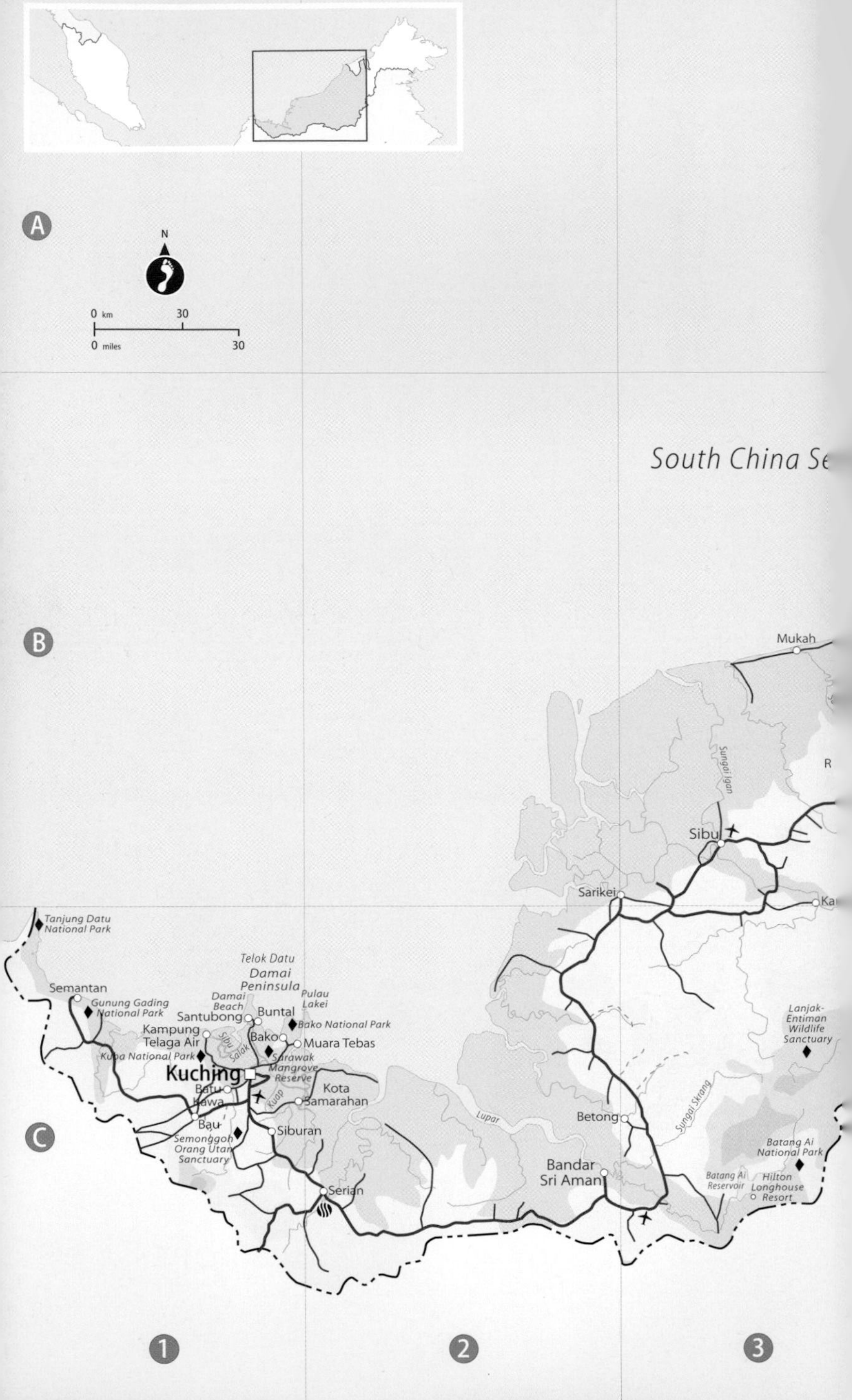

South China Se

Mukah

Sungai Igan

Sibu

R

Sarikei

Ka

Tanjung Datu National Park

Semantan

Gunung Gading National Park

Telok Datu
Damai Peninsula
Damai Beach
Pulau Lakei

Santubong
Buntal
Bako
Bako National Park

Kampung
Telaga Air
Kupa National Park

Sungai Salak

Muara Tebas

Sarawak Mangrove Reserve

Kuching
Batu Kawa

Kota Samarahan

Sungai Kuap

Lupar

Betong

Sungai Skrang

Lanjak-Entiman Wildlife Sanctuary

Bau
Semonggoh Orang Utan Sanctuary

Siburan

Serian

Bandar Sri Aman

Batang Ai Reservoir

Batang Ai National Park

Hilton Longhouse Resort

N

0 km 30
0 miles 30

A

B

C

1 2 3

Map 4

South China Sea

Tempasuk
(Bird Sanctuary)
Kota Beluc
Surusup
Tuaran
Mengkabong   Tamparu
Telipok
Tunku Abdul Rahman
National Park   **Kota Kinaba**
Pulau Gaya   Kun
Tanjung Aru   Raffle
Putatan   Forest Re
Penampang   Gu
Kinarut   Sungai Papar
Pulau Tiga   Mawa
National Park   Papar Manggis   Waterfal
Tambunan
Crocker Range
National Park

L A B U A N
Pulau
Labuan   Beaufort   Keningau

Melalap
Telok Brunei   Tenom   Agricultural
Research Station,
Orchid Centre
Muara
BANDAR SERI   Lawas   Gunung   Tomani
BEGAWAN   Lumaku
BRUNEI & MUARA   Labu   (1,966m)
Tutong   Bangar
Limbang   Kampong
Lutong Kuala Seria Lumut   Batong
Belait   Duri   Sap
Miri Kuala   TUTONG   TEMBURONG
Baram   **BRUNEI**   Partit
Baru
Labi   Amo
Teraja   Sungai Trusan
BELAIT   Ladan Hills   Long
Marudi   Semado
Gunung Mulu
(2,376m)   **KALIMANTAN**
Gunung Mulu
Long   National Park   **(INDONESIA**
Terawan Sungai Tutoh Long
Seridan   Gunung Murudi
Niah   (2,423m)
National
Park   Bukit Batu Bali
Loagan Bunut   (2,082m)
National Park   Bario
Sungai Baram
Sungai Patah   Kelabit Highlands

S A R A W A K

Gunung   Long
Skalap   Peran Sungai Belepeh
Long Muma

N

0 km   30
0 miles   30

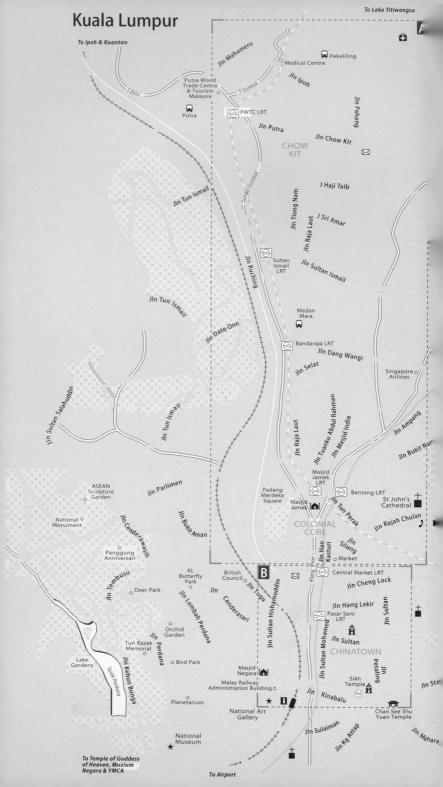

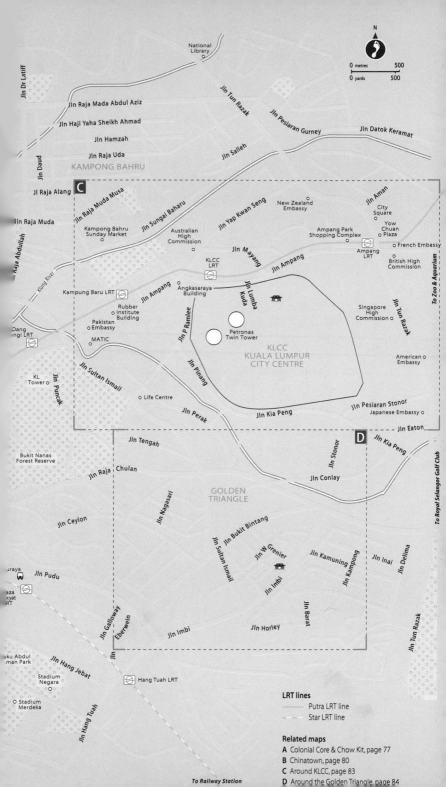

N

0 metres 500
0 yards 500

National Library

Jln Dr Latiff

Jln Raja Mada Abdul Aziz

Jln Haji Yaha Sheikh Ahmad

Jln Hamzah

Jln Raja Uda

Jln Tun Razak

Jln Pesiaran Gurney

Jln Datok Keramat

Jln Daud

KAMPONG BAHRU

Jln Salleh

Jl Raja Alang

C

Jln Raja Muda Musa

Jln Sungai Baharu

Jln Yap Kwan Seng

New Zealand Embassy

Jln Aman

City Square

Jln Raja Muda

Kampong Bahru Sunday Market

Australian High Commission

KLCC LRT

Jln Mayang

Jln Ampang

Ampang Park Shopping Complex

Yow Chuan Plaza

Ampang LRT

French Embassy

nja Abdullah

Klang River

Kampung Baru LRT

Jln Ampang

Angkasaraya Building

Jln Lumba Kuda

British High Commission

Dang ngi LRT

Rubber Institute Building

Pakistan Embassy

MATIC

Jln P Ramlee

Petronas Twin Tower

Singapore High Commission

Jln Tun Razak

KLCC
KUALA LUMPUR
CITY CENTRE

American Embassy

To Zoo & Aquarium

KL Tower

Jln Puncak

Jln Sultan Ismail

Life Centre

Jln Pinang

Jln Perak

Jln Kia Peng

Jln Pesiaran Stonor

Japanese Embassy

Jln Eaton

D

Jln Kia Peng

Bukit Nanas Forest Reserve

Jln Tengah

Jln Raja Chulan

Jln Stonor

Jln Conlay

Jln Ceylon

Jln Nagasari

GOLDEN TRIANGLE

Jln Bukit Bintang

Jln W Grenier

Jln Kamuning

Jln Inai

Jln Sultan Ismail

Jln Imbi

Jln Kampong

Jln Delima

uraya

Jln Pudu

aza kyat RT

Jln Barat

Jln Galloway

Eberwein

Jln Imbi

Jln Horley

Jln Tun Razak

ku Abdul man Park

Jln Hang Jebat

Stadium Negara

Hang Tuah LRT

Stadium Merdeka

Jln Hang Tuah

To Royal Selangor Golf Club

LRT lines

Putra LRT line

Star LRT line

Related maps

A Colonial Core & Chow Kit, page 77

B Chinatown, page 80

C Around KLCC, page 83

D Around the Golden Triangle, page 84

To Railway Station

Footprint travel list

Footprint publish travel guides to over 120 countries worldwide. Each guide is packed with practical, concise and colourful information for everybody from first-time travellers to travel aficionados . The list is growing fast and current titles are noted below. For further information check out the website **www.footprintbooks.com**

Andalucía Handbook
Argentina Handbook
Bali & the Eastern Isles Hbk
Bangkok & the Beaches Hbk
Bolivia Handbook
Brazil Handbook
Cambodia Handbook
Caribbean Islands Handbook
Chile Handbook
Colombia Handbook
Cuba Handbook
Dominican Republic Handbook
East Africa Handbook
Ecuador & Galápagos Handbook
Egypt Handbook Handbook
Goa Handbook
India Handbook
Indian Himalaya Handbook
Indonesia Handbook
Ireland Handbook
Israel Handbook
Jordan Handbook
Jordan, Syria & Lebanon Hbk
Laos Handbook
Libya Handbook
Malaysia Handbook
Myanmar Handbook
Mexico Handbook
Mexico & Central America Hbk
Morocco Handbook
Namibia Handbook
Nepal Handbook
Pakistan Handbook

Peru Handbook
Rio de Janeiro Handbook
Scotland Handbook
Singapore Handbook
South Africa Handbook
South American Handbook
South India Handbook
Sri Lanka Handbook
Sumatra Handbook
Thailand Handbook
Tibet Handbook
Tunisia Handbook
Venezuela Handbook
Vietnam Handbook

In the pipeline – Turkey, London, Edinburgh, Rajasthan, Scotland Highlands & Islands, Syria & Lebanon

Also available from Footprint
Traveller's Handbook
Traveller's Healthbook

Available at all good bookshops

Will you help us?

We try as hard as we can to make each Footprint Handbook as up-to-date and accurate as possible but, of course, things always change. Many people write to us - with corrections, new information, or simply comments.

If you want to let us know about an experience or adventure - hair-raising or mundane, good or bad, exciting or boring or simply something rather special - we would be delighted to hear from you. Please give us as precise information as possible, quoting the edition number (you'll find it on the front cover) and page number of the Handbook you are using.

Your help will be greatly appreciated, especially by other travellers. In return we will send you details about our special guidebook offer.

email Footprint at:
MAS3_online@footprintbooks.com

or write to:
Elizabeth Taylor
Footprint Handbooks
6 Riverside Court
Lower Bristol Road
Bath
BA2 3DZ
England

What the papers say

"I carried the South American Handbook in my bag from Cape Horn to Cartagena and consulted it every night for two and a half months. And I wouldn't do that for anything else except my hip flask."

Michael Palin

"Footprint's India Handbook told me everything from the history of the region to where to get the best curry.

Jennie Bond, BBC correspondent

"Of all the main guidebook series this is genuinely the only one we have never received a complaint about."

The Bookseller

Awards
Wanderlust Readers' Award for Top Guidebook Series
Bronze Award

Literati Club
Outstanding Achievement

Mail order
Available worldwide in good bookstores, Footprint Handbooks can also be ordered directly from us in Bath, via our website or from the address on page 2.

Website
www.footprintbooks.com
Take a look for the latest news, to order a book or to join our mailing list.

Acknowledgements

Specialist contributor:

Dan Harlow
After deciding there must be more to the world than southeast England, Dan travelled to Africa, teaching in Kenya before travelling to Cape Town. Other trips have taken in the contrasting cultures of the Americas and Middle East. Currently studying for an MA in International Relations, this was his first foray into Southeast Asia.

Many more people have been extremely helpful during the preparation of this edition. In particular, we would like to thank:

Lisa Steer, for her contributions on updating Kuala Lumpur.

For their contributions to the Singapore chapter:

Kar Tiang and Peter, Singapore
Debjani Ghosh, UK
P Alberts, UK
Carl Gay
Karel Soumillion, The Netherlands

Thanks also to the following travellers who wrote to us with comments and suggestions:

Ralph Arnoldussen, The Netherlands
Tony Bing, UK
Audrey Bradford, Spain
Veronica Coad, UK
Keith Davies, Australia
Andreas Engekmayer, Germany
Carol Evans, UK
Roy Faulkner, UK
Gary Geller, USA
Kenny Ng, Malaysia
Piergiorgio Pescali, Italy
Tom Reynolds, UK

Joshua Eliot, Kate Renshaw & Jane Bickersteth

Joshua Eliot first visited Malaysia as a teenager. Since then he has taken a degree in Asian Studies at London's School of Oriental and African Studies, written children's books and academic papers, lectured on cruise liners, familiarised businessmen working in the country, advised military personnel, and given radio broadcasts. He travels regularly to Malaysia and Singapore to keep tabs on developments.

Kate Renshaw first travelled to Southeast Asia in 1995. She graduated in Psychology from Durham University but as an inveterate traveller she was unwilling to settle down. She eagerly accepted the opportunity to spend several months in Malaysia researching this edition.

Jane Bickersteth first visited Malaysia in the early '80s when she accompanied an intrepid band of mothers and children on a journey upriver into the interior. Since then she has returned on several occasions. She also knows Singapore well, and is the co-author of Footprint's Singapore Handbook.